Your full-circle solution— from assessment to instruction

McDougal Littell Assessment System

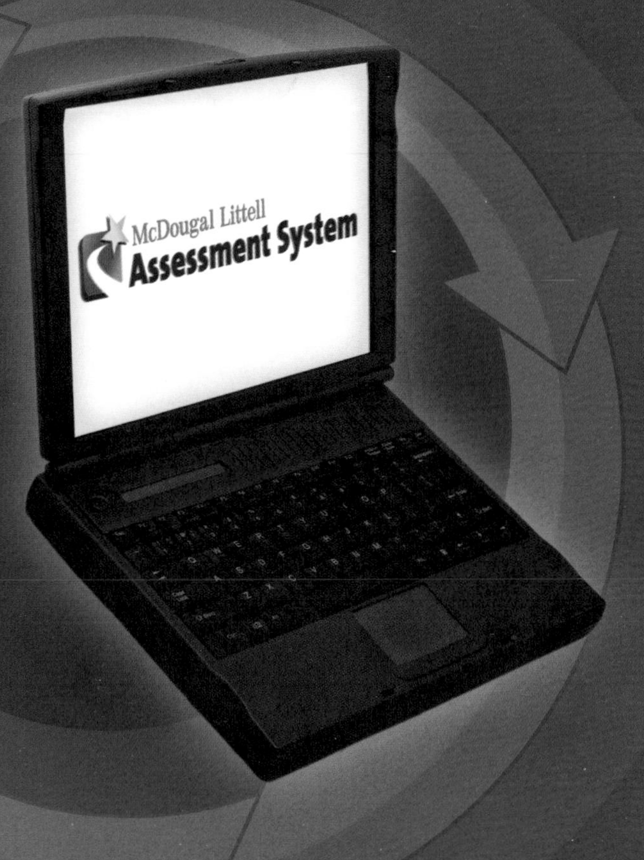

Test

- Access pre-made lesson and benchmark tests correlated to standards
- Create custom tests using the McDougal Littell Test Generator

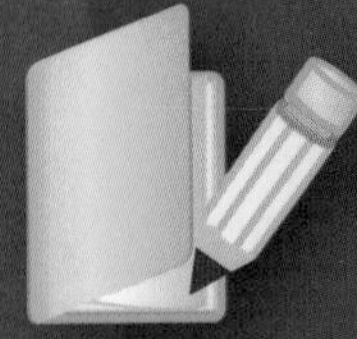

Score

- Score tests online or use our unique plain-paper scanner system
- Avoid expensive scan cards and other impractical answer sheets

Report

- Generate instant progress reports for individual students or for groups of students
- Track students' performance over time to measure and monitor improvement

Reteach

- Access a complete library of worksheets, study guides, and enrichment exercises tied to standards
- Identify at-risk students and target reteaching based on individual needs

McDougal Littell
Where Great Lessons Begin

1

Bleu

TEACHER'S EDITION

Discovering FRENCH *Nouveau!*

Jean-Paul Valette
Rebecca M. Valette

From the Authors

DEDICATION

On June 6, 1944, shortly after 6:30 a.m., Private John Nedelka of the 16th Regiment, First Division (the Big Red One), came ashore on a stretch of the Normandy Coast now known as Omaha Beach. Pinned down under a deluge of fire, he spent the next hour crawling his way to the relative safety of a seawall just one hundred yards inland. As he scrambled up the cliffs off the beach later that afternoon, he suddenly realized that he was one of the few survivors of his company.

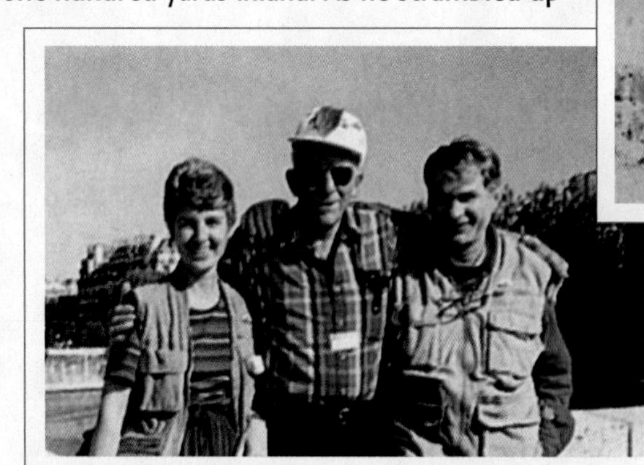

This book is dedicated to our friend John Nedelka, to the hundreds of thousands of young Americans who, like him, risked their lives, and, above all, to the tens of thousands who lost theirs in the liberation of France.

IN MEMORIAM

Roger Coulombe (*1940–2001*)

We would like to dedicate ***Discovering French, Nouveau!*** to the memory of our long-time associate, Roger Coulombe. For twenty-five years, he provided his editorial guidance and focused his artistic flair on the production and design of our language books–books which have encouraged millions of American young people to discover the beauty of French language and culture. May his commitment to quality and education inspire new generations of foreign language editors.

Jean-Paul Valette Rebecca M. Valette

Printed in the United States of America

ISBN-13: 978-0-618-65657-8

ISBN-10: 0-618-65657-X X 2 3 4 5 6 7 8 9 10 – VJM – 12 11 10 09 08 07 06

Internet: www.mcdougallittell.com

Dear French Teachers,

We take this opportunity to welcome you to **Discovering French, Nouveau!** In fact, this is really your program, for it has been revised and expanded thanks to the suggestions, critiques, and encouragement we have received from the many hundreds of secondary school teachers who have enjoyed success getting their students to communicate with *Discovering French.*

Discovering French, Nouveau! emphasizes communication with accuracy and stresses meaningful cultural contexts. With **Discovering French, Nouveau!** your students will:

- **Experience France and the Francophone world**
- **Communicate with confidence**
- **Extend and enhance their learning through integrated technology**

Teachers who have already begun using the book are enthusiastic about its new features, such as the end-of-unit *Tests de contrôle* and thematic vocabulary lists. In addition, this 2007 edition contains creative *Tête à tête* pair activities designed to stimulate interpersonal exchanges.

In conclusion, we would like to stress that our program is a flexible one, which allows teachers to take into account the needs of their students and build their own curriculum focusing on specific skills or topics.

We wish you the best of success with **Discovering French, Nouveau!** It is our hope that for you and your students, teaching and learning French with this program will be an enjoyable as well as a rewarding experience.

Jean-Paul Valette Rebecca M. Valette

Contents

Contributors to the 2007 Edition

Pre-AP Consultant

Mary L. Diehl
Specialist–Department of Spanish and Portuguese
Master Teacher and Project Coordinator–UTeach-Liberal Arts
University of Texas at Austin

Inclusion Consultants

Leonore Ganschow, Ed.D.
Professor Emeritus
Miami University
Oxford, OH

Richard L. Sparks, Ed.D.
Professor
College of Mt. St. Joseph
Cincinnati, OH

Lorin Pritikin
French Instructor
Francis W. Parker School
Chicago, IL

Program Consultants

- Dan Battisti
- Dr. Teresa Carrera-Hanley
- David Kleinbeck
- Bill Lionetti
- Patty Murguía Bohannan
- Lorena Richins Layser

Discovering FRENCH *Nouveau!*

Explores France and the distinctive French-speaking cultures

- Photos and illustrations reflect the cultural diversity of the French-speaking world.
- *Connexions* offer real-world activities that promote cultural awareness.
- *En bref* features familiarize students with the wide variety of countries in the French-speaking world.
- *Notes culturelles* provide more in-depth cultural information about France and the French-speaking world.

Builds skills and develops strategies for more accurate communication

- Strategies for developing reading and writing skills are included in each unit.
- Writing hints provide further support to help students write accurately in French.
- Distinguishing features provide strategies for communication and help students understand how language functions.

Integrates technology for engaging, real-world instruction

- Extensive video program presents and practices vocabulary and grammar in authentic cultural contexts.
- Online Workbook offers leveled practice on the Internet.
- EasyPlanner CD-ROM gives teachers the flexibility of having all ancillaries available in an electronic format.
- McDougal Littell Assessment System is an innovative skills-based system that helps you test, score, and track results. It provides ready-made materials for reteaching and remediation. The scannable tests and answer sheets can be printed out on plain paper.
- Test Generator allows teachers to customize their assessments by editing existing questions or adding their own.
- ClassZone.com presents a variety of engaging resources, from WebQuests to test preparation tools, all correlated to **Discovering French, *Nouveau!***
- Take-Home Tutor CD-ROM provides extra skills support with video and audio clips, flashcards, and self-check exercises for at-home guided practice.

Program Resources

Extensive resources tailored to the needs of today's students!

TEACHER'S EDITION

TEACHER'S RESOURCE PACKAGE

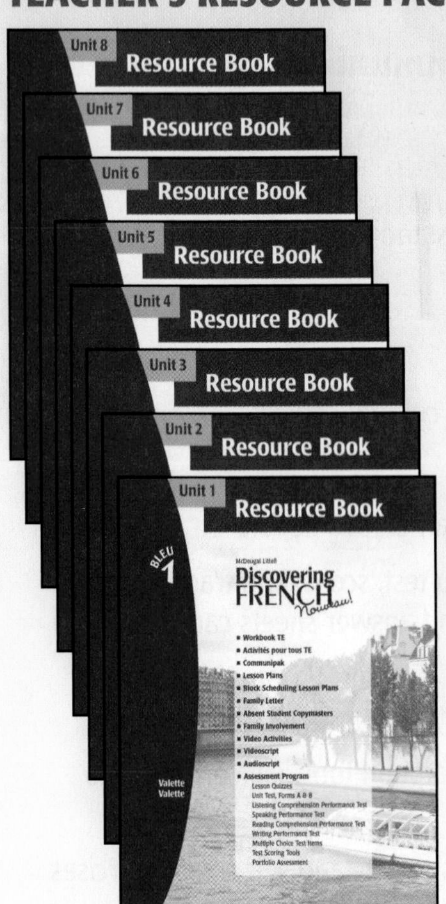

Unit Resource Books

Per Lesson –
- Workbook TE
- *Activités pour tous* TE
- Lesson Plans
- Block Scheduling Lesson Plans
- Absent Student Copymasters
- Family Involvement
- Video Activities
- Videoscripts
- Audioscripts

Per Unit –
- Family Letter
- Communipak
- *Activités pour tous* TE Reading
- Workbook TE Reading and Culture Activities

Assessment Options
- Lesson Quiz
- Portfolio Assessment
- Unit Test Form A
- Unit Test Form B
- Unit Test Part III (Alternate) Cultural Awareness
- Listening Comprehension Performance Test
- Speaking Performance Test
- Reading Comprehension Performance Test
- Writing Performance Test
- Multiple Choice Test Items
- Test Scoring Tools
- Audioscripts
- Answer Keys

- **Block Scheduling Copymasters** Work in a block schedule with projects, learning scenarios, and homework assignments
- **Teacher to Teacher Copymasters** Provide enrichment with classroom-proven games, puzzles, extension activities, and teaching tips

ADDITIONAL RESOURCES

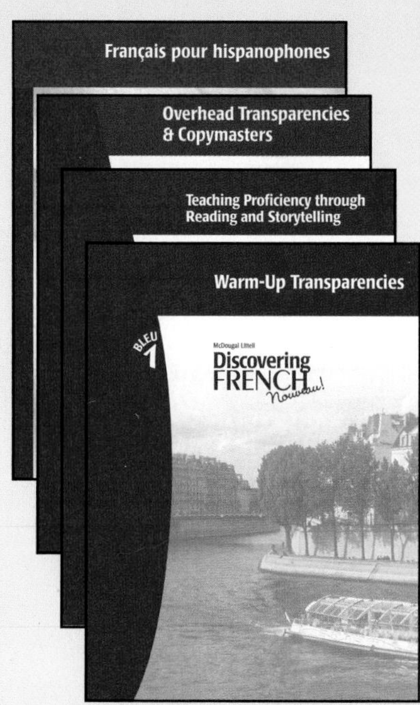

- ***Français pour hispanophones***
- **Overhead Transparencies & Copymasters**
  - Color Overhead Visuals (including Supplementary Situational Transparencies)
  - Fine Art Transparencies
  - Black and White Copymasters
  - Suggested Expansion Activities
- **Teaching Proficiency through Reading and Storytelling**
- **Warm-Up Transparencies**

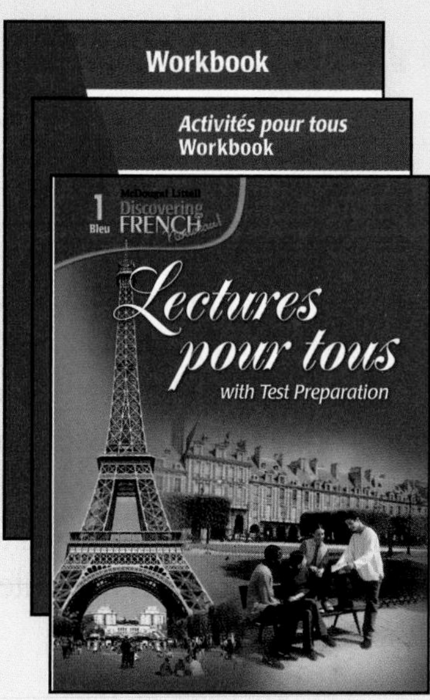

Student Workbooks

- **Workbook**
- ***Activités pour tous***
  Leveled practice
  - Vocabulary
  - Grammar
  - Reading
- ***Lectures pour tous***

INTERNET RESOURCES

- **McDougal Littell Assessment System**
  - Innovative skills-based system
  - Helps you test, score, and track results
  - Provides ready-made materials for reteaching and remediation
  - Scannable tests and answer sheets can be printed out on plain paper
- **Online Workbook**
  Leveled, self-scoring practice
- **ClassZone.com**
  WebQuests, test preparation, flashcards and more

MIDDLE SCHOOL RESOURCES

- **Middle School Bridging Packet**
  - Reprise Workbook TE
  - Reprise Audioscript
  - Middle School Copymasters
  - Middle School Audio CD

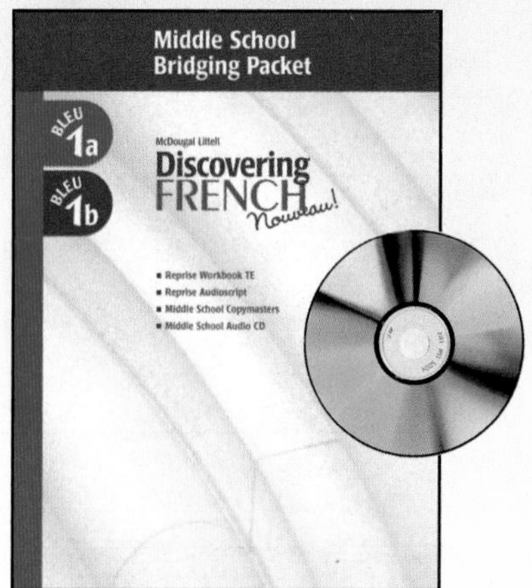

TECHNOLOGY RESOURCES

- **Audio CD Program**
- ***Chansons* Audio CD**
- **Sing Along: Grammar and Vocabulary Songs**
- **Video Program DVD**
- **Test Generator CD-ROM**
- **McDougal Littell Assessment System**
- **EasyPlanner CD-ROM**
- **Power Presentations CD-ROM**
- **eEdition CD-ROM**
- **Take-Home Tutor CD-ROM**

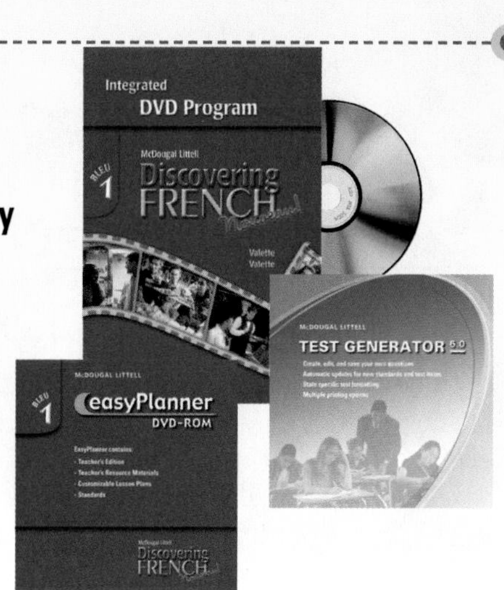

Book Organization

Discovering French, *Nouveau!* BLEU

Basic Structure The Student Text contains eight units and two *Images* photo essays. It can be divided into three categories: Introduction, Core Material, and Further Development. The *Invitation au français* section builds student confidence and quickly develops basic conversation skills. Units 3-6 form the core of study at level 1, and focus on the formal development of language for accurate communication. Units 7-8 introduce somewhat more complex language functions. Although it's desirable to complete the last two units, it's not critical to do so, since the material is reviewed in *Discovering French, Nouveau! – Blanc*.

INTRODUCTION

Invitation au français emphasizes speaking and listening to French.

UNITÉ 1 • Faisons connaissance
UNITÉ 2 • La vie courante

TOPICS COVERED
- greeting people
- introducing oneself
- talking about friends and family
- ordering in a café
- numbers 0–100
- telling time
- days of the week
- months and dates
- weather and seasons

CORE MATERIAL

These units provide the linguistic base needed for basic communication skills.
Emphasis is on asking and answering questions. (Students should complete these units.)

UNITÉ 3 • Qu'est-ce qu'on fait?
IMAGES ***À l'école en France***
UNITÉ 4 • Le monde personnel et familier
UNITÉ 5 • En ville
IMAGES ***À Paris***
UNITÉ 6 • Le shopping

TOPICS COVERED
- discussing daily activities and leisure pastimes
- talking about people and possessions
- getting around town
- describing where one lives
- shopping for clothes

FURTHER DEVELOPMENT

Units 7 and 8 introduce somewhat more complex language functions. (It is not critical to finish these units since the material is reviewed and expanded in the first part of *Discovering French, Nouveau! – Blanc*.)

UNITÉ 7 • Le temps libre
UNITÉ 8 • Les repas

TOPICS COVERED
- describing weekend activities
- talking about vacation plans
- planning meals
- shopping for food

Easy Articulation

▶ *Discovering French, Nouveau!* is a carefully articulated three-level sequence of French instruction. Each level has its own special focus, which builds a spiraling progression across levels.

	CONVERSATION	DESCRIPTION	NARRATION	EXPLANATION
BLEU	Basic communication with learned phrases; simple questions and answers	Simple descriptions of people and things	Simple narration in the present; introduction to past narration	Simple explanations as to why something is done
BLANC	Creative conversation; asking and answering questions	More detailed descriptions, including simple comparisons	Basic narration in the past (*passé composé* and imperfect) and future	Expression of personal wishes and needs
ROUGE	Extended conversation using complex sentences and appropriate pronouns	More complex comparisons of people, things and actions	Extended narration of past, present and future events and corresponding conditions	Expression of emotions, wishes and hypotheses in complex sentences

▶ This chart shows the articulation of basic communication themes and topics across levels. (Only the major entry and reentry points are shown.) These themes and topics are recycled throughout the program in the various exercises, readings and communication activities.

THEMES AND TOPICS	BLEU	BLANC	ROUGE
Greeting and meeting people	Unit 1	Reprise: Rappel 1	–
Time and weather	Unit 2	Reprise: Rappel 1	Unit 3
Family and friends; Family relationships	Unit 1	Unit 1	Reprise A; Unit 9
Food and restaurants	Unit 2 Unit 8	Units 1, 3	Reprise A
Money and shopping	Units 2, 6	Reprise: Rappel 2	Reprise B; Unit 4
School and education	Images: À l'école en France	Reprise: Faisons connaissance	Unit 10
Daily activities	Unit 3	Reprise: Rappel 3	Reprise A
Getting around the city	Unit 3 Unit 5	Unit 2	Unit 8
Describing oneself	Unit 4	Units 1, 7	Unit 1
Home and furnishings	Units 4, 5	Unit 6	Unit 6
Possessions and their description	Unit 4	Reprise: Rappel 2 Unit 2	Reprise A; Unit 2
Sports, fitness, daily routine	Unit 5	Units 5, 8	Unit 1
Medical and dental care	–	Unit 5	Unit 7
Clothing and personal appearance	Unit 6	Unit 7	Reprise A; Unit 4
Leisure activities, music, entertainment	Unit 7	Unit 4	Interlude 4
Vacation and travel	Unit 7	Unit 8	Reprise B; Unit 3
Transportation	Unit 7	Units 8, 9	Unit 5
Jobs and professions	–	Unit 1	Units 2, 10
Helping around the house	–	Unit 2	Unit 2
Nature and the environment	–	Unit 2	Unit 3
Services and repairs	–	–	Unit 4
Hotel accommodations	–	–	Unit 6

FUNCTION	BLEU	BLANC	ROUGE
Greeting people and socializing	Units 1, 2	Reprise: Rappel 1	–
Talking about the present Asking and answering questions Describing people, places and things Describing future plans (Simple description)	Units 3, 4, 5, 6	Reprise: Rappels 2, 3; Unit 1	Reprise A
Narrating past events (Simple narration)	Unit 7	Unit 2	Reprise B
Discussing daily routines (Simple narration)	–	Unit 5	Unit 1
Describing people, places, things (Extended description)	Unit 8	Units 3, 4, 5	Reprise C Units 2, 4
Describing past conditions and narrating past events (Extended narration)	–	Unit 6	Reprise B Units 3, 7
Comparing and discussing people, things and actions (Complex description)	–	Unit 7	Units 6, 9
Discussing future events (Extended narration)	–	Unit 8	Unit 5, 8
Discussing hypothetical conditions and events (Complex discussion)	–	Unit 8	Units 5, 8
Expressing wishes and obligations (Direct statements)	–	Unit 9	Unit 2
Expressing doubts and emotions (Complex discussion)	–	–	Unit 7
Expressing cause and purpose (Complex discussion)	–	–	Unit 10

LEVEL 1

Unité 4

Leçon 10
- Optional presentation of the **passé composé** appears in the Teacher's Edition.

Unité 7

Leçon 21
- **Faire de** + sport

Leçon 22
- The **passé composé** of **-er** verbs
- Expressions with **avoir**

Leçon 23
- The **passé composé** of **-ir** verbs
- The **passé composé** of **-re** verbs
- The **passé composé** of irregular verbs
- The verb **voir**

Leçon 24
- The **passé composé** with **être**

Unité 8

Leçon 26
- The verb **prendre**
- The verb **vouloir**
- The verb **boire**
- Partitive article

Leçon 27
- The verbs **pouvoir** and **devoir**
- Pronouns **me, te, nous, vous**
- Pronouns with commands

Leçon 28
- The verb **connaître**
- The verbs **dire** and **écrire**
- Pronouns **le, la, les, lui, leur**

LEVEL 2

Unité 1

Leçon 3
- The verb **faire**
- The verb **avoir**

Leçon 4
- The verb **aller**
- The verb **venir**
- The construction **aller** + infinitive

Unité 2

Leçon 6
- The **passé composé** with **avoir**
- The verbs **mettre, permettre,** and **promettre**
- The verb **prendre**

Leçon 7
- The **passé composé** with **avoir** *(cont.)*
- The **passé composé** with **être**
- The verb **voir**

Leçon 8
- The **passé composé** with **être** *(cont.)*

Unité 3

Leçon 10
- The verb **vouloir**
- Partitive article
- The verbs **pouvoir** and **devoir**

Leçon 11
- The verb **préférer**
- The verb **boire**
- The verb **acheter**
- The verb **payer**

Unité 4

Leçon 14
- Object pronouns **me, te, nous, vous**
- Object pronouns in commands

Leçon 15
- The verb **connaître**
- Object pronouns **le, la, les**

Leçon 16
- The verbs **écrire, lire,** and **dire**
- Object pronouns **lui, leur**

Unité 5

Leçon 18
- The pronouns **en** and **y**

Leçon 19
- Definite article with parts of the body
- Reflexive verbs: present tense

Leçon 20
- Reflexive verbs: infinitive constructions

LEVEL 3

Unité 1

Partie 1
- Definite article with parts of the body
- Reflexive verbs: present tense
- Reflexive verbs: infinitive constructions

Partie 2
- Reflexive verbs: **passé composé**
- Reflexive verbs: idiomatic usage

Recycles some topics from Blanc *Unité 5*

Unité 2 — Recycles *Blanc* Unité 9

Partie 1
- Present subjunctive: regular forms
- Usage of the subjunctive after **il faut que**

Partie 2
- Present subjunctive: irregular forms
- Usage of the subjunctive after certain impersonal expressions and **vouloir que**

Unité 3

Partie 1
- Review of the **passé composé**
- Review of the imperfect
- Contrasting the imperfect and the **passé composé**

Partie 2
- Describing an event using the imperfect and the **passé composé**
- Using the imperfect and the **passé composé** in the same sentence
- The **passé simple**

Recycles some topics from Blanc *Unité 6*

Unité 4

Partie 1
- Review of the pronouns **en** and **y**
- Indefinite expressions of quantity

Partie 2
- Review of the pronouns **le, la, les, lui, leur**
- The order of pronouns
- The construction **faire** + infinitive

Recycles some topics from Blanc *Unité 4*

Unité 5 — Recycles *Blanc* Unité 8

Partie 1
- Negative expressions
- The expression **ne … que**

Partie 2
- The future tense
- The future with **si**-clauses
- The future with **quand**
- The conditional

Grammar Across Levels

Discovering French, *Nouveau!* addresses the challenges of articulation between levels by providing a unique instructional overlap. Much of the grammar and vocabulary taught in Units 7 and 8 of ***Bleu*** are covered again in ***Blanc,*** so teachers can choose how far into the grammatical and functional sequence they wish to go. Since the units of ***Rouge*** are self-contained, they can be taught in any order. Students' study of French can continue seamlessly!

Unité 6	Unité 7	Unité 8	Unité 9
Leçon 23 • The imperfect • Contrasting the imperfect and the **passé composé** **Leçon 24** • Contrasting the imperfect and the **passé composé** *(cont.)*	**Leçon 27** • Comparisons with adjectives • Comparisons with adverbs • Superlative constructions **Leçon 28** • Pronouns **lequel** and **celui**	**Leçon 31** • The future tense • The future with **si**-clauses • The future with **quand** **Leçon 32** • The conditional	**Leçon 35** • Present subjunctive: regular forms • Usage of the subjunctive after **il faut que** **Leçon 36** • Present subjunctive: irregular forms • Usage of the subjunctive after **vouloir que**

Unité 6 Recycles *Blanc* Unité 7	Unité 7	Unité 8	Unité 9	Unité 10
Partie 1 • Comparisons with adjectives • Comparisons with adverbs • The superlative **Partie 2** • The pronouns **lequel** and **celui** • Possessive pronouns	**Partie 1** • Concept of the subjunctive • The verbs **croire** and **craindre** • Usage of the subjunctive: emotions, feelings, doubt **Partie 2** • The past subjunctive	**Partie 1** • The construction **si** + imperfect • The **plus-que-parfait** **Partie 2** • Review of the conditional • The conditional in phrases with **si** • Other uses of the conditional **Partie 3** • The past conditional • Summary of tenses with **si**	**Partie 1** • Using reflexive verbs to express reciprocal action • Review of the relative pronouns **qui** and **que** • The construction preposition + relative pronoun • The relative pronoun **dont** **Partie 2** • Summary of relative pronouns • **Ce qui, ce que,** and **ce dont**	**Partie 1** • The construction preposition + infinitive • The past infinitive • The present participle **Partie 2** • The construction conjunction + subjunctive

Level 1 Scope and Sequence

INVITATION AU FRANÇAIS

UNITÉ 1 Faisons connaissance • CULTURAL CONTEXT Meeting people

Communication: Functions and Activities COMPREHENSION AND SELF-EXPRESSION	**Communication Topics** THEMATIC VOCABULARY	**Linguistic Goals** ACCURACY OF EXPRESSION
Meeting people • Introducing oneself **(Leçon 1A)** • Spelling one's name **(Leçon 1A)** • Asking someone's name **(Leçon 1A)** • Saying where you are from **(Leçon 1B)**	• Adjectives of nationality **(Leçon 1B)**	**• L'alphabet (Leçon 1A)** **• Français / française (Leçon 1B)**
Greeting people • Saying hello **(Leçon 1A)** • Asking how people feel **(Leçon 1C)** • Saying good-bye **(Leçon 1C)**	• Expressions with **ça va (Leçon 1C)** • Counting 0 to 10 **(Leçon 1A)** • Counting 10 to 20 **(Leçon 1B)** • Counting 20 to 60 **(Leçon 1C)**	
Talking about other people • Pointing people out **(Leçon 2A)** • Finding out someone's name **(Leçon 2B)** • Saying where a person is from **(Leçon 2B)**	• People **(Leçon 2A)**	**• Un garçon / une fille (Leçon 2A)** **• Le garçon / la fille (Leçon 2B)**
Introducing one's family • Giving their names **(Leçon 2B)** • Giving their ages **(Leçon 2C)**	• Family members **(Leçon 2C)** • Counting 60 to 79 **(Leçon 2A)** • Counting 80 to 100 **(Leçon 2B)**	**• Mon cousin / ma cousine (Leçon 2C)** **• Ton cousin / ta cousine (Leçon 2C)**

UNITÉ 2 La vie courante • CULTURAL CONTEXT Having a snack in France

Communication: Functions and Activities	**Communication Topics**	**Linguistic Goals**
Saying you are hungry • Offering a friend something to eat **(Leçon 3A)** • Asking a friend for something to eat **(Leçon 3A)**	• Foods **(Leçon 3A)**	**• Un sandwich / une pizza (Leçon 3A)**
Saying you are thirsty • Ordering a beverage in a café **(Leçon 3B)** • Asking an adult for something to eat or drink **(Leçon 3B)**	• Beverages **(Leçon 3B)**	**• S'il te plaît / s'il vous plaît (Leçon 3B)**
Paying at a café in France • Asking what something costs **(Leçon 3C)** • Asking a friend to lend you money **(Leçon 3C)**		
Talking about time • Asking for the time **(Leçon 4A)** • Indicating the time **(Leçon 4A)** • Saying when certain events are scheduled **(Leçon 4A)**	• Expressions of time **(Leçon 4A)**	
Talking about dates • Asking the day of the week **(Leçon 4B)** • Giving the date **(Leçon 4B)** • Talking about birthdays **(Leçon 4B)**	• Days of the week **(Leçon 4B)** • Months of the year **(Leçon 4B)**	
Talking about the weather	• Weather expressions **(Leçon 4C)** • Seasons **(Leçon 4C)**	

UNITÉ 3 Qu'est-ce qu'on fait? • CULTURAL CONTEXT Daily activities at home, at school, on weekends

COMMUNICATION: FUNCTIONS AND ACTIVITIES COMPREHENSION AND SELF-EXPRESSION	COMMUNICATION TOPICS THEMATIC VOCABULARY	LINGUISTIC GOALS ACCURACY OF EXPRESSION
Describing daily activities • What people do and don't do **(Leçon 5)** • What people like to do and don't like to do **(Leçon 5)** • What you want and don't want to do **(Leçon 5)**	• Daily activities **(Leçon 5)** • Expressions with **faire (Leçon 8)**	• Subject pronouns **(Leçon 6)** • The negative **ne... pas (Leçon 6)** • Verb + infinitive **(Leçon 7)** • Regular **-er** verbs **(Leçon 7)** • The verb **faire (Leçon 8)**
Talking about where people are	• Places **(Leçon 6)**	• The verb **être (Leçon 6)**
Finding out what is going on • Asking yes/no questions **(Leçon 6)** • Asking information questions **(Leçon 8)**	• Question words **(Leçon 8)**	• Yes/no questions with **est-ce que (Leçon 6)** • Information questions with **est-ce que (Leçon 8)** • Questions with inversion **(Leçon 8)**
Inviting friends to do things with you • Extending an invitation **(Leçon 5)** • Accepting an invitation **(Leçon 5)** • Turning down an invitation **(Leçon 5)**		• Verb + infinitive **(Leçon 7)**
Expanding one's conversational skills • Answering yes/no questions **(Leçon 6)** • Expressing approval or regret **(Leçon 7)** • Expressing mild doubt or surprise **(Leçon 8)**	• Affirmative and negative expressions **(Leçon 6)**	

UNITÉ 4 Le monde personnel et familier • CULTURAL CONTEXT People and their possessions

COMMUNICATION: FUNCTIONS AND ACTIVITIES COMPREHENSION AND SELF-EXPRESSION	COMMUNICATION TOPICS THEMATIC VOCABULARY	LINGUISTIC GOALS ACCURACY OF EXPRESSION
Describing yourself and others • Physical appearance **(Leçon 9)** • Age **(Leçons 9, 10)** • Character traits **(Leçon 11)** • Nationality **(Leçon 11)**	• People **(Leçon 9)** • Adjectives of physical description **(Leçon 9)** • Adjectives of personality **(Leçon 11)** • Adjectives of nationality **(Leçon 11)** • Adjectives of aspect **(Leçon 12)**	• Singular and plural nouns **(Leçon 10)** • Definite and indefinite articles **(Leçon 10)** • The expression **avoir... ans (Leçon 10)** • Adjective formation **(Leçon 11)** • Adjective position **(Leçons 11, 12)** • Use of **c'est** and **il est (Leçon 12)**
Describing your room • What is in it **(Leçon 9)** • Where things are located **(Leçon 9)**	• Room furnishings **(Leçon 9)** • Prepositions of place **(Leçon 9)**	• The expression **il y a (Leçon 9)**
Talking about possessions • Things that one owns and doesn't own **(Leçons 9, 10)** • Whether they work or not **(Leçon 9)** • Where they were made **(Leçon 11)** • What they look like **(Leçon 12)**	• Everyday objects **(Leçon 9)** • Color **(Leçon 12)** • Aspect **(Leçon 12)**	• The verb **avoir (Leçon 10)** • The negative article **pas de (Leçon 10)**
Expanding one's conversational skills • Getting someone's attention **(Leçon 12)** • Making generalizations **(Leçon 10)** • Expressing opinions **(Leçon 12)** • Talking about regular events **(Leçon 10)** • Contradicting a negative statement or question **(Leçon 10)** • Introducing a conclusion **(Leçon 11)**	• Attention getters **(Leçon 12)** • Expressions of opinion **(Leçon 12)**	• Use of the definite article: in general statements to indicate repeated events **(Leçon 10)** • Impersonal **c'est (Leçon 12)**
optional: Talking about past events **(Leçons 10, 11, 12)**		• Conversational introduction: answering questions in the **passé composé (Leçons 10, 11, 12)**

UNITÉ 5 En ville • CULTURAL CONTEXT City life–the home, the family and urban activities

COMMUNICATION: FUNCTIONS AND ACTIVITIES COMPREHENSION AND SELF-EXPRESSION	COMMUNICATION TOPICS THEMATIC VOCABULARY	LINGUISTIC GOALS ACCURACY OF EXPRESSION
Describing your city • Streets and public buildings **(Leçon 13)** • Places you often go to **(Leçon 14)** • How you get around **(Leçon 14)**	• City places and buildings **(Leçon 13)** • Transportation **(Leçon 14)**	• The verb **aller (Leçon 14)** • Contractions with **à (Leçon 14)**
Finding your way around • Asking and giving directions **(Leçon 13)** • Indicating the floor **(Leçon 16)**	• Giving directions **(Leçon 13)**	• Ordinal numbers **(Leçon 16)**
Describing your home and your family • Your address **(Leçon 13)** • The inside and outside of your home **(Leçon 13)** • Your family **(Leçon 16)**	• Neighborhood **(Leçon 13)** • Rooms of the house **(Leçon 13)** • Family members **(Leçon 16)**	• The expression **chez (Leçon 14)** • Stress pronouns **(Leçon 15)** • The construction noun + **de** + noun **(Leçon 15)** • Possession with **de (Leçon 16)** • Possessive adjectives **(Leçon 16)**
Making plans to do things in town • What you are going to do **(Leçon 14)** • Asking others to come along **(Leçon 15)** • Saying where you have been **(Leçon 15)**	• Activities: sports, games, etc. **(Leçon 15)**	• **Aller** + infinitive **(Leçon 14)** • The verb **venir (Leçon 15)** • Contractions with **de (Leçon 15)**
Expanding one's conversational skills: • Contradicting someone **(Leçon 15)** • Expressing doubt **(Leçon 16)** • Expressing surprise **(Leçon 15)**		
optional: Talking about past events **(Leçons 13, 14, 15, 16)**		• Conversational introduction: answering questions in the **passé composé (Leçons 13, 14, 15, 16)**

UNITÉ 6 Le shopping • CULTURAL CONTEXT Buying clothes

COMMUNICATION: FUNCTIONS AND ACTIVITIES	COMMUNICATION TOPICS	LINGUISTIC GOALS
Talking about clothes • What people are wearing **(Leçon 17)** • Whether the clothes fit **(Leçon 17)** • What they look like **(Leçons 17, 19)** • What one's preferences are **(Leçon 17)**	• Clothing and accessories **(Leçon 17)** • Descriptive adjectives **(Leçon 17)** • Adjectives **beau, nouveau, vieux (Leçon 19)** • Expressions of opinion **(Leçon 17)**	• The verb **mettre (Leçon 18)** • The verb **préférer (Leçon 18)** • The demonstrative **ce (Leçon 18)** • The interrogative **quel? (Leçon 18)**
Discussing shopping plans • Where to go **(Leçons 17, 20)** • What to buy **(Leçon 18)**	• Stores that sell clothes **(Leçon 17)** • Verbs like **vendre (Leçon 20)**	• The verb **acheter (Leçon 18)** • Regular **-re** verbs **(Leçon 20)** • The pronoun **on (Leçon 20)**
Buying clothes • Asking for help **(Leçon 17)** • Finding out prices **(Leçons 17, 20)** • Deciding what to choose **(Leçon 19)** • Comparing items **(Leçon 19)** • Talking about what you need and what you like **(Leçon 20)** • Giving advice **(Leçon 20)**	• Numbers 100–1000 **(Leçon 17)** • Money-related expressions **(Leçon 20)** • Verbs like **choisir (Leçon 19)** • Expressions **avoir besoin de** and **avoir envie de (Leçon 20)**	• Regular **-ir** verbs **(Leçon 19)** • The verb **payer (Leçon 20)** • Comparisons **(Leçon 19)** • The imperative **(Leçon 20)**
Expanding one's conversational skills • Emphasizing a remark **(Leçon 18)** • Indicating approval **(Leçon 20)** • Introducing an opinion **(Leçon 19)**		
optional: Talking about past events **(Leçons 17, 18, 19, 20)**		• Conversational introduction:answering questions in the **passé composé (Leçons 17, 18, 19, 20)**

UNITÉ 7 Le temps libre • CULTURAL CONTEXT Leisure-time activities

COMMUNICATION: FUNCTIONS AND ACTIVITIES COMPREHENSION AND SELF-EXPRESSION	COMMUNICATION TOPICS THEMATIC VOCABULARY	LINGUISTIC GOALS ACCURACY OF EXPRESSION
Discussing leisure activities • Going out with friends **(Leçon 21)** • Sports **(Leçon 21)** • Helping around the house **(Leçon 21)** • How you and others feel **(Leçon 22)** • Things you never do **(Leçon 24)**	• Common weekend activities **(Leçon 21)** • Individual summer and winter sports **(Leçon 21)** • Household chores **(Leçon 21)**	• **Faire de** + sport **(Leçon 21)** • Expressions with **avoir (Leçon 22)** • **Ne … jamais (Leçon 24)**
Describing vacation travel plans • Travel dates **(Leçons 21, 24)** • How to travel **(Leçon 21)** • How long to stay **(Leçons 21, 23)** • What to see **(Leçon 23)**	• Means of transportation **(Leçon 21)** • Divisions of time **(Leçon 21)** • Periods of future time **(Leçon 23)** • Verbs of movement **(Leçon 24)**	• The verb **voir (Leçon 23)**
Narrating what happened • What you did and didn't do **(Leçons 22, 23)** • Where you went and when you returned **(Leçon 24)** • The sequence in which you did these things **(Leçon 22)** • Remaining vague about certain details **(Leçon 24)**	• Adverbs of sequence **(Leçon 22)** • Periods of past time **(Leçon 23)**	• **Passé composé** of **-er** verbs **(Leçon 22)** • **Passé composé** of **-ir** verbs **(Leçon 23)** • **Passé composé** of **-re** verbs **(Leçon 23)** • **Passé composé** of irregular verbs **(Leçon 23)** • **Passé composé** with **être (Leçon 24)** • **Quelqu'un, quelque chose** and their opposites **(Leçon 24)**

UNITÉ 8 Les repas • CULTURAL CONTEXT Food and meals

COMMUNICATION: FUNCTIONS AND ACTIVITIES COMPREHENSION AND SELF-EXPRESSION	COMMUNICATION TOPICS THEMATIC VOCABULARY	LINGUISTIC GOALS ACCURACY OF EXPRESSION
Talking about your favorite foods • What you like and don't like **(Leçon 25)** • What you can, should and want to eat **(Leçons 25, 26, 27)**	• Names of foods and beverages **(Leçon 25)** • Verbs of preference **(Leçon 25)**	• The verb **vouloir (Leçon 26)** • The verbs **pouvoir** and **devoir (Leçon 27)**
Shopping for food • Making a shopping list **(Leçon 25)** • Interacting with vendors **(Leçon 25)** • Asking prices **(Leçon 25)**	• Quantities **(Leçon 25)** • Fruits and vegetables **(Leçon 25)**	• Partitive article **(Leçon 26)**
Planning a meal • Asking others to help you **(Leçon 27)** • Setting the table **(Leçon 25)**	• Meals **(Leçon 25)** • Verbs asking for service **(Leçon 27)** • Place setting **(Leçon 25)**	• Pronouns **me, te, nous, vous (Leçon 27)** • Pronouns with commands **(Leçon 27)**
Eating out with friends • Ordering food **(Leçon 25)** • Asking the waiter/waitress to bring things for others **(Leçon 28)** • Talking about people you know **(Leçon 27)** • Talking about what others have said or written **(Leçon 28)**	• Verbs using indirect objects **(Leçon 28)**	• The verb **prendre (Leçon 26)** • The verb **boire (Leçon 26)** • The verb **connaître (Leçon 28)** • The verbs **dire** and **écrire (Leçon 28)** • Pronouns **le, la, les, lui, leur (Leçon 28)**

Level 2 Scope and Sequence

REPRISE (REVIEW) Entre amis • CULTURAL CONTEXT Getting acquainted

Communication: Functions and Activities COMPREHENSION AND SELF-EXPRESSION	Communication Topics THEMATIC VOCABULARY	Linguistic Goals ACCURACY OF EXPRESSION
Talking about school and classes (Faisons connaissance!)	• School subjects **(Faisons connaissance!)**	
Expressing oneself on familiar topics • Giving the date **(Rappel-1)** • Telling time **(Rappel-1)** • Describing the weather **(Rappel-1)**	• Review: numbers 1-100 **(Appendix A)** • Review: days, months **(Appendix A)** • Review: times of day **(Appendix A)** • Review: weather **(Appendix A)**	
Talking about places and things • Describing things you own **(Rappel-2)** • Saying where things are **(Rappel-2)** • Pointing things out **(Rappel-2)** • Expressing preferences **(Rappel-2)**	• Review: common objects and items of clothing **(Appendix A)** • Prepositions of location **(Rappel-2)** • Review: place names **(Appendix A)**	• Review: articles and contractions, **ce** and **quel** **(Appendix A)** • Review: possessive adjectives **(Appendix A)**
Carrying out simple conversations • Asking and answering questions **(Rappel-3)** • Talking about daily activities **(Rappel-3)** • Talking about places where you go **(Rappel-3)** • Saying what you like **(Rappel-3)**	• Review: question words **(Rappel-3)** • Review: common **–er**, **-ir**, **-re** verbs **(Appendix A)**	• Review: present tense of regular verbs **(Appendix A)** • Review: interrogative and negative constructions **(Appendix A)** • Review: subject pronouns and stress pronouns **(Rappel-3)** • Review: the imperative **(Appendix A)**

UNITÉ 1 Qui suis-je? • CULTURAL CONTEXT Oneself and others

Communication: Functions and Activities	Communication Topics	Linguistic Goals
Presenting oneself and others • Providing personal data **(Leçon 1)** • Identifying one's family **(Leçon 1)** • Talking about professions **(Leçon 1)**	• Adjectives of nationality **(Leçon 1)** • Family and friends **(Leçon 1)** • Professions **(Leçon 1)**	• The verb **être (Leçon 2)** • **C'est** and **il est (Leçon 2)**
Interacting with others • Introducing people **(Leçon 1)** • Making phone calls **(Leçon 1)** • Reading birth and wedding announcements **(Leçon 1)**		
Talking about oneself and others • Describing looks and personality **(Leçon 2)** • Talking about age **(Leçon 3)** • Describing feelings and needs **(Leçon 3)**	• Descriptive adjectives **(Leçon 2)** • Expressions with **avoir (Leçon 3)** • Expressions with **faire (Leçon 3)**	• Regular and irregular adjectives **(Leçon 2)** • The verb **avoir (Leçon 3)** • The verb **faire (Leçon 3)** • Inverted questions **(Leçon 3)**
Describing one's plans • Saying where people are going and what they are going to do **(Leçon 4)** • Saying where people are coming from **(Leçon 4)** • Saying how long people have been doing things **(Leçon 5)**	• Expressions with **depuis (Leçon 4)**	• The verb **aller (Leçon 4)** • The construction **aller** + infinitive **(Leçon 4)** • The verb **venir (Leçon 4)** • The present with **depuis (Leçon 4)**
READING Getting the gist		

UNITÉ 2 Le week-end, enfin! • CULTURAL CONTEXT Weekend activities

COMMUNICATION: FUNCTIONS AND ACTIVITIES COMPREHENSION AND SELF-EXPRESSION	COMMUNICATION TOPICS THEMATIC VOCABULARY	LINGUISTIC GOALS ACCURACY OF EXPRESSION
Talking about weekend plans • Describing weekend plans in the city **(Leçon 5)** • Planning a visit to the country **(Leçon 5)**	• Going out with friends **(Leçon 5)** • Helping at home **(Leçon 5)** • The country and the farm **(Leçon 5)** • Domestic and other animals **(Leçon 5)** • Expressions of present and future time **(Leçon 7)**	• The verbs **mettre**, **permettre**, and **promettre (Leçon 6)** • The verb **voir (Leçon 7)** • The verbs **sortir**, **partir**, and **dormir (Leçon 8)**
Getting from one place to another • Getting around in Paris **(Leçon 5)** • Visiting the countryside **(Leçon 5)**	• Getting around by subway **(Leçon 5)**	• The verb **prendre (Leçon 6)**
Narrating past weekend activities • Talking about where one went **(Leçons 7, 8)** • Talking about what one did and did not do **(Leçons 6, 7, 8)**	• Expressions of past time **(Leçon 6)**	• The **passé composé** with **avoir (Leçons 6, 7)** • The **passé composé** with **être (Leçons 7, 8)** • Impersonal expressions: **quelqu'un**, **quelque chose**, **personne**, **rien (Leçon 7)** • **Il y a** + elapsed time **(Leçon 8)**
READING Recognizing word families		

UNITÉ 3 Bon appétit! • CULTURAL CONTEXT Meals and food shopping

COMMUNICATION: FUNCTIONS AND ACTIVITIES COMPREHENSION AND SELF-EXPRESSION	COMMUNICATION TOPICS THEMATIC VOCABULARY	LINGUISTIC GOALS ACCURACY OF EXPRESSION
Planning a meal • Talking about where to eat **(Leçon 9)** • Setting the table **(Leçon 9)**	• Meals **(Leçon 9)** • Place setting **(Leçon 9)**	
Going to a café • Ordering in a café **(Leçon 9)**	• Café foods and beverages **(Leçon 9)**	• The verb **boire (Leçon 11)**
Talking about favorite foods • Discussing preferences **(Leçon 9)** • Expressing what one wants **(Leçon 12)**	• Mealtime foods and beverages **(Leçon 9)** • Fruits and vegetables **(Leçon 9)**	• The verb **préférer (Leçon 11)** • The verb **vouloir (Leçon 10)**
Shopping for food at a market • Interacting with vendors and asking prices **(Leçon 9)** • Asking for specific quantities **(Leçon 9)** • Discussing what one can get **(Leçon 12)** • Talking about what one should buy or do **(Leçon 12)**	• Common quantities **(Leçon 12)** • Expressions of quantity **(Leçon 12)**	• Partitive article **(Leçon 10)** • The verbs **acheter** and **payer (Leçon 11)** • Expressions of quantity with **de (Leçon 12)** • The adjective **tout (Leçon 12)** • The verbs **devoir** and **pouvoir (Leçon 10)** • The expression **il faut (Leçon 12)**
READING Reading by phrase groups		

UNITÉ 4 Loisirs et spectacles! • CULTURAL CONTEXT Free time and entertainment

COMMUNICATION: FUNCTIONS AND ACTIVITIES COMPREHENSION AND SELF-EXPRESSION	COMMUNICATION TOPICS THEMATIC VOCABULARY	LINGUISTIC GOALS ACCURACY OF EXPRESSION
Planning one's free time • Going out with friends **(Leçon 13)** • Extending, accepting, and turning down invitations **(Leçon 13)** • Talking about concerts and movies **(Leçon 13)**	• Places to go and things to do **(Leçon 13)** • Types of movies **(Leçon 13)**	
Talking about your friends and your neighborhood • Describing people and places you know **(Leçon 15)**		• The verb **connaître (Leçon 15)** • Object pronouns **le, la, les (Leçon 15)** • The verb **savoir (Leçon 16)**
Discussing relations with others • Asking others for assistance **(Leçon 14)** • Describing services of others **(Leçon 16)**	• Verbs asking for a service **(Leçon 14)** • Verbs using indirect objects **(Leçon 16)**	• Object pronouns **me, te, nous, vous (Leçon 14)** • Object pronouns **lui, leur (Leçon 16)** • Object pronouns in commands **(Leçon 14)** • Double object pronouns **(Leçon 16)**
Reading and writing about daily events • Writing a letter to a friend **(Leçon 14)** • Discussing what you like to read **(Leçon 16)** • Talking about what others have written or said **(Leçon 16)**	• Expressions used in letters **(Leçon 14)** • Reading materials **(Leçon 16)**	• The verbs **écrire, lire,** and **dire (Leçon 16)**
Narrating what happened • Talking about losing and finding things **(Leçon 15)**	• Verbs used to talk about possessions **(Leçon 15)**	• Object pronouns in the **passé composé (Leçon 15)**
READING Inferring meaning		

UNITÉ 5 Vive le sport! • CULTURAL CONTEXT Sports and health

COMMUNICATION: FUNCTIONS AND ACTIVITIES	COMMUNICATION TOPICS	LINGUISTIC GOALS
Discussing sports • Finding out what sports your friends like **(Leçon 17)** • Talking about where you practice sports and when **(Leçon 18)** • Giving your opinion **(Leçon 18)**	• Individual sports **(Leçon 17)** • Adverbs of frequency **(Leçon 18)** • Expressions of opinion **(Leçon 18)**	• The verb **courir (Leçon 17)** • The expression **faire du (Leçon 17)** • The pronouns **en** and **y (Leçon 18)**
Discussing fitness and health • Describing exercise routines **(Leçon 17)** • Describing common pains and illnesses **(Leçon 17)**	• Parts of the body **(Leçon 17)** • Health **(Leçon 17)**	• The expression **avoir mal à (Leçon 17)** • Definite article with parts of the body **(Leçon 19)**
Talking about one's daily activities • Describing the daily routine **(Leçon 19)** • Caring for one's appearance **(Leçon 19)** • Giving others advice **(Leçon 20)** • Asking about tomorrow's plans **(Leçon 20)**	• Daily occupations **(Leçon 19)** • Hygiene and personal care **(Leçon 19)**	• Reflexive verbs: present tense **(Leçon 19)** • Reflexive verbs: imperative **(Leçon 20)** • Reflexive verbs: infinitive constructions **(Leçon 20)**
Narrating past activities • Describing one's daily routine in the past **(Leçon 20)**	• Common activities **(Leçon 20)**	• Reflexive verbs: **passé composé (Leçon 20)**
READING Recognizing prefixes		

UNITÉ 6 Chez nous • CULTURAL CONTEXT House and home

COMMUNICATION: FUNCTIONS AND ACTIVITIES COMPREHENSION AND SELF-EXPRESSION	COMMUNICATION TOPICS THEMATIC VOCABULARY	LINGUISTIC GOALS ACCURACY OF EXPRESSION
Discussing where you live • Describing the location of your house or apartment **(Leçon 21)** • Explaining what your house or apartment looks like **(Leçon 21)**	• Location of one's home **(Leçon 21)** • Rooms of the house **(Leçon 21)** • Furniture and appliances **(Leçon 21)**	• The verb **vivre (Leçon 22)**
Renting an apartment or house • Reading classified ads **(Leçon 21)** • Asking about a rental **(Leçon 21)** • Giving more complete descriptions **(Leçon 22)**		• Relative pronouns **qui** and **que (Leçon 22)**
Talking about the past • Explaining what you used to do in the past and when **(Leçon 23)** • Describing ongoing past actions **(Leçon 23)** • Giving background information about specific past events **(Leçon 24)**	• Prepositions of time **(Leçon 23)** • An accident **(Leçon 24)**	• The imperfect **(Leçon 23)** • Contrasting the imperfect and the **passé composé (Leçons 23, 24)**
READING Recognizing partial cognates		

UNITÉ 7 Soyez à la mode! • CULTURAL CONTEXT Clothes and accessories

COMMUNICATION: FUNCTIONS AND ACTIVITIES COMPREHENSION AND SELF-EXPRESSION	COMMUNICATION TOPICS THEMATIC VOCABULARY	LINGUISTIC GOALS ACCURACY OF EXPRESSION
Talking about clothes • Saying what people are wearing **(Leçon 25)** • Describing clothes and accessories **(Leçon 25)**	• Clothes and accessories **(Leçon 25)** • Colors **(Leçon 25)** • Fabric, design, materials **(Leçon 25)**	
Shopping for clothes • Talking with the sales clerk **(Leçon 25)** • Expressing opinions **(Leçon 25)**	• Types of clothing stores **(Leçon 25)** • Sizes, looks, and price **(Leçon 25)** • Numbers 100-1,000,000 **(Leçon 26)** • Adjectives **beau, nouveau, vieux (Leçon 26)**	
Comparing people and things • Ranking items in a series **(Leçon 26)** • Expressing comparisons **(Leçon 27)** • Saying who or what is the best **(Leçon 27)** • Referring to specific items **(Leçon 28)**	• Descriptive adjectives **(Leçon 27)**	• Ordinal numbers **(Leçon 26)** • Comparisons with adjectives **(Leçon 27)** • Superlative constructions **(Leçon 27)** • Pronouns **lequel?** and **celui (Leçon 28)**
Talking about how things are done • Describing how things are done **(Leçon 26)** • Comparing how things are done **(Leçon 27)**	• Common adverbs **(Leçon 27)**	• Adverbs ending in **-ment (Leçon 26)** • Comparisons with adverbs **(Leçon 27)**
READING Understanding the context		

LEVEL 2 CONTINUED

UNITÉ 8 Bonnes vacances • CULTURAL CONTEXT Travel and summer vacations

COMMUNICATION: FUNCTIONS AND ACTIVITIES COMPREHENSION AND SELF-EXPRESSION	COMMUNICATION TOPICS THEMATIC VOCABULARY	LINGUISTIC GOALS ACCURACY OF EXPRESSION
Discussing summer vacations • Talking about vacation plans **(Leçon 29)** • Planning a camping trip **(Leçon 29)**	• Destinations, lodging, travel documents **(Leçon 29)** • Foreign countries **(Leçon 29)** • Camping equipment **(Leçon 29)**	• Prepositions with names of countries **(Leçon 30)** • The verbs **recevoir** and **apercevoir (Leçon 30)**
Making travel arrangements • Buying tickets **(Leçon 29)** • Checking schedules **(Leçon 29)** • Expressing polite requests **(Leçon 32)**	• At the train station, at the airport **(Leçon 29)**	• The use of the conditional to make polite requests **(Leçon 32)**
Talking about what you would do under various circumstances	• Verbs followed by infinitives **(Leçon 30)**	• The constructions verb **+ à +** infinitive, verb **+ de +** infinitive **(Leçon 30)**
Making future plans • Talking about the future **(Leçon 31)** • Setting forth conditions **(Leçon 31)**		• The future tense **(Leçon 31)** • The future with **si**-clauses **(Leçon 31)** • The future with **quand (Leçon 31)**
Talking about what one would do under certain circumstances • Discussing what would occur **(Leçon 32)** • Describing conditions **(Leçon 32)**		• The conditional **(Leçon 32)** • The conditional with **si**-clauses **(Leçon 32)**

READING Recognizing false cognates

UNITÉ 9 Bonne route • CULTURAL CONTEXT Getting around by car

COMMUNICATION: FUNCTIONS AND ACTIVITIES COMPREHENSION AND SELF-EXPRESSION	COMMUNICATION TOPICS THEMATIC VOCABULARY	LINGUISTIC GOALS ACCURACY OF EXPRESSION
Talking about cars • Describing cars **(Leçon 33)** • Having one's car serviced **(Leçon 33)** • Getting one's license **(Leçon 33)** • Rules of right of way **(Leçon 33)**	• Types of vehicles **(Leçon 33)** • Parts of a car **(Leçon 33)** • Car maintenance **(Leçon 33)**	• The verbs **conduire** and **suivre (Leçon 33)**
Expressing how one feels about certain events		• Adjective **+ de +** infinitive **(Leçon 34)**
Talking about past and present events • Describing purpose and sequence **(Leçon 34)** • Describing simultaneous actions and cause and effect **(Leçon 34)**	• Prepositions **pour, sans, avant de,** and **en (Leçon 34)**	• Preposition + infinitive **(Leçon 34)** • Present participle constructions **(Leçon 34)**
Discussing what has to be done • Expressing necessity and obligation **(Leçon 35)** • Letting others know what you want them to do **(Leçon 36)**	• **Il faut que (Leçon 35)** • **Je veux que (Leçon 36)**	• Present subjunctive: regular forms **(Leçon 35)** • Present subjunctive: irregular forms **(Leçon 36)**

READING Recognizing figures of speech

Level 3 Scope and Sequence

REPRISE • OBJECTIVE Light Review of Basic Material (from Levels One and Two)

BASIC REVIEW		CULTURE AND READING
Structures	**Vocabulary**	**Vacation Options** Travel, sports, archaeology, helping others
A. La vie courante Describing the present • Present of regular verbs • **Être, avoir, aller, faire, venir** and expressions used with these verbs • Other common irregular verbs • Use of present with **depuis** • Regular and irregular adjectives • Use of the partitive article	• Daily activities • Food and beverages	The French-speaking world: Its people
B. Hier et avant Describing the past • **Passé composé** with **avoir** and **être** • Imperfect and its basic uses	• Clothes	The French-speaking world: Cultural background
C. Nous et les autres Referring to people, things, and places • Object pronouns • Negative expressions • **Connaître** and **savoir** • Other irregular verbs		**Lecture: *Les trois bagues***

UNITÉ 1 Au jour le jour • MAIN THEMES Looking good; one's daily routine

COMMUNICATION OBJECTIVES		READING AND CULTURAL OBJECTIVES		**Interlude Culturel 1** Le monde des arts
Communication: Functions and Contexts LE FRANÇAIS PRATIQUE	**Linguistic Goals** LANGUE ET COMMUNICATION	**Daily life** INFO MAGAZINE	**Reading** LECTURE	GENERAL CULTURAL BACKGROUND
Describing people • Their physical appearance **Caring for one's appearance** • Personal care and hygiene • Looking good **Describing the various aspects of one's daily routine** **Expressing how one feels and inquiring about other people**	**Describing people and their ailments** • The use of the definite article **Describing what people do for themselves** • Reflexive verbs **Explaining one's daily activities** • Reflexive verbs: different tenses and uses	**How important is personal appearance for French young people and what do they do to enhance it?** • The importance of **le look** • Clothing and personal style **How have artists expressed their concept of beauty?** **How do people begin their daily routine?**	**Ionesco, *Conte pour enfants de moins de trois ans***	**French modern art** • **Impressionism** and impressionist artists: **Monet, Degas, Renoir, Manet, B. Morisot** • Artists of the **post-impressionist** era: **Van Gogh, Gauguin, Matisse, Rousseau, Toulouse-Lautrec** • **Surrealism** as an artistic and literary movement: **Magritte** **Poems** • **Desnos, *La fourmi*** • **Prévert, *Pour faire le portrait d'un oiseau***

UNITÉ 2 Soyons utiles! • MAIN THEME Being helpful around the house

COMMUNICATION OBJECTIVES		READING AND CULTURAL OBJECTIVES		Interlude Culturel 2 Les grands moments de l'histoire de France (jusqu'en 1453)
COMMUNICATION: FUNCTIONS AND CONTEXTS LE FRANÇAIS PRATIQUE	**LINGUISTIC GOALS** LANGUE ET COMMUNICATION	**DAILY LIFE** INFO MAGAZINE	**READING** LECTURE	GENERAL CULTURAL BACKGROUND
Helping around the house • In the house itself • Outside **Asking for help and offering to help** • Accepting or refusing help • Thanking people for their help **Describing an object** • Shape, weight, length, consistency, appearance, etc. • The material it is made of	**Explaining what has to be done** • **Il faut que** + subjunctive **Telling people what you would like them to do** • **Vouloir que** + subjunctive	**Why do French people enjoy do-it-yourself activities?** • What is **bricolage?** • What is **jardinage?** **How should you take care of your plants?** **How do French young people earn money by helping their neighbors?**	***La Couverture*** *(Une fable médiévale)*	**Early French history** • Important events The Roman conquest The Holy Roman Empire The Norman Conquest of England The Hundred Years War • Important people **Vercingétorix** **Charlemagne** **Guillaume le Conquérant** **Aliénor d'Aquitaine** **Jeanne d'Arc** **Literature: *La Chanson de Roland***

UNITÉ 3 Vive la nature! • MAIN THEMES Vacation and outdoor activities; the environment and its protection

COMMUNICATION: FUNCTIONS AND CONTEXTS	LINGUISTIC GOALS	DAILY LIFE	READING	Interlude Culturel 3 Les grands moments de l'histoire de France (1453-1715) — GENERAL CULTURAL BACKGROUND
Talking about outdoor activities • What to do • What not to do **Describing the natural environment and how to protect it** **Talking about the weather and natural phenomena** **Relating a sequence of past events** **Describing habitual past actions**	**Talking about the past** • The **passé composé** • The imperfect • The **passé simple** • Contrastive uses of the **passé composé** and the imperfect **Narrating past events** • Differentiating between specific actions **(passé composé)** and the circumstances under which they occurred (imperfect) • Providing background information (imperfect)	**How do the French feel about nature and their land?** • What is **le tourisme vert?** • What is an **éco-musée?** **How do the French protect their environment?** • What rules to observe on camping trips • What young people do to protect the environment • Who was **Jacques-Yves Cousteau?** **Why do the French people love the sun?**	**Sempé / Goscinny, *King***	**The classical period of French history** • Important periods: **la Renaissance, le Grand Siècle** • Important people: **François Ier, Louis XIV** • French castles, as witnesses of French history **Literature** • **La Fontaine, *Le Corbeau et le renard*** • **Prévert, *Soyons polis*** **Film: Rostand, *Cyrano de Bergerac***

UNITÉ 4 Aspects de la vie quotidienne • MAIN THEME Going shopping and asking for services

COMMUNICATION OBJECTIVES		READING AND CULTURAL OBJECTIVES		Interlude Culturel 4 Vive la musique!
Communication: Functions and Contexts LE FRANÇAIS PRATIQUE	**Linguistic Goals** LANGUE ET COMMUNICATION	**Daily Life** INFO MAGAZINE	**Reading** LECTURE	GENERAL CULTURAL BACKGROUND
Shopping for various items • in a stationery store • in a pharmacy • in a convenience store **Buying stamps and mailing items at the post office** **Having one's hair cut** **Asking for a variety of services** • at the cleaners • at the shoe repair shop • at the photo shop	**Answering questions and referring to people, things, and places using pronouns** • Object pronouns • Two-pronoun sequence **Talking about quantities** • The pronoun **en** • Indefinite expressions of quantity **Describing services that you have done by other people** • The construction **faire +** infinitive	**How are certain aspects of daily life different in France?** • Shopping on the Internet • Shopping in a supermarket • Services at the post office • When to tip and not to tip	***Histoire de cheveux***	**The musical landscape of France and the French-speaking world** • Classical musicians: **Lully, Chopin, Bizet, Debussy** • Historical overview of French songs • Famous French singers of yesterday and today • The multicultural aspect of music from the francophone world: **zouk** (Antilles); **raï** (North Africa); **cajun, zydéco** (Louisiana) **Song: Vigneault, *Mon pays*** **Opera: Bizet, *Carmen***

UNITÉ 5 Bon voyage! • MAIN THEME Travel

COMMUNICATION OBJECTIVES		READING AND CULTURAL OBJECTIVES		Interlude Culturel 5 Les grands moments de l'histoire de France (1715-1870)
				GENERAL CULTURAL BACKGROUND
Planning a trip abroad **Going through customs** **Making travel arrangements** • Purchasing tickets **Travel in France** • at the train station • at the airport	**Making negative statements** • Affirmative and negative expressions **Describing future plans** • Future tense • Use of future after **quand** **Hypothesizing about what one would do** • Introduction to the conditional	**What are the advantages of visiting France by train?** • The **TGV** • The **Eurotunnel** **Why do French people like to travel abroad and what do they do on their vacations?** • Impressions of young people visiting the United States	***Le mystérieux homme en bleu***	**The historical foundation of modern France** • Important periods the **French Revolution** the **Napoleonic era** • Important contemporary French institutions • Important people **Louis XVI et Marie-Antoinette** **Napoléon** **Song: Rouget de Lisle, *La Marseillaise*** **Literature: Victor Hugo, *Les Misérables***

UNITÉ 6 Séjour en France • MAIN THEME Hotels and other places to stay when traveling

COMMUNICATION OBJECTIVES		READING AND CULTURAL OBJECTIVES		**Interlude Culturel 6** Les grands moments de l'histoire de France (1870 au présent)
COMMUNICATION: FUNCTIONS AND CONTEXTS LE FRANÇAIS PRATIQUE	**LINGUISTIC GOALS** LANGUE ET COMMUNICATION	**DAILY LIFE** INFO MAGAZINE	**READING** LECTURE	GENERAL CULTURAL BACKGROUND
Deciding where to stay when traveling **Reserving a room in a hotel** **Asking for services in a hotel**	**Comparing people, things, places and situations** • The comparative • The superlative **Asking for an alternative** • The interrogative pronoun **lequel?** **Pointing out people or things** • The demonstrative pronoun **celui** **Indicating possession** • The possessive pronoun **le mien**	**What inexpensive accommodations are available to students?** • **Auberges de jeunesse** • **Séjour à la ferme** **How does one use the *Guide Michelin* when traveling in France?** • To find a hotel • To choose a restaurant	***Une étrange aventure***	**France in the 20th century** • Important events the two World Wars the economic union of Europe • Important people **Marie Curie** **Charles de Gaulle** **Simone Veil** **Literature: Éluard, *Liberté*** **Film: L. Malle, *Au revoir, les Enfants***

UNITÉ 7 La forme et la santé • MAIN THEME Health and medical care

COMMUNICATION: FUNCTIONS AND CONTEXTS	LINGUISTIC GOALS	DAILY LIFE	READING	**Interlude Culturel 7** Les Français d'aujourd'hui — GENERAL CULTURAL BACKGROUND
Going to the doctor's office • Describing your symptoms • Explaining what is wrong • Giving information about your medical history • Understanding the doctor's prescriptions **Going to the dentist** **Going to the emergency ward**	**Expressing how you and others feel about certain facts or events** • Use of the subjunctive after expressions of emotion **Expressing fear, doubt or disbelief** • Use of the subjunctive after expressions of doubt and uncertainty **Expressing feelings or attitudes about past actions and events** • The past subjunctive	**How do the French take care of their health?** • How does the French health system work? • What is the **Sécurité sociale?** • Why do the French consume so much mineral water? • What is **thermalisme?** **How do French doctors participate in humanitarian missions around the world?** • What is **Médecins sans frontières?**	**Maupassant, *En voyage***	**Modern France as a multi-ethnic and multi-cultural society** • The French as citizens of Europe • The new French mosaic: the impact of immigration on French society • The **Maghrébins** – their culture and their religion • **SOS Racisme** • Two French humanitarians: **L'abbé Pierre** and **Coluche** **Song: *Éthiopie***

UNITÉ 8 En ville • MAIN THEME Cities and city life

COMMUNICATION: FUNCTIONS AND CONTEXTS	LINGUISTIC GOALS	DAILY LIFE	READING	**Interlude Culturel 8** Les Antilles francophones — GENERAL CULTURAL BACKGROUND
Making a date and fixing the time and place **Explaining where one lives and how to get there** **Discussing the advantages and disadvantages of city life**	**Narrating past actions in sequence** • The pluperfect **Formulating polite requests** • The conditional **Hypothesizing about what one would do under certain circumstances** • The conditional and its uses • The past conditional • Sequence of tenses in **si**-clauses	**What does a typical French city look like?** • Its historical development • Its various neighborhoods • Its buildings • The **villes nouvelles** **Why do French people love to stroll in the streets?** • Various street shows • Sculptures to view while walking in Paris	**Theuriet, *Les Pêches***	**The French-speaking Caribbean islands** • Historical background • Important people **Toussaint Louverture** **Joséphine de Beauharnais** **Aimé Césaire** • Haitian art as an expression of life **Literature: Césaire, *Pour saluer le Tiers-Monde*** **Film: Palcy, *Rue Cases-nègres***

UNITÉ 9 Les relations personnelles • MAIN THEME Personal relationships, friendships, and family life

COMMUNICATION OBJECTIVES		READING AND CULTURAL OBJECTIVES		Interlude Culturel 9 L'Afrique dans la communauté francophone
Communication: Functions and Contexts LE FRANÇAIS PRATIQUE	**Linguistic Goals** LANGUE ET COMMUNICATION	**Daily Life** INFO MAGAZINE	**Reading** LECTURE	GENERAL CULTURAL BACKGROUND
Describing degrees of friendship **Expressing different feelings towards other people** **Discussing the state of one's relationship with other people** **Congratulating, comforting, and expressing sympathy for other people** **Describing the various phases of a person's life**	**Describing how people interact** • Reciprocal use of reflexive verbs **Describing people and things in complex sentences** • Relative pronouns • Relative clauses	**How important are friends and family to French people?** • The meaning of friendship • Family relationships **How socially concerned are French young people and what type of social outreach do they do?** **What is a typical French wedding like?** • Where French spouses meet one another • Planning the wedding • A French wedding ceremony	**M. Maurois, *Le Bracelet***	**The place of Western and Central Africa in the francophone world** • Historical periods and events: prehistory, the **African empires,** colonization, and independence • Basic facts about Western Africa language and culture religions and traditions • **African art** and its influence on European art **African Fable: *La Gélinotte et la Tortue*** **Literature** • **D. Diop, *Afrique*** • **Dadié, *La légende baoulé***

UNITÉ 10 Vers la vie active • MAIN THEME University studies and careers

COMMUNICATION: FUNCTIONS AND CONTEXTS	LINGUISTIC GOALS	DAILY LIFE	READING	Interlude Culturel 10 La France et le Nouveau Monde GENERAL CULTURAL BACKGROUND
Deciding on a college major • University courses **Planning for a career** • Professions • The work environment • Different types of industries **Looking for a job** • Preparing a résumé • Describing one's qualifications at a job interview	**Describing simultaneous actions** • The present participle **Explaining the purpose of an action** • **Pour** + infinitive • **Pour que** + subjunctive **Explaining the timing, conditions, and constraints of an action** • The use of the infinitive or the subjunctive after certain prepositions and conjunctions	**How important is academic success to French young people?** • The French school system: high schools and universities • **Le bac:** its history and its importance **What does one do after graduation?** • Choosing a profession • **Le service militaire** **How does one interview for a job?** • Preparing for the interview • Writing a résumé in French	**Thériault, *Le Portrait***	**The French presence in North America** • Historical background The French in Canada and Louisiana • Important people **Jacques Cartier, Jeanne Mance, Cavelier de La Salle** • Why certain American cities have French names **Song: Richard, *Réveille*** **Literature: La Fayette, *Lettre à sa femme***

Setting the Stage for Communication

The Unit Opener presents the unit theme and communicative objectives.

There are **four thematically-linked lessons** in each unit. Vocabulary presented in the first lesson (*Le français pratique*) is then used throughout the next three lessons as structure is taught, reinforcing the unit theme.

Unit Theme and Objectives preview for the students what they will be able to do at the end of the unit.

DVD and audio icons indicate the variety of resources that support lesson content.

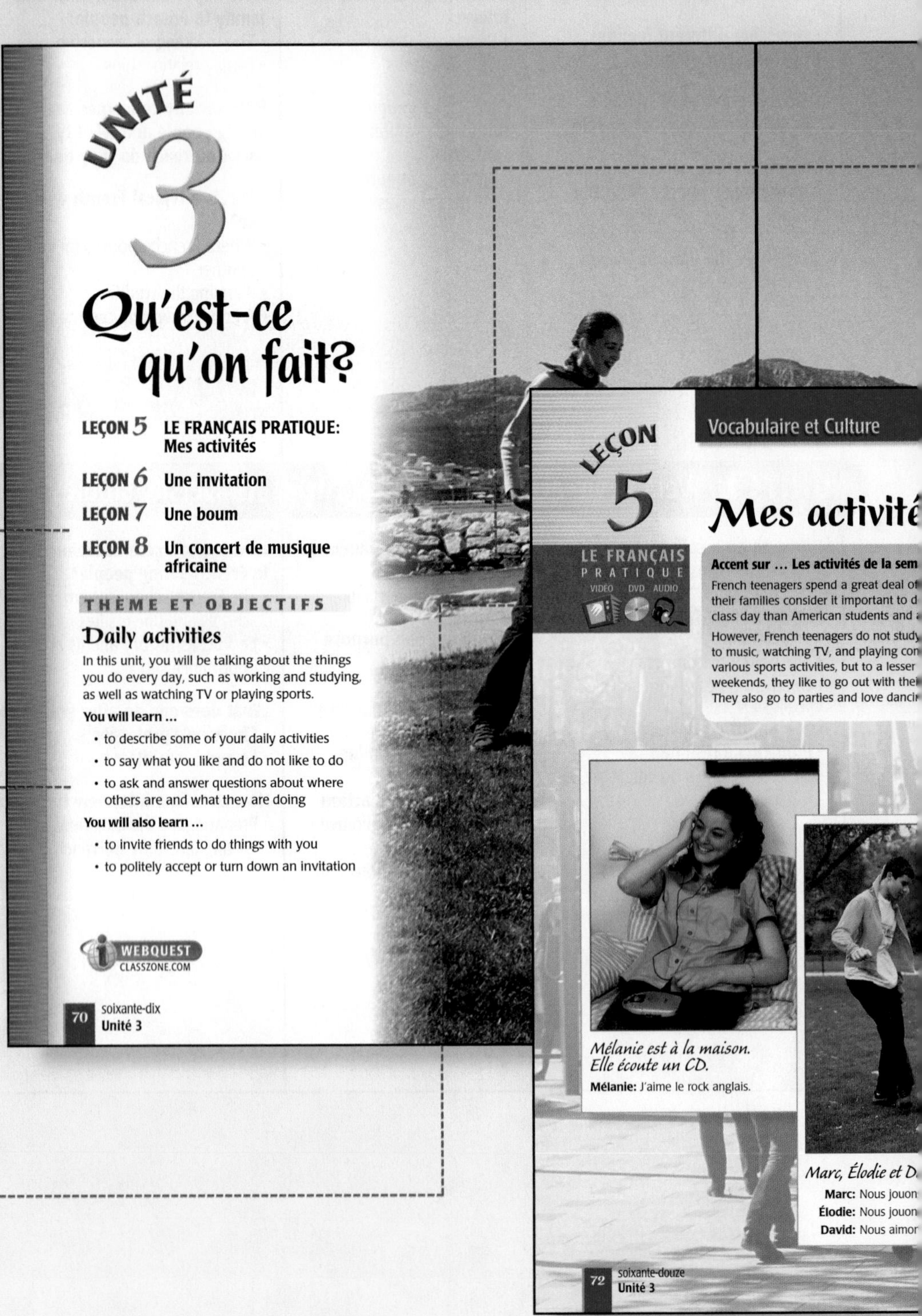

UNITÉ 3
Qu'est-ce qu'on fait?
LEÇON 5 LE FRANÇAIS PRATIQUE: Mes activités
LEÇON 6 Une invitation
LEÇON 7 Une boum
LEÇON 8 Un concert de musique africaine
THÈME ET OBJECTIFS
Daily activities
In this unit, you will be talking about the things you do every day, such as working and studying, as well as watching TV or playing sports.
You will learn ...
• to describe some of your daily activities
• to say what you like and do not like to do
• to ask and answer questions about where others are and what they are doing
You will also learn ...
• to invite friends to do things with you
• to politely accept or turn down an invitation
WEBQUEST
CLASSZONE.COM
70 soixante-dix
Unité 3
LEÇON 5
LE FRANÇAIS PRATIQUE
VIDÉO DVD AUDIO
Vocabulaire et Culture
Mes activité
Mélanie est à la maison. Elle écoute un CD.
Mélanie: J'aime le rock anglais.
72 soixante-douze
Unité 3

The Lesson Opener provides cultural and linguistic background and a visual overview of the contents of the lesson.

Le français pratique presents the communicative focus and functional language of the unit. Students immediately get and give information in French.

The **thematic presentation** introduces students to the lesson content. The video program provides additional cross-cultural interactions.

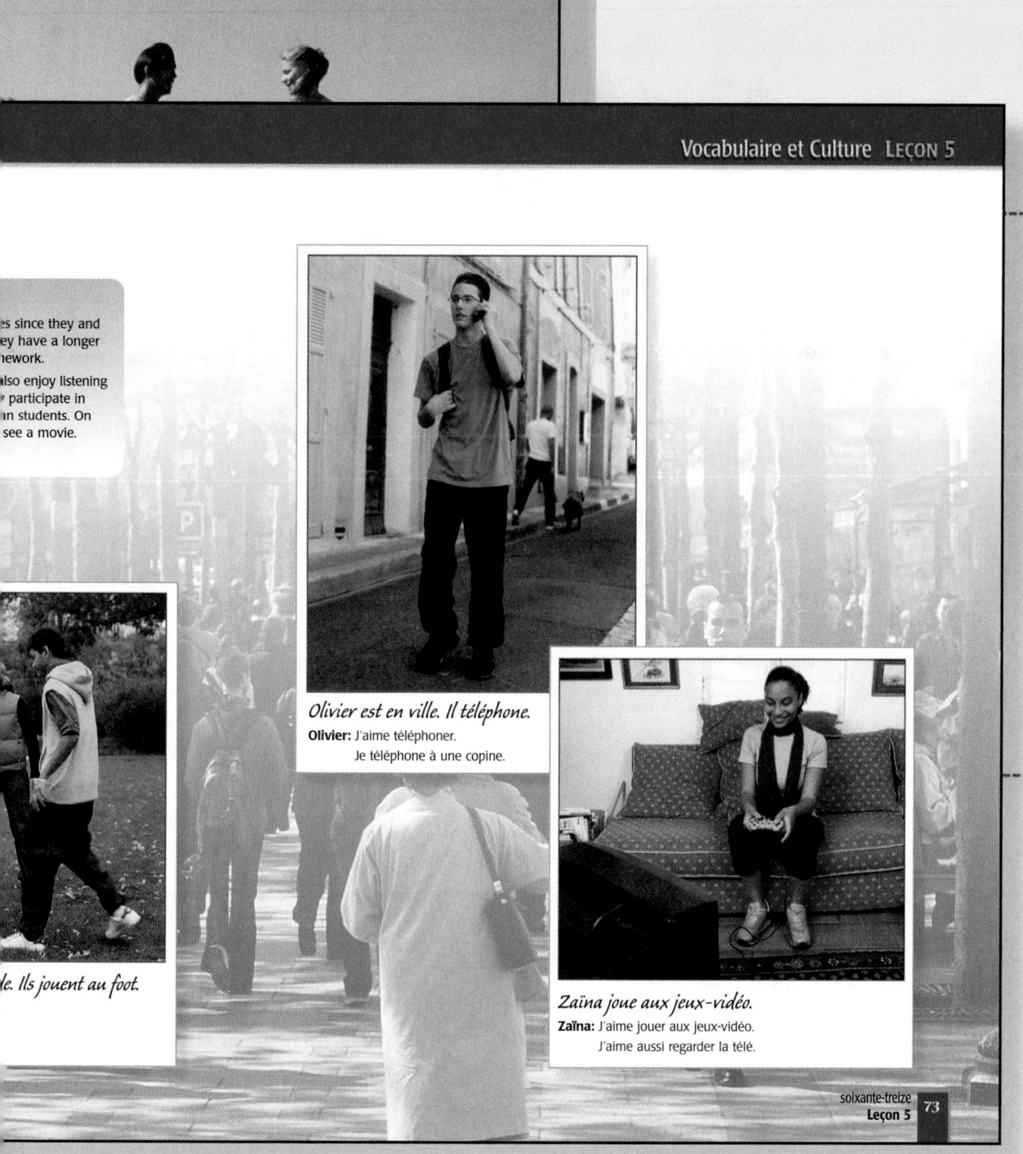

Vocabulaire et Culture LEÇON 5
es since they and
ey have a longer
nework.
also enjoy listening
participate in
an students. On
see a movie.
Olivier est en ville. Il téléphone.
Olivier: J'aime téléphoner.
Je téléphone à une copine.
le. Ils jouent au foot.
Zaïna joue aux jeux-vidéo.
Zaïna: J'aime jouer aux jeux-vidéo.
J'aime aussi regarder la télé.
soixante-treize
Leçon 5 73

Students are introduced to the **language** patterns of the unit **in context**.

Discovering FRENCH Nouveau!

Strengthen proficiency

The *Vocabulaire et communication* sections of *Le français pratique* lessons present new conversational patterns by function.

New vocabulary and related conversational patterns are introduced in **thematic context**. All vocabulary is coded in yellow; functions are highlighted with a red triangle and darker yellow band.

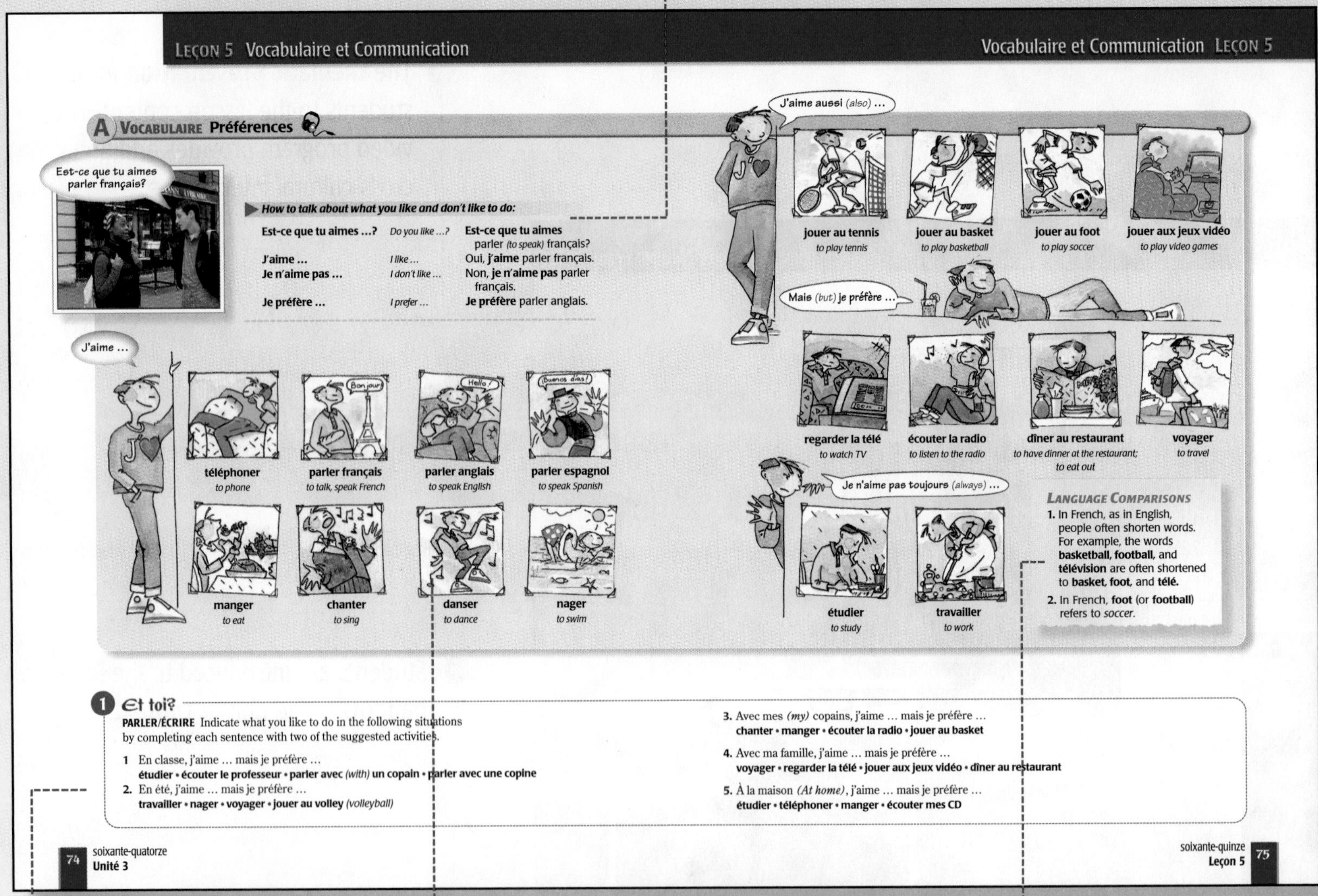

LEÇON 5 Vocabulaire et Communication

Vocabulaire et Communication LEÇON 5

A VOCABULAIRE Préférences

▶ *How to talk about what you like and don't like to do:*

Est-ce que tu aimes ...?	*Do you like ...?*	**Est-ce que tu aimes** parler *(to speak)* français?
J'aime ...	*I like ...*	Oui, **j'aime** parler français.
Je n'aime pas ...	*I don't like ...*	Non, **je n'aime pas** parler français.
Je préfère ...	*I prefer ...*	**Je préfère** parler anglais.

téléphoner *to phone*
parler français *to talk, speak French*
parler anglais *to speak English*
parler espagnol *to speak Spanish*
manger *to eat*
chanter *to sing*
danser *to dance*
nager *to swim*

jouer au tennis *to play tennis*
jouer au basket *to play basketball*
jouer au foot *to play soccer*
jouer aux jeux vidéo *to play video games*

regarder la télé *to watch TV*
écouter la radio *to listen to the radio*
dîner au restaurant *to have dinner at the restaurant; to eat out*
voyager *to travel*

étudier *to study*
travailler *to work*

LANGUAGE COMPARISONS

1. In French, as in English, people often shorten words. For example, the words **basketball, football,** and **télévision** are often shortened to **basket, foot,** and **télé.**
2. In French, **foot** (or **football**) refers to *soccer.*

1 Et toi?

PARLER/ÉCRIRE Indicate what you like to do in the following situations by completing each sentence with two of the suggested activities.

1. En classe, j'aime ... mais je préfère ...
   étudier • écouter le professeur • parler avec *(with)* **un copain • parler avec une copine**
2. En été, j'aime ... mais je préfère ...
   travailler • nager • voyager • jouer au volley *(volleyball)*
3. Avec mes *(my)* copains, j'aime ... mais je préfère ...
   chanter • manger • écouter la radio • jouer au basket
4. Avec ma famille, j'aime ... mais je préfère ...
   voyager • regarder la télé • jouer aux jeux vidéo • dîner au restaurant
5. À la maison *(At home)*, j'aime ... mais je préfère ...
   étudier • téléphoner • manger • écouter mes CD

74 soixante-quatorze Unité 3

soixante-quinze Leçon 5 75

Student-centered activities practice new vocabulary in contexts ranging from structured to open-ended self-expression.

Art-cued vocabulary is used to help the visual learner and provide a functional cultural context. Since the artists used in *Discovering French, Nouveau!* are actually French, students are exposed to authentic cultural detail in every drawing.

Language comparisons help students understand how language functions.

Each *Le français pratique* lesson moves through functional introduction of language practice activities, and culminates in the *À votre tour* review section.

- ***À votre tour*** activities recombine material from each lesson as well as previous units. These open-ended activities allow students to demonstrate what they can do with the language and to monitor their own progress through critical thinking and self-expression.

- ***Objectifs*** remind students of what they've learned and why.

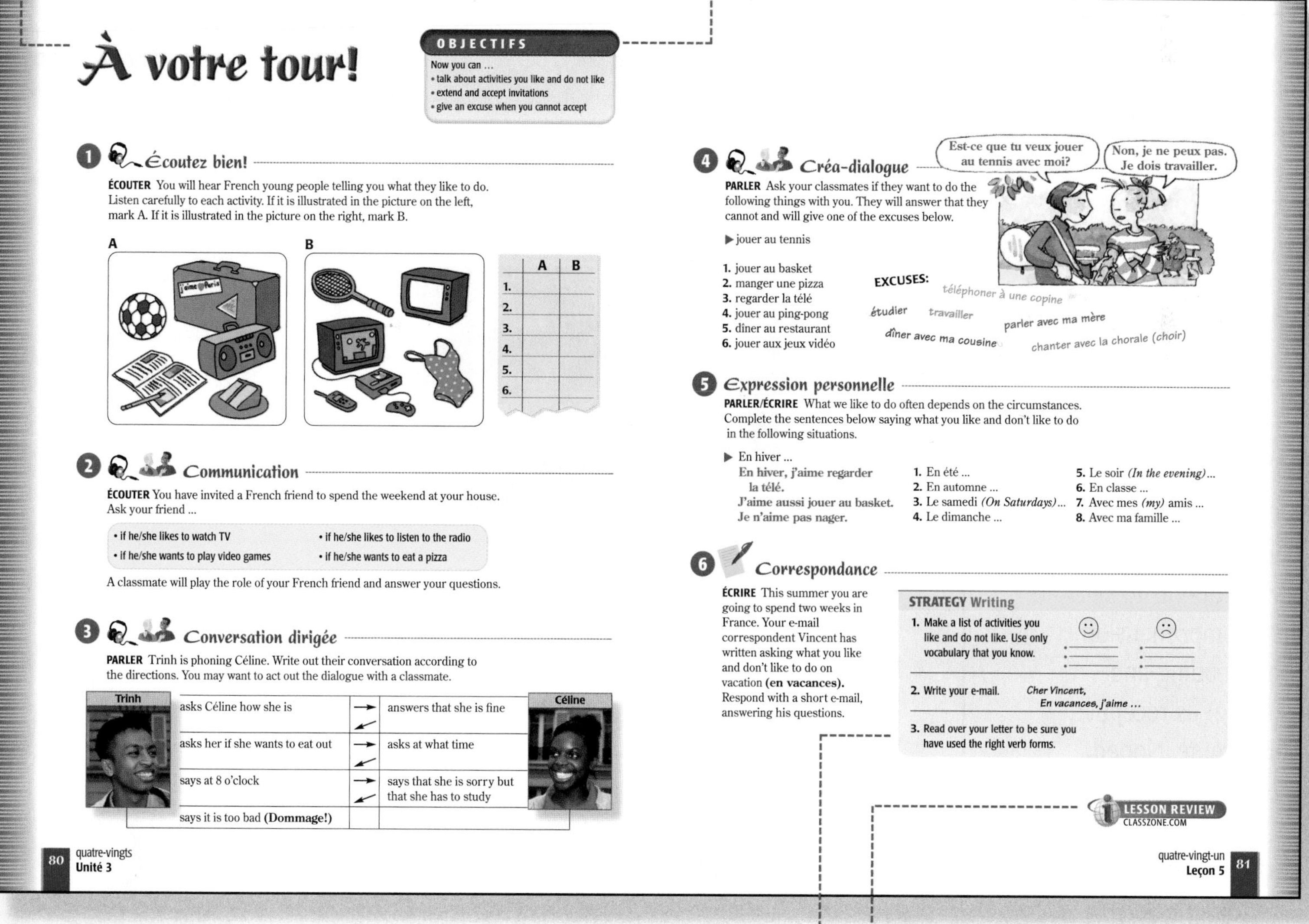

À votre tour!

OBJECTIFS
Now you can ...
- talk about activities you like and do not like
- extend and accept invitations
- give an excuse when you cannot accept

1 Écoutez bien!

ÉCOUTER You will hear French young people telling you what they like to do. Listen carefully to each activity. If it is illustrated in the picture on the left, mark A. If it is illustrated in the picture on the right, mark B.

A | B

	A	B
1.		
2.		
3.		
4.		
5.		
6.		

2 Communication

ÉCOUTER You have invited a French friend to spend the weekend at your house. Ask your friend ...

- if he/she likes to watch TV
- if he/she wants to play video games
- if he/she likes to listen to the radio
- if he/she wants to eat a pizza

A classmate will play the role of your French friend and answer your questions.

3 Conversation dirigée

PARLER Trinh is phoning Céline. Write out their conversation according to the directions. You may want to act out the dialogue with a classmate.

Trinh		Céline
asks Céline how she is	→ ←	answers that she is fine
asks her if she wants to eat out	→ ←	asks at what time
says at 8 o'clock	→ ←	says that she is sorry but that she has to study
says it is too bad **(Dommage!)**		

4 Créa-dialogue

PARLER Ask your classmates if they want to do the following things with you. They will answer that they cannot and will give one of the excuses below.

▶ jouer au tennis

1. jouer au basket
2. manger une pizza
3. regarder la télé
4. jouer au ping-pong
5. dîner au restaurant
6. jouer aux jeux vidéo

EXCUSES: téléphoner à une copine, étudier, travailler, parler avec ma mère, dîner avec ma cousine, chanter avec la chorale (choir)

5 Expression personnelle

PARLER/ÉCRIRE What we like to do often depends on the circumstances. Complete the sentences below saying what you like and don't like to do in the following situations.

▶ En hiver ...
En hiver, j'aime regarder la télé. J'aime aussi jouer au basket. Je n'aime pas nager.

1. En été ...
2. En automne ...
3. Le samedi *(On Saturdays)*...
4. Le dimanche ...
5. Le soir *(In the evening)*...
6. En classe ...
7. Avec mes *(my)* amis ...
8. Avec ma famille ...

6 Correspondance

ÉCRIRE This summer you are going to spend two weeks in France. Your e-mail correspondent Vincent has written asking what you like and don't like to do on vacation **(en vacances).** Respond with a short e-mail, answering his questions.

STRATEGY Writing
1. Make a list of activities you like and do not like. Use only vocabulary that you know.
2. Write your e-mail. *Cher Vincent, En vacances, j'aime ...*
3. Read over your letter to be sure you have used the right verb forms.

LESSON REVIEW CLASSZONE.COM

80 quatre-vingts Unité 3

quatre-vingt-un Leçon 5 81

- **Writing strategies** offer important tips for improving writing skills.

- **Web icons** guide students to relevant online materials at ClassZone.com

Build accuracy

***Conversation et Culture* lesson openers present reading and culture as they recycle the communicative functions of *Le français pratique* vocabulary and provide grammar support and explanation.**

The opening **reading and/or video dialog** provides a context for the communicative functions and presentation of linguistic structures. You may vary your presentation of the new language according to the needs of your students, addressing a variety of learner types.

Comprehension checks allow students to self-check their comprehension (both reading and listening) as receptive skills are developed.

LEÇON 7 Conversation et Culture

AUDIO

Une boum

Jean-Marc has been invited to a party. He is trying to decide whether to bring Béatrice or Valérie.

LEÇON 6 Conversation et Culture

VIDÉO DVD AUDIO

Une invitation

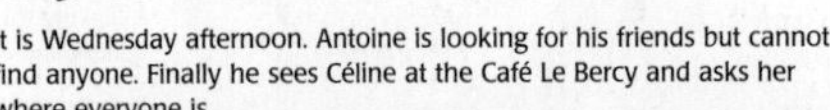

It is Wednesday afternoon. Antoine is looking for his friends but cannot find anyone. Finally he sees Céline at the Café Le Bercy and asks her where everyone is.

Antoine:	Où est Léa?	*Where*
Céline:	Elle est à la maison.	*at home*
Antoine:	Et Mathieu? Il est là?	*here*
Céline:	Non, il n'est pas là.	
Antoine:	Où est-il?	
Céline:	Il est en ville avec une copine.	*in town*
Antoine:	Et Julie et Stéphanie? Est-ce qu'elles sont ici?	*here*
Céline:	Non, elles sont au restaurant.	
Antoine:	Alors, qui est là?	*So*
Céline:	Moi, je suis ici.	
Antoine:	C'est vrai, tu es ici! Eh bien, puisque tu es là, je t'invite au cinéma. D'accord?	*true / since* *I'll invite you to the movies.*
Céline:	Super! Antoine, tu es un vrai copain!	*real*

Compréhension

Indicate where the following people are by selecting the appropriate completions.

1. Léa est ...
2. Mathieu est ...
3. Julie et Stéphanie sont ...
4. Antoine et Céline sont ...

en ville · au café · à la maison · au restaurant

NOTE culturelle

Le mercredi après-midi

French middle school students do not usually have classe[s] Wednesday afternoons. Some young people use this free time to go out with their friends or to catch up on their homework. For other students, Wednesday afternoon is the time for music and dance lessons as well as sports activities. Many students play soccer with their school tea[m] with their local sports club. Other popular activities inclu[de] tennis, skateboarding, and in-line skating.

COMPARAISONS CULTURELLES

How does the school week in France compare to the school week in the United States?

- Do you see any differences in the ways French and American teenagers spend their free time? Explain.
- Do American and French teenagers like the same sports? Explain.

Conversation et Culture

Conversation et Culture LEÇON 8

LEÇON 8

Un concert de musique africaine

VIDÉO DVD AUDIO

Nicolas is at a café with his new friend Fatou. He is interviewing her for an article in his school newspaper.

Conversation et Culture LEÇON 7

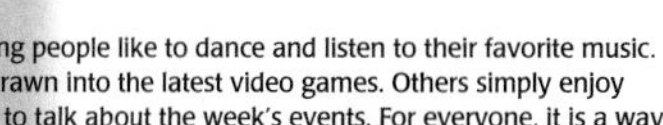

Une boum

On weekends, French teenagers like to go to parties that are organized at a friend's home. These informal parties have different names according to the age group of the participants. For students at a **collège** (middle school), a party is sometimes known as **une boum** or **une fête.** For older students at a **lycée** (high school), it is called

...ents are usually around to help out and set up a ...en features items contributed by the guests. Pizza ...ery popular. There may also be homemade ...Chinese food. Preferred beverages are sodas and

...ng people like to dance and listen to their favorite music. ...drawn into the latest video games. Others simply enjoy ... to talk about the week's events. For everyone, it is a way ...o spend a relaxing evening with friends.

et Culture LEÇON 6

COMPARAISONS CULTURELLES

How do French parties compare to parties that you and your friends organize? Explain.

quatre-vingt-treize
Leçon 7 93

Dakar, Sénégal

Le Sénégal
* Dakar

EN BREF: Le Sénégal
Capitale: Dakar
Population: 10 000 000
Langue officielle: français

A former French colony, Senegal became an independent republic in 1960. Its population is divided into about a dozen ethnic groups, each with its own language, the most important being **wolof** and **pulaar.**

Youssou N'Dour

Youssou N'Dour is an internationally known musician from Senegal who combines traditional African music with pop, rock, and jazz. He sings in French and English, as well as in three Senegalese dialects. His lyrics promote African unity and human dignity. In many of his songs, he also plays the **tama**, a traditional Senegalese drum covered with reptile skins.

Le tama

Des jeunes Sénégalais

CONNEXIONS Senegal and African Music

- As a class project, make a display board on Senegal, using information and pictures from travel brochures or from the Internet.
- Obtain a CD of Youssou N'Dour or of music from another French-African country and play your favorite selection for the class.

cent cinq
Leçon 8 105

Connexions offer real world activities that engage students and promote cultural awareness.

quatre-vingt-trois
Leçon 6 83

Notes culturelles, coded in blue throughout the program, expand on the cultural content of the lesson opener. Further cultural expansion is also available on video, correlated at point-of-use in the Teacher's Edition.

Langue et communication **pages present grammatical structures in a variety of formats appropriate to varied learning styles, including model sentences, visual representations, cartoons, summary boxes, and charts.**

Listening icons highlight the listening strand in the student books.

Coded in green, the **structure sections** clearly and concisely summarize essential grammar points. Sample sentences are provided to present material in meaningful context.

Pair and group activities allow students to communicate and exchange information while practicing new structures in both guided and open-ended activities.

LEÇON 8 Langue et Communication

A Les questions d'information

The questions below ask for specific information and are called INFORMATION QUESTIONS. The INTERROGATIVE EXPRESSIONS in heavy print indicate what kind of information is requested.

—**Où** est-ce que tu habites?	***Where*** *do you live?*
—J'habite **à Nice.**	*I live* ***in Nice.***
—**À quelle heure** est-ce que vous dînez?	***At what time*** *do you eat dinner?*
—Nous dînons **à sept heures.**	*We eat* ***at seven.***

→ In French, information questions may be formed according to the pattern:

INTERROGATIVE EXPRESSION	+ **est-ce que**	+ SUBJECT	+ VERB ... ?
À quelle heure	**est-ce que**	vous	travaillez?

→ **Est-ce que** becomes **est-ce qu'** before a vowel sound.

Quand **est-ce qu'**Alice et Roger dînent?

→ In information questions, your voice rises on the interrogative expression and then falls until the last syllable.

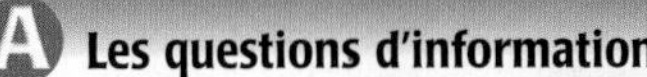

Quand est-ce que tu travailles? **À quelle heure** est-ce que vous dînez?

Observation In casual conversation, French speakers frequently form information questions by placing the interrogative expression at the end of the sentence. The voice rises on the interrogative expression.

Vous habitez **où?** Vous dînez **à quelle heure?**

VOCABULAIRE Expressions interrogatives

où	*where?*	**Où** est-ce que vous travaillez?
quand?	*when?*	**Quand** est-ce que ton copain organise une boum?
à quelle heure?	*at what time?*	**À quelle heure** est-ce que tu regardes la télé?
comment?	*how?*	**Comment** est-ce que tu chantes? Bien ou mal?
pourquoi?	*why?*	—**Pourquoi** est-ce que tu étudies le français?
parce que	*because*	—**Parce que** je veux voyager en France.

→ **Parce que** becomes **parce qu'** before a vowel sound.

Juliette invite Olivier **parce qu'**il danse bien.

106 cent six
Unité 3

B Les e...
To ask abou...

1  É...

STRATEG...
Understan...
attention t...
expressio...
informatio...

ÉCOUTER Th...
hear can be...
only one of...
Listen caref...
and select t...

a. à sept he...
b. à Paris

VOCABULA...
How to expres...
Ah bon?

3 PARLER Jac...
his plans.
▶ organiser

1. organise...
2. dîner ave...
3. dîner ave...
4. regarder...
5. inviter B...

4 Questi...
1. Où est-ce...
2. Où est-ce...
3. À quelle...
4. À quelle...
5. Quand e...

Listening strategies give students a variety of tips to improve their listening skills.

interrogatives avec *qui*

:h speakers use the following interrogative expressions:

n!

?ay
:ive
ype of

at you will
ered by
ptions.
estion
er.

tobre
bien

2 Curiosité

PARLER At a party in Paris, Nicolas meets Béatrice, a Canadian student. He wants to know more about her. Play both roles.

▶ où / habiter? (à Québec)

NICOLAS: **Où est-ce que tu habites?**
BÉATRICE: **J'habite à Québec.**

1. où/étudier? (à Montréal)
2. où/travailler? (dans *[in]* une pharmacie)
3. quand/parler français? (toujours)
4. quand/parler anglais? (souvent)
5. comment/jouer au tennis? (bien)
6. comment/danser? (très bien)
7. pourquoi/être en France? (parce que j'aime voyager)
8. pourquoi/être à Paris? (parce que j'étudie ici)

sions pour la conversation

ild doubt:

–Stéphanie organise une soirée.
–Ah bon? Quand?

ne

ie to tell her about

and? samedi)
e (quand? dimanche)
nd? lundi)
? au restaurant Belcour)
uelle heure? à 9 heures)
concert)

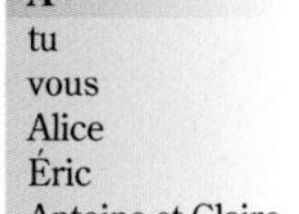

J'organise une soirée.
Ah bon? Quand est-ce que tu organises une soirée?
Samedi.

6. parler espagnol (comment? assez bien)
7. étudier l'italien (pourquoi? je veux voyager en Italie)

nelles PARLER/ÉCRIRE

? *(name of your city)*
? *(name of your school)*
e tu dînes?
e tu regardes la télé?
es? (en été? en hiver?)

6. Quand est-ce que tu joues au volley? (en mai? en juillet?)
7. Comment est-ce que tu chantes? (bien? très bien? mal?)
8. Comment est-ce que tu nages?

7 Questions

PARLER/ÉCRIRE For each illustration, prepare a short dialogue with a classmate using the suggested cues.

où?

à la maison

▶ **—Où est-ce que tu dînes?**
—Je dîne à la maison.

1. à quelle heure?
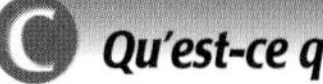
à 8 heures

2. quand?

en septembre

3. comment?

BONJOUR!
très bien

4. avec qui?
avec Denise

5. à qui?

à mon cousin

6. de qui?

BLA BLA BLA...
de toi

7. pour qui?

pour M. Lambert

C *Qu'est-ce que?*

Note the use of the interrogative expression **qu'est-ce que** *(what)* in the questions below.

Qu'est-ce que tu regardes?	Je regarde un match de tennis.
Qu'est-ce qu'Alice mange?	Elle mange une pizza.

To ask *what people are doing,* the French use the following construction:

qu'est-ce que + SUBJECT + VERB + ...?	**Qu'est-ce que** tu regardes?
qu'est-ce qu' (+ VOWEL SOUND)	**Qu'est-ce qu'**elle mange?

8 À la FNAC

PARLER People in Column A are at the FNAC, a store that sells books and recordings. Use a verb from Column B to ask what they are listening to or looking at. A classmate will answer you, using an item from Column C.

A	B	C
tu	écouter?	un livre de photos
vous	regarder?	un poster
Alice		un CD de rock
Éric		un CD de jazz
Antoine et Claire		un album de Youssou N'Dour

Qu'est-ce qu'Éric écoute?
Il écoute un album de Youssou N'Dour.

Whenever possible, **authentic French drawings, photos, and realia** are used to increase comprehension and success for all students.

After students have become comfortable with material in context, **formal charts** help them analyze forms and structure.

Learning about language notes focus on strategies for authentic language production, explain terminology, and help students understand how language functions.

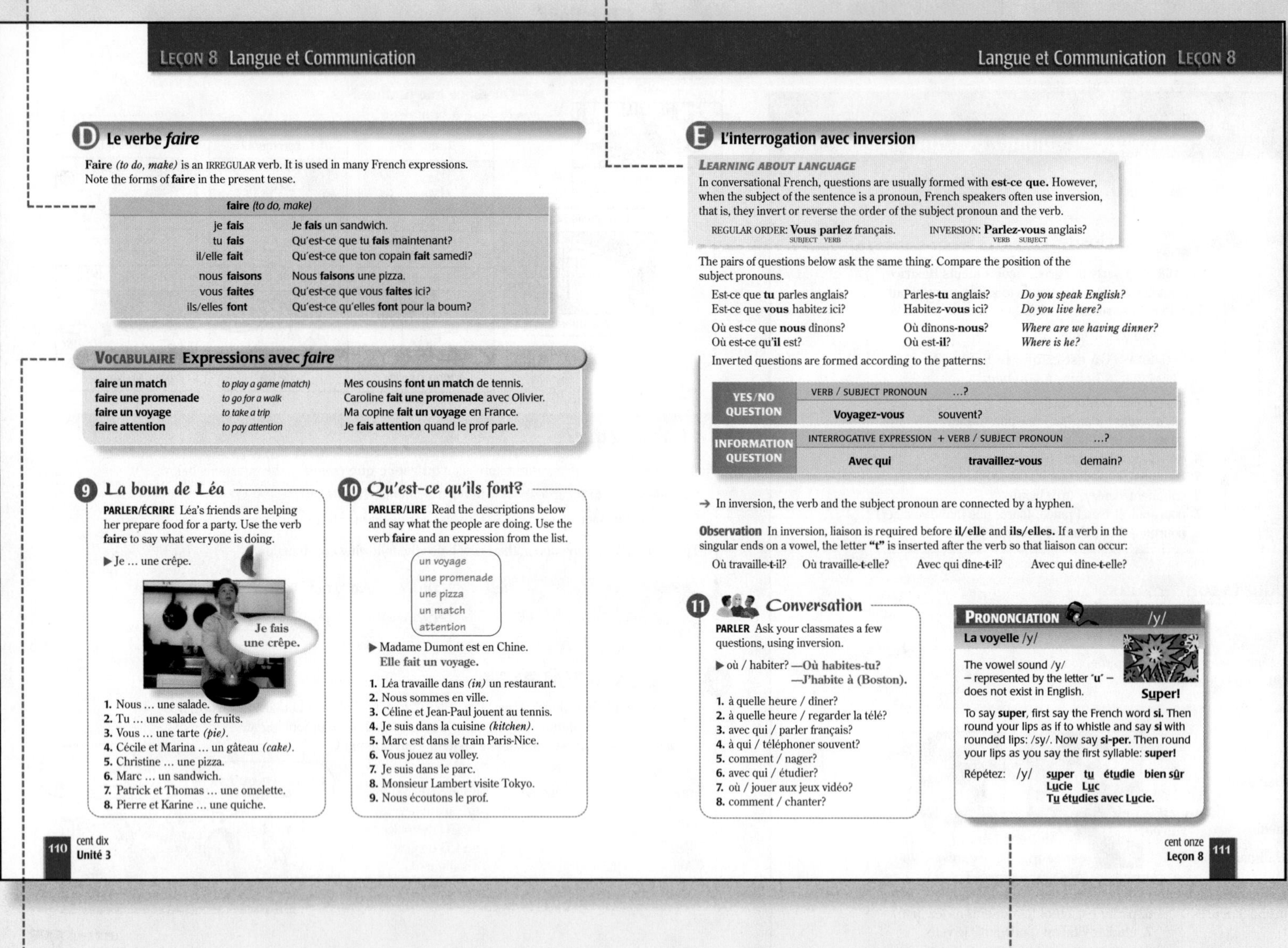

LEÇON 8 Langue et Communication

Langue et Communication LEÇON 8

D Le verbe *faire*

Faire *(to do, make)* is an IRREGULAR verb. It is used in many French expressions. Note the forms of **faire** in the present tense.

faire *(to do, make)*	
je **fais**	Je **fais** un sandwich.
tu **fais**	Qu'est-ce que tu **fais** maintenant?
il/elle **fait**	Qu'est-ce que ton copain **fait** samedi?
nous **faisons**	Nous **faisons** une pizza.
vous **faites**	Qu'est-ce que vous **faites** ici?
ils/elles **font**	Qu'est-ce qu'elles **font** pour la boum?

VOCABULAIRE Expressions avec *faire*

faire un match	*to play a game (match)*	Mes cousins **font un match** de tennis.
faire une promenade	*to go for a walk*	Caroline **fait une promenade** avec Olivier.
faire un voyage	*to take a trip*	Ma copine **fait un voyage** en France.
faire attention	*to pay attention*	Je **fais attention** quand le prof parle.

9 La boum de Léa

PARLER/ÉCRIRE Léa's friends are helping her prepare food for a party. Use the verb **faire** to say what everyone is doing.

▶ Je ... une crêpe.

Je fais une crêpe.

1. Nous ... une salade.
2. Tu ... une salade de fruits.
3. Vous ... une tarte *(pie)*.
4. Cécile et Marina ... un gâteau *(cake)*.
5. Christine ... une pizza.
6. Marc ... un sandwich.
7. Patrick et Thomas ... une omelette.
8. Pierre et Karine ... une quiche.

10 Qu'est-ce qu'ils font?

PARLER/LIRE Read the descriptions below and say what the people are doing. Use the verb **faire** and an expression from the list.

un voyage
une promenade
une pizza
un match
attention

▶ Madame Dumont est en Chine.
Elle fait un voyage.

1. Léa travaille dans *(in)* un restaurant.
2. Nous sommes en ville.
3. Céline et Jean-Paul jouent au tennis.
4. Je suis dans la cuisine *(kitchen)*.
5. Marc est dans le train Paris-Nice.
6. Vous jouez au volley.
7. Je suis dans le parc.
8. Monsieur Lambert visite Tokyo.
9. Nous écoutons le prof.

E L'interrogation avec inversion

LEARNING ABOUT LANGUAGE

In conversational French, questions are usually formed with **est-ce que.** However, when the subject of the sentence is a pronoun, French speakers often use inversion, that is, they invert or reverse the order of the subject pronoun and the verb.

REGULAR ORDER: **Vous parlez** français. (SUBJECT VERB) INVERSION: **Parlez-vous** anglais? (VERB SUBJECT)

The pairs of questions below ask the same thing. Compare the position of the subject pronouns.

Est-ce que **tu** parles anglais?	Parles-**tu** anglais?	*Do you speak English?*
Est-ce que **vous** habitez ici?	Habitez-**vous** ici?	*Do you live here?*
Où est-ce que **nous** dînons?	Où dînons-**nous**?	*Where are we having dinner?*
Où est-ce qu'**il** est?	Où est-**il**?	*Where is he?*

Inverted questions are formed according to the patterns:

YES/NO QUESTION	VERB / SUBJECT PRONOUN	...?	
	Voyagez-vous	souvent?	
INFORMATION QUESTION	INTERROGATIVE EXPRESSION	+ VERB / SUBJECT PRONOUN	...?
	Avec qui	**travaillez-vous**	demain?

→ In inversion, the verb and the subject pronoun are connected by a hyphen.

Observation In inversion, liaison is required before **il/elle** and **ils/elles.** If a verb in the singular ends on a vowel, the letter **"t"** is inserted after the verb so that liaison can occur:

Où travaille-t-il? Où travaille-t-elle? Avec qui dîne-t-il? Avec qui dîne-t-elle?

11 Conversation

PARLER Ask your classmates a few questions, using inversion.

▶ où / habiter? —**Où habites-tu?**
—**J'habite à (Boston).**

1. à quelle heure / dîner?
2. à quelle heure / regarder la télé?
3. avec qui / parler français?
4. à qui / téléphoner souvent?
5. comment / nager?
6. avec qui / étudier?
7. où / jouer aux jeux vidéo?
8. comment / chanter?

PRONONCIATION /y/

La voyelle /y/

The vowel sound /y/ – represented by the letter "u" – does not exist in English.

Super!

To say **super**, first say the French word **si.** Then round your lips as if to whistle and say **si** with rounded lips: /sy/. Now say **si-per.** Then round your lips as you say the first syllable: **super!**

Répétez: /y/ **super tu étudie bien sûr Lucie Luc**
Tu étudies avec Lucie.

110 cent dix Unité 3

cent onze Leçon 8 111

Supplementary vocabulary, coded in yellow, offers students communicative functions for immediate implementation in dialogs.

Prononciation features give students the opportunity to practice single "key" words and then to use them in context. All pronunciation sections, coded in purple, are available on the audio program.

Culminating the lesson, the *À votre tour* activities provide opportunities for self assessment in a variety of contextualized formats.

Culminating **listening and speaking activities** are ideal for expanding students' use of language beyond the classroom setting.

The ***Créa-dialogue*** provides models to guide but not limit students' creative language use. Recombination and re-entry of previously-learned material provide students with opportunities to demonstrate how well they can communicate in French.

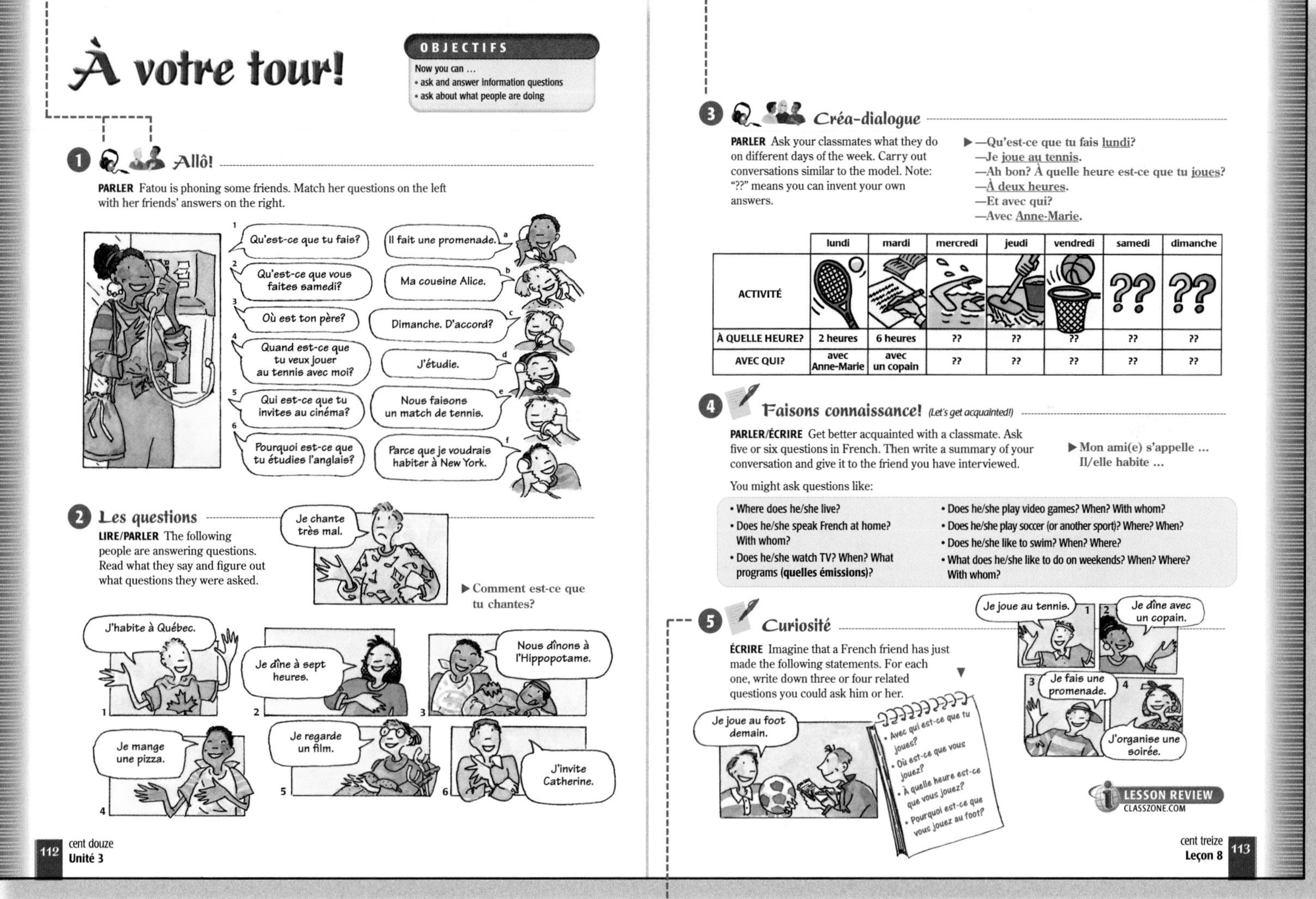

À votre tour!

OBJECTIFS
Now you can ...
- ask and answer information questions
- ask about what people are doing

1 Allô!

PARLER Fatou is phoning some friends. Match her questions on the left with her friends' answers on the right.

1. Qu'est-ce que tu fais?
2. Qu'est-ce que vous faites samedi?
3. Où est ton père?
4. Quand est-ce que tu veux jouer au tennis avec moi?
5. Qui est-ce que tu invites au cinéma?
6. Pourquoi est-ce que tu étudies l'anglais?

a. Il fait une promenade.
b. Ma cousine Alice.
c. Dimanche. D'accord?
d. J'étudie.
e. Nous faisons un match de tennis.
f. Parce que je voudrais habiter à New York.

2 Les questions

LIRE/PARLER The following people are answering questions. Read what they say and figure out what questions they were asked.

Je chante très mal.

▶ Comment est-ce que tu chantes?

1. J'habite à Québec.
2. Je dîne à sept heures.
3. Nous dînons à l'Hippopotame.
4. Je mange une pizza.
5. Je regarde un film.
6. J'invite Catherine.

112 cent douze
Unité 3

3 Créa-dialogue

PARLER Ask your classmates what they do on different days of the week. Carry out conversations similar to the model. Note: "??" means you can invent your own answers.

▶ —Qu'est-ce que tu fais lundi?
—Je joue au tennis.
—Ah bon? À quelle heure est-ce que tu joues?
—À deux heures.
—Et avec qui?
—Avec Anne-Marie.

	lundi	mardi	mercredi	jeudi	vendredi	samedi	dimanche
ACTIVITÉ						??	??
À QUELLE HEURE?	2 heures	6 heures	??	??	??	??	??
AVEC QUI?	avec Anne-Marie	avec un copain	??	??	??	??	??

4 Faisons connaissance! *(Let's get acquainted!)*

PARLER/ÉCRIRE Get better acquainted with a classmate. Ask five or six questions in French. Then write a summary of your conversation and give it to the friend you have interviewed.

▶ Mon ami(e) s'appelle ...
Il/elle habite ...

You might ask questions like:
- Where does he/she live?
- Does he/she speak French at home? With whom?
- Does he/she watch TV? When? What programs **(quelles émissions)**?
- Does he/she play video games? When? With whom?
- Does he/she play soccer (or another sport)? Where? When?
- Does he/she like to swim? When? Where?
- What does he/she like to do on weekends? When? Where? With whom?

5 Curiosité

ÉCRIRE Imagine that a French friend has just made the following statements. For each one, write down three or four related questions you could ask him or her.

▼ Je joue au foot demain.
- Avec qui est-ce que tu joues?
- Où est-ce que vous jouez?
- À quelle heure est-ce que vous jouez?
- Pourquoi est-ce que vous jouez au foot?

1. Je joue au tennis.
2. Je dîne avec un copain.
3. Je fais une promenade.
4. J'organise une soirée.

LESSON REVIEW
CLASSZONE.COM

cent treize 113
Leçon 8

Writing activities encourage students to present their thoughts and ideas in written form and provide material for student portfolios.

Follow up with Diagnostic Review

Tests de contrôle provide comprehensive review activities that students can use to check their comprehension.

The **"learning tabs"** in the side column help students self diagnose and review what they can do and where to go for help.

UNITÉ 3 Tests de contrôle

Tests de contrôle UNITÉ 3

Tests de contrôle

By taking the following tests, you can check your progress in French and also prepare for the unit test. Write your answers on a separate sheet of paper.

Review ...
- the uses and forms of -er verbs: pp. 94, 95, 96, and 98

1 The right activity

Complete each of the following sentences by filling in the blank with the appropriate form of one of the verbs in the box. Be logical in your choice of verbs.

chanter	manger	écouter	habiter
jouer	parler	regarder	travailler

1. Jean-Paul — une pizza.
2. Vous — aux jeux vidéo.
3. Isabelle — un CD de rock.
4. Monsieur Mercier — pour une banque (*bank*).
5. Mon cousin — à Chicago.
6. Ils — dans une chorale (*choir*).
7. Nous — une comédie à la télé.
8. Est-ce que tu — français ou anglais?

Review ...
- être and faire: pp. 84 and 110

2 Être and faire

For each item, fill in the first blank with the appropriate form of **être** and the second blank with the appropriate form of **faire.**

1. Je — en classe. Je — attention.
2. Léa — dans la cuisine (*kitchen*). Elle — un sandwich.
3. Nous — en ville. Nous — une promenade.
4. Les touristes — en France. Ils — un voyage.
5. Vous — au stade (*stadium*). Vous — un match de foot.

Review ...
- negative sentences: pp. 88 and 98

3 Non!

Rewrite the following sentences in the negative, replacing the underlined words with the words in parentheses.

▶ Thomas parle français. **(anglais)** — **Thomas ne parle pas anglais.**

1. Léa est française. **(américaine)**
2. Nous jouons au foot. **(au basket)**
3. Vous dînez au restaurant. **(à la maison)**
4. Tu invites Céline. **(Isabelle)**
5. Ils habitent à Québec. **(à Montréal)**

114 cent quatorze **Unité 3**

Review ...
- information questions: pp. 106 and 108

4 The right question

Write out the questions that correspond to the answers below. Make sure to begin your sentences with the question words that correspond to the underlined information. Use **tu** in your questions.

▶ J'habite à Paris. — **Où est-ce que tu habites?**

1. Je téléphone à Marc.
2. Je dîne à sept heures.
3. Je mange une pizza.
4. Je voyage en juillet.
5. J'écoute un CD.
6. Je joue très bien au foot.

Review ...
- vocabulary: pp. 77, 78, 85, 89, 95, 100, 106

5 The right choice

Choose the word or expression in parentheses which logically completes each of the following sentences.

1. François habite — France. **(à, au, en)**
2. Isabelle est au café — Céline. **(et, avec, pour)**
3. Nicolas parle français, — il ne parle pas espagnol. **(pourquoi, mal, mais)**
4. Pierre écoute — radio. **(à, la, à la)**
5. Je n'habite pas ici. J'habite —. **(où, aussi, là-bas)**
6. Tu ne chantes pas bien. Tu chantes —. **(mal, souvent, beaucoup)**
7. Philippe aime beaucoup jouer au foot. Il joue —. **(pour, mais non, souvent)**
8. Je ne peux pas dîner avec toi. Je — étudier pour l'examen. **(dois, veux, n'aime pas)**
9. J'étudie l'espagnol — je voudrais visiter Madrid. **(où, comment, parce que)**
10. Qui est-ce? Jérôme — Patrick? **(pour, ou, aussi)**

6 Composition: Les vacances

Write a short paragraph of five or six sentences saying what you and your friends do and don't do during summer vacation. Use only vocabulary and expressions that you know in French.

STRATEGY Writing

a. Make a list of activities that you do and a second list of things that you don't do. Use infinitives.
b. Organize your ideas and write your paragraph, using **je** or **nous.**
c. Check each sentence to be sure that the verb endings agree with the subject.

oui	non
• nager	•
•	•
•	•
•	•
•	•

cent quinze **Tests de contrôle** 115

Pre-writing strategies and **graphic organizers** help students become successful writers.

Thematic French-English vocabulary presentation brings together all unit vocabulary for easy review.

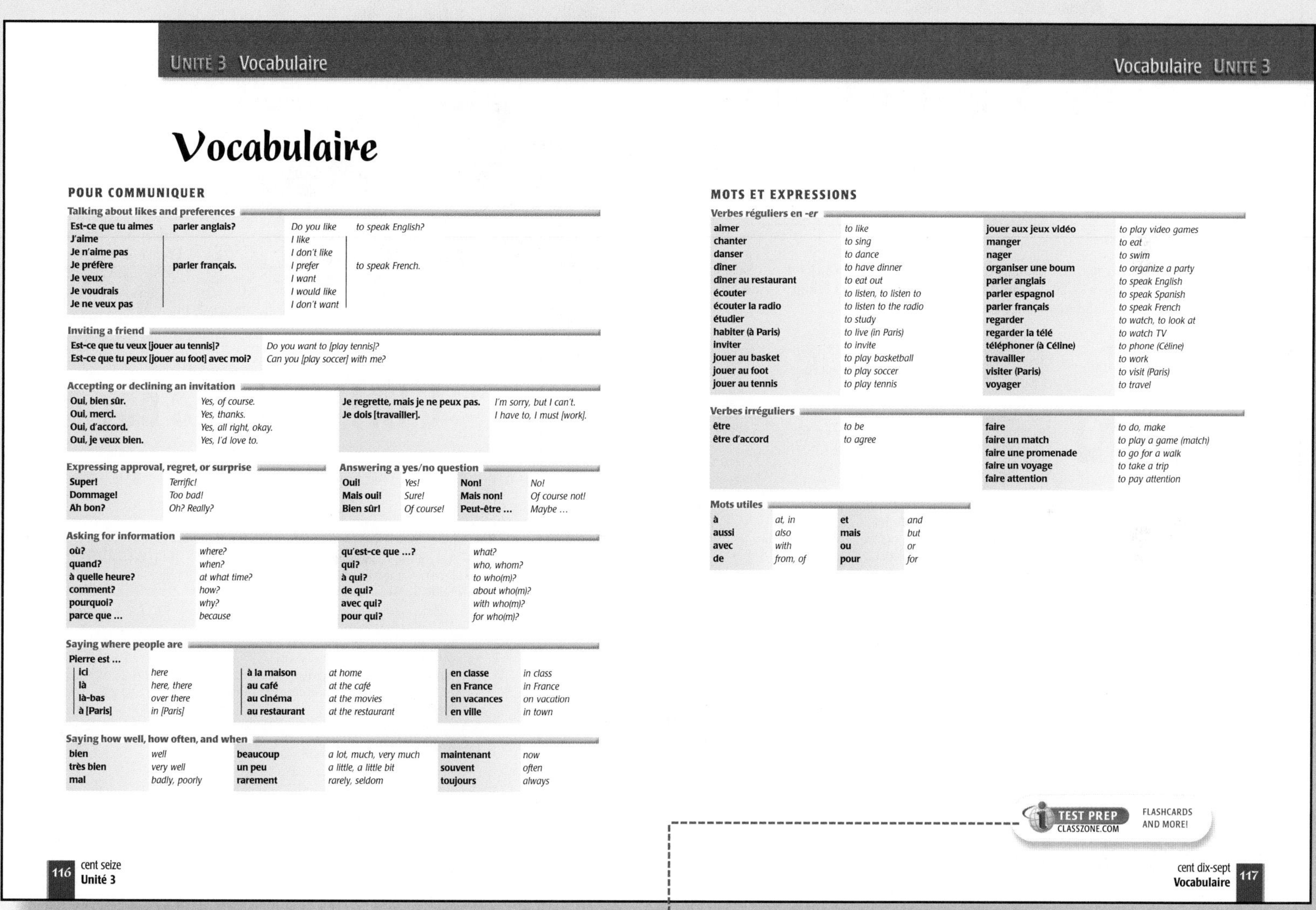

Vocabulaire

POUR COMMUNIQUER

Talking about likes and preferences

Est-ce que tu aimes	**parler anglais?**	*Do you like*	*to speak English?*
J'aime		*I like*	
Je n'aime pas		*I don't like*	
Je préfère	**parler français.**	*I prefer*	*to speak French.*
Je veux		*I want*	
Je voudrais		*I would like*	
Je ne veux pas		*I don't want*	

Inviting a friend

Est-ce que tu veux [jouer au tennis]?	*Do you want to [play tennis]?*
Est-ce que tu peux [jouer au foot] avec moi?	*Can you [play soccer] with me?*

Accepting or declining an invitation

Oui, bien sûr.	*Yes, of course.*	**Je regrette, mais je ne peux pas.**	*I'm sorry, but I can't.*
Oui, merci.	*Yes, thanks.*	**Je dois [travailler].**	*I have to, I must [work].*
Oui, d'accord.	*Yes, all right, okay.*		
Oui, je veux bien.	*Yes, I'd love to.*		

Expressing approval, regret, or surprise

Super!	*Terrific!*
Dommage!	*Too bad!*
Ah bon?	*Oh? Really?*

Answering a yes/no question

Oui!	*Yes!*	**Non!**	*No!*
Mais oui!	*Sure!*	**Mais non!**	*Of course not!*
Bien sûr!	*Of course!*	**Peut-être ...**	*Maybe ...*

Asking for information

où?	*where?*	**qu'est-ce que ...?**	*what?*
quand?	*when?*	**qui?**	*who, whom?*
à quelle heure?	*at what time?*	**à qui?**	*to who(m)?*
comment?	*how?*	**de qui?**	*about who(m)?*
pourquoi?	*why?*	**avec qui?**	*with who(m)?*
parce que ...	*because*	**pour qui?**	*for who(m)?*

Saying where people are

Pierre est ...

ici	*here*	**à la maison**	*at home*	**en classe**	*in class*
là	*here, there*	**au café**	*at the café*	**en France**	*in France*
là-bas	*over there*	**au cinéma**	*at the movies*	**en vacances**	*on vacation*
à [Paris]	*in [Paris]*	**au restaurant**	*at the restaurant*	**en ville**	*in town*

Saying how well, how often, and when

bien	*well*	**beaucoup**	*a lot, much, very much*	**maintenant**	*now*
très bien	*very well*	**un peu**	*a little, a little bit*	**souvent**	*often*
mal	*badly, poorly*	**rarement**	*rarely, seldom*	**toujours**	*always*

MOTS ET EXPRESSIONS

Verbes réguliers en *-er*

aimer	*to like*	**jouer aux jeux vidéo**	*to play video games*
chanter	*to sing*	**manger**	*to eat*
danser	*to dance*	**nager**	*to swim*
dîner	*to have dinner*	**organiser une boum**	*to organize a party*
dîner au restaurant	*to eat out*	**parler anglais**	*to speak English*
écouter	*to listen, to listen to*	**parler espagnol**	*to speak Spanish*
écouter la radio	*to listen to the radio*	**parler français**	*to speak French*
étudier	*to study*	**regarder**	*to watch, to look at*
habiter (à Paris)	*to live (in Paris)*	**regarder la télé**	*to watch TV*
inviter	*to invite*	**téléphoner (à Céline)**	*to phone (Céline)*
jouer au basket	*to play basketball*	**travailler**	*to work*
jouer au foot	*to play soccer*	**visiter (Paris)**	*to visit (Paris)*
jouer au tennis	*to play tennis*	**voyager**	*to travel*

Verbes irréguliers

être	*to be*	**faire**	*to do, make*
être d'accord	*to agree*	**faire un match**	*to play a game (match)*
		faire une promenade	*to go for a walk*
		faire un voyage	*to take a trip*
		faire attention	*to pay attention*

Mots utiles

à	*at, in*	**et**	*and*
aussi	*also*	**mais**	*but*
avec	*with*	**ou**	*or*
de	*from, of*	**pour**	*for*

TEST PREP CLASSZONE.COM FLASHCARDS AND MORE!

Online test prep at ClassZone.com prepares students to be successful test takers.

Develop Reading Skills and Experience Francophone Culture

UNITÉ 3 ENTRACTE Lecture et Culture

Ce week-end, à la télé

Le week-end, les jeunes Français regardent souvent la télé. Ils aiment regarder les films et le sport. Ils regardent aussi les jeux et les séries américaines et françaises. Les principales chaînes° sont TF1, France 2, France 3, Cinquième Arte, M6 et Canal Plus. Voici le programme de télévision pour ce week-end.

chaînes *channels*

Note In French TV listings, times are expressed using a 24-hour clock. In this system, 8 p.m. is 20.00 **(vingt heures)**, 9 p.m. is 21.00 **(vingt et une heures)**, 10 p.m. is 22 heures **(vingt-deux heures)**, etc.

SÉLECTION DE LA SEMAINE	VENDREDI	SAMEDI
TF1	20.50 Magazine **SUCCÈS** Émission présentée par Julien Courbet et Anne Magnien 23.15 MAGAZINE • **Célébrités**	20.50 Jeu **QUI VEUT GAGNER DES MILLIONS?** avec Jean-Pierre Foucault 21.50 SÉRIE • **Les Soprano**
France 2	20.55 Série **HÔTEL DE POLICE** **Le gentil Monsieur** de Claude Barrois avec Cécile Magnet 23.20 DOCUMENTAIRE • **Histoires Naturelles**	21.00 Variétés **CHAMPS-ÉLYSÉES** Invités: Ricky Martin, Juliette Binoche, Ben Affleck 22.35 SÉRIE • **Buffy contre les Vampires**
france 3	21.00 Film **LE CINQUIÈME ÉLÉMENT** de Luc Besson avec Bruce Willis et Milla Jovovich 22.15 CONCERT • **Viva Latino**	20.40 Série **INSPECTEUR BARNABY** avec Daniel Casey 22.50 SPORT • **Grand Prix d'Italie** Motocyclisme
france 5 arte	20.45 Documentaire **CATHÉDRALES** de Jean-François Delassus 22.20 FILM • **Quasimodo, le bossu de Notre Dame**	20.50 Documentaire **ARCHITECTURES** La Tour Eiffel 20.05 CONCERT • **Le Philharmonique de Vienne**
M6 	20.50 Variétés **GRAINES DE STAR** émission présentée par Laurent Boyer 22.20 THÉÂTRE • **Rhinocéros**	20.35 Film **LE MARIAGE DE MON MEILLEUR AMI** avec Julia Roberts 22.15 SÉRIE • **Police District**
CANAL+	20.50 Football **MARSEILLE-NICE** Championnat de France 22.50 FILM • **Air Force One** avec Harrison Ford	20.45 Film **MON PÈRE, CE HÉROS** avec Gérard Depardieu 23.15 RUGBY • **Toulouse-Biarritz**

118 cent dix-huit
Unité 3

Lecture

COMPARAISONS CULTURELLE
The TV schedule on the opposite pag
featured programs which are broadca
evening news on the major French ch
the United States, French viewers als
to numerous cable and satellite chann
similarities and differences do you se
French and American prime time TV?

UNITÉ 3 ENTRACTE Lecture et Culture

L'INTERNET, c'est co

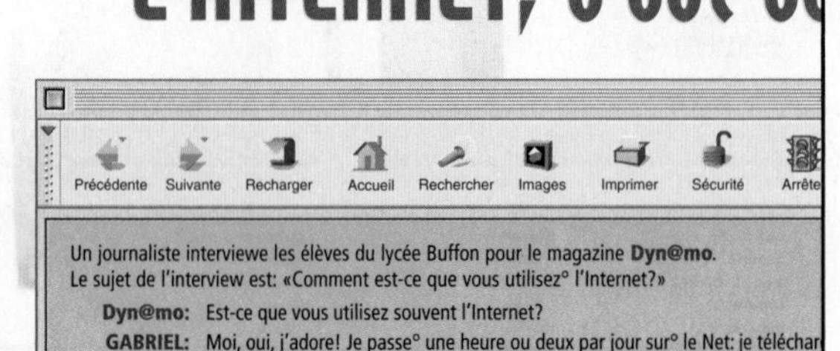

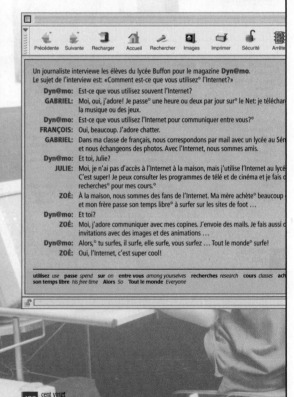

Un journaliste interviewe les élèves du lycée Buffon pour le magazine **Dyn@mo**.
Le sujet de l'interview est: «Comment est-ce que vous utilisez° l'Internet?»

Dyn@mo: Est-ce que vous utilisez souvent l'Internet?
GABRIEL: Moi, oui, j'adore! Je passe° une heure ou deux par jour sur° le Net: je téléchar la musique ou des jeux.
Dyn@mo: Est-ce que vous utilisez l'Internet pour communiquer entre vous?°
FRANÇOIS: Oui, beaucoup. J'adore chatter.
GABRIEL: Dans ma classe de français, nous correspondons par mail avec un lycée au Sén et nous échangeons des photos. Avec l'Internet, nous sommes amis.
Dyn@mo: Et toi, Julie?
JULIE: Moi, je n'ai pas d'accès à l'Internet à la maison, mais j'utilise l'Internet au lycé C'est super! Je peux consulter les programmes de télé et de cinéma et je fais d recherches° pour mes cours.°
ZOÉ: À la maison, nous sommes des fans de l'Internet. Ma mère achète° beaucoup et mon frère passe son temps libre° à surfer sur les sites de foot …
Dyn@mo: Et toi?
ZOÉ: Moi, j'adore communiquer avec mes copines. J'envoie des mails. Je fais aussi d invitations avec des images et des animations …
Dyn@mo: Alors,° tu surfes, il surfe, elle surfe, vous surfez … Tout le monde° surfe!
ZOÉ: Oui, l'Internet, c'est super cool!

utilisez *use* **passe** *spend* **sur** *on* **entre vous** *among yourselves* **recherches** *research* **cours** *classes* **ach**
son temps libre *his free time* **Alors** *So* **Tout le monde** *Everyone*

120 cent vingt
Unité 3

122 cent vi
Unité

Reading Strategies develop students' skills by emphasizing different ways to approach a variety of texts.

Entracte: Lecture et Culture **supports the development of reading skills, cultural awareness, and vocabulary in context.**

ENTRACTE UNITÉ 3

Cultural comparisons help students appreciate the similarities and differences between American and French cultures.

Lecture et Culture ENTRACTE UNITÉ 3

NOTE culturelle

3 ENTRACTE Lecture et Culture

Lecture et Culture ENTRACTE UNITÉ 3

our, Trinh!

Bonjour!

te | Écrire un mail | Priorité | Annuler | Envoyer

r!

guyen. J'ai 14 ans. J'habite à Paris avec ma famille. Je suis élève
ège. J'étudie beaucoup, mais je n'étudie pas tout le temps.°
aire.

ce que j'adore danser.

me surtout le rock, le rap et le reggae.
a guitare, mais je ne sais pas.

hiver je fais du snowboard et en été
tennis. (Je ne suis pas un champion,
en.) J'aime jouer au basket, mais je
. Le week-end, quand il fait beau,
° avec mes copains.

aime l'anglais parce que le prof est sympa.° J'aime aussi l'histoire, mais
es maths.

couter mes CD de rock. J'aime aussi regarder la télé. J'aime le sport et

vidéo. Et, j'aime jouer aux jeux d'ordinateur sur l'ordinateur de ma mère
nander la permission. J'aime surfer sur l'Internet et télécharger de la musique.
ails à mes copains. Je n'aime pas chatter en ligne parce que je n'aime pas parler
connais° pas.

na copine, mais je ne téléphone pas souvent. (Mon père n'aime pas ça.°)
vous aimez faire? Répondez-moi vite.°

e **aimerais** *would like* **faire du roller** *to go in-line skating* **sympa(thique)** *nice*
eople **connais** *know* **ça** *that* **vite** *quickly* **Amicalement** *In friendship*

dy discovered
ds in French
ords and have
are called
ou increase your
effortlessly. Be
the French way!

- Sometimes the spelling is the same, or almost the same:

un champion	*champion*
la permission	*permission*

- Sometimes the spelling is a little different:

les maths	*math*

Activité écrite: Une lettre à Trinh

You are writing an e-mail to Trinh in which you introduce yourself and explain what you like to do. Be sure to use only vocabulary that you know in French. You may tell him:

- if you like music (and what kind)
- what sports you like to do in fall or winter
- what sports you like to do in spring or summer
- which school subjects you like and which you do not like
- what you like to do at home
- which programs you like to watch on TV
- what you like to do on the Internet and what you do not like to do

Writing Hint Use Trinh's letter as a model.

NOTE culturelle

Les Vietnamiens en France

Vietnam and other Southeast Asian countries like Laos and Cambodia have a long civilization. For a period of about eighty years until the mid-1950s, these countries were occupied and administered by France which established schools and promoted the use of the French language among their populations.

In recent years, many Vietnamese people like Trinh's family have emigrated to France. Vietnamese restaurants are very popular with French students because of their fine yet inexpensive cuisine.

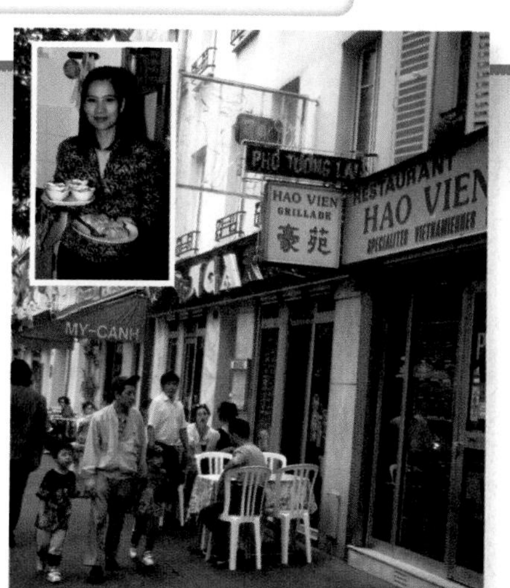

cent vingt-trois
Lecture et Culture 123

Note culturelle **features the variety of cultures that make up the French-speaking world.**

Implement ideas and lesson plans easily and effectively

The Expansion Activities, Planning Guide and Pacing Guide in the Teacher's Edition offer outstanding support to make teaching French adaptable to every situation.

Expansion Activities spark students' excitement with new ways to learn language and culture.

UNITÉ
3

Expansion activities PLANNING AHEAD

Games

• Charades
Divide the class into two or three teams. Choose one of the vocabulary words from pages 74–75, and tell one member from each team the word for that round. These team members alternate acting out clues until one team guesses the correct word. The first team to guess the word gets a point and starts the next round with a new member from each team as performer. Set a 1-minute time limit for each round. The team with the most points is the winner.

Pacing Suggestion: Upon completion of Leçon 5.

• Mais non!
First, have each student draw a quick illustration of a person in one of the places taught in **Vocabulaire** on page 85. Ask students to write a true or false caption for their illustration. For example, if a student draws a boy near the Eiffel Tower, the caption might read either **Jean est à Paris** (true), or **Jean est à la maison** (false). Then divide the class into two teams. Have a student from one team show his or her illustration to the class and read the caption aloud. The first student to raise his or her hand gets the opportunity to respond **«Oui, c'est vrai»** or **«Mais non!»** If they respond **«Mais non!»** they must correct the sentence using **ne . . . pas** and name the place the illustration really portrays to earn a point. Have teams alternate presenting their drawings.

Pacing Suggestion: Upon completion of Leçon 6.

Projects

• Invitation à une boum
Have students create a party invitation. The invitations should tell when and where the party will be and who is throwing the party. Using vocabulary they have learned, students may wish to list the refreshments that will be served. The invitations should be decorated with markers, stickers, glitter, beads, etc. As a variation, you may want to have students create invitations online.

Pacing Suggestion: Upon completion of Leçon 7.

• Le Sénégal
Divide the class into small groups. Have each group find information about Senegal. Groups may:

- create a map that shows where Senegal is located
- find information about activities that are common among young people in Senegal
- find or create illustrations that show what Senegal looks like
- find information about the weather, people, politics, industry, etc., of Senegal

Each group should create a colorful booklet or pamphlet they can use to present the information they obtained to the rest of the class. Students can create these by hand or on the computer.

Pacing Suggestion: Upon completion of Leçon 8.

Bulletin Boards

• La musique francophone
Have students search the Internet to find out what singers, musical groups, and songs are currently popular in France or in francophone countries. (You could assign a different country to pairs or groups of students and suggest specific Web sites for their search.) Ask students to find photos of some of these artists and create a bulletin board about francophone music. You can expand the activity by having students draw comparisons between their findings and some of their favorite popular music groups and performers in the United States.

Pacing Suggestion: Upon completion of Leçon 5.

69A • Expansion activities Unité 3

Storytelling

• Une mini-histoire
Model a brief conversation in which you call a friend. Invite your friend to do something you both enjoy, acting out the conversation with stuffed animals or puppets. Pass out copies of your conversation and say it aloud with pauses, allowing students to repeat after you, or fill in the words. Then have them work in pairs to expand on their versions. Ask students to write out their conversations, practice them for intonation, and perform them for the class.

Pacing Suggestion: Upon completion of Leçon 6.

• Écrire un poème
Explain to students that French is rich in rhyme. (You can point out, for example, that the infinitive form of all verbs ending in *-er* rhyme.) Have students brainstorm some rhyming words they have learned in French. Then have them use their lists of words to create a short poem. You may wish to ask for volunteers to share their poems with the class.

MODEL: Je n'aime pas nager, je préfère danser.
Mais je veux bien parler français.
Maintenant je ne peux pas nager,
Je ne peux pas danser.
Je dois étudier le français!

Pacing Suggestion: Upon completion of Leçon 7.

Recipe

• Fondue au chocolat
Fondue, which originated in Switzerland, is a typical French party food. Fondue can be made of melted cheese, chocolate, caramel, etc. You may wish to tell students that fondue is traditionally served in a fondue pot and that guests dip their foods using fondue forks.

Pacing Suggestion: Upon completion of Leçon 7.

Hands-on Crafts

• Le tama
Have pairs of students make a collage inspired by the **tama,** a traditional Senegalese drum, like the one pictured on this page. Suggest that students begin with colored or construction paper as a base. Ask them to bring in twine, rope, and other decorative materials to build up their two-dimensional drum designs into layers. When they have finished, have students set up a display of their drums.

Pacing Suggestion: Upon completion of Leçon 8.

End of Unit

• C'est moi!
Each student will create a poster to tell about his or her activities. First, have students write several sentences with their name, age, and several activities in which they participate. Then ask them to exchange papers with a classmate. Once they have corrected any errors, have students write their sentences on a poster, and use magazine photos or drawings to illustrate each sentence. You may want to have students give oral presentations to the class using their posters. As an alternative, have students act out and videotape their self-portraits.

Rubric **A** = 13–15 pts. **B** = 10–12 pts. **C** = 7–9 pts. **D** = 4–6 pts. **F** = < 4 pts.

Criteria	Scale
Vocabulary Use	1 2 3 4 5
Grammar/Spelling Accuracy	1 2 3 4 5
Creativity	1 2 3 4 5

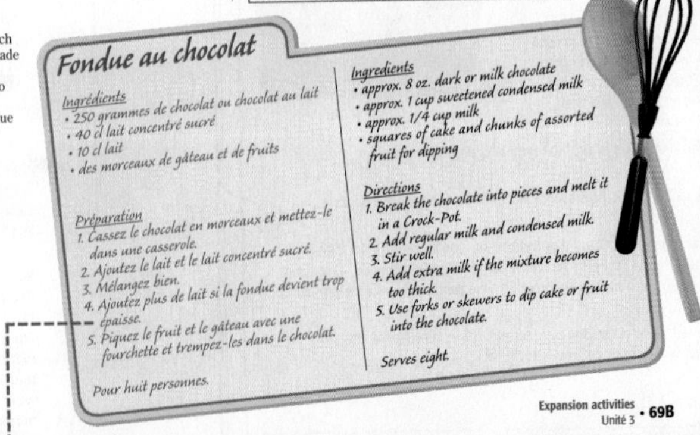
Fondue au chocolat
Ingrédients
• 250 grammes de chocolat ou chocolat au lait
• 40 cl lait concentré sucré
• 10 cl lait
• des morceaux de gâteau et de fruits
Préparation
1. Cassez le chocolat en morceaux et mettez-le dans une casserole.
2. Ajoutez le lait et le lait concentré sucré.
3. Mélangez bien.
4. Ajoutez plus de lait si la fondue devient trop épaisse.
5. Piquez le fruit et le gâteau avec une fourchette et trempez-les dans le chocolat.
Pour huit personnes.
Ingredients
• approx. 8 oz. dark or milk chocolate
• approx. 1 cup sweetened condensed milk
• approx. 1/4 cup milk
• squares of cake and chunks of assorted fruit for dipping
Directions
1. Break the chocolate into pieces and melt it in a Crock-Pot.
2. Add regular milk and condensed milk.
3. Stir well.
4. Add extra milk if the mixture becomes too thick.
5. Use forks or skewers to dip cake or fruit into the chocolate.
Serves eight.

Expansion activities Unité 3 • 69B

Easy-to-prepare recipes give students a delicious opportunity to experience cuisine from France and the French-speaking world.

At-a-glance overviews outline the objectives and program resources for at-a-glance support.

Listening scripts in the Teacher's Edition provide the practical information needed for easier lesson preparation.

UNITÉ 3

Student Text Listening Activity Scripts

AUDIO PROGRAM

▶ **LEÇON 5** LE FRANÇAIS PRATIQUE Mes activités

• **Préférences** *p. 74* CD 2, TRACK 1

How to talk about what you like and don't like to do. Écoutez et répétez.

Est-ce que tu aimes . . . ? # / J'aime . . . # / Je n'aime pas . . . # / Je préfère . . . #

Est-ce que tu aimes parler français? # / Oui, j'aime parler français. # / Non, je n'aime pas parler français. # / Je préfère parler anglais. #

Now practice the names of the activities.

téléphoner # / parler français # / parler anglais # / parler espagnol # / manger # / chanter # / danser # / nager # / jouer au tennis # / jouer au basket # / jouer au foot # / jouer aux jeux vidéo # / regarder la télé # / écouter la radio # / dîner au restaurant # / voyager # / étudier # / travailler #

J'aime téléphoner. # / J'aime parler français. # / J'aime parler anglais. # / J'aime parler espagnol. # / J'aime manger. # / J'aime chanter. # / J'aime danser. # / J'aime nager. # / J'aime aussi jouer au tennis. # / J'aime aussi jouer au basket. # / J'aime aussi jouer au foot. # / J'aime aussi jouer aux jeux vidéo. # / Mais je préfère regarder la télé. # / Mais je préfère écouter la radio. # / Mais je préfère dîner au restaurant. # / Mais je préfère voyager. # / Je n'aime pas toujours étudier. #

• **Créa-dialogue** *p. 81* CD 2, TRACK 5

Listen to the following sample *Créa-dialogue*. Ecoutez les conversations.

Modèle: –Est-ce que tu veux jouer au tennis avec moi? –Non, je ne peux pas. Je dois travailler.

Here are some sample dialogues.

1. –Est-ce que tu veux jouer au basket avec moi? –Non, je ne peux pas. Je dois téléphoner à une copine. #
2. –Est-ce que tu veux manger une pizza? –Non, je ne peux pas. Je dois dîner avec ma cousine. #
3. –Est-ce que tu veux regarder la télé? –Non, je ne peux pas. Je dois parler avec ma mère. #
4. –Est-ce que tu veux jouer au ping-pong? –Non, je ne peux pas. Je dois étudier. #
5. –Est-ce que tu veux dîner au restaurant? –Non, je ne peux pas. Je dois chanter avec la chorale. #
6. –Est-ce que tu veux jouer aux jeux vidéo? –Non, je ne peux pas. Je dois étudier. #

▶ **LEÇON 6** Une invitation

• **Une invitation** *p. 82*

A. **Compréhension orale** CD 2, TRACK 6

Please turn to page 82 for complete *Compréhension orale* text.

B. **Écoutez et répétez.**

▶ **LEÇON 7** Une boum

• **Une boum** *p. 92*

A. **Compréhension orale** CD 2, TRACK 11

Please turn to page 92 for complete *Compréhension orale* text.

B. **Écoutez et répétez.** CD 2, TRACK 12

You will now hear a paused version of the dialog. Listen to the speaker and repeat right after he or she has completed the sentence.

• **Écoutez bien!** *p. 99* CD 2, TRACK 13

You will hear French young people tell you what they do and do not do. Listen carefully to what they each say and determine if they do the following activities.

Modèle: Je ne joue pas au foot. Je joue au basket. #

Let's begin.

1. Je parle anglais. Je ne parle pas espagnol. #
2. Je n'habite pas à Tours. J'habite à Paris. #
3. Je dîne à la maison. Je ne dîne pas au restaurant. #
4. Je téléphone à un copain. Je ne téléphone pas à une copine. #
5. Je ne mange pas une pizza. Je mange un sandwich. #
6. J'étudie l'espagnol. Je n'étudie pas l'anglais. #
7. Je n'écoute pas la radio. J'écoute un CD. #

• **Prononciation** *p. 101* CD 2, TRACK 14

Les voyelles /i/ **et** /u/

Écoutez: /u/ **où?** /i/ **ici!**

Be sure to pronounce the French "i" as in **Mimi.**

1. Où est-ce que tu habites? #
2. À quelle heure est-ce que vous dînez? #
3. Comment est-ce que vous parlez français? #
4. Quand est-ce que vous visitez Dakar? #
5. Où est-ce que ton oncle travaille? #
6. Quand est-ce que ton copain voyage en France? #
7. À quelle heure est-ce que vous regardez la télé? #
8. Comment est-ce que tu chantes? #

• **Prononciation** *p. 111* CD 2, TRACK 20

La voyelle /y/

Écoutez: Super!

The vowel sound /y/—represented by the letter "u"—does not e… first say the French word **si.** Then round your lips as if to whistle… lips: /sy/. Now say **si-per.** Then round your lips as you say the fi…

Répétez: /y/ # super # tu # étudie # bien sûr # Lucie # Luc…

À votre tour!

• **Allô!** *p. 112* CD 2, TRACK 21

Fatou is phoning some friends. Match her questions on the left … answers on the right.

1. Qu'est-ce que tu fais?
2. Qu'est-ce que vous faites samedi?
3. Où est ton père?
4. Quand est-ce que tu veux jouer …

J'étudie. / Nous faisons un … / Il fait une promena… / Dimanche. D'accor…

UNITÉ 3

Planning Guide CLASSROOM MANAGEMENT

OBJECTIVES

Communication
- Describe some of your daily activities *pp. 72–73, 95*
- Say what you like and do not like to do *pp. 74–75, 77*
- Ask and answer questions about where others are and what they are doing *pp. 85–86, 89*
- Invite friends to do things with you *p. 78*
- Politely accept or turn down an invitation *p. 78*

Grammar
- Le verbe *être* et les pronoms sujets *pp. 84–85*
- Les questions à réponse affirmative ou négative *pp. 86–87*
- La négation *p. 88*
- Les verbes en *-er*: le singulier *p. 94*
- Les verbes en *-er*: le pluriel *p. 96*
- Le présent des verbes en *-er*: forme affirmative et forme négative *p. 98*
- La construction: verbe + infinitif *p. 101*
- Les questions d'information *p. 106*
- Les expressions interrogatives avec *qui p. 108*
- *Qu'est-ce que? p. 109*
- Le verbe *faire p. 110*
- L'interrogation avec inversion *p. 111*

Vocabulary
- Préférences *pp. 74–75*
- Souhaits *p. 77*
- Invitations *p. 78*
- Où? *p. 85*
- Expressions pour la conversation *pp. 87, 100, 107*
- Mots utiles *pp. 89, 100*
- Les verbes en *-er p. 95*
- Expressions interrogatives *p. 106*
- Expressions avec *faire p. 110*

Pronunciation
- La voyelle /a/ *p. 89*
- Les voyelles /i/ et /u/ *p. 101*
- La voyelle /y/ *p. 111*

Culture
- Le téléphone *p. 79*
- Le mercredi après-midi *p. 83*
- Une boum *p. 93*
- Le Sénégal *p. 105*
- Les jeunes Français et l'Internet *p. 121*
- Les Vietnamiens en France *p. 123*

PROGRAM RESOURCES

Print
- Workbook PE, *pp. 59–84*
- *Activités pour tous* PE, *pp. 33–49*
- Block Scheduling Copymasters, *pp. 33–64*
- *Français pour hispanophones*
- *Lectures pour tous*
- Teacher to Teacher Copymasters
- Teaching Proficiency through Reading and Storytelling
- Unit 3 Resource Book
  - Lessons 5–8 Resources
    - Workbook TE
    - *Activités pour tous* TE
    - Family Letter
    - Absent Student Copymasters
    - Family Involvement
    - Video Activities
    - Videoscripts
    - Audioscripts
    - Assessment Program
  - Unit 3 Resources
    - Communipak
    - *Activités pour tous* TE Reading
    - Workbook TE Reading and Culture Activities
    - Assessment Program
    - Answer Keys

Audiovisual
- Audio Program PE CD 2 Tracks 1–23
- Audio Program Workbook CD 7 Tracks 1–21
- *Chansons* Audio CD
- Sing Along: Grammar and Vocabulary Songs CD
- Video Program Modules 5, 6, 7, 8
- Warm-Up Transparencies

- Overhead Transparencies
  - 15 *Où sont-ils?*;
  - 12 Menu from "Le Select";
  - 16 Subject Pronouns;
  - 14a, 14b, 17 *-er* Verbs;
  - 16 Subject Pronouns;
  - 6 Clock face *Quelle heure est-il?*;
  - 8 Expressions with *faire*

Technology
- Online Workbook
- ClassZone.com
- McDougal Littell Assessment System/Test Generator CD-ROM
- EasyPlanner CD-ROM
- Power Presentations on CD-ROM
- Take-Home Tutor CD-ROM

Assessment Program Options
- Lesson Quizzes
- Portfolio Assessment
- Unit Test Form A
- Unit Test Form B
- Unit Test Part III (Alternate) Cultural Awareness
- Listening Comprehension Performance Test
- Speaking Performance Test
- Reading Comprehension Performance Test
- Writing Performance Test
- Multiple Choice Test Items
- Test Scoring Tools
- Audio Program CD 14 Tracks 1–16
- Answer Keys
- McDougal Littell Assessment System/ Test Generator CD-ROM

Pacing Guide SAMPLE LESSON PLAN

DAY	DAY	DAY	DAY	DAY
1 Unité 3 Opener Leçon 5 • Vocabulaire et Culture–Mes activités • Vocabulaire–Préférences	**2** Leçon 5 • Vocabulaire–Préférences *(continued)* • Vocabulaire–Souhaits	**3** Leçon 5 • Vocabulaire–Invitations • Note culturelle–Le téléphone	**4** Leçon 5 • À votre tour!	**5** Leçon 6 • Une invitation • Note culturelle–Le mercredi après-midi • Le verbe *être* et les pronoms sujets
6 Leçon 6 • Vocabulaire–Où? • Les questions à réponse affirmative ou négative	**7** Leçon 6 • Vocabulaire–Expressions pour la conversation • La négation	**8** Leçon 6 • La négation *(continued)* • Vocabulaire–Mots utiles • Prononciation–Le voyelle /a/	**9** Leçon 6 • À votre tour!	**10** Leçon 7 • Une boum • Note culturelle–Une boum • Les verbes en *-er*: le singulier • Vocabulaire–Les verbes en *-er*
11 Leçon 7 • Vocabulaire–Les verbes en *-er (continued)* • Les verbes en *-er*: le pluriel	**12** Leçon 7 • Le présent des verbes en *-er*: forme affirmative et forme négative	**13** Leçon 7 • Vocabulaire–Mots utiles • Vocabulaire–Expressions pour la conversation • La construction: verbe + infinitif	**14** Leçon 7 • Prononciation–Les voyelles /i/ et /u/ • À votre tour!	**15** Leçon 8 • Un concert de musique africaine • Note culturelle–Le Sénégal • Les questions d'information
16 Leçon 8 • Vocabulaire–Expressions interrogatives • Vocabulaire–Expressions pour la conversation	**17** Leçon 8 • Les expressions interrogatives avec *qui* • *Qu'est-ce que?*	**18** Leçon 8 • Le verbe *faire* • Vocabulaire–Expressions avec *faire* • L'interrogation avec inversion	**19** Leçon 8 • Prononciation–La voyelle /y/ • À votre tour!	**20** • Tests de contrôle
21 • Unit 3 Test	**22** • Entracte: Lecture et culture			

69C • Planning Guide Unité 3

Pacing Guide Unité 3 • 69D

Time-saving lessons present sequenced teaching suggestions and suggest appropriate pacing.

Suggests practical teaching ideas

The comprehensive Teacher's Edition and resource materials provide the support you need to introduce, explain, and expand your lessons.

- **Point-of-use** references to program components help you integrate a variety of resources into your lessons with ease.

- **Answers for every activity** are included in the wrap.

À VOTRE TOUR

Main Topic
- Recapitulation and review

Teaching Resource Options

PRINT

Workbook PE, pp. 59–63
Unit 3 Resource Book
Audioscript, pp. 27–28
Communipak, pp. 128–143
Family Involvement, pp. 19–20
Workbook TE, pp. 1–5
Assessment
Lesson 5 Quiz, pp. 31–32
Portfolio Assessment, Unit 1 URB pp. 155–164
Audioscript for Quiz 5, p. 30
Answer Keys, pp. 216–219

AUDIO & VISUAL

Audio Program
CD 2 Tracks 2–5
CD 14 Track 1

TECHNOLOGY

Test Generator CD-ROM/McDougal Littell Assessment System

1 LISTENING COMPREHENSION

1. A
2. B
3. A
4. B
5. B
6. B
7. A
8. A
9. B
10. A

2 GUIDED ORAL EXPRESSION

Answers will vary.
- –Est-ce que tu aimes regarder la télé?
  –Oui, j'aime regarder la télé.
- –Est-ce que tu aimes écouter la radio?
  –Oui, j'aime écouter la radio.
- –Est-ce que tu veux jouer aux jeux vidéo?
  –Non, je ne veux pas jouer aux jeux vidéo.
- –Est-ce que tu veux manger une pizza?
  –Non, je ne veux pas manger de pizza.

3 ORAL EXPRESSION

Trinh: (Salut, Céline.) Ça va?
Céline: Oui, ça va (merci).
Trinh: Tu veux dîner au restaurant?
Céline: À quelle heure?
Trinh: À 8 heures.
Céline: Je regrette, mais je dois étudier.
Trinh: Dommage!

80 • À votre tour! Unité 3 LEÇON 5

À votre tour!

OBJECTIFS
Now you can ...
- talk about activities you like and do not like
- extend and accept invitations
- give an excuse when you cannot accept

1 Écoutez bien!

ÉCOUTER You will hear French young people telling you what they like to do. Listen carefully to each activity. If it is illustrated in the picture on the left, mark A. If it is illustrated in the picture on the right, mark B.

A

B

	A	B
1.		
2.		
3.		
4.		
5.		
6.		

2 Communication

ÉCOUTER You have invited a French friend to spend the weekend at your house. Ask your friend ...

- if he/she likes to watch TV
- if he/she wants to play video games
- if he/she likes to listen to the radio
- if he/she wants to eat a pizza

A classmate will play the role of your French friend and answer your questions.

3 Conversation dirigée

PARLER Trinh is phoning Céline. Write out their conversation according to the directions. You may want to act out the dialogue with a classmate.

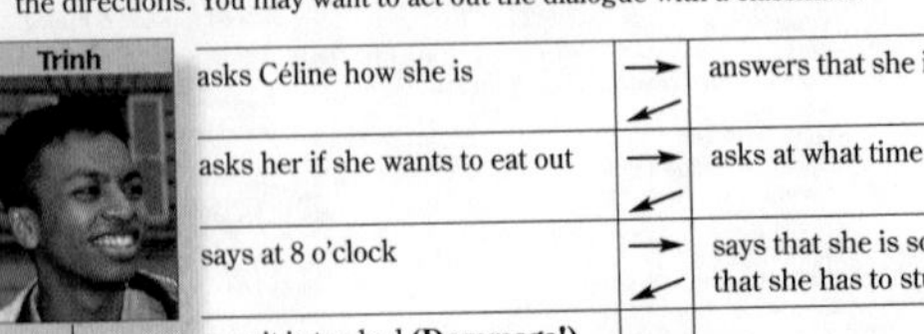
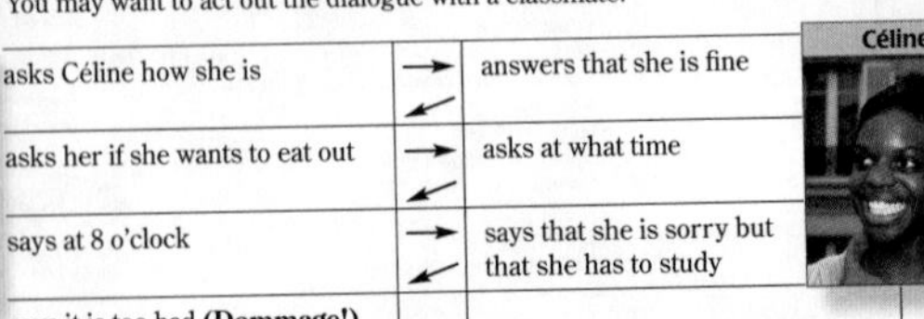

Trinh		Céline
asks Céline how she is	→ ←	answers that she is fine
asks her if she wants to eat out	→ ←	asks at what time
says at 8 o'clock	→ ←	says that she is sorry but that she has to study
says it is too bad **(Dommage!)**		

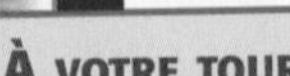

80 quatre-vingts Unité 3

À VOTRE TOUR

Beginning with this lesson, the **À votre tour!** sections have both oral and written communication activities. Depending on your goals and objectives, you may or may not wish to assign all of the activities in the **À votre tour** section.

INCLUSION

Structured Have students practice the full conjugation **aimer** orally, with question/answer format of verb only **Tu aimes?/Oui, j'aime; elle aime/oui, elle aime; vou aimez/oui, nous aimons;** etc. Have students practice answering in the negative, too.

Cumulative Have students practice the construct of **vouloir + aimer** orally. Have them pose questions in t **tu** form. Have them write an example.

4 Créa-dialogue

PARLER Ask your classmates if they want to do the following things with you. They will answer that they cannot and will give one of the excuses below.

▶ jouer au tennis

Est-ce que tu veux jouer au tennis avec moi?
Non, je ne peux pas. Je dois travailler.

1. jouer au basket
2. manger une pizza
3. regarder la télé
4. jouer au ping-pong
5. dîner au restaurant
6. jouer aux jeux vidéo

EXCUSES: téléphoner à une copine · étudier · travailler · parler avec ma mère · dîner avec ma cousine · chanter avec la chorale (choir)

5 Expression personnelle

PARLER/ÉCRIRE What we like to do often depends on the circumstances. Complete the sentences below saying what you like and don't like to do in the following situations.

▶ En hiver ...
En hiver, j'aime regarder la télé. J'aime aussi jouer au basket. Je n'aime pas nager.

1. En été ...
2. En automne ...
3. Le samedi *(On Saturdays)*...
4. Le dimanche ...
5. Le soir *(In the evening)*...
6. En classe ...
7. Avec mes *(my)* amis ...
8. Avec ma famille ...

6 Correspondance

ÉCRIRE This summer you are going to spend two weeks in France. Your e-mail correspondent Vincent has written asking what you like and don't like to do on vacation **(en vacances).** Respond with a short e-mail, answering his questions.

STRATEGY Writing

1. Make a list of activities you like and do not like. Use only vocabulary that you know.

2. Write your e-mail. *Cher Vincent,*
En vacances, j'aime ...

3. Read over your letter to be sure you have used the right verb forms.

LESSON REVIEW
CLASSZONE.COM

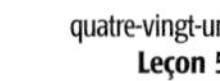

Portfolio Assessment

Beginning with Unit 3, students may start a Written Portfolio.

You will perhaps want to do only one oral portfolio recording and one written composition per unit. In this lesson, a good written portfolio topic is Act. 6.

Inclusion

Multisensory Have students write complete conjugations of the verbs **pouvoir** and **devoir**. Then have them practice all the forms orally. Next, ask them to students practice **pouvoir** in the negative for all forms.

Cumulative Have students review the seasons. Have them write out seasons with the proper preposition. Have students make a list of activities and sports for each season.

4 Written Self-Expression

Answers will vary.
1. –Est-ce que tu veux jouer au basket avec moi?
–Non, je ne peux pas. Je dois (téléphoner à une copine).
2. –Est-ce que tu veux manger une pizza avec moi?
–Non, je ne peux pas. Je dois (dîner avec ma cousine).
3. –Est-ce que tu veux regarder la télé avec moi?
–Non, je ne peux pas. Je dois (parler avec ma mère).
4. –Est-ce que tu veux jouer au ping-pong avec moi?
–Non, je ne peux pas. Je dois (étudier).
5. –Est-ce que tu veux dîner au restaurant avec moi?
–Non, je ne peux pas. Je dois (chanter avec la chorale).
6. –Est-ce que tu veux jouer aux jeux vidéo avec moi?
–Non, je ne peux pas. Je dois (étudier).

Variation Using the audio, have students match numbers 1–6 with the excuses given by the speakers.

5 Written Self-Expression

Answers will vary.
1. En été, j'aime (nager). J'aime aussi (voyager). Je n'aime pas (travailler).
2. En automne, j'aime (jouer au basket). J'aime aussi (chanter). Je n'aime pas (nager).
3. Le samedi, j'aime (danser). J'aime aussi (téléphoner). Je n'aime pas (travailler).
4. Le dimanche, j'aime (jouer au volley). J'aime aussi chanter. Je n'aime pas (regarder la télé).
5. Le soir, j'aime (écouter la radio). J'aime aussi (téléphoner). Je n'aime pas (étudier).
6. En classe, j'aime (parler français). J'aime aussi (étudier). Je n'aime pas (danser).
7. Avec mes amis, j'aime (aller au restaurant). J'aime aussi (danser). Je n'aime pas (étudier).
8. Avec ma famille, j'aime (aller au restaurant). J'aime aussi voyager. Je n'aime pas (jouer au basket).

6 Written Self-Expression

Answers will vary.

1. | **J'aime** | **Je n'aime pas** |
|---|---|
| • voyager | • étudier |
| • danser | • regarder la télé |
| • nager | • parler anglais |

2. Cher Vincent,
En vacances, j'aime voyager, danser, nager, jouer au volley et parler français. Je n'aime pas étudier, regarder la télé, parler anglais et jouer au basket.
Paul (Carole)

Pre-AP skill: Peer-edit and self-edit.

Group Reading Practice Have students prepare a writing activity for homework. Then, in class, divide students into small groups and let them read one another's compositions.

Throughtout the Teacher's Edition you will find activities that have been correlated to a listening, spaeking, reading, or writing **Pre-AP skill.**

Inclusion activities provide clarification and reinforcement of grammar concepts, vocabulary review, and pronunciation lessions to address the needs of all students.

Cultural Reference Guide

Note: *Page numbers in bold type refer to the Teacher's Edition.*

METROPOLITAIN

BRASSERIE

Note: *Page numbers in bold type refer to the Teacher's Edition.*

entrée
entrée
du Musée d'Orsay

Teaching to the Standards

General Background: Questions and Answers

What are the Goals and Standards for Foreign Language Learning?

Over the past several years, the federal government has supported the development of Standards in many K-12 curriculum areas such as math, English, fine arts, and geography. These Standards are "content" standards and define what students should "know and are able to do" at the end of grades 4, 8 and 12. Moreover, the Standards are meant to be challenging, and their attainment should represent a strengthening of the American educational system.

In some subject matter areas, these Standards have formed the basis for building tests used in the National Assessment of Education Progress (NAEP). At that point, it was necessary to develop "performance" standards which define "how well" students must do on the assessment measure to demonstrate that they have met the content standards.

As far as states and local school districts are concerned, both implementation of the Standards and participation in the testing program are voluntary. However, the very existence of these standards is seen as a way of improving our educational system so as to make our young people more competitive on the global marketplace.

How are the Goals and Standards for Foreign Language Learning defined?

The Goals and Standards for Foreign Language Learning contain five general goals which focus on communication, culture, and the importance of second language competence in enhancing the students' ability to function more effectively in the global community of the 21st century. These five goals, each with their accompanying standards, are shown in the chart below. In the formal report, these standards are defined in greater detail with the addition of sample "benchmarks" or learning outcomes for grades 4, 8 and 12, and are illustrated with sample learning scenarios.

Standards for the Learning of French

Goal 1: Communication Communicate in French	Standard 1.1 **Interpersonal Communication** Students engage in conversations or correspondence in French to provide and obtain information, express feelings and emotions, and exchange opinions. Standard 1.2 **Interpretive Communication** Students understand and interpret spoken and written French on a variety of topics. Standard 1.3 **Presentational Communication** Students present information, concepts, and ideas in French to an audience of listeners or readers.
Goal 2: Cultures Gain Knowledge and Understanding of the Cultures of the Francophone World	Standard 2.1 **Practices of Culture** Students demonstrate an understanding of the relationship between the practices and perspectives of the cultures of the francophone world. Standard 2.2 **Products of Culture** Students demonstrate an understanding of the relationship between the products and perspectives of the cultures of the francophone world.
Goal 3: Connections Use French to Connect with Other Disciplines and Expand Knowledge	Standard 3.1 **Making Connections** Students reinforce and further their knowledge of other disciplines through French. Standard 3.2 **Acquiring Information** Students acquire information and recognize the distinctive viewpoints that are available through francophone cultures.
Goal 4: Comparisons Develop Insight through French into the Nature of Language and Culture	Standard 4.1 **Language Comparisons** Students demonstrate understanding of the nature of language through comparisons of French and their native language. Standard 4.2 **Cultural Comparisons** Students demonstrate understanding of the concept of culture through comparisons of francophone cultures and their own.
Goal 5: Communities Use French to Participate in Communities at Home and Around the World	Standard 5.1 **School and Community** Students use French both within and beyond the school setting. Standard 5.2 **Lifelong Learning** Students show evidence of becoming life-long learners by using French for personal enjoyment and enrichment.

Teaching to the Standards

With **Discovering French, *Nouveau!*** teachers can effectively teach towards these goals and standards while at the same time maintaining realistic expectations for their students.

The new Standards for Foreign Language Learning focus on the outcomes of long K-12 sequences of instruction. In most schools, however, French programs begin at the Middle School or Secondary level. With **Discovering French, *Nouveau!*** teachers can effectively teach toward these goals and standards while at the same time maintaining realistic expectations for their students.

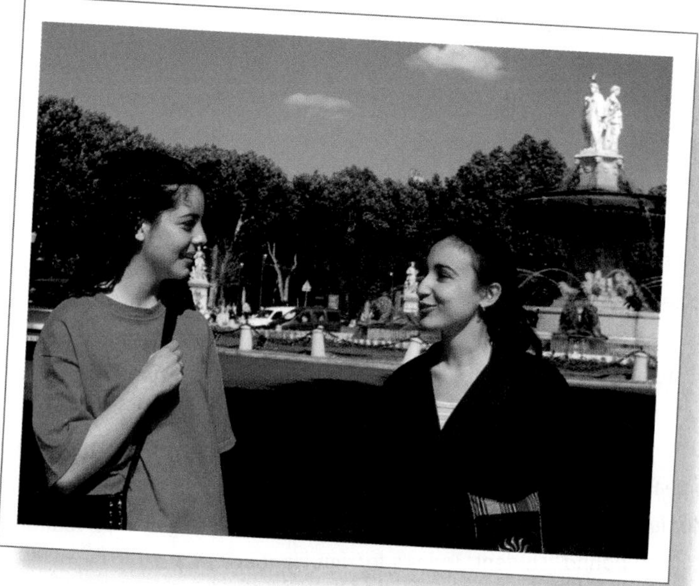

Goal One: Communicate in French

From the outset, **Discovering French, *Nouveau!*** students learn to communicate in French. In the *Invitation au français* opening section of **DFN-Bleu**, the focus is on understanding what French young people are saying (on video, DVD, and audio) and on exchanging information in simple conversations. In units 3–6, the oral skills are supplemented by the written skills, and students learn to read and express themselves in writing.

As students progress through **DFN-Blanc** and **DFN-Rouge**, they learn to engage in longer conversations, read and interpret more challenging texts, and understand French-language films and videos. Teachers who incorporate portfolio assessment into their programs will have the opportunity to keep samples of both written and recorded student presentations.

Goal Two: Gain Knowledge and Understanding of the Cultures of the Francophone World

In **Discovering French, *Nouveau!*** students are introduced to the diversity of the French-speaking world. In **DFN-Bleu**, the emphasis is on contemporary culture – in France, of course, but also in Quebec, the Caribbean, and Africa. Students learn to observe and analyze cultural differences in photographs and on the video program.

Goal Three: Use French to Connect with Other Disciplines and Expand Knowledge

It is especially in **DFN-Rouge** that students have the opportunity to use the French language to learn about history, art, music, social concerns and civic responsibilities. Topics suggested in the student text can be coordinated with colleagues across the school curriculum.

Goal Four: Develop Insight through French into the Nature of Language and Culture

From the outset, **Discovering French, *Nouveau!*** draws the students' attention to the way in which French speakers communicate with one another, and how some of these French patterns differ from American ones (for example, shaking hands or greeting friends with a *bise*). Notes in the Teacher's Edition provide suggestions for encouraging cross-cultural observation. English and French usage are also compared and contrasted, as appropriate.

Goal Five: Use French to Participate in Communities at Home and Around the World

In **Discovering French, *Nouveau!*** beginning students are invited to exchange letters with French-speaking pen pals. In addition, students are encouraged to participate in international student exchanges. The Teacher's Edition has a listing of addresses of organizations that can provide these types of services. In addition, teachers are given information on where to obtain French-language publications for their classes, and where to find French-language material on the Internet. In **DFN-Rouge**, students are invited to discover French-language videos which in many parts of the country can be found in a local video store. As students experience the satisfaction of participating in authentic cultural situations, they become more confident in their ability to use their skills in the wider global community.

For more information on the National Standards project and its publications, contact: **National Standards in Foreign Language Education, 6 Executive Plaza, Yonkers, NY 10701-6801; phone: (914) 963-8830 or on the Internet go to: www.actfl.org**

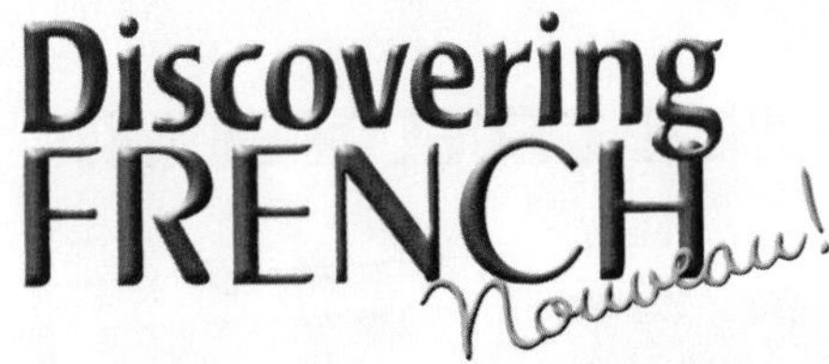

Inclusion in the French Classroom

by Leonore Ganschow, Ed.D. and Richard L. Sparks, Ed.D.

The acquisition of a foreign language in our increasingly multilingual society has emerged as a major goal for today's students. Across the country, states require or are starting to require foreign language study by all students, sometimes beginning as early as middle school. Further, in our public schools the movement towards inclusion–placing students with exceptionalities (special education) in regular classrooms–has received increasing emphasis since the early 1990s. These are real changes from the days when the study of a foreign language was largely reserved for the "college-bound" student. Today's foreign language instructors face increasing teaching challenges as more and more learners of diverse abilities and cultures come together in their classrooms.

In this introduction, an approach is presented for addressing the needs of diverse learners. The term "at-risk language learners" is used to describe students who struggle with languages, native or foreign. The introduction is divided into two themes, both of which are important as underpinnings for helping teachers build successful adaptation strategies in their classroom. The themes are (1) there are well-supported assumptions about at-risk language learners and (2) there are solid principles of instruction for at-risk language learners. Both the assumptions and the principles are based on an extensive body of research and input from numerous foreign language and native language teachers who have had years of experience working specifically with at-risk native language learners.

Assumptions

Why do some students learn a foreign language so easily? They learn the meanings of new vocabulary words quickly and begin to read and spell words in the foreign language easily. They quickly comprehend phrases and questions and sometimes even pronounce words in the foreign language as if they had previously spoken the language. They appear to incorporate most aspects of the new language naturally and without extensive effort. In contrast, foreign language teachers encounter other students who cannot read words in the new language and constantly misspell words even after extensive review. They confuse the meanings of vocabulary words and cannot say or understand simple basic foreign language phrases or basic questions. Despite dogged attempts to learn the language, there is nothing that comes naturally to them.

In past years, most foreign language educators assumed that students who did poorly in language classes displayed low motivation, negative attitudes, or lack of effort. While some poor language learners exhibit these characteristics, foreign language teachers often are baffled because these students want to succeed but simply are unable to do so despite spending extra time studying the course material or even participating in tutoring. Moreover, many of the students who have problems in foreign language classes are otherwise good students who do reasonably well (and even exceptionally) in their other courses.

Over the years, researchers have studied why students with average to above-average intelligence struggle with foreign language learning. The emergence of an extensive body of research on native language learning problems has enabled researchers to draw parallels between native and foreign language learning. Findings indicate that "at-risk" students who have difficulty with foreign language learning exhibit overt or subtle problems with their native language skills. Their problems with native language learning usually occurred when they were much younger (i.e., in the primary or intermediate grades) and affected their skills when they were learning to read, spell, and write their native language. Many of these students then struggled in high school with reading comprehension, and they were poor and/or slow readers. Some of these "at-risk" students may have exhibited speech articulation (pronunciation) deficits that required speech therapy. Others had difficulty learning phonics (i.e., letter-sound relationships) and may have received tutoring to learn how to read and spell their native language. Some "at-risk" students learned to read and spell their native language well but have always had difficulty with comprehending oral and/or written language. Still others have weak vocabulary skills in their native language and do not know the meanings of words that their peers seem to know.

It is not surprising that "at-risk" students who had difficulty learning to read, spell, and write their native language or had previous difficulty with speech articulation or who have weak vocabulary skills have similar difficulties when attempting to learn a foreign language. After all, learning to read, spell, write, speak, and listen to a foreign language is the learning of *language,* albeit a new language. And therein lies the problem. The difficulties that these "at-risk" learners encountered in learning their first language are "re-created" when they face the task of learning a second language.

Generally, "at-risk" students who have difficulty with foreign language learning have language-based problems. These problems can occur in the phonological (sound and sound-symbol), syntactic (grammar), and/or semantic (meaning) components of language. For example, a student who had problems in the phonological component of English in elementary school may have had difficulty learning phonics, i.e., the sounds that letters make. This student will probably have difficulty learning to read and spell words in a foreign language and may also have some problems with the pronunciation of words in the new language. In some cases, for example, a student with serious phonological problems may not even notice that some consonant sounds or most vowel sounds in the foreign language are different from the sounds in their native language. Another student may have had problems with the syntactic component of the native language. He or she may have experienced problems with subject-verb agreement or the understanding of adjectives and adverbs. This student will likely have difficulty with grammatical learning in the foreign language. For example, he or she may struggle conjugating verbs, matching the correct masculine or feminine article with a noun, or placing the adjective in the proper order in a spoken or written sentence in the new language. A third type of student may have adequate phonological skills but have weak native language syntactic (grammar) and semantics (meaning) skills. In the native language, this student has difficulty using appropriate grammar when writing and speaking and also has problems with the efficient comprehension of language when listening to others speak or when reading. In the foreign language, this student may have difficulty comprehending oral questions and written text even though he or she knows the meaning of the vocabulary words. Sometimes, students with semantic difficulties do well in the first semester or year of foreign language learning but begin to struggle when the amount and complexity of listening comprehension, speaking, reading comprehension, and writing increase.

New research findings from several languages show that most "at-risk" language learners have problems primarily in the phonological (sound and sound-symbol) and sometimes syntactic (grammatical) components of language. Generally, students who have problems with foreign language learning do not have the same degree of difficulty learning the semantic (meaning) aspects of the new language as they do learning the new phonological and grammar systems. For example, they tend to learn the meaning of new vocabulary words or basic phrases and questions fairly well. However, their problems with the phonology and grammar of the native language cause them to have problems with reading and spelling words, pronouncing sounds, comprehending questions and sentences, and writing grammatically correct sentences in the foreign language. Most of the time, the problems of these "at-risk" learners become apparent early in the first weeks of the first semester of the foreign language course. Other "at-risk" learners may do average work in the first quarter of the course but begin to exhibit problems soon thereafter.

Foreign language teachers play a crucial role in helping their at-risk language learners attain success in their classrooms.

Researchers have found that "at-risk" students who struggle to learn the phonology and grammar of a new language not only exhibit poor skills in the written aspects (reading and writing) of the foreign language, but also achieve low scores on the oral aspects (i.e., speaking and listening) of learning a new language. That is, they do not learn to speak and interpret the foreign language as well as students who have stronger phonological and syntactic skills. Researchers speculate that students with lower levels of phonology and grammar will be hindered in both the written and oral aspects of foreign language learning.

Each year, foreign language teachers encounter increasing numbers of students in their classrooms classified as learning disabled, at risk, language impaired, or even dyslexic. While each student is unique, most students with language learning problems exhibit similar types of difficulties. Their difficulties are *language-based;* that is, the students have problems with the phonological, syntactic, and/or semantic components of language. Because their problems with the learning of a foreign language originate in weak language skills, the large majority of these "at-risk" learners will benefit from instruction that follows several basic principles.

Principles of Instruction

What can foreign language teachers learn from these findings that apply in their inclusion classrooms? This question can be answered by tying these findings to principles derived from an extensive body of literature on language instruction (listening, speaking, reading, writing) with at-risk language learners in the native language. Further, there is a small body of research indicating that principles of instruction that apply to at-risk learners in the native language are effective with at-risk foreign language learners as well. Drawing upon this research base, foreign language teachers can apply the following eight principles of instruction in working with at-risk language learners by making the learning of a foreign language:

Multisensory use multiple input/output strategies and involve all of the learning channels–visual, auditory, tactile, and kinesthetic
Repetitive provide ample opportunities for students to "overlearn" a concept through frequent practice and reviews
Structured teach language concepts in logical order and help students organize the language into logical categories
Sequential organize language concepts from simple to complex. Note that the term sequential also applies to the phonological level of language, where at-risk language learners have difficulty learning the sound and sound-symbol system of the foreign language, and to the grammatical level of language, where at-risk language learners have problems recognizing parts of speech (nouns, verbs, adjectives)
Cumulative build on what at-risk language learners already know
Alphabetic/phonetic teach students directly and explicitly the sounds of the language and the letters those sounds/sound sequences represent
Metacognitive teach students how to think about or reflect on the language; thinking about how the language is structured is especially important in grasping grammar concepts (e.g., word order in a sentence)
Synthetic/analytic help students break language into parts (analytic) and put the parts together again (synthetic). For example, help them recognize parts in a chunk of language (a syllable, a word, a phrase, a sentence) (analytic). Help them put together the sounds of the language to form words and chunk parts of words (prefixes, suffixes, roots) together to form larger words (synthetic).

Instructional adaptations for at-risk language learners, then, should reflect one or more of these guiding principles.

These eight principles provide some direction for teachers, but can these principles really be applied successfully in inclusion settings? In our view, the extent to which instruction can be modified and the types of lesson adaptations that are feasible and desirable depend to a large extent on the *severity* of the at-risk learner's language difficulties and on the *nature* of the learner's language difficulties. In terms of severity, it is helpful to think of a continuum of difficulty/lack of difficulty with language. The following figure visually presents an outline of a severity continuum in relation to the degree of adaptations that might be necessary in inclusion classrooms.

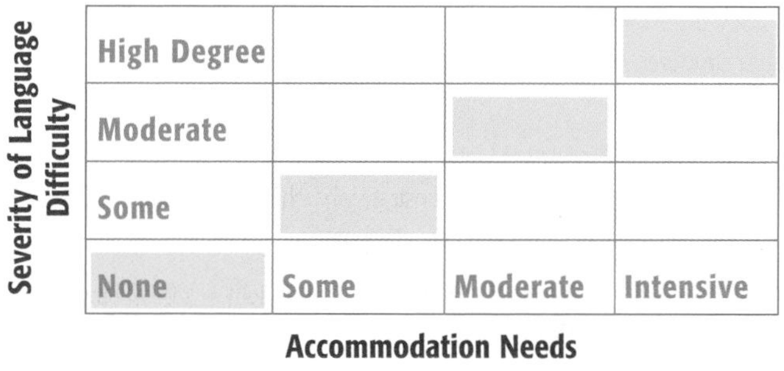

Severity of Language Difficulty

High Degree			
Moderate			
Some			
None	Some	Moderate	Intensive

Accommodation Needs

In inclusion classrooms, foreign language teachers are likely to experience the most success using accommodations for students with some to moderate difficulties. As the severity of the language difficulty becomes more of an issue, the need for adaptation strategies becomes increasingly critical. For students with a high degree of language difficulty and intensive accommodation needs, teachers should consult with the learning specialist at their school as more intensive modifications may be necessary.

Foreign language teachers play a crucial role in helping their at-risk language learners attain success in their classrooms. In order to do so, however, teachers need an understanding of the nature of these students' learning difficulties and help in developing accommodations that can be successful in helping them learn the foreign language.

General Suggestions for Making Classroom Accommodations

- Provide a simple study guide of the day's activities (structured).
- Present major points simultaneously orally and on overheads; have students repeat important words and phrases and say them again as they write them in their notebooks (multisensory).
- Provide guided pair activities to practice/reinforce a concept (pair strong/weaker language learners) (repetitive).
- Analyze the concept to be learned and talk students through the sequence of steps needed to master the concept (especially important in teaching grammar concepts); have written samples available to work as guides (sequential).
- Require students to keep a notebook and help them organize it (structured).
- Speak slowly and with clear pronunciation, using the same phrases repeatedly (alphabetic/phonetic).
- Provide daily structured written reviews of material covered that day (repetitive, cumulative).
- Use verbal/visual (pictorial) mnemonic devices to assist in memory; let students design their own mnemonic devices and discuss the value of this strategy (metacognitive).
- Show students how parts are added to words to change meaning and how long words can be broken down into parts (i.e., prefixes, suffixes, roots) (synthetic/analytic).
- Use color coding to illustrate grammar and pronunciation (alphabetic/phonetic).
- Provide an opportunity to demonstrate mastery of smaller chunks of information prior to longer, unit exams (sequential, repetitive).
- Provide time for students to reflect on how they best learn and remember language concepts; teach them strategies to help them remember (metacognitive).

Inclusion of Accelerated Language Learners in the French Classroom

Gifted and talented learners have the potential to move through the foreign language curriculum at an accelerated pace; some excel in one language area, such as reading or speaking; others may excel in all language areas. Typically, these students learn new language concepts quickly; they don't need repetition and once they learn something, they remember. They're highly curious, find new information challenging and stimulating, and often ask probing questions. They're also creative and enjoy tackling the unfamiliar. Their approach to problem-solving, including the challenge of a new language, is often unusual because they tend to think "outside the box." On the flip side, if these students are not challenged, they might tune out, stop doing their homework, and become a problem to the teacher.

Principles of Instruction

How, then, might foreign language teachers address the special needs of the accelerated language learner? Educators of the gifted commonly recommend that teachers differentiate their classroom curriculum. Classroom teachers can differentiate the foreign language curriculum by modifying (1) course content, (2) the learning process, (3) the learning environment, and (4) the product or outcome expectations. The following examples demonstrate how teachers can differentiate curriculum in their foreign language classes.

Course Content

Enrichment Through Curriculum Expansion Develop structured opportunities for students to explore the language through an expansion or extension of activities related to a given language concept or topic. Educators of the gifted can be very helpful in setting up these learning experiences.

Enrichment Through In-depth Exploration Develop opportunities for students to deepen their understanding of a language concept or topic through a more in-depth focus. Again, teachers might solicit guidance from an educator of the gifted.

Learning Process

Self-pacing Allow students to move through the textbook and their assignments at an accelerated pace. Allow them to competency-test out of units.

Individualized Learning Once they have mastered a language concept, provide structured opportunities for students to work on their own. Short- and long-term projects can be negotiated through teacher-student contracts.

Self-directed Learning Encourage students to initiate or create their own enrichment activities. The role of teacher becomes negotiating, structuring, and monitoring the learning experience.

Learning Environment

Higher-Level Thinking Encourage students to think about language concepts in increasingly complex ways. In helping students design activities, use the three highest levels of Bloom's taxonomy (analysis, synthesis, evaluation).

Creative Thinking Encourage students to develop unusual or unique approaches to language study. Invite them to problem-solve in figuring out language structures such as grammar concepts and vocabulary connections.

Product/Outcome Expectations

Product Variation Allow students to demonstrate what they are learning in different ways and through a variety of verbal and nonverbal media.

Self-Evaluation Provide opportunities for students to participate in evaluating their own progress and their products.

Initially, implementing these principles will necessitate some extra work by the teacher. However, the experience of providing a motivating and enriched environment will ultimately be fulfilling for the student and allow the foreign language teacher to experience the satisfaction of having challenged the student. Further, the task will become easier as the teacher increases his or her understanding of the specialized needs and capabilities of accelerated language learners and uses this knowledge to build a repertoire of appropriate differentiated curriculum options.

Related References

General

Ganschow, L., & Sparks, R. (2001). Learning difficulties and foreign language learning: A review of research and instruction. *Language Teaching, 34,* 79–98.

Ganschow, L., & Sparks, R. (2000). Reflections on foreign language study for students with language learning problems: Research, issues, and challenges. *Dyslexia, 6,* 87–100.

Sparks, R., & Ganschow, L. (1991). Foreign language learning difficulties: Affective or native language aptitude differences? *Modern Language Journal, 75,* 3–16.

Research

Sparks, R., Artzer, M., Patton, J., Ganschow, L., Miller, K., Hordubay, D., & Walsh, G. (1998). Benefits of multisensory language instruction for at-risk learners: A comparison study of high school Spanish students. *Annals of Dyslexia, 48,* 239–270.

Sparks, R., Ganschow, L., Javorsky, J., Pohlman, J., & Patton, J. (1992). Test comparisons among students identified as high-risk, low-risk, and learning disabled in high school foreign language courses. *Modern Language Journal, 76,* 142–159.

Sparks, R., Ganschow, L., Javorsky, J., Pohlman, J., & Patton, J. (1992). Identifying native language deficits in high and low-risk foreign language learners in high school. *Foreign Language Annals, 25,* 403–418.

Teaching

Ganschow, L., & Schneider, E. (1997). Teaching all students: From research to reality. In A. Vogely (Ed.), *Celebrating languages, opening all minds!* Annual Meeting Series – NO. 14, New York State Association of Foreign Language Teachers, Fall, 1997.

Pritikin, L. (1999). *A policy of inclusion: Alternative foreign language curriculum for high-risk and learning disabled students.* ERIC Clearinghouse on Languages and Linguistics, Center for Applied Linguistics. ED 428 486.

Schneider, E., & Ganschow, L. (2000). Dynamic assessment and instructional strategies for learners who struggle to learn a foreign language. *Dyslexia, 6,* 72–82.

Sparks, R., Ganschow, L., & Schneider, E. (2002). Teaching foreign (second) languages to at-risk learners: Research and practice. In J. H. Sullivan (Ed.), *Literacy and the second language learner* (pp. 55–83). Greenwich, CT: Information Age Publishing.

Sparks, R., & Miller, K. (2000). Teaching a foreign language using multisensory structured language techniques to at-risk learners: A review. *Dyslexia, 6,* 124–132.

Strategies for Pre-AP Students

by Mary L. Diehl

Integrating Pre-AP strategies into the *Discovering French, Nouveau!* series

The standards-based goals of the **Discovering French, *Nouveau!*** series address the skills necessary for success in Advanced Placement French Language. While many instructional approaches exist for developing the skills required in AP, certain strategies prepare students to meet the objectives of the AP course and examination in French language. The **Discovering French, *Nouveau!*** series uses an integrated, thematic approach that combines listening, speaking, reading, and writing. Vertical teaming, beginning with French 1 and continuing through the highest level offered (AP language and/or literature), is essential in ensuring success. In other words, teachers work together to provide sequential programs that develop language proficiency and challenge all students. **Discovering French, *Nouveau!*** offers important tools for teachers to do just that.

Background Information: The Advanced Placement French Language Course and Examination

The AP French Language Course prepares students for the French Language Examination, which evaluates proficiency in listening comprehension, grammar and vocabulary, reading, speaking and writing. The skills of listening and reading comprehension are tested as multiple-choice items while speaking and writing are assessed in a free-response format. A group of questions based on a picture or picture sequence evaluates speaking proficiency. Fill-ins that require a grammatically correct, logical answer and a composition assess writing ability. The examination is timed and students must learn to work within the time limits. Note that the AP exam weighs the reading, writing, listening, and speaking sections at 25% each. Begin to prepare students in French 1–3 by using strategies that reflect the goals of the AP course and examination.

Grammar and vocabulary

Students must develop a command of many grammatical structures and a wide range of vocabulary in order to be proficient in listening, reading, speaking, and writing. Teaching students *about* grammar is not the same as having students *use* the grammar and vocabulary they have learned to carry on conversations, understand what they hear, read and comprehend what they have read, and write coherent sentences, paragraphs, and, later on, compositions. Incorporate the new grammar and vocabulary students learn into the different types of activities students perform. You can provide learner-centered opportunities for Pre-AP students to:

- use a variety of structures and vocabulary, which increase in complexity as the students move from level 1 through level 3.
- recognize errors in forms or usage. On the speaking portion of the Advanced Placement Examination, for example, awareness of error which leads to self-correction shows that the student is cognizant of what is "correct" usage. This student will score at a higher level than one who does not self-correct because he/she is unaware of errors.
- demonstrate knowledge and use of devices that link meaning (transitions).
- use circumlocution. Encourage students to describe in French rather than use English when they don't know a certain word or phrase.
- use a variety of structures and vocabulary at the same time rather than always dealing with one tense, structure, or set of vocabulary items at a time.

Discovering French, *Nouveau!* 1–3 teaches structures and includes many topics ideal for Pre-AP courses. The exercises requiring that the students create with the language rather than merely following a pattern are crucial. Exercises that provide practice in the same format as the AP exam are also important (examples: **Discovering French, *Nouveau!–Blanc,*** p. 132, Activity 9; **Discovering French, *Nouveau!–Rouge,*** p. 206, Activity 10). Pre-AP students, especially in level 3, need practice exercises that "mix" a variety of structures and vocabulary. Make students aware of tense usage and the complexities of language structure as their proficiency level increases.

Listening

The AP listening section requires students to listen and respond to two types of speech. First, they listen to short exchanges between two speakers and choose the logical response from a list. Second, they hear dialogues or short monologues and answer questions that are given on the audio. In order to prepare students for these tasks, Pre-AP courses should include a wide variety of listening passages on many different topics. The passages should become longer and more complicated as the student progresses through levels 1, 2, and 3. For example, in **Discovering French, *Nouveau!–Bleu,*** students learn to get the "gist" of passages and then more details as their proficiency increases. By the time students use **Discovering French, *Nouveau!–Rouge,*** listening passages stress both the main idea and details and involve more complicated material.

You can help Pre-AP students organize information by incorporating sequencing, sorting, and categorizing activities. First, the Pre-AP students learn to summarize what they have heard and later analyze, compare and contrast, and evaluate the information.

Ask questions that range from the concrete and factual to those that ask for implied or inferred information. From the beginning, the Pre-AP student should be given the opportunity to tell "why" and to use higher order thinking skills.

Incorporate these specific strategies to help the Pre-AP student get ready for the listening portion of the AP Examination:

- Conduct your classes in the target language to the greatest extent possible.
- Provide practice in a multiple-choice format as well as the question/answer type free response.
- Have students listen only and not read the text at the same time.
- Teach students to use context cues to determine unknown words or phrases they hear. Encourage students to "guess."
- Teach students to listen for intonation patterns and stress to determine whether they are hearing a question, a statement, and so on. By listening for stress patterns they can also determine if the speaker is talking about the past, present, or future.
- Teach students to listen for background noises or sounds that help determine where a dialogue takes place.
- Provide opportunities for students to practice note-taking skills when listening or viewing.
- Design or choose activities that require the class to listen to classmates (as well as tapes, videos or DVDs, CDs, and you, their teacher). Elicit a written or spoken response to what is heard. (Example: Students do oral presentations on travel brochures they have created and classmates list reasons for going to each place. This encourages listening for both general ideas and details.)

Reading

On the reading section of the AP exam, students read for the main idea, details, and inferred meaning. The passages vary in length and generally are cultural in nature. Students must have command of grammar and vocabulary in order to understand the reading selections which come from a wide range of sources (examples: fiction, journalistic articles, essays). Teach your Pre-AP students to:

- identify the main idea and as many details as possible.
- use pre-reading skills such as establishing the purpose, making predictions, looking for cognates, and so on.
- skim and scan.
- read increasingly longer, more complicated passages.
- sequence information.
- use context clues.
- analyze language used (formal, informal, metaphors, similes, etc.)
- make predictions and inferences based on what they have read.
- draw conclusions.
- recreate the text in their own words.
- elaborate when summarizing.
- distinguish fact from opinion.
- determine cause and effect.
- indicate where in the text the answer to a certain question is found. The questions and the answers may express ideas in language using synonyms or circumlocution.

Writing

The writing section of the AP has two parts. The first is a fill-in section that requires students to have sufficient command of grammar and vocabulary to understand the sentences they read before "filling-in," to choose the correct form, to spell words correctly and to put accents in the right place. This is an "all or nothing" section. Students will do well on this portion of the AP if they have been trained from French I in the way they will be evaluated.

The second part of the writing section is a composition on a general topic. Students are to write a "well-organized essay." The essay is evaluated holistically "for appropriateness and range of vocabulary, grammatical accuracy, idiomatic usage, organization, and style." (French Course Description, College Board, 2004, p. 18) In order to prepare your Pre-AP students for these tasks, provide opportunities for them to:

- write in a timed situation.
- use pre-writing skills such as brainstorming, organizing ideas, making outlines.
- organize thoughts and then essays. Know how to write introductions, supporting paragraphs and conclusions.
- write thesis statements.
- support ideas with details.
- use transitions and ways to link paragraphs.
- write relevant and thorough compositions.
- consider the audience (voice) and establish purpose.

- write relevant and thorough responses.
- practice combining sentences
- use a variety of vocabulary and structures to form cohesive sentences, paragraphs and essays.
- show command of the conventions of written language.
- control both simple and complex structures.
- evaluate the writing of others as well as their own writing. (peer-edit and self-edit)
- practice writing in a variety of formats: journals, letters, articles, dialogues, and essays.

Begin with very guided writing. In level 1, students write simple information with learned phrases, structures and vocabulary. In level 2, students begin to create with the language, while level 3 students can write about a wider variety of topics using a greater number of structures and transitions. The most important point is to provide many writing opportunities.

Composition

Have students use the **Vive la différence** dialogue as a point of departure for writing a composition about themselves and one of their friends. Suggest that they write their descriptions in two columns, using as a model Léa's and Céline's text on p. 150. Students should complete their compositions in 15 minutes. **Pre-AP skill:** Write in a timed situation.

Pre-reading

Have students look quickly at the menu and decide what meal is presented.

How can they tell? **Pre-AP skill:** Skim and scan.

Speaking

In the speaking section of the AP exam, students are asked questions based on a picture or series of pictures. They have ninety seconds to study the picture(s), read the questions, and prepare their answers. They are then given sixty seconds to record their answer for each question. In order to prepare students for this task, have them:

- retell information or stories (move from simple to complex in levels 1–3).
- use pictures as a basis for telling stories or describing.
- respond to questions with thorough answers that are increasingly more complex and correct.
- plan for what will be said by brainstorming answers.
- organize ideas and sequence information.
- vary vocabulary and circumlocute.
- expand, elaborate.
- use intonation and pronounce with care.
- self-correct.
- agree, disagree; approve, disapprove; encourage, discourage.
- give directions, orders, advice.
- relate opinions.
- communicate preferences.
- persuade.
- relate what happened before, what is happening, what will happen next
- participate in pair activities, information gap activities where one student has the information another needs.
- answer within a given time frame.
- take risks and not be afraid to make errors.
- feel comfortable speaking. In linguistic terms, this is "lowering the affective filter."

General Comments

The **Discovering French, *Nouveau!*** series contains many activities that will prepare the Pre-AP student for the AP French course. Many of the sections involving speaking (*Tête à tête,* for example) could easily be targeted for Pre-AP, especially those involving storytelling (Expansion activities). The *À votre tour!* sections could be emphasized for the Pre-AP students. Writing should occur frequently so that the students are ready for what follows in the AP courses. At times, you may redesign activities with the Advanced Placement Language Course and Examination in mind so they go a step further in preparing students. Many of the strategies presented above are used in combination. The skills of listening, reading, speaking and writing do not develop isolated from each other. This way, the job of the AP teacher is facilitated and the students benefit. Our goal is not only success on the AP French Language Examination but also to produce students who understand what they read and hear and who can communicate ideas through speaking and writing.

Technology in the Classroom

Introduction

Technology—whether it is on the Internet, CD-ROM, or DVD—provides additional resources, enrichment, and excitement to the French classroom, and makes teachers' lives easier. **Discovering French, *Nouveau!*** provides technology resources that make your teaching easier, more effective, and more enjoyable. Components include:

- Online Workbook
- ClassZone.com
- DVD Program
- Audio Program
- Power Presentations on CD-ROM
- McDougal Littell Assessment System/Test Generator CD-ROM
- EasyPlanner CD-ROM

In order to select technology products that enhance and complement your own teaching style, consider the following checklist:

- Easy to use
- Fully integrated into the student text and teacher's materials
- Offer full use of the strongest features of each particular medium
- Interactive to motivate student interest
- Flexibly structured for individual and pair/group use
- Suitable for your particular teaching style

Technology should always be the means to a more effective language presentation, and not an end in itself. In addition, good technology products should never be intimidating!

Integrating well-designed technology into the French curriculum gives both students and teachers access to the French-speaking world no matter where their classroom is located! The **Discovering French, *Nouveau!*** program provides technology components that are fun, practical, focused, and easy-to-use.

Online Workbook and ClassZone.com

The Internet has opened an exciting new environment for language teaching and learning. **Discovering French, *Nouveau!*** has taken advantage of the best capabilities of the Internet to offer teachers and students leveled, self-scoring practice in the *Online Workbook* as well as webquests, test preparation, flashcards, and more on *ClassZone.com.*

Integrating the wide range of Internet resources available for **Discovering French, *Nouveau!*** on *ClassZone.com* into your classroom can revitalize your teaching and provide you and your students with a personalized connection to French speakers worldwide.

Audio and DVD

The **Discovering French, *Nouveau!*** Audio and DVD Program motivates students from the first day of class, and provides a complete cultural and linguistic experience.

Objectives

- Foster cross-cultural connections
- Develop listening skills using dozens of different voices in varied contexts
- Promote communication skills in real-life situations
- Encourage vocabulary acquisition in context
- Provide materials suitable for a variety of learners
- Provide authentic music from the francophone world

Discovering French, *Nouveau!* provides technology resources that make your teaching easier, more effective, and more enjoyable.

Power Presentations on CD-ROM

This CD-ROM offers a complete array of grammar and vocabulary PowerPoint™ presentations to support **Discovering French, *Nouveau!*** Teachers can present animated grammar slide shows directly through PowerPoint™ or print out overhead transparencies. The **Discovering French, *Nouveau!*** *Overhead Transparencies* are already included, plus Clip Art is available to help you create and customize your own presentations.

Test Generator CD-ROM and McDougal Littell Assessment System

The **Discovering French, *Nouveau!*** *Test Generator CD-ROM* gives teachers the capability to edit tests and quizzes, create new items or create whole tests. Teachers may use the existing tests, adapt them by adding, deleting, or changing items, or create a completely personalized testing program. Answer keys are generated automatically. The Internet-based *McDougal Littell Assessment System* helps you test, score, and track results. It provides ready-made materials for reteaching and remediation. The scannable tests and answer sheets can be printed out on plain paper.

eEdition CD-ROM

The **Discovering French, *Nouveau!*** CD-ROM provides teachers the complete text of the Pupil Edition in PDF format. Each page of the printed text is included in the easy-to-use electronic version for anytime, anywhere access.

EasyPlanner CD-ROM

The *EasyPlanner CD-ROM* gives teachers the flexibility of having all the ancillaries for **Discovering French, *Nouveau!*** in a convenient electronic format. Teachers can view and print, plus plan their lessons with an easy-to-use calendar feature.

Take-Home Tutor CD-ROM

The Take-Home Tutor CD-ROM provides extra skills support with at-home guided practice. Video clips, audio recordings, flashcards, and self-check exercises reinforce the four skills with point-of-use aids for all students.

Classroom Management

The Role of Listening Comprehension

Listening comprehension provides a very effective introduction to second-language learning. More specifically, listening activities in which students respond physically in some way (moving around, pointing, handling objects, etc.) are not only excellent ways of establishing comprehension of new phrases, but material learned in this manner is remembered longer. This explains why students learn the parts of the body more quickly by playing "Simon Says" than by repeating the same vocabulary words after the teacher.

How is an effective comprehension activity structured?

In a typical comprehension activity, the teacher gives commands to the students, either as a full class, a small group, or individually. The activity often consists of four steps:

STEP 1 Group performance with a teacher model

The teacher gives a command and then performs the action. The students listen, watch and imitate the teacher. Three to five new commands are presented in this way.

STEP 2 Group performance without a teacher model

When the teacher feels the students understand the new phrases, he or she gives the command without moving. It is the students who demonstrate their comprehension by performing the desired action. If the students seem unsure about what to do, the teacher will model the action again.

STEP 3 Individual performance without a teacher model

Once the group can perform the new commands easily, the teacher gives these commands to individual students. If an individual student does not remember a given command, the teacher calls on the group to perform the command. It is important to maintain a relaxing atmosphere where all students feel comfortable.

STEP 4 Individual performance of a series of commands

When the class is comfortable with the new commands, the teacher gives an individual student a series of two or more commands. This type of activity builds retention and encourages more careful listening.

These four steps are repeated each time new commands are introduced. As the activities progress, the new commands are intermingled with those learned previously.

How many new commands are introduced at any one time?

Generally three to five new commands are introduced and then practiced. It is important not to bring in new items until all the students are comfortable with the current material. Practice can be made more challenging by giving the commands more rapidly.

There are essentially two kinds of comprehension activities:

- **TEXT-RELATED ACTIVITIES** These activities introduce material which will be immediately activated in the corresponding lesson of the book. The comprehension activity helps students build their listening comprehension before being asked to produce this new material in speaking and writing. Then, when students are presented with this material formally, they can concentrate on details such as pronunciation and spelling because they will already know what all the new words mean.

- **COMPREHENSION-EXPANSION ACTIVITIES** These activities are designed to expand the students' listening proficiency and introduce vocabulary and structures which will not be formally presented until later in the program. Since this approach is fun, and since the material presented is not formally "tested," comprehension activities can be effectively used for vocabulary expansion and for introduction of new material.

Sample classroom commands

Here is a listing of some sample commands in both the "tu" and the "vous" forms. As a teacher, you have two options:

- You can use the formal "vous" form for both group and individual commands.
- You can address the class and small groups with the plural "vous" form and then address individual students as "tu."

Category	English	Tu form	Vous form
Movements	Stand up.	**Lève-toi.** **Debout.**	**Levez-vous.** **Debout.**
	Sit down.	**Assieds-toi.**	**Asseyez-vous.**
	Walk.	**Marche.**	**Marchez.**
	Jump.	**Saute.**	**Sautez.**
	Stop.	**Arrête.**	**Arrêtez.**
	Turn around.	**Tourne-toi.**	**Tournez-vous.**
	Turn right / left.	**Tourne à droite/à gauche.**	**Tournez à droite/à gauche.**
	Go …	**Va** (au tableau).	**Allez** (à la fenêtre).
	Come …	**Viens** (au bureau).	**Venez** (au tableau).
	Raise …	**Lève** (la main).	**Levez** (le bras).
	Lower …	**Baisse** (la tête).	**Baissez** (les yeux).
Pointing out and manipulating objects	Point out …	**Montre** (le cahier).	**Montrez** (le livre).
	Touch …	**Touche** (la porte).	**Touchez** (la fenêtre).
	Pick up / Take …	**Prends** (le crayon).	**Prenez** (le stylo).
	Put …	**Mets** (le livre sur la table).	**Mettez** (le cahier sous la chaise).
	Take away …	**Enlève** (le livre).	**Enlevez** (le cahier).
	Empty …	**Vide** (le sac).	**Videz** (la corbeille).
	Give …	**Donne** (la cassette à Anne).	**Donnez** (le CD à Paul).
	Give back …	**Rends** (la cassette à Marie).	**Rendez** (le CD à Michel).
	Pass …	**Passe** (le stylo à Denise).	**Passez** (le crayon à Marc).
	Keep …	**Garde** (la cassette).	**Gardez** (la cassette).
	Open …	**Ouvre** (la porte).	**Ouvrez** (le livre).
	Close …	**Ferme** (la fenêtre).	**Fermez** (le cahier).
	Throw …	**Lance** (la balle à Jean).	**Lancez** (le ballon à Claire).
	Bring me …	**Apporte-moi** (la balle).	**Apportez-moi** (le ballon).
Activities with pictures and visuals	Look at …	**Regarde** (la carte).	**Regardez** (le plan de Paris).
	Look for / Find …	**Cherche** (la Suisse).	**Cherchez** (la tour Eiffel).
	Show me …	**Montre-moi** (Genève).	**Montrez-moi** (Notre-Dame).
Paper or chalkboard activities	Draw …	**Dessine** (une maison).	**Dessinez** (un arbre).
	Write …	**Écris** (ton nom).	**Écrivez** (votre nom).
	Erase …	**Efface** (le dessin).	**Effacez** (la carte).
	Color …	**Colorie** (le chat en noir).	**Coloriez** (le chien en jaune).
	Put an "x" on …	**Mets un "x" sur** (le garçon).	**Mettez un "x" sur** (la fille).
	Circle …	**Trace un cercle autour de** (la chemise rouge).	**Tracez un cercle autour de** (la jupe blanche).
	Cut out …	**Découpe** (un coeur).	**Découpez** (un cercle).

Professional Reference Information

Professional Language Organizations

American Association of Teachers of French (AATF)

Mailcode 4510
Southern Illinois University
Carbondale, IL 62901-4510

Phone: (618) 453-5731

www.frenchteachers.org

As an AATF member:

- you will receive subscriptions to the French Review and the AATF National Bulletin.
- you will be able to attend local, regional, and national AATF meetings where you can share ideas and meet new colleagues.
- you have the opportunity to apply for one of the many summer scholarships to France and Quebec offered to AATF members.
- you may sponsor a chapter of the *Société Honoraire de Français* at your school so that your students will then be eligible to compete for study abroad travel grants and participate in the SHF creative writing contest.
- you can have your students participate in the National French Contest and be considered for local, regional, and national awards.
- you can obtain pen pals for your students through the *Bureau de Correspondance Scolaire.*

American Council on the Teaching of Foreign Languages (ACTFL)

700 S. Washington St., Suite 210
Alexandria, VA 22314

Phone: (703) 894-2900

Fax: (703) 894-2905

headquarters@actfl.org

www.actfl.org

Governmental Organizations

Alliance Française

The *Alliance Française* is a French organization dedicated to the promotion of French language and culture.

To obtain the address of the Alliance Française nearest you, write:

Federation of Alliances Françaises USA
1800 E. Capitol Drive
Milwaukee, WI 53211

Phone: 800-6-FRANCE (800-637-2623)

Fax: 1-800-491-6980

federation@afusa.org

www.afusa.org

French Cultural Services

The French Cultural Services are very supportive of French teaching in the United States. For more information, contact the French Cultural Officer at the French Consulate nearest you or write the New York office.

To obtain information about available French cultural materials, write:

Cultural Services of the French Embassy
972 Fifth Avenue
New York, NY 10021

Phone: (212) 439-1400

Fax: (212) 439-1455

www.frenchculture.org

Other Useful Addresses

Sister Cities International

If your town has a Sister City in a French-speaking country, you might want to explore the possibility of initiating a youth or education exchange program. If your town does not yet have a French-speaking Sister City, you might want to encourage your community to set up such an affiliation.

For information on both youth exchanges and the establishment of a sister-city association, contact:

Sister Cities International
1301 Pennsylvania Ave, NW
Suite 850
Washington, DC 20004

Phone: (202) 347-8630

www.sister-cities.org

info@sister-cities.org

Nacel Open Door

Nacel Open Door is a nonprofit organization sponsoring cultural exchanges between American and foreign families and students. If you have students who would like to host a French-speaking student for a month during the summer, or who would themselves like to stay with a family in France or Senegal, have them contact the non-profit organization Nacel Open Door.

Nacel Open Door
1536 Hewitt Avenue, Box 268
St. Paul, MN 55104

Phone: 800-NACELLE (800-622-3553)

info@nacelopendoor.org

www.nacelopendoor.org

1

Bleu

Discovering FRENCH Nouveau!

Jean-Paul Valette
Rebecca M. Valette

McDougal Littell
A DIVISION OF HOUGHTON MIFFLIN COMPANY
Evanston, Illinois • Boston • Dallas

Teacher Reviewers

Paul Giles
Forsyth Central High School, Georgia

Thierry Gustave
Lincoln School, Rhode Island

David Miller
Davis High School, Utah

Teacher Panel for Revised Edition

Linda Davisson
Wilbur Middle School, Kansas

Korey Dugger
Austin-East Magnet High School, Tennessee

Carolyn Fletcher
Bonita High School, California

Paul Giles
Forsyth Central High School, Georgia

Carole Lapointe-Prospère
West Roxbury High School, Massachusetts

Paul J. Maher
West Seneca East Senior High School, New York

Ann Minor
St. Andrew's Episcopal School, Mississippi

Dr. Mary Schense
Manzano High School, New Mexico

Martha Schillerstrom
Glenbard East High School, Illinois

Jennifer Schoenfeld
Lawton Community Schools, Michigan

Student Reviewers

Rebecca Lange
Washington

Donald Medor
Massachusetts

Native Reader

Sophie Masliah
Saint-Germain-en-Laye, France

Teacher Review Board

Steve Covey
Sunnyvale Junior High School, California

Dianne Hopen
Humboldt High School, Minnesota

Patricia McCann
Lincoln-Sudbury High School, Massachusetts

T. Jeffrey Richards
Roosevelt High School, South Dakota

Margie Ricks
Dulles High School, Texas

Frank Strell
La Salle-Peru Township High School, Illinois

Susan Wildman
Western Albemarle High School, Virginia

Cover photography

Cover design by Studio Montage **Front cover** Eiffel Tower illuminated at night, Paris, France; **Back cover** Level 1a: Palace of Versailles, Versailles, France; Level 1b: Martinique; Level 1: Eiffel Tower illuminated at night, Paris, France; Level 2: Chateau Frontenac, Quebec Old Town, Quebec, Canada; Level 3: Port Al-Kantaoui, Sousse, Tunisia
Photography credits appear on page R52.

Printed in the United States of America

ISBN-13: 978-0-618-65651-6
ISBN-10: 0-618-65651-0 X 2 3 4 5 6 7 8 9 10 - VJM - 12 11 10 09 08 07 06

Internet: www.mcdougallittell.com

Faisons connaissance

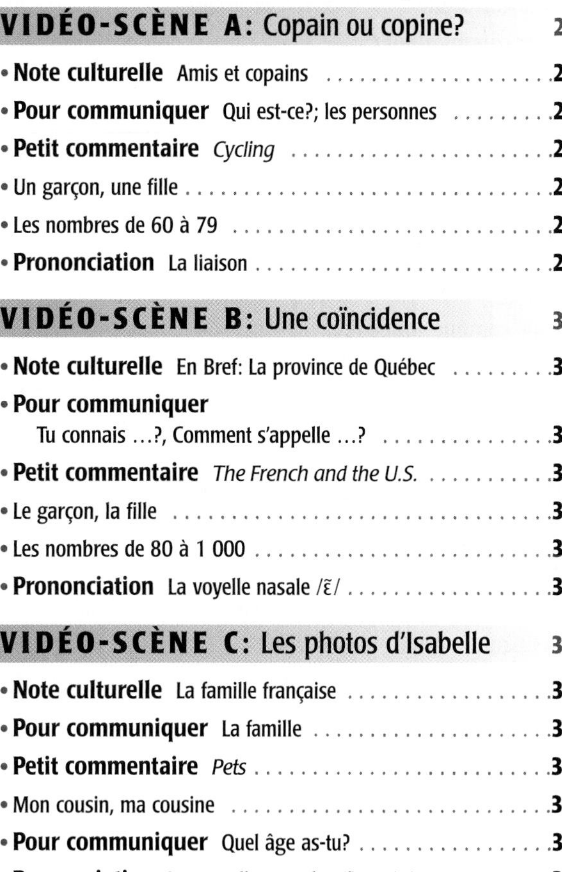

iii

UNITÉ 2 *Invitation au français*

La vie courante

LEÇON 3 Bon appétit!

LEÇON 4 De jour en jour

iv

UNITÉ 3

Qu'est-ce qu'on fait?

Thème Daily activities

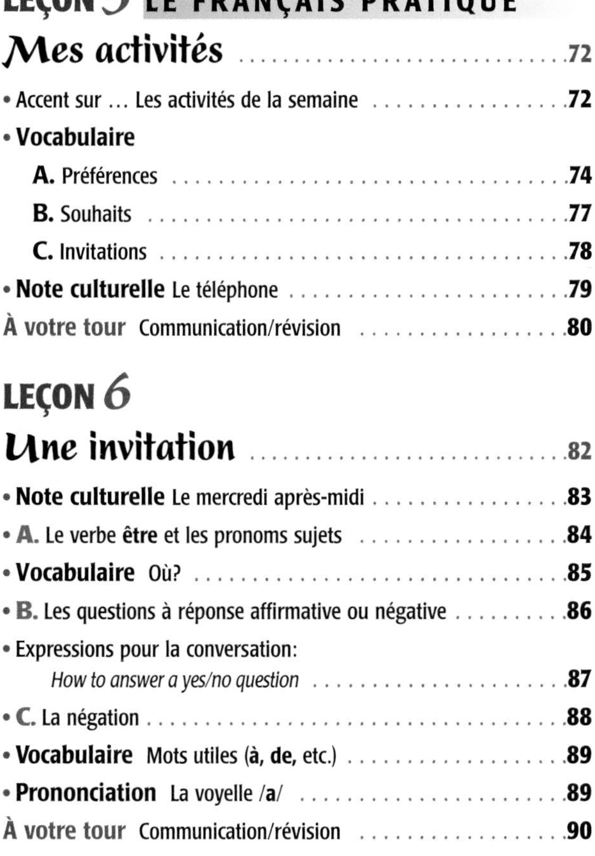

v

UNITÉ 4

Le monde personnel et familier

vi

Unité 5

vii

Le shopping

viii

ix

Les repas

Bienvenue ... and welcome!

Chers amis,

Welcome to *Discovering French-Nouveau!* and congratulations on your choice of French as a foreign language! Perhaps someone in your family speaks French. Maybe you know people who are of French-speaking origin — from France or Canada or Louisiana or Haiti or western Africa — and you want to better appreciate their heritage. Or perhaps you are hoping to travel to Quebec or Martinique or Paris, and want to be able to get around easily on your own. Perhaps simply you were influenced by the fact that French is a beautiful language. Or maybe you have studied ballet and already know quite a few French expressions. Or you like to bicycle and enjoy watching the **Tour de France.** Or you love the Internet and want to explore the many exciting French sites. Or perhaps your friends have told you that French class is fun and opens doors to a whole new world. Whatever the reason or reasons, welcome and **bienvenue!**

By learning French, you will get to know and communicate with people who use French in their daily lives. These millions of French speakers or **francophones** come from a wide variety of ethnic and cultural backgrounds. As you will see, they live not only in France and other parts of Europe, but also in Africa, in North and South America, in Asia . . . in fact, on all continents.

By studying French, you will also develop a better understanding of your own language and how it works. And by exploring cultural similarities and differences, you will grow to appreciate your own culture and value the culture of others.

On the pages of this book and in the accompanying video, you will meet many young people who speak French. Listen carefully to what they say and how they express themselves. They will help you understand not only their language but also the way they live.

Bonne chance!

Jean-Paul Valette Rebecca M. Valette

Teaching Resource Options

PRINT 

Unit 1 Resource Book
Videoscript, pp. 193–194

VIDEO PROGRAM

VIDÉO DVD

IMAGES
Parlons français!

TOTAL TIME: 6:42 min.
DVD Disk 1
Videotape 1 (COUNTER: 00:00 min.)

A.1 Introduction (0:00-0:48 min.)

A.2 La France (0:49-2:34 min.)

A.3 Le monde francophone (2:35-4:42 min.)

A.4 Des francophones aux États-Unis (4:43-6:42 min.)

Photo cultural notes

- **L'Opéra National de Paris** This building was designed by Charles Garnier and was completed in 1874. It is also known as **l'Opéra de Paris, le palais Garnier,** and simply **l'Opéra.** In addition to operas, spectators can see concerts, ballets, and modern dance performances.
- **Le musée du Louvre** Probably the most well-known pieces of the Louvre's collection are the Mona Lisa **(La Joconde)** by Leonardo da Vinci and the **Vénus de Milo,** but the museum also houses ancient and medieval artifacts, and paintings and sculptures from around the world and of many eras. The pyramid is the main entrance to the Louvre. At night, the pyramid and the facades of the Louvre are illuminated.

Pourquoi parler français?

WHY SPEAK FRENCH?

Here are ten good reasons.

1. ***French is an international language.***
French is the first or second language in about fifty countries or regions in Europe, Africa, North and South America, Asia, and Oceania. It is spoken by over 100 million people around the world.

2. ***French is an important diplomatic language.***
French is one of the five official languages of the United Nations and one of the two main languages of the European Union.

3. ***French is the second language on the Internet.***
With French, you have immediate access to Internet sites in France and Quebec, as well as sites in Belgium, Switzerland, and French-speaking countries of Africa.

4. ***France is a technologically advanced country.***
Historically, French inventors have contributed significantly to the advancement of science. Today, France is a leader in areas such as aero-space technology, high-speed transportation, automotive design, and medical research.

5. ***France is a leader in the world of art and literature.***
Over the past 400 years, Paris has been an important cultural center, attracting artists and writers from around the world. France has won more Nobel Prizes in literature than any other country.

▲ un cybercafé à Paris

▲ l'Opéra National de Paris

le musée du Louvre ▶

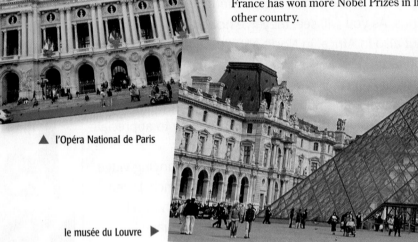

le TGV (train à grand vitesse) ▶
high-speed train

6. ***France is a prime tourist destination.***
If you like to travel, it will not surprise you to learn that millions of tourists visit France every year — and speaking French makes their vacations much more meaningful and more enjoyable.

7. ***For many people, France evokes style and elegance.***
When people think of high fashion, beauty products, perfumes, or gourmet cuisine, they think of France . . . and rightly so.

8. ***Knowing French will enrich your English.***
In 1066, William the Conqueror, a French nobleman, invaded England and became king, bringing with him his court and his language: French. Today over one-third of all English words are derived from French. As you study French, you will increase your English vocabulary.

9. ***Knowing French will help you with your university studies.***
University admissions officers look for candidates who have foreign language skills. In addition, research by the College Board shows that the longer students study a foreign language, the higher their math and verbal SAT scores.

10. ***Knowing French will be useful for your career.***
Many jobs require the knowledge of another language. France and Canada are major trading partners of the United States. In addition, about 1,000 French companies have subsidiaries in this country.

▲ l'Université Paris-Sorbonne

Et vous? *(And you?)*

Which three reasons for speaking French are most important to you? Take a class poll comparing your answers with those of your classmates. Which are the most popular reasons?

Photo cultural notes

- The top photo of the **TGV** was taken at the **Gare de Lyon** in Paris.
- The bottom photo is of the **Église de la Sorbonne.** The Sorbonne was founded in 1257 by Robert de Sorbon, but today the Église is the oldest part of the university. It was built by Lemercier between 1635 and 1642. The Sorbonne is located in the **Quartier latin,** which is full of cafés, bookstores, and shops that cater to the student population.

Teaching note Have students brainstorm about what types of jobs might require being able to speak another language.

Teaching Resource Options

PRINT 

Unit 1 Resource Book
Videoscript, pp. 193–194

AUDIO & VISUAL

Overhead Transparencies
1 Map of France

VIDEO PROGRAM

VIDÉO DVD

IMAGES

A.2 La France
(0:49-2:34 min.)

Cultural notes France

- **Les Alpes et Chamonix**
  Chamonix is located in a valley in the Alps at the foot of the **Massif du Mont Blanc.** (**Mont Blanc** is the highest mountain in Europe.) Chamonix is a famous ski resort. The first Winter Olympics were held there in 1924.
- **La Côte d'Azur**
  The French Riviera, or **la Côte d'Azur,** stretches about 100 miles along the Mediterranean, from the Toulon area to the Italian border. For the French, the Côte d'Azur is their favorite summer vacation place.
- **Les Pyrénées**
  The **Pyrénées** are a high mountain chain which separates France from Spain (**l'Espagne**).
- **Les Châteaux de la Loire**
  There are many castles located in the Loire Valley. **Les Châteaux de la Loire,** such as the Château de Chenonceau, were built by the French kings nearly 500 years ago.

Bonjour, la France!

CONNAISSEZ-VOUS LA FRANCE? *(Do you know France?)*

- In area, France is the second-largest country in Western Europe. It is smaller than Texas, but bigger than California.
- Geographically, France is a very diversified country, with the highest mountains in Europe (**les Alpes** and **les Pyrénées**) and an extensive coastline along the Atlantic (**l'océan Atlantique**) and the Mediterranean (**la Méditerranée**).
- France consists of many different regions which have maintained their traditions, their culture, and — in some cases — their own language. Some of the traditional provinces are Normandy and Brittany (**la Normandie** and **la Bretagne**) in the west, Alsace (**l'Alsace**) in the east, Touraine (**la Touraine**) in the center, and Provence (**la Provence**) in the south.

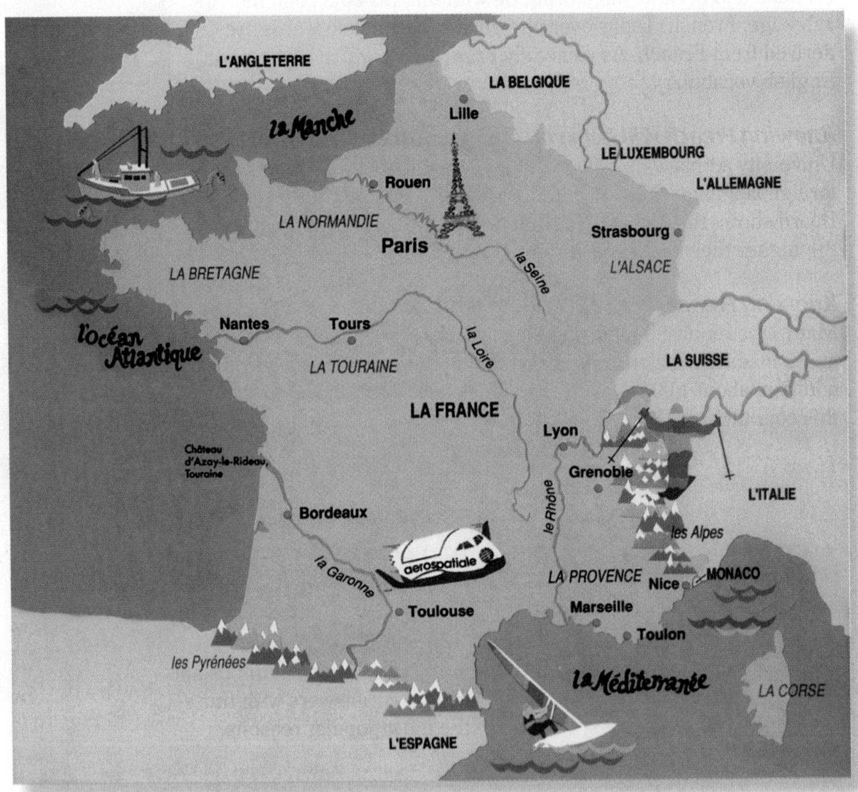

CLASSROOM PROJECT

You might have students prepare a bulletin board display about France using maps, postcards, travel brochures, etc.

Paris: Montmartre
Paris, the capital of France, is also its economic, intellectual, and artistic center. For many people, Paris is the most beautiful city in the world.

Snowboarding in the Alps
During winter vacation, many French young people enjoy snowboarding or skiing. The most popular destinations are the Alps and the Pyrenees.

Château de Chenonceau
The long history of France is evident in its many castles and monuments. This chateau, built in the 16th century, attracts nearly one million visitors a year.

Home in Provence
The French love flowers and take pride in making their homes beautiful. This house is built in the traditional style of Provence, a region in southern France.

Photo cultural notes

- The Paris neighborhood of **Montmartre** is well-known as a haven for artists. The white, domed Sacré-Coeur church sits atop the hill and can be seen from many parts of Paris.
- The **Château de Chenonceau** was completed in 1521. It is picturesque because part of the castle sits on a bridge over the river Cher. This addition was made by Catherine de Médicis in the late 1500s.
- This house is located in Moustier, Provence. Note the typically French shutters.

Bonjour, les Français!

Cultural notes

- **Size:** In area, one can compare France to:
  (a) 4/5 of Texas, or
  (b) Wyoming plus Oregon, or
  (c) New England plus New York, Pennsylvania and Ohio.
- **Technology:** The French Ariane rockets are launched from French Guiana (**la Guyane française**) in South America.
- **French cultural tradition:**
  –Philosophers: Voltaire, Montesquieu, Rousseau, Jean-Paul Sartre
  –Writers: Victor Hugo, Albert Camus, Colette, Baudelaire
  –Musicians: composers Debussy and Ravel, flutist Jean-Pierre Rampal
  –Artists: Gauguin, Renoir, Matisse
- **Pre-history:** the Cro-Magnon caveman and the caves of Lascaux
- **Roman times:** Julius Caesar conquered France (Gaul) in 43 B.C.; one can still visit the Roman ruins in Provence: Nîmes, Orange, Pont du Gard.

Bonjour, les Français!

Here are some facts about France and the French people.

LA FRANCE

Capitale: Paris
Population: 60 (soixante) millions d'habitants
Drapeau: bleu, blanc, rouge

Devise: Liberté, Égalité, Fraternité
Monnaie: l'euro

BLEU BLANC ROUGE

LE DRAPEAU FRANÇAIS

L'EURO

LA MONNAIE FRANÇAISE

LES FRANÇAIS

Origine de la population: multi-ethnique
- européenne (majorité)
- nord-africaine
- africaine
- asiatique

Principales religions pratiquées:
- catholique (majorité)
- musulmane
- juive
- protestante

STRATEGY Comparing Cultures

How does France compare to the United States or to your country of origin? Make a chart like the one above. Include the capital, the population, the flag, the motto, and the currency.

These are some of the young French people you will meet in the video.

Jean-Paul âge: 14 ans

Céline âge: 15 ans

Léa âge: 15 ans

François âge: 14 ans

Isabelle âge: 14 ans

Stéphanie âge: 14 ans

Philippe âge: 15 ans

Trinh âge: 14 ans

Antoine âge: 14 ans

Bonjour, le monde francophone!

Teaching Resource Options

PRINT

Unit 1 Resource Book
Videoscript pp. 193–194

AUDIO & VISUAL 

Overhead Transparencies
2b Map of the French-speaking world (page R2)
2c Map of the French-speaking world (page R3)

VIDEO PROGRAM

VIDÉO DVD **IMAGES**

A.3 Le monde francophone (2:35-4:42 min.)

A.4 Des francophones aux États-Unis (4:43-6:42 min.)

Cultural note There are also two small French islands in the Atlantic, off the Canadian coast: Saint Pierre and Miquelon. Since 1985, Saint Pierre and Miquelon (**Saint-Pierre-et-Miquelon**) are considered as a "collectivité territoriale" and not as a "départment".

Teaching note Before students look at the map, ask them whether they know in which parts of the United States French is spoken.

Bonjour, le monde francophone!

CANADA
About one-third of the population speaks French. These French speakers live mainly in the province of Quebec (**le Québec**). They are descendants of French settlers who came to Canada in the 17th and 18th centuries.

HAITI
Haïti is the first Black Republic. Its people speak Creole and French.

MARTINIQUE AND GUADELOUPE
These two Caribbean islands (**la Martinique** and **la Guadeloupe**) are part of France. Their inhabitants, primarily of African ancestry, are French citizens.

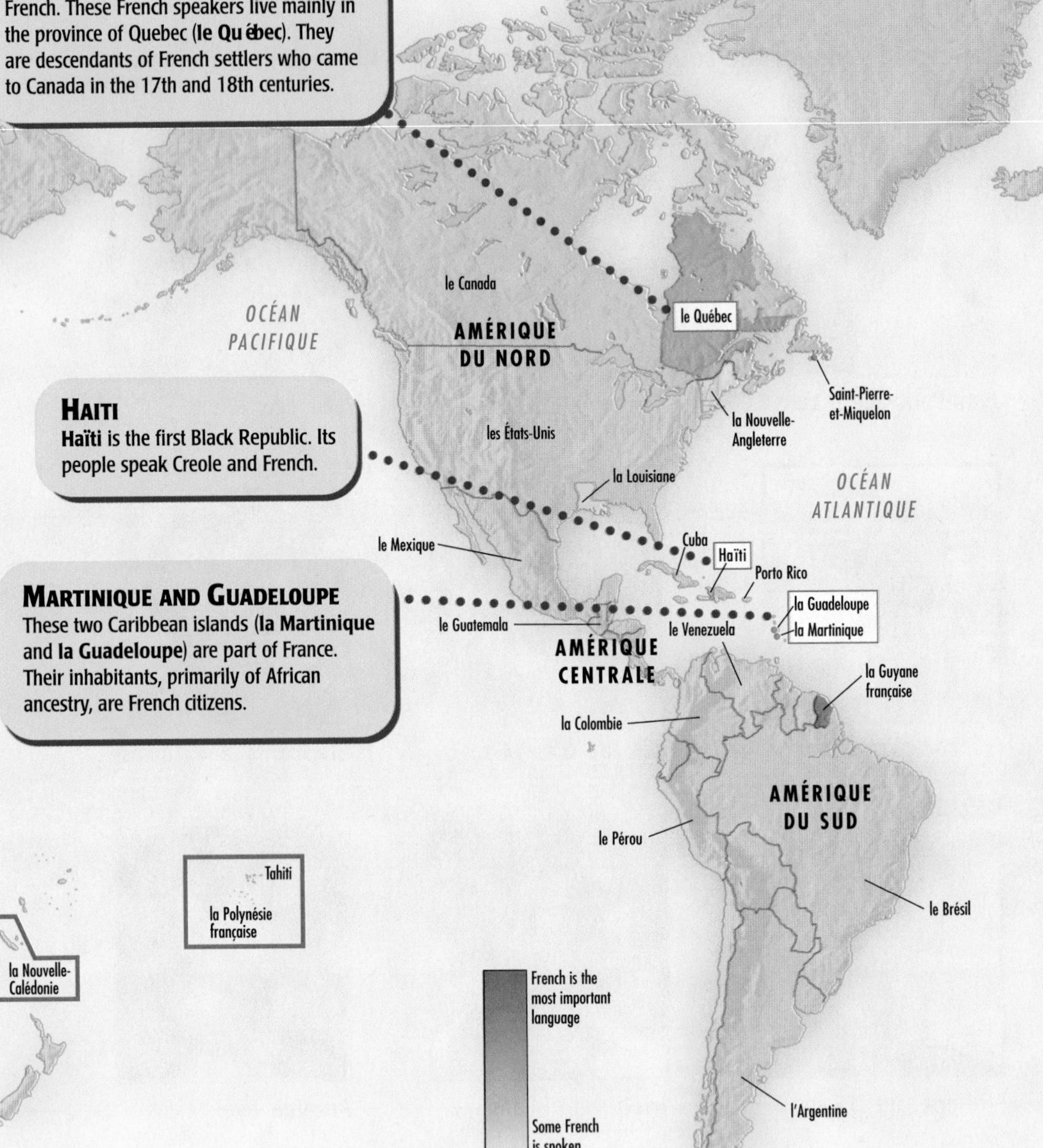

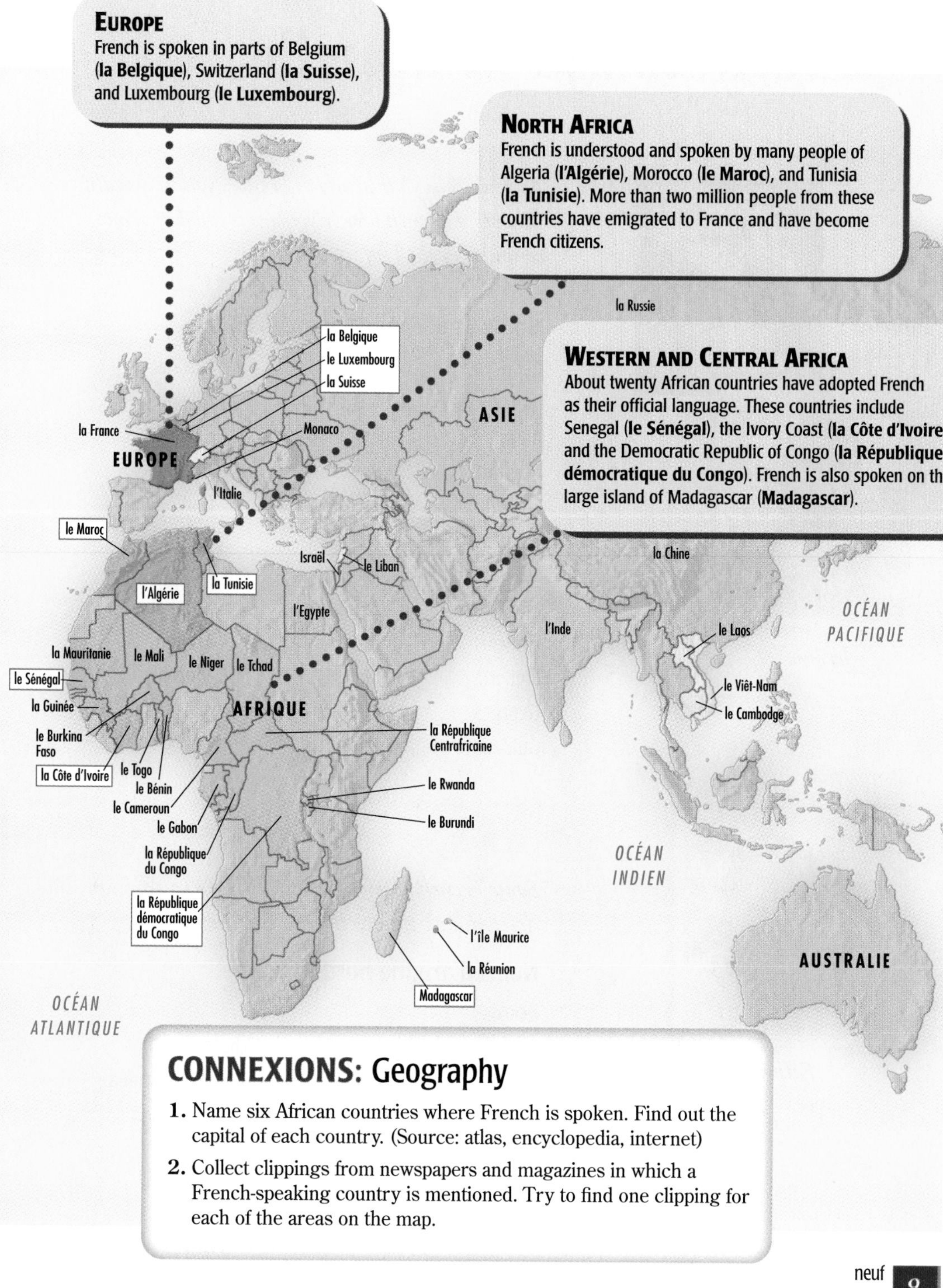

EUROPE

French is spoken in parts of Belgium (**la Belgique**), Switzerland (**la Suisse**), and Luxembourg (**le Luxembourg**).

NORTH AFRICA

French is understood and spoken by many people of Algeria (**l'Algérie**), Morocco (**le Maroc**), and Tunisia (**la Tunisie**). More than two million people from these countries have emigrated to France and have become French citizens.

WESTERN AND CENTRAL AFRICA

About twenty African countries have adopted French as their official language. These countries include Senegal (**le Sénégal**), the Ivory Coast (**la Côte d'Ivoire**), and the Democratic Republic of Congo (**la République démocratique du Congo**). French is also spoken on the large island of Madagascar (**Madagascar**).

CONNEXIONS: Geography

1. Name six African countries where French is spoken. Find out the capital of each country. (Source: atlas, encyclopedia, internet)
2. Collect clippings from newspapers and magazines in which a French-speaking country is mentioned. Try to find one clipping for each of the areas on the map.

Cultural note Two African countries are named after the Congo river, one of the longest rivers in the world. In size, **la République démocratique du Congo** is the largest French-speaking country of Africa. It was known as **le Congo belge** before its independence in 1960, and as **le Zaïre** until 1997. Its eastern neighbor, **la République du Congo,** is a former French colony.

Cultural expansion

Names of African countries where French is an important language (capitals are given in parentheses):

- Algérie (Alger)
- Bénin (Porto-Novo)
- Burkina Faso (Ougadougou)
- Burundi (Bujumbura)
- Cameroun (Yaoundé)
- Côte d'Ivoire (Yamoussoukro)
- Djibouti (Djibouti)
- Gabon (Libreville)
- Guinée (Conakry)
- Madagascar (Antananarivo)
- Mali (Bamako)
- Maroc (Rabat)
- Mauritanie (Nouakchott)
- Niger (Niamey)
- République Centrafricaine (Bangui)
- République Démocratique du Congo (Kinshasa)
- République du Congo (Brazzaville)
- Ruanda [Rwanda] (Kigali)
- Sénégal (Dakar)
- Tchad (N'Djamena)
- Togo (Lomé)
- Tunisie (Tunis)

English equivalents of French boys' names

- Alain (Alan)
- André (Andrew)
- Antoine (Anthony)
- Christophe (Christopher)
- Édouard (Edward)
- Étienne (Steven)
- François (Francis, Frank)
- Frédéric (Frederick)
- Geoffroy (Jeffrey)
- Guillaume (William)
- Henri (Henry)
- Jacques (James)
- Jean (John)
- Julien (Julian)
- Laurent (Lawrence)
- Marc (Mark)
- Mathieu (Matthew)
- Michel (Michael)
- Olivier (Oliver)
- Philippe (Phillip)
- Pierre (Peter)
- Raoul (Ralph)

Bonjour, je m'appelle . . .

Antoine

Jérôme

As you begin your study of French, you may want to "adopt" a French identity. Here is a list of some common French names.

Noms traditionnels (garçons):

Alain	Henri	Nicolas
André	Jacques	Olivier
Antoine	Jean	Patrick
Bernard	Jean-Louis	Paul
Christophe	Jean-Paul	Philippe
Clément	Jérôme	Pierre
Édouard	Joseph	Robert
Éric	Julien	Stéphane
François	Laurent	Thomas
Frédéric	Marc	Vincent
Georges	Mathieu	
Guillaume	Michel	

Fatima

Some French people of North African or African descent have names that reflect their origin.

Noms d'origine nord-africaine

GARÇONS		FILLES	
Ali	Latif	Aïcha	Leila
Ahmed	Mustapha	Fatima	Yasmina
Habib	Youcef	Jamila	Zaïna

TEACHING NOTE Choosing French names

Let students adopt a new French identity. Some may want to find a French version of their English name. Others may want to pick a completely original name.

If some students do not want to choose a French name, teach them how to pronounce their own name with a French accent.

INCLUSION

Repetitive Explain how certain final consonants are pronounced, and how some aren't. Have students listen t you as you model, and they will then repeat the names. A students to find names ending in "c", "r", or "l", pronounc them, and write them in their notebooks.

Structured Explain how "ll" is sometimes pronounced like Have students listen as you model words with "ll". Students will repeat the words and write them in their notebooks.

Léa

Mélanie

Noms traditionnels (filles):

Anne	Florence	Michèle
Anne-Marie	Françoise	Monique
Aurélie	Hélène	Nathalie
Béatrice	Isabelle	Nicole
Caroline	Jeanne	Pauline
Cécile	Julie	Sophie
Céline	Laure	Stéphanie
Charlotte	Léa	Suzanne
Christine	Louise	Sylvie
Claire	Marie	Thérèse
Élisabeth	Marie-Christine	Véronique
Élodie	Mathilde	Virginie
Émilie	Mélanie	

Ousmane

Noms d'origine africaine

GARÇONS		FILLES	
Abdou	Kouamé	Adjoua	Latifah
Amadou	Moussa	Asta	Malika
Koffi	Ousmane	Aya	Mariama

English equivalents of French girls' names

Andrée (Andrea)
Cécile (Cecilia)
Diane (Diana)
Éléonore (Eleanor)
Émilie (Emily)
Françoise (Frances)
Hélène (Helen)
Jeanne (Jean)
Laure (Laura)
Lise (Lisa)
Lucie (Lucy)
Marguerite (Margaret)
Marie (Mary)
Marthe (Martha)
Michèle (Michelle)
Monique (Monica)
Nathalie (Natalie)
Suzanne (Susan)
Sylvie (Sylvia)
Thérèse (Teresa)
Virginie (Virginia)

EACHING NOTE Pronunciation

ead the above lists aloud and have students repeat the ames after you. Be sure they always let the accent fall the last syllable of each name.

INCLUSION

Synthetic/analytic Tell students to use desktops to beat out all syllables of each name, stressing the last syllable. (You may use rhythm sticks, drums, pens, pencils, etc. to demonstrate.)

Alphabetic/phonetic Ask students to say the name for each vowel. Explain that the name gives a clue to the sound. Model a sound and have the class say it three times. Provide phonetic transcriptions for sounds with a list of easy words. Have students practice in pairs, and save the list in their notebooks.

Expansion activities PLANNING AHEAD

Games

• À la pêche!

Divide students into groups of four. Give each group two decks of cards. Have students remove the face cards and shuffle the remaining cards of the two decks together. One student deals five cards to each player. Players remove any pairs they have in their hand. The dealer then asks another player for a specific card. If the player has that card, he or she passes it to the dealer, and the dealer's turn continues. If the player does not have that card, he or she tells the dealer *«À la pêche!»* The dealer draws a card from the pile, and the turn passes to the next player. The game is over when there are no more cards left to draw from the stack. The player with the most pairs wins.

Pacing Suggestion: Upon completion of Leçon 1.

• Dix

Have students stand up at their desks. Begin in one corner of the room. The first student starts with the number **«Un»** and has the option to name up to three numbers in sequence. (For example, the student who begins has the option to say **«Un,» «Un, Deux,»** or **«Un, Deux, Trois.»**) The next student continues, and again may name up to three sequential numbers, following from where the first student left off. The student who arrives at the point where he or she must say **«Dix»** is automatically out and has to sit down. The game then starts again at **«Un»** and continues as long as there are players left standing.

Pacing Suggestion: Upon completion of Leçon 1.

Projects

• Allons au Québec

Students will plan a vacation to Quebec. Divide the class into groups. Each group should choose a place in Quebec to visit. Suggest to students that they might consult travel agents or use the Internet. (You might suggest a specific search engine.) They should plan the following:

- the best way to get there (plane, train, car)
- historic and cultural sites they wish to visit
- where they will stay
- what activities they will try while they are there

Ask students to provide visuals—such as maps and travel posters—with the information they accumulate to give oral presentations of their itinerary to the rest of the class.

Pacing Suggestion: Upon completion of Leçon 2.

Bulletin Boards

• L'alphabet

Assign a letter of the alphabet to each student in the class and have students work together to create an alphabet bulletin board. Have each student write a French word that begins with his or her assigned letter on the bulletin board. Encourage students to use words they've already learned and the glossary at the back of the book to find cognates for the rest. Students may wish to design the bulletin board with a theme in mind, such as French first names or city names. The bulletin board should be colorful and visually appealing.

Pacing Suggestion: Upon completion of Leçon 1.

• Couleurs

List the names of the colors at the end of Unité 1 in French at the top of the board. Have students create a poster of francophone flags with labels for the colors and the countries.

Pacing Suggestion: Upon completion of Leçon 2.

Music

• *Frère Jacques*

Distribute the lyrics of the traditional French folk song *Frère Jacques* to students. Have them look up any unfamiliar words, and then discuss the general meaning. You may want to use the song lyrics for pronunciation practice.

Frère Jacques,
Frère Jacques,
Dormez-vous?
Dormez-vous?
Sonnez les matines,
Sonnez les matines,
Ding, ding, dong!
Ding, ding, dong!

Pacing Suggestion: Upon completion of Leçon 2.

Storytelling

• La famille

Make up a story about a fictional family. In the story, list the members of the family, their ages, their nationalities, and where they're from. Give students a script to read along, and have comprehension questions prepared in English to discuss with the students. Then, have students write a short story about their family to present to a partner. Once pair work has ended, select a few students to present their stories to the class.

Pacing Suggestion: Upon completion of Leçon 2.

Recipe

• Les tartines

Tartines are slices of bread or toast with a topping commonly served at breakfast or as an after-school snack. Encourage students to try toppings they've never had before. You may wish to include beverages that are typically served at a French breakfast: hot chocolate and café au lait.

Pacing Suggestion: Upon completion of Leçon 2.

Hands-on Crafts

• Une boite mosaïque

Have students use cardboard to fold into a cube. Then, on each side, have students create mosaic images of six of the flags found on pages 40–41. They can do this by tearing colored construction paper into very small pieces and pasting them onto the outer surface of the box. Each side should have a different flag representing one of the various francophone countries. Ask for volunteers to talk about their boxes to the class. Students can say which countries their box represents, where the countries are located, and what colors were chosen for their flags. Teachers may wish to make a small hole in one corner of each box and tie string or fishing line on them in order to hang the boxes from the ceiling.

Pacing Suggestion: Upon completion of Leçon 2.

End of Unit

• Une famille

Students will use what they've learned in Unité 1 to introduce either their real families or an invented "famous family" to the class. First assign a medium for students to use: videotape, a photo album and an audio recording, a booklet and audio recording, etc. Each presentation should include an audio and a visual component. Ask students to introduce each family member, give each person's name and age, and relation to the student. Have students introduce themselves as well. You may want to suggest supplementary vocabulary, such as **beau-père** and **belle-mère.**

Rubric **A** = 13–15 pts. **B** = 10–12 pts. **C** = 7–9 pts. **D** = 4–6 pts. **F** = < 4 pts.

Criteria	Scale
Vocabulary Use	1 2 3 4 5
Grammar/Spelling Accuracy	1 2 3 4 5
Creativity	1 2 3 4 5

Les tartines

Ingrédients
- *2–3 baguettes*
- *confiture (de fraises, de framboises, d'abricots, d'oranges)*
- *pâte de noisettes et cacao*
- *beurre*

Préparation
1. *Coupez une baguette en tranches.*
2. *Sur chaque tranche de pain, étalez de la confiture, du beurre ou de la pâte de noisettes et cacao.*

Ingredients
- *2–3 loaves of French bread*
- *jam (strawberry, raspberry, apricot, orange)*
- *chocolate-hazelnut spread*
- *butter*

Directions
1. *Cut a loaf of French bread into several slices.*
2. *Top each slice of bread with the spread of your choice.*

Planning Guide CLASSROOM MANAGEMENT

OBJECTIVES

Communication
- Say hello and good-bye *pp. 15, 23*
- Introduce yourself and say where you are from *pp. 15, 19*
- Introduce friends, family, and relatives *pp. 27, 35*
- Count to 100 *pp. 17, 21, 25, 29, 33*
- Say how old you are and find out someone's age *p. 37*

Pronunciation
- Les signes orthographiques *p. 17*
- Les lettres muettes *p. 21*
- Les consonnes finales *p. 25*
- La liaison *p. 29*
- La voyelle nasale /ɛ̃/ *p. 33*
- Les voyelles nasales /ɑ̃/ and /ɔ̃/ *p. 37*

Culture
- Salutations *p. 13*
- La rentrée *p. 15*
- Les prénoms français *p. 15*
- La Martinique *p. 19*
- Bonjour ou Salut? *p. 23*
- Amis et copains *p. 27*
- La province de Québec *p. 31*
- La famille française *p. 35*

PROGRAM RESOURCES

Print

- Workbook PE, *pp. 1–28*
- *Activités pour tous* PE, *pp. 1–15*
- Block Scheduling Copymasters *pp. 1–16*
- *Français pour hispanophones*
- *Lectures pour tous*
- Teacher to Teacher Copymasters
- Teaching Proficiency through Reading and Storytelling
- Unit 1 Resource Book
  - Lessons 1–2 Resources
    - Workbook TE
    - *Activités pour tous* TE
    - Family Letter
    - Absent Student Copymasters
    - Family Involvement
    - Video Activities
    - Videoscripts
    - Audioscripts
    - Assessment Program
  - Unit 1 Resources
    - Communipak
    - *Activités pour tous* TE Reading
    - Workbook TE Reading and Culture Activities
    - Assessment Program
    - Answer Keys

Audiovisual

- Audio Program PE CD 1 Tracks 1–27
- Audio Program Workbook CD 5 Tracks 1–34
- *Chansons* Audio CD
- Sing Along: Grammar and Vocabulary Songs CD
- Video Program Modules 1A, 1B, 1C, 2A, 2B, 2C
- Warm-Up Transparencies
- Overhead Transparencies
  - 4 U.S., Canada, England, France *Les nationalités*;
  - 5 Expressions with ***ça va***;
  - 7 People *Les personnes*;
  - 8 Family Tree *La famille*

Technology

- Online Workbook
- ClassZone.com
- McDougal Littell Assessment System/Test Generator CD-ROM
- EasyPlanner CD-ROM
- Power Presentations on CD-ROM
- Take-Home Tutor CD-ROM

Assessment Program Options

Lesson Quizzes
Portfolio Assessment
Unit Test Form A
Unit Test Form B
Unit Test Part III Cultural Awareness
Listening Comprehension Performance Test
Speaking Performance Test
Reading Comprehension Performance Test
Writing Performance Test
Multiple Choice Test Items
Test Scoring Tools
Audio Program CD 13 Tracks 1–11
Answer Keys
McDougal Littell Assessment System/ Test Generator CD-ROM

Pacing Guide SAMPLE LESSON PLAN

DAY	DAY	DAY	DAY	DAY
1 **Unité 1 Opener** **Introduction culturelle– Salutations** **Leçon 1A** • Vidéo-scène–La rentrée • Pour communiquer • Notes culturelles– La rentrée, Les prénoms français	**2** **Leçon 1A** • L'alphabet • Prononciation–Les signes orthographiques • Les nombres de 0 à 10	**3** **Leçon 1B** • Vidéo-scène– Tu es français? • Pour communiquer • Note culturelle– La Martinique • Français, française	**4** **Leçon 1B** • Les nombres de 10 à 20 • Prononciation– Les lettres muettes **Leçon 1C** • Vidéo-scène–Salut! Ça va? • Pour communiquer • Note culturelle– Bonjour ou Salut?	**5** **Leçon 1C** • Pour communiquer • Les nombres de 20 à 60 • Prononciation– Les consonnes finales **Leçon 2A** • Vidéo-scène– Copain ou copine? • Un garçon, une fille
6 **Leçon 2A** • Pour communiquer • Note culturelle– Amis et copains • Les nombres de 60 à 79 • Prononciation–La liaison	**7** **Leçon 2B** • Vidéo-scène– Une coïncidence • Pour communiquer • Note culturelle– La province de Québec • Le garçon, la fille	**8** **Leçon 2B** • Les nombres de 80 à 100 et 1000 • Prononciation– La voyelle nasale /ɛ̃/ **Leçon 2C** • Vidéo-scène– Les photos d'Isabelle • Pour communiquer	**9** **Leçon 2C** • Note culturelle– La famille française • Mon cousin, ma cousine • Pour communiquer • Prononciation– Les voyelles nasales /ɑ̃/ and /ɔ̃/	**10** • À votre tour!
11 • Unit 1 Test	**12** • Entracte–Lecture et Culture	**13**	**14**	**15**
16	**17**	**18**	**19**	**20**

Student Text Listening Activity Scripts

AUDIO PROGRAM

▶ LEÇON 1 Bonjour!

• Vidéo-scène A: La rentrée *p. 14*

A. Compréhension orale CD 1, TRACK 1

This is the first day of school. Students are greeting their friends and meeting new classmates. Écoutez.

Trinh: Bonjour! Je m'appelle Trinh.
Céline: Et moi, je m'appelle Céline.

Marc: Je m'appelle Marc. Et toi?
Isabelle: Moi, je m'appelle Isabelle.

Jean-Paul: Comment t'appelles-tu?
Nathalie: Je m'appelle Nathalie.
Jean-Paul: Bonjour.
Nathalie: Bonjour.

B. Écoutez et répétez. CD 1, TRACK 2

You will now hear a paused version of the dialog. Listen to the speaker and repeat right after he or she has completed the sentence.

• L'alphabet *p. 17* CD 1, TRACK 3

Écoutez et répétez.

A # B # C # D # E # F # G # H # I # J # K # L # M #
N # O # P # Q # R # S # T # U # V # W # X # Y # Z #

• Prononciation *p. 17* CD 1, TRACK 4

Les signes orthographiques

French uses accents and spelling marks that do not exist in English. These marks are part of the spelling and cannot be left out.

In French, there are four accents that may appear on vowels.

l'accent aigu # Cécile # Stéphanie #
l'accent grave # Michèle # Hélène #
l'accent circonflexe # Jérôme #
le tréma # Noël # Joëlle #

There is only one spelling mark used with a consonant. It occurs under the letter "**c.**"

la cédille # François #

• Les nombres de 0 à 10 *p. 17* CD 1, TRACK 5

Écoutez et répétez.

zéro # un # deux # trois # quatre # cinq # six # sept # huit # neuf # dix #

• Vidéo-scène B: Tu es français? *p. 18*

A. Compréhension orale CD 1, TRACK 6

It is the opening day of school and several of the students meet in the cafeteria (**la cafétéria** or **la cantine**) at lunchtime. Marc discovers that not everyone is French.

Marc: Tu es français?
Jean-Paul: Oui, je suis français.

Marc: Et toi, Patrick, tu es français aussi?
Patrick: Non! Je suis américain. Je suis de Boston.

Marc: Et toi, Stéphanie, tu es française ou américaine?
Stéphanie: Je suis française.
Marc: Tu es de Paris?
Stéphanie: Non, je suis de Fort-de-France.
Marc: Tu as de la chance!

B. Écoutez et répétez. CD 1, TRACK 7

You will now hear a paused version of the dialog. Listen to the speaker and repeat right after he or she has completed the sentence.

• Les nombres de 10 à 20 *p. 21* CD 1, TRACK 8

Écoutez et répétez.

dix # onze # douze # treize # quatorze # quinze #
seize # dix-sept # dix-huit # dix-neuf # vingt #

• Prononciation *p. 21* CD 1, TRACK 9

Les lettres muettes

Écoutez: Paris

In French, the last letter of a word is often not pronounced.

- Final "**e**" is always silent.

Répétez: Céline # Philippe # Stéphanie # anglaise # française #
onze # douze # treize # quatorze # quinze # seize #

- Final "**s**" is almost always silent.

Répétez: Paris # Nicolas # Jacques # anglais # français # trois #

- The letter "**h**" is always silent.

Répétez: Hélène # Henri # Thomas # Nathalie # Catherine # Thérèse #

• Vidéo-scène C: Salut! Ça va? *p. 22*

A. Compréhension orale CD 1, TRACK 10

Please turn to page 22 for complete *vidéo-scène* text.

B. Écoutez et répétez. CD 1, TRACK 11

You will now hear a paused version of the dialog. Listen to the speaker and repeat right after he or she has completed the sentence.

• Les nombres de 20 à 60 *p. 25* CD 1, TRACK 12

Écoutez et répétez.

20 # 21 # 22 # 23 # . . . 29 #   30 # 31 # 32 # 33 # . . . 39 #
40 # 41 # 42 # 43 # . . . 49 #   50 # 51 # 52 # 53 # . . . 59 # 60 #

• Prononciation *p. 25* CD 1, TRACK 13

Les consonnes finales

Écoutez: un deux trois

In French, the last consonant of a word is often not pronounced.

- Remember: Final "**s**" is usually silent.

Répétez: trois # français # anglais

- Most other final consonants are usually silent.

Répétez: Richard # Albert # Robert # salut # américain # canadien # bien # deux #

EXCEPTION: The following final consonants are usually pronounced: "**c,**" "**f,**" "**l,**" and sometimes "**r.**"

Répétez: Éric # Daniel Lebeuf # Pascal # Victor #

However, the ending **-er** is usually pronounced /e/.

Répétez: Roger # Olivier #

▶ LEÇON 2 Famille et copains

• Vidéo-scène A: Copain ou copine? *p. 26*

A. Compréhension orale CD 1, TRACK 14

In French there are certain girls' and boys' names that sound the same. Occasionally this can be confusing.

SCÈNE 1 **Philippe et Jean-Paul**
Philippe is at home with his friend Jean-Paul. He seems to be expecting someone. Who could it be . . . ? The doorbell rings.

Philippe: Tiens! Voilà Dominique!
Jean-Paul: Dominique? Qui est-ce? Un copain ou une copine?
Philippe: C'est une copine.

pause for oral response

SCÈNE 2 **Philippe, Jean-Paul, Dominique**
Philippe: Salut, Dominique! Ça va?
Dominique: Oui, ça va! Et toi?
Jean-Paul: *(thinking)* C'est vrai! C'est une copine!

B. Écoutez et répétez. CD 1, TRACK 15

You will now hear a paused version of the dialog. Listen to the speaker and repeat right after he or she has completed the sentence.

• Les nombres de 60 à 79 *p. 29* CD 1, TRACK 16

Écoutez et répétez.

60 # 61 # 62 # 63 # 64 # 65 # 66 # 67 # 68 # 69 #
70 # 71 # 72 # 73 # 74 # 75 # 76 # 77 # 78 # 79 #

• Prononciation *p. 29* CD 1, TRACK 17

La liaison

Écoutez: un ami

un ami # un Américain # un Anglais # un artiste #

In general, the "**n**" of **un** is silent. However, in the above words, the "**n**" of **un** is pronounced as if it were the *first* letter of the next word. This is called LIAISON.

Liaison occurs between two words when the second one begins with a VOWEL SOUND, that is, with "**a**," "**e**," "**i**," "**o**," "**u**," and sometimes "**h**" and "**y**."

Contrastez et répétez:

LIAISON: un ami # un Américain # un Italien # un artiste #
NO LIAISON: un copain # un Français # un Canadien # un prof #

• Vidéo-scène B: Une coïncidence *p. 30*

A. Compréhension orale CD 1, TRACK 18

Isabelle is at a party with her new Canadian friend Marc. She wants him to meet some of the other guests.

Isabelle: Tu connais la fille là-bas?
Marc: Non. Qui est-ce?
Isabelle: C'est une copine. Elle s'appelle Juliette Savard.
Marc: Elle est française?
Isabelle: Non, elle est canadienne. Elle est de Montréal.
Marc: Moi aussi!
Isabelle: Quelle coïncidence!

B. Écoutez et répétez. CD 1, TRACK 19

You will now hear a paused version of the dialog. Listen to the speaker and repeat right after he or she has completed the sentence.

• Les nombres de 80 à 1000 *p. 33* CD 1, TRACK 20

Écoutez et répétez.

80 # 81 # 82 # 83 # 84 # 85 # 86 # 87 # 88 # 89 #
90 # 91 # 92 # 93 # 94 # 95 # 96 # 97 # 98 # 99 #
100 # 1000 #

• Prononciation *p. 33* CD 1, TRACK 21

La voyelle nasale /ɛ̃/

In French, there are three nasal vowel sounds:

Écoutez: /ɛ̃/ **cinq** (5) /ɔ̃/**onze** (11) /ɑ̃/ **trente** (30)

Practice the sound /ɛ̃/ in the following words.

Be sure not to pronounce an "**n**" or "**m**" after the nasal vowel.

Répétez: "in" # cinq # quinze # vingt # vingt-cinq # quatre-vingt-quinze #
"ain" # américain # Alain # copain #
"(i)en" # bien # canadien # tiens! #
"un" # un #
Tiens! Voilà Alain. Il est américain. Et Julien? Il est canadien. #

• Vidéo-scène C: Les photos d'Isabelle *p. 34*

A. Compréhension orale CD 1, TRACK 22

Isabelle is showing her family photo album to her friend Jean-Paul.

Isabelle: Voici ma mère.
Jean-Paul: Et le monsieur, c'est ton père?
Isabelle: Non, c'est mon oncle Thomas.
Jean-Paul: Et la fille, c'est ta cousine?
Isabelle: Oui, c'est ma cousine Béatrice. Elle a seize ans.
Jean-Paul: Et le garçon, c'est ton cousin?
Isabelle: Non, c'est un copain.
Jean-Paul: Un copain ou ton copain?
Isabelle: Dis donc, Jean-Paul, tu es vraiment trop curieux!

B. Écoutez et répétez. CD 1, TRACK 23

You will now hear a paused version of the dialog. Listen to the speaker and repeat right after he or she has completed the sentence.

• Prononciation *p. 37* CD 1, TRACK 24

Les voyelles nasales /ɑ̃/ **et** /ɔ̃/

Écoutez: tante oncle

The letters "**an**" and "**en**" usually represent the nasal vowel /ɑ̃/. Be sure not to pronounce an "**n**" after the nasal vowel.

Répétez: ans # tante # français # quarante # trente # comment # Henri Laurent #

The letters "**on**" represent the nasal vowel /ɔ̃/. Be sure not to pronounce an "**n**" after the nasal vowel.

Répétez: non # bonjour # oncle # garçon #

Contrastez: an–on # tante–ton # onze ans # Mon oncle François a trente ans. #

À votre tour!

• Écoutez bien! *p. 38* CD 1, TRACK 25

Loto is a French version of Bingo. You will hear a series of numbers. If the number is on Card A, raise your left hand. If it is on Card B, raise your right hand.

19, 19 # 67, 67 # 15, 15 # 8, 8 # 72, 72 # 12, 12 # 42, 42 # 93, 93 # 5, 5 # 82, 82 # 33, 33 # 48, 48 # 25, 25 # 3, 3 # 17, 17 # 61, 61 # 98, 98 # 89, 89 # 70, 70 # 55, 55 #

• Et toi? *p. 38* CD 1, TRACK 26

You and Nathalie meet at a sidewalk café. Respond to her greetings and questions. Répondez aux questions de Nathalie.

1. Salut! Ça va? #
2. Comment t'appelles-tu? #
3. Tu es canadien (canadienne)? #
4. Quel âge as-tu? #
5. Comment s'appelle ton copain (ta copine)? #
6. Quel âge a ton copain (ta copine)?

• Conversation dirigée *p. 38* CD 1, TRACK 27

Two students, Jean-Pierre and Janet, have met on the Paris-Lyon train. Écoutez leur conversation.

Jean-Pierre: Bonjour.
Janet: Bonjour. Ça va?
Jean-Pierre: Oui, ça va.
Janet: Comment t'appelles-tu?
Jean-Pierre: Je m'appelle Jean-Pierre. Et toi?
Janet: Je m'appelle Janet.
Jean-Pierre: Tu es anglaise?
Janet: Non, je suis américaine.
Jean-Pierre: Tu es de New York?
Janet: Non, je suis de San Francisco.

Complete videoscripts, plus Workbook and Assessment audioscripts, are available in the Unit Resource Books.

Main Theme
- Getting acquainted

COMMUNICATION
- Saying hello and good-bye
- Introducing yourself
- Saying where you're from
- Introducing friends, family, and relatives
- Counting to 100
- Saying how old you are and finding out someone else's age

CULTURES
- Learning about French salutations
- Learning about going back to school in France
- Learning about French names
- Learning about Astérix
- Learning about Martinique
- Learning about French friendships
- Learning about Quebec
- Learning about the French family

CONNECTIONS
- Connecting to Math: Counting in French
- Connecting to History: The history of the Statue of Liberty and the Eiffel Tower
- Connecting to Geography: Learning about Martinique and the province of Quebec
- Connecting to Geography: Studying the flags, populations, and capitals of some French-speaking countries

COMPARISONS
- Comparing French and American salutations
- Comparing the French and American ideas of friends and family

continued on next page

Invitation au français

Faisons connaissance

LEÇON 1 Bonjour!

VIDÉO-SCÈNES

A La rentrée
B Tu es français?
C Salut! Ça va?

LEÇON 2 Famille et copains

VIDÉO-SCÈNES

A Copain ou copine?
B Une coïncidence
C Les photos d'Isabelle

THÈME ET OBJECTIFS

Getting acquainted

In this unit, you will be meeting French people.

You will learn ...

- to say hello and good-bye
- to introduce yourself and say where you are from
- to introduce friends, family, and relatives

You will also learn ...

- to count to 100
- to say how old you are and find out someone's age

OVERVIEW OF Invitation au français

Invitation au français begins **Discovering French, *Nouveau!–Bleu*** with a focus on oral communication, both listening comprehension and speaking. Basic conversational skills are introduced without a formal presentation of structure.

- New conversational patterns are grouped by function in the **Pour communiquer** sections.
- Students will learn how to greet people, introduce themselves, talk about their friends and family, and even order in a café.
- Telling time, talking about the days of the week, months and dates, the weather and seasons, and the numbers from 0–100 are introduced.

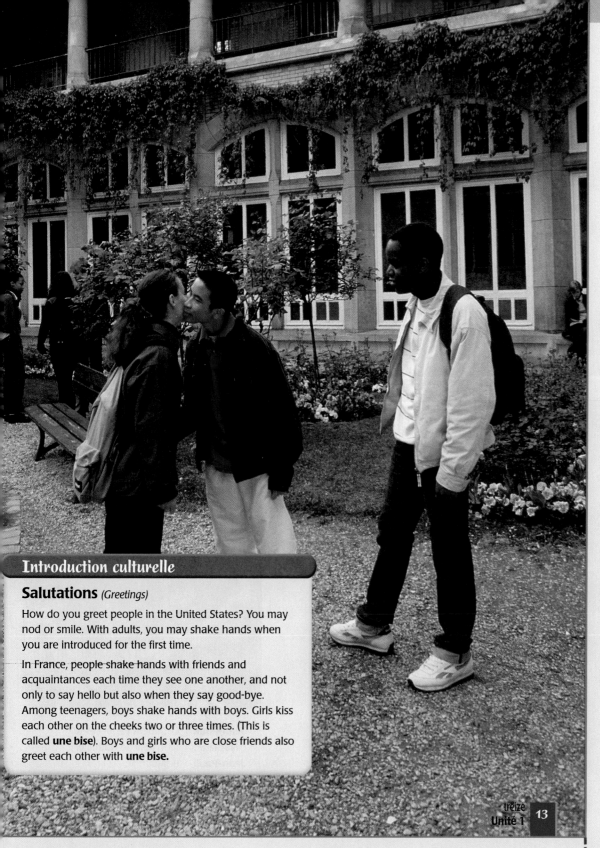

Introduction culturelle

Salutations *(Greetings)*

How do you greet people in the United States? You may nod or smile. With adults, you may shake hands when you are introduced for the first time.

In France, people shake hands with friends and acquaintances each time they see one another, and not only to say hello but also when they say good-bye. Among teenagers, boys shake hands with boys. Girls kiss each other on the cheeks two or three times. (This is called **une bise**). Boys and girls who are close friends also greet each other with **une bise.**

treize
Unité 1 13

UNIT OVERVIEW

- **Communication Goals:** Students will learn greetings and basic phrases. They will also learn how to count and tell time.
- **Linguistic Goals:** Students will begin to recognize what French sounds like and learn how French words are pronounced.
- **Critical Thinking Goals:** Students will encounter the concept of linguistic differences. They will discover that often there is no word-for-word correspondence between French and English.
- **Cultural Goals:** Students will discover that in France people greet one another and interact differently than in the U.S.

STANDARDS *continued*

- Learning about American influence on French teenagers

COMMUNITIES

- Using French for personal enjoyment
- Increasing awareness of the francophone world in the classroom

Teaching Resource Options

PRINT 

Unit 1 Resource Book
Family Letter, p. 31
Français pour hispanophones
Conseils, pp. 5–8
Vocabulaire, pp. 38–39

AUDIO & VISUAL 

Audio Program
Chansons CD

TECHNOLOGY

EasyPlanner CD-ROM

Cultural Note

French children kiss their parents good morning and good night.

Cross-cultural observation

Have students study the pictures carefully, looking at the young people, their dress, and their way of greeting one another.

- Which elements in the pictures seem to be definitely French?
- Which elements could also be American?

Pacing

Try to move through this unit rather quickly, concentrating on listening and speaking.

In the units following **Invitation au français,** students will encounter the same vocabulary again. At that time they will be expected to master the material in writing.

Leçon 1A

Main Topic Greeting and meeting friends

Teaching Resource Options

PRINT

Workbook PE, pp. 1–4
Activités pour tous PE, pp. 1–2
Block Scheduling Copymasters, pp. 1–8
Unit 1 Resource Book
- *Activités pour tous* TE, pp. 13–14
- Audioscript, pp. 54, 56–58
- Communipak, pp. 128–146
- Lesson Plans, pp. 19–20
- Block Scheduling Lesson Plans, pp. 25–26
- Absent Student Copymasters, p. 32
- Video Activities, pp. 38–41
- Videoscript, p. 50
- Workbook TE, pp. 1–4

AUDIO & VISUAL 

Audio Program
CD 1 Tracks 1, 2
CD 5 Tracks 1–9

TECHNOLOGY

Online Workbook

VIDEO PROGRAM

MODULE 1A
La rentrée

TOTAL TIME: 3:46 min.
DVD Disk 1
Videotape 1 (COUNTER: 6:53 min.)

1A.1 Dialogue: La rentrée (6:53-7:54 min.)

1A.2 Mini-scenes: Meeting people (7:55-9:14 min.)

1A.3 Vignette culturelle: Bonjour! (9:15-10:39 min.)

Comprehension practice Play the entire module through as an introduction to the lesson.

Cultural note **Trinh** is a Vietnamese first name. Many people of Vietnamese and Cambodian origin live in France.

Some common Vietnamese names:

boys		girls	
Trinh	Chau	Kim	Hoa
Minh	Tam	Mai	Anh
My	Tan		

LEÇON 1

VIDÉO-SCÈNE 

Bonjour!

A La rentrée

This is the first day of school. Students are greeting their friends and meeting new classmates.

Trinh: Bonjour! Je m'appelle Trinh.
Céline: Et moi, je m'appelle Céline.

Marc: Je m'appelle Marc. Et toi?
Isabelle: Moi, je m'appelle Isabelle.

Comment t'appelles-tu?
Je m'appelle Nathalie.

Jean-Paul: Comment t'appelles-tu?
Nathalie: Je m'appelle Nathalie.
Jean-Paul: Bonjour.
Nathalie: Bonjour.

USING THE VIDEO AND THE AUDIO PROGRAM

For each vidéo-scène of **Invitation au français,** the opening text corresponds to part 1 of the video.

First play the entire video module through as an introduction to the lesson. Have students observe how young people greet one another in France.

Then play the opening scene several more times and have students practice repeating the new phrases.

POUR COMMUNIQUER

▶ How to say hello:

Bonjour!	*Hello!*	–**Bonjour**, Nathalie! –**Bonjour**, Jean-Paul!

▶ How to ask a classmate's name:

Comment t'appelles-tu?	*What's your name?*	–**Comment t'appelles-tu?**
Je m'appelle ...	*My name is ...*	–**Je m'appelle** Céline.

Other Expressions

moi	*me*	**Moi**, je m'appelle Marc.
et toi?	*and you?*	**Et toi**, comment t'appelles-tu?

NOTES culturelles

1 La rentrée *(Back to school)*

French and American students have about the same number of days of summer vacation. In France, summer vacation usually begins at the end of June and classes resume in early September. The first day back to school in fall is called **la rentrée.**

2 Les prénoms français *(French first names)*

Many traditional French names have corresponding equivalents in English.

For boys:	For girls:
Jean *(John)*	**Marie** *(Mary)*
Pierre *(Peter)*	**Monique** *(Monica)*
Marc *(Mark)*	**Cécile** *(Cecilia)*
Philippe *(Philip)*	**Véronique** *(Veronica)*
Nicolas *(Nicholas)*	**Virginie** *(Virginia)*

Often the names **Jean** and **Marie** are combined in double names such as **Jean-Paul** and **Marie-Christine.** In recent years, names of foreign origin, like **Kevin** and **Laura**, have become quite popular.

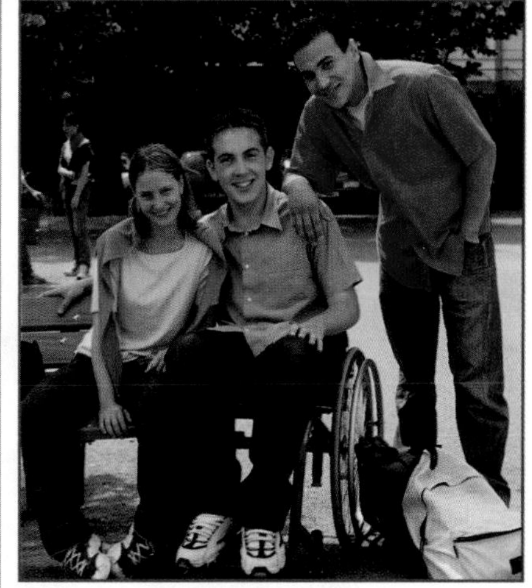

POUR COMMUNIQUER

Language note Literally, **bonjour** means *good day* and corresponds to *good morning* or *good afternoon.*

In the evening, **bonjour** may be replaced by **bonsoir** *(good evening).*

Bonne nuit *(good night)* is used when someone is going to bed.

Also: **Comment est-ce que tu t'appelles?**

Language note When speaking among themselves, French people often use casual speech. Since these forms are spoken (and not written), they are not formally presented in the students' textbook. If you wish, you may introduce them orally in class for recognition. For example, to ask someone's name in casual French one may say:

Tu t'appelles comment? or **Comment tu t'appelles?**

Notes culturelles

There are four grades in a French **collège:**

- **sixième** (sixth grade),
- **cinquième** (seventh grade),
- **quatrième** (eighth grade) and
- **troisième** (ninth grade).

CHOOSING NAMES

Assign students French names or let them choose names for themselves from the list on pp. 10-11. Have students introduce themselves to the class. First practice the pronunciation of **je m'appelle** and then model the correct pronunciation of their French names. If you do not wish to use French names, help students pronounce their own names with a French accent.

INCLUSION

Multisensory Model the sound of words ending in vowel + "n" (as in the name **Jean**) and have students practice the sound, noting the open mouth/feeling in nose. Provide a list of easy words so that students can model pronunciation. Have students practice in pairs, and then put the list in their notebooks.

Teaching Resource Options

PRINT 

Workbook PE, pp. 1–4
Unit 1 Resource Book
- Audioscript, p. 54
- Communipak, pp. 128–146
- Video Activities, pp. 39–40
- Videoscript, p. 50
- Workbook TE, pp. 1–4

AUDIO & VISUAL 

Audio Program
CD 1 Tracks 3, 4, 5

VIDEO PROGRAM

VIDÉO DVD

MODULE 1A

1A.2 Mini-scenes: Meeting people
(7:55–9:14 min.)

Petit commentaire
- Julius Caesar invaded Gaul around 50 B.C.
- The title of the book *Le tour de Gaule d'Astérix* is a take-off on the Tour de France bicycle race (see p. 28).

1 EXCHANGES greetings
- Bonjour! – Bonjour!

2 COMMUNICATION identifying oneself
- Je m'appelle (Robert). – Je m'appelle (Anne).

3 COMMUNICATION asking someone's name
- Comment t'appelles-tu? – Je m'appelle (Daniel).

4 PRACTICE greetings
1. Bonjour, Céline!
2. Bonjour, Jean-Paul!
3. Bonjour, Isabelle!
4. Bonjour, François!
5. Bonjour, Stéphanie!
6. Bonjour, Nathalie!
7. Bonjour, Trinh!

Chain activity in small groups
Student 1 asks Student 2 his/her name. Then Student 2 asks the name of Student 3, and so on. **Je m'appelle [Stéphanie]. Et toi? Moi, je m'appelle [David]. Et toi?** etc.

PETIT COMMENTAIRE
Astérix le Gaulois is one of the best-loved cartoon characters in France. Small in size but extremely clever and courageous, he represents the "little man" defending his country Gaul (the ancient name of France) against the invading Roman legions led by Julius Caesar.

1 Bonjour!
PARLER Say hello to the student nearest to you.

2 Je m'appelle ...
PARLER Introduce yourself to your classmates.

▶ **Je m'appelle (Paul).**

▶ **Je m'appelle (Denise).**

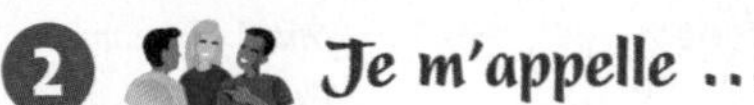

3 Et toi?
PARLER Ask a classmate his or her name.

▶ **—Comment t'appelles-tu?**
—Je m'appelle (Christine).

4 Bonjour, les amis! *(Hello everyone!)*
PARLER Say hello to the following students.

▶ **Bonjour, Marc!**

▶ Marc

1. Céline

2. Jean-Paul

3. Isabelle

4. François

5. Stéphanie

6. Nathalie

7. Trinh

TEACHING THE ALPHABET
Say each letter of the alphabet and have students repeat as you write it on the board. Then, have a volunteer come and point to the letters as you say them in random order. The others can point to the corresponding letters in their textbook.

INCLUSION
Metacognitive, Gifted & Talented Have students look at different alphabets (Greek, Cyrillic) and discuss the role of letters in the Roman alphabet as symbols for sounds. Review vowel sounds. Have students listen to you as you say the name of each letter. Have students write phonetic transcriptions for the names of letters.

L'alphabet

A	B	C	D	E	F	G	H	I	J	K	L	M
a	bé	cé	dé	e	effe	gé	hache	i	ji	ka	elle	emme

N	O	P	Q	R	S	T	U	V	W	X	Y	Z
enne	o	pé	ku	erre	esse	té	u	vé	double vé	ixe	i grec	zède

PRONONCIATION

Les signes orthographiques *(Spelling marks)*

French uses accents and spelling marks that do not exist in English. These marks are part of the spelling and cannot be left out.

In French, there are four accents that may appear on vowels.

´	**l'accent aigu** *(acute accent)*	C**é**cile, St**é**phanie
`	**l'accent grave** *(grave accent)*	Mich**è**le, Hél**è**ne
^	**l'accent circonflexe** *(circumflex)*	Jér**ô**me
¨	**le tréma** *(diaeresis)*	No**ë**l, Jo**ë**lle

There is only one spelling mark used with a consonant. It occurs under the letter "**c.**"

¸	**la cédille** *(cedilla)*	Fran**ç**ois

5 La rentrée

PARLER It is the first day of class. The following students are introducing themselves. Act out the dialogues with your classmates.

▶ Hélène et Philippe — **—Je m'appelle Hélène. Et toi?** **—Moi, je m'appelle Philippe.**

1. Stéphanie et Marc
2. Cécile et Frédéric
3. Michèle et François
4. Anaïs et Clément
5. Céline et Jérôme
6. Mélanie et Noël

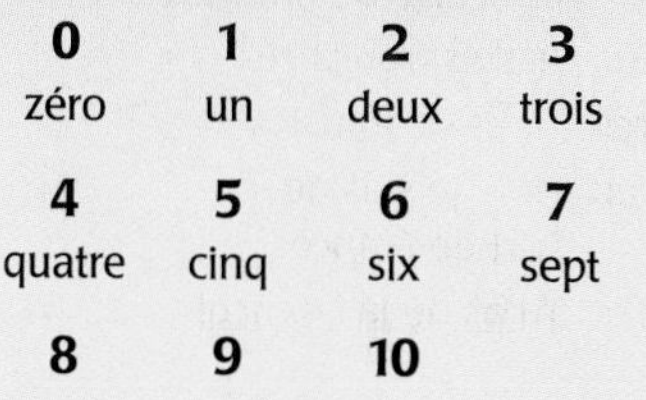

Les nombres de 0 à 10

0	1	2	3
zéro	un	deux	trois
4	**5**	**6**	**7**
quatre	cinq	six	sept
8	**9**	**10**	
huit	neuf	dix	

6 Numéros de téléphone

PARLER Imagine you are visiting a family in Quebec. Give them your American phone number in French.

617-963-4028 — **six, un, sept — neuf, six, trois — quatre, zéro, deux, huit**

COMPREHENSION Numbers 0 to 10

With your right hand, demonstrate the numbers 0 to 5 as you say them:

Voici 0. [closed fist]
Voici 1. [thumb extended]
Voici 2. [thumb and index finger] ...

Have students respond to commands with the same gestures:

Montrez-moi 0, 1, 2 ...

Practice the numbers in random order:

Montrez-moi 3, 5, 2, ...

Continue with numbers 6 through 10, using both hands.

PRONUNCIATION

Language notes

- The acute accent ´ occurs only on **e** to show it is pronounced /e/.
- The grave accent ` occurs mainly on **e** to show it is pronounced /ɛ/, and in the words **à**, **là**, and **où**.
- The circumflex ^ can occur on all vowels; often the corresponding English word has an "s": **forêt, hôpital, mât.**
- The diaeresis ¨ is placed on the second of two vowels to show that they are pronounced separately: **naïf.**
- The c-cedilla ç is used before **a, o, u** to show it is pronounced /s/: **ça, garçon, reçu.** Otherwise, **c** before **a, o, u** is pronounced /k/: **café, collège, culturel.**
- Note Accent marks are often not placed on capital letters. In this book, however, we will show accents on capital letters to make it easier for students.

5 EXCHANGES making introductions

– Moi, je m'appelle ... Et toi?
– Je m'appelle...

1. Stéphanie/Marc.
2. Cécile/Frédéric.
3. Michèle/François.
4. Anaïs/Clément.
5. Céline/Jérôme.
6. Mélanie/Noël.

Speaking activity To practice the numbers 0-10, knock loudly on your desk. Have the students identify the number of knocks in French. For example: (toc! toc!) **Deux!**, etc.

If students ask

un nombre = number or numeral, in the mathematical sense
un numéro = number, in a series; e.g., phone number, house number

6 COMMUNICATION giving one's telephone number

617-963-4028 (six, un, sept - neuf, six, trois - quatre, zéro, deux, huit)

Cultural note In Quebec, as in the United States, phone numbers are given digit by digit.

Leçon 1B

Main Topic Stating one's nationality and where one is from

Teaching Resource Options

PRINT 

Workbook PE, pp. 5–8
Activités pour tous PE, pp. 3–4
Unit 1 Resource Book
- *Activités pour tous* TE, pp. 15–16
- Audioscript, pp. 55, 58–59
- Communipak, pp. 128–146
- Lesson Plans, pp. 21–22
- Block Scheduling Lesson Plans, pp. 27–28
- Absent Student Copymasters, pp. 33–34
- Video Activities, pp. 42–45
- Videoscript, pp. 51–52
- Workbook TE, pp. 5–8

AUDIO & VISUAL 

Audio Program
CD 1 Tracks 6, 7
CD 5 Tracks 10–14

Overhead Transparencies
4 U.S., Canada, England, France
Les nationalités

TECHNOLOGY 

Online Workbook

VIDEO PROGRAM

VIDÉO

DVD

MODULE 1B
Tu es français?

TOTAL TIME: 7:09 min.
DVD Disk 1
Videotape 1 (COUNTER: 10:49 min.)

1B.1 Dialogue: Tu es français? (10:49–12:15 min.)

1B.2 Mini-scenes: Finding out where people are from (12:16–13:48 min.)

1B.3 Vignette culturelle: Qui est français? (13:49–17:58 min.)

Comprehension practice Play the entire module through as an introduction to the lesson.

Cultural note Marc tells Stéphanie **Tu as de la chance!** because he thinks she is lucky to live in Martinique, a tropical island with beautiful beaches and exotic flowers. For French people, Martinique evokes the kinds of images that "Hawaii" evokes for Americans.

LEÇON 1

VIDÉO-SCÈNE

VIDÉO DVD AUDIO

B Tu es français?

It is the opening day of school and several of the students meet in the cafeteria (**la cafétéria** or **la cantine**) at lunchtime. Marc discovers that not everyone is French.

Tu es français?

Oui, je suis français.

Marc: Tu es français?
Jean-Paul: Oui, je suis français.

Non! Je suis américain.

Marc: Et toi, Patrick, tu es français aussi?
Patrick: Non! Je suis américain. Je suis de Boston.

Je suis française.

Marc: Et toi, Stéphanie, tu es française ou américaine?
Stéphanie: Je suis française.
Marc: Tu es de Paris?
Stéphanie: Non, je suis de Fort-de-France.
Marc: Tu as de la chance! *You're lucky!*

CLASSROOM MANAGEMENT Groups

Play the entire video module as an introduction to the lesson.

Divide the class into groups and name one person in each group as **secrétaire** *(recorder)*. Play Part 1 of the video again.

Have the groups list things they observed in the French school that are similar to their own school, as well as things that are different.

Have the recorders come forward to read their lists. The team with the most complete list is the winner. For confirmation, play the video once more.

POUR COMMUNIQUER

▶ *How to talk about where people are from:*

Tu es de ...?	*Are you from ...?*	–**Tu es de** Nice?
Je suis de ...	*I'm from ...*	–Non, **je suis de** Paris.

▶ *How to talk about one's nationality:*

Tu es ...?	*Are you ...?*	–Pierre, **tu es** français?
Je suis ...	*I am ...*	–Oui, **je suis** français.

Les nationalités

français	**française**
anglais	**anglaise**
américain	**américaine**
canadien	**canadienne**

Other Expressions

oui	*yes*	Tu es français? **Oui,** je suis français.
non	*no*	Tu es canadien? **Non,** je suis américain.
et	*and*	Je suis de Paris. **Et** toi?
ou	*or*	Tu es français **ou** canadien?
aussi	*also, too*	Moi **aussi,** je suis française.

NOTE culturelle

EN BREF

Capitale: Fort-de-France
Population: 400 000
Langues: créole, français

La Martinique

Martinique is a small French island located in the Caribbean, southeast of Puerto Rico. Because Martinique is part of the French national territory, its inhabitants are French citizens. Most of them are of African origin. They speak French as well as a dialect called **créole.**

POUR COMMUNIQUER

Teaching note This is the students' first introduction to adjective agreement, and should be kept as simple as possible. The key objective is that students hear the sound differences and pronounce the masculine and feminine forms correctly.

Notes from the authors Please note that students are now being introduced to the verb **être.** This is also the first time they encounter subject-verb agreement and adjective agreement. These concepts will be explored in depth in later units. Here, they are to be used conversationally.

Pronunciation Be sure students notice that the final consonant sound (/z/, /n/) is pronounced in the feminine forms but is silent in the masculine forms.

Cultural note As students have learned in **Bonjour, le monde francophone!** (pp. 8-9), the French national territory extends beyond continental France **(la France métropolitaine).**

Martinique is one of the five French overseas departments **(Départements d'Outre-Mer).**

Have students go on the Internet to find out the names of the other four French overseas departments.

LISTENING COMPREHENSION ACTIVITY

Read the following eight sentences. Have students raise their hands (or stand) if the sentence refers to a girl.

Tu es français?	**Tu es américaine?**
Tu es canadienne?	**Tu es anglaise?**
Tu es anglais?	**Tu es américain?**
Tu es française?	**Tu es canadien?**

INCLUSION

Sequential Have students prepare large index cards of nationality vocabulary, with only endings in capital letters, marking feminine forms in red: AIS/AISE, IEN/IENNE, AIN/AINE. Have students put cards in a pile and take turns practicing endings only. Move to full words: **français(e), anglais(e), américain(e), italien (italienne).**

Teaching Resource Options

PRINT

Workbook PE, pp. 5–8
Unit 1 Resource Book
Audioscript, p. 55
Communipak, pp. 128–146
Workbook TE, pp. 5–8

AUDIO & VISUAL

Audio Program
CD 1 Tracks 8, 9

TECHNOLOGY

Power Presentations

Petit commentaire
The Statue of Liberty was sculpted by Auguste Bartholdi, who called upon Gustave Eiffel to design the interior metal framework. Although the arm and torch were exhibited at the World's Fair in Philadelphia in 1876, the statue itself was not inaugurated until ten years later. Gustave Eiffel built the Eiffel Tower for the Paris World's Fair in 1889. Have students think of a gift the United States could give France that would reflect the same spirit of freedom as the Statue of Liberty.

1 COMMUNICATION identifying oneself

- Bonjour! Je m'appelle (Karen Babcock). Je suis (américaine). Je suis de (Cleveland).
- Bonjour! Je m'appelle (Randy Bergholz). Je suis (américain). Je suis de (Palo Alto).

Pronunciation If your students are from a city that begins with a vowel sound, have them use **d': Je suis d'(Atlanta).** (The concept of elision is presented formally in Lesson 6.)

2 ROLE PLAY discussing where people are from

– (x), tu es français(e)?
– Oui, je suis français(e). Je suis de ...

1. Pierre/français/Paris
2. Paul/français/ Bordeaux
3. Éric/français/Lyon
4. Marial/française/Marseille
5. Nicole/française/Nice

Extra speaking activity Ask students to pretend they are a famous English, French, Canadian, or American person. Have them introduce themselves to the class, say where they are from, and give their nationalities.

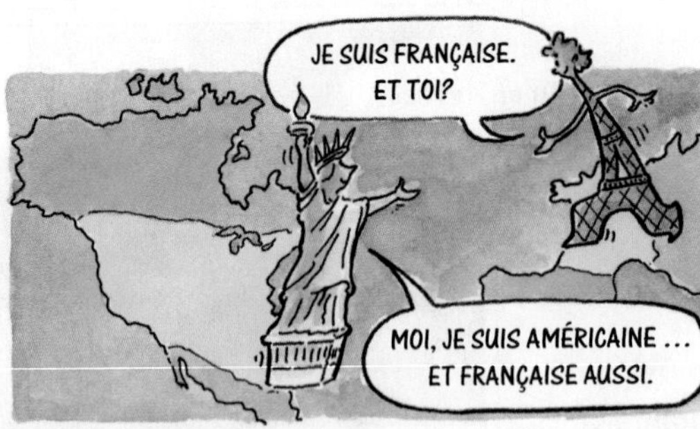

PETIT COMMENTAIRE
The Statue of Liberty **(la statue de la Liberté)** was a gift to the United States from the French people on the occasion of the 100th anniversary of American independence. The Eiffel Tower **(la tour Eiffel)** was built to celebrate the 100th anniversary of the French Revolution.

français, française

Names of nationalities may have two different forms, depending on whom they refer to:

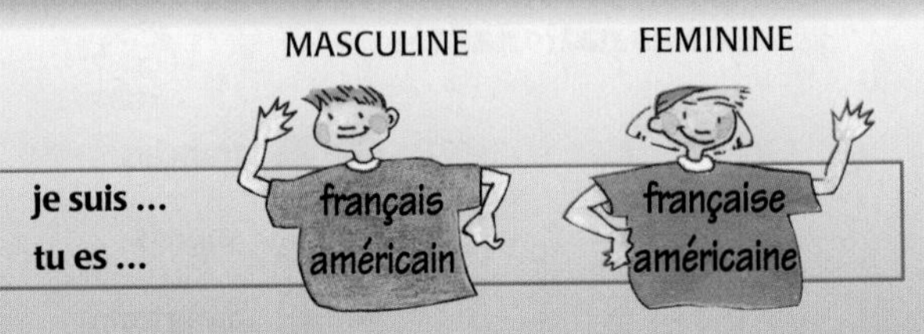

	MASCULINE	FEMININE
je suis ...	français	française
tu es ...	américain	américaine

Note In written French the feminine forms always end in **-e.**

1 Et toi?

PARLER Give your name, your nationality, and your city of origin.

▼

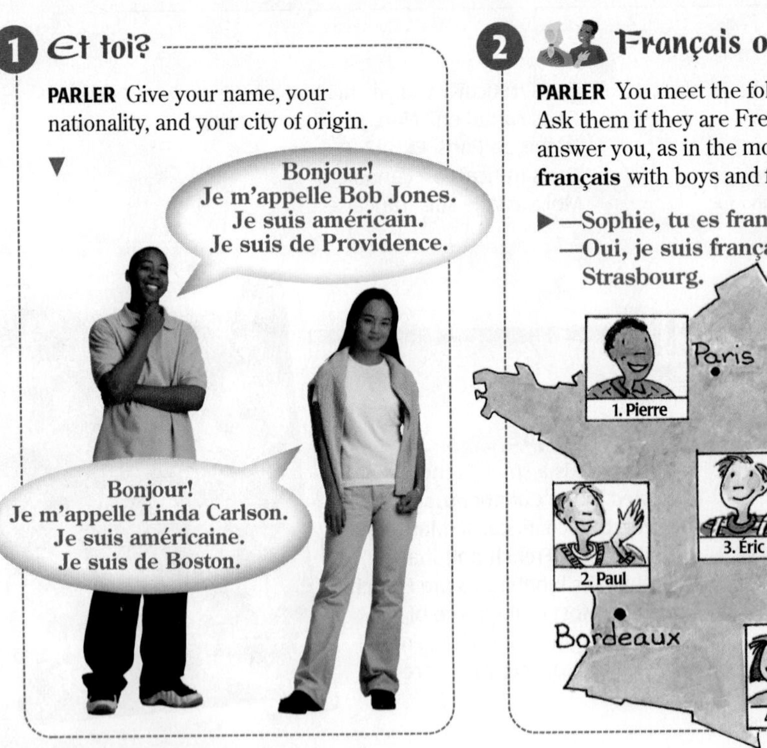

Je suis de Providence.

Je m'appelle Linda Carlson.

2 Français ou française?

PARLER You meet the following young people. Ask them if they are French. A classmate will answer you, as in the model. (Be sure to use **français** with boys and **française** with girls.)

▶ **—Sophie, tu es française?**
—Oui, je suis française. Je suis de Strasbourg.

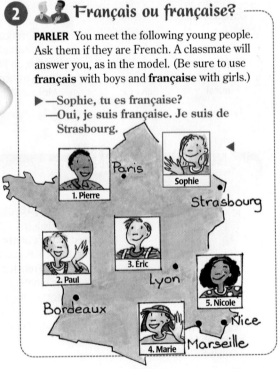

CLASSROOM MANAGEMENT Pair Practice

In pair practice, students do activities together with a partner. Introduce the class to pair practice with Act. 2 and 3. Be sure each student has a partner.

First do the exercise with the entire class, having half the group give the first cue, and the other half the response.

Then let the students do the same activity again in pairs. For the odd numbered cues, Student A asks the question and Student B responds. For the even-numbered cues, the roles are reversed.

3  *Quelle nationalité?* *(Which nationality?)*

PARLER Greet the following young people and find out each one's nationality. A classmate will answer you, according to the model.

▶ **—Bonjour, Marc. Tu es canadien?**
—Oui, je suis canadien.
Je suis de Montréal.

▶ Marc Montréal	1. Claire Québec	2. Patrick Boston

3. Denise Liverpool	4. Donna Memphis	5. Paul Cambridge

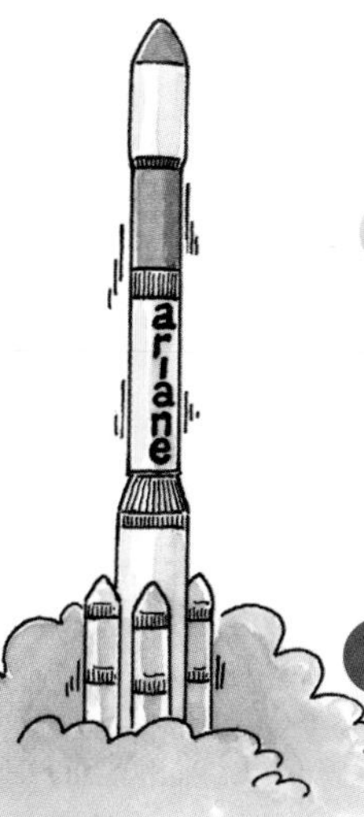

Les nombres de 10 à 20

10	11	12	13	14	15
dix	onze	douze	treize	quatorze	quinze
16	**17**	**18**	**19**	**20**	
seize	dix-sept	dix-huit	dix-neuf	vingt	

4 *La fusée Ariane* *(The Ariane rocket)*

PARLER Give the countdown for the liftoff of the French rocket Ariane, from 20 to 0.

PRONONCIATION

Les lettres muettes *(Silent letters)*

In French, the last letter of a word is often not pronounced.

Paris

- Final "**e**" is always silent.
  Répétez: **Céline Philippe Stéphanie anglaise française onze douze treize quatorze quinze seize**
- Final "**s**" is almost always silent.
  Répétez: **Paris Nicolas Jacques anglais français trois**
- The letter "**h**" is always silent.
  Répétez: **Hélène Henri Thomas Nathalie Catherine Thérèse**

3 ROLE PLAY discussing one's nationality

1. – Bonjour, Claire. Tu es canadienne?
   – Oui, je suis canadienne. Je suis de Québec.
2. – Bonjour, Patrick. Tu es américain?
   – Oui, je suis américain. Je suis de Boston.
3. – Bonjour, Denise. Tu es anglaise?
   – Oui, je suis anglaise. Je suis de Liverpool.
4. – Bonjour, Donna. Tu es américaine?
   – Oui, je suis américaine. Je suis de Memphis.
5. – Bonjour, Paul. Tu es anglais?
   – Oui, je suis anglais. Je suis de Cambridge.

Language note People from the province of Quebec will often say: **Je suis québécois(e).**

Pronunciation Note the pronunciation of **vingt** /vɛ̃/.

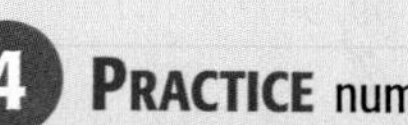

4 PRACTICE numbers 0 to 20

Vingt, dix-neuf, dix-huit, dix-sept, seize, quinze, quatorze, treize, douze, onze, dix, neuf, huit, sept, six, cinq, quatre, trois, deux, un, zéro!

Language note In French, a countdown is **un compte à rebours.**

Cultural note All the French Ariane rockets are launched from Kourou in French Guiana (South America). France is the only country in Europe with an on-going space program.

PRONUNCIATION

- Have students pronounce the French /r/ in Paris as if they were clearing their throats.
- In later lessons, students will encounter a few common words where the final "s" is pronounced: **un fils, mars, tennis**
- The letters "ph" represent the sound /f/, as in English: **Philippe, Stéphanie.**
- The letters "ch" usually represent the sound /ʃ/, as in: **Chicago, Michèle.**
- The letters "chr" represent the sound /kr/ as in: **Christophe, Christine.**

COMPREHENSION Numbers 11 to 20

PROPS: index cards with numbers 11 to 20

Place the first five index cards on the chalkboard tray. Point to the numbers as you name them: 11, 12, 13, 14, 15.

Have students come forward to point out and touch the numbers as you name them.
X, montre le 12. Touche le 15.

Present the second five cards.

Place all cards randomly on the tray. Ask students to pass numbers to their classmates.
Y, prends le 20 et donne-le à Z.

Leçon 1C

Main Topic Saying hello and good-bye

Teaching Resource Options

PRINT  

Workbook PE, pp. 9–12
Activités pour tous PE, pp. 5–6
Unit 1 Resource Book
- *Activités pour tous* TE, pp. 17–18
- Audioscript, pp. 55–56, 59–60
- Communipak, pp. 128–146
- Lesson Plans, pp. 23–24
- Block Scheduling Lesson Plans, pp. 29–30
- Absent Student Copymasters, p. 35
- Video Activities, pp. 46–49
- Videoscript, pp. 52–53
- Workbook TE, pp. 9–12

AUDIO & VISUAL 

Audio Program
CD 1 Tracks 10, 11
CD 5 Tracks 15–20

TECHNOLOGY 

Online Workbook

VIDEO PROGRAM

VIDÉO DVD

MODULE 1C
Salut! Ça va?

TOTAL TIME: 4:38 min.
DVD Disk 1
Videotape 1 (COUNTER: 18:08 min.)

1C.1 Dialogue: Salut! Ça va? (18:31–18:50 min.)

1C.2 Mini-scenes: Greeting people (18:51–21:26 min.)

1C.3 Vignette culturelle: Bonjour ou Salut? (21:27–22:46 min.)

Comprehension practice Play the entire module through as an introduction to the lesson, asking students to take notes.
Pre-AP skill: Practice note-taking skills when listening or viewing.

LEÇON 1

VIDÉO-SCÈNE

VIDÉO DVD AUDIO

C Salut! Ça va?

On the way to school, François meets his friends.

François also meets his teachers.

Monsieur Masson

Madame Chollet

Mademoiselle Lacour

After class, François says good-bye to his teacher and his friends.

SETTING THE SCENE

Ask students how they greet their teachers when they meet them before school or in the hall.

Have them watch the video to see if French students greet their teachers with the same formality or informality.

INCLUSION

Cumulative Pair Practice: Have students write expressions from the dialogue on large index cards with phonetic transcriptions and color-coded silent letters. Have students practice orally from the cards, not the text. Have students practice each dialogue three times, exchanging roles. Have students practice dialogues from the cards at home and record their renditions. Have them act out one dialogue from memory in front of the class.

POUR COMMUNIQUER

▶ *How to greet a friend or classmate:*

Salut! *Hi!*

▶ *How to greet a teacher or another adult:*

Bonjour! *Hello!* **Bonjour, monsieur.**
Bonjour, madame.
Bonjour, mademoiselle.

▶ *How to say good-bye:*

Au revoir! *Good-bye!* **Au revoir, Philippe.**
Au revoir, monsieur.

→ In written French, the following abbreviations are commonly used:

M. Masson	Monsieur Masson
Mme Chollet	Madame Chollet
Mlle Lacour	Mademoiselle Lacour

→ Young people often use **Salut!** to say good-bye to each other.

NOTE culturelle

Bonjour ou Salut?

French young people may greet one another with **Bonjour**, but they often prefer the less formal **Salut.** When they meet their teachers, however, they always use **Bonjour.** French young people are generally much more formal with adults than with their friends. This is especially true in their relationships with teachers, whom they treat with respect.

Have you noticed that in France adults are addressed as **monsieur, madame,** or **mademoiselle?** The last name is usually not used in greeting people.

POUR COMMUNIQUER

Language note When used alone, the titles **monsieur, madame,** and **mademoiselle** are not capitalized.

Casual speech Young people often use **salut** or the Italian **ciao** / tʃau / to say good-bye.

If students ask The French have no equivalent for "Ms." Instead they usually use **Madame**.

Abbreviations

- When an abbreviation includes only the first letter of a word, a period is used: **Monsieur = M.**
- When an abbreviation consists of the first and last letters of a word, no period is needed: **Madame = Mme, Mademoiselle = Mlle**

Note culturelle In France, young people almost never call adults by their first names. Have students imagine that they are staying with a host family in France. Ask how they think their French host father might react if they were to call him by his first name and why he would react that way. You might have students act out this scenario.

TEACHING STRATEGY Greeting adults

To activate **Monsieur, Madame,** and **Mademoiselle,** give names of other teachers in your school. Ask students to imagine they see these people in the hall. Have them greet the teachers in French.

Mrs. Mills – **Bonjour, Madame!**
Mr. Tower – **Bonjour, Monsieur!**
Miss Swenson – **Bonjour, Mademoiselle!**

INCLUSION

Alphabetic/phonetic Explain how the "n" and "r" of **monsieur** are not pronounced. Have students copy the pronunciation key of this word from a French dictionary into their notebooks. Then have students write the phonetic pronunciation on the board and say it aloud three times.

Teaching Resource Options

PRINT

Workbook PE, pp. 9–12
Unit 1 Resource Book
- Audioscript, pp. 56, 61
- Communipak, pp. 128–146
- Family Involvement, pp. 36–37
- Video Activities, pp. 46–47
- Videoscript, pp. 52–53
- Workbook TE, pp. 9–12

Assessment
- Lesson 1 Quiz, pp. 62–63
- Audioscript for Quiz 1, p. 61
- Answer Keys, pp. 195–197

AUDIO & VISUAL

Audio Program
CD 1 Tracks 12, 13
CD 13 Tracks 1, 2

Overhead Transparencies
5 Expressions with ***ça va***

TECHNOLOGY

Test Generator CD-ROM/McDougal Littell Assessment System

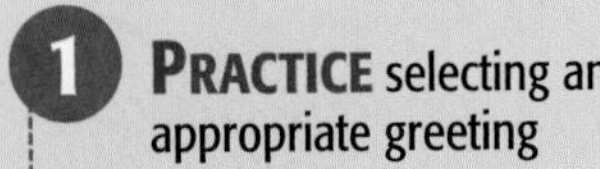

VIDEO PROGRAM

VIDÉO DVD

MODULE 1C

1C.2 Mini-scenes: Greeting people
(18:51–21:26 min.)

1 PRACTICE selecting an appropriate greeting

1. Salut, Céline!
2. Bonjour, monsieur!
3. Salut, Nathalie!
4. Salut, Marc!
5. Bonjour, madame!
6. Bonjour, mademoiselle!

Variation Say good-bye.
- **Au revoir, Valérie.**
- **Au revoir, mademoiselle.**

2 EXCHANGES greetings

Answers will vary.
- Salut, (Anne)! Ça va?
- Ça va (bien)! Et toi?
- Ça va (très bien). Merci.
- Salut, (Éric)! Ça va?
- (Non), ça va (mal). Et toi?
- Ça va (comme ci, comme ça). Merci.

1 Bonjour ou salut?

PARLER You are enrolled in a French school. Greet your friends and teachers.

Valérie

▶ Salut, Valérie!

Mademoiselle Pinot

▶ Bonjour, mademoiselle!

1. Céline

2. Monsieur Masson

3. Nathalie

4. Marc

5. Madame Albert

6. Mademoiselle Boucher

POUR COMMUNIQUER

▶ ***How to ask people how they feel:***

—**Ça va?** *How are you? How are things going? How's everything?*
—**Ça va!** *(I'm) fine. (I'm) okay. Everything's all right.*

Ça va ...

très bien

bien

comme ci, comme ça

mal

très mal

▶ ***How to express one's feelings of frustration and appreciation:***

Zut! *Darn!* **Zut!** Ça va mal! **Merci!** *Thanks!* Ça va, **merci.**

→ **Ça va?** *(How are you?)* is an informal greeting that corresponds to the following expressions:
- **Comment vas-tu?** (when addressing a friend)
  - **Bonjour, Paul. Comment vas-tu?**
- **Comment allez-vous?** (when addressing an adult)
  - **Bonjour, madame. Comment allez-vous?**

2 Dialogue

PARLER Exchange greetings with your classmates and ask how they are doing.

▶ —Salut, (Thomas)! Ça va?
—Ça va! Et toi?
—Ça va bien. Merci.

ÇA VA?
OUI, ÇA VA TRÈS BIEN!

ÇA VA?
AH NON! ÇA VA MAL!

TEACHING NOTE Spoken and written numbers

The emphasis in **Invitation au français** is on functional language use. In order to get around in a French-speaking country, it is very important to be able to understand and use numbers in communicative situations.

At the basic level, students need a great deal of practice in order to understand and use numbers easily.

As a challenge activity, some students may want to learn to spell the numbers, but spelling is not necessary at this level. Most French people use digits to write numbers, especially numbers over 20.

3 Situations

PARLER Sometimes we feel good and sometimes we don't. How would you respond in the following situations?

▶ You have the flu.
—**Ça va?**
—**Ça va mal!**

1. You just received an "A" in French.
2. You lost your wallet.
3. Your uncle gave you five dollars.
4. Your grandparents sent you a check for 100 dollars.
5. You bent the front wheel of your bicycle.
6. Your parents bought you a new video game.
7. Your little brother broke your cell phone.
8. It's your birthday.
9. You have a headache.
10. You just had an argument with your best friend.
11. Your French teacher has just canceled a quiz.

4 Ça va?

PARLER How would the following people answer the question **Ça va?**

Les nombres de 20 à 60

20 vingt	**30** trente	**40** quarante	**50** cinquante	**60** soixante
vingt et un	trente et un	quarante et un	cinquante et un	
vingt-deux	trente-deux	quarante-deux	cinquante-deux	
vingt-trois	trente-trois	quarante-trois	cinquante-trois	
...	...	...	...	
vingt-neuf	trente-neuf	quarante-neuf	cinquante-neuf	

Note Use **et** before **un: vingt et un.**

5 Séries

PARLER Read the following number series out loud.

13 21 37 42 55 60

16 20 29 31 48 56

PRONONCIATION

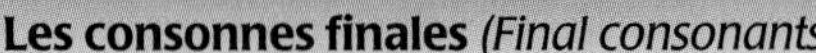

Les consonnes finales *(Final consonants)*

1 2 3

In French, the last consonant of a word is often not pronounced. **un deux trois**

- Remember: Final "**s**" is usually silent.
  Répétez: **trois français anglais**
- Most other final consonants are usually silent.
  Répétez: **Richard Albert Robert salut américain canadien bien deux**

EXCEPTION: The following final consonants are usually pronounced: "**c**," "**f**," "**l**," and sometimes "**r**."
Répétez: **Éric Daniel Lebeuf Pascal Victor**

However, the ending **-er** is usually pronounced /e/.
Répétez: **Roger Olivier**

COMPREHENSION Numbers and prepositions

PROPS: Index cards for 10, 20, 30, 40, 50, 60

Spread out the index cards on a table. Place three cards in a row on the chalktray.
Je mets les nombres 10-20-30 en ligne droite.

Then have students perform similar actions.
X, mets les nombres 40-50-60 en ligne droite.

Introduce new numbers with **après** *(after).*
Maintenant, je mets le 30 après le 20.
Y, mets le 10 après le 30. ...

Similarly introduce **avant** *(before),* **derrière** *(behind),* **devant** *(in front of).*
Je mets le 40 avant le 10. ...
Je mets le 50 derrière le 20. ...
Je mets le 60 devant le 40. ...

3 ROLE PLAY expressing one's feelings

– Ça va?
– Ça va (très) ...!

1. bien!
2. mal!
3. bien! (comme ci, comme ça.)
4. bien!
5. mal!
6. bien!
7. mal!
8. bien!
9. mal! (comme ci, comme ça.)
10. mal!
11. bien!

4 PRACTICE selecting an appropriate response

1. Ça va (très) bien!
2. Ça va (très) bien!
3. Ça va (très) bien!
4. Ça va (trés) mal!
5. Ça va (trés) mal!
6. Ça va (trés) mal!

Les nombres de 20 à 60

Pronunciation Remind students that there is no liaison after **et**: 31 / trãteɛ̃ /, etc.

Speaking activity Have the class say numbers in series.
- counting by 3s: 30 - 33 - 36 - 39 - 42 - 45 - 48 - 51 ...
- by 4s: 28 - 32 - 36 - 40 - 44 ...
- by 5s: 25 - 30 - 35 - 40 - 45 ...

5 PRACTICE reading numbers up to 60

(top) treize, vingt et un, trente-sept, quarante-deux, cinquante-cinq, soixante
(bottom) seize, vingt, vingt-neuf, trente et un, quarante-huit, cinquante-six

Listening comprehension Read a number from one of the tickets and have students indicate whether the number appears on the top or bottom ticket.

PRONUNCIATION

Exceptions
- The final consonant is pronounced in **zut!** and numbers used in counting like **six, sept, huit, dix.**
- The "r" in **monsieur** is silent.

Memory aid These final consonants are found in the word: CaReFuL.

Leçon 2A

Main Topics Pointing out people and finding out who they are

Teaching Resource Options

PRINT

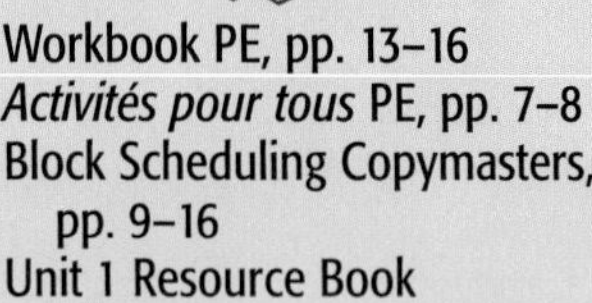

Workbook PE, pp. 13–16
Activités pour tous PE, pp. 7–8
Block Scheduling Copymasters, pp. 9–16
Unit 1 Resource Book
- *Activités pour tous* TE, pp. 77–78
- Audioscript, pp. 118, 120–121
- Communipak, pp. 128–146
- Lesson Plans, pp. 83–84
- Block Scheduling Lesson Plans, pp. 89–90
- Absent Student Copymasters, p. 95
- Video Activities, pp. 102–105
- Videoscript, p. 114
- Workbook TE, pp. 65–68

AUDIO & VISUAL

Audio Program
CD 1 Tracks 14, 15
CD 5 Tracks 21–25

Overhead Transparencies
7 People *Les personnes*

TECHNOLOGY

Online Workbook

VIDEO PROGRAM

VIDÉO
DVD

MODULE 2A
Copain ou copine?

TOTAL TIME: 3:34 min.
DVD Disk 1
Videotape 1 (COUNTER: 22:57 min.)

2A.1 Dialogue: Copain ou copine? (23:42–24:18 min.)

2A.2 Mini-scenes: Listening –Pointing out people (24:19–25:17 min.)

2A.3 Vignette culturelle: La bande de copains (25:18–26:31 min.)

Comprehension practice Play the entire module through as an introduction to the lesson.

LEÇON 2

VIDÉO-SCÈNE

VIDÉO DVD AUDIO

Famille et copains

A Copain ou copine?

In French, there are certain girls' and boys' names that sound the same. Occasionally this can be confusing.

Dominique? Qui est-ce?
Un copain ou une copine?

SCÈNE 1 **Philippe et Jean-Paul**

Philippe is at home with his friend Jean-Paul. He seems to be expecting someone. Who could it be ... ? The doorbell rings.

Philippe: Tiens! Voilà Dominique!
Jean-Paul: Dominique? Qui est-ce? Un copain ou une copine?
Philippe: C'est une copine.

Salut, Dominique!
Ça va?

SCÈNE 2 **Philippe, Jean-Paul, Dominique**

Philippe: Salut, Dominique! Ça va?
Dominique: Oui, ça va! Et toi?
Jean-Paul: *(thinking)* C'est vrai! C'est une copine! — *It's true!*

SETTING THE STAGE

Ask students to think of names for boys and girls that sound the same.

For example: Kim, Lynn, Marty, Bobby/Bobbie, Gene/Jean.

In French, also, there are many boy's and girl's names that are pronounced alike.

Names spelled the same:
Dominique, Claude.

Names spelled differently:
René/Renée, André/Andrée, Joël/Joëlle, Noël/Noëlle, Michel/Michèle, Daniel/Danielle, Gabriel/Gabrielle, Frédéric/Frédérique.

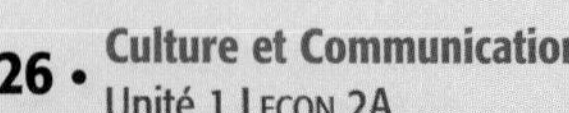

POUR COMMUNIQUER

Tiens! Voilà Caroline! C'est une copine!

How to introduce or point out someone:

Voici ...	*This is ..., Here come(s) ...*	**Voici** Jean-Paul. **Voici** Nathalie et François.
Voilà ...	*This (That) is ..., There's ...*	**Voilà** Isabelle. **Voilà** Philippe et Dominique.

How to find out who someone is:

Qui est-ce?	*Who's that? Who is it?*	—**Qui est-ce?**
C'est ...	*It's ..., That's ..., He's ..., She's ...*	—**C'est** Patrick. **C'est** un copain.

How to get someone's attention or to express surprise:

Tiens!	*Look! Hey!*	**Tiens,** voilà Dominique!

Les personnes

un garçon	*boy*
un ami	*friend (male)*
un copain	*friend (male)*
un monsieur	*gentleman*
un prof	*teacher*

une fille	*girl*
une amie	*friend (female)*
une copine	*friend (female)*
une dame	*lady*
une prof	*teacher*

NOTE culturelle

Amis et copains

French young people, like their American counterparts, enjoy spending time with their friends. They refer to their friends as **un ami** (for a boy) and **une amie** (for a girl) or — more commonly — as **un copain** or **une copine.** Note that the words **copain, copine** can also have special meanings. When a boy talks about **une copine**, he is referring to a friend who is a girl. However, when he says **ma** (*my*) **copine**, he may be referring to his girlfriend. Similarly, a girl would call her boyfriend **mon copain.**

Le Luco

POUR COMMUNIQUER

Language notes

- The expression **voilà** may also mean *That is, There is, There are.*
- One can say:

  C'est qui? Qui c'est?

Cultural note There are several ways of referring to one's boyfriend or girlfriend:

- **mon petit ami, ma petite amie** (though these terms are not as commonly used as several years ago)
- **mon petit copain, ma petite copine**
- **mon ami, mon amie**

The possessive is used to signal a more personal relationship.

Hold up magazine photos of popular celebrities and have volunteers introduce them as their boyfriends or girlfriends.

Language note

Un prof/une prof. In casual speech, both teachers and students in France use the terms **un prof** and **une prof.** These expressions are easier for beginners and are therefore introduced here in **Invitation au français.** The more formal term **un professeur,** which refers to both men and women, is introduced in Lesson 19.

COMPREHENSION Nouns with un/une

PROPS: Transparency 7: People *Les personnes*
Red and blue index cards

Model new words on the transparency.
Voici un garçon. Voici une fille. ...

Have students come point out the words.
X, viens ici. Montre-nous une fille.

Distribute two cards to each student.
Voici "un". [Hold up the blue card.]
Voici "une". [Hold up the red card.]

As you make statements using the new words, have students hold up their cards.
C'est un copain. Levez la carte bleue.
C'est une amie. Levez la carte rouge.
C'est un ami. [blue cards.]

Teaching Resource Options

PRINT  

Workbook PE, pp. 13–16
Unit 1 Resource Book
Audioscript, p. 118
Communipak, pp. 128–146
Workbook TE, pp. 65–68

AUDIO & VISUAL  

Audio Program
CD 1 Tracks 16, 17

TECHNOLOGY 

Power Presentations

Petit commentaire

- The **Tour de France,** which was created in 1904, is a month-long bicycle race that takes cyclists around France, with particularly grueling stages **(étapes)** in the Alps and the Pyrenees. Every year the route is somewhat different, but the finish line is always in Paris at the bottom of the Champs-Élysées.
- The **Tour de France féminin** began in 1984. From 1987 to 1989, it was dominated by the French cyclist Jeannie Longo.

Teaching note This is the first time students see indefinite articles. They are introduced to the concept of gender in that they discover that articles agree with the nouns they introduce.

1 PRACTICE identifying male and female friends

1. Alice est une copine.
2. Cécile est une copine.
3. Trinh est un copain.
4. Robert est un copain.
5. Céline est une copine.

Pronunciation

- Insist that students do not pronounce the "n" in **un** or **copain.**
- Note that liaison is common after **est: Christine est une copine.**

2 ROLE PLAY meeting and identifying friends

–Tiens, voilà ... !
–Qui est-ce?
–C'est ...

1. Alice/une amie.
2. Cécile/une amie.
3. Trinh/un ami.
4. Robert/un ami.
5. Céline/une amie.

3 PRACTICE choosing genders

1. une 2. un 3. une 4. une 5. un
6. un 7. une 8. une 9. un 10. une

C'EST UN CHAMPION!

MAIS NON! C'EST UNE CHAMPIONNE!

PETIT COMMENTAIRE

Cycling is a popular competitive sport throughout France. The most popular races are the **Tour de France** *for men and the* **Grande Boucle Féminine Internationale** *for women. French women cyclists have won many titles.*

un garçon, une fille

In French, all NOUNS are either MASCULINE or FEMININE.
Nouns referring to boys or men are almost always MASCULINE.
They are introduced by **un** *(a, an).*
Nouns referring to girls or women are almost always FEMININE.
They are introduced by **une** *(a, an).*

MASCULINE		FEMININE	
un garçon	*a boy*	**une** fille	*a girl*
un ami	*a friend (male)*	**une** amie	*a friend (female)*

1 Copain ou copine?

PARLER Say that the following people are your friends. Use **un copain** or **une copine,** as appropriate.

▶ **Élodie est une copine.**

Élodie

1. Alice

2. Cécile

3. Trinh 4. Robert 5. Céline

2 Les amis

PARLER The same young people are visiting your school. Point them out to your classmates, using **un ami** or **une amie,** as appropriate.

▶ **—Tiens, voilà Élodie!**
—Qui est-ce?
—C'est une amie.

3 Un ou une?

PARLER Identify the people below by completing the sentences with **un** or **une.**

1. Voici ... fille.
2. Voilà ... garçon.
3. Voici ... dame.
4. C'est ... amie.
5. Nicolas est ... ami.
6. Jean-Paul est ... copain.
7. Cécile est ... copine.
8. Voici Mlle Lacour. C'est ... prof.
9. Voici M. Masson. C'est ... prof.
10. Voici Mme Chollet. C'est ... prof.

TEACHING NOTES un/une

The concept of gender is presented formally in Lesson 10. The focus in this lesson is on sound discrimination between **un** and **une.**

▶ Saying **un:** Be sure that students pronounce **un** without a final /n/ – except in liaison.

▶ Saying **une:** Have students think of **une** as "een" (and not "oon"). Then ask them to round their lips as they say "een." (This way students will begin to acquire the French pronunciation.)

4  À la fenêtre *(At the window)*

PARLER You and a friend are walking down the street and you see the following people at their windows. Identify them in short dialogues.

▶ —Tiens, voilà un monsieur!
—Qui est-ce?
—C'est Monsieur Mercier.

Monsieur Mercier

1. Nicole

2. Mademoiselle Lasalle

3. Éric

4. Madame Albert

5. Monsieur Lavie

6. Alain

Les nombres de 60 à 79 

60 soixante
61 soixante et un
62 soixante-deux
63 soixante-trois
64 soixante-quatre
65 soixante-cinq
66 soixante-six
67 soixante-sept
68 soixante-huit
69 soixante-neuf

70 soixante-dix
71 soixante et onze
72 soixante-douze
73 soixante-treize
74 soixante-quatorze
75 soixante-quinze
76 soixante-seize
77 soixante-dix-sept
78 soixante-dix-huit
79 soixante-dix-neuf

5 Numéros de téléphone

PARLER Read aloud the phone numbers of Jean-Paul's friends in Paris.

▶ Philippe zéro un, quarante-deux, soixante et un, dix-neuf, soixante-quinze

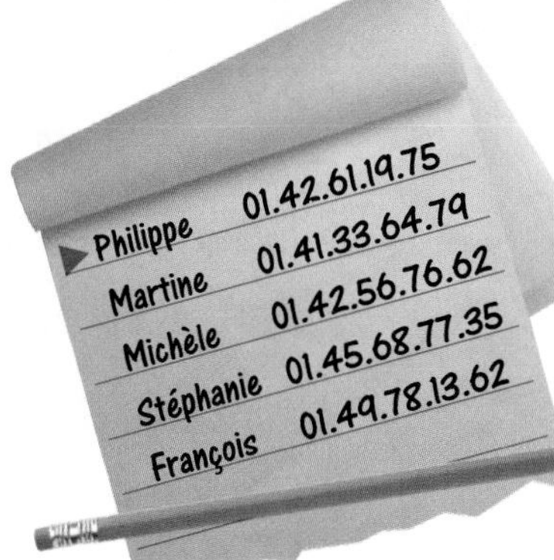

PRONONCIATION 

La liaison

un‿ami

Pronounce the following words:

un‿ami un‿Américain un‿Anglais un‿artiste

In general, the "**n**" of **un** is silent. However, in the above words, the "**n**" of **un** is pronounced as if it were the *first* letter of the next word. This is called LIAISON.

Liaison occurs between two words when the second one begins with a VOWEL SOUND, that is, with "**a**", "**e**", "**i**", "**o**", "**u**", and sometimes "**h**" and "**y**".

➔ Although liaison is not marked in written French, it will be indicated in your book by the symbol ‿ where appropriate.

Contrastez et répétez:

LIAISON: **un‿ami un‿Américain un‿Italien un‿artiste**

NO LIAISON: **un copain un Français un Canadien un prof**

GAME Mini-loto (Numbers 60-79)

PREPARATION: Write the numbers from 60-79 on slips of paper (or use commercial bingo numbers).

Have students draw a tic-tac-toe grid and fill the nine squares with numbers of their choice between 60 and 79.

Call out the numbers as you draw the slips in random order. When a student has three numbers in a row in any direction, have him/her call out "Loto."

4 ROLE PLAY discussing the identity of people

– Tiens, voilà ... !
– Qui est-ce?
– C'est ...

1. une fille (une copine, une amie)/Nicole.
2. une dame/Mademoiselle Lasalle.
3. un garçon (un ami, un copain)/Éric.
4. une dame (une prof)/Madame Albert.
5. un monsieur (un prof)/Monsieur Lavie.
6. un garçon (un copain, un ami)/Alain.

Encourage varied responses.

If students ask From 1 to 60, French uses the Roman system of counting by 10s. However, from 60 to 100, the French count by scores (or 20s). This system was brought to England and Normandy in the tenth century by the Vikings or Norsemen.

Pronunciation Remind students that there is no liaison after **et: soixante et un, soixante et onze.**

Note that in counting from 70-79, the French continue adding numbers to 60:

70 = 60 + 10
71 = 60 + 11
72 = 60 + 12

5 PRACTICE reading numbers up to 79

- Martine: zéro un, quarante et un, trente-trois, soixante-quatre, soixante-dix-neuf
- Michèle: zéro un, quarante-deux, cinquante-six, soixante-seize, soixante-deux
- Stéphanie: zéro un, quarante-cinq, soixante-huit, soixante-dix-sept, trente-cinq
- François: zéro un, quarante-neuf, soixante-dix-huit, treize, soixante-deux

Cultural note Paris phone numbers consist of 10 digits read in groups of two. The first digit for Paris is always 01.

Listening comprehension Have students close their books. Slowly dictate the numbers from the phone list. Then have students open their books to correct their work as you read the numbers once more.

PRONUNCIATION

You may want to point out that similar linking occurs in English after *an: an apple, an uncle, an hour.*

If students ask Adjectives of nationality are capitalized when they are used as nouns referring to people.

Leçon 2B

Main Topic Talking about other people

Teaching Resource Options

PRINT 

Workbook PE, pp. 17–20
Activités pour tous PE, pp. 9–10
Unit 1 Resource Book
Activités pour tous TE, pp. 79–80
Audioscript, pp. 118–119, 121–122
Communipak, pp. 128–146
Lesson Plans, pp. 85–86
Block Scheduling Lesson Plans, pp. 91–92
Absent Student Copymasters, pp. 96–97
Video Activities, pp. 106–109
Videoscript, pp. 115–116
Workbook TE, pp. 69–72

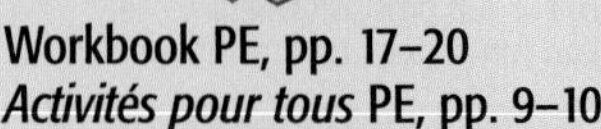

AUDIO & VISUAL 

Audio Program
CD 1 Tracks 18, 19
CD 5 Tracks 26–30

Overhead Transparencies
4 U.S., Canada, England, France *Les nationalités*

TECHNOLOGY 

Online Workbook

VIDEO PROGRAM

VIDÉO DVD

MODULE 2B
Une coïncidence

TOTAL TIME: 4:50 min.
DVD Disk 1
Videotape 1 (COUNTER: 26:42 min.)

2B.1 Dialogue: Une coïncidence
(27:11–27:40 min.)

2B.2 Mini-scenes: Listening
– Describing people
(27:41–29:19 min.)

2B.3 Vignette culturelle: Le Québec
(29:20–31:32 min.)

Comprehension practice Play the entire module through as an introduction to the lesson.

LEÇON 2

VIDÉO-SCÈNE 

VIDÉO DVD AUDIO

B Une coïncidence

Isabelle is at a party with her new Canadian friend Marc. She wants him to meet some of the other guests.

Isabelle:	Tu connais la fille là-bas?	*over there*
Marc:	Non. Qui est-ce?	
Isabelle:	C'est une copine. Elle s'appelle Juliette Savard.	
Marc:	Elle est française?	
Isabelle:	Non, elle est canadienne. Elle est de Montréal.	
Marc:	Moi aussi!	
Isabelle:	Quelle coïncidence!	*What a coincidence!*

WARM-UP AND REVIEW Nationalities

PROP: Transparency 4: U.S., Canada, England, France, *Les nationalités*

Ask students to give names to the 8 people, and write these names on the transparency next to each of the figures.

Pointing to the figures, have the students identify them.
Qui est-ce? [C'est Marie.]

Then, having the students take the role of the figure, ask their nationalities.
Marie, tu es française?
[Oui, je suis française.]
Marie, tu es anglaise?
[Non, je suis française.]

POUR COMMUNIQUER

Tu connais la dame?
Oui, elle s'appelle Madame Leblanc.

▶ *How to inquire about people:*

Tu connais ...?	*Do you know ...?*	**Tu connais** Jean-Paul?

▶ *How to describe people and give their nationalities:*

Il est ...	*He is ...*	**Il est** canadien.
Elle est ...	*She is ...*	**Elle est** canadienne.

▶ *How to find out another person's name:*

Comment s'appelle ...?	*What's the name of ...?*	**Comment s'appelle** le garçon? **Comment s'appelle** la fille?
Il s'appelle ...	*His name is ...*	**Il s'appelle** Marc.
Elle s'appelle ...	*Her name is ...*	**Elle s'appelle** Juliette.

NOTE culturelle

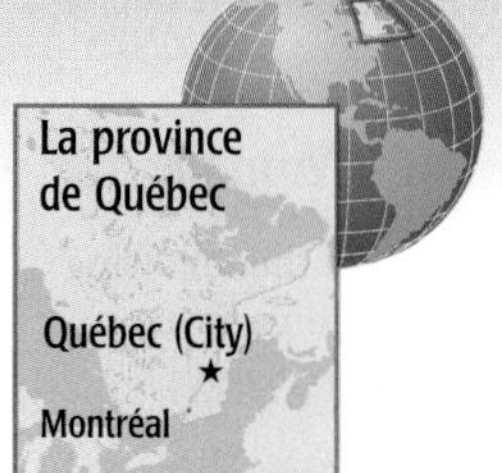

EN BREF
Capitale: Québec *(Quebec City)*
Population: 7 500 000
Langues: français, anglais

La province de Québec

The province of **Québec** is located in the eastern part of Canada. French speakers represent about 75% of its population. Most of them are descendants of French settlers who came to Canada in the 17th and 18th centuries. There are also a large number of Haitian immigrants who are of African origin.

Montréal (population 2 million) is the largest city in the province of Quebec. In population, it is the second-largest French-speaking city in the world after Paris.

POUR COMMUNIQUER

Language note Current usage often replaces **la dame/le monsieur** with **la/cette femme, le/ce/homme.**

If students ask The largest city in Canada is Toronto.

Photo culture note

Le Vieux Montréal Place Jacques Cartier in the heart of Old Montreal. The building in the background with the green roof is the Hôtel de Ville. It is here that Charles de Gaulle made his famous proclamation, "Vive le Québec! Vive le Québec libre!"

Have a contest to see which student can most quickly find out why Charles de Gaulle made this impassioned proclamation.

INCLUSION

Synthetic/analytic Explain the difference between nasal "u" and "ou." You can use **tu** and **vous** as examples. Model nasal "u" as students repeat the sound and read easy words with "u." Model "ou" as students repeat the sound and read a list of words that you have prepared. Then have students put the list in their notebooks.

Multisensory Write 10 easy words with "u" or "ou" and place a number (1-10) next to each one. Ask students to make 10 number cards, with one number on each card. Have students hold up the appropriate number card for each word that they hear. Then practice saying each word. (Suggestion: Pair a strong and an at-risk student.)

Teaching Resource Options

PRINT  

Workbook PE, pp. 17–20
Unit 1 Resource Book
Audioscript, p. 119
Communipak, pp. 128–146
Workbook TE, pp. 69–72

AUDIO & VISUAL 

Audio Program
CD 1 Tracks 20, 21
Overhead Transparencies
7 People *Les personnes*

TECHNOLOGY 

Power Presentations

Petit commentaire
Cross-cultural understanding If students want to host a French student, they may contact Nacel (a non-profit organization that arranges student exchanges). Refer to page T64 for contact information.

1 PRACTICE asking about people, using definite article

Qui est ... ?
1. le monsieur
2. la dame
3. la fille
4. le garçon
5. le prof
6. l'ami
7. l'amie
8. la copine

2 EXCHANGES identifying people

– Tu connais ... ?
– Oui, c'est ...

1. le prof/M. Simon
2. le garçon/Christophe
3. la fille/Charlotte
4. la dame/Mlle Lenoir
5. la prof/Mme Boucher
6. le monsieur/M. Duval

Expansion Have each student bring in a picture of a known personality:
– **Tu connais ce monsieur?** (holding up picture of a man)
– **Oui, c'est Jay Leno.** (Non, qui est-ce?)

3 EXCHANGES discussing people's names

– Comment s'appelle ... ?
1. le garçon/Il s'appelle Marc.
2. la fille/Elle s'appelle Céline.
3. le garçon/Il s'appelle François.
4. le garçon/Il s'appelle Jean-Paul.
5. la fille/Elle s'appelle Nathalie.
6. le garçon/Il s'appelle Trinh.
7. la fille/Elle s'appelle Isabelle.

If students ask
- The dropping of a final "e" (or "a," in the case of **la**) is called elision.
- A word that begins with **a, e, i, o,** or **u** is said to begin with a vowel sound.

PETIT COMMENTAIRE
Most French teenagers study English in school. They are generally very much interested in the United States. They love American music, American movies, and American fashions.

le garçon, la fille

The French equivalent of *the* has two basic forms: **le** and **la.**

MASCULINE		FEMININE	
le garçon	*the boy*	**la** fille	*the girl*
le copain	*the friend*	**la** copine	*the friend*

Note Both **le** and **la** become **l'** before a vowel sound.

un copain → le copain   une copine → la copine
un ami → l'ami   une amie → l'amie

1 Qui est-ce?

PARLER Ask who the following people are, using **le, la,** or **l'.**

▶ une prof
Qui est la prof?

1. un monsieur
2. une dame
3. une fille
4. un garçon
5. un prof
6. un ami
7. une amie
8. une copine

2 Tu connais ... ?

PARLER Ask your classmates if they know the following people. They will answer that they do.

▶ une dame / Madame Vallée

1. un prof / Monsieur Simon
2. un garçon / Christophe
3. une fille / Charlotte
4. une dame / Mademoiselle Lenoir
5. une prof / Madame Boucher
6. un monsieur / Monsieur Duval

3 Comment s'appelle ... ?

PARLER Ask the names of the following people, using the words **le garçon, la fille.** A classmate will respond.

▶ **—Comment s'appelle la fille?**
—Elle s'appelle Stéphanie.

Stéphanie

1. Marc

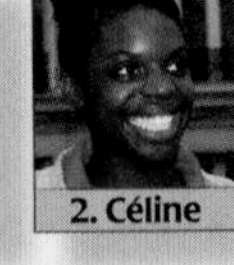
2. Céline

3. François

4. Jean-Paul

5. Nathalie

6. Trinh

7. Isabelle

COMPREHENSION Nouns with le/la

PROPS: Cards with people of Transparency 7: People *Les personnes*. Optional: red and blue index cards

Place the picture cards on the chalkboard tray. To review, have students point out people.
X, viens ici. Montre-nous un garçon.
Montre-nous une dame ....

Hand out the pictures to the class.
Voici le prof. Je donne le prof à Y.
Qui a le prof? [answer: Y]

Have students pass around the cards.
Y, prends le garçon et donne-le à Z.

OPTIONAL: Describe classroom objects; have students raise blue **(le)** or red **(la)** cards:
Voici le bureau. [blue] **Voici la porte.** [red]

4 Français, anglais, canadien ou américain?

PARLER Give the nationalities of the following people.

▶ Julia Roberts?
Elle est américaine.

1. le prince Charles?
2. Céline Dion?
3. Juliette Binoche?
4. Catherine Deneuve?
5. Pierre Cardin?
6. Matt Damon?
7. Oprah Winfrey?
8. Brad Pitt?
9. Elton John?

Les nombres de 80 à 1000

80 quatre-vingts
81 quatre-vingt-un
82 quatre-vingt-deux
83 quatre-vingt-trois
84 quatre-vingt-quatre
85 quatre-vingt-cinq
86 quatre-vingt-six
87 quatre-vingt-sept
88 quatre-vingt-huit
89 quatre-vingt-neuf

90 quatre-vingt-dix
91 quatre-vingt-onze
92 quatre-vingt-douze
93 quatre-vingt-treize
94 quatre-vingt-quatorze
95 quatre-vingt-quinze
96 quatre-vingt-seize
97 quatre-vingt-dix-sept
98 quatre-vingt-dix-huit
99 quatre-vingt-dix-neuf

100 cent **1000 mille**

➔ Note that in counting from 80 to 99, the French add numbers to the base of **quatre-vingts** *(fourscore)*:

$80 = 4 \times 20$ $90 = 4 \times 20 + 10$
$85 = 4 \times 20 + 5$ $99 = 4 \times 20 + 19$

5 Au téléphone

PARLER In France, the telephone area code **(l'indicatif)** is always a four-digit number. Your teacher will name a city **(une ville)** from the chart. Give the area code.

▶ Nice? **C'est le zéro quatre quatre-vingt-treize.**

VILLE	INDICATIF
Albi	05-63
Avignon	04-90
Dijon	03-80
Marseille	04-91
Montpellier	04-67
Nancy	03-83
Nice	04-93
Nîmes	04-66
Rennes	02-99
Saint-Tropez	04-94
Strasbourg	03-88
Vichy	04-70

PRONONCIATION

La voyelle nasale /ɛ̃/

/ɛ̃/ **5** cinq

In French, there are three nasal vowel sounds:

/ɛ̃/ **cinq** (5) /ɔ̃/ **onze** (11) /ɑ̃/ **trente** (30)

Practice the sound /ɛ̃/ in the following words.

➔ Be sure not to pronounce an "**n**" or "**m**" after the nasal vowel.

Répétez: **"in"** **cinq quinze vingt vingt-cinq quatre-vingt-quinze**
"ain" **américain Alain copain**
"(i)en" **bien canadien tiens!**
"un" **un**
Tiens! Voilà Alain. Il est américain. Et Julien? Il est canadien.

4 DESCRIPTION discussing people's nationalities

1. Il est anglais.
2. Elle est canadienne.
3. Elle est française.
4. Elle est française.
5. Il est français.
6. Il est américain.
7. Elle est américaine.
8. Il est américain.
9. Il est anglais.

Pronunciation There is no liaison between **quatre-vingt** and the numbers **un, huit, onze.**

Language note
Mille is presented for recognition. Numbers between 100 and 1,000 are not activated. If students ask:

101 **cent un** 102 **cent deux**
111 **cent onze** 120 **cent vingt**

5 COMPREHENSION identifying telephone area codes

- (Albi?) C'est le zéro cinq soixante-trois.
- (Avignon?) … zéro quatre quatre-vingt-dix.
- (Dijon?) … zéro trois quatre-vingts.
- (Marseille?) … zéro quatre quatre-vingt-onze.
- (Montpellier?) … zéro quatre soixante-sept.
- (Nancy?) … zéro trois quatre-vingt-trois.
- (Nice?) … zéro quatre quatre-vingt-treize.
- (Nîmes?) … zéro quatre soixante-six.
- (Rennes?) … zéro deux quatre-vingt-dix-neuf.
- (Saint-Tropez?) … zéro quatre quatre-vingt-quatorze.
- (Strasbourg?) … zéro trois quatre-vingt-huit.
- (Vichy?) … zéro quatre soixante-dix.

Cultural notes

- Outside of Paris, the **indicatif** is now part of the local phone number. (All numbers have 10 digits.)
- For the Paris area, the **indicatif** is "01" and is used only for long distance calls.

PRONUNCIATION

Some French people still distinguish between /ɛ̃/ **(in)** and /œ̃/ **(un)**. However, most French speakers use only the nasal vowel /ɛ̃/. For simplicity, we are not introducing the nasal /œ̃/ at this level.

Point out to students that the nasal vowel /ɛ̃/ can have several different spellings.

INCLUSION

Repetitive Point out the change in pronunciation of **est** preceding a word beginning with a vowel **(Elle est américaine.)**. Prepare a worksheet of phrases with this rule, and ask students to read the phrases out loud. Ask them to pair off and repeat the reading with a partner.

GAME Numbers 11 to 99

You will need four sets of the numbers 0–9 on index cards. Divide the class into two teams. Have two students from each team come to the front, stand side by side, and face the class. Give each student a set of the numbers 0–9. Say a number in French: e.g., **vingt-cinq!** The first pair to hold up the correct cards [2 and 5] wins a point for its team. You may wish to teach your students the expressions **Bravo!** *(Great!)*, **Allez-y!** *(Go for it!)*, and **C'est dommage!** *(That's too bad!)*.

Leçon 2C

Main Topics Introducing one's family and talking about how old people are

Teaching Resource Options

PRINT 

Workbook PE, pp. 21–24
Activités pour tous PE, pp. 11–12
Unit 1 Resource Book
- *Activités pour tous* TE, pp. 81–82
- Audioscript, pp. 119, 122–123
- Communipak, pp. 128–146
- Lesson Plans, pp. 87–88
- Block Scheduling Lesson Plans, pp. 93–94
- Absent Student Copymasters, pp. 98–99
- Video Activities, pp. 110–113
- Videoscript, pp. 116–117
- Workbook TE, pp. 73–76

AUDIO & VISUAL 

Audio Program
CD 1 Tracks 22, 23
CD 5 Tracks 31–34

Overhead Transparencies
8 Family tree *La famille*

VIDEO PROGRAM

VIDÉO DVD

MODULE 2C
Les photos d'Isabelle

TOTAL TIME: 6:46 min.
DVD Disk 1
Videotape 1 (COUNTER: 31:34 min.)

2C.1 Dialogue: Les photos d'Isabelle
(32:02–32:32 min.)

2C.2 Monologue: La famille d'Isabelle
(32:33–33:50 min.)

2C.3 Mini-scenes: How old are you?
(33:51–35:27 min.)

2C.4 Vignette culturelle: La famille française: un mariage
(35:28–38:20 min.)

Comprehension practice Play the entire module through as an introduction to the lesson.

LEÇON 2

VIDÉO-SCÈNE

VIDÉO DVD AUDIO

C Les photos d'Isabelle

Isabelle is showing her family photo album to her friend Jean-Paul.

Isabelle:	Voici ma mère.	
Jean-Paul:	Et le monsieur, c'est ton père?	*the man / your*
Isabelle:	Non, c'est mon oncle Thomas.	
Jean-Paul:	Et la fille, c'est ta cousine?	*your*
Isabelle:	Oui, c'est ma cousine Béatrice. Elle a seize ans.	*She's sixteen.*
Jean-Paul:	Et le garçon, c'est ton cousin?	
Isabelle:	Non, c'est un copain.	
Jean-Paul:	Un copain ou ton copain?	
Isabelle:	Dis donc, Jean-Paul, tu es vraiment trop curieux!	*Hey there, Jean-Paul, you are really too curious!*

ma mère

mon oncle Thomas

ma cousine Béatrice

? ?

WARM-UP AND REVIEW Copains et copines

Ask questions about students in the class:

[Point to a girl] **Qui est-ce?** [C'est Anne.]
Est-ce que c'est un garçon ou une fille?
[C'est une fille.]
C'est un copain ou une copine?
[C'est une copine.]

Address a boy in the class:
Et toi, est-ce qu'Anne est une copine ou ta copine?
[C'est une copine. or: C'est ma copine.]

Ask similar questions about other students.

Voici mon chien Malice.

POUR COMMUNIQUER

▶ ***How to introduce your family:***

Voici mon père.	*This is my father.*
Et voici ma mère.	*And this is my mother.*

La famille *(Family)*

un frère	*brother*	**une soeur**	*sister*
un cousin	*cousin*	**une cousine**	*cousin*
un père	*father*	**une mère**	*mother*
un oncle	*uncle*	**une tante**	*aunt*
un grand-père	*grandfather*	**une grand-mère**	*grandmother*

Les animaux domestiques *(Pets)*

un chat

un chien

NOTE culturelle

La famille française

When you and your friends talk about your families, you usually are referring to your brothers, sisters, and parents. In French, however, **la famille** refers not only to parents and children but also to grandparents, aunts, uncles, cousins, as well as a whole array of more distant relatives related by blood and marriage.

Since the various members of a family often live in the same region, French teenagers see their grandparents and cousins fairly frequently. Even when relatives do not live close by, the family finds many occasions to get together: for weekend visits, during school and summer vacations, on holidays, as well as on special occasions such as weddings and anniversaries.

Supplementary vocabulary

FAMILY
un beau-père *stepfather*
une belle-mère *stepmother*
un beau-frère *stepbrother*
une belle-soeur *stepsister*
un demi-frère *halfbrother*
une demi-soeur *halfsister*

PETS
un hamster /ɛ̃amster /, no liaison
un cochon d'Inde *Guinea pig*
un poisson rouge *goldfish*
une souris blanche *white mouse*
un oiseau *bird*
une perruche *parakeet*
un serpent *snake*

Cross-cultural observation

Ask students what the different definitions of "family" in French and American cultures might say about the two cultures' attitudes towards family life. Then have volunteers create and act out a humorous skit called "My Big, Fat French Wedding" in which an American with a very small family weds a French person with a very large and extended family.

INCLUSION

Structured Remind students that double "ll" makes two different sounds (**famille** vs. **Mallet**). Prepare a worksheet with two columns of words (each column representing one of the two "ll" sounds), and have students read the words in each column. Then point to words from each list, and have students say the words aloud.

COMPREHENSION The family

PROP: Transparency 8: Family tree *La famille*

Describe the various family relationships, pointing to the transparency.

François Mallet est le père de Véronique.
M. Mallet est aussi le père de Frédéric ...

Ask students to point out family members.

X, viens à l'écran. Montre-nous la cousine de Catherine. ...

Teaching Resource Options

PRINT

Workbook PE, pp. 21–24
Unit 1 Resource Book
Audioscript, p. 119
Communipak, pp. 128–146
Video Activities, p. 112
Videoscript, p. 117
Workbook TE, pp. 73–76

Assessment
Lesson 2 Quiz, pp. 125–126
Audioscript for Quiz 2, p. 124
Answer Keys, pp. 195–197

AUDIO & VISUAL

Audio Program
CD 1 Track 24
CD 13 Track 3

Overhead Transparencies
8 Family tree *La famille*

TECHNOLOGY

Power Presentations

VIDEO PROGRAM

VIDÉO DVD

MODULE 2C

2C.3 Mini-scenes: How old are you? (33:51–35:27 min.)

1 PRACTICE talking about friends, relatives, and pets

Voici ...

1. mon frère.
2. ma soeur.
3. ma tante Monique.
4. mon oncle Pierre.
5. mon père.
6. ma mère.
7. mon copain Nicolas.
8. mon ami Jérôme.
9. ma copine Pauline.
10. mon amie Florence.
11. ma grand-mère Michèle.
12. mon grand-père Robert.
13. mon chien Toto.
14. mon chat Minou.
15. ma cousine Émilie.
16. mon cousin Marc.

Pronunciation album /albɔm/

2 COMMUNICATION discussing the names of relatives, friends, and pets

– Comment s'appelle ... ?
– ... s'appelle ...

1. ton oncle/Mon oncle
2. ta tante/Ma tante
3. ton cousin/Mon cousin
4. ta cousine/Ma cousine
5. ta copine/Ma copine
6. ton ami/Mon ami
7. ton grand-père/Mon grand-père
8. ta grand-mère/Ma grand-mère
9. ton chien/Mon chien
10. ton chat/Mon chat

PETIT COMMENTAIRE

The French people love pets, especially cats and dogs. What is important is the animal's personality and friendliness rather than its pedigree. Some common names given to animals are:
Minou, Pompon, Fifi (*cats*)
Titus, Milou, Azor (*dogs*)

mon cousin, ma cousine

The French equivalents of *my* and *your* have the following forms:

MASCULINE		FEMININE	
mon cousin	*my cousin (male)*	**ma** cousine	*my cousin (female)*
mon frère	*my brother*	**ma** soeur	*my sister*
ton cousin	*your cousin (male)*	**ta** cousine	*your cousin (female)*
ton frère	*your brother*	**ta** soeur	*your sister*

→ Note that the feminine **ma** becomes **mon** and the feminine **ta** becomes **ton** before a vowel sound. Liaison is required.

une amie → **mon** amie **ton** amie

1 L'album de photos

PARLER You are showing a friend your photo album. Identify the following people, using **mon** and **ma,** as appropriate.

▶ cousine Jacqueline **Voici ma cousine Jacqueline.**

1. frère
2. soeur
3. tante Monique
4. oncle Pierre
5. père
6. mère
7. copain Nicolas
8. ami Jérôme
9. copine Pauline
10. amie Florence
11. grand-mère Michèle
12. grand-père Robert
13. chien Toto
14. chat Minou
15. cousine Émilie
16. cousin Marc

2 Comment s'appelle ... ?

PARLER Ask your classmates to name some of their friends, relatives, and pets. They can invent names if they wish.

▶ le copain **—Comment s'appelle ton copain?**
—Mon copain s'appelle Bob.

1. l'oncle
2. la tante
3. le cousin
4. la cousine
5. la copine
6. l'ami
7. le grand-père
8. la grand-mère
9. le chien
10. le chat

WARM-UP AND REVIEW Numbers

Divide the class in half: side A and side B.

Point to side A and say a number. Then point to side B and say another number. Students on the side with the higher number raise their hands.

A–22. B–35. [Students on Side B raise their hands.]

A–89. B–64. [Students on Side A raise their hands.]

Teaching notes

- This lesson provides an initial introduction to adjective agreement with the singular forms **mon/ma** and **ton/ta.**
- It is important that students learn to differentiate clearly between the pronunciation of **mon** and **ma, ton** and **ta.** They should pronounce the "n" of **mon** and **ton** only in liaison.
- In Lesson 16, students will encounter all the forms of the possessive adjectives.

POUR COMMUNIQUER

▶ ***How to find out how old a friend is:***

Quel âge as-tu?	*How old are you?*	**–Quel âge as-tu?**
J'ai ... ans.	*I'm ... (years old).*	**–J'ai quinze ans.**

▶ ***How to ask about how old others are:***

–Quel âge a ton père?	*How old is your father?*
–Il a quarante-deux ans.	*He is 42 (years old).*
–Quel âge a ta mère?	*How old is your mother?*
–Elle a trente-neuf ans.	*She is 39 (years old).*

➔ Although *years old* may be left out in English, the word **ans** must be used in French when talking about someone's age.

Il a vingt ans. *He's twenty. (He's twenty years old.)*

3  *Quel âge as-tu?*

PARLER Ask your classmates how old they are.

▶ **—Quel âge as-tu?**
—J'ai (treize) ans.

 4  *Joyeux anniversaire!*

(Happy birthday!)

PARLER Ask your classmates how old the following people are.

▶ **—Quel âge a Stéphanie?**
—Elle a quatorze ans.

Stéphanie

1. Éric **2. Mademoiselle Doucette** **3. Monsieur Boucher**

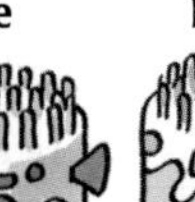

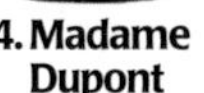

4. Madame Dupont **5. Monsieur Camus** **6. Madame Simon**

 5  *Curiosité*

PARLER Find out the ages of your classmates' friends and relatives. If they are not sure, they can guess or invent an answer.

▶ la copine **—Quel âge a ta copine?**
—Ma copine a (treize) ans.

1. le père
2. la mère
3. l'oncle
4. la tante
5. le cousin
6. la cousine
7. le grand-père
8. la grand-mère

PRONONCIATION 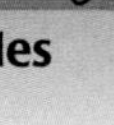 /ɑ̃/ /ɔ̃/

Les voyelles nasales
/ɑ̃/ et /ɔ̃/

The letters "**an**" and "**en**" usually represent the nasal vowel /ɑ̃/. Be sure not to pronounce an "**n**" after the nasal vowel.

Répétez: **ans tante français quarante trente comment Henri Laurent**

The letters "**on**" represent the nasal vowel /ɔ̃/. Be sure not to pronounce an "**n**" after the nasal vowel.

Répétez: **non bonjour oncle garçon**

Contrastez: **an–on tante–ton onze–ans**
Mon oncle François a trente ans.

TEACHING STRATEGY Ages

PROP: Transparency 8: Family tree *La famille*

Ask students to determine the ages of the people on the transparency.

- **Quel âge a Frédéric?**
- [Student X]: Il a quinze ans.
- **Vous êtes d'accord?** Do you agree?

Write "15" in the box next to Frédéric.

Have students assign ages to the other members of the family. Then ask questions about the transparency.

Qui a quarante ans?
Quel âge a la soeur de Frédéric?

POUR COMMUNIQUER

Common colloquial alternatives Tu as quel âge? Quel âge as-tu?

If students ask Literally, these sentences mean: What age do you have? I have thirteen years.

3 COMMUNICATION asking how old someone is

- Quel âge as-tu?
- J'ai (quatorze) ans.

4 PRACTICE discussing people's ages

- Quel âge a ... ?
- ... ans.

1. Éric/dix-huit
2. Mademoiselle Doucette/vingt-cinq
3. Monsieur Boucher/trente-deux
4. Madame Dupont/soixante-quatre
5. Monsieur Camus/soixante-quinze
6. Madame Simon/quatre-vingt-trois

Listening comprehension Ask the ages of these people in random order. Students write down the number of the corresponding birthday cake.

Qui a soixante-quatre ans? (4)
Qui a trente-deux ans? (3)
Qui a dix-huit ans? (1)
Qui a quatre-vingt-trois ans? (6)
Qui a vingt-cinq ans? (2)
Qui a soixante-quinze ans? (5)

5 COMMUNICATION discussing friends' and relatives' ages

- Quel âge a ... ?
- ... a (X) ans.

1. ton père/Mon père
2. ta mère/Ma mère
3. ton oncle/Mon oncle
4. ta tante/Ma tante
5. ton cousin/Mon cousin
6. ta cousine/Ma cousine
7. ton grand-père/Mon grand-père
8. ta grand-mère/Ma grand-mère

If students have trouble guessing ages, put sample ages on the board. **E.g.** 1. le père: 42 2. la mère: 39, etc.

PRONUNCIATION

- The combination **ien** is pronounced /jɛ̃/: **bien**
- Remind students that they should not pronounce an "n" after the nasal vowel.

À VOTRE TOUR

Main Topic
- Recapitulation and review

Teaching Resource Options

PRINT 

Workbook PE, pp. 1–24
Unit 1 Resource Book
  Audioscript, pp. 119–120
  Communipak, pp. 128–146

Assessment
Unit 1 Test, pp. 165–172
Portfolio Assessment, pp. 155–164
Multiple Choice Test Items, pp. 184–188
Listening Comprehension Performance Test, pp. 173–174
Reading Performance Test, pp. 179–181
Speaking Performance Test, pp. 175–178
Writing Performance Test, pp. 182–183
Test Scoring Tools, p. 189
Audioscript for Tests, pp. 190–192
Answer Keys, pp. 195–197

AUDIO & VISUAL 
Audio Program
CD 1 Tracks 25–27
CD 13 Tracks 4–11

TECHNOLOGY 
Test Generator CD-ROM/McDougal Littell Assessment System

1 COMPREHENSION

19-B, 67-B, 15-B, 8-A, 72-A, 12-A, 42-A, 93-A, 5-B, 82-A, 33-B, 48-B, 25-A, 3-A, 17-A, 61-A, 98-B, 89-B, 70-B, 55-B,

À votre tour!

OBJECTIFS

Now you can...
- greet people and say where you are from
- introduce friends and relatives
- give your age and ask how old people are
- understand and use numbers up to 100

1 Écoutez bien!

STRATEGY Listening

Numbers As you hear each number, repeat it over and over in your head until you find the corresponding number on the card.

ÉCOUTER Loto is a French version of Bingo. You will hear a series of numbers. If the number is on Card A, raise your left hand. If it is on Card B, raise your right hand.

A
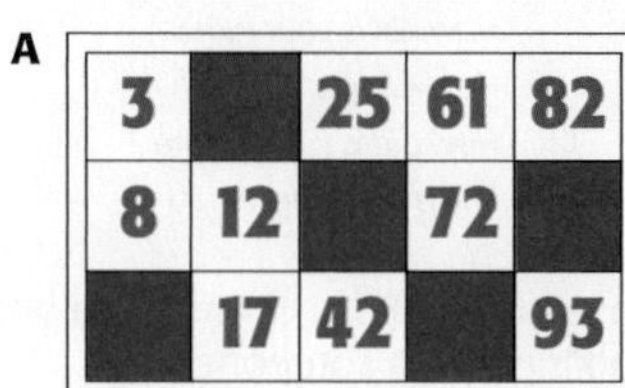

3		25	61	82
8	12		72	
	17	42		93

B

5		48	67	
	19	55		89
15	33		70	98

2 Et toi?

ÉCOUTER ET PARLER You and Nathalie meet at a sidewalk café. Respond to her greetings and questions.

1. Salut! Ça va?
2. Comment t'appelles-tu?
3. Tu es canadien (canadienne)?
4. Quel âge as-tu?
5. Comment s'appelle ton copain (ta copine)?
6. Quel âge a ton copain (ta copine)?

3 Conversation dirigée

ÉCOUTER ET PARLER Two students, Jean-Pierre and Janet, meet on the Paris-Lyon train. With a partner, compose and act out their dialogue according to the suggested script.

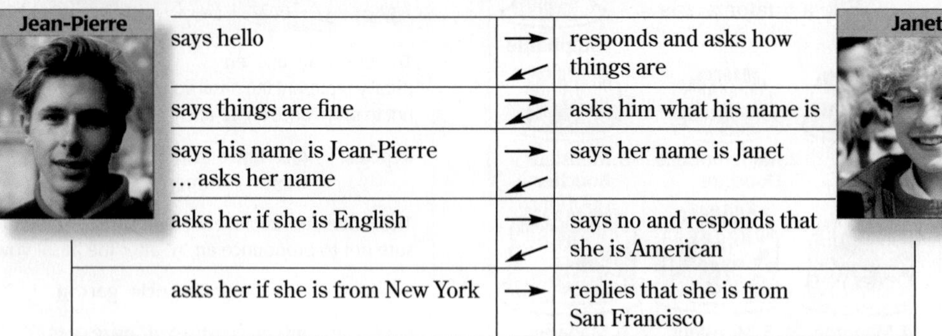

Jean-Pierre		Janet
says hello	→ ↙	responds and asks how things are
says things are fine	→ ↙	asks him what his name is
says his name is Jean-Pierre … asks her name	→ ↙	says her name is Janet
asks her if she is English	→ ↙	says no and responds that she is American
asks her if she is from New York	→	replies that she is from San Francisco

À VOTRE TOUR

The communicative activities in this section move from closely structured (Act. 1) to more open-ended (Act. 5).

Select those activities which are most appropriate for your students. You may or may not wish to do them all.

PAIR AND GROUP PRACTICE

PAIR WORK: Students do the activities in pairs. For Act. 1, 2, and 3, they can check their work by listening to the audio.

TRIOS: Students work in groups of 3. Two students perform a dialogue. The third acts as monitor.

4 Ma famille *(My family)*

PARLER You are showing your friends pictures of your family. Introduce everyone, giving their ages. If you prefer, show your classmates a picture of your own family and give each person's age.

▶ **Voici ma soeur. Elle a douze ans.**

▶ 

1 

2 

3 

4 

5 

6 

5  En scène

PARLER With a classmate, act out the following scene.

CHARACTERS:

You and a French guest

SITUATION:

You are in France. Your French friends have invited you to a picnic. You meet one of the guests and have a conversation.

- Greet the guest.
- Ask how things are.
- Tell the guest that you are American and ask the guest if he/she is French.
- Tell the guest how old you are and ask his/her age.
- *(The guest waves to a friend.)* Ask the guest the name of his/her friend.
- *(It is the end of the picnic.)* Say good-bye.

6 Les nombres

PARLER

1. Select any number between 0 and 15 and give the next five numbers in sequence.
2. Select a number between 1 and 9. Use that number as a starting point and count by tens to 100.

▶ deux...
douze, vingt-deux, trente-deux, etc.

ORAL PORTFOLIOS

For an introduction to oral portfolio assessment, see the Unit 1 Resource Book for a complete description.

Divide the class into pairs. Either assign all students the same activity, or let each pair select an activity at the appropriate level of challenge.

Have the pairs prepare their dialogues and make an audio (or video) recording. (Be sure they introduce themselves on the recording: **Je m'appelle X. Moi, je m'appelle Y.**)

If time allows, play all the recordings for the entire class. Store the audio as part of each student's oral portfolio.

2 GUIDED ORAL EXPRESSION

1. Oui, ça va (très) bien. (Non, ça va [très] mal.) (Ça va comme ci, comme ça.)
2. Je m'appelle (Tom Banks / Lora Andrews).
3. Oui, je suis canadien (canadienne). (Non, je suis américain[e].)
4. J'ai (dix-sept) ans.
5. Mon copain s'appelle Pierre.
6. Il a (dix-huit) ans.

Speaking practice
- Play the audio, stopping after each question to elicit various student answers.
- Play the audio activity straight through, having students whisper their answers quickly in the pauses.
- Play the audio again, pointing to individual students to give their answers in the pauses.

3 GUIDED ORAL EXPRESSION

Jean-Pierre: Bonjour.
Janet: Bonjour. Ça va?
Jean-Pierre: Oui, ça va.
Janet: Comment t'appelles-tu?
Jean-Pierre: Je m'appelle Jean-Pierre. Et toi?
Janet: Je m'appelle Janet.
Jean-Pierre: Tu es anglaise?
Janet: Non, je suis américaine.
Jean-Pierre: Tu es de New York?
Janet: Non, je suis de San Francisco.

4 GUIDED ORAL EXPRESSION

1. Voici mon frère. Il a dix-sept ans.
2. Voici ma soeur. Elle a neuf ans.
3. Voice mon copain. Il a quinze ans.
4. Voici mon oncle. Il a quarante-deux ans.
5. Voici ma mère. Elle a quarante et un ans.
6. Voici mon grand-père. Il a soixante-six ans.

Listening practice Play the sample exchanges.

Pair Practice Have students in pairs prepare their own exchanges.

5 GUIDED ORAL EXPRESSION

Answers will vary.
élève 1: Salut! (Bonjour!)
élève 2: Salut! (Bonjour!)
élève 1: Ça va?
élève 2: Oui, ça va (très) bien, (merci).
élève 1: Je suis américain(e). Tu es français(e)?
élève 2: Oui, je suis français(e).
élève 1: J'ai dix-sept ans. Et toi?
élève 2: J'ai dix-huit ans.
élève 1: Comment s'appelle ton amie?
élève 2: Elle s'appelle Cécile.
élève 1: Au revoir!
élève 2: Au revoir!

6 GUIDED ORAL EXPRESSION

Answers will vary.
1. sept: huit, neuf, dix, onze, douze
2. trois: treize, vingt-trois, trente-trois, quarante-trois, cinquante-trois, soixante-trois, soixante-treize, quatre-vingt-trois, quatre-vingt-treize

ENTRACTE

- Increasing students' awareness of the francophone world
- Introducing colors

Teaching Resource Options

PRINT  

Workbook PE, pp. 25–28
Activités pour tous PE, pp. 13–15
Unit 1 Resource Book
Activités pour tous TE, pp. 147–149
Workbook TE, pp. 151–154

Le drapeau des pays francophones

Answers

Le Luxembourg: Le drapeau est rouge, blanc et bleu.

La Suisse: Le drapeau est rouge et blanc.

Le Canada: Le drapeau est rouge et blanc.

Haïti: Le drapeau est bleu, rouge, blanc, vert et jaune.

Le Cameroun: Le drapeau est vert, rouge et jaune.

La Côte d'Ivoire: Le drapeau est orange, blanc et vert.

Le Maroc: Le drapeau est rouge et vert.

Le Mali: Le drapeau est vert, jaune et rouge.

La République démocratique du Congo: Le drapeau est bleu et jaune.

Le Sénégal: Le drapeau est vert, jaune et rouge.

Les Couleurs

rouge | orange | jaune | vert | bleu | violet | blanc | noir

Le drapeau des pays francophones

In the following countries, many people use French in their daily lives. Locate each country on the map on pages 8–9 and then describe the colors of its flag.

▶ La Belgique: **Le drapeau est noir, jaune et rouge.**

Europe

LA BELGIQUE
Population: 10 millions
Capitale: Bruxelles

LE LUXEMBOURG
Population: 0,5 million
Capitale: Luxembourg

LA SUISSE
Population: 7 millions
Capitale: Berne

Amérique

LE CANADA
Population: 31 millions
Capitale: Ottawa

HAÏTI
Population: 8 millions
Capitale: Port-au-Prince

Afrique

LE CAMEROUN
Population: 15 millions
Capitale: Yaoundé

LA CÔTE D'IVOIRE
Population: 16 millions
Capitale: Yamoussoukro

LE MAROC
Population: 28 millions
Capitale: Rabat

LE MALI
Population: 10 millions
Capitale: Bamako

LA RÉPUBLIQUE DÉMOCRATIQUE DU CONGO
Population: 42 millions
Capitale: Kinshasa

LE SÉNÉGAL
Population: 9 millions
Capitale: Dakar

CONNEXIONS World Geography

Increase your awareness of the francophone world. Select one of the countries mentioned and make a poster which includes the flag and a map showing the capital city. Complete the poster with pictures or other information of interest (sources: atlas, encyclopedia, Internet, travel ads, newspapers, and magazines).

Language Learning Benchmarks

FUNCTION
- Greet and respond to greetings pp. 16, 24
- Engage in conversations pp. 16, 24
- Obtain information pp. 20, 28, 32
- Begin to provide information pp. 37

CONTEXT
- Converse in face-to-face social interactions pp. 16, 17, 24
- Listen to audio and video texts pp. 14, 17, 18, 22, 26, 30, 34
- Use authentic materials when reading: charts p. 33

TEXT TYPE
- Use short sentences when speaking pp. 17, 20, 25, 29
- Use learned words and phrases when speaking pp. 16, 28
- Use simple questions when speaking pp. 16, 24, 32, 36, 37
- Understand some ideas and familiar details presented in clear, uncomplicated speech when listening pp. 14, 18, 22, 26, 30, 34

CONTENT
- Understand and convey information about family pp. 36, 37
- Understand and convey information about friends pp. 28, 36, 37
- Understand and convey information about health p. 25
- Understand and convey information about numbers pp. 21, 25, 29, 33

ASSESSMENT
- Demonstrate culturally acceptable behavior for greeting and responding to greetings p. 38
- Demonstrate culturally acceptable behavior for engaging in conversations p. 38
- Demonstrate culturally acceptable behavior for obtaining information p. 39
- Demonstrate culturally acceptable behavior for providing information p. 39

Expansion activities PLANNING AHEAD

Games

• Chassez l'intrus

Ask each student to select three words related to a specific category (colors, numbers, family members, foods, beverages, days, months, and so on). Then have each student add a fourth word that does not belong to the category. Ask students to write the words in random order on a sheet of paper and collect them. Divide the class into two teams. Give one of the sheets of paper to the first member of Team A, who will read the words aloud. If the first player on Team B correctly identifies **l'intrus,** he or she wins a point for the team. Set a ten-second time limit and have teams take turns reading the lists for their opponents.

Pacing Suggestion: Upon completion of Leçon 4.

Projects

• Mon café

Have each student create a café menu complete with a restaurant name, food and beverages served there, and prices. Be sure they use only familiar vocabulary. Students may use colored pencils, cardboard, construction paper, photos, and illustrations to make their menus appealing. As an alternative, you may give students the option of creating menus on a computer.

Pacing Suggestion: Upon completion of Leçon 3.

• L'euro

Have students work in small groups to investigate the images found on euro coins. Explain to students that euro notes are the same for all the countries that use them. While the coins have one common face, each country selected individual images to use on the reverse. Each group will research the images selected by one of the countries using the euro. Have the groups give class presentations in which they show what the coins look like and explain what they have learned about the images. As an alternative, have students draw or download copies of the coins and put them on a map of the Euro-zone countries.

Pacing Suggestion: Upon completion of Leçon 3.

Bulletin Boards

• Le temps

Have students research current weather conditions in France. Assign groups different French cities and have students make a bulletin board with illustrations of a five-day forecast. Students might also include a five-day forecast of their own city or town. As a way of extending this exercise, you could change the city weekly and have groups alternate being responsible for the week's weather report. Post the best, funniest, clearest drawings on the bulletin board.

Pacing Suggestion: Upon completion of Leçon 4.

Music

• L'hymne national

Teach your students *O Canada,* the national anthem of Canada. The lyrics are provided below in French. You may also want to give students a list of vocabulary words from the song in English. You can download the music from the Internet.

The music for *O Canada* was composed in the 1880s by Calixa Lavallée to accompany a French poem written by Sir Adolphe-Basile Routhier. In 1968 an official English version was adopted. *O Canada* became the Canadian national anthem in 1980.

O Canada

O Canada! Terre de nos aïeux,
Ton front est ceint de fleurons glorieux.
Car ton bras sait porter l'épée,
Il sait porter la croix.
Ton histoire est une épopée,
Des plus brillants exploits.
Et ta valeur, de foi trempée,
Protégera nos foyers et nos droits.

Pacing Suggestion: Upon completion of Leçon 4.

Storytelling

• Tu as faim?

Use two puppets to portray a client and a server at a café. Develop a dialogue and act it out for the students. Make sure to include an entertaining twist in the dialogue, such as someone ordering strange combinations, a conflict between the server and customer, or someone ordering too much food. Then, have students work in pairs to recreate a similar dialogue to act out in small groups or for the class.

Pacing Suggestion: Upon completion of Leçon 3.

Hands-on Crafts

• Mon calendrier

Have students make calendars or twelve-month agendas using one sheet of paper for each month of the year. Students should label the days and months in French. Have each student work with a partner to choose important events to add to their calendars, such as holidays and birthdays, school activities, games, and proms. Have students complete the project by making colorful covers for their calendars/agendas.

Pacing Suggestion: Upon completion of Leçon 4.

End of Unit

• Au café

Have students work in pairs or small groups to write and perform a café scene. In each scene, students will greet one another, order and pay for their food, and make small talk. (For example, they can discuss how they are, the weather, what they want to eat, places they would like to go, and times for appointments.) Students may wish to create menus and use other props to make their scenes more realistic. Have students present their scenes to the class live or on videotape.

Rubric **A** = 13–15 pts. **B** = 10–12 pts. **C** = 7–9 pts. **D** = 4–6 pts. **F** = < 4 pts.

Criteria	Scale
Vocabulary Use	1 2 3 4 5
Grammar/Spelling Accuracy	1 2 3 4 5
Creativity	1 2 3 4 5

Recipe

• Croque-monsieur

Croque-monsieur, a toasted ham and cheese sandwich, has become a staple in French cafés. There are several variations: the sandwich may be served with a béchamel sauce or a slice of tomato. One variation is the **croque-madame,** a croque-monsieur topped with an egg.

Pacing Suggestion: Upon completion of Leçon 3.

Croque-monsieur

Ingrédients
- *2 tranches de pain de mie*
- *1 tranche de jambon*
- *25 grammes de Gruyère râpé*
- *du beurre*

Préparation
1. *Beurrez une tranche de pain.*
2. *Ajoutez le jambon et le Gruyère.*
3. *Beurrez l'autre tranche de pain et mettez-la sur le dessus du sandwich.*
4. *Faites cuire au four jusqu'à ce que le pain soit bien grillé.*

Ingredients
- *2 slices of bread*
- *1 slice of ham*
- *approx. 1 oz. of grated Gruyère (Swiss cheese)*
- *butter*

Directions
1. *Butter one slice of bread.*
2. *Add the ham and cheese.*
3. *Butter the second slice of bread and use it to top the sandwich.*
4. *Cook under the broiler or in a toaster oven until bread is browned.*

Planning Guide CLASSROOM MANAGEMENT

OBJECTIVES

Communication
- Order snacks and beverages in a café *p. 49*
- Ask about prices and pay for your food/drink *p. 53*
- Use French money *pp. 52–53*
- Tell time *pp. 56–58*
- Give the date and the day of the week *pp. 61–63*
- Talk about the weather *p. 65*

Pronunciation
- L'intonation *p. 47*
- L'accent final *p. 51*
- La consonne «r» *p. 55*

Culture
- Bon appétit! *p. 43*
- Les jeunes et la nourriture *p. 45*
- Le café *p. 49*
- L'argent européen *pp. 52–53*

PROGRAM RESOURCES

Print

- Workbook PE, *pp. 29–58*
- *Activités pour tous* PE, *pp. 17–31*
- Block Scheduling Copymasters, *pp. 17–32*
- *Français pour hispanophones*
- *Lectures pour tous*
- Teacher to Teacher Copymasters
- Teaching Proficiency through Reading and Storytelling
- Unit 2 Resource Book
  - Lessons 3–4 Resources
    - Workbook TE
    - *Activités pour tous* TE
    - Family Letter
    - Absent Student Copymasters
    - Family Involvement
    - Video Activities
    - Videoscripts
    - Audioscripts
    - Assessment Program
  - Unit 2 Resources
    - Communipak
    - *Activités pour tous* TE Reading
    - Workbook TE Reading and Culture Activities
    - Assessment Program
    - Answer Keys

Audiovisual

- Audio Program PE CD 1 Tracks 28–49
- Audio Program Workbook CD 6 Tracks 1–31
- *Chansons* Audio CD
- Sing Along: Grammar and Vocabulary Songs CD
- Video Program Modules 3A, 3B, 3C, 4A, 4B, 4C
- Warm-Up Transparencies
- Overhead Transparencies
  - 10 Foods;
  - 11 Beverages;
  - 12 Menu from "Le Select";
  - 6 Clock face;
  - 9 Calendar;
  - 13 Weather

Technology

- Online Workbook
- ClassZone.com
- McDougal Littell Assessment System/Test Generator CD-ROM
- EasyPlanner CD-ROM
- Power Presentations on CD-ROM
- Take-Home Tutor CD-ROM

Assessment Program Options

Lesson Quizzes
Portfolio Assessment
Unit Test Form A
Unit Test Form B
Unit Test Part III Cultural Awareness
Listening Comprehension Performance Test
Speaking Performance Test
Reading Comprehension Performance Test
Writing Performance Test
Multiple Choice Test Items
Test Scoring Tools
Audio Program CD 13 Tracks 12–22
Answer Keys
McDougal Littell Assessment System/ Test Generator CD-ROM

Pacing Guide SAMPLE LESSON PLAN

DAY	DAY	DAY	DAY	DAY
1 Unité 2 Opener Introduction culturelle–Bon appétit! Leçon 3A • Vidéo-scène–Tu as faim? • Pour communiquer • Note culturelle–Les jeunes et la nourriture	**2** Leçon 3A • Un sandwich, une pizza • Prononciation–L'intonation Leçon 3B • Vidéo-scène–Au café	**3** Leçon 3B • Pour communiquer • Note culturelle–Le café • Prononciation–L'accent final	**4** Leçon 3C • Vidéo-scène–Ça fait combien? • Note culturelle–L'argent européen	**5** Leçon 3C • Pour communiquer • Prononciation–La consonne «r» Leçon 4A • Vidéo-scène–L'heure
6 Leçon 4A • Pour communiquer • Vidéo-scène–À quelle heure est le film?	**7** Leçon 4B • Pour communiquer • Vidéo-scène–Le jour et la date • Pour communiquer	**8** Leçon 4B • Vidéo-scène–Anniversaire • Pour communiquer • La date	**9** Leçon 4C • Vidéo-scène–Le temps • Pour communiquer	**10** • À votre tour!
11 • Unit 2 Test	**12** • Entracte: Lecture et Culture	**13**	**14**	**15**
16	**17**	**18**	**19**	**20**

Student Text Listening Activity Scripts
AUDIO PROGRAM

▶ LEÇON 3 Bon appétit!

• Vidéo-scène A: Tu as faim? *p. 44*

A. Compréhension orale CD 1, TRACK 28

Pierre, Philippe, and Nathalie are on their way home from school. They stop by a street vendor who sells sandwiches and pizza. Today it is Pierre's turn to treat his friends.

SCÈNE 1 **Pierre et Nathalie**
Pierre: Tu as faim?
Nathalie: Oui, j'ai faim.
Pierre: Tu veux un sandwich ou une pizza?
Nathalie: Donne-moi une pizza, s'il te plaît.
Pierre: Voilà.
Nathalie: Merci.

SCÈNE 2 **Pierre et Philippe**
Pierre: Et toi, Philippe, tu as faim?
Philippe: Oh là, là, oui, j'ai faim.
Pierre: Qu'est-ce que tu veux? Un sandwich ou une pizza?
Philippe: Je voudrais un sandwich . . . euh . . . et donne-moi aussi une pizza.
Pierre: C'est vrai! Tu as vraiment faim!

B. Écoutez et répétez. CD 1, TRACK 29

You will now hear a paused version of the dialog. Listen to the speaker and repeat right after he or she has completed the sentence.

• Prononciation *p. 47* CD 1, TRACK 30

L'intonation

Écoutez: Voici un steak . . . et une salade.

When you speak, your voice rises and falls. This is called INTONATION. In French, as in English, your voice goes down at the end of a statement. However, in French, your voice rises after each group of words in the middle of a sentence. (This is the opposite of English, where your voice drops a little when you pause in the middle of a sentence.)

Répétez: Je voudrais une pizza. #
Je voudrais une pizza et un sandwich. #
Je voudrais une pizza, un sandwich et un hamburger. #
Voici un steak. #
Voici un steak et une salade. #
Voici un steak, une salade et une glace. #

• Vidéo-scène B: Au café *p. 48*

A. Compréhension orale CD 1, TRACK 31

This afternoon Trinh and Céline went shopping. They are now tired and thirsty. Trinh invites Céline to a café.

SCÈNE 1 **Trinh, Céline**
Trinh: Tu as soif?
Céline: Oui, j'ai soif.
Trinh: On va dans un café? Je t'invite.
Céline: D'accord!

SCÈNE 2 **Le garçon, Céline, Trinh**
Le garçon: Vous désirez, mademoiselle?
Céline: Un jus d'orange, s'il vous plaît.
Le garçon: Et pour vous, monsieur?
Trinh: Donnez-moi une limonade, s'il vous plaît.

SCÈNE 3 **Le garçon, Céline, Trinh**
Le garçon: *(à Céline)* La limonade, c'est pour vous, mademoiselle?
Trinh: Non, c'est pour moi.
Le garçon: Ah, excusez-moi. Voici le jus d'orange, mademoiselle.
Céline: Merci.

B. Écoutez et répétez. CD 1, TRACK 32

You will now hear a paused version of the dialog. Listen to the speaker and repeat right after he or she has completed the sentence.

• Prononciation *p. 51* CD 1, TRACK 33

L'accent final

Écoutez: un chocolat

In French, the rhythm is very even and the accent always falls on the ***last*** syllable of a word or a group of words.

Répétez: Philippe # Thomas # Alice # Sophie # Dominique #
un café # Je voudrais un café. #
une salade # Donnez-moi une salade. #
un chocolat # Donne-moi un chocolat. #

• Vidéo-scène C: Ça fait combien? *p. 52*

A. Compréhension orale CD 1, TRACK 34

At the café, Trinh and Céline have talked about many things. It is now time to go. Trinh calls the waiter so he can pay the check.

Trinh: S'il vous plaît?
Le garçon: Oui, monsieur.
Trinh: Ça fait combien?
Le garçon: Voyons, un jus d'orange, 2 euros 50, et une limonade, 1 euro 50. Ça fait 4 euros.
Trinh: 4 euros . . . Très bien . . . Mais, euh . . . Zut! Où est mon porte-monnaie . . . ? Dis, Céline, prête-moi 5 euros, s'il te plaît.

B. Écoutez et répétez. CD 1, TRACK 35

You will now hear a paused version of the dialog. Listen to the speaker and repeat right after he or she has completed the sentence.

• Prononciation *p. 55* CD 1, TRACK 36

La consonne «r»

Écoutez: Marie

The French consonant "**r**" is not at all like the English "**r.**" It is pronounced at the back of the throat. In fact, it is similar to the Spanish "jota" sound of José.

Répétez: Marie # Paris # orange # Henri #
franc # très # croissant # fromage #
bonjour # pour # Pierre # quart #
Robert # Richard # Renée # Raoul #
Marie, prête-moi trente euros. #

▶ LEÇON 4 De jour en jour

• Vidéo-scène A: L'heure *p. 56*

1. Un rendez-vous

A. Compréhension orale CD 1, TRACK 37

Jean-Paul and Stéphanie are sitting in a café. Stéphanie seems to be in a hurry to leave.

Stéphanie: Quelle heure est-il?
Jean-Paul: Il est trois heures.
Stéphanie: Trois heures?
Jean-Paul: Oui, trois heures.
Stéphanie: Oh là là. J'ai un rendez-vous avec David dans vingt minutes. Au revoir, Jean-Paul.
Jean-Paul: Au revoir, Stéphanie. À bientôt!

B. Écoutez et répétez. CD 1, TRACK 38

You will now hear a paused version of the dialog. Listen to the speaker and repeat right after he or she has completed the sentence.

pause for oral response

• Écoutez bien! *p. 57* CD 1, TRACK 39

Listen as people talk about the time. For each dialog, indicate which of the watches below corresponds to the time you hear.

1. –Quelle heure est-il?
   –Il est sept heures. #
2. –Quelle heure est-il?
   –Il est deux heures. #
3. –Quelle heure est-il?
   –Il est huit heures. #
4. –Quelle heure est-il?
   –Il est midi. #
5. –Quelle heure est-il?
   –Il est dix heures. #
6. –Quelle heure est-il?
   –Il est cinq heures. #

2. À quelle heure est le film? *p. 58*

A. Compréhension orale CD 1, TRACK 40

Stéphanie and David have decided to go to a movie.

Stéphanie: Quelle heure est-il?
David: Il est trois heures et demie.
Stéphanie: Et à quelle heure est le film?
David: À quatre heures et quart.
Stéphanie: Ça va. Nous avons le temps.

B. Écoutez et répétez. CD 1, TRACK 41

You will now hear a paused version of the dialog. Listen to the speaker and repeat right after he or she has completed the sentence.

• Vidéo-scène B: Le jour et la date *p. 60*

1. Quel jour est-ce?

A. Compréhension orale CD 1, TRACK 42

For many people, the days of the week are not all alike.

DIALOGUE 1 **Vendredi**
Philippe: Quel jour est-ce?
Stéphanie: C'est vendredi.
Philippe: Super! Demain, c'est samedi!

DIALOGUE 2 **Mercredi**
Nathalie: Ça va?
Marc: Pas très bien.
Nathalie: Pourquoi?
Marc: Aujourd'hui, c'est mercredi.
Nathalie: Et alors?
Marc: Demain, c'est jeudi! Le jour de l'examen.
Nathalie: Zut! C'est vrai! Au revoir, Marc.
Marc: Au revoir, Nathalie. À demain!

B. Écoutez et répétez. CD 1, TRACK 43

You will now hear a paused version of the dialog. Listen to the speaker and repeat right after he or she has completed the sentence.

2. Anniversaire *p. 62*

A. Compréhension orale CD 1, TRACK 44

François and Isabelle are on their way to Nathalie's birthday party. As they are talking, François wants to know when Isabelle's birthday is.

François: C'est quand, ton anniversaire?
Isabelle: C'est le 18 mars!
François: Le 18 mars? Pas possible!
Isabelle: Si! Pourquoi?
François: C'est aussi mon anniversaire.
Isabelle: Quelle coïncidence!

B. Écoutez et répétez. CD 1, TRACK 45

You will now hear a paused version of the dialog. Listen to the speaker and repeat right after he or she has completed the sentence.

• Vidéo-scène C: Le temps *p. 64*

A. Compréhension orale CD 1, TRACK 46

It is nine o'clock Sunday morning. Cécile and her brother Philippe have planned a picnic for the whole family. Cécile is asking about the weather.

Cécile: Quel temps fait-il?
Philippe: Il fait mauvais!
Cécile: Il fait mauvais?
Philippe: Oui, il fait mauvais! Regarde! Il pleut!
Cécile: Zut, zut et zut!
Philippe: !!!???
Cécile: Et le pique-nique?
Philippe: Le pique-nique? Ah, oui, le pique-nique! . . . Écoute, ça n'a pas d'importance.
Cécile: Pourquoi?
Philippe: Pourquoi? Parce que Papa va nous inviter au restaurant.
Cécile: Super!

B. Écoutez et répétez. CD 1, TRACK 47

You will now hear a paused version of the dialog. Listen to the speaker and repeat right after he or she has completed the sentence.

À votre tour!

• Ecoutez bien! *p. 66* CD 1, TRACK 48

Isabelle is in a café talking to Jean-Paul. You will hear Isabelle asking questions. For each of Isabelle's questions, select Jean-Paul's response from the suggested answers. She will repeat each question. Écoutez.

1. Quel temps fait-il? #
2. Tu veux un sandwich? #
3. Tu veux un jus d'orange? #
4. Quelle heure est-il? #
5. C'est quand, ton anniversaire? #
6. Combien coûte le sandwich? #

• Conversation dirigée *p. 66* CD 1, TRACK 49

Stéphanie is in a café called Le Select. The waiter is taking her order. Écoutez leur conversation.

Le garçon: Bonjour, mademoiselle! Vous désirez?
Stéphanie: Je voudrais un croissant, s'il vous plaît. Combien coûte un jus d'orange?
Le garçon: 2 euros.
Stéphanie: Donnez-moi un jus d'orange, s'il vous plaît! . . . Monsieur, s'il vous plaît! Ça fait combien?
Le garçon: Ça fait 4 euros cinquante.
Stéphanie: Voici 5 euros.
Le garçon: Merci, mademoiselle.

Complete videoscripts, plus Workbook and Assessment audioscripts, are available in the Unit Resource Books.

Main Theme
- Daily Activities

COMMUNICATION
- Ordering snacks and beverages in a café
- Asking about prices and paying for food/drink
- Using French money
- Telling time
- Giving the date and day of the week
- Talking about the weather

CULTURES
- Learning about the euro
- Learning where French teens eat with their friends
- Learning about the café

CONNECTIONS
- Connecting to Math: Tallying a restaurant check
- Connecting to Science: Learning about the weather
- Connecting to Music: Singing "Alouette"

COMPARISONS
- Comparing the difference in sound of the French "r" and the English "r"
- Comparing where teens in France and the U.S. go for a snack
- Comparing what teens in France and the U.S. eat
- Learning about the influence of the "euro" countries on other countries in regards to travel

COMMUNITIES
- Using French to order in a restaurant
- Using French to perform for people in the community

UNITÉ 2 Invitation au français

La vie courante

LEÇON 3 Bon appétit!

VIDÉO-SCÈNES

- **A** Tu as faim?
- **B** Au café
- **C** Ça fait combien?

LEÇON 4 De jour en jour

VIDÉO-SCÈNES

- **A** L'heure
- **B** Le jour et la date
- **C** Le temps

THÈME ET OBJECTIFS

Everyday life in France

In this unit, you will learn how to get along in France. In particular, you may want to know how to buy something to eat or drink.

You will learn ...

- to order snacks and beverages in a café
- to ask about prices and pay for your food/drink
- to use French money

You will also learn ...

- to tell time
- to give the date and the day of the week
- to talk about the weather

UNIT OVERVIEW

- **Communication Goals:** Students will learn to order something to eat or drink in a café or fast food restaurant. They will also learn to talk about weather.
- **Linguistic Goals:** Students will begin to acquire features of the French sound system, particularly rhythm, stress, intonation, and the French / r /.
- **Critical Thinking Goals:** Students will discover that all nouns – even those referring to things – have gender. They will observe that in French it is expressed as either **il** or **elle.**
- **Cultural Goals:** Students will become aware of types of eating establishments and the French monetary system.

Introduction culturelle

Bon appétit!

Where do you go when you want something to eat or drink? Maybe to a fast-food restaurant or an ice cream place?

French teenagers also have a large choice of places to go when they are hungry or thirsty. Some go to a bakery **(une boulangerie)** or a pastry shop **(une pâtisserie)** to buy **croissants, éclairs,** or other small pastries. Some may buy pizzas, **crêpes,** hot dogs, or ice-cream cones from street vendors. Still others may go to a fast-food restaurant **(un fast-food).** But the favorite place to get something to eat or drink is the **café.** There are **cafés** practically everywhere in France. As you will see, the **café** plays an important role in the social life of all French people.

Teaching Resource Options

PRINT 

Unit 2 Resource Book
Family Letter, p. 31
Français pour hispanophones
Conseils, p. 8
Vocabulaire, pp. 40–41

AUDIO & VISUAL 

Audio Program
Chansons CD

TECHNOLOGY 

EasyPlanner CD-ROM

Cultural note

Fast-food restaurants (**les fast-foods,** or technically, **les restaurants de restauration rapide**) have multiplied in France in recent years and are now very popular with French teenagers. One can order:

- hamburgers (**des hamburgers**)
- hot dogs (**des saucisses, des hot dogs**)
- French fries (**des frites**)
- salads (**des salades**)

A typical meal at a fast-food restaurant costs about 6 euros. Popular chains are *Quick, Free Time, Le Duff,* and *La Croissanterie.*

PACING

▶ Try to move through this unit rather quickly, focusing on listening and speaking.

In later lessons, students will encounter the same vocabulary again. At that time they will be expected to master the material in writing.

CRITICAL THINKING The French Connection

Ask students which of the food names in the ***Pour communiquer*** box on p. 45 have English cognates.

LANGUAGE NOTES

- The expression **Bon appétit!** is used as people sit down to eat. It means *Enjoy the meal!*
- The term for "drive-up" is **service au volant** *(service at the steering wheel).*

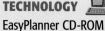

Leçon 3A

Main Topics Offering and asking for food

Teaching Resource Options

PRINT  

Workbook PE, pp. 29–32
Activités pour tous PE, pp. 17–18
Block Scheduling Copymasters, pp. 17–24
Unit 2 Resource Book
- *Activités pour tous* TE, pp. 13–14
- Audioscript, pp. 56, 57–59
- Communipak, pp. 132–156
- Lesson Plans, pp. 19–20
- Block Scheduling Lesson Plans, pp. 25–26
- Absent Student Copymasters, pp. 32–33
- Video Activities, pp. 38–41
- Videoscript, pp. 50–51
- Workbook TE, pp. 1–4

AUDIO & VISUAL 

Audio Program
CD 1 Tracks 28, 29
CD 6 Tracks 1–5
Overhead Transparencies
10 Foods

TECHNOLOGY 

Online Workbook

VIDEO PROGRAM

MODULE 3A
Tu as faim?

TOTAL TIME: 5:51 min.
DVD Disk 1
Videotape 1 (COUNTER: 38:31 min.)

3A.1 Dialogue: Tu as faim? (38:40–39:35 min.)

3A.2 Mini-scenes: Ordering food (39:36–41:29 min.)

3A.3 Vignette culturelle: Qu'est-ce qu'on mange? (41:30–44:22 min.)

Comprehension practice Play the entire module through as an introduction to the lesson.

LEÇON 3

VIDÉO-SCÈNE (VIDÉO DVD AUDIO)

Bon appétit!

A Tu as faim?

Pierre, Philippe, and Nathalie are on their way home from school. They stop by a street vendor who sells sandwiches and pizza. Today it is Pierre's turn to treat his friends.

SCÈNE 1 Pierre et Nathalie

Pierre: Tu as faim?
Nathalie: Oui, j'ai faim.
Pierre: Tu veux un sandwich ou une pizza?
Nathalie: Donne-moi une pizza, s'il te plaît.
Pierre: Voilà.
Nathalie: Merci.

SCÈNE 2 Pierre et Philippe

Pierre: Et toi, Philippe, tu as faim?
Philippe: Oh là là, oui, j'ai faim.
Pierre: Qu'est-ce que tu veux? Un sandwich ou une pizza?
Philippe: Je voudrais un sandwich ... euh ... et donne-moi aussi une pizza. — *er ...*
Pierre: C'est vrai! Tu as vraiment faim! — *really*

CROSS-CULTURAL OBSERVATION

Have students look at the foods pictured in **Pour communiquer.**

The only word that may be unfamiliar to them is **frites** *(French fries).*

Model the words and have students repeat them with a French accent.

Observation questions:
- Which of the food names are originally American words?
- Which of the food names are French?
- Which food name is Italian?

POUR COMMUNIQUER

J'ai faim!
Tu as faim?

▶ *How to say that you are hungry:*

J'ai faim.	*I'm hungry.*
Tu as faim?	*Are you hungry?*

▶ *How to offer a friend something:*

Tu veux ... ?	*Do you want ...?*	**Tu veux** un sandwich?
Qu'est-ce que tu veux?	*What do you want?*	**Qu'est-ce que tu veux?** Un sandwich ou une pizza?

▶ *How to ask a friend for something:*

Je voudrais ...	*I would like ...*	**Je voudrais** un sandwich.
Donne-moi ...	*Give me ...*	**Donne-moi** une pizza.
S'il te plaît ...	*Please ...*	**S'il te plaît**, François, donne-moi une pizza.

Les nourritures *(Foods)*

un croissant, un sandwich, un steak, un steak-frites, un hamburger, un hot dog

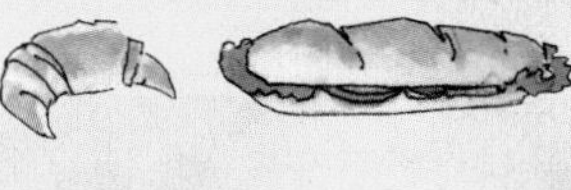

une salade, une pizza, une omelette, une crêpe, une glace

NOTE culturelle

Les jeunes et la nourriture

In general, French teenagers eat their main meals at home with their families. On weekends or after school, however, when they are with friends, they often stop at a fast-food restaurant or a café for something to eat.

At fast-food restaurants, French teenagers order pretty much the same types of foods as Americans: hamburgers, hot dogs, and pizza.

At a café, teenagers may order a croissant, a sandwich, or a dish of ice cream. Some favorite sandwiches are ham **(un sandwich au jambon)**, Swiss cheese **(un sandwich au fromage)**, or salami **(un sandwich au saucisson).** And, of course, they are made with French bread, which has a crunchy crust. Another traditional quick café meal is a small steak with French fries **(un steak-frites).**

COMPREHENSION Foods

PROPS: Pictures of the foods (above)

Present the French names of the foods.

[Hold up "croissant."] **Voici un croissant.**
[Hold up "sandwich."] **Voici un sandwich.**
Est-ce que c'est un croissant? [Non.]
Est-ce que c'est un sandwich? [Oui.]

Have students distribute the "foods."

X, prends le croissant et donne-le à Y.
Qui a le croissant? [Y.]

You may give more complex commands.

X, prends une pizza et un steak.
Donne la pizza à Y et le steak à Z.

POUR COMMUNIQUER

Photo culture note

Les pizzas In France, pizzas are sold:
- at pizzerias **(une pizzéria)**
- at certain bakeries **(une boulangerie)**
- at deli shops **(une charcuterie)**.

One can buy individual mini-pizzas about 5 inches in diameter. (These are sometimes served at home as an **hors-d'oeuvre**.)

Pizzas may have the following ingredients as toppings:
- cheese **(du fromage)**
- anchovies **(des anchois)**
- pepperoni **(du chorizo)**
- green peppers **(des poivrons)**
- mushrooms **(des champignons)**

Note the sign for take-out pizza **(pizza à emporter)**.

If students ask Literally, **j'ai faim** means *I have hunger.*

Pronunciation Be sure the students say the American words with a French accent: nasal "a" and no "n" or "m" in **sandwich, hamburger**; no liaison and a silent "h" in **un hot dog**.

Les nourritures Another traditional sandwich is **un croque-monsieur** which is a toasted ham and cheese sandwich.

Supplementary vocabulary

FOODS
une salade verte
une salade de tomates
une tarte *pie*
un gâteau *cake*
un éclair
une glace à la vanille
une glace au chocolat

Cross-cultural observation

Have students note similarities and differences in where French young people stop for food and what they eat.

Cultural note In France, **les fast-foods** are not drive-ins, but are located in downtown areas and shopping malls. They often have only stand-up counters and are not designed for simply sitting and talking with friends.

Teaching Resource Options

PRINT 

Workbook PE, pp. 29–32
Unit 2 Resource Book
Audioscript, p. 56
Communipak, pp. 132–156
Workbook TE, pp. 1–4

AUDIO & VISUAL 

Audio Program
CD 1 Track 30

TECHNOLOGY 

Power Presentations

Petit commentaire
Two popular sandwiches sold in cafés are **le croque-monsieur** and **le croque-madame**.

- The **croque-monsieur** is a grilled ham and cheese sandwich made with American-style bread.
- The **croque-madame** is similar, but with a fried egg on top.

1 EXCHANGES offering food and making a selection

– Qu'est-ce que tu veux? ...?
– Donne-moi ... s'il te plaît.

1. Un hamburger ou un steak?/un hamburger (un steak)
2. Un hot dog ou un sandwich?/un hot dog (un sandwich)
3. Une salade ou une omelette?/ une salade (une omelette)
4. Un steak-frites ou une pizza?/un steak-frites (une pizza)
5. Une crêpe ou un croissant?/une crêpe (un croissant)
6. Une glace à la vanille ou une glace au chocolat?/une glace à la vanille (une glace au chocolat)

Variation To simplify this activity, have students choose one of the two foods in each item.
– Donne-moi une pizza, s'il te plaît.
– Voilà.
– Merci.

Challenge (dialogue format)
– Tu as faim?
– Oui, j'ai faim.
– Tu veux un hamburger?
– Oui, donne-moi un hamburger, s'il te plaît.

PETIT COMMENTAIRE
In France, sandwiches are traditionally very simple: a piece of French bread with a slice of ham or cheese. However, nowadays one can buy fancier sandwiches made with different breads, such as "panini", and a variety of ingredients.

un sandwich, une pizza

You may have noted that the names of some foods are masculine and others are feminine. In French, ALL NOUNS, whether they designate people or things, are either MASCULINE or FEMININE.

MASCULINE NOUNS		FEMININE NOUNS	
un sandwich	**le** sandwich	**une** pizza	**la** pizza
un croissant	**le** croissant	**une** salade	**la** salade

1  Au choix *(Your choice)*

PARLER Offer your classmates a choice between the following items. They will decide which one they would like.

▶ une pizza ou un sandwich?

1. un hamburger ou un steak?
2. un hot dog ou un sandwich?
3. une salade ou une omelette?
4. un steak-frites ou une pizza?
5. une crêpe ou un croissant?
6. une glace à la vanille ou une glace au chocolat?

2 Au café

PARLER You are in a French café. Ask for the following dishes.

▶ 

1  2  3 

4 5  6 

▶ **Je voudrais un croissant.**

LISTENING PRACTICE Gender identification

PROPS: Red and blue index cards for each student

Quickly read aloud sentences containing masculine and feminine nouns. Have the students hold up the blue card for masculine nouns and the red card for feminine nouns.

1. **Voici une salade.** [R]
2. **Voici le sandwich.** [B]
3. **Voici la glace.** [R]
4. **Voici une crêpe.** [R]
5. **Voici un steak.** [B]
6. **Voici le croissant.** [B]
7. **Voici la pizza.** [R]
8. **Voici un hot dog.** [B]

3  *Tu as faim?*

PARLER You have invited French friends to your home. Ask if they are hungry and offer them the following foods.

▶ —Tu as faim?
—Oui, j'ai faim.
—Tu veux un hamburger?
—Oui, merci.

1

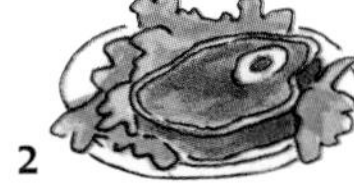
2

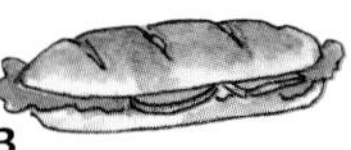
3

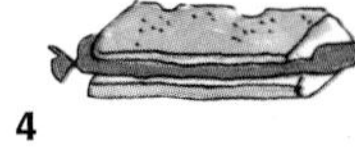
4

5

6

4  *Qu'est-ce que tu veux?*

PARLER Say which foods you would like to have in the following circumstances.

▶ You are very hungry.

1. You are at an Italian restaurant.
2. You are on a diet.
3. You are a vegetarian.
4. You are having breakfast.
5. You would like a dessert.
6. You want to eat something light for supper.

PRONONCIATION

L'intonation

When you speak, your voice rises and falls. This is called INTONATION. In French, as in English, your voice goes down at the end of a statement. However, in French, your voice rises after each group of words in the middle of a sentence. (This is the opposite of English, where your voice drops a little when you pause in the middle of a sentence.)

Voici un steak . . . et une salade.

Répétez: **Je voudrais une pizza.**

Je voudrais une pizza et un sandwich.

Je voudrais une pizza, un sandwich et un hamburger.

Voici un steak.

Voici un steak et une salade.

Voici un steak, une salade et une glace.

SOUNDING FRENCH

A key outcome of **Invitation au français** is that students begin to "sound French" so that they can be easily understood by French speakers.

One of the most important parts of "sounding French" is to acquire the intonation patterns of the language.

An effective technique is to have students say English sentences using French intonation. Use English equivalents of the above sentences to practice. For example:

I would like a pizza.

I would like a pizza and a sandwich.

I would like a pizza, a sandwich, and a hamburger.

2 COMMUNICATION ordering food

Je voudrais...
1. un sandwich.
2. une salade.
3. une pizza.
4. une glace.
5. une omelette.
6. un steak-frites.

3 ROLE PLAY offering food and accepting it

1. – Tu as faim?
   – Oui, j'ai faim.
   – Tu veux une pizza?
   – Oui, merci.
2. – Tu as faim?
   – Oui, j'ai faim.
   – Tu veux un steak?
   – Oui, merci.
3. – Tu as faim?
   – Oui, j'ai faim.
   – Tu veux un sandwich?
   – Oui, merci.
4. – Tu as faim?
   – Oui, j'ai faim.
   – Tu veux un hot dog?
   – Oui, merci.
5. – Tu as faim?
   – Oui, j'ai faim.
   – Tu veux une glace?
   – Oui, merci.
6. – Tu as faim?
   – Oui, j'ai faim
   – Tu veux une crêpe?
   – Oui, merci.

4 COMPREHENSION selecting food according to specific circumstances

Answers will vary.
1. Je voudrais une pizza.
2. Je voudrais une salade.
3. Je voudrais une salade (un sandwich, un croissant, une crêpe).
4. Je voudrais un croissant (une omelette).
5. Je voudrais une crêpe (une glace).
6. Je voudrais un sandwich (une salade, un hot dog, une omelette, un croissant).

Leçon 3B

Main Topic Ordering something to drink

Teaching Resource Options

PRINT

Workbook PE, pp. 33–36
Activités pour tous PE, pp. 19–20
Unit 2 Resource Book
- *Activités pour tous* TE, pp. 15–16
- Audioscript, pp. 56–57, 59–60
- Communipak, pp. 132–156
- Lesson Plans, pp. 21–22
- Block Scheduling Lesson Plans, pp. 27–28
- Absent Student Copymasters, p. 34
- Video Activities, pp. 42–45
- Videoscript, pp. 52–53
- Workbook TE, pp. 5–8

AUDIO & VISUAL

Audio Program
CD 1 Tracks 31, 32
CD 6 Tracks 6–10
Overhead Transparencies
11 Beverages

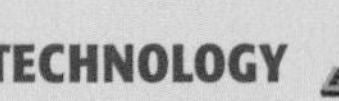

TECHNOLOGY

Online Workbook

VIDEO PROGRAM

VIDÉO DVD

MODULE 3B
Au café

TOTAL TIME: 4:34 min.
DVD Disk 1
Videotape 1 (COUNTER: 44:33 min.)

3B.1 Dialogue: Au café
(44:41–45:38 min.)

3B.2 Mini-scenes: Saying please
(45:39–47:27 min.)

3B.3 Vignette culturelle: Qu'est-ce qu'on boit?
(47:28–49:07 min.)

Comprehension practice Play the entire module through as an introduction to the lesson.

Photo culture note **Le garçon de café** French waiters **(un garçon de café)** are usually dressed formally: black pants, white shirt and bow tie, vest or jacket.

LEÇON 3

VIDÉO-SCÈNE

VIDÉO DVD AUDIO

B Au café

This afternoon Trinh and Céline went shopping. They are now tired and thirsty. Trinh invites Céline to a café.

SCÈNE 1 Trinh, Céline

Trinh: Tu as soif?
Céline: Oui, j'ai soif.
Trinh: <u>On va dans un café?</u> *Shall we go to a café?* <u>Je t'invite.</u> *I'm treating (inviting).*
Céline: <u>D'accord!</u> *Okay!*

SCÈNE 2 Le garçon, Céline, Trinh

Le garçon: Vous désirez, mademoiselle?
Céline: Un jus d'orange, s'il vous plaît.
Le garçon: Et <u>pour</u> vous, monsieur? *for*
Trinh: Donnez-moi une limonade,* s'il vous plaît.

SCÈNE 3 Le garçon, Céline, Trinh

Le garçon: *(à Céline)* La limonade, c'est pour vous, mademoiselle?
Trinh: Non, c'est pour moi.
Le garçon: <u>Ah, excusez-moi.</u> *Oh, excuse me.* Voici le jus d'orange, mademoiselle.
Céline: Merci.

****Une limonade** is a popular inexpensive soft drink with a slight lemon flavor.*

WARM-UP AND REVIEW Forms of address

PROPS: Magazine pictures of individual men, women, and teenagers.

Have students greet one another saying:

– Salut, X! Comment vas-tu?

– Ça va très bien (comme ci, comme ça).

Hold up the magazine pictures; point out that students do not know these people.

Ask them to greet each person in the picture formally:

Bonjour, madame (monsieur, mademoiselle). Comment allez-vous?

Then have them observe how people address one another in the café scene from the video.

POUR COMMUNIQUER

Donnez-moi une limonade, s'il vous plaît!

▶ *How to say that you are thirsty:*

J'ai soif.	*I'm thirsty.*
Tu as soif?	*Are you thirsty?*

▶ *How to order in a café:*

Vous désirez?	*May I help you?*	**—Vous désirez?**
Je voudrais ...	*I would like ...*	**—Je voudrais** un jus d'orange.

▶ *How to request something ...*

from a friend:	*from an adult:*	
S'il te plaît, donne-moi ...	**S'il vous plaît, donnez-moi ...**	*Please, give me ...*

→ Note that French people have two ways of saying please. They use
s'il te plaît with friends, and
s'il vous plaît with adults.

As we will see later, young people address their friends as **tu** and adults that they do not know very well as **vous**.

Les boissons *(Beverages)*

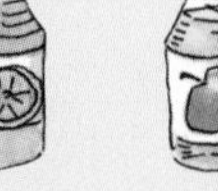

un soda · un jus d'orange · un jus de pomme · un jus de tomate · un jus de raisin* · une limonade · un café · un thé · un chocolat

NOTE culturelle

Le café

The café is a favorite gathering place for French young people. They go there not only when they are hungry or thirsty but also to meet their friends. They can sit at a table and talk for hours over a cup of coffee or a glass of juice. French young people also enjoy mineral water and soft drinks. In a French café, a 15% service charge is included in the check. However, most people also leave some small change as an added tip.

**Jus de raisin* *is a golden-colored juice made from grapes.*

Language notes

- When calling a waiter, one may also say **"Garçon!"** It is becoming common, however, to use the more polite **"Monsieur!"**
- The traditional term **un garçon** is slowly being replaced by **un serveur.**
- A waitress is **une serveuse.**

POUR COMMUNIQUER

Language note Literally, **tu as soif** means *you have thirst.*

Supplementary vocabulary

BEVERAGES

un café crème *coffee with cream*
un jus d'ananas *pineapple juice*
un jus de pamplemousse *grapefruit juice*
un citron pressé *freshly squeezed lemon juice, served with water and sugar on the side*
une orange pressée *freshly squeezed orange juice, served with water and sugar on the side*

Teaching notes

- Have students read the dialogue on page 48 while listening to the audio recording. Then, have them break into groups of three to write similar dialogues in which they play the roles of waiter/waitress and customers.
- Ask students if they have been to any local French cafés or restaurants. If so, ask them if the menus were printed in both French and English or if the wait staff spoke French.

Cross-cultural observation

Have students note similarities and differences in where French young people like to eat and drink.

COMPREHENSION Beverages

PROPS: Transparency 11: Beverages
red and blue transparency markers

Point out beverages on the transparency.
Voici un café. Voici un soda. etc.

Have students point out beverages.
X, viens ici. Montre-nous un café.

Hold up the blue and the red markers.
Voici un stylo bleu et un stylo rouge. Si vous entendez un, prenez le stylo bleu. Si vous entendez une, prenez le rouge.

Dessinez un cercle autour de la boisson.

Écoutez. «Je voudrais un thé.»

[Draw a blue circle around the tea.]

Teaching Resource Options

PRINT 

Workbook PE, pp. 33–36
Unit 2 Resource Book
Audioscript, p. 57
Communipak, pp. 132–156
Workbook TE, pp. 5–8

AUDIO & VISUAL

CD 1 Track 33

Petit commentaire
French young people often order mineral water mixed with a **sirop** or flavored concentrate, such as **menthe** *(mint)*, **orange, citron, grenadine** *(pomegranate)*, or **fraise** *(strawberry)*. These drinks are named according to the mineral water used.

1 EXCHANGES offering and selecting beverages

- Tu veux ...
- Donne-moi ..., s'il te plaît.

1. un thé ou un café?/un thé (un café)
2. une limonade ou un soda?/une limonade (un soda)
3. un jus de pomme ou un jus d'orange?/ un jus de pomme (un jus d'orange)
4. un jus de raisin ou un jus de tomate?/ un jus de raisin (un jus de tomate)

2 ROLE PLAY placing an order at a café

- Monsieur (Mademoiselle), s'il vous plaît!
- Vous désirez?
- ..., s'il vous plaît!

1. Un chocolat
2. Une limonade
3. Un jus de pomme
4. Un thé
5. Un café
6. Un jus de tomate

Variation (more basic): You may want to do the exercise quickly with the whole class, having students give just a one-sentence response: **Un jus d'orange, s'il vous plaît.** Then have students in pairs practice the dialogue format as indicated in the text.

VOUS DÉSIREZ?
UN JUS DE TOMATE, S'IL VOUS PLAÎT.

PETIT COMMENTAIRE
At a café, French young people often order carbonated soft drinks. They also enjoy natural beverages, such as flavored mineral water or juice. In the larger cities, one can find inviting juice bars that offer a wide selection of freshly blended fruit drinks.

1 Tu as soif?

PARLER You have invited a French friend to your house. You offer a choice of beverages and your friend (played by a classmate) responds.

▶ un thé ou un chocolat?
—**Tu veux un thé ou un chocolat?**
—**Donne-moi un chocolat, s'il te plaît.**

Chocolat

1. un thé ou un café?
2. une limonade ou un soda?
3. un jus de pomme ou un jus d'orange?
4. un jus de raisin ou un jus de tomate?

2 Au café

PARLER You are in a French café. Get the attention of the waiter **(Monsieur)** or the waitress **(Mademoiselle)** and place your order. Act out the dialogue with a classmate.

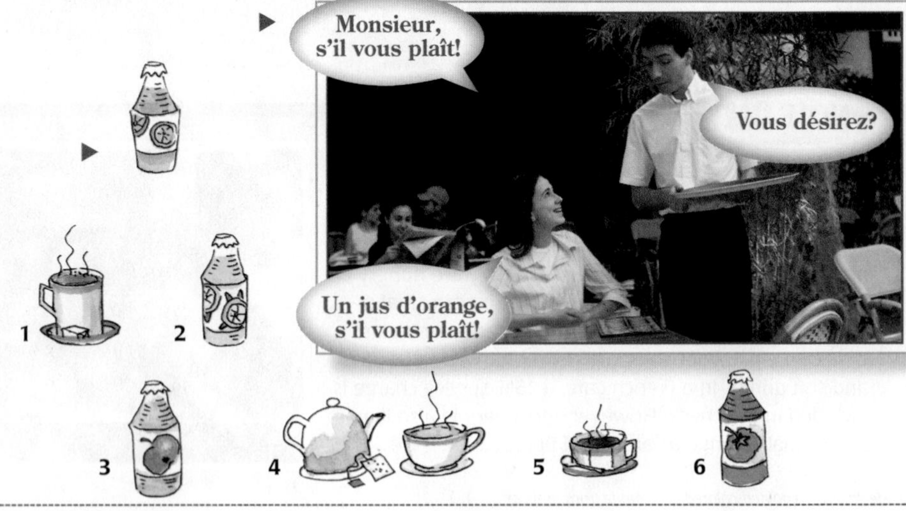
Monsieur, s'il vous plaît!
Vous désirez?
Un jus d'orange, s'il vous plaît!
1
2
3
4
5
6

GAME C'est logique?

PREPARATION: Prepare 2 bags of cards:

- (Bag A: 10 cards) On 5 cards, write **J'ai faim.** On the other 5, write **J'ai soif.**
- (Bag B: 21 cards) Begin each card with **Je voudrais, Donne-moi,** or **Donnez-moi** and add a food or beverage from pages 45 and 49.

Divide the class into two teams: **logique** and **illogique.**

A player from each team comes up. One reads a card from Bag A, the other reads one from Bag B. If the sentences fit logically, the **logique** team earns a point. If not, a point goes to the **illogique** team. For example:

J'ai soif. Donne-moi une pizza. = illogique

3 Que choisir? *(What to choose?)*

PARLER You are in a French café. Decide what beverage you are going to order in each of the following circumstances.

▶ You are very thirsty.
S'il vous plaît, une limonade (un jus de pomme) ...

1. It is very cold outside.
2. You do not want to spend much money.
3. You like juice but are allergic to citrus fruits.
4. It is breakfast time.
5. You have a sore throat.

4 La faim et la soif *(Hungry and thirsty)*

PARLER You are having a meal in a French café. Order the food suggested in the picture. Then order something to drink with that dish. A classmate will play the part of the waiter.

Note: **Et avec ça?** means *And with that?*

1
2
3
4

Vous désirez?
Je voudrais un steak-frites.
Et avec ça?
Un jus de tomate, s'il vous plaît!

PRONONCIATION

L'accent final

In French, the rhythm is very even and the accent always falls on the *last* syllable of a word or group of words.

Répétez: **Philippe Thomas Alice Sophie Dominique**

un café — **Je voudrais un café.**
une salade — **Donnez-moi une salade.**
un chocolat — **Donne-moi un chocolat.**

un chocolat

3 COMPREHENSION selecting an appropriate beverage

Answers will vary.
1. S'il vous plaît, un thé (un chocolat, un café).
2. S'il vous plaît, une limonade (un café).
3. S'il vous plaît, un jus de raisin (de tomate, de pomme).
4. S'il vous plaît, un thé (un café, un chocolat).
5. S'il vous plaît, un jus d'orange (un thé).

Variation
Donnez-moi une limonade (un jus de pomme), s'il vous plaît.

4 ROLE PLAY ordering food and a beverage

1. – Vous désirez?
   – Je voudrais une omelette.
   – Et avec ça?
   – (Un thé), s'il vous plaît.
2. – Vous désirez?
   – Je voudrais une glace.
   – Et avec ça?
   – (Un chocolat), s'il vous plaît.
3. – Vous désirez?
   – Je voudrais un hot dog.
   – Et avec ça?
   – (Un jus de pomme), s'il vous plaît.
4. – Vous désirez?
   – Je voudrais une salade.
   – Et avec ça?
   – (Un jus de raisin), s'il vous plaît.

PRONUNCIATION

For the sample sentences, you may want to tap out the syllables evenly making the last one somewhat longer than the rest.

Language note Since the French terms for milk and water are generally used with the partitive, they have not been included in this lesson.

Optional expansion You may want to teach:
du lait
de l'eau
de l'eau minérale

SOUNDING FRENCH

Along with intonation, one of the most important parts of "sounding French" is to acquire the rhythm and stress patterns of the language.

Let students mimic a French accent in English. Have them speak in a staccato rhythm, ending each group of words with a longer syllable, and using rising intonation at the end of phrases in the middle of a sentence.

INCLUSION

Metacognitive Have students generate a rule to help them remember **l'accent final**. Prepare a list of words, and ask students to beat out each syllable of each word on the list, stressing the last syllable. You may use rhythm sticks, drums, pencils, etc. to illustrate the sound.

Leçon 3C

Main Topic Asking about prices

Teaching Resource Options

PRINT 

Workbook PE, pp. 37–40
Activités pour tous PE, pp. 21–22
Unit 2 Resource Book
- *Activités pour tous* TE, pp. 17–18
- Audioscript, pp. 57, 60–62
- Communipak, pp. 132–156
- Lesson Plans, pp. 23–24
- Block Scheduling Lesson Plans, pp. 29–30
- Absent Student Copymasters. p. 35
- Video Activities, pp. 46–49
- Videoscript, pp. 54–55
- Workbook TE, pp. 9–12

AUDIO & VISUAL 

Audio Program
CD 1 Tracks 34, 35
CD 6 Tracks 11–15

TECHNOLOGY

Online Workbook

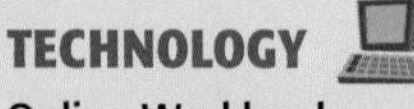

VIDEO PROGRAM

VIDÉO DVD

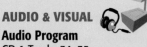

MODULE 3C
Ça fait combien?

TOTAL TIME: 7:10 min.
DVD Disk 1
Videotape 1 (COUNTER: 49:19 min.)

3C.1 Dialogue: Ça fait combien? (49:38–50:15 min.)

3C.2 Mini-scenes: Asking what one owes (50:16–52:15 min.)

3C.3 Vignette culturelle: L'argent français (52:16–56:29 min.)

Comprehension practice Play the entire module through as an introduction to the lesson.

LEÇON 3

VIDÉO-SCÈNE

C Ça fait combien?

At the café, Trinh and Céline have talked about many things. It is now time to go. Trinh calls the waiter so he can pay the check.

Trinh: S'il vous plaît?
Le garçon: Oui, monsieur.
Trinh: Ça fait combien?
Le garçon: Voyons, un jus d'orange, 2 euros 50, et une limonade, 1 euro 50. Ça fait 4 euros.
Trinh: 4 euros ... Très bien ... Mais, euh ... Zut! Où est mon porte-monnaie ...? Dis, Céline, prête-moi 5 euros, s'il te plaît.

euh: uh ...
Où est mon porte-monnaie: Where is my wallet?
Dis: Hey

NOTE culturelle

L'argent européen *(European money)*

Since 2002, twelve European countries have been using a new currency: the euro (**l'euro**). These countries include France, as well as Germany, Ireland, Austria, Italy, Spain, Portugal, Greece, Finland, Belgium, Luxembourg, and the Netherlands. The euro has the same value in all of these countries. It is also very convenient since you do not need to change money when you travel from one country to another.

The euro is divided into 100 cents or **centimes**. The euro currency consists of 7 different bills and 8 different coins. The euro bills are of different colors and different sizes. The largest is worth 500 euros and the smallest 5 euros.

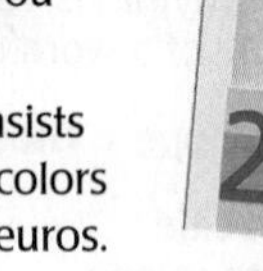

WARM-UP Numbers

Teach the students the following phrase:
Combien font deux plus deux?
(Note that the "s" on **plus** is pronounced /plys/.)
Have the class solve arithmetic problems.
Combien font quatorze plus seize?
[Trente] or
[Quatorze plus seize font trente.]

POUR COMMUNIQUER

How to ask how much something costs:

C'est combien?	*How much is it?*	—**C'est combien?**
Ça fait combien?	*How much does that come to (make)?*	—**Ça fait combien?**
Ça fait ...	*That's ..., That comes to ...*	—**Ça fait** 10 euros.
Combien coûte ...?	*How much does ... cost?*	—**Combien coûte** le sandwich?
Il/Elle coûte ...	*It costs ...*	—**Il coûte** 5 euros.

How to ask a friend to lend you something:

Prête-moi ...	*Lend me ..., Loan me ...*	**Prête-moi** 30 euros, s'il te plaît.

➔ Note that masculine nouns can be replaced by **il** and feminine nouns can be replaced by **elle.**

Voici **une glace.**	**Elle** coûte 2 euros.	***It** costs 2 euros.*
Voici **un sandwich.**	**Il** coûte 5 euros.	***It** costs 5 euros.*

STRATEGY Speaking

Linking words When counting in euros, be sure to use the proper liaisons and elisions.

un euro (n)	trois euros (z)	cinq euros (k)	sept euros (t)	neuf euros
deux euros (z)	quatre euros	six euros (z)	huit euros (t)	dix euros (z)

GAME

Divide the class into teams A and B. Two players come forward.

Player A asks a math question.

If player B answers correctly, both teams get a point.

If player B is wrong, and player A can answer his/her own question correctly, team A gets a point.

Then the next two players have their turn. This time player B asks the question. Etc.

POUR COMMUNIQUER

Language note In asking for prices, the casual speech forms given are much more common than **Combien est-ce que c'est?** or **Combien est-ce que ça fait?**

Cultural note The exchange rate between the dollar and the euro fluctuates daily. For the purposes of the activities, an exchange rate of 1 dollar = 1 euro can be used, unless there is a substantial variation in that parity.

Teaching note Tell students to research and make a list of which French and francophone companies have branches in the United States. Have them look at the companies' job postings periodically to see what types of jobs are available to those who speak French. Keep copies of the listings in a help wanted bulletin board or binder.

Note culturelle

The denominations of the euro bills are: 5, 10, 20, 50, 100, 200 and 500 euros. The face of a euro bill shows an archway, door or window to symbolize opportunity and opening to new ideas. The bridge on the back of each bill emphasizes the strong links among the various European countries shown in the map underneath the bridge.

The eight euro coins are issued in the following values: 1, 2, 5, 10, 20 and 50 cents, and 1 and 2 euros.

If students ask

French-speaking countries each have their own currency:

Quebec: le dollar canadien

Switzerland: le franc suisse

Algeria and Tunisia: le dinar

Morocco: le dirham

Senegal, Ivory Coast, etc.: le franc CFA (de la Communauté financière africaine)

Teaching Resource Options

PRINT 

Workbook PE, pp. 37–40
Unit 2 Resource Book
- Audioscript, p. 57
- Communipak, pp. 132–156
- Family Involvement, pp. 36–37
- Workbook TE, pp. 9–12

Assessment
- Lesson 3 Quiz, pp. 63–64
- Audioscript for Quiz 3, p. 62
- Answer Keys, pp. 195–198

AUDIO & VISUAL 

Audio Program
CD 1 Track 36
CD 13 Track 12
Overhead Transparencies
12 Menu from "Le Select"

TECHNOLOGY

Test Generator CD-ROM/McDougal Littell Assessment System

Petit commentaire
The **Guide Michelin,** the classic guide to restaurants in France, annually grants "stars" for outstanding cuisine. About 575 restaurants are given one star, 85 restaurants receive two stars, and about 20 truly outstanding restaurants are awarded the coveted three stars.

1 PRACTICE asking someone for a loan

1. S'il te plaît, prête-moi deux euros.
2. S'il te plaît, prête-moi trois euros.
3. S'il te plaît, prête-moi dix euros.
4. S'il te plaît, prête-moi vingt euros.
5. S'il te plaît, prête-moi trente euros.
6. S'il te plaît, prête-moi quarante euros.
7. S'il te plaît, prête-moi vingt-cinq euros.
8. S'il te plaît, prête-moi quinze euros.
9. S'il te plaît, prête-moi cinquante euros.

Teaching note You may wish to project **Transparency 12** as students do the activities on this page.

Realia note Ask the students: **Comment s'appelle le café/restaurant? [Le Select]**

PETIT COMMENTAIRE
French people of all ages love to eat out, and French restaurants have the reputation of offering the best cuisine in the world. Of course, there are all kinds of restaurants for all kinds of budgets, ranging from the simple country inn **(l'auberge de campagne)** with its hearty regional food to the elegant three-star restaurant **(restaurant trois étoiles)** with its exquisite—and expensive—menu.

1 S'il te plaît ...

PARLER You have been shopping in Paris and discover that you did not exchange enough money. Ask a friend to loan you the following sums.

▶ 5 euros
S'il te plaît, prête-moi cinq euros.

1. 2 euros
2. 3 euros
3. 10 euros
4. 20 euros
5. 30 euros
6. 40 euros
7. 25 euros
8. 15 euros
9. 50 euros

2  Décision

PARLER Before ordering at a café, Charlotte and Fatima are checking the prices. Act out the dialogues.

▶ le chocolat

1. le thé
2. le jus d'orange
3. la salade de tomates
4. la glace à la vanille
5. le café
6. le steak-frites
7. le hot dog
8. l'omelette
9. la salade mixte
10. le jus de raisin

LE SELECT
CAFÉ RESTAURANT

BOISSONS

café...1€50
chocolat...2€50
thé...2€
limonade...2€50
jus d'orange...2€70
jus de raisin...2€70

GLACES

glace au chocolat...2€50
glace à la vanille...2€50

SANDWICHS

sandwich au jambon...3€50
sandwich au fromage...3€50

ET AUSSI . . .

steak-frites...8€
salade mixte...3€50
salade de tomates...4€
omelette...4€25
hot dog...4€
croissant...1€40
pizza...8€

PROJECT Un menu

Using the "Le Select" menu as a model, have the students prepare menus in French. They should include the name, address, and telephone number of the café/restaurant and illustrate with original drawings or cut-out pictures. Display the finished products on the bulletin board and/or around the room. If you choose to have your students do the Challenge activity on p. 67, they can use the menus in their café conversations.

3  Ça fait combien?

PARLER You have gone to Le Select with your friends and have ordered the following items. Now you are ready to leave the café, and each one wants to pay. Check the prices on the menu for Le Select, and act out the dialogue.

▶ —Ça fait combien, s'il vous plaît?
—Ça fait deux euros cinquante.
—Voici deux euros cinquante.
—Merci.

  Au «Select»

PARLER You are at Le Select. Order something to eat and drink. Since you are in a hurry, ask for the check right away. Act out the dialogue with a classmate who will play the part of the waiter/waitress.

Monsieur, s'il vous plaît!
Vous désirez?
Je voudrais un sandwich au jambon et un café. Ça fait combien?
Ça fait 5 euros.

PRONONCIATION  /r/

La consonne «r»

The French consonant "**r**" is not at all like the English "**r.**" It is pronounced at the back of the throat. In fact, it is similar to the Spanish "jota" sound of José.

Répétez: **Marie Paris orange Henri**
franc très croissant fromage
bonjour pour Pierre quart
Robert Richard Renée Raoul

Marie, prête-moi trente euros.

Marie

INCLUSION

Cumulative Ask students to practice saying **frites** first with an American "r" and then with a French guttural "r" (back of throat). Prepare a list of appropriate words from previous lessons, and have students read these words aloud.

2 EXCHANGES asking how much things cost

1. – Combien coûte le thé?
   – Il coûte deux euros.
2. – Combien coûte le jus d'orange?
   – Il coûte deux euros soixante-dix.
3. – Combien coûte la salade de tomates?
   – Elle coûte quatre euros.
4. – Combien coûte la glace à la vanille?
   – Elle coûte deux euros cinquante.
5. – Combien coûte le café?
   – Il coûte un euro cinquante.
6. – Combien coûte le steak-frites?
   – Il coûte huit euros.
7. – Combien coûte le hot dog?
   – Il coûte quatre euros.
8. – Combien coûte l'omelette?
   – Elle coûte quatre euros vingt-cinq.
9. – Combien coûte la salade mixte?
   – Elle coûte trois euros cinquante.
10. – Combien coûte le jus de raisin?
    – Il coûte deux euros soixante-dix.

3 EXCHANGES asking the price of something and paying for it

1. – Ça fait combien, s'il vous plaît?
   – Ça fait un euro quarante.
   – Voici un euro quarante.
   – Merci.
2. – Ça fait combien, s'il vous plaît?
   – Ça fait huit euros.
   – Voici huit euros.
   – Merci.
3. – Ça fait combien, s'il vous plaît?
   – Ça fait trois euros cinquante.
   – Voici trois euros cinquante.
   – Merci.
4. – Ça fait combien, s'il vous plaît?
   – Ça fait deux euros soixante-dix.
   – Voici deux euros soixante-dix.
   – Merci.
5. – Ça fait combien, s'il vous plaît?
   – Ça fait deux euros.
   – Voici deux euros.
   – Merci.

4 ROLE PLAY ordering something to eat and drink

Answers will vary.
– Monsieur (Mademoiselle), s'il vous plaît!
– Vous désirez?
– Je voudrais (une omelette et un jus de raisin). Ça fait combien?
– Ça fait (6 euros 95).

Pre-AP skill: Pronounce with care.

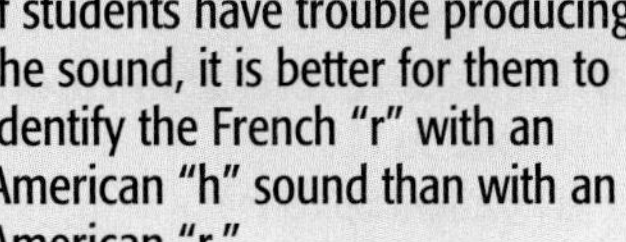
PRONUNCIATION

If students have trouble producing the sound, it is better for them to identify the French "r" with an American "h" sound than with an American "r."

Leçon 4A

Main Topic Telling time

Teaching Resource Options

PRINT

Workbook PE, pp. 41–44
Activités pour tous PE, pp. 23–24
Block Scheduling Copymasters, pp. 25–32
Unit 2 Resource Book
- *Activités pour tous* TE, pp. 79–80
- Audioscript, pp. 121, 123–124
- Communipak, pp. 132–156
- Lesson Plans, pp. 85–86
- Block Scheduling Lesson Plans, pp. 91–92
- Absent Student Copymasters, pp. 97–98
- Video Activities, pp. 103–106
- Videoscript, pp. 115–116
- Workbook TE, pp. 65–68

AUDIO & VISUAL 

Audio Program
CD 1 Tracks 37–39
CD 6 Tracks 16–21

TECHNOLOGY 

Online Workbook

VIDEO PROGRAM

MODULE 4A
Le français pratique
L'heure

TOTAL TIME: 7:30 min.
DVD Disk 1
Videotape 1 (COUNTER: 56:39 min.)

4A.1 Dialogue: Un rendez-vous (56:47–57:13 min.)

4A.2 Mini-scenes: Telling time (57:17–1:01:40 min.)

4A.3 À quelle heure est le film? (1:01:41–1:02:00 min.)

4A.4 Mini-scenes: Indicating at what time an event occurs (1:02:01–1:02:37 min.)

4A.5 Vignette culturelle: L'heure officielle (1:02:38–1:05:09 min.)

Comprehension practice Play the entire module of the video through as an introduction to the lesson.

LEÇON 4

VIDÉO-SCÈNE

De jour en jour

A L'heure

1. Un rendez-vous

Jean-Paul and Stéphanie are sitting in a café. Stéphanie seems to be in a hurry to leave.

Stéphanie: Quelle heure est-il?
Jean-Paul: Il est trois heures.
Stéphanie: Trois heures?
Jean-Paul: Oui, trois heures.
Stéphanie: Oh là là. J'ai un rendez-vous (*I have a date*) avec (*with*) David dans vingt minutes. Au revoir, Jean-Paul.
Jean-Paul: Au revoir, Stéphanie. À bientôt! (*See you soon!*)

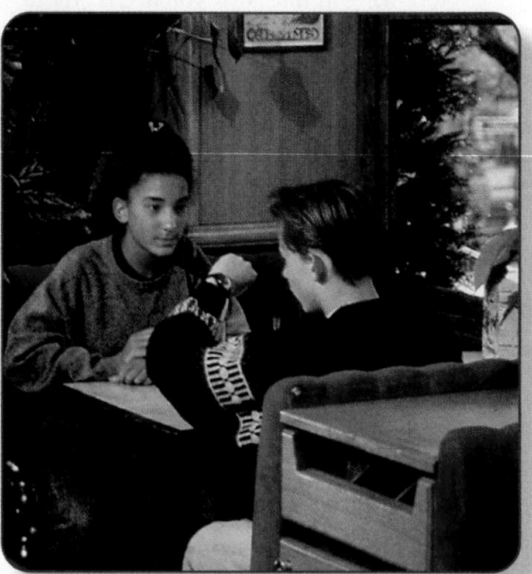

POUR COMMUNIQUER

How to talk about the time:

Quelle heure est-il? *What time is it?*
Il est ... *It's ...*

une heure	deux heures	trois heures	quatre heures	cinq heures	six heures

sept heures	huit heures	neuf heures	dix heures	onze heures	midi	minuit

WARM-UP Reviewing numbers

Have the students each write their phone numbers on a slip of paper and place them in a box.

Draw the first number and read it out loud (Quebec style: digit by digit).

The student whose number is read stands up and recites his/her phone number back. Then that student comes forward, draws a new number, and reads it aloud. The game continues until no numbers are left in the box.

1  Écoutez bien!

ÉCOUTER Listen as people talk about the time. For each dialog, indicate which of the watches below corresponds to the time you hear.

2 Quelle heure est-il?

PARLER Ask your classmates what time it is.

1  2  3  4  5  6  7 

→ Although *o'clock* may be left out in English, the expression **heure(s)** must be used in French when giving the time.

It's ten. (It's ten o'clock.) **Il est dix heures.**

→ To distinguish between A.M. and P.M., the French use the following expressions:

du matin	*in the morning*	Il est dix heures **du matin.**
de l'après-midi	*in the afternoon*	Il est deux heures **de l'après-midi.**
du soir	*in the evening*	Il est huit heures **du soir.**

NOTE DE PRONONCIATION: In telling time, the NUMBER and the word **heure(s)** are linked together. Remember, in French the letter "**h**" is always silent.

une heure **deux heures** **trois heures** **quatre heures** **cinq heures** **six heures**

sept heures **huit heures** **neuf heures** **dix heures** **onze heures**

COMPREHENSION Telling time

PROP: Clock with movable hands

Move the hands of the clock to show the hours and give the corresponding times.

Quelle heure est-il? Il est une heure.
Il est deux heures. etc.

Call on individual students to move the hands of the clock as you give the time.

Il est cinq heures.
X, viens ici. Montre-nous cinq heures.

1 PRACTICE understanding the spoken time

1. A
2. E
3. D
4. F
5. C
6. B

2 PRACTICE asking and telling the time

1. – Quelle heure est-il?
   – Il est trois heures.
2. – Quelle heure est-il?
   – Il est six heures.
3. – Quelle heure est-il?
   – Il est une heure.
4. – Quelle heure est-il?
   – Il est neuf heures.
5. – Quelle heure est-il?
   – Il est onze heures.
6. – Quelle heure est-il?
   – Il est midi.
7. – Quelle heure est-il?
   – Il est minuit.

Cross-cultural observation

As is described in the video, the French use a 24-hour clock on timetables and TV schedules:

1 p.m. = **13h (treize heures)**

8 p.m. = **20h (vingt heures)**

- To go from p.m. to the 24-hour clock, add 12 hours:
  1 p.m. = 1 + 12 = **13 heures**
- To go from the 24-hour clock to p.m., simply subtract 12 hours:
  20 heures = 20 – 12 = 8 p.m.

Teaching Resource Options

PRINT 

Workbook PE, pp. 41–44
Unit 2 Resource Book
- Audioscript, p. 121
- Communipak, pp. 132–156
- Video Activities, pp. 104–106
- Videoscript, p. 116
- Workbook TE, pp. 65–68

AUDIO & VISUAL 

Audio Program
CD 1 Tracks 40, 41
Overhead Transparencies
6 Clock face, *Quelle heure est-il?*
1 Map of France

VIDEO PROGRAM

VIDÉO DVD

MODULE 4A

4A.3 À quelle heure est le film?
(1:01:41–1:02:00 min.)

4A.4 Mini-scenes: Indicating at what time an event occurs
(1:02:01–1:02:37 min.)

4A.5 Vignette culturelle: L'heure officielle
(1:02:38–1:05:09 min.)

If students ask To refer to clock time, the French use the word **heure:**
Quelle heure est-il?
To talk about time in the general sense, they use the word **temps:**
Nous avons le temps.

POUR COMMUNIQUER

Language notes

- It is correct to use either **avoir un rendez-vous** or **avoir rendez-vous** to discuss dates and appointments. **Avoir un rendez-vous** is used in this program since it parallels English usage (have **a** date, **an** appointment).
- Since people use digits when writing out times, students at the basic level do not need to spell these phrases out. (Therefore, the spelling **demi** as in **midi et demi**, is not shown.)
- **Expansion** You may want to introduce **moins** + minutes, as in **deux heures moins dix**. At the basic level, students can simply say **une heure cinquante**. This is more and more common with the increased use of digital clocks in France.

2. À quelle heure est le film?

Stéphanie and David have decided to go to a movie.

Stéphanie: Quelle heure est-il?
David: Il est trois heures et demie.
Stéphanie: Et à quelle heure est le film?
David: À quatre heures et quart.
Stéphanie: Ça va. Nous avons le temps.

That's okay. / We have time.

À quelle heure est le dîner?

POUR COMMUNIQUER

▶ How to ask at what time something is scheduled:

À quelle heure est ...? — *At what time is ...?*
—À quelle heure est le concert? — *At what time is the concert?*
—Le concert est à huit heures. — *The concert is at eight.*

▶ How to say that you have an appointment or a date:

J'ai un rendez-vous à ... — *I have an appointment (a date) at ...* — **J'ai un rendez-vous à** deux heures.

▶ How to indicate the minutes:

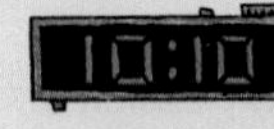

Il est ... dix heures dix — six heures vingt-cinq — sept heures trente-cinq — deux heures cinquante-deux

▶ How to indicate the half hour and the quarter hours:

 **et quart**
 **et demie**
 **moins le quart**

 Il est une heure **et quart.**
 Il est deux heures **et demie.**
 Il est trois heures **moins le quart.**

COMPREHENSION Quarter hours and minutes practice

PROP: clock with movable hands

Model the quarter hours and minutes, moving the hands on the clock.
Il est trois heures et quart. etc.

Have students show the times on the clock.
X, montre-nous cinq heures dix.

Send two students to the board to write the times as you say them.
Y et Z, venez au tableau.
Il est dix heures vingt. Écrivez l'heure. [Students write: "10h20".]

Students at their desks can also write down the times.

3 L'heure

PARLER Give the times according to the clocks.

▶ **Il est une heure et quart.**

▶  1  2  3  4  5 

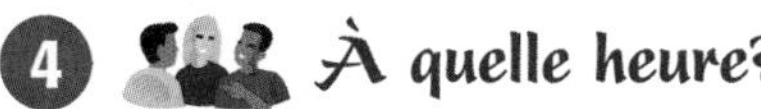

4 À quelle heure?

PARLER Ask your classmates at what time certain activities are scheduled. They will answer according to the information below.

▶ 8h 50 le film —**À quelle heure est le film?**
—**Le film est à huit heures cinquante.**

1. 7h 15 le concert
2. 2h 30 le match de football *(soccer)*
3. 3h 45 le match de tennis
4. 5h 10 le récital
5. 7h 45 le dîner

5 Rendez-vous

PARLER Isabelle has appointments with various classmates and teachers. Look at her notebook and act out her dialogues with Philippe.

▶ ISABELLE: **J'ai un rendez-vous avec Marc.**
PHILIPPE: **À quelle heure?**
ISABELLE: **À onze heures et demie.**

▶ 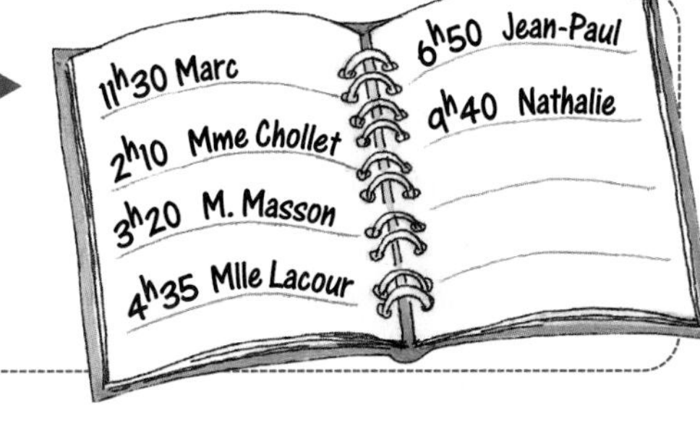

6 À la gare *(At the train station)*

PARLER You are at the information desk of a French train station. Travelers ask you the departure times for the following trains. Answer them according to the posted schedule.

▶ le train pour Nice

À quelle heure est le train pour Nice?

Le train pour Nice est à six heures dix.

INFORMATIONS

▶

DÉPARTS			
NICE	♦ 6h 10	TOULON	♦ 9h 35
LYON	♦ 7h 15	COLMAR	♦ 10h 40
CANNES	♦ 7h 30	TOULOUSE	♦ 10h 45
TOURS	♦ 8h 12	MARSEILLE	♦ 10h 50
DIJON	♦ 8h 25	BORDEAUX	♦ 10h 55

GEOGRAPHY SKILLS

PROP: Transparency 1: Map of France
As a warm-up, have individual students point to the cities in Act. 6 on the transparency.

X, viens ici et montre-nous Nice. [Voici Nice.]

Have the other students point to the same cities on the map of France in their book, p. R4.

INCLUSION

Multisensory Review the link between **est à** and the open sound of **est** with liaison. Write contrasting examples on the board: **Le film est** ... vs. **Le film est à huit heures**. / **À quelle heure est le train?** vs. **Le train est à huit heures**. Have students model pronunciations and write the examples in their notebooks.

3 PRACTICE telling time

1. Il est deux heures et demie (deux heures trente).
2. Il est quatre heures moins le quart (trois heures quarante-cinq).
3. Il est quatre heures et quart (quatre heures quinze).
4. Il est six heures et demie (six heures trente).
5. Il est onze heures moins le quart (dix heures quarante-cinq).

4 EXCHANGES asking and answering questions about time of events

– À quelle heure est ...?
– ... est à ...
1. le concert?/sept heures (et quart/quinze).
2. le match de football?/deux heures (et demie/trente).
3. le match de tennis?/quatre heures moins le quart (trois heures quarante-cinq).
4. le récital?/cinq heures dix.
5. le dîner?/huit heures moins le quart (sept heures quarante-cinq).

If students ask
- The "h" dividing the hours from the minutes in French stands for **heures** and corresponds to the colon used in English.
- U.S. football is **le football américain**.

5 EXCHANGES discussing appointment times

Isabelle: J'ai un rendez-vous avec ...
Philippe: À quelle heure?
Isabelle: À ...
- Mme Chollet/deux heures dix
- M. Masson/trois heures vingt
- Mlle Lacour/quatre heures trente-cinq
- Jean-Paul/six heures cinquante
- Nathalie/neuf heures quarante

6 ROLE PLAY asking and answering questions about train schedules

– À quelle heure est le train pour ... ?
– Le train pour ... est à ...
- Lyon/sept heures (et quart/quinze)
- Cannes/sept heures (et demie/trente)
- Tours/huit heures douze
- Dijon/huit heures vingt-cinq
- Toulon/neuf heures trente-cinq
- Colmar/dix heures quarante
- Toulouse/onze heures moins le quart (dix heures quarante-cinq)
- Marseille/dix heures cinquante
- Bordeaux/dix heures cinquante-cinq.

Variation (easier format):
– **À quelle heure est le train pour Nice?**
– **À six heures dix.**

VIDÉO-SCÈNE

VIDÉO DVD AUDIO

B Le jour et la date

1. Quel jour est-ce?

For many people, the days of the week are not all alike.

DIALOGUE 1 Vendredi

Philippe: Quel jour est-ce?
Stéphanie: C'est vendredi.
Philippe: Super! Demain, c'est samedi!

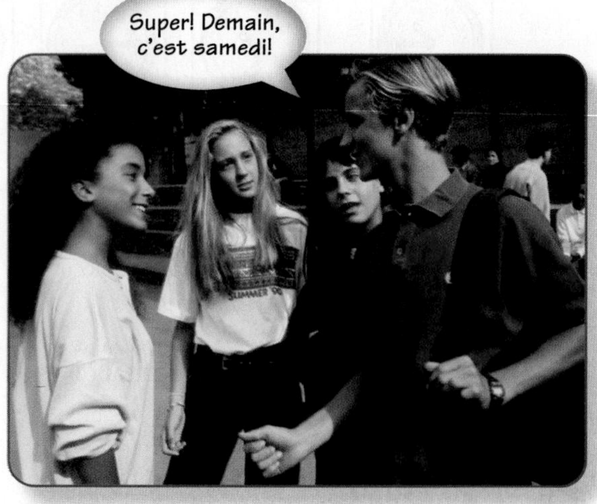
Super! Demain, c'est samedi!

DIALOGUE 2 Mercredi

Nathalie: Ça va?
Marc: Pas très bien.
Nathalie: Pourquoi? — *Why?*
Marc: Aujourd'hui, c'est mercredi.
Nathalie: Et alors? — *So?*
Marc: Demain, c'est jeudi! Le jour de l'examen.
Nathalie: Zut! C'est vrai! — *Darn! /That's right!* Au revoir, Marc.
Marc: Au revoir, Nathalie. À demain!

Demain, c'est jeudi! Le jour de l'examen.

Leçon 4B

Main Topics Talking about days of the week and dates

Teaching Resource Options

PRINT 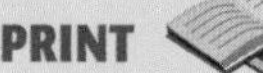 

Workbook PE, pp. 45–49
Activités pour tous PE, pp. 25–26
Unit 2 Resource Book
- *Activités pour tous* TE, pp. 81–82
- Audioscript, pp. 121–122, 124–126
- Communipak, pp. 132–156
- Lesson Plans, pp. 87–88
- Block Scheduling Lesson Plans, pp. 93–94
- Absent Student Copymasters, p. 99
- Video Activities, pp. 107–110
- Videoscript, pp. 117–118
- Workbook TE, pp. 69–73

AUDIO & VISUAL 

Audio Program
CD 1 Tracks 42, 43
CD 6 Tracks 22–27

TECHNOLOGY 

Online Workbook

VIDEO PROGRAM

MODULE 4B
Le français pratique
Le jour et la date

TOTAL TIME: 5:48 min.
DVD Disk 1
Videotape 1 (COUNTER: 1:05:21 min.)

4B.1 Dialogues:
1. Quel jour est-ce? (1:05:28–1:06:23 min.)
2. Anniversaire (1:06:24–1:06:41 min.)

4B.2 Mini-scenes: Dates and birthdays (1:06:42–1:09:20 min.)

4B.3 Vignette culturelle: Joyeux anniversaire! (1:09:21–1:11:09 min.)

Comprehension practice Play the entire module of the video through as an introduction to the lesson.

WARM-UP AND REVIEW Ça va?

Ask students how they are feeling, reviewing the expressions from Lesson 3. For example:
Bonjour, X. Ça va? [Oui, ça va très bien.]
Et toi, Y, ça va bien ou ça va mal? [Ça va mal.]
Z, demande à W si ça va. [–Bonjour W, ça va? –Ça va comme ci, comme ça.]

INCLUSION

Metacognitive, Gifted & Talented After reviewing, ask students how they plan to practice these expressions.

POUR COMMUNIQUER

How to talk about days of the week:

Quel jour est-ce?	*What day is it?*
Aujourd'hui, c'est mercredi.	*Today is Wednesday.*
Demain, c'est jeudi.	*Tomorrow is Thursday.*

How to tell people when you will see them again:

À samedi!	*See you Saturday!*
À demain!	*See you tomorrow!*

Les jours de la semaine *(Days of the week)*

lundi	*Monday*	**vendredi**	*Friday*	**aujourd'hui**	*today*
mardi	*Tuesday*	**samedi**	*Saturday*	**demain**	*tomorrow*
mercredi	*Wednesday*	**dimanche**	*Sunday*		
jeudi	*Thursday*				

1 Questions

PARLER

1. Quel jour est-ce aujourd'hui?
2. Et demain, quel jour est-ce?

2  Un jour de retard *(One day behind)*

PARLER Georges has trouble keeping track of the date. He is always one day behind. Monique corrects him.

▶ samedi

1. lundi
2. mardi
3. jeudi
4. vendredi
5. dimanche
6. mercredi

3 Au revoir!

PARLER You are on the phone with the following friends. Say good-bye and tell them when you will see them.

▶ Christine/lundi
Au revoir, Christine. À lundi.

1. David/dimanche
2. Nicolas/samedi
3. Céline/mercredi
4. Julie/vendredi
5. Thomas/mardi
6. Pierre/jeudi

LANGUAGE NOTE Days of the week

You may wish to tell your students that the days are named for the Roman gods. The suffix **di** comes from the Latin **dies** *(day)*.

lun-di	(moon-day)
mar-di	(Mars-day)
mercre-di	(Mercury-day)
jeu-di	(Jupiter-day)
vendre-di	(Venus-day)
same-di	(Saturn-day)

Dimanche comes from the Latin **Dominus** *(the Lord).*

POUR COMMUNIQUER

Language note Also: **Quel jour sommes-nous? Quel jour est-on?**

Casual speech One can say: **C'est quel jour? On est quel jour?**

Supplementary vocabulary
À bientôt! *See you soon!*

Cultural note On French calendars, the week traditionally begins with **lundi**. On Canadian calendars, however, the week begins with **dimanche**.

If students ask The days of the week are usually not capitalized in French.

1 COMMUNICATION stating today's and tomorrow's dates

Answers will vary
1. Aujourd'hui, c'est (lundi).
2. Demain, c'est (mardi).

2 EXCHANGES getting the date right

1. – Aujourd'hui, c'est lundi?
   – Non, aujourd'hui, c'est mardi!
2. – Aujourd'hui, c'est mardi?
   – Non, aujourd'hui, c'est mercredi!
3. – Aujourd'hui, c'est jeudi?
   – Non, aujourd'hui, c'est vendredi!
4. – Aujourd'hui, c'est vendredi?
   – Non, aujourd'hui, c'est samedi!
5. – Aujourd'hui, c'est dimanche?
   – Non, aujourd'hui, c'est lundi!
6. – Aujourd'hui, c'est mercredi?
   – Non, aujourd'hui, c'est jeudi!

Variation Philippe is one day ahead.
– Aujourd'hui, c'est samedi?
– Non, aujourd'hui, c'est vendredi.

3 ROLE PLAY telling people good-bye and when you will see them again

1. Au revoir, David. À dimanche!
2. Au revoir, Nicolas. À samedi!
3. Au revoir, Céline. À mercredi!
4. Au revoir, Julie. À vendredi!
5. Au revoir, Thomas. À mardi!
6. Au revoir, Pierre. À jeudi!

Challenge (dialogue format)
– Au revoir, Christine.
– Au revoir. À lundi.

Teaching Resource Options

PRINT 

Workbook PE, pp. 45–49
Unit 2 Resource Book
 Audioscript, p. 122
 Communipak, pp. 132–156
 Video Activities, pp. 107–109
 Videoscript, pp. 117–118
 Workbook TE, pp. 69–73

AUDIO & VISUAL 

Audio Program
CD 1 Tracks 44, 45
Overhead Transparencies
9 Calendar

TECHNOLOGY 

Power Presentations

VIDEO PROGRAM

VIDÉO  DVD 

MODULE 4B

4B.1 Dialogue: Anniversaire
(1:06:24–1:06:41 min.)

4B.2 Mini-scenes: Dates and birthdays
(1:06:42–1:09:20 min.)

If students ask Explain that **si** *(yes)* is used to respond to a negative statement or question.

POUR COMMUNIQUER

Language note To ask for the date, one can also say:
Quel jour est-ce?
Quel jour est-on? or
Quel jour sommes-nous?

Common colloquial alternative
On est quelle date?

If students ask The months are usually not capitalized in French.

2. Anniversaire

François and Isabelle are on their way to Nathalie's birthday party. As they are talking, François wants to know when Isabelle's birthday is.

François: C'est quand, ton anniversaire?
Isabelle: C'est le 18 mars!
François: Le 18 mars? Pas possible! — *That's not possible!*
Isabelle: Si! Pourquoi? — *Yes, it is! Why?*
François: C'est aussi mon anniversaire.
Isabelle: Quelle coïncidence! — *What a coincidence!*

POUR COMMUNIQUER

How to talk about the date:

Quelle est la date?	*What's the date?*
C'est le 12 (douze) octobre.	*It's October 12.*
C'est le premier juin.	*It's June first.*

How to talk about birthdays:

–C'est quand, ton anniversaire?	*When is your birthday?*
–Mon anniversaire est le 2 (deux) mars.	*My birthday is March 2.*

Les mois de l'année *(Months of the year)*

janvier	**avril**	**juillet**	**octobre**
février	**mai**	**août**	**novembre**
mars	**juin**	**septembre**	**décembre**

CASUAL SPEECH PRACTICE

In French, casual speech is often heard, but rarely written. (This is like English, where people often say: *You coming?* and write: *Are you coming?*)

In this textbook, students are introduced to standard written French.

Some forms of casual speech are so common that they have been accepted into general usage. Two examples of this are **un prof** and **jouer au foot.**

In this lesson, students learn the casual **C'est quand, ton anniversaire?** which is simpler than **Quand est-ce, ton anniversaire?**

La date

To express a date in French, the pattern is:

le	+	NUMBER	+	MONTH
le		11 (onze)		novembre
le		20 (vingt)		mai

EXCEPTION: The first of the month is **le premier.**

→ In front of numbers, the French use **le** (and never **l'**): **le onze, le huit.**

→ Note that when dates are abbreviated in French, the day always comes first.

2/8 **le deux août** 1/11 **le premier novembre**

4 Anniversaires

PARLER Ask your classmates when their birthdays are.

5 Quelle est la date?

PARLER Ask what the date is.

▶ —Quelle est la date?
—C'est le douze septembre.

6 Dates importantes

PARLER Give the following dates in French.

▶ Noël *(Christmas)*: 25/12 **C'est le vingt-cinq décembre.**

1. le jour de l'An *(New Year's Day)*: 1/1
2. la fête *(holiday)* de Martin Luther King: 15/1
3. la Saint-Valentin: 14/2
4. la Saint-Patrick: 17/3
5. la fête nationale américaine: 4/7
6. la fête nationale française: 14/7
7. la fête de Christophe Colomb: 12/10

INCLUSION

Sequential You may wish to have your students prepare a calendar of the month of their next birthday. Have them label the month, the days of the week, and their birthday in French. Ask them to illustrate the top of the calendar with an original drawing.

This activity is particularly appropriate for younger learners.

Repetitive Have students write numerals 1-31 in a notebook. Next to each numeral, write authentic spelling and a phonetic transcription. Have students practice numbers orally. Show numeral on card and ask individual students to say the number. Practice with **le** in front of the number. Show cards numbered 1-12 and ask students which month corresponds to the numeral (e.g. 8 = **août**). Then ask day and month.

Language notes

- You may wish to introduce the year:
  2004 deux mille quatre
  2006 deux mille six, etc.
  Aujourd'hui, nous sommes le vingt septembre deux mille cinq.
- Also: **le un** (when **un** is a number and not a pronoun).
- Abbreviations of dates may also be punctuated with hyphens or periods.
  – The months are sometimes expressed in roman numerals: **le 2.VIII.**
  – Note: **le premier** may be abbreviated as **le 1er**.

4 COMMUNICATION discussing birthdays

Answers will vary
– C'est quand, ton anniversaire?
– Mon anniversaire est le (8 mai).

Variation
Have students walk around the room grouping themselves according to the month of their birth.

– C'est quand, ton anniversaire?
– Mon anniversaire est le 1er mai. Et toi?

As a follow-up, begin with January, and have students in each group give their birthdays before sitting back down.

5 EXCHANGES asking today's date

1. – Quelle est la date?
   – C'est le trente juin.
2. – Quelle est la date?
   – C'est le huit mai.
3. – Quelle est la date?
   – C'est le quatre mars.
4. – Quelle est la date?
   – C'est le vingt et un novembre.
5. – Quelle est la date?
   – C'est le premier avril.
6. – Quelle est la date?
   – C'est le vingt-cinq août.

6 PRACTICE telling the date of certain events

1. C'est le premier janvier.
2. C'est le quinze janvier.
3. C'est le quatorze février.
4. C'est le dix-sept mars.
5. C'est le quatre juillet.
6. C'est le quatorze juillet.
7. C'est le douze octobre.

Leçon 4C

Main Topic Talking about the weather

Teaching Resource Options

PRINT 

Workbook PE, pp. 51–54
Activités pour tous PE, pp. 27–28
Unit 2 Resource Book
Activités pour tous TE, pp. 83–84
Audioscript, pp. 122, 126–128
Communipak, pp. 132–156
Lesson Plans, pp. 89–90
Block Scheduling Lesson Plans, pp. 95–96
Absent Student Copymasters, p. 100
Family Involvement, pp. 101–102
Video Activities, pp. 111–114
Videoscript, pp. 119–120
Workbook TE, pp. 75–78

Assessment
Lesson 4 Quiz, pp. 129–130
Audioscript for Quiz 4, p. 128
Answer Keys, pp. 195–198

AUDIO & VISUAL 

Audio Program
CD 1 Tracks 46, 47
CD 6 Tracks 28–31
CD 13 Tracks 13, 14
Overhead Transparencies
13 Weather

TECHNOLOGY 

Online Workbook
Test Generator CD-ROM/McDougal Littell Assessment System

VIDEO PROGRAM

VIDÉO
DVD

MODULE 4C
Le français pratique
Le temps

TOTAL TIME: 5:29 min.
DVD Disk 1
Videotape 1 (COUNTER: 1:11:21 min.)

4C.1 Dialogue: Le temps (1:11:30–1:12:10 min.)

4C.2 Mini-scenes: Talking about weather (1:12:11–1:13:53 min.)

4C.3 Vignette culturelle: La géographie de la France (1:13:54–1:16:50 min.)

Comprehension practice Play the entire module through as an introduction to the lesson.

LEÇON
4

VIDÉO-SCÈNE

VIDÉO DVD AUDIO

C Le temps

It is nine o'clock Sunday morning. Cécile and her brother Philippe have planned a picnic for the whole family. Cécile is asking about the weather.

Quel temps fait-il?

Il fait mauvais.

Zut, zut et zut!

Papa va nous inviter au restaurant.

Cécile:	Quel temps fait-il?	
Philippe:	Il fait mauvais!	
Cécile:	Il fait mauvais?	
Philippe:	Oui, il fait mauvais! Regarde! Il pleut!	*Look!*
Cécile:	Zut, zut et zut!	
Philippe:	!!!???	
Cécile:	Et le pique-nique?	*picnic*
Philippe:	Le pique-nique? Ah oui, le pique-nique! … Écoute, ça n'a pas d'importance.	*Listen, it doesn't matter. (It's not important.)*
Cécile:	Pourquoi?	*Why?*
Philippe:	Pourquoi? Parce que Papa va nous inviter au restaurant.	*Because Dad is going to take us out (invite us) to a restaurant.*
Cécile:	Super!	

WARM-UP AND REVIEW Months and dates

Have the class name the months of the year as you write their abbreviations across the top of the chalkboard.

Then go around the class asking all the students to give their birthdays.

Sue, c'est quand, ton anniversaire?
[Sue: C'est le 21 août.]

Write the student's name and abbreviated birthdate under the appropriate month.

[août] Sue: le 21/8.

Have students read the dates. Ask:

C'est quand, l'anniversaire de Sue?

Note: In a class of 25 the odds are 50/50 that two people will share the same birthday.

POUR COMMUNIQUER

Quel temps fait-il?

▶ **How to talk about the weather:**

Quel temps fait-il? *How's the weather?*

Il fait beau.

Il fait bon.

Il fait chaud.

Il fait frais.

Il fait froid.

Il fait mauvais.

Il pleut.

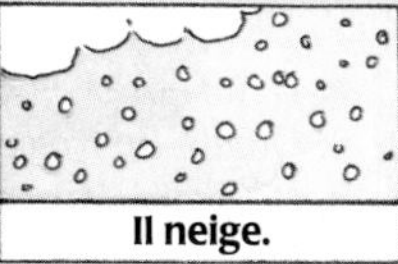
Il neige.

Les saisons *(Seasons)*

le printemps	*spring*	**au printemps**	*in (the) spring*
l'été	*summer*	**en été**	*in (the) summer*
l'automne	*fall, autumn*	**en automne**	*in (the) fall*
l'hiver	*winter*	**en hiver**	*in (the) winter*

1 Ta région

PARLER Say what the weather is like in your part of the country.

▶ en juillet

En juillet,
il fait chaud.

1. en août
2. en septembre
3. en novembre
4. en janvier
5. en mars
6. en mai

2 Les quatre saisons

PARLER Describe what the weather is like in each of the four seasons in the following cities.

▶ à Miami

En été, il fait chaud.
En automne, il fait chaud aussi. En hiver, il fait frais.
Au printemps, il fait bon.
Miami

1. à Chicago
2. à San Francisco
3. à Denver
4. à Boston
5. à Seattle
6. à Dallas

COMPREHENSION Weather

PROPS: Transparency 13: Weather, *Quel temps fait-il?*
Teach the weather expressions by pointing to the pictures on the overhead.
Quel temps fait-il? Il fait beau. Et maintenant, quel temps fait-il? Il pleut. Est-ce qu'il fait beau? [Non.]
Have students point out the weather.
X, viens ici. Montre-nous le temps.
Il pleut. [points to rain] **Il neige.** [points to snow] etc.

INCLUSION

Alphabetic/phonetic Have the class pronounce nasal sounds and ask them to explain how they remember pronunciation. Have students say **printemps** three times, and write the word in their notebooks. Then have them write the phonetic transcription. (Refer students to the "Nasal vowels" section on p. R5 of their textbooks.)

POUR COMMUNIQUER

Language note Contrast:

Il fait beau. *It's beautiful weather, the sun is out.*
Il fait bon. *It's nice weather, comfortable, warm.*

Expansion **Il fait très beau, très froid,** etc.

Pronunciation notes
- Be sure students do not pronounce the silent letters in **temps** and **printemps**.
- Be sure students make the following liaisons: **en‿hiver, en‿été, en‿automne**.

1 COMMUNICATION talking about the weather

Answers will vary.
1. En août, il fait beau (chaud).
2. En septembre, il fait bon (beau).
3. En novembre, il fait mauvais (il fait froid, il pleut).
4. En janvier, il neige (il fait froid).
5. En mars, il pleut (il fait frais, il neige).
6. En mai, il fait frais (bon, beau).

Variation (dialogue format)
– Quel temps fait-il en juillet?
– Il fait chaud.

2 DESCRIPTION giving details about the weather

Answers will vary.
1. (à Chicago) En été, il fait chaud. En automne, il fait bon (beau). En hiver, il fait froid (il fait mauvais, il neige). Au printemps, il fait frais (beau).
2. (à San Francisco) En été, il fait beau (chaud, bon). En automne, il fait bon (frais, beau). En hiver, il fait beau (il fait frais, il pleut). Au printemps, il fait beau (il fait bon, il pleut).
3. (à Denver) En été, il fait chaud. En automne, il fait beau (frais). En hiver, il fait froid (et il neige). Au printemps, il fait bon (beau, frais).
4. (à Boston) En été, il fait chaud. En automne, il fait beau (frais). En hiver, il fait froid (il fait mauvais, il neige). Au printemps, il fait frais (il fait beau, il fait bon, il pleut).
5. (à Seattle) En été, il fait chaud (beau, bon). En automne, il fait beau (il fait frais, il pleut). En hiver, il fait froid (il pleut, il neige). Au printemps, il fait beau (il fait bon, il fait frais, il pleut).
6. (à Dallas) En été, il fait (très) chaud. En automne, il fait chaud. En hiver, il fait beau (bon). Au printemps, il fait chaud (il fait beau, il pleut).

Geography activity/Pre-viewing activity In preparation for the **Vignette culturelle**, have students turn to page 4 and locate the following provinces on the map of France: Touraine, Alsace, Provence.

À VOTRE TOUR

Main Focus

- Recapitulation and review

Teaching Resource Options

PRINT 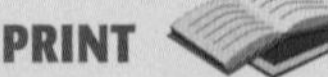

Workbook PE, pp. 55–58
Unit 2 Resource Book
Audioscript, p. 122
Communipak, pp. 132–156

Assessment
Unit 2 Test, pp. 165–170
Portfolio Assessment, Unit 1 URB pp. 155–164
Multiple Choice Test Items, pp. 185–190
Listening Comprehension Performance Test, pp. 171–172
Reading Performance Test, pp. 177–180
Speaking Performance Test, pp. 173–176
Writing Performance Test, pp. 181–184
Test Scoring Tools, p. 191
Audioscript for Tests, pp. 192–194
Answer Keys, pp. 195–198

AUDIO & VISUAL 

Audio Program
CD 1 Tracks 48, 49
CD 13 Tracks 15–22

TECHNOLOGY

Test Generator CD-ROM/McDougal Littell Assessment System

1 COMPREHENSION

1. Quel temps fait-il? [f]
2. Tu veux un sandwich? [e]
3. Tu veux un jus d'orange? [c]
4. Quelle heure est-il? [b]
5. C'est quand, ton anniversaire? [d]
6. Combien coûte le sandwich? [a]

2 ORAL EXPRESSION

Answers will vary.

1. Il est deux heures.
2. Il est trois heures (quinze/et quart).
3. Il est onze heures (et demie/trente).
4. Il est midi.
5. Il est quatre heures quarante-cinq (cinq heures moins le quart).
6. Il est huit heures cinq.

À votre tour!

OBJECTIFS

Now you can...
- order snacks and beverages in a café
- ask about prices and pay for your food/drink
- tell time and give the date
- talk about the weather

1 Écoutez bien!

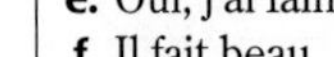

ÉCOUTER Isabelle is in a café talking to Jean-Paul. You will hear Isabelle asking questions. For each of Isabelle's questions, select Jean-Paul's response from the suggested answers.

- **a.** Deux euros cinquante.
- **b.** Quatre heures et demie.
- **c.** Oui, j'ai soif.
- **d.** C'est le 3 novembre.
- **e.** Oui, j'ai faim.
- **f.** Il fait beau.

2 Quelle heure est-il?

PARLER Give the times indicated on the following clocks.

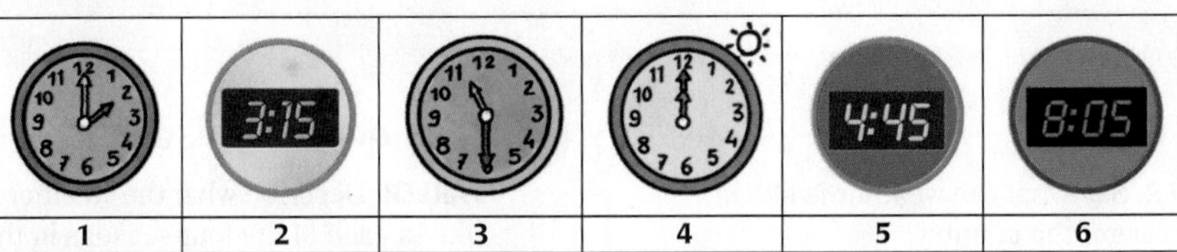

3 Conversation dirigée

ÉCOUTER ET PARLER Stéphanie is in a café called Le Select. The waiter is taking her order. With a partner, compose and act out a dialogue according to the script suggested below.

le garçon		Stéphanie
greets client and asks if he may help her	→ ↙	says that she would like a croissant and asks how much an orange juice costs
answers 2 euros	→ ↙	asks for an orange juice… calls the waiter and asks how much she owes
says 4 euros cinquante	→ ↙	gives waiter 5 euros **(Voici…)**
says thank you		

À VOTRE TOUR

For specific teaching suggestions, see the **Teacher Notes** in Unit 1, page 38.

You will want to select those activities which are most appropriate for your students. Encourage them to work in pairs and in trios (where one acts as monitor).

The first and third activities are on CD.

Act. 1: Play Track 48 of CD 1 so that students can check their answers.
Act. 3: Play Track 49 of CD 1 as a model. Then have students act out their own dialogues.

4 Au café

PARLER You are in a French café. Call the waiter/waitress and order the following items. A classmate will play the part of the waiter/waitress.

▶ —**Monsieur (Mademoiselle), s'il vous plaît!**
—**Vous désirez?**
—**Un croissant, s'il vous plaît!**
(Donnez-moi un croissant, s'il vous plaît!)
(Je voudrais un croissant, s'il vous plaît!)

5 En scène

STRATEGY Speaking

Sounding French If you want French people to understand you, the most important thing is to speak with an even rhythm and to stress the last syllable in each group of words. (Try speaking English this way: people will think you have a French accent!)

PARLER With two other classmates, act out the following scene.

CHARACTERS:
You, a French friend, and the waiter in the café

SITUATION:
A French friend has been showing you around Paris. You invite your friend to a café and discover too late that you have not changed enough money. Your friend will respond to your questions.

- Ask your friend if he/she is thirsty.
- Ask if he/she wants a soft drink.
- Ask if he/she is hungry.
- Ask if he/she wants a sandwich.
- When the waiter comes, your friend orders and you ask for a croissant and a cup of hot chocolate.
- Ask the waiter how much everything is.
- Ask your friend to please lend you 20 euros.

6 La date, la saison et le temps

PARLER Look at the calendar days. For each one, give the day and the date, the season, and the weather.

▶ **C'est mardi, le dix avril.**
C'est le printemps.
Il pleut.

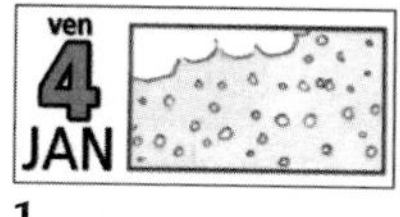

1

2

3

4

5

Portfolio Assessment

For more specific guidelines, see the Teacher Notes in Unit 1, page 39.

The café conversations of the **Challenge** activity on the right could be recorded for the oral portfolio.

Inclusion

Cumulative Students in groups of 3 or 4 prepare original café conversations. One person is the waiter, and the others are teenage customers who are talking to one another. Encourage them to use expressions they learned in Units 1 and 2: greetings, introductions, time, etc.

3 Guided Oral Expression

G: Bonjour, mademoiselle! Vous désirez?
S: (Donnez-moi, Je voudrais) un croissant, s'il vous plaît. Combien coûte un jus d'orange?
G: (Un jus d'orange coûte) 2 euros.
S: (Donnez-moi, Je voudrais) un jus d'orange, s'il vous plaît! . . . Monsieur, s'il vous plaît! Ça fait combien?
G: (Ça fait) 4 euros 50.
S: Voici 5 euros.
G: Merci, mademoiselle.

4 Guided Oral Expression

– Monsieur (Mademoiselle), s'il vous plaît!
– Vous désirez?
– (Je voudrais/Donnez-moi) ..., s'il vous plaît!
1. une glace
2. une pizza
3. un chocolat
4. un jus de raisin
5. un steak-frites

Challenge You are leaving the café and want to know what you owe. Your classmate will invent a reasonable price.

Pre-AP skill: Expand, elaborate.

– Monsieur/Mademoiselle, s'il vous plaît! Ça fait combien?
– Ça fait huit euros cinquante.

5 Guided Oral Expression

Answers will vary.
1: Tu as soif, (Paul / Nicole)?
2: Oui, j'ai soif!
1: Tu veux un soda?
2: Oui, je voudrais un soda, s'il te plaît.
1: Tu as faim?
2: Oui, j'ai faim!
1: Tu veux un sandwich?
2: Oui, je voudrais un sandwich au jambon. (The waiter [waitress] comes.)
2: Donnez-moi un soda et un sandwich au jambon, s'il vous plaît!
1: Je voudrais un croissant et un chocolat . . . Ça fait combien?
3: Ça fait 20 euros.
1: Prête-moi 20 euros, s'il te plaît!
2: Voila.
1: Merci, (Paul / Nicole).

6 Guided Oral Expression

1. C'est vendredi, le quatre janvier. C'est l'hiver. Il neige.
2. C'est jeudi, le cinq juillet. C'est l'été. Il fait chaud.
3. C'est mercredi, le vingt-six septembre. C'est l'automne. Il fait mauvais (froid, frais).
4. C'est samedi, le dix-neuf mai. C'est le printemps. Il fait beau (bon).
5. C'est lundi, le premier octobre. C'est l'automne. Il fait frais.

ENTRACTE 2

Objectives
- Development of cross-cultural awareness
- Vocabulary expansion

Teaching Resource Options

PRINT

Workbook PE, pp. 55–58
Activités pour tous PE, pp. 29–31
Unit 2 Resource Book
Activités pour tous TE, pp. 157–159
Workbook TE, pp. 161–164

Les parties du corps

Objective
- Learning parts of the body

Game Vrai ou faux? When the teacher mentions a part of the body and points to it correctly, students respond by saying **vrai**. When the teacher points to the wrong part, students respond by saying **faux.** E.g.,
Voici ma jambe. (point to leg) **vrai**
Voici mon pied. (point to arm) **faux**

Jacques a dit
Expansion
Les mains sur les épaules *(shoulders)*.
Les mains sur la taille *(waist)*.
Les mains sur les genoux *(knees)*.

Une chanson: Alouette

Objectives
- Introducing a popular French-Canadian folksong
- Introducing parts of the body

Cultural note
- **In Canada,** the lark was formerly hunted as a game bird. In this song, the cook is plucking the bird's feathers before preparing to roast it.
- **English equivalent**
Lark, sweet lark, I will pluck you
I will pluck your head ..., your beak ..., your neck ..., your wings ..., your back ..., your legs ..., your tail ...

Les parties du corps

(Parts of the body)

la tête
les cheveux
l'oeil (les yeux)
l'oreille
le nez
la bouche
le cou
la main
le bras
le ventre
le dos
la jambe
le pied

Un jeu: Jacques a dit

The French sometimes play a game called **Jacques a dit** *(Jim said)*. The rules are the same as the English game of *Simon Says.* Everyone stands up to play.

The game leader says: **Jacques a dit: Les mains sur la tête!** placing her hands on her head. The other players also place their hands on their heads.

Then the game leader may say: **Les mains sur le dos!** placing her hands on her back. This time, however, the other players should not move, because the game leader did not first say **Jacques a dit**. Any player that did move must sit down, but may continue playing.

The game continues until only one player is left standing.

COMPREHENSION Parts of the body

PROP: Halloween skeleton
Introduce the class to the skeleton, to whom you have given a name.
Qui est-ce? C'est mon ami Victor.

Shake hands with the skeleton.
Je donne la main à Victor.

Call on individual students to come up.
X, viens ici et donne la main à Victor.
Touche-lui l'épaule.
Montre-nous sa bouche. ...

Optional: Have students contort Victor.
Y, viens et mets-lui le pied sur la tête.
Mets-lui la main gauche sur le cou.

Une chanson: Alouette

ALOUETTE *(The Lark)* is a popular folk song of French-Canadian origin. As the song leader names the various parts of the bird's anatomy, he points to his own body. The chorus repeats the refrain with enthusiasm.

Alouette
G D7 G
A - lou - et - te, gen - tille a - lou - et - te,
D7 G
a - lou - et - te, je te plu - me - rai.
G D7 G
Je te plu - me - rai la tête, je te plu - me - rai la tête.
D7
Et la tête, et la tête, a - lou - ett', a - lou - ett', oh!

1. *Alouette, gentille alouette,*
   Alouette, je te plumerai.

   Je te plumerai la tête,
   Je te plumerai la tête.

   Et la tête—et la tête
   Alouette—Alouette
   Oh oh oh oh

2. *Alouette, gentille alouette*
   Alouette, je te plumerai.

   Je te plumerai le bec,
   Je te plumerai le bec.

   Et le bec—et le bec
   Et la tête—et la tête
   Alouette—Alouette
   Oh oh oh oh

3. *Je te plumerai le cou ...*
4. *Je te plumerai les ailes ...*
5. *Je te plumerai le dos ...*
6. *Je te plumerai les pattes ...*
7. *Je te plumerai la queue ...*

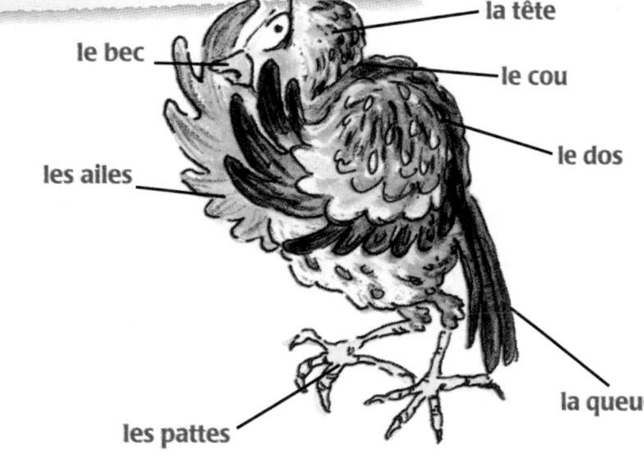
la tête
le bec
le cou
le dos
les ailes
la queue
les pattes

COMMUNAUTÉS: French song

As a class project, you might want to memorize *Alouette* and perform it at a senior center or teach the song to a local grade school class.

CLASSROOM MANAGEMENT

Pre-reading activity

Ask how many students know the song "Alouette."
- What country is the song from? [Canada]
- What kind of bird is an **alouette?** [lark]
- What is the song all about? [telling a lark what parts of its body the singer is going to pluck]

Post-reading activity

Ask students if they know other French songs. Perhaps they can sing "Frère Jacques."
Frère Jacques / Dormez-vous? / Sonnez les matines. / Din din don. /
(Are you sleeping / Brother John? / Morning bells are ringing / Ding dang dong)

...g

...ions p. 59
...50, 51, 55
... pp. 57, 59, 63
... formation
pp. ...

CONTEXT
- Converse in face-to-face social interactions pp. 47, 51, 54, 55, 59, 61, 63
- Listen during social interactions p. 63
- Listen to audio and video texts pp. 44, 47, 48, 51, 52, 55, 56, 60, 64
- Use authentic materials when reading
  - –menus pp. 54, 55
  - –posters p. 63
  - –schedules p. 59

TEXT TYPE
- Use short sentences when speaking p. 55
- Use learned words and phrases when speaking pp. 46, 54
- Use simple questions when speaking pp. 47, 55, 57
- Use commands when speaking p. 50
- Understand some ideas and familiar details presented in clear, uncomplicated speech when listening p. 57

CONTENT
- Understand and convey information about
  - –schedules p. 59
  - –prices pp. 54, 55
  - –weather and seasons p. 65
  - –days p. 61
  - –dates p, 63
  - –months p. 63
  - –time p. 57, 58
  - –food and customs pp. 46, 47, 50, 51

ASSESSMENT
- Communicate effectively with some hesitation and errors, which do not hinder comprehension p. 66
- Demonstrate culturally acceptable behavior for
  - –engaging in conversations p. 67
  - –making requests pp. 66, 67
  - –providing information pp. 66, 67

UNITÉ 3 Expansion activities PLANNING AHEAD

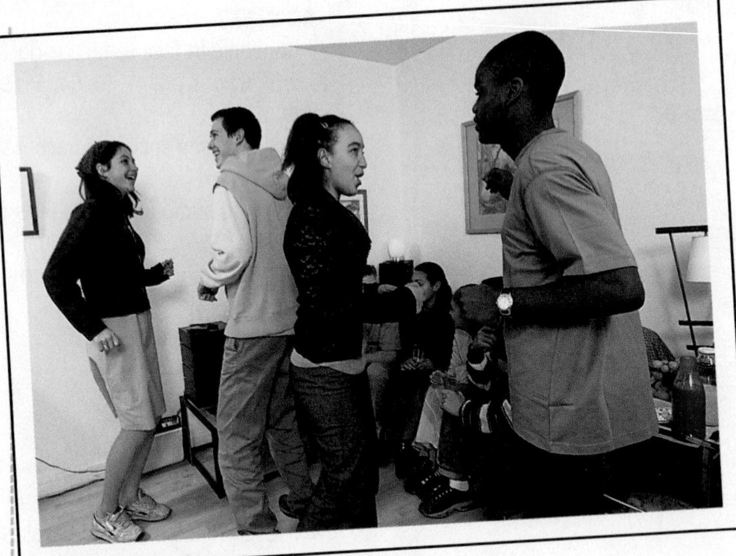

Games

• Charades

Divide the class into two or three teams. Choose one of the vocabulary words from pages 74–75, and tell one member from each team the word for that round. These team members alternate acting out clues until one team guesses the correct word. The first team to guess the word gets a point and starts the next round with a new member from each team as performer. Set a 1-minute time limit for each round. The team with the most points is the winner.

Pacing Suggestion: Upon completion of Leçon 5.

• Mais non!

First, have each student draw a quick illustration of a person in one of the places taught in **Vocabulaire** on page 85. Ask students to write a true or false caption for their illustration. For example, if a student draws a boy near the Eiffel Tower, the caption might read either **Jean est à Paris** (true), or **Jean est à la maison** (false). Then divide the class into two teams. Have a student from one team show his or her illustration to the class and read the caption aloud. The first student to raise his or her hand gets the opportunity to respond **«Oui, c'est vrai»** or **«Mais non!»** If they respond **«Mais non!»** they must correct the sentence using **ne . . . pas** and name the place the illustration really portrays to earn a point. Have teams alternate presenting their drawings.

Pacing Suggestion: Upon completion of Leçon 6.

Projects

• Invitation à une boum

Have students create a party invitation. The invitations should tell when and where the party will be and who is throwing the party. Using vocabulary they have learned, students may wish to list the refreshments that will be served. The invitations should be decorated with markers, stickers, glitter, beads, etc. As a variation, you may want to have students create invitations online.

Pacing Suggestion: Upon completion of Leçon 7.

• Le Sénégal

Divide the class into small groups. Have each group find information about Senegal. Groups may:

- create a map that shows where Senegal is located
- find information about activities that are common among young people in Senegal
- find or create illustrations that show what Senegal looks like
- find information about the weather, people, politics, industry, etc., of Senegal

Each group should create a colorful booklet or pamphlet they can use to present the information they obtained to the rest of the class. Students can create these by hand or on the computer.

Pacing Suggestion: Upon completion of Leçon 8.

Bulletin Boards

• La musique francophone

Have students search the Internet to find out what singers, musical groups, and songs are currently popular in France or in francophone countries. (You could assign a different country to pairs or groups of students and suggest specific Web sites for their search.) Ask students to find photos of some of these artists and create a bulletin board about francophone music. You can expand the activity by having students draw comparisons between their findings and some of their favorite popular music groups and performers in the United States.

Pacing Suggestion: Upon completion of Leçon 5.

Storytelling

• Une mini-histoire

Model a brief conversation in which you call a friend. Invite your friend to do something you both enjoy, acting out the conversation with stuffed animals or puppets. Pass out copies of your conversation and say it aloud with pauses, allowing students to repeat after you, or fill in the words. Then have them work in pairs to expand on their versions. Ask students to write out their conversations, practice them for intonation, and perform them for the class.

Pacing Suggestion: Upon completion of Leçon 6.

• Écrire un poème

Explain to students that French is rich in rhyme. (You can point out, for example, that the infinitive form of all verbs ending in *-er* rhyme.) Have students brainstorm some rhyming words they have learned in French. Then have them use their lists of words to create a short poem. You may wish to ask for volunteers to share their poems with the class.

Model: Je n'aime pas nager, je préfère danser.
Mais je veux bien parler français.
Maintenant je ne peux pas nager,
Je ne peux pas danser.
Je dois étudier le français!

Pacing Suggestion: Upon completion of Leçon 7.

Recipe

• Fondue au chocolat

Fondue, which originated in Switzerland, is a typical French party food. Fondue can be made of melted cheese, chocolate, caramel, etc. You may wish to tell students that fondue is traditionally served in a fondue pot and that guests dip their foods using fondue forks.

Pacing Suggestion: Upon completion of Leçon 7.

Hands-on Crafts

• Le tama

Have pairs of students make a collage inspired by the **tama,** a traditional Senegalese drum, like the one pictured on this page. Suggest that students begin with colored or construction paper as a base. Ask them to bring in twine, rope, and other decorative materials to build up their two-dimensional drum designs into layers. When they have finished, have students set up a display of their drums.

Pacing Suggestion: Upon completion of Leçon 8.

End of Unit

• C'est moi!

Each student will create a poster to tell about his or her activities. First, have students write several sentences with their name, age, and several activities in which they participate. Then ask them to exchange papers with a classmate. Once they have corrected any errors, have students write their sentences on a poster, and use magazine photos or drawings to illustrate each sentence. You may want to have students give oral presentations to the class using their posters. As an alternative, have students act out and videotape their self-portraits.

Rubric A = 13–15 pts. B = 10–12 pts. C = 7–9 pts. D = 4–6 pts. F = < 4 pts.

Criteria	Scale
Vocabulary Use	1 2 3 4 5
Grammar/Spelling Accuracy	1 2 3 4 5
Creativity	1 2 3 4 5

Fondue au chocolat

Ingrédients
- 250 grammes de chocolat ou chocolat au lait
- 40 cl lait concentré sucré
- 10 cl lait
- des morceaux de gâteau et de fruits

Préparation
1. Cassez le chocolat en morceaux et mettez-le dans une casserole.
2. Ajoutez le lait et le lait concentré sucré.
3. Mélangez bien.
4. Ajoutez plus de lait si la fondue devient trop épaisse.
5. Piquez le fruit et le gâteau avec une fourchette et trempez-les dans le chocolat.

Pour huit personnes.

Ingredients
- approx. 8 oz. dark or milk chocolate
- approx. 1 cup sweetened condensed milk
- approx. 1/4 cup milk
- squares of cake and chunks of assorted fruit for dipping

Directions
1. Break the chocolate into pieces and melt it in a Crock-Pot.
2. Add regular milk and condensed milk.
3. Stir well.
4. Add extra milk if the mixture becomes too thick.
5. Use forks or skewers to dip cake or fruit into the chocolate.

Serves eight.

Planning Guide CLASSROOM MANAGEMENT

OBJECTIVES

Communication
- Describe some of your daily activities *pp. 72–73, 95*
- Say what you like and do not like to do *pp. 74–75, 77*
- Ask and answer questions about where others are and what they are doing *pp. 85–86, 89*
- Invite friends to do things with you *p. 78*
- Politely accept or turn down an invitation *p. 78*

Grammar
- Le verbe *être* et les pronoms sujets *pp. 84–85*
- Les questions à réponse affirmative ou négative *pp. 86–87*
- La négation *p. 88*
- Les verbes en *-er:* le singulier *p. 94*
- Les verbes en *-er:* le pluriel *p. 96*
- Le présent des verbes en *-er:* forme affirmative et forme négative *p. 98*
- La construction: verbe + infinitif *p. 101*
- Les questions d'information *p. 106*
- Les expressions interrogatives avec *qui p. 108*
- *Qu'est-ce que? p. 109*
- Le verbe *faire p. 110*
- L'interrogation avec inversion *p. 111*

Vocabulary
- Préférences *pp. 74–75*
- Souhaits *p. 77*
- Invitations *p. 78*
- Où? *p. 85*
- Expressions pour la conversation *pp. 87, 100, 107*
- Mots utiles *pp. 89, 100*
- Les verbes en *-er p. 95*
- Expressions interrogatives *p. 106*
- Expressions avec *faire p. 110*

Pronunciation
- La voyelle /a/ *p. 89*
- Les voyelles /i/ et /u/ *p. 101*
- La voyelle /y/ *p. 111*

Culture
- Le téléphone *p. 79*
- Le mercredi après-midi *p. 83*
- Une boum *p. 93*
- Le Sénégal *p. 105*
- Les jeunes Français et l'Internet *p. 121*
- Les Vietnamiens en France *p. 123*

PROGRAM RESOURCES

Print
- Workbook PE, *pp. 59–84*
- *Activités pour tous* PE, *pp. 33–49*
- Block Scheduling Copymasters, *pp. 33–64*
- *Français pour hispanophones*
- *Lectures pour tous*
- Teacher to Teacher Copymasters
- Teaching Proficiency through Reading and Storytelling
- Unit 3 Resource Book
  - Lessons 5–8 Resources
    - Workbook TE
    - *Activités pour tous* TE
    - Family Letter
    - Absent Student Copymasters
    - Family Involvement
    - Video Activities
    - Videoscripts
    - Audioscripts
    - Assessment Program
  - Unit 3 Resources
    - Communipak
    - *Activités pour tous* TE Reading
    - Workbook TE Reading and Culture Activities
    - Assessment Program
    - Answer Keys

Audiovisual
- Audio Program PE CD 2 Tracks 1–23
- Audio Program Workbook CD 7 Tracks 1–21
- *Chansons* Audio CD
- Sing Along: Grammar and Vocabulary Songs CD
- Video Program Modules 5, 6, 7, 8
- Warm-Up Transparencies
- Overhead Transparencies
  - 15 *Où sont-ils?*;
  - 12 Menu from "Le Select";
  - 16 Subject Pronouns;
  - 14a, 14b, 17 ***-er*** Verbs;
  - 16 Subject Pronouns;
  - 6 Clock face *Quelle heure est-il?*;
  - 8 Expressions with ***faire***

Technology
- Online Workbook
- ClassZone.com
- McDougal Littell Assessment System/Test Generator CD-ROM
- EasyPlanner CD-ROM
- Power Presentations on CD-ROM
- Take-Home Tutor CD-ROM

Assessment Program Options
Lesson Quizzes
Portfolio Assessment
Unit Test Form A
Unit Test Form B
Unit Test Part III (Alternate) Cultural Awareness
Listening Comprehension Performance Test
Speaking Performance Test
Reading Comprehension Performance Test
Writing Performance Test
Multiple Choice Test Items
Test Scoring Tools
Audio Program CD 14 Tracks 1–16
Answer Keys
McDougal Littell Assessment System/ Test Generator CD-ROM

Pacing Guide SAMPLE LESSON PLAN

DAY	DAY	DAY	DAY	DAY
1 Unité 3 Opener Leçon 5 • Vocabulaire et Culture–Mes activités • Vocabulaire–Préférences	**2** Leçon 5 • Vocabulaire–Préférences *(continued)* • Vocabulaire–Souhaits	**3** Leçon 5 • Vocabulaire–Invitations • Note culturelle–Le téléphone	**4** Leçon 5 • À votre tour!	**5** Leçon 6 • Une invitation • Note culturelle–Le mercredi après-midi • Le verbe *être* et les pronoms sujets
6 Leçon 6 • Vocabulaire–Où? • Les questions à réponse affirmative ou négative	**7** Leçon 6 • Vocabulaire–Expressions pour la conversation • La négation	**8** Leçon 6 • La négation *(continued)* • Vocabulaire–Mots utiles • Prononciation–Le voyelle /a/	**9** Leçon 6 • À votre tour!	**10** Leçon 7 • Une boum • Note culturelle–Une boum • Les verbes en *-er:* le singulier • Vocabulaire–Les verbes en *-er*
11 Leçon 7 • Vocabulaire–Les verbes en *-er (continued)* • Les verbes en *-er:* le pluriel	**12** Leçon 7 • Le présent des verbes en *-er:* forme affirmative et forme négative	**13** Leçon 7 • Vocabulaire–Mots utiles • Vocabulaire–Expressions pour la conversation • La construction: verbe + infinitif	**14** Leçon 7 • Prononciation–Les voyelles /i/ et /u/ • À votre tour!	**15** Leçon 8 • Un concert de musique africaine • Note culturelle–Le Sénégal • Les questions d'information
16 Leçon 8 • Vocabulaire–Expressions interrogatives • Vocabulaire–Expressions pour la conversation	**17** Leçon 8 • Les expressions interrogatives avec *qui* • *Qu'est-ce que?*	**18** Leçon 8 • Le verbe *faire* • Vocabulaire–Expressions avec *faire* • L'interrogation avec inversion	**19** Leçon 8 • Prononciation–La voyelle /y/ • À votre tour!	**20** • Tests de contrôle
21 • Unit 3 Test	**22** • Entracte: Lecture et culture			

Student Text Listening Activity Scripts

AUDIO PROGRAM

▶ LEÇON 5 LE FRANÇAIS PRATIQUE Mes activités

• Préférences *p. 74* CD 2, TRACK 1

How to talk about what you like and don't like to do. Écoutez et répétez.

Est-ce que tu aimes . . . ? #	Est-ce que tu aimes parler français? #
J'aime . . . #	Oui, j'aime parler français. #
Je n'aime pas . . . #	Non, je n'aime pas parler français. #
Je préfère . . . #	Je préfère parler anglais. #

Now practice the names of the activities.

téléphoner #	J'aime téléphoner. #
parler français #	J'aime parler français. #
parler anglais #	J'aime parler anglais. #
parler espagnol #	J'aime parler espagnol. #
manger #	J'aime manger. #
chanter #	J'aime chanter. #
danser #	J'aime danser. #
nager #	J'aime nager. #
jouer au tennis #	J'aime aussi jouer au tennis. #
jouer au basket #	J'aime aussi jouer au basket. #
jouer au foot #	J'aime aussi jouer au foot. #
jouer aux jeux vidéo #	J'aime aussi jouer aux jeux vidéo. #
regarder la télé #	Mais je préfère regarder la télé. #
écouter la radio #	Mais je préfère écouter la radio. #
dîner au restaurant #	Mais je préfère dîner au restaurant. #
voyager #	Mais je préfère voyager. #
étudier #	Je n'aime pas toujours étudier. #
travailler #	Je n'aime pas toujours travailler. #

À votre tour!

• Écoutez bien! *p. 80* CD 2, TRACK 2

You will hear French young people telling you what they like to do. Listen carefully to each activity. If it is illustrated in the picture on the left, mark A. If it is illustrated in the picture on the right, mark B.

1. J'aime écouter la radio.
2. J'aime téléphoner.
3. J'aime manger.
4. J'aime jouer au tennis.
5. J'aime nager.
6. J'aime regarder la télé.
7. J'aime étudier.
8. J'aime voyager.
9. J'aime jouer aux jeux vidéo.
10. J'aime jouer au foot.

• Communication *p. 80* CD 2, TRACK 3

Listen to the following conversation.

1. –Est-ce que tu aimes regarder la télé?
   –Oui, j'aime regarder la télé.
2. –Est-ce que tu veux jouer aux jeux vidéo?
   –Oui, je veux jouer aux jeux vidéo. (Non, je ne veux pas jouer aux jeux vidéo.)
3. –Est-ce que tu aimes écouter la radio?
   –Oui, j'aime écouter la radio. (Non, je n'aime pas écouter la radio.)
4. –Est-ce que tu veux manger une pizza?
   –Oui, je veux manger un pizza. (Non, je ne veux pas manger de pizza.)

• Conversation dirigée *p. 80* CD 2, TRACK 4

Écoutez la conversation entre Trinh et Céline.

Trinh: Salut, Céline. Ça va?
Céline: Oui, ça va, merci.
Trinh: Tu veux dîner au restaurant?
Céline: À quelle heure?
Trinh: À huit heures.
Céline: Je regrette, mais je dois étudier.
Trinh: Dommage!

• Créa-dialogue *p. 81* CD 2, TRACK 5

Listen to the sample *Créa-dialogue*. Ecoútez les conversations.

Modèle: –Est-ce que tu veux jouer au tennis avec moi?
–Non, je ne peux pas. Je dois travailler.

Here are some sample dialogs.

1. –Est-ce que tu veux jouer au basket avec moi?
   –Non, je ne peux pas. Je dois téléphoner à une copine. #
2. –Est-ce que tu veux manger une pizza?
   –Non, je ne peux pas. Je dois dîner avec ma cousine. #
3. –Est-ce que tu veux regarder la télé?
   –Non, je ne peux pas. Je dois parler avec ma mère. #
4. –Est-ce que tu veux jouer au ping-pong?
   –Non, je ne peux pas. Je dois étudier. #
5. –Est-ce que tu veux dîner au restaurant?
   –Non, je ne peux pas. Je dois chanter avec la chorale. #
6. –Est-ce que tu veux jouer aux jeux vidéo?
   –Non, je ne peux pas. Je dois étudier. #

▶ LEÇON 6 Une invitation

• Une invitation *p. 82*

A. Compréhension orale CD 2, TRACK 6

Please turn to page 82 for complete *Compréhension orale* text.

B. Écoutez et répétez. CD 2, TRACK 7

You will now hear a paused version of the dialog. Listen to the speaker and repeat right after he or she has completed the sentence.

• Prononciation *p. 89* CD 2, TRACK 8

La voyelle /a/

Écoutez: chat

The letter "**a**" alone always represents the sound /a/ as in the English word *ah.* It never has the sound of "*a*" as in English words like *class, date,* or *cinema.*

Répétez: chat # ça va # à # la # là-bas # avec # ami # voilà #
classe # café # salade # dame # date # Madame # Canada #
Anne est au Canada avec Madame Laval. #

À votre tour!

• Allô! *p. 90* CD 2, TRACK 9

Jacques is phoning some friends. Match his questions on the left with his friends' answers on the right.

1. Où es-tu?	Je suis à la maison.
2. Où est ta soeur?	Elle est en classe.
3. Est-ce que ton frère est à la maison?	Non, il est au cinéma.
4. Tes parents sont en vacances, n'est-ce pas?	Oui! Ils sont à Paris.
5. Ta soeur est avec une copine?	Oui, elles sont au restaurant.

• Créa-dialogue *p. 91* CD 2, TRACK 10

Listen to some sample *Créa-dialogues.* Écoutez les conversations.

Modèle: –Bonjour. Vous êtes anglaise?
–Oui, je suis anglaise.
–Est-ce que vous êtes de Londres?
–Mais non, je ne suis pas de Londres. Je suis de Liverpool.

Maintenant, écoutez le dialogue numéro 1.

–Bonjour. Vous êtes américaine?
–Oui, je suis américaine.
–Est-ce que vous êtes de New York?
–Mais non, je ne suis pas de New York. Je suis de Washington.

pause for oral response

▶ LEÇON 7 Une boum

• Une boum *p. 92*

A. Compréhension orale CD 2, TRACK 11

Please turn to page 92 for complete *Compréhension orale* text.

B. Écoutez et répétez. CD 2, TRACK 12

You will now hear a paused version of the dialog. Listen to the speaker and repeat right after he or she has completed the sentence.

• Écoutez bien! *p. 99* CD 2, TRACK 13

You will hear French young people tell you what they do and do not do. Listen carefully to what they each say and determine if they do the following activities.

Modèle: Je ne joue pas au foot. Je joue au basket. #

Let's begin.

1. Je parle anglais. Je ne parle pas espagnol. #
2. Je n'habite pas à Tours. J'habite à Paris. #
3. Je dîne à la maison. Je ne dîne pas au restaurant. #
4. Je téléphone à un copain. Je ne téléphone pas à une copine. #
5. Je ne mange pas une pizza. Je mange un sandwich. #
6. J'étudie l'espagnol. Je n'étudie pas l'anglais. #
7. Je n'écoute pas la radio. J'écoute un CD. #

• Prononciation *p. 101* CD 2, TRACK 14

Les voyelles /i/ **et** /u/

Écoutez: /u/ **où?** /i/ **ici!**

Be sure to pronounce the French "**i**" as in **Mimi.**

Répétez: /i/ # ici # Philippe # il # Mimi # Sylvie # visite #
Alice visite Paris avec Sylvie. #
/u/ # où # nous # vous # écoute # joue # toujours #
Vous jouez au foot avec nous? #

À votre tour!

• Allô! *p. 102* CD 2, TRACK 15

Sophie is phoning some friends. Match her questions on the left with her friends' answers on the right.

1. Est-ce que Marc est canadien?	Oui, il habite à Montréal.
2. Est-ce que tu joues au tennis?	Oui, mais pas très bien.
3. Ton frère est à la maison?	Non, il dîne au restaurant avec un copain.
4. Ta mère est en vacances?	Non, elle travaille.
5. Tu invites Christine et Juliette à la boum?	Bien sûr! Elles aiment beaucoup danser.

• Créa-dialogue *p. 102* CD 2, TRACK 16

Listen to some sample *Créa-dialogues.* Écoutez les conversations.

Modèle: –Robert, est-ce que tu joues au tennis? –Non, je ne joue pas au tennis.
–Est-ce que tu écoutes la radio? –Oui, j'écoute souvent la radio.

Maintenant, écoutez un autre dialogue.

–Louise, est-ce que tu nages? –Non, je ne nage pas.
–Est-ce que tu chantes? –Oui, je chante un peu.

▶ LEÇON 8 Un concert de musique africaine

• Un concert de musique africaine *p. 104*

A. Compréhension orale CD 2, TRACK 17

Please turn to page 104 for complete *Compréhension orale* text.

B. Écoutez et répétez. CD 2, TRACK 18

You will now hear a paused version of the dialog. Listen to the speaker and repeat right after he or she has completed the sentence.

• Écoutez bien! *p. 107* CD 2, TRACK 19

The questions that you will hear can be logically answered by only one of the following options. Listen carefully to each question and select the logical answer. You will hear each question twice. Let's begin.

1. Où est-ce que tu habites? #
2. À quelle heure est-ce que vous dînez? #
3. Comment est-ce que vous parlez français? #
4. Quand est-ce que vous visitez Dakar? #
5. Où est-ce que ton oncle travaille? #
6. Quand est-ce que ton copain voyage en France? #
7. À quelle heure est-ce que vous regardez la télé? #
8. Comment est-ce que tu chantes? #

• Prononciation *p. 111* CD 2, TRACK 20

La voyelle /y/

Écoutez: Super!

The vowel sound /y/–represented by the letter "**u**"–does not exist in English. To say **super,** first say the French word **si.** Then round your lips as if to whistle and say **si** with rounded lips: /sy/. Now say **si-per.** Then round your lips as you say the first syllable: **super!**

Répétez: /y/ # super # tu # étudie # bien sûr # Lucie # Luc # Tu étudies avec Lucie. #

À votre tour!

• Allô! *p. 112* CD 2, TRACK 21

Fatou is phoning some friends. Match her questions on the left with her friends' answers on the right.

1. Qu'est-ce que tu fais?	J'étudie.
2. Qu'est-ce que vous faites samedi?	Nous faisons un match de tennis.
3. Où est ton père?	Il fait une promenade.
4. Quand est-ce que tu veux jouer au tennis avec moi?	Dimanche. D'accord?
5. Qui est-ce que tu invites au cinéma?	Ma cousine Alice.
6. Pourquoi est-ce que tu étudies l'anglais?	Parce que je voudrais habiter à New York.

• Créa-dialogue *p. 113* CD 2, TRACK 22

Listen to some sample *Créa-dialogues.* Écoutez les conversations.

Modèle: –Qu'est-ce que tu fais lundi? –Je joue au tennis.
–Ah bon? À quelle heure est-ce que tu joues? –À deux heures.
–Et avec qui? –Avec Anne-Marie.

Maintenant, écoutez un autre dialogue.

–Qu'est-ce que tu fais mardi? –J'étudie.
–Ah bon? À quelle heure est-ce que tu étudies? –À six heures.
–Et avec qui? –Avec un copain.

• Écoutez bien! *p. 133* CD 2, TRACK 23

Imagine you are in a school in France. Listen carefully to what different French teachers ask you to do and carry out their instructions. If you have trouble understanding the commands, your teacher will mime the actions for you.

1. Prends ton crayon.
2. Prends ton livre.
3. Ouvre ton livre.
4. Ouvre ton cahier.
5. Montre-moi ton cahier.
6. Montre-moi ton stylo.
7. Montre-moi ton sac.
8. Lève-toi.
9. Va au tableau.
10. Montre-moi un morceau de craie.
11. Va à la porte.
12. Va à la fenêtre.
13. Assieds-toi.
14. Prends une feuille de papier.
15. Écris avec ton crayon.

Très bien!

Complete videoscripts, plus Workbook and Assessment audioscripts, are available in the Unit Resource Books.

Main Theme
- Daily Activities

COMMUNICATION
- Describing daily activities
- Saying what you like and don't like to do
- Asking and answering questions about where others are and what they're doing
- Inviting friends to do things
- Accepting and turning down invitations

CULTURES
- Learning how French teens spend their leisure time
- Learning about what French young people do at parties
- Learning about Senegal and African music
- Learning how the French use the Internet
- Learning about the Vietnamese in France

CONNECTIONS
- Connecting to English: Learning grammar terms
- Connecting to Math: Understanding the 24-hour clock
- Connecting to English: Recognizing cognates

COMPARISONS
- Comparing French and American attitudes toward cell phones
- Comparing the school schedule in France and the U.S.
- Comparing parties in France and the U.S.
- Comparing t.v. schedules in France and the U.S.

continued on next page

UNITÉ 3

Qu'est-ce qu'on fait?

THÈME ET OBJECTIFS

Daily activities

In this unit, you will be talking about the things you do every day, such as working and studying, as well as watching TV or playing sports.

You will learn ...
- to describe some of your daily activities
- to say what you like and do not like to do
- to ask and answer questions about where others are and what they are doing

You will also learn ...
- to invite friends to do things with you
- to politely accept or turn down an invitation

UNIT OVERVIEW

- **Communication Goals:** Students will learn to talk about their daily activities and how to extend and respond to invitations.
- **Linguistic Goals:** The primary focus is on the present tense (affirmative, negative) and question formation.
- **Critical Thinking Goals:** Students are introduced to the concept of subject-verb agreement and the importance of verb endings in French.
- **Cultural Goals:** This unit focuses on the daily activities of French young people: school and homework, as well as sports and leisure activities.

STANDARDS *continued*

- Comparing Internet use of teens in France and the U.S.
- Learning about cross-cultural influences in Youssou N'Dour's music

COMMUNITIES

- Using French when making a phone call
- Using French when writing e-mail
- Listening to French-African music for personal enrichment

Teaching Resource Options

PRINT 

Unit 3 Resource Book
Family Letter, p. 14
Français pour hispanophones
Conseils, p. 9
Vocabulaire, pp. 42–43

AUDIO & VISUAL 

Audio Program
Chansons CD

TECHNOLOGY 

EasyPlanner CD-ROM

PACING

Beginning with Unit 3, the lessons are longer and there is a dual emphasis on both oral and written skills.

For specific suggestions on pacing, turn to page 69D.

CROSS-CULTURAL OBSERVATION

This picture was taken in France.

As usual, have students look at the photo and answer the following questions:

- Could this photo have been taken in the United States?
- Why or why not?
- Which elements in the picture seem to be definitely French?

Leçon 5

Main Topics
- Describing daily activities
- Offering and receiving invitations

Teaching Resource Options

PRINT

Workbook PE, pp. 59–63
Activités pour tous PE, pp. 33–35
Block Scheduling Copymasters, pp. 33–40
Unit 3 Resource Book
Activités pour tous TE, pp. 7–9
Audioscript, pp. 28–30
Communipak, pp. 128–143
Lesson Plans, pp. 10–11
Block Scheduling Lesson Plans, pp. 12–13
Absent Student Copymasters, pp. 15–18
Video Activities, pp. 21–24
Videoscript, pp. 25–26
Workbook TE, pp. 1–5

AUDIO & VISUAL

Audio Program
CD 7 Tracks 1-5

TECHNOLOGY

Online Workbook

VIDEO PROGRAM

VIDÉO DVD

MODULE 5
Le français pratique
Mes activités

TOTAL TIME: 5:59 min.
DVD Disk 1
Videotape 2 (COUNTER: 5:50 min.)

5.1 Mini-scenes: Listening
– J'aime téléphoner
(6:44–7:28 min.)

5.2 Mini-scenes: Speaking
– Tu aimes écouter la radio?
(7:29–8:30 min.)

5.3 Mini-scenes: Listening
– Invitations
(8:31–8:52 min.)

5.4 Dialogue: Tennis
(8:53–10:00 min.)

5.5 Vignette culturelle: Le téléphone
(10:01–11:49 min.)

Comprehension practice Play the entire module through as an introduction to the lesson.

LEÇON 5

LE FRANÇAIS PRATIQUE
VIDÉO DVD AUDIO

Mes activités

Accent sur ... Les activités de la semaine

French teenagers spend a great deal of time on their studies since they and their families consider it important to do well in school. They have a longer class day than American students and are given more homework.

However, French teenagers do not study all the time. They also enjoy listening to music, watching TV, and playing computer games. Many participate in various sports activities, but to a lesser extent than American students. On weekends, they like to go out with their friends to shop or see a movie. They also go to parties and love dancing.

Mélanie est à la maison. Elle écoute un CD.
Mélanie: J'aime le rock anglais.

Marc, Élodie et David sont au stade. Ils jouent au foot.
Marc: Nous jouons au foot.
Élodie: Nous jouons aussi au basket.
David: Nous aimons les sports.

USING THE VIDEO

Beginning with this lesson, there is more variety in the sequencing of the video modules.

Play the entire module through as an introduction to the cultural themes and new linguistic material of the lesson.

The various parts of the video are closely correlated to specific sections in the lesson. Notes in the Teacher's Edition (prefaced with the video logo) indicate points at which you may want to use certain video segments.

Language note French teens use the words **une boum, une soirée** and **une fête** to refer to a party.

Teaching tip You can help students understand the text by reading it aloud and mimicking the activities mentioned. You can also invite them to guess the meanings of the words from the photographs. This page can also be used as a reading activity at the end of the lesson to help recap the vocabulary.

Olivier est en ville. Il téléphone.

Olivier: J'aime téléphoner.
Je téléphone à une copine.

Zaïna joue aux jeux vidéo.

Zaïna: J'aime jouer aux jeux vidéo.
J'aime aussi regarder la télé.

Teaching strategy Le français pratique

Beginning with Unit 3, the first lesson of each unit introduces the communication theme and the related vocabulary. All of these new words and phrases are then re-entered in a variety of situations in the remainder of the unit.

Try to move rather quickly through **Le français pratique** because students will have ample opportunity to master the new material as they do the many activities in the next three lessons.

SECTION A

Communicative function
Expressing likes and dislikes

Teaching Resource Options

PRINT  

Workbook PE, pp. 59–63
Unit 3 Resource Book
Audioscript, p. 27
Communipak, pp. 128–143
Video Activities, pp. 21–22
Videoscript, p. 25
Workbook TE, pp. 1–5

AUDIO & VISUAL 

Audio Program
CD 2 Track 1

Overhead Transparencies
14a, 14b 17 *-er* Verbs

VIDEO PROGRAM

VIDÉO DVD

MODULE 5

5.1 Mini-scenes: J'aime téléphoner (6:44–7:28 min.)

5.2 Mini-scenes: Tu aimes écouter la radio? (7:29–8:30 min.)

Pronunciation practice This audio activity models the new vocabulary in sentence context.

Looking ahead In this lesson, students will become familiar with the meaning of these verbs in the infinitive form. In Lesson 7, they will learn how to use them in the present tense.

Teaching note Have students identify the true and false cognates in the new vocabulary.

A VOCABULAIRE Préférences 

How to talk about what you like and don't like to do:

Est-ce que tu aimes ...?	*Do you like ...?*	**Est-ce que tu aimes** parler *(to speak)* français?
J'aime ...	*I like ...*	Oui, **j'aime** parler français.
Je n'aime pas ...	*I don't like ...*	Non, **je n'aime pas** parler français.
Je préfère ...	*I prefer ...*	**Je préfère** parler anglais.

téléphoner
to phone

parler français
to talk, speak French

parler anglais
to speak English

parler espagnol
to speak Spanish

manger
to eat

chanter
to sing

danser
to dance

nager
to swim

1 Et toi?

PARLER/ÉCRIRE Indicate what you like to do in the following situations by completing each sentence with two of the suggested activities.

1 En classe, j'aime ... mais je préfère ...
étudier • écouter le professeur • parler avec *(with)* **un copain • parler avec une copine**

2. En été, j'aime ... mais je préfère ...
travailler • nager • voyager • jouer au volley *(volleyball)*

COMPREHENSION Everyday activities

PROPS: Transparencies 14a, 14b, 17: *-er* Verbs
Develop a gesture for each verb.

Model the sentences in the verb charts and have the class mimic the action with you.
J'aime téléphoner. [Gesture "dialing"]
J'aime manger. [Gesture "eating"]
J'aime jouer au foot. [Gesture "kicking"]

Say sentences with students acting out verbs. Have students point out the actions on the transparency:
X, montre-nous l'action: J'aime chanter. ,etc.

Have students repeat each sentence with you as they gesture the action. Do the action and have the class say the sentence.

LANGUAGE COMPARISONS

1. In French, as in English, people often shorten words. For example, the words **basketball**, **football**, and **télévision** are often shortened to **basket**, **foot**, and **télé**.
2. In French, **foot** (or **football**) refers to *soccer*.

3. Avec mes *(my)* copains, j'aime ... mais je préfère ...
   chanter • manger • écouter la radio • jouer au basket
4. Avec ma famille, j'aime ... mais je préfère ...
   voyager • regarder la télé • jouer aux jeux vidéo • dîner au restaurant
5. À la maison *(At home)*, j'aime ... mais je préfère ...
   étudier • téléphoner • manger • écouter mes CD

1 COMMUNICATION indicating preferences

Answers will vary.

1. En classe, j'aime (écouter le professeur), mais je préfère (parler avec un copain).
2. En été, j'aime (nager), mais je préfère (jouer au volley).
3. Avec mes copains, j'aime (écouter la radio), mais je préfère (jouer au basket).
4. Avec ma famille, j'aime (dîner au restaurant), mais je préfère (voyager).
5. À la maison, j'aime (étudier), mais je préfère (écouter mes CD).

Oral introduction

- Model the options in each question for listening comprehension, asking for a show of hands.
  En classe, qui aime étudier?
  Qui aime écouter le professeur?
  Qui préfère parler avec un copain?
  Qui préfère parler avec une copine?
- Ask individual students who have raised their hands to respond orally:
  X, en classe, est-ce que tu aimes étudier?
  X: Oui, j'aime étudier.

CLASSROOM MANAGEMENT Group Practice

As a preparation for group work, first introduce Activity 1 orally. (See side note.)

Then divide the class into groups, each with a recorder **(un/une secrétaire).**

Individual group members take turns indicating their preferences (Act. 1).

En classe, je préfère étudier.

The **secrétaire** tallies the group's responses.

#1. La majorité préfère étudier.
(La majorité préfère écouter le professeur.)

The results can be reported back to the class, or handed in to the teacher.

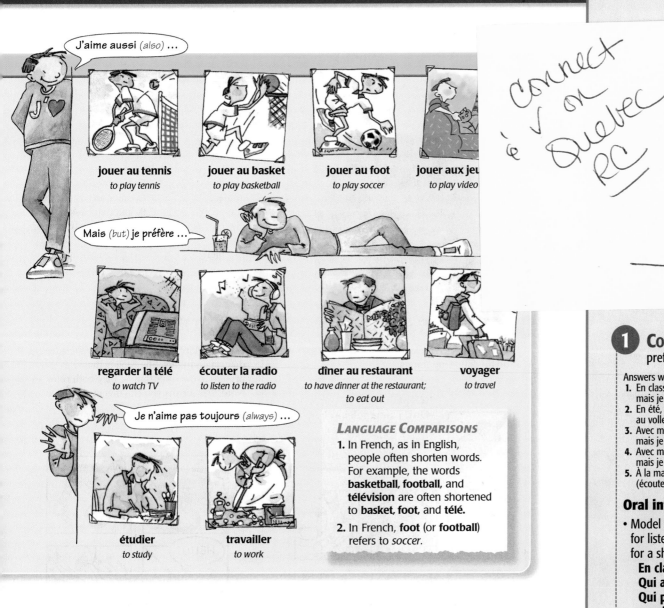

Teaching Resource Options

PRINT

Workbook PE, pp. 59–63
Unit 3 Resource Book
Communipak, pp. 128–143
Workbook TE, pp. 1–5

2 COMMUNICATION expressing likes and dislikes

Answers will vary.
1. J'aime manger. (Je n'aime pas manger.)
2. J'aime étudier. (Je n'aime pas étudier.)
3. J'aime danser. (Je n'aime pas danser.)
4. J'aime téléphoner. (Je n'aime pas téléphoner.)
5. J'aime voyager. (Je n'aime pas voyager.)
6. J'aime travailler. (Je n'aime pas travailler.)
7. J'aime regarder la télé. (Je n'aime pas regarder la télé.)
8. J'aime dîner au restaurant. (Je n'aime pas dîner au restaurant.)
9. J'aime jouer au basket. (Je n'aime pas jouer au basket.)
10. J'aime jouer aux jeux vidéo. (Je n'aime pas jouer aux jeux vidéo.)
11. J'aime écouter la radio. (Je n'aime pas écouter la radio.)
12. J'aime parler français. (Je n'aime pas parler français.)

3 EXCHANGES asking friends what they like to do

–Est-ce que tu aimes ...?
–Oui, j'aime ... (Non, je n'aime pas ...)

1. jouer au tennis
2. écouter la radio
3. jouer au foot
4. voyager
5. étudier
6. nager
7. chanter
8. dîner au restaurant
9. travailler

4 ROLE PLAY discussing preferred activities

Mark: Est-ce que tu aimes ...?
Léa: Oui, mais je préfère ...

1. jouer au basket/jouer au foot
2. parler anglais/parler espagnol
3. chanter/danser
4. écouter la radio/regarder la télé
5. étudier/(voyager, téléphoner)

Variation Have "Léa" ask the question using the activity in the bottom row. Philippe answers, using the activity in the top row.

L: Est-ce que tu aimes jouer au tennis?
M: Oui, mais je préfère nager.

2 *Tu aimes ou tu n'aimes pas?*

PARLER/ÉCRIRE Say whether or not you like to do the following things.

▶ chanter?

1. manger?
2. étudier?
3. danser?
4. téléphoner?
5. voyager?
6. travailler?
7. regarder la télé?
8. dîner au restaurant?
9. jouer au basket?
10. jouer aux jeux vidéo?
11. écouter la radio?
12. parler français?

3  *Préférences*

PARLER Ask your classmates if they like to do the following things.

▶ —**Est-ce que tu aimes téléphoner?**
—**Oui, j'aime téléphoner. (Non, je n'aime pas téléphoner.)**

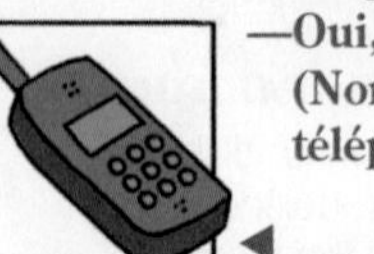

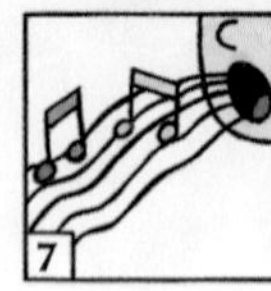

4 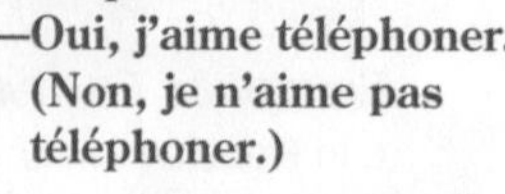 *Dialogue*

PARLER Marc is asking Léa if she likes to do certain things. She replies that she prefers to do other things. Play both roles. Note: "??" means you can invent an answer.

▶ MARC: **Est-ce que tu aimes nager?**
LÉA: **Oui, mais je préfère jouer au tennis.**

TEACHING NOTE Writing activities

Beginning with Unit 3, students will be developing both their writing and speaking skills. Activities which lend themselves to written (as well as oral) practice will be signaled in the Pupil Edition with the skill indicator **PARLER/ÉCRIRE**.

The Student Workbook provides a wide variety of additional writing activities.

B VOCABULAIRE Souhaits *(Wishes)*

Je voudrais voyager en France.

▶ *How to talk about what you want, would like, and do not want to do:*

Je veux ...	*I want ...*	**Je veux** parler français.
Je voudrais ...	*I would like ...*	**Je voudrais** voyager en France.
Je ne veux pas ...	*I don't want ...*	**Je ne veux pas** étudier aujourd'hui.

5 Ce soir *(Tonight)*

PARLER/ÉCRIRE Say whether or not you want to do the following things tonight.

▶ étudier?
Oui, je veux étudier.
(Non, je ne veux pas étudier.)

1. parler français?
2. travailler?
3. jouer aux jeux vidéo?
4. chanter?
5. danser?
6. regarder la télé?
7. écouter la radio?
8. dîner avec une copine?
9. manger une pizza?
10. téléphoner à mon cousin?

6 Week-end

PARLER/ÉCRIRE Léa and her friends are discussing their weekend plans. What do they say they would like to do?

▶ LÉA: **Je voudrais jouer au tennis.**

7 Trois souhaits *(Three wishes)*

ÉCRIRE Read the list of suggested activities and select the three that you would like to do most.

parler français
parler espagnol
parler avec *(with)* Oprah Winfrey
dîner avec le Président
dîner avec Matt Damon
voyager avec ma cousine
voyager en France
chanter comme *(like)* Britney Spears
jouer au tennis comme Venus Williams
jouer au basket comme Shaquille O'Neal

▶ **Je voudrais parler espagnol.**
Je voudrais chanter comme Britney Spears.
Je voudrais voyager en France.

INCLUSION

Synthetic/analytic Explain the pronuncation of the **-er** verb ending. Make a list of words ending in **-er** and have students model the words. Point out the similarity between the endings **-ais** and **-er**. Prepare a word list for students, and have students read the list and save it in their notebooks.

Synthetic/analytic Contrast **"eu"** with **"ou"** {**Je veux**} {**Je voudrais**}. Have students model and practice the sounds, and have them write the examples in their notebooks.

Cumulative Have students say **Je ne veux pas...** three times. Ask them to practice saying and writing all the verbs in **Activité 5** before completing the exercise.

SECTION B

Communicative function
Expressing wishes

5 COMMUNICATION indicating what you want/don't want to do

Oui, je veux ... (Non, je ne veux pas ...)

1. parler français
2. travailler
3. jouer aux jeux vidéo
4. chanter
5. danser
6. regarder la télé
7. écouter la radio
8. dîner avec une copine
9. manger une pizza
10. téléphoner à mon cousin

Language note In French, one must say **téléphoner à,** *to phone "to" someone.*

6 DESCRIPTION indicating what people would like to do

1. Jérôme: Je voudrais nager.
2. Monique: Je voudrais dîner au restaurant.
3. Jean-Louis: Je voudrais danser.
4. Caroline: Je voudrais jouer au basket.
5. Patrick: Je voudrais écouter la radio.

Challenge Add **Et toi?** The next student replies with an alternative activity.
Léa: **Je voudrais jouer au tennis. Et toi?**
Élève A: **Je voudrais jouer au foot (chanter, etc.).**

7 COMMUNICATION indicating what you would like to do

Answers will vary.

- Je voudrais parler français.
  Je voudrais dîner avec le Président.
  Je voudrais jouer au tennis comme Venus Williams.
- Je voudrais dîner avec Matt Damon.
  Je voudrais voyager avec ma cousine.
  Je voudrais parler espagnol.
- Je voudrais parler avec Oprah Winfrey.
  Je voudrais jouer au basket comme Shaquille O'Neal.
  Je voudrais chanter comme Britney Spears.

Variation Have students substitute other names in their responses.
Je voudrais parler avec Chris Rock.

Variation Have the students select the three activities they would like to do least. Then have them compare their responses with a partner.
Je ne voudrais pas voyager avec ma cousine., etc.

SECTION C

Communicative function
Extending invitations

Teaching Resource Options

PRINT

Workbook PE, pp. 59–63
Unit 3 Resource Book
- Communipak, pp. 128–143
- Video Activities, pp. 23–24
- Videoscript, pp. 25–26
- Workbook TE, pp. 1–5

VIDEO PROGRAM

VIDÉO DVD

MODULE 5

5.3 Mini-scenes: Invitations (8:31–8:52 min.)

5.4 Dialogue: Tennis? (8:53–10:00 min.)

5.5 Vignette culturelle: Le téléphone (10:01–11:49 min.)

8 ROLE PLAY extending and accepting invitations

1. –Thomas, est-ce que tu veux parler français avec moi?
   –Oui, d'accord, je veux bien parler français avec toi.
2. –Simon, est-ce que tu veux étudier avec moi?
   –Oui, d'accord, je veux bien étudier avec toi.
3. –Céline, est-ce que tu veux jouer au tennis avec moi?
   –Oui, d'accord, je veux bien jouer au tennis avec toi.
4. –Anne, est-ce que tu veux manger une pizza avec moi?
   –Oui, d'accord, je veux bien manger une pizza avec toi.
5. –Jean-Claude, est-ce que tu veux chanter avec moi?
   –Oui, d'accord, je veux bien chanter avec toi.
6. –Caroline, est-ce que tu veux danser avec moi?
   –Oui, d'accord, je veux bien danser avec toi.

Challenge Students can use other phrases as they accept the invitations: e.g., **D'accord / Oui, merci / Oui, bien sûr.**

C VOCABULAIRE Invitations

Est-ce que tu veux jouer au tennis?

How to invite a friend:

Est-ce que tu veux ...?	*Do you want to ...?*	**Est-ce que tu veux** jouer au tennis?
Est-ce que tu peux ...?	*Can you ...?*	**Est-ce que tu peux** parler à mon copain?
avec moi/toi	*with me/you*	Est-ce que tu veux dîner **avec moi?**

How to accept an invitation:

Oui, bien sûr ...	*Yes, of course ...*	
Oui, merci ...	*Yes, thanks ...*	
Oui, d'accord ...	*Yes, all right, okay ...*	
je veux bien.	*I'd love to.*	**Oui, bien sûr, je veux bien.**
je veux bien ...	*I'd love to ...*	**Oui, merci, je veux bien** dîner avec toi.

How to turn down an invitation:

Je regrette, mais je ne peux pas ...	*I'm sorry, but I can't ...*	**Je regrette, mais je ne peux pas** dîner avec toi.
Je dois ...	*I have to, I must ...*	**Je dois** étudier.

8 Oui, d'accord

PARLER Invite the following French students (played by your classmates) to do things with you. They will accept.

▶ Monique / dîner

Monique, est-ce que tu veux dîner avec moi?

Oui, d'accord, je veux bien dîner avec toi.

1. Thomas / parler français
2. Simon / étudier
3. Céline / jouer au tennis
4. Anne / manger une pizza
5. Jean-Claude / chanter
6. Caroline / danser

9 Conversation

PARLER Ask your classmates if they want to do the following things. They will answer that they cannot and explain why.

▶ jouer au basket? (étudier)
— **Est-ce que tu veux jouer au basket?**
— **Non, je ne peux pas. Je dois étudier.**

1. jouer aux jeux vidéo? (travailler)
2. jouer au ping-pong? (téléphoner à ma cousine)
3. étudier avec moi? (étudier avec ma copine)
4. dîner avec moi? (dîner avec ma famille)
5. nager? (jouer au foot à deux heures)

TEACHING THE VIDEO DIALOGUE

For Lesson 5, the video (part 5.4) contains a series of conversations.

Step 1: Set the scene. Tell students: In this scene Jean-Claude is looking for a tennis partner. **Regardez. (Écoutez.)**

Step 2: Play the video segment.

Step 3: Have students in small groups try to recall the scenes.
Écrivez l'invitation de Jean-Claude et les réponses de ses amis.

Step 4: Play the segment again to let groups check their work.

Step 5: Compare the group answers.

NOTE culturelle

Le téléphone

French teenagers, like their American counterparts, love to talk with their friends on the phone. At home, they can use the family phone, but now more and more young people also have a cell phone which is called **un téléphone portable** or simply **un portable** for short. (**Portable** comes from the French verb **porter**, which means *to carry*.)

Europeans have been ahead of Americans in the use of mobile phones. In France, for instance, almost half of the people own a cell phone. This proportion is higher with teenagers and college students. Cell phones have many advantages. You can call your friends from wherever you are and whenever you want, and if you are going to be late for dinner, you can call and let your parents know. Cell phones, however, can be annoying and even distracting. In France, it is illegal to make cell phone calls while driving a car. Moreover, students are not allowed to bring cell phones to class. It is also considered impolite to use them in restaurants, cinemas, and concert halls.

COMPARAISONS CULTURELLES

Compare the French and American attitudes toward the use of cell phones.

How do you feel about people using cell phones in the following circumstances? Indicate whether you think it is appropriate or not by saying: **C'est acceptable.** or **Ce n'est pas acceptable.**

- au café
- au cinéma
- au restaurant
- pendant *(during)* la classe de français
- pendant un concert de rock
- en conduisant *(while driving)*

L'étiquette téléphonique

- to introduce yourself when phoning a friend, you say:
  Allô … Ici Thomas. Bonjour. Ça va?
- if your friend is not home and if a parent answers, you say:
  Allô … Ici Thomas Rémi. Bonjour, monsieur (madame).
  Est-ce que je pourrais *(May I)* parler à Mélanie?
- if you would like to leave a message, you ask:
  Est-ce que je peux *(Can I)* laisser un message?
- before hanging up, you say:
  Merci, monsieur (madame). Au revoir.

10 Allô!

PARLER Céline is phoning Trinh to ask him if he wants to go to a movie. Trinh's mother says that he is not home. Céline asks her to take a message. Act out the conversation between Céline and Trinh's mother.

INCLUSION

Repetitive Review liaison and the change in pronuncation between **c'est acceptable** vs. **ce n'est pas acceptable**. Have students repeat three times, and write the words/phonetic transcriptions in their notebooks.

Cells -
chat
+ cult

...o?
...g?
...er à
...vec
...ec ma
...foot à

...nted
...re not
considered active vocabulary.

10 ROLE PLAY engaging in a phone conversation

- Allô . . . Ici Céline (Renoir). Bonjour, madame. Est-ce que je pourrais parler à Trinh?
- Trinh n'est pas à la maison. Il est en ville.
- Est-ce que je peux laisser un message?
- Oui, bien sûr.
- Je vais aller au cinéma ce soir, et je veux inviter Trinh.
- D'accord, Céline.
- Merci, madame. Au revoir.

À VOTRE TOUR

Main Topic
- Recapitulation and review

Teaching Resource Options

PRINT 

Workbook PE, pp. 59–63
Unit 3 Resource Book
- Audioscript, pp. 27–28
- Communipak, pp. 128–143
- Family Involvement, pp. 19–20
- Workbook TE, pp. 1–5

Assessment
- Lesson 5 Quiz, pp. 31–32
- Portfolio Assessment, Unit 1 URB pp. 155–164
- Audioscript for Quiz 5, p. 30
- Answer Keys, pp. 216–219

AUDIO & VISUAL 

Audio Program
CD 2 Tracks 2–5
CD 14 Track 1

TECHNOLOGY 

Test Generator CD-ROM/McDougal Littell Assessment System

1 Listening Comprehension

1.	A	**6.**	B
2.	B	**7.**	A
3.	A	**8.**	A
4.	B	**9.**	B
5.	B	**10.**	A

2 Guided Oral Expression

Answers will vary.
- –Est-ce que tu aimes regarder la télé?
  –Oui, j'aime regarder la télé.
- –Est-ce que tu aimes écouter la radio?
  –Oui, j'aime écouter la radio.
- –Est-ce que tu veux jouer aux jeux vidéo?
  –Non, je ne veux pas jouer aux jeux vidéo.
- –Est-ce que tu veux manger une pizza?
  –Non, je ne veux pas manger de pizza.

3 Oral Expression

Trinh: (Salut, Céline.) Ça va?
Céline: Oui, ça va (merci).
Trinh: Tu veux dîner au restaurant?
Céline: À quelle heure?
Trinh: À 8 heures.
Céline: Je regrette, mais je dois étudier.
Trinh: Dommage!

À votre tour!

OBJECTIFS

Now you can ...
- talk about activities you like and do not like
- extend and accept invitations
- give an excuse when you cannot accept

1 *Écoutez bien!*

ÉCOUTER You will hear French young people telling you what they like to do. Listen carefully to each activity. If it is illustrated in the picture on the left, mark A. If it is illustrated in the picture on the right, mark B.

A

B

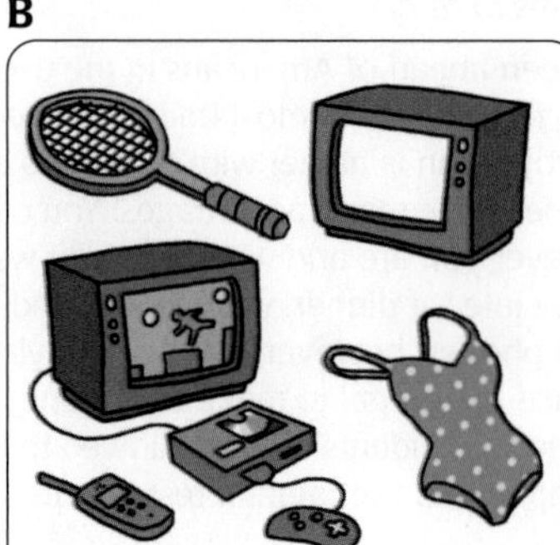

	A	B
1.		
2.		
3.		
4.		
5.		
6.		

2 *Communication*

ÉCOUTER You have invited a French friend to spend the weekend at your house. Ask your friend ...

- if he/she likes to watch TV
- if he/she wants to play video games
- if he/she likes to listen to the radio
- if he/she wants to eat a pizza

A classmate will play the role of your French friend and answer your questions.

3 *Conversation dirigée*

PARLER Trinh is phoning Céline. Write out their conversation according to the directions. You may want to act out the dialogue with a classmate.

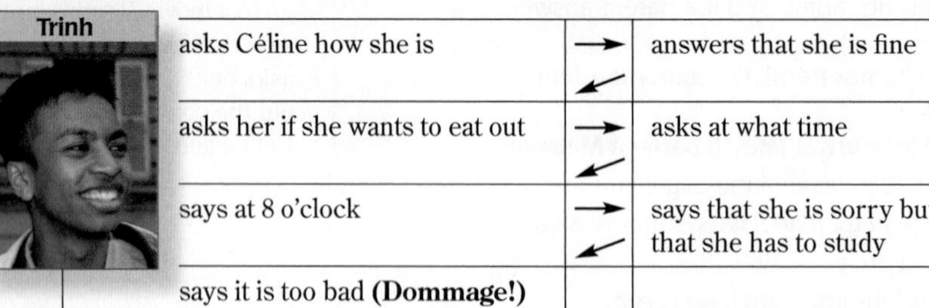

Trinh		Céline
asks Céline how she is	→ ←	answers that she is fine
asks her if she wants to eat out	→ ←	asks at what time
says at 8 o'clock	→ ←	says that she is sorry but that she has to study
says it is too bad **(Dommage!)**		

À votre tour

Beginning with this lesson, the **À votre tour!** sections have both oral and written communication activities. Depending on your goals and objectives, you may or may not wish to assign all of the activities in the **À votre tour** section.

Inclusion

Structured Have students practice the full conjugation of **aimer** orally, with question/answer format of verb only: **Tu aimes?/Oui, j'aime; elle aime/oui, elle aime; vous aimez/oui, nous aimons;** etc. Have students practice answering in the negative, too.

Cumulative Have students practice the construct of **vouloir + aimer** orally. Have them pose questions in the **tu** form. Have them write an example.

4  Créa-dialogue

Est-ce que tu veux jouer au tennis avec moi?

Non, je ne peux pas. Je dois travailler.

PARLER Ask your classmates if they want to do the following things with you. They will answer that they cannot and will give one of the excuses below.

▶ jouer au tennis

1. jouer au basket
2. manger une pizza
3. regarder la télé
4. jouer au ping-pong
5. dîner au restaurant
6. jouer aux jeux vidéo

EXCUSES: téléphoner à une copine · étudier · travailler · parler avec ma mère · dîner avec ma cousine · chanter avec la chorale (choir)

5 Expression personnelle

PARLER/ÉCRIRE What we like to do often depends on the circumstances. Complete the sentences below saying what you like and don't like to do in the following situations.

▶ En hiver ...
En hiver, j'aime regarder la télé.
J'aime aussi jouer au basket.
Je n'aime pas nager.

1. En été ...
2. En automne ...
3. Le samedi *(On Saturdays)*...
4. Le dimanche ...
5. Le soir *(In the evening)*...
6. En classe ...
7. Avec mes *(my)* amis ...
8. Avec ma famille ...

6  Correspondance

ÉCRIRE This summer you are going to spend two weeks in France. Your e-mail correspondent Vincent has written asking what you like and don't like to do on vacation **(en vacances).** Respond with a short e-mail, answering his questions.

STRATEGY Writing

1. Make a list of activities you like and do not like. Use only vocabulary that you know.

2. Write your e-mail. *Cher Vincent,*
En vacances, j'aime ...

3. Read over your letter to be sure you have used the right verb forms.

Portfolio assessment

Beginning with Unit 3, students may start a Written Portfolio.

You will perhaps want to do only one oral portfolio recording and one written composition per unit. In this lesson, a good written portfolio topic is Act. 6.

Inclusion

Multisensory Have students write complete conjugations of the verbs **pouvoir** and **devoir**. Then have them practice all the forms orally. Next, ask them to students practice **pouvoir** in the negative for all forms.

Cumulative Have students review the seasons. Have them write out seasons with the proper preposition. Have students make a list of activities and sports for each season.

4 Written Self-Expression

Answers will vary.

1. –Est-ce que tu veux jouer au basket avec moi?
   –Non, je ne peux pas. Je dois (téléphoner à une copine).
2. –Est-ce que tu veux manger une pizza avec moi?
   –Non, je ne peux pas. Je dois (dîner avec ma cousine).
3. –Est-ce que tu veux regarder la télé avec moi?
   –Non, je ne peux pas. Je dois (parler avec ma mère).
4. –Est-ce que tu veux jouer au ping-pong avec moi?
   –Non, je ne peux pas. Je dois (étudier).
5. –Est-ce que tu veux dîner au restaurant avec moi?
   –Non, je ne peux pas. Je dois (chanter avec la chorale).
6. –Est-ce que tu veux jouer aux jeux vidéo avec moi?
   –Non, je ne peux pas. Je dois (étudier).

Variation Using the audio, have students match numbers 1–6 with the excuses given by the speakers.

5 Written Self-Expression

Answers will vary.

1. En été, j'aime (nager). J'aime aussi (voyager). Je n'aime pas (travailler).
2. En automne, j'aime (jouer au basket). J'aime aussi (chanter). Je n'aime pas (nager).
3. Le samedi, j'aime (danser). J'aime aussi (téléphoner). Je n'aime pas (travailler).
4. Le dimanche, j'aime (jouer au volley). J'aime aussi chanter. Je n'aime pas (regarder la télé).
5. Le soir, j'aime (écouter la radio). J'aime aussi (téléphoner). Je n'aime pas (étudier).
6. En classe, j'aime (parler français). J'aime aussi (étudier). Je n'aime pas (danser).
7. Avec mes amis, j'aime (aller au restaurant). J'aime aussi (danser). Je n'aime pas (étudier).
8. Avec ma famille, j'aime (aller au restaurant). J'aime aussi voyager. Je n'aime pas (jouer au basket).

6 Written Self-Expression

Answers will vary.

1. | **J'aime** | **Je n'aime pas** |
   |---|---|
   | • voyager | • étudier |
   | • danser | • regarder la télé |
   | • nager | • parler anglais |

2. Cher Vincent,
   En vacances, j'aime voyager, danser, nager, jouer au volley et parler français. Je n'aime pas étudier, regarder la télé, parler anglais et jouer au basket.
   Paul (Carole)

Pre-AP skill: Peer-edit and self-edit.

Group Reading Practice Have students prepare a writing activity for homework. Then, in class, divide students into small groups and let them read one another's compositions.

Leçon 6

Main Topic Finding out where people are

Teaching Resource Options

PRINT 

Workbook PE, pp. 65–68
Activités pour tous PE, pp. 37–39
Block Scheduling Copymasters, pp. 41–48
Unit 3 Resource Book
- *Activités pour tous* TE, pp. 37–38
- Audioscript, pp. 55, 56–57
- Communipak, pp. 128–143
- Lesson Plans, pp. 39–40
- Block Scheduling Lesson Plans, pp. 41–42
- Absent Student Copymasters, pp. 43–46
- Video Activities, pp. 49–52
- Videoscript, pp. 53–54
- Workbook TE, pp. 33–36

AUDIO & VISUAL 

Audio Program
CD 2 Tracks 6, 7
CD 7 Tracks 6–11

TECHNOLOGY 

Online Workbook

VIDEO PROGRAM

VIDÉO DVD

MODULE 6
Une invitation

TOTAL TIME: 4:43 min.
DVD Disk 1
Videotape 2 (COUNTER: 11:59 min.)

6.1 Dialogue: Une invitation (12:37–13:28 min.)

6.2 Mini-scenes: Listening – Je suis en classe (13:29–13:51 min.)

6.3 Mini-scenes: Speaking – Où sont-ils? (13:52–15:05 min.)

6.4 Vignette culturelle: Au café (15:06–16:42 min.)

Comprehension practice Play the entire module through as an introduction to the lesson.

Compréhension

Answers
1. Léa est à la maison.
2. Mathieu est en ville.
3. Julie et Stéphanie sont au restaurant.
4. Antoine et Céline sont au café.

LEÇON 6

Une invitation

VIDÉO DVD AUDIO

It is Wednesday afternoon. Antoine is looking for his friends but cannot find anyone. Finally he sees Céline at the Café Le Bercy and asks her where everyone is.

Antoine:	Où est Léa?	*Where*
Céline:	Elle est à la maison.	*at home*
Antoine:	Et Mathieu? Il est là?	*here*
Céline:	Non, il n'est pas là.	
Antoine:	Où est-il?	
Céline:	Il est en ville avec une copine.	*in town*
Antoine:	Et Julie et Stéphanie? Est-ce qu'elles sont ici?	*here*
Céline:	Non, elles sont au restaurant.	
Antoine:	Alors, qui est là?	*So*
Céline:	Moi, je suis ici.	
Antoine:	C'est vrai, tu es ici! Eh bien, puisque tu es là, je t'invite au cinéma. D'accord?	*true / since* *I'll invite you to the movies.*
Céline:	Super! Antoine, tu es un vrai copain!	*real*

Compréhension

Indicate where the following people are by selecting the appropriate completions.

1. Léa est ...
2. Mathieu est ...
3. Julie et Stéphanie sont ...
4. Antoine et Céline sont ...

en ville
au café
au restaurant
à la maison

SETTING THE STAGE

You may want to introduce the opening text by having students listen to the audio with their books closed. They will hear a conversation between Antoine et Céline. Antoine is looking for **Léa, Mathieu,** and **Julie et Stéphanie.**

Draw three sets of stick figures (a girl, a boy, two girls) and identify them, as above.

Then label line drawings of three places: **en ville, au restaurant, à la maison.**

Tell students they are to listen to the conversation carefully and determine who is where.

NOTE culturelle

Le mercredi après-midi

French middle school students do not usually have classes on Wednesday afternoons. Some young people use this free time to go out with their friends or to catch up on their homework. For other students, Wednesday afternoon is also the time for music and dance lessons as well as sports activities. Many students play soccer with their school team or with their local sports club. Other popular activities include tennis, skateboarding, and in-line skating.

COMPARAISONS CULTURELLES

- How does the school week in France compare to the school week in the United States?
- Do you see any differences in the ways French and American teenagers spend their free time? Explain.
- Do American and French teenagers like the same sports? Explain.

Oral comprehension Read each statement and have students indicate whether it is true **(vrai)** or false **(faux).**

1. Léa est à la maison. (vrai)
2. Mathieu est à la maison. (faux)
3. Julie est au restaurant. (vrai)
4. Stéphanie est au cinéma. (faux)
5. Céline est au café. (vrai)

Note culturelle For more information about the French school system, turn to the photo essay on pp. 124–131, **À l'école en France.**

Cross-cultural observation After showing the video segment, have students in pairs make a list of similarities and differences between the French **café** and similar places where teens go in the United States.

Supplementary Vocabulary

le skate *skateboarding*
un skate(board) *skateboard*
faire du skate *to go skateboarding*
le roller *in-line skating*
des rollers *in-line skates*
faire du roller *to go in-line skating*

INCLUSION

Metacognitive, Gifted & Talented Have students think about what they might do if they had an afternoon with no classes. Have them make a list of activities in English. Have students translate the English list into French and have them use a French dictionary to find activities that they may not yet have learned. Ask students to explain how the activity helped them learn French vocabulary.

Structured Have students interview two friends outside of French class. Have them ask their friends how they like to spend their free time. Have them record their answers in a notebook. Have them translate answers into French, looking up new vocabulary in a French dictionary.

SECTION A

Communicative function
Identifying people and where they are

Teaching Resource Options

PRINT 

Workbook PE, pp. 65–68
Unit 3 Resource Book
- Communipak, pp. 128–143
- Video Activities, pp. 50–51
- Videoscript, p. 53
- Workbook TE, pp. 33–36

AUDIO & VISUAL 

Overhead Transparencies
15 *Où sont-ils?*

TECHNOLOGY 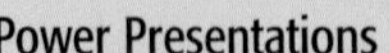

Power Presentations

VIDEO PROGRAM

VIDÉO DVD

MODULE 6

6.2 Mini-scenes: Je suis en classe (13:29–13:51 min.)

6.3 Mini-scenes: Où sont-ils? (13:52–15:05 min.)

Teaching note
Why begin with **être**?

The conjugation of the verb **être** is presented in Leçon 6, ahead of the **–er** verbs for the following reasons:
- **Être** is the most frequently used verb in the French language.
- Students are introduced to the concept of conjugation (in the affirmative, negative and interrogative) with a single verb.

In Leçon 7, students will learn about infinitives, stems and endings.

 **Re-entry and review**

Remind students that they have already been using the singular forms of **être:**

Je suis américain.
Tu es français.
Il est canadien.

Pronunciation note There is usually liaison after **est**: Elle **est**‿ici. Liaison is optional after other forms of **être**: Ils **sont**‿ici. or Ils **sont** ici.

A Le verbe *être* et les pronoms sujets

Être *(to be)* is the most frequently used verb in French. Note the forms of **être** in the chart below.

	être	*to be*	
SINGULAR	je **suis**	*I am*	Je **suis** américain.
	tu **es**	*you are*	Tu **es** canadienne.
	il/elle **est**	*he/she is*	Il **est** anglais.
PLURAL	nous **sommes**	*we are*	Nous **sommes** à Paris.
	vous‿**êtes**	*you are*	Vous‿**êtes** à San Francisco.
	ils/elles **sont**	*they are*	Ils **sont** à Genève.

→ Note the liaison in the **vous** form:

Vous‿êtes français?

→ Note the expression **être d'accord** *(to agree)*:

—Tu **es d'accord** avec moi?	*Do you agree with me?*
—Oui, je **suis d'accord!**	*Yes, I agree!*

TU or VOUS?

When talking to ONE person, the French have two ways of saying *you*:
- **tu** ("familiar *you*") is used to talk to someone your own age (or younger) or to a member of your family
- **vous** ("formal *you*") is used when talking to anyone else

When talking to TWO or more people, the French use **vous.**

 **RAPPEL** You should use ...
- **vous** to address your teacher
- **tu** to address a classmate

LEARNING ABOUT LANGUAGE
- The words **je** *(I)*, **tu** *(you)*, **il** *(he)*, **elle** *(she)*, etc. are called SUBJECT PRONOUNS.
  - SINGULAR pronouns refer to one person (or object).
  - PLURAL pronouns refer to two or more people (or objects).
- The VERB **être** *(to be)* is IRREGULAR because its forms do not follow a predictable pattern.
- A chart showing the subject pronouns and their corresponding verb forms is called a CONJUGATION.

Tu es français?

Vous êtes français?

Vous êtes français?

INCLUSION

Synthetic/analytic Ask students to copy the verb **être** in their notebooks. Next to each verb form, have students add the adjective **américain** and and all appropriate liaisons. They can also add phonetic transcriptions of the verb forms. Have students check their work in pairs and say the words to each other three times each.

ILS or ELLES?

The French have two ways of saying *they*:

- **ils** refers to two or more males or to a mixed group of males and females
- **elles** refers to two or more females

Ils sont à Paris.
Ils sont à Bordeaux.
Ils sont à Lyon.
Elles sont à Nice.

1 En France

PARLER/ÉCRIRE The following students are on vacation in France. Which cities are they in?

▶ Sophie … à Nice. **Sophie est à Nice.**

1. Antoine … à Tours.
2. Nous … à Toulouse.
3. Vous … à Marseille.
4. Je … à Strasbourg.
5. Julie et Marie … à Lille.
6. Éric et Vincent … à Lyon.
7. Ma cousine … à Paris.
8. Tu … à Bordeaux.

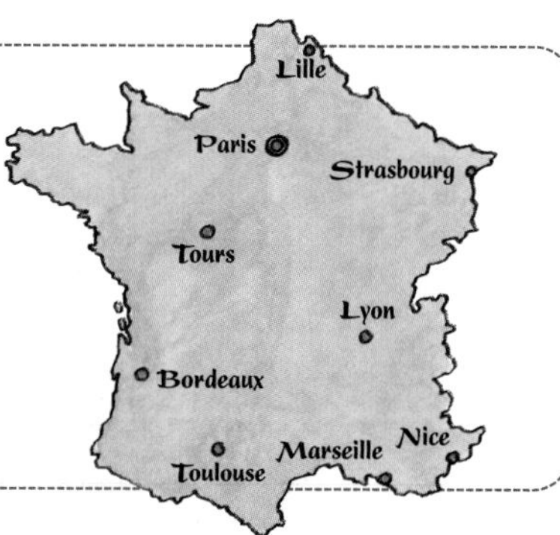
Lille
Paris
Strasbourg
Tours
Lyon
Bordeaux
Nice
Marseille
Toulouse

VOCABULAIRE Où?

Où est Cécile? *Where is Cécile?*

Elle est …

ici *(here)*	**là** *(here, there)*	**là-bas** *(over there)*
à Paris *(in Paris)*	**à** Boston	**à** Québec
en classe *(in class)*	**en ville** *(in town)*	
en vacances *(on vacation)*	**en** France *(in France)*	
au café *(at the café)*	**au restaurant**	**au cinéma** *(at the movies)*
à la maison *(at home)*		

2 À Tours

PARLER/ÉCRIRE You are spending your summer vacation in Tours at the home of your friend Léa. Ask the following people questions using **Tu es** or **Vous êtes** as appropriate.

▶ *(the mailman)* … français? **Vous êtes français?**

1. *(Léa's mother)* … de Tours?
2. *(Léa's best friend)* … française?
3. *(Léa's brother)* … en vacances?
4. *(a lady in the park)* … française?
5. *(Léa's cousin)* … de Paris?
6. *(a little girl)* … avec ta mère?
7. *(Léa's teacher)* … strict?
8. *(a tourist)* … américain?

COMPREHENSION In France

PROPS: signs: Paris, Bordeaux, Lyon, Nice

Place signs dividing class into 4 "cities."

Voici Paris. Voici Bordeaux. etc.

Ask in which city students are.

Où est X? [À Bordeaux.]
Où sont Y et Z? [À Paris.]

Then have students move around.

X, où es-tu? [À Bordeaux.]
Lève-toi et va à Nice.
Où es-tu maintenant? [À Nice.] ...
Y et Z, levez-vous et allez à Lyon.
Où êtes-vous? [À Lyon.] ...

Optional, with full answers:

[Je suis à Nice.]

If students ask The pronouns **il** and **elle** may also mean *it*.

Remind them that in **Invitation au français** they used sentences like:

[le sandwich] Il coûte 5 euros.

Learning aid Always use **vous** with people you address as **Monsieur, Madame,** or **Mademoiselle.**

Teaching tip Use **Transparency 16** (Subject pronouns) as a visual aid to present and practice verb forms throughout this program.

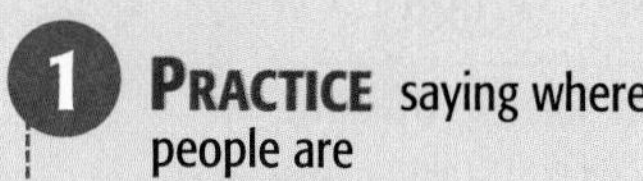

1 PRACTICE saying where people are

1. Antoine est à Tours.
2. Nous sommes à Toulouse.
3. Vous êtes à Marseille.
4. Je suis à Strasbourg.
5. Julie et Marie sont à Lille.
6. Éric et Vincent sont à Lyon.
7. Ma cousine est à Paris.
8. Tu es à Bordeaux.

2 COMPREHENSION using tu and vous

1. Vous êtes de Tours?
2. Tu es française?
3. Tu es en vacances?
4. Vous êtes française?
5. Tu es de Paris?
6. Tu es avec ta mère?
7. Vous êtes strict?
8. Vous êtes américain?

If students ask In French, the word for vacation **(les vacances)** is always plural.

Teaching note
To meet the needs of different learners, **Discovering French, *Nouveau!–Bleu*** presents French structures in several ways:

- Structures in context (in dialogues)– for those who learn best by hearing and repeating.
- Charts and brief explanations–for those who need to understand a pattern before practicing it.
- Cartoon drawings (where appropriate)–for those who find it helpful to visualize a concept in picture form.

Comprehension Variation Use places from the **Vocabulaire** section: en classe, au café, au cinéma, à la maison ...

Teaching Resource Options

PRINT 

Workbook PE, pp. 65–68
Unit 3 Resource Book
Communipak, pp. 128–143
Video Activities, p. 51
Videoscript, p. 53
Workbook TE, pp. 33–36

VIDEO PROGRAM

VIDÉO DVD

MODULE 6

6.3 Mini-scenes: Où sont-ils? (13:52–15:05 min.)

3 PRACTICE saying where people are

1. Oui, elle est à Lyon.
2. Oui, il est à San Francisco.
3. Oui, elles sont à la maison.
4. Oui, elles sont au café.
5. Oui, elle est en ville.
6. Oui, il est en vacances.
7. Oui, ils sont au cinéma.
8. Oui, ils sont à Montréal.

Variation Respond in the negative, naming another location of your choice.
– Ta cousine est à Chicago?
– Non, elle est à Saint Louis (à Boston, etc.).

4 EXCHANGES finding out where people are

– Où est ... ?

1. Daniel/Il est à Paris.
2. Caroline/Elle est au cinéma.
3. Jean-Louis/Il est au café.
4. Robert/Il est en classe (à l'école).
5. Florence/Elle est en vacances.
6. Hélène/Elle est au restaurant.
7. Julien/Il est en ville.

Challenge Have students imagine that they are with the people in Act. 4.
a) Statement: **Je suis avec Céline. Nous sommes à New York.**
b) Dialogue format: First teach the question **Où êtes-vous?**
– Je suis avec Céline.
– Où êtes-vous?
– Nous sommes à New York.

3 Où sont-ils?

PARLER Corinne is wondering if some of the people she knows are in certain places. Tell her she is right, using **il, elle, ils,** or **elles** in your answers.

▶ Ta cousine est à Chicago? **Oui, elle est à Chicago.**

1. Stéphanie est à Lyon?
2. Monsieur Thomas est à San Francisco?
3. Léa et Céline sont à la maison?
4. Cécile et Charlotte sont au café?
5. Ta soeur est en ville?
6. Ton cousin est en vacances?
7. Claire, Alice et Éric sont au cinéma?
8. Monsieur et Madame Joli sont à Montréal?

4 Où?

PARLER You want to know where certain people are. A classmate will answer you.

▶ **—Où est Céline?**
—Elle est à New York.

Céline

1. Daniel

2. Caroline

3. Jean-Louis

4. Robert

5. Florence

6. Hélène

7. Julien

B Les questions à réponse affirmative ou négative

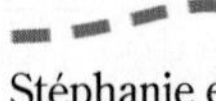

The sentences on the left are statements. The sentences on the right are questions. These questions are called YES/NO QUESTIONS because they can be answered by *yes* or *no*. Note how the French questions begin with **est-ce que.**

STATEMENTS	YES/NO QUESTIONS	
Stéphanie est ici.	**Est-ce que** Stéphanie est ici?	*Is Stéphanie here?*
Tu es français.	**Est-ce que** tu es français?	*Are you French?*
Paul et Marc sont au café.	**Est-ce qu'**ils sont au café?	*Are they at the café?*
Tu veux jouer au foot.	**Est-ce que** tu veux jouer au foot?	*Do you want to play soccer?*

Yes/no questions can be formed according to the pattern:

est-ce que + STATEMENT?	**Est-ce que** Pierre est ici?
est-ce qu' (+ VOWEL SOUND)	**Est-ce qu'**il est en ville?

TEACHING NOTE Elision

The dropping of the final letter (usually "e") of a one-syllable word, as in **que → qu'**, is called ELISION.

Students have seen examples of elision already with **le, la → l'**. In this lesson they will also encounter **ne → n'** and **de → d'**. The term "elision" is not used in the student text. Note, however, that words which have an elision form will be pointed out in the appropriate grammar sections.

INCLUSION

Synthetic/analytic Model the pronunciation **est-ce que** and have students repeat three times. Ask students to write the expression and its phonetic transcription in their notebooks.

Repetitive Model elision by saying **est-ce qu'il / est-ce qu'elle** aloud. Ask students to repeat each expression three times. Students will then draw liaisons in their notebooks.

→ In yes/no questions, the voice goes up at the end of the sentence.

Est-ce que Paul et Florence sont au café?

→ In casual conversation, yes/no questions can be formed without **est-ce que** simply by letting your voice rise at the end of the sentence.

Tu es français? Cécile est en ville?

Observation When you expect someone to agree with you, another way to form a yes/no question is to add the tag **n'est-ce pas** at the end of the sentence.

Tu es américain, **n'est-ce pas?**	*You are American,* ***aren't you?***
Tu aimes parler français, **n'est-ce pas?**	*You like to speak French,* ***don't you?***
Vous êtes d'accord, **n'est-ce pas?**	*You agree,* ***don't you?***

5 Nationalités

PARLER/ÉCRIRE You are attending an international music camp. Ask about other people's nationalities.

▶ Marc/canadien? **Est-ce que Marc est canadien?**

1. Jim / américain?
2. Luisa / mexicaine?
3. Paul et Philippe / français?
4. tu / canadien?
5. vous / anglais?
6. Anne / française?
7. Ellen et Carol / américaines?

VOCABULAIRE Expressions pour la conversation

How to answer a yes/no question:

Oui!	*Yes!*	**Peut-être ...**	*Maybe ...*	**Non!**	*No!*
Mais oui!	*Sure!*			**Mais non!**	*Of course not!*
Bien sûr!	*Of course!*				

6 Conversation

PARLER Ask your classmates the following questions. They will answer, using an expression from **Expressions pour la conversation.**

▶ Ton cousin est français?

1. Ta mère est à la maison?
2. Ta cousine est en France?
3. Ton copain est en classe?
4. Tu veux manger une pizza avec moi?
5. Tu veux jouer aux jeux vidéo avec moi?

Alice, est-ce que ton cousin est français?
Mais oui! (Mais non!)

LANGUAGE COMPARISON

You may want to draw the students' attention to the fact that French uses only one tag question **(n'est-ce pas?)** whereas English has a very complex system of tags. Let students generate the following tags, and then reflect on how difficult it must be to learn tags in English.

you can	can't you?
he works	doesn't he?
she will	won't she?
they won't come	will they?
you understood	didn't you?

SECTION B

Communicative function
Asking questions

Language note Point out that **est-ce que** literally means *is it that?*

Pronunciation As in English, your voice goes up at the end of the tag.

5 PRACTICE asking questions about nationality

1. Est-ce que Jim est américain?
2. Est-ce que Luisa est mexicaine?
3. Est-ce que Paul et Philippe sont français?
4. Est-ce que tu es canadien (canadienne)?
5. Est-ce que vous êtes anglais(e/es)?
6. Est-ce qu'Anne est française?
7. Est-ce qu'Ellen et Carol sont américaines?

Re-entry and review
Nationalities from Unit 1, Leçon 1B.

Challenge Answer each question affirmatively.
– Est-ce que Marc est canadien?
– Oui, il est canadien.

Note Help students differentiate between singular and plural in items 4 and 5:
4. Oui, je suis ...
5. Oui, nous sommes ...

Variation Formulate tag questions with **n'est-ce pas.**
Marc est canadien, n'est-ce pas?

Supplementary vocabulary
Bien sûr que oui! *Why, of course!*
Bien sûr que non! *Why, of course not!*

6 COMMUNICATION asking personal questions

1. – (Diane), est-ce que ta mère est à la maison?
   – Mais oui! (Bien sûr! / Peut-être ... / Mais non!)
2. – (Paul), est-ce que ta cousine est en France?
   – Mais oui! (Bien sûr! / Peut-être ... / Mais non!)
3. – (Anne), est-ce que ton copain est en classe?
   – Mais oui! (Bien sûr! / Peut-être ... / Mais non!)
4. – (Philippe), est-ce que tu veux manger une pizza avec moi?
   – Mais oui! (Bien sûr! / Peut-être ... / Mais non!)
5. – (Marie), est-ce que tu veux jouer aux jeux vidéo avec moi?
   – Mais oui! (Bien sûr! / Peut-être ... / Mais non!)

SECTION C

Communicative function
Expressing negation

Teaching Resource Options

PRINT 

Workbook PE, pp. 65–68
Unit 3 Resource Book
- Audioscript, p. 55
- Communipak, pp. 128–143
- Video Activities, p. 49
- Videoscript, p. 53
- Workbook TE, pp. 33–36

AUDIO & VISUAL 

Audio Program
CD 2 Track 8
Overhead Transparencies
15 *Où sont-ils?*

TECHNOLOGY 

Power Presentations

VIDEO PROGRAM

VIDÉO DVD

MODULE 6

6.1 Dialogue: Une invitation
(12:37–13:28 min.)

Language note **Ne → n'** is another example of elision.

7 DESCRIPTION answering questions in the negative

1. Non, je ne suis pas canadien (canadienne).
2. Non, je ne suis pas à Québec.
3. Non, je ne suis pas à la maison.
4. Non, je ne suis pas au café.
5. Non, je ne suis pas en vacances.
6. Non, je ne suis pas au cinéma.

Expansion Continue your answer with a positive statement.
– Est-ce que tu es français?
– Non, je ne suis pas français(e). Je suis américain(e).

8 PRACTICE saying who does/doesn't agree

1. Nous sommes d'accord.
2. Je suis d'accord.
3. Tu n'es pas d'accord.
4. Vous n'êtes pas d'accord.
5. Patrick et Marc sont d'accord.
6. Claire et Stéphanie ne sont pas d'accord.
7. Ma copine est d'accord.
8. Mon frère n'est pas d'accord.

C La négation

Compare the affirmative and negative sentences below:

AFFIRMATIVE	NEGATIVE	
Je **suis** américain.	Je **ne suis pas** français.	*I'm **not** French.*
Nous **sommes** en classe.	Nous **ne sommes pas** en vacances.	*We **are not** on vacation.*
Claire **est** là-bas.	Elle **n'est pas** ici.	*She **is not** here.*
Tu **es** d'accord avec moi.	Tu **n'es pas** d'accord avec Marc.	*You **do not** agree with Marc.*

Negative sentences are formed as follows:

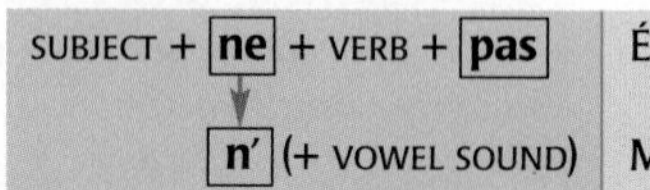

SUBJECT + **ne** + VERB + **pas**	Éric et Anne **ne** sont **pas** là.
n' (+ VOWEL SOUND)	Michèle **n'**est **pas** avec moi.

Nous sommes en ville.
Nous ne sommes pas à la maison.

7 Non!

PARLER Answer the following questions negatively.

▶ **—Est-ce que tu es français (française)?**
—Non, je ne suis pas français (française).

1. Est-ce que tu es canadien (canadienne)?
2. Est-ce que tu es à Québec?
3. Est-ce que tu es à la maison?
4. Est-ce que tu es au café?
5. Est-ce que tu es en vacances?
6. Est-ce que tu es au cinéma?

8 D'accord

PARLER It is raining. François suggests to his friends that they go to the movies. Say who agrees and who does not, using the expression **être d'accord.**

▶ Philippe

Philippe n'est pas d'accord.

▶ Hélène

Hélène est d'accord.

1. ☺ nous
2. ☺ je
3. ☹ tu
4. ☹ vous
5. ☺ Patrick et Marc
6. ☹ Claire et Stéphanie
7. ☺ ma copine
8. ☹ mon frère

SPEAKING PRACTICE

PROP: Transparency 15: *Où sont-ils?* with names written in the boxes below each picture.
Point to the picture of the café.
Qui est-ce? [C'est Sophie.]
Est-ce que Sophie est au café?
[Mais oui, elle est au café.]

Similarly introduce each picture.

Then practice negatives. Point to Sophie.
Qui est-ce? C'est Marc?
[Non, ce n'est pas Marc. C'est Sophie.]
Est-ce que Sophie est en classe?
[Non, elle n'est pas en classe.]
Est-ce que Sophie est à la maison?
[Mais non, elle n'est pas à la maison.]
Où est Sophie? [Elle est au café.]

VOCABULAIRE Mots utiles *(Useful words)*

à	*at*	Je suis **à** la maison **à** dix heures.
	in	Nous sommes **à** Paris.
de	*from*	Vous êtes **de** San Francisco.
	of	Voici une photo **de** Paris.
et	*and*	Anne **et** Sophie sont en vacances.
ou	*or*	Qui est-ce? Juliette **ou** Sophie?
avec	*with*	Philippe est **avec** Pauline.
pour	*for*	Je veux travailler **pour** Monsieur Martin.
mais	*but*	Je ne suis pas français, **mais** j'aime parler français.

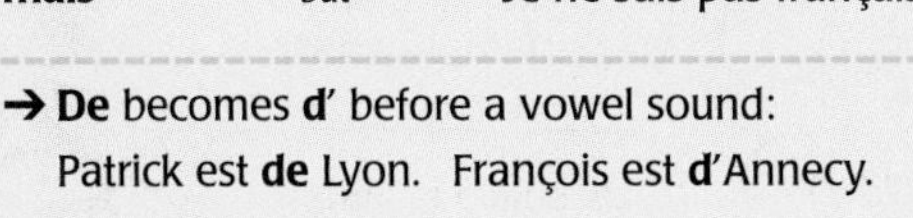

→ **De** becomes **d'** before a vowel sound:
Patrick est **de** Lyon. François est **d'**Annecy.

9 Le mot juste *(The right word)*

PARLER/ÉCRIRE Complete each sentence with the word in parentheses that fits logically.

1. Monsieur Moreau est en France. Aujourd'hui, il est ... Lyon. (à/de)
2. Martine est canadienne. Elle est ... Montréal. (de/et)
3. Florence n'est pas ici. Elle est ... Jean-Claude. (et/avec)
4. Léa ... Paul sont en ville. (avec/et)
5. Jean-Pierre n'est pas à la maison. Il est au café ... au cinéma. (ou/et)
6. J'aime jouer au tennis ... je ne veux pas jouer avec toi. (ou/mais)
7. Je travaille ... mon père. (pour/à)

10 Être ou ne pas être

PARLER/ÉCRIRE We cannot be in different places at the same time. Express this according to the model.

▶ Aline est en ville. (ici)
Aline n'est pas ici.

1. Frédéric est là-bas. (à la maison)
2. Nous sommes en classe. (au restaurant)
3. Tu es à Nice. (à Tours)
4. Vous êtes au café. (au cinéma)
5. Jean est avec Sylvie. (avec Julie)
6. Juliette et Sophie sont avec Éric. (avec Marc)

PRONONCIATION  /a/

La voyelle /a/

The letter "**a**" alone always represents the sound /a/ as in the English word *ah*. It never has the sound of *"a"* as in English words like *class, date,* or *cinema*.

Répétez: **chat ça va à la là-bas avec ami voilà**
classe café salade dame date Madame Canada
Anne est au Canada avec Madame Laval.

chat

Language note You may wish to point out the spelling difference between **ou** *(or)* and **où** *(where)*:
Où est Juliette?
Au café ou au cinéma?

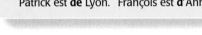

Cultural realia Ask your students:
- What event is taking place in Paris? [the national holiday]
- What is the date of this event? [Tuesday, July 14]
- **Quelle est la date de la Fête Nationale? [le mardi 14 juillet]**
- **À quelle heure est la fête? [À 22h.]**
- Are there any local celebrations of **la Fête Nationale française** (Bastille Day) in their area? If so, encourage them to participate.

9 COMPREHENSION choosing prepositions and conjunctions

1. Monsieur Moreau est en France. Aujourd'hui, il est à Lyon.
2. Martine est canadienne. Elle est de Montréal.
3. Florence n'est pas ici. Elle est avec Jean-Claude.
4. Léa et Paul sont en ville.
5. Jean-Pierre n'est pas à la maison. Il est au café ou au cinéma.
6. J'aime jouer au tennis mais je ne veux pas jouer avec toi.
7. Je travaille pour mon père.

10 DESCRIPTION saying where people are not

1. Frédéric n'est pas à la maison.
2. Nous ne sommes pas au restaurant.
3. Tu n'es pas à Tours.
4. Vous n'êtes pas au cinéma.
5. Jean n'est pas avec Julie.
6. Juliette et Sophie ne sont pas avec Marc.

LISTENING GAME Une invitation

Prepare a cloze version of the video script of **Une invitation** with selected words deleted.

Play the video dialogue.

Divide the class into teams of three and distribute one script to each team.

The teams all try to fill in as many missing words as they can remember.

Replay the video, pausing after each sentence so that the teams can try to complete their texts.

Have teams exchange and correct their scripts. The team with the most correct completions is the winner.

À votre tour

Main Topic
- Recapitulation and review

Teaching Resource Options

PRINT 

Workbook PE, pp. 65–68
Unit 3 Resource Book
  Audioscript, p. 55
  Communipak, pp. 128–143
  Family Involvement, pp. 47–48
  Workbook TE, pp. 33–36
  Assessment
  Lesson 6 Quiz, pp. 59–60
  Portfolio Assessment, Unit 1 URB pp. 155–164
  Audioscript for Quiz 6, p. 58
  Answer Keys, pp. 216–219

AUDIO & VISUAL 

Audio Program
CD 2 Tracks 9, 10
CD 14 Track 2

TECHNOLOGY 

Test Generator CD-ROM/McDougal Littell Assessment System

1 Comprehension

1. Où es-tu?
   (c) Je suis à la maison.
2. Où est ta soeur?
   (d) Elle est en classe.
3. Est-ce que ton frère est à la maison?
   (a) Non, il est au cinéma.
4. Tes parents sont en vacances, n'est-ce pas?
   (e) Oui! Ils sont à Paris.
5. Ta soeur est avec une copine?
   (b) Oui, elles sont au restaurant.

2 Comprehension

1. Nous sommes au cinéma.
2. Les touristes sont en vacances (en ville).
3. Vous êtes au restaurant.
4. Tu es à la maison.
5. Valérie est en classe.

À votre tour!

OBJECTIFS
Now you can ...
- say where people are
- ask and answer simple yes/no questions

1 Allô!

PARLER Jacques is phoning some friends. Match his questions on the left with his friends' answers on the right.

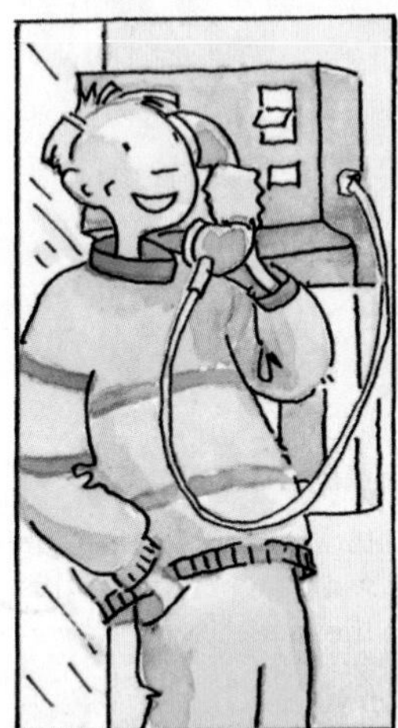

1. Où es-tu?
2. Où est ta soeur?
3. Est-ce que ton frère est à la maison?
4. Tes parents sont en vacances, n'est-ce pas?
5. Ta soeur est avec une copine?

a. Non, il est au cinéma.
b. Oui, elles sont au restaurant.
c. Je suis à la maison.
d. Elle est en classe.
e. Oui! Ils sont à Paris.

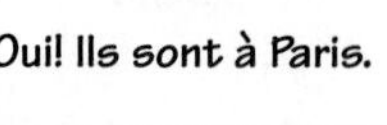

2 Où sont-ils?

LIRE Read what the following people are saying and decide where they are.

▶ Anne et Éric sont au café.

Une limonade, s'il vous plaît.

▶ Anne et Éric

Le film est génial (*great*).

1. nous

Où est le musée (*museum*)?

2. les touristes

Une pizza, s'il vous plaît.

3. vous

Bonjour, maman.

4. tu

Aujourd'hui, c'est le jour de l'examen!

5. Valérie

À votre tour

Depending on your goals and objectives, you may or may not wish to assign all of the activities in the **À votre tour!** section.

Pair and Group Practice

Act. 1 and 3 lend themselves to pair practice.

For Act. 3, you may prefer to have students work in trios, with two performing while the other acts as a monitor.

3 Créa-dialogue

PARLER You are working for a student magazine in France. Your assignment is to interview tourists who are visiting Paris. Ask them where they are from. (Make sure to address the people appropriately as **tu** or **vous**.) Remember: The symbol "??" means you may invent your own responses.

Nationalité	Villes *(Cities)*
▶ anglaise	Londres? *(London)* Liverpool

▶ —Bonjour. Vous êtes anglaise?
—Oui, je suis anglaise.
—Est-ce que vous êtes de Londres?
—Mais non, je ne suis pas de Londres. Je suis de Liverpool.

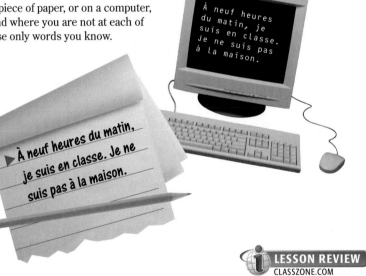

Nationalité	Villes
1 américaine	New York? Washington
2 canadien	Québec? Montréal
3 française	Paris? Nice
4 mexicain	Mexico? Puebla
5 ??	?? ??
6 ??	?? ??

4 Composition: Personnellement

ÉCRIRE On a separate piece of paper, or on a computer, write where you are and where you are not at each of the following times. Use only words you know.

▶ à 9 heures du matin

- à 4 heures
- à 7 heures du soir
- samedi
- dimanche
- en juillet

À neuf heures du matin, je suis en classe. Je ne suis pas à la maison.

▶ À neuf heures du matin, je suis en classe. Je ne suis pas à la maison.

LESSON REVIEW
CLASSZONE.COM

3 Guided Oral Expression

1. – Bonjour. Vous êtes américaine?
   – Oui, je suis américaine.
   – Est-ce que vous êtes de New York?
   – Mais non, je ne suis pas de New York. Je suis de Washington.
2. – Bonjour. (Salut!) Tu es canadien?
   – Oui, je suis canadien.
   – Est-ce que tu es de Québec?
   – Mais non, je ne suis pas de Québec. Je suis de Montréal.
3. – Bonjour. (Salut!) Tu es française?
   – Oui, je suis française.
   – Est-ce que tu es de Paris?
   – Mais non, je ne suis pas de Paris. Je suis de Nice.
4. – Bonjour. Vous êtes mexicain?
   – Oui, je suis mexicain.
   – Est-ce que vous êtes de Mexico?
   – Mais non, je ne suis pas de Mexico. Je suis de Puebla.
5. – Bonjour. (Salut!) Tu es (française)?
   – Oui, je suis (française).
   – Est-ce que tu es de (Bordeaux)?
   – Mais non, je ne suis pas de (Bordeaux). Je suis de (Marseille).
6. – Bonjour. Vous êtes (anglais)?
   – Oui, je suis (anglais).
   – Est-ce que vous êtes de (Manchester)?
   – Mais non, je ne suis pas de (Manchester). Je suis de (Londres).

4 Written Self-Expression

Answers will vary.

- À 4 heures, je suis (au café). Je ne suis pas (au restaurant).
- À 7 heure du soir, je suis (au cinéma). Je ne suis pas (au café).
- Samedi, je suis (à Paris). Je ne suis pas (à Nice).
- Dimanche, je suis (à la maison). Je ne suis pas (en ville).
- En juillet, je suis (en vacances). Je ne suis pas (en classe).

Portfolio Assessment

You will probably select only one speaking activity and one writing activity to go into the students' portfolios for Unit 3.

In this lesson, Act. 3 lends itself well to an oral portfolio recording. Act. 4 is a good writing portfolio topic. (Encourage your students to invent their own responses as in items 5 and 6 in Act. 3.)

Inclusion

Multisensory Model the pronunciation of **À votre tour**. Have students repeat this expression three times and ask them to draw the necessary liaisons. Prepare a list of words with liaisons, and have the students mark where they occur.

Leçon 7

Main Topic Talking about one's activities

Teaching Resource Options

PRINT 

Workbook PE, pp. 69–74
Activités pour tous PE, pp. 39–41
Block Scheduling Copymasters, pp. 49–55
Unit 3 Resource Book
- *Activités pour tous* TE, pp. 67–69
- Audioscript, pp. 87, 88–89
- Communipak, pp. 128–143
- Lesson Plans, pp. 70–71
- Block Scheduling Lesson Plans, pp. 72–73
- Absent Student Copymasters, pp. 74–78
- Video Activities, pp. 81–84
- Videoscript, pp. 85–86
- Workbook TE, pp. 61–66

AUDIO & VISUAL 

Audio Program
CD 2 Tracks 11, 12
CD 7 Tracks 12–17

TECHNOLOGY 

Online Workbook

VIDEO PROGRAM

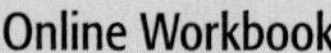

VIDÉO DVD

MODULE 7
Une boum

TOTAL TIME: 4:38 min.
DVD Disk 1
Videotape 2 (COUNTER: 16:53 min.)

7.1 Mini-scenes: Listening
– J'étudie (17:15–18:06 min.)

7.2 Mini-scenes: Listening
– Tu téléphones? (18:07–18:41 min.)

7.3 Mini-scenes: Speaking
– Est-ce qu'il travaille? (18:42–19:45 min.)

7.4 Dialogue: Jean-Paul à la boum
(19:46–20:38 min.)

7.5 Vignette culturelle: Une boum
(20:39–21:31 min.)

Compréhension: Vrai ou faux? Answers
1. C'est vrai!
2. C'est vrai!
3. C'est faux! (Elle ne danse pas très bien.)
4. C'est faux! (Il ne sait pas danser.)
5. C'est vrai!
6. C'est vrai!

LEÇON 7

Une boum

AUDIO

Jean-Marc has been invited to a party. He is trying to decide whether to bring Béatrice or Valérie.

Jean-Marc:	Dis, Béatrice, tu aimes danser?	*Hey*
Béatrice:	Oui, j'adore danser. Je danse très, très bien.	*very well*
Jean-Marc:	Et toi, Valérie, tu danses bien?	
Valérie:	Non, je ne danse pas très bien.	
Jean-Marc:	Est-ce que tu veux aller à une boum avec moi samedi?	*to go*
Valérie:	Oui, d'accord, mais pourquoi est-ce que tu n'invites pas Béatrice? Elle adore danser …	*why*
Jean-Marc:	Oui, mais moi, je ne sais pas danser et je ne veux pas être ridicule …	*don't know how* / *ridiculous*
Béatrice:	Écoute. Entre copains, on n'est jamais ridicule.	*Among / one is never*
Jean-Marc:	C'est vrai! Alors, je vous invite toutes les deux!	*Then / invite both of you*
Béatrice:	Super!	

Compréhension: Vrai ou faux?

Say whether the following statements are true **(C'est vrai!)** or false **(C'est faux!).**

1. Béatrice aime danser.
2. Elle danse bien.
3. Valérie danse très bien.
4. Jean-Marc adore danser.
5. Jean-Marc ne veut pas être ridicule.
6. Jean-Marc invite Béatrice et Valérie.

SETTING THE STAGE

Ask students if they organize informal parties at home for their friends.

What do they serve to eat and drink?

What do they do? Talk? Dance? Sing?

Tell them that in this lesson they will learn about French parties.

INCLUSION

Alphabetic/phonetic Have students copy the dialogue in their notebooks. Then ask them to underline or highlight five difficult words and write phonetic guides to these words.

Repetitive Model the pronunciation of **aimes**. Ask students to model this pronunciation three times. Then have them write this word in their notebooks with a phonetic transcription.

Comprehension practice Play the entire module through as an introduction to the lesson.

NOTE culturelle

Une boum

On weekends, French teenagers like to go to parties that are organized at a friend's home. These informal parties have different names according to the age group of the participants. For students at a **collège** (middle school), a party is sometimes known as **une boum** or **une fête.** For older students at a **lycée** (high school), it is called **une soirée.**

At a **boum**, parents are usually around to help out and set up a buffet which often features items contributed by the guests. Pizza and chips are very popular. There may also be homemade sandwiches or Chinese food. Preferred beverages are sodas and mineral waters.

Most of the young people like to dance and listen to their favorite music. Some may get drawn into the latest video games. Others simply enjoy getting together to talk about the week's events. For everyone, it is a way to spend a relaxing evening with friends.

COMPARAISONS CULTURELLES

How do French parties compare to parties that you and your friends organize? Explain.

Cross-cultural understanding

Have students watch the video (or look at the above photographs).

What kinds of similarities and differences do they notice between parties in France and parties that they go to?

SECTION A

Communicative function
Describing what one person is doing

Teaching Resource Options

PRINT 

Workbook PE, pp. 69–74
Unit 3 Resource Book
Communipak, pp. 128–143
Video Activities, p. 81
Videoscript, p. 85
Workbook TE, pp. 61–66

AUDIO & VISUAL 

Overhead Transparencies
16 Subject Pronouns
14a, 14b, 17 ***-er*** Verbs

TECHNOLOGY

Power Presentations

VIDEO PROGRAM

VIDÉO DVD

MODULE 7

7.1 Mini-scenes: J'étudie (17:15–18:06 min.)

7.2 Mini-scenes: Tu téléphones? (18:07–18:41 min.)

Teaching notes

Why present the singular forms of **parler** and **habiter** separately from the plural forms?

The initial presentation of **-er** verbs has been divided into two parts for pedagogical reasons.

- First the students learn the concept of "stem" and "endings" and practice with the most commonly used singular forms, where these endings are silent.
- Then, two pages later, when the students are comfortable handling the singular forms, they are introduced to the plural forms. They learn that the endings **-ons** and **-ez** are pronounced while **-ent** is silent. They also learn that liaison is required before verbs beginning with a vowel sound.

If you feel that your students can handle all of these concepts at once, you may want to present the whole paradigm immediately.

A Les verbes en *-er:* le singulier

The basic form of a verb is called the infinitive. Many French infinitives end in **-er.** Most of these verbs are conjugated like **parler** *(to speak)* and **habiter** *(to live)*. Note the forms of the present tense of these verbs in the singular. Pay attention to their endings.

INFINITIVE	parler	habiter	ENDINGS
STEM	parl-	habit-	
PRESENT TENSE (SINGULAR)	Je **parle** français. Tu **parles** anglais. Il/Elle **parle** espagnol.	J' **habite** à Paris. Tu **habites** à Boston. Il/Elle **habite** à Madrid.	**-e** **-es** **-e**

The present tense forms of **-er** verbs consist of two parts:

STEM + ENDING

- The STEM does not change. It is the infinitive minus **-er**:

  parler **parl-** **habiter** **habit-**

- The ENDINGS change with the subject:

  je → **-e** **tu** → **-es** **il/elle** → **-e**

→ The above endings are silent.
→ **Je** becomes **j'** before a vowel sound.
je parle **j'**habite

LEARNING ABOUT LANGUAGE
Verbs conjugated like **parler** and **habiter** follow a *predictable pattern.*
They are called REGULAR VERBS.

1 Curiosité

PARLER At the party, Olivier wants to learn more about Isabelle. She answers his questions affirmatively. Play both roles.

Tu parles anglais?
Oui, je parle anglais.

▶ parler anglais?

1. parler espagnol?
2. habiter à Paris?
3. danser bien?
4. jouer aux jeux vidéo?
5. jouer au basket?
6. chanter?
7. téléphoner à ton copain?
8. travailler en été?

CRITICAL THINKING ABOUT LANGUAGE

In this lesson, students are encouraged to think about how verbs work in French.

In Section A, they will learn the singular forms, which sound the same, but which are not all spelled the same.

In Section B, they will learn the plural forms with their endings, and notice how liaison helps link subject and verb together.

Finally in Section C, they will see the complete verb charts with both affirmative and negative forms. They will learn what a paradigm for regular verbs looks like, and how it can serve as a model.

VOCABULAIRE Les verbes en *-er*

▶ ***Verbs you already know:***

chanter	*to sing*	**nager**	*to swim*
danser	*to dance*	**parler**	*to speak, talk*
dîner	*to have dinner*	**regarder**	*to watch, look at*
écouter	*to listen (to)*	**téléphoner (à)**	*to phone, call*
étudier	*to study*	**travailler**	*to work*
jouer	*to play*	**voyager**	*to travel*
manger	*to eat*		

▶ ***New verbs:***

aimer	*to like*	Tu **aimes** Paris?
habiter (à)	*to live (in + city)*	Philippe **habite** à Toulouse?
inviter	*to invite*	J'**invite** un copain.
organiser	*to organize*	Sophie **organise** une **boum**/ une **soirée**/une **fête** *(party).*
visiter	*to visit (places)*	Céline **visite** Québec.

➔ **Regarder** has two meanings:
to look (at) Paul **regarde** Cécile.
to watch Cécile **regarde** la télé.

➔ Note the construction **téléphoner à:**

Céline **téléphone**	**à**	Marc.
Céline calls	...	*Marc.*

➔ Note the constructions with **regarder** *(to look at)* and **écouter** *(to listen to)*:

Philippe **regarde**	...	Alice.
Philippe looks	*at*	*Alice.*

Alice **écoute**	...	le professeur.
Alice listens	*to*	*the teacher.*

2 Quelle activité?

PARLER/ÉCRIRE Describe what the following people are doing by completing the sentences with one of the verbs below. Be logical.

chanter écouter parler travailler manger voyager regarder inviter habiter

1. Je ... un sandwich. Tu ... une pizza.
2. Tu ... anglais. Je ... français.
3. Éric ... la radio. Claire ... un CD.
4. Jean-Paul ... la télé. Tu ... un match de tennis.
5. M. Simon ... en *(by)* bus. Mme Dupont ... en train.
6. Nicolas ... Marie à la boum. Tu ... Alain.
7. Mlle Thomas ... dans *(in)* un hôpital. Je ... dans un supermarché *(supermarket)*.
8. La chorale *(choir)* ... bien. Est-ce que tu ... bien?
9. Tu ... en France. Aya ... en Afrique.

INCLUSION

Cumulative Have students review the list of **-er** verbs and beat out the syllables of each verb.

Metacognitive Model how to move from the infinitive form of the verb to the **je/tu** forms, noting the dropping of the {ay} sound. Prepare a list of ten paired words (e.g., **parler** -- **parle**), and have students read the list. Then ask them to write phonetic transcriptions for at least three of the word pairs. Ask students what they will do to remember this concept.

Multisensory Explain how certain first person verb forms use elision (e.g. **aimer** -- **j'aime**). Hand out a list of words with elision, and ask students to repeat the words aloud. Then have them write phonetic transcriptions in their notebooks as needed.

Teaching Tip You may point out that in French dictionaries, verbs are listed in the infinitive form.

Pronunciation You may want to point out that the singular forms of **-er** verbs all sound the same. There is a difference in spelling in the **tu-** form.

Language comparison English has many two-word verbs. Usually these two-word verbs are expressed in one word in French.

to look at	**regarder**
to look for	**chercher**
to listen to	**écouter**

Have students try to think of other English two-word verbs. (E.g., to look after, to look into, to look up; to go after, to go over, etc.)

1 ROLE PLAY getting acquainted

1. – Tu parles espagnol?
   – Oui, je parle espagnol.
2. – Tu habites à Paris?
   – Oui, j'habite à Paris.
3. – Tu danses bien?
   – Oui, je danse bien.
4. – Tu joues aux jeux vidéo?
   – Oui, je joue aux jeux vidéo.
5. – Tu joues au basket?
   – Oui, je joue au basket.
6. – Tu chantes?
   – Oui, je chante.
7. – Tu téléphones à ton copain?
   – Oui, je téléphone à mon copain.
8. – Tu travailles en été?
   – Oui, je travaille en été.

2 COMPREHENSION saying what people are doing

1. Je mange un sandwich. Tu manges une pizza.
2. Tu parles anglais. Je parle français.
3. Éric écoute la radio. Claire écoute un CD.
4. Jean-Paul regarde la télé. Tu regardes un match de tennis.
5. M. Simon voyage en bus. Mme Dupont voyage en train.
6. Nicolas invite Marie à la boum. Tu invites Alain.
7. Mlle Thomas travaille dans un hôpital. Je travaille dans un supermarché.
8. La chorale chante bien. Est-ce que tu chantes bien?
9. Tu habites en France. Aya habite en Afrique.

Teaching Resource Options

PRINT  

Workbook PE, pp. 69–74
Unit 3 Resource Book
Communipak, pp. 128–143
Workbook TE, pp. 61–66

TECHNOLOGY 

Power Presentations

3 DESCRIPTION describing what people are doing

1. Monsieur Dupin regarde la télé.
2. Madame Ménard écoute la radio.
3. Patrick étudie.
4. Florence chante.
5. Coco parle.

4 EXCHANGES discussing where people are

1. – Où est Pauline?
   – Elle est au restaurant. Elle dîne.
2. – Où est Véronique?
   – Elle est à la maison. Elle téléphone.
3. – Où est Madame Dupont?
   – Elle est en ville. Elle travaille.
4. – Où est Monsieur Lemaire?
   – Il est en France. Il voyage.
5. – Où est Léa?
   – Elle est à Paris. Elle visite la tour Eiffel.
6. – Où est André?
   – Il est au stade. Il joue au foot.
7. – Où est Alice?
   – Elle est à l'Olympic Club. Elle nage.

Variation Divide the class into three sections: A, B, C. Elicit part-choral or individual responses from the students in each section.
A: **Où est Jacques?**
B: **Il est en classe.**
C: **Il étudie.**

SECTION B

Communicative function
Describing what several people are doing

Pronunciation Note that **il parle** and **ils parlent** sound the same.

Language notes

- The "e" is inserted to keep the soft "g" sound.
- This spelling change is presented mainly for recognition.

3 Les voisins *(The neighbors)*

PARLER/ÉCRIRE Simon is explaining what his neighbors are doing. Describe each person's activity.

▶ **Madame Dumas téléphone.**

4 Où sont-ils?

PARLER You want to know where the following people are. A classmate tells you and says what they are doing.

▶ Jacques? (en classe/étudier)

1. Pauline? (au restaurant/dîner)
2. Véronique? (à la maison/téléphoner)
3. Mme Dupont? (en ville/travailler)
4. M. Lemaire? (en France/voyager)
5. Léa? (à Paris/visiter la tour Eiffel)
6. André? (au stade/jouer au foot)
7. Alice? (à l'Olympic Club/nager)

B Les verbes en *-er:* le pluriel

Note the plural forms of **parler** and **habiter**, paying attention to the endings.

INFINITIVE	parler	habiter	ENDINGS
STEM	parl-	habit-	
PRESENT TENSE (PLURAL)	Nous **parlons** français. Vous **parlez** anglais. Ils/Elles **parlent** espagnol.	Nous **habitons** à Québec. Vous **habitez** à Chicago. Ils/Elles **habitent** à Caracas.	-ons -ez -ent

➔ In the present tense, the plural endings of **-er** verbs are:

nous → **-ons** vous → **-ez** ils / elles → **-ent**

➔ The **-ent** ending is silent.

➔ Note the liaison when the verb begins with a vowel sound:

Nous étudions. Vous invitez Thomas. Ils habitent en France. Elles aiment Paris.

Observation When the infinitive of the verb ends in **-ger**, the **nous** form ends in **-geons**.

nager: nous na**geons** **manger:** nous man**geons** **voyager:** nous voya**geons**

COMPREHENSION Subject pronouns

Teach students gestures for each pronoun.
Montrez-moi "je". [point to self]
Montrez-moi "tu". [point straight ahead, somewhat down, as if to a child]
Montrez-moi "il" ou "elle" [stretch one arm out to the side, hand open]
Add: **"nous"** [both hands point to self]
"vous" [both hands point straight ahead]
"ils/elles" [both arms stretched to side]

Have students identify subjects.
Nous organisons une boum. ["nous"]

The subjects **il(s)/elle(s)** may be ambiguous.
Il(s) joue(nt) au tennis. ["il" or "ils"]

Clarify: **Pierre joue au tennis. ["il"]**

5 Qui?

PARLER/ÉCRIRE Élodie is speaking to or about her friends. Complete her sentences with **tu, elle, vous,** or **ils.**

▶ … étudient à Toulouse.
Ils étudient à Toulouse.

1. … habitez à Tours.
2. … joue aux jeux vidéo.
3. … étudiez à Bordeaux.
4. … aiment danser.
5. … organisent une boum.
6. … parlez espagnol.
7. … téléphone à Jean-Pierre.
8. … invites un copain.
9. … dîne avec Cécile.
10. … invitent Monique.

6 À la boum

PARLER At a party, Olivier is talking to two Canadian students, Monique and her friend. Monique answers yes to his questions.

▶ parler français?

Vous parlez français, n'est-ce pas?
Oui, nous parlons français.

1. parler anglais?
2. habiter à Québec?
3. étudier à Montréal?
4. voyager en France?
5. voyager en train?
6. visiter Paris?
7. aimer Paris?
8. aimer la France?

7 En colonie de vacances *(At summer camp)*

PARLER/ÉCRIRE Describe the activities of the following campers by completing the sentences.

▶ À cinq heures, Alice et Marc … **À cinq heures, Alice et Marc jouent au foot.**

▶   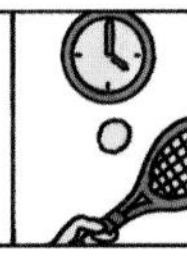    

1. À neuf heures, nous …
2. À quatre heures, vous …
3. À huit heures, Véronique et Pierre …
4. À sept heures, nous …
5. À trois heures, Thomas et François …
6. À six heures, vous …

8 Un voyage à Paris

PARLER/ÉCRIRE A group of American students is visiting Paris. During their stay, they do all of the following things:

voyager en bus	téléphoner à un copain	inviter une copine
visiter la tour Eiffel	dîner au restaurant	parler français

Describe the trips of the following people.

▶ Jim **Il voyage en bus, il visite la tour Eiffel …**

1. Linda 2. Paul et Louise 3. nous 4. vous 5. Jen et Sarah

CLASSROOM MANAGEMENT Writing Practice

Act. 8 lends itself to pair and group writing practice. First go through the entire model paragraph with the whole class.

Then group students in pairs and assign each pair a number (1, 2, 3, or 4). Each pair then writes out the paragraph corresponding to its number. When all are done, have each pair pass its paper to the next pair.

The pairs then read and check the new paragraph they have received. (For example, pair 2 passes its paper to pair 3 and reads the paper it receives from pair 1.)

5 PRACTICE selecting subject pronouns

1. Vous
2. Elle
3. Vous
4. Ils
5. Ils
6. Vous
7. Elle
8. Tu
9. Elle
10. Ils

Be sure students make the liaison in 1, 3, 4, 5, and 10.

6 ROLE PLAY getting to know people

– Vous ..., n'est-ce pas?
– Oui, nous ...

1. – parlez/parlons anglais
2. – habitez/habitons à Québec
3. – étudiez/étudions à Montréal
4. – voyagez/voyageons en France
5. – voyagez/voyageons en train
6. – visitez/visitons Paris
7. – aimez/aimons Paris
8. – aimez/aimons la France

Variation Ask questions with **est-ce que;** respond with **bien sûr.**
– Est-ce que vous parlez français?
– Bien sûr, nous parlons français.

7 COMPREHENSION describing what people do at various times of day

1. téléphons
2. jouez au tennis
3. regardent la télé
4. dînons
5. jouent au basket
6. nagez

Re-entry and review
Before doing this exercise you may want to review telling time (Unit 2, Leçon 4A).

8 PRACTICE describing activities on a trip

1. Elle voyage en bus. Elle visite la tour Eiffel. Elle téléphone à un copain. Elle dîne au restaurant. Elle invite une copine. Elle parle français.
2. Ils voyagent en bus. Ils visitent la tour Eiffel. Ils téléphonent à un copain. Ils dînent au restaurant. Ils invitent une copine. Ils parlent français.
3. Nous voyageons en bus. Nous visitons la tour Eiffel. Nous téléphonons à un copain. Nous dînons au restaurant. Nous invitons une copine. Nous parlons français.
4. Vous voyagez en bus. Vous visitez la tour Eiffel. Vous téléphonez à un copain. Vous dînez au restaurant. Vous invitez une copine. Vous parlez français.
5. Elles voyagent en bus. Elles visitent la tour Eiffel. Elles téléphonent à un copain. Elles dînent au restaurant. Elles invitent une copine. Elles parlent français.

Pronunciation **bus** /bys/

SECTION C

Communicative function
Describing what people do and don't do

Teaching Resource Options

PRINT

Workbook PE, pp. 69–74
Unit 3 Resource Book
- Audioscript, p. 87
- Communipak, pp. 128–143
- Video Activities, p. 82
- Videoscript, p. 85
- Workbook TE, pp. 61–66

AUDIO & VISUAL

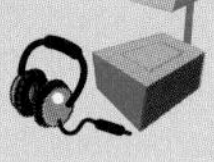

Audio Program
CD 2 Track 13

Overhead Transparencies
16 Subject Pronouns

TECHNOLOGY

Power Presentations

VIDEO PROGRAM

VIDÉO DVD

MODULE 7

7.3 Mini-scenes: Est-ce qu'il travaille? (18:42–19:45 min.)

Language note Be sure students notice that the one word **parle** in French may correspond to two words in English:

is speaking, does speak.

Point out that **is** corresponds to **est** only when it represents the main verb.

Teaching note
Use Transparency 16: Subject Pronouns to help students learn to spell the verb endings and say the forms. First have the students identify the pronoun cartoons **(je, tu, ...).**

With a washable transparency marker, write the forms of **dîner** below each picture.

With a second color, box the endings.

Have students read the verbs aloud, first in sequence **(je dîne, tu dînes, ...)** and then randomly as you point to them **(nous dînons, elle dîne, ...).**

Erase the forms of **dîner.** Have volunteers come write the forms of other verbs.

C Le présent des verbes en *-er:* forme affirmative et forme négative

Compare the affirmative and negative forms of **parler.**

AFFIRMATIVE	NEGATIVE
je **parle**	je **ne parle pas**
tu **parles**	tu **ne parles pas**
il/elle **parle**	il/elle **ne parle pas**
nous **parlons**	nous **ne parlons pas**
vous **parlez**	vous **ne parlez pas**
ils/elles **parlent**	ils/elles **ne parlent pas**

RAPPEL The negative form of the verb follows the pattern:

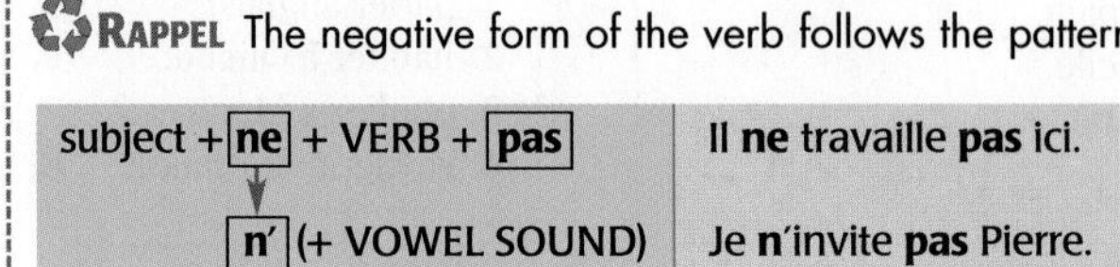

subject + **ne** + VERB + **pas** ↓ **n'** (+ VOWEL SOUND)	Il **ne** travaille **pas** ici. Je **n'**invite **pas** Pierre.

Il ne travaille pas.

Ils n'écoutent pas.

Elle ne chante pas bien.

LANGUAGE COMPARISONS

English has several verb forms for expressing actions in the present.
In French there is only one form. Compare:

Je **joue** au tennis. — ***I play** tennis.* / ***I do play** tennis.* / ***I am playing** tennis.*

Je **ne joue pas** au tennis. — ***I do not play** tennis. (**I don't play** tennis.)* / ***I am not playing** tennis. (**I'm not playing** tennis.)*

INCLUSION

Multisensory Have students copy the full conjugation of **parler** in their notebooks, putting asterisks next to all forms that are pronounced identically. Have students repeat this exercise using 3-5 **-er** verbs of their choice. Remind students to include asterisks for identical sounding forms. (Students can also use different color inks or highlighters to note the identical sounding forms.)

Synthetic/analytic Ask students to model your pronunciation of the dialogue in Act. 11. Then have students then practice this exercise in pairs.

9 Non!

PARLER One cannot do everything. From the following list of activities, select at least three that you do *not* do.

▶ **Je ne joue pas au bridge.**

parler espagnol
parler italien
danser le tango
jouer au hockey
jouer au water-polo
jouer au bridge
étudier à Paris
habiter à Québec
étudier le japonais
nager en hiver
dîner avec le prof
travailler dans un restaurant

10 Écoutez bien!

STRATEGY Listening

Negative sentences To know if a sentence is negative, listen for the word **pas** immediately after the verb.

ÉCOUTER You will hear French young people tell you what they do and do not do. Listen carefully to what they each say and determine if they do the following activities.

▶ Marc: jouer au foot?
Non. Marc ne joue pas au foot.

1. Sophie: parler espagnol?
2. Vincent: habiter à Tours?
3. Mélanie: dîner à la maison?
4. Nicolas: téléphoner à un copain?
5. Julie: manger une pizza?
6. Jean: étudier l'anglais?
7. Marie: écouter un CD?

11 Un jeu: Week-end!

PARLER/ÉCRIRE On weekends, people like to do different things. For each person, pick an activity and say what that person does. Select another activity and say what that person does not do.

▶ Antoine et Isabelle
Antoine et Isabelle dansent.
Ils ne regardent pas la télé.

1. je
2. tu
3. ma cousine
4. nous
5. Nicolas et Élodie
6. Madame Jolivet
7. vous
8. le professeur

GAME Week-end!

You can treat Act. 11 as a game. Divide the class into teams of three. Each team picks a person from the list and decides what that subject is doing and not doing. All three team members must write the same two sentences correctly.

Then the team chooses another subject plus two other activities. All three write down the next two sentences.

The game is played against the clock. For example, you may set a 5-minute time limit. The team whose three members have written the greatest number of correct sentences in that time is the winner.

9 COMMUNICATION stating activities that one does not do

Answers will vary.
Je ne parle pas (espagnol, italien).
Je ne danse pas le tango.
Je ne joue pas au (hockey, water-polo, bridge).
Je n'étudie pas (à Paris, le japonais).
Je n'habite pas à Québec.

Dice game
give verb
Δ sujets

1. Non. Sophie ne parle pas espagnol.
2. Non. Vincent n'habite pas à Tours.
3. Oui. Mélanie dîne à la maison.
4. Oui. Nicolas téléphone à un copain.
5. Non. Julie ne mange pas de pizza.
6. Non. Jean n'étudie pas l'anglais.
7. Oui. Marie écoute un CD.

Teaching Suggestion First play the recording for this activity and have students respond with "**oui**" or "**non**". Then, play the recording again, pausing after each cue so that students can reply with a full sentence.

Teaching Note Number 5 requires "pas de," which the students have not yet learned. You may want to mention it in passing.

11 COMPREHENSION stating what people do and don't do

Answers will vary.
1. Je danse. Je ne dîne pas au restaurant.
2. Tu écoutes la radio. Tu ne regardes pas la télé.
3. Ma cousine joue aux jeux vidéo. Elle ne danse pas.
4. Nous étudions. Nous ne nageons pas.
5. Nicolas et Élodie regardent la télé. Ils ne jouent pas au basket.
6. Madame Jolivet travaille. Elle n'écoute pas la radio.
7. Vous jouez au basket. Vous ne nagez pas.
8. Le professeur nage. Il (Elle) ne travaille pas.

Teaching Resource Options

PRINT  

Workbook PE, pp 69–74
Unit 3 Resource Book
- Audioscript, p. 87
- Communipak, pp. 128–143
- Video Activities, p. 83
- Videoscript, pp. 85–86
- Workbook TE, pp. 61–66

AUDIO & VISUAL 

Audio Program
CD 2 Track 14

TECHNOLOGY 

Power Presentations

VIDEO PROGRAM

VIDÉO DVD

MODULE 7

7.4 Mini-scenes: Jean-Paul à la boum (19:46–20:38 min)

12 COMMUNICATION describing how well or often one does things

Answers will vary.

1. mal (bien, très bien, souvent, toujours, rarement, un peu, beaucoup)
2. bien (mal, très bien, souvent, toujours, rarement, un peu, beaucoup)
3. souvent (toujours, rarement, un peu, beaucoup)
4. beaucoup (bien, mal, très bien, souvent, toujours, rarement, un peu)
5. rarement (souvent, toujours, beaucoup)
6. très bien (bien, souvent, toujours, rarement)
7. un peu (toujours, souvent, rarement)
8. un peu (toujours, souvent, rarement)
9. bien (très bien, toujours, beaucoup)

13 COMMUNICATION expressing approval or regret

– Est-ce que tu ... ?
– Oui, je ... (Non, je ne ... pas ...)
– Super! (Dommage!)

1. parles/parle/ne parle pas (espagnol)
2. joues/joue/ne joue pas (au basket)
3. chantes/chante/ne chante pas (bien)
4. voyages/voyage/ne voyage pas (beaucoup)
5. dînes/dîne/ne dîne pas (au restaurant)
6. invites souvent ton copain/invite mon copain/n'invite pas mon copain

Variation Address two or more students.
– Est-ce que vous chantez?
– Oui, nous aimons chanter. (Non, nous n'aimons pas chanter.)

VOCABULAIRE Mots utiles

bien	*well*	Je joue **bien** au tennis.
très bien	*very well*	Je ne chante pas **très bien.**
mal	*badly, poorly*	Tu joues **mal** au volley.
beaucoup	*a lot, much, very much*	Paul aime **beaucoup** voyager.
un peu	*a little, a little bit*	Nous parlons **un peu** français.
souvent	*often*	Thomas joue **souvent** aux jeux vidéo.
toujours	*always*	Charlotte travaille **toujours** en été.
aussi	*also, too*	Je téléphone à Marc. Je téléphone **aussi** à Véronique.
maintenant	*now*	J'étudie **maintenant.**
rarement	*rarely, seldom*	Vous voyagez **rarement.**

➔ In French, the above expressions *never* come *between* the subject and the verb. They usually come *after* the verb. Compare their positions in French and English.

Nous parlons **toujours** français.	*We **always** speak French.*
Tu joues **bien** au tennis.	*You play tennis **well**.*

12 Expression personnelle

PARLER/ÉCRIRE Complete the following sentences with one of the suggested expressions.

bien   mal   très bien   toujours   souvent   rarement   un peu   beaucoup

1. Je chante …
2. Je nage …
3. Je regarde … la télé.
4. Je mange …
5. Je voyage … en bus.
6. Le prof parle … français.
7. Mes copains surfent … sur l'Internet.
8. Mon ami joue … aux jeux vidéo.
9. Les Yankees jouent … au baseball.

VOCABULAIRE Expressions pour la conversation

How to express approval or regret:

Super!	*Terrific!*	Tu parles français? **Super!**
Dommage!	*Too bad!*	Tu ne joues pas au tennis? **Dommage!**

13  Conversation

PARLER Ask your classmates if they do the following things. Then express approval or regret.

▶ parler français?

Est-ce que tu parles français?
Oui, je parle français. (Non, je ne parle pas français.)
Super! (Dommage!)

1. parler espagnol?
2. jouer au basket?
3. chanter bien?
4. voyager beaucoup?
5. dîner souvent au restaurant?
6. inviter souvent ton copain?

TEACHING TIP

Have students notice the two-column (French-English) format in the **Vocabulaire** sections. Encourage them to practice the vocabulary by covering one of the two columns with a slip of paper and then saying or writing the corresponding expression in the other language. They can verify their responses by sliding the paper down the page as they go through the list.

D La construction: verbe + infinitif

Note the use of the infinitive in the following French sentences.

J'aime **parler** français.	*I like **to speak** French. I like **speaking** French.*
Ils n'aiment pas **danser.**	*They don't like **to dance.** They don't like **dancing.***

To express what they like and don't like to do, the French use these constructions:

SUBJECT + PRESENT TENSE + INFINITIVE ... of **aimer**			SUBJECT + **n'** + PRESENT TENSE + **pas** + INFINITIVE ... of **aimer**		
Nous	**aimons**	**voyager.**	Nous	**n'aimons pas**	**voyager.**

Note that in this construction, the verb **aimer** may be affirmative or negative:

AFFIRMATIVE: Jacques **aime** voyager. NEGATIVE: Philippe **n'aime pas** voyager.

→ The infinitive is also used after the following expressions:

Je préfère ...	*I prefer ...*	**Je préfère travailler.**
Je voudrais ...	*I would like ...*	**Je voudrais voyager.**
Je (ne) veux (pas) ...	*I (don't) want ...*	**Je veux jouer** au foot.
Est-ce que tu veux ...	*Do you want ...*	**Est-ce que tu veux danser?**
Je (ne) peux (pas) ...	*I can (I can't) ...*	**Je ne peux pas dîner** avec toi.
Je dois ...	*I have to ...*	**Je dois étudier.**

14  Dialogue

PARLER Ask your friends if they like to do these things.

▶ nager?
—**Est-ce que tu aimes nager?**
—**Oui, j'aime nager. (Non, je n'aime pas nager.)**

1. étudier?
2. voyager?
3. chanter?
4. téléphoner?
5. manger?
6. danser?
7. jouer au foot?
8. jouer au basket?
9. travailler en été?

15 Une excellente raison *(An excellent reason)*

PARLER/ÉCRIRE The following people are doing certain things. Say that they like these activities.

▶ Thomas joue au tennis. **Il aime jouer au tennis.**

1. Alice chante.
2. Pierre voyage.
3. Céline joue au foot.
4. Tu téléphones.
5. Nous travaillons.
6. Julie et Paul dansent.
7. Nous jouons au frisbee.
8. Éric et Lise nagent.
9. Vous surfez sur l'Internet.
10. Léa organise la boum.

PRONONCIATION

Les voyelles /i/ et /u/

/u/ **où?** /i/ **ici!**

Be sure to pronounce the French "**i**" as in **Mimi.**

Répétez:

/i/ **ici Philippe il Mimi Sylvie visite**
Alice visite Paris avec Sylvie.

/u/ **où nous vous écoute joue toujours**
Vous jouez au foot avec nous?

JEAN-PAUL À LA BOUM

- Divide the class into teams of four.
- Play the video segment **Jean-Paul à la boum.**
- Replay the first scene and pause so that each team can write as many phrases from the conversation as they can remember. Do the same for the second scene.
- Then play both scenes once more so the teams can try to complete their texts.
- Distribute a copy of the video script to each team so that they can circle all the phrases they listed correctly. Play the scenes a final time for confirmation.

SECTION D

Communicative function
Talking about what people like and don't like to do

14 COMMUNICATION discussing likes and dislikes

1. –Est-ce que tu aimes étudier?
   –Oui, j'aime étudier. (Non, je n'aime pas étudier.)
2. –Est-ce que tu aimes voyager?
   –Oui, j'aime voyager. (Non, je n'aime pas voyager.)
3. –Est-ce que tu aimes chanter?
   –Oui, j'aime chanter. (Non, je n'aime pas chanter.)
4. –Est-ce que tu aimes téléphoner?
   –Oui, j'aime téléphoner. (Non, je n'aime pas téléphoner.)
5. –Est-ce que tu aimes manger?
   –Oui, j'aime manger. (Non, je n'aime pas manger.)
6. –Est-ce que tu aimes danser?
   –Oui, j'aime danser. (Non, je n'aime pas danser.)
7. –Est-ce que tu aimes jouer au foot?
   –Oui, j'aime jouer au foot. (Non, je n'aime pas jouer au foot.)
8. –Est-ce que tu aimes jouer au basket?
   –Oui, j'aime jouer au basket. (Non, je n'aime pas jouer au basket.)
9. –Est-ce que tu aimes travailler en été?
   –Oui, j'aime travailler en été. (Non, je n'aime pas travailler en été.)

Expansion In the event of an affirmative answer, a follow-up question could be asked with **bien** or **souvent.**
Est-ce que tu chantes bien?

15 PRACTICE saying what people like to do

1. Elle aime chanter.
2. Il aime voyager.
3. Elle aime jouer au foot.
4. Tu aimes téléphoner.
5. Nous aimons travailler.
6. Ils aiment danser.
7. Nous aimons jouer au frisbee.
8. Ils aiment nager.
9. Vous aimez surfer sur l'Internet.
10. Elle aime organiser la boum.

Challenge Continue the response by inventing an activity that the person does not like to do.
Il aime voyager mais il n'aime pas parler anglais.

PRONUNCIATION

/i/ Spelled **i, y.**
Be sure students pronounce /i/ like "ee" of *beet* and not the "i" of *bit.*
/u/ Spelled **ou, où.**

À VOTRE TOUR

Main Topic

- Recapitulation and review

Teaching Resource Options

PRINT 

Workbook PE, pp. 69–74
Unit 3 Resource Book
Audioscript, pp. 87–88
Communipak, pp. 128–143
Family Involvement, pp. 79–80
Workbook TE, pp. 61–66

Assessment
Lesson 7 Quiz, pp. 91–92
Portfolio Assessment, Unit 1 URB pp. 155–164
Audioscript for Quiz 7, p. 90
Answer Keys, pp. 216–219

AUDIO & VISUAL 

Audio Program
CD 2 Tracks 15, 16
CD 14 Track 3

TECHNOLOGY 

Test Generator CD-ROM/McDougal Littell Assessment System

1 COMPREHENSION

1. Est-ce que Marc est canadien?
(d) Oui, il habite à Montréal.
2. Est-ce que tu joues au tennis?
(b) Oui, mais pas très bien.
3. Ton frère est à la maison?
(e) Non, il dîne au restaurant avec un copain.
4. Ta mère est en vacances?
(a) Non, elle travaille.
5. Tu invites Christine et Juliette à la boum?
(c) Bien sûr! Elles aiment beaucoup danser.

2 GUIDED ORAL EXPRESSION

Answers will vary.
- Est-ce que tu nages?
- Oui, je nage (souvent). (Non, je ne nage pas.)
- Est-ce que tu voyages?
- Oui, je voyage (beaucoup). (Non, je ne voyage pas.)
- Est-ce que tu chantes?
- Oui, je chante (un peu). (Non, je ne chante pas.)
- Est-ce que tu regardes la télé?
- Oui, je regarde (souvent) la télé. (Non, je ne regarde pas la télé.)
- Est-ce que tu étudies?
- Oui, j'étudie (beaucoup). (Non, je n'étudie pas.)
- Est-ce que tu travailles?
- Oui, je travaille (souvent). (Non, je ne travaille pas.)

À votre tour!

OBJECTIFS

Now you can ...
- describe what you and other people are doing and not doing
- talk about what you and other people like and don't like to do

1 Allô!

PARLER Sophie is phoning some friends. Match her questions on the left with her friends' answers on the right.

1. Est-ce que Marc est canadien?
2. Est-ce que tu joues au tennis?
3. Ton frère est à la maison?
4. Ta mère est en vacances?
5. Tu invites Christine et Juliette à la boum?

a. Non, elle travaille.
b. Oui, mais pas très bien.
c. Bien sûr! Elles aiment beaucoup danser.
d. Oui, il habite à Montréal.
e. Non, il dîne au restaurant avec un copain.

2 Créa-dialogue

PARLER Find out how frequently your classmates do the following activities. They will respond using one of the expressions on the scale.

NON	OUI			
	rarement →	un peu →	souvent →	beaucoup

▶ —Robert, est-ce que tu joues au tennis?
—Non, je ne joue pas au tennis.
—Est-ce que tu écoutes la radio?
—Oui, j'écoute souvent la radio.

À VOTRE TOUR

Depending on your goals and objectives, you may or may not wish to assign all of the activities in the **À votre tour** section.

PAIR AND GROUP PRACTICE

In Acts. 1 and 2, you may want to have students work together in trios, with two performing and one acting as monitor.

INCLUSION

Repetitive Read aloud the dialogue from Act. 1. Then have the class repeat along with you as you model the dialogue a second time. Students can then practice in pairs.

3 Qu'est-ce qu'ils font?

(What do they do?)

PARLER/ÉCRIRE Look at what the following students have put in their lockers and say what they like to do.

Éric aime jouer au tennis.
Il aime aussi ...
ÉRIC
HÉLÈNE & ANNE
LE FRANÇAIS PRATIQUE
NOUS
VOUS
¿QUÉ TAL?

4 Message illustré

ÉCRIRE Marc wrote about certain activities, using pictures. On a separate sheet, write out his description replacing these pictures with the missing words.

À la maison, ma soeur Catherine
à une copine. Mon frère
Éric . En général, nous
à sept heures et
demie. Après° le dîner, mes°
parents . Moi, j'
pour la classe de français.
En vacances, nous .
Je . Éric et Catherine
. Parfois° mes parents
au restaurant.

Après *After* **mes** *my* **Parfois** *Sometimes*

5 Point de vue personnel

ÉCRIRE Write a short composition in which you describe some of the activities you do and don't do in different situations: at home, in class, on vacation, with your friends, and with your family. If appropriate, you may indicate how frequently you engage in certain activities.

STRATEGY Writing

- First list the activities you want to mention, using infinitives.
- Write out your paragraph describing your activities and those that you do not do.
- Check your composition to be sure all verb forms are correct.

	☺	☹
• à la maison	• ________	• ________
• en classe	• ________	• ________
• en vacances	• ________	• ________
• avec mes copains	• ________	• ________
• avec ma famille	• ________	• ________

LESSON REVIEW
CLASSZONE.COM

3 COMPREHENSION

Éric aime jouer au tennis. Il aime aussi parler (étudier le) français.
Hélène et Anne aiment danser. Elles aiment aussi écouter la radio.
Nous aimons jouer au basket. Nous aimons aussi parler (étudier l') espagnol.
Vous aimez nager. Vous aimez aussi jouer au foot.

4 COMPREHENSION

À la maison, ma soeur Catherine téléphone à une copine. Mon frère Éric écoute la radio. En général, nous dînons à sept heures et demie. Après le dîner, mes parents regardent la télé. Moi, j'étudie pour la classe de français. En vacances, nous n'étudions pas. Je nage. Éric et Catherine jouent au tennis. Parfois mes parents dînent au restaurant.

Challenge De nouveaux messages
Have students, alone or in pairs, prepare their own **messages illustrés** (complete with an answer key on the back). Let them exchange their messages with each other. On a separate sheet of paper, have them replace the pictures with the missing words and check their answers using the answer key provided.

5 WRITTEN SELF-EXPRESSION

Answers will vary.

- écouter le prof
- étudier
- regarder la télé
- dîner
- parler avec mon ami
- écouter la radio
- jouer au volley
- jouer au tennis

À la maison, je regarde la télé et je dîne. Je n'écoute pas la radio.

En classe, j'écoute le prof et j'étudie. Je ne parle pas avec mon ami.

En vacances, je nage et je parle au téléphone. Je n'étudie pas.

Avec mes copains, je joue au basket et je joue au foot. Je ne joue pas au volley.

Avec mes parents, je dîne au restaurant et je voyage. Je ne joue pas au tennis.

PORTFOLIO ASSESSMENT

You will probably only select one speaking activity and one writing activity to go into the students' portfolios for Unit 3.

In this lesson, Act. 2 can be the basis of an oral portfolio recording. (You may want to use the Challenge version of Act. 4 for the written portfolio.)

Leçon 8

Main Topic Finding out information

Teaching Resource Options

PRINT  

Workbook PE, pp. 75–79
Activités pour tous PE, pp. 43–45
Block Scheduling Copymasters, pp. 57–64
Unit 3 Resource Book
- *Activités pour tous* TE, pp. 99–101
- Audioscript, pp. 120, 121–122
- Communipak, pp. 128–143
- Lesson Plans, pp. 102–103
- Block Scheduling Lesson Plans, pp. 104–106
- Absent Student Copymasters, pp. 107–111
- Video Activities, pp. 114–117
- Videoscript, pp. 118–119
- Workbook TE, pp. 93–97

AUDIO & VISUAL 

Audio Program
CD 2 Tracks 17, 18
CD 7 Tracks 18–21

TECHNOLOGY 

Online Workbook

VIDEO PROGRAM

MODULE 8
Un concert de musique africaine

TOTAL TIME: 6:14 min.
DVD Disk 1
Videotape 2 (COUNTER: 21:45 min.)

8.1 Mini-scenes: Listening
– Où est-ce qu'il va?
(22:39–24:04 min.)

8.2 Mini-scenes: Listening
– Qu'est-ce que tu fais?
(24:05–24:53 min.)

8.3 Mini-scenes: Speaking
– Questions
(24:54–25:35 min.)

8.4 Dialogue: Un concert de musique africaine
(25:36–26:26 min.)

8.5 Vignette culturelle: Le Sénégal
(26:27–27:59 min.)

LEÇON 8

Un concert de musique africaine

VIDÉO DVD AUDIO

Nicolas is at a café with his new friend Fatou. He is interviewing her for an article in his school newspaper.

Nicolas: Bonjour, Fatou. Ça va?
Fatou: Oui, ça va.
Nicolas: Tu es sénégalaise, n'est-ce pas? — *from Senegal*
Fatou: Oui, je suis sénégalaise.
Nicolas: Où est-ce que tu habites?
Fatou: Je suis de Dakar, mais maintenant j'habite à Paris avec ma famille.
Nicolas: Est-ce que tu aimes Paris?
Fatou: J'adore Paris.
Nicolas: Qu'est-ce que tu fais le week-end?
Fatou: Ça dépend. En général, je regarde la télé ou je sors avec mes copains. Dis, Nicolas! Est-ce que je peux te poser une question? — *That / go out; ask you*
Nicolas: Oui, bien sûr!
Fatou: Qu'est-ce que tu fais ce week-end? — *this*
Nicolas: Euh, ... je ne sais pas. — *I don't know*
Fatou: Est-ce que tu veux aller avec nous à un concert de Youssou N'Dour, le musicien sénégalais?
Nicolas: Oui, bien sûr! Où? Quand? Et à quelle heure? — *Where? / When?*

Compréhension:

1. Est-ce que Fatou est française?
2. Où est-ce qu'elle habite maintenant?
3. Qu'est-ce que *(What)* Fatou aime faire *(to do)* le week-end?
4. Qui est-ce qu'elle invite au concert de musique africaine?

SETTING THE SCENE

Ask students how many African countries they can name. Write these on the board. Do they remember which of these countries use French as an official language? Circle these countries. (If necessary, have them turn back to the photo essay on pages 8–9.)

Locate these French-speaking countries on the map. In particular, have students locate Senegal and its capital city Dakar. Tell them that in this chapter they will meet a student from Dakar.

NOTE culturelle

EN BREF: Le Sénégal
Capitale: Dakar
Population: 10 000 000
Langue officielle: français

A former French colony, Senegal became an independent republic in 1960. Its population is divided into about a dozen ethnic groups, each with its own language, the most important being **wolof** and **pulaar.**

Dakar, Sénégal

Des jeunes Sénégalais

Le tama

Youssou N'Dour

Youssou N'Dour is an internationally known musician from Senegal who combines traditional African music with pop, rock, and jazz. He sings in French and English, as well as in three Senegalese dialects. His lyrics promote African unity and human dignity. In many of his songs, he also plays the **tama**, a traditional Senegalese drum covered with reptile skins.

CONNEXIONS Senegal and African Music

- As a class project, make a display board on Senegal, using information and pictures from travel brochures or from the Internet.
- Obtain a CD of Youssou N'Dour or of music from another French-African country and play your favorite selection for the class.

USING THE VIDEO

In this lesson, the opening text corresponds to the video interview. However, the printed text is somewhat different from the video version.

First, have students follow in their books as you read the text aloud.

Tell the class that the recorded version will not be exactly the same, and play it for them.

Then play the video a second time. Have students find those sentences which are different from those in the recorded dialogue.

Photo culture note Un café à Paris

On the table you can see:
- a ham and cheese sandwich (**un sandwich au jambon et au fromage**) made from half a loaf of French bread (**une baguette**).
- a plate of mixed vegetable salads (**des crudités**) including grated carrots (**des carottes râpées**) and beets (**des betteraves**).

Comprehension practice Play the entire module through as an introduction to the lesson.

Compréhension
Answers
1. Non, Fatou est sénégalaise.
2. Fatou habite à Paris.
3. Fatou aime regarder la télé ou sortir avec ses copains.
4. Fatou invite Nicolas au concert de musique africaine.

Teaching note For number four, tell students that the infinitive of **sors** is **sortir**.

Cross-cultural observation

Have
simil
Sene

SECTION A

Communicative function
- Asking for information
- The video/audio sequence includes questions with **qui.**

Teaching Resource Options

PRINT 

Workbook PE, pp. 75–79
Unit 3 Resource Book
 Audioscript, p. 120
 Communipak, pp. 128–143
 Video Activities, p. 114
 Videoscript, p. 118
 Workbook TE, pp. 93–97

AUDIO & VISUAL 

Audio Program
CD 2 Track 19

Overhead Transparencies
6 Clock face *Quelle heure est-il?*

TECHNOLOGY 

Power Presentations

VIDEO PROGRAM

VIDÉO DVD

MODULE 8

8.1 Mini-scenes: Où est-ce qu'il va?
(22:39–24:04 min.)

1 LISTENING COMPREHENSION

1. b 2. a 3. d 4. c
5. b 6. c 7. a 8. d

Pronunciation Note that the "t" is not pronounced in **Montréal** since it is considered as the final consonant of a word: **Mont Réal** *(Mount Royal).*

A Les questions d'information

The questions below ask for specific information and are called INFORMATION QUESTIONS. The INTERROGATIVE EXPRESSIONS in heavy print indicate what kind of information is requested.

—**Où** est-ce que tu habites?	***Where** do you live?*
—J'habite **à Nice.**	*I live **in Nice.***
—**À quelle heure** est-ce que vous dînez?	***At what time** do you eat dinner?*
—Nous dînons **à sept heures.**	*We eat **at seven.***

→ In French, information questions may be formed according to the pattern:

INTERROGATIVE EXPRESSION +	**est-ce que** +	SUBJECT +	VERB ... ?
À quelle heure	**est-ce que**	vous	travaillez?

→ **Est-ce que** becomes **est-ce qu'** before a vowel sound.

Quand **est-ce qu'**Alice et Roger dînent?

→ In information questions, your voice rises on the interrogative expression and then falls until the last syllable.

Quand est-ce que tu travailles?   **À quelle heure** est-ce que vous dînez?

Observation In casual conversation, French speakers frequently form information questions by placing the interrogative expression at the end of the sentence. The voice rises on the interrogative expression.

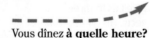

Vous habitez **où?**   Vous dînez **à quelle heure?**

VOCABULAIRE Expressions interrogatives

où	*where?*	**Où** est-ce que vous travaillez?
quand?	*when?*	**Quand** est-ce que ton copain organise une boum?
à quelle heure?	*at what time?*	**À quelle heure** est-ce que tu regardes la télé?
comment?	*how?*	**Comment** est-ce que tu chantes? Bien ou mal?
pourquoi?	*why?*	—**Pourquoi** est-ce que tu étudies le français?
parce que	*because*	—**Parce que** je veux voyager en France.

→ **Parce que** becomes **parce qu´** before a vowel sound.

Juliette invite Olivier **parce qu'**il danse bien.

INCLUSION

Multisensory Make hand movements to demonstrate the rise and fall of your voice when asking the following questions: **À quelle heure est-ce que tu dînes? / Tu dînes à quelle heure?** Ask students to say and imitate the movements. (Have them imagine that they are conducting an orchestra.) Then have them chant the words, as if they were singing, noting how the sentences rise and fall.

1  Écoutez bien!

STRATEGY Listening

Understanding questions Pay attention to the interrogative expression. It tells what type of information is asked for.

ÉCOUTER The questions that you will hear can be logically answered by only one of the following options. Listen carefully to each question and select the logical answer.

a. à sept heures
b. à Paris
c. en octobre
d. assez bien

2  Curiosité

PARLER At a party in Paris, Nicolas meets Béatrice, a Canadian student. He wants to know more about her. Play both roles.

▶ où / habiter? (à Québec)

NICOLAS: **Où est-ce que tu habites?**
BÉATRICE: **J'habite à Québec.**

1. où/étudier? (à Montréal)
2. où/travailler? (dans *[in]* une pharmacie)
3. quand/parler français? (toujours)
4. quand/parler anglais? (souvent)
5. comment/jouer au tennis? (bien)
6. comment/danser? (très bien)
7. pourquoi/être en France? (parce que j'aime voyager)
8. pourquoi/être à Paris? (parce que j'étudie ici)

VOCABULAIRE Expressions pour la conversation

How to express surprise or mild doubt:

Ah bon? *Oh? Really?* —Stéphanie organise une soirée.
—Ah bon? Quand?

3 Au téléphone

PARLER Jacques calls Élodie to tell her about his plans.

▶ organiser une soirée (quand? samedi)

1. organiser un pique-nique (quand? dimanche)
2. dîner avec Pauline (quand? lundi)
3. dîner avec Caroline (où? au restaurant Belcour)
4. regarder «Batman» (à quelle heure? à 9 heures)
5. inviter Brigitte (où? à un concert)
6. parler espagnol (comment? assez bien)
7. étudier l'italien (pourquoi? je veux voyager en Italie)

4 Questions personnelles PARLER/ÉCRIRE

1. Où est-ce que tu habites? *(name of your city)*
2. Où est-ce que tu étudies? *(name of your school)*
3. À quelle heure est-ce que tu dînes?
4. À quelle heure est-ce que tu regardes la télé?
5. Quand est-ce que tu nages? (en été? en hiver?)
6. Quand est-ce que tu joues au volley? (en mai? en juillet?)
7. Comment est-ce que tu chantes? (bien? très bien? mal?)
8. Comment est-ce que tu nages?

WARM-UP AND REVIEW

PROP: Transparency 6: Clock face *Quelle heure est-il?* or clock with hands

Review times by asking students at what time they do certain things. Then ask a classmate to show the corresponding time on the clock face.

Dis-moi, W, à quelle heure est-ce que tu dînes?

[Je dîne à six heures et quart.]

X, viens ici et montre-nous six heures et quart.

Y, à quelle heure est-ce que tu étudies? ...

Z, à quelle heure est-ce que tu écoutes la radio? ...

4. **N:** Quand est-ce que tu ...?
B: Je parle souvent anglais.
5. **N:** Comment est-ce que tu joues au tennis?
B: Je joue bien au tennis.
6. **N:** Comment est-ce que tu danses?
B: Je danse très bien.
7. **N:** Pourquoi est-ce que tu es en France?
B: Je suis en France parce que j'aime voyager.
8. **N:** Pourquoi est-ce que tu es à Paris?
B: Je suis à Paris parce que j'étudie ici.

3 ROLE PLAY asking for information

1. – J'organise un pique-nique.
– Ah bon? Quand est-ce que tu organises un pique-nique?
– Dimanche.
2. – Je dîne avec Pauline.
– Ah bon? Quand est-ce que tu dînes avec Pauline?
– Lundi.
3. – Je dîne avec Caroline.
– Ah bon? Où est-ce que tu dînes avec Caroline?
– Au restaurant Belcour.
4. – Je regarde «Batman».
– Ah bon? À quelle heure est-ce que tu regardes «Batman»?
– À 9 heures.
5. – J'invite Brigitte.
– Ah bon? Où est-ce que tu invites Brigitte?
– À un concert.
6. – Je parle espagnol.
– Ah bon? Comment est-ce que tu parles espagnol?
– Assez bien.
7. – J'étudie l'italien.
– Ah bon? Pourquoi est-ce que tu étudies l'italien?
– Je veux voyager en Italie.

4 COMMUNICATION answering personal questions

Answers will vary.
1. J'habite à (Boston).
2. J'étudie à (Jefferson High School).
3. Je dîne à (6 h 30).
4. Je regarde la télé à (8h).
5. Je nage (en été).
6. Je joue au volley en mai (en juillet).
7. Je chante très bien (bien, mal).
8. Je nage mal (bien, très bien).

Variation

Have students describe themselves by answering the questions in writing. They may vary the sequence of their answers and add additional information for extra credit.

SECTION B

Communicative function
Asking about people

Teaching Resource Options

PRINT 

Workbook PE, pp. 75–79
Unit 3 Resource Book
Communipak, pp. 128–143
Video Activities, pp. 114–115
Videoscript, pp. 118–119
Workbook TE, pp. 93–97

TECHNOLOGY
Power Presentations

VIDEO PROGRAM

VIDÉO DVD

MODULE 8

8.2 Mini-scenes: Qu'est-ce que tu fais? (24:05–24:53 min.)

8.3 Mini-scenes: Questions (24:54–25:35 min.)

5 ROLE PLAY finding out information about others

1. – Jean-Pierre téléphone.
 – Ah bon? À qui est-ce qu'il téléphone?
 – Il téléphone à Sylvie.
2. – Frédéric étudie.
 – Ah bon? Avec qui est-ce qu'il étudie?
 – Il étudie avec un copain.
3. – Madame Masson parle.
 – Ah bon? À qui est-ce qu'elle parle?
 – Elle parle à Madame Bonnot.
4. – Monsieur Lambert travaille.
 – Ah bon? Avec qui est-ce qu'il travaille?
 – Il travaille avec Monsieur Dumont.
5. – Juliette danse.
 – Ah bon? Avec qui est-ce qu'elle danse?
 – Elle danse avec Georges.
6. – François parle à Michèle.
 – Ah bon? De qui est-ce qu'il parle à Michèle? (De qui est-ce qu'ils parlent?)
 – Il parle (Ils parlent) de toi.

Language note Unlike their English equivalents, the two words in expressions like **à qui** and **avec qui** cannot be separated.

Avec qui est-ce que tu travailles?
Who(m) do you work with?

Language note In French as in English, the verb in **qui** questions is singular even if the expected answer is plural.

– **Qui joue au tennis?** *(Who is playing tennis?)*
– **Paul et Monique.**

B Les expressions interrogatives avec *qui*

To ask about PEOPLE, French speakers use the following interrogative expressions:

qui?	*who(m)?*	**Qui** est-ce que tu invites au concert?
à qui?	*to who(m)?*	**À qui** est-ce que tu téléphones?
de qui?	*about who(m)?*	**De qui** est-ce que vous parlez?
avec qui?	*with who(m)?*	**Avec qui** est-ce que Pierre étudie?
pour qui?	*for who(m)?*	**Pour qui** est-ce que Laure organise la boum?

To ask *who is doing something*, French speakers use the construction:

qui + VERB ... ?	
Qui habite ici?	***Who** lives here?*
Qui organise la boum?	***Who** is organizing the party?*

5   Curiosité

PARLER Anne is telling Élodie what certain people are doing. Élodie asks for more details. Play both roles.

▶ Alice dîne. (avec qui? avec une copine)

1. Jean-Pierre téléphone. (à qui? à Sylvie)
2. Frédéric étudie. (avec qui? avec un copain)
3. Madame Masson parle. (à qui? à Madame Bonnot)
4. Monsieur Lambert travaille. (avec qui? avec Monsieur Dumont)
5. Juliette danse. (avec qui? avec Georges)
6. François parle à Michèle. (de qui? de toi)

Alice dîne.
Ah bon? Avec qui est-ce qu'elle dîne?
Elle dîne avec une copine.

6   Un sondage *(A poll)*

PARLER Take a survey to find out how your classmates spend their free time. Ask who does the following things.

Europe 2
La radio
LA MUSIQUE

▶ écouter la radio
Qui écoute la radio?

1. voyager souvent
2. aimer chanter
3. nager
4. aimer danser
5. regarder la télé
6. jouer au tennis
7. parler italien
8. travailler
9. regarder les clips *(music videos)*
10. jouer aux jeux vidéo
11. étudier beaucoup
12. visiter souvent New York

GAME Getting acquainted

On a separate sheet of paper, have each student copy the model and 12 cues of Act. 6.

Students then move around asking classmates one by one if they do an activity on the list.

Annie: **Marc, est-ce que tu nages?**
Marc: **Oui, je nage.**

Annie writes Marc's name next to **nager**. If Marc says no, Annie asks someone else.

The first person to complete his/her sheet with 13 different names is the winner.

7 Questions

PARLER/ÉCRIRE For each illustration, prepare a short dialogue with a classmate using the suggested cues.

où?

à la maison

▶ —**Où est-ce que tu dînes?**
—**Je dîne à la maison.**

1. à quelle heure? — à 8 heures

2. quand? — en septembre

BONJOUR!

3. comment? — très bien

4. avec qui? — avec Denise

5. à qui? — à mon cousin

BLA
BLA
BLA...

6. de qui? — de toi

7. pour qui? — pour M. Lambert

C Qu'est-ce que?

Note the use of the interrogative expression **qu'est-ce que** *(what)* in the questions below.

Qu'est-ce que tu regardes? Je regarde un match de tennis.
Qu'est-ce qu'Alice mange? Elle mange une pizza.

To ask *what people are doing,* the French use the following construction:

qu'est-ce que + SUBJECT + VERB + ...?	**Qu'est-ce que** tu regardes?
qu'est-ce qu' (+ VOWEL SOUND)	**Qu'est-ce qu'**elle mange?

8 À la FNAC

PARLER People in Column A are at the FNAC, a store that sells books and recordings. Use a verb from Column B to ask what they are listening to or looking at. A classmate will answer you, using an item from Column C.

A	B	C
tu	écouter?	un livre de photos
vous	regarder?	un poster
Alice		un CD de rock
Éric		un CD de jazz
Antoine et Claire		un album de Youssou N'Dour

Qu'est-ce qu'Éric écoute?
Il écoute un album de Youssou N'Dour.

VARIATION Un jeu

Using the cues from Activitiy 8, have teams of students see how many correct dialogues they can write in five minutes.

Casual speech In casual conversation, the entire interrogative expression may go to the end of the sentence: **Tu travailles avec qui?**

6 COMMUNICATION taking a survey

1. Qui voyage souvent?
2. Qui aime chanter?
3. Qui nage?
4. Qui aime danser?
5. Qui regarde la télé?
6. Qui joue au tennis?
7. Qui parle italien?
8. Qui travaille?
9. Qui regarde les clips?
10. Qui joue aux jeux vidéo?
11. Qui étudie beaucoup?
12. Qui visite souvent New York?

Pronunciation clips /klips/
Note **un clip** is a music video.

7 EXCHANGES asking and answering questions

1. – À quelle heure est-ce que tu regardes la télé?
   – Je regarde la télé à 8 (huit) heures.
2. – Quand est-ce que tu visites Paris?
   – Je visite Paris en septembre.
3. – Comment est-ce que tu parles français?
   – Je parle très bien français.
4. – Avec qui est-ce que tu joues au tennis?
   – Je joue au tennis avec Denise.
5. – À qui est-ce que tu téléphones?
   – Je téléphone à mon cousin.
6. – De qui est-ce que tu parles (vous parlez)?
   – Je parle (Nous parlons) de toi.
7. – Pour qui est-ce que tu travailles?
   – Je travaille pour Monsieur Lambert.

Expansion Have students make up their own answers to the questions.
– Où est-ce que tu dînes?
– Je dîne au restaurant. (etc.)

SECTION C

Communicative function
Asking what people are doing

Casual speech Note how **quoi** is used instead of **qu'est-ce que** in casual questions.
Tu regardes quoi?
Alice mange quoi?

8 EXCHANGES asking and answering questions

Answers will vary.
- – Qu'est-ce que tu écoutes?
  – J'écoute (un CD de rock).
- – Qu'est-ce que vous regardez?
  – Nous regardons (Je regarde) (un poster).
- – Qu'est-ce qu'Alice (écoute)?
  – Alice écoute (un CD de jazz).
- – Qu'est-ce qu'Éric (regarde)?
  – Éric regarde (un livre de photos).
- – Qu'est-ce qu'Antoine et Claire (écoutent)?
  – Antoine et Claire écoutent (un album de Youssou N'Dour).

SECTION D

Communicative function
Describing what people are doing

Teaching Resource Options

PRINT 
Workbook PE, pp. 75–79
Unit 3 Resource Book
Audioscript, p. 120
Communipak, pp. 128–143
Workbook TE, pp. 93–97

AUDIO & VISUAL 
Audio Program
CD 2 Track 20
Overhead Transparencies
18 Expressions with ***faire***

TECHNOLOGY 
Power Presentations

Teaching strategy Ask students what other irregular verb they have learned (**être**). Have them point out the similarities between **être** and **faire**: singular forms end in **-s, -s, -t**; **vous**-form ends in **-tes**; **ils**-form ends in **-ont**.

Practice drill Have students practice sentences with **faire**.
Je fais une pizza.
(Tu) Tu fais une pizza., etc.
Qu'est-ce que je fais?
(Vous) Qu'est-ce que vous faites?, etc.

Supplementary vocabulary
faire un pique-nique *to have a picnic*
faire un tour *to go for a short walk or ride*
Note: **faire une promenade** may also mean *to go for a ride:* **faire une promenade à vélo, en voiture.** (This is re-entered in Lesson 14.)

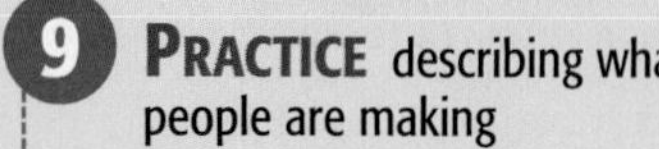

Review Remind students that **faire** is used in many weather expressions: **Il fait beau. Il fait bon.**

9 PRACTICE describing what people are making

1. faisons **2.** fais **3.** faites **4.** font
5. fait **6.** fait **7.** font **8.** font

D Le verbe *faire*

Faire *(to do, make)* is an IRREGULAR verb. It is used in many French expressions. Note the forms of **faire** in the present tense.

faire *(to do, make)*	
je **fais**	Je **fais** un sandwich.
tu **fais**	Qu'est-ce que tu **fais** maintenant?
il/elle **fait**	Qu'est-ce que ton copain **fait** samedi?
nous **faisons**	Nous **faisons** une pizza.
vous **faites**	Qu'est-ce que vous **faites** ici?
ils/elles **font**	Qu'est-ce qu'elles **font** pour la boum?

VOCABULAIRE Expressions avec *faire*

faire un match	*to play a game (match)*	Mes cousins **font un match** de tennis.
faire une promenade	*to go for a walk*	Caroline **fait une promenade** avec Olivier.
faire un voyage	*to take a trip*	Ma copine **fait un voyage** en France.
faire attention	*to pay attention*	Je **fais attention** quand le prof parle.

9 La boum de Léa

PARLER/ÉCRIRE Léa's friends are helping her prepare food for a party. Use the verb **faire** to say what everyone is doing.

▶ Je ... une crêpe.

1. Nous ... une salade.
2. Tu ... une salade de fruits.
3. Vous ... une tarte *(pie)*.
4. Cécile et Marina ... un gâteau *(cake)*.
5. Christine ... une pizza.
6. Marc ... un sandwich.
7. Patrick et Thomas ... une omelette.
8. Pierre et Karine ... une quiche.

10 Qu'est-ce qu'ils font?

PARLER/LIRE Read the descriptions below and say what the people are doing. Use the verb **faire** and an expression from the list.

un voyage
une promenade
une pizza
un match
attention

▶ Madame Dumont est en Chine.
Elle fait un voyage.

1. Léa travaille dans *(in)* un restaurant.
2. Nous sommes en ville.
3. Céline et Jean-Paul jouent au tennis.
4. Je suis dans la cuisine *(kitchen)*.
5. Marc est dans le train Paris-Nice.
6. Vous jouez au volley.
7. Je suis dans le parc.
8. Monsieur Lambert visite Tokyo.
9. Nous écoutons le prof.

INCLUSION

Structured Ask students to copy the full conjugation of **faire** in their notebooks. Have them color code, using one color for each pronunciation. Call out a color, and have students recite the corresponding verb form(s) (including pronoun).

L'interrogation avec inversion

LEARNING ABOUT LANGUAGE

In conversational French, questions are usually formed with **est-ce que.** However, when the subject of the sentence is a pronoun, French speakers often use inversion, that is, they invert or reverse the order of the subject pronoun and the verb.

REGULAR ORDER: **Vous parlez** français. (SUBJECT VERB) INVERSION: **Parlez-vous** anglais? (VERB SUBJECT)

The pairs of questions below ask the same thing. Compare the position of the subject pronouns.

Est-ce que **tu** parles anglais?	Parles-**tu** anglais?	*Do you speak English?*
Est-ce que **vous** habitez ici?	Habitez-**vous** ici?	*Do you live here?*
Où est-ce que **nous** dînons?	Où dînons-**nous**?	*Where are we having dinner?*
Où est-ce qu'**il** est?	Où est-**il**?	*Where is he?*

Inverted questions are formed according to the patterns:

YES/NO QUESTION	VERB / SUBJECT PRONOUN	...?	
	Voyagez-vous	souvent?	
INFORMATION QUESTION	INTERROGATIVE EXPRESSION	+ VERB / SUBJECT PRONOUN	...?
	Avec qui	**travaillez-vous**	demain?

→ In inversion, the verb and the subject pronoun are connected by a hyphen.

Observation In inversion, liaison is required before **il/elle** and **ils/elles.** If a verb in the singular ends on a vowel, the letter **"t"** is inserted after the verb so that liaison can occur:

Où travaille-**t**-il? Où travaille-**t**-elle? Avec qui dîne-**t**-il? Avec qui dîne-**t**-elle?

  *Conversation*

PARLER Ask your classmates a few questions, using inversion.

▶ où / habiter? —**Où habites-tu?**
—**J'habite à (Boston).**

1. à quelle heure / dîner?
2. à quelle heure / regarder la télé?
3. avec qui / parler français?
4. à qui / téléphoner souvent?
5. comment / nager?
6. avec qui / étudier?
7. où / jouer aux jeux vidéo?
8. comment / chanter?

PRONONCIATION /y/

La voyelle /y/

The vowel sound /y/ – represented by the letter "**u**" – does not exist in English.

Super!

To say **super**, first say the French word **si.** Then round your lips as if to whistle and say **si** with rounded lips: /sy/. Now say **si-per.** Then round your lips as you say the first syllable: **super!**

Répétez: /y/ **super tu étudie bien sûr**
Lucie Luc
Tu étudies avec Lucie.

TEACHING STRATEGY

If students have trouble producing /y/, have them pronounce the sound as /i/. They should not pronounce it as /u/.

10 COMPREHENSION describing what people are doing

1. Elle fait une pizza.
2. Nous faisons une promenade.
3. Ils font un match.
4. Je fais une pizza.
5. Il fait un voyage.
6. Vous faites un match.
7. Je fais une promenade.
8. Il fait un voyage.
9. Nous faisons attention.

SECTION E

Communicative function
Asking questions

Teaching note Inversion is taught mainly for recognition here. It is not emphasized in Book One.

11 COMMUNICATION getting acquainted

Answers will vary.

1. – À quelle heure dînes-tu?
   – Je dîne à (6 [six]) heures.
2. – À quelle heure regardes-tu la télé?
   – Je regarde la télé à (8 [huit]) heures.
3. – Avec qui parles-tu français?
   – Je parle français avec (mon copain).
4. – À qui téléphones-tu souvent?
   – Je téléphone souvent à (ma cousine).
5. – Comment nages-tu?
   – Je nage (très bien).
6. – Avec qui étudies-tu?
   – J'étudie avec (ma copine).
7. – Où joues-tu aux jeux vidéo?
   – Je joue aux jeux vidéo (à la maison).
8. – Comment chantes-tu?
   – Je chante (bien).

For additional practice, use the cues of this activity to practice other subject pronouns.

a) Address your questions to several students:
–Où habitez-vous?
–Nous habitons à (San Francisco).
b) Ask questions about Mélanie:
–Où habite-t-elle?
–Elle habite à (Lille).
c) Ask questions about Pierre:
–Où habite-t-il?
–Il habite à (Fort-de-France).
d) Ask questions about Trinh and Céline:
–Où habitent-ils?
–Ils habitent à (Paris).

Additional practice To practice inversion with **il/elle**, have the students redo Act. 5, p. 108 using inversion instead of **est-ce que.**

– Alice dîne.
– Ah bon? Avec qui dîne-t-elle?
– Elle dîne avec une copine.

À votre tour

Main Topic
- Recapitulation and review

Teaching Resource Options

PRINT 

Workbook PE, pp. 75–79
Unit 3 Resource Book
Audioscript, pp. 120–121
Communipak, pp. 128–143
Family Involvement, pp. 112–113
Workbook TE, pp. 93–97

Assessment
Lesson 8 Quiz, pp. 124–125
Portfolio Assessment, Unit 1 URB pp. 155–164
Audioscript for Quiz 8, p. 123
Answer Keys, pp. 216–219

AUDIO & VISUAL 

Audio Program
CD 2 Tracks 21, 22
CD 14 Track 4

TECHNOLOGY 

Test Generator CD-ROM/McDougal Littell Assessment System

1 Comprehension

1. Qu'est-ce que tu fais?
   (d) J'étudie.
2. Qu'est-ce que vous faites samedi?
   (e) Nous faisons un match de tennis.
3. Où est ton père?
   (a) Il fait une promenade.
4. Quand est-ce que tu veux jouer au tennis avec moi?
   (c) Dimanche. D'accord?
5. Qui est-ce que tu invites au cinéma?
   (b) Ma cousine Alice.
6. Pourquoi est-ce que tu étudies l'anglais?
   (f) Parce que je voudrais habiter à New York.

2 Comprehension

1. Où est-ce que tu habites?
2. À quelle heure est-ce que tu dînes?
3. Où est-ce que vous dînez?
4. Qu'est-ce que tu manges?
5. Qu'est-ce que tu regardes?
6. Qui est-ce que tu invites?

À votre tour!

OBJECTIFS

Now you can …
- ask and answer information questions
- ask about what people are doing

1 Allô!

PARLER Fatou is phoning some friends. Match her questions on the left with her friends' answers on the right.

1. Qu'est-ce que tu fais?
2. Qu'est-ce que vous faites samedi?
3. Où est ton père?
4. Quand est-ce que tu veux jouer au tennis avec moi?
5. Qui est-ce que tu invites au cinéma?
6. Pourquoi est-ce que tu étudies l'anglais?

a. Il fait une promenade.
b. Ma cousine Alice.
c. Dimanche. D'accord?
d. J'étudie.
e. Nous faisons un match de tennis.
f. Parce que je voudrais habiter à New York.

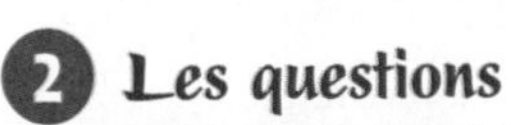

2 Les questions

LIRE/PARLER The following people are answering questions. Read what they say and figure out what questions they were asked.

▶ Comment est-ce que tu chantes?

2 Je dîne à sept heures.

6 J'invite Catherine

À votre tour

Depending on your goals and objectives, you may or may not wish to assign all of the activities in the **À votre tour** section.

Pair practice

Act. 1–4 lend themselves to pair practice.

3 Créa-dialogue

PARLER Ask your classmates what they do on different days of the week. Carry out conversations similar to the model. Note: "??" means you can invent your own answers.

▶ **—Qu'est-ce que tu fais lundi?**
—Je joue au tennis.
—Ah bon? À quelle heure est-ce que tu joues?
—À deux heures.
—Et avec qui?
—Avec Anne-Marie.

	lundi	mardi	mercredi	jeudi	vendredi	samedi	dimanche
ACTIVITÉ						??	??
À QUELLE HEURE?	2 heures	6 heures	??	??	??	??	??
AVEC QUI?	avec Anne-Marie	avec un copain	??	??	??	??	??

4 Faisons connaissance! *(Let's get acquainted!)*

PARLER/ÉCRIRE Get better acquainted with a classmate. Ask five or six questions in French. Then write a summary of your conversation and give it to the friend you have interviewed.

▶ **Mon ami(e) s'appelle …**
Il/elle habite …

You might ask questions like:

- Where does he/she live?
- Does he/she speak French at home? With whom?
- Does he/she watch TV? When? What programs (**quelles émissions**)?
- Does he/she play video games? When? With whom?
- Does he/she play soccer (or another sport)? Where? When?
- Does he/she like to swim? When? Where?
- What does he/she like to do on weekends? When? Where? With whom?

5 Curiosité

ÉCRIRE Imagine that a French friend has just made the following statements. For each one, write down three or four related questions you could ask him or her.

▼

Je joue au foot demain.

1
Je joue au tennis.
2
Je dîne avec un copain.

3
Je fais une promenade.
4
J'organise une soirée.

PORTFOLIO ASSESSMENT

You will probably only select one speaking activity and one writing activity to go into the students' portfolios for Unit 3.

In this lesson, Act. 3 and 4 are good oral portfolio conversation topics.

3 Guided Oral Expression

Answers will vary.
– Qu'est-ce que tu fais?
– Je ...
– Ah bon? À quelle heure est-ce que tu ... ?
– À ... heure(s).
– Et avec qui?
– Avec ...

- mardi / J'étudie / étudies / 6 / un copain
- mercredi / nage / nages / 3 h 30 / Anne-Marie
- jeudi / travaille / travailles / 5 / mon oncle
- vendredi / joue au basket / joues au basket / 4 / les copains
- samedi / fais une promenade / fais une promenade /2 / Paul et Éric
- dimanche / regarde la télé / regardes la télé / 6 / ma soeur

4 Guided Conversation

- Où est-ce que tu habites? (Où habites-tu?)
- Est-ce que tu parles français à la maison? (Parles-tu français à la maison?) Avec qui?
- Est-ce que tu regardes la télé? (Regardes-tu la télé?) Quand? Quelles émissions?
- Est-ce que tu joues aux jeux vidéo? (Joues-tu aux jeux vidéo?) Quand? Avec qui?
- Est-ce que tu joues au foot? (Joues-tu au foot?) Où? Quand?
- Est-ce que tu aimes nager? (Aimes-tu nager?) Quand? Où?
- Qu'est-ce que tu aimes faire le week-end? (Qu'aimes-tu faire le week-end?) Quand? Où? Avec qui?

5 Written Self-Expression

Answers will vary.

1. • Avec qui est-ce que tu joues?
   • Où est-ce que vous jouez?
   • À quelle heure est-ce que vous jouez?
   • Pourquoi est-ce que vous jouez au tennis?
2. • Où est-ce que vous dînez?
   • À quelle heure est-ce que vous dînez?
   • Pourquoi est-ce que vous dînez?
   • Quand est-ce que vous dînez?
3. • Avec qui est-ce que tu fais une promenade?
   • Où est-ce que vous faites une promenade?
   • Quand est-ce que vous faites une promenade?
   • Pourquoi est-ce que vous faites une promenade?
4. • Pourquoi est-ce que tu organises une soirée?
   • Quand est-ce que tu organises une soirée?
   • Où est-ce que tu organises une soirée?
   • Avec qui est-ce que tu organises une soirée?

Variation

Have students write this activity out as a dialogue with a partner.

TESTS DE CONTRÔLE

Teaching Resource Options

PRINT

Unit 3 Resource Book
Communipak, pp. 128–143

Assessment
Unit 3 Test, pp. 157–165
Portfolio Assessment, Unit 1 URB pp. 155–164
Multiple Choice Test Items, pp. 177–184
Listening Comprehension Performance Test, pp. 166–167
Reading Performance Test, pp. 172–174
Speaking Performance Test, pp. 168–171
Writing Performance Test, pp. 175–176
Comprehensive Test 1, Units 1–3, pp. 185–204
Test Scoring Tools, pp. 205–207
Audioscript for Tests, pp. 208–213
Answer Keys, pp. 216–219

AUDIO & VISUAL

Audio Program
CD 14 Tracks 5–16

TECHNOLOGY

Test Generator CD-ROM/McDougal Littell Assessment System

1 COMPREHENSION

1. Jean-Paul mange une pizza.
2. Vous jouez aux jeux vidéo.
3. Isabelle écoute un CD de rock.
4. Monsieur Mercier travaille pour une banque.
5. Mon cousin habite à Chicago.
6. Ils chantent dans une chorale.
7. Nous regardons une comédie à la télé.
8. Est-ce que tu parles français ou anglais?

2 COMPREHENSION

1. Je suis en classe. Je fais attention.
2. Léa est dans la cuisine. Elle fait un sandwich.
3. Nous sommes en ville. Nous faisons une promenade.
4. Les touristes sont en France. Ils font un voyage.
5. Vous êtes au stade. Vous faites un match de foot.

Tests de contrôle

By taking the following tests, you can check your progress in French and also prepare for the unit test. Write your answers on a separate sheet of paper.

Review ...
- the uses and forms of -er verbs: pp. 94, 95, 96, and 98

1 The right activity

Complete each of the following sentences by filling in the blank with the appropriate form of one of the verbs in the box. Be logical in your choice of verbs.

chanter	manger	écouter	habiter
jouer	parler	regarder	travailler

1. Jean-Paul — une pizza.
2. Vous — aux jeux vidéo.
3. Isabelle — un CD de rock.
4. Monsieur Mercier — pour une banque (*bank*).
5. Mon cousin — à Chicago.
6. Ils — dans une chorale (*choir*).
7. Nous — une comédie à la télé.
8. Est-ce que tu — français ou anglais?

Review ...
- être and faire: pp. 84 and 110

2 Être and faire

For each item, fill in the first blank with the appropriate form of **être** and the second blank with the appropriate form of **faire.**

1. Je — en classe. Je — attention.
2. Léa — dans la cuisine (*kitchen*). Elle — un sandwich.
3. Nous — en ville. Nous — une promenade.
4. Les touristes — en France. Ils — un voyage.
5. Vous — au stade (*stadium*). Vous — un match de foot.

Review ...
- negative sentences: pp. 88 and 98

3 Non!

Rewrite the following sentences in the negative, replacing the underlined words with the words in parentheses.

▶ Thomas parle français. **(anglais)** **Thomas ne parle pas anglais.**

1. Léa est française. **(américaine)**
2. Nous jouons au foot. **(au basket)**
3. Vous dînez au restaurant. **(à la maison)**
4. Tu invites Céline. **(Isabelle)**
5. Ils habitent à Québec. **(à Montréal)**

4 The right question

Write out the questions that correspond to the answers below. Make sure to begin your sentences with the question words that correspond to the underlined information. Use **tu** in your questions.

▶ J'habite à Paris. **Où est-ce que tu habites?**

1. Je téléphone à Marc.
2. Je dîne à sept heures.
3. Je mange une pizza.
4. Je voyage en juillet.
5. J'écoute un CD.
6. Je joue très bien au foot.

Review ...
- information questions: pp. 106 and 108

5 The right choice

Choose the word or expression in parentheses which logically completes each of the following sentences.

1. François habite — France. **(à, au, en)**
2. Isabelle est au café — Céline. **(et, avec, pour)**
3. Nicolas parle français, — il ne parle pas espagnol. **(pourquoi, mal, mais)**
4. Pierre écoute — radio. **(à, la, à la)**
5. Je n'habite pas ici. J'habite —. **(où, aussi, là-bas)**
6. Tu ne chantes pas bien. Tu chantes —. **(mal, souvent, beaucoup)**
7. Philippe aime beaucoup jouer au foot. Il joue —. **(pour, mais non, souvent)**
8. Je ne peux pas dîner avec toi. Je — étudier pour l'examen. **(dois, veux, n'aime pas)**
9. J'étudie l'espagnol — je voudrais visiter Madrid. **(où, comment, parce que)**
10. Qui est-ce? Jérôme — Patrick? **(pour, ou, aussi)**

Review ...
- vocabulary: pp. 77, 78, 85, 89, 95, 100, 106

6 Composition: Les vacances

Write a short paragraph of five or six sentences saying what you and your friends do and don't do during summer vacation. Use only vocabulary and expressions that you know in French.

STRATEGY Writing

a Make a list of activities that you do and a second list of things that you don't do. Use infinitives.

b Organize your ideas and write your paragraph, using **je** or **nous**.

c Check each sentence to be sure that the verb endings agree with the subject.

oui	non
• *nager*	•
•	•
•	•
•	•
•	•

3 COMPREHENSION

1. Léa n'est pas américaine.
2. Nous ne jouons pas au basket.
3. Vous ne dînez pas à la maison.
4. Tu n'invites pas Isabelle.
5. Ils n'habitent pas à Montréal.

4 COMPREHENSION

1. À qui est-ce que tu téléphones?
2. À quelle heure est-ce que tu dînes?
3. Qu'est-ce que tu manges?
4. Quand est-ce que tu voyages?
5. Qu'est-ce que tu écoutes?
6. Comment est-ce que tu joues au foot?

5 COMPREHENSION

1. François habite en France.
2. Isabelle est au café avec Céline.
3. Nicolas parle français, mais il ne parle pas espagnol.
4. Pierre écoute la radio.
5. Je n'habite pas ici. J'habite là-bas.
6. Tu ne chantes pas bien. Tu chantes mal.
7. Philippe aime beaucoup jouer au foot. Il joue souvent.
8. Je ne peux pas dîner avec toi. Je dois étudier pour l'examen.
9. J'étudie l'espagnol parce que je voudrais visiter Madrid.
10. Qui est-ce? Jérôme ou Patrick?

6 WRITTEN SELF-EXPRESSION

Answers will vary.

a.

oui	non
nager	étudier
regarder la télé	dîner avec la famille
écouter la radio	parler anglais
jouer au tennis	jouer au foot
jouer au volley	manger au restaurant

b. En été, j'aime regarder la télé avec mes copains. Nous jouons au tennis mais nous ne jouons pas au foot. Je n'étudie pas quand je suis en vacances et je nage avec mes copains. Nous jouons au volley souvent et nous écoutons la radio.

Vocabulaire

Language Learning Benchmarks

FUNCTION
- Engage in conversations pp. 87, 107
- Express likes and dislikes p. 76
- Obtain information pp. 88, 97, 100
- Begin to provide information p. 88

CONTEXT
- Converse in face-to-face social interactions pp. 88, 96, 101
- Listen during social interactions p. 108
- Listen to audio and video texts pp. 72-73, 89, 99, 101, 107, 111, 124
- Use authentic materials when reading: schedules pp. 118, 131
- Use authentic materials when reading: short narratives p. 121
- Write lists pp. 103, 115, 121
- Write short letters p. 123

TEXT TYPE
- Use short sentences when speaking p. 76
- Use short sentences when writing pp. 74, 97
- Use learned words and phrases when speaking p. 76
- Use learned words and phrases when writing pp. 77, 99
- Use simple questions when speaking pp. 78, 86, 95, 111
- Use simple questions when writing pp. 87, 109
- Understand some ideas and familiar details presented in clear, uncomplicated speech when listening p. 107

Vocabulaire

POUR COMMUNIQUER

Talking about likes and preferences

Est-ce que tu aimes	**parler anglais?**	*Do you like*	*to speak English?*
J'aime		*I like*	
Je n'aime pas		*I don't like*	
Je préfère	**parler français.**	*I prefer*	*to speak French.*
Je veux		*I want*	
Je voudrais		*I would like*	
Je ne veux pas		*I don't want*	

Inviting a friend

Est-ce que tu veux [jouer au tennis]?	*Do you want to [play tennis]?*
Est-ce que tu peux [jouer au foot] avec moi?	*Can you [play soccer] with me?*

Accepting or declining an invitation

Oui, bien sûr.	*Yes, of course.*	**Je regrette, mais je ne peux pas.**	*I'm sorry, but I can't.*
Oui, merci.	*Yes, thanks.*	**Je dois [travailler].**	*I have to, I must [work].*
Oui, d'accord.	*Yes, all right, okay.*		
Oui, je veux bien.	*Yes, I'd love to.*		

Expressing approval, regret, or surprise

Super!	*Terrific!*
Dommage!	*Too bad!*
Ah bon?	*Oh? Really?*

Answering a yes/no question

Oui!	*Yes!*	**Non!**	*No!*
Mais oui!	*Sure!*	**Mais non!**	*Of course not!*
Bien sûr!	*Of course!*	**Peut-être ...**	*Maybe ...*

Asking for information

où?	*where?*	**qu'est-ce que ...?**	*what?*
quand?	*when?*	**qui?**	*who, whom?*
à quelle heure?	*at what time?*	**à qui?**	*to who(m)?*
comment?	*how?*	**de qui?**	*about who(m)?*
pourquoi?	*why?*	**avec qui?**	*with who(m)?*
parce que ...	*because*	**pour qui?**	*for who(m)?*

Saying where people are

Pierre est ...

ici	*here*	**à la maison**	*at home*	**en classe**	*in class*
là	*here, there*	**au café**	*at the café*	**en France**	*in France*
là-bas	*over there*	**au cinéma**	*at the movies*	**en vacances**	*on vacation*
à [Paris]	*in [Paris]*	**au restaurant**	*at the restaurant*	**en ville**	*in town*

Saying how well, how often, and when

bien	*well*	**beaucoup**	*a lot, much, very much*	**maintenant**	*now*
très bien	*very well*	**un peu**	*a little, a little bit*	**souvent**	*often*
mal	*badly, poorly*	**rarement**	*rarely, seldom*	**toujours**	*always*

MOTS ET EXPRESSIONS

Verbes réguliers en *-er*

aimer	*to like*	**jouer aux jeux vidéo**	*to play video games*
chanter	*to sing*	**manger**	*to eat*
danser	*to dance*	**nager**	*to swim*
dîner	*to have dinner*	**organiser une boum**	*to organize a party*
dîner au restaurant	*to eat out*	**parler anglais**	*to speak English*
écouter	*to listen, to listen to*	**parler espagnol**	*to speak Spanish*
écouter la radio	*to listen to the radio*	**parler français**	*to speak French*
étudier	*to study*	**regarder**	*to watch, to look at*
habiter (à Paris)	*to live (in Paris)*	**regarder la télé**	*to watch TV*
inviter	*to invite*	**téléphoner (à Céline)**	*to phone (Céline)*
jouer au basket	*to play basketball*	**travailler**	*to work*
jouer au foot	*to play soccer*	**visiter (Paris)**	*to visit (Paris)*
jouer au tennis	*to play tennis*	**voyager**	*to travel*

Verbes irréguliers

être	*to be*	**faire**	*to do, make*
être d'accord	*to agree*	**faire un match**	*to play a game (match)*
		faire une promenade	*to go for a walk*
		faire un voyage	*to take a trip*
		faire attention	*to pay attention*

Mots utiles

à	*at, in*	**et**	*and*
aussi	*also*	**mais**	*but*
avec	*with*	**ou**	*or*
de	*from, of*	**pour**	*for*

TEST PREP CLASSZONE.COM FLASHCARDS AND MORE!

CONTENT

- Understand and convey information about leisure activities pp. 74, 76, 77
- Understand and convey information about campus life pp. 127, 131
- Understand and convey information about likes and dislikes p. 76

ASSESSMENT

- Communicate effectively with some hesitation and errors, which do not hinder comprehension pp. 91, 103
- Demonstrate culturally acceptable behavior for greeting and responding to greetings p. 80
- Demonstrate culturally acceptable behavior for engaging in conversations pp. 80, 103, 113
- Demonstrate culturally acceptable behavior for expressing likes and dislikes p. 81
- Demonstrate culturally acceptable behavior for obtaining information pp. 80, 91, 113, 115
- Demonstrate culturally acceptable behavior for providing information p. 91

ENTRACTE 3

Objectives

- Reading skill development
- Re-entry of materials in the unit
- Development of cultural awareness
- Vocabulary expansion

À la télé

Objectives

- Reading for information
- Selecting programs from a French TV guide

Teaching Resource Options

Workbook PE, pp. 81–84
Activités pour tous PE, pp. 47–49
Unit 3 Resource Book
Activités pour tous TE, pp. 145–147
Workbook TE, pp. 149–152

Sélection de la semaine

émission *TV show*
hôtel de police *police department*
bossu *hunchback*

Teaching Suggestion Have students note which American programs (TV shows/movies) are listed on this TV guide. Students can also visit online versions of French television guides to see how American TV influences French TV.

Ce week-end, à la télé

Le week-end, les jeunes Français regardent souvent la télé. Ils aiment regarder les films et le sport. Ils regardent aussi les jeux et les séries américaines et françaises. Les principales chaînes° sont TF1, France 2, France 3, Cinquième Arte, M6 et Canal Plus. Voici le programme de télévision pour ce week-end.

chaînes *channels*

Note In French TV listings, times are expressed using a 24-hour clock. In this system, 8 p.m. is 20.00 **(vingt heures)**, 9 p.m. is 21.00 **(vingt et une heures)**, 10 p.m. is 22 heures **(vingt-deux heures)**, etc.

SÉLECTION DE LA SEMAINE	VENDREDI	SAMEDI
TF1	**20.50** Magazine **SUCCÈS** Émission présentée par Julien Courbet et Anne Magnien **23.15** MAGAZINE • **Célébrités**	**20.50** Jeu **QUI VEUT GAGNER DES MILLIONS?** avec Jean-Pierre Foucault **21.50** SÉRIE • **Les Soprano**
France 2	**20.55** Série **HÔTEL DE POLICE** **Le gentil Monsieur** de Claude Barrois avec Cécile Magnet **23.20** DOCUMENTAIRE • **Histoires Naturelles**	**21.00** Variétés **CHAMPS-ÉLYSÉES** Invités: Ricky Martin, Juliette Binoche, Ben Affleck **22.35** SÉRIE • **Buffy contre les Vampires**
france 3	**21.00** Film **LE CINQUIÈME ÉLÉMENT** de Luc Besson avec Bruce Willis et Milla Jovovich **22.15** CONCERT • **Viva Latino**	**20.40** Série **INSPECTEUR BARNABY** avec Daniel Casey **22.50** SPORT • **Grand Prix d'Italie** Motocyclisme
france 5 arte	**20.45** Documentaire **CATHÉDRALES** de Jean-François Delassus **22.20** FILM • **Quasimodo, le bossu de Notre Dame**	**20.50** Documentaire **ARCHITECTURES** La Tour Eiffel **20.05** CONCERT • **Le Philharmonique de Vienne**
M6	**20.50** Variétés **GRAINES DE STAR** émission présentée par Laurent Boyer **22.20** THÉÂTRE • **Rhinocéros**	**20.35** Film **LE MARIAGE DE MON MEILLEUR AMI** avec Julia Roberts **22.15** SÉRIE • **Police District**
CANAL+	**20.50** Football **MARSEILLE-NICE** Championnat de France **22.50** FILM • **Air Force One** avec Harrison Ford	**20.45** Film **MON PÈRE, CE HÉROS** avec Gérard Depardieu **23.15** RUGBY • **Toulouse-Biarritz**

CLASSROOM MANAGEMENT

Pre-reading

Ask pairs of students to name their favorite TV programs.

Quelle est votre émission favorite?
Nous aimons [les matchs de football].

Group reading activity

Divide the class into groups of 4 or 5. Each group must decide on which early and which late show they will watch each night. Then they report their decision to the class.

Vendredi nous allons regarder ... et ...
Samedi nous allons regarder ... et ...

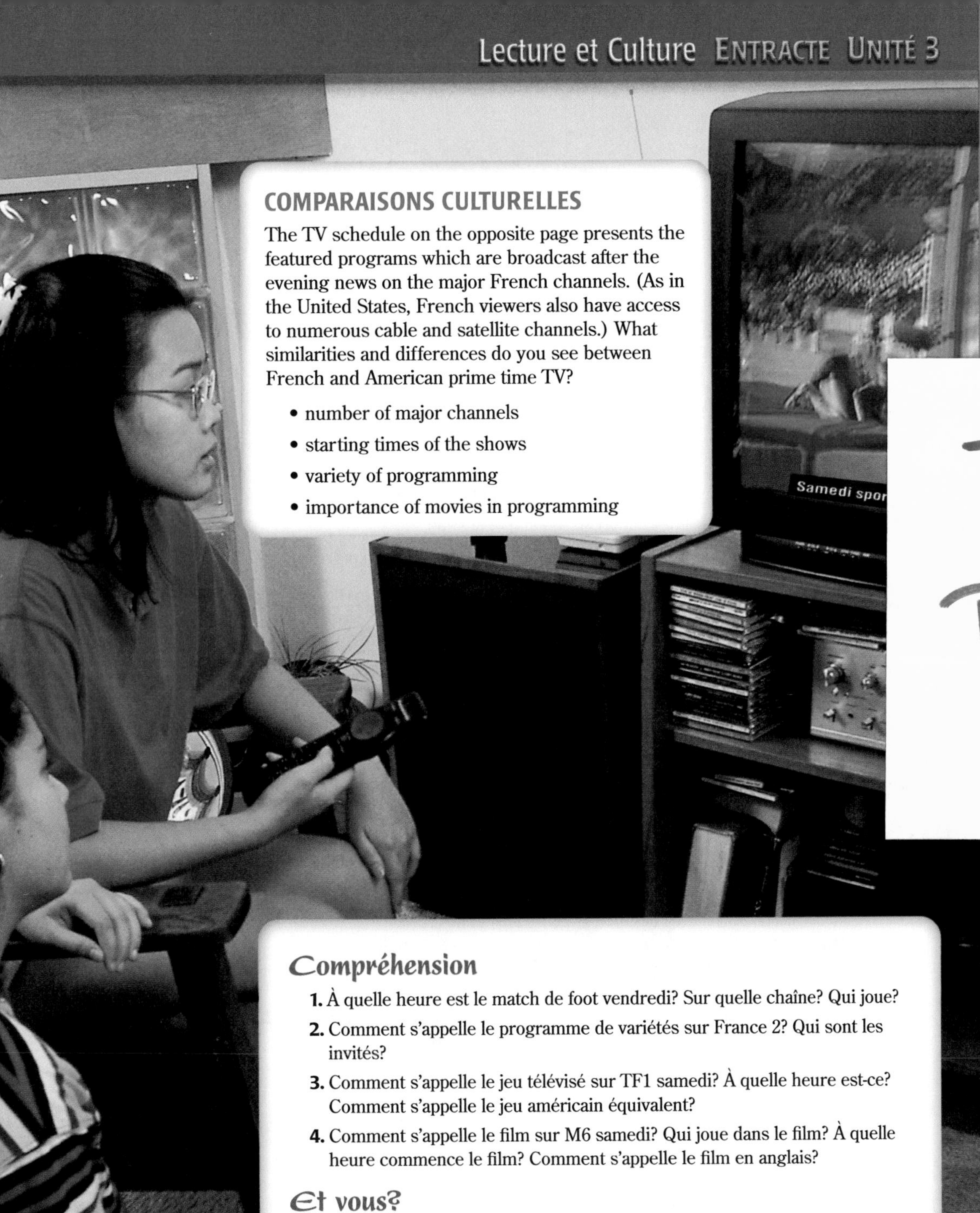

COMPARAISONS CULTURELLES

The TV schedule on the opposite page presents the featured programs which are broadcast after the evening news on the major French channels. (As in the United States, French viewers also have access to numerous cable and satellite channels.) What similarities and differences do you see between French and American prime time TV?

- number of major channels
- starting times of the shows
- variety of programming
- importance of movies in programming

Compréhension

1. À quelle heure est le match de foot vendredi? Sur quelle chaîne? Qui joue?
2. Comment s'appelle le programme de variétés sur France 2? Qui sont les invités?
3. Comment s'appelle le jeu télévisé sur TF1 samedi? À quelle heure est-ce? Comment s'appelle le jeu américain équivalent?
4. Comment s'appelle le film sur M6 samedi? Qui joue dans le film? À quelle heure commence le film? Comment s'appelle le film en anglais?

Et vous?

Vous êtes en France et vous aimez les films. Quel film est-ce que vous voudriez *(would like)* regarder à la télé ce week-end? Sur quelle chaîne? À quelle heure? Est-ce que c'est un film français ou américain?

Teaching note Tell students to look for French language broadcasts on local radio or television stations. Cable TV may offer stations from France or Quebec. Public and college radio stations often play world music. Of course, many French language radio and television stations can be accessed on the Internet.

Compréhension

Answers.

1. Le match de foot est à 20.50 (à 8 h 50) sur Canal Plus. Marseille et Nice jouent.
2. Le programme de variétés s'appelle «Champs-Élysées». Les invités sont Ricky Martin, Juliette Binoche et Ben Affleck.
3. Le jeu télévisé sur TF1 samedi s'appelle «Qui veut gagner des millions?» Il est à 20.50. Le jeu américain équivalent s'appelle «Who Wants to Be a Millionaire?»
4. Le film sur M6 samedi s'appelle «Le mariage de mon meilleur ami». Julia Roberts joue dans le film. Le film commence à 20.35. En anglais, le film s'appelle «My Best Friend's Wedding».

Et vous?

Answers will vary.
Je voudrais regarder «Mon père, ce héros» sur Canal Plus à 20.45. C'est un film français.

L'internet, c'est cool!

Objectives

- Reading a longer text
- Develop logical thinking

Teaching Resource Options

PRINT  

Workbook PE, pp. 81–84
Activités pour tous PE, pp. 47–49
Unit 3 Resource Book
Activités pour tous TE, pp. 145–147
Workbook TE, pp. 149–152

Teaching strategy

Do not have students read aloud since they will have difficulty pronouncing the new words and cognates. Have them follow along silently as you read the text.

Cultural note

Êtes vous branché(e)?

In France, people who like to "surf the Net," **surfer sur le Net,** are called **les cybernautes** or **les internautes.** With the Web, we can make a reservation in a Parisian hotel . . . or visit Mont-Saint-Michel . . . or take an African safari . . . **tout est possible avec l'Internet!** Young French people love to play computer games or **les jeux d'ordinateur.** Some games are on CD-ROM and are interactive. One game even allows students to visit the Louvre, with photos of paintings, and commentary (**les récits**). Also included may be sound clips **(les citations sonores),** animations **(les animations),** text, and illustrations.

Teaching Suggestions

- Have students choose one of the four students interiewed in the reading, and ask them to write an email to that person to find out more information about how he / she uses the Internet.
- You may wish to moderate a classroom "epal" exchange with students in francophone countries. This moderated activity could be done in your own classroom or in a language lab. Also, refer to p. T64 for more information about connecting your students to penpal/epal resources.

L'INTERNET, c'est cool!

Précédente Suivante Recharger Accueil Rechercher Images Imprimer Sécurité Arrêter

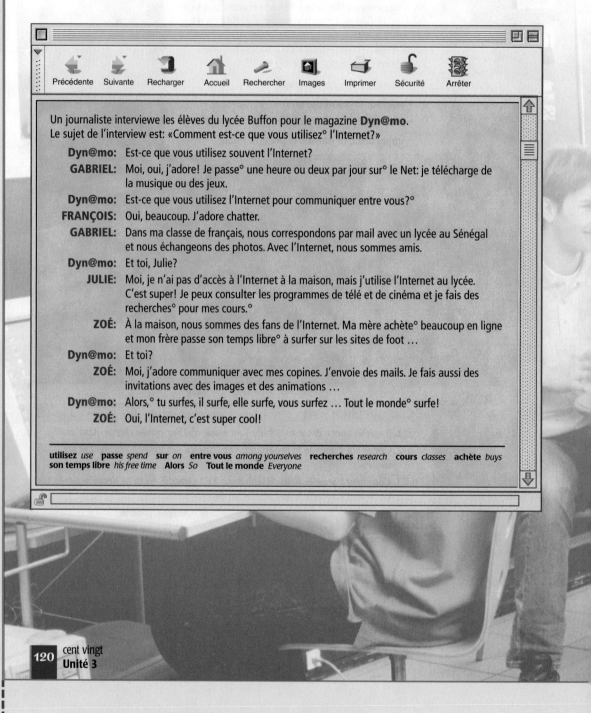

Un journaliste interviewe les élèves du lycée Buffon pour le magazine **Dyn@mo.**
Le sujet de l'interview est: «Comment est-ce que vous utilisez° l'Internet?»

Dyn@mo: Est-ce que vous utilisez souvent l'Internet?

GABRIEL: Moi, oui, j'adore! Je passe° une heure ou deux par jour sur° le Net: je télécharge de la musique ou des jeux.

Dyn@mo: Est-ce que vous utilisez l'Internet pour communiquer entre vous?°

FRANÇOIS: Oui, beaucoup. J'adore chatter.

GABRIEL: Dans ma classe de français, nous correspondons par mail avec un lycée au Sénégal et nous échangeons des photos. Avec l'Internet, nous sommes amis.

Dyn@mo: Et toi, Julie?

JULIE: Moi, je n'ai pas d'accès à l'Internet à la maison, mais j'utilise l'Internet au lycée. C'est super! Je peux consulter les programmes de télé et de cinéma et je fais des recherches° pour mes cours.°

ZOÉ: À la maison, nous sommes des fans de l'Internet. Ma mère achète° beaucoup en ligne et mon frère passe son temps libre° à surfer sur les sites de foot ...

Dyn@mo: Et toi?

ZOÉ: Moi, j'adore communiquer avec mes copines. J'envoie des mails. Je fais aussi des invitations avec des images et des animations ...

Dyn@mo: Alors,° tu surfes, il surfe, elle surfe, vous surfez ... Tout le monde° surfe!

ZOÉ: Oui, l'Internet, c'est super cool!

utilisez *use* **passe** *spend* **sur** *on* **entre vous** *among yourselves* **recherches** *research* **cours** *classes* **achète** *buys* **son temps libre** *his free time* **Alors** *So* **Tout le monde** *Everyone*

NOTE culturelle

Les jeunes Français et l'Internet

French people are technologically very sophisticated. They developed the **Minitel**, a precursor of the Internet, many years before this newer system of transmitting information became universally adopted.

At school, French students learn how to use the Internet in their computer science classes (**les cours d'informatique**). Many have Internet connections at home. Those who do not can go to a **cybercafé** where they can surf the Net while having a sandwich or a soda.

PETIT DICTIONNAIRE DE L'INTERNET

- **chatter** = *to chat*
- **envoyer un mail (un mél)** = *to send an e-mail*
- **surfer sur l'Internet (le Net)** = *to surf the Internet*
- **télécharger** = *to download*
- **être en ligne** = *to be online*

COMPARAISONS CULTURELLES

Read the **Dyn@mo** interview again and make a list of the different ways students at the lycée Buffon use the Internet. Then list the ways in which you use the Internet. Do you engage in some of the same activities as the French teenagers?

les jeunes Français	moi
•	•
•	•
•	•

Language note

In 2004, the French Ministry of Culture declared that the term **un courriel** should be used in official documents to refer to *e-mail* instead of the English-derived words **un mail** and **un mél**. **Un courriel**, which is a blend of another term meaning *e-mail*, **courrier électronique**, is already widely used in Quebec, Canada, but many French people continue to use the words **un mail** and **un mél**.

Note culturelle

Many French schools have their own web sites which are often created by the students themselves. Locate URLs for several French *collèges* and *lycées*. Have students visit the schools' web sites and answer the question: What can you tell from the web sites about the attitudes and interests of young French students?

Teaching notes

- After the students have read **L'Internet, c'est cool!,** divide the class into teams of three. Have them compete to see which group can find the most cognates.
- Have students look at the websites for the consulates of several francophone countries. They should note what services and cultural activities these offices offer to their citizens who are living in the United States and to the general public.

Comparaisons culturelles

Answers.
les jeunes Français
(Ils utilisent l'Internet pour ...)
- télécharger de la musique
- télécharger des jeux
- chatter
- correspondre par mail avec un lycée au Sénégal
- échanger des photos
- consulter les programmes de télé et de cinéma
- faire des recherches
- (acheter des choses en ligne)
- surfer
- envoyer des mails (communiquer avec des amis)
- faire des invitations

Bonjour, Trinh!

Objective

- Reading at the paragraph level

Teaching Resource Options

PRINT

Workbook PE, pp. 81–84
Activités pour tous PE, pp. 47–49
Unit 3 Resource Book
Activités pour tous TE, pp. 145–147
Workbook TE, pp. 149–152

Language notes

- Trinh writes in a casual style. Point out the shortened words:
  un prof (professeur)
  sympa (sympathique)

Teaching note

If your school has computer capabilities, you may want to explore the possibility of using the Internet to facilitate instruction. You may also consider linking your class with an English class in France through e-mail correspondance. Contact the American Association of Teachers of French (AATF) for more information and ideas.

Questions sur le texte

1. Pourquoi est-ce que Trinh aime les boums? [Il adore danser.]
2. Quelle sorte de musique est-ce qu'il aime? [le rock, le rap, le reggae]
3. Quels sports est-ce qu'il pratique en hiver? Et en été? [En hiver, il fait du snowboard. En été, il nage et il joue au tennis.]
4. Comment est-ce qu'il joue au tennis? [assez bien]
5. Pourquoi est-ce qu'il aime l'anglais? [Le prof est sympa.]
6. Qu'est-ce qu'il aime regarder à la télé? [le sport et les films d'aventures]
7. À qui est-ce qu'il téléphone? [à sa copine]
8. Pourquoi est-ce qu'il ne téléphone pas souvent? [Son père n'aime pas ça.]

Bonjour, Trinh!

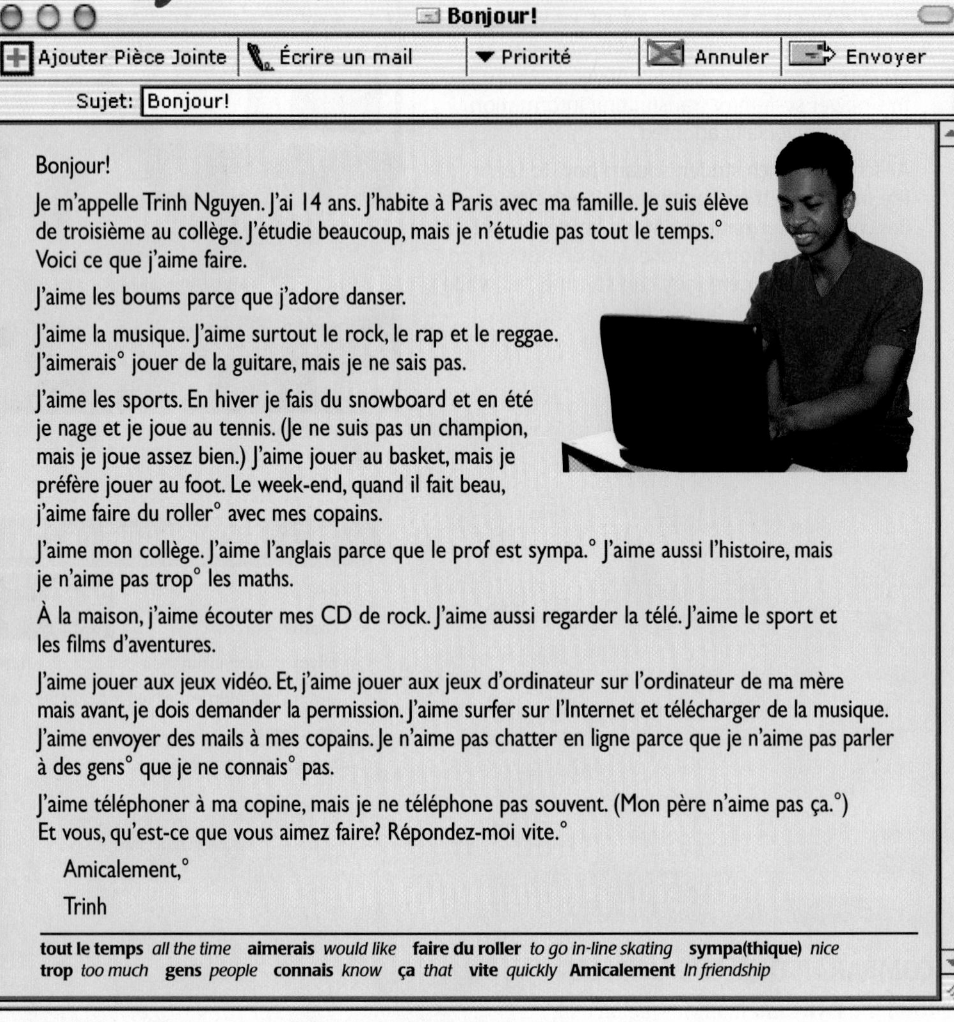

Bonjour!

Ajouter Pièce Jointe | Écrire un mail | Priorité | Annuler | Envoyer

Sujet: Bonjour!

Bonjour!

Je m'appelle Trinh Nguyen. J'ai 14 ans. J'habite à Paris avec ma famille. Je suis élève de troisième au collège. J'étudie beaucoup, mais je n'étudie pas tout le temps.° Voici ce que j'aime faire.

J'aime les boums parce que j'adore danser.

J'aime la musique. J'aime surtout le rock, le rap et le reggae. J'aimerais° jouer de la guitare, mais je ne sais pas.

J'aime les sports. En hiver je fais du snowboard et en été je nage et je joue au tennis. (Je ne suis pas un champion, mais je joue assez bien.) J'aime jouer au basket, mais je préfère jouer au foot. Le week-end, quand il fait beau, j'aime faire du roller° avec mes copains.

J'aime mon collège. J'aime l'anglais parce que le prof est sympa.° J'aime aussi l'histoire, mais je n'aime pas trop° les maths.

À la maison, j'aime écouter mes CD de rock. J'aime aussi regarder la télé. J'aime le sport et les films d'aventures.

J'aime jouer aux jeux vidéo. Et, j'aime jouer aux jeux d'ordinateur sur l'ordinateur de ma mère mais avant, je dois demander la permission. J'aime surfer sur l'Internet et télécharger de la musique. J'aime envoyer des mails à mes copains. Je n'aime pas chatter en ligne parce que je n'aime pas parler à des gens° que je ne connais° pas.

J'aime téléphoner à ma copine, mais je ne téléphone pas souvent. (Mon père n'aime pas ça.°) Et vous, qu'est-ce que vous aimez faire? Répondez-moi vite.°

Amicalement,°

Trinh

tout le temps *all the time* **aimerais** *would like* **faire du roller** *to go in-line skating* **sympa(thique)** *nice* **trop** *too much* **gens** *people* **connais** *know* **ça** *that* **vite** *quickly* **Amicalement** *In friendship*

STRATEGY Reading

Cognates You have already discovered that there are many words in French that look like English words and have similar meanings. These are called cognates. Cognates let you increase your reading comprehension effortlessly. Be sure to pronounce them the French way!

- Sometimes the spelling is the same, or almost the same:

  un champion *champion*
  la permission *permission*

- Sometimes the spelling is a little different:

  les maths *math*

PRE-READING

Ask if any of the students in the class have pen pals.

Est-ce que vous avez un correspondant ou une correspondante?

Où habite votre correspondant(e)?

Tell them this is an e-mail from a French pen pal.

Activité écrite: Une lettre à Trinh

You are writing an e-mail to Trinh in which you introduce yourself and explain what you like to do. Be sure to use only vocabulary that you know in French. You may tell him:

- if you like music (and what kind)
- what sports you like to do in fall or winter
- what sports you like to do in spring or summer
- which school subjects you like and which you do not like
- what you like to do at home
- which programs you like to watch on TV
- what you like to do on the Internet and what you do not like to do

Writing Hint Use Trinh's letter as a model.

NOTE culturelle

Les Vietnamiens en France

Vietnam and other Southeast Asian countries like Laos and Cambodia have a long civilization. For a period of about eighty years until the mid-1950s, these countries were occupied and administered by France which established schools and promoted the use of the French language among their populations.

In recent years, many Vietnamese people like Trinh's family have emigrated to France. Vietnamese restaurants are very popular with French students because of their fine yet inexpensive cuisine.

Questions personnelles

1. Est-ce que tu aimes la musique? Quelle sorte de musique est-ce que tu aimes écouter? [Oui, j'aime la musique. (Non, je n'aime pas la musique.) J'aime écouter le rap.]
2. Est-ce que tu joues d'un instrument? [Oui, je joue (de la guitare). (Non, je ne joue pas d'un instrument.)]
3. Quels sports est-ce que tu pratiques en hiver? en été? [En éte, je (nage). En hiver, je (joue au basketball).]
4. Est-ce que tu aimes ton école? Quelles matières est-ce que tu aimes? Quelle matières est-ce que tu n'aimes pas? [Oui, j'aime mon école. (Non, je n'aime pas mon école.) J'aime (le français et les maths). Je n'aime pas (l'anglais et l'histoire).]
5. Est-ce que tu aimes étudier le français? (Pourquoi ou pourquoi pas?) [J'aime étudier le français parce que (j'aime parler avec les Français). Je n'aime pas étudier le français parce que (mes copains ne sont pas dans la classe).]
6. Est-ce que tu téléphones souvent? À qui? Est-ce que tu aimes téléphoner? [Oui, je téléphone souvent. (Non, je ne téléphone pas souvent.) Je téléphone à (des copains). Oui, j'aime téléphoner. (Non, je n'aime pas téléphoner.)]

Additional cognates

adore
la musique
le rock
la guitare
les sports
le tennis
le week-end
mes CD
les maths ...

Teaching note

Have students use a French search engine **(un portail)** to find and set up free "French" e-mail accounts and have their own French e-mail boxes **(boîtes aux lettres).** They can even use instant messaging **(la messagerie instantanée)** to talk to their new French friends.

IMAGES

Cultural Theme

• School in France

À l'école en France

Teaching Resource Options

PRINT 

Workbook PE, pp. 81–84
Activités pour tous PE, pp. 47–49
Unit 3 Resource Book
Activités pour tous TE, pp. 145–147
Lesson Plans, pp. 153–154
Block Scheduling Lesson Plans, pp. 155–156
Videoscript, p. 215
Workbook TE, pp. 149–152

VIDEO PROGRAM

VIDÉO DVD

IMAGES
À l'école en France

TOTAL TIME: 5:36 min.
DVD Disk 1
Videotape 2 (COUNTER: 00:00 min.)

B.1 Visite avec Nathalie Aubin (0:00-1:00 min.)

B.2 Le lycée Jean-Baptiste Corot (1:01-3:31 min.)

B.3 Mini-scenes: Quel est ton sujet favori? (3:32-4:04 min.)

B.4 Conclusion de la visite (4:05-5:36 min.)

IMAGES

À l'école en France

Bonjour, Nathalie!

Bonjour!
Je m'appelle Nathalie Aubin.
J'ai 15 ans et j'habite à Savigny-sur-Orge avec ma famille. (Savigny est une petite° ville à 20 kilomètres au sud° de Paris.)
J'ai un frère, Christophe, 17 ans, et deux soeurs, Céline, 13 ans, et Florence, 7 ans.
Mon père est programmeur. (Il travaille à Paris.)
Ma mère est dentiste. (Elle travaille à Savigny.)
Je vais au lycée Jean-Baptiste Corot.
Je suis élève° de seconde°.
Et vous?

Nathalie

petite *small* **sud** *south* **élève** *student* **seconde** *tenth grade*

USING THE VIDEO

This **Images, À l'école en France,** was filmed at the Lycée Jean-Baptiste Corot in Savigny-sur-Orge, near Paris. Play the entire module as an introduction to the photo essay.

Les photos de Nathalie

Voici ma famille.

moi

ma mère ma soeur Céline

mon père

mon frère Christophe et ma soeur Florence

Voici ma maison. (C'est une maison confortable, mais ce n'est pas un château!)

Voici mon école.°
Le lycée Jean-Baptiste Corot est dans° un château!°

école *school* **dans** *in* **château** *castle*

Classroom Management Groups

After showing the video, have students in groups discuss the similarities and differences between their school and the Lycée Corot. Let each group name a recorder (**secrétaire**) who will list their findings.

As a full class activity, ask the recorders to read their lists and compare the findings. Which group was most observant?

As a follow-up, you may want to play the video a second time.

Le lycée Jean-Baptiste Corot

Teaching Resource Options

PRINT 

Workbook PE, pp. 81–84
Activités pour tous PE, pp. 47–49
Unit 3 Resource Book
Activités pour tous TE, pp. 145–147
Videoscript, p. 215
Workbook TE, pp. 149–152

VIDEO PROGRAM

VIDÉO DVD

IMAGES

B.2 Le lycée Jean-Baptiste Corot (1:01-3:31 min.)

B.3 Mini-scenes: Quel est ton sujet favori? (3:32-4:04 min.)

Teaching suggestion You may want to play these two segments again, having students focus on the school itself rather than on Nathalie.

Cultural notes

- **Savigny-sur-Orge** The construction of the **R.E.R. (Réseau Express Régional)**, a fast commuter train, has brought Savigny-sur-Orge within easy commuting distance of Paris. It takes only half an hour to get from Savigny to the center of the capital.
- Paintings
  - –The top painting is a self-portrait of Jean-Baptiste Corot.
  - –The bottom painting by Corot is a view of Chatelaine, Geneva.

Le lycée Jean-Baptiste Corot

Jean-Baptiste Corot

The lycée Jean-Baptiste Corot is located in Savigny-sur-Orge, a small town about 12 miles south of Paris. Like many French schools, it is named after a famous French person. Jean-Baptiste Corot was a 19th century painter, remembered especially for his landscapes.

The lycée Jean-Baptiste Corot is both old and modern. It was created in the 1950s on the grounds of a historical castle dating from the 12th century. The castle, which serves as the administrative center, is still surrounded by a moat. The lycée itself has many modern facilities which include:

- **les salles de classe** *(classrooms)*
- **la cantine** *(cafeteria)*
- **le stade** *(stadium)* **et le terrain de sport** *(playing field)*

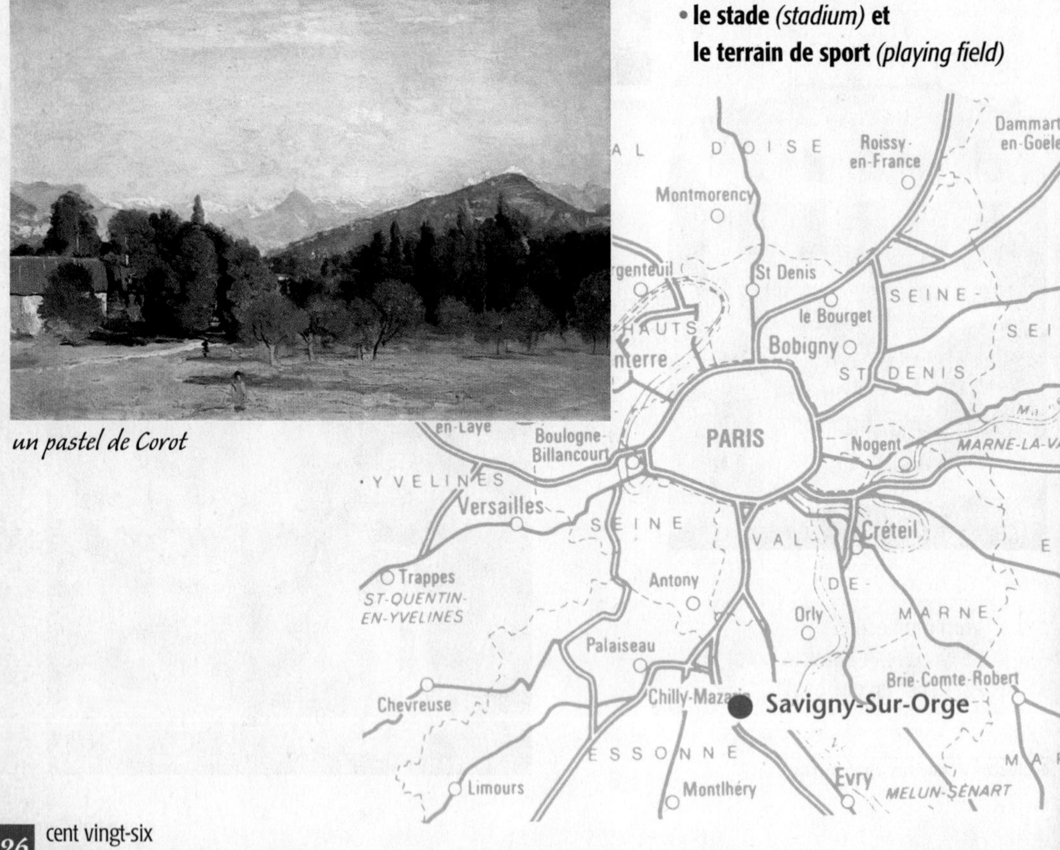

un pastel de Corot

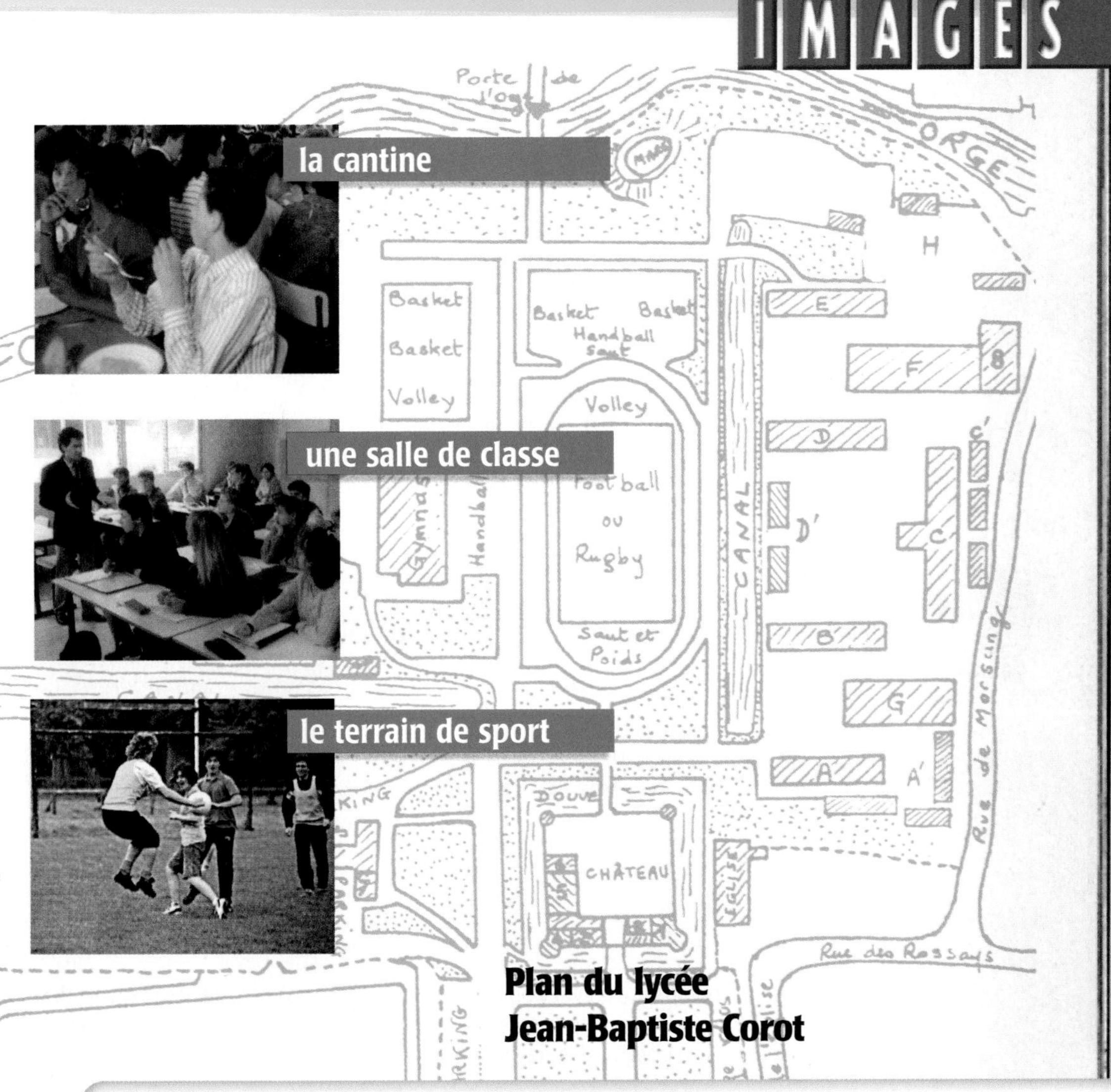

Plan du lycée Jean-Baptiste Corot

Comparaisons Culturelles

1. Compare your school to the lycée Jean-Baptiste Corot.

- Is your school named after somebody? If so, why is this person famous?
- Is your school older or more modern than the lycée Jean-Baptiste Corot? When was it built (approximately)?
- Does your school have the same facilities as the lycée Jean-Baptiste Corot? Does it have other facilities?

2. Make a map of your school, giving French names to its facilities. (Ask for your teacher's help for words you do not know.)

Supplementary vocabulary

réfectoires élèves *student cafeteria*
réfectoire professeurs *teachers' cafeteria*

L'école secondaire en France

Teaching Resource Options

PRINT 

Workbook PE, pp. 81–84
Activités pour tous PE, pp. 47–49
Unit 3 Resource Book
Activités pour tous TE, pp. 145–147
Workbook TE, pp. 149–152

Supplementary Vocabulary

le proviseur *principal*
le proviseur adjoint *vice principal*
le conseiller principal d'éducation *guidance counselor*
le professeur principal *homeroom teacher*

Teaching suggestion Ask students to think of various careers in which knowledge of French would be useful or necessary. Have them look at job postings online and ask them to make a list of positions in which knowledge of French is a requirement.

L'école secondaire en France

There are two types of secondary schools in France:

- **le collège,** which corresponds to the U.S. middle school (grades 6 to 9)
- **le lycée,** which corresponds to the U.S. high school (grades 10 to 12)

On the following chart, you will notice that each grade **(une classe)** is designated by a number (as in the United States): **sixième (6e), cinquième (5e), quatrième (4e),** etc. However, the progression from grade to grade is the opposite in France. The secondary school begins in France with **sixième** and ends with **terminale.**

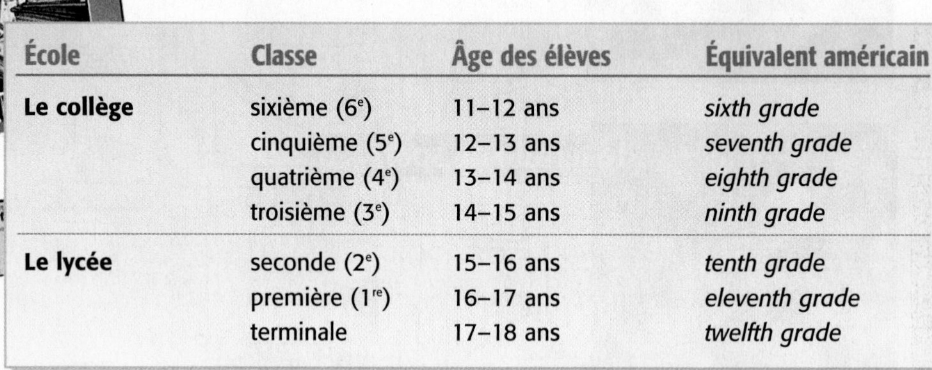

École	Classe	Âge des élèves	Équivalent américain
Le collège	sixième (6e)	11–12 ans	*sixth grade*
	cinquième (5e)	12–13 ans	*seventh grade*
	quatrième (4e)	13–14 ans	*eighth grade*
	troisième (3e)	14–15 ans	*ninth grade*
Le lycée	seconde (2e)	15–16 ans	*tenth grade*
	première (1re)	16–17 ans	*eleventh grade*
	terminale	17–18 ans	*twelfth grade*

A student **(un/une élève)** who does not do well in a given grade has to repeat that grade the next year. This is called **redoubler.** About 50% of the French students are kept back at least once during their secondary school studies.

At the end of high school, French students take a two-part national examination called **le baccalauréat,** or **le bac** for short, which they have to pass in order to enter the university.

- The first part, which focuses on the French language, is administered at the end of **première.**
- The second part, which is given at the end of **terminale,** offers students over twenty options reflecting their area of specialization.

Only 75% of the students who take the **bac** in a given year pass the exam. Of those who are successful, about 85% continue their studies either at the university or at a specialized professional school. Since education in France is considered a responsibility of the government, tuition is free at all public universities.

Des élèves vous parlent

David Souliac, 14 ans

J'habite à Bergerac, une petite ville
dans le sud-ouest° de la France. *southwest*
Je suis élève de 4e au collège Jacques Prévert.
Là, j'étudie l'anglais et l'espagnol.

Antoine Restaut, 14 ans

J'habite à Paris.
Je suis élève au collège Jeannine Manuel.
C'est un collège international.
J'aime les maths et les sciences.
Je voudrais être pilote comme° mon père. *like*

Pauline Lescure, 16 ans

Je suis élève de première au lycée Schoelcher
à Fort-de-France en Martinique.
J'étudie les sciences.
Je veux être médecin.° *doctor*
Je voudrais aller° à l'université à Paris. *to go*
Mais d'abord,° je dois être reçue° au bac. *first/pass*

Le programme scolaire

Teaching Resource Options

PRINT 

Workbook PE, pp. 81–84
Activités pour tous PE, pp. 47–49
Unit 3 Resource Book
Activités pour tous TE, pp. 145–147
Workbook TE, pp. 149–152

IMAGES

Le programme scolaire (School curriculum)

At the middle school **(au collège)**, all French students take certain required subjects **(des matières obligatoires)**. In **quatrième,** for instance, these subjects include French, math, one foreign language, history and geography, science **(sciences de la vie et de la terre** – life and earth sciences), and art. Depending on their preferences and career plans, they can also choose among a certain number of electives **(des matières facultatives)**. Many opt for a second foreign language **(une langue).**

Here is a list of subjects taught in French middle schools. (Note that no school offers all the languages listed, but most schools offer three or four.) How many of the subjects can you identify?

Matières obligatoires	Matières facultatives	Langues modernes
français	latin	allemand
maths	grec	anglais
1ère langue moderne	2ème langue moderne	arabe
histoire		espagnol
géographie		hébreu
physique-chimie		italien
sciences de la vie et de la terre		portugais
technologie		russe
éducation civique		
éducation physique et sportive		
arts plastiques		
éducation musicale		

Comparaisons Culturelles

Compare the curriculum of an eighth grader in the United States with that of a French teenager in the equivalent grade **(quatrième).** You may first want to list the subjects offered in your school system for grades six through nine.

a) Matières obligatoires
b) Matières facultatives
c) Langues modernes

Do you prefer the French or the American curriculum? Explain.

L'emploi du temps de Nathalie

Nathalie Aubin est en seconde au lycée Jean-Baptiste Corot. Voici son emploi du temps.

LYCÉE JEAN-BAPTISTE COROT

Étudiante: AUBIN, Nathalie

	LUNDI	MARDI	MERCREDI	JEUDI	VENDREDI	SAMEDI
8h30 à 9h30	Histoire	Allemand		Informatique°		Français
9h30 à 10h30	Anglais	Français	Anglais	Physique	Allemand	Français
10h30 à 11h30	Sport	Français	Informatique	Maths	Latin	Latin
11h30 à 12h30	Français	Latin	Maths		Sciences vie et terre	Histoire ou civilisation
13h00 à 14h00						
14h00 à 15h00	Sciences vie et terre	Maths		Allemand		
15h00 à 16h00	Géographie	Maths				
16h00 à 17h00	Physique	Anglais		Sport		

informatique *computer science*

Comparaisons Culturelles

Compare Nathalie's schedule with that of an American student in the same grade (tenth grade). You may want to make a chart:

	France	United States
number of classes per week		
number of foreign languages		
number of hours per week for sports		
other differences		

On the basis of your comparisons, do you prefer the French system or the American system? Explain.

Mon emploi du temps
Write out your own school schedule in French.

L'emploi du temps de Nathalie

Comparaisons Culturelles
Answers
Number of classes per week: 12 (Allemand, Anglais, Français, Latin, Physique, Sciences vie et terre, Informatique, Maths, Civilisation Géographie, Histoire, Sport)

Number of foreign languages: 3 (Anglais, Allemand, Latin)

Number of hours per week for sports: 2

Expressions pour la classe

Teaching Resource Options

PRINT

Workbook PE, pp. 81–84
Activités pour tous PE, pp. 47–49
Unit 3 Resource Book
Activités pour tous TE, pp. 145–147
Audioscript, p. 214
Workbook TE, pp. 149–152

AUDIO & VISUAL

Audio Program
CD 2 Track 23

Overhead Transparencies
S1 *La technologie*
S2 *Une classe branchée*
50 Classroom Objects

Expressions pour la classe

Le professeur dit ...

à une élève / **à un élève**

Regarde! *(Look!)*
Regarde la vidéo.
Écoute! *(Listen!)*
Écoute la cassette *(tape)*.
Parle! *(Speak!)*
Parle plus fort *(louder)*.
Réponds! *(Answer!)*
Réponds à la question.
Répète! *(Repeat!)*
Répète la phrase *(sentence)*.
Lis! *(Read!)*
Lis l'exercice.
Écris! *(Write!)*
Écris dans ton cahier.

Prends *(Take)*	une feuille de papier. un crayon
Ouvre *(Open)*	ton livre. la porte
Ferme *(Close)*	ton cahier. la fenêtre

Viens! *(Come!)*
Viens ici.
Va! *(Go!)*
Va au tableau.
Lève-toi! *(Stand up!)*
Assieds-toi! *(Sit down!)*

Apporte-moi *(Bring me)* **Donne-moi** *(Give me)* **Montre-moi** *(Show me)*	ton devoir.

à la classe

Regardez!
Regardez la vidéo.
Écoutez!
Écoutez la cassette.
Parlez!
Parlez plus fort.
Répondez!
Répondez à la question.
Répétez!
Répétez la phrase.
Lisez!
Lisez l'exercice.
Écrivez!
Écrivez dans vos cahiers.

Prenez	une feuille de papier. un crayon
Ouvrez	vos livres. la porte
Fermez	vos cahiers. la fenêtre

Venez!
Venez ici.
Allez!
Allez au tableau.
Levez-vous!
Asseyez-vous!

Apportez-moi **Donnez-moi** **Montrez-moi**	vos devoirs.

Teaching Note

Le professeur dit

These phrases are primarily for listening comprehension. Try to use these regularly in class so that students can internalize them and acquire a feeling for French rhythm and intonation patterns.

Quelques objets; Tu dis

These words and phrases are active. Students will be using them to express themselves in class and ask questions.

Quelques objets

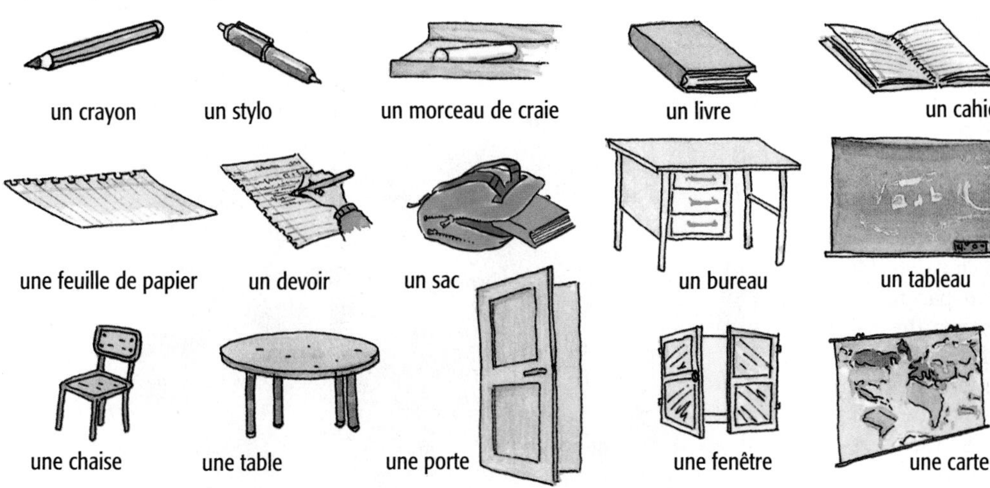

Tu dis ...

Je sais.
Je ne sais pas.
Je ne comprends pas.
Que veut dire ... ?
Comment dit-on ... en français?

I know.

I don't know.

I don't understand.

What does ... mean?

How does one say ... in French?

Écoutez bien!

Imagine you are in a school in France. Listen carefully to what different French teachers ask you to do and carry out their instructions. If you have trouble understanding the commands, your teacher will mime the actions for you.

Supplementary vocabulary

l'adresse *f.* électronique *e-mail address*
l'autoroute *f.* de l'information, l'Inforoute *the information highway*
un casque *headphones*
le clavier *keyboard*
le disque dur *hard drive (computer)*
un écran *screen (computer)*
envoyer quelque chose par e-mail (courrier électronique), par messagerie vocale *send an e-mail message, send a voice mail message*
un fax-modem *the machine that sends* **un fax**
faxer (envoyer un fax) *to fax*
une imprimante *printer*
un lecteur de CD *CD player*
un mail (un mél) *e-mail*
la messagerie vocale *voice mail*
le répondeur *answering machine*
le tapis souris *mouse pad*

COMPREHENSION Classroom objects

You may want to introduce these words with gestures.

Montrez-moi une feuille de papier. etc.
Mettez un stylo sur la feuille de papier.
Mettez un livre sur le stylo.
Mettez un morceau de craie sur le bureau.

Expansion activities PLANNING AHEAD

Games

• Vous rappelez-vous? *(Do you remember?)*

Place a covered transparency of the items presented on pages 140, 142, or 147 on an overhead projector. Uncover the transparency for 30 seconds and have students look at it. Then, recover the items and have students write down, in French, all of the items they can remember seeing. The student who remembers the most objects on the transparency, and spells them correctly, is the winner. You can expand the activity by having students practice prepositions of location and write down the positions of the objects in relation to each other.

Pacing Suggestion: Upon completion of Leçon 9.

• La course aux verbes

After reviewing the conjugation of *-er* verbs, *être, faire,* and *avoir,* divide the class into two or three teams. Announce an infinitive and a subject pronoun. The first member of each team should hurry to the board, write the conjugation, and then use the verb form in a simple sentence (i.e., subject/verb/object.) The first player to finish writing the correct form in a correct sentence wins a point for his or her team.

Pacing Suggestion: Upon completion of Leçon 10.

• Qui est-ce?

Select one person in the class to be the mystery person and don't tell the other students whom you have chosen. Students will try to guess who the mystery person is by asking you *oui/non* questions. You may want to give students some sample questions to get them started. The first student to correctly guess the mystery person gets to select someone else. His or her classmates then try to guess the new mystery student.

Model: —C'est un garçon?
—Non.

—C'est une fille?
—Oui!

—Elle est grande?
—Oui.

—Elle aime jouer au tennis?
—Oui.

—C'est Lucie?
—Oui.

Pacing Suggestion: Upon completion of Leçon 11.

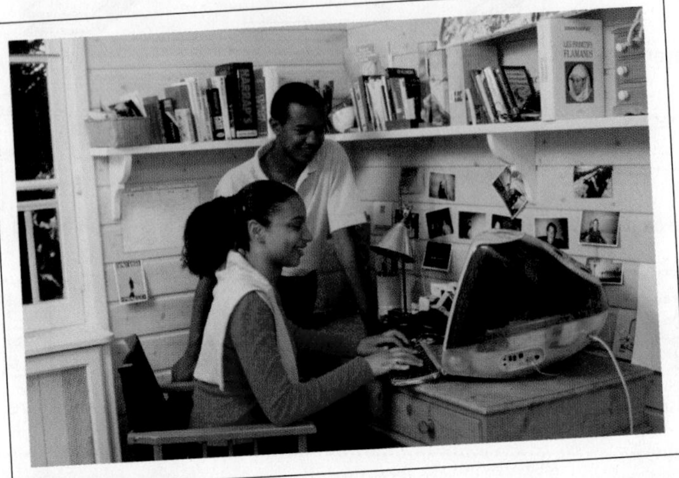

Projects

• Mon site Internet

Have students visit several French Web sites. You may want to give them clues for an effective search using a French word such as *musée* as the basis of their search. Ask them to find the French words for the buttons normally found on a Web page, such as "Home," "Help," and "Back." (You may also have students refer to the Web page found on page 120.) Then have students use these words to create their own French Web page layout. Select a topic for the Web page or have students make a personal Web page telling who they are and what they do. Then have them create a visual model of what the Web page would look like. Students may create their layouts by hand or on the computer.

Pacing Suggestion: Upon completion of Leçon 12.

Bulletin Boards

• Favorite Celebrities

Suggest that students create posters profiling their favorite celebrities. Divide the class into small groups. Have the students in each group compile a list of their favorite celebrities with descriptions of each. Groups may:

- look for information about the backgrounds of their chosen celebrities
- find out what they like to do and where they like to go
- bring photos from magazines or the internet to illustrate their posters
- use adjectives and the verb *avoir* in their descriptions

Each group should create a colorful poster they can use to present the information to the rest of the class. As an alternative, you may want to have students create personal profiles and posters illustrating **Notre Classe** or **Notre École.**

Pacing Suggestion: Upon completion of Leçon 10.

Storytelling

• Mini-histoire

Ask students to use the vocabulary on page 144 to create a description of their real bedrooms or of their "dream" bedrooms. First, have students draw a simple picture of their rooms and have them write out a description of the objects in it. Then have them elaborate on their image, adding details and changing the sentences.

Pacing Suggestion: Upon completion of Leçon 9.

Recipe

• Gratin de pommes de terre

This tasty side dish combines the flavors of potatoes, onions, and cheese. Serve with a main dish of fish, meat, or chicken.

Since *crème fraîche* is not widely available in the United States, it is possible to create your own using any of the following combinations:

- half sour cream and half heavy cream
- heavy cream with some lemon juice or buttermilk added to it
- skim of the heavy cream layer of a large container of organic plain whole milk yogurt

Pacing Suggestion: Upon completion of Leçon 11.

Hands-on Crafts

• Les voitures françaises

Have students investigate what French cars look like. They may want to visit the Web sites of Renault, Peugeot-Citroën, and other car manufacturers. Then have each student create a model of one of the French cars using clay. Display the finished models and have students vote on the car they would most like to buy.

Pacing Suggestion: Upon completion of Leçon 12.

End of Unit

• Mobile

First, have students brainstorm a list of words to describe themselves. Students may wish to include information about their families, favorite colors, favorite activities, etc. (Encourage students to provide positive information.) Next, have them cut out photos or create illustrations to represent each of their descriptive words and mount the photos or illustrations on pieces of construction paper or cardboard. Have students write a sentence caption for each image. For example «**Je suis blonde.**» «**J'aime regarder la télé.**» Finally, have students use string and dowel rods or straws to connect their illustrated sentences and create a mobile. You may wish to display the mobiles by hanging them from the classroom ceiling.

Rubric **A** = 13–15 pts. **B** = 10–12 pts. **C** = 7–9 pts. **D** = 4–6 pts. **F** = < 4 pts.

Criteria	Scale
Vocabulary Use	1 2 3 4 5
Grammar/Spelling Accuracy	1 2 3 4 5
Creativity	1 2 3 4 5

Gratin de pommes de terre

Ingrédients
- 120 g de Gruyère râpé
- 1 oeuf
- 15 cl de crème fraîche
- 30 g de beurre
- 1 oignon, coupé finement
- 700 g de pommes de terres moyennes, épluchées et coupées en tranches

Préparation
1. Préchauffez le four à 180° C et beurrez un plat à four.
2. Mettez les tranches de pommes de terres dans un bol d'eau.
3. Mettez le beurre et l'oignon dans une casserole, et cuisez à feu doux jusqu'à ce que l'oignon soit mou.
4. Mettez une couche de pommes de terres dans la casserole. Ajoutez une cuillère d'oignon dessus.
5. Saupoudrez de fromage. Continuez à ajouter des couches de pommes de terre, d'oignons et de fromage.
6. Battez l'œuf dans la crème. Versez sur les pommes de terre. Saupoudrez de fromage.
7. Mettez une heure et demie au four.

Ingredients
- approx. 1/2 cup grated Gruyère (Swiss) cheese
- 1 egg
- approx. 3 tsp. crème fraîche (1/2 sour cream, 1/2 heavy cream)
- approx. 2 tbsp. butter
- 1 onion, cut in thin slices
- approx. 3 cups medium-sized potatoes, peeled and cut in slices

Directions
1. Preheat the oven to 356° F. Butter a baking dish.
2. Put the potato slices in a bowl of water.
3. Cook the onions in butter on low heat until they soften.
4. Put a layer of potatoes in the baking dish. Top with a spoonful of onion.
5. Sprinkle with cheese. Continue to add layers of potatoes, onions, and cheese.
6. Beat the egg with the crème fraîche. Pour over the potatoes and add more cheese.
7. Bake for an hour and a half.

Planning Guide CLASSROOM MANAGEMENT

OBJECTIVES

Communication
- Talk about yourself: your personality and what you look like *pp. 138–139, 165, 167*
- Describe your friends and how old they are *pp. 138–139*
- Describe your room *p. 144*
- Talk about everyday objects that you own or use *pp. 140, 142, 147*
- Describe these objects: their color and size *pp. 174, 175*

Grammar
- Le verbe *avoir p. 152*
- Les noms et les articles: masculin et féminin *p. 153*
- Les noms et les articles: le pluriel *pp. 154–155*
- L'article indéfini dans les phrases négatives *p. 156*
- L'usage de l'article défini dans le sens général *p. 158*
- L'usage de l'article défini avec les jours de la semaine *p. 159*
- Les adjectifs: masculin et féminin *p. 164*
- Les adjectifs: le pluriel *p. 166*
- La place des adjectifs *p. 168*
- Les couleurs *p. 174*
- La place des adjectifs avant le nom *p. 175*
- *Il est* ou *c'est*? *p. 177*
- Les expressions impersonnelles avec *c'est p. 178*

Vocabulary
- La description des personnes *pp. 138–139*
- Les objets *p. 140*
- Les affaires personnelles *p. 142*
- Ma chambre *p. 144*
- Mon ordinateur *p. 147*
- Expressions pour la conversation *pp. 157, 167, 176*
- La description *p. 165*
- Les adjectifs de nationalité *p. 167*
- Les couleurs *p. 174*
- Les adjectifs qui précèdent le nom *p. 175*
- Opinions *p. 178*

Pronunciation
- Les articles *le* et *les p. 159*
- Les consonnes finales *p. 169*
- Les lettres «ch» *p. 179*

Culture
- Haïti *p. 151*
- L'amitié et la bande de copains *p. 163*
- Les Français et la voiture *p. 173*
- La mobylette et le scooter *p. 189*
- Toulouse *p. 191*

PROGRAM RESOURCES

Print
- Workbook PE, *pp. 85–116*
- *Activités pour tous* PE, *pp. 51–69*
- Block Scheduling Copymasters, *pp. 65–96*
- *Français pour hispanophones*
- *Lectures pour tous*
- Teacher to Teacher Copymasters
- Teaching Proficiency through Reading and Storytelling
- Unit 4 Resource Book
  - Lessons 9–12 Resources
    - Workbook TE
    - *Activités pour tous* TE
    - Family Letter
    - Absent Student Copymasters
    - Family Involvement
    - Video Activities
    - Videoscripts
    - Audioscripts
    - Assessment Program
  - Unit 4 Resources
    - Communipak
    - *Activités pour tous* TE Reading
    - Workbook TE Reading and Culture Activities
    - Assessment Program
    - Answer Keys

Audiovisual
- Audio Program PE CD 2 Tracks 24–45
- Audio Program Workbook CD 8 Tracks 1–24
- *Chansons* Audio CD
- Sing Along: Grammar and Vocabulary Songs CD
- Video Program Modules 9, 10, 11, 12
- Warm-Up Transparencies
- Overhead Transparencies
  - 2a Map of the French-Speaking World;
  - 19 *La description physique;*
  - 20 *Quelques objets (a);*
  - 21 *Quelques objets (b);*
  - 22 *Dans ma chambre;*
  - 23 *Les prépositions;*
  - 24 *Le grenier;*
  - 25 Class schedule;
  - 26 *La description;*
  - 27 *Les adjectifs de nationalité;*
  - 28 *Les couleurs;*

Technology
- Online Workbook
- ClassZone.com
- McDougal Littell Assessment System/Test Generator CD-ROM
- EasyPlanner CD-ROM
- Power Presentations on CD-ROM
- Take-Home Tutor CD-ROM

Assessment Program Options
Lesson Quizzes
Portfolio Assessment
Unit Test Form A
Unit Test Form B
Unit Test Part III (Alternate) Cultural Awareness
Listening Comprehension Performance Test
Speaking Performance Test
Reading Comprehension Performance Test
Writing Performance Test
Multiple Choice Test Items
Test Scoring Tools
Audio Program CD 14 Tracks 17–24
Answer Keys
McDougal Littell Assessment System/ Test Generator CD-ROM

Pacing Guide SAMPLE LESSON PLAN

DAY	DAY	DAY	DAY	DAY
1 Unité 4 Opener Leçon 9 • Vocabulaire et Culture–Les personnes et les objets • Vocabulaire–La description des personnes	**2** Leçon 9 • Vocabulaire–La description des personnes *(continued)* • Vocabulaire–Les objets	**3** Leçon 9 • Vocabulaire–Les affaires personnelles • Vocabulaire–Ma chambre	**4** Leçon 9 • Vocabulaire–Ma chambre *(continued)* • Vocabulaire–Mon ordinateur	**5** Leçon 9 • À votre tour!
6 Leçon 10 • Vive la différence! • Note culturelle–Haïti • Le verbe *avoir* • Vocabulaire–Expressions avec *avoir*	**7** Leçon 10 • Les noms et les articles: masculin et féminin • Les noms et les articles: le pluriel	**8** Leçon 10 • L'article indéfini dans les phrases négatives	**9** Leçon 10 • Vocabulaire–Expressions pour la conversation • L'usage de l'article défini dans le sens général	**10** Leçon 10 • L'usage de l'article défini avec les jours de la semaine • Prononciation–Les articles *le* et *les*
11 Leçon 10 • À votre tour!	**12** Leçon 11 • Le copain de Mireille • Note culturelle–L'amitié et la bande de copains • Les adjectifs: masculin et féminin	**13** Leçon 11 • Vocabulaire–La description • Les adjectifs: le pluriel	**14** Leçon 11 • Vocabulaire–Les adjectifs de nationalité • Vocabulaire–Expressions pour la conversation • La place des adjectifs • Prononciation–Les consonnes finales	**15** Leçon 11 • À votre tour!
16 Leçon 12 • La voiture de Roger • Note culturelle–Les Français et la voiture • Les couleurs • Vocabulaire–Les couleurs	**17** Leçon 12 • La place des adjectifs avant le nom • Vocabulaire–Les adjectifs qui précèdent le nom • Vocabulaire–Expressions pour la conversation	**18** Leçon 12 • *Il est* ou *c'est*? • Les expressions impersonnelles avec *c'est* • Vocabulaire–Opinions • Prononciation–Les lettres «ch»	**19** Leçon 12 • À votre tour!	**20** • Tests de contrôle
21 • Unit 4 Test	**22** • Entracte–Lecture et culture			

Student Text Listening Activity Scripts
AUDIO PROGRAM

▶ LEÇON 9 LE FRANÇAIS PRATIQUE Les personnes et les objets

• La description des personnes *p. 138* CD 2, TRACK 24

How to describe someone. Écoutez et répétez.

Qui est-ce? #	C'est un copain. #
Qui est-ce? #	C'est une copine. #
Comment s'appelle-t-il? #	Il s'appelle Marc. #
Comment s'appelle-t-elle? #	Elle s'appelle Sophie. #
Quel âge a-t-il? #	Il a seize ans. #
Quel âge a-t-elle? #	Elle a quinze ans. #
Comment est-il? #	Il est petit. # Il est blond. #
Comment est-elle? #	Elle est grande. # Elle est brune. #

Les personnes

une personne #	
un étudiant #	une étudiante #
un élève #	une élève #
un camarade #	une camarade #
un homme #	une femme #
un professeur, un prof #	un professeur, une prof #
un voisin #	une voisine #

La description physique

Il est grand. #	Elle est grande. #
Il est petit. #	Elle est petite. #
Il est brun. #	Elle est brune. #
Il est blond. #	Elle est blonde. #
Il est beau. #	Elle est belle. # Elle est jolie. #
Il est jeune. #	Elle est jeune. #

À votre tour!

• Écoutez bien! *p. 148* CD 2, TRACK 25

You will hear a series of sentences. In each one an object is mentioned. If you see the object only in Léa's room, mark A. If you see the object only in Pierre's room, mark B. If you see the object in the two rooms, mark both A and B. You will hear each sentence twice. Listen carefully. Écoutez bien.

1. Tu as un ordinateur. #
2. Regarde l'affiche. #
3. La fenêtre est grande. #
4. Montre-moi ton baladeur, s'il te plaît. #
5. Où est la radiocassette? #
6. Qu'est-ce qu'il y a sur le lit? #
7. C'est derrière la porte. #
8. Tu joues de la guitare? #
9. La table n'est pas très grande. #
10. Est-ce que l'appareil-photo marche bien? #
11. Est-ce que je peux utiliser le téléphone? #
12. Où est ton livre de français? #
13. Est-ce que tu as un portable? #
14. La chaise est assez confortable. #
15. J'écoute souvent la chaîne hi-fi. #
16. Le bureau est assez petit. #
17. C'est une raquette anglaise. #
18. Zut! La lampe ne marche pas. #

• Conversation dirigée *p. 148* CD 2, TRACK 26

Écoutez la conversation entre André et Marie.

André: Est-ce que tu as un ordinateur?
Marie: Oui.
André: Est-ce qu'il marche bien?
Marie: Oui, il marche très bien. Pourquoi?
André: Je voudrais envoyer un mail à un copain.
Marie: L'ordinateur est sur le bureau dans ma chambre.

• Créa-dialogue *p. 149* CD 2, TRACK 27

Listen to the sample *Créa-dialogues*. Écoutez les conversations.

Modèle: –Qui est-ce?	–C'est un copain.
–Comment s'appelle-t-il?	–Il s'appelle Éric.
–Quel âge a-t-il?	–Il a quatorze ans.

Maintenant, écoutez le dialogue numéro 1.

–Qui est-ce?	–C'est une cousine.
–Comment s'appelle-t-elle?	–Elle s'appelle Valérie.
–Quel âge a-t-elle?	–Elle a vingt ans.

▶ LEÇON 10 Vive la différence!

• Vive la différence! *p. 150*

A. Compréhension orale CD 2, TRACK 28

Please turn to page 150 for complete *Compréhension orale* text.

B. Écoutez et répétez. CD 2, TRACK 29

You will now hear a paused version of the dialog. Listen to the speaker and repeat right after he or she has completed the sentence.

• Prononciation *p. 159* CD 2, TRACK 30

Les articles *le* et *les*

Écoutez: le sac les sacs

Be sure to distinguish between the pronunciation of **le** and **les.** In spoken French, that is often the only way to tell the difference between a singular and a plural noun.

Répétez: /lə/ le # le sac # le vélo # le portable # le copain # le voisin #
/le/ les # les sacs # les vélos # les portables # les copains # les voisins #

À votre tour!

• Allô! *p. 160* CD 2, TRACK 31

Jean-Marc is phoning some friends. Match his questions on the left with his friends' answers on the right.

1. Quel âge a ton copain?	Quatorze ans.
2. Est-ce qu'Éric a un scooter?	Non, mais il a une moto.
3. Où est l'appareil-photo?	Il est sur la table.
4. Tu as un baladeur?	Oui, mais je n'ai pas de chaîne hi-fi.
5. Est-ce que tu aimes étudier l'anglais?	Oui, mais je préfère l'espagnol.
6. Tu as soif?	Oui, je voudrais une limonade.

• Créa-dialogue *p. 161* CD 2, TRACK 32

Listen to some sample *Créa-dialogues.* Écoutez les conversations.

Modèle: –Tu aimes le tennis?	–Oui, j'aime le tennis.
–Tu as une raquette?	–Oui, j'ai une raquette.
–Tu aimes le tennis?	–Non, je n'aime pas le tennis.
–Tu as une raquette?	–Non, je n'ai pas de raquette.

Maintenant, écoutez le dialogue numéro 1.

–Tu aimes la musique?	–Oui, j'aime la musique.
–Tu as une radiocassette?	–Non, je n'ai pas de radiocassette.

▶ LEÇON 11 Le copain de Mireille

• Le copain de Mireille *p. 162*

A. Compréhension orale CD 2, TRACK 33

Please turn to page 162 for complete *Compréhension orale* text.

pause for oral response

B. Écoutez et répétez. CD 2, TRACK 34

You will now hear a paused version of the dialog. Listen to the speaker and repeat right after he or she has completed the sentence.

• Vocabulaire *p. 165* CD 2, TRACK 35

La description

Listen and repeat the descriptions after the speaker. Écoutez et répétez.

Il est **amusant.** #	Elle est **amusante.** #
Il est **intelligent.** #	Elle est **intelligente.** #
Il est **intéressant.** #	Elle est **intéressante.** #
Il n'est pas **méchant.** #	Elle n'est pas **méchante.** #
Il n'est pas **bête.** #	Elle n'est pas **bête.** #
Il est **sympathique.** #	Elle est **sympathique.** #
Il est **timide.** #	Elle n'est pas **timide.** #
Il est **gentil.** #	Elle est **gentille.** #
Il est **mignon.** #	Elle est **mignonne.** #
Il est **sportif.** #	Elle est **sportive.** #
assez #	Nous sommes **assez** intelligents. #
très #	Vous n'êtes pas **très** sportifs! #

• Prononciation *p. 169* CD 2, TRACK 36

Les consonnes finales

Écoutez: blond blonde

As you know, when the last letter of a word is a consonant, that consonant is often silent. But when a word ends in **"e,"** the consonant before it is pronounced. As you practice the following adjectives, be sure to distinguish between the masculine and the feminine forms.

Répétez: blond #	blonde #
grand #	grande #
petit #	petite #
amusant #	amusante #
français #	française #
anglais #	anglaise #
américain #	américaine #
canadien #	canadienne #

À votre tour!

• Allô! *p. 170* CD 2, TRACK 37

Listen to the phone conversations. Écoutez les conversations.

1. Ton frère aime jouer au foot?	Oui, il est très sportif.
2. Cécile et Sophie sont mignonnes, n'est-ce pas?	Oui, et intelligentes aussi!
3. Pourquoi est-ce que tu invites Olivier?	Parce qu'il est amusant et sympathique.
4. Tu aimes la classe?	Oui, j'ai un professeur très intéressant.
5. Tu as des cousins?	Oui, mais ils ne sont pas très sympathiques.

• Créa-dialogue *p. 170* CD 2, TRACK 38

Listen to some sample *Créa-dialogues.* Écoutez les conversations.

Modèle: –J'ai des cousins mexicains.
–Ils sont mignons?
–Oui, ils sont très mignons.

Maintenant, écoutez le dialogue numéro 1.

–J'ai une voisine anglaise.
–Elle est blonde?
–Non, elle est brune.

▶ LEÇON 12 La voiture de Roger

• Dialogue *p. 172*

A. Compréhension orale CD 2, TRACK 39

Please turn to page 172 for complete *Compréhension orale* text.

B. Écoutez et répétez. CD 2, TRACK 40

You will now hear a paused version of the dialog. Listen to the speaker and repeat right after he or she has completed the sentence.

• Vocabulaire *p. 174* CD 2, TRACK 41

Les couleurs

Écoutez et répétez.

blanc #	blanche #
noir #	noire #
bleu #	bleue #
rouge #	rouge #
jaune #	jaune #
vert #	verte #
gris #	grise #
marron #	marron #
orange #	orange #
rose #	rose #

• Vocabulaire *p. 175* CD 2, TRACK 42

Les adjectifs qui précèdent le nom

Écoutez et répétez.

beau # **belle** #	Regarde la **belle** voiture!
joli #	Qui est la **jolie** fille avec André?
grand #	Nous habitons dans un **grand** appartement.
petit #	Ma soeur a un **petit** ordinateur.
bon # **bonne** #	Tu es un **bon** copain.
mauvais #	Patrick est un **mauvais** élève.

• Prononciation *p. 179* CD 2, TRACK 43

Les lettres «ch»

Écoutez: chien

The letters **"ch"** are usually pronounced like the English *"sh."*

Répétez: chien # chat # chose # marche #
chouette # chocolat # affiche #
Michèle a un chat et deux chiens. #

À votre tour

• Allô! *p. 180* CD 2, TRACK 44

Listen to the phone conversations. Écoutez les conversations.

1. De quelle couleur est ton vélo?	Il est vert.
2. Ta raquette est bleue?	Non, elle est blanche.
3. Tu aimes regarder la télé?	Oui, c'est amusant.
4. C'est un magazine français?	Non, il est canadien.
5. Philippe n'aime pas parler en public?	C'est vrai! Il est très timide.

• Créa-dialogue *p. 180* CD 2, TRACK 45

Listen to some sample *Créa-dialogues.* Écoutez les conversations.

Modèle: **Détective 1:** Qu'est-ce qu'il y a devant le café?
Détective 2: Il y a une voiture.
Détective 1: Elle est grande ou petite?
Détective 2: C'est une petite voiture.

Maintenant, écoutez le dialogue numéro 1.

Détective 1: Qu'est-ce qu'il y a devant la phamarcie?
Détective 2: Il y a une moto.
Détective 1: Elle est rouge ou bleue?
Détective 2: C'est une moto rouge.

Complete videoscripts, plus Workbook and Assessment audioscripts, are available in the Unit Resource Books.

Main Theme
- People and possessions

COMMUNICATION
- Asking people about what they have and telling them what you have
- Telling others about yourself
- Describing friends
- Giving people's ages
- Describing a bedroom
- Talking about and describing everyday objects

CULTURES
- Learning about how French teens spend their free time
- Learning about Haiti
- Learning how to get a driver's license in France
- Learning how French teenagers use scooters or mopeds.

CONNECTIONS
- Connecting to Art: Learning about Haitian art
- Connecting to Music: Learning about Haitian music styles
- Connecting to English: Learning grammar terms

COMPARISONS
- Comparing attitudes toward friendship in France and the U.S.
- Comparing animal expressions in French and English
- Learning about the influence of the American way of life on French teenagers

COMMUNITIES
- Using French for personal enjoyment
- Using French to write a letter

Le monde personnel et familier

THÈME ET OBJECTIFS

People and possessions

When you meet French teenagers, you will want to share information about yourself, your friends, and your possessions.

In this unit, you will learn ...

- to talk about yourself: your personality and what you look like
- to describe your friends and how old they are
- to describe your room
- to talk about everyday objects that you own or use
- to describe these objects: their size and color

UNIT OVERVIEW

- **Communication Goals:** Students will learn to describe themselves and their family, friends, and personal possessions.
- **Linguistic Goals:** The focus is on the noun group: articles, nouns, and adjectives. The passé composé is introduced informally.
- **Critical Thinking Goals:** Students are introduced to the concepts of gender and noun-adjective agreement. They learn to observe and apply these patterns in French.
- **Cultural Goals:** This unit presents the multi-cultural reality of contemporary France, while highlighting the common interests of French and American youth.

cent trente-cinq 135
Unité 4

Teaching Resource Options

PRINT 

Unit 4 Resource Book
Family Letter, p. 17
Français pour hispanophones
Conseils, pp. 10–12
Vocabulaire, pp. 44–45

AUDIO & VISUAL 

Audio Program
Chansons CD

TECHNOLOGY 

EasyPlanner CD-ROM

Pacing

Unit 4 reviews and expands considerably on Unit 1 of **Invitation au français**. As in Unit 3, there is a dual emphasis on both oral and written skills.

For specific suggestions on pacing, turn to p. 133D TE.

Leçon 9

Main Topic Describing people and things

Teaching Resource Options

PRINT 

Workbook PE, pp. 85–92
Activités pour tous PE, pp. 51–53
Block Scheduling Copymasters, pp. 65–72
Unit 4 Resource Book
- *Activités pour tous* TE, pp. 9–11
- Audioscript, pp. 32–34
- Communipak, pp. 140–160
- Lesson Plans, pp. 12–13
- Block Scheduling Lesson Plans, pp. 14–16
- Absent Student Copymasters, pp. 18–22
- Video Activities, pp. 25–28
- Videoscript, pp. 29–30
- Workbook TE, pp. 1–8

AUDIO & VISUAL 

Audio Program
CD 8 Tracks 1–6

Overhead Tranparencies
2a Map of the French-Speaking World

TECHNOLOGY 

Online Workbook

VIDEO PROGRAM

VIDÉO DVD

MODULE 9
Le français pratique
Les personnes et les objets

TOTAL TIME: 7:28 min.
DVD Disk 1
Videotape 2 (COUNTER: 28:10 min.)

9.1 Mini-scenes: Listening
– J'ai une guitare (29:20–30:31 min.)

9.2 Mini-scenes: Speaking
– Qu'est-ce que c'est? (30:32–31:39 min.)

9.3 Dialogue: Tu as un portable? (31:40–32:57 min.)

9.4 Mini-scenes: Speaking
– Où est-il? (32:58–34:13 min.)

9.5 Vignette culturelle: La chambre de Catherine (34:14–35:38 min.)

Comprehension practice Play the entire module through as an introduction to the lesson.

LEÇON 9

LE FRANÇAIS PRATIQUE
VIDÉO DVD AUDIO

Les personnes et les objets

Accent sur ... les jeunes Français

France is a young country. One quarter of the population is under the age of twenty. In their daily lives outside school, young people in France are not that different from their counterparts in the United States. They enjoy listening to music and going to the movies. On weekends, they go to the mall or into the city to check out the newest teen fashions and the latest in video games and sound equipment. As computers become more and more widespread, French young people often spend their free time surfing the Internet and participating in chat rooms and forums.

Since almost everyone studies English in school, French teenagers are very much aware of the American way of life. They have a generally positive attitude towards the United States and many would like to visit our country.

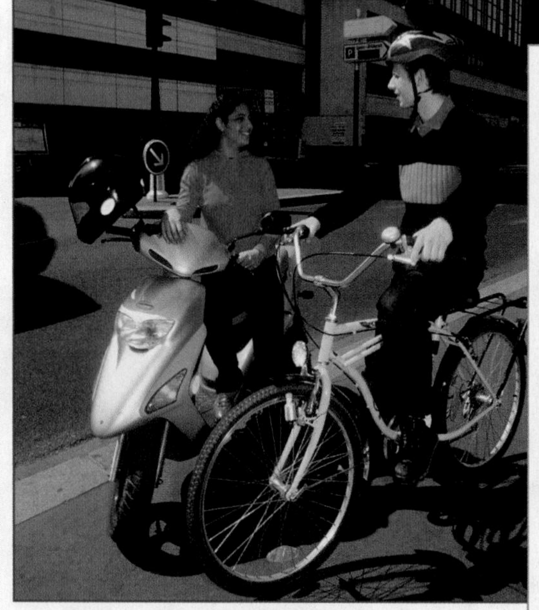

Thomas a un vélo. C'est un vélo anglais. Michèle n'a pas de vélo. Elle a un scooter.

Élodie et Paul font une promenade en ville. Paul a un baladeur. Il écoute un CD. Élodie a un portable. Elle téléphone à une copine.

SETTING THE SCENE

Ask students what kinds of things they buy, other than food and clothes: school supplies, books, posters, CDs, audio equipment, etc.

Ask what other possessions they have: a watch, a camera, a bicycle, etc.

As they watch **Video Module 9,** they will meet many French young people who will talk about their own possessions.

In the last segment, Olivier invites them to his room and points out some of his favorite things.

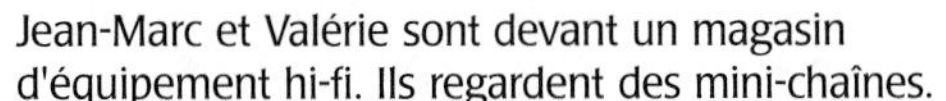
Jean-Marc et Valérie sont devant un magasin d'équipement hi-fi. Ils regardent des mini-chaînes.

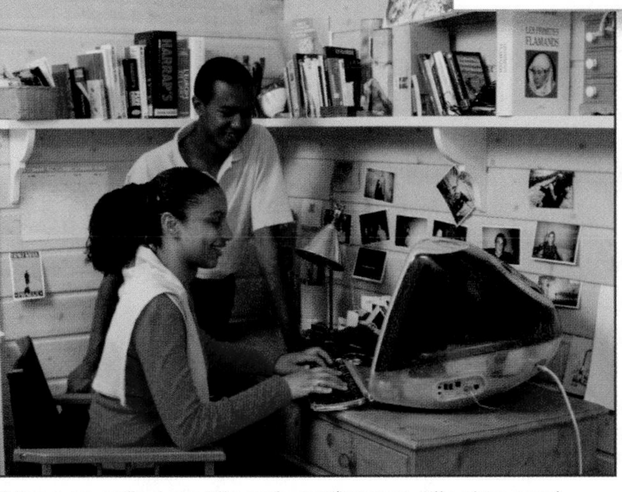
Zaïna a un ordinateur. Elle surfe sur l'Internet. Elle aime aussi jouer aux jeux d'ordinateur avec Ousmane.

Cultural notes

- The U.S. population is about 290 million. Less than 20% percent of the U.S. population is under 20.
- North Africa, French-speaking West Africa, Vietnam, Laos, and Cambodia are all former French colonies.

Photo cultural note

- **Le baladeur** Like their American counterparts, French teenagers love to listen to music through headphones (**des écouteurs**) on their portable players **(un baladeur).** Find a French music web site and print a list of current hit music CDs that shows the popularity of American singers. Show the list to students and then ask them to name as many French-speaking singers as they can. Ask students to give possible reasons why more of the French listen to American music than vice versa.

MULTICULTURALISM IN FRANCE

PROP: Transparency 2a: Map of the French-Speaking World

French society is becoming increasingly multicultural as the country attracts immigrants representing many different traditions and backgrounds.

On the world map on pp. R2–R3, have students find the main countries of origin of these French immigrant groups:

Les Arabes et les Musulmans: l'Algérie, la Tunisie, le Maroc

Les Noirs: l'Afrique occidentale – la Côte d'Ivoire, le Sénégal, le Mali ...

Les Orientaux: le Viêt-Nam, le Cambodge

SECTION A

Communicative function
Describing people

Teaching Resource Options

PRINT 

Workbook PE, pp. 85–92
Unit 4 Resource Book
  Audioscript, p. 31
  Communipak, pp. 140–160
  Workbook TE, pp. 1–8

AUDIO & VISUAL 

Audio Program
CD 2 Track 24

Overhead Transparencies
19 *La description physique*

 **Review and expansion**
Phrases from **Invitation au français.**

Casual speech Questions can be formed using a rising intonation:

C'est qui?

Il/Elle s'appelle comment?

Il/Elle a quel âge?

Language note The term **un étudiant (une étudiante)** refers to college students, although it is now sometimes used in talking about high school students, especially older ones. The traditional term for high school students is **un lycéen (une lycéenne)**.

Teaching strategy To help students differentiate between the sound of **un** and **une**, point to various students and ask:

Est-ce que c'est un élève ou une élève?

Est-ce que c'est un camarade ou une camarade?

A VOCABULAIRE La description des personnes

Qui est-ce?
C'est un copain.

▶ ***How to describe someone:***

Qui est-ce?
C'est un copain.

Comment s'appelle-t-il?
Il s'appelle Marc.

Quel âge a-t-il?
Il a seize ans.

Comment est-il?
Il est petit.
Il est blond.

Qui est-ce?
C'est une copine.

Comment s'appelle-t-elle?
Elle s'appelle Sophie.

Quel âge a-t-elle?
Elle a quinze ans.

Comment est-elle?
Elle est grande.
Elle est brune.

Les personnes

une **personne** 

une **personne** 

un **étudiant**	*student*	une **étudiante**
un **élève**	*pupil*	une **élève**
un **camarade**	*classmate*	une **camarade**
un **homme**	*man*	une **femme** *woman*
un **professeur**, un **prof**	*teacher*	un **professeur**, une **prof**
un **voisin**	*neighbor*	une **voisine**

→ **Une personne** is always feminine whether it refers to a male or female person.

→ **Un professeur** is always masculine whether it refers to a male or female teacher. However, in casual French, one distinguishes between **un prof** (male) and **une prof** (female).

COMPREHENSION Descriptive adjectives

PROPS: Blue and red index cards

Give each student a blue and a red card.

On the board, draw a stick figure of a boy (labeled Michel) and a girl (labeled Michelle).

Voici Michel. C'est un copain.
Et voilà Michelle. C'est une copine.

Hold a blue card next to Michel, and a red card next to Michelle.

La carte bleue est pour Michel.
La carte rouge est pour Michelle.

Read descriptions using new vocabulary and have students hold up the right card.

Michel est grand. [blue card]
Michelle est belle. [red card]
Michel(le) est jeune. [either: both cards]

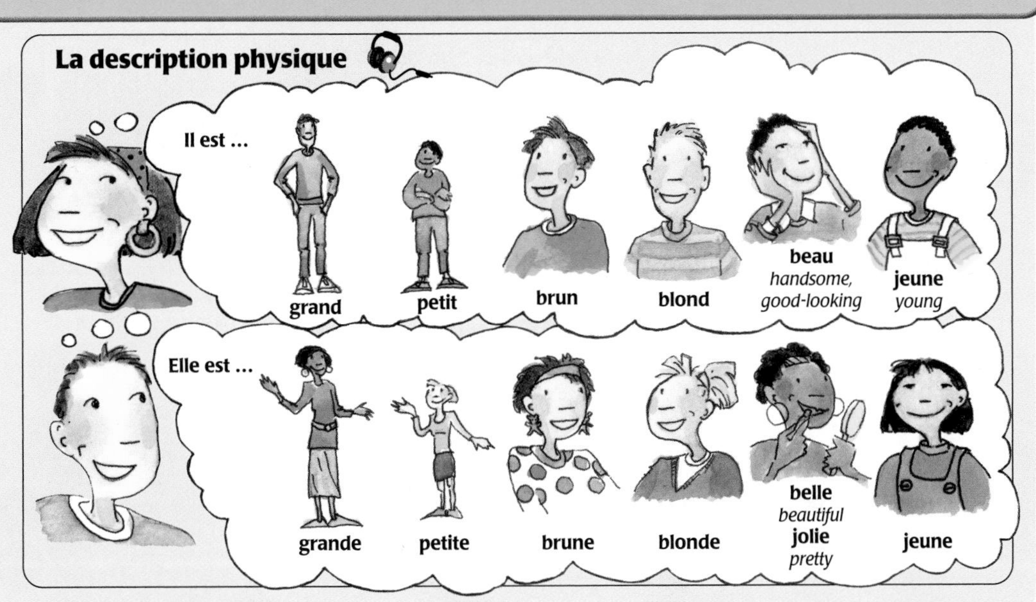

1 Oui ou non?

PARLER Describe the people below in affirmative or negative sentences.

▶ Frankenstein / beau?
Frankenstein n'est pas beau.

1. Shaquille O'Neal / grand?
2. Brad Pitt / brun?
3. Dracula / beau?
4. mon copain / blond?
5. mon père / petit?
6. mon voisin / jeune?
7. Britney Spears / belle?
8. le président / jeune?
9. Oprah Winfrey / grande?
10. ma copine / petite?
11. ma mère / brune?
12. ma voisine / jolie?

2 Vacances à Québec

PARLER/ÉCRIRE You spent last summer in Quebec and have just had your photographs developed. Describe each of the people, giving name, approximate age, and two or three characteristics.

Alain

blond(e)	petit(e)
brun(e)	beau (belle)
grand(e)	jeune

▶ **Il s'appelle Alain.**
Il est blond.
Il a seize ans.
Il n'est pas grand.
Il est petit.

1. Anne-Marie

2. Jean-Pierre

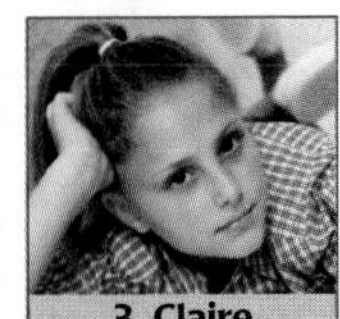
3. Claire

4. Mademoiselle Lévêque

5. Madame Paquette

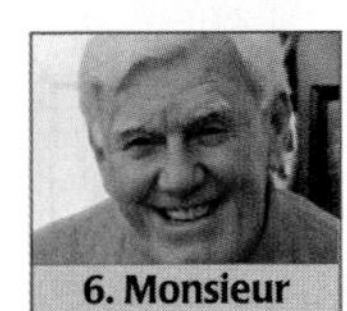
6. Monsieur Beliveau

GAME Qui est-ce?

PROPS: Magazine pictures showing a variety of individuals with different looks

Tape the pictures across the chalkboard. Have the class identify each one. Write the names.

Voici une femme. Comment s'appelle-t-elle? [Elle s'appelle Mme Duroc.] ...

Each student stands and describes one of the people without mentioning his/her name. The others try to guess who it is.

C'est une femme. Elle est blonde. Elle est grande. Elle n'est pas jeune. Qui est-ce? [C'est Madame Duroc.]

Variation Use well-known personalities.

La description physique

Looking ahead
- Noun-adjective agreement is formally presented in Lesson 11.
- The masculine form **joli** is introduced in Lesson 12. Note that **joli** is not used to describe men and boys.

Extra practice Have students describe similar-looking twins:
Marc et Sophie.
Marc est grand. Sophie est grande.
Sophie est belle. Marc est beau., etc.

Supplementary vocabulary

roux (rousse) *red-head*
fort (forte) *strong*
faible *weak*
laid (laide) *ugly*
moche *plain*
âgé (âgée) *old*
vieux (vieille) *old*

1 DESCRIPTION describing people

1. Shaquille O'Neal (est/n'est pas) grand.
2. Brad Pitt (est/n'est pas) brun.
3. Dracula (est/n'est pas) beau.
4. Mon copain (est/n'est pas) blond.
5. Mon père (est/n'est pas) petit.
6. Mon voisin (est/n'est pas) jeune.
7. Britney Spears (est/n'est pas) belle.
8. Le président (est/n'est pas) jeune.
9. Oprah Winfrey (est/n'est pas) grande.
10. Ma copine (est/n'est pas) petite.
11. Ma mère (est/n'est pas) brune.
12. Ma voisine (est/n'est pas) jolie.

2 COMMUNICATION describing appearance and age

Answers will vary.
1. Elle s'appelle Anne-Marie. Elle est brune. Elle a (seize) ans. Elle n'est pas petite. Elle est grande.
2. Il s'appelle Jean-Pierre. Il est brun. Il a (six) ans. Il est petit. Il est jeune. Il n'est pas grand.
3. Elle s'appelle Claire. Elle a (onze) ans. Elle est blonde. Elle n'est pas grande. Elle est petite.
4. Elle s'appelle Mlle Lévêque. Elle a (trente-cinq) ans. Elle est jeune. Elle est grande. Elle n'est pas petite. Elle est belle.
5. Elle s'appelle Mme Paquette. Elle a (soixante-cinq) ans. Elle n'est pas jeune. Elle est petite.
6. Il s'appelle M. Beliveau. Il a (soixante) ans. Il est grand. Il n'est pas beau.

Teaching strategy If you do not introduce **âgé** *(old)* at this point, students can describe an older person by saying:
Il/Elle n'est pas jeune.

SECTION B

Communicative function
Identifying objects

Teaching Resource Options

PRINT 

Workbook PE, pp. 85–92
Unit 4 Resource Book
  Communipak, pp. 140–160
  Workbook TE, pp. 1–8

AUDIO & VISUAL 

Overhead Transparencies
20 *Quelques objets (a)*

B VOCABULAIRE Les objets

▶ *How to identify something:*

Qu'est-ce que c'est? — *What is it? What's that?*
C'est ... — *It's ..., That's ...*

—**Qu'est-ce que c'est?**
—**C'est** un livre.

▶ *How to say that you know or do not know:*

Je sais. — *I know.*
Je ne sais pas. — *I don't know.*

▶ *How to point out something:*

—**Regarde ça.** — *Look at that.*
—**Quoi?** — *What?*
—**Ça,** là-bas. — *That, over there.*

Quelques objets *(A few objects)*

un objet **un stylo** **un crayon** **un téléphone**

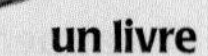

un livre **un cahier** **un sac**

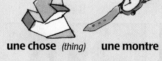

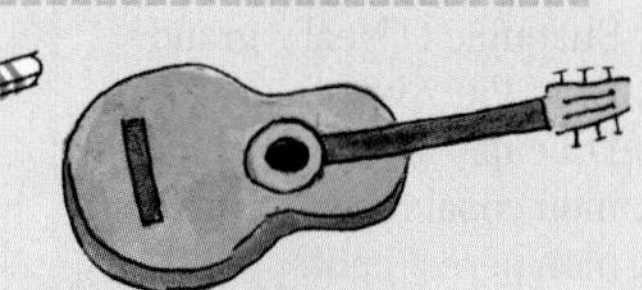

une chose *(thing)* **une montre** **une raquette** **une guitare**

une affiche *(un poster)*

une calculatrice

RAPPEL
In French, the names of objects are MASCULINE or FEMININE.
Masculine objects can be introduced by **un** or **le (l'): un stylo, le stylo, l'objet.**
Feminine objects can be introduced by **une** or **la (l'): une montre, la montre, l'affiche.**

COMPREHENSION Everyday objects

PROPS: Objects from the above vocabulary

Hold up the objects (or corresponding pictures), identifying them one by one.
  Voici un stylo.
  Voici un cahier. ...

Go over the objects, misidentifying some.
  Voici un stylo. [holding a pencil]
  Ah non, ce n'est pas un stylo.
  Est-ce que c'est un livre? [non]
  Est-ce que c'est un crayon? [oui]

Have students manipulate the objects.
  X, viens ici. Montre-nous le sac.
  Y, prends la raquette et donne-la à Z.

—QU'EST-CE QUE C'EST QUE ÇA?
—QUOI?
—ÇA, LÀ-BAS!
—C'EST UNE TÉLÉ.
—OH LÀ LÀ, NON! REGARDE! C'EST UN EXTRA-TERRESTRE!

3 *Qu'est-ce que c'est?*

PARLER Ask a classmate to identify the following objects.

▶ **Qu'est-ce que c'est?**
C'est un stylo.

4 *S'il te plaît*

PARLER Ask a classmate to give you the following objects.

▶ **—S'il te plaît, donne-moi le livre.**
—Voilà le livre.
—Merci.

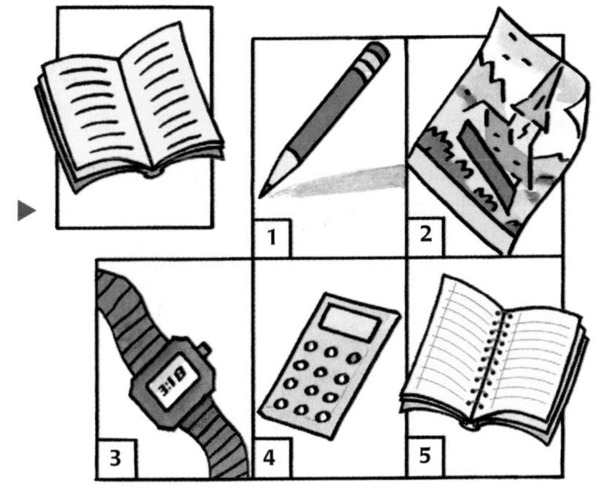

Teaching strategy Have students note the use of **ça** and **quoi** in the cartoon at left.

3 DESCRIPTION identifying objects

1. – Qu'est-ce que c'est?
   – C'est un téléphone.
2. – Qu'est-ce que c'est?
   – C'est une affiche.
3. – Qu'est-ce que c'est?
   – C'est une guitare.
4. – Qu'est-ce que c'est?
   – C'est une raquette.
5. – Qu'est-ce que c'est?
   – C'est un sac.

Variation Go around the classroom holding up or pointing to objects students can identify.

– Regardez ça. Qu'est-ce que c'est?
– C'est [un crayon].
– Et ça? Qu'est-ce que c'est?
– C'est [un stylo].

4 EXCHANGES asking for things

1. – S'il te plaît, donne-moi le crayon.
   – Voilà le crayon.
   – Merci.
2. – S'il te plaît, donne-moi l'affiche.
   – Voilà l'affiche.
   – Merci.
3. – S'il te plaît, donne-moi la montre.
   – Voilà la montre.
   – Merci.
4. – S'il te plaît, donne-moi la calculatrice.
   – Voilà la calculatrice.
   – Merci.
5. – S'il te plaît, donne-moi le cahier.
   – Voilà le cahier.
   – Merci.

INCLUSION

Repetitive Have students draw objects on slips of paper, labeling each one. Have them jot down the phonetic transcription to help them remember how each one sounds. Then have them work in pairs, asking each other for objects – (**Donne-moi le stylo, s'il te plaît. Voilà le stylo.**). Remind students to say thank you (**Merci**).

SECTION C

Communicative function
Discussing possessions

Teaching Resource Options

 **PRINT** 

Workbook PE, pp. 85–92
Unit 4 Resource Book
- Communipak, pp. 140–160
- Video Activities, pp. 25–26
- Videoscript, p. 29
- Workbook TE, pp. 1–8

AUDIO & VISUAL

Overhead Transparencies
21 *Quelques objets (b)*

VIDEO PROGRAM

VIDÉO DVD

MODULE 9

9.1 Mini-scenes: J'ai une guitare (29:20–30:31 min.)

9.2 Mini-scenes: Qu'est-ce que c'est? (30:32–31:39 min.)

Looking ahead The negative **pas de (je n'ai pas de guitare)** is taught in Lesson 10.

Supplementary vocabulary

un appareil-photo numérique *digital camera*
une caméra *movie camera*
un caméscope *camcorder*
un radio-réveil *clock radio*
une radiocassette/CD *boombox with CD player*
une chaîne stéréo, une stéréo *stereo set*
une micro-chaîne *mini stereo*
un casque *head set*
un lecteur de CD *CD player*
un lecteur de DVD *DVD player*
un lecteur de MP3 *MP3 player*
un magnétoscope *VCR*
un téléviseur *TV set*
une console de jeux vidéo *video game console*
un cédérom *CD-ROM*
un VTT *mountain bike*
un skate *skateboard*
des rollers *in-line skates*
une trottinette *scooter*

Est-ce que tu as une moto?
Oui, j'ai une moto.

C VOCABULAIRE Les affaires personnelles *(personal belongings)*

▶ ***How to talk about things you have:***

Est-ce que tu as ... ?	*Do you have ... ?*	–**Est-ce que tu as** une moto?
Oui, j'ai ...	*Yes, I have ...*	–**Oui, j'ai** une moto.

Quelques objets

un portable

un appareil-photo

un baladeur

un CD

une télé

un DVD

une cassette vidéo

un ordinateur

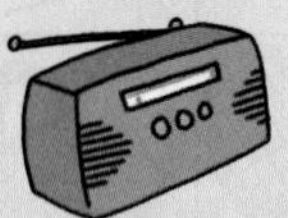
une radio

une radiocassette

une chaîne hi-fi (une mini-chaîne)

une voiture (une auto)

un vélo (une bicyclette)

une mobylette

un scooter

une moto

▶ ***How to ask if an object works:***

–Est-ce que la radio **marche?** *Does the radio work?*
–Oui, elle **marche.** *Yes, it works.*

➔ The verb **marcher** has two meanings:

for people:	*to walk*	Nous **marchons.**
for things:	*to work, to run*	Le scooter ne **marche** pas bien.

RAPPEL

Masculine nouns can be replaced by **il.**
Le vélo marche.
Il marche bien.

Feminine nouns can be replaced by **elle.**
La voiture marche.
Elle marche bien.

SPEAKING PRACTICE

Have students bring in a picture of one of the above vocabulary items. Ask each one to describe his/her object and say if it works.

Voici un baladeur. Il est petit.
Il marche bien.

LANGUAGE NOTES

- You might want to mention that **VTT** stands for **vélo tout terrain.**
- Remind students that *to work* in the sense of *doing work* is **travailler.** You may want to point out that in English something "runs" well, whereas in French it "walks."
- **Casual speech** Common shortened forms: **un appareil, un magnéto, une mob, une chaîne**

5 Et toi?

PARLER

1. J'ai ... *(Name 3 objects you own.)*
2. Je voudrais ... *(Name 3 things you would like to have.)*
3. Pour Noël / Hanoukka, je voudrais ... *(Name 2 gifts you would like to receive.)*

6 Joyeux anniversaire *(Happy birthday)*

PARLER/ÉCRIRE For your birthday, a rich aunt is giving you the choice between different possible gifts. Indicate your preferences.

▶ vélo ou scooter?

1. mobylette ou moto?
2. portable ou baladeur?
3. appareil-photo ou radio?
4. radiocassette ou chaîne hi-fi?
5. télé ou ordinateur?
6. DVD ou cassette vidéo?

Je préfère le vélo.
Je préfère le scooter.

7  Qu'est-ce que tu as?

PARLER Éric asks Léa if she has the following objects. She says that she does. Play both roles.

▶ ÉRIC: **Est-ce que tu as une guitare?**
LÉA: **Oui, j'ai une guitare.**

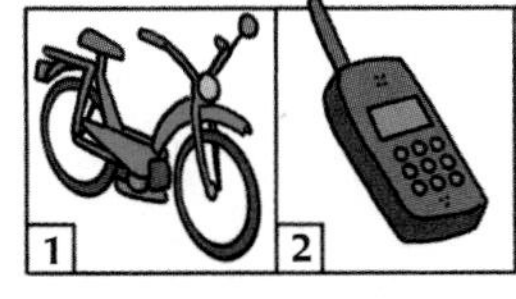

8   Est-ce qu'il marche bien?

PARLER Tell your classmates that you own the following objects. They will ask you if the objects are working. Answer according to the illustrations.

▶ **—J'ai un vélo.**
—Est-ce qu'il marche bien?
—Non, il ne marche pas bien.

▶ **—J'ai une télé.**
—Est-ce qu'elle marche bien?
—Oui, elle marche très bien.

LANGUAGE NOTE

The word **mobylette** was originally a brand name. The word has become the generic term for *motorbike* in French, replacing **vélomoteur**. Other common examples of brand names that have become generic terms are:

un frigidaire or **un frigo** (replacing **un réfrigérateur**)
un bic (replacing **un stylo à bille**)

Have students guess possible reasons why the brand names conquered the generic names (perhaps one brand of an item was overwhelmingly preferred by French consumers over another until that brand became synonymous with the item itself).

5 COMMUNICATION talking about what one has and what one wants

Answers will vary.
1. J'ai (un baladeur, une affiche et une montre).
2. Je voudrais (un vélo, un stylo et une télé).
3. Pour Noël / Hanoukka, je voudrais (un téléphone et une calculatrice).

Expansion Ask students if the objects they mentioned in number 1 of Act. 5 work well.
– J'ai une chaîne hi-fi.
– Est-ce qu'elle marche bien?
– Non, elle ne marche pas bien.

6 COMMUNICATION indicating preferences

1. Je préfère la mobylette. (la moto)
2. Je préfère le portable. (le baladeur)
3. Je préfère l'appareil-photo. (la radio)
4. Je préfère la radiocassette. (la chaîne hi-fi)
5. Je préfère la télé. (l'ordinateur)
6. Je préfère le DVD. (la cassette vidéo)

Photo cultural note Scooters are an increasingly popular mode of transportation among French young people. To drive a scooter you must be 14 years old, carry a license (**un permis**), and wear a helmet (**un casque**). However, **le vélo, la mobylette** and **la moto** are most popular.

7 ROLE PLAY discussing what one has

Éric: Est-ce que tu as ... ?
Léa: Oui, j'ai ...
1. une mobylette
2. un portable
3. un vélo (une bicyclette)
4. un ordinateur
5. un appareil-photo
6. une chaîne hi-fi

8 EXCHANGES talking about whether things work

1. – J'ai un appareil-photo.
   – Est-ce qu'il marche bien?
   – Non, il ne marche pas bien.
2. – J'ai un scooter.
   – Est-ce qu'il marche bien?
   – Oui, il marche très bien.
3. – J'ai une chaîne hi-fi.
   – Est-ce qu'elle marche bien?
   – Oui, elle marche très bien.
4. – J'ai une mobylette.
   – Est-ce qu'elle marche bien?
   – Non, elle ne marche pas bien.
5. – J'ai une radio.
   – Est-ce qu'elle marche bien?
   – Oui, elle marche très bien.
6. – J'ai une montre.
   – Est-ce qu'elle marche bien?
   – Non, elle ne marche pas bien.

SECTION D

Communicative function
Describing one's room

Teaching Resource Options

PRINT 

Workbook PE, pp. 85–92
Unit 4 Resource Book
Communipak, pp. 140–160
Video Activities, p. 27
Videoscript, pp. 29–30
Workbook TE, pp. 1–8

AUDIO & VISUAL 

Overhead Transparencies
22 *Dans ma chambre*
23 *Les prépositions*

VIDEO PROGRAM

MODULE 9

9.3 Dialogue: Tu as un portable? (31:40–32:57 min.)

9.4 Mini-scenes: Où est-il? (32:58–34:13 min.)

Looking ahead Plural nouns are presented in Lesson 10.

Language note **Une chambre** is a *bedroom.* The general word for *room* is **une pièce.**

Supplementary vocabulary

un meuble *piece of furniture*
un fauteuil *armchair*
un placard *closet*
un tapis *rug, carpet*
une bibliothèque *bookcase*
une étagère *shelf*
une commode *dresser*

D VOCABULAIRE Ma chambre *(My room)*

How to talk about what there is in a place:

il y a	*there is* *there are*	Dans *(In)* ma chambre, **il y a** une télé. Dans le garage, **il y a** deux voitures.
est-ce qu'il y a ... ?	*is/are there ... ?*	**Est-ce qu'il y a** un ordinateur dans la classe?
qu'est-ce qu'il y a ... ?	*what is there ... ?*	**Qu'est-ce qu'il y a** dans le garage?

Dans ma chambre

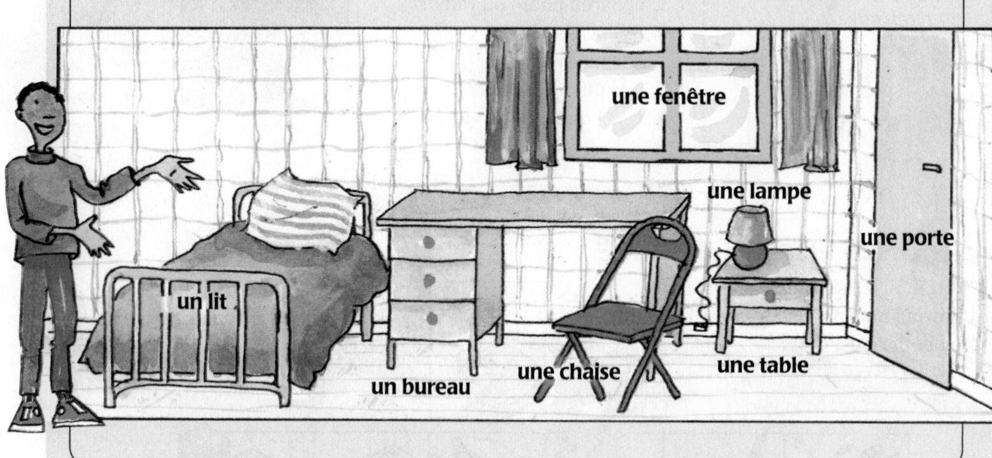

How to say where something or someone is:

INCLUSION

Cumulative Write a list of vocabulary words on the board. Ask students to describe their room to a partner (**Dans ma chambre, il y a...**). Have partners take notes and then describe the room to the class or write a paragraph describing the partner's room. Have students switch roles and repeat.

9 Qu'est-ce qu'il y a?

PARLER Describe the various objects that are in the pictures.

1. Sur la table, il y a ... **2.** Sous le lit, il y a ... **3.** Dans le garage, il y a ...

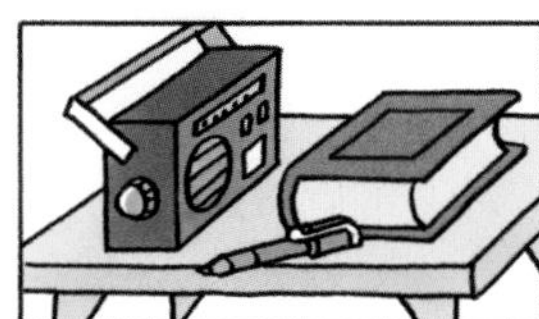

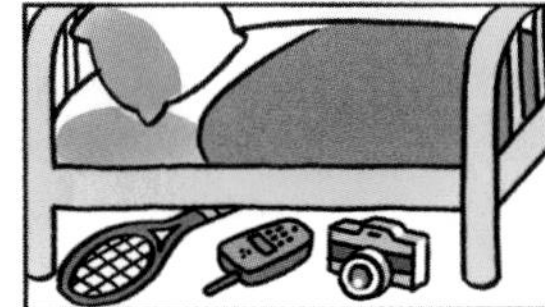

10 Ma chambre

PARLER/ÉCRIRE Describe the various objects (pieces of furniture and personal belongings) that are in your room.

▶ **Dans ma chambre, il y a une radio, ...**
Il y a aussi ...

11 Où est le téléphone?

PARLER Michèle is looking for the telephone. Jean-Claude tells her where it is.

▶ MICHÈLE: **Où est le téléphone?**
JEAN-CLAUDE: **Il est sur la table.**

12 C'est étrange! *(It's strange!)*

PARLER/ÉCRIRE Funny things sometimes happen. Describe these curious happenings by selecting an item from Column A and putting it in one of the places listed in Column B.

▶

Il y a un éléphant sous le lit!

▶ Il y a ...

A	B
un rhinocéros	dans la classe
un éléphant	sur le bureau
une girafe	sous la table
un crabe	sous le lit
une souris *(mouse)*	derrière la porte
un ami de King Kong	sur la tour Eiffel
un extra-terrestre	dans le jardin *(garden)*
	devant le restaurant

9 DESCRIPTION saying where things are

1. Sur la table, il y a une radio, un stylo et un livre.
2. Sous le lit, il y a une raquette, un portable et un appareil-photo.
3. Dans le garage, il y a un scooter, une voiture (une auto) et un vélo (une bicyclette).

10 COMMUNICATION describing one's room

Answers will vary.
Dans ma chambre, il y a un lit et une chaise. Il y a aussi un bureau, une table, un téléphone, un livre et un sac.

11 ROLE PLAY saying where something is

1. **M:** Où est le téléphone?
   JC: Il est sur le bureau.
2. **M:** Où est le téléphone?
   JC: Il est sur la chaise.
3. **M:** Où est le téléphone?
   JC: Il est sous le lit.
4. **M:** Où est le téléphone?
   JC: Il est devant la fenêtre.
5. **M:** Où est le téléphone?
   JC: Il est derrière la porte.

12 COMMUNICATION describing improbable locations

Answers will vary.
Il y a un rhinocéros (derrière la porte)!
Il y a un éléphant (dans le jardin)!
Il y a une girafe (sur le bureau)!
Il y a un crabe (sous la table)!
Il y a une souris (sous le lit)!
Il y a un ami de King Kong (sur la tour Eiffel)!
Il y a un extra-terrestre (devant le restaurant)!

Expansion Have students invent other improbable statements using known vocabulary.

COMPREHENSION Location

PROPS: Objects from the lesson

Demonstrate prepositions of place:
Je mets le CD dans le sac.
Je mets la raquette sur la chaise.
Je mets la guitare sous la table.
Je mets le stylo derrière le livre. ...

Have students move the objects around.
X, viens ici. Mets le CD dans le sac.
Y, viens et mets le crayon devant le sac.
Z, prends le livre et mets-le derrière le sac.

Optional give more complex commands.
X, mets le crayon dans le sac.
Et puis mets le sac sous la chaise de Y.

Teaching Resource Options

PRINT  

Workbook PE, pp. 85–92
Unit 4 Resource Book
Communipak, pp. 140–160
Video Activities, p. 28
Videoscript, p. 30
Workbook TE, pp. 1–8

VIDEO PROGRAM

VIDÉO DVD

MODULE 9

9.5 Vignette culturelle: La chambre de Catherine (34:14–35:38 min.)

13 ROLE PLAY asking where things are

1. **F:** Où est la raquette?
   N: Elle est sous le lit.
2. **F:** Où est la guitare?
   N: Elle est derrière la chaise.
3. **F:** Où est le livre?
   N: Il est dans le sac.
4. **F:** Où est le vélo?
   N: Il est devant la fenêtre.
5. **F:** Où est l'ordinateur?
   N: Il est sur le bureau.
6. **F:** Où est le sac?
   N: Il est devant la télé (sur la table).
7. **F:** Où est la radio?
   N: Elle est sur le bureau.
8. **F:** Où est le CD?
   N: Il est sur la table.
9. **F:** Où est le portable?
   N: Il est sur la chaise.

14 COMPREHENSION describing where someone is

1. M. Vénard est dans la voiture.
2. M. Vénard est sous la voiture.
3. M. Vénard est derrière la voiture.
4. La contractuelle est devant la voiture.

Cultural note **La contractuelle** is an auxiliary police officer who is authorized to write tickets (**une contravention**) for illegally parked vehicles. The traffic sign in the cartoon signals a no parking zone (**stationnement interdit**).

13  La chambre de Nicole

PARLER Florence wants to borrow a few things from Nicole's room. Nicole tells her where each object is.

▶ la télé
FLORENCE: **Où est la télé?**
NICOLE: **Elle est sur la table.**

1. la raquette
2. la guitare
3. le livre
4. le vélo
5. l'ordinateur
6. le sac
7. la radio
8. le CD
9. le portable

14 Pauvre Monsieur Vénard *(Poor Mr. Vénard)*

PARLER/ÉCRIRE Today Monsieur Vénard left on vacation, but he soon ran out of luck. Describe the four cartoons by completing the sentences below.

Le voyage de Monsieur Vénard

1. M. Vénard est ____ la voiture.

2. M. Vénard est ____ la voiture.

3. M. Vénard est ____ la voiture.

4. La contractuelle° est ____ la voiture.

la contractuelle *meter maid*

E VOCABULAIRE Mon ordinateur

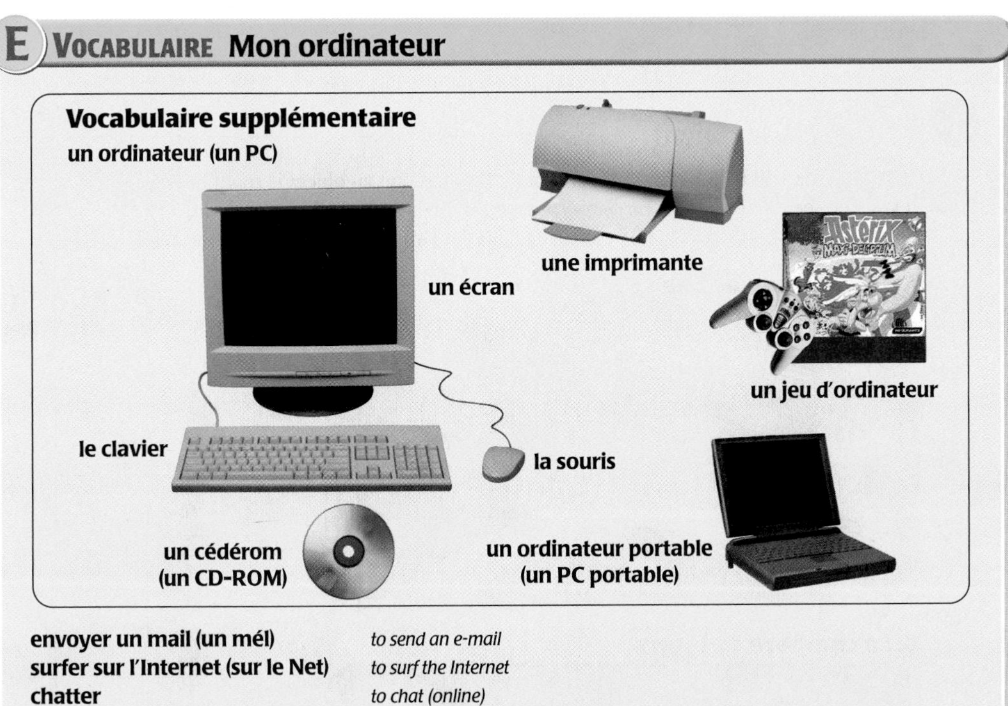

envoyer un mail (un mél) *to send an e-mail*
surfer sur l'Internet (sur le Net) *to surf the Internet*
chatter *to chat (online)*
télécharger *to download*

COMPARAISONS INTERPERSONNELLES

Here is a list of various activities that you can do with a computer. List the four activities you like to do best, ranking them in order of preference. Compare your lists with your classmates.

- chatter
- faire mes devoirs *(homework)*
- écouter de la musique
- envoyer un mail à un copain / une copine
- surfer sur le Net
- regarder les nouvelles *(news)*
- télécharger de la musique
- faire des recherches *(research)* pour la classe de français
- jouer aux jeux d'ordinateur

UN SONDAGE

Conduct a poll in your class to determine which two of the above computer activities students like the best and which two they like the least.

SECTION E

The vocabulary in this section "Mon ordinateur" is presented primarily for recognition. Students should not be expected to memorize and/or produce these expressions independently.

Teaching note **Envoyer** is presented for recognition. If appropriate, you may introduce the present tense forms:

j'**envoie**	nous **envoyons**
tu **envoies**	vous **envoyez**
il/elle **envoie**	ils/elles **envoient**

Supplementary vocabulary

graver un CD *to burn a CD*
un graveur de CD *CD burner*
le disque dur *hard drive*
le logiciel *software*
le modem *modem*
un scanner *scanner*

Teaching note French borrows many English high technology terms. Make an overhead transparency listing the vocabulary on PE page 142 and the supplementary vocabulary from PE page 147 and TE pages 142 and 147. Have the students figure out which of these words were borrowed from English.

À VOTRE TOUR

Main Topic
- Recapitulation and review

Teaching Resource Options

PRINT 

Workbook PE, pp. 85–92
Unit 4 Resource Book
- Audioscript, pp. 31–32
- Communipak, pp. 140–160
- Family Involvement, pp. 23–24
- Workbook TE, pp. 1–8

Assessment
- Lesson 9 Quiz, pp. 35–36
- Portfolio Assessment, Unit 1 URB, pp. 155–164
- Audioscript for Quiz 9, p. 34
- Answer Keys, pp. 201–205

AUDIO & VISUAL 

Audio Program
CD 2 Tracks 25, 26, 27
CD 14 Track 17

TECHNOLOGY 

Test Generator CD-ROM/McDougal Littell Assessment System

1 LISTENING COMPREHENSION

1. A	7. B	13. A
2. B	8. B	14. A
3. A	9. B	15. B
4. A	10. A	16. A
5. B	11. B	17. A
6. A, B	12. B	18. A, B

2 GUIDED ORAL EXPRESSION

A: Est-ce que tu as (As-tu) un ordinateur?
M: Oui.
A: Est-ce qu'il marche bien?
M: Oui, il marche très bien. Pourquoi?
A: Je voudrais envoyer un mail à un copain.
M: L'ordinateur est sur le bureau dans ma chambre.

Variation Have students write out the dialogue with a partner.

À votre tour!

OBJECTIFS
Now you can ...
- describe your belongings
- talk about people and give their ages

1 Écoutez bien!

ÉCOUTER You will hear a series of sentences. In each one an object is mentioned. If you see the object only in Léa's room, mark A. If you see the object only in Pierre's room, mark B. If you see the object in the two rooms, mark both A and B.

A. La chambre de Léa

B. La chambre de Pierre

	A Léa	B Pierre
1.		
2.		
3.		
4.		
5.		
6.		
7.		
8.		
9.		
10.		
11.		
12.		
13.		
14.		
15.		
16.		
17.		
18.		

2 Conversation dirigée

PARLER André is visiting his cousin Marie. Act out the dialogue according to the instructions.

André

André		Marie
asks Marie if she has a computer	→ ↙	answers affirmatively
asks her if it works well	→ ↙	says that it works very well and asks why
says he would like to send an e-mail to a friend	→	says that the computer is on the desk in her room

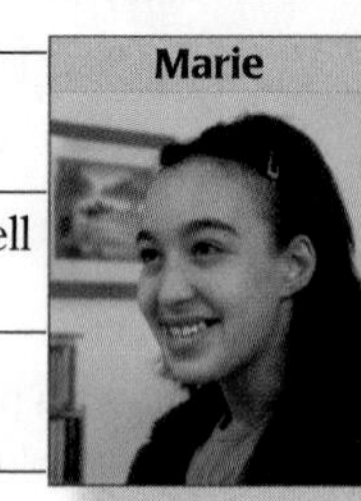
Marie

À VOTRE TOUR

Select those activities which are most appropriate for your students.

GROUP PRACTICE

In Act. 2 and 3, you may want to have students work in trios, with two performing and one acting as monitor.

3  Créa-dialogue

PARLER Daniel is showing Nathalie his recent photographs, and she is asking questions about the various people. Create similar dialogues and act them out in class.

▶ **un copain**

Éric/14

▶ —Qui est-ce?
—C'est un copain.
—Comment s'appelle-t-il?
—Il s'appelle Éric.
—Quel âge a-t-il?
—Il a quatorze ans.

1. une cousine	2. un camarade	3. une camarade	4. un voisin	5. une voisine	6. un professeur
Valérie/20	Philippe Boucher/13	Nathalie Masson/15	Monsieur Dumas/70	Madame Smith/51	Monsieur Laval/35

4  Mes affaires

ÉCRIRE Imagine that your family is going to move to another city. Prepare for the move by making a checklist of your things. Write out your list by hand or on a computer.

5  Ma chambre

ÉCRIRE A French student is going to spend two weeks at your house. Write him/her a short e-mail describing your room. In your note, mention …

- at least 3 pieces of furniture
- at least 3 school-related objects
- 4 personal belongings

If you wish, you can add some descriptive comments.

6  Un ordinateur

ÉCRIRE Imagine that you have just won a brand new computer in a contest at your school. Write a short paragraph in which you …

- describe its various components
- mention 3 ways in which you want to use it

Portfolio Assessment

You will probably select only one speaking activity and one writing activity to go into the students' portfolios for Unit 4.

In this lesson, Activities 5 and 6 are appropriate writing portfolio topics.

3 Guided Oral Expression

1. – Qui est-ce?
   – C'est une cousine.
   – Comment s'appelle-t-elle?
   – Elle s'appelle Valérie.
   – Quel âge a-t-elle?
   – Elle a vingt ans.
2. – Qui est-ce?
   – C'est un camarade.
   – Comment s'appelle-t-il?
   – Il s'appelle Philippe Boucher.
   – Quel âge a-t-il?
   – Il a treize ans.
3. – Qui est-ce?
   – C'est une camarade.
   – Comment s'appelle-t-elle?
   – Elle s'appelle Nathalie Masson.
   – Quel âge a-t-elle?
   – Elle a quinze ans.
4. – Qui est-ce?
   – C'est un voisin.
   – Comment s'appelle-t-il?
   – Il s'appelle Monsieur Dumas.
   – Quel âge a-t-il?
   – Il a soixante-dix ans.
5. – Qui est-ce?
   – C'est une voisine.
   – Comment s'appelle-t-elle?
   – Elle s'appelle Madame Smith.
   – Quel âge a-t-elle?
   – Elle a cinquante et un ans.
6. – Qui est-ce?
   – C'est un professeur.
   – Comment s'appelle-t-il?
   – Il s'appelle Monsieur Laval.
   – Quel âge a-t-il?
   – Il a trente-cinq ans.

4 Written Self-Expression

Answers will vary.
Mes affaires:
- un lit
- un bureau
- un vélo
- une chaise
- une guitare
- un CD

5 Written Self-Expression

Chère Carole,
Dans ma chambre, il y a un lit, un petit bureau et une chaise. En général, sur le bureau, il y a un cahier, un stylo et des crayons. Il y a aussi une chaîne hi-fi, un ordinateur et beaucoup de CD dans ma chambre.
–Julie

6 Written Self-Expression

Answers will vary.
L'ordinateur est génial! C'est un ordinateur portable. Il a une souris, un modem et un graveur de CD! Je voudrais télécharger de la musique (française, bien sûr!), chatter avec mes copains et surfer sur le Net.

Leçon 10

Main Topic Talking about possessions and preferences

Teaching Resource Options

PRINT 

Workbook PE, pp. 93–100
Activités pour tous PE, pp. 55–57
Block Scheduling Copymasters, pp. 73–79
Unit 4 Resource Book
- *Activités pour tous* TE, pp. 45–47
- Audioscript, pp. 66, 67–68
- Communipak, pp. 140–160
- Lesson Plans, pp. 48–49
- Block Scheduling Lesson Plans, pp. 50–51
- Absent Student Copymasters, pp. 52–57
- Video Activities, pp. 60–63
- Videoscript, pp. 64–65
- Workbook TE, pp. 37–44

AUDIO & VISUAL 

Audio Program
CD 2 Tracks 28, 29
CD 8 Tracks 7–13

TECHNOLOGY 

Online Workbook

VIDEO PROGRAM

MODULE 10
Tu as un vélo?

TOTAL TIME: 5:15 min.
DVD Disk 1
Videotape 2 (COUNTER: 35:48 min.)

10.1 Mini-scenes: Listening
–Tu as un vélo? (36:21–37:02 min.)

10.2 Mini-scenes: Listening
–Qu'est-ce que tu as? (37:03–38:06 min.)

10.3 Mini-scenes: Speaking
–Est-ce que tu as un vélo? (38:07–39:08 min.)

10.4 Dialogue: J'organise une boum (39:09–39:42 min.)

10.5 Vignette culturelle: La mobylette (39:43–41:03 min.)

Language note In French, **pas de** is often followed by a singular noun.

Il n'a pas de frère. = *He doesn't have a brother. (He has no brothers.)*

LEÇON 10

Vive la différence!

AUDIO

We are not necessarily like our friends. Léa describes herself and her best friend Céline. Both of them live in Paris and are quite different.

Léa

Céline

Je m'appelle Léa.	Elle s'appelle Céline.
Je suis française.	Elle est haïtienne.
J'ai des frères, mais je n'ai pas de soeur.	Elle n'a pas de frère, mais elle a deux soeurs.
J'ai un chien.	Elle n'a pas de chien, mais elle a un chat très mignon.
J'ai un scooter.	Elle a un vélo.
J'aime la musique classique.	Elle préfère le compas.
J'aime le basket et le tennis.	Elle préfère le foot.

Céline et moi, nous sommes très différentes ... mais nous sommes copines. C'est l'essentiel, non?

Compréhension

Answer the questions below with the appropriate names: **Léa, Céline,** or **Léa et Céline.**

1. Qui habite en France?
2. Qui a deux soeurs?
3. Qui n'a pas de frère?
4. Qui a un vélo?
5. Qui aime la musique classique?
6. Qui aime les sports?

SETTING THE SCENE

The theme of this opening text is that friends do not always have identical tastes and backgrounds.

TEACHING NOTE Census Information

According to the 2000 census, French ranks third after Spanish and Chinese as the non-English language most spoken at home in the United States. Have students go to the the website for the United States Census Bureau to see the current percentage of people who speak a language other than English at home.

NOTE culturelle

EN BREF: Haïti
Capitale: Port-au-Prince
Population: 8 millions d'habitants
Langues: créole, français

Un marché à Pétionville (près de Port-au-Prince)

Une peinture haïtienne

Haiti occupies the western part of the large Caribbean island on which the Dominican Republic is also located. Its inhabitants are of African origin. Their enslaved ancestors revolted against their French masters in 1805 and established the first independent Black nation in modern history. Today many Haitians have emigrated to France, Canada, and especially to the United States. There are sizable Haitian communities in Florida and in cities along the northeastern seaboard.

Haitians are friendly, industrious, and artistic people. In the twentieth century, Haitian painters developed their own widely appreciated folk art style and Haitian paintings are now in collections around the world. The Haitians also love music, especially **compas** or **kompas** which highlights a variety of instruments including conga drums, guitar, and keyboard. Its creole lyrics are expressed against a background of African, Caribbean, reggae, and rock rhythms.

Haitian creole cuisine, which features rice dishes, pork, and shellfish, is often quite spicy. Typical Haitian dishes include **griots** (fried pork), **riz djon-djon** (rice with mushrooms), and **pain patate** (sweet potato cake).

CONNEXIONS Haïti

Learn more about Haiti. Divide the class into several groups, each with a different assignment. For example:

- Create a bulletin board display with pictures, maps, and newspaper clippings about Haiti.
- Find books on Haitian paintings and Haitian artists and make a presentation to the class.
- Find examples of **compas** music and play a selection for the class.

USING THE VIDEO

Video Module 10 prepares students to talk about various things they own. They will meet a wide variety of French people who will describe their possessions. The **Vignette culturelle** is about the moped.

COMPOSITION

Have students use the **Vive la différence** dialogue as a point of departure for writing a composition about themselves and one of their friends. Suggest that they write their descriptions in two columns, using as a model Léa's and Céline's text on p. 150. Students should complete their compositions in 15 minutes.
Pre-AP skill: Write in a timed situation.

Compréhension

Answers

1. Léa et Céline habitent en France.
2. Céline a deux soeurs.
3. Céline n'a pas de frère.
4. Céline a un vélo.
5. Léa aime la musique classique.
6. Léa et Céline aiment les sports.

Teaching strategy Have students give short answers since they do not know the plural forms of **avoir**.

Note culturelle

Photo cultural notes

- Top: This is a photograph of the outdoor market in Petionville, Haiti. Ask students if they have ever shopped at an outdoor market. Discuss the advantages and disadvantages of buying food at an outdoor market (advantages: festive atmosphere, fresh produce; disadvantages: market only open certain days, some products may not be available).
- Bottom: This painting is entitled *Boys Flying Kites.* It was painted by J. Charlemagne.

Teaching note According to a 2003 report by the Association for Canadian Studies, Florida is second only to Quebec in the number of North Americans who speak French at home. Have students research the possible causes. (It is because of the growth of the state's Haitian and French-Canadian populations.)

SECTION A

Communicative function
Talking about what one has

Teaching Resource Options

PRINT 

Workbook PE, pp. 93–100
Unit 4 Resource Book
Communipak, pp. 140–160
Workbook TE, pp. 37–44

TECHNOLOGY 

Power Presentations

Review and expansion

Students learned the singular forms of **avoir** in **Invitation au français.** Point out that the plural form **ont** is similar to **sont** and **font**.

Teaching note Use flash cards for subject pronouns and known objects to practice the forms of **avoir**.

On the chalkledge place 2 cards, e.g., card [**nous**] + card [*tennis racket*]

Response: **Nous avons une raquette.**

1 PRACTICE saying what people have

1. Tu as une raquette.
2. Il a un baladeur.
3. Tu as une télé.
4. Vous avez un portable.
5. Nous avons un baladeur.
6. Vous avez un ordinateur.
7. Elles ont une raquette.
8. Ils ont un ordinateur.

2 COMMUNICATION giving people's ages

1. J'ai (quinze) ans.
2. Tu as (seize) ans.
3. Vous avez (trente-huit) ans.
4. Mon copain a (seize) ans.
5. Ma copine a (quinze) ans.
6. La voisine a (soixante-huit) ans.

Expansion Have students guess the ages of well-known sports and TV figures.

Language note The French always use **ans** after the number when giving someone's age.

A Le verbe *avoir*

The verb **avoir** *(to have, to own)* is irregular. Note the forms of this verb in the present tense.

avoir	*to have*	
j' **ai**	*I have*	J'**ai** une copine à Québec.
tu **as**	*you have*	Est-ce que tu **as** un frère?
il/elle **a**	*he/she has*	Philippe **a** une cousine à Paris.
nous **avons**	*we have*	Nous **avons** un ordinateur.
vous **avez**	*you have*	Est-ce que vous **avez** une moto?
ils/elles **ont**	*they have*	Ils n'**ont** pas ton appareil-photo.

→ There is liaison in the forms: **nous avons, vous avez, ils ont, elles ont.**

VOCABULAIRE Expressions avec *avoir*

avoir faim	*to be hungry*	**J'ai faim.** Et toi, est-ce que tu **as faim?**
avoir soif	*to be thirsty*	Paul **a soif.** Sylvie n'**a** pas **soif.**
avoir ... ans	*to be ... (years old)*	**J'ai** 14 **ans.** Le prof **a** 35 **ans.**

1 Qu'est-ce qu'ils ont?

PARLER From what the people are doing, say which object in the box they have.

un baladeur
un ordinateur
un portable
une raquette
une télé

▶ Léa regarde un film.
Elle a une télé.

1. Tu joues au tennis.
2. Éric écoute du rock.
3. Je regarde un film.
4. Vous téléphonez.
5. Nous écoutons un CD.
6. Vous envoyez un mail.
7. Elles jouent au tennis.
8. Ils surfent sur le Net.

2 Expression personnelle

PARLER/ÉCRIRE How old are the following people? Complete the sentences below. If you don't know their ages, guess.

1. J'ai ...
2. *(A classmate)* Tu as ...
3. *(The teacher)* Vous ...
4. Mon copain ...
5. Ma copine ...
6. La voisine ...

3 Faim ou soif?

PARLER You are at a party with your classmates. Offer them the following foods and beverages. They will accept or refuse by saying whether they are hungry or thirsty.

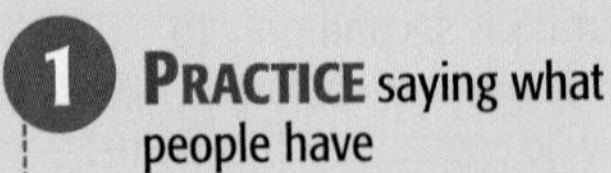

Tu veux un sandwich?
Oui, merci! J'ai faim.
(Non, merci! Je n'ai pas faim.)

▶ un sandwich

1. une crêpe
2. un soda
3. un hamburger
4. un jus d'orange
5. un croissant
6. un jus de raisin
7. une pizza
8. une limonade

152 cent cinquante-deux
Unité 4

TEACHING NOTE Introducing the past tense

Once students learn the present tense forms of **avoir**, you may want to introduce the PASSÉ COMPOSÉ for conversation practice. (The tense is presented formally in Unit 7.)

Beginning with this lesson, you will find optional oral questions about past events.

To talk about what happened yesterday (**hier**), the French use the PASSÉ COMPOSÉ:
present of **avoir** + past participle

For **-er** verbs, the past participle ends in **-é**. (You may want to use the chart on p. 321.)

Unit 10 form quiz

B Les noms et les articles: masculin et féminin

NOUNS

- Nouns designating PEOPLE

  Nouns that designate male persons are almost always *masculine:*

  un garçon **un ami**

  Nouns that designate female persons are almost always *feminine:*

  une fille **une amie**

→ EXCEPTIONS:

une personne is always feminine (even when it refers to a male)

un professeur is always masculine (even when it refers to a woman)

- Nouns designating ANIMALS, OBJECTS, and THINGS

  There is no systematic way to determine whether these nouns are masculine or feminine. Therefore, it is very important to learn these nouns with their articles.

MASCULINE:	**un** portable	**un** vélo	**un** ordinateur
FEMININE:	**une** chaîne hi-fi	**une** moto	**une** affiche

LEARNING ABOUT LANGUAGE

NOUNS are words that designate people, animals, objects, and things.

In French, all nouns have GENDER: they are either MASCULINE or FEMININE.

ARTICLES

Note the forms of the articles in the chart below.

	MASCULINE		FEMININE			
INDEFINITE ARTICLE	**un**	*a, an*	**une**	*a, an*	**un** garçon	**une** fille
DEFINITE ARTICLE	**le**	*the*	**la**	*the*	**le** garçon	**la** fille

→ Both **le** and **la** become **l'** before a vowel sound:

le garçon **l'ami**

la fille **l'amie**

LEARNING ABOUT LANGUAGE

Nouns are often introduced by ARTICLES. In French, ARTICLES have the *same* gender as the nouns they introduce.

PRONOUNS

Note the forms of the pronouns in the chart below.

MASCULINE	**il**	*he* *it*	Où est **le** garçon? Où est **le** portable?	**Il** est en classe. **Il** est sur la table.
FEMININE	**elle**	*she* *it*	Où est **la** fille? Où est **la** voiture?	**Elle** est en ville. **Elle** est là-bas.

LEARNING ABOUT LANGUAGE

Nouns may be replaced by PRONOUNS. In French, PRONOUNS have the *same* gender as the nouns they replace.

TALKING ABOUT PAST EVENTS

▶ Let's talk about what you did yesterday.

Est-ce que tu as étudié hier? Oui, j'ai étudié hier. (Non, je n'ai pas étudié hier.)

- **Est-ce que tu as étudié hier?**
- **Est-ce que tu as travaillé hier?**
- **Est-ce que tu as regardé la télé hier?**
- **Est-ce que tu as écouté la radio?**
- **Est-ce que tu as parlé français?**
- **Est-ce que tu as joué au tennis?**
- **Est-ce que tu as dîné au restaurant?**
- **Est-ce que tu as mangé un steak?** (Reminder: use **pas de** in the negative.)
- **Est-ce que tu as mangé une omelette?**

Communicative function
Designating people and things

Language notes

- For the more common farm animals, the gender of the noun does correspond to the sex of the animal: **un taureau, une vache.**
- Be sure students understand that gender is linked to the NOUN and not to the object itself. For example, a *bicycle* can be referred to as **une bicyclette** or **un vélo.**

Re-entry and review

Definite and indefinite articles from Unit 1, Lessons 2A and 2B; pronouns from Unit 2, Lesson 3C and Unit 3, Lesson 6.

Critical thinking: Pronouns

Have students look at the sentences in the pronoun chart. How can they tell if **il** means *he* or *it?*

Il est en classe. *He is in class.*

Il est sur la table. *It is on the table.*

[They look at the context to see what **il** is referring to: **le garçon? le CD?**]

Similarly, how can they tell if **elle** means *she* or *it?*

Teaching Resource Options

PRINT 

Workbook PE, pp. 93–100
Unit 4 Resource Book
Communipak, pp. 140–160
Workbook TE, pp. 37–44

TECHNOLOGY 

Power Presentations

SECTION C

Communicative function
Identifying people and things

Language note Note the following plural: **des appareils-photo**
There is no "s" on **photo** since this is a shortened form of **photographique(s)**.

Vocabulary note **gens** is masculine.

Realia note The **Galeries Lafayette** is a well-known Parisian department store.

4 EXCHANGES identifying celebrities

– Tiens, voilà ... !
– Qui est-ce?
– Un(e) ...

1. Dan Rather/Un journaliste.
2. Julia Roberts/Une actrice.
3. Brad Pitt/Un acteur.
4. Will Smith/Un chanteur.
5. Britney Spears/Une chanteuse.
6. Tiger Woods/Un athlète.
7. Venus Williams/Une athlète.
8. Whoopi Goldberg/Une comédienne.

Expansion Have students suggest other names for each of the categories in Act. 4: e.g., **Leslie Stahl est une journaliste.**

5 ROLE PLAY describing location

Caroline: Où est ... ?
Cécile: (Le/La) ... ? (Il/Elle) est (sur/sous) la table.

1. (l'ordinateur) Il est sur la table.
2. (le sac) Il est sur la table.
3. (l'affiche) Elle est sur la table.
4. (la calculatrice) Elle est sous la table.
5. (la raquette) Elle est sous la table.
6. (l'appareil-photo) Il est sous la table.
7. (la radiocassette) Elle est sous la table.
8. (la télé) Elle est sous la table.

Expansion Use classroom objects.
– Où est le livre?
– Il est sur le bureau.

4 Les célébrités

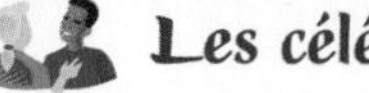

PARLER You and Jean-Pierre have been invited to a benefit attended by many American celebrities. Jean-Pierre asks you who each person is. Answer him using **un** or **une**, as appropriate.

▶ Katie Couric/journaliste
—Tiens, voilà Katie Couric!
—Qui est-ce?
—Une journaliste.

1. Dan Rather/journaliste
2. Julia Roberts/actrice
3. Brad Pitt/acteur
4. Will Smith/chanteur *(singer)*
5. Britney Spears/chanteuse
6. Tiger Woods/athlète
7. Venus Williams/athlète
8. Whoopi Goldberg/comédienne

5 Sur la table ou sous la table?

PARLER Caroline is looking for the following objects. Cécile tells her where each one is: on or under the table.

▶ baladeur
CAROLINE: **Où est le baladeur?**
CÉCILE: **Le baladeur?**
Il est sur la table.

1. ordinateur
2. sac
3. affiche
4. calculatrice
5. raquette
6. appareil-photo
7. radiocassette
8. télé

C Les noms et les articles: le pluriel

Compare the singular and plural forms of the articles and nouns in the sentences below.

SINGULAR	PLURAL
Tu as **le livre?**	Tu as **les livres?**
Qui est **la fille** là-bas?	Qui sont **les filles** là-bas?
Voici **un sac.**	Voici **des sacs.**
J'invite **une copine.**	J'invite **des copines.**

PLURAL NOUNS

In written French, the plural of most nouns is formed as follows:

→ If the noun ends in **-s** in the singular, the singular and plural forms are the same.

Voici **un Français.** Voici **des Français.**

→ In spoken French, the final **-s** of the plural is always silent.

→ NOTE: **des gens** *(people)* is always plural. Compare:

une personne	*person*	Qui est **la personne** là-bas?
des gens	*people*	Qui sont **les gens** là-bas?

COMPREHENSION Singular and plural forms

PROPS: Classroom objects

Point out either one or two common objects.
Voici un crayon.
Voici des crayons.
Voilà une fenêtre.
Voilà des fenêtres.
Où sont les livres? Où est le livre?

Then have individual students point out one or several objects.
X, montre-nous un stylo.
Maintenant, montre-nous des stylos.
Y, montre-nous le livre de français.
Où sont les livres de français?
Z, montre-nous des élèves.
Maintenant, montre-nous une élève.

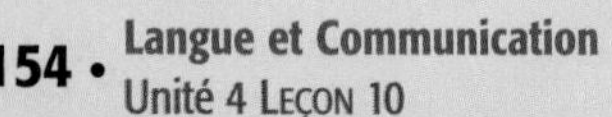

SINGULAR AND PLURAL ARTICLES

The forms of the articles are summarized in the chart below.

	SINGULAR		PLURAL			
DEFINITE ARTICLE	**le (l')** **la (l')**	*the*	**les**	*the*	**les** garçons **les** filles	**les** ordinateurs **les** affiches
INDEFINITE ARTICLE	**un** **une**	*a, an*	**des**	*some*	**des** garçons **des** filles	**des** ordinateurs **des** affiches

→ There is liaison after **les** and **des** when the next word begins with a vowel sound.

→ **Des** corresponds to the English article *some.* While *some* is often omitted in English, **des** MUST be expressed in French. Contrast:

Il y a	**des**	**livres sur la table.**
There are	*some*	*books on the table.*

Je dîne avec	**des**	**amis.**
I'm having dinner with	...	*friends.*

6 Pluriel, s'il vous plaît

PARLER/ÉCRIRE Give the plurals of the following nouns.

▶ une copine
des copines

▶ l'ami
les amis

1. un copain
2. une amie
3. un homme
4. une femme
5. un euro
6. une affiche
7. le voisin
8. l'élève
9. la cousine
10. le livre
11. l'ordinateur
12. la voiture

7   Shopping

PARLER You are in a department store looking for the following items. Ask the salesperson if he or she has these items. The salesperson will answer affirmatively.

▶ **—Pardon, monsieur (madame). Est-ce que vous avez des sacs?**
—Bien sûr, nous avons des sacs.

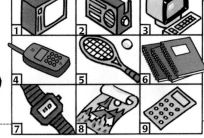

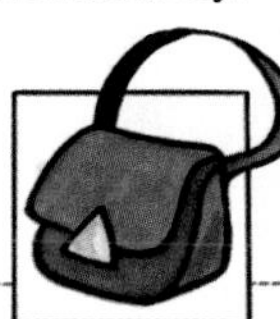

8 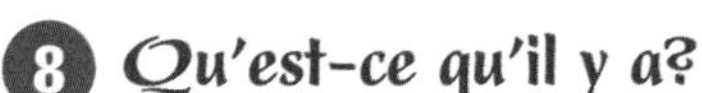 Qu'est-ce qu'il y a?

PARLER/ÉCRIRE Explain what there is in the following places. Complete the sentences with **il y a** and at least two nouns of your choice. Be sure to use the appropriate articles: **un, une, des.**

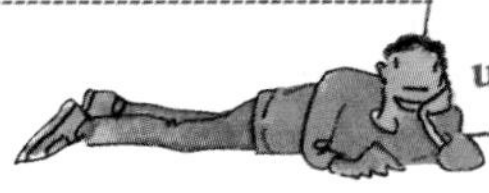

Dans le garage, il y a une moto (des voitures ...).

▶ Dans le garage, ...

1. Sur le bureau, ...
2. À la boum, ...
3. Dans la classe, ...
4. Au café, sur la table, ...
5. Dans ma chambre, ...
6. Dans mon sac, ...

LISTENING ACTIVITY

Quickly read off sentences containing singular or plural articles. Have students raise one finger if they hear a singular article. Have them extend all fingers if they hear a plural article.

1. **Voici des copines.** [P]
2. **Voici le vélo.** [S]
3. **Voici une affiche.** [S]
4. **Voici les professeurs.** [P]
5. **Voici des ordinateurs.** [P]
6. **Voici un camarade.** [S]
7. **Voici les amis.** [P]
8. **Voici l'appareil-photo.** [S]

6 PRACTICE plural articles and nouns

1. des copains
2. des amies
3. des hommes
4. des femmes
5. des euros
6. des affiches
7. les voisins
8. les élèves
9. les cousines
10. les livres
11. les ordinateurs
12. les voitures

Teaching Tip Do this activity rapidly, focusing on student pronunciation.

7 ROLE PLAY asking for items in a store

1. – Pardon, monsieur (madame). Est-ce que vous avez des télés?
   – Bien sûr, nous avons des télés.
2. – Pardon, monsieur (madame). Est-ce que vous avez des radios?
   – Bien sûr, nous avons des radios.
3. – Pardon, monsieur (madame). Est-ce que vous avez des ordinateurs?
   – Bien sûr, nous avons des ordinateurs.
4. – Pardon, monsieur (madame). Est-ce que vous avez des portables?
   – Bien sûr, nous avons des portables.
5. – Pardon, monsieur (madame). Est-ce que vous avez des raquettes?
   – Bien sûr, nous avons des raquettes.
6. – Pardon, monsieur (madame). Est-ce que vous avez des cahiers?
   – Bien sûr, nous avons des cahiers.
7. – Pardon, monsieur (madame). Est-ce que vous avez des montres?
   – Bien sûr, nous avons des montres.
8. – Pardon, monsieur (madame). Est-ce que vous avez des affiches?
   – Bien sûr, nous avons des affiches.
9. – Pardon, monsieur (madame). Est-ce que vous avez des calculatrices?
   – Bien sûr, nous avons des calculatrices.

Teaching note Be sure students make the required liaisons in items 3 and 8.

Listening activity Read the following sentences aloud and have students mark whether the nouns are singular or plural.
Voici le professeur. [singular]
Voici les élèves. [plural], etc.

8 COMPREHENSION saying where things are

1. Sur le bureau, il y a (un stylo, des livres, un ordinateur).
2. À la boum, il y a (des filles et des garçons).
3. Dans la classe, il y a (des livres, un professeur, des stylos, des élèves, une table).
4. Au café, sur la table, il y a (une limonade et des croissants).
5. Dans ma chambre, il y a (un stylo, des livres, des affiches, un lit, un ordinateur, une table).
6. Dans mon sac, il y a (des stylos, des livres, des cahiers, un portable, une calculatrice).

SECTION D

Communicative function
Expressing negation

Teaching Resource Options

PRINT 

Workbook PE, pp. 93–100
Unit 4 Resource Book
Communipak, pp. 140–160
Video Activities, pp. 60–63
Videoscript, pp. 64–65
Workbook TE, pp. 37–44

AUDIO & VISUAL 

Overhead Transparencies
21 Objects *Quelques objets* (b)
24 *Le grenier*

TECHNOLOGY

Power Presentations

VIDEO PROGRAM

VIDÉO DVD

MODULE 10

10.1 Mini-scenes: Tu as un vélo? (36:21–37:02 min.)

10.2 Mini-scenes: Qu'est-ce que tu as? (37:03–38:06 min.)

10.3 Mini-scenes: Est-ce que tu as un vélo? (38:07–39:08 min.)

10.4 Dialogue: J'organise une boum (39:09–39:42 min.)

10.5 Vignette culturelle: La mobylette (39:43–41:03 min.)

9 EXCHANGES discussing possessions

Answers will vary.
– Est-ce que tu as ... ?
– Oui, j'ai un(e) ... (Non, je n'ai pas de (d') ...)

1. un appareil-photo (pas d'appareil-photo)
2. (une/pas de) moto
3. (une/pas de) mobylette
4. (une/pas de) clarinette
5. (des/pas de) jeux vidéo
6. des affiches (pas d'affiches)
7. (un/pas de) boa
8. un alligator (pas d'alligator)
9. des hamsters (pas de hamsters)
10. (un/pas de) portable

Expansion Ask a third person to report the answer.
X a un ordinateur. (X n'a pas d'ordinateur.)

Variation (with people)

1. un ami à Paris
2. une amie à Québec
3. un oncle riche
4. des cousins à Lille
5. des cousines à Dijon

D L'article indéfini dans les phrases négatives

Compare the forms of the indefinite article in affirmative and negative sentences.

AFFIRMATIVE	NEGATIVE	
Tu as **un** vélo?	Non, je n'ai **pas de** vélo.	*No, I don't have a bike.*
Est-ce que Paul a **une** radio?	Non, il n'a **pas de** radio.	*No, he doesn't have a radio.*
Vous invitez **des** copains demain?	Non, nous n'invitons **pas de** copains.	*No, we are not inviting any friends.*

After a NEGATIVE verb:

pas + un, une, des becomes **pas de**

→ Note that **pas de** becomes **pas d'** before a vowel sound.

Alice a un ordinateur.	Paul n'a **pas d'**ordinateur.
J'ai des amis à Québec.	Je n'ai **pas d'**amis à Montréal.

→ The negative form of **il y a** is **il n'y a pas:**

Dans ma chambre,		
il y a une radio.	**Il n'y a pas de** télé.	*There is no TV.*
il y a des affiches.	**Il n'y a pas de** photos.	*There are no photographs.*

→ After **être,** the articles **un, une,** and **des** do NOT change.

Philippe est un voisin.	Éric n'est **pas un** voisin.
Ce sont des vélos.	Ce ne sont **pas des** mobylettes.

9 Possessions

PARLER Ask your classmates if they own the following.

▶ un ordinateur

Est-ce que tu as un ordinateur?
Oui, j'ai un ordinateur.
(Non, je n'ai pas d'ordinateur.)

1. un appareil-photo
2. une moto
3. une mobylette
4. une clarinette
5. des jeux vidéo
6. des affiches
7. un boa
8. un alligator
9. des hamsters
10. un portable

10 Oui et non

PARLER/ÉCRIRE One cannot have everything. Say that the following people do not have what is indicated in parentheses.

▶ Paul a un vélo. (un scooter)
Il n'a pas de scooter.

1. Julien a un scooter. (une voiture)
2. J'ai une radio. (une télé)
3. Vous avez un baladeur. (une chaîne hi-fi)
4. Léa a une calculatrice. (un ordinateur)
5. Vous avez des frères. (une soeur)
6. Nous avons un chien. (des chats)
7. Tu as des copains à Bordeaux. (des copains à Lyon)
8. Marc a un oncle à Québec. (un oncle à Montréal)
9. Nathalie a des cousins à Paris. (des cousins à Lille)

TEACHING STRATEGY Il y a with objects

PROP: Transparency 21: Objects, *Quelques objets* (b)

Using a transparency marker, draw an "X" through eight of the objects shown. Describe what is and is not in the picture.

Point to the bicycle, saying: **Il y a un vélo.**
Cross out the scooter: **Il n'y a pas de scooter.**
Continue, having students repeat after you.

When eight items have been crossed out, ask questions about the transparency.

Est-ce qu'il y a une voiture?
[Oui, il y a une voiture.]
Est-ce qu'il y a un ordinateur?
[Non, il n'y a pas d'ordinateur.]

11 Le grenier *(The attic)*

PARLER Your friend is cleaning the attic. Ask if the following items are up there. Your friend (a classmate) will answer according to the illustration.

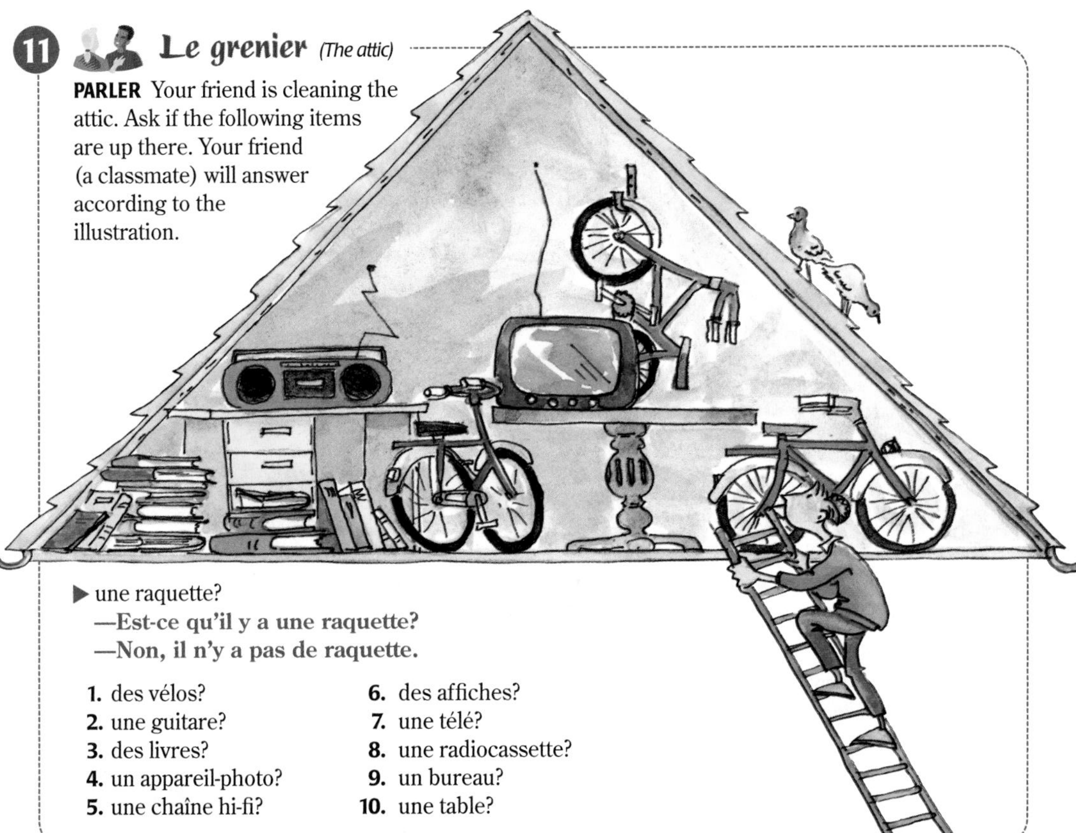

▶ une raquette?
—**Est-ce qu'il y a une raquette?**
—**Non, il n'y a pas de raquette.**

1. des vélos?
2. une guitare?
3. des livres?
4. un appareil-photo?
5. une chaîne hi-fi?
6. des affiches?
7. une télé?
8. une radiocassette?
9. un bureau?
10. une table?

VOCABULAIRE Expression pour la conversation

Tu n'as pas de chaîne hi-fi?
Si! J'ai une chaîne hi-fi.

▶ ***How to contradict a negative statement or question:***

Si! *Yes!* –Tu n'as pas de chaîne hi-fi?
–**Si!** J'ai une chaîne hi-fi.

12 Contradictions!

PARLER/ÉCRIRE Contradict all of the following negative statements.

▶ Tu ne parles pas anglais! **Si, je parle anglais!**

1. Tu ne parles pas français!
2. Tu n'étudies pas!
3. Tu ne joues pas au basket!
4. Tu n'aimes pas les sports!
5. Tu n'aimes pas la musique!
6. Tu n'écoutes pas le professeur!

INCLUSION

Synthetic/analytic Have students review the forms of the indefinite article, writing them out on the board. Create a sentence for each of the articles and write out its negative form. As you recite the sentences, ask students to beat on the desk each time they hear the negative **pas de**. Then create sentences that use articles following **être**, where the article does not change in the negative. After reinforcing this difference to students, read all the sentences, having them beat on the desk only for sentences where the article changes to **de**.

10 PRACTICE saying what people don't have

1. Il n'a pas de voiture.
2. Je n'ai pas de télé.
3. Vous n'avez pas de chaîne hi-fi.
4. Elle n'a pas d'ordinateur.
5. Vous n'avez pas de soeur.
6. Nous n'avons pas de chats.
7. Tu n'as pas de copains à Lyon.
8. Il n'a pas d'oncle à Montréal.
9. Elle n'a pas de cousins à Lille.

Language note Remind students that in French, the noun after **pas de** may be in the singular.
Je n'ai pas de copain à Lyon.
or: **Je n'ai pas de copains à Lyon.**

11 EXCHANGES locating objects

1. – Est-ce qu'il y a des vélos?
   – Oui, il y a des vélos.
2. – Est-ce qu'il y a une guitare?
   – Non, il n'y a pas de guitare.
3. – Est-ce qu'il y a des livres?
   – Oui, il y a des livres.
4. – Est-ce qu'il y a un appareil-photo?
   – Non, il n'y a pas d'appareil-photo.
5. – Est-ce qu'il y a une chaîne hi-fi?
   – Non, il n'y a pas de chaîne hi-fi.
6. – Est-ce qu'il y a des affiches?
   – Non, il n'y a pas d'affiches.
7. – Est-ce qu'il y a une télé?
   – Oui, il y a une télé.
8. – Est-ce qu'il y a une radiocassette?
   – Oui, il y a une radiocassette.
9. – Est-ce qu'il y a un bureau?
   – Oui, il y a un bureau.
10. – Est-ce qu'il y a une table?
   – Oui, il y a une table.

12 PRACTICE contradicting negative statements

1. Si, je parle français!
2. Si, j'étudie!
3. Si, je joue au basket!
4. Si, j'aime les sports!
5. Si, j'aime la musique!
6. Si, j'écoute le professeur!

Re-entry and review
Verbs from Unit 3.

Teaching strategy Have students contrast the negative question and response in the example with the following affirmative question and response:
– Tu as une chaîne hi-fi?
– Oui, j'ai une chaîne hi-fi.

SECTION E

Communicative function
Making generalizations

Teaching Resource Options

PRINT 

Workbook PE, pp. 93–100
Unit 4 Resource Book
Audioscript, p. 66
Communipak, pp. 140–160
Workbook TE, pp. 37–44

AUDIO & VISUAL 

Audio Program
CD 2 Track 30

Overhead Transparencies
25 Class schedule

TECHNOLOGY 

Power Presentations

Language note Usually, English does not use articles to introduce abstract nouns or nouns used in a general sense.

Realia note Have students read the sign: **J'aime le français.** (They may want to make similar signs of their own.)

13 COMMUNICATION expressing likes and dislikes

Answers will vary.
(J'aime beaucoup) la musique.
(J'aime un peu) la nature.
(Je n'aime pas) les sports.
(J'aime un peu) le camping.
(J'aime beaucoup) le français.
(J'aime un peu) les maths.
(J'aime un peu / Je n'aime pas) les sciences.
(Je n'aime pas) la violence.
(Je n'aime pas) l'injustice.
(J'aime beaucoup) la liberté.
(J'aime un peu) le théâtre.
(J'aime beaucoup) le cinéma.
(J'aime un peu) la danse.
(J'aime beaucoup) la photo.

Teaching hint Model the new words and cognates, being sure that students pronounce them the French way.

14 COMPREHENSION describing what people like

1. Jean-Claude aime le tennis.
2. Léa aime la nature.
3. Vouz aimez l'art.
4. J'aime le cinéma.
5. Nous aimons le français.
6. Véronique et Roger aiment la danse.

E L'usage de l'article défini dans le sens général

In French, the definite article **(le, la, les)** is used more often than in English. Note its use in the following sentences.

J'aime **la musique.**	*(In general) I like* ***music.***
Tu préfères **le tennis** ou **le golf?**	*(Generally) do you prefer* ***tennis*** *or* ***golf?***
Julie aime **les jeux vidéo.**	*(In general) Julie likes* ***video games.***
Nous aimons **la liberté.**	*(In general) we love* ***liberty.***

LANGUAGE COMPARISONS
In contrast with English, French uses the definite article **(le, la, les)** to introduce ABSTRACT nouns, or nouns used in a GENERAL or COLLECTIVE sense.

13 Expression personnelle

PARLER/ÉCRIRE Say how you feel about the following things, using one of the suggested expressions.

Je n'aime pas ...
J'aime un peu ...
J'aime beaucoup ...

▶ **Je n'aime pas la violence.**

la musique	le français	la violence	le théâtre
la nature	les maths	l'injustice	le cinéma
les sports	les sciences	la liberté	la danse
le camping			la photo *(photography)*

14 C'est évident! *(It's obvious!)*

PARLER Read about the following people and say what they like. Choose the appropriate item from the list. (Masculine nouns are in blue. Feminine nouns are in red.)

▶ Sophie écoute des CD.
Sophie aime la musique.

art cinéma danse français musique nature tennis

1. Jean-Claude a une raquette.
2. Léa fait une promenade dans la forêt.
3. Nous visitons un musée *(museum)*.
4. Tu regardes un film.
5. Vous étudiez en classe de français.
6. Véronique et Roger sont dans une discothèque.

TEACHING HINT

Have students memorize the **comptine** that accompanies the daisy petals. (It begins: **Elle m'aime un peu...** and continues clockwise.) Point out that the odds of being "loved" are much greater in the French than in the English version (*he/she loves me, he/she loves me not ...*).

INCLUSION

Structured Ask students to copy the definite articles in their notebooks. Write nouns on the board (**art, musique, tennis,** etc.) and have students write them in their notebooks next to the appropriate article. Pair strong and at-risk students and have them check each other's work and say each of the article/word combinations to each other three times.

F L'usage de l'article défini avec les jours de la semaine

Compare the following sentences.

REPEATED EVENTS	SINGLE EVENT
Le samedi, je dîne avec des copains.	**Samedi,** je dîne avec mon cousin.
***(On) Saturdays** (in general), I have dinner with friends.*	***(On) Saturday** (that is, this Saturday), I am having dinner with my cousin.*

To indicate a repeated or habitual event, French uses the construction:

le + DAY OF THE WEEK

→ When an event happens only once, no article is used.

15 Questions personnelles PARLER

1. Est-ce que tu étudies le samedi?
2. Est-ce que tu dînes au restaurant le dimanche? Si *(If)* oui, avec qui?
3. Est-ce que tu as une classe de français le lundi? le mercredi?
4. Est-ce que tu regardes les matchs de football américain le samedi? le dimanche?
5. Est-ce que tu travailles? Où? *(Name of place or store)* Quand?

16 L'emploi du temps

PARLER/ÉCRIRE

	LUNDI	MARDI	MERCREDI	JEUDI	VENDREDI
9 h	français	physique	sciences	biologie	
10 h		histoire		maths	anglais
11 h	maths	sciences	anglais		français

The following students all have the same morning schedule. Complete the sentences accordingly.

▶ **Nous avons une classe de français <u>le lundi</u> ...**

1. J'ai une classe de maths _______.
2. Tu as une classe de sciences _______.
3. Jacques a une classe de physique _______.
4. Thérèse a une classe d'histoire _______.
5. Vous avez une classe de biologie _______.
6. Les élèves ont une classe d'anglais _______.

PRONONCIATION

Les articles *le* et *les*

le/lə/ les/le/

Be sure to distinguish between the pronunciation of **le** and **les.** In spoken French, that is often the only way to tell the difference between a singular and a plural noun.

<u>le</u> sac

<u>les</u> sacs

Répétez:						
/lə/	**le**	**le sac**	**le vélo**	**le portable**	**le copain**	**le voisin**
/le/	**les**	**les sacs**	**les vélos**	**les portables**	**les copains**	**les voisins**

TALKING ABOUT PAST EVENTS

Let's talk about what you did last Saturday.

Est-ce que tu as étudié samedi dernier? Oui, j'ai étudié samedi dernier. (Non, je n'ai pas étudié samedi dernier.)

- **Est-ce que tu as travaillé?**
- **Est-ce que tu as regardé la télé?**
- **Est-ce que tu as joué au basket?**
- **Est-ce que tu as organisé une boum?**
- **Est-ce que tu as dansé?**
- **Est-ce que tu as dîné au restaurant?**
- **Est-ce que tu as mangé un hot dog?** (Reminder: use **pas de** in the negative.)
- **Est-ce que tu as mangé une pizza?**

SECTION F

Communicative function
Discussing repeated events

Re-entry and review
Days of the week from Lesson 4B.

Language note In French, the word **sur** (*on*) is never used with days of the week.

15 COMMUNICATION answering personal questions

Answers will vary.
1. Oui, j'étudie le samedi. (Non, je n'étudie pas le samedi.)
2. Oui, je dîne au restaurant le dimanche. Je dîne avec (mes parents). (Non, je ne dîne pas au restaurant le dimanche.)
3. Oui, j'ai une classe de français le lundi et le mercredi. (Non, je n'ai pas de classe de français le lundi. J'ai une classe de français le mercredi.) (Non, je n'ai pas de classe de français le lundi et le mercredi.)
4. Oui, je regarde les matchs de football américain le samedi et le dimanche. (Non, je ne regarde pas les matchs de football américain le samedi et le dimanche.)
5. Oui, je travaille. Je travaille (à la maison / à Mini Mart…). Je travaille (le samedi).

Language note Point out that in French, **si** has two meanings:
- *if* (as in **s'il vous plaît:** literally, *if it pleases you*)
- *yes* (to contradict a negative statement)

16 COMPREHENSION describing school schedules

1. J'ai une classe de maths le lundi et le jeudi.
2. Tu as une classe de sciences le mardi et le mercredi.
3. Jacques a une classe de physique le mardi.
4. Thérèse a une classe d'histoire le mardi.
5. Vous avez une classe de biologie le jeudi.
6. Les élèves ont une classe d'anglais le mercredi et le vendredi.

Additional practice Show Transparency 25: Class schedule or have students turn to the **emploi du temps** on p. 131. Let them imagine that they have the same schedule and ask them questions:
–Quel jour avez-vous une classe de français?
–Nous avons une classe de français le lundi, le mardi, etc.

À votre tour!

OBJECTIFS

Now you can …
- talk about what you have and do not have
- describe in general what you like and do not like

1 Allô!

PARLER Jean-Marc is phoning some friends. Match his questions on the left with his friends' answers on the right.

1. Quel âge a ton copain?
2. Est-ce qu'Éric a un scooter?
3. Où est l'appareil-photo?
4. Tu as un baladeur?
5. Est-ce que tu aimes étudier l'anglais?
6. Tu as soif?

a. Oui, mais je n'ai pas de chaîne hi-fi.
b. Il est sur la table.
c. Quatorze ans.
d. Oui, je voudrais une limonade.
e. Oui, mais je préfère l'espagnol.
f. Non, mais il a une moto.

2 Un sondage

PARLER/ÉCRIRE A French consumer research group wants to know what things American teenagers own. Conduct a survey in your class asking who has the objects on the list. Count the number of students who raise their hands for each object, and report your findings on a separate piece of paper.

Qui a un portable? … Quinze élèves ont des portables.

À VOTRE TOUR

Main Topic
- Recapitulation and review

Teaching Resource Options

PRINT 

Workbook PE, pp. 93–100
Unit 4 Resource Book
- Audioscript, pp. 66–67
- Communipak, pp. 140–160
- Family Involvement, pp. 58–59
- Workbook TE, pp. 37–44

Assessment
- Lesson 10 Quiz, pp. 70–71
- Portfolio Assessment, Unit 1 URB, pp. 155–164
- Audioscript for Quiz 10, p. 69
- Answer Keys, pp. 201–205

AUDIO & VISUAL 

Audio Program
CD 2 Tracks 31, 32
CD 14 Track 18

TECHNOLOGY 

Test Generator CD-ROM/McDougal Littell Assessment System

1 COMPREHENSION

1. Quel âge a ton copain?
   (c) Quatorze ans.
2. Est-ce qu'Éric a un scooter?
   (f) Non, mais il a une moto.
3. Où est l'appareil-photo?
   (b) Il est sur la table.
4. Tu as un baladeur?
   (a) Oui, mais je n'ai pas de chaîne hi-fi.
5. Est-ce que tu aimes étudier l'anglais?
   (e) Oui, mais je préfère l'espagnol.
6. Tu as soif?
   (d) Oui, je voudrais une limonade.

2 ORAL EXPRESSION

- Qui a une montre?
  (Dix-sept) élèves ont une montre.
- Qui a un vélo?
  (Treize) élèves ont un vélo.
- Qui a une radio?
  (Douze) élèves ont une radio.
- Qui a un baladeur?
  (Seize) élèves ont un baladeur.
- Qui a des affiches?
  (Dix) élèves ont des affiches.
- Qui a un ordinateur?
  (Huit) élèves ont un ordinateur.
- Qui a des CD?
  (Neuf) élèves ont des CD.

À VOTRE TOUR

Depending on your goals and objectives, you may or may not wish to assign all of the activities in the **À votre tour** section.

PAIR AND GROUP PRACTICE

Act. 1 lends itself to pair practice. It can also be done in trios, with two students performing and the third acting as monitor.

3  Créa-dialogue

PARLER Ask your classmates if they like the following things. Then ask if they own the corresponding object.

1. la musique	2. le jogging	3. les maths	4. la photo	5. les matchs de baseball	6. l'exercice

▶ —Tu aimes le tennis?
—Oui, j'aime le tennis.
(Non, je n'aime pas le tennis.)

—Tu as une raquette?
—Oui, j'ai une raquette.
(Non, je n'ai pas de raquette.)

4 Quelle est la différence?

PARLER/ÉCRIRE Sophie went away with her family for the weekend and she took some of her belongings with her. Describe what is in her room on Friday and what is missing on Saturday.

▶ Il y a ...

▶ Il n'y a pas de ...

5  Composition: Ma semaine

ÉCRIRE In a short paragraph, describe what you do (or do not do) regularly on various days of the week. Select three days and two different activities for each day. Use only vocabulary that you know. Perhaps you might want to exchange paragraphs with a friend by e-mail.

PORTFOLIO ASSESSMENT

You will probably select only one speaking activity and one writing activity to go into the students' portfolios for Unit 4.

In this lesson, Act. 5 is a good written portfolio topic. You might also wish to use the composition suggested at the bottom of page 151 of the TE.

3 GUIDED ORAL EXPRESSION

1. – Tu aimes la musique?
– Oui, j'aime la musique.
(Non, je n'aime pas la musique.)
– Tu as une radiocassette?
(Non, je n'ai pas de radiocassette.)

2. – Tu aimes le jogging?
– Oui, j'aime le jogging.
(Non, je n'aime pas le jogging.)
– Tu as un baladeur?
– Oui, j'ai un baladeur.
(Non, je n'ai pas de baladeur.)

3. – Tu aimes les maths.
– Oui, j'aime les maths.
(Non, je n'aime pas les maths.)
– Tu as une calculatrice?
– Oui, j'ai une calculatrice.
(Non, je n'ai pas de calculatrice.)

4. – Tu aimes la photo?
– Oui, j'aime la photo.
(Non, je n'aime pas la photo.)
– Tu as un appareil-photo?
– Oui, j'ai un appareil-photo.
(Non, je n'ai pas d'appareil-photo.)

5. – Tu aimes les matchs de baseball?
– Oui, j'aime les matchs de baseball.
(Non, je n'aime pas les matchs de baseball.)
– Tu as une télé?
– Oui, j'ai une télé.
(Non, je n'ai pas de télé.)

6. – Tu aimes l'exercice?
– Oui, j'aime l'exercice.
(Non, je n'aime pas l'exercice.)
– Tu as un vélo?
– Oui, j'ai un vélo.
(Non, je n'ai pas de vélo.)

4 COMPREHENSION

- Vendredi, il y a une affiche, une raquette, une guitare, une télé, un lit, un sac, des CD, des livres, un portable, une radiocassette, une chaîne hi-fi, une chaise, un bureau, un appareil-photo, des crayons, des stylos un baladeur et un chat.
- Samedi, il n'y a pas d'appareil-photo, de raquette, de radiocassette, de CD, de sac, de chat, de portable.

5 WRITTEN SELF-EXPRESSION

Answers will vary.

- Le mardi, j'ai une classe de sciences. Je dîne avec ma famille à sept heures.
- Le mercredi je joue au tennis à quatre heures avec ma copine. Après le dîner, j'étudie.
- Le dimanche, j'écoute la radio et je regarde un film à la télé.

Leçon 11

Main Topic Describing people

Teaching Resource Options

PRINT 

Workbook PE, pp. 101–106
Activités pour tous PE, pp. 59–61
Block Scheduling Copymasters, pp. 81–88
Unit 4 Resource Book
- *Activités pour tous* TE, pp. 79–81
- Audioscript, pp. 100, 101–102
- Communipak, pp. 140–160
- Lesson Plans, pp. 82–83
- Block Scheduling Lesson Plans, pp. 84–85
- Absent Student Copymasters, pp. 86–89
- Video Activities, pp. 92–97
- Videoscript, pp. 98–99
- Workbook TE, pp. 73–78

AUDIO & VISUAL 

Audio Program
CD 2 Tracks 33, 34
CD 8 Tracks 14–18

TECHNOLOGY 

Online Workbook

VIDEO PROGRAM

MODULE 11
Le copain de Mireille

TOTAL TIME: 4:56 min.
DVD Disk 1
Videotape 2 (COUNTER: 41:15 min.)

11.1 Introduction: Listening
–Je suis américain
(41:50–42:08 min.)

11.2 Mini-scenes: Listening
–Qui est-ce? (42:09–43:01 min.)

11.3 Mini-scenes: Speaking
– Comment sont-ils?
(43:02–43:54 min.)

11.4 Dialogue: Le copain de Mireille
(43:55–44:42 min.)

11.5 Vignette culturelle: La France et ses voisins (44:43–46:11 min.)

Compréhension
Answers
1. Nicolas regarde une fille.
2. Elle s'appelle Mireille Labé.
3. Oui, elle est jolie (elle est mignonne).
4. Oui! Elle est amusante, intelligente et sympathique.
5. Oui, elle a un copain.
6. C'est Jean-Claude.

LEÇON 11

Le copain de Mireille

Nicolas and Jean-Claude are having lunch at the school cafeteria. Nicolas is looking at the students seated at the other end of their table.

Nicolas:	Regarde la fille là-bas!	
Jean-Claude:	La fille blonde?	
Nicolas:	Oui! Qui est-ce?	
Jean-Claude:	C'est Mireille Labé.	
Nicolas:	Elle est mignonne!	*cute*
Jean-Claude:	Elle est aussi amusante, intelligente et sympathique.	*fun/nice*
Nicolas:	Est-ce qu'elle a un copain?	
Jean-Claude:	Oui, elle a un copain.	
Nicolas:	Il est sympathique?	
Jean-Claude:	Oui … Très sympathique!	
Nicolas:	Et intelligent?	
Jean-Claude:	Aussi!	
Nicolas:	Dommage! … Qui est-ce?	
Jean-Claude:	C'est moi!	
Nicolas:	Euh … oh … Excuse-moi et félicitations!	*congratulations*

Compréhension

1. Qui est-ce que Nicolas regarde?
2. Comment s'appelle la fille?
3. Est-ce qu'elle est jolie?
4. Est-ce qu'elle a d'autres *(other)* qualités?
5. Est-ce qu'elle a un copain?
6. Qui est le copain de Mireille *(Mireille's boyfriend)*?

SETTING THE SCENE

The opening text introduces several students having lunch at the Lycée Corot. Not untypically, they are engaged in people-watching. (For more background on this **lycée,** have students turn to pp. 124–127.)

To help students develop listening comprehension skills, have them keep their books closed as they watch the video. Then have them open their books and read the text.

NOTE culturelle

L'amitié et la bande de copains

French people believe in friendship **(l'amitié)** and family life and rank these values far above money, material comfort, and personal success. The friendships they establish at an early age tend to be durable. Since French people move much less frequently than Americans, and since distances are much smaller, they remain in close contact with their high school friends throughout their entire lives.

French teenagers, like their American counterparts, are very sociable. They have a close-knit group of friends, known as **la bande de copains**, with whom they share common interests. They go out together, especially to movies, concerts, and parties. This group may include classmates, cousins, other young people whom they have met during vacations, as well as the children of family friends. When young people invite their friends to the house, it is customary to introduce them to their parents.

COMPARAISONS CULTURELLES

What similarities and differences do you see between the French and American attitudes towards friendship?

- les similarités
- les différences

In your opinion, are these attitudes basically the same? Explain.

OPINION PERSONNELLE

Rank the following values mentioned in the text from 1 (the highest) to 5.

- l'amitié
- l'argent *(money)*
- le confort matériel
- la famille
- le succès personnel

Compare your rankings with your classmates.

MULTICULTURALISM IN FRANCE

The opening segments of **Video Module 11** focus on the diversity of the French population. The final **Vignette culturelle** presents the various national origins of the people of contemporary France.

INCLUSION

Synthetic/analytic Tell students to use desktops to beat out all syllables of each adjective (**mignonne, amusante, intelligente**), including one light beat for the mute "e". Explain the pronunciation difference between these feminine adjectives and their masculine counterparts. Then have them pronounce each masculine adjective, and beat out its syllables.

SECTION A

Communicative function
Describing people and objects

Teaching Resource Options

PRINT 

Workbook PE, pp. 101–106
Unit 4 Resource Book
- Audioscript, p. 100
- Communipak, pp. 140–160
- Workbook TE, pp. 73–78

AUDIO & VISUAL 

Audio Program
CD 2 Track 35

Overhead Transparencies
26a *La description*
26b *La description* (overlay)

TECHNOLOGY 

Power Presentations

Teaching hint Use **Transparencies 26a** and **26b**, *La description* and the overlay, to present the descriptive adjectives.

1 PRACTICE adjective forms

1. Carole n'est pas blonde.
2. Mireille n'est pas petite.
3. Marthe n'est pas belle.
4. Louise n'est pas grande.
5. Émilie n'est pas riche.
6. Lisa n'est pas française.
7. Céline n'est pas espagnole.
8. Julie n'est pas américaine.

Language note Point out that nationalities are adjectives.

Expansion (dialogue format)
Jean-Marc est blond. (Mélanie)
– Jean-Marc est blond.
– Et Mélanie? Elle est blonde?
– Mais non, elle n'est pas blonde.

2 COMMUNICATION describing people

Answers will vary.
1. Il est sympathique. (Il n'est pas sympathique.)
2. Elle est sportive. (Elle n'est pas sportive.)
3. Elle est gentille. (Elle n'est pas gentille.)
4. Elle est mignonne. (Elle n'est pas mignonne.)
5. Elle est intelligente. (Elle n'est pas intelligente.)
6. Il n'est pas bête. (Il est bête.)
7. Il est amusant. (Il n'est pas amusant.)
8. Il n'est pas méchant. (Il est méchant.)

Variation (dialogue format)
– Est-ce que le prince Charles est intéressant?
– Oui, il est intéressant. (Non, il n'est pas intéressant.)

A Les adjectifs: masculin et féminin

Compare the forms of the adjectives in heavy print as they describe masculine and feminine nouns.

MASCULINE	FEMININE
Le scooter est **petit.**	La voiture est **petite.**
Patrick est **intelligent.**	Caroline est **intelligente.**
L'ordinateur est **moderne.**	La télé est **moderne.**

LEARNING ABOUT LANGUAGE

ADJECTIVES are words that describe people, places, and things.

In French, MASCULINE adjectives are used with masculine nouns, and FEMININE adjectives are used with feminine nouns. This is called NOUN-ADJECTIVE AGREEMENT.

In written French, feminine adjectives are usually formed as follows:

MASCULINE ADJECTIVE + **-e** = FEMININE ADJECTIVE

→ If the masculine adjective ends in **-e,** there is no change in the feminine form.

Jérôme est **timide.** Juliette est **timide.**

→ Adjectives that follow the above patterns are called REGULAR adjectives. Those that do not are called IRREGULAR adjectives. For example:

Marc est **beau.** Sylvie est **belle.**
Paul est **canadien.** Marie est **canadienne.**

NOTE French dictionaries list adjectives by their masculine forms. For irregular adjectives, the feminine form is indicated in parentheses.

NOTES DE PRONONCIATION:

- If the masculine form of an adjective ends in a silent consonant, that consonant is pronounced in the feminine form.
- If the masculine form of an adjective ends in a vowel or a pronounced consonant, the masculine and feminine forms sound the same.

DIFFERENT PRONUNCIATION		SAME PRONUNCIATION	
petit	petite	timide	timide
blond	blonde	joli	jolie
français	française	espagnol	espagnole

Vive la différence!

PARLER/ÉCRIRE People can be friends and yet be quite different. Describe the girls named in parentheses, indicating that they are not like their friends.

▶ Jean-Marc est blond. (Mélanie) **Mélanie n'est pas blonde.**

1. Jean-Louis est blond. (Carole)
2. Paul est petit. (Mireille)
3. Éric est beau. (Marthe)
4. Jérôme est grand. (Louise)
5. Michel est riche. (Émilie)
6. André est français. (Lisa)
7. Antonio est espagnol. (Céline)
8. Bill est américain. (Julie)

COMPREHENSION Descriptions

PROPS: Blue and red index cards

On the board, draw a stick figure of a boy (labeled René) and a girl (labeled Renée).

Voici René. C'est un voisin. [blue]
Et ici Renée. C'est une voisine. [red]

Give each student a blue and a red card.

As you read descriptions using the new vocabulary, they raise the appropriate card.

René est amusant. [blue card]
Renée est mignonne. [red card]
René(e) est timide. [either: both cards]
Renée est assez sportive. [red card]
René est très intelligent. [blue card] ...

VOCABULAIRE La description

Voici Olivier.

Voici Sophie.

ADJECTIFS		Voici Olivier.	Voici Sophie.
amusant	*amusing, fun*	Il est **amusant.**	Elle est **amusante.**
intelligent	*intelligent*	Il est **intelligent.**	Elle est **intelligente.**
intéressant	*interesting*	Il est **intéressant.**	Elle est **intéressante.**
méchant	*mean, nasty*	Il n'est pas **méchant.**	Elle n'est pas **méchante.**
bête	*silly, dumb*	Il n'est pas **bête.**	Elle n'est pas **bête.**
sympathique	*nice, pleasant*	Il est **sympathique.**	Elle est **sympathique.**
timide	*timid*	Il est **timide.**	Elle n'est pas **timide.**
gentil (gentille)	*nice, kind*	Il est **gentil.**	Elle est **gentille.**
mignon (mignonne)	*cute*	Il est **mignon.**	Elle est **mignonne.**
sportif (sportive)	*athletic*	Il est **sportif.**	Elle est **sportive.**

ADVERBES		
assez	*rather*	Nous sommes **assez** intelligents.
très	*very*	Vous n'êtes pas **très** sportifs!

2 Oui ou non?

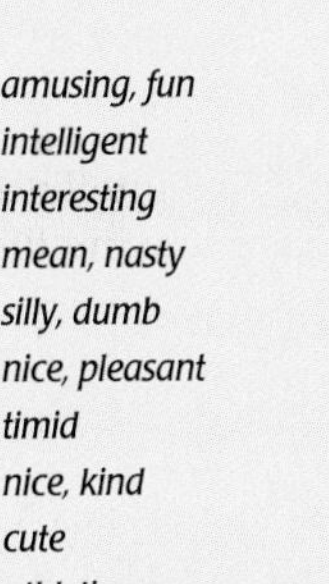
Il est intéressant.
Il n'est pas intéressant.

PARLER In your opinion, do the following people have the suggested traits? (Note: These traits are given in the masculine form only.)

▶ le prince William / intéressant?

1. le Président / sympathique?
2. Venus Williams / sportif?
3. ma copine / gentil?
4. Britney Spears / mignon?
5. Oprah Winfrey / intelligent?
6. Einstein / bête?
7. Jay Leno / amusant?
8. le prof / méchant?

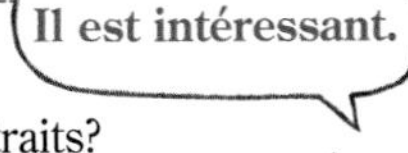

3 Descriptions

PARLER Select one of the following characters. Using words from the **Vocabulaire,** describe this character in two affirmative or negative sentences.

▶ Frankenstein
Il est très méchant.
Il n'est pas très mignon.

1. Tarzan
2. King Kong
3. Big Bird
4. Batman
5. Miss Piggy
6. Wonder Woman
7. Charlie Brown
8. Blanche-Neige *(Snow White)*
9. Garfield
10. Snoopy

4 L'idéal

PARLER/ÉCRIRE Now you have the chance to describe your ideal people. Use two adjectives for each one.

1. Le copain idéal est ... et ...
2. La copine idéale est ... et ...
3. Le professeur idéal est ... et ...
4. L'étudiant idéal est ... et ...
5. L'étudiante idéale est ... et ...

GAME Descriptions

Have students in pairs pick one of the characters in Act. 3 and write a description in two identical copies.

Then ask each pair to give one copy of the description to the pair on their left, and the other to the pair on their right.

Each pair now has two new descriptions to read. They read the two descriptions and at the bottom of each they write down the name of the person they think is being described.

The descriptions are then returned to the "original authors." The winners are those pairs who had both copies of their descriptions identified correctly.

Language notes

- In conversational speech, **sympathique** is often shortened to **sympa.** This shortened form is invariable and does not take adjective endings.
- Adverbs like **assez** and **très** often modify adjectives. Note that liaison is required after **très**. In conversation, there is usually no liaison after **assez**.

Pronunciation

gentil /ʒ ɑ̃ti/ **gentille** /ʒ ɑ̃tij/

Supplementary vocabulary

content ≠ **triste** *happy ≠ sad*
fort ≠ **faible** *strong ≠ weak*
riche ≠ **pauvre** *rich ≠ poor*
fatigué ≠ **énergique** *tired ≠ energetic*
génial ≠ **stupide** *brilliant ≠ dumb*
poli ≠ **impoli** *polite ≠ impolite*
drôle ≠ **pénible** *funny ≠ "a pain"*
optimiste ≠ **pessimiste**
sincère **athlétique**
indépendant **dynamique**

3 COMMUNICATION describing people

Answers will vary.
1. Il est (très sportif). Il est (assez bête).
2. Il n'est pas (très mignon). Il est (assez timide).
3. Il est (grand). Il n'est pas (très intelligent).
4. Il n'est pas (timide). Il est (très intelligent).
5. Elle est (très bête). Elle est (assez amusante).
6. Elle est (très intelligente). Elle est (très sportive).
7. Il est (sympathique). Il n'est pas (très sportif).
8. Elle est (belle). Elle est (assez timide).
9. Il est (amusant). Il n'est pas (très sportif).
10. Il est (sympathique). Il n'est pas (méchant).

4 COMMUNICATION describing ideal people

Answers will vary.
1. (amusant, intéressant)
2. (intelligente, amusante)
3. (sympathique, intéressant)
4. (intelligent, intéressant)
5. (intelligente, intéressante)

Variation (in the negative)
Le copain idéal n'est pas (méchant) ...

Expansion le père idéal, la mère idéale, le frère idéal, la soeur idéale

B Les adjectifs: le pluriel

Compare the forms of the adjectives in heavy print as they describe singular and plural nouns.

SINGULAR	PLURAL
Paul est **intelligent** et **timide.**	Paul et Éric sont **intelligents** et **timides.**
Alice est **intelligente** et **timide.**	Alice et Claire sont **intelligentes** et **timides.**

In written French, plural adjectives are usually formed as follows:

SINGULAR ADJECTIVE + -s = PLURAL ADJECTIVE

→ If the masculine singular adjective already ends in **-s**, there is no change in the plural form.

Patrick est **français.**	Patrick et Daniel sont **français.**
BUT: Anne est **française.**	Anne et Alice sont **françaises.**

NOTE DE PRONONCIATION: Because the final **-s** of plural adjectives is silent, singular and plural adjectives sound the same.

SUMMARY: Forms of regular adjectives

	MASCULINE	FEMININE	*also:*	
SINGULAR	- grand	-e grand**e**	timide	timide
PLURAL	-s grand**s**	-es grand**es**	français	français**es**

5 Une question de personnalité

PARLER/ÉCRIRE Indicate whether or not the following people exhibit the personality traits in parentheses. (These traits are given in the masculine singular form only. Make the necessary agreements.)

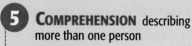

Elles ne sont pas timides.

▶ Alice et Thérèse aiment parler en public. (timide?)

1. Claire et Valérie sont très populaires. (amusant?)
2. Robert et Jean-Luc n'aiment pas danser. (timide?)
3. Catherine et Martine aiment jouer au foot. (sportif?)
4. Laure et Léa ont un «A» en français. (intelligent?)
5. Thomas et Vincent n'aiment pas le jogging. (sportif?)
6. Les voisins n'aiment pas parler avec nous. (sympathique?)

SECTION B

Communicative function
Describing people and objects

Teaching Resource Options

PRINT 

Workbook PE, pp. 101–106
Unit 4 Resource Book
Communipak, pp. 140–160
Video Activities, pp. 92–93
Videoscript, p. 98
Workbook TE, pp. 73–78

AUDIO & VISUAL 

Overhead Transparencies
27 *Les adjectifs de nationalité*

TECHNOLOGY 

Power Presentations

VIDEO PROGRAM

VIDÉO DVD

MODULE 11

11.1 Introduction: Je suis américain (41:50–42:08 min.)

11.2 Mini-scenes: Qui est-ce? (42:09–43:01 min.)

11.3 Mini-scenes: Comment sont-ils? (43:02–43:54 min.)

Language note When a plural adjective describes two or more nouns, one of which is masculine, the masculine plural is used.
Patrick et Anne sont français.
Ils ne sont pas américains.

Looking ahead Irregular plural forms like **beau-beaux** are taught in Lesson 11.

5 COMPREHENSION describing more than one person

1. Elles sont amusantes.
2. Ils sont timides.
3. Elles sont sportives.
4. Elles sont intelligentes.
5. Ils ne sont pas sportifs.
6. Ils ne sont pas sympathiques.

TALKING ABOUT PAST EVENTS

Let's talk about what you did last summer.

▶ **Est-ce que tu as voyagé l'été dernier?**
Oui, j'ai voyagé l'été dernier.
(Non, je n'ai pas voyagé l'été dernier.)

- **Est-ce que tu as visité Paris l'été dernier?**
- **Est-ce que tu as visité Québec?**
- **Est-ce que tu as étudié?**
- **Est-ce que tu as travaillé?**
- **Est-ce que tu as joué au volley?**
- **Est-ce que tu as joué au tennis?**
- **Est-ce que tu as nagé?**
- **Est-ce que tu as dîné au restaurant?**

VOCABULAIRE Les adjectifs de nationalité

américain	*American*	**italien (italienne)**	*Italian*
mexicain	*Mexican*	**canadien (canadienne)**	*Canadian*
français	*French*	**japonais**	*Japanese*
anglais	*English*	**chinois**	*Chinese*
espagnol	*Spanish*		
suisse	*Swiss*		

SILC PASSEPORT POUR LE MONDE

→ Words that describe nationality are adjectives and take adjective endings.

Monsieur Katagiri est **japonais.**
Kumi et Michiko sont **japonaises.**

VOCABULAIRE Expression pour la conversation

J'habite à Québec.
Alors, tu es canadien.

How to introduce a conclusion:

alors *so, then* —J'habite à Québec.
—Alors, tu es canadien!

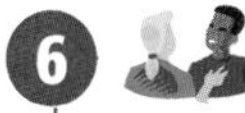

6 Quelle nationalité?

PARLER Ask where the following people live and what their nationalities are. A friend will answer you.

▶ **—Où habitent Lois et Kim?**
—Elles habitent à Miami.
—Alors, elles sont américaines?
—Mais oui, elles sont américaines.

▶ Lois et Kim	1. Jim et Bob	2. Léa et Aline
Miami	Liverpool	Toulouse
américain	anglais	français

3. Clara et Tere	4. Luc et Paul	5. ??
Madrid	Montréal	??
espagnol	??	??

7 Les nationalités

PARLER/ÉCRIRE Give the nationalities of the following people.

▶ Silvia et Maria sont de Rome.
Elles sont italiennes.

1. Lise et Nathalie étudient à Québec.
2. Michael et Dennis sont de Liverpool.
3. Luis et Paco étudient à Madrid.
4. Isabel et Carmen travaillent à Acapulco.
5. Yoko et Kumi sont de Tokyo.
6. Monsieur et Madame Chen habitent à Beijing.
7. Jean-Pierre et Claude sont de Genève.
8. Françoise et Sylvie travaillent à Paris.

Review and expansion

Adjectives of nationality from Lesson 1B.

Language note Remind students that adjectives of nationality are not capitalized in French.

Supplementary vocabulary

allemand *German*
hollandais *Dutch*
portugais *Portuguese*
libanais *Lebanese*
russe *Russian*
grec (grecque) *Greek*
égyptien(ne) *Egyptian*
israëlien(ne) *Israeli*
brésilien(ne) *Brazilian*
péruvien(ne) *Peruvian*
coréen(ne) *Korean*
vietnamien(ne) *Vietnamese*

6 EXCHANGES discussing nationalities

1. – Où habitent Jim et Bob?
   – Ils habitent à Liverpool.
   – Alors, ils sont anglais?
   – Mais oui, ils sont anglais.
2. – Où habitent Léa et Aline?
   – Elles habitent à Toulouse.
   – Alors, elles sont françaises?
   – Mais oui, elles sont françaises.
3. – Où habitent Clara et Tere?
   – Elles habitent à Madrid.
   – Alors, elles sont espagnoles?
   – Mais oui, elles sont espagnoles.
4. – Où habitent Luc et Paul?
   – Ils habitent à Montréal.
   – Alors, ils sont canadiens?
   – Mais oui, ils sont canadiens.
5. – Où habitent (Kim et Ted)?
   – (Ils) habitent à (Seattle).
   – Alors, ils sont (américains)?
   – Mais oui, il sont (américains).

7 COMPREHENSION identifying nationality

1. Elles sont canadiennes.
2. Ils sont anglais.
3. Ils sont espagnols.
4. Elles sont mexicaines.
5. Elles sont japonaises.
6. Ils sont chinois.
7. Ils sont suisses.
8. Elles sont françaises.

Now you will learn to talk about what others did last summer. (First ask one student what he/she did. Then ask the class to reaffirm.)

▶ **X, est-ce que tu as voyagé l'été dernier?**
Oui, j'ai voyagé.
(to the class) **Est-ce que X a voyagé?**
Oui, il a voyagé.

Z, est-ce que tu as visité Paris?
Non, je n'ai pas visité Paris.
(to the class) **Est-ce que Z a visité Paris?**
Non, elle n'a pas visité Paris.

(Use the questions on the facing page.)

SECTION C

Communicative function
Using adjectives to describe people and things

Teaching Resource Options

PRINT 

Workbook PE, pp. 101–106
Unit 4 Resource Book
- Audioscript, p. 100
- Communipak, pp. 140–160
- Video Activities, pp. 95–97
- Videoscript, p. 99
- Workbook TE, pp. 73–78

AUDIO & VISUAL 

Audio Program
CD 2 Track 36

TECHNOLOGY 

Power Presentations

VIDEO PROGRAM

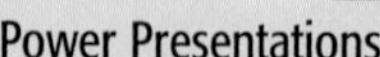

VIDÉO DVD

MODULE 11

11.5 Vignette culturelle: La France et ses voisins (44:43–46:11 min.)

Looking ahead Adjectives which precede the noun will be presented in Lesson 12.

Realia note
Ask students to read the pen pal ad.
- Was it written by a boy or a girl? [a boy]
- How do you know? [from the word **étudiant** and the masculine adjectives]
- Is the person looking for a male or female pen pal? [a female pen pal]
- How do you know? [from the word **étudiante** and the feminine adjectives]

Expansion: Have students write their own pen pal ads.

C La place des adjectifs

Note the position of the adjectives in the sentences on the right.

Philippe a une voiture.	Il a une voiture **anglaise.**
Denise invite des copains.	Elle invite des copains **américains.**
Voici un livre.	Voici un livre **intéressant.**
J'ai des amies.	J'ai des amies **sympathiques.**

In French, adjectives usually come AFTER the noun they modify, according to the pattern:

ARTICLE +	NOUN +	ADJECTIVE
une	voiture	**française**
des	copains	**intéressants**

R.S.V.P.
Le Club de Correspondance

Étudiant français, 16 ans, brun, grand, sportif, assez intelligent, un peu timide, voudrait correspondre avec étudiante américaine sportive et sympathique.

8 Préférences personnelles

PARLER For each person or object below, choose among the characteristics in parentheses. Indicate your preference.

▶ avoir un copain (sympathique, intelligent, sportif)
Je préfère avoir un copain intelligent.

1. avoir une copine (amusante, mignonne, intelligente)
2. avoir un professeur (gentil, intelligent, amusant)
3. avoir des voisins (sympathiques, intéressants, riches)
4. avoir une voiture (moderne, confortable, rapide)
5. avoir une calculatrice (japonaise, américaine, française)
6. avoir une montre (suisse, japonaise, française)
7. dîner dans un restaurant (italien, chinois, français)
8. regarder un film (intéressant, amusant, intelligent)
9. travailler avec des personnes (gentilles, amusantes, sérieuses)
10. faire un voyage avec des gens (amusants, riches, sympathiques)

9 Qui se ressemble ...

(Birds of a feather ...)

PARLER Say that the following people have friends, relatives, or acquaintances with the same personality or nationality.

▶ Claire est anglaise. (un copain)
Elle a un copain anglais.

1. Jean-Pierre est sympathique. (des cousines)
2. La prof est intelligente. (des étudiants)
3. Madame Simon est intéressante. (des voisines)
4. Alice est américaine. (des copines)
5. Véronique est amusante. (un frère)
6. Michel est sportif. (une soeur)
7. Pedro est espagnol. (des camarades)
8. Antonio est mexicain. (une copine)
9. Bernard est sportif. (un voisin)

Birds of a feather flock together.

TALKING ABOUT PAST EVENTS

Let's talk about what you and your friends did last weekend.

–W et X, est-ce que vous avez étudié le week-end dernier?
–Oui, nous avons étudié.
(Non, nous n'avons pas étudié.)

- **Est-ce que vous avez regardé la télé?**
- **Est-ce que vous avez joué au foot?**
- **Est-ce que vous avez joué au tennis?**
- **Est-ce que vous avez nagé?**
- **Est-ce que vous avez organisé une boum?**
- **Est-ce que vous avez invité des copains?**
- **Est-ce que vous avez dansé?**
- **Est-ce que vous avez chanté?**

10 Préférences internationales

PARLER/ÉCRIRE Choose an item from Column A and indicate your preference as to country of origin by choosing an adjective from Column B. Be sure to make the necessary agreement.

	A	B
	la musique	anglais
	la cuisine	américain
	les voitures	français
Je préfère …	les ordinateurs	mexicain
	les appareils-photo	chinois
	les CD	japonais
	les restaurants	italien

Je préfère les voitures italiennes.

PRONONCIATION

Les consonnes finales

/-/ blo~~n~~~~d~~ /d/ blo~~n~~de

As you know, when the last letter of a word is a consonant, that consonant is often silent. But when a word ends in "**e**," the consonant before it is pronounced. As you practice the following adjectives, be sure to distinguish between the masculine and the feminine forms.

	MASCULINE ADJECTIVE *(no final consonant sound)*		FEMININE ADJECTIVE *(final consonant sound)*
Répétez:	**blo~~nd~~**	/d/	**blo~~n~~de**
	gra~~nd~~		**gra~~n~~de**
	peti~~t~~	/t/	**petite**
	amusa~~nt~~		**amusa~~n~~te**
	françai~~s~~	/z/	**française**
	anglai~~s~~		**anglaise**
	américai~~n~~	/n/	**américaine**
	canadie~~n~~		**canadienne**

▶ Now you will learn to talk about what others did last weekend. (First ask one pair what they did. Then ask the class to reaffirm.)

W et X, est-ce que vous avez étudié le week-end dernier?

Oui, nous avons étudié. (Turn to class:)
Est-ce que W et X ont étudié?
Oui, ils/elles ont étudié.

Y et Z, est-ce que vous avez étudié?
Non, nous n'avons pas étudié.

(Then ask the class:)
Est-ce que Y et Z ont étudié?
Non, ils/elles n'ont pas étudié.

(Use the questions on the facing page.)

8 COMMUNICATION expressing preferences

Answers will vary.
1. Je préfère avoir une copine (intelligente).
2. Je préfère avoir un professeur (amusant).
3. Je préfère avoir des voisins (sympathiques).
4. Je préfère avoir une voiture (confortable).
5. Je préfère avoir une calculatrice (américaine).
6. Je préfère avoir une montre (suisse).
7. Je préfère dîner dans un restaurant (italien).
8. Je préfère regarder un film (amusant).
9. Je préfère travailler avec des personnes (sérieuses).
10. Je préfère faire un voyage avec des gens (amusants).

9 PRACTICE pointing out similarities

1. Il a des cousines sympathiques.
2. Elle a des étudiants intelligents.
3. Elle a des voisines intéressantes.
4. Elle a des copines américaines.
5. Elle a un frère amusant.
6. Il a une soeur sportive.
7. Il a des camarades espagnol(e)s.
8. Il a une copine mexicaine.
9. Il a un voisin sportif.

10 COMPREHENSION expressing preferences

Answers will vary.
- Je préfère la musique (mexicaine).
- Je préfère la cuisine (française).
- Je préfère les voitures (italiennes).
- Je préfère les ordinateurs (américains).
- Je préfère les appareils-photo (japonais).
- Je préfère les CD (anglais).
- Je préfère les restaurants (chinois).

Language note Remind students that the plural of **l'appareil-photo** is **les appareils-photo.**

Expansion (dialogue format)
– **Je préfère les voitures anglaises. Et toi?**
– **Moi, je préfère les voitures américaines.**

Teaching strategy Be sure students end the masculine adjectives on a vowel sound. In contrast, have them exaggerate the final consonants on the feminine adjectives.

Main Topic
- Recapitulation and review

Teaching Resource Options

PRINT 

Workbook PE, pp. 101–106
Unit 4 Resource Book
- Audioscript, pp. 100–101
- Communipak, pp. 140–160
- Family Involvement, pp. 90–91
- Workbook TE, pp. 73–78

Assessment
- Lesson 11 Quiz, pp. 103–104
- Portfolio Assessment, Unit 1 URB, pp. 155–164
- Audioscript for Quiz 11, p. 102
- Answer Keys, pp. 201–205

AUDIO & VISUAL 

Audio Program
CD 2 Tracks 37, 38
CD 14 Track 19

TECHNOLOGY 

Test Generator CD-ROM/McDougal Littell Assessment System

1 COMPREHENSION

1. Ton frère aime jouer au foot?
   (d) Oui, il est très sportif.
2. Cécile et Sophie sont mignonnes, n'est-ce pas?
   (a) Oui, et intelligentes aussi!
3. Pourquoi est-ce que tu invites Olivier?
   (b) Parce qu'il est amusant et sympathique.
4. Tu aimes la classe?
   (e) Oui, j'ai un professeur très intéressant.
5. Tu as des cousins?
   (e) Oui, mais ils ne sont pas très sympathiques.

À votre tour!

OBJECTIFS

Now you can …
- describe your personality
- describe other people: their nationality, their physical appearance and their personality

1 Allô!

PARLER Valérie is phoning some friends. Match her questions on the left with her friends' answers on the right.

1. Ton frère aime jouer au foot?
2. Cécile et Sophie sont mignonnes, n'est-ce pas?
3. Pourquoi est-ce que tu invites Olivier?
4. Tu aimes la classe?
5. Tu as des cousins?

a. Oui, et intelligentes aussi!
b. Parce qu'il est amusant et sympathique.
c. Oui, j'ai un professeur très intéressant.
d. Oui, il est très sportif.
e. Oui, mais ils ne sont pas très sympathiques.

2 Créa-dialogue

PARLER With your classmates, talk about the people of different nationalities you may know or objects you may own.

▶ des cousins

mignon?

▶ —J'ai des <u>cousins mexicains</u>.
—<u>Ils sont mignons</u>?
—<u>Oui, ils sont très mignons</u>.

1. une voisine	2. un prof	3. des copines	4. un livre	5. une voiture
blond?	sympathique?	sportif?	intéressant?	grand?

À VOTRE TOUR

Depending on your goals and objectives, you may or may not wish to assign all of the activities in the **À votre tour** section.

PAIR AND GROUP PRACTICE

Act. 1 and 2 lend themselves to pair practice. They can also be done in trios, with two students performing and the third acting as monitor.

3 Avis de recherche *(Missing person's bulletin)*

ÉCRIRE The two people in the pictures to the right have been reported missing. Describe each one as well as you can, using your imagination. Mention:

- the (approximate) age of the person
- the way he/she looks
- personality traits
- other features or characteristics

4 Descriptions

PARLER Give an oral presentation describing your favorite actor **(un acteur)** and actress **(une actrice).** In your descriptions, include:

- the person's name
- approximate age
- nationality
- physical appearance
- personality traits
- a film he/she plays in (*Il/elle joue dans …*)

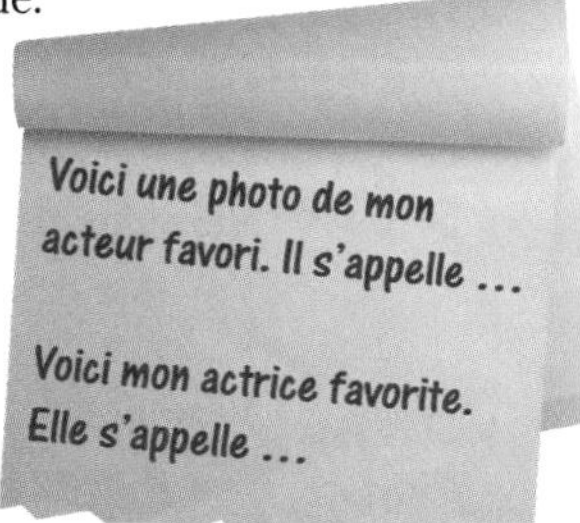

Voici une photo de mon acteur favori. Il s'appelle ...
Voici mon actrice favorite. Elle s'appelle ...

You may wish to show photos of the two actors you have chosen to talk about.

5 Composition: Fête d'anniversaire

ÉCRIRE You have invited Jean-Pierre, a French exchange student, to your upcoming birthday party. Write him an e-mail describing two of the guests that he will meet at the party: a boy and a girl. For each person (who may be real or imaginary), provide such information as name, age, nationality, physical appearance, and personality traits.

PORTFOLIO ASSESSMENT

You will probably select only one speaking activity and one writing activity to go into the students' portfolios for Unit 4.

In this lesson, Act. 2 and 4 are good oral portfolio topics.

Act. 3 and 5 lend themselves well to written portfolio compositions.

2 GUIDED ORAL EXPRESSION

1. – J'ai une voisine anglaise.
   – Elle est blonde?
   – Non, elle est brune. (Non, elle n'est pas blonde. [Elle est brune.])
2. – J'ai un prof canadien.
   – Il est sympathique?
   – Oui, il est sympathique. (Non, il n'est pas sympathique.)
3. – J'ai des copines suisses.
   – Elles sont sportives?
   – Oui, elles sont sportives.
4. – J'ai un livre français.
   – Il est intéressant?
   – Oui, il est intéressant. (Non, il n'est pas intéressant.)
5. – J'ai une voiture japonaise.
   – (Est-ce qu') elle est grande?
   – Non, elle n'est pas grande. (Non, elle est petite.)

Teaching tip As a preliminary activity, have students identify the flags.

C'est un drapeau ...

1. anglais
2. canadien
3. suisse
4. français
5. japonais

3 WRITTEN EXPRESSION

Answers will vary.
Elle a dix-sept ans. Elle est blonde et sportive. Elle est grande. Elle n'est pas timide. Elle a un chien.

Il a cinquante ans. Il est brun. Il est grand. Il n'est pas sportif. Il est timide et très gentil.

4 ORAL EXPRESSION

Answers will vary.
Mon actrice favorite est Juliette Binoche. Elle a (X) ans. Elle est française. Elle n'est pas grande et elle est brune. Elle est très intelligente et sympathique. Elle joue dans «Chocolat».

Mon acteur favori est Jean-Claude Van Damme. Il a (X) ans. Il est belge. Il est petit, sportif et beau. Il est intéressant et drôle. Il joue dans «Time Cop».

5 WRITTEN SELF-EXPRESSION

Answers will vary.
Il y a un garçon qui s'appelle Alex. Il a quatorze ans et il est américain. Il est petit, blond et beau. Alex est timide et très sympathique.

Il y a une fille qui s'appelle Heather. Elle a treize ans et elle est américaine. Elle est grande, brune et mignonne. Heather est très intelligente et intéressante.

+ video

Leçon

Main To
color and

Teachi

PRINT 

Workbook PE, pp. 107–112
Activités pour tous PE, pp. 63–65
Block Scheduling Copymasters, pp. 89–96
Unit 4 Resource Book
- *Activités pour tous* TE, pp. 111–113
- Audioscript, pp. 132, 133–135
- Communipak, pp. 140–160
- Lesson Plans, pp. 114–115
- Block Scheduling Lesson Plans, pp. 116–118
- Absent Student Copymasters, pp. 119–123
- Video Activities, pp. 126–129
- Videoscript, pp. 130–131
- Workbook TE, pp. 105–110

AUDIO & VISUAL 

Audio Program
CD 2 Tracks 39, 40
CD 8 Tracks 19–24

TECHNOLOGY 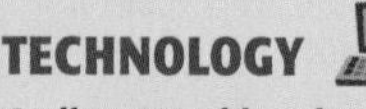

Online Workbook

VIDEO PROGRAM

VIDÉO DVD

MODULE 12
La voiture de Roger

TOTAL TIME: 6:46 min.
DVD Disk 1
Videotape 2 (COUNTER: 46:26 min.)

12.1 Introduction: Listening – Les couleurs (46:39–48:35 min.)

12.2 Mini-scenes: Listening – De quelle couleur? (48:36–48:59 min.)

12.3 Mini-scenes: Speaking – Qu'est-ce que tu préfères? (49:00–50:23 min.)

12.4 Dialogue: La voiture de Roger (50:24–51:28 min.)

12.5 Vignette culturelle: Les Français et l'auto (51:29–53:12 min.)

Compréhension

Answers

1. Il y a une voiture dans la rue.
2. Non, elle n'est pas grande (elle est petite).
3. Il s'appelle Roger.
4. Il est dans le café.
5. Elle s'appelle Véronique.
6. La voiture est rouge.

LEÇON 12 La voiture de Roger

VIDÉO DVD AUDIO

Dans la <u>rue</u>, il y a une voiture <u>rouge</u>. — *street/red*
C'est une petite voiture. C'est une voiture de sport.
Dans la rue, il y a aussi un café. Au café, il y a un jeune homme.
Il s'appelle Roger.
C'est le <u>propriétaire</u> de la voiture rouge. — *owner*
Une jeune fille <u>entre dans</u> le café. — *enters*
Elle s'appelle Véronique.
C'est <u>l'amie de Roger</u>. — *Roger's friend*
Véronique parle à Roger.

Véronique: Tu as une <u>nouvelle</u> voiture, n'est-ce pas? — *new*
Roger: Oui, j'ai une nouvelle voiture.
Véronique: Est-ce qu'elle est grande ou petite?
Roger: C'est une petite voiture.
Véronique: De quelle couleur est-elle?
Roger: C'est une voiture rouge.
Véronique: Est-ce que c'est une voiture italienne?
Roger: Oui, c'est une voiture italienne. Mais <u>dis donc</u>, Véronique, tu es <u>vraiment</u> très curieuse! — *hey there / really*
Véronique: Et toi, tu n'es pas <u>assez curieux</u>! — *curious enough*
Roger: Ah bon? Pourquoi?
Véronique: Pourquoi?! ... Regarde la <u>contractuelle</u> là-bas! — *meter maid*
Roger: Ah, zut alors!

Compréhension

1. Qu'est-ce qu'il y a dans la rue?
2. Est-ce que la voiture est grande?
3. Comment s'appelle le jeune homme?
4. Où est-il?
5. Comment s'appelle la jeune fille?
6. De quelle couleur est la voiture?

SETTING THE SCENE

Video Module 12 prepares students for the introductory dialogue by first teaching the colors.

The scene with Roger and his car constitutes Segment 4 of the video.

The *Vignette culturelle* develops the *Note culturelle* on the facing page about the French and their cars.

NOTE culturelle

Les Français et la voiture

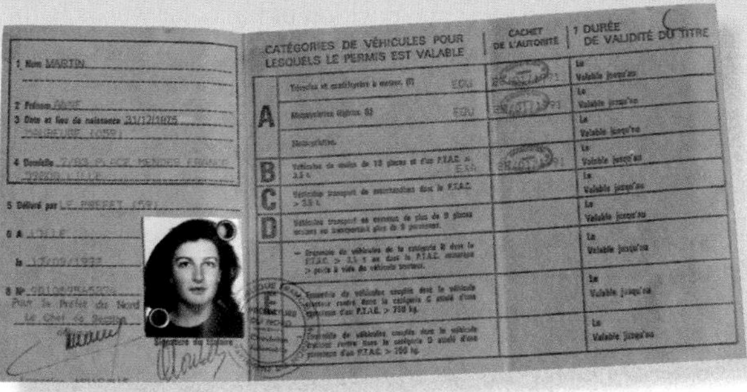

France is one of the leading producers of automobiles in the world. The two automakers, **Renault** and **Peugeot-Citroën**, manufacture a variety of models ranging from sports cars to mini-vans and buses.

To obtain a driver's license **(un permis de conduire)** in France, you must be eighteen years old and pass a very difficult driving test. French teenagers can, however, begin to drive at the age of sixteen, as long as they take lessons at an accredited driving school **(auto-école)** and are accompanied by an adult. Lessons in these schools are expensive and it may cost you 300 euros before you pass the exam and get your official license.

The French driver's license is a **permis à points** (license with points). A new license carries with it 12 points. When a driver commits a traffic violation, such as speeding or not wearing a seat belt, a corresponding number of points is subtracted from the license. If a driver loses all 12 points, the license is revoked and that person can no longer drive.

OPINION PERSONNELLE

Do you think that the **permis à points** is a good idea? Explain your position.

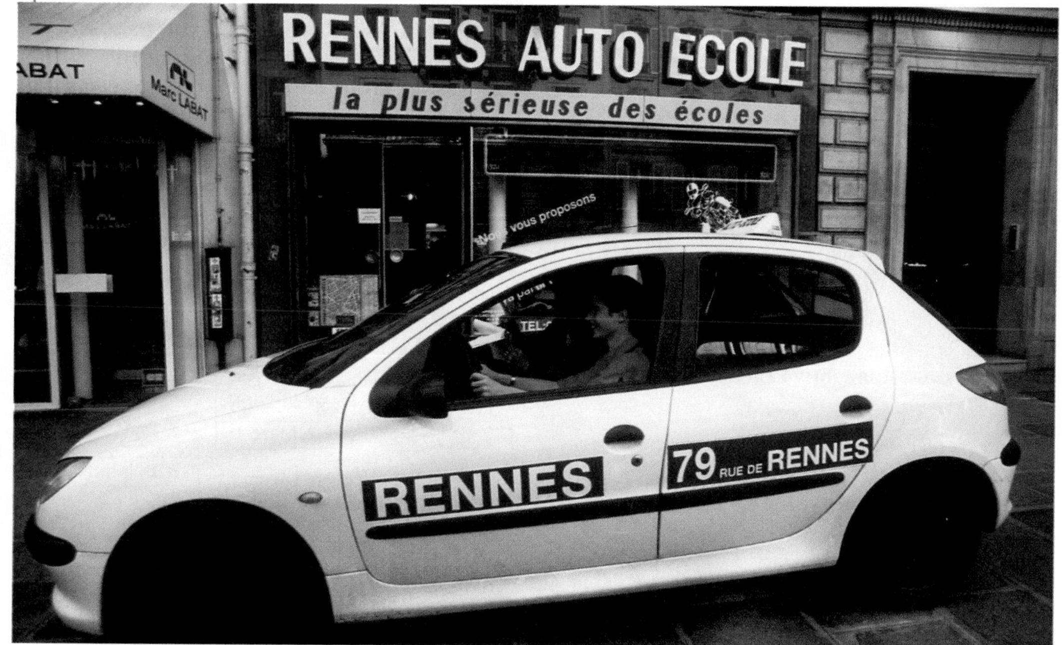

TALKING ABOUT PAST EVENTS

Let's talk about what you did last weekend.

Note that the past participle of **faire** is **fait.**

Est-ce que tu as fait une promenade le week-end dernier?
Oui, j'ai fait une promenade.
(Non, je n'ai pas fait de promenade.)

- **Est-ce que tu as fait un match de tennis?**
- **Est-ce que tu as fait un match de basket?**
- **Est-ce que tu as fait un match de foot?**
- **Est-ce que tu as fait un pique-nique?**

(Remember to use **pas de** in the negative.)

Photo cultural note

Saint-Germain-des-Prés

The neighborhood around Saint-Germain-des-Prés **(le quartier Saint-Germain)** is one of the oldest areas of Paris. Because of its numerous shops and movie theaters, **le boulevard Saint-Germain** is a favorite strolling place for Parisians. There are also many cafés, including the famous **Café des Deux Magots.**

Cultural background

- Gasoline costs about 1 euro a liter, which comes to about 4 dollars a gallon.
- With a production of nearly 2 million vehicles per year, Renault is one of the leading European automobile manufacturers. It is owned by the French government (**régie nationale** = government enterprise).

Language note In Quebec, a driving school is **une école de conduite**.

Note culturelle

Cultural note Once a driver has reached 12 points, his or her license is revoked and he or she cannot drive for at least six months. In order to get his or her license back, the driver has to take a written test. If the driver has had his or her license for less than three years, he or she must also take a road test.

SECTION A

Communicative function
Describing colors

Teaching Resource Options

PRINT 

Workbook PE, pp. 107–112
Unit 4 Resource Book
- Audioscript, p. 132
- Communipak, pp. 140–160
- Video Activities, pp. 126–127
- Videoscript, p. 130
- Workbook TE, pp. 105–110

AUDIO & VISUAL 

Audio Program
CD 2 Tracks 41, 42

Overhead Transparencies
28 *Les couleurs*
21 Objects (b) *Quelques objets*

TECHNOLOGY 

Power Presentations

VIDEO PROGRAM

VIDÉO  DVD 

MODULE 12

12.1 Introduction: Les couleurs (46:39–48:35 min.)

12.2 Mini-scenes: De quelle couleur? (48:36–48:59 min.)

12.3 Mini-scenes: Qu'est-ce que tu préfères? (48:60–50:23 min.)

Language notes

- When colors are used as nouns they are always masculine. J'aime **le noir.** Je déteste **le rose.**
- Another word for *brown* is **brun(e),** which is used to describe hair and eyes.

Teaching strategy To activate colors, use names of articles of clothing, especially **tee-shirt** which is a cognate. **De quelle couleur est le tee-shirt de Jim? Il est bleu et jaune.**

Looking ahead In conjunction with colors, you may want to pre-teach selected items of clothing:

un pantalon	**une chemise**
un tee-shirt	**une robe**
un sweater	**une jupe**
un polo	**des chaussures**

(Clothes are taught in Lesson 17.)

A Les couleurs

Note the form and position of the color words in the following sentences:

Alice a un vélo **bleu.**	*Alice has a **blue** bicycle.*
Nous avons des chemises **bleues.**	*We have **blue** shirts.*

Names of colors are ADJECTIVES and take adjective ENDINGS. They come *after* the noun.

VOCABULAIRE Les couleurs 

De quelle couleur ... ? *What color ... ?* —**De quelle couleur** est la moto?
—Elle est rouge.

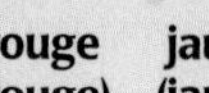
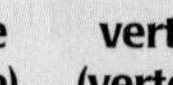

blanc (blanche)	noir (noire)	bleu (bleue)	rouge (rouge)	jaune (jaune)	vert (verte)	gris (grise)	marron (marron)	orange (orange)	rose (rose)

➔ The colors **orange** and **marron** are INVARIABLE. They do not take any endings.

un sac **orange**	des sacs **orange**
un tee-shirt **marron**	une chemise **marron**

1 De quelle couleur? 

PARLER Ask your classmates to name the colors of things they own. (They may invent answers.)

▶ ta chambre?

De quelle couleur est ta chambre?
Elle est blanche et bleue.

1. ta bicyclette?
2. ton tee-shirt?
3. ton appareil-photo?
4. ta montre?
5. ta raquette de tennis?
6. ton livre de français?
7. ton chien (chat)?

2 Possessions 

PARLER Ask what objects or pets the following people own. A classmate will answer, giving the color.

▶ —**Est-ce que Léa a un chat?**
—**Oui, elle a un chat jaune.**

▶ Léa

1. Mme Mercier

2. Marc

3. Delphine

4. Sophie

5. Éric

COMPREHENSION Colors

PROPS: For each student: scissors and colored paper (red, yellow, blue, green, orange, pink, brown, white, black, gray)

Have students cut out shapes.
Découpez un cercle, un carré *(square),* **un triangle.**

(Or distribute precut colored paper shapes.)

Have students hold up a shape.
Montrez-moi un cercle.

Take one student's circle and name its color.
Voici un cercle vert.
Si vous avez un cercle vert, levez la main.

Continue, teaching other colors and shapes.
X a un carré noir. Qui a un carré blanc?
Y a un triangle gris. Qui a un cercle gris?

3 L'arche de Noé

PARLER/ÉCRIRE Noah's ark has just landed. Give the colors of the animals as they get off the ship.

▶ le chien **Le chien est blanc.**

1. le chat
2. l'éléphant *(m.)*
3. la panthère
4. le zèbre
5. le flamant
6. le cardinal
7. le lion
8. le perroquet

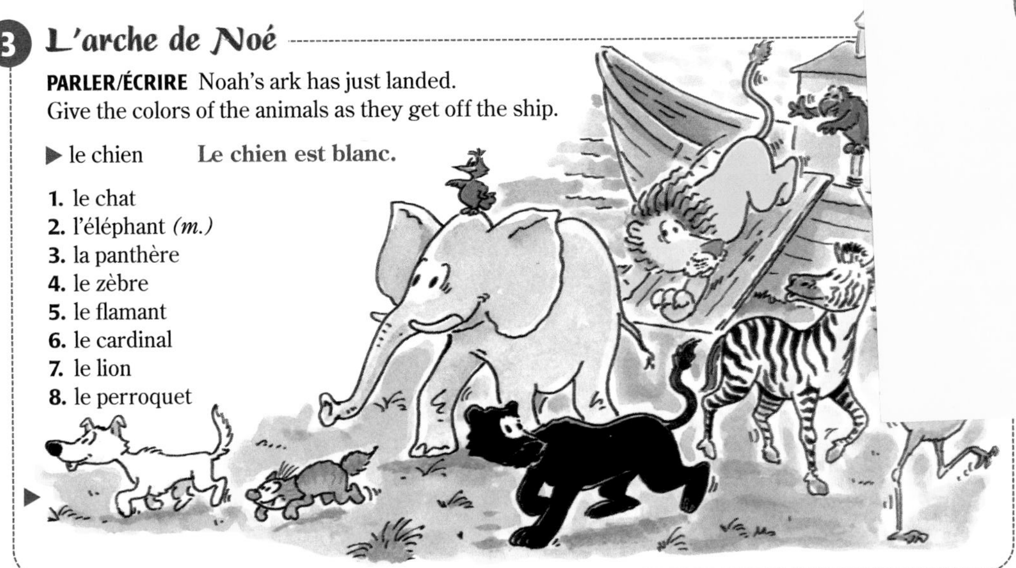

B La place des adjectifs avant le nom

Compare the position of the adjectives in the following sentences.

Voici une voiture **française.**	Voici une **petite** voiture.
Paul est un garçon **intelligent.**	Pierre est un **beau** garçon.

A few adjectives like **petit** and **beau** come BEFORE the noun they modify.

→ The article **des** often becomes **de** before an adjective. Compare:

des voitures → **de** petites voitures

VOCABULAIRE Les adjectifs qui précèdent le nom

beau (belle)	*beautiful, handsome*	Regarde la **belle** voiture!
joli	*pretty*	Qui est la **jolie** fille avec André?
grand	*big, large, tall*	Nous habitons dans un **grand** appartement.
petit	*little, small, short*	Ma soeur a un **petit** ordinateur.
bon (bonne)	*good*	Tu es un **bon** copain.
mauvais	*bad*	Patrick est un **mauvais** élève.

→ There is a LIAISON after the above adjectives when the noun which follows begins with a vowel sound. Note that in liaison:

- the "**d**" of **grand** is pronounced /t/: **un grand appartement**
- **bon** is pronounced like **bonne: un bon élève**

INCLUSION

Metacognitive, Gifted & Talented Explain the placement of adjectives that precede the noun. Ask students to then explain the rule in their own words. Prepare a fill-in-the-blank worksheet on which they will insert the adjectives in the proper place.

ON asking

ire).

(noir).
on).
e est (grise).
t (bleu).

cribing colors

1. – Est-ce que Mme Mercier a une voiture?
   – Oui, elle a une voiture rouge.
2. – Est-ce que Marc a un scooter?
   – Oui, il a un scooter jaune.
3. – Est-ce que Delphine a un vélo?
   – Oui, elle a un vélo noir (gris).
4. – Est-ce que Sophie a une guitare?
   – Oui, elle a une guitare orange.
5. – Est-ce qu'Éric a un chien?
   – Oui, il a un chien blanc.

Game One person describes what one of the people in the picture has, mentioning its color. The other students identify the person.

3 DESCRIPTION describing colors of animals

1. Le chat est orange.
2. L'éléphant est gris.
3. La panthère est noire.
4. Le zèbre est noir et blanc.
5. Le flammant est rose.
6. Le cardinal est rouge.
7. Le lion est jaune.
8. Le perroquet est vert.

Teaching strategy Model the pronunciation of the animal names for students.

SECTION B

Communicative function
Describing objects

Language notes

- In current French, it is becoming more and more common to use **des** before the adjective. Therefore, students should be able to recognize the **de** construction when they encounter it, but should not be penalized for failing to produce it.
- **Jeune** comes before the noun in expressions like **un jeune homme** and **une jeune fille**.

Teaching Resource Options

PRINT 

Workbook PE, pp. 107–112
Unit 4 Resource Book
Communipak, pp. 140–160
Workbook TE, pp. 105–110

TECHNOLOGY 

Power Presentations

4 COMMUNICATION expressing opinions

1. *Titanic* est un bon (mauvais) film.
2. «60 Minutes» est un bon (mauvais) programme de télé.
3. Britney Spears est une bonne (mauvaise) chanteuse.
4. Matt Damon est un bon (mauvais) acteur.
5. Dracula est une bonne (mauvaise) personne.
6. Les Yankees sont une bonne (mauvaise) équipe de baseball.
7. Les Lakers sont une bonne (mauvaise) équipe de basket.
8. Je suis un bon (mauvais) élève/Je suis une bonne (mauvaise) élève.
9. *Discovering French* est un bon (mauvais) livre.

Language note If students ask, the **plural** forms are **Dites!** and **Dites donc!**

5 ROLE PLAY discussing and describing possessions

– Dis,Thomas, tu as ... ?
– Oui, j'ai ...

1. une télé/une petite télé.
2. une guitare/une guitare espagnole.
3. un vélo/un vélo rouge.
4. une calculatrice/une petite calculatrice.
5. un sac/ un grand sac.
6. des livres/des livres intéressants.
7. une copine/une copine amusante.
8. une mobylette/une mobylette bleue.
9. une montre/une belle montre.
10. un copain/un bon copain.
11. une cousine/une jolie cousine.
12. une radio/une radio japonaise.

Expansion Have students use adjectives and write three original sentences about their possessions and friends.

J'ai une bicyclette rouge.
J'ai un bon copain.
J'ai une montre suisse.

4 Opinions personnelles

PARLER/ÉCRIRE Give your opinion about the following people and things, using the adjectives **bon** or **mauvais.**

▶ Julia Roberts est (une) actrice *(actress).*
Julia Roberts est une bonne actrice (une mauvaise actrice).

1. *Titanic* est un film.
2. «60 Minutes» est un programme de télé.
3. Britney Spears est (une) chanteuse.
4. Matt Damon est (un) acteur.
5. Dracula est une personne.
6. Les Yankees sont une équipe *(team)* de baseball.
7. Les Lakers sont une équipe de basket.
8. Je suis un(e) élève.
9. *Discovering French* est un livre.

VOCABULAIRE Expressions pour la conversation

▶ ***How to get someone's attention:***

Dis!	*Say! Hey!*	**Dis**, Éric, est-ce que tu as une voiture?
Dis donc!	*Hey there!*	**Dis donc**, est-ce que tu veux faire une promenade avec moi?

5 Dialogue

PARLER Christine asks her cousin Thomas if he has certain things. He responds affirmatively, describing each one. Play both roles.

▶ une chaîne hi-fi (petite) ▶ un scooter (italien)

1. une télé (petite)
2. une guitare (espagnole)
3. un vélo (rouge)
4. une calculatrice (petite)
5. un sac (grand)
6. des livres (intéressants)
7. une copine (amusante)
8. une mobylette (bleue)
9. une montre (belle)
10. un copain (bon)
11. une cousine (jolie)
12. une radio (japonaise)

TEACHING STRATEGY Using chants

Certain grammatical constructions, such as the use of **c'est** vs. **il est**, can be internalized through the use of chants.

For example, the phrase **c'est un** can be chanted to the "Mexican Hat Dance" tune.

C'est un, c'est un, c'est un...
C'est un ami mexicain.
C'est une, c'est une, c'est une...
C'est une amie mexicaine.
C'est un, c'est un, c'est un...
C'est un vélo italien.
C'est une, c'est une, c'est une...
C'est une voiture italienne.

Il est ou c'est?

When describing a person or thing, French speakers use two different constructions, **il est (elle est)** and **c'est.**

			Il est + ADJECTIVE Elle est + ADJECTIVE	C'est + ARTICLE + NOUN (+ ADJECTIVE)
	Roger	*He is ...*	**Il est** amusant.	**C'est** un copain. **C'est** un copain amusant.
	Véronique	*She is ...*	**Elle est** sportive.	**C'est** une amie. **C'est** une bonne amie.
	un scooter	*It is ...*	**Il est** joli.	**C'est** un scooter français. **C'est** un bon scooter.
	une voiture	*It is ...*	**Elle est** petite.	**C'est** une voiture anglaise. **C'est** une petite voiture.

→ Note the corresponding plural forms:

(Pierre et Marc)	*They are ...*	**Ils sont** amusants.	**Ce sont** des copains.
(Claire et Anne)	*They are ...*	**Elles sont** timides.	**Ce sont** des copines.

→ In negative sentences, **c'est** becomes **ce n'est pas.**

Ce n'est pas un mauvais élève. — ***He's not** a bad student.*

Ce n'est pas une Peugeot. — ***It's not** a Peugeot.*

→ **C'est** is also used with names of people

C'est Véronique. — **C'est** Madame Lamblet.

Descriptions

PARLER/ÉCRIRE Complete the following descriptions with **Il est, Elle est,** or **C'est,** as appropriate.

A. Roger
1. ____ grand.
2. ____ brun.
3. ____ un garçon sympathique.
4. ____ un mauvais élève.

B. Véronique
5. ____ une fille brune.
6. ____ une amie sympathique.
7. ____ très amusante.
8. ____ assez grande.

C. La voiture de Roger
9. ____ une voiture moderne.
10. ____ une petite voiture.
11. ____ rouge.
12. ____ très rapide.

D. Le scooter de Véronique
13. ____ bleu et blanc.
14. ____ très économique.
15. ____ un joli scooter.
16. ____ assez confortable.

SECTION C

Communicative function
Describing people and things

Language notes

- The adjective may either follow or precede the noun.
- **C'est** is also used when a possessive adjective introduces the noun:
  C'est mon frère. *He's my brother.*
- In negative sentences with **être,** the articles **un, une,** and **des** remain unchanged. Compare:
  Ce **n'est pas un** copain.
  Je **n'ai pas de** copain.
  Ce **ne sont pas des** motos japonaises.
  Nous **n'avons pas de** motos japonaises.

Teaching note French is often used in advertisements. Ask students to keep track of ads that use French that they see around town, in the newspaper, in magazines, or on TV.

6 DESCRIPTION pointing out people and things

A. Roger
1. Il est
2. Il est
3. C'est
4. C'est

B. Véronique
5. C'est
6. C'est
7. Elle est
8. Elle est

C. La voiture de Roger
9. C'est
10. C'est
11. Elle est
12. Elle est

D. Le scooter de Véronique
13. Il est
14. Il est
15. C'est
16. Il est

SPEAKING ACTIVITY Show and tell

Have students bring an object to class and describe it using **il/elle est..., c'est...** and appropriate adjectives.

J'ai une montre.
C'est une montre suisse.
Elle est rouge et noire.
C'est une jolie montre; elle marche très bien.
J'aime beaucoup ma montre!

Variation This can also be done as a written activity with students illustrating their objects.

Note This works particularly well after the holiday season when students have gifts to talk about.

SECTION D

Communicative function
Expressing opinions

Teaching Resource Options

PRINT  

Workbook PE, pp. 107–112
Unit 4 Resource Book
Audioscript, p. 132
Communipak, pp. 140–160
Workbook TE, pp. 105–110

AUDIO & VISUAL 

Audio Program
CD 2 Track 43

TECHNOLOGY 

Power Presentations

Language note This construction is not used to describe specific people and things.
Paul? Il est amusant.
Les livres? Ils sont intéressants.

Casual speech It is very common to drop the **ne** in negative expressions:
C'est pas amusant.
C'est pas vrai.

Language notes
- The French often tend to use negative constructions in a positive sense:
  Ce (n')est pas mal.
  That's not bad. = That's very good.
  Ce (n')est pas bête. *That's not stupid = That's a smart idea.*
- A current popular anglicism is:
  C'est cool.
- **Super** may be used in combination with other expressions:
  C'est super-chouette.
  C'est super-difficile.
- **Extra** is the short form of **extraordinaire.**

7 COMPREHENSION geographic locations

1. C'est faux! (Paris est en France.)
2. C'est vrai!
3. C'est faux! (Genève est en Suisse.)
4. C'est vrai!
5. C'est faux! (Fort-de-France est à la Martinique.)
6. C'est faux! (Québec est au Canada.)
7. C'est vrai!
8. C'est vrai!

Additional cues
Casablanca est en Afrique. (vrai)
Rome est en France. (faux: en Italie)
Vancouver est en France. (faux: au Canada)
Strasbourg est en France. (vrai)
Bordeaux est en Italie. (faux: en France)

D Les expressions impersonnelles avec *c'est*

Note the use of **c'est** in the following sentences.

J'aime parler français.	**C'est** intéressant.	*It's interesting.*
Je n'aime pas travailler le week-end.	**Ce n'est pas** amusant.	*It's no(t) fun.*

To express an opinion on a general topic, French speakers use the construction:

C'est / **Ce n'est pas** } + MASCULINE ADJECTIVE

VOCABULAIRE Opinions

C'est ... *It's ..., That's ...*
Ce n'est pas ... *It's not ..., That's not ...*

vrai	*true*	**chouette**	*neat*
faux	*false*	**super**	*great*
		génial	*terrific*
facile	*easy*	**pénible**	*a pain, annoying*
difficile	*hard, difficult*	**drôle**	*funny*

→ To express an opinion, French speakers also use adverbs like **bien** and **mal.**

C'est bien.	*That's good.*	Tu étudies? **C'est bien.**
C'est mal.	*That's bad.*	Alain n'étudie pas. **C'est mal.**

7  Vrai ou faux?

PARLER Imagine that your little sister is talking about where certain cities are located. Tell her whether her statements are right or wrong.

Miami est en Californie.
C'est faux!
Miami est en Floride.
C'est vrai!

1. Paris est en Italie.
2. Los Angeles est en Californie.
3. Genève est en Italie.
4. Dakar est en Afrique.
5. Fort-de-France est au Canada.
6. Québec est en France.
7. Port-au-Prince est en Haïti.
8. Montréal est au Canada.

TALKING ABOUT PAST EVENTS

▶ **V, qu'est-ce que tu as fait hier soir?**
J'ai étudié (regardé la télé, travaillé...).
▶ **W et X, qu'est-ce que vous avez fait?**
Nous avons joué aux jeux vidéo (...).

Ask individuals what they did. Have others report back. Ask if they did the same thing.

- **V, qu'est-ce que tu as fait hier soir?**
- **Y, qu'est-ce que V a fait hier soir? Est-ce que tu as fait la même chose?**
- **W et X, qu'est-ce que vous avez fait?**
- **Z, qu'est-ce que W et X ont fait hier soir? Est-ce que tu as fait la même chose?**

8 Opinion personnelle

PARLER Ask your classmates if they like to do the following things. They will answer, using an expression from the **Vocabulaire.**

▶ nager

1. téléphoner
2. parler en public
3. parler français
4. danser
5. voyager
6. dîner en ville
7. jouer aux jeux vidéo
8. étudier le week-end
9. écouter la musique classique
10. surfer sur l'Internet
11. télécharger de la musique

PRONONCIATION  ch /ʃ/

Les lettres «ch»

The letters "**ch**" are usually pronounced like the English *"sh."*

Répétez: **chien chat chose marche**
chouette chocolat affiche
Michèle a un chat et deux chiens.

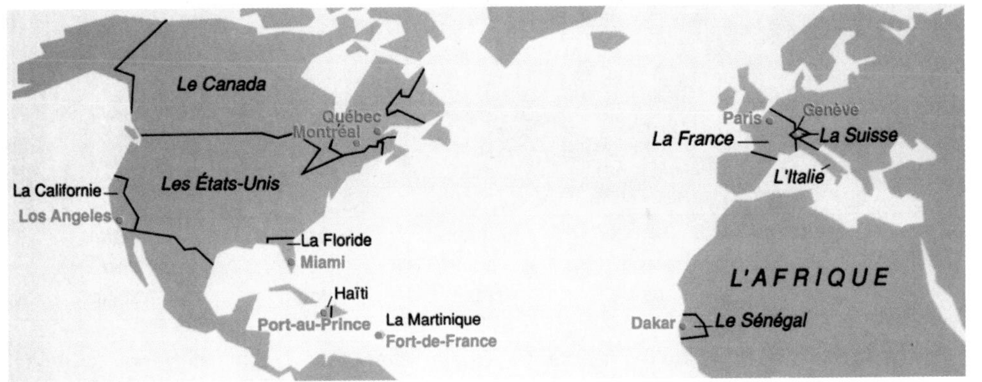

INCLUSION

Structured Draw two columns on board - the first one will have **C'est/Ce n'est pas** and the second will have adjectives such as **vrai, faux, facile,** etc. Point to each column while modeling sample sentences aloud. Ask students to repeat. Then, give them a prompt and ask them to pair from columns to respond (**–Le ski? –C'est facile!; –La musique? –C'est chouette.**)

8 COMMUNICATION talking about what one likes to do

Answers will vary.

1. – Tu aimes téléphoner?
   – Oui, c'est (chouette)!
   (Non, c'est [pénible]!)
2. – Tu aimes parler en public?
   – Oui, c'est (facile)!
   (Non, c'est [difficile]!)
3. – Tu aimes parler français?
   – Oui, c'est (génial)!
   (Non, c'est [difficile]!)
4. – Tu aimes danser?
   – Oui, c'est (facile)!
   (Non, c'est [difficile]!)
5. – Tu aimes voyager?
   – Oui, c'est (super)!
   (Non, c'est [pénible]!)
6. – Tu aimes dîner en ville?
   – Oui, c'est (génial)!
   (Non, c'est [pénible]!)
7. – Tu aimes jouer aux jeux vidéo?
   – Oui, c'est (drôle)!
   (Non, c'est [pénible]!)
8. – Tu aimes étudier le week-end?
   – Oui, c'est (génial)!
   (Non, c'est [pénible]!)
9. – Tu aimes écouter la musique classique?
   – Oui, c'est (super)!
   (Non, c'est [pénible]!)
10. – Tu aimes surfer sur l'Internet?
    – Oui, c'est (génial)!
    (Non, c'est [pénible]!)

Re-entry and review

Verbs from Unit 3.

Challenge The second student asks the same question of the first student, who must respond using another adjective.

– Tu aimes nager?
– Oui, c'est génial! Et toi, tu aimes nager?
– Non, c'est difficile.

PRONUNCIATION

- Although "ch" is usually pronounced /tʃ/ in English, as in *march* and *chocolate,* the letters do represent the sound /ʃ/ in words and names that came directly from French: **Chef, chauffeur, chic, touché,** etc.
- Sometimes the letters "ch" are pronounced /k/ in French, just as they are in the corresponding English cognates: **orchestre, Christine, écho.** Exception: **architecte,** which has the sound /ʃ/.

À VOTRE TOUR

Main Topic
- Recapitulation and review

Teaching Resource Options

PRINT 

Workbook PE, pp. 107–112
Unit 4 Resource Book
Audioscript, pp. 132–133
Communipak, pp. 140–160
Family Involvement, pp. 124–125
Workbook TE, pp. 105–110

Assessment
Lesson 12 Quiz, pp. 136–137
Portfolio Assessment, Unit 1 URB pp. 136–137
Audioscript for Quiz 12, p. 135
Answer Keys, pp. 201–205

AUDIO & VISUAL 

Audio Program
CD 2 Tracks 44, 45
CD 14 Track 20

TECHNOLOGY 

Test Generator CD-ROM/McDougal Littell Assessment System

1 COMPREHENSION

1. De quelle couleur est ton vélo?
   (e) Il est vert.
2. Ta raquette est bleue?
   (c) Non, elle est blanche.
3. Tu aimes regarder la télé?
   (d) Oui, c'est amusant.
4. C'est un magazine français?
   (a) Non, il est canadien.
5. Philippe n'aime pas parler en public?
   (b) C'est vrai! Il est très timide.

2 GUIDED ORAL EXPRESSION

1. **D1:** Qu'est-ce qu'il y a devant la pharmacie?
   D2: Il y a une moto.
   D1: Elle est rouge ou bleue?
   D2: C'est une moto rouge.
2. **D1:** Qu'est-ce qu'il y a devant la librairie?
   D2: Il y a une fille.
   D1: Elle est grande ou petite?
   D2: C'est une petite fille.
3. **D1:** Qu'est-ce qu'il y a devant le restaurant?
   D2: Il y a un homme.
   D1: Il est brun ou blond?
   D2: C'est un homme blond.
4. **D1:** Qu'est-ce qu'il y a devant le cinéma?
   D2: Il y a un garçon.
   D1: Il est anglais ou français?
   D2: C'est un garçon anglais.
5. **D1:** Qu'est-ce qu'il y a devant la fontaine?
   D2: Il y a un chien.
   D1: Il est noir ou jaune?
   D2: C'est un chien jaune.

À votre tour!

OBJECTIFS

Now you can ...
- express your opinions about people and activities
- describe everyday objects: their size and color

1 Allô!

PARLER Christophe is phoning some friends. Match his questions on the left with his friends' answers on the right.

1. De quelle couleur est ton vélo?
2. Ta raquette est bleue?
3. Tu aimes regarder la télé?
4. C'est un magazine français?
5. Philippe n'aime pas parler en public?

a. Non, il est canadien.
b. C'est vrai! Il est très timide.
c. Non, elle est blanche.
d. Oui, c'est amusant.
e. Il est vert.

2 Créa-dialogue

PARLER There has been a burglary in the rue Saint-Pierre. By walkie-talkie, two detectives are describing what they see. Play both roles.

▶ (le)	1. (la)	2. (la)	3. (le)	4. (le)	5. (la)
CAFÉ	PHARMACIE+	LIBRAIRIE	Restaurant	CINÉMA	fontaine
grande ou petite?	rouge ou bleue?	grande ou petite?	brun ou blond?	anglais ou français?	noir ou jaune?

▶ DÉTECTIVE 1: **Qu'est-ce qu'il y a devant le café?**
DÉTECTIVE 2: **Il y a une voiture.**
DÉTECTIVE 1: **Elle est grande ou petite?**
DÉTECTIVE 2: **C'est une petite voiture.**

À VOTRE TOUR

Depending on your goals and objectives, you may or may not wish to assign all of the activities in the **À votre tour** section.

PAIR PRACTICE

Act. 1, 2, 3, and 4 lend themselves to pair practice.

3 Faisons connaissance!

PARLER Try to find out which students have the same interests you do. Select two activities you enjoy from Column A and ask a classmate if he/she likes to do them. Your classmate will answer yes or no, using an appropriate expression from Column B.

A	B
téléphoner	chouette
envoyer des mails	super
surfer sur l'Internet	génial
jouer aux jeux vidéo	amusant
jouer au foot	intéressant
voyager	pénible
organiser des boums	drôle
parler avec les voisins	difficile
parler français en classe	facile
étudier pour l'examen	
travailler dans le jardin	

Tu aimes voyager?
Oui, c'est amusant.
Tu aimes étudier pour l'examen?
Non, c'est difficile.

4 Dialogue: Un chien!

PARLER Imagine that your classmate has just received a dog for his/her birthday. You want to know more about this new pet. Ask your classmate ...

- what the dog's name is
- how old he is
- what color he is
- if he is a small dog or a big dog
- if he is cute
- if he is a mean dog (*un chien méchant*)

5 Composition: Une voiture

ÉCRIRE Describe your parents' car or any other car you have seen recently. Provide the following information, writing a sentence for each of these points.

- make/model
- color
- age
- country of origin
- size (*petit? grand?*)
- other characteristics (*confortable? rapide? économique?*)

LESSON REVIEW
CLASSZONE.COM

Portfolio Assessment

You will probably select only one speaking activity and one writing activity to go into the students' portfolios for Unit 4.

In this lesson, Act. 5 is a good written portfolio topic.

3 Conversation

Answers will vary.

- – Tu aimes téléphoner?
  – Oui, c'est (amusant).
  (Non, c'est [pénible].)
- – Tu aimes envoyer des mails?
  – Oui, c'est (chouette).
  (Non, c'est [difficile].)
- – Tu aimes surfer sur l'Internet?
  – Oui, c'est (facile).
  (Non, c'est [difficile].)
- – Tu aimes jouer aux jeux vidéo?
  – Oui, c'est (amusant).
  (Non, c'est [pénible].)
- – Tu aimes jouer au foot?
  – Oui, c'est (super).
  (Non, c'est [difficile].)
- – Tu aimes voyager?
  – Oui, c'est (amusant).
  (Non, c'est [pénible].)
- – Tu aimes organiser des boums?
  – Oui, c'est (génial).
  (Non, c'est [difficile].)
- – Tu aimes parler avec les voisins?
  – Oui, c'est (intéressant).
  (Non, c'est [pénible].)
- – Tu aimes parler français en classe?
  – Oui, c'est (facile).
  (Non, c'est [difficile].)
- – Tu aimes étudier pour l'examen?
  – Oui, c'est (chouette).
  (Non, c'est [pénible].)
- – Tu aimes travailler dans le jardin?
  – Oui, c'est (chouette).
  (Non, c'est [pénible].)

4 Oral Self-Expression

Answers will vary.
– Comment s'appelle-t-il, ton chien?
– Il s'appelle Ernie.
– Est-ce que c'est un chien grand ou petit?
– Il est petit.
– Quel âge a ton chien?
– Il a trois ans.
– Est-ce qu'il est mignon?
– Oui, il est très mignon.
– De quelle couleur est-il?
– Il est noir.
– Est-ce que c'est un chien méchant?
– Non, il est très gentil.

5 Written Self-Expression

Answers will vary.
Mes parents ont une Renault. Elle est verte. Elle a deux ans. Elle est française. Elle est assez grande. Elle est très confortable et assez rapide.

TESTS DE CONTRÔLE

Teaching Resource Options

PRINT 

Unit 4 Resource Book
Communipak, pp. 140–160

Assessment
Unit 4 Test, pp. 169–177
Portfolio Assessment, Unit 1 URB, pp. 155–164
Multiple Choice Test Items, pp. 190–197
Listening Comprehension Performance Test, pp. 178–179
Reading Performance Test, pp. 184–186
Speaking Performance Test, pp. 180–183
Writing Performance Test, pp. 187–189
Test Scoring Tools, p. 198
Audioscript for Tests, pp. 199–200
Answer Keys, pp. 201–205

AUDIO & VISUAL 

CD 14 Tracks 21–24

TECHNOLOGY 

Test Generator CD-ROM/McDougal Littell Assessment System

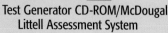

1 COMPREHENSION

1. un stylo
2. une montre
3. un cahier
4. un ordinateur
5. un baladeur
6. une bicyclette (un vélo)
7. une voiture (une auto)
8. un appareil-photo
9. un lit
10. une fenêtre

2 COMPREHENSION

1. Tu as une chaîne hi-fi.
2. Tu es français.
3. Céline a quinze ans.
4. Nous avons soif.
5. Thomas est sympathique.
6. Mes copains sont amusants.
7. Vous avez un portable.
8. Est-ce que vous avez faim?

Tests de contrôle

By taking the following tests, you can check your progress in French and also prepare for the unit test. Write your answers on a separate sheet of paper.

1 The right object

Review…
- names of objects: pp. 140, 142, and 144

Name the following objects. Make sure to use the appropriate article: **un** or **une.**

2 Être and avoir

Review …
- être and avoir: pp. 84 and 152

Complete the following sentences with the appropriate forms of **être** or **avoir.**

1. Tu — une chaîne hi-fi.
2. Tu — français.
3. Céline — quinze ans.
4. Nous — soif.
5. Thomas — sympathique.
6. Mes copains — amusants.
7. Vous — un portable.
8. Est-ce que vous — faim?

3 The right adjectives

Review …
- adjectives: pp. 164-165, 166-167

Complete the following descriptions with the appropriate forms of the adjectives in parentheses.

1. (français)	une amie …	des copains …
2. (américain)	des filles …	des garçons …
3. (sympathique)	une copine …	des personnes …
4. (intelligent)	une personne …	des amies …
5. (sportif)	une fille …	des copines …
6. (gentil)	des amies …	des copains …
7. (rouge)	une voiture …	un vélo …
8. (blanc)	une moto …	des bicyclettes …
9. (japonais)	une mini-chaîne …	des ordinateurs …

4 The right choice

Complete the following sentences with the appropriate option suggested in parentheses.

(Note: ∅ means that no word is needed.)

1. Qui est — fille là-bas? **(le, la, l')**
2. — ordinateur est sur la table. **(L', Le, La)**
3. Jean-Paul aime — musique classique. **(∅, la, une)**
4. Léa a — copines canadiennes. **(∅, une, des)**
5. Philippe n'a pas — portable. **(∅, un, de)**

Review...
- definite and indefinite articles: pp. 153-156, 158

6. Ma mère a une voiture — . **(jaune, jolie, grande)**
7. Nous avons un — professeur. **(bon, sympathique, intéressant)**

Review ...
- position of adjectives: pp. 168, 175

8. Voici Catherine. — une amie sympathique. **(Il est, Elle est, C'est)**
9. Voici Marc. — canadien. **(Il est, Elle est, C'est)**

Review ...
- il est or c'est: p. 177

5 Composition: Mon cousin / Ma cousine

Write a paragraph of five or six sentences describing one of your cousins, real or imaginary. Give your cousin's name, nationality and age, plus a brief description. Say why your cousin is interesting (or not interesting). Use only vocabulary and expressions that you know in French.

STRATEGY Writing

a) Make a list of the things you want to say about your cousin.

b) Organize your ideas and write your description.

c) Check that all the adjectives have the right endings.

nom: ____________

nationalité: ____________

âge: ____________

description physique: ____________

personnalité: ____________

intéressant(e)? (pourquoi) ____________

3 COMPREHENSION

1. une amie française
   des copains français
2. des filles américaines
   des garçons américains
3. une copine sympathique
   des personnes sympathiques
4. une personne intelligente
   des amies intelligentes
5. une fille sportive
   des copines sportives
6. des amies gentilles
   des copains gentils
7. une voiture rouge
   un vélo rouge
8. une moto blanche
   des bicyclettes blanches
9. une mini-chaîne japonaise
   des ordinateurs japonais

4 COMPREHENSION

1. Qui est la fille là-bas?
2. L'ordinateur est sur la table.
3. Jean-Paul aime la musique classique.
4. Léa a des copines canadiennes.
5. Philippe n'a pas de portable.
6. Ma mère a une voiture jaune.
7. Nous avons un bon professeur.
8. Voici Catherine. C'est une amie sympathique.
9. Voici Marc. Il est canadien.

5 WRITTEN SELF-EXPRESSION

Answers will vary.
nom: Christine
nationalité: américaine
âge: 12 ans
description physique: brune, petite
personnalité: amusante, gentille, intelligente
intéressante parce qu'elle voyage beaucoup et parle français & espagnol

Ma cousine s'appelle Christine.
Elle est américaine. Elle a douze ans. Elle est brune et petite. Elle est amusante, gentille et intelligente. C'est une personne intéressante. Elle voyage beaucoup et elle parle français et espagnol.

VOCABULAIRE

Language Learning Benchmarks

FUNCTION

- Engage in conversations pp. 157, 167
- Express likes and dislikes p. 158
- Make requests p. 141
- Obtain information p. 143
- Understand some ideas and familiar details p. 150

CONTEXT

- Converse in face-to-face social interactions pp. 143, 146, 157, 175, 176
- Listen during social interactions p. 156
- Listen to audio and video texts pp. 136-137, 150, 159, 162, 165, 169, 172, 174, 175, 179
- Use authentic materials when reading: schedules p. 159
- Use authentic materials when reading: short narratives p. 190
- Write lists p .149
- Write short letters pp. 149, 191

TEXT TYPE

- Use short sentences when speaking pp. 154, 168, 179
- Use short sentences when writing pp. 145, 155, 167, 175
- Use learned words and phrases when speaking pp. 145, 165
- Use learned words and phrases when writing pp. 139, 165
- Use simple questions when speaking pp. 152, 154, 167, 174
- Understand some ideas and familiar details presented in clear, uncomplicated speech when listening pp. 150, 162, 172

Vocabulaire

POUR COMMUNIQUER

Talking about people

Qui est-ce?	*Who is it?*
Comment est il/elle?	*What is he/she like?*
Quel âge a-t-il/elle?	*How old is he/she?*

Talking about things

Qu'est-ce que c'est?	*What is it? What's that?*
C'est ...	*It's ...*
Est-ce que tu as ...?	*Do you have ...?*
Oui, j'ai ...	*Yes, I have ...*
Regarde ça.	*Look at that.*
Quoi?	*What?*
Ça, là-bas.	*That, over there.*
Il y a ...	*There is ..., There are ...*
Est-ce qu'il y a ...?	*Is there ...? Are there ...?*
Qu'est-ce qu'il y a ...?	*What is there ...?*
De quelle couleur ...?	*What color ...?*

Expressing opinions

C'est ... *It's ...*

bien	*good*
chouette	*neat*
difficile	*hard, difficult*
drôle	*funny*
facile	*easy*
faux	*false*
génial	*terrific*
mal	*bad*
pénible	*a pain, annoying*
super	*great*
vrai	*true*

MOTS ET EXPRESSIONS

Les personnes

un camarade	*classmate*
un élève	*pupil, student*
un étudiant	*student*
une camarade	*classmate*
une élève	*pupil, student*
une étudiante	*student*
un prof	*teacher*
un professeur	*teacher*
un voisin	*neighbor*
une prof	*teacher*
une personne	*person*
une voisine	*neighbor*

Quelques possessions

un appareil-photo	*camera*
un baladeur	*portable CD player*
un cahier	*notebook*
un CD	*CD*
un crayon	*pencil*
un DVD	*DVD*
un livre	*book*
un objet	*object*
un ordinateur	*computer*
un portable	*cell phone*
un sac	*bag*
un scooter	*motor scooter*
un stylo	*pen*
un téléphone	*phone*
un vélo	*bicycle, bike*
une affiche	*poster*
une auto	*car*
une bicyclette	*bicycle*
une calculatrice	*calculator*
une cassette vidéo	*videotape*
une chaîne hi-fi	*stereo set*
une chose	*thing*
une guitare	*guitar*
une mini-chaîne	*compact stereo*
une mobylette	*motorbike, moped*
une montre	*watch*
une moto	*motorcycle*
une radio	*radio*
une radiocassette	*boom box*
une raquette	*tennis racket*
une télé	*TV set*
une voiture	*car*

La chambre

un bureau	*desk*	**une chaise**	*chair*	**une porte**	*door*
un lit	*bed*	**une fenêtre**	*window*	**une table**	*table*
		une lampe	*lamp*		

Où?

dans	*in*	**devant**	*in front of*	**sur**	*on, on top of*
derrière	*behind, in back of*	**sous**	*under*		

La description

amusant(e)	*amusing, fun*	**jeune**	*young*		
beau (belle)*	*beautiful, handsome*	**joli(e)***	*pretty*		
bête	*silly, dumb*	**mauvais(e)***	*bad*		
blond(e)	*blonde*	**méchant(e)**	*mean, nasty*		
bon (bonne)*	*good*	**mignon (mignonne)**	*cute*	**assez**	*rather*
brun(e)	*brown, dark-haired*	**petit(e)***	*small, little, short*	**très**	*very*
gentil (gentille)	*nice, kind*	**sportif (sportive)**	*athletic*		
grand(e)*	*big, large, tall*	**sympathique**	*nice, pleasant*		
intelligent(e)	*intelligent, smart*	**timide**	*timid, shy*		
intéressant(e)	*interesting*				

* *Adjectives that come before the noun*

Les adjectifs de nationalité

américain(e)	*American*	**espagnol(e)**	*Spanish*	**mexicain(e)**	*Mexican*
anglais(e)	*English*	**français(e)**	*French*	**suisse**	*Swiss*
canadien (canadienne)	*Canadian*	**italien (italienne)**	*Italian*		
chinois(e)	*Chinese*	**japonais(e)**	*Japanese*		

Les couleurs

blanc (blanche)	*white*	**jaune**	*yellow*	**orange***	*orange*	**vert(e)**	*green*
bleu(e)	*blue*	**marron***	*brown*	**rose**	*pink*		
gris(e)	*grey*	**noir(e)**	*black*	**rouge**	*red*		

* *Invariable adjectives*

Verbes réguliers en *-er*

marcher	*to work, to run (to function)*
	to walk

Verbes irréguliers

avoir	*to have*
avoir faim	*to be hungry*
avoir soif	*to be thirsty*
avoir ... ans	*to be ... (years old)*

Expressions utiles

Dis!	*Say! Hey!*	**Je sais.**	*I know.*	**lundi**	*on Monday*
Dis donc!	*Hey there!*	**Je ne sais pas.**	*I don't know.*	**le lundi**	*on Mondays*
alors	*so, then*	**Si!**	*Yes!*	**le week-end**	*on weekends*

VOCABULAIRE SUPPLÉMENTAIRE: L'informatique

un CD-ROM (cédérom)	*CD-ROM*	**une imprimante**	*printer*	**chatter**	*to chat (online)*
un clavier	*keyboard*	**une souris**	*mouse*	**envoyer un mail**	*to send an e-mail*
un écran	*screen*			**surfer sur l'Internet**	*to surf the Internet*
un jeu d'ordinateur	*computer game*			**télécharger**	*to download*
un mail (un mél)	*e-mail*				
un ordinateur portable	*laptop*				
un PC	*PC*				

TEST PREP CLASSZONE.COM FLASHCARDS AND MORE!

CONTENT

- Understand and convey information about friends p. 139
- Understand and convey information about rooms p. 145
- Understand and convey information about pets and animals p. 187
- Understand and convey information about geography p. 178
- Understand and convey information about colors p. 174, 175

ASSESSMENT

- Communicate effectively with some hesitation and errors, which do not hinder comprehension p. 181
- Demonstrate culturally acceptable behavior for engaging in conversations pp. 148, 181
- Demonstrate culturally acceptable behavior for expressing likes and dislikes p. 161
- Demonstrate culturally acceptable behavior for obtaining information pp. 160, 180, 181
- Demonstrate culturally acceptable behavior for understanding some ideas and familiar details pp. 170, 171
- Demonstrate culturally acceptable behavior for providing information pp. 149, 171, 183
- Understand most important information. pp. 160, 170, 180

ENTRACTE 4

Objectives

- Reading skills development
- Re-entry of materials in the unit
- Development of cultural awareness

Teaching Resource Options

PRINT 

Workbook PE, pp. 113–116
Activités pour tous PE, pp. 67–69
Unit 4 Resource Book
Activités pour tous TE, pp. 161–163
Workbook TE, pp. 165–168

Le monde personnel

Objectives

- Reading for fun and vocabulary enrichment

Casual speech For **sensationnel(le)** one can also say **sensas** /sãsas/

Petit catalogue des compliments ... et des insultes

1
Il est cool!
Il est génial!
Il est super!
Il est sensationnel!
C'est un champion!
2
CONCERT
Elle est extra!
Elle est cool!
Elle est sensationnelle!
Elle est super!
Elle est géniale!
3
Crétin!
Idiot!
Imbécile!

LANGUAGE COMPARISONS

Over the centuries, French and English have influenced one another.

- Which of the compliments and insults did French borrow from English? Which word has English borrowed from French? Sometimes French and English express themselves in different ways.
- Which of the animal comparisons on the next page are the same in French and English? Which are different?

PRE-READING

Have students suggest English sayings about personality traits that mention animals. E.g.,

Blind as a bat.
Sly as a fox.
An elephant never forgets.
More fun than a barrel of monkeys.
Stubborn as a mule.

POST-READING

Which of the French sayings are similar to American sayings? Which are different?

LES ANIMAUX et LE LANGAGE

Selon° toi, est-ce que les animaux ont une personnalité? Pour les Français, les animaux ont des qualités et des défauts,° comme° nous. Devine° comment on° complète les phrases suivantes° en français.

1 Philippe n'aime pas étudier. Il préfère dormir.° Il est paresseux° comme° …

un tigre

un chat

un lézard

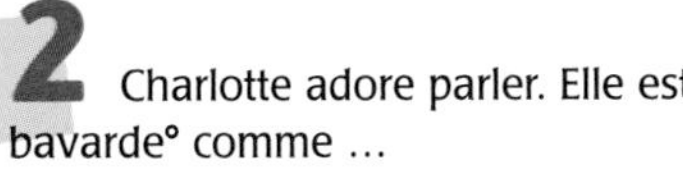

2 Charlotte adore parler. Elle est bavarde° comme …

une poule

une pie

un lion

3 Isabelle est une excellente élève. Elle a une mémoire extraordinaire. Elle a une mémoire de (d') …

éléphant

hippopotame

kangourou

4 Le petit frère de Christine est jeune, mais il est très intelligent. Il est malin° comme …

un cheval

un singe

une girafe

5 Où est Jacques? Il n'est pas prêt!° Oh là là! Il est lent° comme …

une tortue

un poisson

un rhinocéros

6 Nicole a très, très faim. Elle a une faim de (d') …

lion

ours

loup

Selon *According to* **défauts** *shortcomings* **comme** *like* **Devine** *Guess* **on** *one* **phrases suivantes** *following sentences* **dormir** *to sleep* **paresseux** *lazy* **comme** *as* **bavarde** *talkative* **malin** *clever* **prêt** *ready* **lent** *slow*

Voici les réponses:
1. *un lézard* 2. *une pie* 3. *éléphant* 4. *un singe* 5. *une tortue* 6. *loup*

Teaching note

Comptines are simple poems that are similar to nursery rhymes. You can find them on the Internet or at a library or bookstore that carries children's books in French. Once you have some *comptines,* you can have your students memorize and recite them in small groups.

CLASSROOM MANAGEMENT GAME Pair Reading

Be sure all students cover the answers at the bottom of the page. (If you prefer, you can make a transparency of the questions and project it on the overhead.)

Divide the class into pairs. How many groups can complete the six expressions correctly?

Le scooter, c'est génial!

Objectives

- Rapid reading at the sentence level
- Reading for cultural information about personal possessions and attitudes of French people

Teaching Resource Options

PRINT  

Workbook PE, pp. 113–116
Activités pour tous PE, pp. 67–69
Unit 4 Resource Book
Activités pour tous TE, pp. 161–163
Videoscript, p. 65
Workbook TE, pp. 165–168

VIDEO PROGRAM

VIDÉO DVD

MODULE 10

10.5 Vignette culturelle: La mobylette
(39:43–41:03 min.)

Language note

Whereas one can say **à moto** or **en moto, à vélo** or **en vélo**, the only correct preposition with **scooter** is **en** – because one's legs are inside the structure of the scooter, and do not straddle it the way one straddles a motorcycle.

Compréhension

Answers
1 vrai
2 faux
3 vrai
4 faux
5 vrai

Et vous?

Answers will vary.
1 Advantages: Wouldn't have to walk or ride a bike; faster; fun. Disadvantages: It's expensive to buy gas. It can be dangerous
2 I would ride to school instead of walking or taking the bus.

Le scooter, c'est génial!

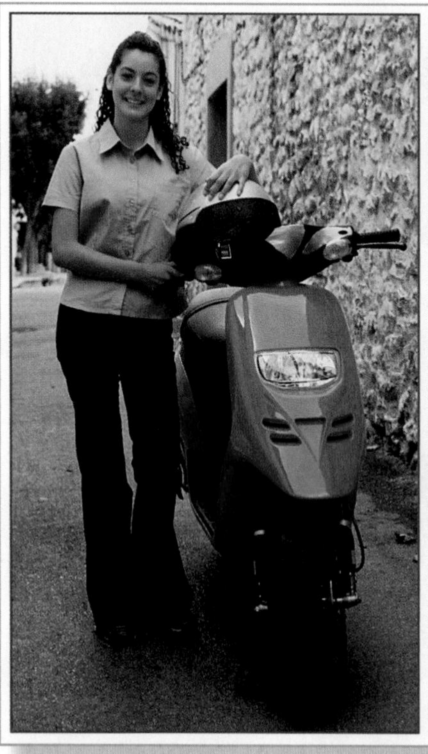

Je m'appelle Mélanie et j'ai 15 ans. J'ai un scooter. C'est un cadeau° d'anniversaire de ma grand-mère. Il est rouge et il est très confortable.

Ma copine Élodie a une mobylette. C'est une MBK. Nous allons° au collège ensemble.° Nous avons le BSR et nous sommes prudentes.° Nous portons° un casque° et nous respectons la limite de vitesse:° 45 kilomètres l'heure.

Le week-end, nous allons au centre-ville. Nous n'avons pas de problème de stationnement.° Quand il fait beau, nous allons à la campagne.° Quand nous sommes sur nos° petites machines, nous avons l'impression de liberté. Le scooter, c'est génial!

cadeau *gift* **allons** *go* **ensemble** *together* **prudentes** *careful* **portons** *wear* **casque** *helmet* **vitesse** *speed* **stationnement** *parking* **campagne** *country* **nos** *our*

Compréhension: vrai ou faux

1. Mélanie a un scooter.
2. Élodie a un scooter aussi.
3. Quand Mélanie est en scooter, elle porte un casque.
4. Avec un scooter, on a souvent un problème de stationnement.
5. En scooter, Mélanie a l'impression de liberté.

Et vous?

1. What are the advantages or disadvantages of owning a moped or a scooter?
2. What would you do if you had a motor scooter? How would this change your habits?

CONNEXIONS

Go to the Internet site of a French manufacturer of mopeds and scooters and make a poster showing some of the products you find.

PRE-READING

Ask students what kinds of two-wheelers they have.
Qui a un vélo?
Qui a un VTT (vélo tout terrain: *mountain bike*)?
Qui a une mobylette?

Mobylette . . . ou scooter?

Modèle: MBK Club
Couleurs: noir, gris, bleu
Prix: 680 €

Modèle: MBK Booster Spirit
Couleurs: rouge, bleu, noir
Prix: 1 600 €

Et vous?

1. Which of the above would you choose? Use the following in your response:
modèle *couleur* *prix en €* *prix en $*

2. Is it expensive? *(cher, chère)*

3. Why did you choose it?

NOTE culturelle

La mobylette et le scooter

Mopeds and motor scooters are very popular among French teenagers. To drive one, you must be at least 14 years old. If you are under 16, you cannot go over 45 kilometers (about 30 miles) per hour. You must also have a license known as the **BSR** or **Brevet de Sécurité Routière** *(Certificate of Highway Safety)* which you get after a short course of driver's education. And, of course, whenever you are riding, you must wear a helmet!

The most popular makes of mopeds and scooters include Peugeot, Renault, and MBK, all manufactured in France. The term **mobylette** was originally a brand name which French students shortened to **mob.** It now is used to refer to any type of moped.

French teens love their mopeds and their scooters, and they take great care of them. During the week, many students ride them to school. On weekends, they use them to go into town, to get to their sports clubs, or to go for a ride in the country with their friends.

Mobylette...ou scooter?

Objectives
- Reading for information

As an introduction, play the **Vignette culturelle** about the mobylette from Video Module 10.

Et vous?
Answers will vary.
1 Je voudrais avoir le MBK Booster Spirit. Il est bleu. Il coûte 1 600€ ($1 600).
2 Oui, il est assez cher.
3 Il est génial et il est rapide.

Bonjour, Brigitte!

Objectives

- Reading a complete text
- Building reading skills

Teaching Resource Options

PRINT

Workbook PE, pp. 113–116
Activités pour tous PE, pp. 67–69
Unit 4 Resource Book
Activités pour tous TE, pp. 161–163
Workbook PE, pp. 165–168

Questions sur le texte

1. Quel âge a Brigitte? (Elle a quatorze ans.)
2. Comment est-elle physiquement? (Elle est de taille moyenne. Elle est brune et elle a les yeux verts.)
3. Quels sports est-ce qu'elle aime? (Elle aime le ski, le jogging et la danse moderne.)
4. Où est-ce qu'elle habite? (Elle habite à Toulouse.)
5. Où travaille son père? Qu'est-ce qu'il fait? (Son père travaille dans l'industrie aéronautique. Il est ingénieur.)
6. Où travaille sa mère? Qu'est-ce qu'elle fait? (Sa mère travaille dans une banque. Elle est directrice du personnel.)
7. Comment s'appelle la soeur de Brigitte? Quel âge a-t-elle? Comment est-elle? (Elle s'appelle Élodie. Elle a cinq ans. Elle est très mignonne.)
8. Comment s'appelle le frère de Brigitte? Quel âge a-t-il? Comment est-il? (Il s'appelle Mathieu. Il a treize ans. Il est pénible.)
9. Est-ce que Brigitte a des animaux? (Elle a un chien, Attila. Elle a aussi deux poissons rouges.)
10. Quelles choses est-ce qu'elle a? (Elle a un baladeur et des CD. Elle a un ordinateur et une mob.)
11. Est-ce qu'elle a un petit copain? (Non, elle n'a pas de petit copain.)

Bonjour, Brigitte!

Chers° copains américains,

Je m'appelle Brigitte Lavie. J'ai quatorze ans. Voici ma photo. Je ne suis pas très grande, mais je ne suis pas petite. Je suis de taille° moyenne.° Je suis brune, mais j'ai les yeux verts. Je suis sportive. J'aime le ski, le jogging et la danse moderne.

J'habite à Toulouse avec ma famille. Mon père travaille dans l'industrie aéronautique. Il est ingénieur.° Ma mère travaille dans une banque. Elle est directrice° du personnel.

J'ai une soeur et un frère. Ma petite soeur s'appelle Élodie. Elle a cinq ans. Elle est très mignonne. Mon frère s'appelle Mathieu. Il a treize ans. Il est pénible. J'ai un chien. Il s'appelle Attila mais il est très gentil. (Il est plus gentil que° mon frère!) J'ai aussi deux poissons rouges.° Ils n'ont pas de nom.°

J'ai un baladeur et des quantités de CD. Je n'ai pas de mini-chaîne. J'ai un ordinateur. C'est un cadeau° de ma marraine.° Je surfe sur l'Internet et j'envoie des mails. Je n'ai pas de scooter mais j'ai une mob.

J'ai beaucoup de copains, mais je n'ai pas de «petit copain».° Ça n'a pas d'importance!° Je suis heureuse° comme ça.°

Amitiés,
Brigitte

Chers *Dear* **taille** *size* **moyenne** *average* **ingénieur** *engineer* **directrice** *director* **plus gentil que** *nicer than* **poissons rouges** *goldfish* **nom** *name* **cadeau** *gift* **marraine** *godmother* **petit copain** *boyfriend* **Ça n'a pas d'importance!** *It doesn't matter!* **heureuse** *happy* **comme ça** *like that*

TEACHING NOTE

Ask if students know in which American city NASA (National Aeronautic and Space Agency) is headquartered. [Houston]

Then ask if they know where the French space center is located. [Toulouse]

Tell them they will be reading a letter from Toulouse.

STRATEGY Reading

Guessing from context As you read French, try to guess the meanings of unfamiliar words before you look at the English equivalents. Often the context provides good hints. For example, Brigitte writes:

Je ne suis pas très grande, mais je ne suis pas petite.
Je suis de taille moyenne.

She is neither tall nor short. She must be about average:

de taille moyenne = *of medium height or size*

Sometimes you know what individual words in an expression mean, but the phrase does not seem to make sense. Then you have to guess at the real meaning. For example, Brigitte writes that she has:

deux poissons rouges *?? red fish??*

If you guessed that these are most likely *goldfish*, you are right!

Activité écrite: Une lettre à Brigitte

Write a letter to Brigitte in which you describe yourself and your family. You may tell her:

- your name and how old you are
- if you are tall or short
- if you like sports, and which ones
- if you have brothers and sisters (and if so, their names and ages)
- if you have pets (and if so, give their names)
- a few things you own
- a few things you like to do

Writing Hint Use Brigitte's letter as a model.

Pour écrire une lettre

To write to a boy, begin with:	**Cher**	**Cher Patrick,**
To write to a girl, begin with:	**Chère**	**Chère Brigitte,**
End your letter with:	**Amicalement,** *(In friendship,)*	
	Amitiés, *(Best regards,)*	

NOTE culturelle

Toulouse

Toulouse, with a population of nearly one million people, is the center of the French aeronautic and space industry. It is in Toulouse that the Airbus planes and the Ariane rockets are being built in cooperation with other European countries.

Questions personnelles

Answers will vary.

1. Quel âge as-tu? [J'ai (quinze) ans.]
2. Est-ce que tu es grand(e), petit(e) ou de taille moyenne? [Je suis (grand).]
3. Est-ce que tu as les yeux bleus ou marron *(brown)* ou noirs? [J'ai les yeux (bleus).]
4. Est-ce que tu as des frères ou des soeurs? [J'ai (une soeur).]
5. (Pour chaque frère ou chaque soeur): Comment est-ce qu'il/elle s'appelle? [Il/Elle s'appelle ...] Quel âge est-ce qu'il/elle a? Comment est-il/elle? [Il est (grand). / Elle est (petite).] [Il/Elle a ... ans.]
6. Est-ce que tu as un chien? un chat? un poisson rouge? Comment est-ce qu'il s'appelle? [J'ai (un chien). Il s'appelle (Spot).]
7. Est-ce que tu as un vélo? Est-ce que tu aimes faire des promenades à vélo? [Oui, j'ai un vélo. J'aime faire des promenades à vélo.]
8. Quels autres *(other)* objets est-ce que tu as? [J'ai (un baladeur et une guitare).]

POST-READING ACTIVITY

Maybe your class would like to exchange letters (or e-mail) with a French class in another school in your area. (The advantage of cross-city exchanges is that letters can be exchanged easily.)

Have your students each write letters introducing themselves.

Place these in a large envelope and exchange packets with a French teacher in another school. The first set of correspondence will be distributed randomly. From then on, however, students will have a specific pen pal to correspond with during the year.

Expansion activities PLANNING AHEAD

Games

• Les directions

Give each student a copy of a simple city map in French from the Internet, or use an overhead projector to project an image of a map for the students. Divide the class into two teams. Have Team A give directions from a designated starting point and have Team B identify where the directions lead. As an alternative, you may want to give students a copy of a map of your school and the area around it, and have one team give directions while the other identifies specific locations.

Pacing Suggestion: Upon completion of Leçon 13.

• Le jeu de la mémoire

Before class, create pairs of cards for the vocabulary on page 220: the first card will be the French vocabulary word, and the second card will be an illustration or an English translation of the word. Tape the cards on the blackboard in random order so they form a 5 x 5 card grid. Create a second set of note cards numbered 1–25. Tape a numbered card over each of the vocabulary cards, so the words and illustrations are not visible. Divide the class into two teams. Have a player from the first team call out two numbers. Lift the numbered cards to reveal the vocabulary cards underneath. If they match and the team uses the word correctly in a sentence, they receive a point. Those cards are then removed from the board. If they don't match, the cards are covered again, and the turn passes to the other team.

Pacing Suggestion: Upon completion of Leçon 15.

Projects

• Où est-ce?

Have students work in pairs to write a dialogue in which one student asks for directions and the other gives directions. (You may want to specify the length of the exchange.) Have students exchange and proofread each other's work. Finally, have students act out their dialogues for the class.

Pacing Suggestion: Upon completion of Leçon 13.

Bulletin Boards

• À Paris

Divide the class into several small groups. Assign different tourist attractions in Paris and have each group create a bulletin board with the following information:

- a map that shows where the attraction is located
- the days and hours when the attraction is open
- what there is to see and do there
- illustrations or photos to show what the attraction looks like
- street signs for famous streets in the vicinity of the attraction, such as the **Champs-Élysées**

Pacing Suggestion: Upon completion of Leçon 14.

• Ma famille

Have each student use a poster board to create a real or imagined family tree. Have students include a picture for each family member and a paragraph explaining their relationship to the student. Imaginary family members can be cut out of magazines. You may wish to provide students with additional vocabulary for extended families.

Pacing Suggestion: Upon completion of Leçon 16.

Music

• *Au clair de la lune*

You may wish to teach students the traditional French song *Au clair de la lune,* which includes some of the possessive adjectives presented in Leçon 16. You can find the lyrics and music on the Internet.

«Au clair de la lune,
Mon ami, Pierrot,
Prête-moi ta plume
Pour écrire un mot!
Ma chandelle est morte,
Je n'ai plus de feu;
Ouvre-moi ta porte,
Je suis très peureux!»

Pacing Suggestion: Upon completion of Leçon 16.

• *Les grands boulevards*

Play *Les grands boulevards* from the *Chansons* CD for students. Give students a copy of the lyrics and have them listen first to get the gist of the song. Play it a second time and have students list all the words they hear that they recognize. Have the class discuss the general meaning of the song. As an alternative, you may wish to have students listen for and underline forms of the possessive adjectives they hear in the song.

Pacing Suggestion: Upon completion of Leçon 16.

Storytelling

• Une mini-histoire

Distribute a copy of a map of a French town, or if unavailable, use the map of *Villeneuve* on page 202. Model a short story about where one character goes and what he or she does while in the town. Add details to your story like date, time, and what the weather is like. When you are finished, hand out copies of your story with blanks for students to fill in. Have students fill in the blanks individually, with details they recall from your version, and review the story as a group.

Pacing Suggestion: Upon completion of Leçon 14.

• Diabolo menthe

The *diabolo menthe* is a popular café beverage among French teenagers. The bright green drink is made using *limonade,* which is similar to a lemon-lime soda, and mint syrup. You may be able to find traditional French *limonade* at the grocery store. If necessary, substitute a sweetened lemon-lime–flavored soda. Variations on the *diabolo menthe* are made using different flavored syrups, such as strawberry, raspberry, and red or black currant.

Pacing Suggestion: Upon completion of Leçon 15.

Hands-on Crafts

• Les modèles

Allow students to choose a Parisian landmark (historical monument, cathedral, museum, or other well-known structure). Have students learn more about their landmark, through library or Internet research, and then construct a small model of it. Students may use whatever materials they deem appropriate to create their models. Once their reproductions are complete, have them add a brief paragraph about the landmark and a map showing where it is located. Have students present their models to the class. As a variation, you may expand the project to include landmarks from anywhere in the francophone world.

Pacing Suggestion: Upon completion of Leçon 14.

End of Unit

• Une maison

Students will create an audiovisual home tour. Students can use their own home, a friend's or a relative's home, or a home featured in a magazine. First, have students select three rooms they wish to present and write short paragraphs describing each room. Students should then proofread each other's work. Next, have students make audio recordings of their paragraphs and select appropriate photographs for them. Students may show slides, create a poster, or enlarge individual photographs to accompany their audio recordings. Finally, have students present their tours to the class. You may wish to give students the options of videotaping or creating computer audiovisuals of their presentations.

Rubric **A** = 13–15 pts. **B** = 10–12 pts. **C** = 7–9 pts. **D** = 4–6 pts. **F** = < 4 pts.

Criteria	Scale
Vocabulary Use	1 2 3 4 5
Grammar/Spelling Accuracy	1 2 3 4 5
Creativity	1 2 3 4 5

Diabolo menthe
Ingrédients
• 150 ml limonade
• 30 ml sirop de menthe
Préparation
1. Versez la limonade froide dans un verre.
2. Ajoutez le sirop de menthe et remuez.
Pour une personne.
Ingredients
• approx. 5 oz. of limonade (lemon-lime soda)
• approx. 1 oz. of mint syrup
Directions
1. Pour the chilled limonade into a glass.
2. Add the mint syrup and stir.
Serves one person.

Planning Guide CLASSROOM MANAGEMENT

OBJECTIVES

Communication
- Describe your city, its public buildings, and places of interest *pp. 196, 197*
- Ask and give directions *p. 199*
- Talk about the various places you go to during the week and on weekends *pp. 197, 210*
- Describe your house or apartment *p. 200*
- Discuss your future plans and say what you are going to do *p. 212*
- Talk about your friends and their families *p. 229*

Grammar
- Le verbe *aller* *p. 206*
- La préposition *à; à* + l'article défini *p. 208*
- La préposition *chez* *p. 211*
- La construction *aller* + l'infinitif *p. 212*
- Le verbe *venir* *p. 218*
- La préposition *de; de* + l'article défini *p. 219*
- Les pronoms accentués *p. 221*
- La construction: nom + *de* + nom *p. 223*
- La possession avec *de* *p. 228*
- Les adjectifs possessifs: *mon, ton, son* *p. 230*
- Les adjectifs possessifs: *notre, votre, leur* *p. 232*
- Les nombres ordinaux *p. 233*

Vocabulary
- Où habites-tu? *p. 196*
- Ma ville *p. 197*
- Pour demander un renseignement *p. 199*
- Ma maison *p. 200*
- En ville *p. 210*
- Les sports, les jeux et la musique *p. 220*
- Expressions pour la conversation *pp. 222, 231*
- La famille *p. 229*

Pronunciation
- Les semi-voyelles /w/ et /j/ *p. 213*
- Les voyelles /ø/ et /œ/ *p. 223*
- Les voyelles /o/ et /ɔ/ *p. 233*

Culture
- Le nom des rues *p. 196*
- À Paris *p. 205*
- Au café *p. 217*
- Les animaux domestiques en France *p. 227*

PROGRAM RESOURCES

Print

- Workbook PE, *pp. 117–148*
- *Activités pour tous* PE, *pp. 71–89*
- Block Scheduling Copymasters, *pp. 97–128*
- *Français pour hispanophones*
- *Lectures pour tous*
- Teacher to Teacher Copymasters
- Teaching Proficiency through Reading and Storytelling
- Unit 5 Resource Book
  - Lessons 13–16 Resources
    - Workbook TE
    - *Activités pour tous* TE
    - Family Letter
    - Absent Student Copymasters
    - Family Involvement
    - Video Activities
    - Videoscripts
    - Audioscripts
    - Assessment Program
  - Unit 5 Resources
    - Communipak
    - *Activités pour tous* TE Reading
    - Workbook TE Reading and Culture Activities
    - Assessment Program
    - Answer Keys

Audiovisual

- Audio Program PE CD 3 Tracks 1–19
- Audio Program Workbook CD 9 Tracks 1–32
- *Chansons* Audio CD
- Sing Along: Grammar and Vocabulary Songs CD
- Video Program Modules 13, 14, 15, 16, *Images À Paris*
- Warm-Up Transparencies
- Overhead Transparencies
  30a, 30b *Ma ville*;
  31 *La maison*;
  32 Map of Villeneuve;
  33 Means of transportation;
  16 Subject pronouns;
  34 Apartment building;
  8 Family tree

Technology

- Online Workbook
- ClassZone.com
- McDougal Littell Assessment System/ Test Generator CD-ROM
- EasyPlanner CD-ROM
- Power Presentations on CD-ROM
- Take-Home Tutor CD-ROM

Assessment Program Options

Lesson Quizzes
Portfolio Assessment
Unit Test Form A
Unit Test Form B
Unit Test Part III (Alternate) Cultural Awareness
Listening Comprehension Performance Test
Speaking Performance Test
Reading Comprehension Performance Test
Writing Performance Test
Multiple Choice Test Items
Test Scoring Tools
Audio Program CD 15 Tracks 1–8
Answer Keys
McDougal Littell Assessment System/ Test Generator CD-ROM

Pacing Guide SAMPLE LESSON PLAN

DAY	DAY	DAY	DAY	DAY
1 Unité 5 Opener Leçon 13 • Vocabulaire et Culture–La ville et la maison • Vocabulaire et Culture–Ici à Tours • Vocabulaire–Où habites-tu?	**2** Leçon 13 • Note culturelle–Le nom des rues • Vocabulaire–Ma ville	**3** Leçon 13 • Vocabulaire–Pour demander un renseignement • Vocabulaire–Ma maison	**4** Leçon 13 • À votre tour!	**5** Leçon 14 • Conversation et Culture–Week-end à Paris • Note culturelle–À Paris • Le verbe *aller*
6 Leçon 14 • La préposition *à;* *à* + l'article défini	**7** Leçon 14 • Vocabulaire–En ville • La préposition *chez*	**8** Leçon 14 • La construction *aller* + l'infinitif • Prononciation–Les semi-voyelles /w/ et /j/	**9** Leçon 14 • À votre tour!	**10** Leçon 15 • Conversation et Culture–Au Café de l'Univers • Note culturelle–Au café
11 Leçon 15 • Le verbe *venir* • La préposition *de;* *de* + l'article défini	**12** Leçon 15 • Vocabulaire–Les sports, les jeux et la musique • Les pronoms accentués	**13** Leçon 15 • Vocabulaire–Expressions pour la conversation • La construction: nom + *de* + nom • Prononciation–Les voyelles /ø/ et /œ/	**14** Leçon 15 • À votre tour!	**15** Leçon 16 • Conversation et Culture–Mes voisins • Note culturelle–Les animaux domestiques en France • La possession avec *de*
16 Leçon 16 • La possession avec *de* *(continued)* • Vocabulaire–La famille • Les adjectifs possessifs: *mon, ton, son*	**17** Leçon 16 • Les adjectifs possessifs: *mon, ton, son (continued)* • Vocabulaire–Expressions pour la conversation • Les adjectifs possessifs: *notre, votre, leur*	**18** Leçon 16 • Les adjectifs possessifs: *notre, votre, leur (continued)* • Les nombres ordinaux • Prononciation–Les voyelles /o/ et /ɔ/	**19** Leçon 16 • À votre tour!	**20** • Tests de contrôle
21 • Unit 5 Test	**22** • Entracte–Lecture et culture			

Student Text Listening Activity Scripts
AUDIO PROGRAM

▶ LEÇON 13 LE FRANÇAIS PRATIQUE La ville et la maison

À votre tour!

• Écoutez bien! *p. 202* CD 3, TRACK 1

Look at the map of Villeneuve. You will hear where certain people are. If they are somewhere on the left side of the map, mark A. If they are on the right side of the map, mark B.

Listen carefully. Do not worry if you do not understand every word. Pay attention to the place name that is mentioned. You will hear each sentence twice. Let's begin.

1. Isabelle joue au foot au stade municipal. #
2. Catherine passe à la bibliothèque pour prendre des livres. #
3. Mon petit frère joue dans le parc de la ville. #
4. Ma mère travaille à l'hôpital Sainte-Anne. #
5. Julie et Thomas voient un film au Ciné-Rex.
6. Nous sommes au musée pour l'exposition d'art moderne. #
7. Qu'est-ce que vous faites au supermarché? #
8. Ma soeur travaille dans un magasin de sport. #

• Créa-dialogue *p. 203* CD 3, TRACK 2

Listen to some sample *Créa-dialogues.* Écoutez les conversations.

Modèle: –Pardon, monsieur. Où est-ce qu'il y a un hôtel?
–Il y a un hôtel avenue de Bordeaux.
–Est-ce que c'est loin?
–Non, c'est près.
–Merci beaucoup!

Maintenant, écoutez le dialogue numéro 1.

–Pardon, madame. Où est-ce qu'il y a un café?
–Il y a un café avenue de Bordeaux.
–Est-ce que c'est loin?
–Non, c'est près.
–Merci beaucoup!

• Où est-ce? *p. 203* CD 3, TRACK 3

Listen to the conversation with the tourist. Écoutez la conversation avec le touriste.

Modèle: –Pardon, monsieur. Où est l'hôpital Sainte-Anne?
–C'est tout droit, mademoiselle.
–Merci bien, monsieur.

Voici une autre conversation:

–Pardon, mademoiselle. Où est le musée La Salle?
–Tournez à gauche, rue Danton, monsieur.

▶ LEÇON 14 Week-end à Paris

• Week-end à Paris *p. 204*

A. Compréhension orale CD 3, TRACK 4

Aujourd'hui c'est samedi. Les élèves ne vont pas en classe. Où est-ce qu'ils vont alors? Ça dépend!

Thomas va au café. Il a un rendez-vous avec une copine.

Florence et Karine vont aux Champs-Élysées. Elles vont regarder les vêtements dans les magasins. Après, elles vont aller au cinéma.

Daniel va chez son copain Laurent. Les garçons vont jouer aux jeux vidéo. Après, ils vont aller au musée des sciences de la Villette. Ils vont jouer avec les machines électroniques.

Béatrice a un grand sac et des lunettes de soleil. Est-ce qu'elle va à un rendez-vous secret? Non! Elle va au Centre Pompidou. Elle va regarder les acrobates. Et après, elle va aller à un concert.

Et Jean-François? Qu'est-ce qu'il va faire aujourd'hui? Est-ce qu'il va visiter le Centre Pompidou? Est-ce qu'il va regarder les acrobates? Est-ce qu'il va aller à un concert? Hélas, non! Il va rester à la maison. Pourquoi? Parce qu'il est malade. Pauvre Jean-François! Il fait si beau dehors!

B. Écoutez et répétez. CD 3, TRACK 5

You will now hear a paused version of the dialog. Listen to the speaker and repeat right after he or she has completed the sentence.

• Prononciation *p. 213* CD 3, TRACK 6

Les semi-voyelles /w/ **et** /j/

Écoutez: oui très bien

In French, the semi-vowels /w/ and /j/ are pronounced very quickly, almost like consonants.

Répétez: /w/ # oui # chouette # Louise #
/wa/, /wɛ̃/ # moi # toi # pourquoi # voiture # loin #
Chouette! La voiture de Louise n'est pas loin. #
/j/ # bien # chien # radio # piano # Pierre # Daniel # violon # pied # étudiant #
Pierre écoute la radio avec Daniel. #

À votre tour!

• Allô! *p. 214* CD 3, TRACK 7

Listen to the phone conversation. Écoutez la conversation entre Anne et Jérôme.

Anne: Tu restes chez toi samedi?
Jérôme: Non, j'ai un rendez-vous avec Christine.
Anne: Qu'est-ce que vous allez faire?
Jérôme: Nous allons faire une promenade en ville.
Anne: Est-ce que vous allez aller au cinéma?
Jérôme: Peut-être! Il y a un très bon film au Rex.
Anne: À quelle heure est-ce que tu vas rentrer?
Jérôme: À dix heures.

• Créa-dialogue *p. 214* CD 3, TRACK 8

Listen to some sample *Créa-dialogues.* Écoutez les conversations.

Modèle: –Salut, Alison. Ça va?
–Oui, ça va!
–Où vas-tu?
–Je vais au restaurant.
–Ah bon? Qu'est-ce que tu vas faire là-bas?
–Je vais dîner avec un copain.
–Avec qui?
–Avec Chris.

Maintenant, écoutez le dialogue numéro 1.

–Salut, Tom.
–Ça va?
–Oui, ça va!
–Où vas-tu?
–Je vais au café.
–Ah bon? Qu'est-ce que tu vas faire là-bas?
–Je vais manger une pizza.
–Avec qui?
–Avec Sally.

▶ LEÇON 15 Au Café de l'Univers

• Au Café de l'Univers *p. 216*

A. Compréhension orale CD 3, TRACK 9

Où vas-tu après les cours? Est-ce que tu vas directement chez toi? Valérie, elle, ne va pas directement chez elle. Elle va au Café de l'Univers avec ses copines Fatima et Zaïna. Elle vient souvent ici avec elles.

À la table de Valérie, la conversation est toujours très animée. De quoi parlent les filles aujourd'hui?

Est-ce qu'elles parlent de l'examen d'histoire? du problème de maths? de la classe de sciences?

pause for oral response

Non!

Est-ce qu'elles parlent du week-end prochain? des vacances?

Non plus!

Est-ce qu'elles parlent du nouveau copain de Marie-Claire? de la cousine de Pauline? des amis de Véronique?

Pas du tout!

Aujourd'hui, les filles parlent d'un sujet beaucoup plus important! Elles parlent du nouveau prof d'anglais! (C'est un jeune professeur américain. Il est très intéressant, très amusant, très sympathique . . . et surtout il est très mignon!)

B. Écoutez et répétez. CD 3, TRACK 10

You will now hear a paused version of the dialog. Listen to the speaker and repeat right after he or she has completed the sentence.

• Prononciation *p. 223* CD 3, TRACK 11

Les voyelles /ø/ **et** /œ/

Écoutez: deux neuf

The letters "**eu**" and "**oeu**" represent vowel sounds that do not exist in English but that are not very hard to pronounce.

Répétez: /ø/ # deux # eux # je veux # un peu # jeux #
il pleut # un euro #
Tu peux aller chez eux. #
/œ/ # neuf # soeur # heure # professeur # jeune #
Ma soeur arrive à neuf heures. #

À votre tour!

• Conversation *p. 224* CD 3, TRACK 12

Listen to the conversation. Écoutez la conversation entre Henri et Stéphanie.

Henri: Salut, Stéphanie! D'où viens-tu?
Stéphanie: Du supermarché.
Henri: Et où vas-tu maintenant?
Stéphanie: Je rentre chez moi.
Henri: Tu ne veux pas venir au cinéma avec moi?
Stéphanie: Je ne peux pas. Je dois étudier.
Henri: Ah bon? Pourquoi?
Stéphanie: J'ai un examen d'anglais lundi.

• Créa-dialogue *p. 224* CD 3, TRACK 13

Listen to the sample *Créa-dialogues.* Écoutez les conversations.

Modèle: –Où vas-tu?
–Je vais chez Jean-Claude. Tu viens?
–Ça dépend! Qu'est-ce que tu vas faire chez lui?
–Nous allons jouer au ping-pong.
–D'accord, je viens!

Maintenant, écoutez le dialogue numéro 1.

–Où vas-tu?
–Je vais chez Françoise. Tu viens?
–Ça dépend! Qu'est-ce que tu vas faire chez elle?
–Nous allons regarder la télé.
–D'accord, je viens!

▶ LEÇON 16 Mes voisins

• Mes voisins *p. 226*

A. Compréhension orale CD 3, TRACK 14

Bonjour! Je m'appelle Frédéric Mallet. J'habite à Paris avec ma famille. Nous habitons dans un immeuble de six étages. Voici mon immeuble et voici mes voisins.

Monsieur Lacroche habite au sixième étage avec sa femme. Ils sont musiciens. Lui, il joue du piano et elle, elle chante. Oh là là, quelle musique!

Mademoiselle Jolivet habite au cinquième étage avec son oncle et sa tante. Paul, mon meilleur ami, habite au quatrième étage avec sa soeur et ses parents.

Mademoiselle Ménard habite au troisième étage avec son chien Pomme, ses deux chats Fritz et Arthur, son perroquet Coco et son canari Froufrou. (Je pense que c'est une personne très intéressante, mais mon père pense qu'elle est un peu bizarre.)

Monsieur et Madame Boutin habitent au deuxième étage avec leur fils et leurs deux filles.

Et qui habite au premier étage? C'est un garçon super-intelligent, super-cool et très sympathique! Et ce garçon . . . c'est moi!

B. Écoutez et répétez. CD 3, TRACK 15

You will now hear a paused version of the dialog. Listen to the speaker and repeat right after he or she has completed the sentence.

• Vocabulaire *p. 229* CD 3, TRACK 16

La famille

Écoutez et répétez. Repeat the names of the family members after the speaker.

la famille #

les grands-parents #	le grand-père # la grand-mère #
les parents #	le père # la mère # le mari # la femme
les enfants #	un enfant # une enfant # le frère # la soeur # le fils # la fille #
les parents #	l'oncle # la tante # le cousin # la cousine

• Prononciation *p. 233* CD 3, TRACK 17

Les voyelles /o/ **et** /ɔ/

Écoutez: vélo téléphone

The French vowel /o/ is pronounced with more tension than in English. It is usually the last sound in a word.

Répétez: /o/ # vélo # radio # nos # vos # eau # château # chaud #
Nos vélos sont au château. #

The French vowel /ɔ/ occurs in the middle of a word. Imitate the model carefully.

Répétez: /ɔ/ # téléphone # école # Nicole # notre # votre # copain #
prof # dommage #
Comment s'appelle votre prof? #

À votre tour!

• Allô! *p. 234* CD 3, TRACK 18

Listen to the phone conversation. Écoutez la conversation entre Émilie et Bernard.

Émilie: Avec qui est-ce que tu vas au cinéma?
Bernard: Avec mon copain Marc.
Émilie: C'est le cousin de Monique?
Bernard: Non, c'est son frère.
Émilie: Tu connais leurs parents?
Bernard: Bien sûr, ils sont très sympathiques.
Émilie: Ils sont canadiens, n'est-ce pas?
Bernard: Non, mais leurs voisins sont de Québec.

• Créa-dialogue *p. 234* CD 3, TRACK 19

Listen to some sample *Créa-dialogues.* Écoutez les conversations.

Modèle: –C'est le vélo de Paul?
–Non, ce n'est pas son vélo.
–Tu es sûr?
–Mais oui. Son vélo est bleu.

Maintenant, écoutez le dialogue numéro 1.

–C'est la guitare d'Alice?
–Non, ce n'est pas sa guitare.
–Tu es sûr?
–Mais oui. Sa guitare est brune.

Complete videoscripts, plus Workbook and Assessment audioscripts, are available in the Unit Resource Books.

Main Theme
- City Life

COMMUNICATION
- Describing a city, public buildings, and places of interest
- Asking for and giving directions
- Talking about the places you go
- Describing a house or apartment
- Discussing future plans and saying what you're going to do
- Talking about friends and their families

CULTURES
- Learning about French cities in general
- Learning about Tours
- Learning about Paris and its monuments
- Learning about street names
- Learning about cafés
- Learning about pets in France
- Learning about French movie-going habits
- Learning about *Tintin*
- Learning about Belgium
- Learning about francophone music

CONNECTIONS
- Connecting to Geography: Reading and creating maps
- Connecting to English: Making language comparisons between French and English
- Connecting to Math: Using ordinal numbers
- Connecting to Music: Creating a project on franchophone music

continued on next page

UNITÉ 5

En ville

THÈME ET OBJECTIFS

Visiting a French city

There are many things to do in a city: places to visit, concerts to attend, sports to play.

In this unit, you will learn ...

- to describe your city, its public buildings, and places of interest
- to ask for and give directions
- to talk about the various places you go to during the week and on weekends
- to describe your house or apartment

You will also be able ...

- to discuss your future plans and say what you are going to do
- to talk about your friends and their families

192 cent quatre-vingt-douze
Unité 5

UNIT OVERVIEW

- **Communication Goals:** Students will be able to ask and give directions, and to describe their city and their home. They will also learn to talk about future plans.
- **Linguistic Goals:** Students will learn to use the verbs **aller** and **venir,** and the possessive adjectives.
- **Critical Thinking Goals:** Students will observe both linguistic similarities (use of **aller** to express future time) and differences (use of possessive adjectives) between French and English.
- **Cultural Goals:** This unit introduces students to two French cities: Paris (in the student text) and Tours (in the video).

STANDARDS *continued*

COMPARISONS
- Comparing houses in France and the U.S.
- Comparing building floors in France and the U.S.
- Comparing movie-going preferences of teens in France and the U.S.
- Learning about the influence of American movies on the French

COMMUNITIES
- Using French to prepare a map for French-speaking visitors to your city
- Using French to host a *fête Tintin* at your school
- Using francophone music to entertain other classes or local senior citizens
- Listening to French music, like MC Solaar, for personal enrichment

Teaching Resource Options

PRINT 

Unit 5 Resource Book
  Family Letter, p. 14
Français pour hispanophones
  Conseils, pp. 13–14
  Vocabulaire, pp. 46–47

AUDIO & VISUAL 

Audio Program
Chansons CD

TECHNOLOGY 

EasyPlanner CD-ROM

PHOTO CULTURAL NOTE

The teens are at **La Place des Vosges** in Paris. The buildings of stone and faux brick were home to many famous people, such as Richelieu and Victor Hugo.

People can visit the museum at **Maison de Victor Hugo** 6, place des Vosges, where he lived from 1832–1848.

Leçon 13

Main Topic Getting around in a French city

Teaching Resource Options

PRINT 

Workbook PE, pp. 117–121
Activités pour tous PE, pp. 71–73
Block Scheduling Copymasters, pp. 97–104
Unit 5 Resource Book
- *Activités pour tous* TE PE, pp. 7–9
- Audioscript, pp. 30–31
- Communipak, pp. 140–163
- Lesson Plans, pp. 10–11
- Block Scheduling Lesson Plans, pp. 12–13
- Absent Student Copymasters, pp. 15–18
- Video Activities, pp. 21–26
- Videoscript, pp. 27–28
- Workbook TE, pp. 1–5

AUDIO & VISUAL 

Audio Program
CD 9 Tracks 1–7

TECHNOLOGY 

Online Workbook

VIDEO PROGRAM

VIDÉO DVD

MODULE 13
Le français pratique
La ville et la maison

TOTAL TIME: 7:02 min.
DVD Disk 2
Videotape 3 (COUNTER: 00:00 min.)

13.1 Introduction: Listening
– Les villes de France
(0:10–1:09 min.)

13.2 Dialogue: La ville de Tours
(1:10–4:06 min.)

13.3 Mini-scenes: Speaking
– Qu'est-ce que c'est?
(4:07–5:10 min.)

13.4 Mini-scenes: Listening
– Pardon! Excusez-moi!
(5:11–6:02 min.)

13.5 Vignette culturelle: La maison d'Olivier
(6:03–7:02 min.)

LEÇON 13

LE FRANÇAIS PRATIQUE
VIDÉO DVD AUDIO

La ville et la maison

Accent sur ... les villes françaises

- Today 80% of the French population lives in cities and their surrounding suburbs.
- French cities have a long history. Paris, Lyon, Marseille, and Nice were founded well over two thousand years ago!
- Cities in France differ in urban design from cities in the United States.
  - –The downtown area **(le centre-ville)** is the historical district with buildings and monuments dating back several centuries. Usually no buildings are taller than six stories. With the many cafés, restaurants, stores, and movie houses, it is a very animated area that attracts many young people.
  - –The suburbs **(la banlieue)** is where the tall apartment buildings and office buildings are located. Young people who live in the Parisian suburbs often get together in the local shopping mall **(le centre commercial)** which offers shops, cafés, and cinemas.

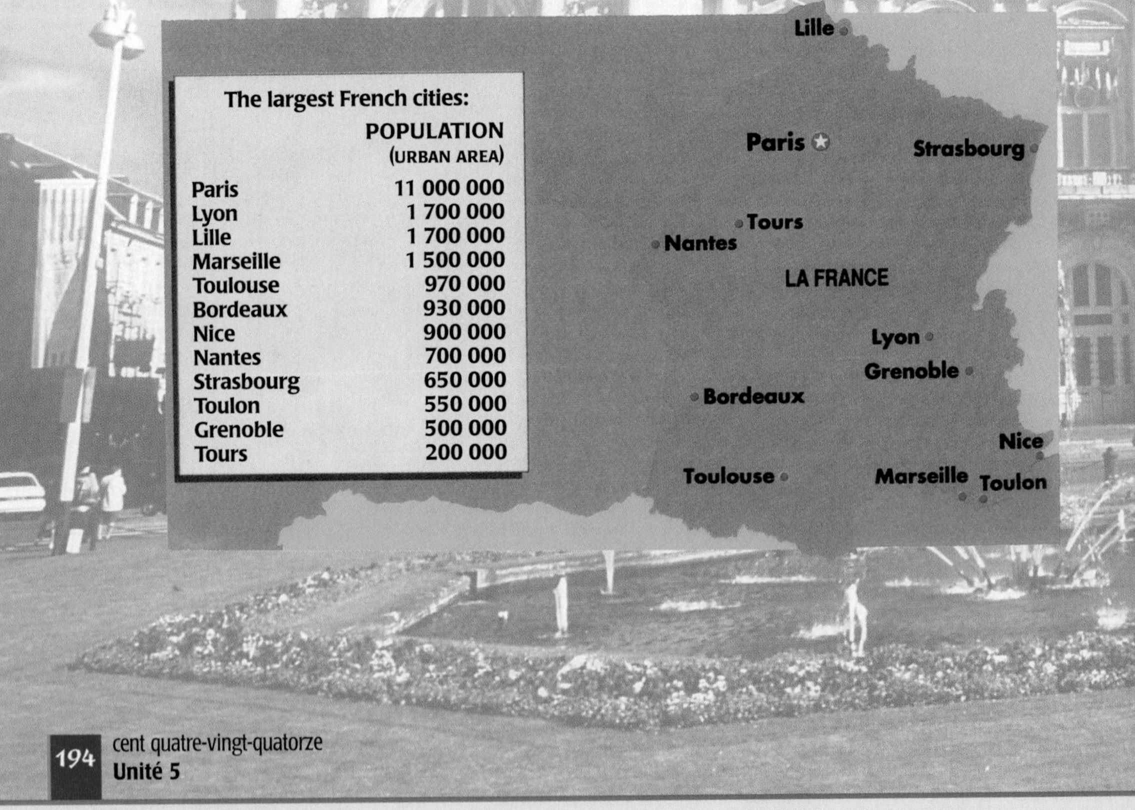

The largest French cities:

	POPULATION (URBAN AREA)
Paris	11 000 000
Lyon	1 700 000
Lille	1 700 000
Marseille	1 500 000
Toulouse	970 000
Bordeaux	930 000
Nice	900 000
Nantes	700 000
Strasbourg	650 000
Toulon	550 000
Grenoble	500 000
Tours	200 000

SETTING THE SCENE

PROPS: Worksheets with a map of France and 11 dots representing the above cities. Names of the 11 cities are listed at bottom.

Have students keep their books closed. Divide the class into teams of 4 or 5. Have the teams try to locate the cities on the map.

Have the teams open their books to correct their maps.

- How many cities did they find correctly?
- Have they heard about any of these cities?

Tell students that in the video they will visit the city of Tours, in the Loire valley.

Ici, à Tours

Tours est une ville de 200 000 (deux cent mille) habitants située à 200 kilomètres au sud-ouest de Paris. C'est une ville française typique.

L'Hôtel de Ville

Au centre, il y a l'hôtel de ville qui est le bâtiment administratif principal. C'est ici que les gens viennent se marier.

bâtiment: building; viennent: come; se marier: to get married

La place Plumereau

La place Plumereau est située dans un quartier très ancien. Il y a beaucoup de maisons historiques, et aussi beaucoup de cafés où viennent les jeunes de Tours. C'est un endroit très animé.

quartier: district; endroit: place

Le Château de Tours

Comme beaucoup de villes françaises, Tours a un château historique. Ce château est une ancienne forteresse royale. Aujourd'hui, c'est un bâtiment administratif.

ancienne: former

Une maison près de Tours

Les Français qui n'habitent pas dans le centre-ville préfèrent habiter dans une maison individuelle. Cette maison de la région de Tours a deux étages.

étages: floors

Comprehension practice Play the entire module through as an introduction to the lesson.

Cultural note Marseille was founded by the Phoenicians in 600 B.C. Paris and Lyon were founded by the Romans at the time of Julius Caesar around 43 B.C.

Photo culture note

- L'Hôtel de Ville is located at Place Jean-Jaurès.

TALKING ABOUT PAST EVENTS

Let's talk about what time you did certain things. (Review times, if needed.)

▶ **À quelle heure est-ce que tu as dîné hier?**
J'ai dîné à sept heures et quart.

- **X, à quelle heure est-ce que tu as étudié?**
- **À quelle heure est-ce que tu as téléphoné à des amis?**
- **Y et Z, à quelle heure est-ce que vous avez dîné samedi soir?**
- **À quelle heure est-ce que vous avez regardé la télé?**

SECTION A

Communicative function
Talking about where one lives

Teaching Resource Options

PRINT 

Workbook PE, pp. 117–121
Unit 5 Resource Book
Communipak, pp. 140–163
Video Activities, p. 23
Videoscript, pp. 27–28
Workbook TE, pp. 1–5

AUDIO & VISUAL

Overhead Transparencies
30a, 30b *Ma ville*

VIDEO PROGRAM

VIDÉO DVD

MODULE 13

13.3 Mini-scenes: Qu'est-ce que c'est? (4:07–5:10 min.)

Vocabulary note Point out that **adresse** is feminine.

Supplementary vocabulary
au centre-ville *downtown*
dans la banlieue *in the suburbs*
à la campagne *in the country*
dans un immeuble *in an apartment house*

1 COMMUNICATION describing where you live

Answers will vary.
1. J'habite à (Boston).
2. Ma ville est (grande).
(Ma ville [n'est pas moderne].)
Mon village est (joli).
(Mon village [n'est pas grand].)
3. Mon quartier est (moderne).
(Mon quartier n'est pas [joli].)
4. Mon adresse est (150 Willow Avenue).
5. Ma ville favorite est (Chicago).
6. Un jour, je voudrais visiter (Paris).

Language note In item 4, help students with numbers.
In France, P.O. Box = **B.P. (Boîte postale).**
In Canada, P.O. Box = **C.P. (Case postale).**

A VOCABULAIRE Où habites-tu?

How to talk about where one lives:

Où habites-tu?
J'habite | à Tours.
à Villeneuve
dans **une grande ville** *(city, town)*
dans **un petit village**
dans **un joli quartier** *(neighborhood)*
dans **une rue** *(street)* intéressante

Quelle est **ton adresse?**
J'habite | 32, **avenue** Victor Hugo.
14, **rue** La Fayette
50, **boulevard** Wilson

NOTE culturelle

Le nom des rues

En France, les rues ont très souvent le nom de personnes célèbres,° en particulier écrivains,° artistes et personnalités politiques.

- **Victor Hugo** (1802-1885) est un très grand poète. Il a aussi écrit° *Les Misérables* qui° a inspiré une comédie musicale moderne.
- **La Fayette** (1757-1834) est un aristocrate français. Ami de Georges Washington, il a joué un rôle important pendant la Révolution américaine.

célèbres *famous* **écrivains** *writers* **a écrit** *wrote* **qui** *which*

1 Expression personnelle

PARLER/ÉCRIRE Describe where you live by completing the following sentences.

1. J'habite à ...
2. Ma ville est (n'est pas) ...
(grande? petite? moderne? jolie?)
Mon village est (n'est pas) ...
(grand? petit? joli?)
3. Mon quartier est (n'est pas) ...
(intéressant? joli? moderne?)
4. Mon adresse est ...
5. Ma ville favorite est ...
6. Un jour, je voudrais visiter ... *(name of city)*

2 Interview

PARLER/ÉCRIRE You are a French journalist writing an article about living conditions in the United States. Interview a classmate and find out the following information.

1. Where does he/she live?
2. Is his/her city large or small?
3. Is his/her city pretty?
4. What is his/her address?

COMPREHENSION Places

PROPS: Vocabulary cards of the places on p. 197: blue borders on masculine nouns, red borders on feminine nouns.

Model nouns as you place them on chalktray.
Voici un théâtre. Voici une église. ...

Hold up a picture. [museum card]
Est-ce un café? [non]
Est-ce un musée? [oui]

Ask students to pass cards to classmates.
X, prends le parc et donne-le à Y. ...
Qui a le parc? [Y] ...

Have all students with cards hold them up.
Montrez-nous vos cartes.

B VOCABULAIRE Ma ville

▶ *How to talk about one's hometown:*

Note two cards on either side of the room.
Qui a l'hôtel? [X] **Qui a la piscine?** [Z]
Oh là là! L'hôtel est loin de la piscine! [gesture distance]

Note two cards that are close together.
Où est le stade? Où est le parc?
Est-ce que le stade est loin du parc? [non]
Non, le stade est près du parc. ...

If time allows, have students pass around the cards. For example, have X give the hotel card to a student who is near Z.
X, lève-toi et donne l'hôtel à Y.
Et maintenant, est-ce que l'hôtel est loin de la piscine? [non]
L'hôtel est près de la piscine.

Photo cultural note

Le "Vieux Tours" In the background you see the **Place Plumereau** with its houses dating back to the 16th and 17th centuries. The exposed wooden beams and the steep slate roofs are typical of the period. Since its renovation in the 1960s, this area of Tours with its cafés and outdoor concerts has become very popular with young people.

2 ROLE PLAY asking where people live

Answers will vary.
1. Elle habite à Cambridge.
2. Sa ville n'est pas grande.
3. Sa ville est jolie.
4. Son adresse est 1020 Massachusetts Avenue.

Expansion Ask students questions about the person they were interviewing.
X, où est-ce que Y habite?

SECTION B

Communicative function
Identifying places in one's hometown

Supplementary vocabulary

un aéroport *airport*
un collège *junior high school*
un fast-food *fast-food restaurant*
un lycée *senior high school*
un terrain de sport *athletic field*
une banque *bank*
une boutique *shop*
un centre sportif *sport center*
une gare *(train) station*
une grande surface *combination giant supermarket/discount store*
un hypermarché *giant supermarket*
un jardin public *public garden*
une mairie *city hall*
une Maison des jeunes *youth center*
une pharmacie *drugstore*
la poste *post office*
une station-service *gas station*
une université *university*
une mosquée *mosque*
un temple *Protestant church*
une synagogue *Jewish temple or synagogue*

Teaching Resource Options

PRINT 

Workbook PE, pp. 117–121
Unit 5 Resource Book
- Communipak, pp. 140–163
- Video Activities, p. 24
- Videoscript, p. 28
- Workbook TE, pp. 1–5

VIDEO PROGRAM

VIDÉO DVD

MODULE 13

13.4 Mini-scenes: Pardon! Excusez-moi!
(5:11–6:02 min.)

3 COMMUNICATION describing your town

Answers will vary.

1. Il y a un restaurant. Il s'appelle Chez Bob. (Il n'y a pas de restaurant.)
2. Il y a un cinéma. Il s'appelle The Capitol. (Il n'y a pas de cinéma.)
3. Il y a une église. Elle s'appelle St. Paul's. (Il n'y a pas d'église.)
4. Il y a un centre commercial. Il s'appelle Chestnut Hill Mall. (Il n'y a pas de centre commercial.)
5. Il y a une bibliothèque. Elle s'appelle The Wilson Memorial Library. (Il n'y a pas de bibliothèque.)
6. Il y a un café. Il s'appelle Cappuccino's. (Il n'y a pas de café.)
7. Il y a une plage. Elle s'appelle Ellis Beach. (Il n'y a pas de plage.)
8. Il y a un supermarché. Il s'appelle Shop Till You Drop. (Il n'y a pas de supermarché.)
9. Il y a un hôpital. Il s'appelle Boston Medical Center. (Il n'y a pas d'hôpital.)
10. Il y a un parc. Il s'appelle Boston Common. (Il n'y a pas de parc.)
11. Il y a un stade. Il s'appelle Veterans' Memorial Stadium. (Il n'y a pas de stade.)
12. Il y a un musée. Il s'appelle The Museum of Contemporary Art. (Il n'y a pas de musée.)
13. Il y a un hôtel. Il s'appelle The Traveller's Repose. (Il n'y a pas d'hôtel.)
14. Il y a une piscine. Elle s'appelle The Local Dip. (Il n'y a pas de piscine.)
15. Il y a un théâtre. Il s'appelle Center Stage. (Il n'y a pas de théâtre.)

4 ROLE PLAY asking about various places in a city

–Pauline, est-ce qu'il y a ... dans ton quartier?

1. un café	6. un théâtre
2. un cinéma	7. un supermarché
3. une piscine	8. un musée
4. un stade	9. un parc
5. une bibliothèque	10. un hôpital

Teaching strategy Be sure students use expressions they have learned in the lesson.

3 Mon quartier

PARLER Say whether the following places are located in the area where you live. If so, you may want to give the name of the place.

▶ école **Il y a une école. Elle s'appelle «Washington School». (Il n'y a pas d'école.)**

1. restaurant	6. café	11. stade
2. cinéma	7. plage	12. musée
3. église	8. supermarché	13. hôtel
4. centre commercial	9. hôpital	14. piscine
5. bibliothèque	10. parc	15. théâtre

CHATEAU
BELLEVUE
HÔTEL CHÂTEAU BELLEVUE
16, rue de La Porte, Vieux-Québec,
Qc Canada G1R 4M9
Tél. : 418.692.2573
Téléc. : 418.692.4876
bellevue@vieuxquebec.com

4 À Montréal

PARLER You are visiting your friend Pauline in Montreal. For each of the situations below, decide where you would like to go. Ask Pauline if there is such a place in her neighborhood.

▶ You are hungry.

Pauline, est-ce qu'il y a un restaurant dans ton quartier?

1. You want to have a soft drink.
2. You want to see a movie.
3. You want to swim a few laps.
4. You want to run on a track.
5. You want to read a book about Canada.
6. You want to see a French play.
7. You want to buy some fruit and crackers.
8. You want to see an art exhibit.
9. You want to play frisbee on the grass.
10. You slipped and you're afraid you sprained your ankle.

COMMUNAUTÉS

Do French-speaking visitors sometimes come to your community? As a class project, prepare a map of your city on which you label key places and buildings in French. Maybe your local chamber of commerce would like to make such a map available for tourists.

TEACHING NOTE Sounding French

An aim of Act. 3 is to get students to sound French as they use the new words.

Warm-up: First, have students imagine that they live in a large city. Ask the class:
Est-ce qu'il y a une école?
Oui, il y a une école. ...

Be sure to correct pronunciation problems.
Then ask them to imagine they live in the desert, and have them answer negatively.
Est-ce qu'il y a une école?
Non, il n'y a pas d'école. ...

When they can handle the place names fluently, have students describe the area where they actually live.

C VOCABULAIRE Pour demander un renseignement *(information)*

▶ *How to ask for directions:*

Pardon, | monsieur. Où est l'hôtel Normandie?
Excusez-moi, | madame
| mademoiselle

Il est dans la rue Jean Moulin.

Pardon, monsieur, Où est l'hôtel Normandie?

Il est dans la rue Jean Moulin.

Où est-ce qu'il y a un café?

Il y a un café | **rue** Saint Paul. | **une rue**
| **boulevard** Masséna | **un boulevard**
| **avenue** de Lyon | **une avenue**

Où est-ce? *(Where is it?)*
Est-ce que c'est **loin** *(far)*?

Non, ce n'est pas loin.
C'est **près** *(nearby)*.

Où est-ce? Est-ce que c'est loin?

Non, ce n'est pas loin. C'est près.

C'est | **à gauche** *(to the left)*. **Tournez** | à gauche.
| **à droite** *(to the right)* | à droite
| **tout droit** *(straight ahead)* **Continuez** tout droit.

Merci beaucoup!

5  En ville

PARLER A tourist who is visiting a French city asks a local resident how to get to the following places. Act out the dialogues.

▶ —**Pardon, mademoiselle (monsieur). Où est le Café de la Poste?**
—**Le Café de la Poste? Il est dans la rue Pascal.**
—**Où est-ce?**
—**Continuez tout droit!**
—**Merci, mademoiselle (monsieur).**

▶ 

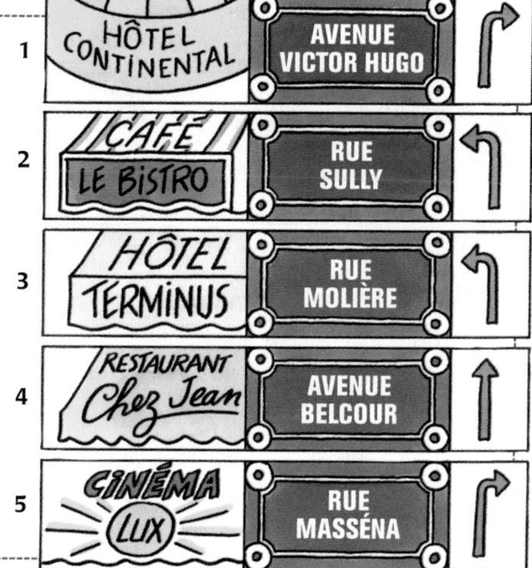

SECTION C

Communicative function
Asking for directions

Cultural notes

- Jean Moulin (1899–1943) was a hero of the French resistance against the Nazi occupation in World War II.
- Masséna (1758–1817) was one of Napoleon's marshals.

Supplementary vocabulary

C'est près d'ici. **C'est à côté.**
C'est tout près. **C'est en face.**
C'est loin d'ici.

5 ROLE PLAY asking and giving directions

1. – Pardon, mademoiselle (monsieur). Où est l'hôtel Continental?
   – L'hôtel Continental? Il est dans l'avenue Victor Hugo.
   – Où est-ce?
   – Tournez à droite!
   – Merci, mademoiselle (monsieur).
2. – Pardon, mademoiselle (monsieur). Où est le café «Le Bistro»?
   – Le café «Le Bistro»? Il est dans la rue Sully.
   – Où est-ce?
   – Tournez à gauche!
   – Merci, mademoiselle (monsieur).
3. – Pardon, mademoiselle (monsieur). Où est l'hôtel Terminus?
   – L'hôtel Terminus? Il est dans la rue Molière.
   – Où est-ce?
   – Tournez à gauche!
   – Merci, mademoiselle (monsieur).
4. – Pardon, mademoiselle (monsieur). Où est le restaurant «Chez Jean»?
   – Le restaurant «Chez Jean»? Il est dans l'avenue Belcour.
   – Où est-ce?
   – Continuez tout droit!
   – Merci, mademoiselle (monsieur).
5. – Pardon, mademoiselle (monsieur). Où est le cinéma Lux?
   – Le cinéma Lux? Il est dans la rue Masséna.
   – Où est-ce?
   – Tournez à droite!
   – Merci, mademoiselle (monsieur).

Variation Have students write out the dialogue with a partner.

Cultural notes

- Blaise Pascal (1623–1662), mathematician and philosopher.
- Duc de Sully (1559–1641), finance minister of Henri IV.
- Molière (1622–1673), classical author, writer of comedies.

EXPANSION Communautés

Have students use the maps they created for the *Communautés* activity (p. 198) for role-play activities in which they show visitors how to get around.

INCLUSION

Cumulative, Gifted & Talented Have students use the maps they created for the *Communautés* activity (p. 198) to reinforce vocabulary. Have students generate vocabulary lists and ask them to write them on the board (names for streets, directions, etc.). Each student picks a point on the map. Then have pairs of students ask each other questions about getting directions from one place to another.

SECTION D

Communicative function
Describing one's home

Teaching Resource Options

PRINT

Workbook PE, pp. 117–121
Unit 5 Resource Book
- Communipak, pp. 140–163
- Video Activities, pp. 25–26
- Videoscript, p. 28
- Workbook TE, pp. 1–5

AUDIO & VISUAL

Overhead Transparencies
31 *La maison*

VIDEO PROGRAM

VIDÉO DVD

MODULE 13

13.5 Vignette culturelle: La maison d'Olivier (6:03–7:02 min.)

Pronunciation Be sure students do NOT pronounce an "n" in **en haut**: /ã o/. The word **haut** begins with an *aspirate h*. There is never liaison or elision before an *aspirate h*.

Language notes
- **Les toilettes:** also **les WC** (called **double vécé** or simply **vécé**); or **les cabinets**. Tell students that **WC** stands for 'water closet.'
- **Une chambre** is a *room,* in the sense of *bedroom.*
- **Une pièce** is the more general word for *room of a house.*

Cultural notes
- Traditionally in a French home the toilet is in a small room separate from the bathroom.
- **Un salon** is a traditional formal living room. In modern, less formal homes, one may find **un séjour (une salle de séjour),** also referred to as **un living (un living-room).**
- In French homes, the shutters **(les volets)** are usually closed every night.

Supplementary vocabulary
une entrée
un escalier *staircase*
un ascenseur *elevator*
le toit *roof*
le grenier *attic*
le sous-sol *basement*
la cave *cellar*

D VOCABULAIRE Ma maison

How to describe one's home:

J'habite dans | **une maison** *(house).* / **un appartement** / **un immeuble** *(apartment building)*

Ma maison/mon appartement est | **moderne.** / **confortable**

Ma chambre est | **en haut** *(upstairs).* / **en bas** *(downstairs)*

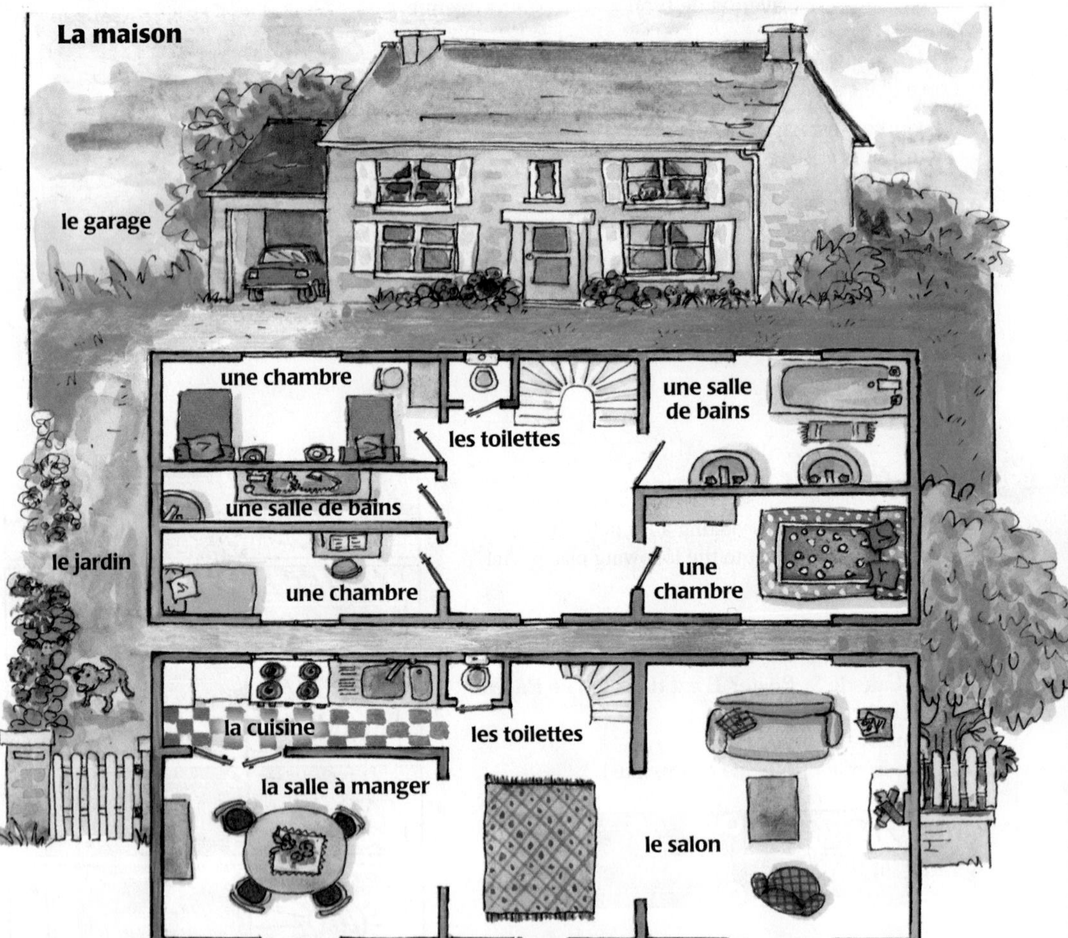

COMPREHENSION The house

PROPS: Transparency 31: *La maison*; magazine pictures of various rooms

Identify the new words on the transparency.

Voici le salon. Voilà la cuisine. ...
X, viens ici et montre-nous le jardin. ...

Place the magazine pictures on the desk. Have students pick up specific pictures and place themselves around the room.

X, prends le salon et mets-toi près de la porte.
Y, prends la salle à manger et mets-toi devant le tableau noir.

6 Ma maison

PARLER/ÉCRIRE Describe your home by completing the following sentences.

1. J'habite dans … (une maison? un appartement?)
2. Mon appartement est … (grand? petit? confortable? joli?)
   Ma maison est … (grande? petite? confortable? jolie?)
3. La cuisine est … (grande? petite? moderne?)
4. La cuisine est peinte *(painted)* en … (jaune? vert? gris? blanc? ??)
5. Ma chambre est peinte en … (bleu? rose? ??)
6. Dans le salon, il y a … (une télé? un sofa? des plantes vertes? ??)
7. En général, nous dînons dans … (la cuisine? la salle à manger?)
8. Ma maison/mon appartement a … (un jardin? un garage? ??)

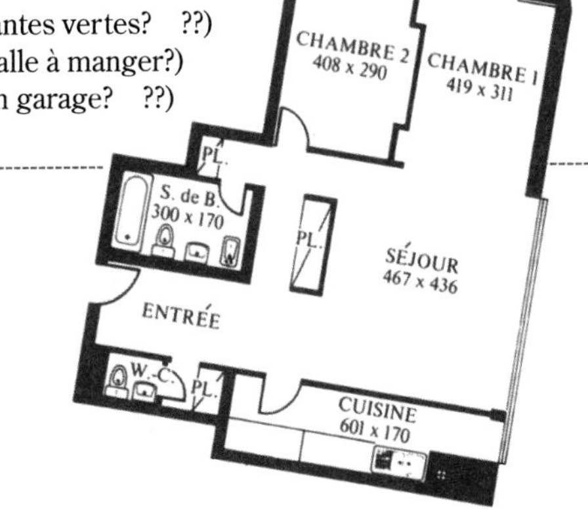

7 En haut ou en bas?

PARLER Imagine that you live in a two-story house. Indicate where the following rooms are located.

▶ ma chambre

1. la cuisine
2. la salle à manger
3. les toilettes
4. la salle de bains
5. la chambre de mes *(my)* parents
6. le salon

COMPARAISON CULTURELLE

In traditional French homes, the toilet (**WC**) is in a small room separate from the main bathroom.

8 Où sont-ils?

PARLER/ÉCRIRE From what the following people are doing, guess where they are — in or around the house.

▶ Madame Martin répare *(is repairing)* la voiture.
Elle est dans le garage.

1. Nous dînons.
2. Tu regardes la télé.
3. Antoine et Juliette jouent au frisbee.
4. J'étudie le français.
5. Monsieur Martin prépare le dîner.
6. Henri se lave *(is washing up)*.
7. Ma soeur téléphone à son copain.

6 COMMUNICATION describing your home

Answers will vary.
1. J'habite dans un appartement (une maison).
2. Mon appartement est (joli). Ma maison est (petite).
3. La cuisine est (grande).
4. La cuisine est peinte en (blanc et rouge).
5. Ma chambre est peinte en (bleu).
6. Dans le salon, il y a (un sofa et une télé).
7. En général, nous dînons dans (la salle à manger).
8. Mon appartement a (un garage).

7 DESCRIPTION indicating where rooms are located

Answers will vary.
1. La cuisine est en haut. (La cuisine est en bas.)
2. La salle à manger est en haut. (La salle à manger est en bas.)
3. Les toilettes sont en haut. (Les toilettes sont en bas.)
4. La salle de bains est en haut. (La salle de bains est en bas.)
5. La chambre de mes parents est en haut. (La chambre de mes parents est en bas.)
6. Le salon est en haut. (Le salon est en bas.)

Language note Be sure students use the plural in item 3: Les toilettes **sont...**

8 COMPREHENSION describing where people are

1. Vous êtes dans la salle à manger.
2. Je suis dans le salon.
3. Ils sont dans le jardin.
4. Tu es dans ta chambre. (Tu es dans le salon.)
5. Il est dans la cuisine.
6. Il est dans la salle de bains.
7. Elle est dans le salon.

Realia note Ask questions about the floor plan:

Trouvez l'entrée, le séjour, les deux chambres, la cuisine, la salle de bains, les toilettes (les WC).

Est-ce qu'il y a aussi des toilettes dans la salle de bains?

Combien de placards *(closets)* **y a-t-il?**

Once the layout of the house has been set, have other students go to various rooms.

Z, tu as faim. Va à la cuisine.
Qui est dans la cuisine? [Z]
W, tu veux regarder la télé. Va au salon.
V, tu dois te laver les mains [gesture].
Va dans la salle de bains. ...

INCLUSION

Sequential To reinforce and build vocabulary, have students draw floor plans of their apartments/homes. Write a list of vocabulary on the board and color code it (red for **cuisine**, green for **salle de bain**, etc.) Have students use a different color crayon for each room. Write model sentences on the board, and have them work in pairs to describe their apartments or homes.

À VOTRE TOUR

Main Topic
- Recapitulation and review

Teaching Resource Options

PRINT 

Workbook PE, pp. 117–121
Unit 5 Resource Book
- Audioscript, p. 29
- Communipak, pp. 140–163
- Family Involvement, pp. 19–20
- Workbook TE, pp. 1–5

Assessment
- Lesson 13 Quiz, pp. 33–34
- Portfolio Assessment, Unit 1 URB, pp. 155–164
- Audioscript for Quiz 13, p. 32
- Answer Keys, pp. 210–213

AUDIO & VISUAL 

Audio Program
CD 3 Tracks 1–3
CD 15 Track 1

Overhead Transparencies
32 Map of Villeneuve

TECHNOLOGY 

Test Generator CD-ROM/McDougal Littell Assessment System

1 Listening Comprehension

1. B **2.** A **3.** B **4.** B **5.** A
6. A **7.** B **8.** B

2 Written Self-Expression

Answers will vary.
Dans mon quartier, il y a un parc. C'est le parc Menotomy Rocks.
Il y a une église. C'est l'église Holy Trinity.
Il y a une bibliothèque. C'est la bibliothèque d'Arlington.
Il y a un cinéma. C'est le cinéma Orson Wells.
Il y a un centre commercial. Il s'appelle The Burlington Mall.

À votre tour!

OBJECTIFS
Now you can …
- describe your town and your neighborhood
- ask and give directions

1 Écoutez bien!

ÉCOUTER Look at the map of Villeneuve. You will hear where certain people are. If they are somewhere on the left side of the map, mark A. If they are on the right side of the map, mark B.

A								
B								
	1	2	3	4	5	6	7	8

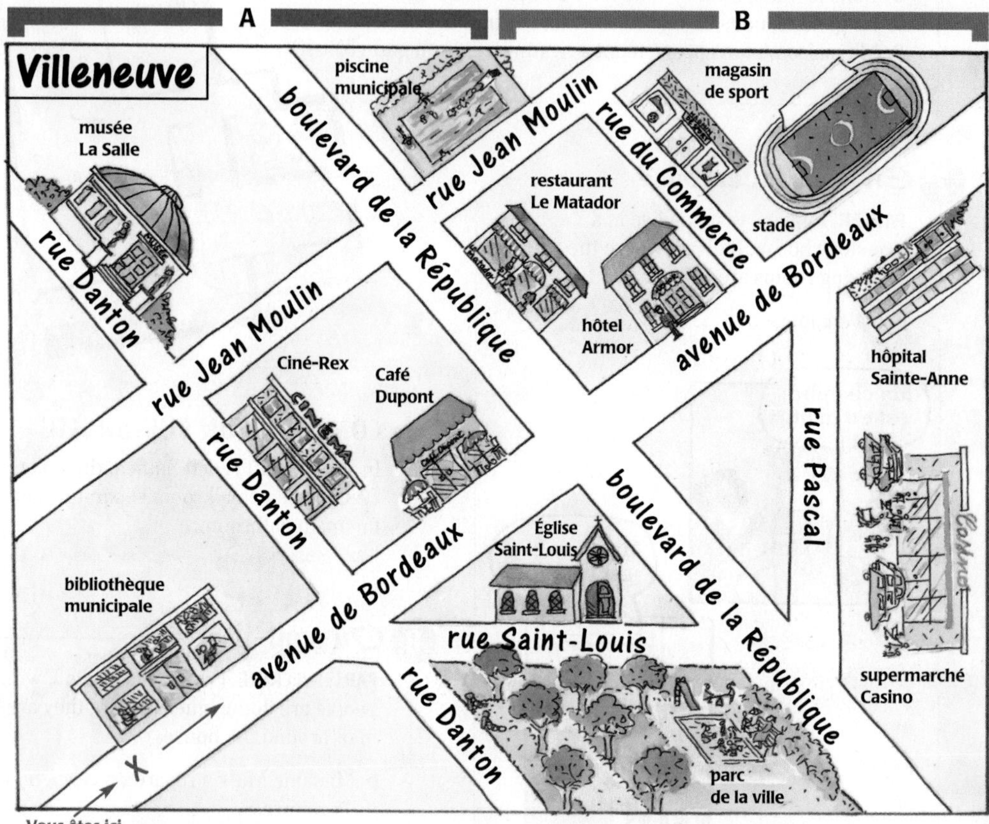

2 Mon quartier

ÉCRIRE Describe your neighborhood, listing five places and giving their names.

▶ **Dans mon quartier, il y a un supermarché. C'est le supermarché Casino.**

À VOTRE TOUR

Select those activities which are most appropriate for your students.

GROUP PRACTICE

In Act. 3 and 4, you may want to have students work in trios, with two performing and one acting as monitor.

PORTFOLIO ASSESSMENT

You will probably select only one speaking activity and one writing activity to go into the students' portfolios for Unit 5.

In this lesson, Act. 5 offers an excellent writing portfolio topic.

3 Créa-dialogue

PARLER You have just arrived in Villeneuve, where you will spend the summer. Ask a pedestrian where you can find the places represented by the symbols. He (She) will give you the location of each place, according to the map.

▶ —Pardon, monsieur (madame). Où est-ce qu'il y a un hôtel?
—Il y a un hôtel avenue de Bordeaux.
—Est-ce que c'est loin?
—Non, c'est près.
—Merci beaucoup!

▶ 

1
2
3
4
5
6
7
8
9

4 Où est-ce?

PARLER Now you have been in Villeneuve for several weeks and are familiar with the city. You meet a tourist on the **avenue de Bordeaux** at the place indicated by an X on the map. The tourist asks you where certain places are and you indicate how to get there.

▶ l'hôpital Sainte-Anne

1. le musée La Salle
2. le supermarché Casino
3. l'hôtel Armor
4. le restaurant Le Matador
5. l'église Saint-Louis

Pardon, monsieur. Où est l'hôpital Sainte-Anne?
C'est tout droit, mademoiselle.
Merci bien, monsieur.

5 Composition: La maison idéale

ÉCRIRE Briefly describe your dream house. You may use the following adjectives to describe the various rooms: **grand, petit, moderne, confortable, joli,** as well as colors. If you wish, sketch and label a floor plan.

▶ 

La maison idéale est grande et moderne. Le salon est ...

LESSON REVIEW
CLASSZONE.COM

3 Guided Oral Expression

–Pardon, monsieur (madame). Où est-ce qu'il y a ...?
–Il y a ...
–Est-ce que c'est loin?
– ...
–Merci beaucoup!

1. un café/avenue de Bordeaux/Non, c'est près.
2. un restaurant/boulevard de la République/ Non, c'est près. (Oui, c'est loin.)
3. une église/rue Saint-Louis/Non, c'est près.
4. un supermarché/rue Pascal/Oui, c'est loin.
5. une bibliothèque/avenue de Bordeaux/Non, c'est près.
6. un stade/avenue de Bordeaux/Oui, c'est loin.
7. une piscine/rue Jean Moulin/Oui, c'est [très] loin.
8. un cinéma/rue Danton/Non, c'est près.
9. un hôpital/avenue de Bordeaux/Oui, c'est loin.

4 Guided Oral Expression

1. –Pardon, monsieur (mademoiselle). Où est le musée La Salle?
   –Tournez à gauche (rue Danton), monsieur (mademoiselle).
   –Merci bien, monsieur.
2. –Pardon, monsieur (mademoiselle). Où est le supermarché Casino?
   –Continuez tout droit et tournez à droite (rue Pascal), monsieur (mademoiselle).
   –Merci bien, monsieur.
3. –Pardon, monsieur (mademoiselle). Où est l'hôtel Armor?
   –C'est tout droit, monsieur (mademoiselle).
   –Merci bien, monsieur.
4. –Pardon, monsieur (mademoiselle). Où est le restaurant le Matador?
   –Continuez tout droit et tournez a gauche, monsieur (mademoiselle).
   –Merci bien, monsieur.
5. –Pardon, monsieur (mademoiselle). Où est l'église Saint-Louis?
   –Tournez à droite (rue Saint-Louis), monsieur (mademoiselle).
   –Merci bien, monsieur.

5 Written Self-Expression

Answers will vary.
Ma maison idéale est confortable et jolie. Elle a deux chambres, une salle de bains, des toilettes, un salon, une salle à manger et un jardin. Le garage n'est pas grand. Les chambres sont grandes mais la salle à manger est petite. Le salon est très confortable. Le jardin est joli.

Challenge Activities Villeneuve

If appropriate, you can introduce additional challenge activities using the map of Villeneuve.

Have students give more complex directions, using **continuez tout droit, tournez à gauche dans la rue Pascal, ...**

Getting around: Have students give directions from one place to the next, e.g., from **l'hôtel Armor** to **le musée La Salle**, from **le musée** to **le supermarché,** etc.

Mystery destination: Tell students that they are at place "x" on the map. Give them instructions in French to get to a new location. **Maintenant, où êtes-vous?**

Leçon 14

Main Topics Going to places, Talking about future plans

Teaching Resource Options

PRINT

Workbook PE, pp. 123–130
Activités pour tous PE, pp. 75–77
Block Scheduling Copymasters, pp. 105–112
Unit 5 Resource Book
- *Activités pour tous* TE, pp. 43–45
- Audioscript, pp. 64, 65–67
- Communipak, pp. 140–163
- Lesson Plans, pp. 46–47
- Block Scheduling Lesson Plans, pp. 48–49
- Absent Student Copymasters, pp. 50–53
- Video Activities, pp. 56–61
- Videoscript, pp. 62–63
- Workbook TE, pp. 35–42

AUDIO & VISUAL

Audio Program
CD 3 Tracks 4, 5
CD 9 Tracks 8–16

TECHNOLOGY

Online Workbook

VIDEO PROGRAM

MODULE 14
Une promenade en ville

TOTAL TIME: 6:55 min.
DVD Disk 2
Videotape 3 (COUNTER: 7:14 min.)

14.1 Mini-scenes: Listening – Où allez-vous? (7:47–8:20 min.)

14.2 Mini-scenes: Listening – Où est-ce que tu vas? (8:21–8:46 min.)

14.3 Mini-scenes: Speaking – Où vont-ils? (8:47–9:41 min.)

14.4 Mini-scenes: Listening – Qu'est-ce que vous allez faire? (9:42–11:00 min.)

14.5 Mini-scenes: Speaking – Tu vas nager? (11:01–11:49 min.)

14.6 Dialogue: Julien travaille (11:50–12:40 min.)

14.7 Vignette culturelle: Le métro (12:41–14:09 min.)

LEÇON 14

Week-end à Paris

AUDIO

Aujourd'hui c'est samedi.
Les élèves ne vont pas en classe. — *are not going*
Où est-ce qu'ils vont alors?
Ça dépend!

Thomas va au café. — *is going*
Il a un rendez-vous avec une copine. — *date*

Florence et Karine vont aux Champs-Élysées.
Elles vont regarder les vêtements dans les magasins. — *clothes*
Après, elles vont aller au cinéma. — *Afterward / to go*

Daniel va chez son copain Laurent. — *to the house of / his*
Les garçons vont jouer aux jeux vidéo.
Après, ils vont aller au musée des sciences de la Villette.
Ils vont jouer avec les machines électroniques.

Béatrice a un grand sac et des lunettes de soleil. — *sunglasses*
Est-ce qu'elle va à un rendez-vous secret?
Non! Elle va au Centre Pompidou.
Elle va regarder les acrobates.
Et après, elle va aller à un concert.

Et Jean-François? Qu'est-ce qu'il va faire aujourd'hui?
Est-ce qu'il va visiter le Centre Pompidou?
Est-ce qu'il va regarder les acrobates?
Est-ce qu'il va aller à un concert?
Hélas, non! — *Alas (Unfortunately)*
Il va rester à la maison. — *to stay*
Pourquoi? Parce qu'il est malade. — *sick*
Pauvre Jean-François! — *Poor*
Il fait si beau dehors! — *so / outside*

TALKING ABOUT PAST EVENTS

Let's talk about where you have been recently. Note that the past participle of **être** is **été**.

▶ **Est-ce que tu as été en ville le week-end dernier?**
Oui, j'ai été en ville.
(Non, je n'ai pas été en ville.)
- **Est-ce que tu as été à la piscine samedi?**
- **Est-ce que tu as été à la bibliothèque?**
- **Est-ce que tu as été au centre commercial? au musée? au parc?**
- **Est-ce que tu as été au théâtre samedi soir?**
- **Est-ce que tu as été à l'hôpital?**
- **Où est-ce que tu as été dimanche dernier?**

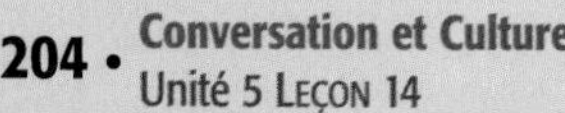

Compréhension

1. Quel jour est-ce aujourd'hui?
2. Pourquoi est-ce que Thomas va au café?
3. Avec qui est-ce que Florence va au cinéma?
4. Où va Daniel? Qu'est-ce qu'il fait avec Laurent?
5. Où va Béatrice?
6. Pourquoi est-ce que Jean-François ne va pas en ville?
7. Quel temps fait-il aujourd'hui?

NOTE culturelle

À Paris

Paris offre beaucoup d'attractions diverses pour les jeunes.

Les Champs-Élysées

Les Champs-Élysées sont une très longue et très large° avenue avec beaucoup de cafés, de restaurants, de cinémas et de boutiques élégantes.

Le Centre Pompidou

Le Centre Pompidou est un grand musée d'art moderne. C'est aussi un centre culturel avec un grand nombre de salles° multimédia pour les jeunes. Devant le musée, il y a une place où les acrobates, les mimes, les jongleurs° et les musiciens démontrent leurs° talents. Ici, le spectacle est permanent.

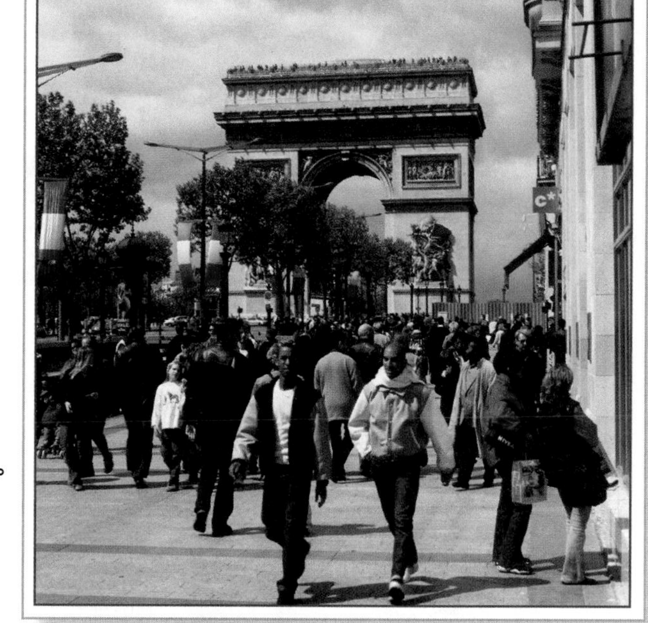

Le Parc de la Villette

Le Parc de la Villette est un musée scientifique pour les jeunes. À la Géode, ils peuvent° voir° des films sur un grand écran panoramique Omni. Au Zénith, ils peuvent assister à° des concerts de rock et de musique techno.

large *wide* **salles** *large rooms* **jongleurs** *jugglers* **leurs** *their* **peuvent** *can* **voir** *see* **assister à** *attend*

Compréhension

Answers

1. Aujourd'hui, c'est samedi.
2. Il a un rendez-vous avec une copine.
3. Elle va au cinéma avec Karine.
4. Daniel va chez son copain Laurent. Ils jouent aux jeux vidéo.
5. Béatrice va au Centre Pompidou.
6. Il est malade.
7. Il fait (très) beau.

Note culturelle Paris

- **La Seine** flows through Paris. As you face downstream, the part of the city on your left is called the Left Bank **(la rive gauche),** while the part on your right, is called the Right Bank **(la rive droite).**
- **Les Champs-Élysées** is the most famous avenue of Paris and a favorite place for strolling with friends. The avenue runs from the **Arc de Triomphe** to the **Place de la Concorde**. The **Champs-Élysées** is also the scene of the **Défilé** (parade) **du Quatorze Juillet** and the **Arrivée** (finish) **du Tour de France** bicycle race.
- **Le Centre Pompidou,** was named in honor of Georges Pompidou who was President of France (1969–1974).
- In the photo of **le Parc de la Villette,** on p. 204, you see a large steel sphere, **La Géode,** which houses the Omni theater and its circular panoramic screen.

Critical thinking activity

Write on the chalkboard:

Elles vont aux Champs-Élysées.
Elles vont regarder les magasins.

Ask: How would you express these sentences in English?

- In which sentence does **vont** mean that the girls are actually going to *a place*? Is the place mentioned?
- In which sentence does **vont** mean that the girls are going to *do something*? Is the activity mentioned?

Read the opening text and look for examples of **va** and **vont.**

- Which ones refer to movement?
- Which ones refer to future activities?

Teaching strategy

- Have students read the cultural notes and look at the photos.
- Play the audio of the opening text (books closed).
- On the board, write words and phrases students remembered.
- Have students write a postcard describing the fun things they did the first week of an imaginary vacation in Paris.

COMPREHENSION Visiting Paris

PROPS: 3 signs that read
"Le Parc de la Villette"
"Le Centre Pompidou"
"Les Champs-Élysées"

Place the signs around the classroom.

Voici le Parc de la Villette., etc.
(Pronunciation: Villette /vilɛt/)

Have students go to these places.

X, lève-toi et va aux Champs-Élysées.
Où va X? Il va aux Champs-Élysées.
Y et Z, allez au Centre Pompidou.
Où vont Y et Z? aux Champs-Élysées?
[non] **Ils vont au Centre Pompidou. ...**

Follow-up questions:

Où est X? Qu'est-ce qu'il va visiter?

SECTION A

Communicative function
Talking about where one is going

Teaching Resource Options

PRINT 

Workbook PE, pp. 123–130
Unit 5 Resource Book
Communipak, pp. 140–163
Workbook TE, pp. 35–42

TECHNOLOGY 

Power Presentations

Language note Remind students of the elision (with **ne**) in the negative forms:
nous n'allons pas, vous n'allez pas

Language usage The verb **aller** is usually accompanied by a word or phrase indicating a place. (After the verb *to go* in English, the place is often left out.) Compare:

Quand est-ce que tu vas à Paris?
When are you going to Paris?

Je vais à Paris en mai.
I am going (to Paris) in May.

Pronunciation Be sure that students use liaison in **vas-y** and **allons-y.**

Vocabulary expansion

When speaking to several people:
Allez-y!
Allez-vous-en!
Note also:
On y va! *Let's go!*

A Le verbe *aller*

Aller *(to go)* is the only IRREGULAR verb that ends in **-er.** Note the forms of **aller** in the present tense.

aller	*to go*	J'aime **aller** au cinéma.
je **vais**	*I go, I am going*	Je **vais** à un concert.
tu **vas**	*you go, you are going*	**Vas**-tu à la boum?
il/elle **va**	*he/she goes, he/she is going*	Paul **va** à l'école.
nous **allons**	*we go, we are going*	Nous **allons** au café.
vous **allez**	*you go, you are going*	Est-ce que vous **allez** là-bas?
ils/elles **vont**	*they go, they are going*	Ils ne **vont** pas en classe.

→ Remember that **aller** is used in asking people how they feel.

Ça **va?**	Oui, ça **va.**
Comment **vas**-tu?	Je **vais** bien, merci.
Comment **allez**-vous?	Très bien.

→ **Aller** is used in many common expressions.

- To encourage someone to do something:
  Vas-y! *Come on! Go ahead! Do it!*

- To tell someone to go away:
  Va-t'en! *Go away!*

- To tell friends to start doing something:
  Allons-y! *Let's go!*

TEACHING NOTE Listening activities

A. Review gestures for the subject pronouns (see Lesson 7, Comprehension activity, p. 96).
Make statements about where people are going; have students identify the subject.
Il va au stade.
[signal **il/elle**]
Elles vont au cinéma.
[signal **ils/elles**] ...

B. On the board, write **aller/avoir/être/faire.**
Make statements using the four verbs. Students say which one they heard.
Mes amis sont à Tours. [être]
Ils ont des vélos. [avoir]
Ils font une promenade. [faire]
Ils vont à la piscine. [aller]
Ils vont nager. [aller] ...

1 Les vacances

PARLER/ÉCRIRE The following students at a boarding school in Nice are going home for vacation. Indicate to which of the cities they are going, according to the luggage tags shown below.

▶ Jean-Michel est canadien.

1. Je suis suisse.
2. Charlotte est américaine.
3. Nous sommes italiens.
4. Tu es français.
5. Vous êtes espagnols.
6. Michiko est japonaise.
7. Mike et Shelley sont anglais.
8. Ana et Carlos sont mexicains.

Jean-Michel va à Québec.

▶

2 Jamais le dimanche! *(Never on Sunday!)*

PARLER/ÉCRIRE On Sundays, French students do not go to class. They all go somewhere else. Express this according to the model.

▶ nous / en ville
Le dimanche, nous n'allons pas en classe.
Nous allons en ville.

1. Philippe / au café
2. vous / au cinéma
3. Céline et Michèle / à un concert
4. Jérôme / au restaurant
5. je / à un match de foot
6. tu / à la piscine
7. Éric et Léa / à la plage
8. Mes copains / au stade
9. Hélène / au centre commercial
10. Vous / dans les magasins

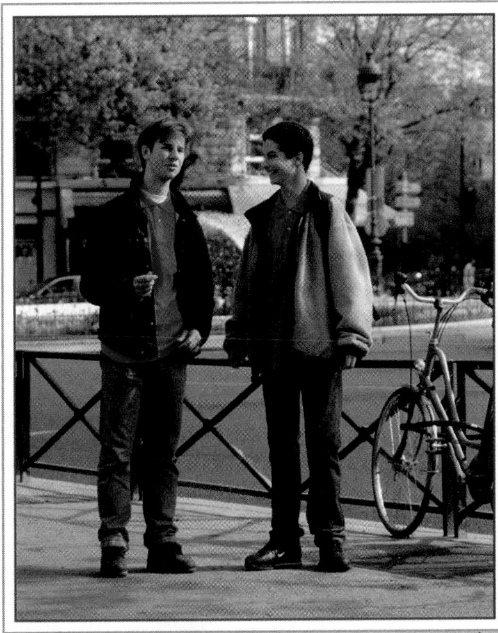

1 COMPREHENSION telling people what cities to go to

1. Je vais à Genève.
2. Charlotte va à Chicago.
3. Nous allons à Rome.
4. Tu vas à Lyon.
5. Vous allez à Madrid.
6. Michiko va à Tokyo.
7. Mike et Shelley vont à Londres.
8. Ana et Carlos vont à Acapulco.

Re-entry and review
Adjectives of nationality (from Lesson 11).

Challenge Let students name another city in the appropriate country.
Jean-Michel va à Montréal.

2 PRACTICE describing where people are going/not going

1. Le dimanche, Philippe ne va pas en classe. Il va au café.
2. Le dimanche, vous n'allez pas en classe. Vous allez au cinéma.
3. Le dimanche, Céline et Michèle ne vont pas en classe. Elles vont à un concert.
4. Le dimanche, Jérôme ne va pas en classe. Il va au restaurant.
5. Le dimanche, je ne vais pas en classe. Je vais à un match de foot.
6. Le dimanche, tu ne vas pas en classe. Tu vas à la piscine.
7. Le dimanche, Éric et Léa ne vont pas en classe. Ils vont à la plage.
8. Le dimanche, mes copains ne vont pas en classe. Ils vont au stade.
9. Le dimanche, Hélène ne va pas en classe. Elle va au centre commercial.
10. Le dimanche, vous n'allez pas en classe. Vous allez dans les magasins.

WARM-UP Cities and nationalities

Review nationalities, with books closed.

Indicate where people live, and have students give their nationalities. First use masculine singular subjects.
Henri habite à Paris. [Il est français.]
Bill habite à Boston. [Il est américain.]

Practice with the cities of Act. 1.

Then continue with feminine singular subjects.
Marie habite à Genève. [Elle est suisse.]

Finally practice with plural subjects.
Tatsuo et Michiko habitent à Kyoto. [Ils sont japonais.]
Sally et Susie habitent à Liverpool. [Elles sont anglaises.]

SECTION B

Communicative function
Talking about going places

Teaching Resource Options

PRINT  

Workbook PE, pp. 123–130
Unit 5 Resource Book
- Communipak, pp. 140–163
- Video Activities, pp. 56–57
- Videoscript, p. 62
- Workbook TE, pp. 35–42

TECHNOLOGY 

Power Presentations

VIDEO PROGRAM

VIDÉO DVD

MODULE 14

14.1 Mini-scenes: Où allez-vous? (7:47–8:20 min.)

14.2 Mini-scenes: Où est-ce que tu vas? (8:21–8:46 min.)

14.3 Mini-scenes: Où vont-ils? (8:47–9:41 min.)

3 EXCHANGES asking where people are going

1. –Tu vas au stade?
   –Non, je vais à la piscine.
2. –Tu vas au cinéma?
   –Non, je vais au théâtre.
3. –Tu vas à l'hôtel?
   –Non, je vais au supermarché.
4. –Tu vas à la bibliothèque?
   –Non, je vais au musée.
5. –Tu vas à l'école?
   –Non, je vais au parc.

Variation Have students write out the dialogue with a partner.

Teaching note: Be sure students realize that the words in heavy print in the green chart correspond to *at the* and *to the.*

Teaching note: You may want to point out the use of **à** with certain verbs.

téléphoner à:
- **Je téléphone à Pierre.**
- **Je téléphone au professeur.**

jouer à:
- **Je joue au tennis.**
- **Nous jouons à la balle.**

B La préposition *à*; *à* + l'article défini

The preposition **à** has several meanings:

in	Patrick habite **à** Paris.	*Patrick lives* ***in*** *Paris.*
at	Nous sommes **à** la piscine.	*We are* ***at*** *the pool.*
to	Est-ce que tu vas **à** Toulouse?	*Are you going* ***to*** *Toulouse?*

CONTRACTIONS

Note the forms of **à** + DEFINITE ARTICLE in the sentences below.

Voici **le** café.	Marc est **au** café.	Corinne va **au** café.
Voici **les** Champs-Élysées.	Tu es **aux** Champs-Élysées.	Je vais **aux** Champs-Élysées.
Voici **la** piscine.	Anne est **à la** piscine.	Éric va **à la** piscine.
Voici **l'**hôtel.	Je suis **à l'**hôtel.	Vous allez **à l'**hôtel.

The preposition **à** contracts with **le** and **les,** but not with **la** and **l'.**

CONTRACTION	NO CONTRACTION		
à + le → **au**	à + la = **à la**	**au** cinéma	**à la** piscine
à + les → **aux**	à + l' = **à l'**	**aux** Champs-Élysées	**à l'**école

→ There is liaison after **aux** when the next word begins with a vowel sound.
Le professeur parle **aux élèves.** Je téléphone **aux amis** de Claire.

3 Dans la rue

PARLER Two friends meet in the street and talk about where they are going.

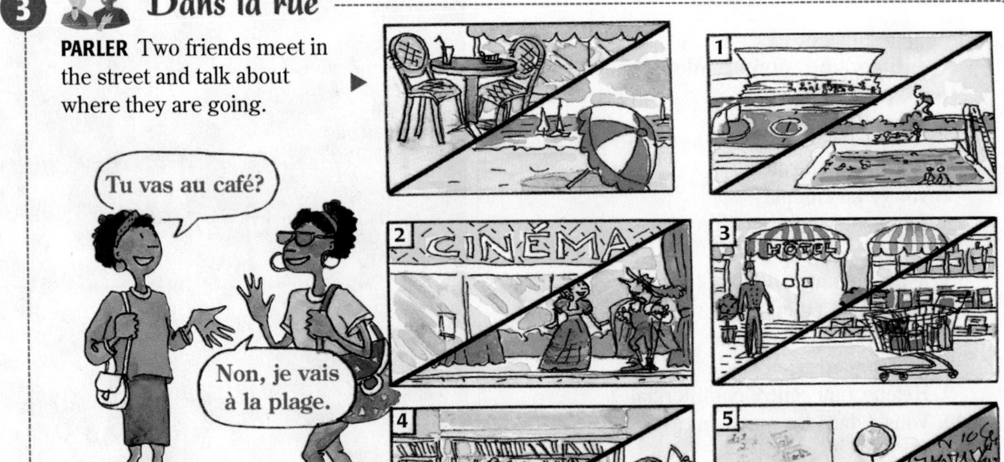
Tu vas au café?
Non, je vais à la plage.
1
2
CINÉMA
3
HOTEL
4
5

TEACHING NOTE Additional practice

Although contractions are not hard to learn, students often fail to use them in conversation. Sometimes extra drill practice helps them internalize the patterns.

Je suis au café.

(le cinéma)	**Je suis au cinéma.**
(la piscine)	**Je suis à la piscine.**
(l'hôpital)	**Je suis à l'hôpital.**
(le stade)	**Je suis au stade.**
(l'appartement)	**Je suis à l'appartement.**
(le musée)	**Je suis au musée.**
(la maison)	**Je suis à la maison.**
(le restaurant)	**Je suis au restaurant.**

4 Préférences

PARLER Ask your classmates about their preferences. Be sure to use contractions when needed.

▶ aller à (le concert ou le théâtre?)

1. dîner à (la maison ou le restaurant)?
2. étudier à (la bibliothèque ou la maison)?
3. nager à (la piscine ou la plage)?
4. regarder un match de foot à (la télé ou le stade)?
5. aller à (le cinéma ou le musée)?

Tu préfères aller au concert ou au théâtre?
Je préfère aller au concert.
(Je préfère aller au théâtre.)

5 À Paris

PARLER You are living in Paris. A friend asks you where you are going and why. Act out the dialogues with a classmate.

▶ —Où vas-tu?
—**Je vais à l'Opéra.**
—Pourquoi?
—**Parce que j'aime la danse classique.**

OÙ?	POURQUOI?
▶ l'Opéra	J'aime la danse classique.
1. l'Alliance Française	J'ai une classe de français.
2. le Centre Pompidou	J'aime l'art moderne.
3. le musée d'Orsay	C'est un musée intéressant.
4. les Champs-Élysées	J'ai un rendez-vous là-bas.
5. la tour Eiffel	Il y a une belle vue *(view)* sur Paris.
6. le Zénith	Il y a un concert de rock.
7. la Villette	Il y a une exposition *(exhibit)* intéressante.
8. le stade de France	Il y a un match de foot.

6 Où vont-ils?

PARLER/ÉCRIRE Say where the following people are going, according to what they like to do.

▶ Daniel aime danser.
Il va à la discothèque.

1. Corinne aime l'art moderne.
2. Jean-François aime manger.
3. Delphine aime les westerns.
4. Marina aime nager.
5. Éric aime regarder les magazines.
6. Denise aime faire des promenades.
7. Philippe aime la musique.
8. Alice aime le football.
9. Cécile aime le shopping.
10. Léa aime surfer sur l'Internet.

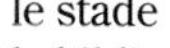

le stade
la bibliothèque
le cinéma
le centre commercial
la discothèque
le musée
le cybercafé
le parc
le restaurant
la piscine
le concert

INCLUSION

Multisensory Ask students to make 3x5 cards with **à** + article on side 1 and the contracted version on side 2. Have students place the cards on desk (side 2 facing up) and point, repeating the words after you. Do this three times. Ask students to turn cards to side 1 and give the contracted version. Mix cards and have students drill with partners. Then say contractions as students repeat and write them.

4 COMMUNICATION expressing preferences

1. –Tu préfères dîner à la maison ou au restaurant?
   –Je préfère dîner à la maison (dîner au restaurant).
2. –Tu préfères étudier à la bibliothèque ou à la maison?
   –Je préfère étudier à la bibliothèque (à la maison).
3. –Tu préfères nager à la piscine ou à la plage?
   –Je préfère nager à la piscine (à la plage).
4. –Tu préfères regarder un match de foot à la télé ou au stade?
   –Je préfère regarder un match de foot à la télé (au stade).
5. –Tu préfères aller au cinéma ou au musée?
   –Je préfère aller au cinéma (au musée).

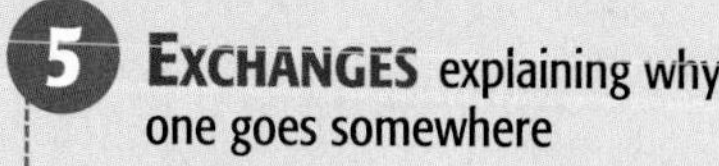

Expansion Additional cues:
aller à (le musée ou la bibliothèque)?
aller à (le café ou le restaurant)?
aller à (l'école ou le parc)?

5 EXCHANGES explaining why one goes somewhere

–Où vas-tu?
–Je vais ...
–Pourquoi?
–Parce que (qu') ...

1. –à l'Alliance Française/j'ai une classe de français.
2. –au Centre Pompidou/j'aime l'art moderne.
3. –au musée d'Orsay/c'est un musée intéressant.
4. –aux Champs-Élysées/j'ai un rendez-vous là-bas.
5. –à la tour Eiffel/une belle vue sur Paris.
6. –au Zénith/il y a un concert de rock.
7. –à la Villette/il y a une exposition intéressante.
8. –au stade de France/il y a un match de foot.

Teaching note Have students find as many of these places as possible on the map of Paris in the photo essay on p. 250.

Cultural background L'Opéra
There are two opera buildings in Paris:
- **L'Opéra Garnier,** the old opera house, now home of the Paris ballet.
- **L'Opéra de la Bastille,** concert hall built in 1989, home of the Paris opera.

6 COMPREHENSION concluding where people are going

1. Corinne va au musée.
2. Jean-François va au restaurant.
3. Delphine va au cinéma.
4. Marina va à la piscine.
5. Éric va à la bibliothèque.
6. Denise va au parc.
7. Philippe va au concert.
8. Alice va au stade.
9. Cécile va au centre commercial.
10. Léa va au cybercafé.

Teaching Resource Options

PRINT  

Workbook PE, pp. 123–130
Unit 5 Resource Book
- Communipak, pp. 140–163
- Video Activities, pp. 56–61
- Videoscript, pp. 62–63
- Workbook TE, pp. 35–42

AUDIO & VISUAL 

Overhead Transparencies
33 Means of transportation

TECHNOLOGY 

Power Presentations

VIDEO PROGRAM

VIDÉO DVD 

MODULE 14

14.7 Vignette culturelle: Le métro
(12:41–14:09 min.)

Supplementary vocabulary
une exposition *exhibit*

Language notes
- **Un bus (un autobus)** is a city bus that follows a regular route.
- An intercity or tour bus is **un car** or **un autocar.**
- A school bus is **un car scolaire.**

7 COMMUNICATION answering personal questions

Answers will vary.

1. En général, j'arrive à l'école à (huit heures et demie).
2. Je rentre à la maison à (cinq heures). Quand je rentre à la maison, je (joue au football et j'étudie).
3. Je vais à l'école (à pied / en vélo / en bus / en métro).
4. Le week-end, je reste à la maison. (Le week-end, je ne reste pas à la maison. Je vais [à la plage / au cinéma].)
5. Je vais à la piscine (à pied). Je vais à la plage (en voiture). Je vais au cinéma (à vélo).
6. Oui, j'aime faire des promenades à pied. Je vais (au parc) avec (un[e] ami[e] / ma soeur / des copains, etc.). (Non, je n'aime pas faire de promenades à pied.)
7. Oui j'aime faire des promenades à vélo. Je vais (au parc / en ville / au stade, etc.). (Non, je n'aime pas faire de promenades à vélo.)
8. Oui, j'aime regarder des films à la télé. Je préfère (les comédies). (Non, je n'aime pas regarder de films à la télé.)
9. Quand j'ai un rendez-vous avec une copine (un copain), je vais (au café).
10. J'aime aller (aux concerts / aux matchs de football, etc.)

VOCABULAIRE En ville

▶ *Quelques endroits et quelques événements où aller*

un endroit	*place*	**un match**	*game*	**une boum**	*party*
un événement	*event*	**un pique-nique**	*picnic*	**une fête**	*party*
un concert	*concert*	**un rendez-vous**	*appointment, date*	**une soirée**	*evening party*
un film	*movie*				

Verbes

arriver	*to arrive, come*	**J'arrive** à l'école à 9 heures.
rentrer	*to go back, come back*	À quelle heure **rentres**-tu à la maison?
rester	*to stay*	Les touristes **restent** à l'hôtel.

Expressions

à pied	*on foot*	**en voiture**	*by car*	**en métro**	*by subway*
à vélo	*by bicycle*	**en bus**	*by bus*	**en taxi**	*by taxi*
		en train	*by train*		

faire une promenade à pied	*to go for a walk*
faire une promenade à vélo	*to go for a ride (by bike)*
faire une promenade en voiture	*to go for a drive*

7 Questions personnelles PARLER/ÉCRIRE

1. En général, à quelle heure est-ce que tu arrives à l'école?
2. À quelle heure est-ce que tu rentres à la maison? Qu'est-ce que tu fais quand tu rentres à la maison?
3. Comment vas-tu à l'école? à pied, à vélo, en voiture ou en bus?
4. Le week-end, est-ce que tu restes à la maison? Où vas-tu?
5. Comment vas-tu à la piscine? à la plage? au cinéma?
6. Est-ce que tu aimes faire des promenades à pied? Où vas-tu? avec qui?
7. Est-ce que tu aimes faire des promenades à vélo? Où vas-tu?
8. En général, est-ce que tu aimes regarder les films à la télé? Quels films est-ce que tu préfères? (les films d'action? les films de science-fiction? les comédies?)
9. Quand tu as un rendez-vous avec un copain ou une copine, où allez-vous?
10. À quels événements aimes-tu aller? Pourquoi?

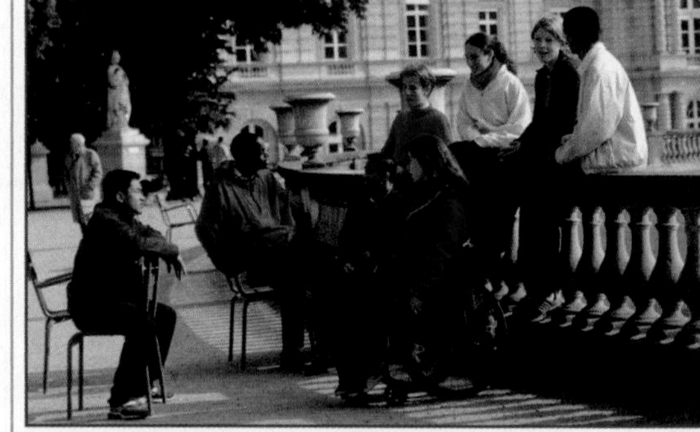

TALKING ABOUT PAST EVENTS

Let's talk about where you went yesterday. We will use the passé composé of **aller:**

present of **être + allé(e)**

(Note: since the focus is on spoken French, there is no need to introduce the agreement of the past participle at this time.)

▶ **Est-ce que tu es allé(e) en ville hier?**
Oui, je suis allé(e) en ville.
(Non, je ne suis pas allé(e) en ville.)

- **X, est-ce que tu es allé(e) au cinéma hier? à l'école? au supermarché?**

C La préposition *chez*

Note the use of **chez** in the following sentences.

Paul est **chez Céline.**	*Paul is* ***at Céline's (house).***
Je dîne **chez un copain.**	*I am having dinner* ***at a friend's (home).***
Nathalie va **chez Juliette.**	*Nathalie is going* ***to Juliette's (apartment).***
Tu vas **chez ta cousine.**	*You are going* ***to your cousin's (place).***

The French equivalent of *to* or *at someone's (house, home)* is the construction:

chez + PERSON	**chez** Béatrice	**chez** ma cousine

→ Note the interrogative expression: **chez qui?**
Chez qui vas-tu? ***To whose house*** *are you going?*

8 En vacances

PARLER/ÉCRIRE When we are on vacation, we often like to visit friends and relatives. Say where the following people are going.

▶ Claire / Marc
Claire va chez Marc.

1. Hélène / Jérôme
2. Jean-Paul / Lucie
3. tu / un copain
4. Corinne / une cousine
5. vous / des copines à Québec
6. nous / un cousin à Paris

9 Week-end

PARLER On weekends, we often like to visit friends and do things together. Say how the following people are spending Sunday afternoon.

▶ Cécile / jouer au ping-pong / Robert

1. Julie / aller / Béatrice
2. Claire / dîner / des cousins
3. Antoine / jouer au croquet / Sylvie
4. Marc / écouter des CD / un copain
5. Mathieu / regarder la télé / une copine
6. Élodie / jouer aux jeux vidéo / Thomas
7. Nous / manger une pizza / Léa
8. Vous / regarder un DVD / Éric
9. Tu / jouer au basket / Alice

- **Y, est-ce que tu es allé(e) chez des amis? chez des cousins?**
- **Est-ce que tu es allé(e) à un pique-nique? à la bibliothèque?**
- **Z, où est-ce que tu es allé(e) hier matin? hier après-midi? hier soir?**

Follow-up: Ask students what others did.

- **Est-ce que X est allé(e) au cinéma hier?**
- **Est-ce que Y est allé(e) chez des amis hier?**
- **Où est-ce que Z est allé(e) hier matin?**

Language note The word **rendez-vous** includes all types of appointments with friends, teachers, as well as professional appointments with doctors, dentists, etc. The term means that people have arranged to meet somewhere.

SECTION C

Communicative function
Talking about going to someone's house

Language notes

- **Chez** also means at *the office of*: **Je vais chez le docteur.**
- Be sure students see that the word **chez** means *to* or *at someone's place.* The preposition **à** is NEVER used with **chez.**

Looking ahead **Chez** + stress pronouns is presented in Lesson 15.

Pronunciation There is no liaison between **chez** and the name of a person:
chez Alice, chez Éric
However there is liaison with **un/une:**
chez un(e) ami(e)

8 PRACTICE saying whom people are visiting

1. Hélène va chez Jérôme.
2. Jean-Paul va chez Lucie.
3. Tu vas chez un copain.
4. Corinne va chez une cousine.
5. Vous allez chez des copines à Québec.
6. Nous allons chez un cousin à Paris.

9 DESCRIPTION stating at whose home people do certain activities

1. Julie va chez Béatrice.
2. Claire dîne chez des cousins.
3. Antoine joue au croquet chez Sylvie.
4. Marc écoute des CD chez un copain.
5. Mathieu regarde la télé chez une copine.
6. Élodie joue aux jeux vidéo chez Thomas.
7. Nous mangeons une pizza chez Léa.
8. Vous regardez un DVD chez Éric.
9. Tu joues au basket chez Alice.

SECTION D

Communicative function
Talking about future plans

Teaching Resource Options

PRINT

Workbook PE, pp. 123–130
Unit 5 Resource Book
- Audioscript, p. 64
- Communipak, pp. 140–163
- Video Activities, pp. 58–60
- Videoscript, pp. 62–63
- Workbook TE, pp. 35–42

AUDIO & VISUAL

Audio Program
CD 3 Track 6

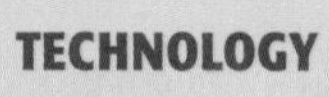

TECHNOLOGY

Power Presentations

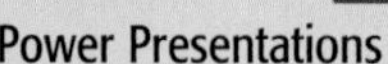

VIDEO PROGRAM

VIDÉO DVD

MODULE 14

14.4 Mini-scenes: Qu'est-ce que vous allez faire? (9:42–11:00 min.)

14.5 Mini-scenes: Tu vas nager? (11:01–11:49 min.)

14.6 Dialogue: Julien travaille (11:50–12:40 min.)

Casual speech One can also say: **Vous allez rentrer quand?**

Note that **Tu vas faire quoi?** is less common than **Qu'est-ce que tu vas faire?**

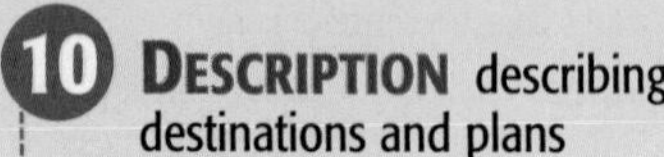

10 DESCRIPTION describing destinations and plans

1. Alice va à New York. Elle va visiter la statue de la Liberté.
2. Nous allons en Égypte. Nous allons visiter les pyramides.
3. Vous allez à Rome. Vous allez visiter le Colisée.
4. Tu vas à la Nouvelle Orléans. Tu vas visiter le Vieux Carré.
5. Je vais à San Francisco. Je vais visiter Chinatown.
6. Les élèves vont à San Antonio. Ils vont visiter l'Alamo.
7. Madame Lambert va à Beijing. Elle va visiter la Cité interdite.
8. Les touristes vont à Kyoto. Ils vont visiter les temples.

D La construction *aller* + l'infinitif

The following sentences describe what people are *going to do*.
Note how the verb **aller** is used to describe these FUTURE events.

Nathalie **va nager.**	*Nathalie **is going to swim.***
Paul et Marc **vont jouer** au tennis.	*Paul and Marc **are going to play** tennis.*
Nous **allons rester** à la maison.	***We are going to stay** home.*
Je **vais aller** en ville.	***I am going to go** downtown.*

To express the NEAR FUTURE, the French use the construction:

PRESENT of **aller** + INFINITIVE

→ In negative sentences, the construction is:

SUBJECT + **ne** + PRESENT of **aller** + **pas** + INFINITIVE ...				
Sylvie	**ne**	va	**pas**	écouter le concert avec nous.

→ Note the interrogative forms:

Qu'est-ce que tu vas faire?	***What are you going** to do?*
Quand est-ce que vous allez rentrer?	***When are you going** to come back?*

LANGUAGE COMPARISON

To talk about FUTURE plans and intentions, French and English frequently use similar verbs: **aller** *(to be going to).*

10 Tourisme

PARLER/ÉCRIRE Say where the following people are going this summer and what they are going to visit.

▶ Monique (à Paris / le Louvre)
Monique va à Paris. Elle va visiter le Louvre.

1. Alice (à New York / la statue de la Liberté)
2. nous (en Égypte / les pyramides)
3. vous (à Rome / le Colisée)
4. tu (à La Nouvelle Orléans / le Vieux Carré)
5. je (à San Francisco / Chinatown)
6. les élèves (à San Antonio / l'Alamo)
7. Madame Lambert (à Beijing / la Cité interdite *[Forbidden City]*)
8. les touristes (à Kyoto / les temples)

CULTURAL NOTES

- The coliseum **(le Colisée)** is a large stadium built by the Romans.
- The **Vieux Carré** is the part of the French Quarter known for its jazz clubs and its picturesque old buildings with wrought iron balconies.
- Historically, Kyoto was the capital of Japan; one can still visit the many Buddhist temples there as well as the Emperor's palace.

INCLUSION

Synthetic/analytic Review the conjugation of **aller**, and write the forms on board. Have 8 students go to the board and make sentences by writing infinitives after each **aller** verb form. Have the other students do this exercise in their notebooks.

11 Qu'est-ce que tu vas faire?

PARLER Ask your classmates if they are going to do the following things this weekend.

▶ étudier

1. travailler
2. surfer sur le Net
3. regarder la télé
4. aller au cinéma
5. inviter des amis
6. aller à une boum
7. jouer aux jeux vidéo
8. rester à la maison
9. faire une promenade à vélo

Est-ce que tu vas étudier?
Oui, je vais étudier.
(Non, je ne vais pas étudier.)

12 Un jeu: Descriptions

PARLER/ÉCRIRE Choose a person from Column A and say where the person is, what he or she has, and what he or she is going to do. Use the verbs **être, avoir,** and **aller** with the phrases in columns B, C, and D. How many logical descriptions can you make?

▶ **Monique est en ville. Elle a un vélo. Elle va faire une promenade.**

A	B (être)	C (avoir)	D (aller)
tu	sur le court	des livres	aller dans les magasins
Monique	à la bibliothèque	un vélo	étudier
je	au salon	20 euros	faire une promenade
les amis	en ville	une télé	regarder un film
nous	à la maison	une chaîne hi-fi	faire un match
vous	au café	une raquette	écouter des CD

PRONONCIATION

Les semi-voyelles /w/ et /j/

In French, the semi-vowels /w/ and /j/ are pronounced very quickly, almost like consonants.

/w/

oui

/j/

très bien

Répétez:

/w/ **oui chouette Louise**

/wa/, /wɛ̃/ **moi toi pourquoi voiture loin**
Chouette! La voiture de Louise n'est pas loin.

/j/ **bien chien radio piano Pierre Daniel violon pied étudiant**
Pierre écoute la radio avec Daniel.

GAME Un jeu

Act. 12 can be done as a team game. Divide the class into groups of 3 or 4 students. Have each group take out a sheet of paper and choose a recorder **(un/une secrétaire)**. As the group creates a description, the recorder will write it down.

Give a signal for the groups to start. At the end of the time limit, stop the groups. Have them exchange papers (Group 1 passes its paper to Group 2, Group 2 to Group 3, etc.).

Each group checks the paper it received for accuracy and records the number of correct and logical descriptions. The group with the highest score wins.

Realia note See if the students can guess that it is the Mona Lisa's eye that appears in the **Carte musée et monuments**. Then ask if they remember the name of the museum where the Mona Lisa is located **(le Louvre).** The **Carte musée et monuments** allows the bearer to visit 70 museums and monuments for 1, 3, or 5 days.

11 EXCHANGES talking about weekend plans

–Est-ce que tu vas ... ?
–Oui, je vais ... (Non, je ne vais pas ...)

1. travailler
2. surfer sur le Net
3. regarder la télé
4. aller au cinéma
5. inviter des amis
6. aller à une boum
7. jouer aux jeux vidéo
8. rester à la maison
9. faire une promenade à vélo

Variation (with **vous** and **nous**)
– **Est-ce que vous allez étudier?**
– **Oui, nous allons étudier. (Non, nous n'allons pas étudier.)**

Teaching strategy: Act. 11 may be conducted as a classroom survey. See *Game: Getting acquainted* on p. 108.

12 DESCRIPTION describing people and their plans

Answers will vary.

- Tu es (au salon). Tu as (une télé). Tu vas (regarder un film).
- Je suis (en ville). J'ai (20 euros). Je vais (aller dans les magasins).
- Les amis sont (à la maison). Ils ont (une chaîne hi-fi). Ils vont (écouter des CD).
- Nous sommes (à la bibliothèque). Nous avons (des livres). Nous allons (étudier).
- Vous êtes (sur le court). Vous avez (une raquette). Vous allez (faire un match).

Re-entry and review
This activity reviews the forms of **être, avoir,** and **aller.**

PRONUNCIATION

- Be sure students pronounce the /j/ very quickly. The following words should sound like two (and not three) syllables:
  pia-no **Da-niel**
  ra-dio **vio-lon**
  These words are pronounced in one syllable:
  Pierre /ɛer/ **pied** /ɛe/
- You may want to present the other French semi vowel /ɥ/, which is not formally introduced at this level: It is spelled **u** + vowel, as in **lui, suis, juillet** and **aujourd'hui.**

À VOTRE TOUR

Main Topic

- Recapitulation and review

Teaching Resource Options

PRINT  

Workbook PE, pp. 123–130
Unit 5 Resource Book
Audioscript, pp. 64–65
Communipak, pp. 140–163
Family Involvement, pp. 54–55
Workbook TE, pp. 35–42

Assessment
Lesson 14 Quiz, pp. 69–70
Portfolio Assessment, Unit 1 URB, pp. 155–164
Audioscript for Quiz 14, p. 68
Answer Keys, pp. 210–213

AUDIO & VISUAL 

Audio Program
CD 3 Tracks 7, 8
CD 15 Track 2

TECHNOLOGY 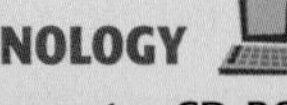

Test Generator CD-ROM/McDougal Littell Assessment System

1 COMPREHENSION

1. Tu restes chez toi samedi?
   (d) Non, j'ai un rendez-vous avec Christine.
2. Qu'est-ce que vous allez faire?
   (c) Nous allons faire une promenade en ville.
3. Est-ce que vous allez aller au cinéma?
   (b) Peut-être! Il y a un très bon film au Rex.
4. À quelle heure est-ce que tu vas rentrer?
   (a) À dix heures.

À votre tour!

OBJECTIFS

Now you can ...
- talk about places you go to
- discuss what you are going to do in the future

1 Allô!

PARLER Anne is calling Jérôme. Match Jérôme's answers with Anne's questions. Then act out the dialogue with a friend.

2 Créa-dialogue

PARLER As you are going for a walk in town, you meet several friends. Ask them where they are going and what they are going to do there.

OÙ?	ACTIVITÉ
	dîner avec un copain

▶ —Salut, Alison. Ça va?
—Oui, ça va!
—Où vas-tu?
—Je vais au restaurant.
—Ah bon? Qu'est-ce que tu vas faire là-bas?
—Je vais dîner avec un copain.
—Avec qui?
—Avec Chris.

OÙ?	ACTIVITÉ
1	manger une pizza
2	faire une promenade
3	jouer au foot
4	nager
5	jouer au volley
6	travailler
7	??

À VOTRE TOUR

Select those activities which are most appropriate for your students.

PAIR PRACTICE

Act 1–3 lend themselves well to pair practice. For preparation, have the class listen to the corresponding audio recordings.

PORTFOLIO ASSESSMENT

You will probably select only one speaking activity and one writing activity to go into the students' portfolios for Unit 5.

In this lesson, Act. 2 can be the basis for an oral portfolio dialogue. Act. 5 can be used as a writing portfolio topic.

3 Conversation libre

PARLER Have a conversation with a classmate. Ask your classmate questions about what he/she plans to do on the weekend. Try to find out as much as possible, using yes/no questions.

4 Qu'est-ce que vous allez faire?

ÉCRIRE Leave a note for your friend Jean-Marc, telling him three things that you and your friends are going to do tonight and three things that you are going to do this weekend.

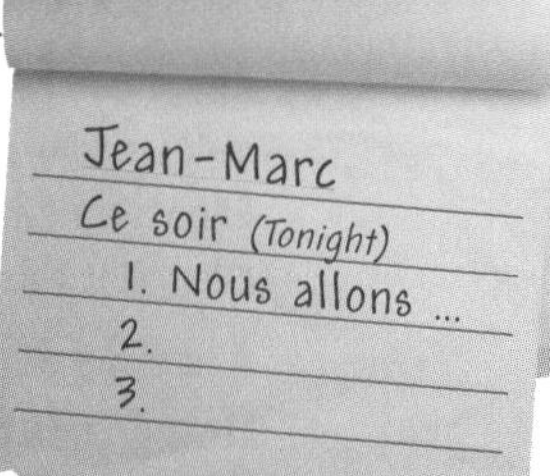

Jean-Marc
Ce soir (Tonight)
1. Nous allons ...
2.
3.

5 Bonnes résolutions

ÉCRIRE Imagine that it is January 1 and you are making up New Year's resolutions. On a separate sheet of paper, describe six of your resolutions by saying what you are going to do and what you are not going to do in the coming year.

CLASSROOM MANAGEMENT Group reading and writing practice

Have all students prepare Act. 5 as homework. Then, divide the class into groups of 4.

Ask students to share their lists of resolutions with those in their group. Then have each group compare the 4 lists and vote on the 6 best resolutions.

The recorder **(le/la secrétaire)** rewrites the 6 resolutions in the **nous**-form.

1. **Nous allons toujours parler français en classe.**
2. **Nous n'allons pas être pénibles avec nos copains.**, etc.

The reporter **(le reporter)** will read the group's list to the rest of the class.

2 GUIDED ORAL EXPRESSION

–Salut, (X). Ça va?
–Oui, ça va!
–Où vas-tu?
–Je vais ...
–Ah bon, qu'est-ce que tu vas faire là-bas?
–Je vais ...
–Avec qui?
–Avec (X).

1. Thomas/au café/manger une pizza/Sandrine
2. Jean-Paul/au parc/faire une promenade/Karine
3. Robert/au stade/jouer au foot/mes copains
4. Nancy/à la piscine/nager/Caroline
5. Sylvie/à la plage/jouer au volley/mes amis
6. Patrick/au supermarché/travailler/Julien
7. Claire/au centre commercial/(regarder des vêtements / aller dans les magasins)/(Julie)

Teaching strategy If students have difficulty with item 7, you may wish to suggest possible activities: **retrouver des amis, aller dans les magasins, manger un hot-dog,** etc.

(The verb **acheter** is introduced in Lesson 17.)

Variation Have students write out the dialogue with a partner.

3 CONVERSATION

Answers will vary.

- –Est-ce que tu vas aller à la plage?
  –Oui, je vais aller à la plage. (Non, je ne vais pas aller à la plage.)
- –Est-ce que tu vas aller au restaurant?
  –Oui, je vais aller au restaurant. (Non, je ne vais pas aller au restaurant.)
- –Est-ce que tu vas aller au centre commercial?
  –Oui, je vais aller au centre commercial. (Non, je ne vais pas aller au centre commercial.)
- –Est-ce que tu vas aller au match de foot?
  –Oui, je vais aller au match de foot. (Non, je ne vais pas aller au match de foot.)

Variation Have students write out the conversation with a partner.

4 WRITTEN SELF-EXPRESSION

Answers will vary.

Ce soir
1. Nous allons dîner chez Paul.
2. Nous allons faire une promenade en ville.
3. Nous allons étudier.

Ce week-end
1. Nous allons organiser une boum.
2. Nous allons danser.
3. Nous allons regarder un film.

5 WRITTEN SELF-EXPRESSION

Answers will vary.
1. Je vais travailler à la maison.
2. Je ne vais pas regarder la télé.
3. Je vais écouter le professeur en classe.
4. Je vais étudier.
5. Je ne vais pas être pénible avec mon frère.
6. Je vais jouer au tennis avec ma soeur.

Leçon 15

Main Topic Finding out what people are talking about

Teaching Resource Options

PRINT 

Workbook PE, pp. 131–136
Activités pour tous PE, pp. 79–81
Block Scheduling Copymasters, pp. 113–120
Unit 5 Resource Book
- *Activités pour tous* TE, pp. 77–79
- Audioscript, pp. 97, 98–99
- Communipak, pp. 140–163
- Lesson Plans, pp. 80–81
- Block Scheduling Lesson Plans, pp. 82–83
- Absent Student Copymasters, pp. 84–88
- Video Activities, pp. 91–94
- Videoscript, pp. 95–96
- Workbook TE, pp. 71–76

AUDIO & VISUAL 

Audio Program
CD 3 Tracks 9, 10
CD 9 Tracks 17–24

TECHNOLOGY

Online Workbook

VIDEO PROGRAM

VIDÉO DVD 

MODULE 15
Sports et musique

TOTAL TIME: 6:03 min.
DVD Disk 2
Videotape 3 (COUNTER: 14:20 min.)

15.1 Mini-scenes: Listening
–Quels sports est-ce que vous pratiquez? (15:43–16:11 min.)

15.2 Mini-scenes: Listening
–Tu veux jouer au volley? (16:12–16:32 min.)

15.3 Mini-scenes: Speaking
–Est-ce que Paul joue au tennis? (16:33–17:21 min.)

15.4 Mini-scenes: Listening
–De quel instrument est-ce que tu joues? (17:22–18:20 min.)

15.5 Dialogue: Interview avec Éric
(18:21–18:55 min.)

15.6 Vignette culturelle: À la Maison des jeunes
(18:56–20:23 min.)

Comprehension practice Play the entire module through as an introduction to the lesson.

LEÇON 15

Au Café de l'Univers

AUDIO

Où vas-tu après les cours?	*after school*
Est-ce que tu vas directement chez toi?	*straight/home*
Valérie, elle, ne va pas directement chez elle.	*to her house*
Elle va au Café de l'Univers avec ses copines Fatima et Zaïna.	
Elle vient souvent ici avec elles.	*comes*
À la table de Valérie, la conversation est toujours très animée.	*lively*
De quoi parlent les filles aujourd'hui?	*About what*
Est-ce qu'elles parlent de l'examen d'histoire? / du problème de maths? / de la classe de sciences?	*history test*
Non!	
Est-ce qu'elles parlent du week-end prochain? / des vacances?	*next*
Non plus!	*Not that either!*
Est-ce qu'elles parlent du nouveau copain de Marie-Claire? / de la cousine de Pauline? / des amis de Véronique?	*new*
Pas du tout!	*Not at all!*
Aujourd'hui, les filles parlent d'un sujet beaucoup plus important! Elles parlent du nouveau prof d'anglais! (C'est un jeune professeur américain. Il est très intéressant, très amusant, très sympathique … et surtout il est très mignon!)	*subject/more* … *above all*

SETTING THE STAGE

With books closed, ask students what they talk about when they get together. List the topics (in English) on the board.

Then play the audio recording of the above text. Have students listen to see what topics of conversation are mentioned in the text.

Which of the topics on the students' list are the same as those mentioned by the speaker? Which are new?

Play the audio again, and ask them to try to get additional information.

Finally have them open their books and follow along as you play the audio once more.

Compréhension

1. Où va Valérie après les cours?
2. Avec qui est-ce qu'elle va au café?
3. Qu'est-ce que les filles font au café?
4. Est-ce qu'elles parlent de l'école?
5. Est-ce qu'elles parlent des activités du week-end?
6. De quelle *(which)* personne parlent-elles aujourd'hui?
7. De quelle nationalité est le professeur d'anglais?
8. Comment est-il?

Et toi?

Describe what you do by completing the following sentences.

1. En général, après les cours,
   je vais ...
   je ne vais pas ...

   • à la bibliothèque • au café
   • chez mes *(my)* copains • directement chez moi

2. Avec mes copains,
   je parle ...
   je ne parle pas ...

   • de la classe de français • des examens
   • du prof de français • du week-end

3. Avec mes parents,
   je parle ...
   je ne parle pas ...

   • de l'école • de mes notes *(grades)*
   • de la classe de français • de mes copains

4. Avec mon frère ou ma soeur,
   je parle ...
   je ne parle pas ...

   • de mes copains • de mes problèmes
   • du week-end • des vacances

NOTE culturelle

Au café

On peut° faire beaucoup de choses différentes dans un café français. On peut manger un sandwich. On peut commander° un jus de fruits. On peut étudier. On peut jouer aux jeux électroniques. Dans les cybercafés, on peut aussi surfer sur l'Internet. Les jeunes Français vont au café principalement pour retrouver° leurs° copains et passer° un bon moment avec eux.°

Un café français est divisé en deux parties: l'intérieur et la terrasse.° Au printemps et en été, les Français préfèrent s'asseoir° à la terrasse. Là, ils peuvent° profiter du soleil° et regarder les gens qui passent dans la rue.

On peut *One can* **commander** *order* **retrouver** *meet* **leurs** *their* **passer** *spend* **eux** *them*
la terrasse *terrace (outdoor section of a café)* **s'asseoir** *to sit* **peuvent** *can* **profiter du soleil** *enjoy the sun*

TALKING ABOUT PAST EVENTS

Let's talk about where you went Saturday.

X et Y, est-ce que vous êtes allé(e)s au cinéma samedi soir?

Oui, nous sommes allé(e)s au cinéma.

(Non, nous ne sommes pas allé(e)s au cinéma.)

- **Est-ce que vous êtes allé(e)s en ville? chez des amis? à un concert?**
- **Où êtes-vous allé(e)s samedi matin? samedi après-midi?**

Let's say where others went last weekend.

Est-ce que X et Y sont allé(e)s au cinéma samedi soir?

Oui, ils/elles sont allé(e)s au cinéma.

(Non, ils/elles ne sont pas allé(e)s au cinéma.)

Compréhension

Answers

1. Valérie va au Café de l'Univers.
2. Elle va au café avec Fatima et Zaïna.
3. Elles parlent.
4. non
5. non
6. Elles parlent du nouveau prof d'anglais.
7. Il est américain.
8. Il est intéressant, amusant, sympathique et... mignon.

Et toi?

Answers will vary.

1. En général, après les cours, je vais (chez mes copains).
   Je ne vais pas (directement chez moi).
2. Avec mes copains, je parle (du week-end).
   Je ne parle pas (de la classe de français).
3. Avec mes parents, je parle (de l'école).
   Je ne parle pas (de mes notes).
4. Avec mon frère et ma soeur, je parle (de mes problèmes).
   Je ne parle pas (des vacances).

Teaching strategy With their books closed, have students raise their hands as you read through the items in **Et toi?**

(Note: Read only the affirmative sentences.)

En général, après les classes, qui va à la bibliothèque?

Qui va chez ses copains?, etc.

Pre-AP skill: Listen without reading.

Critical thinking activity Have students give the English equivalents of the following phrases in the dialogue on p. 216.

le nouveau copain de Marie-Claire
[Marie-Claire's new boyfriend]

la cousine de Pauline
[Pauline's cousin]

Ask: Is the word order the same in French and English?

Does French use an apostrophe to express relationship?

What is a word-for-word translation of the French construction?

Looking ahead Possession with **de** is formally introduced in Lesson 16.

SECTION A

Communicative function
Saying who is coming

Teaching Resource Options

PRINT 

Workbook PE, pp. 131–136
Unit 5 Resource Book
Communipak, pp. 140–163
Workbook TE, pp. 71–76

TECHNOLOGY 

Power Presentations

Pronunciation note Be sure that students pronounce the third person plural form correctly: **viennent** /vjɛn/.

Language note If someone is waiting for you and calls out: **Tu viens?** the usual French response is: **J'arrive** (which means *I'm just about ready and I'm coming*). However, if the person is simply asking if you are planning to join them, the French response is: **Oui, je viens** (which means, *Yes I'm coming along with you*).

1 EXCHANGES inviting friends to come along

1. –Je vais au café. Tu viens avec moi?
   –D'accord, je viens. (Non, je ne viens pas.)
2. –Je vais à la bibliothèque. Tu viens avec moi?
   –D'accord, je viens. (Non, je ne viens pas.)
3. –Je vais à la piscine. Tu viens avec moi?
   –D'accord, je viens. (Non, je ne viens pas.)
4. –Je vais au cybercafé. Tu viens avec moi?
   –D'accord, je viens. (Non, je ne viens pas.)
5. –Je vais au centre commercial. Tu viens avec moi?
   –D'accord, je viens. (Non, je ne viens pas.)
6. –Je vais au magasin de CD. Tu viens avec moi?
   –D'accord, je viens. (Non, je ne viens pas.)
7. –Je vais au stade. Tu viens avec moi?
   –D'accord, je viens. (Non, je ne viens pas.)
8. –Je vais en classe. Tu viens avec moi?
   –D'accord, je viens. (Non, je ne viens pas.)

Challenge For negative answers, explain why you cannot come.
Non, je ne viens pas.
Je dois dîner avec Michelle.

2 PRACTICE saying who is coming to an event

1. Alice vient.
2. Jean-Pierre ne vient pas.
3. Paul et Caroline viennent.
4. Vous ne venez pas.
5. Je viens.
6. Nous ne venons pas.
7. Tu ne viens pas.
8. Le prof de français vient.
9. Le prof d'anglais vient.

A Le verbe *venir*

The verb **venir** *(to come)* is irregular. Note the forms of **venir** in the present tense.

venir	Nous allons **venir** avec des amis.
je **viens** tu **viens** il/elle **vient**	Je **viens** avec toi. Est-ce que tu **viens** au cinéma? Monique ne **vient** pas avec nous.
nous **venons** vous **venez** ils/elles **viennent**	Nous **venons** à cinq heures. À quelle heure **venez**-vous à la boum? Ils **viennent** de Paris, n'est-ce pas?

→ **Revenir** *(to come back)* is conjugated like **venir.**
—À quelle heure **revenez**-vous?
—Nous **revenons** à dix heures.

→ Note the interrogative expression: **d'où?** *(from where?)*

D'où viens-tu? *__Where__ do you come __from?__*

1  Tu viens?

PARLER Tell a friend where you are going and ask him or her to come along.

▶ à la pizzeria

1. au café
2. à la bibliothèque
3. à la piscine
4. au cybercafé
5. au centre commercial
6. au magasin de CD
7. au stade
8. en classe

2 Le pique-nique du Club français

PARLER/ÉCRIRE The French Club has organized a picnic. Say who is coming and who is not.

▶ Philippe (non)
Philippe ne vient pas.

1. Alice (oui)
2. Jean-Pierre (non)
3. Paul et Caroline (oui)
4. vous (non)
5. je (oui)
6. nous (non)
7. tu (non)
8. le prof de français (oui)
9. le prof d'anglais (oui)

TOURING PARIS

PROPS: Paper and pencils or crayons

Name and sketch on the board four Paris sites:
1. le Louvre
2. la tour Eiffel
3. les Champs-Élysées
4. l'Arc de Triomphe

Have the class count off by four's. Then have each student draw and label a site.
Si vous avez le numéro 1, dessinez le Louvre.
Si vous avez le numéro 2, dessinez...

Ask about tourist plans.
Qui va visiter la tour Eiffel aujourd'hui?
Levez le dessin.

B La préposition *de; de* + l'article défini

The preposition **de** has several meanings:

from	Nous venons **de** la bibliothèque.	*We are coming **from** the library.*
of	Quelle est l'adresse **de** l'école?	*What is the address **of** the school?*
about	Je parle **de** mon copain.	*I am talking **about** my friend.*

CONTRACTIONS

Note the forms of **de** + DEFINITE ARTICLE in the sentences below.

Voici **le** café.	Marc vient **du** café.
Voici **les** Champs-Élysées.	Nous venons **des** Champs-Élysées.
Voici **la** piscine.	Tu reviens **de la** piscine.
Voici **l'**hôtel.	Les touristes arrivent **de l'**hôtel.

The preposition **de** contracts with **le** and **les,** but not with **la** and **l'.**

CONTRACTION	NO CONTRACTION		
de + le → **du**	de + la = **de la**	**du** café	**de la** plage
de + les → **des**	de + l' = **de l'**	**des** magasins	**de l'**école

→ There is liaison after **des** when the next word begins with a vowel sound.
Où sont les livres **des étudiants?**

3 Rendez-vous

PARLER The following students live in Paris. On a Saturday afternoon they are meeting in a café. Say where each one is coming from.

▶ Jacques: le musée d'Orsay

1. Sylvie: le Louvre
2. Isabelle: le parc de la Villette
3. Jean-Paul: le Centre Pompidou
4. François: le Quartier latin
5. Cécile: l'avenue de l'Opéra
6. Nicole: la tour Eiffel
7. Marc: le jardin du Luxembourg
8. André: les Champs-Élysées
9. Pierre: les Galeries Lafayette
10. Corinne: la rue Bonaparte

Jacques vient du musée d'Orsay.

Review **aller** and contractions with **à.**

Ask each group where they are going.

Qui va au Louvre?
[Nous, nous allons au Louvre.]
Vous allez à l'Arc de Triomphe?
[Non, nous allons au Louvre!]...

On the board write: **au Louvre, aux Champs-Élysées, à la tour Eiffel, à l'Arc de Triomphe.**

Practice **venir** and contractions with **de.**

Qui vient des Champs-Élysées?
[Moi, je viens des Champs-Élysées.]
Et X, est-ce qu'il vient des Champs-Élysées?
[Non, il vient de la tour Eiffel.] ...

On the board write: **du Louvre, des Champs-Élysées, de la tour Eiffel, de l'Arc de Triomphe.**

SECTION B

Communicative function
Talking about where people are coming from

Teaching strategy Be sure students realize that the words in heavy print in the sentences on the left correspond to *the* and that those in the sentences on the right correspond to *from the.*

3 PRACTICE saying where people are coming from

1. Sylvie vient du Louvre.
2. Isabelle vient du parc de la Villette.
3. Jean-Paul vient du Centre Pompidou.
4. François vient du Quartier latin.
5. Cécile vient de l'avenue de l'Opéra.
6. Nicole vient de la tour Eiffel.
7. Marc vient du jardin de Luxembourg.
8. André vient des Champs-Élysées.
9. Pierre vient des Galeries Lafayette.
10. Corinne vient de la rue Bonaparte.

Cultural background
The **Quartier latin** is the historical students' quarter on the Left Bank. One of the streets is **la rue Bonaparte,** named in honor of Napoleon.

Le jardin du Luxembourg is also in that part of Paris.

Les Galeries Lafayette is a well-known Paris department store.

Teaching strategy This exercise should be done quickly with the rhythm of a practice drill. Be sure to read the cues aloud, carefully modeling the pronunciation of the new place names.

Variation Repeat the drill, changing the subjects orally.
nous: le musée d'Orsay
Nous venons du musée d'Orsay.

Re-entry and review Say that the people are going to these places.

Jacques va au musée d'Orsay.

Teaching Resource Options

PRINT 

Workbook PE, pp. 131–136
Unit 5 Resource Book
- Communipak, pp. 140–163
- Video Activities, pp. 91–94
- Videoscript, pp. 95–96
- Workbook TE, pp. 71–76

AUDIO & VISUAL 

Overhead Transparencies
16 Subject pronouns

TECHNOLOGY 

Power Presentations

VIDEO PROGRAM

MODULE 15
Sports et musique
(14:20–20:23 min.)

4 ROLE PLAY finding out where people are coming from

–D'où viens-tu?
–Je viens ...
1. du restaurant
2. de la bibliothèque
3. du concert de rock
4. de la boum de Christine
5. du pique-nique de Monique
6. de l'opéra

Language notes

- **Le foot (le football)** is soccer; American football is **le football américain.**
- In the expressions **jouer du piano** and **jouer de la flûte, du** and **de la** represent the preposition **de** plus a definite article. Therefore, in the negative one does not use **de.** Compare:
  Je n'ai pas de clarinette.
  Je ne joue pas de la clarinette.

Supplementary vocabulary

SPORTS
le croquet **le golf**
le frisbee **le rugby**
le hockey sur glace, sur gazon
INSTRUMENTS
le cor anglais *French horn*
le synthé, synthétiseur
le trombone
le tuba
la flûte à bec *recorder*
la guitare électrique
la trompette
le violoncelle *cello*

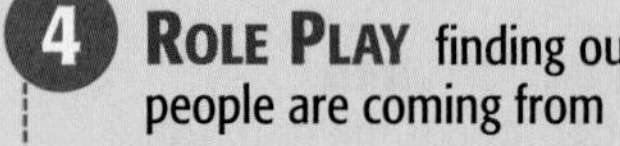

4  D'où viens-tu?

PARLER During vacation, Olivier goes out every day. When he gets home, his sister Sophie asks him where he is coming from.

▶ mardi

1. lundi
2. mercredi
3. vendredi
4. dimanche
5. samedi
6. jeudi

LUNDI	le restaurant
▶ MARDI	le cybercafé
MERCREDI	la bibliothèque
JEUDI	l'opéra
VENDREDI	le concert de rock
SAMEDI	le pique-nique de Monique
DIMANCHE	la boum de Christine

VOCABULAIRE Les sports, les jeux et la musique

▶ Les sports

le foot(ball) **le basket(ball)** **le ping-pong** **le volley(ball)** **le tennis** **le baseball**

▶ Les jeux *(games)*

les échecs *(chess)* **les jeux vidéo** **les jeux d'ordinateur** **les dames** *(checkers)* **les cartes** *(cards)*

▶ Les instruments de musique

le piano **le violon** **le saxo(phone)** **le clavier** *(keyboard)* **la flûte** **la guitare** **la clarinette** **la batterie** *(drums)*

jouer à + le, la, les + SPORT or GAME	*to play*	Nous **jouons au** tennis.
jouer de + le, la, les + INSTRUMENT	*to play*	Alice **joue du** piano.

5  Activités

PARLER Ask your classmates if they play the following instruments and games.

▶ —Est-ce que tu joues au ping-pong?
—Oui, je joue au ping-pong.
(Non, je ne joue pas au ping-pong.)

▶ —Est-ce que tu joues du piano?
—Oui, je joue du piano.
(Non, je ne joue pas du piano.)

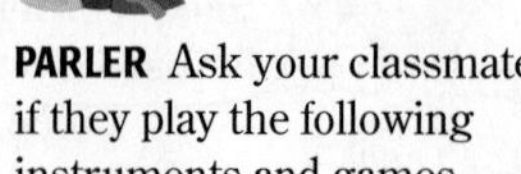

USING THE VIDEO

The entire video module for this lesson develops the themes of sports and music, and utilizes the expressions **jouer à** and **jouer de.**

If you do not want to present the whole module at once, you can show some of the segments at the end of the lesson for review.

INCLUSION

Metacognitive Write all the stress pronouns on the board. Explain the rules of forming pronouns. Ask students to repeat using their own words. Then point to each one as you model the pronunciation. Give students a noun and ask them to generate a pronoun.

Les pronoms accentués

In the answers to the questions below, the nouns in heavy print are replaced by pronouns. These pronouns are called STRESS PRONOUNS. Note their forms.

—François dîne avec **Florence?** *Is François having dinner with* ***Florence?***
—Oui, il dîne avec **elle.** *Yes, he is having dinner with* ***her.***

—Tu parles de **Jean-Paul?** *Are you talking about* ***Jean-Paul?***
—Non, je ne parle pas de **lui.** *No, I'm not talking about* ***him.***

FORMS

(SUBJECT PRONOUNS)	STRESS PRONOUNS	(SUBJECT PRONOUNS)	STRESS PRONOUNS
(je)	**moi**	(nous)	**nous**
(tu)	**toi**	(vous)	**vous**
(il)	**lui**	(ils)	**eux**
(elle)	**elle**	(elles)	**elles**

USES

Stress pronouns are used:

- to reinforce a subject pronoun
  Moi, je parle français. *I speak French.*
  Vous, vous parlez anglais. ***You*** *speak English.*
- after **c'est** and **ce n'est pas**
  —C'est Paul là-bas?
  —Non, ce n'est pas **lui.** *No, it's not* ***him.***
- in short sentences where there is no verb
  —Qui parle français ici?
  —**Moi!** ***I do!***
- before and after **et** and **ou**
  Lui et moi, nous sommes copains. ***He and I,*** *(we) are friends.*
- After prepositions such as **de, avec, pour, chez**
  Voici Marc et Paul. Je parle souvent **d'eux.** *I often talk* ***about them.***
  Voici Isabelle. Je vais au cinéma **avec elle.** *I go to the movies* ***with her.***
  Voici M. Mercier. Nous travaillons **pour lui.** *We work* ***for him.***

→ Note the meaning of **chez** + STRESS PRONOUN:
Je vais **chez moi.** *I am going* ***home.***
Paul étudie **chez lui.** *Paul is studying* ***at home.***
Tu viens **chez nous?** *Are you coming* ***to our house?***
Je suis chez Alice. Je dîne **chez elle.** *I am having dinner* ***at her place.***

TALKING ABOUT PAST EVENTS

Let's talk about what sports and games you and your friends played last weekend.

X et Y, est-ce que vous avez joué au tennis le week-end dernier?

Oui, nous avons joué au tennis.

(Non, nous n'avons pas joué au tennis.)

- **Est-ce que vous avez joué au football? au baseball? au ping-pong? au volley? aux échecs? aux cartes? aux dames? au Monopoly?**

Additional challenge questions

- **Où est-ce que vous avez joué?**
- **Avec qui est-ce que vous avez joué?**
- **Qui a gagné?** (Who won?)

5 COMMUNICATION talking about leisure activities

–Est-ce que tu joues ... ?
–Oui, je joue ... (Non, je ne joue pas ...)

1. de la guitare
2. de la flûte
3. au basket[ball]
4. de la clarinette
5. de la batterie
6. aux échecs
7. aux dames
8. aux cartes
9. du violon
10. au tennis

SECTION C

Communicative function
Referring to people

Language notes

- One can also reinforce the subject as follows:
  Je parle français, moi.
  Vous parlez anglais, vous.
- The stress form of **que** *(what)* is **quoi.**
  It is used:
  - alone: **Quoi?**
  - after a preposition: **De quoi** est-ce que tu parles?
  - in casual questions: Tu fais **quoi**?

Teaching strategy

- Use **Transparency 16: Subject pronouns** to introduce stress pronouns, writing the corresponding pronoun in the box below each drawing.
- Erase the words from the transparency. As you make statements, have a student volunteer point to the corresponding pronouns.
  Qui vient? Lui! Toi! Nous! Qui joue au tennis? Eux! Vous! etc.
- Then point to the pronouns and let the students respond.
  Qui parle français? [point to "je"]
  Moi.
  Qui parle anglais? [point to "il"]
  Lui. etc.

Teaching Resource Options

PRINT 

Workbook PE, pp. 131–136
Unit 5 Resource Book
Audioscript, p. 97
Communipak, pp. 140–163
Workbook TE, pp. 71–76

AUDIO & VISUAL 

Audio Program
CD 3 Track 11

TECHNOLOGY

Power Presentations

6 COMPREHENSION stating who is home and who isn't

1. Il est chez lui. (Il n'est pas chez lui.)
2. Elle n'est pas chez elle.
3. Ils ne sont pas chez eux.
4. Elles sont chez elles. (Elles ne sont pas chez elles.)
5. Ils ne sont pas chez eux.
6. Je suis chez moi. (Je ne suis pas chez moi.)
7. Tu n'es pas chez toi.
8. Nous ne sommes pas chez nous.
9. Tu es chez toi. (Tu n'est pas chez toi.)

Expansion The first model and items 1, 4, 6, 9 could be either: the people could be at home or at another person's home. If students give a negative response, ask them to clarify.

Alice étudie.

Elle n'est pas chez elle.

Elle étudie (chez Sophie, à la bibliothèque, etc.).

7 COMMUNICATION answering personal questions

1. Oui, j'étudie souvent avec eux. (Non, je n'étudie pas souvent avec eux.)
2. Oui, je vais souvent chez elle. (Non, je ne vais pas souvent chez elle.)
3. Oui, je travaille pour eux. (Non, je ne travaille pas pour eux.)
4. Oui, je parle français avec lui. (Non, je ne parle pas français avec lui.)
5. Oui, je vais souvent au cinéma avec elles. (Non, je ne vais pas souvent au cinéma avec elles.)
6. Oui, je reste chez moi le week-end. (Non, je ne reste pas chez moi le week-end.)
7. Oui, je reste chez moi pendant les vacances. (Non, je ne reste pas chez moi pendant les vacances.)
8. Oui, je voyage avec mes parents. (Non, je ne voyage pas avec mes parents.)
9. Oui, je joue aux jeux vidéo avec lui. (Non, je ne joue pas aux jeux vidéo avec lui.)
10. Oui, je vais souvent chez eux. (Non, je ne vais pas souvent chez eux.)

6 Samedi soir *(Saturday night)*

PARLER/ÉCRIRE On Saturday night, some people stay home and others do not. Read what the following people are doing and say whether or not they are at home.

▶ Alice étudie.
Elle est chez elle.

▶ Paul va au cinéma.
Il n'est pas chez lui.

1. François regarde la télé.
2. Mélanie va au cinéma.
3. Marc et Pierre dînent en ville.
4. Léa et Pauline écoutent des CD.
5. Les voisins font une promenade.
6. Je travaille avec mon père.
7. Tu vas au théâtre.
8. Nous allons à la bibliothèque.
9. Tu prépares le dîner.

7 Questions personnelles

PARLER/ÉCRIRE Use stress pronouns in your answers.

1. Tu étudies souvent avec tes *(your)* copains?
2. Tu vas souvent chez ta cousine?
3. Tu travailles pour les voisins?
4. Tu parles français avec ton père?
5. Tu vas souvent au cinéma avec tes copines?
6. Tu restes chez toi le week-end?
7. Tu restes chez toi pendant *(during)* les vacances?
8. Tu voyages avec tes parents?
9. Tu joues aux jeux vidéo avec ton copain?
10. Tu vas souvent chez tes voisins?

VOCABULAIRE Expressions pour la conversation

▶ ***How to express surprise:***

Vraiment?! *Really?!*
–Je parle chinois.
–**Vraiment?!**

▶ ***How to contradict someone:***

Pas du tout! *Not at all! Definitely not!*
–Tu es anglais?
–**Pas du tout!** Je suis français!

8  Commérage *(Gossip)*

PARLER Élodie likes to gossip. Act out the dialogues between her and her friend Thomas.

▶ Marina dîne avec Jean-Pierre.

1. Éric dîne avec Alice.
2. Thérèse va chez Paul.
3. Jérôme est au cinéma avec Delphine.
4. Monsieur Mercier travaille pour Mademoiselle Duval.
5. Philippe travaille pour le voisin.
6. Marc et Vincent dansent avec Mélanie et Juliette.

D La construction: nom + *de* + nom

Compare the word order in French and English.

J'ai une raquette.	C'est une **raquette de tennis.**	*It's a **tennis racket.***
Paul a une voiture.	C'est une **voiture de sport.**	*It's a **sports car.***

When one noun is used to modify another noun, the French construction is:

MAIN NOUN + **de** + MODIFYING NOUN	**une classe de français.**
d' (+ VOWEL SOUND)	**une classe d'espagnol.**

→There is no article after **de.**

LANGUAGE COMPARISON

In French, when one noun modifies another, the main noun comes FIRST.

In English, the main noun comes SECOND.

un **jeu** d'ordinateur — *a computer **game***

9 Précisions

PARLER/ÉCRIRE Complete the following sentences with an expression consisting of **de** + underlined noun.

▶ J'aime le sport. J'ai une voiture …

J'ai une voiture de sport!

1. Claire aime le ping-pong. Elle a une raquette …
2. Nous adorons le rock. Nous écoutons un concert …
3. Jacques aime le jazz. Il écoute un programme …
4. Vous étudiez l'anglais. Vous avez un livre …
5. Tu étudies le piano. Aujourd'hui, tu as une leçon …
6. Léa étudie l'espagnol. Elle a un bon prof …
7. Je regarde mes photos. J'ai un album …
8. Pierre joue au baseball. Il a une batte …
9. J'aime la musique africaine. J'ai des CD …
10. Paul est bon en maths. Il fait un problème …

PRONONCIATION

Les voyelles /ø/ et /œ/

The letters "**eu**" and "**oeu**" represent vowel sounds that do not exist in English but that are not very hard to pronounce.

/ø/ **deux** — /œ/ **neuf**

Répétez:

/ø/ **deux eux je veux je peux un peu jeux il pleut un euro**
Tu peux aller chez eux.

/œ/ **neuf soeur heure professeur jeune**
Ma soeur arrive à neuf heures.

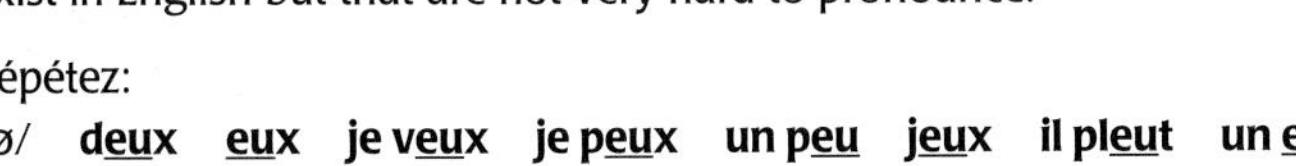

INCLUSION

Alphabetic/phonetic Model the sounds of words containing the vowel combinations in *Prononciation* to make the difference clear. Ask students to practice the sounds, noting the degree of mouth aperture for each. Provide a list of easy words and ask students to pronounce them as a group. Have students pair off and practice; then put list in their notebooks.

8 ROLE PLAY talking about others

1. –Éric dîne avec Alice.
   –Vraiment?
   –Mais oui! Il dîne avec elle!
2. –Thérèse va chez Paul.
   –Vraiment?
   –Mais oui! Elle va chez lui!
3. –Jérôme est au cinéma avec Delphine.
   –Vraiment?
   –Mais oui! Il est au cinéma avec elle!
4. –M. Mercier travaille pour Mlle Duval.
   –Vraiment?
   –Mais oui! Il travaille pour elle!
5. –Philippe travaille pour le voisin.
   –Vraiment?
   –Mais oui! Il travaille pour lui!
6. –Marc et Vincent dansent avec Mélanie et Juliette.
   –Vraiment?
   –Mais oui! Ils dansent avec elles!

SECTION D

Communicative function
Describing objects and people

Critical thinking Point out that in English, the main noun comes second: *tennis racket, sports car.*

In French, the main noun comes first: **une raquette de tennis, une voiture de sport.**

How do the French say:
orange juice **[un jus d'orange]**
tomato salad **[une salade de tomates]**
bathroom **[une salle de bains]**

9 PRACTICE describing objects using de + noun

1. Elle a une raquette de ping-pong.
2. Nous écoutons un concert de rock.
3. Jacques écoute un programme de jazz.
4. Vous avez un livre d'anglais.
5. Aujourd'hui, tu as une leçon de piano.
6. Elle a un bon prof d'espagnol.
7. J'ai un album de photos.
8. Il a une batte de baseball.
9. J'ai des CD de musique africaine.
10. Il fait un problème de maths.

Pronunciation Item 7: **album** /albɔm/

À VOTRE TOUR

Main Topic
- Recapitulation and review

Teaching Resource Options

PRINT 

Workbook PE, pp. 131–136
Unit 5 Resource Book
 Audioscript, pp. 97–98
 Communipak, pp. 140–163
 Family Involvement, pp. 89–90
 Workbook TE, pp. 71–76
 Assessment
 Lesson 15 Quiz, pp. 101–102
 Portfolio Assessment, Unit 1 URB, pp. 155–164
 Audioscript for Quiz 15, p. 100
 Answer Keys, pp. 210–213

AUDIO & VISUAL 

Audio Program
CD 3 Tracks 12, 13
CD 15 Track 3

TECHNOLOGY 

Test Generator CD-ROM/McDougal Littell Assessment System

1 COMPREHENSION

1. Salut, Stéphanie! D'où viens-tu?
 (b) Du supermarché.
2. Et où vas-tu maintenant?
 (c) Je rentre chez moi.
3. Tu ne veux pas venir au cinéma avec moi?
 (d) Je ne peux pas. Je dois étudier.
4. Ah bon? Pourquoi?
 (a) J'ai un examen d'anglais lundi.

2 GUIDED ORAL EXPRESSION

–Où vas-tu?
–Je vais ... Tu viens?
–Ça dépend! Qu'est-ce que tu vas faire chez ... ?
–Nous allons ...
–D'accord, je viens! (Non, je ne viens pas.)

1. chez Françoise / elle / regarder la télé.
2. chez Corinne et Claire / elles / dîner.
3. chez Nicolas et Patrick / eux / jouer aux cartes.
4. chez mon cousin / lui / jouer aux échecs.
5. chez ma cousine / elle / jouer du piano.
6. chez des copains / eux / écouter la radio.

À votre tour!

OBJECTIFS

Now you can ...
- let people know if you are coming with them or not
- talk about the musical instruments, sports, and games that you play

1 Conversation

PARLER Saturday afternoon, Henri meets Stéphanie downtown. Match Henri's questions with Stéphanie's answers. Then act out the conversation with a classmate.

1 Salut, Stéphanie! D'où viens-tu?
2 Et où vas-tu maintenant?
3 Tu ne veux pas venir au cinéma avec moi?
4 Ah bon? Pourquoi?
a J'ai un examen d'anglais lundi.
b Du supermarché.
c Je rentre chez moi.
d Je ne peux pas. Je dois étudier.

2 Créa-dialogue

PARLER Ask your classmates whom they are going to visit and what they are going to do. Then decide if you are going to come along.

▶ —Où vas-tu?
—Je vais chez Jean-Claude. Tu viens?
—Ça dépend! Qu'est-ce que tu vas faire chez lui?
—Nous allons jouer au ping-pong.
—D'accord, je viens!
(Non, je ne viens pas.)

▶ Jean-Claude 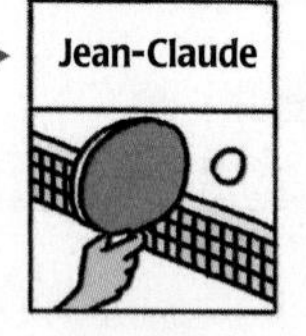

CHEZ QUI?	1. Françoise	2. Corinne et Claire	3. Nicolas et Patrick	4. mon cousin	5. ma cousine	6. des copains
ACTIVITÉ						

3 Retour à la maison

PARLER This afternoon, the following people went downtown. Say which places they are coming from.

▶ Nous venons de l'école.

▶ 

nous

1 tu
2 vous
3 Madame Simon
4 Monsieur Dupont
5 Claire et Diane
6 Daniel et Philipp

À VOTRE TOUR

Depending on your goals and objectives, you may or may not wish to assign all of the activities in the **À votre tour** section.

PAIR PRACTICE

Act. 1–4 lend themselves to pair practice.

For Act. 2 and 4, you may have students work in trios, with two performing while the other holds the Answer Key and acts as monitor.

Message illustré

ÉCRIRE Frédéric likes to use illustrations in his diary. Transcribe what he has written about himself and others, replacing the pictures with the corresponding missing words.

Je joue
J'aime aussi
aller
Ma soeur Catherine
joue très bien
Elle est musicienne
aussi. Elle joue
et
Mon frère Marc
préfère jouer
Tiens, voilà ma
copine Stéphanie.
Elle vient
Elle joue très
bien

Un mail à Sandrine

ÉCRIRE In a recent e-mail, Sandrine, your French pen pal, mentioned various hobbies she enjoys. In a short e-mail, tell her …

- which sports you play
- which musical instruments you play
- which games you play

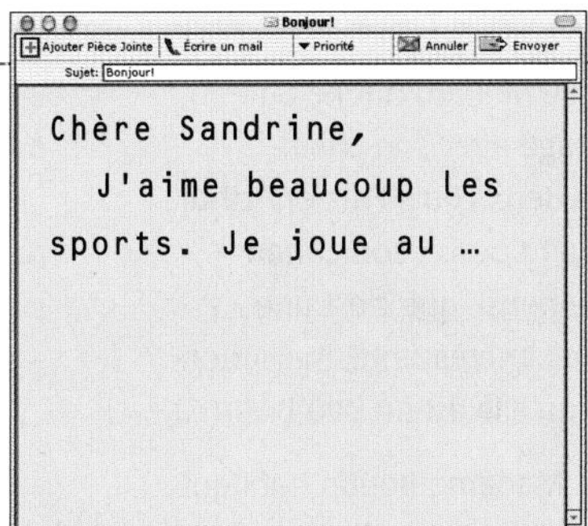
Bonjour!
Ajouter Pièce Jointe
Écrire un mail
Priorité
Annuler
Envoyer
Sujet: Bonjour!
Chère Sandrine,
J'aime beaucoup les
sports. Je joue au …

parc
supermarché
stade
école
bibliothèque
piscine

LESSON REVIEW
CLASSZONE.COM

Comprehension

1. Tu viens de l'école.
2. Vous venez de la bibliothèque.
3. Madame Simon vient du parc.
4. Monsieur Dupont vient du supermarché.
5. Claire et Diane viennent du stade (du parc).
6. Daniel et Philippe viennent de la piscine.

Reading Comprehension

Je joue au volleyball.

J'aime aussi aller à la piscine.

Ma soeur Catherine joue très bien au tennis.

Elle est musicienne aussi. Elle joue de la clarinette et du violon.

Mon frère Marc préfère jouer aux cartes.

Tiens, voilà ma copine Stéphanie. Elle vient du stade.

Elle joue très bien au foot[ball].

Challenge You may wish to have the students prepare their own **"messages illustrés."** (See *Challenge* ***De nouveaux messages***, p. 103.)

Written Self-Expression

Answers will vary.
Chère Sandrine,
J'aime beaucoup les sports. Je joue au tennis et au volley. J'aime nager. Je joue du piano. J'aime jouer aux cartes et aux échecs avec mes copines. Et toi?

Amitiés,

Anne

Portfolio Assessment

You will probably select only one speaking activity and one writing activity to go into the students' portfolios for Unit 5.

In this lesson, Act. 2 lends itself well to an oral portfolio recording.

Act. 5 offers an excellent writing portfolio topic.

Leçon 16

Main Topic Talking about one's family

Teaching Resource Options

PRINT 

Workbook PE, pp. 137–143
Activités pour tous PE, pp. 83–85
Block Scheduling Copymasters, pp. 121–128
Unit 5 Resource Book
- *Activités pour tous* TE, pp. 111–113
- Audioscript, pp. 132, 133–135
- Communipak, pp. 140–163
- Lesson Plans, pp. 114–115
- Block Scheduling Lesson Plans, pp. 116–118
- Absent Student Copymasters, pp. 119–122
- Video Activities, pp. 125–128
- Videoscript, pp. 129–131
- Workbook TE, pp. 103–109

AUDIO & VISUAL 

Audio Program
CD 3 Tracks 14, 15
CD 9 Tracks 25–32

Overhead Transparencies
34 Apartment building

TECHNOLOGY

Online Workbook

VIDEO PROGRAM

MODULE 16
Où habitez-vous?

TOTAL TIME: 5:12 min.
DVD Disk 2
Videotape 3 (COUNTER: 20:35 min.)

16.1 Presentation: Listening – C'est ma maison (21:28–22:29 min.)

16.2 Mini-scenes: Listening – C'est ta voiture? (22:30–23:27 min.)

16.3 Dialogue: C'est ta famille? (23:28–24:27 min.)

16.4 Vignette culturelle: Un immeuble à Paris (24:28–25:47 min.)

Comprehension practice Play the entire module through as an introduction to the lesson.

LEÇON 16 Mes voisins

AUDIO

Bonjour!
Je m'appelle Frédéric Mallet.
J'habite à Paris avec ma famille.
Nous habitons dans un immeuble (*building*) de six étages (*floors*).
Voici mon immeuble et voici mes (*my*) voisins.

Monsieur Lacroche habite au sixième (*sixth*) étage avec sa femme. Ils sont musiciens. Lui, il joue du piano et elle, elle chante. Oh là là, quelle (*what*) musique!

Mademoiselle Jolivet habite au cinquième (*fifth*) étage avec son (*her*) oncle et sa (*her*) tante.
Paul, mon meilleur (*best*) ami, habite au quatrième (*fourth*) étage avec sa (*his*) soeur et ses (*his*) parents.

Mademoiselle Ménard habite au troisième (*third*) étage avec son chien Pomme, ses deux chats Fritz et Arthur, son perroquet (*parrot*) Coco et son canari Froufrou. (Je pense (*think*) que (*that*) c'est une personne très intéressante, mais mon père pense qu'elle est un peu bizarre.)

Monsieur et Madame Boutin habitent au deuxième (*second*) étage avec leur (*their*) fils (*son*) et leurs deux filles (*daughters*).

Et qui habite au premier étage?
C'est un garçon super-intelligent, super-cool et très sympathique!
Et ce garçon … c'est moi!

SETTING THE STAGE

PROPS: Transparency 34: Apartment Building
(Have students keep their books closed.)
Describe the building on the transparency.
Voici un immeuble.
Voici le rez-de-chaussée.
Voici le premier étage, le deuxième étage, …

On the chalkboard, write the following list:
Paul
Frédéric Mallet
Mademoiselle Jolivet
Mademoiselle Ménard
Monsieur et Madame Boutin
Monsieur et Madame Lacroche

Compréhension

1. Où habite Frédéric Mallet?
2. Combien *(How many)* d'étages a son immeuble?
3. Qui habite à chaque *(each)* étage?
4. Quelle est la profession des Lacroche?
5. Selon toi *(In your opinion)*, est-ce que Mademoiselle Ménard est une personne bizarre ou intéressante? Pourquoi?

COMPARAISONS CULTURELLES

The floors of buildings are numbered differently in France and in the United States. Compare:

- **rez-de-chaussée** — *ground floor or first floor*
- **premier étage (1er étage)** — *second floor*
- **deuxième étage (2ème étage)** — *third floor*

NOTE: In the older downtown areas of French cities, apartment houses have a maximum of six stories. This is because until the twentieth century there were no elevators and people had to use the stairs.

NOTE culturelle

Les animaux domestiques en France

La France a une population de 60 millions d'habitants et de 42 millions d'animaux domestiques.° Les Français adorent les animaux. Une famille sur deux° a un animal domestique. Par ordre de préférence, les principaux animaux domestiques sont les chiens (39%: trente-neuf pour cent), les chats (35%), les poissons (12%), les oiseaux (5%) et les hamsters (4%). Il y a aussi un certain nombre de serpents, de tortues et de lapins.

un hamster

un lapin

une tortue

un poisson

un poisson rouge

un oiseau

animaux domestiques *pets* **une ... sur deux** *one out of two*

Tell students to listen carefully to determine who lives on which floor. You may want to play the audio recording more than once.

Then have students open their books and follow along as you play the recording once more.

Answers:
Paul (4e)
Frédéric Mallet (1er)
Mademoiselle Jolivet (5e)
Mademoiselle Ménard (3e)
Monsieur et Madame Boutin (2e)
Monsieur et Madame Lacroche (6e)

Compréhension
Answers

1. Il habite à Paris.
2. Son immeuble a six étages.
3. Les Lacroche habitent au 6e étage. Mlle Jolivet, son oncle et sa tante habitent au 5e étage. Paul et sa famille habitent au 4e étage. Mlle Ménard et ses animaux habitent au 3e étage. Les Boutin habitent au 2e étage. Frédéric Mallet habite au premier étage.
4. Ils sont musiciens.
5. Mlle Ménard est bizarre (intéressante) parce qu'elle a un chien, deux chats et deux oiseaux.

Language note You may want to point out the irregular plural forms:

un animal des animaux
un oiseau des oiseaux

Prononciation note **Un hamster** is pronounced almost as in English, but with a silent "h" and no liaison: /amstɛr/

Teaching suggestion Take a class poll of pet ownership. **Qui a un chat? Qui a un chien?** Tabulate your results in percentages and compare them with the percentages in France.

Note culturelle Tell students that there are many organizations in France dedicated to protect both wild and domesticated animals. Have students find the name of one of these organizations and research its history, its goals, and other information, and report their findings to the class.

SECTION A

Communicative function
Talking about possessions

Teaching Resource Options

PRINT 

Workbook PE, pp. 137–143
Unit 5 Resource Book
Audioscript, p. 132
Communipak, pp. 140–163
Workbook TE, pp. 103–109

AUDIO & VISUAL 

Audio Program
CD 3 Track 16

Overhead Transparencies
8 Family tree

TECHNOLOGY 

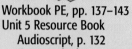

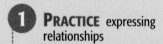

Power Presentations

Teaching strategy To help students remember the word order, have them think of **de** as meaning *of* or *which belongs to.*

1 PRACTICE expressing relationships

1. Carole est la cousine de Jacques.
2. Michel est le copain de Caroline.
3. Philippe est le camarade de Charles.
4. Robert est le frère de Guillaume.
5. Marina est la copine de Paul.
6. Pauline est l'amie d'Éric.
7. Alice est la soeur de Karine.

2 DESCRIPTION describing ownership

- Marc a la guitare d'Alice et la radio d'Éric.
- Alice a le vélo de Laure et le baladeur de Marc.
- Éric a la raquette de Marc et l'appareil-photo de Laure.
- Laure a le scooter d'Alice et les CD d'Éric.

A La possession avec *de*

Note the words in heavy print:

Voici une moto.	C'est la moto **de Frédéric.**	*It's **Frédéric's** motorcycle.*
Voici un vélo.	C'est le vélo **de Sophie.**	*It's **Sophie's** bike.*

To express POSSESSION, French speakers use the construction:

le/la/les + NOUN + **de** + OWNER	la radio **de** Thomas
↓	les livres **de** Claire
d'(+ VOWEL SOUND)	la maison **d'**Émilie

→ The same construction is used to express RELATIONSHIP:

C'est **le copain de Daniel.**	*That's **Daniel's friend.***
C'est **la mère de Paul.**	*That's **Paul's mother.***

→ Remember that **de** contracts with **le** and **les:**

Où est le chat **du voisin?**	*Where is the **neighbor's** cat?*
C'est la chambre **des enfants.**	*This is the **children's** room.*

→ While English often indicates possession with ***'s,*** French always uses **de.**

la copine **de Monique**	***Monique's** friend (the friend **of Monique**)*

1 Présentations *(Introductions)*

PARLER Imagine that you are hosting a party in France. Introduce the following people.

▶ Jean-Marc (cousin/Sylvie)

Jean-Marc est le cousin de Sylvie.

1. Carole (cousine/Jacques)
2. Michel (copain/Caroline)
3. Philippe (camarade/Charles)
4. Robert (frère/Guillaume)
5. Marina (copine/Paul)
6. Pauline (amie/Éric)
7. Alice (soeur/Karine)

2 Échanges

PARLER/ÉCRIRE The following friends have decided to trade a few of their possessions. On a separate sheet of paper, write out what each person has, once the exchange has been completed.

TALKING ABOUT PAST EVENTS

Let's talk about what you and your friends did last weekend.

(Reminder: If the question contains **tu as...,** students should answer with **j'ai...** or **je n'ai pas...** If it contains **tu es...,** they should answer with **je suis...** or **je ne suis pas...**)

Est-ce que tu es allé(e) à la plage?
Oui, je suis allé(e) à la plage.
(Non, je ne suis pas allé(e) à la plage.)
Est-ce que tu as nagé?
Oui, j'ai nagé.
(Non, je n'ai pas nagé.)

VOCABULAIRE La famille 

la famille *(family)*

les grands-parents

le grand-père	**la grand-mère**		
les parents *(parents)*		**les parents** *(relatives)*	
le père	**la mère**	**l'oncle**	**la tante** *(aunt)*
le mari *(husband)*	**la femme** *(wife)*		
les enfants *(children)*			
un enfant	**une enfant**		
le frère	**la soeur**	**le cousin**	**la cousine**
le fils *(son)*	**la fille** *(daughter)*		

3 La famille de Frédéric

PARLER/ÉCRIRE Frédéric has drawn his family tree. Study it and explain the relationships between the people below.

▶ Éric/Alice Vidal
Éric est le fils d'Alice Vidal.

1. Léa/Frédéric
2. Martine Mallet/Léa
3. Albert et Julie Mallet/Éric
4. Alice Vidal/Frédéric
5. Jean Mallet/Martine Mallet
6. Alice Vidal/Maurice Vidal
7. Julie Mallet/Éric
8. Élodie/Maurice Vidal
9. Léa/Éric
10. Frédéric/Élodie

▶ Marc a la guitare d'Alice et ...

- **Est-ce que tu es allé(e) à la plage?**
- **Est-ce que tu as nagé?**
- **Est-ce que tu es allé(e) au restaurant?**
- **Est-ce que tu as mangé une pizza?**
- **Est-ce que tu es allé(e) en ville?**
- **Est-ce que tu as acheté des vêtements?**
- **Est-ce que tu es allé(e) au parc?**
- **Est-ce que tu as joué au frisbee?**
- **Où est-ce que tu es allé(e)?**
- **Qu'est-ce que tu as fait?**

 Re-entry and review

The following words were taught in Lesson 2C: **père, mère, frère, soeur, cousin, cousine.**

Pronunciation Make sure that students pronounce the following nouns correctly:

femme /fam/

fils /fis/

cousin /kuzɛ̃/ and **cousine** /kuzin/

Supplementary vocabulary

les petits-enfants *grandchildren*
le petit-fils / la petite-fille *grandson/granddaughter*
les jumeaux *twins*
un jumeau / une jumelle *male twin/female twin*
un frère aîné / une soeur aînée *older brother / sister*
un frère cadet / une soeur cadette *younger brother / sister*
un(e) enfant unique *only child*
le neveu / la nièce *nephew / niece*
le beau-père / la belle-mère *stepfather, father-in-law / stepmother, mother-in-law*
le beau-frère / la belle-soeur *stepbrother, brother-in-law / stepsister, sister-in-law*
le demi-frère / la demi-soeur *half-brother / half-sister*
le parrain / la marraine *godfather / godmother*

3 COMPREHENSION describing family relationships

1. Léa est la soeur de Frédéric.
2. Martine Mallet est la mère de Léa.
3. Albert et Julie Mallet sont les grands-parents d'Éric.
4. Alice Vidal est la tante de Frédéric.
5. Jean Mallet est le mari de Martine Mallet.
6. Alice Vidal est la femme de Maurice Vidal.
7. Julie Mallet est la grand-mère d'Éric.
8. Élodie est la fille de Maurice Vidal.
9. Léa est la cousine d'Éric.
10. Frédéric est le cousin d'Élodie.

SECTION B

Communicative function
Talking about possessions

Teaching Resource Options

PRINT 

Workbook PE, pp. 137–143
Unit 5 Resource Book
Communipak, pp. 140–163
Workbook TE, pp. 103–109

TECHNOLOGY 

Power Presentations

Re-entry and review

Mon/ma and **ton/ta** were introduced in Lesson 2c.

Critical thinking Point out that just as **ma** becomes **mon** before a vowel sound in French, the article *a* in English also changes form.

Contrast: *a pear, an apple.*

B Les adjectifs possessifs: *mon, ton, son*

LEARNING ABOUT LANGUAGE

French, like English, shows possession and relationship with POSSESSIVE ADJECTIVES:

ma voiture (***my** car*), **mon** père (***my** father*)

In French, possessive adjectives AGREE with the nouns they introduce.

Note the forms of the possessive adjectives in the chart below:

		SINGULAR		PLURAL			
(POSSESSOR)		MASCULINE	FEMININE				
(je)	*my*	**mon**	**ma**	**mes**	**mon** frère	**ma** soeur	**mes** copains
(tu)	*your*	**ton**	**ta**	**tes**	**ton** oncle	**ta** tante	**tes** cousins
(il)	*his*	**son**	**sa**	**ses**	**son** père	**sa** mère	**ses** parents
(elle)	*her*	**son**	**sa**	**ses**	**son** père	**sa** mère	**ses** parents

→ The feminine singular forms **ma, ta, sa** become **mon, ton, son** before a vowel sound.

une amie	**mon** amie	**ton** amie	**son** amie
une auto	**mon** auto	**ton** auto	**son** auto

→ There is liaison after **mon, ton, son, mes, tes, ses** before a vowel sound.

mon oncle   **mes** amis

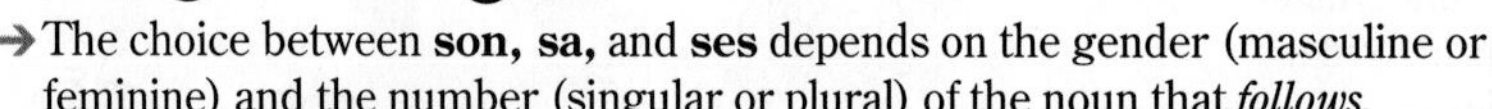

→ The choice between **son, sa,** and **ses** depends on the gender (masculine or feminine) and the number (singular or plural) of the noun that *follows.*

It does NOT depend on the gender of the possessor (that is, whether the owner is male or female). Compare:

PERSONNALISE TON PORTABLE

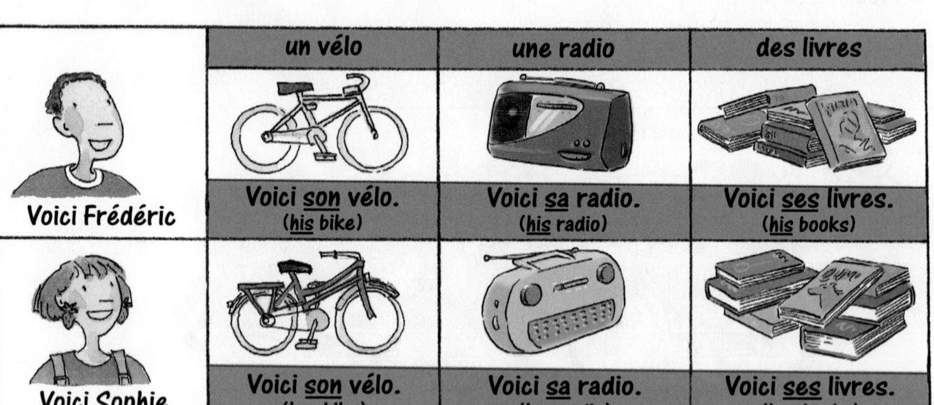

un vélo
une radio
des livres
Voici Frédéric
Voici son vélo.
(his bike)
Voici sa radio.
(his radio)
Voici ses livres.
(his books)
Voici Sophie
Voici son vélo.
(her bike)
Voici sa radio.
(her radio)
Voici ses livres.
(her books)

COMPREHENSION Possessions

PROPS: Books, watches, etc.

Hold up your own textbook, saying:
Voici un livre de français.
C'est mon livre.
X, montre-nous ton livre de français.

Continue with **ma/ta montre.**

Walk around holding up students' items.
C'est le livre de X [boy]?
Oui, c'est son livre.
C'est le livre de Y [girl]?
Oui, c'est son livre.
C'est la montre de Z?
Oui, c'est sa montre.

Follow-up (pointing out items):
Comment dit-on: *his book? her book?*

4 Marc et Hélène

PARLER Marc never knows where his things are, but Hélène does. Play both roles.

▶ le vélo/dans le garage
—**Où est mon vélo?**
—**Ton vélo? Il est dans le garage.**

1. les CD/ici
2. la raquette/là-bas
3. la montre/sur toi
4. les livres/dans le sac
5. le portable/sur le bureau
6. le chat/derrière la porte
7. l'appareil-photo/dans la chambre
8. le baladeur/sur la table

5 Invitations

PARLER/ÉCRIRE Say whom each person is inviting to the school party, using the appropriate possessive adjectives.

▶ Michel/la copine
Michel invite sa copine.

1. André/la cousine
2. Jean-Claude/la soeur
3. Marie-Noëlle/les frères
4. Pascal/l'amie Sophie
5. Monique/les cousins
6. Nathalie/l'ami Marc
7. Georges/l'amie Cécile
8. Paul/l'amie Thérèse

6 Chez Marie et Christophe Boutin

PARLER/ÉCRIRE Items 1 to 8 belong to Marie. Items 9 to 16 belong to Christophe. Point these things out.

Marie		Christophe	
▶ le vélo	**C'est son vélo.**	▶ les CD	**Ce sont ses CD.**
1. le baladeur	5. l'ordinateur	9. la guitare	13. les livres
2. le sac	6. la guitare	10. la chaîne hi-fi	14. la montre
3. le chien	7. les CD	11. le chat	15. les photos
4. l'album	8. les cassettes	12. le scooter	16. les skis

VOCABULAIRE Expression pour la conversation

▶ ***How to question a statement or express a doubt:***

Tu es sûr(e)? *Are you sure?* —C'est mon pantalon *(pants)!*
—Tu es sûr?

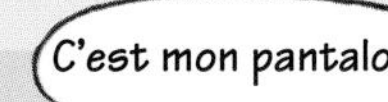
C'est mon pantalon!

Tu es sûr?

7 Après la soirée

PARLER Last night Frédéric and Paul gave a party. They realize that their friends left certain things behind. Frédéric thinks he knows what belongs to whom.

▶ le sac/Claire
FRÉDÉRIC: **Voici le sac de Claire.**
PAUL: **Tu es sûr?**
FRÉDÉRIC: **Mais oui, c'est son sac!**

1. le sac/Jean-Pierre
2. la guitare/Antoine
3. l'appareil-photo/Cécile
4. le baladeur/Stéphanie
5. les CD/Léa
6. le portable/Thomas

TALKING ABOUT PAST EVENTS

Let's talk about a recent party.

Imaginez que vous avez organisé une boum le week-end dernier avec des amis.

Est-ce que tu as organisé une boum le week-end dernier?
Oui, j'ai organisé une boum.

- **Avec qui est-ce que tu as organisé la boum?**
- **À qui est-ce que vous avez téléphoné?**
- **Qui est-ce que vous avez invité?**
- **Est-ce que vous avez dansé?**
- **Est-ce que vous avez chanté?**
- **Qu'est-ce que vous avez mangé?**

4 ROLE PLAY finding one's things

1. –Où sont mes CD?
–Tes CD? Ils sont ici.
2. –Où est ma raquette?
–Ta raquette? Elle est là-bas.
3. –Où est ma montre?
–Ta montre? Elle est sur toi.
4. –Où sont mes livres?
–Tes livres? Ils sont dans le sac.
5. –Où est mon portable?
–Ton portable? Il est sur le bureau.
6. –Où est mon chat?
–Ton chat? Il est derrière la porte.
7. –Où est mon appareil-photo?
–Ton appareil-photo? Il est dans la chambre.
8. –Où est mon baladeur?
–Ton baladeur? Il est sur la table.

Language note Be sure students use plural forms in items 1 and 4.

5 PRACTICE identifying friends and relatives

1. André invite sa cousine.
2. Jean-Claude invite sa soeur.
3. Marie-Noëlle invite ses frères.
4. Pascal invite son amie Sophie.
5. Monique invite ses cousins.
6. Nathalie invite son ami Marc.
7. Georges invite son amie Cécile.
8. Paul invite son amie Thérèse.

6 PRACTICE identifying possessions

1. C'est son baladeur.
2. C'est son sac.
3. C'est son chien.
4. C'est son album.
5. C'est son ordinateur.
6. C'est sa guitare.
7. Ce sont ses CD.
8. Ce sont ses cassettes.
9. C'est sa guitare.
10. C'est sa chaîne hi-fi.
11. C'est son chat.
12. C'est son scooter.
13. Ce sont ses livres.
14. C'est sa montre.
15. Ce sont ses photos.
16. Ce sont ses skis.

7 ROLE PLAY identifying ownership

1. Frédéric: Voici le sac de Jean-Pierre.
Paul: Tu es sûr?
Frédéric: Mais oui, c'est son sac!
2. Frédéric: Voici la guitare d'Antoine.
Paul: Tu es sûr?
Frédéric: Mais oui, c'est sa guitare!
3. Frédéric: Voici l'appareil-photo de Cécile.
Paul: Tu es sûr?
Frédéric: Mais oui, c'est son appareil-photo!
4. Frédéric: Voici le baladeur de Stéphanie.
Paul: Tu es sûr?
Frédéric: Mais oui, c'est son baladeur!
5. Frédéric: Voici les CD de Léa.
Paul: Tu es sûr?
Frédéric: Mais oui, ce sont ses CD!
6. Frédéric: Voici le portable de Thomas.
Paul: Tu es sûr?
Frédéric: Mais oui, c'est son portable!

Language note Be sure students use the plural **Ce sont** in item 5.

SECTION C

Communicative function
Talking about possessions

Teaching Resource Options

PRINT  

Workbook PE, pp. 137–143
Unit 5 Resource Book
Audioscript, p. 132
Communipak, pp. 140–163
Video Activities, pp. 125–126
Videoscript, p. 129
Workbook TE, pp. 103–109

AUDIO & VISUAL 

Audio Program
CD 3 Track 17

TECHNOLOGY
Power Presentations

VIDEO PROGRAM

VIDÉO DVD

MODULE 16

16.1 Mini-scenes: C'est ma maison (21:28–22:29 min.)

16.2 Mini-scenes: C'est ta voiture? (22:30–23:27 min.)

16.3 Dialogue: C'est ta famille? (23:28–24:27 min.)

Language note Be sure students note that **notre, votre,** and **leur** are used with singular nouns and that **nos, vos,** and **leurs** are used with plural nouns. Contrast:

leur frère *their brother*
leurs frères *their brothers*

8 ROLE PLAY asking for items in a store

1. –S'il vous plaît, où sont vos livres?
–Nos livres sont à gauche.
2. –S'il vous plaît, où sont vos affiches?
–Nos affiches sont à droite.
3. –S'il vous plaît, où est votre restaurant?
–Notre restaurant est en haut.
4. –S'il vous plaît, où est votre garage?
–Notre garage est en bas.
5. –S'il vous plaît, où sont vos ordinateurs?
–Nos ordinateurs sont ici.
6. –S'il vous plaît, où est votre cafétéria?
–Notre cafétéria est tout droit.

C Les adjectifs possessifs: *notre, votre, leur*

Note the forms of the possessive adjectives in the chart below:

(POSSESSOR)		SINGULAR	PLURAL		
(nous)	*our*	**notre**	**nos**	**notre** prof	**nos** livres
(vous)	*your*	**votre**	**vos**	**votre** ami	**vos** copains
(ils/elles)	*their*	**leur**	**leurs**	**leur** radio	**leurs** amies

→ There is liaison after **nos, vos, leurs** when the next word begins with a vowel sound.

nos amis **vos** amies **leurs** ordinateurs

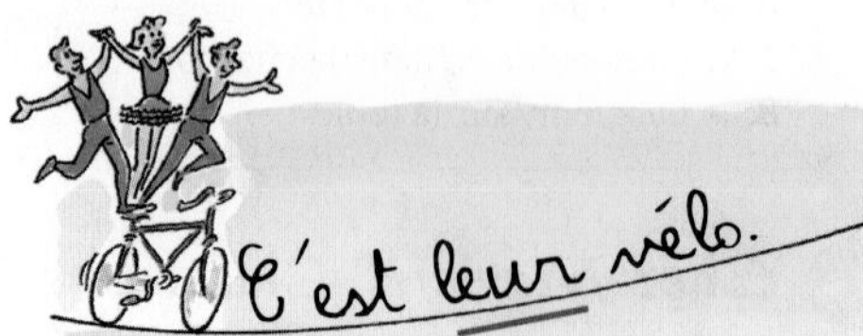

8 Aux Galeries Lafayette

PARLER At the Galeries Lafayette department store, a customer is looking for various things. The person at the information desk indicates where they can be found. Play both roles.

▶ les CD/là-bas

1. les livres/à gauche
2. les affiches/à droite
3. le restaurant/en haut
4. le garage/en bas
5. les ordinateurs/ici
6. la cafétéria/tout droit

9 Les millionnaires

PARLER/ÉCRIRE Imagine you are showing a millionaire's estate to French visitors.

▶ la maison
Voici leur maison.

1. la piscine
2. la Rolls Royce
3. les chiens
4. le parc
5. l'hélicoptère
6. les courts de tennis

10 En famille

PARLER/ÉCRIRE We often do things with our family. Complete each sentence with a possessive adjective: **son, sa, ses, leur,** or **leurs.**

▶ **Pascal joue au tennis avec sa cousine.**
▶ **Éric et Paul jouent aux cartes avec leurs cousins.**

1. Frédéric dîne chez ... oncle.
2. André dîne chez ... grands-parents.
3. Caroline et Paul vont chez ... grand-mère.
4. Mlle Vénard fait une promenade avec ... chien.
5. Antoine va à la piscine avec ... soeur.
6. Stéphanie et Céline vont au cinéma avec ... parents.
7. M. et Mme Boutin voyagent avec ... fille.
8. Mme Denis visite Paris avec ... fils, Marc et Frédéric.

GAME Possessions

PREPARATION: Prepare 2 bags.

Bag A contains 12 sentence cards.
- (6 cards with names of single people)
Voici Pierre. Voici Michelle. Voici...
- (6 cards with names of two people)
Voici Anne et Paul. Voici Éric et Sylvie. ...

Bag B contains 12 sentence cards.
- (6 cards with singular nouns)
Voici son crayon, ...son stylo, sa montre.
Voici leur crayon, ...leur stylo, leur montre.
- (6 cards with plural nouns)
Voici ses crayons, ...ses stylos, ses montres.
Voici leurs crayons, ...leurs stylos, leurs montres.

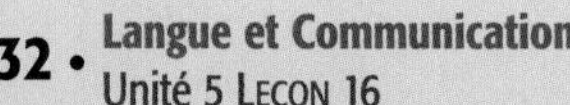

D Les nombres ordinaux

Compare the following regular numbers and the ordinal numbers in French:

(2)	deux	**deuxième**	Février est le **deuxième** mois de l'année.
(3)	trois	**troisième**	Mercredi est le **troisième** jour de la semaine.
(4)	quatre	**quatrième**	J'habite au **quatrième** étage *(floor)*.

To form ordinal numbers, French speakers use the following pattern:

NUMBER (minus final **-e**, if any) + **-ième**						
(6)	six	:	**six**	+ **-ième**	→	**sixième**
(11)	onze	:	**onz-**	+ **-ième**	→	**onzième**

→ EXCEPTIONS: (1) un (une) → **premier (première)**
(5) cinq → **cinquième**
(9) neuf → **neuvième**

→ Ordinal numbers are adjectives and come BEFORE the noun.

LEARNING ABOUT LANGUAGE

Numbers like *first, second, third, fourth, fifth* are used to rank persons or things—to put them in a given order.

They are called ORDINAL NUMBERS.

In English, most ordinal numbers end in *-th.*

11 La course *(The race)*

PARLER/ÉCRIRE Frédéric and his friends are participating in a five-kilometer race. Announce the order of arrival of the following runners.

▶ Paul (6)

1. Frédéric (4)
2. Jérôme (7)
3. Christophe (8)
4. Sophie (2)
5. Christine (1)
6. Claire (10)
7. Karine (11)
8. Olivier (12)

PRONONCIATION

Les voyelles /o/ et /ɔ/

/o/ vélo — /ɔ/ téléphone

The French vowel /o/ is pronounced with more tension than in English. It is usually the last sound in a word.

Répétez: /o/ **vélo radio nos vos eau château chaud**
Nos vélos sont au château.

The French vowel /ɔ/ occurs in the middle of a word. Imitate the model carefully.

Répétez: /ɔ/ **téléphone école Nicole notre votre copain prof dommage**
Comment s'appelle votre prof?

PROCEDURE: Divide the class into two teams: **logique** and **illogique.** Each team names a scorekeeper.

Two players (one from each team) come to the front. One reads a card from Bag A, the other reads a card from Bag B.

If the sentences fit logically, the **logique** team earns a point. If not, a point goes to the **illogique** team. For example:

Voici Marc. Voici leur stylo. = illogique

Have students at their seats decide if the sentences are logical or not.

9 PRACTICE pointing out possessions

1. Voici leur piscine.
2. Voici leur Rolls-Royce.
3. Voici leurs chiens.
4. Voici leur parc.
5. Voici leur hélicoptère.
6. Voici leurs courts de tennis.

Challenge To practice adjectives, have students make a comment on each thing they are pointing out.
Voici leur maison.
Elle est belle (grande, super, extra, etc.), n'est-ce pas?

10 COMPREHENSION indicating family relationships

1. son 2. ses 3. leur 4. son
5. sa 6. leurs 7. leur 8. ses

SECTION D

Communicative function
Indicating sequence

Language notes
- For **deuxième,** one can also say **second(e)**, pronounced /səgɔ̃(d)/
- 21st = **vingt et unième**
31st = **trente et unième,** etc.
Note that the "u" of **unième** is pronounced /y/.

Extra practice Write the numbers 1 to 20 on the board. Point to a number and have students give the corresponding ordinal number.
For example: 15 **[quinzième]**, etc.

11 PRACTICE ranking people

1. Frédéric est quatrième.
2. Jérôme est septième.
3. Christophe est huitième.
4. Sophie est deuxième.
5. Christine est première.
6. Claire est dixième.
7. Karine est onzième.
8. Olivier est douzième.

PRONUNCIATION

- Have students pronounce the /o/ with tension and clip off the ending before the glide /oᵘ/ of the English *go.*
- Be sure students do not pronounce these words with the vowel /o/. The French /ɔ/ is close to the "o" sound of the English *orange.*

À votre tour!

OBJECTIFS

Now you can ...
- talk about your family and your relatives
- identify things as belonging to you or to someone else
- talk about your pets

1 Allô!

PARLER Émilie is on the phone with Bernard. Match Émilie's questions with Bernard's answers. Then act out the dialogue with a classmate.

2 Créa-dialogue

PARLER We often identify objects by their color. Create conversations with your classmates according to the model.

le vélo / Paul?

▶ —C'est le vélo de Paul?
—Non, ce n'est pas son vélo.
—Tu es sûr?
—Mais oui. Son vélo est bleu.

1. la guitare / Alice?
2. le scooter / Paul et Anne?
3. le chien / tes cousins?
4. la mobylette / Isabelle?
5. la maison / M. et Mme Lavoie?
6. la voiture / ton oncle?

À VOTRE TOUR

Main Topic
- Recapitulation and review

Teaching Resource Options

PRINT 

Workbook PE, pp. 137–143
Unit 5 Resource Book
 Audioscript, p. 133
 Communipak, pp. 140–163
 Family Involvement, pp. 123–124
 Assessment
 Lesson 16 Quiz, pp. 137–138
 Portfolio Assessment, Unit 1 URB, pp. 155–164
 Audioscript for Quiz 16, p. 136
 Answer Keys, pp. 210–213

AUDIO & VISUAL

Audio Program
CD 3 Tracks 18, 19
CD 15 Track 4

TECHNOLOGY 

Test Generator CD-ROM/McDougal Littell Assessment System

1 Comprehension

1. Avec qui est-ce que tu vas au cinéma?
 (c) Avec mon copain Marc.
2. C'est le cousin de Monique?
 (a) Non, c'est son frère.
3. Tu connais leurs parents?
 (b) Bien sûr, ils sont très sympathiques.
4. Ils sont canadiens, n'est-ce pas?
 (d) Non, mais leurs voisins sont de Québec.

2 Guided Oral Expression

1. –C'est la guitare d'Alice?
 –Non, ce n'est pas sa guitare.
 –Tu es sûr?
 –Mais oui. Sa guitare est orange.
2. –C'est le scooter de Paul et Anne?
 –Non, ce n'est pas leur scooter.
 –Tu es sûr?
 –Mais oui. Leur scooter est vert.
3. –C'est le chien de tes cousins?
 –Non, ce n'est pas leur chien.
 –Tu es sûr?
 –Mais oui. Leur chien est noir.
4. –C'est la mobylette d'Isabelle?
 –Non, ce n'est pas sa mobylette.
 –Tu es sûr?
 –Mais oui. Sa mobylette est rouge.
5. –C'est la maison de M. et Mme Lavoie?
 –Non, ce n'est pas leur maison.
 –Tu es sûr?
 –Mais oui. Leur maison est blanche.
6. –C'est la voiture de ton oncle?
 –Non, ce n'est pas sa voiture.
 –Tu es sûr?
 –Mais oui. Sa voiture est jaune.

Variation Have students write out the dialogue with a partner.

À votre tour

Depending on your goals and objectives, you may or may not wish to assign all of the activities in the **À votre tour** section.

Inclusion

Cumulative Prepare students for Act. 2 by reviewing possessive adjectives. Write the adjectives on the board and have students repeat them three times. Have them look at the book and identify the colors of each object. Then have them work in pairs to complete the dialogues.

3 Composition: un animal domestique

ÉCRIRE Write a short composition about a pet: either your own pet, a pet belonging to a friend, or an imaginary pet. You may mention …

- the type of animal
- its name
- its age
- its colors
- its size
- its eating habits
- some physical and personality traits

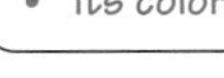

4 Composition: Ma famille

ÉCRIRE Select five people in your family and write one to three sentences about each person.

Mon cousin s'appelle
John. Il habite
à San Francisco.
Il a seize ans.

5 Arbre généalogique *(Family tree)*

ÉCRIRE On a separate sheet of paper, draw your own (real or imaginary) family tree. Label the people and indicate their relationships to you.

3 Written Self-Expression

Answers will vary.
J'ai un chat. Mon chat s'appelle Trotter. Il a trois ans. Mon chat est petit et blanc. Il mange trop. Trotter est gentil. J'aime mon chat!

4 Written Self-Expression

Answers will vary.
- Mon frère s'appelle Jay. Il a quinze ans. Il aime beaucoup les sports.
- Ma mère n'aime pas faire la cuisine. Elle a beaucoup de soeurs. J'ai beaucoup de tantes!
- Mon grand-père a quatre-vingt-cinq ans. Il aime beaucoup la musique. Il a un baladeur!
- Ma cousine Jen a treize ans. Elle habite à Cincinnati. J'aime parler avec elle.
- Mon père s'appelle Paul. Il a quarante-deux ans. Il voyage souvent.

5 Written Self-Expression

Answers will vary.

Marc Dubois (mon grand-père) — Alice Dubois (ma grand-mère)

- Marc Dubois (mon grand-père): Laure Dubois (ma mère), Bernard Dubois (mon père)
- Alice Dubois (ma grand-mère): Sylvie Trocmé (ma tante), Daniel Trocmé (mon oncle)
- Laure Dubois / Bernard Dubois: Catherine (moi), Georges (mon frère)
- Sylvie Trocmé / Daniel Trocmé: Alice (ma cousine), Jean (mon cousin), Marc (mon cousin)

Teaching strategy Some students may prefer preparing the family tree of a TV family or a family in the public eye.

Photo culture note French people of African ancestry come principally from the French Carribean islands of **Martinique** and **Guadeloupe,** and from countries of western Africa, especially **Mali, Sénégal, Cameroun, Congo,** and **Côte d'Ivoire.**

Portfolio Assessment

You will probably select only one speaking activity and one writing activity to go into the students' portfolios for Unit 5.

In this lesson, Act. 2 lends itself well to an oral portfolio recording. Act. 3, 4, and 5 are appropriate writing portfolio topics.

Inclusion

Sequential to prepare students for the writing in Act. 5, have them review names of family members. Draw a family tree on the board, and label the members. Have students copy the tree into their notebooks. Have them work in pairs to generate short sentences about family members, one person dictating while the other writes down the sentences.

TESTS DE CONTRÔLE

Teaching Resource Options

PRINT 

Unit 5 Resource Book
Communipak, pp. 140–163

Assessment
Unit 5 Test, pp. 177–185
Portfolio Assessment, Unit 1, URB, pp. 155–164
Multiple Choice Test Items, pp. 198–206
Listening Comprehension, pp. 137–143 Performance Test, pp. 186–187
Reading Performance Test, pp. 192–194
Speaking Performance Test, pp. 188–191
Writing Performance Test, pp. 195–197
Test Scoring Tools, p. 207
Audioscripts for Tests, pp. 208–209
Answer Keys, pp. 210–213

AUDIO & VISUAL 

Audio Program
CD 15 Tracks 5–8

Test Generator CD-ROM/McDougal Littell Assessment System

1 COMPREHENSION

1. Le réfrigérateur est dans la cuisine.
2. Quand il y a des invités, nous dînons dans la salle à manger.
3. Dans le jardin, il y a un lilas.
4. Dans le complexe sportif où nous allons, il y a une piscine olympique.
5. Il y a beaucoup de livres à la bibliothèque de la ville.
6. Dans ma chambre, il y a une table et un grand lit.
7. En été, nous allons en vacances sur une plage de l'Atlantique.
8. Il y a une église catholique dans notre quartier.
9. Le samedi, les élèves américains ne vont pas à l'école.
10. Le shampooing est dans la salle de bains.
11. Mes cousins habitent dans un grand immeuble moderne.
12. Je vais acheter un ordinateur dan un magasin d'équipement électronique.

Tests de contrôle

By taking the following tests, you can check your progress in French and also prepare for the unit test. Write your answers on a separate sheet of paper.

Review...
- places and rooms of the house: pp. 197 and 200

1 The right place

Complete each of the following sentences by filling in the blank with one of the places in the box. Be logical and do not use the same word more than once.

bibliothèque	chambre	cuisine	école	église	immeuble
jardin	magasin	piscine	plage	salle de bains	salle à manger

1. Le réfrigérateur est dans la —.
2. Quand il y a des invités *(guests)*, nous dînons dans la —.
3. Dans le —, il y a un lilas *(lilac tree)*.
4. Dans le complexe sportif où nous allons, il y a une — olympique.
5. Il y a beaucoup de livres à la — de la ville.
6. Dans ma —, il y a une table et un grand lit.
7. En été, nous allons en vacances sur une — de l'Atlantique.
8. Il y a une — catholique dans notre quartier.
9. Le samedi, les élèves américains ne vont pas à l'—.
10. Le shampooing *(shampoo)* est dans la —.
11. Mes cousins habitent dans un grand — moderne.
12. Je vais acheter un ordinateur dans un — d'équipement électronique.

Review...
- use of **à**, **de**, and **chez** pp. 208, 210, 211, 219, 220, and 223

2 The right choice

Choose the word or expression in parentheses which logically completes each of the following sentences.

1. Marc dîne — restaurant. **(à, au)**
2. Thomas nage — piscine. **(la, à la)**
3. Le professeur parle — élèves. **(aux, les)**
4. Les élèves vont — école en bus. **(à la, à l')**
5. Nous faisons une promenade — pied. **(à, au)**
6. Pauline va — sa copine Isabelle. **(à, chez)**
7. Nous revenons — école à trois heures. **(à l', de l')**
8. Les touristes arrivent — musée. **(du, de l')**
9. J'aime jouer — football. **(au, du)**
10. Est-ce que tu joues — clarinette? **(à la, de la)**
11. Comment s'appelle la copine — Monique? **(de, à)**
12. Voici la maison — voisins. **(des, de)**

3 The right owner

Complete each of the following sentences with the possessive adjective that corresponds to the underlined subject.

▶ Jean-Paul regarde **ses** photos.

1. Tu téléphones à — copine.
2. Je vais souvent au cinéma avec — amis.
3. Marc dîne chez — tante.
4. Alice invite — voisins à la boum.
5. Isabelle n'a pas — appareil-photo avec elle.
6. Thomas et Charlotte sont en vacances chez — oncle.
7. Les élèves respectent — professeurs.
8. Vous parlez avec — amie Mélanie.
9. Nous allons visiter Paris avec — professeur de français.
10. Est-ce que vous écoutez toujours — parents?

Review...
- possessive adjectives: pp. 230 and 232

4 Aller and venir

Complete the following sentences with the appropriate forms of **aller** or **venir.**

1. Attendez-moi *(Wait for me)*! Je —.
2. Thomas et Céline — très souvent au cinéma.
3. Qu'est-ce que tu — faire samedi?
4. Nous — aller à une boum.
5. Le professeur est canadien. Il — de Montréal.
6. Je — souvent à la piscine parce que j'aime nager.
7. Nicolas n'a pas faim. Il — du restaurant.
8. D'où est-ce que vous —?

Review...
- aller and venir: pp. 206, 212, and 218

5 Composition: La maison idéale

Write a short paragraph of five or six sentences describing your ideal house and its rooms. Does it have a garden? Where is it located? What do you especially like about it?

STRATEGY Writing

a	b	c
Sketch out a floor plan of your ideal house, labelling the rooms.	Organize your paragraph, concluding with why you like this house.	Reread your composition to be sure you have spelled all the names of the rooms correctly.

2 COMPREHENSION

1. Marc dîne au restaurant.
2. Thomas nage à la piscine.
3. Le professeur parle aux élèves.
4. Les élèves vont à l'école en bus.
5. Nous faisons une promenade à pied.
6. Pauline va chez sa copine Isabelle.
7. Nous revenons de l'école à trois heures.
8. Les touristes arrivent du musée.
9. J'aime jouer au football.
10. Est-ce que tu joues de la clarinette?
11. Comment s'appelle la copine de Monique?
12. Voici la maison des voisins.

3 COMPREHENSION

1. Tu téléphones à ta copine.
2. Je vais souvent au cinéma avec mes amis.
3. Marc dîne chez sa tante.
4. Alice invite ses voisins à la boum.
5. Isabelle n'a pas son appareil-photo avec elle.
6. Thomas et Charlotte sont en vacances chez leur oncle.
7. Les élèves respectent leurs professeurs.
8. Vous parlez avec votre amie Mélanie.
9. Nous allons visiter Paris avec notre professeur de français.
10. Est-ce que vous écoutez toujours vos parents?

4 COMPREHENSION

1. Je viens!
2. Thomas et Céline vont très souvent au cinéma.
3. Qu'est-ce que tu vas faire samedi?
4. Nous allons aller à une boum.
5. Il vient de Montréal.
6. Je vais souvent à la piscine parce que j'aime nager.
7. Il vient du restaurant.
8. D'où est-ce que vous venez?

5 WRITTEN SELF-EXPRESSION

Answers will vary.
Ma maison idéale est à Paris. Elle est très grande et moderne. Il y a un salon, une salle à manger, une cuisine, quatre chambres, deux salles de bain, deux toilettes et un garage. Ma chambre est confortable. Il y a une piscine et beaucoup de fleurs dans le jardin. J'aime ma maison parce qu'elle est à Paris!

VOCABULAIRE

Language Learning Benchmarks

FUNCTION
- Introduce and respond to introductions p. 228
- Engage in conversations p. 199, 213
- Make requests pp. 218, 232
- Obtain information pp. 196, 199
- Understand some ideas and familiar details pp 205, 217
- Begin to provide information p. 199, 201, 210, 222

CONTEXT
- Converse in face-to-face social interactions pp. 199, 209, 213, 220, 222
- Listen during social interactions p. 196
- Listen to audio and video texts pp. 194-195, 216, 226
- Use authentic materials when reading: posters p. 211
- Use authentic materials when reading: charts p. 201
- Use authentic materials when reading: signs pp. 196, 198, 247
- Use authentic materials when reading: short narratives pp. 243, 244
- Write notes pp. 215, 235
- Write lists p. 215
- Write short letters p. 225

TEXT TYPE
- Use short sentences when speaking pp. 198, 229, 232
- Use short sentences when writing pp. 198. 207, 231
- Use learned words and phrases when speaking pp. 196, 220, 222, 231
- Use learned words and phrases when writing pp. 196, 223
- Use simple questions when speaking pp. 198, 209, 213, 231

Vocabulaire

POUR COMMUNIQUER

Asking where people are going

Où vas-tu?		*Where are you going?*
Je vais à + PLACE, EVENT	**Je vais au concert.**	*I am going to the concert.*
Je vais chez + PERSON	**Je vais chez Pierre.**	*I am going to Pierre's house.*
Je vais chez + STRESS PRONOUN	**Je vais chez moi.**	*I am going to my house.*

Asking where people are coming from

D'où est-ce que tu viens?		*Where are you coming from?*
Je viens de + PLACE	**Je viens de la piscine.**	*I am coming from the pool.*

Asking for directions

Excusez-moi, où est [le théâtre]? *Excuse me, where is [the theater]?*	**Est-ce que c'est loin? / près?**	*Is it far? / nearby, close?*
	Tournez à gauche. / à droite.	*Turn to the left. / to the right.*
	Continuez tout droit.	*Continue straight ahead.*
Pardon, où sont [les toilettes]? *Excuse me, where are [the toilets]?*	**Elles sont en haut. / en bas**	*They are upstairs. / downstairs.*

Talking about future plans

Qu'est-ce que tu vas faire?	*What are you going to do?*
Je vais [travailler].	*I am going [to work].*

Expressing possession

C'est mon (ton, son ...) livre.	*That's my (your, his/her, ...) book.*

MOTS ET EXPRESSIONS

Moyens de transport *(means of transportation)*

à pied	*on foot*
à vélo	*by bicycle*
en bus	*by bus*
en métro	*by subway*
en taxi	*by taxi*
en train	*by train*
en voiture	*by car*

La ville

un boulevard	*boulevard*
un café	*café*
un centre commercial	*mall, shopping center*
un cinéma	*movie theater*
un hôpital	*hospital*
un hôtel	*hotel*
un magasin	*store*
un musée	*museum*
un parc	*park*
un quartier	*neighborhood*
un restaurant	*restaurant*
un stade	*stadium*
un supermarché	*supermarket*
un théâtre	*theater*
un village	*town, village*
une adresse	*address*
une avenue	*avenue*
une bibliothèque	*library*
une école	*school*
une église	*church*
une piscine	*(swimming) pool*
une plage	*beach*
une rue	*street*
une ville	*city, town*

La maison

un appartement	*apartment*	**une chambre**	*bedroom*
un garage	*garage*	**une cuisine**	*kitchen*
un immeuble	*apartment building*	**une maison**	*house*
un jardin	*garden, yard*	**une salle à manger**	*dining room*
un salon	*living room*	**une salle de bains**	*bathroom*
		les toilettes	*bathroom, toilet*

Quelques endroits où aller

un concert	*concert*	**un film**	*movie*	**une boum**	*party (casual)*
un endroit	*place*	**un pique-nique**	*picnic*	**une fête**	*party*
un événement	*event*	**un rendez-vous**	*date, appointment*	**une soirée**	*party (evening)*

La famille

les parents	*parents; relatives*	**la famille**	*family*
les grands-parents	*grandparents*		
le grand-père	*grandfather*	**la grand-mère**	*grandmother*
le père	*father*	**la mère**	*mother*
le mari	*husband*	**la femme**	*wife*
un enfant	*child*	**une enfant**	*child*
le fils	*son*	**la fille**	*daughter*
le frère	*brother*	**la soeur**	*sister*
l'oncle	*uncle*	**la tante**	*aunt*
le cousin	*cousin*	**la cousine**	*cousin*

Verbes en *-er*

arriver	*to arrive, to come*
rentrer	*to go back, come back*
rester	*to stay*
jouer à + SPORT, GAME	*to play (a sport, game)*
jouer de + INSTRUMENT	*to play (an instrument)*

Verbes irréguliers

aller	*to go*
faire une promenade à pied	*to go for a walk*
faire une promenade à vélo	*to go for a bike ride*
faire une promenade en voiture	*to go for a drive*
venir	*to come*
revenir	*to come back*

Les sports

le baseball	*baseball*
le basket(ball)	*basketball*
le foot(ball)	*soccer*
le ping-pong	*ping-pong*
le tennis	*tennis*
le volley(ball)	*volleyball*

Les jeux

les échecs	*chess*	**les cartes**	*cards*
les jeux d'ordinateur	*computer games*	**les dames**	*checkers*
les jeux vidéo	*video games*		

Les instruments de musique

le clavier	*keyboard*	**la batterie**	*drums*
le piano	*piano*	**la clarinette**	*clarinet*
le saxo(phone)	*saxophone*	**la flûte**	*flute*
le violon	*violin*	**la guitare**	*guitar*

Expressions utiles

Pas du tout!	*Not at all! Definitely not!*
Vraiment?!	*Really?!*
Tu es sûr(e)?	*Are you sure?*
Vas-y!	*Go on!*
Va-t'en!	*Go away!*

Les nombres ordinaux

premier (première)	*first*	**septième**	*seventh*
deuxième	*second*	**huitième**	*eighth*
troisième	*third*	**neuvième**	*ninth*
quatrième	*fourth*	**dixième**	*tenth*
cinquième	*fifth*	**onzième**	*eleventh*
sixième	*sixth*	**douzième**	*twelfth*

FLASHCARDS AND MORE!

- Understand some ideas and familiar details presented in clear, uncomplicated speech when listening pp. 204, 217, 226
- Understand short texts enhanced by visual clues when reading pp. 205, 226, 242-243, 248-251

CONTENT
- Understand and convey information about home p. 201
- Understand and convey information about rooms p. 201
- Understand and convey information about directions p. 199
- Understand and convey information about buildings and monuments p. 198
- Understand and convey information about cultural and historical figures p. 245
- Understand and convey information about places and events p, 251
- Understand and convey information about travel pp. 249, 251, 253

ASSESSMENT
- Communicate effectively with some hesitation and errors, which do not hinder comprehension pp. 203, 214, 224
- Demonstrate culturally acceptable behavior for engaging in conversations pp. 203, 215, 225, 234
- Demonstrate culturally acceptable behavior for obtaining information pp. 203, 215
- Demonstrate culturally acceptable behavior for understanding some ideas and familiar details p. 203
- Demonstrate culturally acceptable behavior for providing information pp. 203, 225
- Understand most important information pp. 202, 214, 225, 235

ENTRACTE

Objectives
- Reading skills development
- Re-entry of material in the unit
- Development of cultural awarenesss

Teaching Resource Options

Workbook PE, pp. 145–148
Activités pour tous PE, pp. 87–89
Unit 5 Resource Book
Activités pour tous TE, pp. 165–167
Workbook TE, pp. 169–172

Le cinéma

Objectives
- Reading at the paragraph level
- Reading for cultural information about the cinema

Comparaisons culturelles

Answers will vary.

Les préférences	Les jeunes Français	Moi	Différence ou similarité
jour	samedi	(vendredi)	(différence)
sorte de cinéma	les multiplexes	(les multiplexes)	(similarité)
films	les films d'action, les comédies	(les comédies)	(similarité)

LES JEUNES FRANÇAIS ET *le cinéma*

Le samedi, les jeunes Français adorent aller au cinéma. C'est pour eux l'occasion de voir° un bon film et aussi d'être avec leurs copains. Quand ils sont en ville, ils peuvent° aller dans les cinémas de quartier. Mais en général, ils préfèrent les «multiplexes». Là, ils ont le choix entre 6 et 12 films différents. Dans les grandes multiplexes, il y a aussi des restaurants, des boutiques et des salles de jeux vidéo où ils peuvent aller avant° et après le film. Les jeunes qui vont souvent au cinéma peuvent acheter° une carte de multiplexe.° Avec cette° carte qui coûte dix-huit euros par mois, ils peuvent voir un nombre illimité de films dans leur multiplexe favorite.

Les jeunes Français vont au cinéma pour voir les films français récents. Ils aiment aussi les films américains, en particulier les films d'action, les films de science-fiction et les comédies. Les jeunes qui parlent bien anglais peuvent voir ces films en «version originale» — avec, bien sûr, des sous-titres° en français.

voir *to see* **peuvent** *can* **avant** *before* **acheter** *buy* **carte de multiplexe** *movie pass* **cette** *that* **ces** *these* **sous-titres** *subtitles*

COMPARAISONS CULTURELLES

Compare the movie-going preferences of French and American teenagers by filling in the following chart:

Les préférences	Les jeunes Français	Moi	Différence ou similarité?
• Quel jour?	________	________	________
• Dans quelle sorte de cinéma?	________	________	________
• Quels films?	________	________	________

Films américains, public français

Voici une liste de films américains qui ont eu° beaucoup de succès en France. Est-ce que vous pouvez° identifier ces films? Lisez° le titre° français de chaque° film. Faites correspondre° le titre de ce film avec le titre américain.

ont eu *have had* **pouvez** *can* **Lisez** *Read* **titre** *title* **chaque** *each* **Faites correspondre** *Match*

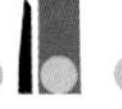

TITRES FRANÇAIS	TITRES AMÉRICAINS
1. Blanche-Neige et les sept nains (1937)	A. E.T. the Extra-Terrestrial
2. Le Magicien d'Oz (1939)	B. The Lion King
3. La mélodie du bonheur (1965)	C. The Godfather
4. Devine qui vient dîner? (1967)	D. Snow White and the Seven Dwarves
5. Le Parrain (1972)	E. Guess Who's Coming to Dinner?
6. Les aventuriers de l'arche perdue (1981)	F. The Perfect Storm
7. E.T. l'extra-terrestre (1982)	G. Raiders of the Lost Ark
8. Le roi Lion (1994)	H. Saving Private Ryan
9. Il faut sauver le soldat Ryan (1998)	I. The Sound of Music
10. En pleine tempête (2000)	J. The Wizard of Oz

CONNEXIONS

Use the Internet to find out which American films are currently playing in Paris. As you read the French titles, can you guess the original English titles?

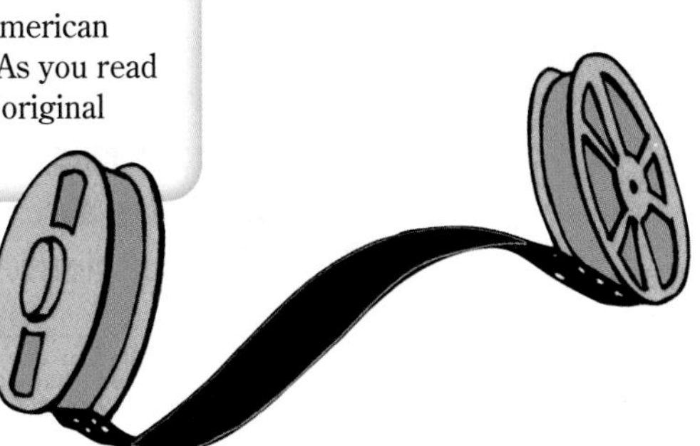

Films américains, public français

Objectives

- Reading for fun
- Deriving meaning by word association

Films américains, public français
Answers

1. d
2. j
3. i
4. e
5. c
6. g
7. a
8. b
9. h
10. f

Variation (books closed)

Write only the French film titles on the chalkboard or on a transparency.

Divide the class into groups and see how many English titles each group can discover.

Teaching note Tell students to watch for French films playing at theaters in the area. They might also be able to see French plays at a local college or university.

PRE-READING

Ask students to look at the illustrations and the title at the top of the page.

- What do they think is the topic of this reading?

Ask pairs of students to name their favorite movies.
Quel est votre film favori?
Notre film favori est [Lord of the Rings].

POST-READING

Ask students which of these movies they have seen.

- Which ones did they like best?

OPTIONAL: Prepare a movie poster in French.

Teaching Resource Options

PRINT 

Workbook PE, pp. 145–148
Activités pour tous PE, pp. 87–89
Unit 5 Resource Book
Activités pour tous TE, pp. 165–167
Workbook TE, pp. 169–172

Tintin et ses amis

Objectives

- Reading a longer text
- Building reading skills

Questions sur le texte

1. Quel âge a Tintin? (17 ans)
2. Est-ce que Tintin est français? (Non, il est belge.)
3. Comment est Tintin? (Il est intelligent et courageux.)
4. Comment s'appelle le chien de Tintin? (Milou)
5. Est-ce que le capitaine Haddock habite dans une maison? (Non, il habite au château de Moulinsart.)
6. Est-ce que Dupont et Dupond sont frères? (Non, mais ils sont presque identiques.)
7. Qui est un génie scientifique? (Le professeur Tournesol)

Teaching tip Students may be interested in getting their own Tintin books. Direct them to an appropriate online store or to a local bookstore that sells foreign books.

Teaching note Have students check their local library to see if it carries French books, videos, or audio recordings. They could also look for French films in a video store.

Tintin et ses amis

Tintin et Milou

Tous° les jeunes Français connaissent° Tintin. Tintin n'est pas une personne réelle. C'est le héros d'une bande dessinée° très populaire en France et dans le monde° entier. «Les Aventures de Tintin» ont été publiées en français, mais aussi en anglais, en espagnol, en italien, en chinois, en japonais ... au total dans 40 langues° différentes.

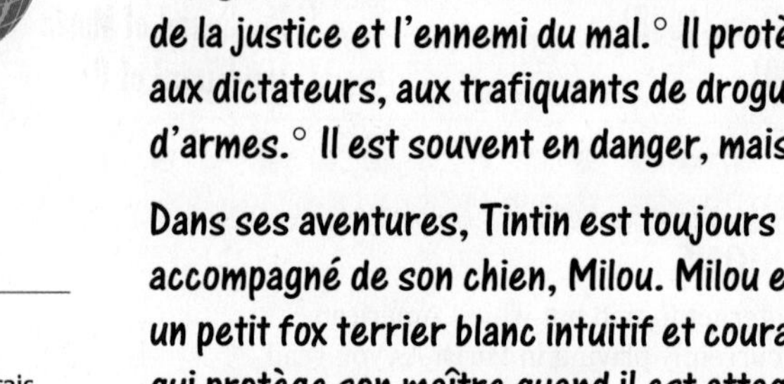

Tintin a dix-sept ans et il est belge.° C'est un journaliste-détective. Il est intelligent et courageux et il adore voyager. Il va en Égypte, au Congo, en Chine, au Tibet, au Mexique et en Amérique. Il va même° sur° la lune, bien avant° les astronautes américains. Dans ses voyages, il connaît° des aventures extraordinaires. Tintin est l'ami de la justice et l'ennemi du mal.° Il protège ses amis et il s'attaque aux dictateurs, aux trafiquants de drogue° et aux marchands d'armes.° Il est souvent en danger, mais il triomphe toujours.

Dans ses aventures, Tintin est toujours accompagné de son chien, Milou. Milou est un petit fox terrier blanc intuitif et courageux qui protège son maître quand il est attaqué. Il accompagne Tintin dans toutes ses aventures. Quand il va avec lui sur la lune, il est équipé d'une combinaison spatiale° pour chiens.

Tous *All* **connaissent** *know* **bande dessinée** *comic strip* **monde** *world* **langues** *languages* **belge** *Belgian* **même** *even* **sur** *on* **avant** *before* **connaît** *experiences* **mal** *evil* **trafiquants de drogue** *drug dealers* **armes** *weapons* **combinaison spatiale** *space suit* **Voila qui est fait.** *There, you're all set.*

EN BREF: LA BELGIQUE

Capitale: Bruxelles
Population: 10 250 000
Langues officielles: français, flamand° et allemand°

La Belgique est une monarchie constitutionnelle avec un roi,° le roi Albert II. Sa capitale, Bruxelles, est le siège° de la Commission Européenne.

flamand *Flemish* **allemand** *German* **roi** *king* **siège** *seat*

PRE-READING

Ask if any students have heard of Tintin. **Est-ce que vous connaissez Tintin?** If yes, ask if they have their own copies of any of the Tintin books. **Est-ce que vous avez des livres de Tintin?**

Tintin a d'autres compagnons d'aventures, très sympathiques, mais un peu bizarres.

le capitaine Haddock

Le capitaine Haddock habite au château° de Moulinsart en Belgique. C'est un ancien° officier de la marine marchande. Il est brave et courageux ... mais il est aussi très irritable.

Garnements! *Rascals!* **Iconoclastes!** *Iconoclasts! (people who attack and seek to overthrow traditional ideas)* **château** *castle* **ancien** *former*

Dupont et Dupond

Dupont et Dupond sont presque° identiques, mais ils ne sont pas frères. Ce sont des policiers méthodiques ... mais incompétents.

presque *almost*

le professeur Tournesol

Le professeur Tournesol est un génie scientifique. Il est modeste et réservé et comme° beaucoup de professeurs, il est très distrait.°

comme *like* **distrait** *absent-minded*

STRATEGY Reading

Recognizing Cognate Patterns Recognizing French-English cognate patterns will help you increase your reading vocabulary and improve your reading comprehension. Here are some common patterns:

FRENCH	ENGLISH	FRENCH	ENGLISH
-aire	*-ar, -ary*	**extraordinaire**	*extraordinary*
-eux, -euse	*-ous*	**courageux**	*courageous*
-ique	*-ic, -ical*	**identique**	*identical*
-iste	*-ist, istic*	**journaliste**	*journalist*
-é	*-ed*	**réservé**	*reserved*

COMMUNAUTÉ

Organize a **fête Tintin** for the language classes in your school. You may display Tintin books in French and other languages and show a video or DVD of some of Tintin's adventures. Encourage your classmates to come dressed as Tintin characters.

Et vous?

Quelle est ta bande dessinée favorite? Qui sont les héros? Pourquoi est-ce que tu aimes cette bande dessinée?

Et vous?
Answers will vary.
Ma bande dessinée favorite est (Garfield).

Le héros est (Garfield).

J'aime cette bande dessinée parce que (j'aime les chats).

Bonjour, Ousmane!

Objectives

- Reading at the paragraph level
- Developing logical thinking

Teaching Resource Options

PRINT 

Workbook PE, pp. 145–148
Activités pour tous PE, pp. 87–89
Unit 5 Resource Book
Activités pour tous TE, pp. 165–169
Workbook TE, pp. 169–172

Compréhension
Answers

1. le rap et le rock
2. de la guitare
3. le mercredi après-midi
4. parce que sa mère déteste ça

Activité écrite
Answers will vary.
J'aime le rock. Je déteste la musique classique. Mon groupe préféré est U2. Ils chantent bien.

Bonjour, Ousmane!

Bonjour! Je m'appelle Ousmane. J'adore la musique. J'aime surtout le rap et le rock. Mon chanteur° préféré est MC Solaar. Il chante très bien. J'ai beaucoup de CD de lui. Ma soeur, elle, préfère le blues et le jazz.

Je suis un peu musicien. Je joue de la guitare. Et je ne joue pas trop mal. J'ai organisé° un petit orchestre° de rock avec des copains. Nous répétons° le mercredi après-midi. Nous ne répétons pas chez moi, parce que ma mère déteste ça°. Parfois°, le week-end, nous jouons à des boums pour nos amis.

chanteur *singer* **ai organisé** *organized* **orchestre** *band*
répétons *rehearse* **ça** *that* **Parfois** *Sometimes*

Compréhension

1. Quelle est la musique préférée d'Ousmane?
2. De quel instrument est-ce qu'il joue?
3. Quand est-ce qu'il répète avec ses copains?
4. Pourquoi est-ce qu'il ne répète pas à la maison?

Activité écrite

Write a short note to Ousmane in which you describe your musical preferences. Use the following suggestions:

- J'aime … (quelles musiques?)
- Je déteste … (quelles musiques?)
- Mon groupe préféré est … (qui?)
- Ils/Elles chantent … (comment?)

MC Solaar, le <<Monsieur Rap>> français

MC Solaar

le «Monsieur Rap» français

MC Solaar est né° à Dakar au Sénégal. Il s'appelle en réalité Claude M'Barali. Ses parents émigrent en France quand il a six mois. Il fait ses études dans la région parisienne. Après° le bac, il s'intéresse à° la musique. Il compose des chansons° françaises sur des rythmes de rap américain. Ses chansons ont beaucoup de succès. MC Solaar donne° des concerts en France, mais aussi en Angleterre,° en Allemagne,° en Russie et dans les pays° d'Afrique.

Aujourd'hui, MC Solaar est le «Monsieur Rap» français! Dans ses chansons, il exprime° des messages positifs contre° la violence et pour la paix.° Voilà pourquoi il est très populaire en France et dans le monde° francophone.

est né *was born* **Après** *After* **s'intéresse à** *becomes interested in* **chansons** *songs* **donne** *gives* **Angleterre** *England* **Allemagne** *Germany* **pays** *countries* **exprime** *expresses* **contre** *against* **la paix** *peace* **monde** *world*

CONNEXIONS

With 2 or 3 classmates, select a French singer, such as MC Solaar. Go on the Internet and obtain as much information as you can about the person you have chosen. If possible, get samples of his or her music. Share your findings with the rest of the class.

COMMUNAUTÉ

Prepare a short program about music from the French-speaking world. You may want to include pictures of the performers, selections of their recordings, and perhaps a world map showing their countries of origin. Present your program to another class at school or at a local senior center.

I M A G E S

À Paris

Bonjour, Paris!

Quelques faits

- Paris est la capitale de la France.
- Paris est une très grande ville. La ville de Paris a deux millions d'habitants. La région parisienne a onze millions d'habitants. Vingt pour cent (20%) des Français habitent dans la région parisienne.
- Paris est situé° sur la Seine. Ce fleuve° divise° la ville en deux parties: la rive° droite (au nord) et la rive gauche (au sud).
- Administrativement, Paris est divisé en vingt arrondissements.°
- Paris est une ville très ancienne.° Elle a plus de° deux mille° ans.
- Paris est aussi une ville moderne et dynamique. C'est le centre économique, industriel et commercial de la France.
- Avec ses musées, ses théâtres, ses bibliothèques et ses écoles d'art, Paris est un centre culturel et artistique très important.
- Avec ses nombreux° monuments et ses larges avenues, Paris est une très belle ville. Pour beaucoup de gens, c'est la plus° belle ville du monde.° Chaque année,° des millions de touristes visitent Paris.

situé *located* **fleuve** *river* **divise** *divides* **rive** *(river)bank* **arrondissements** *districts* **ancienne** *old* **plus de** *more than* **mille** *thousand* **nombreux** *many* **la plus** *the most* **monde** *world* **Chaque année** *Each year*

IMAGES

Cultural Theme
- Paris

À Paris

Objectives
- Reading a complete text
- Building reading skills

Teaching Resource Options

PRINT 

Workbook PE, pp. 145–148
Activités pour tous PE, pp. 87–89
Unit 5 Resource Book
Activités pour tous TE, pp. 165–167
Lesson Plans, pp. 173–174
Block Scheduling Lesson Plans, pp. 175–176
Videoscript, pp. 130–131
Workbook TE, pp. 169–172

VIDEO PROGRAM

VIDÉO DVD

IMAGES
À Paris

TOTAL TIME: 7:18 min.
DVD Disk 2
Videotape 3 (COUNTER: 26:01 min.)

C.1 Introduction à Paris
(26:10–27:23 min.)

C.2 Interview avec Jean-Marc Lacoste
(27:24–28:15 min.)

C.3 Visite de Paris
(28:16–32:22 min.)

C.4 Promenade en bateau-mouche
(32:23–34:19 min.)

deux cent quarante-sept 247
Lecture et Culture

Cultural notes Paris

- The **Place de la Concorde,** at the end of the Champs-Élysées, is one of the largest squares in the world. At the center stands **l'obélisque,** a gift to the king of France (Charles X) from the viceroy of Egypt.
- **Les Invalides** is a former French military hospital (hence its name). Tourists come to **Les Invalides** to see Napoleon's tomb and visit the military museum.
- **Le jardin des Tuileries** is a large public park which extends from the **Place de la Concorde** to the **Louvre.**
- The French legislature has two houses, **l'Assemblée nationale** (similar to the U.S. House of Representatives) and **le Sénat.**

Photo cultural notes

- Top left: artistes à Montmartre
- Bottom left: **Les Champs-Élysées** with **L'arc de Triomphe** in the background
- Bottom right: **un arrêt du Métro**

Using the video

In this Essay, **À Paris,** Jean-Marc Lacoste (see p. 252) takes the students around Paris. Play the entire module as an introduction to the IMAGES.

Le Paris traditionnel

Teaching Resource Options

PRINT 

Workbook PE, pp. 145–148
Activités pour tous PE, pp. 87–89
Unit 5 Resource Book
Activités pour tous TE, pp. 165–167
Workbook TE, pp. 169–172

Cultural background

- The Eiffel Tower was built to commemorate the 100th anniversary of the French Revolution which began July 14, 1789 and lasted ten years.

IMAGES

Le Paris TRADITIONNEL

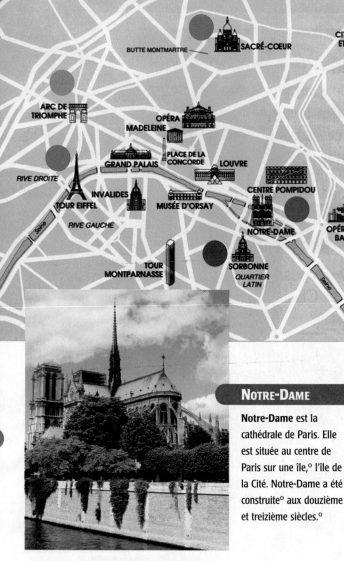

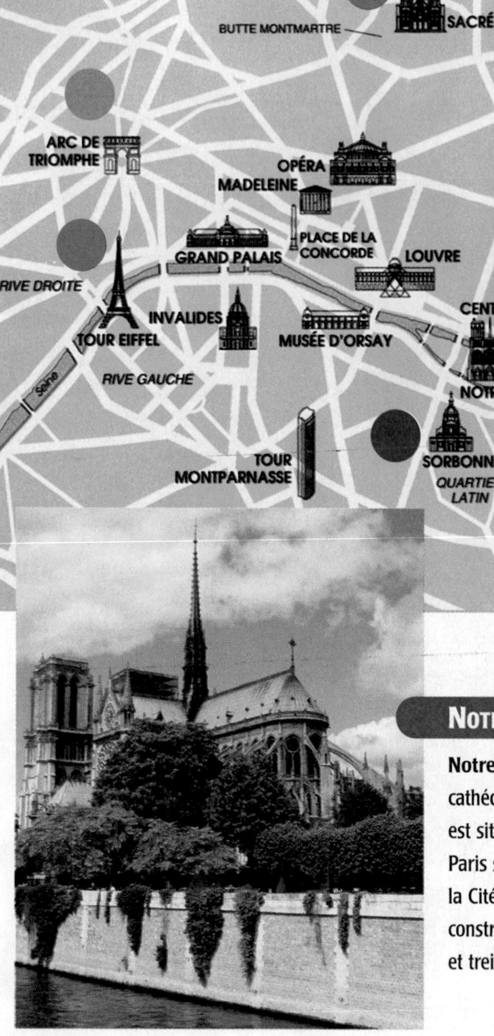

LA TOUR EIFFEL

Pour beaucoup de gens, **la tour Eiffel** est le symbole de Paris. Cette° immense tour de fer° a trois cent mètres de haut.° Elle a été inaugurée en 1889 (dix-huit cent quatre-vingt-neuf) par l'ingénieur Gustave Eiffel. Du sommet de la tour Eiffel, on° a une très belle vue sur Paris.

NOTRE-DAME

Notre-Dame est la cathédrale de Paris. Elle est située au centre de Paris sur une île,° l'île de la Cité. Notre-Dame a été construite° aux douzième et treizième siècles.°

Cette *This* **fer** *iron* **a trois cent mètres de haut** *is 300 meters high* **on** *one*
île *island* **a été construite** *was built* **siècles** *centuries*

Le Sacré-Coeur

Le Sacré-Coeur est une église de pierre° blanche qui domine Paris. Cette église est située sur la butte° Montmartre. Montmartre est un quartier pittoresque. Les artistes viennent ici pour peindre° et les touristes viennent pour regarder les artistes. Si vous voulez° avoir un souvenir personnel de Paris, allez à Montmartre et demandez à° un artiste de faire votre portrait.

Le Quartier latin

Le Quartier latin est le quartier des étudiants. C'est un quartier très animé avec des cafés, des cinémas, des librairies° et des restaurants exotiques et bon marché.° Pourquoi est-ce que ce quartier s'appelle «Quartier latin»? Parce qu'autrefois° les étudiants parlaient° latin ici.

L'Arc de Triomphe et les Champs-Élysées

L'Arc de Triomphe est un monument qui° commémore les victoires de Napoléon (1769–1821). Ce monument est situé en haut° des Champs-Élysées.

Les Champs-Élysées sont une très grande et très belle avenue. Pour les Parisiens, c'est la plus° belle avenue du monde.

Activité Culturelle

Imaginez que vous passez une journée° à Paris. Où allez-vous aller le matin? Où allez-vous aller l'après-midi? Choisissez deux endroits à visiter et expliquez° votre choix.°

pierre *stone* **butte** *hill* **peindre** *to paint* **voulez** *want* **demandez à** *ask* **librairies** *bookstores*
bon marché *inexpensive* **autrefois** *in the past* **parlaient** *used to speak* **qui** *which* **en haut** *at the top*
la plus *the most* **passez une journée** *are spending a day* **expliquez** *explain* **choix** *choice*

Cultural background

- Napoleon came to power after the French Revolution. He declared himself Emperor in 1804 and was defeated at Waterloo in 1815. In France he is remembered as a military genius and an efficient administrator.

Teaching Suggestion Remind students that many jobs require the knowledge of another language. Have students imagine that they are going to pursue studies at **l'Université Paris-Sorbonne** in **le Quartier latin**. Which course of study most interests them? Have them discuss how knowledge of French could potentially help them in their futures when they are ready to begin searching for a job.

Activité Culturelle

Answers will vary.
À Paris, je vais visiter La tour Eiffel. C'est le symbole de la France. Je vais aussi visiter le Quartier latin. Il y a beaucoup de choses à faire là-bas.

Le nouveau Paris

Teaching Resource Options

PRINT 

Workbook PE, pp. 145–148
Activités pour tous PE, pp. 87–89
Unit 5 Resource Book
Activités pour tous TE, pp. 165–167
Workbook TE, pp. 169–172

Cultural background

- Mona Lisa (also known as "la Joconde") was painted by Leonardo da Vinci (1452–1519).
- Le Centre Pompidou was named after Georges Pompidou (1911–1974), President of France (1969–1974).
- Claude Monet (1840–1926), Berthe Morisot (1841–1895), and Auguste Renoir (1841–1919), Impressionist painters; Camille Claudel (1864–1943) sculptor; Henri de Toulouse-Lautrec (1864–1901).

IMAGES

Le NOUVEAU Paris

Le Louvre et la pyramide du Louvre

Le Louvre est une ancienne° résidence royale transformée en musée. C'est dans ce° musée que se trouve° la fameuse «Mona Lisa». On entre dans le Louvre par° une pyramide de verre.° Cette pyramide moderne a été construite° par l'architecte américain I.M. Pei. Avec sa pyramide, le Louvre est le symbole du nouveau° Paris, à la fois° moderne et traditionnel.

Le Centre Pompidou

Le Centre Pompidou est le monument le plus° visité de Paris. C'est un musée d'art moderne. C'est aussi une bibliothèque, une cinémathèque et un centre audio-visuel. À l'extérieur,° sur l'esplanade, il y a des musiciens, des mimes, des acrobates, des jongleurs° … Un peu plus loin,° il y a une place° avec des fontaines, un bassin° et des sculptures mobiles.

Le musée d'Orsay

Autrefois,° c'était° une gare.° Aujourd'hui, c'est un musée. On vient ici admirer les chefs-d'oeuvre° des grands peintres° et sculpteurs français du dix-neuvième siècle.° On peut,° par exemple, admirer les oeuvres° de Monet, de Claudel, de Renoir, de Morisot et de Toulouse-Lautrec. À l'extérieur, il y a des sculptures qui représentent les cinq continents.

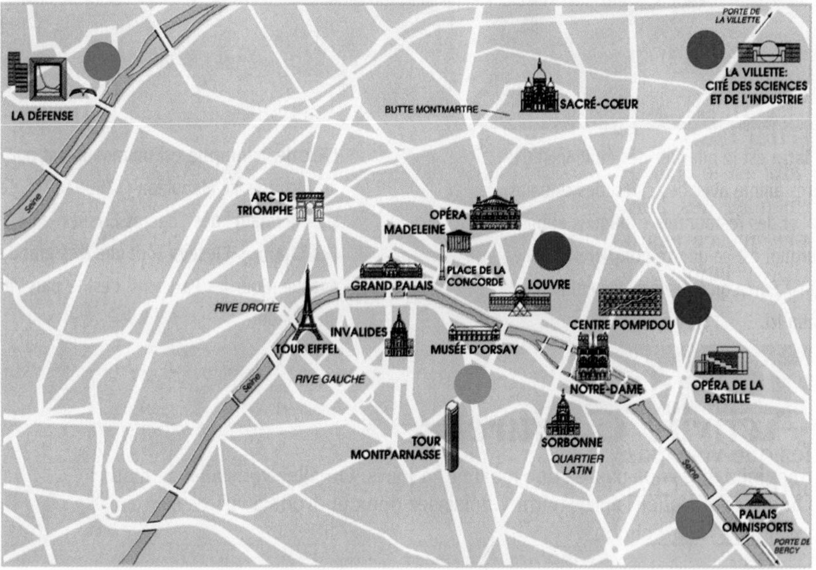

ancienne *former* **ce** *this* **se trouve** *is located* **par** *by* **verre** *glass* **a été construite** *was built* **nouveau** *new* **à la fois** *at the same time* **le plus** *the most* **À l'extérieur** *Outside* **jongleurs** *jugglers* **plus loin** *farther away* **place** *square* **bassin** *ornamental pool* **Autrefois** *Formerly* **c'était** *it used to be* **gare** *train station* **chefs-d'oeuvre** *masterpieces* **peintres** *painters* **siècle** *century* **peut** *can* **oeuvres** *works*

If students ask: Un **gratte-ciel** is a "sky-scratcher." Which term do they find more appropriate: the French word or the English word?

Le Palais Omnisports de Bercy

Sport ou musique? **Bercy** est un stade couvert° pour tous les sports. C'est aussi une immense salle° de concert. On vient ici écouter et applaudir les vedettes° de la chanson° française … et de la chanson américaine.

Le parc de la Villette

Le parc de la Villette est un lieu° de récréation pour les jeunes de tout âge.° On trouve ici des parcs pour enfants,° des terrains de jeu° et différentes° constructions ultra-modernes.

- Le Zénith est une salle de concert où viennent les vedettes du monde° entier.
- La Géode est un cinéma omnimax avec un écran° circulaire géant.
- La Cité des sciences et de l'industrie est un grand musée scientifique où les jeunes peuvent° faire leurs propres° expériences° et jouer avec toutes sortes de gadgets électroniques.

La Défense et son arche

La Défense est le nouveau centre d'affaires° situé à l'ouest de Paris. Chaque° jour, des milliers° de Parisiens viennent travailler dans ses gratte-ciel° de verre. Il y a aussi des magasins, des cinémas, des restaurants et une patinoire.° La Grande Arche a été construite pour commémorer le deux centième anniversaire de la Révolution française.

Activité Culturelle

Vous êtes à Paris pour une semaine. Pendant votre séjour, vous voulez faire les choses suivantes. Dites où vous allez pour cela.

▶ **Lundi, je veux voir une exposition d'art moderne. Je vais au Centre Pompidou.**

Quand?	Pourquoi?	Où?
▶ lundi	voir *(to see)* une exposition d'art moderne	??
mardi	voir une exposition sur les lasers	??
mercredi	voir la «Mona Lisa»	??
jeudi	voir un match de basket	??
vendredi	voir une exposition sur Toulouse-Lautrec	??
samedi	aller dans les magasins et faire du shopping	??

couvert *covered* **salle** *hall* **vedettes** *stars* **chanson** *song* **lieu** *place* **de tout âge** *of all ages* **parcs pour enfants** *playgrounds* **terrains de jeu** *playing fields* **différentes** *several* **monde** *world* **écran** *screen* **peuvent** *can* **propres** *own* **expériences** *experiments* **affaires** *business* **Chaque** *Each* **des milliers** *thousands* **gratte-ciel** *skyscrapers* **patinoire** *skating rink*

Activité Culturelle

Answers

- Mardi, je veux voir une exposition sur les lasers. Je vais au parc de la Villette.
- Mercredi, je veux voir la «Mona Lisa». Je vais au Louvre.
- Jeudi, je veux voir un match de basket. Je vais au palais Omnisports de Bercy.
- Vendredi, je veux voir une exposition sur Toulouse-Lautrec. Je vais au musée d'Orsay.
- Samedi, je veux aller dans les magasins et faire du shopping. Je vais à la Défense.

Salut, les amis!

Teaching Resource Options

PRINT 

Workbook PE, pp. 145–148
Activités pour tous PE, pp. 87–89
Unit 5 Resource Book
Activités pour tous TE, pp. 165–167
Videoscript, pp. 130–131
Workbook TE, pp. 169–172

VIDEO PROGRAM

VIDÉO DVD

IMAGES

C.1 Introduction à Paris (26:10–27:23 min.)

C.2 Interview avec Jean-Marc Lacoste (27:24–28:15 min.)

C.3 Visite de Paris (28:16–32:22 min.)

C.4 Promenade en bateau-mouche (32:23–34:19 min.)

Teaching Suggestion Have students write an e-mail responding to Jean-Marc. Remind them to answer any questions that he may have asked in his e-mail. They should also give as much information about themselves as possible (nationality, where they live, what they do during the week and on weekends, where they like to go, etc.).

Précédente Suivante Recharger Accueil Rechercher Images Imprimer Sécurité Arrêter

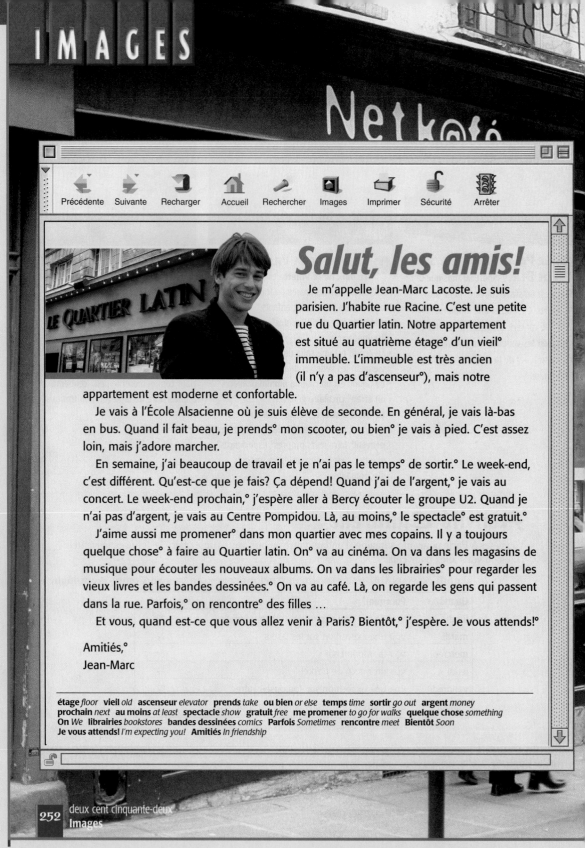

Salut, les amis!

Je m'appelle Jean-Marc Lacoste. Je suis parisien. J'habite rue Racine. C'est une petite rue du Quartier latin. Notre appartement est situé au quatrième étage° d'un vieil° immeuble. L'immeuble est très ancien (il n'y a pas d'ascenseur°), mais notre appartement est moderne et confortable.

Je vais à l'École Alsacienne où je suis élève de seconde. En général, je vais là-bas en bus. Quand il fait beau, je prends° mon scooter, ou bien° je vais à pied. C'est assez loin, mais j'adore marcher.

En semaine, j'ai beaucoup de travail et je n'ai pas le temps° de sortir.° Le week-end, c'est différent. Qu'est-ce que je fais? Ça dépend! Quand j'ai de l'argent,° je vais au concert. Le week-end prochain,° j'espère aller à Bercy écouter le groupe U2. Quand je n'ai pas d'argent, je vais au Centre Pompidou. Là, au moins,° le spectacle° est gratuit.°

J'aime aussi me promener° dans mon quartier avec mes copains. Il y a toujours quelque chose° à faire au Quartier latin. On° va au cinéma. On va dans les magasins de musique pour écouter les nouveaux albums. On va dans les librairies° pour regarder les vieux livres et les bandes dessinées.° On va au café. Là, on regarde les gens qui passent dans la rue. Parfois,° on rencontre° des filles ...

Et vous, quand est-ce que vous allez venir à Paris? Bientôt,° j'espère. Je vous attends!°

Amitiés,°
Jean-Marc

étage *floor* **vieil** *old* **ascenseur** *elevator* **prends** *take* **ou bien** *or else* **temps** *time* **sortir** *go out* **argent** *money* **prochain** *next* **au moins** *at least* **spectacle** *show* **gratuit** *free* **me promener** *to go for walks* **quelque chose** *something* **On** *We* **librairies** *bookstores* **bandes dessinées** *comics* **Parfois** *Sometimes* **rencontre** *meet* **Bientôt** *Soon* **Je vous attends!** *I'm expecting you!* **Amitiés** *In friendship*

PRE-READING ACTIVITY

Replay parts 2 and 3 of the video, so that students get to know Jean-Marc.

Then have them read his letter.

POST-READING ACTIVITY

Have students make a list of the places that Jean-Marc mentions in his e-mail and then locate them on the map of Paris.

Which place or places they would like to visit with him?

IMAGES

PARIS en BATEAU-MOUCHE

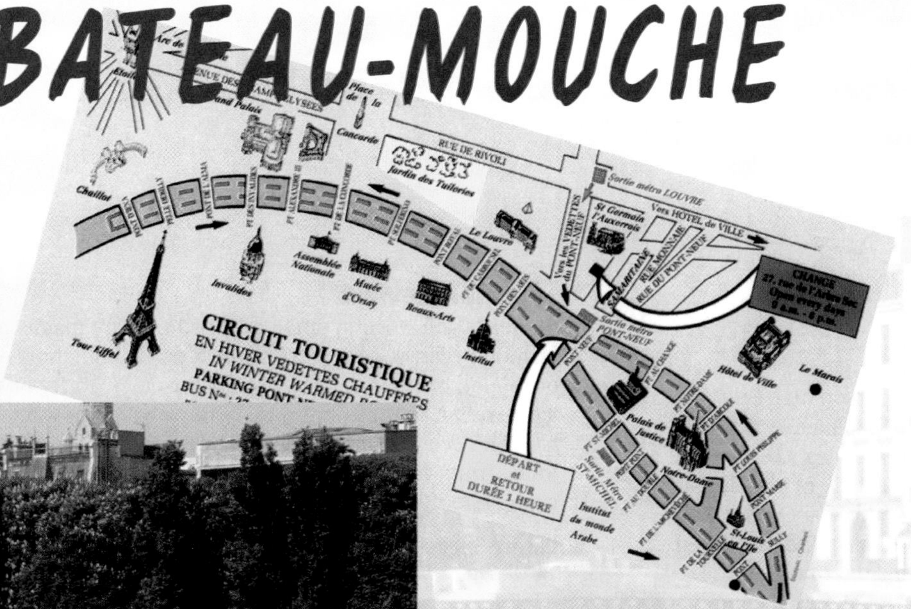

Comment visiter Paris? On peut° visiter Paris en taxi, mais c'est cher.° On peut prendre° le bus. C'est amusant, mais la circulation° à Paris est souvent difficile. On peut prendre le métro. C'est pratique, rapide et bon marché,° mais on ne voit rien.°

Pourquoi ne pas faire une promenade° en bateau-mouche?° Les bateaux-mouches sont des bateaux modernes et confortables qui circulent sur la Seine. Pendant° la promenade, on peut prendre des photos et admirer les monuments le long de° la Seine. Le soir, on peut voir les monuments illuminés!

Activité Culturelle

Vous faites une promenade en bateau-mouche.

- Combien coûte le billet?
- Quels° monuments est-ce que vous pouvez° voir?

On peut *One can* **cher** *expensive* **prendre** *take* **circulation** *traffic* **bon marché** *inexpensive* **ne voit rien** *sees nothing*
Pourquoi ne pas faire une promenade *Why not take a ride* **bateau-mouche** *sight-seeing boat* **Pendant** *During* **le long de** *along*
Quels *Which* **pouvez** *can*

Using the Video

Play Part 4 of the video, in which students are taken on a bateau-mouche ride. Students may look for **Notre Dame, la tour Eiffel,** and the many beautiful bridges and **quais** along the Seine.

Paris en bateau-mouche

Activité Culturelle
Answers

- 15 euros
- la tour Eiffel
  les Invalides
  l'Assemblé Nationale
  le musée d'Orsay
  l'École Nationale des Beaux Arts
  l'Institut de France
  le Palais de Justice
  Notre Dame
  St-Louis-en-l'Île
  l'Hôtel de Ville
  le Louvre
  le jardin des Tuileries
  le Grand Palais.

Teaching Strategy Tell students to imagine that a new park is being planned for the heart of Paris. It will be near one of the city's famous monuments. Have groups of students form committees and choose which monument it should be near. Students will research and report on how that particular monument is of cultural importance to Parisians.

Expansion activities PLANNING AHEAD

Games

• Je fais un voyage et j'apporte . . .

Divide the class into two teams. The first person on Team A begins «**Je fais un voyage et j'apporte...**» plus one article of clothing. The first person on Team B continues «**Je fais un voyage et j'apporte...**», repeats the first article of clothing the person from Team A mentioned, and adds a second article of clothing. Teams will take turns adding items to the list. When someone forgets an item, or gets the items out of order, the turn passes to the other team. The other team gets a point if they list all the items in the correct order. Otherwise, no one gets a point and the game starts over with the person who made the original error. Students could make the game more difficult by adding colors and sizes to the articles of clothing they name.

Pacing Suggestion: Upon completion of Leçon 17.

• L'espionnage

Divide students into three or four groups. Have one student in each group begin by describing what they see someone else in the group is wearing. Students should begin with the phrase, «**Je vois...**» The first person to guess the name of the chosen person correctly will do the next description.

Pacing Suggestion: Upon completion of Leçon 18.

Projects

• Mon magasin

Have students create a catalog page for their own department store. Each student will select the items for his or her catalog page and include a description and price for each item. They will also include photographs or illustrations to accompany each item. Have students lay out the images and descriptions to create an appealing catalog page. As an alternative, you could give students the names of French department stores, such as **Les Galeries Lafayette** and **Le Bon Marché,** and have them do research online in order to create a catalog page for one of these stores.

Pacing Suggestion: Upon completion of Leçon 17.

• Fashion Review

Students will work in small groups to create magazine-style fashion reviews. Members of each group will choose a celebrity or model, bring in photos of the chosen celebrity or model, and agree on an outfit to critique. Groups will then write a short fashion review (For example, «**Nous trouvons cette chemise jolie, mais la jupe est démodée.**») One student from each group should then present their group's review to the class.

Pacing Suggestion: Upon completion of Leçon 19.

Bulletin Boards

• L'Algérie

Divide the class into small groups. Have each group research some aspect of Algeria. Groups may:

- create a map that shows where Algeria is located
- find or create illustrations to show what Algeria looks like
- find information about the cuisine of Algeria
- find information about activities that are common among Algerian young people
- learn about Algerian immigrants in France
- learn about the influence of Algerian culture on the French

Have the groups create a bulletin board and each group present their information to the rest of the class.

Pacing Suggestion: Upon completion of Unité 6.

Music

• *Le Pont d'Avignon*

Teach students the words to the traditional French song «*Le Pont d'Avignon*». The music is available on the Internet and the lyrics are provided below.

«Sur le pont d'Avignon,
L'on y danse, l'on y danse;
Sur le pont d'Avignon,
L'on y danse tout en rond

Les beaux messieurs font comme ça,
Et puis encore comme ça.»
(Repeat first stanza)

Storytelling

• Mini-histoire

Model a brief conversation in which you shop for clothes. In the conversation, get help from a salesperson, compare two similar garments, and discuss the fit of a garment. Act out the conversation using gestures to help convey meaning. Pass out copies of your scripted conversation to students. Repeat the conversation with pauses, allowing students to either repeat after you or fill in the words. Then have them work in pairs to expand on the conversation. Ask students to write out their expanded conversations, practice them aloud for intonation, and perform them for the class.

Pacing Suggestion: Upon completion of Leçon 19.

Recipe

• Omelette au fromage

Omelets, a staple of French cuisine, make a simple but elegant dinner. This recipe is for a plain cheese omelet, but you may want to allow students to try fillings such as ham, green onions, and tomatoes.

Pacing Suggestion: Upon completion of Leçon 20.

Hands-on Crafts

• Flipbook à la mode

Ask students to bring in old magazines to cut figures from. Then, have them cut out separately three heads, three torsos, and three pairs of legs. Next, students will randomly line up the heads, torsos, and pairs of legs and glue them to a rectangular piece of construction paper. Finally, keeping the heads exposed, students should cut out three or four more layers of construction paper and glue three new torsos and pairs of legs to each one in alignment with the three visible heads to create a "fashion" flipbook.

Pacing Suggestion: Upon completion of Leçon 18.

End of Unit

• À la mode

Have students work in pairs to create entries for a fashion show. Students will select one of their own outfits to wear for the fashion show and write a detailed description of it. You may wish to give students vocabulary for additional colors, fabrics, styles, etc. Then partners will trade, read and edit each other's descriptions. Once the final descriptions are written, have students read aloud the description of their partner's outfit to practice intonation. On the day of the fashion show, each student will model for the class while their partner describes the outfit. You may wish to have students vote on the most elegant, bizarre, or trendy outfits. Students may also videotape their fashion show with music as background.

Rubric **A** = 13–15 pts. **B** = 10–12 pts. **C** = 7–9 pts. **D** = 4–6 pts. **F** = < 4 pts.

Criteria	Scale
Vocabulary Use	1 2 3 4 5
Grammar/Spelling Accuracy	1 2 3 4 5
Creativity	1 2 3 4 5

Omelette au fromage

Ingrédients
- 2 oeufs
- 15 grammes de beurre
- 1 cuillère à soupe de lait
- sel et poivre
- 85 grammes de fromage râpé

Préparation
1. Cassez les oeufs dans un saladier.
2. Avec une fourchette, battez les oeufs.
3. Ajoutez le lait, le sel et le poivre.
4. Faites chauffer une poêle et ajoutez le beurre.
5. Versez les oeufs dans la poêle.
6. Inclinez la poêle pour bien étendre les oeufs.
7. Quand les oeufs commencent à devenir solides, levez le bord et laissez couler le liquide au-dessous.
8. Faites cuire jusqu'à ce que les oeufs soient fermes.
9. Ajoutez le fromage au milieu de l'omelette.
10. Pliez l'omelette en deux et servez-la.

Ingredients
- 2 eggs
- approx. 2 teaspoons butter
- 1 tablespoon milk
- salt and pepper
- approx. 3 oz. grated cheese

Directions
1. Crack eggs into a mixing bowl.
2. Beat eggs with a fork.
3. Add milk, salt, and pepper.
4. Heat an 8-inch frying pan over high heat and add butter.
5. Pour egg mixture into pan.
6. Tilt pan to spread egg mixture evenly.
7. As eggs begin to firm, lift the edge of the omelet and allow the liquid to flow underneath.
8. Continue to cook until eggs are mostly firm.
9. Add cheese along the middle of the omelet.
10. Fold the omelet in half or in thirds and tip onto a plate.

Planning Guide CLASSROOM MANAGEMENT

OBJECTIVES

Communication
- Name and describe the clothes you wear *pp. 258–259, 260, 272*
- Discuss style *p. 262*
- Shop for clothes and other items *pp. 262, 268*
- Talk about money *p. 286*
- Make comparisons *p. 280*
- Point out certain people or objects to your friends *p. 270*

Grammar
- Les verbes *acheter* et *préférer* *p. 268*
- L'adjectif démonstratif *ce* *p. 270*
- L'adjectif interrogatif *quel?* *p. 271*
- Le verbe *mettre* *p. 272*
- Les verbes réguliers en *-ir* *p. 278*
- Les adjectifs *beau, nouveau* et *vieux* *p. 279*
- La comparaison avec les adjectifs *p. 280*
- Le pronom *on* *p. 288*
- Les verbes réguliers en *-re* *p. 290*
- L'impératif *p. 291*

Vocabulary
- Les vêtements *pp. 258–259*
- D'autres vêtements et accessoires *p. 260*
- Dans un magasin *p. 262*
- Les nombres de 100 à 1000 *p. 263*
- Verbes comme *acheter* et *préférer* *p. 269*
- Verbes réguliers en *-ir* *p. 278*
- Expressions pour la conversation *pp. 281, 289*
- L'argent *p. 286*
- Verbes réguliers en *-re* *p. 290*

Pronunciation
- Les lettres «e» et «è» *p. 273*
- Les lettres «ill» *p. 281*
- Les lettres «an» et «en» *p. 293*

Culture
- Le grand magasin *p. 266*
- Les jeunes et la mode *p. 276*
- L'argent des jeunes *p. 285*
- Les soldes *p. 303*
- Prénoms arabes *p. 304*
- L'Algérie *p. 305*

PROGRAM RESOURCES

Print
- Workbook PE, *pp. 149–179*
- *Activités pour tous* PE, *pp. 91–109*
- Block Scheduling Copymasters, *pp. 129–159*
- *Français pour hispanophones*
- *Lectures pour tous*
- Teacher to Teacher Copymasters
- Teaching Proficiency through Reading and Storytelling
- Unit 6 Resource Book
  - Lessons 17–20 Resources
    - Workbook TE
    - *Activités pour tous* TE
    - Family Letter
    - Absent Student Copymasters
    - Family Involvement
    - Video Activities
    - Videoscripts
    - Audioscripts
    - Assessment Program
  - Unit 6 Resources
    - Communipak
    - *Activités pour tous* Reading
    - Workbook TE Reading and Culture Activities
    - Assessment Program
    - Answer Keys

Audiovisual
- Audio Program PE CD 3 Tracks 20–43
- Audio Program Workbook CD 10 Tracks 1–27
- *Chansons* Audio CD
- Sing Along: Grammar and Vocabulary Songs CD
- Video Program Modules 17, 18, 19, 20
- Warm-Up Transparencies
- Overhead Transparencies
  35 *Les vêtements*;
  36 *Vêtements et accessoires*;
  12 Menu from *Le Select*
  37 Comparing clothing;
  38 *Au grand magasin*;
  39 **-ir** Verbs;
  6 Clock face *Quelle heure est-il?*
  40 Adjectives *beau, nouveau, vieux*;
  20 Objects (a) *Quelques objets (a)*;
  41 **-re** Verbs

Technology
- Online Workbook
- ClassZone.com
- McDougal Littell Assessment System/ Test Generator CD-ROM
- EasyPlanner CD-ROM
- Power Presentations on CD-ROM
- Take-Home Tutor CD-ROM

Assessment Program Options
Lesson Quizzes
Portfolio Assessment
Unit Test Form A
Unit Test Form B
Unit Test Part III (Alternate) Cultural Awareness
Listening Comprehension Performance Test
Speaking Performance Test
Reading Comprehension Performance Test
Writing Performance Test
Multiple Choice Test Items
Test Scoring Tools
Audio Program CD 15 Tracks 9–22
Answer Keys
McDougal Littell Assessment System/ Test Generator CD-ROM

Pacing Guide SAMPLE LESSON PLAN

DAY	DAY	DAY	DAY	DAY
1 Unité 6 Opener Leçon 17 • Vocabulaire et Culture–L'achat des vêtements • Vocabulaire–Les vêtements	**2** Leçon 17 • Vocabulaire–D'autres vêtements et accessoires • Vocabulaire–Dans un magasin	**3** Leçon 17 • Vocabulaire–Dans un magasin *(continued)* • Les nombres de 100 à 1000	**4** Leçon 17 • À votre tour!	**5** Leçon 18 • Conversation et Culture–Rien n'est parfait! • Note culturelle–Le grand magasin • Les verbes *acheter* et *préférer*
6 Leçon 18 • Vocabulaire–Verbes comme *acheter* et *préférer* • L'adjectif démonstratif *ce*	**7** Leçon 18 • L'adjectif démonstratif *ce (continued)* • L'adjectif interrogatif *quel?*	**8** Leçon 18 • Le verbe *mettre* • Prononciation–Les lettres «e» et «è»	**9** Leçon 18 • À votre tour!	**10** Leçon 19 • Conversation et Culture–Un choix difficile • Note culturelle–Les jeunes et la mode • Les verbes réguliers en *-ir*
11 Leçon 19 • Vocabulaire–Verbes réguliers en *-ir* • Les adjectifs *beau, nouveau* et *vieux*	**12** Leçon 19 • La comparaison avec les adjectifs	**13** Leçon 19 • Vocabulaire–Expressions pour la conversation • Prononciation–Les lettres «ill»	**14** Leçon 19 • À votre tour!	**15** Leçon 20 • Conversation et Culture–Alice a un job • Note culturelle–L'argent des jeunes • Vocabulaire–L'argent
16 Leçon 20 • Vocabulaire–L'argent *(continued)* • Le pronom *on* • Vocabulaire–Expressions pour la conversation	**17** Leçon 20 • Les verbes réguliers en *-re* • Vocabulaire–Verbes réguliers en *-re*	**18** Leçon 20 • L'impératif • Prononciation–Les lettres «an» et «en»	**19** Leçon 20 • À votre tour!	**20** • Tests de contrôle
21 • Unit 6 Test	**22** • Entracte–Lecture et culture	**23** • Entracte–Lecture et culture *(continued)*		

Student Text Listening Activity Scripts

AUDIO PROGRAM

▶ LEÇON 17 LE FRANÇAIS PRATIQUE L'achat des vêtements

• Vocabulaire *p. 263* CD 3, TRACK 20

Les nombres de 100 à 1 000

Repeat the numbers after the speaker. Écoutez et répétez.

100 # 101 # 102 # 200 # 300 # 400 #
500 # 600 # 700 # 800 # 900 # 1 000 #

À votre tour!

• Écoutez bien! *p. 264* CD 3, TRACK 21

Thomas and Frédéric are both getting ready to leave on vacation. Listen to the following sentences which mention items that they are packing. If the item belongs to Thomas, mark A. If the item belongs to Frédéric, mark B. You will hear each sentence twice.

Let's begin. Commençons.

1. Il a une casquette. #
2. Où est sa ceinture? #
3. Quand il pleut, il porte un imperméable. #
4. Il a un blouson noir. #
5. Ses chaussures sont marron. #
6. Le pull est sur le lit. #
7. Il porte souvent des sandales. #
8. Oui, c'est sa cravate. #
9. Ce survêtement est très cher. #
10. J'aime bien la veste. #
11. Il a des chaussettes blanches. #
12. Tiens, voilà ses lunettes de soleil. #
13. Quand il fait chaud, il porte un tee-shirt. #
14. Le pantalon est dans la valise. #

• Créa-dialogue *p. 264* CD 3, TRACK 22

Listen to the sample *Créa-dialogues.* Écoutez les conversations.

Modèle: –Vous désirez, mademoiselle?
–Je cherche un pantalon.
–Comment trouvez-vous le pantalon gris?
–Il est joli. Combien est-ce qu'il coûte?
–Soixante dollars.
–Oh là là, il est cher!

Maintenant, écoutez le dialogue numéro 1.

–Vous désirez, monsieur?
–Je cherche un pull.
–Comment trouvez-vous le pull rouge?
–Il est élégant. Combien est-ce qu'il coûte?
–Trente dollars.
–Il est bon marché.

• Conversation dirigée *p. 265* CD 3, TRACK 23

Listen to the conversation. Écoutez la conversation entre Sophie et Christophe.

Sophie: Qu'est-ce que tu cherches, Christophe?
Christophe: Je cherche une casquette.
Sophie: Comment trouves-tu la casquette jaune?
Christophe: Elle est géniale, mais je vais acheter la casquette bleu.
Sophie: Combien est-ce qu'elle coûte?
Christophe: Elle coûte 5 euros.
Sophie: Elle est bon marché, mais elle est trop petite.

▶ LEÇON 18 Rien n'est parfait!

• Rien n'est parfait! *p. 266*

A. Compréhension orale CD 3, TRACK 24

Please turn to page 266 for complete *Compréhension orale* text.

B. Écoutez et répétez. CD 3, TRACK 25

You will now hear a paused version of the dialog. Listen to the speaker and repeat right after he or she has completed the sentence.

• Grammaire *p. 268* CD 3, TRACK 26

Les verbes *acheter* et *préférer*

Écoutez et répétez. Repeat the sentences after the speaker.

J'**achète** une veste. #
Tu **achètes** une cravate. #
Il **achète** un imper. #
Nous **achetons** un jean. #
Vous **achetez** un short. #
Elles **achètent** un pull. #

Je **préfère** la veste bleue. #
Tu **préfères** la cravate jaune. #
Il **préfère** l'imper gris. #
Nous **préférons** le jean noir. #
Vous **préférez** le short blanc. #
Elles **préfèrent** le pull rouge. #

• Prononciation *p. 273* CD 3, TRACK 27

Les lettres «e» et «è»

Écoutez: chemise chaussette chère

Practice pronouncing "**e**" within a word:

• /ə/ (as in **je**) [. . . "**e**" + *one* CONSONANT + VOWEL]

Répétez: chemise # regarder # Denise # Renée # petit # venir #

Note that in the middle of a word the /ə/ is sometimes silent.

Répétez: acheter # achetons # amener # samedi # rarement # avenue #

• /ɛ/ (as in **elle**) [. . . "**e**" + *two* CONSONANTS + VOWEL]

Répétez: chaussette # veste # quelle # cette # rester # professeur # raquette #

Now practice pronouncing "**è**" within a word:

• /ɛ/ (as in **elle**) [. . . "**e**" + *one* CONSONANT + VOWEL]

Répétez: chère # père # mère # achète # amènent # espère # deuxième #

À votre tour!

• La bonne réponse *p. 274* CD 3, TRACK 28

Listen to the conversation. Écoutez la conversation entre Alice et Jérôme.

Alice: Je vais à la soirée de Delphine. Et toi?
Jérôme: Moi aussi.
Alice: Tu amènes une copine?
Jérôme: Oui, Christine.
Alice: Qu'est-ce que vous allez apporter?
Jérôme: Nous allons acheter des pizzas.
Alice: Qu'est-ce que tu vas mettre?
Jérôme: Mon pull jaune et mon blouson marron.

• Créa-dialogue *p. 274* CD 3, TRACK 29

Listen to some sample *Créa-dialogues.* Écoutez les conversations.

Modèle: –Comment trouves-tu cette fille?
–Quelle fille?
–Cette fille-là!
–Eh bien, je pense qu'elle est jolie.

Maintenant, écoutez le dialogue numéro 1.

–Comment trouves-tu ces livres?
–Quels livres?
–Ces livres-là!
–Eh bien, je pense qu'ils sont intéressants.

▶ LEÇON 19 Un choix difficile

pause for oral response

▶ LEÇON 19 Un choix difficile

• Un choix difficile *p. 276*

A. Compréhension orale CD 3, TRACK 30

Please turn to page 276 for complete *Compréhension orale* text.

B. Écoutez et répétez. CD 3, TRACK 31

You will now hear a paused version of the dialog. Listen to the speaker and repeat right after he or she has completed the sentence.

• Grammaire *p. 278* CD 3, TRACK 32

Les verbes réguliers en *-ir*

Repeat the sentences after the speaker. Écoutez et répétez.

Je finis à deux heures. #
Elle finit à cinq heures. #
Vous finissez à une heure. #
Tu finis à une heure. #
Nous finissons à midi. #
Ils finissent à minuit. #

• Vocabulaire *p. 278* CD 3, TRACK 33

Verbes réguliers en *-ir*

choisir # — Quelle veste **choisis**-tu? #
finir # — Les classes **finissent** à midi. #
grossir # — Marc **grossit** parce qu'il mange beaucoup. #
maigrir # — Je **maigris** parce que je mange peu. #
réussir # — Tu vas **réussir** parce que tu travailles! #
réussir à un examen # — Nous **réussissons à nos examens.** #

• Prononciation *p. 281* CD 3, TRACK 34

Les lettres «ill»

Écoutez: maillot

In the middle of a word, the letters "**ill**" usually represent the sound /j/ like the "**y**" of yes.

Répétez: maillot # travaillez # oreille # vieille # fille # famille # juillet #
En juillet, Mireille va travailler pour sa vieille tante. #

At the end of a word, the sound /j/ is sometimes spelled **il.**

Répétez: appareil-photo # vieil # travail #
Mon oncle a un vieil appareil-photo. #

EXCEPTION: The letters **ill** are pronounced /il/ in the following words:

Répétez: ville # village # mille # Lille #

À votre tour!

• La bonne réponse *p. 282* CD 3, TRACK 35

Listen to the conversation. Écoutez la conversation entre François et Stéphanie.

François: Tu aimes cette veste verte?
Stéphanie: Oui, mais elle est très chère.
François: Combien est-ce qu'elle coûte?
Stéphanie: 300 euros.
François: Et qu'est-ce que tu penses de cette veste rouge?
Stéphanie: À mon avis, elle est moins jolie.
François: Alors, qu'est-ce que tu vas choisir?
Stéphanie: La veste bleue. Elle est meilleur marché et elle est aussi élégante.

• Créa-dialogue *p. 282* CD 3, TRACK 36

Listen to the sample *Créa-dialogues.* Écoutez les conversations.

Modèle: –Tu choisis la voiture rouge ou la voiture noire?
–Je choisis la voiture rouge.
–Pourquoi?
–Parce qu'elle est plus petite et moins chère.

Maintenant, écoutez le dialogue numéro 1.

–Tu achètes la chaîne hi-fi ou le baladeur?
–J'achète la chaîne hi-fi.
–Pourquoi?
–Parce qu'elle est meilleure et plus grande.

▶ LEÇON 20 Alice a un job

• Alice a un job *p. 284*

A. Compréhension orale CD 3, TRACK 37

Please turn to page 284 for complete *Compréhension orale* text.

B. Écoutez et répétez. CD 3, TRACK 38

You will now hear a paused version of the dialog. Listen to the speaker and repeat right after he or she has completed the sentence.

• Grammaire *p. 290* CD 3, TRACK 39

Les verbes réguliers en *-re*

Repeat the sentences with *vendre.* Écoutez et répétez.

Je **vends** ma raquette. #
Il **vend** son ordinateur. #
Vous **vendez** vos CD. #
Tu **vends** ton scooter. #
Nous **vendons** nos livres. #
Elles **vendent** leur voiture. #

• Vocabulaire *p. 290* CD 3, TRACK 40

Verbes réguliers en *-re*

Repeat these sentences containing *-re* verbs.

attendre # — Pierre **attend** Michèle au café. #
entendre # — Est-ce que tu **entends** la radio? #
perdre # — Jean-Claude **perd** le match. #
rendre visite à # — Je **rends visite à** mon oncle. #
répondre à # — Nous **répondons à** la question du prof. #
vendre # — À qui **vends**-tu ton vélo? #

• Prononciation *p. 293* CD 3, TRACK 41

Les lettres «an» et «en»

Écoutez: enfant

The letters "**an**" and "**en**" represent the nasal vowel /ã/. Be sure not to pronounce the sound "**n**" after the vowel.

Répétez: /ã/ # enfant # an # manteau # collants # grand # élégant #
André mange un grand sandwich.
/ã/ # enfant # en # argent # dépenser # attends # entend #
vend # envie #
Vincent dépense rarement son argent. #

À votre tour!

• La bonne réponse *p. 294* CD 3, TRACK 42

Listen to the conversation. Écoutez la conversation entre Anne et Jean-François.

Anne: Est-ce que tu rends visite à tes cousins ce week-end?
Jean-François: Non, je reste ici.
Anne: Tu veux aller dans les boutiques avec moi?
Jean-François: Écoute! Je n'ai pas besoin de vêtements.
Anne: Est-ce que tu as envie d'aller au cinéma?
Jean-François: Bonne idée! Il y a un nouveau film au «Majestic».
Anne: Et après, qu'est-ce qu'on fait?
Jean-François: Eh bien, allons au restaurant!

• Créa-dialogue *p. 294* CD 3, TRACK 43

Listen to some sample *Créa-dialogues.* Écoutez les conversations.

Modèle: –Qu'est-ce qu'on fait samedi?
–Allons au cinéma.
–Je n'ai pas envie d'aller au cinéma.
–Eh bien, rendons visite à nos amis. D'accord?
–Oui, c'est une bonne idée!

Maintenant, écoutez le dialogue numéro 1.

–Qu'est-ce qu'on fait ce soir?
–Étudions.
–Je n'ai pas envie d'étudier.
–Eh bien, regardons la télé. D'accord?
–Oui, c'est une bonne idée!

Complete videoscripts, plus Workbook and Assessment audioscripts, are available in the Unit Resource Books.

Main Theme
- Buying clothes

COMMUNICATION
- Naming and describing clothes
- Discussing style
- Shopping for clothes and other items
- Talking about money
- Making comparisons
- Pointing out certain people and objects

CULTURES
- Learning about French stores, including *le grand magasin*
- Learning about French shopping habits and *les soldes*
- Learning about how French teens buy clothing
- Learning how French teenagers get their spending money
- Learning about North Africa and Algeria

CONNECTIONS
- Connecting to Math: Deciding on purchases within a budget
- Connecting to Computer Science: Using the Internet to do research

COMPARISONS
- Making language comparisons between French and English
- Comparing French and American department stores
- Comparing how teens in France and the U.S. obtain their spending money
- Learning about the Algerian influence on the French way of life

COMMUNITIES
- Surveying people in the community
- Using the Internet to learn about other cultures

Le shopping

THÈME ET OBJECTIFS

Buying clothes

Are you interested in clothes? When you visit France, you will enjoy going window shopping. In fact, you will probably want to try on a few items and buy something special to bring home.

In this unit, you will learn ...
- to name and describe the clothes you wear
- to discuss style
- to shop for clothes and other items
- to talk about money

You will also be able ...
- to make comparisons
- to point out certain people or objects to your friends

UNIT OVERVIEW

- **Communication Goals:** Students will be able to shop for clothing, describe what people are wearing, and make comparisons.
- **Linguistic Goals:** Students will learn the present tense of **-ir** and **-re** verbs, the imperative, and comparative forms of adjectives.
- **Critical Thinking Goals:** Students will observe similarities and differences in the ways French and English make commands and express comparisons.
- **Cultural Goals:** Students will become aware of the French concept of style and the ways in which young people earn and spend their money.

SALAMANDER

deux cent cinquante-cinq
Unité 6 255

Teaching Resource Options

PRINT 

Unit 6 Resource Book
Family Letter, p. 16
Français pour hispanophones
Conseils, p. 15
Vocabulaire, pp. 48–49

AUDIO & VISUAL 

Audio Program
Chansons CD

TECHNOLOGY

EasyPlanner CD-ROM

Leçon 17

Main Topic Shopping for clothing

Teaching Resource Options

PRINT 

Workbook PE, pp. 149–155
Activités pour tous PE, pp. 91–93
Block Scheduling Copymasters, pp. 129–135
Unit 6 Resource Book
- *Activités pour tous* TE, pp. 9–11
- Audioscript, pp. 32–34
- Communipak, pp. 140–158
- Lesson Plans, pp. 12–13
- Block Scheduling Lesson Plans, pp. 14–15
- Absent Student Copymasters, pp. 17–20
- Video Activities, pp. 23–28
- Videoscript, pp. 29–30
- Workbook TE, pp. 1–7

AUDIO & VISUAL 

Audio Program
CD 10 Tracks 1–8

TECHNOLOGY 

Online Workbook

VIDEO PROGRAM

VIDÉO DVD

MODULE 17
Le français pratique
L'achat des vêtements

TOTAL TIME: 7:33 min.
DVD Disk 2
Videotape 3 (COUNTER: 34:31 min.)

17.1 Introduction: Listening
– Le shopping (34:40–35:55 min.)

17.2 Dialogue: Aux Galeries Lafayette
(35:56–37:11 min.)

17.3 Mini-scenes: Listening
– Qu'est-ce que vous cherchez?
(37:12–38:08 min.)

17.4 Mini-scenes: Speaking
– Vous désirez? (38:09–39:08 min.)

17.5 Mini-scenes: Speaking
– Combien coûte la veste?
(39:09–39:52 min.)

17.6 Mini-scenes: Listening
– Comment trouves-tu ma robe?
(39:53–40:28 min.)

17.7 Vignette culturelle: Où acheter les vêtements? (40:29–42:04 min.)

Comprehension practice Play the entire module through as an introduction to the lesson.

LEÇON 17

LE FRANÇAIS PRATIQUE
VIDÉO DVD AUDIO

L'achat des vêtements

Accent sur … l'élégance française

France is a leader in high fashion. French fashion design houses, such as Dior, Chanel, Yves Saint Laurent and Pierre Cardin, are known all over the world for the style and quality of their creations.

French young people like to be in style, even if their clothes are casual and not too expensive. Depending on their budgets, they buy their clothes at …

- **une grande surface** (*low-cost chain store*)
- **un grand magasin** (*department store*)
- **une boutique de vêtements** (*clothing store*)
- **une boutique de soldes** (*discount clothing shop*)
- **le marché aux puces** (*flea market*)

Mélanie cherche une robe pour aller au mariage de sa cousine. Quelle robe est-ce qu'elle va acheter?

SETTING THE STAGE

Ask your students if they like to shop for clothes and where they go.

Est-ce que vous aimez faire du shopping?
Où allez-vous?
Allez-vous dans un grand magasin?
Comment s'appelle-t-il?
Allez-vous dans une boutique de vêtements?
Comment s'appelle-t-elle?
Allez-vous dans une boutique de soldes?
Comment s'appelle-t-elle?
Est-ce qu'il y a une marché aux puces dans notre ville?

Tell students that in the video they will observe French young people shopping for clothes. In the *Vignette culturelle,* they will see various types of clothing stores.

Fatima est dans une boutique de vêtements. Ici les vêtements sont très élégants … et très chers aussi.

Patrick et Béatrice achètent leurs vêtements dans une grande surface. Ici les vêtements sont de bonne qualité et ils ne sont pas trop chers.

Michel est dans un magasin de chaussures. Quelles chaussures est-ce qu'il va acheter? Des baskets ou des chaussures de sport?

CRITICAL THINKING SKILLS

English has borrowed many words pertaining to clothing and fashion: **boutique, eau de cologne, haute couture.**

Ask students to list other borrowed French words relating to fashion and clothes.

For example:

chemise **crêpe**
culottes **maillot**
chic

SECTION A

Communicative function
Talking about clothing

Teaching Resource Options

PRINT 

Workbook PE, pp. 149–155
Unit 6 Resource Book
Communipak, pp. 140–158
Video Activities, p. 25
Videoscript, p. 29
Workbook TE, pp. 1–7

AUDIO & VISUAL 

Overhead Transparencies
35 *Les vêtements*

VIDEO PROGRAM

MODULE 17

17.3 Mini-scenes: Qu'est-ce que vous cherchez? (37:12–38:08 min.)

Looking ahead Students will learn the forms of **acheter** in Lesson 18.

Extra activity To review **euros,** ask the prices of each item.
Combien coûte le blouson?

Language notes

- **Un pull** is a shortened form of **un pull-over,** which is a borrowed word from English. It is used for any sweater which is pulled over the head. French has also borrowed the word **un sweater** /swɛTɛr/.
- In Quebec, **un chandail** /ʃɑ̃daj/ is used for **un pull.**

Pronunciation Be sure students say **pull** /pyl/ with the /y/ of **tu.**

Supplementary vocabulary
faire les magasins *to go shopping (browsing from store to store)*
un anorak *ski jacket*
un costume *man's suit*
un tailleur *woman's suit*

Teaching note Have students identify which vocabulary words on pages 258 and 259 are true and false cognates. (true: *une boutique, un jean, un polo*; false: *un blouson, une robe, une veste*)

A VOCABULAIRE Les vêtements

How to talk about shopping for clothes:

Où vas-tu?
Je vais | dans **une boutique** *(shop).*
dans **un magasin** *(store)*
dans **un grand magasin** *(department store)*
Qu'est-ce que tu vas **acheter** *(to buy)*?
Je vais acheter **des vêtements** *(clothes).*

Les vêtements

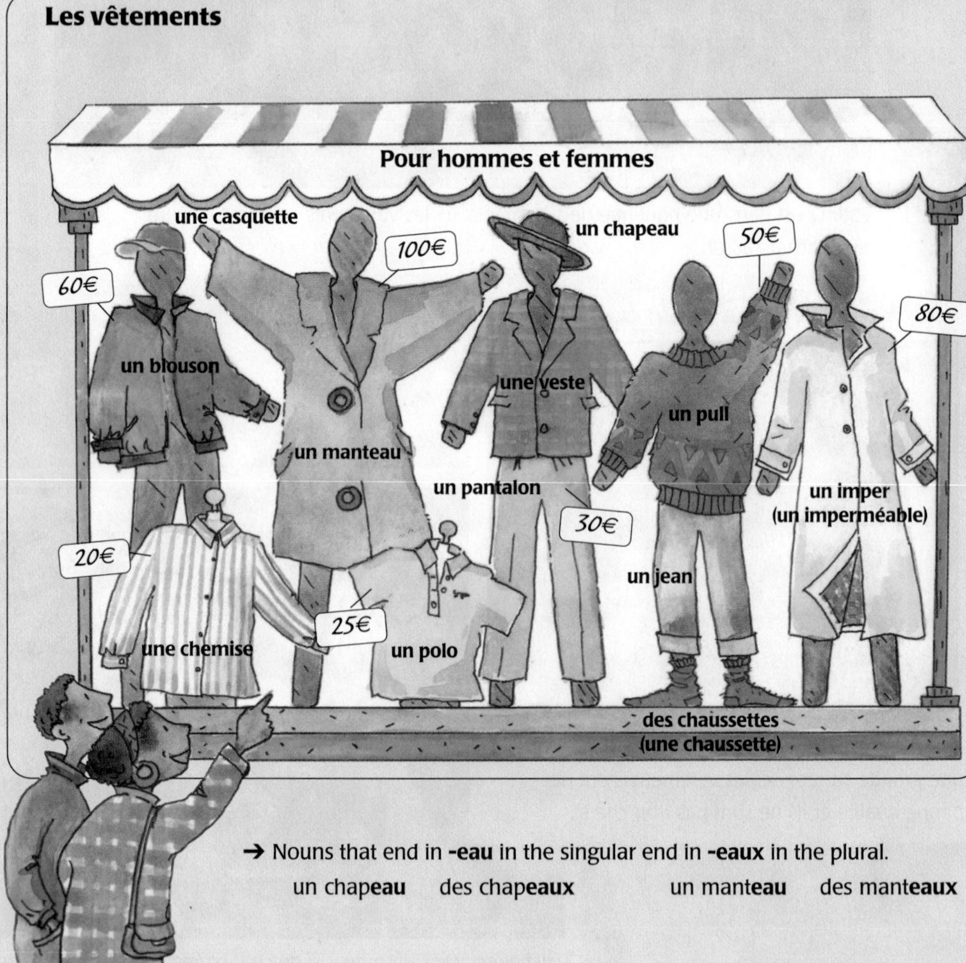

➔ Nouns that end in **-eau** in the singular end in **-eaux** in the plural.
un chap**eau** des chap**eaux** un mant**eau** des mant**eaux**

COMPREHENSION Clothes

PROPS: A bag of old clothes in large sizes

Give students various items of clothing.
X, montre-nous le pull.
Y, montre-nous la cravate. ...
Qui a le pull? [X]...

If appropriate, have students try items on.
Z, mets le chapeau. Ah, c'est très joli!
Qui porte le chapeau? [Z]

Have students move the clothing around.
X, mets le pull sur la chaise de Z.
Où est le pull? [sur la chaise de Z]
Z, donne le pull à W.
Qui a le pull maintenant? [W]

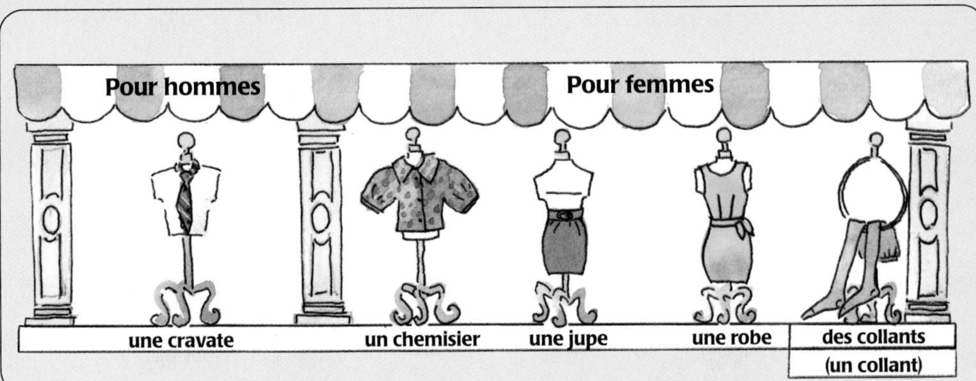

acheter	*to buy*	Je vais **acheter** une cravate.
porter	*to wear*	Qu'est-ce que tu vas **porter** demain?
mettre	*to put on, wear*	Oh là là, il fait froid. Je vais **mettre** un pull.

→ **Mettre** is irregular. (Its forms are presented in Leçon 18.)

1 Shopping

PARLER Below are the names of several Paris stores. Using the illustrations as a guide, talk to a classmate about where you are going shopping and what you plan to buy.

▶ —**Où vas-tu?**
—**Je vais au Monoprix.**
—**Qu'est-ce que tu vas acheter?**
—**Je vais acheter une chemise.**

2 Quels vêtements?

PARLER/ÉCRIRE What we wear often depends on the circumstances: where we are, what we will be doing, what the weather is like. Complete the following sentences with the appropriate items of clothing.

1. Aujourd'hui, je porte …
2. Le professeur porte …
3. L'élève à ma gauche porte …
4. L'élève à ma droite porte …
5. Quand je vais à une boum, je porte …
6. Quand je vais dans un restaurant élégant, je porte …
7. S'il pleut *(If it rains)* demain, je vais mettre …
8. S'il fait chaud demain, je vais mettre …
9. Si *(If)* je vais en ville samedi, je vais mettre …
10. Si je vais à un concert dimanche, je vais mettre …

1 EXCHANGES talking about shopping plans

1. –Où vas-tu?
–Je vais au Printemps.
–Qu'est-ce que tu vas acheter?
–Je vais acheter un pantalon.
2. –Où vas-tu?
–Je vais au Bon Marché.
–Qu'est-ce que tu vas acheter?
–Je vais acheter une robe.
3. –Où vas-tu?
–Je vais chez Kookaï.
–Qu'est-ce que tu vas acheter?
–Je vais acheter des chaussettes.
4. –Où vas-tu?
–Je vais chez Céline.
–Qu'est-ce que tu vas acheter?
–Je vais acheter une jupe.
5. –Où vas-tu?
–Je vais aux Galeries Lafayette.
–Qu'est-ce que tu vas acheter?
–Je vais acheter un blouson.
6. –Où vas-tu?
–Je vais chez Leclerc.
–Qu'est-ce que tu vas acheter?
–Je vais acheter un imper[méable].
7. –Où vas-tu?
–Je vais chez Dior.
–Qu'est-ce que tu vas acheter?
–Je vais acheter un chemisier.
8. –Où vas-tu?
–Je vais à la Samaritaine.
–Qu'est-ce que tu vas acheter?
–Je vais acheter un manteau.

2 COMMUNICATION talking about clothes

Answers will vary.
1. Aujourd'hui, je porte (un pantalon).
2. Le professeur porte (une veste).
3. L'élève à ma gauche porte (un jean).
4. L'élève à ma droite porte (un pull).
5. Quand je vais à une boum, je porte (une jupe / une veste).
6. Quand je vais dans un restaurant élégant, je porte (une cravate / une robe).
7. S'il pleut demain, je vais mettre (un imperméable).
8. S'il fait chaud demain, je vais mettre (un polo).
9. Si je vais en ville samedi, je vais mettre (une chemise et un pantalon élégant).
10. Si je vais à un concert dimanche, je vais mettre (une veste).

Expansion
Quand il neige, je porte...
Quand je vais en ville, je porte...
Quand je vais à un match de football américain, je porte...
Quand je vais au cinéma avec mes copains, je porte...

SUPPLEMENTARY LISTENING PRACTICE

You can build listening comprehension skills by talking about the clothing that students are wearing. Students respond with gestures or one-word answers. Repeat each item of clothing in several different questions and responses.

For example:
Qui porte un polo aujourd'hui?
W et X portent un polo.
Y ne porte pas de polo.
Et toi, Z, tu portes un polo? [oui]
De quelle couleur est le polo de Z? [bleu]
Mais oui, il est bleu...

SECTION B

Communicative function
Talking about clothing and accessories

Teaching Resource Options

PRINT  

Workbook PE, pp. 149–155
Unit 6 Resource Book
Communipak, pp. 140–158
Video Activities, p. 25
Videoscript, pp. 29–30
Workbook TE, pp. 1–7

AUDIO & VISUAL

Overhead Transparencies
36 *Vêtements et accessoires*

VIDEO PROGRAM

VIDÉO DVD

MODULE 17

17.4 Mini-scenes: Vous désirez?
(38:08–39:08 min.)

Pronunciation **Un sweat** is pronounced /swit/.

Casual speech **Un maillot de bain** is often referred to as **un maillot.**

Language note Point out that **des lunettes (de soleil)** is feminine.

3 DESCRIPTION indicating what people are wearing

1. Anne porte des lunettes de soleil, un polo, un short et des sandales.
2. Sophie porte un maillot de bain et des tennis.
3. Michel porte un survêtement (un jogging) et des baskets.
4. Catherine porte un sweat, un short et des lunettes de soleil.
5. Je porte (un tee-shirt, des sandales, et des lunettes de soleil).

Challenge Students say what each person is NOT wearing, using **pas de.**
Paul ne porte pas de tee-shirt.

B VOCABULAIRE D'autres vêtements et accessoires

3 À la plage de Deauville

PARLER/ÉCRIRE You are spending the summer vacation in Deauville, a popular seaside resort in Normandy. Describe what you and your friends are wearing.

▶ **Paul porte un maillot de bain ...**

TALKING ABOUT PAST EVENTS

Let's talk about what you wore yesterday. Remember to use **pas de** in negative answers.

Est-ce que tu as porté un manteau hier?
Oui, j'ai porté un manteau.
(Non, je n'ai pas porté de manteau.)

- **Est-ce que tu as porté un chapeau hier?**
- **Est-ce que tu as porté un survêtement?**
- **Est-ce que tu as porté des lunettes de soleil?**
- **Est-ce que tu as porté des tennis?**
- **Est-ce que tu as porté une cravate?**
- **Est-ce que tu as porté une robe?**

4 Qu'est-ce que tu portes?

PARLER Ask your classmates what they wear in the following circumstances. Let them use their imagination.

▶ jouer au tennis

1. aller à la piscine
2. aller à la plage
3. jouer au basket
4. travailler dans le jardin
5. aller au gymnase *(gym)*
6. faire une promenade dans la forêt *(forest)*
7. faire une promenade dans la neige *(snow)*

Qu'est-ce que tu portes quand tu joues au tennis?
Je porte un tee-shirt, un short et des tennis.

5 Un jeu

PARLER/ÉCRIRE When you see what people are wearing, you can often tell what they are going to do. How many different logical sentences can you make in five minutes using the elements of A, B, and C? Follow the model below.

A	B	C
André	un maillot de bain	nager
Sylvie	des lunettes de soleil	aller à la plage
Paul et Éric	un short	aller à un concert
Michèle et Anne	des chaussettes blanches	jouer au tennis
	un sweat	jouer au volley
	un pantalon très chic	jouer au foot
	des chaussures noires	aller à la campagne *(country)*
	des bottes	faire du jogging *(to jog)*
	un costume *(suit)*	dîner en ville
	une robe	
	une casquette	

Sylvie porte un short. Elle va jouer au foot.

6 Joyeux anniversaire!

PARLER/ÉCRIRE The following people are celebrating their birthdays. Find a present for each person by choosing an item of clothing from pages 258, 259, or 260.

1. Pour mon père (ma mère), je vais acheter ...
2. Pour ma grand-mère (mon grand-père), ...
3. Pour ma petite cousine Élodie (10 ans), ...
4. Pour mon grand frère Guillaume (18 ans), ...
5. Pour le professeur, ...
6. Pour mon meilleur *(best)* ami, ...
7. Pour ma meilleure amie, ...

- **Qu'est-ce que tu as porté hier?**
- **Qu'est-ce que tu as porté vendredi soir? samedi après-midi? dimanche matin?**

Follow-up:
- **Qu'est-ce que X a porté hier?**
- **Qu'est-ce que Y a porté vendredi soir?**
- **Qu'est-ce que Z a porté dimanche matin?**

4 COMMUNICATION talking about what one wears when

Answers will vary.
–Qu'est-ce que tu portes quand tu ... ?
–Je porte ...
1. vas à la piscine/(un maillot de bain)
2. vas à la plage/(un short, un tee-shirt, des sandales, et des lunettes de soleil)
3. joues au basket/(un survêtement et des baskets)
4. travailles dans le jardin/(un tee-shirt et un jean)
5. vas au gymnase/(un survêtement et des tennis)
6. fais une promenade dans la forêt/(des baskets, un jean, un sweat et un blouson)
7. fais une promenade dans la neige/(des bottes, un pantalon, un pull, un chapeau et un manteau)

5 COMPREHENSION describing clothes and related activities

Answers will vary.
André porte un maillot de bain. Il va nager.
Sylvie porte des lunettes de soleil et une casquette. Elle va aller à la plage.
Paul et Éric portent un short. Ils vont jouer au volley.
Michèle et Anne portent des chaussettes blanches. Elles vont jouer au tennis.
André porte un sweat. Il va faire du jogging.

Variation (conversation format)
Student 1 states what someone is wearing. Student 2 asks why. Student 3 gives the reason.
– Sylvie porte un short.
– Pourquoi?
– Elle va jouer au football.

Variation
Have students reverse columns B and C, using **mettre.**
André va nager.
Il va mettre un maillot de bain.

6 COMMUNICATION selecting gifts

Answers will vary.
1. une ceinture
2. un chapeau
3. un tee-shirt
4. un survêtement
5. un polo
6. un sweat
7. un chemisier

Supplementary vocabulary

LES ACCESSOIRES
des gants *(m.) gloves*
un foulard *(silk) scarf*
un mouchoir *handkerchief*
des verres *(m.)* **de contact** *contact lenses*
une écharpe *(winter) scarf*

LES BIJOUX
un bijou *piece of jewelry*
un collier *necklace*
un bracelet
une bague *ring*
une chaîne *chain*
des boucles *(f.)* **d'oreille** *earrings*

SECTION C

Communicative function
Buying clothing in a store

Teaching Resource Options

PRINT 

Workbook PE, pp. 149–155
Unit 6 Resource Book
- Audioscript, p. 31
- Communipak, pp. 140–158
- Video Activities, pp. 23–24, 26
- Videoscript, pp. 29–30
- Workbook TE, pp. 1–7

AUDIO & VISUAL 

Audio Program
CD 3 Track 20

Overhead Transparencies
37 Comparing clothing
12 Menu from *Le Select*

VIDEO PROGRAM

VIDÉO DVD

MODULE 17

17.1 Introduction: Le shopping (34:40–35:55 min.)

17.2 Dialogue: Aux Galeries Lafayette (35:56–37:11 min.)

17.5 Mini-scenes: Combien coûte la veste? (39:09–39:52 min.)

17.6 Mini-scenes: Comment trouves-tu ma robe? (39:53–40:28 min.)

Supplementary vocabulary
trop serré *(too tight)*

Vocabulary note
The masculine plural of **génial** is **géniaux.**

Note: In the text, students will only be using this adjective in the singular.

C VOCABULAIRE Dans un magasin

Pardon, madame.
Vous désirez, mademoiselle?
Je cherche un pantalon.

How to get help from a salesperson:

Pardon, monsieur (madame).
Vous désirez *(May I help you),* **monsieur? / madame / mademoiselle**

Je cherche *(I'm looking for)* ...
un pantalon.
Quel est le prix *(What is the price)* du pantalon?
Combien *(How much)* **coûte** le pantalon?
Combien est-ce qu'il coûte?
Il coûte 40 euros.

Je cherche ... 
une veste.
Quel est le prix de la veste?
Combien coûte la veste?
Combien est-ce qu'elle coûte?
Elle coûte 65 euros.

How to discuss clothes with a friend:

Qu'est-ce que tu penses du pantalon vert? *(What do you think of ...?)*
Comment trouves-tu le pantalon vert? *(What do you think of ...?)*

Qu'est-ce que tu penses de la veste verte?
Comment trouves-tu la veste verte?

Comment trouves-tu le pantalon vert?
Il est trop petit.

Il est	**joli.** / **élégant** / **génial** *(terrific)* / **chouette** *(neat)* / **à la mode** *(in style)*	Elle est	**jolie.** / **élégante** / **géniale** / **chouette** / **à la mode**
Il est	**moche** *(plain, ugly).* / **démodé** *(out of style)*	Elle est	**moche.** / **démodée**
Il est **trop** *(too)*	**petit.** / **grand** *(big)* / **court** *(short)* / **long** *(long)*	Elle est **trop**	**petite.** / **grande** / **courte** / **longue**
Il est	**cher** *(expensive).* / **bon marché** *(cheap)*	Elle est	**chère.** / **bon marché**

→ The expression **bon marché** is INVARIABLE. It does not take adjective endings.
Les chaussures blanches sont **bon marché.**

VERBES

chercher	*to look for*	Je **cherche** un jean.
coûter	*to cost*	Les chaussures **coûtent** 60 euros.
penser	*to think*	Qu'est-ce que tu **penses** de cette *(this)* robe?
penser que	*to think (that)*	Je **pense qu'**elle est géniale!
trouver	*to find*	Je ne **trouve** pas ma veste.
	to think of	Comment **trouves**-tu mes lunettes de soleil?

→ The verb **penser** is often used alone.
Tu **penses?** *Do you think so?* Je **ne pense pas.** *I don't think so.*

GAME Prices

PROPS: Transparency 12: Menu from *Le Select*
Using the menu on the transparency, have each student write an addition problem with an answer that is under 40 euros. For example:

Combien coûtent 2 steak-frites et 2 thés? [22 euros]

Place the problems into a hat. Divide the class into two teams. Draw a problem from the hat and read it aloud. Player A-1 plays against player B-1. The first player from either team to stand and answer correctly wins a point. If the response is incorrect, the other player tries to answer. Continue with players A-2 and B-2, etc.

Les nombres de 100 à 1000 

100	**cent**	200	**deux cents**	500	**cinq cents**	800	**huit cents**
101	**cent un**	300	**trois cents**	600	**six cents**	900	**neuf cents**
102	**cent deux**	400	**quatre cents**	700	**sept cents**	1000	**mille**

7 Au marché aux puces

PARLER You are at the Paris flea market looking for clothes with a French friend. Explain why you are not buying the following items. Use your imagination … and expressions from the **Vocabulaire.**

▶ **—Tu vas acheter le blouson?**
—Non, je ne pense pas.
—Pourquoi pas?
—Il est trop grand.

8 C'est combien?

PARLER Ask your friends how much the following items cost.

▶ **—Combien coûte la veste?**
—Elle coûte cent vingt euros.

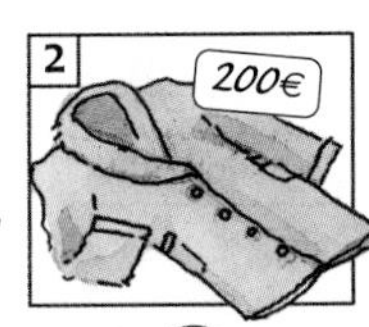

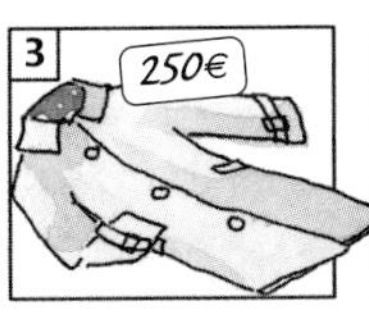

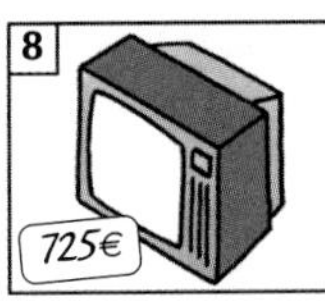

CHALLENGE ACTIVITY Une idole

Une idole is a music superstar. Have students bring in a picture of an American **idole** and describe what he/she is wearing. They can give the approximate prices and comment on the style. For example:

Mon idole est Will Smith. Ici il porte un blouson qui *(which)* **coûte $150 et un pantalon qui coûte $75. Le blouson est trop grand mais le pantalon est très élégant. Il porte aussi des lunettes de soleil. Elles sont chouettes mais chères: elles coûtent $200!**

Les nombres de 100 à 1000
Language notes

- The word **mille** never takes an "s": **deux mille, trois mille,** etc.
- Note: at this level, students are not expected to spell the numbers.

7 EXCHANGES explaining why one is not buying certain items

Answers will vary.

1. –Tu vas acheter la cravate?
   –Non, je ne pense pas.
   –Pourquoi pas?
   –Elle est trop (moche).
2. –Tu vas acheter le pull?
   –Non, je ne pense pas.
   –Pourquoi pas?
   –Il est trop grand.
3. –Tu vas acheter le jean?
   –Non, je ne pense pas.
   –Pourquoi pas?
   –Il est trop court.
4. –Tu vas acheter le chapeau?
   –Non, je ne pense pas.
   –Pourquoi pas?
   –Il est trop (démodé).
5. –Tu vas acheter la veste?
   –Non, je ne pense pas.
   –Pourquoi pas?
   –Elle est trop petite.
6. –Tu vas acheter l'imper[méable]?
   –Non, je ne pense pas.
   –Pourquoi pas?
   –Il est trop (long / grand).
7. –Tu vas acheter les bottes?
   –Non, je ne pense pas.
   –Pourquoi pas?
   – Elles sont (démodées).

8 ROLE PLAY asking about prices

1. – Combien coûte le blouson?
   – Il coûte 150 (cent cinquante) euros.
2. – Combien coûte le manteau?
   – Il coûte 200 (deux cents) euros.
3. – Combien coûte l'impérmeable?
   – Il coûte 250 (deux cent cinquante) euros.
4. – Combien coûte l'appareil-photo?
   – Il coûte 180 (cent quatre-vingts) euros.
5. – Combien coûte la mini-chaîne?
   – Elle coûte 350 (trois cent cinquante) euros.
6. – Combien coûte l'ordinateur?
   – Il coûte 1 400 (mille quatre cents) euros.
7. – Combien coûte le vélo?
   – Il coûte 275 (deux cent soixante-quinze) euros.
8. – Combien coûte le téléviseur?
   – Il coûte 725 (sept cent vingt-cinq) euros.
9. – Combien coûte le scooter?
   – Il coûte 890 (huit cent quatre-vingt-dix) euros.

À VOTRE TOUR

Main Topic
- Recapitulation and review

Teaching Resource Options

PRINT 

Workbook PE, pp. 149–155
Unit 6 Resource Book
- Audioscript, p. 31
- Communipak, pp. 140–158
- Family Involvement, pp. 21–22
- Workbook TE, pp. 1–7

Assessment
- Lesson 17 Quiz, pp. 35–36
- Portfolio Assessment, Unit 1 URB pp. 155–164
- Audioscript for Quiz 17, p. 34
- Answer Keys, pp. 230–234

AUDIO & VISUAL 

Audio Program
CD 3 Tracks 21–23
CD 15 Track 9

TECHNOLOGY 

Test Generator CD-ROM/McDougal Littell Assessment System

1 COMPREHENSION

1. B
2. A
3. A
4. A
5. A
6. B
7. B
8. A
9. B
10. A
11. A
12. B
13. B
14. B

2 GUIDED ORAL EXPRESSION

Answers will vary

1. – Vous désirez, monsieur (mademoiselle)?
   – Je cherche un pull.
   – Comment trouvez-vous le pull rouge?
   – Il est élégant. Combien est-ce qu'il coûte?
   – Trente dollars.
   – Oh là là, il est cher! (Il est bon marché.)
2. – Vous désirez, monsieur (mademoiselle)?
   – Je cherche un imperméable.
   – Comment trouvez-vous l'imperméable bleu?
   – Il est joli. Combien est-ce qu'il coûte?
   – Trois cent cinquante dollars.
   – Oh là là, il est cher!
3. – Vous désirez, monsieur (mademoiselle)?
   – Je cherche une veste.
   – Comment trouvez-vous la veste jaune?
   – Elle est à la mode. Combien est-ce qu'elle coûte?
   – Deux cent cinquante dollars.
   – Oh là là, elle est chère!
4. – Vous désirez, monsieur (mademoiselle)?
   – Je cherche un tee-shirt.
   – Comment trouvez-vous le tee-shirt blanc?
   – Il est génial. Combien est-ce qu'il coûte?
   – Quinze dollars.
   – Il est bon marché.

À votre tour!

OBJECTIFS

Now you can …
- name and describe the clothes you wear
- discuss their style and their fit
- count to 1000

1 Écoutez bien!

ÉCOUTER Thomas and Frédéric are both getting ready to leave on vacation. Listen to the following sentences which mention items that they are packing. If the item belongs to Thomas, mark A. If the item belongs to Frédéric, mark B.

	1	2	3	4	5	6
A: Thomas						
B: Frédéric						

A. Thomas

B. Frédéric

2 Créa-dialogue

PARLER You are at Place Bonaventure in Montreal looking at clothes in various shops. You like what the salesperson shows you and ask how much each item costs. React to the price.

▶ joli / $60

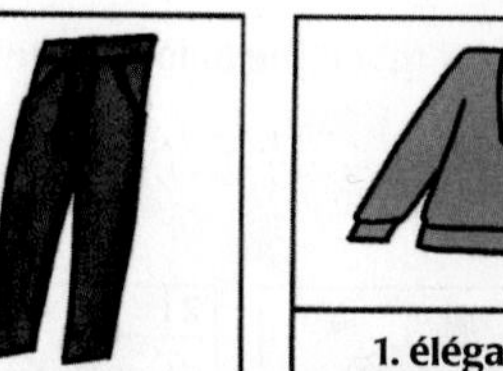

1. élégant / $30

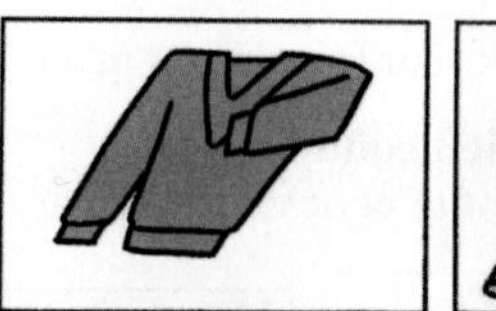

2. joli / $350

3. à la mode / $250

4. génial / $15

▶ —Vous désirez, monsieur (mademoiselle)?
—Je cherche un pantalon.
—Comment trouvez-vous le pantalon gris?
—Il est joli. Combien est-ce qu'il coûte?
—Soixante dollars.
—Oh là là, il est cher! (Il est bon marché.)

À VOTRE TOUR

Depending on your goals and objectives, you may or may not wish to assign all of the activities in the **À votre tour** section.

INCLUSION

Repetitive Prepare students for Activity 1 by having them repeat the names of the clothing items that appear in the pictures. Write the possessive adjectives on the board for the them to refresh their memories as they listen to the dialogue and answer the questions.

3 Conversation dirigée

PARLER Sophie and Christophe are shopping in a department store. Act out their conversation in French.

Sophie

Christophe

Sophie		Christophe
asks Christophe what he is looking for	→ ←	answers that he is looking for a baseball cap
asks him what he thinks of the yellow cap	→ ←	says that it is terrific but adds that he is going to buy the blue cap
asks how much it costs	→ ←	answers 5 euros
says that it is inexpensive but adds that it is too small		

4 Qu'est-ce qui ne va pas? *(What's wrong?)*

PARLER Explain what is wrong with the clothes that these people just bought at a sale.

▶ **Le chapeau de Monsieur Dupont est trop grand.**

Monsieur Dupont

Édouard

5 Les valises

ÉCRIRE You are an exchange student in Paris. Your host family has invited you to spend:

- one weekend in Nice to go sailing
- one weekend in Chamonix to go skiing

Make a list of the different clothes you will take on each trip.

6 À l'aéroport

ÉCRIRE You are flying to Paris tomorrow on an exchange program. Your hosts plan to meet you at the airport, but don't have your picture. Write them an e-mail explaining what you look like and what you will be wearing.

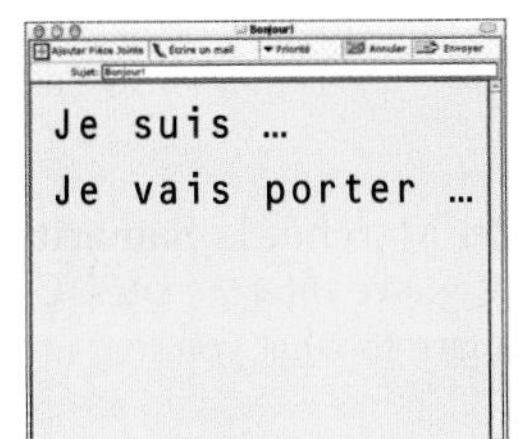

PORTFOLIO ASSESSMENT

You will probably select only one speaking activity and one writing activity to go into the students' portfolios for Unit 6.

In this lesson, Act. 2 lends itself well to an oral portfolio recording.

Act. 6 offers a good writing portfolio topic.

INCLUSION

Cumulative Prepare students for Activity 3 by reviewing the essential vocabulary. Call out the vocabulary mentioned in the direction lines (baseball cap, yellow cap, etc.) and have students call back the French words. Then, have students complete the activity.

3 GUIDED ORAL EXPRESSION

S: Qu'est-ce que tu cherches, Christophe?
C: Je cherche une casquette.
S: Comment trouves-tu la casquette jaune?
C: Elle est géniale, mais je vais acheter la casquette bleue.
S: Combien est-ce qu'elle coûte?
C: Elle coûte cinq euros.
S: Elle est bon marché (elle n'est pas chère), mais elle est trop petite.

4 COMPREHENSION

M. Dupont: La veste de M. Dupont est trop grande. Le pantalon de M. Dupont est trop court.
Édouard: La chemise d'Édouard est trop petite. La cravate d'Édouard est trop longue (grande). Le pantalon d'Édouard est trop long (grand).

5 WRITTEN SELF-EXPRESSION

Answers will vary.

Ma liste de vêtements pour Nice (pour aller à Nice)
un maillot de bain
deux shorts
des lunettes de soleil
un chapeau
une casquette
trois tee-shirts
des tennis
des sandales
un sweat

Ma liste de vêtements pour Chamonix (pour aller à Chamonix)
un jean
un pull
deux pantalons
des bottes
un manteau
deux collants
un chapeau

6 WRITTEN SELF-EXPRESSION

Answers will vary.

Je suis petit(e) et brun(e). (Je suis grand[e] et blond[e].)

Je vais porter un pantalon vert, un pull marron, des chaussures marron et un blouson noir. (Je vais porter un jean bleu, un sweat jaune, une veste grise et des tennis blanches. / Je vais porter une robe rouge et un manteau bleu.)

Cultural note

Place Bonaventure is part of Montreal's unique underground city. Various underground neighborhoods are linked by metro and climate-controlled corridors, a feature which Montrealers greatly appreciate in the wintertime. Between **Place Bonaventure** and **Place du Canada** one can find supermarkets, banks, boutiques, beauty salons, cinemas, theaters, hotels, and two railway stations.

Leçon 18

Main Topics Shopping and talking about clothes

Teaching Resource Options

PRINT

Workbook PE, pp. 157–162
Activités pour tous PE, pp. 95–97
Block Scheduling Copymasters, pp. 137–143
Unit 6 Resource Book
- *Activités pour tous* TE, pp. 43–45
- Audioscript, pp. 62, 63–65
- Communipak, pp. 140–158
- Lesson Plans, pp. 46–47
- Block Scheduling Lesson Plans, pp. 48–49
- Absent Student Copymasters, pp. 50–53
- Video Activities, pp. 56–59
- Videoscript, pp. 60–61
- Workbook TE, pp. 37–42

AUDIO & VISUAL

Audio Program
CD 3 Tracks 24, 25
CD 10 Tracks 9–14

Overhead Transparencies
38 *Au grand magasin*

TECHNOLOGY

Online Workbook

VIDEO PROGRAM

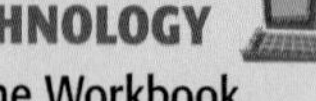

VIDÉO DVD

MODULE 18
Rien n'est parfait!

TOTAL TIME: 5:19 min.
DVD Disk 2
Videotape 3 (COUNTER: 42:15 min.)

18.1 Dialogue: Rien n'est parfait! (42:45–43:44 min.)

18.2 Mini-scenes: Listening – Comment trouves-tu ce pull? (43:45–44:58 min.)

18.3 Mini-scenes: Listening – Quel café? (44:59–45:25 min.)

18.4 Mini-scenes: Speaking – Quelle veste désirez-vous? (45:26–46:09 min.)

18.5 Vignette culturelle: Un grand magasin (46:10–47:34 min.)

Comprehension practice Play the entire module through as an introduction to the lesson.

LEÇON 18

Rien n'est parfait!

VIDÉO DVD AUDIO

<u>Cet</u> après-midi, Frédéric et Jean-Claude vont acheter des vêtements. Ils vont acheter <u>ces</u> vêtements dans un grand magasin. <u>Ce</u> magasin s'appelle le Bon Marché.

This / *these/This*

SCÈNE 1.
Frédéric et Jean-Claude regardent les pulls.

Frédéric: Regarde! Comment trouves-tu ce pull?
Jean-Claude: <u>Quel</u> pull? *Which*
Frédéric: Ce pull bleu.
Jean-Claude: Il est chouette.
Frédéric: C'est vrai, il est très chouette.
Jean-Claude: *(qui regarde le prix)* Il est aussi très cher.
Frédéric: Combien est-ce qu'il coûte?
Jean-Claude: Deux cents euros.
Frédéric: Deux cents euros! <u>Quelle horreur!</u> *What a scandal!*

NOTE culturelle

Le grand magasin

Le grand magasin est un magasin de 4 ou 5 étages où on peut° acheter toutes° sortes de produits différents: vêtements, parfums, meubles,° alimentation° générale, etc. ... Le grand magasin est une idée française. Le premier grand magasin a été créé° en 1852 par Aristide Boucicaut (1810-1877). Ce magasin existe toujours° et s'appelle «le Bon Marché». L'idée de Monsieur Boucicaut était° d'offrir à sa clientèle une marchandise de bonne qualité à des prix bon marché ... d'où° le nom «Bon Marché». Son idée a été vite° copiée dans toutes les villes.

on peut *one can* **toutes** *all* **meubles** *furniture* **alimentation** *food*
a été créé *was created* **toujours** *still* **était** *was* **d'où** *hence* **vite** *quickly*

COMPARAISONS CULTURELLES

French department stores, such as **le Bon Marché, la Samaritaine, le Printemps,** and **les Galeries Lafayette** have Internet sites. Check out one of these stores. How do its products compare to what you find in your local department stores?

WARM-UP AND REVIEW

PROPS: Transparency 38: *Au grand magasin*
Using a transparency marker, fill in prices up to 300 euros in the price tags on the transparency. Then ask questions about the items of clothing and their prices.

Qu'est-ce que c'est?
C'est un pantalon noir.
Combien coûte le pantalon?
Il coûte [cent trente] euros.
C'est cher?
Mais oui, c'est très cher.

SCÈNE 2.

Maintenant Frédéric et Jean-Claude regardent les vestes.

Frédéric: Quelle veste est-ce que tu préfères?

Jean-Claude: Je préfère cette veste jaune. Elle est très élégante et elle n'est pas très chère.

Frédéric: Oui, mais elle est trop grande pour toi!

Jean-Claude: Dommage!

SCÈNE 3.

Frédéric est au rayon (*department*) des chaussures. Quelles chaussures est-ce qu'il va acheter?

Jean-Claude: Alors, quelles chaussures est-ce que tu achètes?

Frédéric: J'achète ces chaussures noires. Elles sont très confortables ... et elles ne sont pas chères. Regarde, elles sont en solde (*on sale*).

Jean-Claude: C'est vrai, elles sont en solde ... mais elles ne sont plus (*are no longer*) à la mode.

Frédéric: Hélas, rien n'est parfait! (*Too bad/nothing is perfect*)

Compréhension

1. Où vont Frédéric et Jean-Claude cet après-midi?
2. Qu'est-ce qu'ils vont faire?
3. Qu'est-ce qu'ils regardent d'abord *(first)*?
4. Combien coûte le pull bleu?
5. Quelle est la réaction de Frédéric?
6. Qu'est-ce que Jean-Claude pense de la veste jaune?
7. Pourquoi est-ce qu'il n'achète pas la veste?
8. Qu'est-ce que Frédéric pense des chaussures noires?
9. Pourquoi est-ce qu'il n'achète pas les chaussures?

Compréhension
Answers

1. Cet après-midi, Frédéric et Jean-Claude vont dans un grand magasin (au Bon Marché).
2. Ils vont acheter des vêtements.
3. Ils regardent d'abord les pulls.
4. Le pull bleu coûte deux cents euros.
5. Frédéric pense que le pull est trop cher. (Il ne va pas acheter le pull.)
6. Jean-Claude pense que la veste jaune est élégante. Elle n'est pas chère.
7. Il n'achète pas la veste parce qu'elle est trop grande.
8. Frédéric pense que les chaussures noires sont confortables (ne sont pas chères).
9. Il n'achète pas les chaussures parce qu'elles ne sont pas à la mode.

Note culturelle

In 1989, **Au Bon Marché** changed its name to **Le Bon Marché.**

SECTION A

Communicative function
Indicating what people prefer and what people are buying

Teaching Resource Options

PRINT 

Workbook PE, pp. 157–162
Unit 6 Resource Book
Audioscript, p. 62
Communipak, pp. 140–158
Workbook TE, pp. 37–42

AUDIO & VISUAL 

Audio Program
CD 3 Track 26

TECHNOLOGY 

Power Presentations

Teaching strategies

- Point out that the stem changes occur only in those forms of the verb where the ending is not pronounced. There is no stem change before **-ons** and **-ez.**
- For your visually-minded students you can present stem-changing verbs as "boot verbs." Within the "boot" the verb endings are not pronounced and there is the same change in the stem. Outside the boot, the endings are pronounced, and there is no stem change.

j'achète	**nous achetons**
tu achètes	**vous achetez**
il achète	**ils achètent**

1 COMPREHENSION describing purchases

Answers will vary.
1. Avec dix dollars, tu achètes (un CD / des lunettes de soleil).
2. Avec quinze dollars, j'achète (des lunettes de soleil / une cravate).
3. Avec trente dollars, nous achetons (un jean / un polo).
4. Avec cinquante dollars, Jean-Claude achète (une veste / un survêtement).
5. Avec cent dollars, vous achetez (un survêtement et une cravate).
6. Avec quinze mille dollars, mes parents achètent (une voiture).
7. Avec vingt-cinq dollars, mon cousin achète (un polo).
8. Avec (soixante dollars), j'achète (des chaussures).

A Les verbes *acheter* et *préférer* 

Verbs like **acheter** *(to buy)* end in: **e** + CONSONANT + **-er.**
Verbs like **préférer** *(to prefer)* end in: **é** + CONSONANT + **-er.**

Note the forms of these two verbs in the chart, paying attention to:
- the **e** of the stem of **ach<u>e</u>ter**
- the **é** of the stem of **préf<u>é</u>rer**

INFINITIVE	acheter	préférer
PRESENT	J' **achète** une veste.	Je **préfère** la veste bleue.
	Tu **achètes** une cravate.	Tu **préfères** la cravate jaune.
	Il/Elle **achète** un imper.	Il/Elle **préfère** l'imper gris.
	Nous **achetons** un jean.	Nous **préférons** le jean noir.
	Vous **achetez** un short.	Vous **préférez** le short blanc.
	Ils/Elles **achètent** un pull.	Ils/Elles **préfèrent** le pull rouge.

→ Verbs like **acheter** and **préférer** take regular endings and have the following changes in the stem:

ach<u>e</u>ter	**e → è**	in the **je, tu, il,** and **ils** forms of the present
préf<u>é</u>rer	**é → è**	

1 Achats *(Purchases)*

PARLER/ÉCRIRE What we buy depends on how much money we have. Complete the sentences below with **acheter** and one or more of the items from the list.

1. Avec dix dollars, tu …
2. Avec quinze dollars, j' …
3. Avec trente dollars, nous …
4. Avec cinquante dollars, Jean-Claude …
5. Avec cent dollars, vous …
6. Avec quinze mille dollars, mes parents …
7. Avec ?? dollars, mon cousin …
8. Avec ?? dollars, j' …

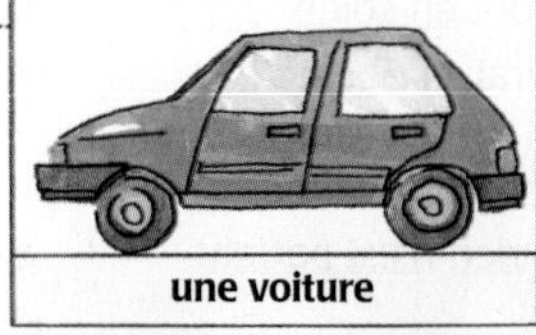
une voiture

des chaussures

une cravate

un survêtement

des lunettes de soleil

un polo

une veste

un CD

un jean

??

TALKING ABOUT PAST EVENTS

Let's talk about what clothes you bought last summer.
Est-ce que tu as acheté un jean l'été dernier?
Oui, j'ai acheté un jean.
(Non, je n'ai pas acheté de jean.)

- **Est-ce que tu as acheté un polo?**
- **Est-ce que tu as acheté des sandales?**
- **Est-ce que tu as acheté un maillot de bain?**
- **Est-ce que tu as acheté une veste?**
- **Qu'est-ce que tu as acheté?**

Follow-up:
Est-ce que X a acheté un jean?

VOCABULAIRE Verbes comme *(like)* *acheter* et *préférer*

acheter	*to buy*	Qu'est-ce que tu **achètes?**
amener	*to bring (a person)*	François **amène** sa copine à la boum.
préférer	*to prefer*	**Préfères**-tu le manteau ou l'imper?
espérer	*to hope*	J'**espère** visiter Paris en été.

➔ In French, there are two verbs that correspond to the English *to bring:*

amener + PEOPLE — J'**amène** une copine au pique-nique.
apporter + THINGS — J'**apporte** des sandwichs au pique-nique.

2 Pique-nique

PARLER/ÉCRIRE Everyone is bringing someone or something to the picnic. Complete the sentences below with the appropriate forms of **amener** or **apporter.**

▶ **Nous amenons un copain.** — **Marc apporte des sandwichs.**

1. Tu ... ta guitare.
2. Philippe ... sa soeur.
3. Nous ... nos voisins.
4. Vous ... un dessert.
5. Michèle ... des sodas.
6. Antoine et Vincent ... leur cousine.
7. Raphaël ... ses CD.
8. Mon cousin ... sa copine.
9. J' ... ma radiocassette.
10. Léa et Émilie ... leurs portables.

3 Expression personnelle

PARLER/ÉCRIRE Complete the sentences below with one of the suggested options or an expression of your choice. Note: You may wish to make some of the sentences negative.

Quand je vais à une fête, j'apporte mon portable.
Et moi, j'apporte ma guitare.

1. Quand je vais à une fête, j'amène ... (des copains, une copine, ma grand-mère, ??)
   J'apporte ... (des sandwichs, ma guitare, mes CD, mon portable, ??)
2. Quand je vais à un pique-nique, j'amène ... (ma soeur, une copine, mon chien, ??)
   J'apporte ... (mon baladeur, mon livre de français, des sandwichs, ??)
3. Le week-end, je préfère ... (étudier, aller au cinéma, rester à la maison, ??)
   Ce *(This)* week-end, j'espère ... (avoir un rendez-vous avec un copain ou une copine, travailler, jouer au volley, ??)
4. Pendant *(During)* les vacances, j'espère ... (rester à la maison, trouver un job, voyager, ??)
5. Un jour, j'espère ... (visiter la France, parler français, aller à l'université, être millionnaire, ??)

Teaching strategy Using subject pronoun cue cards, have students conjugate **amener** and **espérer** orally and in writing.

2 COMPREHENSION describing what and whom people are bringing to a picnic

1. apportes
2. amène
3. amenons
4. apportez
5. apporte
6. amènent
7. apporte
8. amène
9. apporte
10. apportent

3 COMMUNICATION describing what one does and hopes to do

Answers will vary.
1. Quand je vais à une fête, j'amène (une copine).
   J'apporte (mes CD).
2. Quand je vais à un pique-nique, j'amène (ma soeur).
   J'apporte(des sandwichs).
3. Le week-end, je préfère (aller au cinéma).
   Ce week-end, j'espère (jouer au volley).
4. Pendant les vacances, j'espère (voyager).
5. Un jour, j'espère (visiter la France).

Expansion In trios, have students discuss and vote on the choices. The recorder **(secrétaire)** then writes the sentences in the **nous**-form.
1. Quand nous allons à une fête, nous amenons (des copains). Nous apportons (nos portables).
2. Quand nous allons à un pique-nique, nous amenons (des copines).
   Nous apportons (des sandwichs).
3. Le week-end, nous préférons (aller au cinéma).
   Ce week-end, nous espérons (jouer au volley).
4. Pendant les vacances, nous espérons (voyager).
5. Un jour, nous espérons (visiter la France).

Variation (with **amener**)

Est-ce que tu as amené
- **un copain?**
- **une copine?**
- **des amis français?**
- **des cousins?**

TALKING ABOUT PAST EVENTS

Let's talk about what things you brought to a recent party.
Tu es allé(e) à une boum récemment.
Est-ce que tu as apporté des CD?
Oui, j'ai apporté des CD.
(Non, je n'ai pas apporté de CD.)

- **Est-ce que tu as apporté des DVD?**
- **Est-ce que tu as apporté une guitare?**
- **Est-ce que tu as apporté des pizzas?**
- **Est-ce que tu as apporté des sodas?**
- **Qu'est-ce que tu as apporté?**

SECTION B

Communicative function
Pointing out people and things

Teaching Resource Options

PRINT

Workbook PE, pp. 157–162
Unit 6 Resource Book
Communipak, pp. 140–158
Video Activities, pp. 57–58
Videoscript, pp. 60–61
Workbook TE, pp. 37–42

TECHNOLOGY 

Power Presentations

VIDEO PROGRAM

VIDÉO DVD

MODULE 18

18.2 Mini-scenes: Comment trouves-tu ce pull? (43:45–44:58 min.)
18.3 Mini-scenes: Quel café? (44:59–45:25 min.)
18.4 Mini-scenes: Quelle veste désirez-vous? (45:26–46:09 min.)

4 ROLE PLAY commenting on items in a store

1. **N:** Regarde cet imper!
   M: Il est élégant!
2. **N:** Regarde ces bottes!
   M: Elles sont à la mode!
3. **N:** Regarde cette casquette!
   M: Elle est géniale!
4. **N:** Regarde ce survêtement!
   M: Il est chouette!
5. **N:** Regarde ces livres!
   M: Ils sont amusants!
6. **N:** Regarde cet ordinateur!
   M: Il est génial!
7. **N:** Regarde cette télé!
   M: Elle est moderne!
8. **N:** Regarde cette ceinture!
   M: Elle est jolie!
9. **N:** Regarde ces sandales!
   M: Elles sont jolies!

5 ROLE PLAY discussing preferences

–J'aime ...
–Eh bien, moi, je préfère ...
1. cette chemise-ci/cette chemise-là
2. ce blouson-ci/ce blouson-là
3. ces chaussures-ci/ces chaussures-là
4. ces lunettes-ci/ces lunettes-là
5. cette casquette-ci/cette casquette-là
6. cette affiche-ci/cette affiche-là
7. ce stylo-ci/ce stylo-là
8. cet ordinateur-ci/cet ordinateur-là

Point out to students that the French often use **"Eh bien"** to emphasize a question or remark.

– Eh bien, est-ce que tu viens en ville avec nous?
– Eh bien, non!

B L'adjectif démonstratif *ce*

LEARNING ABOUT LANGUAGE

DEMONSTRATIVE ADJECTIVES *(this, that)* are used to point out specific people or things.

In French, the demonstrative adjective **ce** always agrees with the noun it introduces.

Note the forms of the demonstrative adjective **ce** in the chart below.

	SINGULAR *(this, that)*	PLURAL *(these, those)*		
MASCULINE	**ce** ↓ **cet** (+ VOWEL SOUND)	**ces**	**ce** blouson **cet** homme	**ces** blousons **ces** hommes
FEMININE	**cette**	**ces**	**cette** veste **cette** amie	**ces** vestes **ces** amies

→ There is liaison after **cet** and **ces** when the next word begins with a vowel sound.

→ To distinguish between a person or an object that is close by and one that is further away, the French sometimes use **-ci** or **-là** after the noun.

Philippe achète **cette chemise-ci.**	*Philippe is buying **this shirt** (over here).*
François achète **cette chemise-là.**	*François is buying **that shirt** (over there).*

4   À la Samaritaine

PARLER Marc and Nathalie are at the Samaritaine department store. Marc likes everything that Nathalie shows him. Play both roles.

▶ une robe (jolie) NATHALIE: **Regarde cette robe!**
MARC: **Elle est jolie!**

1. un imper (élégant)
2. des bottes (à la mode)
3. une casquette (géniale)
4. un survêtement (chouette)
5. des livres (amusants)
6. un ordinateur (génial)
7. une télé (moderne)
8. une ceinture (jolie)
9. des sandales (jolies)

5  Différences d'opinion

PARLER Whenever they go shopping together, Éric and Brigitte cannot agree on what they like. Play both roles.

▶ un short

1. une chemise
2. un blouson
3. des chaussures
4. des lunettes
5. une casquette
6. une affiche
7. un stylo
8. un ordinateur

J'aime ce short-ci.
Eh bien, moi, je préfère ce short-là.

TEACHING STRATEGIES

- Point out that **ces** (like **les, des, mes**) is used with both masculine and feminine plural nouns. (There is no **cettes.**)
- Tell students that the masculine singular form **cet** is derived from the feminine singular form **cette** minus **-te**: **cette** → **cet.**

LANGUAGE NOTE

The tag **-ci** is related to **ici** *(here)* and **-là** means *there.* The expression **voici** has evolved from **vois ici** *(see here)* and **voilà** from **vois là** *(see there).*

C L'adjectif interrogatif *quel?*

The interrogative adjective **quel** *(what? which?)* is used in questions. It agrees with the noun it introduces and has the following forms:

	SINGULAR	PLURAL		
MASCULINE	quel	quels	**Quel** garçon?	**Quels** cousins?
FEMININE	quelle	quelles	**Quelle** fille?	**Quelles** copines?

→ Note the liaison after **quels** and **quelles** when the next word begins with a vowel sound.
Quelles affiches est-ce que tu préfères?

J'achète un pantalon.
Quel pantalon est-ce que tu achètes?
Ce pantalon noir.

6 Vêtements d'été

PARLER You are shopping for the following items before going on a summer trip to France. A friend is asking you which ones you are buying. Identify each item by color.

▶ un pantalon/noir

1. un maillot de bain/bleu

2. des chaussettes/vertes

3. une jupe/jaune

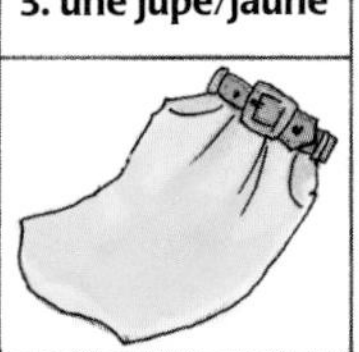

4. une veste/bleue

5. des chaussures/blanches

6. des sandales/marron

7. un sweat/gris

8. une chemise/orange

9. un pull/rouge

7 Questions personnelles PARLER/ÉCRIRE

1. À quelle école vas-tu?
2. Dans quel magasin achètes-tu tes vêtements?
3. Dans quel magasin achètes-tu tes chaussures?
4. Quels CD aimes-tu écouter?
5. Quels programmes aimes-tu regarder à la télé?
6. Quel est ton restaurant préféré?
7. Quelle est ta classe préférée?

LISTENING ACTIVITY Préférences

PROPS: One red and one blue index card for each student

On the board, write **quel(s)** in blue chalk and **quelle(s)** in red chalk. Then read aloud questions containing forms of **quel.** If the form is spelled **quel(s),** students hold up the blue card. If it is spelled **quelle(s),** they hold up the red card.

1. **Quel sweat préfères-tu?** [B]
2. **Quels appareils...?** [B]
3. **Quelle jupe...?** [R]
4. **Quel blouson...?** [B]
5. **Quelles affiches...?** [R]
6. **Quelles chaussettes...?** [R]
7. **Quel pull...?** [B]
8. **Quelle école...?** [R]

SECTION C

Communicative function
Asking for clarification

Language notes

- Point out that all four forms of **quel** sound the same.
- **Quel** may be separated from its noun by **être.**
  Quelle est la date?

Teaching strategy Ask students if they can remember any questions they learned that use **quel.**
Quelle est la date?
Quelle heure est-il?
Quel temps fait-il?
Quel jour est-ce?
De quelle couleur est...?

6 ROLE PLAY discussing purchases

1. – J'achète un maillot de bain.
   – Quel maillot de bain est-ce que tu achètes?
   – Ce maillot de bain bleu.
2. – J'achète des chaussettes.
   – Quelles chaussettes est-ce que tu achètes?
   – Ces chaussettes vertes.
3. – J'achète une jupe.
   – Quelle jupe est-ce que tu achètes?
   – Cette jupe jaune.
4. – J'achète une veste.
   – Quelle veste est-ce que tu achètes?
   – Cette veste bleue.
5. – J'achète des chaussures.
   – Quelles chaussures est-ce que tu achètes?
   – Ces chaussures blanches.
6. – J'achète des sandales.
   – Quelles sandales est-ce que tu achètes?
   – Ces sandales marron.
7. – J'achète un sweat.
   – Quel sweat est-ce que tu achètes?
   – Ce sweat gris.
8. – J'achète une chemise.
   – Quelle chemise est-ce que tu achètes?
   – Cette chemise orange.
9. – J'achète un pull.
   – Quel pull est-ce que tu achètes?
   – Ce pull rouge.

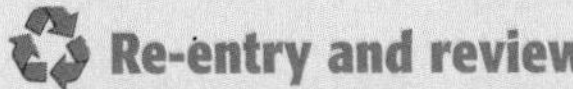

This activity reviews colors from Lesson 20.

7 COMMUNICATION answering personal questions

Answers will vary.
1. Je vais à (North Quincy High School).
2. J'achète mes vêtements à (La Boutique Chic).
3. J'achète mes chaussures chez (Bata).
4. J'aime écouter les CD de (MC Solaar).
5. À la télé, je regarde (les comédies).
6. Mon restaurant préféré est (Chez Antoine).
7. Ma classe préféré est (le français).

SECTION D

Communicative function
Saying where to put things

Teaching Resource Options

PRINT 

Workbook PE, pp. 157–162
Unit 6 Resource Book
Audioscript, pp. 62–63
Communipak, pp. 140–158
Workbook TE, pp. 37–42

AUDIO & VISUAL 

Audio Program
CD 3 Track 27

TECHNOLOGY

Power Presentations

Supplementary vocabulary

VERBS LIKE **METTRE**
mettre la table *to set the table (introduced in Lesson 25)*
permettre *to permit, allow, let*
promettre *to promise*

8 COMPREHENSION describing where people put things

Answers will vary.
Je mets la glace dans le réfrigérateur.
Nous mettons la voiture dans le garage.
Tu mets les livres sur le bureau (sur la table / dans le salon).
Vous mettez le téléphone sur la table (dans le salon / sur le bureau).
Christine met les vêtements dans le placard.
Le professeur met les plantes vertes dans le salon (sur la table / sur le bureau).
Madame Arnaud met une pellicule dans l'appareil-photo.
Marc et Philippe mettent les cartes sur la table (sur le bureau).

Variation Have students give illogical answers.

Mme Arnaud met la voiture dans le salon.

D Le verbe *mettre*

The verb **mettre** *(to put, place)* is irregular. Note its forms in the chart below.

INFINITIVE	mettre	
PRESENT	je **mets**	nous **mettons**
	tu **mets**	vous **mettez**
	il/elle **met**	ils/elles **mettent**

➔ In the singular forms, the "t" of the stem is silent. The "t" is pronounced in the plural forms.

➔ The verb **mettre** has several English equivalents:

to put, place	Je **mets** mes livres sur la table.
to put on, wear	Caroline **met** une robe rouge.
to turn on	Nous **mettons** la télé.

8 Où?

PARLER/ÉCRIRE Say where the people of Column A put the objects of Column B, by choosing a place from Column C. Be logical!

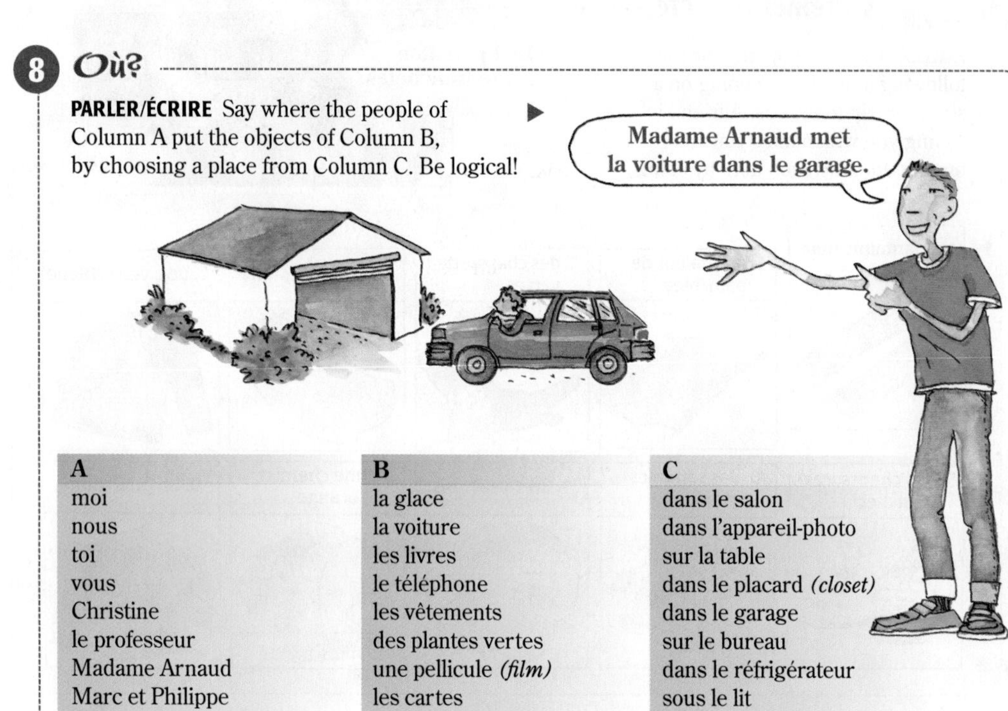
Madame Arnaud met la voiture dans le garage.

A	B	C
moi	la glace	dans le salon
nous	la voiture	dans l'appareil-photo
toi	les livres	sur la table
vous	le téléphone	dans le placard *(closet)*
Christine	les vêtements	dans le garage
le professeur	des plantes vertes	sur le bureau
Madame Arnaud	une pellicule *(film)*	dans le réfrigérateur
Marc et Philippe	les cartes	sous le lit

TEACHING NOTE Un jeu

Divide the students into pairs. Have each student take a sheet of paper. At a given signal, students write a phrase using elements from columns A and B (e.g., **Je mets la glace...**). As soon as they finish, they exchange papers and complete their partner's sentence using an element from column C (**...dans le réfrigérateur**).

Then, they write another phrase using columns A and B, exchange papers, and again complete their partner's sentence using column C.

After you have called time, have the pairs exchange papers for peer correction. The winner is the pair with the most correct sentences.

9 Questions personnelles PARLER/ÉCRIRE

1. Est-ce que tu mets la radio quand tu étudies?
2. Chez vous, est-ce que vous mettez la télé quand vous dînez?
3. Est-ce que tu mets des lunettes de soleil quand tu vas à la plage?
4. Où est-ce que tes parents mettent leur voiture? (dans le garage? dans la rue?)
5. Quels programmes de télé est-ce que tu mets le dimanche? le samedi?
6. Quels CD est-ce que tu mets quand tu vas à une boum?
7. Quels vêtements est-ce que tu mets quand il fait froid?
8. Quels vêtements est-ce que tu mets quand tu joues au basket?

PRONONCIATION

Les lettres «e» et «è»

e = /ə/ **e = /ɛ/** **è = /ɛ/**

chemise

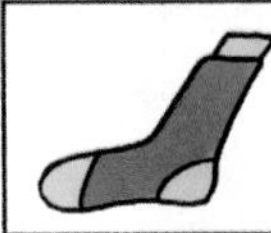

chaussette

chère

Practice pronouncing "**e**" within a word:

- /ə/ (as in **je**) [… "**e**" + *one* CONSONANT + VOWEL]

  Répétez: **chemise regarder Denise Renée petit venir**

  Note that in the middle of a word the /ə/ is sometimes silent.

  Répétez: **acheter achetons amener samedi rarement avenue**

- /ɛ/ (as in **elle**) [… "**e**" + *two* CONSONANTS + VOWEL]

  Répétez: **chaussette veste quelle cette rester professeur raquette**

Now practice pronouncing "**è**" within a word:

- /ɛ/ (as in **elle**) [… "**è**" + *one* CONSONANT + VOWEL]

  Répétez: **chère père mère achète amènent espère deuxième**

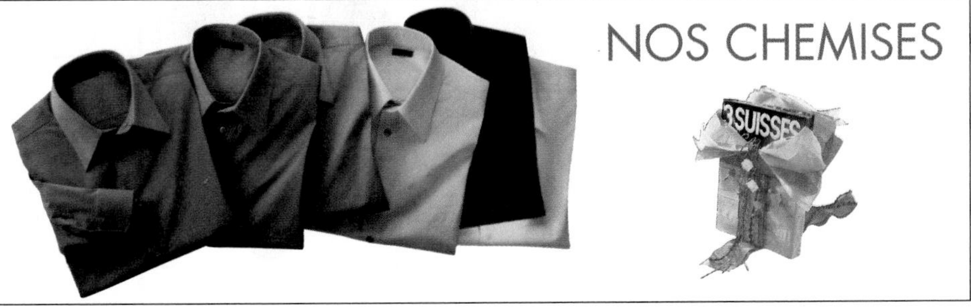

9 COMMUNICATION answering personal questions

Answers will vary.

1. Oui, je mets la radio quand j'étudie. (Non, je ne mets pas la radio quand j'étudie.)
2. Oui, chez nous, nous mettons la télé quand nous dînons. (Non, chez nous, nous ne mettons pas la télé quand nous dînons.)
3. Oui, je mets des lunettes de soleil quand je vais à la plage. (Non, je ne mets pas de lunettes de soleil quand je vais à la plage.)
4. Mes parents mettent leur voiture dans le garage (dans la rue).
5. Le dimanche je mets (le match de football américain). Le samedi, je mets (un film).
6. Quand je vais à une boum, je mets des CD (de MC Solaar et [de] Pascal Obispo).
7. Quand il fait froid, je mets (un manteau, des bottes, et des gants).
8. Quand je joue au basket, je mets (un short, un tee-shirt, des chaussettes et des baskets).

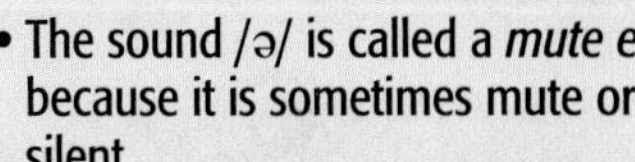

PRONUNCIATION

- The sound /ə/ is called a *mute e* because it is sometimes mute or silent.
- The sound /ɛ/ is called an *open e* because when you say it your mouth is more open than when you say /e/ as in **café.**

Realia note

Les Trois Suisses is a moderately priced chain store that sells clothing, cosmetics, stationery supplies, toys, and housewares. Many of the stores also have a supermarket section.

INCLUSION

Alphabetic/phonetic Model the sound of words with **e** and **è**. Ask students to practice the sound. Write words on the boards and tell students to use desktops to beat out syllables of as you first pronounce words where the **e** is pronounced, and then words where it is mute.

À votre tour!

OBJECTIFS

Now you can ...
- talk about what you plan to buy
- discuss your preferences
- point out certain people or objects

1 La bonne réponse

PARLER Alice is talking to her cousin Jérôme. Match Alice's questions with Jérôme's answers. Act out the dialogue with a classmate.

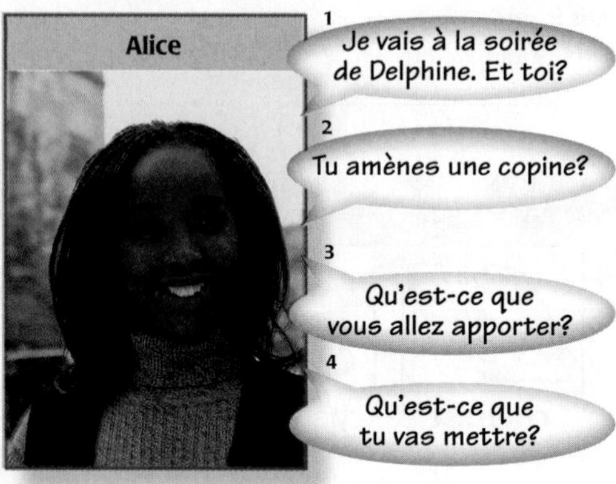

Alice
1 Je vais à la soirée de Delphine. Et toi?
2 Tu amènes une copine?
3 Qu'est-ce que vous allez apporter?
4 Qu'est-ce que tu vas mettre?

Jérôme
a Oui, Christine.
b Mon pull jaune et mon blouson marron.
c Nous allons acheter des pizzas.
d Moi aussi.

2 Créa-dialogue

PARLER Ask your classmates what they think about the following. They will answer affirmatively or negatively.

▶ —Comment trouves-tu <u>cette fille</u>?
—<u>Quelle fille</u>?
—<u>Cette fille-là</u>!
—Eh bien, je pense qu'<u>elle</u> est <u>jolie</u>.
(<u>Elle</u> n'est pas <u>jolie</u>.)

▶ jolie?

1. intéressants?

2. sympathique?

3. courte?

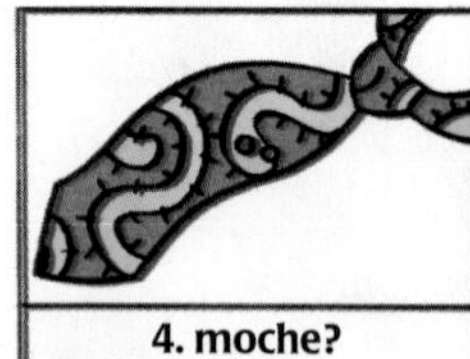
4. moche?

5. bon marché?

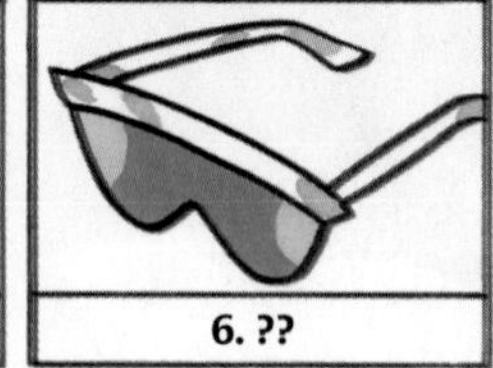
6. ??

7. ??

À VOTRE TOUR

Main Topic
- Recapitulation and review

Teaching Resource Options

PRINT  

Workbook PE, pp. 157–162
Unit 6 Resource Book
- Audioscript, p. 63
- Communipak, pp. 140–158
- Family Involvement, pp. 54–55
- Workbook TE, pp. 37–42

Assessment
- Lesson 18 Quiz, pp. 66–67
- Portfolio Assessment, Unit 1 URB pp. 155–164
- Audioscript for Quiz 18, p. 65
- Answer Keys, pp. 230–234

AUDIO & VISUAL 

Audio Program
CD 3 Tracks 28, 29
CD 15 Track 10

TECHNOLOGY

Test Generator CD-ROM/McDougal Littell Assessment System

1 COMPREHENSION

1. d
2. a
3. c
4. b

2 GUIDED ORAL EXPRESSION

– Comment trouves-tu ... ?
– ... ?
– ... -là!
– Eh bien, je pense qu'...

1. ces livres/Quels livres/Ces livres/ils sont intéressants. (Ils ne sont pas intéressants.)
2. ce monsieur (cet homme)/Quel homme/Cet homme/il n'est pas sympathique. (Il est sympathique.)
3. cette jupe/Quelle jupe/Cette jupe/elle est courte. (Elle n'est pas courte.)
4. cette cravate/Quelle cravate/Cette cravate/elle est moche. (Elle n'est pas moche.)
5. ces chaussures/Quelles chaussures/Ces chaussures/elles ne sont pas bon marché. (Elles sont bon marché.)
6. ces lunettes de soleil/Quelles lunettes de soleil/Ces lunettes de soleil/elles sont (super). (Elles sont moches.)
7. ce manteau/Quel manteau/Ce manteau/il est (cher). (Il n'est pas cher.)

À VOTRE TOUR

Depending on your goals and objectives, you may or may not wish to assign all of the activities in the **À votre tour** section.

PAIR PRACTICE

Act. 1–3 lend themselves to pair practice.

3 Shopping

PARLER You and a friend are shopping by catalog. Choose an object and tell your friend what you are buying. Identify it by color and explain why you like it.

▶ **—Je vais acheter un sac.**
—Quel sac?
—Ce sac rouge.
—Pourquoi?
—Parce qu'il est joli.

4 Composition: La soirée

ÉCRIRE You have been invited to a party by a French friend. In a short paragraph, describe …

- what clothes you are going to wear
- whom you are going to bring along
- what things you are going to bring (food? CDs? boombox? camera?)

Portfolio assessment

You will probably select only one speaking activity and one writing activity to go into the students' portfolios for Unit 6.

Act. 4 offers a good writing portfolio topic.

3 Conversation

Answers will vary.

A. –Je vais acheter un survêtement.
–Quel survêtement?
–Ce survêtement bleu et rouge.
–Pourquoi?
–Parce qu'il est (chouette).

B. –Je vais acheter une casquette.
–Quelle casquette?
–Cette casquette rouge.
–Pourquoi?
–Parce qu'elle est (bon marché).

C. –Je vais acheter des bottes.
–Quelles bottes?
–Ces bottes noires.
–Pourquoi?
–Parce qu'elles sont (chouettes).

D. –Je vais acheter un sac.
–Quel sac?
–Ce sac rouge.
–Pourquoi?
–Parce qu'il est (super).

E. –Je vais acheter un pull.
–Quel pull?
–Ce pull blanc.
–Pourquoi?
–Parce qu'il est (chic).

F. –Je vais acheter une jupe.
–Quelle jupe?
–Cette jupe grise.
–Pourquoi?
–Parce qu'elle (n'est pas chère).

Language note

depuis 20€ = *prices begin at 20€*

4 Written Self-Expression

Answers will vary.
Vendredi, je vais aller à la boum de Nicole. Je vais porter mon nouveau pantalon (ma nouvelle jupe), une jolie chemise et des chaussures noires. Je vais aussi porter mon blouson. Je vais amener mes cousins Brigitte et Paul. Je vais apporter des sandwichs et une salade.
Je vais aussi apporter mes CD de chansons françaises.

Leçon 19

Main Topics Talking about clothes, Making comparisons

Teaching Resource Options

PRINT 

Workbook PE, pp. 163–168
Activités pour tous PE, pp. 99–101
Block Scheduling Copymasters, pp. 145–151
Unit 6 Resource Book
- *Activités pour tous* TE, pp. 75–77
- Audioscript, pp. 94, 95–97
- Communipak, pp. 140–158
- Lesson Plans, pp. 78–79
- Block Scheduling Lessson Plans pp. 80–81
- Absent Student Copymasters, pp. 82–85
- Video Activities, pp. 88–91
- Videoscript, pp. 92–93
- Workbook TE, pp. 69–74

AUDIO & VISUAL 

Audio Program
CD 3 Tracks 30, 31
CD 10 Tracks 15–20

TECHNOLOGY 

Online Workbook

VIDEO PROGRAM

VIDÉO DVD

MODULE 19
Un choix difficile

TOTAL TIME: 5:32 min.
DVD Disk 2
Videotape 3 (COUNTER: 47:47 min.)

19.1 Dialogue: Un choix difficile (48:25–49:35 min.)

19.2 Mini-scenes: Listening – Comparaisons (49:36–51:10 min.)

19.3 Mini-scenes: Speaking – Comparaisons (51:11–51:55 min.)

19.4 Vignette culturelle: Dans un centre commercial (51:56–53:19 min.)

Comprehension practice Play the entire module through as an introduction to the lesson.

LEÇON 19

Un choix difficile

VIDÉO DVD AUDIO

Dans un mois, Delphine va aller au mariage de sa cousine. Elle va acheter une <u>nouvelle</u> (*new*) robe pour cette occasion. Pour cela, elle va dans un magasin de vêtements avec sa copine Véronique. Il y a beaucoup de jolies robes dans ce magasin.

Delphine <u>hésite</u> <u>entre</u> (*is hesitating/between*) une robe jaune et une robe rouge. Quelle robe est-ce que Delphine va <u>choisir</u> (*to choose*)? Ah là là, le <u>choix</u> (*choice*) n'est pas facile.

SCÈNE 1.

Véronique: Alors, quelle robe est-ce que tu choisis?

Delphine: Eh bien, <u>finalement</u> (*finally*) je choisis la robe rouge. Elle est <u>plus jolie que</u> (*prettier than*) la robe jaune.

Véronique: C'est vrai, elle est plus jolie ... mais la robe jaune est <u>moins</u> chère et elle est <u>plus grande</u> (*less/larger*). Regarde. La robe rouge est trop petite pour toi.

Delphine: Mais non, elle n'est pas trop petite.

Véronique: Bon, écoute, <u>essaie-la!</u> (*try it!*)

NOTE culturelle

Les jeunes et la mode

Les jeunes Français aiment être à la mode. Ils dépensent° trente pour cent (30%) de leur budget pour les vêtements. Parce que ce budget est limité, ils font très attention quand ils choisissent leurs vêtements. Heureusement,° il y a des boutiques spécialisées dans la mode des jeunes, comme Zara, Mango et Etam, où les vêtements ne sont pas trop° chers.

Certains jeunes préfèrent la «mode rétro». Ils achètent leurs vêtements au marché aux puces.°

dépensent *spend* **Heureusement** *Fortunately* **trop** *too*
marché aux puces *flea market*

SETTING THE SCENE

Have the class imagine they have all been invited to a wedding. What will they wear?

Imaginez que nous sommes invités à un mariage ce week-end.
Moi, je vais mettre ... [describe the outfit you would plan to wear]

Have various students describe what they are going to wear.

Et toi, X, qu'est-ce que tu vas mettre?
Y, est-ce que tu vas mettre [...] aussi?

Introduce Section 19.1 of the video:

Ce week-end Delphine va à un mariage. Qu'est-ce qu'elle va mettre?

SCÈNE 2.

Delphine sort de la cabine d'essayage. — *comes out/fitting room*

Delphine: C'est vrai, la robe rouge est plus petite mais ce n'est pas un problème. — *smaller*

Véronique: Pourquoi?

Delphine: Parce que j'ai un mois pour maigrir. — *to lose weight*

Véronique: Et si tu grossis? — *if/gain weight*

Delphine: Toi, tais-toi! — *be quiet*

Compréhension

1. Où vont Delphine et Véronique?
2. Qu'est-ce que Delphine va acheter?
3. Pourquoi?
4. Delphine hésite entre deux robes. De quelle couleur sont-elles?
5. Quelle robe est-ce qu'elle choisit?
6. Pourquoi est-ce qu'elle préfère la robe rouge?
7. Selon *(According to)* Véronique, quel est le problème avec la robe rouge?
8. Qu'est-ce que Delphine doit *(must)* faire pour porter la robe?

TALKING ABOUT PAST EVENTS

Let's talk about where you went yesterday and what you wore. Note that the past participle of **mettre** is **mis.**

Imagine que tu es allé(e) à la plage hier. Qu'est-ce que tu as mis?

J'ai mis un maillot de bain et des sandales.

- **Imagine que tu es allé(e) à une boum hier. Qu'est-ce que tu as mis?**
- **Imagine que tu es allé(e) en ville hier. Qu'est-ce que tu as mis?**
- **Imagine que tu es allé(e) au stade hier. Qu'est-ce que tu as mis?**
- **Imagine que tu es allé(e) à un pique-nique hier. Qu'est-ce que tu as mis?**

Compréhension
Answers

1. Elles vont dans un magasin de vêtements.
2. Delphine va acheter une nouvelle robe.
3. Elle va acheter une robe parce qu'elle va aller au mariage de sa cousine.
4. Une robe est jaune et l'autre est rouge.
5. Elle choisit la robe rouge.
6. Elle préfère la robe rouge parce qu'elle est plus jolie que la robe jaune.
7. Elle est trop petite.
8. Elle doit maigrir.

Note culturelle

Cultural note In France, window displays almost always include the prices of the items shown. Only the most expensive designer boutiques do not indicate prices. Ask students to hypothesize why the designer boutiques do not show their prices.

SECTION A

Communicative function
Describing actions

Teaching Resource Options

PRINT 

Workbook PE, pp. 163–168
Unit 6 Resource Book
  Audioscript, p. 94
  Communipak, pp. 140–158
  Workbook TE, pp. 69–74

AUDIO & VISUAL 

Audio Program
CD 3 Tracks 32, 33

Overhead Transparencies
39 **-ir** Verbs
40 Adjectives *beau, nouveau, vieux*
6 Clock face *Quelle heure est-il?*

TECHNOLOGY 

Power Presentations

Teaching strategy Using subject pronoun cue cards, have students conjugate other **-ir** verbs orally and in writing (e.g., **choisir, réussir**). Remind students that in the present tense of **-ir** verbs, all final consonants are silent.

 **PRACTICE** saying who finishes a race

1. Je finis.
2. Tu ne finis pas.
3. Nous finissons.
4. Vous ne finissez pas.
5. Éric finit.
6. Stéphanie ne finit pas.
7. Frédéric et Marc ne finissent pas.
8. Anne et Cécile finissent.

Supplementary vocabulary

a) Some **-ir** verbs correspond to English verbs in **-ish**
  finir *to finish*
  établir *to establish*
  abolir *to abolish*

b) Verbs derived from adjectives often end in **-ir**

COLORS:
  (rouge) rougir *to blush, to turn red*
  (blanc, blanche) blanchir *to blanche, to turn white*
  (jaune) jaunir *to turn yellow*
  (brun) brunir *to turn brown, to tan*

SIZE:
  (grand) grandir *to grow tall*

Note:
  *(***gros, grosse***–fat)* **grossir**
  *(***maigre***–thin)* **maigrir**

A Les verbes réguliers en *-ir* 

Many French verbs end in **-ir.** Most of these verbs are conjugated like **finir** *(to finish)*. Note the forms of this verb in the present tense, paying special attention to the endings.

INFINITIVE	finir	STEM (infinitive minus **-ir**)	ENDINGS
PRESENT	Je **finis** à deux heures.	fin-	**-is**
	Tu **finis** à une heure.		**-is**
	Il/Elle **finit** à cinq heures.		**-it**
	Nous **finissons** à midi.		**-issons**
	Vous **finissez** à une heure.		**-issez**
	Ils/Elles **finissent** à minuit.		**-issent**

1 Le marathon de Paris

PARLER/ÉCRIRE Not all runners finish the Paris marathon. Say who does and who does not.

▶ Philippe (non) **Philippe ne finit pas.**

1. moi (oui)
2. toi (non)
3. nous (oui)
4. vous (non)
5. Éric (oui)
6. Stéphanie (non)
7. Frédéric et Marc (non)
8. Anne et Cécile (oui)

VOCABULAIRE Verbes réguliers en *-ir*

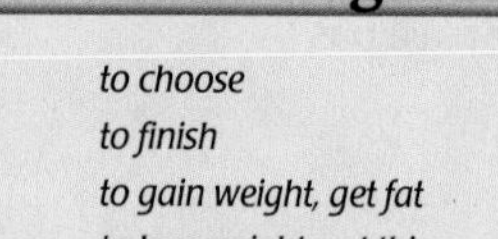

choisir	*to choose*	Quelle veste **choisis**-tu?
finir	*to finish*	Les classes **finissent** à midi.
grossir	*to gain weight, get fat*	Marc **grossit** parce qu'il mange beaucoup.
maigrir	*to lose weight, get thin*	Je **maigris** parce que je mange peu.
réussir	*to succeed*	Tu vas **réussir** parce que tu travailles!
réussir à un examen	*to pass an exam*	Nous **réussissons à nos examens.**

2 Le régime *(Diet)*

PARLER/ÉCRIRE Read about the following people. Say if they are gaining or losing weight.

▶ Philippe mange beaucoup de pizzas.
Il grossit. Il ne maigrit pas.

1. Vous faites des exercices.
2. Nous allons souvent au gymnase.
3. Vous êtes inactifs.
4. Je mange des carottes.
5. Monsieur Moreau adore la bonne cuisine.
6. Vous n'êtes pas très sportifs.
7. Ces personnes mangent trop *(too much)*.
8. Je nage, je joue au volley et je fais des promenades.

WARM-UP AND REVIEW Telling time

PROPS: Clock with movable hands or Transparency 6: Clock face *Quelle heure est-il?*

Review times by changing the hands on the clock.
  Quelle heure est-il?
  Il est deux heures vingt-cinq. ...

Have students practice forms of the verb **finir** together with clock times.
  [moi: 1h30] **Je finis à une heure et demie.**
  [vous: 8h45] **Vous finissez à neuf heures moins le quart.**
  [X: 3h10] **X finit à trois heures dix.**

3 Questions personnelles PARLER/ÉCRIRE

1. À quelle heure finissent les classes?
2. À quelle heure finit la classe de français?
3. Quand finit l'école cette année *(year)*?
4. Tu es invité(e) au restaurant ou au cinéma. Où choisis-tu d'aller?
5. Quand tu vas au cinéma avec ta famille, qui choisit le film?
6. En général, est-ce que tu réussis à tes examens? Est-ce que tu vas réussir à l'examen de français? Et tes copains?

B Les adjectifs *beau, nouveau* et *vieux*

The adjectives **beau** *(beautiful, good-looking)*, **nouveau** *(new)*, and **vieux** *(old)* are irregular.

		beau	nouveau	vieux
SINGULAR	MASC.	le **beau** manteau (le **bel** imper)	le **nouveau** manteau (le **nouvel** imper)	le **vieux** manteau (le **vieil** imper)
	FEM.	la **belle** veste	la **nouvelle** veste	la **vieille** veste
PLURAL	MASC.	les **beaux** manteaux	les **nouveaux** manteaux	les **vieux** manteaux
	FEM.	les **belles** vestes	les **nouvelles** vestes	les **vieilles** vestes

→ The adjectives **beau, nouveau,** and **vieux** usually come BEFORE the noun. If the noun begins with a vowel sound, there is liaison between the adjective and the noun.

les **nouveaux** ordinateurs les **belles** affiches les **vieux** impers

→ In the masculine singular, the liaison forms **bel, nouvel,** and **vieil** are used before a vowel sound. Note that **vieil** is pronounced like **vieille:**

un **vieil** imper une **vieille** robe

4 La collection de printemps

PARLER Mod Boutique is presenting its spring collection. Point out all the items you like to a French friend, using the appropriate forms of **beau.**

▶ une chemise
Regarde la belle chemise!

1. une robe
2. un pantalon
3. des jeans
4. des blousons
5. une veste
6. un imper
7. des sandales
8. un manteau
9. un chapeau
10. des tee-shirts

5 Différences d'opinion

PARLER François is showing the new things he bought to his sister Valérie. She prefers his old things.

▶ des chaussures

1. un polo
2. des lunettes de soleil
3. un imper
4. des affiches
5. une casquette
6. une montre
7. un ordinateur
8. des baskets
9. un survêtement

Tu aimes mes nouvelles chaussures?
En bien, non, je préfère tes vieilles chaussures.

TALKING ABOUT PAST EVENTS

Let's talk about what you ordered when you ate out the last time. Note that the past participle of **-ir** verbs ends in **-i.**

Est-ce que tu as choisi une pizza?
Oui, j'ai choisi une pizza.
(Non, je n'ai pas choisi de pizza.)

- **Est-ce que tu as choisi une salade?**
- **Est-ce que tu as choisi un steak?**
- **Est-ce que tu as choisi une glace?**
- **Est-ce que tu as choisi un soda?**
- **Est-ce que tu as choisi un café?**
- **Qu'est-ce que tu as choisi?**

Follow-up:
- **Est-ce que X a choisi une pizza? ...**

2 COMPREHENSION indicating who is gaining or losing weight

1. Vous maigrissez. Vous ne grossissez pas.
2. Nous maigrissons. Nous ne grossissons pas.
3. Vous grossissez. Vous ne maigrissez pas.
4. Je maigris. Je ne grossis pas.
5. M. Moreau grossit. Il ne maigrit pas.
6. Vous grossissez. Vous ne maigrissez pas.
7. Ces personnes grossissent. Elles ne maigrissent pas.
8. Je maigris. Je ne grossis pas.

3 COMMUNICATION answering personal questions

Answers will vary.
1. Les classes finissent à (trois heures).
2. La classe de français finit à (onze heures et demie).
3. L'école finit cette année le (quinze juin).
4. Je choisis d'aller (au restaurant).
5. Quand je vais au cinéma avec ma famille, (ma petite soeur) choisit le film.
6. En général, je réussis à mes examens. (Je ne réussis pas à mes examens.) Oui, je vais réussir à l'examen de français. (Non, je ne vais pas réussir à l'examen de français.) Mes copains vont réussir à l'examen de français. (Ils ne vont pas réussir à l'examen de français.)

SECTION B

Communicative function
Describing people and things (beautiful, new, old)

Pronunciation notes
- Remind students that in liaison "x" is pronounced /z/; the "il" of **vieil** is pronounced /j/.
- Point out that all three masculine singular liaison forms sound like the corresponding feminine singular forms.

4 PRACTICE saying things are beautiful

Regarde ...
1. la belle robe
2. le beau pantalon
3. les beaux jeans
4. les beaux blousons
5. la belle veste
6. le bel imper
7. les belles sandales
8. le beau manteau
9. le beau chapeau
10. les beaux tee-shirts

5 ROLE PLAY discussing preferences between old and new items

–Tu aimes ...
–Eh bien, non, je préfère ...
1. mon nouveau polo/ton vieux polo
2. mes nouvelles lunettes de soleil/tes vieilles lunettes de soleil
3. mon nouvel imper/ton vieil imper
4. mes nouvelles affiches/tes vieilles affiches
5. ma nouvelle casquette/ta vieille casquette
6. ma nouvelle montre/ta vieille montre
7. mon nouvel ordinateur/ton vieil ordinateur
8. mes nouveaux baskets/tes vieux baskets
9. mon nouveau survêtement/ton vieux survêtement

SECTION C

Communicative function
Expressing comparisons

Teaching Resource Options

PRINT 

Workbook PE, pp. 163–168
Unit 6 Resource Book
Audioscript, p. 95
Communipak, pp. 140–158
Video Activities, p. 89
Videoscript, pp. 92–93
Workbook TE, pp. 69–74

AUDIO & VISUAL 

Audio Program
CD 3 Track 34

TECHNOLOGY 

Power Presentations

VIDEO PROGRAM

VIDÉO DVD

MODULE 19

19.2 Mini-scenes: Comparaisons (49:36–51:10 min.)

19.3 Mini-scenes: Comparaisons (51:11–51:55 min.)

Language notes

- In French as in English, the second part of the comparison may be left out: **Cette robe est plus chère.**
- The comparative form of **bon marché** is **meilleur marché.** This form is not actively presented at this time.
- Remind students that the other comparative forms of **bon** follow the regular pattern:
  Cette cassette est **moins bonne que** ce CD.
  Est-ce que les Red Sox sont **aussi bons que** les Yankees?

C La comparaison avec les adjectifs

Note how COMPARISONS are expressed in French.

Cet imper est **plus cher que** ce manteau.	*... more expensive than ...*
Cette jupe est **plus jolie que** cette robe.	*... prettier than ...*
Paul est **moins sportif que** Patrick.	*... less athletic than ...*
Il est **moins amusant que** lui.	*... less amusing than ...*
Je suis **aussi grand que** toi.	*... as tall as ...*
Tu **n'**es **pas aussi timide que** moi.	*... not as timid as ...*

To make comparisons with adjectives, French speakers use the following constructions:

+ plus		**plus cher (que)**	*more expensive (than)*
− moins	+ ADJECTIVE (+ **que** ...)	**moins cher (que)**	*less expensive (than)*
= aussi		**aussi cher (que)**	*as expensive (as)*

→ Note the irregular **plus**-form of **bon** *(good)*:

plus + bon(ne) → meilleur(e) *(better)*

Ta pizza est **bonne**, mais mon sandwich est **meilleur**.

→ There is liaison after **plus** and **moins** when the next word begins with a vowel sound.

Cette robe-ci est **plus élégante**. Ce livre-là est **moins intéressant**.

→ In comparisons, the adjective always agrees with the noun (or pronoun) it describes.

La jupe est plus **chère** que le chemisier.

Les vestes sont moins **chères** que les manteaux.

→ In comparisons with people, STRESS PRONOUNS are used after **que**.

Paul est plus petit **que moi.** Je suis plus grand **que lui.**

6 Comparaisons

PARLER/ÉCRIRE How much do you think the following pairs of items cost? Give your opinion, saying whether the first one is more expensive, less expensive, or as expensive as the second one.

▶ une guitare/une raquette — **Une guitare est plus (moins, aussi) chère qu'une raquette.**

1. un vélo/un scooter
2. une mobylette/une moto
3. une pizza/un sandwich
4. une télé/un ordinateur
5. des chaussures/des sandales
6. une casquette/des lunettes de soleil
7. des bottes/des tennis
8. un short/un maillot de bain
9. un baladeur/une montre
10. un portable/une mini-chaîne

COMPREHENSION Comparisons

PROPS: Plastic bag with 30 "money cards" (labeled with amounts from $50–$1000)

Have students come up and draw a "prize."

Vous êtes tous riches.
Vous avez gagné à la loterie hier.
Venez chercher vos prix!

Review numbers by asking what they drew.

X, montre-nous ton prix. [holds up $100]
Combien d'argent as-tu? [cent dollars]
Est-ce que X est riche aujourd'hui? [oui!]
Y, montre-nous ton prix. ...

Call up two students with different "prizes."

X et Y, venez ici.
Combien d'argent a X? [$100] **Et Y?** [$500]

VOCABULAIRE Expression pour la conversation

▶ ***How to introduce a personal opinion:***

à mon avis ... *in my opinion ...* **À mon avis,** le français est facile.

7 Expression personnelle

À mon avis, le tennis est plus (moins, aussi) intéressant que le ping-pong.

PARLER/ÉCRIRE Compare the following by using the adjectives suggested. Give your personal opinion.

▶ le tennis/intéressant/le ping-pong

1. le basket/intéressant/le foot
2. l'anglais/facile/le français
3. la classe de français/amusant/la classe d'anglais
4. la Floride/beau/la Californie
5. les Yankees/bon/les Red Sox
6. la cuisine américaine/bon/la cuisine française
7. les filles/intelligent/les garçons
8. l'argent *(money)*/important/l'amitié *(friendship)*

8  Et toi?

PARLER Use the appropriate stress pronouns in answering the questions below.

▶ **—Es-tu plus grand(e) que ton copain?**
—Oui, je suis plus grand(e) que lui.
(Non, je suis moins grand(e) que lui.)
(Je suis aussi grand(e) que lui.)

1. Es-tu plus grand(e) que ta mère?
2. Es-tu aussi riche que Bill Gates?
3. Es-tu plus sportif (sportive) que tes copains?
4. Es-tu plus intelligent(e) qu'Einstein?

PRONONCIATION ill /j/

Les lettres «ill»

In the middle of a word, the letters "**ill**" usually represent the sound /j/ like the "**y**" of *yes*.

Répétez: **maillot travaillez oreille vieille fille famille juillet**
En juillet, Mireille va travailler pour sa vieille tante.

maillot

At the end of a word, the sound /j/ is sometimes spelled **il**.

Répétez: **appareil-photo vieil travail** *(job)*
Mon oncle a un vieil appareil-photo.

EXCEPTION: The letters **ill** are pronounced /il/ in the following words:

Répétez: **ville village mille Lille**

Place Y next to the chalkboard to the left, and place X to the right.

Mais Y est plus riche que X.

Between the two, write: **plus riche que.**

Call on other students to demonstrate the other comparisons, also writing them.

Z est moins riche que B. [$300 < $650]
A est aussi riche que C. [$400 = $400]

Ask all students to hold up their cards.

Montrez-nous vos prix. Qui a $200? [M]
Qui est plus riche que M? Qui est moins riche que lui/elle? Qui est aussi riche?

Have students hand around their "prizes."

En ce moment, Z est moins riche que M.
S'il te plaît, D, va donner tes $1000 à Z.
Maintenant Z est plus riche que B., etc.

6 COMMUNICATION expressing one's opinion about relative prices

Answers will vary.

1. Un vélo est moins cher qu'un scooter.
2. Une mobylette est moins chère qu'une moto.
3. Une pizza est plus (aussi / moins) chère qu'un sandwich.
4. Une télé est moins chère qu'un ordinateur.
5. Des chaussures sont aussi (plus / moins) chères que des sandales.
6. Une casquette est moins (aussi / moins) chère que des lunettes de soleil.
7. Des bottes sont aussi (plus / moins) chères que des tennis.
8. Un short est moins (aussi / plus) cher qu'un maillot de bain.
9. Un baladeur est plus cher qu'une montre.
10. Un portable est moins cher qu'une mini-chaîne.

7 COMMUNICATION comparing people and things

Answers will vary.

1. À mon avis, le basket est moins (plus / aussi) intéressant que le foot.
2. À mon avis, l'anglais est plus (moins / aussi) facile que le français.
3. À mon avis, la classe de français est plus (moins / aussi) amusante que la classe d'anglais.
4. À mon avis, la Floride est aussi (moins / plus) beau que la Californie.
5. À mon avis, les Yankees sont moins bons (meilleurs / aussi bons) que les Red Sox.
6. À mon avis, la cuisine américaine est moins bonne (aussi bonne / meilleure) que la cuisine française.
7. À mon avis, les filles sont aussi (plus / moins) intelligentes que les garçons.
8. À mon avis, l'argent est moins (aussi / plus) important que l'amitié.

Teaching strategies

- Remind students that the adjective must agree with the subject.
- For items 5 and 6, remind students that **plus + bon(ne) → meilleur(e);** as in English, there is no change for **moins bon(ne)** and **aussi bon(ne).**

8 COMMUNICATION comparing oneself to others

1. Oui, je suis plus grand(e) qu'elle. (Non, je suis moins grand[e] qu'elle./ Je suis aussi grand[e] qu'elle.)
2. Non, je suis moins riche que lui. (Oui, je suis plus riche que lui. / Je suis aussi riche que lui.)
3. Oui, je suis plus sportif (sportive) qu'eux. (Non, je suis moins sportif [sportive] qu'eux. / Je suis aussi sportif [sportive] qu'eux.)
4. Je suis aussi intelligent(e) que lui. (Oui, je suis plus intelligent[e] que lui. / Non, je suis moins intelligent[e] que lui.)

PRONUNCIATION

Note that **tranquille** *(quiet)* also contains the sound /il/: /trãkil/

À VOTRE TOUR

Main Topic
- Recapitulation and review

Teaching Resource Options

PRINT 

Workbook PE, pp. 163–168
Unit 6 Resource Book
- Audioscript, p. 95
- Communipak, pp. 140–158
- Family Involvement, pp. 86–87
- Workbook TE, pp. 69–74

Assessment
- Lesson 19 Quiz, pp. 98–99
- Portfolio Assessment, Unit 1 URB pp. 155–164
- Audioscript for Quiz 19, p. 97
- Answer Keys, pp. 230–234

AUDIO & VISUAL 

Audio Program
CD 3 Tracks 35, 36
CD 15 Track 11

TECHNOLOGY

Test Generator CD-ROM/McDougal Littell Assessment System

1 COMPREHENSION

1. d
2. a
3. b
4. c

2 GUIDED ORAL EXPRESSION

Answers will vary.

1. – Tu achètes la chaîne hi-fi ou le baladeur?
   – J'achète le baladeur (la chaîne hi-fi).
   – Pourquoi?
   – Parce qu'il est plus petit et moins cher. (Je préfère la chaîne hi-fi parce qu'elle est meilleure et plus grande.)
2. – Tu préfères les bottes ou les chaussures?
   – Je préfère les chaussures (les bottes).
   – Pourquoi?
   – Parce qu'elles sont plus jolies et plus confortables. (Je préfère les bottes parce qu'elles sont meilleures et moins chères.)
3. – Tu choisis le chien jaune ou le chien blanc?
   – Je choisis le chien jaune (le chien blanc).
   – Pourquoi?
   – Parce qu'il est plus petit et plus mignon. (Je choisis le chien blanc parce qu'il est plus grand et plus joli.)
4. – Tu amènes Alice ou Anne?
   – J'amène Alice (Anne).
   – Pourquoi?
   – Parce qu'elle est plus intéressante (sympathique, mignonne).
5. – Tu invites Paul ou Philippe?
   – J'invite Philippe (Paul).
   – Pourquoi?
   – Parce qu'il est plus amusant (intelligent, beau).

À votre tour!

OBJECTIFS

Now you can …
- make comparisons
- discuss your choices

1 La bonne réponse

PARLER François and Stéphanie are shopping. Match François's questions with Stéphanie's answers. You may act out the dialogue with a friend.

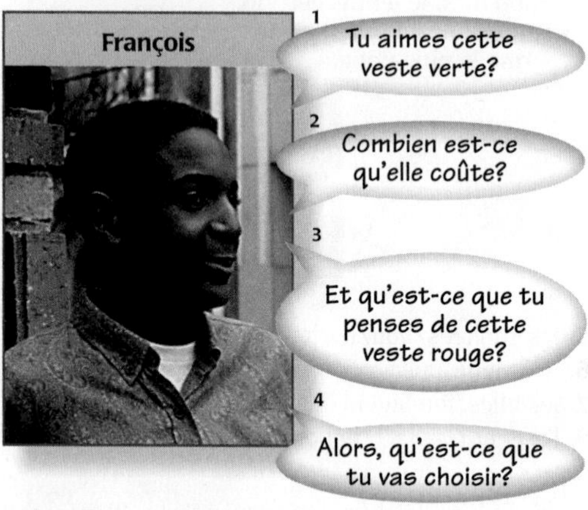

François
1 Tu aimes cette veste verte?
2 Combien est-ce qu'elle coûte?
3 Et qu'est-ce que tu penses de cette veste rouge?
4 Alors, qu'est-ce que tu vas choisir?

Stéphanie
a 300 euros.
b À mon avis, elle est moins jolie.
c La veste bleue. Elle est meilleur marché et elle est aussi élégante.
d Oui, mais elle est très chère.

2 Créa-dialogue

PARLER With a classmate, prepare a dialogue comparing the items in one of the following pictures. Use the suggested verb and some of the suggested adjectives.

▶ —Tu <u>choisis</u> <u>la voiture rouge</u> ou <u>la voiture noire</u>?
—Je <u>choisis</u> <u>la voiture rouge</u>.
—Pourquoi?
—Parce qu'<u>elle</u> est <u>plus petite</u> et <u>moins chère</u>.

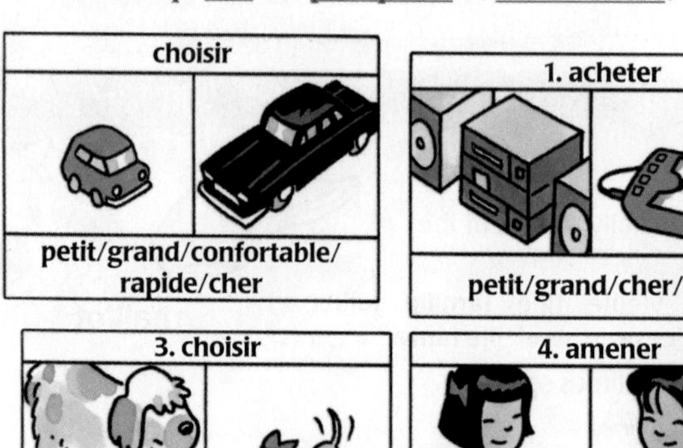

À VOTRE TOUR

Depending on your goals and objectives, you may or may not wish to assign all of the activities in the **À votre tour** section.

INCLUSION

Repetitive Prepare students for Activity 2 by reviewing the vocabulary items, writing them on the board and having students repeat them three times after you. Pair at-risk students with stronger students and have them quiz each other on the vocabulary. Have students complete the dialogue.

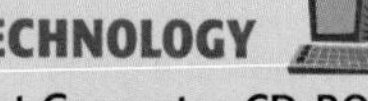

3 Choix personnels

PARLER Select two people or two items in each of the following categories and ask a classmate to indicate which one he/she prefers. You may ask your classmate to explain why.

▶ 2 actors

Tu préfères Tom Hanks ou Brad Pitt?

Parce que Brad Pitt est plus mignon que Tom Hanks.
(plus beau, plus jeune ...)

CATEGORIES:
- ▶ 2 actors
- 2 actresses
- 2 singers (male)
- 2 singers (female)
- 2 baseball teams
- 2 cities
- 2 restaurants in your town
- 2 stores in your town

4 Composition: Portrait comparatif

ÉCRIRE Write a description of yourself, comparing yourself to six other people (your friends, your family, well-known personalities, etc.) You may use some of the following adjectives:

grand petit jeune vieux amusant intelligent bête sportif sympathique timide gentil génial optimiste

▶

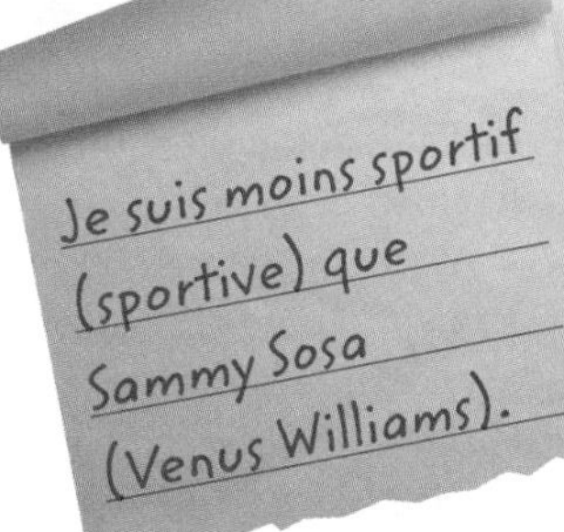

5 Composition: Comparaisons personnelles

▶

Mon cousin s'appelle Patrick. Il a quinze ans. Je suis plus jeune que lui, mais il est moins grand que moi ...

ÉCRIRE Choose a friend or relative about your age. Give this person's name and age. Then, in a short paragraph, compare yourself to that person in terms of physical appearance and personality traits.

Portfolio Assessment

You will probably select only one speaking activity and one writing activity to go into the students' portfolios for Unit 6.

In this lesson, Act. 2 lends itself well to an oral portfolio recording.

Act. 4 and 5 are good writing portfolio topics.

Inclusion

Structured Review the structure of the comparisons, writing out the chart from p. 280 on the board. Ask students to generate sentences using comparisons out loud. Then have them write the composition for Activity 4. (Provide writing prompts as needed.)

3 Guided Oral Expression

Answers will vary.
- –Tu préfères Cameron Diaz ou Julia Roberts?
  –Je préfère Cameron Diaz.
  –Pourquoi?
  –Parce qu'elle est plus intéressante que Julia Roberts.
- –Tu préfères Will Smith ou Rob Thomas?
  –Je préfère Rob Thomas.
  –Pourquoi?
  –Parce qu'il chante mieux que Will Smith.
- –Tu préfères Sheryl Crow ou Jewel?
  –Je préfère Jewel.
  –Pourquoi?
  –Parce qu'elle est plus sympathique que Sheryl Crow.
- –Tu préfères les Red Sox ou les White Sox?
  –Je préfère les Red Sox.
  –Pourquoi?
  –Parce qu'ils sont plus sportifs que les White Sox.
- –Tu préfères Boston ou Pittsburgh?
  –Je préfère Boston.
  –Pourquoi?
  –Parce que Boston est plus belle que Pittsburgh.
- –Tu préfères Chez Joseph ou Maison Albert?
  –Je préfère Maison Albert.
  –Pourquoi?
  –Parce que Maison Albert est moins cher que Chez Joseph.
- –Tu préfères Le Bon Marché ou Le Printemps?
  –Je préfère Le Printemps.
  –Pourquoi?
  –Parce que Le Printemps est moins cher que Le Bon Marché.

4 Written Self-Expression

Answers will vary.
- Je suis moins sportif (sportive) que Sammy Sosa (Venus Williams).
- Je suis plus sportif (sportive) que mon frère.
- Je suis plus grand(e) que ma soeur.
- Je suis plus petit(e) que Ben Affleck.
- Je suis moins jeune que mon frère.
- Je suis plus vieux (vieille) que ma petite soeur.
- Je suis moins amusant(e) que ma meilleure amie.
- Je suis plus intelligent(e) que mon meilleur ami.
- Je suis aussi timide que ma petite soeur.
- Je suis moins élégant(e) que ma meilleure amie.
- Je suis aussi mignon(ne) que ma cousine.

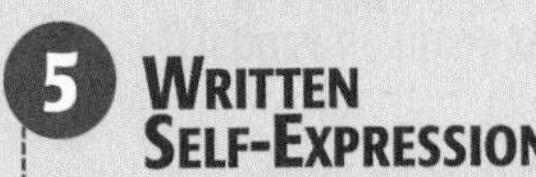

5 Written Self-Expression

Answers will vary.
Mon amie s'appelle Louise. Elle a treize ans. Elle est plus jeune que moi. Elle est aussi plus jolie. Mais moi, je suis plus intélligent(e) et plus drôle qu'elle. Elle est aussi grande que moi. On joue au basket ensemble, mais elle est plus sportive que moi. Elle est aussi plus timide.

Leçon 20

Main Topics Discovering what stores are selling, Giving suggestions and commands

Teaching Resource Options

PRINT 

Workbook PE, pp. 169–175
Activités pour tous PE, pp. 103–105
Block Scheduling Copymasters, pp. 153–159
Unit 6 Resource Book
- *Activités pour tous* TE, pp. 109–111
- Audioscript, pp. 132, 133–135
- Communipak, pp. 140–158
- Lesson Plans, pp. 112–113
- Block Scheduling Lesson Plans, pp. 114–115
- Absent Student Copymasters, pp. 117–121
- Video Activities, pp. 124–129
- Videoscript, pp. 130–131
- Workbook TE, pp. 101–107

AUDIO & VISUAL 

Audio Program
CD 3 Tracks 37, 38
CD 10 Tracks 21–27

Overhead Transparencies
20 Objects (a) *Quelques objets* (a)

TECHNOLOGY 

Online Workbook

VIDEO PROGRAM

VIDÉO DVD

MODULE 20
Alice a un job

TOTAL TIME: 6:39 min.
DVD Disk 2
Videotape 3 (COUNTER: 53:31 min.)

20.1 Dialogue: Alice a un job (54:15–55:10 min.)

20.2 Mini-scenes: Listening – Qu'est-ce qu'on vend? (55:11–55:59 min.)

20.3 Mini-scenes: Speaking – Qu'est-ce qu'on vend ici? (56:00–56:43 min.)

20.4 Mini-scenes: Listening – On dîne? (56:44–57:19 min.)

20.5 Mini-scenes: Speaking – On joue au tennis? (57:20–58:13 min.)

20.6 Vignette culturelle: Au magasin hi-fi (58:14–1:00:00 min.)

Comprehension practice Play the entire module through as an introduction to the lesson.

LEÇON 20

Alice a un job

VIDÉO DVD AUDIO

Alice a un nouveau job. Elle travaille dans un magasin de matériel audio-visuel. Dans ce magasin, on vend toutes sortes de choses: des baladeurs, des chaînes hi-fi, des radiocassettes/CD, des lecteurs de DVD ...

on / vend / toutes: one, they / sell(s) / all

Un jour, son cousin Jérôme lui rend visite. *(lui rend visite: comes to visit her)*

Jérôme: Salut, ça va?
Alice: Oui, ça va.
Jérôme: Et ce nouveau job?
Alice: C'est super.
Jérôme: Qu'est-ce qu'on vend dans ton magasin?
Alice: Eh bien, tu vois, on vend toutes sortes de matériel audio-visuel ... Moi, je vends des mini-chaînes. *(vois: see)*
Jérôme: Tu es bien payée? *(payée: paid)*
Alice: Non, on n'est pas très bien payé, mais on a des réductions sur l'équipement stéréo et sur les CD et les DVD.
Jérôme: Qu'est-ce que tu vas faire avec ton argent? *(argent: money)*
Alice: Je ne sais pas ... J'ai envie de voyager cet été. *(ai envie de: feel like)*
Jérôme: Tu as de la chance. Moi aussi, j'ai envie de voyager, mais je n'ai pas d'argent. *(as de la chance: are lucky)*
Alice: Écoute, Jérôme, si tu as besoin d'argent, fais comme moi. *(besoin / fais comme moi: need / do as I do)*
Jérôme: Comment? *(What?)*
Alice: Cherche un job! *(Find)*

WARM-UP AND REVIEW

PROP: Transparency 20: Objects (a) *Quelques objets* (a)
Review the names of the objects.
Qu'est-ce que c'est? C'est une radio.
X, est-ce que tu as une radio?
Oui, j'ai une radio. (Je n'ai pas de radio.)

Ask where one can buy these objects locally. Introduce the phrase **on achète.**

Ici, à [name of town], **où est-ce qu'on achète des radios?**
On achète des radios à [name of local store].

Tell students that in the opening scene of the video they will visit a hi-fi store.

Compréhension

1. Où travaille Alice?
2. Qu'est-ce qu'elle vend?
3. Qu'est-ce qu'elle espère faire cet été?
4. Pourquoi est-ce que Jérôme ne va pas voyager?
5. Qu'est-ce que Jérôme doit *(must)* faire pour avoir de l'argent?

NOTE culturelle

L'argent° des jeunes

Contrairement à beaucoup de jeunes Américains, les jeunes Français n'ont pas de travail° régulier. Par exemple, ils ne travaillent pas dans les supermarchés, les boutiques ou les stations-service. Occasionnellement, ils font des petits jobs pour leurs voisins: baby-sitting, promenade de chiens,° lavage° de voitures, etc.

En général, ils dépendent de la générosité de leurs parents pour leur argent. Le montant° qu'ils reçoivent varie avec l'âge, les résultats scolaires,° et la situation économique de la famille. Ils reçoivent aussi de l'argent de leur famille et de leurs parrains° et marraines° pour des occasions spéciales: Noël, jour de l'An° et anniversaire.

Voici combien d'argent les jeunes Français ont en moyenne: °

ÂGE	MONTANT PAR MOIS
2-7 ans	5 euros
8-14 ans	15 euros
15-17 ans	100 euros

argent *money* **travail** *work*
promenade de chiens *dog walking* **lavage** *washing*
montant *amount* **résultats scolaires** *report cards*
parrains *godfathers* **marraines** *godmothers*
jour de l'An *New Year's Day* **en moyenne** *on the average*

COMPARAISONS CULTURELLES

- Compare how teenagers in France and in the United States get their spending money.
- Why do you think French teenagers do not have regular jobs?

TALKING ABOUT PAST EVENTS

Let's talk about what you and your family did during a recent vacation.

Toi et ta famille, est-ce que vous avez voyagé pendant les vacances?
Oui, nous avons voyagé.
(Non, nous n'avons pas voyagé.)

- **Où êtes-vous allés?**
- **Est-ce que vous êtes allés à la Maison Blanche?**
- **Est-ce que vous avez trouvé un bon hôtel?**
- **Est-ce que vous avez dîné au restaurant?**
- **Qu'est-ce que vous avez visité?**

Compréhension Answers

1. Alice travaille dans un magasin de matériel audio-visuel.
2. Elle vend des mini-chaînes.
3. Elle espère voyager.
4. Il n'a pas d'argent.
5. Il doit chercher un job.

Teaching Suggestion Give students copies of the dialogue on p. 284. As they are working on the questions for the **Compréhension** activity, ask students to highlight or circle the parts of the dialogue which answer the questions in the activity.

Pre-AP skill: Indicate where in the text the answer to a question is found.

Teaching Suggestion Have students look online at classifed ads in a French newspaper. Which job interests them the most?

Cultural note for **Comparaisons culturelles**

Some reasons why French teenagers do not have regular jobs:

(1) They have to spend a lot of time on their schoolwork.

(2) French laws discourage teenage work.

Teaching note Have students go to a job posting website and enter "French" as a keyword to see what positions are available that require French language skills.

Teaching Resource Options

PRINT 

Workbook PE, pp. 169–175
Unit 6 Resource Book
 Communipak, pp. 140–158
 Workbook TE, pp. 101–107

TECHNOLOGY 

Power Presentations

Language notes

- Point out that **payer** is also a "boot" verb (see p. 268).
- Some students may understand the **avoir** idioms better if they think of them as *I have need of...* and *I have desire of...*

Casual speech One can also say:
Ce CD coûte combien?
Tu as combien d'argent?
Tu as combien de CD?

Supplementary vocabulary

un euro
un centime
un eurocentime
l'argent de poche *allowance, pocket money*
la monnaie *change*
un job *(part-time) job*
économiser *to save money*
par jour *per day, a day*
par semaine *per week, a week*
par heure *per hour, an hour*

1 EXCHANGES asking how many things people have

Answers will vary.
–Combien de (d') ... as tu?
–J'ai (...) ... (Je n'ai pas de [d'] ...)

1. frères/(deux) frères/frères
2. soeurs (deux) soeurs/soeurs
3. casquettes/(trois) casquettes/casquettes
4. affiches/(dix) affiches/affiches
5. tee-shirts/(cinq) tee-shirts/tee-shirts
6. jeans/(deux) jeans/jeans
7. billets d'un dollar/(quatre) billets d'un dollar/billets d'un dollar
8. pièces de dix cents/(trois) pièces de dix cents/pièces de dix cents

Pronunciation Be sure students pronounce the **de** of **combien de** correctly with a mute "e" so that it does not sound like **des.**

Language note There is no elision before **un** when it represents the number *one:*

un billet de un dollar. (cf. item 7)

Variation (using casual speech) **Tu as combien de CD?**

VOCABULAIRE L'argent

NOMS

l'argent *(m.)*	*money*	**une pièce** *coin*
un billet	*bill, paper money*	

ADJECTIFS

riche ≠ pauvre *rich ≠ poor*

VERBES

dépenser	*to spend*	Je n'aime pas **dépenser** mon argent.
gagner	*to earn,*	Je **gagne** 10 dollars par *(per)* jour.
	to win	Tu joues bien. Tu vas **gagner** le match.
payer	*to pay, pay for*	Qui va **payer** aujourd'hui?

EXPRESSIONS

combien + VERB		*how much*	**Combien** coûte cette chaîne hi-fi?
combien de + NOUN		*how much*	**Combien d'**argent as-tu?
		how many	**Combien de** CD as-tu?
avoir besoin de	+ NOUN	*to need*	**J'ai besoin de** 5 dollars.
	+ INFINITIVE	*to need to, have to*	**J'ai besoin de** travailler.
avoir envie de	+ NOUN	*to want*	**J'ai envie d'**une pizza.
	+ INFINITIVE	*to feel like, want to*	**J'ai envie de** manger.

→ Verbs like **payer** that end in **-yer**, have the following stem change:

y → i in the **je, tu, il, ils** forms of the verb

	je **paie**	tu **paies**	il/elle **paie**	ils/elles **paient**
but:	nous **payons**	vous **payez**		

L'ARGENT NE FAIT PAS LE BONHEUR

Money does not buy happiness.

1  Combien?

PARLER Ask your classmates how many of the following they have.

▶ des CD —**Combien de CD as-tu?**
—**J'ai vingt CD.**
(Je n'ai pas de CD.)

1. des frères
2. des soeurs
3. des casquettes
4. des affiches
5. des tee-shirts
6. des jeans
7. des billets d'un dollar
8. des pièces de dix cents

INCLUSION

Metacognitive Model the sounds of each conjugation of the verb **payer** to show students how they are similar. Ask them to repeat what they hear. Write the forms on the board. Have students say and then write phonetic transcriptions for each verb form.

2 Qu'est-ce que tu as envie de faire?

PARLER Ask your classmates if they feel like doing the following things.

▶ aller au cinéma

1. aller au restaurant
2. manger une pizza
3. aller à la piscine
4. parler français
5. écouter un CD
6. visiter Paris
7. jouer au Frisbee
8. acheter une moto
9. faire une promenade
10. surfer sur l'Internet

Est-ce que tu as envie d'aller au cinéma?
Oui, j'ai envie d'aller au cinéma.
Et toi?
Non, je n'ai pas envie d'aller au cinéma.

3 Au restaurant

PARLER/ÉCRIRE The following students are in a restaurant in Quebec. Say what they feel like buying and estimate how much money they need.

▶ Hélène/une pizza
Hélène a envie d'une pizza. Elle a besoin de cinq dollars.

1. Marc/un sandwich
2. nous/une glace
3. moi/un soda
4. toi/un jus d'orange
5. vous/une salade
6. mes copains/un steak

4 Questions personnelles PARLER/ÉCRIRE

1. Est-ce que tu as un job? Où est-ce que tu travailles? Combien est-ce que tu gagnes par *(per)* heure? par semaine?
2. Quand tu vas au cinéma, qui paie? toi ou ton copain (ta copine)?
3. Combien est-ce que tu paies quand tu achètes un hamburger? une pizza? une glace?
4. Est-ce que tu as des pièces dans ta poche *(pocket)*? quelles pièces?
5. Qui est représenté sur le billet d'un dollar? sur le billet de cinq dollars? sur le billet de dix dollars?
6. Est-ce que tu préfères dépenser ou économiser *(to save)* ton argent? Pourquoi?
7. Est-ce que tu espères être riche un jour? Pourquoi?

Le Vendôme
36, Côte de la Montagne
Québec
tél 692.0557
LE VENDÔME

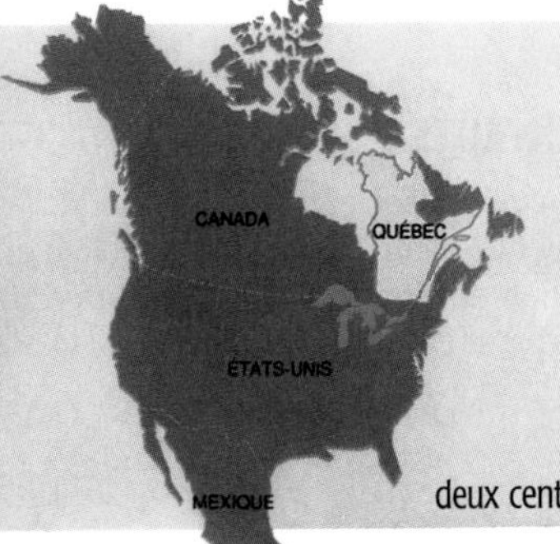

REALIA NOTE

Ask students:
Comment s'appelle ce restaurant? [Le Vendôme]
Quelle est l'adresse du restaurant? [36, Côte de la Montagne]
Quel est son numéro de téléphone? [692.0557]

NOTE: Remind students that in Quebec telephone numbers are given digit by digit.

CULTURE NOTE

The Château Frontenac (a four-star hotel) is located in upper town **(la Haute Ville)** and **Le Vendôme** restaurant is located in lower town **(la Basse Ville).** The oldest part of Quebec City is located around the **Place Royale** in lower town. Here one finds historic houses, restaurants, boutiques, antique stores, and art galleries. A **funiculaire** and the Breakneck Stairs **(l'Escalier Casse-Cou)** connect lower town with upper town.

2 EXCHANGES discussing what one feels like doing

–Est-ce que tu as envie de (d') ...
–Oui, j'ai envie de (d') ...
–Et toi?
–Non, je n'ai pas envie de (d') ...

1. aller au restaurant
2. manger une pizza
3. aller à la piscine
4. parler français
5. écouter un CD
6. visiter Paris
7. jouer au Frisbee
8. acheter une moto
9. faire une promenade
10. surfer sur l'Internet

3 COMPREHENSION describing what people in a restaurant want and what it costs

Answers will vary.

1. Marc a envie d'un sandwich. Il a besoin de (quatre) dollars.
2. Nous avons envie d'une glace. Nous avons besoin de (deux) dollars.
3. J'ai envie d'un soda. J'ai besoin de (deux) dollars.
4. Tu as envie d'un jus d'orange. Tu as besoin de (deux) dollars.
5. Vous avez envie d'une salade. Vous avez besoin de (sept) dollars.
6. Mes copains ont envie d'un steak. Ils ont besoin de (dix) dollars.

Expansion Have students discuss their wants and needs by completing the following open-ended sentences.
J'ai envie de (d')... (réussir en français.)
J'ai besoin de (d')... (étudier souvent.)

4 COMMUNICATION answering personal questions

Answers will vary.

1. Oui, j'ai un job. Je travaille dans un magasin. Je gagne sept dollars par heure et soixante-dix dollars par semaine. (Non, je n'ai pas de job.)
2. Quand je vais au cinéma, je (mon copain / ma copine) paie.
3. Je paie quatre dollars et demi quand j'achète un hamburger. Je paie six dollars quand j'achète une pizza. Je paie un dollar et demi quand j'achète une glace.
4. Oui, j'ai des pièces dans ma poche. J'ai deux «quarters», trois «dimes» et un «nickle». (Non, je n'ai pas de pièces dans ma poche.)
5. George Washington est représenté sur le billet d'un dollar, Abraham Lincoln sur le billet de cinq dollars et Alexander Hamilton sur le billet de dix dollars.
6. Je préfère dépenser mon argent. Je travaille pour avoir de l'argent et pour acheter des choses. (Je préfère économiser mon argent. Je veux être riche un jour.)
7. Oui, j'espère être riche un jour. Avec beaucoup d'argent, je peux beaucoup dépenser et beaucoup économiser! (Non, je n'espère pas être riche un jour. L'argent n'est pas important.)

SECTION A

Communicative function
Talking about people in general

Teaching Resource Options

PRINT

Workbook PE, pp. 169–175
Unit 6 Resource Book
 Communipak, pp. 140–158
 Video Activities, pp. 125–127
 Videoscript, pp. 130–131
 Workbook TE, pp. 101–107

TECHNOLOGY 

Power Presentations

VIDEO PROGRAM

VIDÉO DVD

MODULE 20

20.2 Mini-scenes: Qu'est-ce qu'on vend? (55:11–55:59 min.)

20.3 Mini-scenes: Qu'est-ce qu'on vend ici? (56:00–56:43 min.)

20.4 Mini-scenes: On dîne? (56:44–57:19 min.)

20.5 Mini-scenes: On joue au tennis? (57:20–58:13 min.)

Looking ahead The forms of **vendre** are presented in section B of this lesson.

5 COMPREHENSION discussing what languages are spoken in certain cities

1. À Québec, on parle français (ou anglais).
2. À Boston, on parle anglais.
3. À Madrid, on parle espagnol.
4. À Bruxelles, on parle français.
5. À Genève, on parle français.
6. À Tokyo, on parle japonais.
7. À Buenos Aires, on parle espagnol.
8. À Londres, on parle anglais.
9. À Rome, on parle italien.
10. À Beijing, on parle chinois.

Variation (using the negative in many responses)
– Est-ce qu'on parle français à Acapulco?
– Non, on ne parle pas français.

Challenge Have students turn to the world map on pp. R2–R3. They can ask additional questions: **Est-ce qu'on parle français à Dakar?**, etc.

A Le pronom *on*

Note the use of the subject pronoun **on** in the sentences below.

Qu'est-ce qu'**on** vend ici?	*What do **they** (do **you**) sell here?*
Où est-ce qu'**on** achète ce CD?	*Where does **one** (do **people**) buy that CD?*
En France, **on** parle français.	*In France, **people (you, they)** speak French.*

The pronoun **on** is used in GENERAL statements, according to the construction:

on + il/elle - form of verb	**On** travaille beaucoup.	***One** works a lot.* ***They** work a lot.* ***You** work a lot.* ***People** work a lot.*

▶ There is liaison after **on** when the next word begins with a vowel sound.
 Est-ce qu'on‿invite Stéphanie à la boum?

▶ In conversation, **on** is often used instead of **nous:**

—Est-ce qu'**on** dîne à la maison?	*Are **we** having dinner at home?*
—Non, **on** va au restaurant.	*No, **we** are going to the restaurant.*

Ici on parle ...

PARLER/ÉCRIRE Imagine that you have won a grand prize of a world tour. Say which of the following languages is spoken in each of the cities that you will be visiting.

▶ Acapulco

À Acapulco, on parle espagnol.

1. Québec
2. Boston
3. Madrid
4. Bruxelles
5. Genève
6. Tokyo
7. Buenos Aires
8. Londres *(London)*
9. Rome
10. Beijing

anglais espagnol français
japonais italien chinois

COMMUNAUTÉS

In a multi-cultural society, people speak different languages and have different customs. How many different languages are spoken at home by classmates in your school? What are some of their different customs and different celebrations? As a class project, put up a wall map showing their countries of origin. Do some come from French-speaking areas?

INCLUSION

Cumulative Remind students of the 3rd person singular verb endings. Write 5-6 sentences using this form on the board. Then have students work in pairs to create sentences using **on**. Have them write the sentences in their notebooks, writing out a phonetic transcription of **on** in each sentence to show liaisons.

VOCABULAIRE Expression pour la conversation

▶ *How to indicate approval:*

C'est une bonne idée! *That's a good idea!*

6 Projets de week-end

PARLER Suggest possible weekend activities to your classmates. They will let you know whether they think each idea is a good one or not.

▶ aller au café

1. jouer aux jeux vidéo?
2. aller à la bibliothèque?
3. aller à la plage?
4. téléphoner au professeur?
5. faire une promenade à vélo?
6. aller dans les magasins?
7. acheter des vêtements?
8. écouter des CD?

7 En Amérique et en France

PARLER An American student and a French student are comparing certain aspects of life in their own countries. Play both roles.

▶ jouer au baseball (au foot)

En Amérique, on joue au baseball.
En France, on joue au foot.

1. parler anglais (français)
2. étudier le français (l'anglais)
3. dîner à six heures (à huit heures)
4. manger des hamburgers (des omelettes)
5. voyager souvent en avion *(by plane)* (en train)
6. skier dans le Colorado (dans les Alpes)
7. aller à l'école le mercredi après-midi (le samedi matin)
8. chanter «la Bannière étoilée» *("The Star-Spangled Banner")* («la Marseillaise»)

8 Expression personnelle

PARLER/ÉCRIRE Describe what you, your friends, and your relatives generally do. Complete the following sentences according to your personal routine.

1. À la maison, on dîne … (à quelle heure?)
2. À la télé, on regarde … (quel programme?)
3. À la cafétéria de l'école, on mange … (quoi?)
4. En été, on va … (où?)
5. Le week-end, avec mes copains, on va … (où?)
6. Avec mes copains, on joue … (à quel sport? à quel jeu?)
7. On a une classe de français … (quels jours?)
8. On a un examen de français … (quel jour?)

Supplementary vocabulary
C'est une mauvaise idée.

6 EXCHANGES suggesting weekend activities and indicating one's approval

1. –On joue aux jeux vidéo?
   –Oui, c'est une bonne idée! (Non, ce n'est pas une bonne idée.)
2. –On va à la bibliothèque?
   –Oui, c'est une bonne idée! (Non, ce n'est pas une bonne idée.)
3. –On va à la plage?
   –Oui, c'est une bonne idée! (Non, ce n'est pas une bonne idée.)
4. –On téléphone au professeur?
   –Oui, c'est une bonne idée! (Non, ce n'est pas une bonne idée.)
5. –On fait une promenade à vélo?
   –Oui, c'est une bonne idée! (Non, ce n'est pas une bonne idée.)
6. –On va dans les magasins?
   –Oui, c'est une bonne idée! (Non, ce n'est pas une bonne idée.)
7. –On achète des vêtements?
   –Oui, c'est une bonne idée! (Non, ce n'est pas une bonne idée.)
8. –On écoute des CD?
   –Oui, c'est une bonne idée! (Non, ce n'est pas une bonne idée.)

7 ROLE PLAY describing cultural differences

1. –En Amérique, on parle anglais.
   –En France, on parle français.
2. –En Amérique, on étudie le français.
   –En France, on étudie l'anglais.
3. –En Amérique, on dîne à six heures.
   –En France, on dîne à huit heures.
4. –En Amérique, on mange des hamburgers.
   –En France, on mange des omelettes.
5. –En Amérique, on voyage en avion.
   –En France, on voyage en train.
6. –En Amérique, on skie dans le Colorado.
   –En France, on skie dans les Alpes.
7. –En Amérique, on va à l'école le mercredi après-midi.
   –En France, on va à l'école le samedi matin.
8. –En Amérique, on chante «la Bannière étoilée».
   –En France, on chante «la Marseillaise».

8 COMMUNICATION describing one's usual activities

Answers will vary.

1. À la maison, on dîne (à six heures et demie).
2. À la télé, on regarde (des films).
3. À la cafétéria de l'école, on mange (des sandwichs).
4. En été, on va (à la plage).
5. Le week-end, avec mes copains, on va (au cinéma).
6. Avec mes copains, on joue (au basket).
7. On a une classe de français (le lundi et le mercredi).
8. On a un examen de français (jeudi).

Language note Be sure that students realize that in this activity **on** means *we.*

SECTION B

Communicative function
Describing actions

Teaching Resource Options

PRINT 

Workbook PE, pp. 169–175
Unit 6 Resource Book
- Audioscript, p. 132
- Communipak, pp. 140–158
- Workbook TE, pp. 101–107

AUDIO & VISUAL 

Audio Program
CD 3 Tracks 39, 40

Overhead Transparencies
41 **-re** Verbs

TECHNOLOGY 

Power Presentations

Teaching strategy Point out that the plural endings of **-re** verbs are the same as those of **-er** verbs: **nous vendons, vous vendez,** and **ils vendent.**

Language note You may indicate that **vendre** is a REGULAR verb since many verbs follow the same pattern. However, **mettre** is IRREGULAR since the pattern applies only to verbs that have **mettre** as a root: **permettre, promettre,** etc.

 **Re-entry and review**

The verb chart reviews possessive adjectives (Lesson 16).

9 PRACTICE describing who's waiting for whom

1. Nous attendons nos copains.
2. Vous attendez vos cousines.
3. J'attends Antoine.
4. Tu attends Julie.
5. Olivier et Éric attendent Élodie et Sophie.
6. Les étudiants attendent les étudiantes.
7. Julien et moi, nous attendons Pauline et Mélanie.
8. Annette et toi, vous attendez Jean-Marc.
9. On attend notre copine.
10. Stéphanie attend Léa.

B Les verbes réguliers en *-re* 

Many French verbs end in **-re.** Most of these are conjugated like **vendre** *(to sell)*. Note the forms of this verb in the present tense, paying special attention to the endings.

INFINITIVE	vendre	STEM (infinitive minus **-re**)	ENDINGS
PRESENT	Je **vends** ma raquette.	vend-	-s
	Tu **vends** ton scooter.		-s
	Il/Elle/On **vend** son ordinateur.		–
	Nous **vendons** nos livres.		-ons
	Vous **vendez** vos CD.		-ez
	Ils/Elles **vendent** leur voiture.		-ent

→ The "**d**" of the stem is silent in the singular forms, but it is pronounced in the plural forms.

VOCABULAIRE Verbes réguliers en *-re* 

attendre	*to wait, wait for*	Pierre **attend** Michèle au café.
entendre	*to hear*	Est-ce que tu **entends** la radio?
perdre	*to lose, waste*	Jean-Claude **perd** le match.
rendre visite à	*to visit (a person)*	Je **rends visite à** mon oncle.
répondre à	*to answer*	Nous **répondons à** la question du prof.
vendre	*to sell*	À qui **vends**-tu ton vélo?

→ There are two French verbs that correspond to the English verb *to visit.*

visiter (+ PLACES) — Nous **visitons** Québec.
rendre visite à (+ PEOPLE) — Nous **rendons visite à** nos cousins canadiens.

9 Rendez-vous

PARLER/ÉCRIRE The following people have been shopping and are now waiting for their friends at a café. Express this, using the appropriate forms of the verb **attendre.**

▶ Jérôme (Michèle) **Jérôme attend Michèle.**

1. nous (nos copains)
2. vous (vos cousines)
3. moi (Antoine)
4. toi (Julie)
5. Olivier et Éric (Élodie et Sophie)
6. les étudiants (les étudiantes)
7. Julien et moi, nous (Pauline et Mélanie)
8. Annette et toi, vous (Jean-Marc)
9. on (notre copine)
10. Stéphanie (Léa)

TALKING ABOUT PAST EVENTS

Let's talk about whom you visited last summer. (Note that the past participle of **-re** verbs ends in **-u.**)

Est-ce que tu as rendu visite à ta tante l'été dernier?
Oui, j'ai rendu visite à ma tante.
(Je n'ai pas rendu visite à ma tante.)

- **Est-ce que tu as rendu visite à ton oncle l'été dernier?**
- **As-tu rendu visite à tes cousins?**
- **As-tu rendu visite à tes grands-parents?**
- **Et le week-end dernier, à qui est-ce que tu as rendu visite?**

10 Qui?

PARLER/ÉCRIRE Who is doing what? Answer the following questions, using the suggested subjects.

1. Qui perd le match? (toi, vous, Alice)
2. Qui rend visite à Pierre? (Paul, Léa et Hélène, toi)
3. Qui entend l'avion *(plane)?* (moi, vous, les voisins)
4. Qui vend des CD? (on, ce magasin, ces boutiques)
5. Qui attend le bus? (les élèves, le professeur, on, vous)
6. Qui répond au professeur? (toi, nous, les élèves)

11 Qu'est-ce qu'ils font?

PARLER/ÉCRIRE Say what the following people do by completing each sentence with the appropriate form of one of the verbs from the list. Be logical!

1. Guillaume est patient. Il … ses amis.
2. Vous êtes à Paris. Vous … à vos cousins français.
3. Tu joues mal. Tu … le match.
4. Je suis chez moi. J' … un bruit *(noise)* curieux.
5. Nous sommes en classe. Nous … aux questions du professeur.
6. Julie travaille dans une boutique. Elle … des robes.
7. On est au café. On … nos copains.

attendre entendre rendre visite vendre perdre répondre

C L'impératif

Compare the French and English forms of the imperative.

Écoute ce CD! — ***Listen*** *to this CD!*
Ne vendez pas votre voiture! — ***Don't sell*** *your car!*
Allons au cinéma! — ***Let's go*** *to the movies!*

LEARNING ABOUT LANGUAGE

The IMPERATIVE is used to make suggestions and to give orders and advice. The commands or suggestions may be affirmative or negative.

Note the forms of the imperative in the chart below.

INFINITIVE	parler	finir	vendre	aller
IMPERATIVE				
(tu)	parle	finis	vends	va
(vous)	parlez	finissez	vendez	allez
(nous)	parlons	finissons	vendons	allons

For regular verbs and most irregular verbs, the forms of the imperative are the same as the corresponding forms of the present tense.

→ NOTE: For all **-er** verbs, including **aller,** the **-s** of the **tu** form is dropped. Compare:

Tu **parles** anglais. — **Parle** français, s'il te plaît!
Tu **vas** au café. — **Va** à la bibliothèque!

→ The negative imperative is formed as follows:

ne + VERB + pas ...	**Ne choisis pas** ce blouson.

Follow-up:
- **Est-ce que X a rendu visite à son oncle l'été dernier?**
- **Est-ce que Y a rendu visite à ses cousins?**
- **À qui est-ce que Z a rendu visite le week-end dernier?**

INCLUSION

Synthetic/analytic, Gifted & Talented Ask students to make 3x5 cards with infinitives on one side and imperative forms on the other. Have students repeat both infinitives and imperatives after you. Do this three times. In pairs, have students turn all their cards to the infinitive side. Ask them to then generate the imperatives.

10 PRACTICE describing what people are doing

1. Tu perds le match. (Vous perdez le match. Alice perd le match.)
2. Paul rend visite à Pierre. (Léa et Hélène rendent visite à Pierre. Tu rends visite à Pierre.)
3. J'entends l'avion. (Vous entendez l'avion. Les voisins entendent l'avion.)
4. On rend des CD. (Ce magasin vend des CD. Ces boutiques vendent des CD.)
5. Les élèves attendent le bus. (Le professeur attend le bus. On attend le bus. Vous attendez le bus.)
6. Tu réponds au professeur. (Nous répondons au professeur. Les élèves répondent au professeur.)

11 COMPREHENSION describing people and activities

1. attend
2. perds
3. répondons
4. attend
5. rendez visite à
6. entends
7. vend

SECTION C

Communicative function
Giving commands

Extra practice Have students give the **tu, vous,** and **nous** command forms of the following irregular verbs.

faire une promenade:
fais une promenade
faites une promenade
faisons une promenade
revenir demain:
reviens demain
revenez demain
revenons demain

Language note The irregular imperative forms of **avoir** and **être** are not presented at this level because they are used in only a few phrases. If students ask, you can mention them:

avoir: aie, ayez, ayons
N'aie pas peur.
Don't be afraid.
être: sois, soyez, soyons
Ne sois pas bête.
Don't be silly.

Teaching Resource Options

PRINT 

Workbook PE, pp. 169–175
Unit 6 Resource Book
- Audioscript, pp. 132–133
- Communipak, pp. 140–158
- Workbook TE, pp. 101–107

AUDIO & VISUAL 

Audio Program
CD 3 Track 41

TECHNOLOGY 

Power Presentations

12 ROLE PLAY offering and accepting assistance

1. –Je fais une salade?
   –Mais oui, fais une salade!
2. –J'invite nos copains?
   –Mais oui, invite nos copains!
3. –J'achète des sodas?
   –Mais oui, achète des sodas!
4. –J'apporte des CD?
   –Mais oui, apporte des CD!
5. –Je choisis la musique de danse?
   –Mais oui, choisis la musique de danse!
6. –Je viens à huit heures?
   –Mais oui, viens à huit heures!
7. –Je téléphone aux voisins?
   –Mais oui, téléphone aux voisins!
8. –J'apporte une mini-chaîne?
   –Mais oui, apporte une mini-chaîne!
9. –Je fais des sandwichs?
   –Mais oui, fais des sandwichs!

13 ROLE PLAY giving good and bad advice

1. –Téléphone à ta tante.
   –Ne téléphone pas à ta tante.
2. –Attends tes copains.
   –N'attends pas tes copains.
3. –Fais attention en classe.
   –Ne fais pas attention en classe.
4. –Va à l'école.
   –Ne va pas à l'école.
5. –Finis la leçon.
   –Ne finis pas la leçon.
6. –Écoute tes professeurs.
   –N'écoute pas tes professeurs.
7. –Mets la table.
   –Ne mets pas la table.
8. –Aide tes amis.
   –N'aide pas tes amis.
9. –Rends visite à ta grand-mère.
   –Ne rends pas visite à ta grand-mère.
10. –Choisis des copains sympathiques.
    –Ne choisis pas des copains sympathiques.
11. –Fais tes devoirs.
    –Ne fais pas tes devoirs.
12. –Réussis à l'examen.
    –Ne réussis pas à l'examen.

12  Mais oui!

PARLER You have organized a party at your home. Valérie offers to do the following. You accept.

▶ apporter une pizza?

1. faire une salade?
2. inviter nos copains?
3. acheter des sodas?
4. apporter des CD?
5. choisir la musique de danse?
6. venir à huit heures?
7. téléphoner aux voisins?
8. apporter une mini-chaîne?
9. faire des sandwichs?

J'apporte une pizza?
Mais oui, apporte une pizza!

13  L'ange et le démon *(The angel and the devil)*

PARLER Véronique is wondering whether she should do certain things. The angel gives her good advice. The devil gives her bad advice. Play both roles.

▶ étudier les verbes
Étudie les verbes.
N'étudie pas les verbes.

1. téléphoner à ta tante
2. attendre tes copains
3. faire attention en classe
4. aller à l'école
5. finir la leçon
6. écouter tes professeurs
7. mettre *(set)* la table
8. aider tes amis
9. rendre visite à ta grand-mère
10. choisir des copains sympathiques
11. faire tes devoirs *(homework)*
12. réussir à l'examen

14 Oui ou non?

PARLER For each of the following situations, give your classmates advice as to what to do and what not to do. Be logical.

▶ Nous sommes en vacances. (étudier? voyager?)
N'étudiez pas! Voyagez!

1. Nous sommes à Paris. (parler anglais? parler français?)
2. C'est dimanche. (aller à la bibliothèque? aller au cinéma?)
3. Il fait beau. (rester à la maison? faire une promenade?)
4. Il fait froid. (mettre un pull? mettre un tee-shirt?)
5. Il est onze heures du soir. (rester au café? rentrer à la maison?)
6. Il fait très chaud. (aller à la piscine? regarder la télé?)

GAME Drilling with dice

PROPS: Dice (one for every pair of students). Create a transparency with the verb list at right.

INSTRUCTIONS: (students play in pairs):
Student A rolls the die. For example, 5 spots = **vous.** Student B writes the corresponding form of the first verb: **vous cherchez.**

Then Student B rolls the die and Student A writes the corresponding form of the next verb: 2 spots + **gagner → tu gagnes**.

Keep track of pairs as they finish. Then have teams exchange their papers for peer correction. The first pair with the most correct answers is the winning team.

15 L'esprit de contradiction (Disagreement)

PARLER Make suggestions to your friends about things to do. Your friends will not agree and will suggest something else.

▶ aller au cinéma (à la plage)

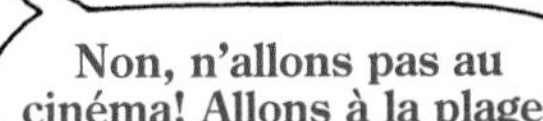

Allons au cinéma!
Non, n'allons pas au cinéma! Allons à la plage!

1. jouer au tennis (aux jeux vidéo)
2. écouter la radio (des CD)
3. regarder la télé (un film vidéo)
4. dîner au restaurant (à la maison)
5. inviter Michèle (Sophie)
6. organiser un barbecue (une boum)
7. faire des sandwichs (une pizza)
8. aller au musée (à la bibliothèque)
9. faire une promenade à pied (en voiture)
10. rendre visite à nos voisins (à nos copains)

PRONONCIATION — an, en /ɑ̃/

Les lettres «an» et «en»

The letters "**an**" and "**en**" represent the nasal vowel /ɑ̃/. Be sure not to pronounce the sound "**n**" after the vowel.

enfant

Répétez:

/ɑ̃/ **enfant an manteau collants grand élégant**
André mange un grand sandwich.

/ɑ̃/ **enfant en argent dépenser attends entend vend envie**
Vincent dépense rarement son argent.

14 COMPREHENSION giving logical advice

1. Ne parlez pas anglais! Parlez français!
2. N'allez pas à la bibliothèque! Allez au cinéma!
3. Ne restez pas à la maison! Faites une promenade!
4. Mettez un pull! Ne mettez pas de tee-shirt!
5. Ne restez pas au café! Rentrez à la maison!
6. Allez à la piscine! Ne regardez pas la télé!

Variation (using the **nous** form)
N'étudions pas! Voyageons!

Challenge For each situation, have students invent additional advice. Encourage them to be creative.
Visitez Québec!
Faites «la route des baleines».
Dînez au Vendôme!

15 EXCHANGES making plans

1. –Jouons au tennis!
   –Non, ne jouons pas au tennis! Jouons aux jeux vidéo!
2. –Écoutons la radio!
   –Non, n'écoutons pas la radio! Écoutons des CD!
3. –Regardons la télé!
   –Non, ne regardons pas la télé! Regardons un film vidéo!
4. –Dînons au restaurant!
   –Non, ne dînons pas au restaurant! Dînons à la maison!
5. –Invitons Michèle!
   –Non, n'invitons pas Michèle! Invitons Sophie!
6. –Organisons un barbecue!
   –Non, n'organisons pas de barbecue! Organisons une boum!
7. –Faisons des sandwichs!
   –Non, ne faisons pas de sandwichs! Faisons une pizza!
8. –Allons au musée!
   –Non, n'allons pas au musée! Allons à la bibliothèque!
9. –Faisons une promenade à pied!
   –Non, ne faisons pas de promenade à pied! Faisons une promenade en voiture!
10. –Rendons visite à nos voisins!
    –Non, ne rendons pas visite à nos voisins! Rendons visite à nos copains!

Note the word 'barbecue' in item 6. Barbecue is pronounced as in English /barbəkju/

Challenge Expand the conversation to include three people. The third one does not like the second suggestion and has another idea.
– Allons au cinéma!
– Non, n'allons pas au cinéma! Allons à la plage.
– Mais non, n'allons pas à la plage. Restons à la maison!

PRONUNCIATION

- Exception: the "**en**" in **examen** represents the sound /ɛ̃/ as in **pain: examen** /egzamɛ̃/
- In the combination **ien,** the letters "**en**" also represent the sound /ɛ̃/ : **italien** /italjɛ̃/

Drilling with dice

1. chercher
2. gagner
3. acheter
4. amener
5. finir
6. grossir
7. maigrir
8. réussir
9. attendre
10. entendre
11. perdre
12. répondre
13. aller
14. avoir
15. être
16. faire
17. mettre
18. permettre (permit)
19. revenir
20. venir

1 = je
2 = tu
3 = elle
4 = nous
5 = vous
6 = ils

À VOTRE TOUR

Main Topic
- Recapitulation and review

Teaching Resource Options

PRINT 

Workbook PE, pp. 169–175
Unit 6 Resource Book
Audioscript, p. 133
Communipak, pp. 140–158
Family Involvement, pp. 122–123
Workbook TE, pp. 101–107

Assessment
Lesson 20 Quiz, pp. 136–137
Portfolio Assessment, Unit 1 URB pp. 155–164
Audioscript for Quiz 20, p. 135
Answer Keys, pp. 230–234

AUDIO & VISUAL 

Audio Program
CD 3 Tracks 42, 43
CD 15 Track 12

TECHNOLOGY 

Test Generator CD-ROM/McDougal Littell Assessment System

1 COMPREHENSION

1. Est-ce que tu rends visite à tes cousins ce week-end?
   (d) Non, je reste ici.
2. Tu veux aller dans les boutiques avec moi?
   (c) Écoute! Je n'ai pas besoin de vêtements.
3. Est-ce que tu as envie d'aller au cinéma?
   (b) Bonne idée! Il y a un nouveau film au «Majestic».
4. Et après qu'est-ce qu'on fait?
   (a) Eh bien, allons au restaurant!

2 GUIDED ORAL EXPRESSION

Answers will vary.
–Qu'est-ce qu'on fait ... ?
–(X)
–Je n'ai pas envie de (d') ....
–Eh bien, (X). D'accord?
–Oui, c'est une bonne idée!

1. ce soir/(Étudions)/étudier/(regardons la télé)
2. dimanche/(Allons en ville)/aller en ville/(dînons au restaurant)
3. après les classes/(Jouons au basket)/jouer au basket/(faisons une promenade)
4. cet été/(Cherchons un job)/chercher un job/(voyageons)
5. ce week-end/(Faisons un pique-nique)/faire un pique-nique/(organisons une boum)
6. demain/(Allons à la bibliothèque)/aller à la bibliothèque/(allons à la piscine)

À votre tour!

OBJECTIFS
Now you can ...
- make suggestions
- tell others what to do

1 La bonne réponse

PARLER Anne is talking to Jean-François. Match Anne's questions with Jean-François's answers. You may act out the conversation with a classmate.

Anne

1. Est-ce que tu rends visite à tes cousins ce week-end?
2. Tu veux aller dans les boutiques avec moi?
3. Est-ce que tu as envie d'aller au cinéma?
4. Et après (*afterwards*) qu'est-ce qu'on fait?

Jean-François

a. Eh bien, allons au restaurant!
b. Bonne idée! Il y a un nouveau film au «Majestic».
c. Écoute! Je n'ai pas besoin de vêtements.
d. Non, je reste ici.

2 Créa-dialogue

PARLER When we are with our friends, it is not always easy to agree on what to do. With your classmates, discuss the following possibilities.

Qu'est-ce qu'on fait samedi?
Allons au cinéma.

Je n'ai pas envie d'aller au cinéma.
Eh bien, rendons visite à nos amis. D'accord?
Oui, c'est une bonne idée.

Quand?	Première suggestion	Deuxième suggestion
▶ samedi	aller au cinéma	rendre visite à nos amis
1. ce soir (*tonight*)	étudier	regarder la télé
2. dimanche	aller en ville	dîner au restaurant
3. après (*after*) les classes	jouer au basket	faire une promenade
4. cet été	chercher un job	voyager
5. ce week-end	faire un pique-nique	??
6. demain	aller à la bibliothèque	??

À VOTRE TOUR

Depending upon your goals and objectives, you may or may not wish to assign all of the activities in the **À votre tour** section.

Conseils

PARLER Your friends tell you what they would like to do. Give them appropriate advice, either positive or negative. Use your imagination.

▶ Je voudrais maigrir. **Alors, mange moins. (Alors, ne mange pas de pizza.)**

1. Je voudrais avoir un «A» en français.
2. Je voudrais gagner beaucoup d'argent.
3. Je voudrais organiser une boum.
4. Je voudrais préparer un barbecue.

Que faire?

PARLER Give a classmate advice about what to do or not to do in the following circumstances.

Pendant *(During)* la classe	Ce soir	Ce week-end	Pendant les vacances
écouter le prof	étudier	rester à la maison	voyager
parler à tes copains	aller au cinéma	aller en ville	travailler
regarder les bandes dessinées *(comics)*	préparer tes leçons	dépenser ton argent	grossir
manger un sandwich	aider *(help)* ta mère	organiser une boum	oublier *(forget)* ton français
répondre en français	surfer sur l'Internet	faire une promenade à pied	??
??	??	??	

▶ **Pendant la classe, écoute le prof. Ne parle pas à tes copains.**

Bon voyage!

ÉCRIRE Your French friend Ariane is going to visit the United States next summer with her cousin. They are traveling on a low budget and are asking you for advice as to how to save money. Make a list of suggestions, including five things they could do and five things they should not do. You may want to use some of the following ideas:

▶ *Voyagez en bus. Ne voyagez pas en train.*

▶
- voyager (comment?)
- rester (dans quels hôtels?)
- dîner (dans quels restaurants?)
- visiter (quelles villes?)
- aller (où?)
- acheter (quelles choses?)
- apporter (quelles choses?)

Portfolio Assessment

You will probably select only one speaking activity and one writing activity to go into the students' portfolios for Unit 6.

In this lesson, Act. 2 lends itself well to an oral portfolio recording.

Act. 5 offers a good writing portfolio topic.

3 Guided Oral Expression

Answers will vary.
1. Alors, parle français en classe. (Alors, étudie bien.)
2. Alors, travaille beaucoup.
3. Alors, invite tes copains.
4. Alors, va au supermarché. (Alors, téléphone à tes amis.)

4 Comprehension

Answers will vary.
- Pendant la classe, ne regarde pas les bandes dessinées. Écoute le prof.
  Pendant la classe, ne mange pas de sandwich. Réponds aux questions en français.
- Ce soir, étudie. Ne va pas au cinéma.
  Ce soir aide ta mère. Ne surfe pas sur l'Internet.
  Prépare tes leçons.
- Ce week-end, ne reste pas à la maison. Va à la campagne.
  Ce week-end, ne va pas en ville. Organise une boum.
  Ce week-end, ne dépense pas ton argent. Fais une promenade à pied.
- Pendant les vacances, n'oublie pas ton français. Voyage.
  Pendant les vacances, travaille à la plage. Ne reste pas à la maison.
  Pendant les vacances, ne grossis pas. Fais du sport.

5 Written Self-Expression

Answers will vary.
Restez dans les hôtels bon marché, ne restez pas dans les hôtels chers.
Dînez dans les restaurants américains. Ne dînez pas dans les restaurants français.
Visitez Québec et Montréal. Ne visitez pas New York.
Allez à la plage et à la montagne. N'allez pas en ville.
Apportez un imper. N'apportez pas de manteau.
Voyagez en train. Ne voyagez pas en avion.
Regardez la télé. N'allez pas au cinéma.
Mangez des hamburgers. Ne mangez pas de steaks.
Allez à la bibliothèque. N'achetez pas de livres.

Tests de contrôle

By taking the following tests, you can check your progress in French and also prepare for the unit test. Write your answers on a separate sheet of paper.

1 The right item

Review...
- items of clothing: pp. 258, 259, and 260

Give the names of the following items of clothing, using the appropriate article: **un, une,** or **des.**

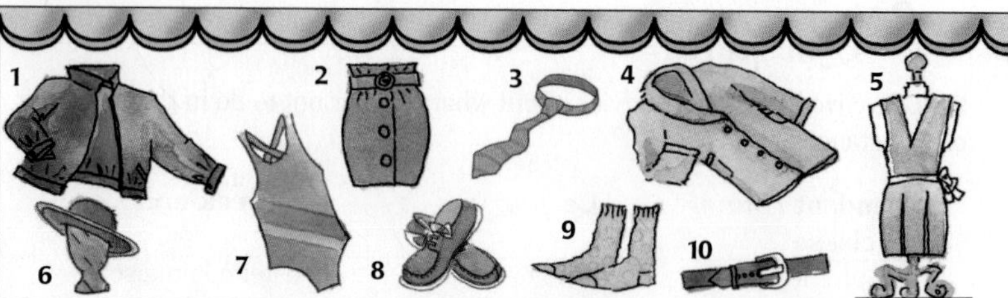

Dans ce magasin, il y a ...

1. —
2. —
3. —
4. —
5. —
6. —
7. —
8. —
9. —
10. —

2 The right activity

Review...
- new verbs: pp. 259, 262, 269, 278, and 290

Complete each of the following sentences with the appropriate forms of the verbs in the box. Be logical in your choice of verbs and do not use the same word more than once.

amener
apporter
attendre
entendre
grossir
porter
rendre visite
répondre
réussir
trouver

1. Philippe — ses CD à la boum.
2. Caroline — sa nouvelle robe.
3. Thomas — parce qu'il mange trop *(too much)*.
4. Léa — un copain au pique-nique.
5. Céline — aux examens parce qu'elle étudie beaucoup.
6. Mélanie ne — pas son stylo. Où est-il?
7. Charlotte est en vacances. Elle — à son oncle.
8. Pierre — à un mail.
9. Je n'— pas bien. Répète, s'il te plaît.
10. Cécile regarde sa montre. Elle — un copain.

3 The right form

Review...
- **beau, nouveau, and vieux:** p. 279

Complete the following sentences with the appropriate forms of **beau, nouveau,** and **vieux.** Be logical in your choices.

1. Dans ce quartier moderne, il y a beaucoup de — immeubles.
2. Ma grand-mère a 82 ans. Elle est —.
3. Catherine est très jolie. C'est une — fille, n'est-ce pas?
4. Mon ordinateur ne marche pas. J'ai besoin d'un — ordinateur.
5. Nicolas va nettoyer *(to clean)* le garage. Il met ses — vêtements.

TESTS DE CONTRÔLE

Teaching Resource Options

PRINT

Unit 6 Resource Book
Communipak, pp. 140–158
Assessment
Unit 6 Test, pp. 166–174
Portfolio Assessment, Unit 1 URB pp. 155–164
Multiple Choice Test Items, pp. 187–195
Listening Comprehension Performance Test, pp. 175–176
Reading Performance Test, pp. 181–183
Speaking Performance Test, pp. 177–180
Writing Performance Test, pp. 184–186
Comprehensive Test 2, Unit 4–6, pp. 197–220
Test Scoring Tools, pp. 221–223
Audioscript for Tests, pp. 224–229
Answer Keys, pp. 230–234

AUDIO & VISUAL 

Audio Program
CD 15 Tracks 13–22

TECHNOLOGY 

Test Generator CD-ROM/McDougal Littell Assessment System

1 COMPREHENSION

1. un blouson
2. une jupe
3. une cravate
4. une veste
5. une robe
6. un chapeau
7. un maillot de bain
8. des chaussures
9. des chaussettes
10. une ceinture

2 COMPREHENSION

1. Philippe apporte ses CD à la boum.
2. Caroline porte sa nouvelle robe.
3. Thomas grossit parce qu'il mange trop.
4. Léa amène un copain au pique-nique.
5. Céline réussit aux examens parce qu'elle étudie beaucoup.
6. Mélanie ne trouve pas son stylo.
7. Elle rend visite à son oncle.
8. Pierre répond à un mail.
9. Je n'entends pas bien.
10. Elle attend un copain.

3 COMPREHENSION

1. Dans ce quartier moderne, il y a beaucoup de nouveaux immeubles.
2. Elle est vieille.
3. C'est une belle fille, n'est-ce pas?
4. J'ai besoin d'un nouvel ordinateur.
5. Il met ses vieux vêtements.

4 The right comparison

Make logical comparisons using the adjectives in parentheses.

(grand) 1. La France est — les États-Unis *(United States)*.
(élégant) 2. Une belle chemise est — un vieux tee-shirt.
(rapide) 3. Les voitures de sport sont — les limousines.
(bon) 4. À l'examen, un «A» est — un «C».

Review...
- comparisons: p. 280

5 *Ce* or *quel*?

Complete the following sentences with the appropriate forms of **ce** or **quel.**

1. — blouson préfères-tu?
2. J'aime — lunettes!
3. — veste est chère!
4. — casquette achetez-vous?
5. — copains invites-tu?
6. — chaussures mets-tu?
7. Comment s'appelle — garçon?
8. Qui est — homme?

Review...
- **ce** and **quel** pp. 270 and 271

6 The right verb

Complete the following sentences with the appropriate forms of the verbs in parentheses.

1. **(acheter)**
   J'— une chemise. Nous — des CD. Qu'est-ce que tu —?
2. **(mettre)**
   Marc — un tee-shirt. Je — un short. Qu'est-ce que vous —?
3. **(choisir)**
   Vous — des vêtements. Ils — des CD. Éric — un polo.
4. **(finir)**
   Nous — les devoirs. Je — un livre. Pauline — la pizza.
5. **(vendre)**
   Ils — leur maison. Je — mon vélo. Claire — sa voiture.
6. **(attendre)**
   Les touristes — le train. J'— le bus. Nous — un copain.

Review...
- verb forms: pp. 268, 272, 278 and 290

7 Composition: Un mariage

Imagine that you are a reporter for the society column of your local newspaper. You are attending an elegant wedding. Describe what the following people are wearing: **la mariée** *(the bride)*, **le marié** *(the groom)*, and **les demoiselles d'honneur** *(the bridesmaids)*. Be imaginative but use only vocabulary and expressions that you know in French.

STRATEGY Writing

a For each of the following, list the clothes and their colors.

la mariée	le marié	les demoiselles d'honneur

b Write three short paragraphs describing what each person is wearing.

c Reread your composition and be sure you have spelled all the items of clothing correctly and have used the correct forms of the color adjectives.

4 COMPREHENSION

1. La France est moins grande que les États-Unis.
2. Une belle chemise est plus élégante qu'un vieux tee-shirt.
3. Les voitures de sport sont plus rapides que les limousines.
4. À l'examen, un «A» est meilleur qu'un «C».

5 COMPREHENSION

1. Quel blouson préfères-tu?
2. J'aime ces lunettes!
3. Cette veste est chère!
4. Quelle casquette achetez-vous?
5. Quels copains invites-tu?
6. Quelles chaussures mets-tu?
7. Comment s'appelle ce garçon?
8. Qui est cet homme?

6 COMPREHENSION

1. J'achète une chemise. Nous achetons des CD. Qu'est-ce que tu achètes?
2. Marc met un tee-shirt. Je mets un short. Qu'est-ce que vous mettez?
3. Vous choisissez des vêtements. Ils choisissent des CD. Éric choisit un polo.
4. Nous finissons les devoirs. Je finis un livre. Pauline finit la pizza.
5. Ils vendent leur maison. Je vends mon vélo. Claire vend sa voiture.
6. Les touristes attendent le train. J'attends le bus. Nous attendons un copain.

7 WRITTEN SELF-EXPRESSION

Answers will vary.
La mariée, Claire Lapointe, porte une belle robe blanche. La robe est très élégante. Mademoiselle Lapointe porte aussi des belles chaussures blanches.

Le marié, Jean-Pierre Letourneau, porte une veste noire et un pantalon noir. Il porte aussi des nouvelles chaussures noires et des belles lunettes.

Les demoiselles d'honneur portent des belles robes bleues. Elles portent des chaussures bleues aussi.

Language Learning Benchmarks

FUNCTION
- Engage in conversations pp. 263, 287
- Express likes and dislikes p. 270
- Obtain information p. 263
- Understand some ideas and familiar details p. 305
- Begin to provide information pp. 261, 271, 273

CONTEXT
- Converse in face-to-face social interactions pp. 270, 271
- Listen to audio and video texts pp. 257-258, 266-267, 276-277, 284
- Use authentic materials when reading: posters p. 287
- Write notes p. 283
- Write lists p. 265
- Write short letters p. 265

TEXT TYPE
- Use short sentences when speaking pp. 272, 278, 289
- Use short sentences when writing pp. 278, 281, 288
- Use learned words and phrases when speaking pp. 259, 260, 269
- Use learned words and phrases when writing pp. 259, 260, 269
- Use simple questions when speaking pp. 279, 281, 289
- Use commands when speaking pp. 279, 292, 293
- Understand some ideas and familiar details presented in clear, uncomplicated speech when listening p. 264
- Understand short texts enhanced by visual clues when reading pp. 256-257

Vocabulaire

POUR COMMUNIQUER

Shopping for clothes

Pardon...	*Excuse me ...*	**Quel est le prix de ...?**	*What is the price of ...?*
Vous désirez, (monsieur)?	*May I help you, (Sir)?*	**Combien coûte ...**	*How much does ... cost?*
Je cherche ...	*I'm looking for ...*		

Expressing opinions and making comparisons

Qu'est-ce que tu penses de [la robe rose]?	*What do you think of [the pink dress]?*
Comment tu trouves [la robe noire]?	*What do you think of [the black dress]?*

La robe rose est	**plus belle que** **moins belle que** **aussi belle que**	**la robe noire.**	*The pink dress is*	*more beautiful than* *less beautiful than* *as beautiful as*	*the black dress.*

MOTS ET EXPRESSIONS

Les magasins

un magasin	*store*	**une boutique**	*shop*
un grand magasin	*department store*		

L'argent

l'argent	*money*	**une pièce**	*coin*
un billet	*bill, paper money*		

Les vêtements et les accessoires

des baskets	*(hightop) sneakers*	**des bottes**	*boots*
un blouson	*jacket*	**une casquette**	*baseball cap*
un chapeau	*hat*	**une ceinture**	*belt*
un chemisier	*blouse*	**des chaussettes**	*socks*
des collants	*tights*	**des chaussures**	*shoes*
un imper(méable)	*raincoat*	**une chemise**	*shirt*
un jean	*jeans*	**une cravate**	*tie*
un jogging	*jogging suit*	**une jupe**	*skirt*
un maillot de bain	*bathing suit*	**des lunettes**	*glasses*
un manteau	*overcoat*	**des lunettes de soleil**	*sunglasses*
un pantalon	*pants*	**une robe**	*dress*
un polo	*polo shirt*	**des sandales**	*sandals*
un pull	*sweater*	**une veste**	*jacket*
un short	*shorts*		
un survêtement	*track suit*		
un sweat	*sweatshirt*		
un tee-shirt	*t-shirt*		
des tennis	*sneakers*		

La description

à la mode	*in style*	**joli(e)**	*pretty*
beau (belle)	*beautiful*	**long(ue)**	*long*
bon marché	*cheap*	**meilleur(e)**	*better*
cher (chère)	*expensive*	**moche**	*ugly*
chouette	*neat*	**nouveau (nouvelle)**	*new*
court(e)	*short*	**pauvre**	*poor*
démodé(e)	*out of style*	**petit(e)**	*small*
élégant(e)	*elegant*	**riche**	*rich*
génial(e)	*terrific*	**vieux (vieille)**	*old*
grand(e)	*big*		

Verbes réguliers en *-er*

chercher	*to look for*
coûter	*to cost*
dépenser	*to spend*
gagner	*to earn; to win*
penser (que)	*to think (that)*
porter	*to wear*
trouver	*to find; to think of*

Verbes avec changements orthographiques

acheter	*to buy*
amener	*to bring (a person)*
espérer	*to hope*
préférer	*to prefer*
payer	*to pay, to pay for*

Verbes réguliers en *-ir*

choisir	*to choose*
finir	*to finish*
grossir	*to gain weight*
maigrir	*to lose weight*
réussir	*to succeed*
réussir à un examen	*to pass an exam*

Verbes réguliers en *-re*

attendre	*to wait, to wait for*
entendre	*to hear*
perdre	*to lose, to waste*
rendre visite à	*to visit (a person)*
répondre à	*to answer*
vendre	*to sell*

Verbes irréguliers

avoir besoin de + *noun*	*to need*	**avoir envie de + *noun***	*to want*
avoir besoin de + *infinitive*	*to need to, to have to*	**avoir envie de + *infinitive***	*to feel like, to want to*
		mettre	*to put, to put on*

Les nombres de 100 à 1000

100	**cent**	**200**	**deux cents**	**500**	**cinq cents**	**800**	**huit cents**
101	**cent un**	**300**	**trois cents**	**600**	**six cents**	**900**	**neuf cents**
102	**cent deux**	**400**	**quatre cents**	**700**	**sept cents**	**1000**	**mille**

Expressions utiles

à mon avis	*in my opinion*	**combien + *verb***	*how much*
Eh bien!	*Well!*	**combien de + *noun***	*how much, how many*
C'est une bonne idée!	*That's a good idea!*	**trop + *adjective***	*too*
ce, cet, cette, ces	*this, that, these, those*		
quel, quelle, quels, quelles	*what, which*		

TEST PREP CLASSZONE.COM FLASHCARDS AND MORE!

CONTENT
- Understand and convey information about shopping p. 259
- Understand and convey information about clothes pp. 259, 260, 261, 268
- Understand and convey information about prices pp. 263, 268, 301
- Understand and convey information about colors pp. 271, 301

ASSESSMENT
- Communicate effectively with some hesitation and errors, which do not hinder comprehension pp. 265, 295
- Demonstrate culturally acceptable behavior for engaging in conversations pp. 265, 275, 282, 294
- Demonstrate culturally acceptable behavior for obtaining information pp. 264, 274, 283
- Demonstrate culturally acceptable behavior for understanding some ideas and familiar details p. 265
- Demonstrate culturally acceptable behavior for providing information pp. 265, 275, 283
- Understand most important information pp. 264, 274, 294

ENTRACTE 6

Objectives
- Reading skill development
- Re-entry of material in the unit
- Development of cultural awareness

Achats par Internet

Objectives
- Reading for information about clothes and fashion

Teaching Resource Options

PRINT 

Workbook PE, pp. 177–179
Activités pour tous PE, pp. 107–109
Unit 6 Resource Book
Activités pour tous TE, pp. 159–161
Workbook TE, pp. 163–165

Achats° par INTERNET

En France, comme° aux États-Unis,° on peut faire beaucoup d'achats par Internet. Ces vêtements figurent° sur le catalogue-en-ligne de «la Redoute», une compagnie française spécialisée dans la vente° de vêtements par correspondance.°

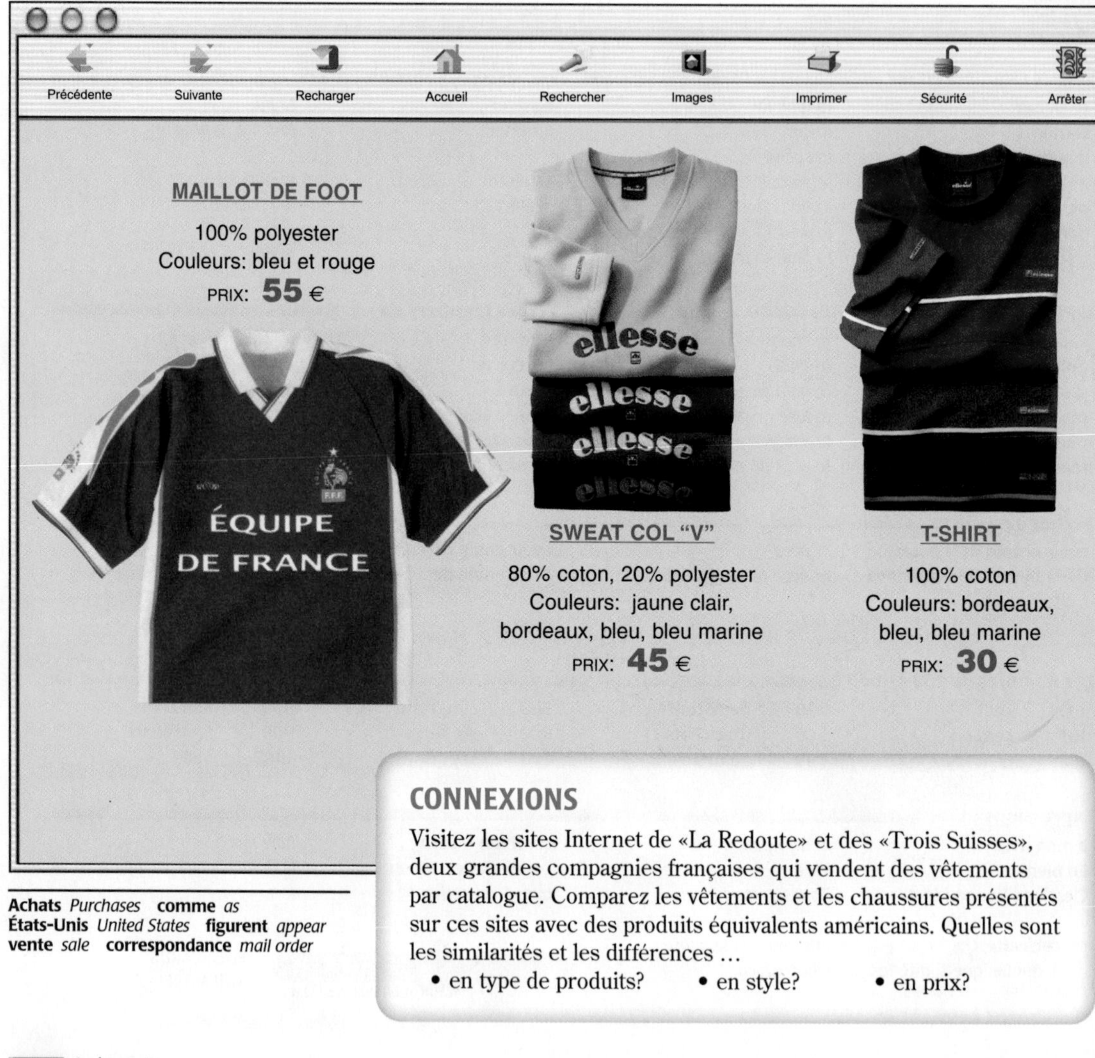

Achats *Purchases* **comme** *as*
États-Unis *United States* **figurent** *appear*
vente *sale* **correspondance** *mail order*

CONNEXIONS

Visitez les sites Internet de «La Redoute» et des «Trois Suisses», deux grandes compagnies françaises qui vendent des vêtements par catalogue. Comparez les vêtements et les chaussures présentés sur ces sites avec des produits équivalents américains. Quelles sont les similarités et les différences …

- en type de produits?
- en style?
- en prix?

PRE-READING

Ask students if they sometimes order clothes from the Internet.

Which websites do they like best?

POST-READING

Have students each select an item they plan to buy (for themselves or as a gift for a friend). In pairs, have students describe their intended purchases to one another.

– Moi, je vais acheter un sweat.
– Ah bon? Pour qui? ...

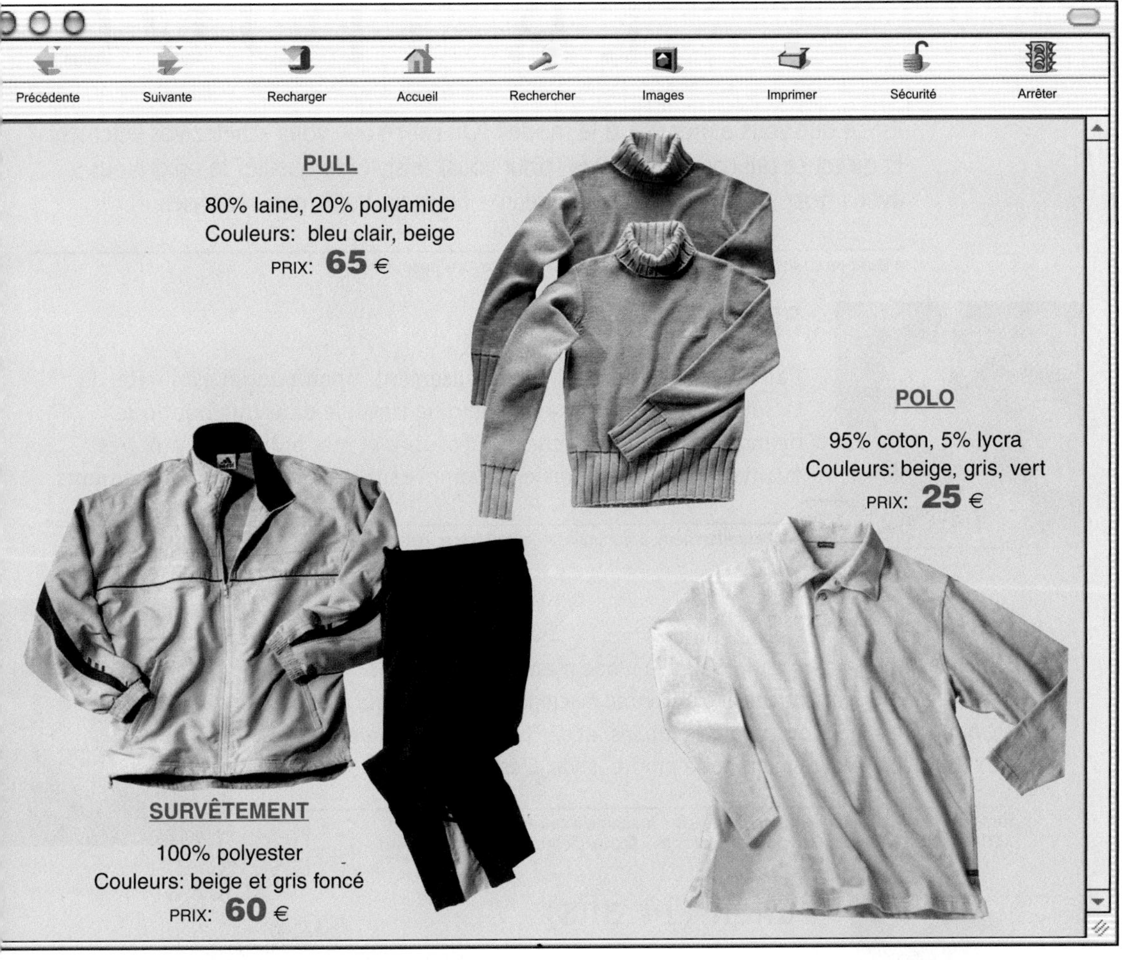

Et vous?

Vous êtes en France et vous voulez acheter deux vêtements différents comme cadeaux *(presents)* pour des amis aux États-Unis. Votre budget est limité à un total de 100 euros. Faites votre sélection.

	Pour qui?	Vêtement	Textile	Couleur	Prix
1.					
2.					
				Prix total:	

Vocabulary notes

jaune clair *light yellow*
bleu marine *navy blue*
bordeaux *maroon*
laine *wool*
gris foncé *dark grey*

Et vous?

Answers will vary.

1. Mon frère
   un polo
   coton et lycra
   gris
   25 euros
2. Ma soeur
   un tee-shirt
   coton
   bleu marine
   30 euros

PAIR PRACTICE

Using the book or the websites for **La Redoute** or **Trois Suisses,** have students do the **Et vous?** activity in pairs. You can increase the spending limit to allow them to “purchase” more items.

Les jeunes Français et la mode

Objectives

- Reading at the paragraph level
- Building reading skills

Teaching Resource Options

PRINT  

Workbook PE, pp. 177–179
Activités pour tous PE, pp. 107–109
Unit 6 Resource Book
Activités pour tous TE, pp. 159–161
Workbook TE, pp. 163–165

Pronunciation Chloé /kloe/

Questions sur le texte

1. Comment est-ce que Florence gagne son argent?
[Elle travaille dans une boutique de mode.]
2. Où est-ce qu'elle achète ses vêtements?
[Elle achète ses vêtements à la boutique où elle travaille.]
3. Est-ce que Chloé achète beaucoup de vêtements?
[Non, elle n'achète pas beaucoup de vêtements.]
4. Qu'est-ce qu'elle fait pour être à la mode?
[Elle coud (met) des rubans et des patchs sur ses vêtements.]
5. Est-ce que Julien aime être à la mode?
[Non, Julien n'aime pas être à la mode.]
6. Qu'est-ce qu'il fait avec son argent?
[Il achète des CD.]
7. Est-ce que Robert aime être bien habillé?
[Oui, il aime être bien habillé.]
8. Est-ce qu'il achète beaucoup de vêtements?
[Non, il achète peu de vêtements mais il fait attention à la qualité.]
9. Qui achète les vêtements d'Éric?
[Sa mère achète ses vêtements.]
10. Où est-ce que la mère d'Éric achète les vêtements de son fils?
[Elle achète ses vêtements sur catalogue.]

Les jeunes Français et LA MODE

Est-ce que vous aimez être à la mode? Où est-ce que vous achetez vos vêtements? Et qu'est-ce qui compte° le plus° pour vous? le style? la qualité? le prix? Nous avons posé° ces questions à cinq jeunes Français. Voilà leurs réponses.

à la mode *in style* **compte** *counts* **le plus** *the most* **avons posé** *asked*

Florence (16 ans)

J'aime être à la mode. Malheureusement,° mon budget est limité. La solution? Le samedi après-midi je travaille dans une boutique de mode. Là, je peux acheter mes jupes et mes pulls à des prix très avantageux.° Pour le reste, je compte sur la générosité de mes parents.

Malheureusement *Unfortunately* **avantageux** *reasonable*

Chloé (15 ans)

Pour moi, le style, c'est tout.° Hélas, la mode n'est pas bon marché. Heureusement,° j'ai une cousine qui a une machine à coudre° et qui est très adroite.° Alors, nous cousons° des rubans° et des patchs sur nos vêtements. De cette façon,° nous créons notre propre° style. C'est génial, non?

tout *everything* **Heureusement** *Fortunately* **machine à coudre** *sewing machine*
adroite *skillful* **cousons** *sew* **rubans** *ribbons* **façon** *manner, way* **propre** *own*

Julien (14 ans)

Vous connaissez° le proverbe: «L'habit ne fait pas le moine*.» Eh bien, pour moi, les vêtements n'ont pas d'importance. Avec mon argent, je préfère acheter des CD. Quand j'ai besoin de jeans ou de tee-shirts, je vais aux puces.° C'est pas cher et c'est marrant!°

connaissez *know* **[marché] aux puces** *flea market* **marrant** *fun*
**Clothes don't make the man. (The habit doesn't make the monk.)*

Robert (15 ans)

Aujourd'hui la présentation extérieure est très importante. Mais il n'est pas nécessaire d'être à la mode pour être bien habillé.° Pour moi, la qualité des vêtements est aussi importante que leur style. En général, j'attends les soldes. J'achète peu de vêtements mais je fais attention à la qualité.

habillé *dressed*

PRE-READING

Have students glance over the reading quickly. What are the questions that were asked in the interview?

POST-READING

Ask each student to decide which of the four people he/she would most want to be introduced to and why.

Imaginez que vous pouvez faire la connaissance d'un de ces jeunes Français.
Qui voulez-vous rencontrer?
Pourquoi?

Éric (12 ans)

Moi, je n'ai pas le choix!° C'est ma mère qui choisit mes vêtements. En ce qui concerne° la mode, elle n'est pas dans le coup.° Elle achète tout sur catalogue et elle choisit ce qui est le moins cher.° C'est pas drôle.

choix *choice* **En ce qui concerne** *As for* **dans le coup** *with it*
le moins cher *the cheapest (the least expensive)*

STRATEGY Reading

Understanding casual French speech

The interviews you read were conducted orally. Notice how casual French speech is different from standard written language.

- Spoken language often contains slang expressions.
  Elle n'est pas dans le coup! C'est marrant! C'est génial!
- Spoken French sometimes drops the **ne** in **ne ... pas**.
  C'est pas cher. = Ce n'est pas cher.

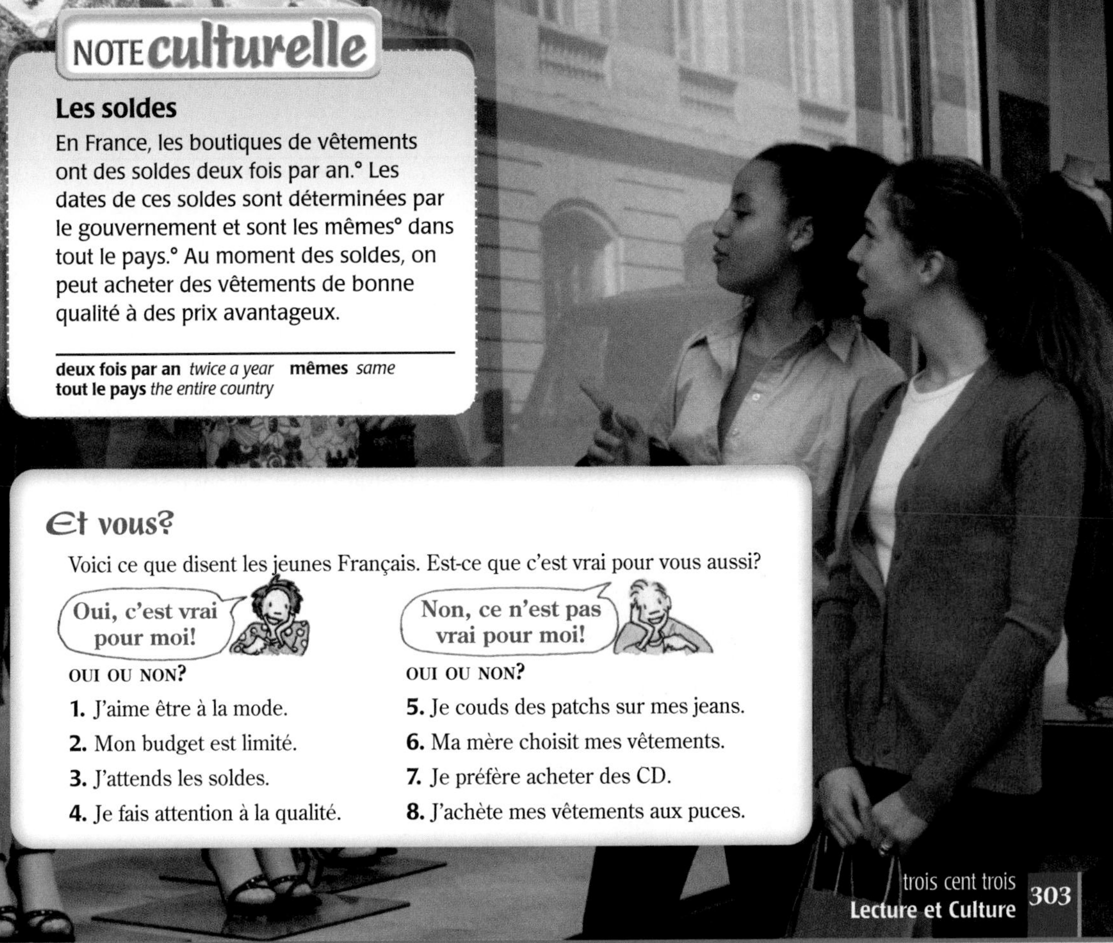

NOTE culturelle

Les soldes

En France, les boutiques de vêtements ont des soldes deux fois par an.° Les dates de ces soldes sont déterminées par le gouvernement et sont les mêmes° dans tout le pays.° Au moment des soldes, on peut acheter des vêtements de bonne qualité à des prix avantageux.

deux fois par an *twice a year* **mêmes** *same*
tout le pays *the entire country*

Et vous?

Voici ce que disent les jeunes Français. Est-ce que c'est vrai pour vous aussi?

Oui, c'est vrai pour moi! — Non, ce n'est pas vrai pour moi!

OUI OU NON?

1. J'aime être à la mode.
2. Mon budget est limité.
3. J'attends les soldes.
4. Je fais attention à la qualité.
5. Je couds des patchs sur mes jeans.
6. Ma mère choisit mes vêtements.
7. Je préfère acheter des CD.
8. J'achète mes vêtements aux puces.

Questions personnelles

Answers will vary.

1. Comment est-ce que tu gagnes ton argent? (Je fais du baby-sitting.)
2. Est-ce que tu travailles? Où? (Oui, je travaille dans une boutique.)
3. Où est-ce que tu achètes tes vêtements? (J'achète mes vêtements au centre commercial.)
4. Est-ce que tu attends les soldes pour acheter tes vêtements? (Oui, j'attends les soldes pour acheter mes vêtements.)
5. Qu'est-ce que tu achètes sur catalogue/sur Internet? (J'achète des CD.)
6. Robert dit: «La présentation extérieure est très importante.» Est-ce que tu es d'accord avec cette opinion? (Oui, je suis d'accord.)
7. Julien dit: «L'habit ne fait pas le moine.» Est-ce que tu es d'accord avec ce proverbe? (Non, je ne suis pas d'accord.)

Et vous?

Answers will vary.

1. Oui, c'est vrai pour moi. (Non, ce n'est pas vrai pour moi.)
2. Oui, c'est vrai pour moi. (Non, ce n'est pas vrai pour moi.)
3. Oui, c'est vrai pour moi. (Non, ce n'est pas vrai pour moi.)
4. Oui, c'est vrai pour moi. (Non, ce n'est pas vrai pour moi.)
5. Non, ce n'est pas vrai pour moi. (Oui, c'est vrai pour moi.)
6. Non, ce n'est pas vrai pour moi. (Oui, c'est vrai pour moi.)
7. Oui, c'est vrai pour moi. (Non, ce n'est pas vrai pour moi.)
8. Non, ce n'est pas vrai pour moi. (Oui, c'est vrai pour moi.)

Bonjour, Fatima!

Objectives

- Reading a complete text
- Building reading skills

Teaching Resource Options

PRINT  

Workbook PE, pp. 177–179
Activités pour tous PE, pp. 107–109
Unit 6 Resource Book
Activités pour tous TE, pp. 159–161
Workbook TE, pp. 163–165

Bonjour, Fatima!

Je m'appelle Fatima et j'ai quinze ans. J'habite dans la banlieue° de Paris. Mes parents sont généreux mais ils ne sont pas très riches. Alors, je n'ai pas beaucoup d'argent de poche: cinquante euros par mois. Ce n'est pas une fortune! Heureusement,° je fais du baby-sitting pour les voisins quand ils vont au cinéma le week-end. Je gagne cinq euros par heure.

J'adore les vêtements. Avec ma copine Djemila, on achète des magazines de mode et on va dans les magasins. Quand on entre dans une boutique, c'est généralement plus pour regarder que pour acheter. J'achète mes nouveaux pulls pendant la période des soldes. Par contre,° j'achète assez souvent des bracelets et des boucles d'oreille.° On trouve des choses géniales dans les petites boutiques de mon quartier. Quand je veux changer de «look», je change de boucles d'oreille et je change de vernis à ongles° et de rouge à lèvres.° C'est facile et ça ne coûte pas cher!

banlieue *suburbs* **Heureusement** *Fortunately* **Par contre** *On the other hand* **boucles d'oreille** *earrings* **vernis à ongles** *nail polish* **rouge à lèvres** *lipstick*

NOTE culturelle

Prénoms arabes

Fatima et **Djemila** sont des jeunes filles d'origine «maghrébine». Elles portent° des noms typiquement arabes.

Le Maghreb est une région géographique constituée par **le Maroc,° l'Algérie** et **la Tunisie**. Quatre millions de Français (sur une population totale de soixante millions) sont d'origine maghrébine. Beaucoup parlent arabe et pratiquent la religion musulmane.°

portent = ont **Maroc** *Morocco* **musulmane** *Moslem*

PRE-READING

Ask students to look at this page and decide what type of reading it is. [a letter]

POST-READING

Have students use their answers to the **Et vous?** activity as the basis for writing a letter to Fatima, explaining how similar or different their lives are from hers.

Compréhension

1. Comment est-ce que Fatima gagne son argent?
2. Qu'est-ce qu'elle fait avec sa copine?
3. Qu'est-ce qu'elle achète avec son argent?
4. Qu'est-ce qu'elle fait pour changer de look?

Et vous?

Quelles ressemblances *(similarities)* et quelles différences est-ce que vous trouvez entre Fatima et vous? Faites une liste de ces ressemblances et de ces différences.

- âge
- parents
- argent de poche
- achats de vêtements
- achats d'accessoires
- comment changer de look

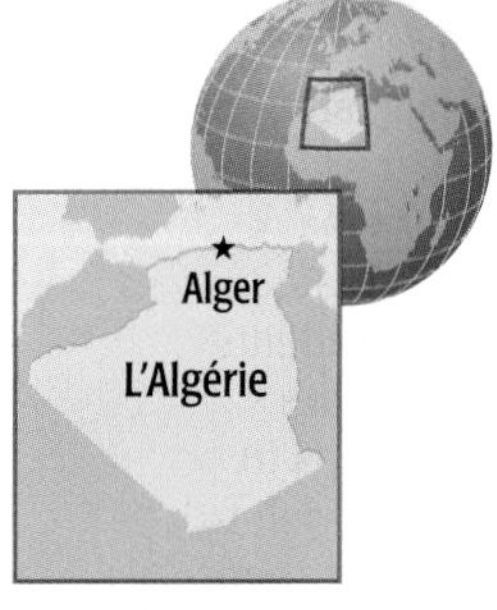

EN BREF: L'ALGÉRIE

Population: 32 millions
Capitale: Alger
Langues: arabe, berbère, français

L'Algérie est un pays° d'Afrique du Nord. Colonie française pendant plus de 100 ans, l'Algérie est devenue indépendante en 1962. La majorité des Algériens sont arabes et pratiquent la religion musulmane. Des millions d'Algériens ont immigré en France et sont devenus Français. Pour cette raison,° la France est maintenant le pays avec la plus grande population musulmane d'Europe.

La présence algérienne influence la vie° ordinaire des Français. Par exemple, les Français mangent du couscous* qui est une spécialité d'Afrique du Nord, et beaucoup de jeunes écoutent le raï qui est une musique d'origine algérienne.

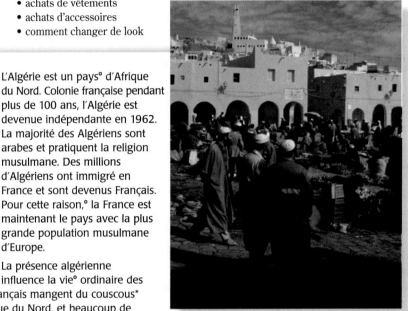

pays *country* **raison** *reason* **vie** *life*

* **Couscous** *is a type of semolina (white gritty wheat) which is usually cooked with meat and vegetables as a main dish, but which can also be steamed and served cold in salads.*

COMMUNAUTÉS

Explore Internet sources to find out more about the Muslim religion. Or perhaps there is a Muslim person in your school or in your community whom you could invite to talk to your class. Use the information you gather to make a bulletin board display explaining the basic tenets of the Muslim faith.

Compréhension
Answers

1. Elle fait du baby-sitting.
2. Elles achètent des magazines de mode et elles vont dans les magasins.
3. Fatima achète des pulls, des bracelets, et des boucles d'oreille.
4. Pour changer le look, elle change de boucles d'oreille, de vernis à ongles et de rouge à lèvres.

Et vous?
Answers will vary.

Ressemblances

1. Nos parents sont généreux, mais ils ne sont pas très riches.
2. Nous faisons du baby-sitting pour gagner de l'argent de poche.
3. Nous n'achetons pas beaucoup de vêtements.
4. Nous changeons de vernis à ongles et de rouge à lèvres pour changer le look.

Différences

1. Elle a quinze ans. J'ai (quatorze) ans.
2. Elle achète plus d'accessoires que moi.

Photo cultural note
The people in the photo are shopping at an outdoor market in the M'Zab in Ghardaia, Algeria.

Expansion activities PLANNING AHEAD

Games

• Dessinez, c'est gagné

After reviewing the vocabulary from pages 310–313, divide the class into two or three teams. Tell one member from each team, the artist, the word for that round. Have the artists draw pictures for their teams until one team guesses the word. The first team to guess the correct word gets one point and a new member of each team becomes the artist. Set a two-minute time limit for each round and let the artists know that they should not use any words to help their teammates guess. The team with the most points wins.

Pacing Suggestion: Upon completion of Leçon 21.

• Attrapez et répondez!

Have students stand in a circle. Announce a subject and a verb (for example, **je** and **choisir**) and toss a ball to one player. That player must conjugate the verb in **passé composé** for that subject pronoun (**j'ai choisi**), pass the ball to another player, and change either the subject pronoun or verb for that player (**nous** and **choisir** or **je** and **parler,** for example). Any player who answers incorrectly is out and must stand outside the circle. For larger classes, you may want to divide the class into two circles. You may want to impose a time limit of five seconds for the student with the ball to respond. As an added challenge, allow students the option of alternating between **passé composé** and present tense.

Pacing Suggestion: Upon completion of Leçon 23.

Projects

• Les fêtes

Have students work in small groups to learn more about holidays and celebrations in France. Students may wish to investigate *Mardi Gras, Premier Avril, 14 Juillet, Chandeleur,* and *Saint Nicolas.* Each group will present a holiday to the class. They will tell when the holiday is celebrated and what traditions and foods are associated with the holiday. The presentations should include a visual component, such as photographs of people celebrating the holiday. Students may also wish to include some of the foods or music associated with the holiday as part of their presentations. Expand the project by having students investigate holidays in other French-speaking areas of the world.

Pacing Suggestion: Upon completion of Leçon 21.

© Robert Fried

Bulletin Boards

• Les cartes postales

Each student will design a postcard. First, have each student choose a French-speaking country that he or she might like to visit and locate pictures, or create an image, for the front of the card. Have students then use the vocabulary in the lesson to create a message for the back of the card and ask a classmate to proofread their message. Students may also research and recreate French or francophone stamps to put on their cards. You may wish to compile the cards and display them on a bulletin board.

Pacing Suggestion: Upon completion of Leçon 21.

• Le Maroc

Divide the class into small groups. Have each group research a piece of information about Morocco. Groups can:

- create a colorful map that shows where Morocco is located
- find or create illustrations of what Morocco looks like
- learn about activities that are common in Morocco
- find information about the weather, people, politics, industry, crafts, music, etc. of Morocco
- learn how Morocco gained its independence from France

Each group will create a colorful poster they can use to present the information they obtained to the rest of the class.

Pacing Suggestion: Upon completion of Leçon 24.

Music

• *Le dernier qui a parlé*

Play *Le dernier qui a parlé* for students. (The song is on the *Chansons* CD.) Give students a copy of the lyrics and have them listen to the song. Play it a second time and have students list all the words that they recognize. Have the class discuss the general meaning of the song. As alternatives, you may wish to have students listen for, and underline, verbs in the **passé composé** or hand out a version of the song with blanks that the students have to fill in as they listen.

Pacing Suggestion: Upon completion of Leçon 22.

Storytelling

• Les expressions avec *avoir*

Have each student write a story based on the vocabulary on page 320 using expressions with *avoir.* You may wish to choose several of the better stories to have students read aloud in class. The class can then vote on the best story and best use of each expression with *avoir.*

Pacing Suggestion: Upon completion of Leçon 22.

Recipe

• Soupe à l'oignon

Easy to make and delicious, **soupe à l'oignon** is a French classic. This soup is best served with salad and French bread.

Pacing Suggestion: Upon completion of Leçon 22.

Soupe à l'oignon

Ingrédients

- *4 oignons coupés en tranches*
- *8 gousses d'ail écrasées*
- *1 cuillère à soupe de farine*
- *1 litre de bouillon (de légumes ou de boeuf)*
- *6 tranches de pain*
- *1/2 tasse de Gruyère râpé*

Préparation

1. *Cuisez les oignons avec un peu de beurre à petit feu. Remuez doucement pendant 20 minutes.*
2. *Quand les oignons commencent à faire une pâte, ajoutez l'ail et cuisez jusqu'à ce que la préparation commence à dorer.*
3. *Ajoutez la farine et cuisez 2 minutes, puis ajoutez le bouillon. Faites bouillir.*
4. *Réduisez le feu et cuire, couvert, à petit feu pendant 20 minutes.*
5. *Mettez les tranches de pain à dorer au four. Retournez-les une fois. Mettez un peu de fromage râpé sur les tranches de pain grillé et faites-les griller jusqu'à ce que le fromage fonde.*
6. *Servez la soupe avec le pain grillé au-dessus. Saupoudrez avec le reste du fromage râpé.*

Ingredients

- *4 onions, sliced*
- *8 cloves garlic, chopped*
- *1 tbsp. flour*
- *approx. 4 cups of broth (vegetable or beef)*
- *6 slices of bread*
- *1/2 cup of grated Gruyère (Swiss cheese)*

Directions

1. *Cook onions in a little bit of butter over low heat for 20 minutes. Stir occasionally.*
2. *When the onions begin to form a paste, add the garlic and cook until the mix begins to brown.*
3. *Add the flour and cook for 2 minutes, then add the broth and bring to a boil.*
4. *Reduce the heat and cook, covered, on low heat for 20 minutes.*
5. *Toast bread in oven. Turn once. Cover with grated cheese. Grill until the cheese begins to melt.*
6. *Top the soup with the toasted bread slices and more grated cheese.*

Hands-on Crafts

• Vacation Scrapbook

Have students create a scrapbook from a favorite or an "ideal" vacation. Ask students to bring in photos or illustrations of a favorite place that they have visited or would like to visit. Then using construction paper, have them build up a scrapbook of images and text. Encourage students to write a brief paragraph describing the scene or the activities shown in each photo or illustration. Have students use thick cardboard or book backing to cover their scrapbooks. Finally, they should decorate the front cover of their books with collages made from stamps, postcards, and other objects, either picked up en route or that relate to their vacation.

Pacing Suggestion: Upon completion of Leçon 22.

End of Unit

• Les infos

Students will work in pairs or in small groups to create a segment for a news broadcast in French. Assign each pair the type of segment they will need to create: a news story, a commercial, a segment on the weather, a sports story, or an interview. You may want to give students vocabulary lists to use for their specific segments. Also, make sure that all the segments contain enough parts so that each student has the opportunity to speak. Students will write a first draft of their segment, and ask another pair or group to proofread it. Have students read their segments out loud to practice intonation. Encourage students to use props to make their news segments more realistic. Finally, have students perform their news segments for the rest of the class. You may wish to videotape the segments to create an entire news program.

Rubric

A = 13–15 pts. **B** = 10–12 pts. **C** = 7–9 pts. **D** = 4–6 pts. **F** = < 4 pts.

Criteria	Scale
Vocabulary Use	1 2 3 4 5
Grammar/Spelling Accuracy	1 2 3 4 5
Creativity	1 2 3 4 5

Planning Guide CLASSROOM MANAGEMENT

OBJECTIVES

Communication
- Discuss your weekend activities *p. 310*
- Talk about individual summer and winter sports *p. 313*
- Describe your vacation and travel plans *p. 312*
- Describe what you did and where you went yesterday, last week, or last summer *pp. 321, 333, 335, 336, 342*
- Narrate what occurred at any time in the past *pp. 321, 333, 335, 336, 342*

Grammar
- Les expressions avec *avoir p. 320*
- Le passé composé des verbes en *-er p. 321*
- Le passé composé: forme négative *p. 324*
- Les questions au passé composé *p. 326*
- Le verbe *voir p. 332*
- Le passé composé des verbes réguliers en *-ir* et *-re p. 333*
- Le passé composé des verbes *être, avoir, faire, mettre* et *voir p. 335*
- Le passé composé avec *être p. 342*
- La construction négative *ne . . . jamais p. 346*
- Les expressions *quelqu'un, quelque chose* et leurs contraires *p. 347*

Vocabulary
- Le week-end *p. 310*
- Les vacances *p. 312*
- Activités sportives *p. 313*
- Expressions avec *avoir p. 320*
- Expressions pour la conversation *p. 323*
- *Quand? p. 336*
- Quelques verbes conjugués avec *être* au passé composé *p. 344*

Pronunciation
- Les lettres «ain» et «in» *p. 327*
- Les lettres «gn» *p. 337*
- Les lettres «qu» *p. 347*

Culture
- Les sports d'hiver *p. 313*
- Le week-end *p. 319*
- Les jeunes Français et la télé *p. 331*
- Les jeunes Français et la musique *p. 341*
- Le Maroc *p. 357*

PROGRAM RESOURCES

Print

- Workbook PE, *pp. 181–212*
- *Activités pour tous* PE, *pp. 111–129*
- Block Scheduling Copymasters *pp. 161–191*
- *Français pour hispanophones*
- *Lectures pour tous*
- Teacher to Teacher Copymasters
- Teaching Proficiency through Reading and Storytelling
- Unit 7 Resource Book
  - Lessons 21–24 Resources
    - Workbook TE
    - *Activités pour tous* TE
    - Family Letter
    - Absent Student Copymasters
    - Family Involvement
    - Video Activities
    - Videoscripts
    - Audioscripts
    - Assessment Program
  - Unit 7 Resources
    - Communipak
    - *Activités pour tous* TE Reading
    - Workbook TE Reading and Culture Activities
    - Assessment Program
    - Answer Keys

Audiovisual

- Audio Program PE CD 4 Tracks 1–20
- Audio Program Workbook CD 11 Tracks 1–25
- *Chansons* Audio CD
- Sing Along: Grammar and Vocabulary Songs CD
- Video Program Modules 21, 22, 23, 24
- Warm-Up Transparencies
- Overhead Transparencies
  42 Weekend Activities;
  43 Les *activités sportives*;
  44 Expressions with ***avoir***;
  16 Subject Pronouns

Technology

- Online Workbook
- ClassZone.com
- McDougal Littell Assessment System/ Test Generator CD-ROM
- Easy Planner CD-ROM
- Power Presentations on CD-ROM
- Take-Home Tutor CD-ROM

Assessment Program Options

Lesson Quizzes
Portfolio Assessment
Unit Test Form A
Unit Test Form B
Unit Test Part III (Alternate) Cultural Awareness
Listening Comprehension Performance Test
Speaking Performance Test
Reading Comprehension Performance Test
Writing Performance Test
Multiple Choice Test Items
Test Scoring Tools
Audio Program CD 16 Tracks 1–8
Answer Keys
McDougal Littell Assessment System/ Test Generator CD-ROM

Pacing Guide SAMPLE LESSON PLAN

DAY	DAY	DAY	DAY	DAY
1 Unité 7 Opener Leçon 21 • Vocabulaire et Culture–Le week-end et les vacances • Vocabulaire–Le week-end	**2** Leçon 21 • Vocabulaire–Les vacances • Vocabulaire–Activités sportives	**3** Leçon 21 • Vocabulaire–Activités sportives *(continued)* • Note culturelle–Les sports d'hiver	**4** Leçon 21 • À votre tour!	**5** Leçon 22 • Conversation et Culture–Vive le week-end! • Note culturelle–Le week-end
6 Leçon 22 • Les expressions avec *avoir* • Vocabulaire–Expressions avec *avoir*	**7** Leçon 22 • Le passé composé des verbes en *-er*	**8** Leçon 22 • Vocabulaire–Expressions pour la conversation • Le passé composé: forme négative	**9** Leçon 22 • Les questions au passé composé • Prononciation–Les lettres «ain» et «in»	**10** Leçon 22 • À votre tour!
11 Leçon 23 • Conversation et Culture–L'alibi • Note culturelle–Les jeunes Français et la télé	**12** Leçon 23 • Le verbe *voir* • Le passé composé des verbes réguliers en *-ir* et *-re*	**13** Leçon 23 • Le passé composé des verbes réguliers en *-ir* et *-re (continued)* • Le passé composé des verbes *être, avoir, faire, mettre* et *voir*	**14** Leçon 23 • Vocabulaire–Quand? • Prononciation–Les lettres «gn»	**15** Leçon 23 • À votre tour!
16 Leçon 24 • Conversation et Culture–Qui a de la chance? • Note culturelle–Les jeunes Français et la musique	**17** Leçon 24 • Le passé composé avec *être*	**18** Leçon 24 • Le passé composé avec *être (continued)* • Vocabulaire–Quelques verbes conjugués avec *être* au passé composé	**19** Leçon 24 • La construction négative *ne . . . jamais* • Les expressions *quelqu'un, quelque chose* et leurs contraires • Prononciation–Les lettres «qu»	**20** Leçon 24 • À votre tour!
21 • Tests de contrôle	**22** • Unit 7 Test	**23** • Entracte–Lecture et culture		

Student Text Listening Activity Scripts

AUDIO PROGRAM

▶ LEÇON 21 LE FRANÇAIS PRATIQUE Le week-end et les vacances

À votre tour!

• Écoutez bien! *p. 316* CD 4, TRACK 1

On weekends, you can stay in and take care of things at home, or you can go out and have fun. Listen carefully to what the people are saying. If they refer to an indoor activity, mark A. If they refer to an outdoor activity, mark B. You will hear each sentence twice. Commençons. Let's begin.

1. Est-ce que tu vas faire du roller? #
2. Je dois aider ma mère. #
3. Pauline lave son pantalon. #
4. Nous allons faire de la natation. #
5. J'aime bien faire du skate. #
6. Guillaume va ranger sa chambre. #
7. Léa va faire du VTT à la campagne. #
8. Alice aime beaucoup faire de la planche à voile. #
9. Monsieur Martin va nettoyer le garage. #
10. Sophie fait ses devoirs. #
11. Où est-ce que vous allez faire de l'escalade? #
12. Thomas va réparer la chaîne hi-fi de son cousin. #

• Créa-dialogue *p. 317* CD 4, TRACK 2

Listen to the sample *Créa-dialogues.* Écoutez les conversations.

Modèle: –Où vas-tu vendredi? –Je vais en ville.
–Qu'est-ce que tu vas faire là-bas? –Je vais faire des achats.

Maintenant, écoutez le dialogue numéro 1.

–Où vas-tu samedi matin? –Je vais à la campagne.
–Qu'est-ce que tu vas faire là-bas? –Je vais faire une promenade à vélo.

• Conversation dirigée *p. 317* CD 4, TRACK 3

Listen to the conversation. Écoutez la conversation entre Thomas et Hélène.

Thomas: Où vas-tu cet été?
Hélène: Je vais à la mer avec des amis.
Thomas: Est-ce que vous allez voyager en voiture?
Hélène: Non, on va voyager en train parce qu'on n'a pas de voiture.
Thomas: Est-ce que tu vas faire de la voile?
Hélène: Oui, et je vais aussi faire de la planche à voile.
Thomas: Au revoir, Hélène, et bonnes vacances!
Hélène: Au revoir!

▶ LEÇON 22 Vive le week-end!

• Vive le week-end! *p. 318*

A. Compréhension orale CD 4, TRACK 4

Le week-end, nous avons nos occupations préférées. Certaines personnes aiment aller en ville et rencontrer leurs amis.

D'autres préfèrent rester à la maison et bricoler. Qu'est-ce que les personnes suivantes ont fait le week-end dernier?

J'aime acheter des vêtements.	J'ai acheté des vêtements.
Tu aimes réparer ton vélo.	Tu as réparé ton vélo.
M. Lambert aime travailler dans le jardin.	Il a travaillé dans le jardin.
Nous aimons organiser des boums.	Nous avons organisé une boum.
Vous aimez jouer au foot.	Vous avez joué au foot.
Pluton et Philibert aiment rencontrer leurs amis.	Ils ont rencontré leurs amis.

B. Écoutez et répétez. CD 4, TRACK 5

You will now hear a paused version of the dialog. Listen to the speaker and repeat right after he or she has completed the sentence.

• Vocabulaire *p. 320* CD 4, TRACK 6

Expressions avec *avoir*

Repeat the sentences after the speaker.

avoir chaud #	Quand j'**ai chaud** en été, je vais à la plage. #
avoir froid #	Est-ce que tu **as froid?** Voici ton pull. #
avoir faim #	Tu **as faim?** Est-ce que tu veux une pizza? #
avoir soif #	**J'ai soif.** Je voudrais une limonade. #
avoir raison #	Est-ce que les profs **ont** toujours **raison?** #
avoir tort #	Marc ne fait pas ses devoirs. Il **a tort!** #
avoir de la chance #	**J'ai de la chance.** J'ai des amis sympathiques. #

• Prononciation *p. 327* CD 4, TRACK 7

Les lettres «ain» et «in»

Écoutez: sa main semaine magasin magazine

When the letters **"ain," "aim," "in,"** and **"im"** are at the end of a word or are followed by a *consonant*, they represent the nasal vowel /ɛ̃/.

REMEMBER: Do not pronounce an /n/ after the nasal vowel /ɛ̃/.

Répétez: /ɛ̃/ # demain # faim # train # main # voisin # cousin # jardin # magasin # maintenant # intelligent # intéressant # important #

When the letters **"ain," "aim," "in(n),"** and **"im"** are followed by a *vowel,* they do NOT represent a nasal sound.

Répétez: /ɛn/ # semaine # américaine #
/ɛm/ # j'aime #
/in/ # voisine # cousine # cuisine # magazine # cinéma # Corinne # finir #
/im/ # timide # dimanche # Mimi # centime #
Alain Minime a un rendez-vous important demain matin, avenue du Maine. #

À votre tour!

• Allô! *p. 328* CD 4, TRACK 8

Listen to the conversation. Écoutez la conversation entre Alain et Christine.

Alain: À quelle heure est-ce que tu as dîné hier soir?
Christine: À sept heures et demie.
Alain: Et après, tu as regardé la télé?
Christine: Oui, mais d'abord j'ai aidé ma mère.
Alain: Qu'est-ce que tu as regardé après?
Christine: Le match Marseille-Nice.
Alain: Qui a gagné?
Christine: Nice. Par un score de trois à un.
Alain: Dis, tu a préparé la leçon pour demain?
Christine: Mais oui! J'ai étudié avant le dîner!

• Créa-dialogue *p. 328* CD 4, TRACK 9

Listen to some sample *Créa-dialogues.* Écoutez les conversations.

Modèle: –Est-ce que tu as dîné au restaurant?
–Oui, j'ai dîné au restaurant.
–Avec qui?
–Avec mes cousins.
–Où est-ce que vous avez dîné?
–Nous avons dîné Chez Tante Lucie.

Maintenant, écoutez le dialogue numéro 1.

–Est-ce que tu as joué au tennis?
–Oui, j'ai joué au tennis.
–Avec qui?
–Avec Tom, Lucie et Karen.
–Quand est-ce que vous avez joué au tennis?
–Nous avons joué au tennis dimanche après-midi.

pause for oral response

▶ LEÇON 23 L'alibi

• L'alibi *p. 330* CD 4, TRACK 10

A. Compréhension orale

Êtes-vous bon détective? Pouvez-vous trouver la solution du mystère suivant?

Samedi dernier à deux heures de l'après-midi, il y a eu une panne d'électricité dans la petite ville de Marcillac-le-Château. La panne a duré une heure. Pendant la panne, un cambrioleur a pénétré dans la Banque Populaire de Marcillac-le-Château. Bien sûr, l'alarme n'a pas fonctionné et c'est seulement lundi matin que le directeur de la banque a remarqué le cambriolage: un million d'euros.

Lundi après-midi, l'inspecteur Leflic a interrogé quatre suspects, mais chacun a un alibi.

Sophie Filou: Euh . . . excusez-moi, Monsieur l'Inspecteur. Ma mémoire n'est pas très bonne. Voyons, qu'est-ce que j'ai fait samedi après-midi? Ah oui, j'ai fini un livre. Le titre du livre? *Le crime ne paie pas!*

Marc Laroulette: Qu'est-ce que j'ai fait samedi? J'ai rendu visite à mes copains. Nous avons joué aux cartes. C'est moi qui ai gagné!

Patrick Lescrot: Voyons, samedi dernier . . . Ah oui . . . cet après-midi-là, j'ai invité des amis chez moi. Nous avons regardé la télé. Nous avons vu le match de foot France-Allemagne. Quel match! Malheureusement, c'est la France qui a perdu! Dommage!

Pauline Malin: Ce n'est pas moi, Monsieur l'Inspecteur! Samedi j'ai fait un pique-nique à la campagne avec une copine. Nous avons choisi un coin près d'une rivière. Ensuite, nous avons fait une promenade à vélo. Nous avons eu de la chance! Il a fait un temps extraordinaire!

Lisez attentivement les quatre déclarations. À votre avis, qui est le cambrioleur ou la cambrioleuse? Pourquoi? (Vous pouvez comparer votre réponse avec la réponse de l'inspecteur à la page 337.)

B. Écoutez et répétez. CD 4, TRACK 11

You will now hear a paused version of the dialog. Listen to the speaker and repeat right after he or she has completed the sentence.

• Grammaire *p. 332* CD 4, TRACK 12

Le verbe *voir*

Repeat the sentences after the speaker.

Je **vois** Marc. #
Il **voit** un accident. #
Vous **voyez** un match de baseball. #
Tu **vois** ton copain. #
Nous **voyons** un film. #
Elles **voient** le professeur. #

• Prononciation *p. 337* CD 4, TRACK 13

Les lettres «gn»

Écoutez: espagnol

The letters "**gn**" represent a sound similar to the "**ny**" in *canyon.* First, practice with words you know.

Répétez: espagnol # gagner # mignon # la montagne # la campagne

Now try saying some new words. Make them sound French!

Répétez: Champagne # Espagne # un signe # la vigne # la ligne # un signal # la dignité # ignorer # magnétique # magnifique # Agnès # Agnès Mignard a gagné son match. C'est magnifique! #

À votre tour!

• Allô! *p. 338* CD 4, TRACK 14

Listen to the conversation. Écoutez la conversation entre Robert et Julien.

Robert: Tu as fini tes devoirs de français?
Julien: Non, je n'ai pas étudié cet après-midi.
Robert: Qu'est-ce que tu as fait alors?
Julien: J'ai joué au tennis avec Caroline.
Robert: Tu as gagné?
Julien: Non, j'ai perdu!
Robert: Mais d'habitude tu joues bien?
Julien: C'est vrai, mais aujourd'hui, je n'ai pas eu de chance . . .
Robert: Peut-être que Caroline a joué mieux que toi?
Julien: Tu as raison. Elle a joué comme une championne.

• Créa-dialogue *p. 338* CD 4, TRACK 15

Listen to the sample *Créa-dialogues*. Écoutez les conversations.

Modèle: –Qu'est-ce que tu as fait dimanche après-midi?
–J'ai joué au tennis avec ma soeur.
–Est-ce que tu as gagné?
–Non, j'ai perdu!
–Dommage!

Maintenant écoutez un autre dialogue.

–Qu'est-ce que tu as fait hier soir?
–J'ai eu un rendez-vous.
–Avec qui est-ce que tu as eu un rendez-vous?
–Avec Thomas, mon meilleur ami.
–C'est chouette!

▶ LEÇON 24 Qui a de la chance?

• Qui a de la chance? *p. 340*

A. Compréhension orale CD 4, TRACK 16

Please turn to page 340 for complete *Compréhension orale* text.

B. Écoutez et répétez. CD 4, TRACK 17

You will now hear a paused version of the dialog. Listen to the speaker and repeat right after he or she has completed the sentence.

• Prononciation *p. 347* CD 4, TRACK 18

Les lettres «qu»

Écoutez: un bouquet

The letters "**qu**" represent the sound /k/.

Répétez: qui # quand # quelque chose # quelqu'un # quatre # quatorze # Québec # Monique # Véronique # sympathique # un pique-nique # le ski nautique # Véronique pense que Monique aime la musique classique. #

À votre tour!

• Allô! *p. 348* CD 4, TRACK 19

Listen to the conversation. Écoutez la conversation entre Sophie et Charlotte.

Sophie: Tu es restée chez toi samedi soir?
Charlotte: Non! J'ai téléphoné à une copine et nous sommes allées au cinéma.
Sophie: Qu'est-ce que vous avez vu?
Charlotte: Un vieux western avec Gary Cooper.
Sophie: Qu'est-ce que vous avez fait ensuite?
Charlotte: Nous sommes allées dans un café sur le boulevard Saint Michel.
Sophie: Vous avez mangé quelque chose?
Charlotte: Oui, des sandwichs.
Sophie: À quelle heure es-tu rentrée chez toi?
Charlotte: À onze heures et demie.

• Créa-dialogue *p. 348* CD 4, TRACK 20

Listen to some sample *Créa-dialogues.* Écoutez les conversations.

Modèle: –Tu es resté chez toi hier matin?
–Oui, je suis resté chez moi.
–Qu'est-ce que tu as fait?
–J'ai rangé ma chambre.

–Tu es resté chez toi hier matin?
–Non, je ne suis pas resté(e) chez moi.
–Qu'est-ce que tu as fait?
–Je suis allé à l'école.

Maintenant, écoutez le dialogue numéro 1.

–Tu es allé en ville samedi après-midi?
–Oui, je suis allé en ville samedi après-midi.
–Qu'est-ce que tu as fait?
–J'ai fait des achats.

–Tu es allée en ville samedi après-midi?
–Non, je ne suis pas allée en ville.
–Qu'est-ce que tu as fait?
–Je suis allée à la plage!

Complete videoscripts, plus Workbook and Assessment audioscripts, are available in the Unit Resource Books.

Main Theme
- Leisure-time activities

COMMUNICATION
- Discussing weekend activities
- Talking about individual summer and winter sports
- Describing vacation and travel plans
- Telling what you did and where you went yesterday, last week, or last summer
- Narrating what happened at any time in the past

CULTURES
- Learning how the French spend their leisure time
- Learning about the sports the French enjoy
- Learning what the French do on weekends
- Learning about the variety of music French teens enjoy
- Learning about the **Fête de la Musique**
- Learning about Morocco

CONNECTIONS
- Connecting to Social Studies: Learning about the history and culture of Morocco
- Connecting to Physical Education: Learning about the benefits and safety equipment of in-line skating
- Connecting to Computer Science: Using the Internet to research exchange programs in French-speaking regions

COMPARISONS
- Comparing television-watching habits of teens in France and the U.S.
- Comparing French and American teenagers' attitude toward and taste in music

continued on next page

Le temps libre

THÈME ET OBJECTIFS

Leisure-time activities

We work hard during the week, but we also need time to relax.

In this unit, you will learn ...

- to discuss your weekend activities
- to talk about individual summer and winter sports
- to describe your vacation and travel plans

You will also be able ...

- to describe what you did and where you went yesterday, last week, or last summer
- more generally, to narrate what happened at any time in the past

UNIT OVERVIEW

- **Communication Goals:** Students will be able to talk about individual sports, helping out at home, and what they did over the weekend or during vacation.
- **Linguistic Goals:** Students will learn to describe and narrate past events using the passé composé.
- **Critical Thinking Goals:** Students will observe the similarities and differences between the passé composé in French and the past tense in English.
- **Cultural Goals:** Students will learn about weekend and sports activities popular in France and the importance of leisure time to the French people.

STANDARDS *continued*

- Making language comparisons between French and English
- Finding out about the influence of certain American television programs on French teenagers.
- Learning about the influence of Moroccan culture on French cuisine

COMMUNITIES

- Using French to do volunteer work in a French-speaking region
- Using French for personal enjoyment

Teaching Resource Options

PRINT 

Unit 7 Resource Book
Family Letter, p. 15
Français pour hispanophones
Conseils, p. 16
Vocabulaire, pp. 50–51

AUDIO & VISUAL 

Audio Program
Chansons CD

TECHNOLOGY

EasyPlanner CD-ROM

PACING

Your pacing of Units 7 and 8 depends on what point in the academic year you begin these units.

Since this material is reintroduced in **Discovering French, *Nouveau!–Blanc*,** you may wish to present the material of Units 7 and 8 primarily for student recognition. Or you may wish to focus on Unit 7 so that the students have a solid introduction to the **passé composé**.

For further suggestions on pacing, see page 305D TE.

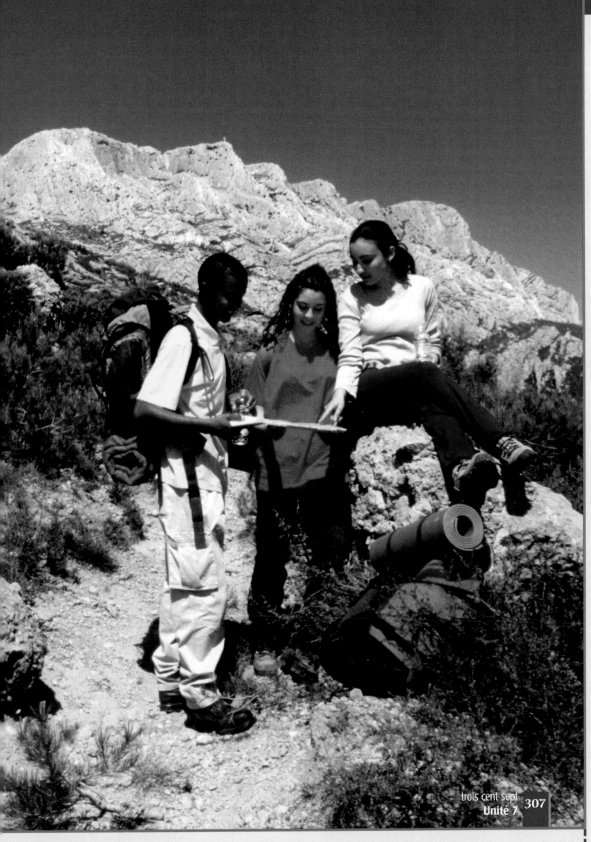

Leçon 21

Main Topic Talking about vacations, sports, and weekend activities

Teaching Resource Options

PRINT 

Workbook PE, pp. 181–186
Activités pour tous PE, pp. 111–113
Block Scheduling Copymasters, pp. 161–168
Unit 7 Resource Book
- *Activités pour tous* TE, pp. 7–9
- Audioscript, pp. 30–31
- Communipak, pp. 148–170
- Lesson Plans, pp. 10–11
- Block Scheduling Lesson Plans, pp. 12–14
- Absent Student Copymasters, pp. 16–18
- Video Activities, pp. 21–26
- Videoscript, pp. 27–28
- Workbook TE, pp. 1–6

AUDIO & VISUAL 

Audio Program
CD 11 Tracks 1–6

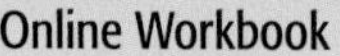

TECHNOLOGY
Online Workbook

VIDEO PROGRAM

VIDÉO DVD

MODULE 21
Le français pratique: Le week-end et les vacances

TOTAL TIME: 6:21 min.
DVD Disk 2
Videotape 4 (COUNTER: 00:00 min.)

21.1 Introduction: Listening – Le week-end (0:10–0:35 min.)

21.2 Mini-scenes: Listening – Que faites-vous le week-end? (0:36–1:42 min.)

21.3 Dialogue: Le week-end (1:43–2:07 min.)

21.4 Mini-scenes: Speaking – Samedi (2:08–3:11 min.)

21.5 Introduction: Listening – Les vacances (3:12–3:45 min.)

21.6 Dialogue: Les vacances (3:46–4:17 min.)

21.7 Mini-scenes: Speaking – Qu'est-ce qu'il fait? (4:18–4:59 min.)

21.8 Vignette culturelle: La planche à voile (5:00–6:21 min.)

Comprehension practice Play the entire module through as an introduction to the lesson.

LEÇON 21

LE FRANÇAIS PRATIQUE
VIDÉO DVD AUDIO

Le week-end et les vacances

Accent sur ... les loisirs

When given the choice, French people would rather have more free time than more money. For them, leisure time is an essential component of what they call **la qualité de la vie** (*quality of life*). By law, they work only thirty-five hours per week and they have a minimum of five weeks of vacation per year.

Like their parents, French teenagers value their leisure time and try to make the most of it. What are their favorite activities? Here is what they do when they have a free evening.

Qu'est-ce que tu aimes faire le soir?	GARÇONS	FILLES
Je regarde la télé.	24%	18%
Je sors° avec mes copains.	20%	18%
Je vais au cinéma.	16%	14%
Je lis.°	14%	20%
Je vais au concert ou au théâtre.	10%	12%
Je vais danser.	8%	12%
Je fais du sport.	6%	4%
Je bricole.°	2%	2%

sors *go out* **lis** *read* **bricole** *do things around the house*

Michèle est très sportive. Elle fait souvent du jogging dans le parc de la ville.

Thomas adore faire du skate. Le samedi, il va au skatepark avec ses copains.

USING THE VIDEO

The main focus of Video Module 21 is on what French people do in their leisure time, both on weekends and on vacation. As students watch, have them look for similarities and differences in the ways the French and Americans spend their leisure time.

The **Vignette culturelle** introduces students to the sport of windsurfing **(la planche à voile),** which is very popular throughout metropolitan France, as well as in the overseas departments of Martinique and Guadeloupe.

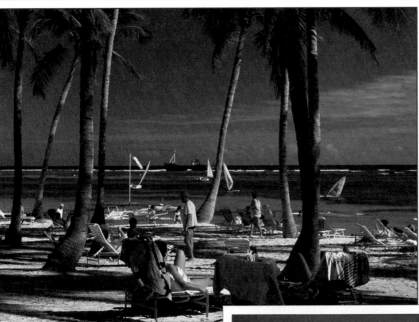

À la Martinique il fait beau tout le temps.
À la plage, on fait du surfing ou de la planche à voile.

En hiver, beaucoup de jeunes Français vont à la montagne avec leur famille ou leur école. Le snowboard — ou le surf — est un sport très populaire.

Cultural notes

Les vacances

You may want to point out that for French people from all walks of life, vacation time is sacred. Often they enjoy a week of winter sports or travel, plus a longer vacation in July or August.

Les examens

French students are concerned about doing well on their final **baccalauréat** exams in the last two years at the **lycée**. Younger students work hard to score well on the **entrée en sixième** (to enter the right secondary school sequence) and the **entrée en seconde** (to enter the right **lycée** sequence). See chart on p. 128.)

CROSS-CULTURAL COMPARISONS

Ask your students what they like to do when they have a free evening, using the suggestions in the **sondage** on p. 308. Then analyze your results and compare them to those in the reading.

You can review numbers by tallying the results in French, using a calculator.

Dans la classe, il y a [12] garçons et [16] filles.
[4] garçons regardent la télé.
Ça fait [25% – vingt-cinq pour cent].
[4] filles regardent la télé.
Ça fait [33 % – trente-trois pour cent].

SECTION A

Communicative function
Discussing weekend activities

Teaching Resource Options

PRINT 

Workbook PE, pp. 181–186
Unit 7 Resource Book
  Communipak, pp. 148–170
  Video Activities, pp. 21–23
  Videoscript, pp. 27–28
  Workbook TE, pp. 1–6

AUDIO & VISUAL 

Overhead Transparencies
42 Weekend activities

VIDEO PROGRAM

VIDÉO DVD

MODULE 21

21.1 Introduction: Le week-end (0:10–0:35 min.)

21.2 Mini-scenes: Que faites-vous le week-end? (0:36–1:42 min.)

21.3 Dialogue: Le week-end (1:43–2:07 min.)

21.4 Mini-scenes: Samedi (2:08–3:11 min.)

Supplementary vocabulary
ranger (sa chambre) *to clean (one's room)*
Compare:
ranger *to straighten up, to pick up*
nettoyer *to dust and vacuum*

Like **manger**, which the students already know, the verb **ranger** has a spelling change in the **nous** form: **nous rangeons**.

retrouver (des amis) *to meet (friends)*
Compare:
retrouver *to meet as arranged*
rencontrer *to run into (by chance)*

Teaching strategy Like **payer, nettoyer** is also a "boot" verb. Have students draw a boot and write the appropriate forms of **nettoyer** inside and outside their drawing.

A VOCABULAIRE Le week-end

METROPOLITAIN
Qu'est-ce que tu vas faire samedi?
Je vais rester chez moi pour réparer mon vélo.

▶ ***How to plan your weekend activities:***

Qu'est-ce que tu vas faire | samedi?
samedi **matin**
dimanche **après-midi**
demain **soir**
ce **week-end**
le week-end **prochain** *(next)*

le matin *morning*
l'après-midi *(m.) afternoon*
le soir *evening*

Je vais rester chez moi **pour** *(in order to)* | faire mes **devoirs** *(homework).*
réparer *(to fix)* mon vélo
préparer le dîner
aider *(to help)* mes parents
laver *(to wash)* la voiture
nettoyer *(to clean)* le garage
ranger *(to pick up)* ma chambre

Je vais aller ... | pour ...
en ville / dans les magasins / au centre commercial | **faire des achats** *(to go shopping).* **louer** *(to rent)* un film
au cinéma / au café / au stade | **voir** *(to see)* un film, **rencontrer** *(to meet)* des copains, **assister à** *(to go to, attend)* un match de foot
à la campagne *(countryside)* | **faire un pique-nique** *(to have a picnic)*

Moi, je vais aller en ville pour faire des achats.

PRINTEMPS

Je vais aller à une boum.
Avant *(Before)* la boum, je vais faire des achats.
Pendant *(During)* la boum, je vais écouter des CD.
Après *(After)* la boum, je vais faire mes devoirs.

→ The verb **nettoyer** is conjugated like **payer:**

je **nettoie** tu **nettoies** il/elle/on **nettoie** ils/elles **nettoient**
but: nous **nettoyons** vous **nettoyez**

WARM-UP AND REVIEW

Review the gestures for the subject pronouns (page 96). Have students identify the forms of **faire.**

C'est le week-end.
Je fais une promenade. [gesture **je**]
Vous faites une promenade. [vous]
Ils font une promenade aussi., etc.

Review times and possessive adjectives, asking when students do their homework.

X, à quelle heure est-ce que tu fais tes devoirs?
[Je fais mes devoirs à sept heures et demie.]
Y, à quelle heure est-ce que X fait ses devoirs?
[Il fait ses devoirs à sept heures et demie.]

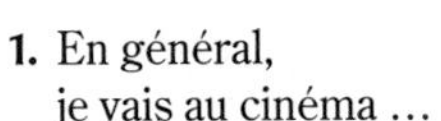

1 Et toi?

PARLER/ÉCRIRE Décris tes activités. Pour cela, complète les phrases suivantes.

1. En général, je vais au cinéma …	• le vendredi soir • le samedi soir	• le dimanche après-midi • … ?
2. En général, je fais mes devoirs …	• avant le dîner • après le dîner	• pendant la classe • … ?
3. Je préfère assister à …	• un match de foot • un match de baseball	• un concert de rock • … ?
4. En général, quand je rentre chez moi après les classes, …	• je fais mes devoirs • je regarde la télé	• j'aide ma mère ou mon père • … ?
5. J'aime aller en ville pour …	• voir un film • rencontrer mes copains	• faire des achats • … ?
6. En général, je préfère faire mes achats …	• seul(e) *(by myself)* • avec mes copains	• avec mes frères et mes soeurs • … ?
7. En été, je préfère faire un pique-nique …	• dans mon jardin • à la campagne	• à la plage • … ?
8. Pour aider mes parents à la maison, je préfère …	• ranger le salon • laver la voiture	• nettoyer le garage • … ?

2 Qu'est-ce qu'ils font?

PARLER/ÉCRIRE Informez-vous sur les personnes suivantes. Décrivez ce qu'elles font ou ce qu'elles vont faire. Pour cela, complétez les phrases avec une expression du **Vocabulaire** à la page 310.

▶ Sandrine est au garage.
Elle répare son vélo (sa mobylette).

1. Mme Jolivet est dans la cuisine. Elle …
2. Vincent Jolivet est aussi dans la cuisine. Il …
3. Anne et Sylvie sont au Bon Marché. Elles …
4. Je suis dans ma chambre et je regarde mon livre de français. Je …
5. Olivier et ses copains achètent des billets *(tickets)* de cinéma. Ils vont …
6. Mes amis vont à Yankee Stadium. Ils vont …
7. Tu vas au café. Tu vas …
8. Vous faites des sandwichs. Vous allez … à la campagne.

3 Mon calendrier personnel

PARLER/ÉCRIRE Décrivez ce que vous allez faire.

MERCREDI

1. Après la classe, je vais …
2. Avant le dîner, …
3. Après le dîner, …
4. Demain soir, …
5. Vendredi soir, …
6. Samedi après-midi, …
7. Samedi soir, …
8. Dimanche après-midi, …
9. Pendant les vacances, …

TEACHING NOTE Directions to activities

From now on, direction lines for the activities are given in French. You may want to present the key verbs listed here. Encourage your students to guess the meanings of other new words and expressions from context.

With more challenging activities, you may wish to have a volunteer paraphrase the instructions in English.

Key verbs for direction lines:

- **décrire** *to describe*
- **demander** *to ask*
- **dire** *to say*
- **expliquer** *to explain*
- **indiquer** *to indicate*
- **lire** *to read*
- **poser une question** *to ask a question*
- **utiliser** *to use*

Language notes

- Expressions used in Quebec:
  un centre d'achats *(a shopping center)*
  un mail */maj/* *(a mall)*
  magasiner/faire du magasinage *(to go shopping)*
- The French also say: **louer une cassette vidéo, louer un DVD**

Looking ahead The present tense forms of **voir** are presented in Lesson 23.

1 COMMUNICATION describing leisure activities

Answers will vary.

1. En général, je vais au cinéma (le samedi soir).
2. En général, je fais mes devoirs (après le dîner).
3. Je préfère assister à (un concert de rock).
4. En général, quand je rentre chez moi après les classes, (je regarde la télé).
5. J'aime aller en ville pour (faire des achats).
6. En général, je préfère faire mes achats (avec mes copains).
7. En été, je préfère faire un pique-nique (à la plage).
8. Pour aider mes parents à la maison, je préfère (ranger le salon).

Variations

- In pairs: Have students work in pairs, sharing their answers.
- In small groups: (See suggested activity on p. 75.)

2 COMPREHENSION describing what people are doing

1. Elle prépare le dîner.
2. Il (aide sa mère / fait ses devoirs).
3. Elles (font des achats / rencontrent leurs copains).
4. Je fais mes devoirs.
5. Ils vont voir un film.
6. Ils vont assister à un match de baseball.
7. Tu vas rencontrer des copains.
8. Vous allez faire un pique-nique à la campagne.

3 COMMUNICATION describing future plans

Answers will vary.

1. Après la classe, je vais (rencontrer des copains).
2. Avant le dîner, je vais (nettoyer ma chambre).
3. Après le dîner, je vais (faire mes devoirs).
4. Demain soir, je vais (aller au café).
5. Vendredi soir, je vais (assister à un concert).
6. Samedi après-midi, je vais (faire des achats).
7. Samedi soir, je vais (voir un film).
8. Dimanche après-midi, je vais (réparer ma mobylette).
9. Pendant les vacances, je vais (aller à la campagne).

SECTION B

Communicative function
Discussing vacations

Teaching Resource Options

PRINT 

Workbook PE, pp. 181–186
Unit 7 Resource Book
- Communipak, pp. 148–170
- Video Activities, pp. 24–25
- Videoscript, p. 28
- Workbook TE, pp. 1–6

AUDIO & VISUAL 

Overhead Transparencies
43 *Les activités sportives*

VIDEO PROGRAM

VIDÉO DVD

MODULE 21

21.5 Introduction: Les vacances (3:12–3:45 min.)

21.6 Dialogues: Les vacances (3:46–4:17 min.)

21.7 Mini-scenes: Qu'est-ce qu'il fait? (4:18–4:59 min.)

Supplementary vocabulary

HOLIDAYS
la Hanoukka
la Pâque *(Passover)*

SPORTS AND ACTIVITIES
faire du ballet
faire du bateau
faire du deltaplane *(hang gliding)*
faire du motocross
faire du ski alpin
faire du ski de fond *(cross-country)*
faire du vélo
faire de la danse moderne
faire de la gymnastique
faire de la marche *(fast walking)*
faire de la moto
faire de la natation *(swimming)*
faire du skate *(skateboarding)*

Looking ahead The negative construction **(Je ne fais pas de ski)** will be presented in Unit 8 when students learn the partitive.

B VOCABULAIRE Les vacances

Qu'est-ce que tu vas faire cet été?
Je vais aller à la mer.

▶ ***How to plan your vacation activities:***

Qu'est-ce que tu vas faire | à **Noël?**
à **Pâques**
pendant *(during)* **les vacances** de printemps
pendant **les grandes vacances**
cet été

Noël *Christmas*
Pâques *Easter*
les vacances *vacation*
les grandes vacances *summer vacation*

Je vais aller | à **la mer** *(ocean, shore).*
à **la montagne** *(mountains)*

Je vais voyager | en avion.
en train
en autocar
en bateau
en voiture

un avion *plane*
un train *train*
un autocar, un car *touring bus*
un bateau *boat, ship*

Je vais voyager | **seul(e)** *(alone).*
avec ma famille

Je vais **passer** *(to spend)* | dix jours
six semaines
deux mois
| là-bas.

un jour *day*
une semaine *week*
un mois *month*

J'aime | **le ski** *(skiing).*
le ski nautique *(water-skiing)*

En hiver, je vais à la montagne pour **faire du ski** *(to ski).*
En été, je vais à la mer pour **faire du ski nautique** *(to water-ski).*

J'aime le ski!

COMPREHENSION Sports

PROPS: Blue cards with logos for jogging, skiing, waterskiing, mountain climbing; red cards with logos for sailing, swimming, and windsurfing

Identify the cards: **Ces cartes représentent des sports différents. Voici l'escalade.**
Hand out the sports cards.

Moi, j'aime le ski. Qui aime le ski ici?
X et Y, vous aimez le ski? [Oui.]
Give them "skiing" card.
Talk about who does what sport.
X et Y, vous faites du ski en hiver? [Oui]
Ils font du ski.

VOCABULAIRE Activités sportives

le sport	*sport(s)*	Je **fais du sport.**	*I practice sports.*
le jogging	*jogging*	Nous **faisons du jogging.**	*We jog.*
la natation	*swimming*	Tu **fais de la natation?**	*Do you go swimming?*
l'escalade *(f.)*	*rock climbing*	J'aime **faire de l'escalade.**	*I like to go rock climbing.*
le ski	*skiing*	Tu **fais du ski?**	*Do you ski?*
le ski nautique	*water-skiing*	Anne **fait du ski nautique.**	*Anne water-skis.*
la voile	*sailing*	Paul **fait de la voile.**	*Paul sails.*
la planche à voile	*windsurfing*	Vous **faites de la planche à voile?**	*Do you windsurf?*

le roller	*in-line skating*	**des rollers**	*in-line skates*
le skate	*skateboarding*	**un skate**	*skateboard*
le snowboard	*snowboarding*	**un snowboard**	*snowboard*
le VTT	*mountain biking*	**un VTT**	*mountain bike*

➔ To describe participation in individual sports or other activities, the French use the construction:

faire { **du** / **de la** / **de l'** } + *SPORT* or *ACTIVITY*

le roller → **faire du roller**
la voile → **faire de la voile**
l'escalade → **faire de l'escalade**

NOTE culturelle

Les sports d'hiver

À Noël et pendant les vacances de février, beaucoup de jeunes Français vont à la montagne avec leur famille pour faire des sports d'hiver. Certaines écoles organisent des «classes de neige». Les élèves étudient le matin et font du sport l'après-midi.

Le ski est un sport très populaire. Mais beaucoup de jeunes préfèrent faire du snowboard, une spécialité dans laquelle° plusieurs° Françaises ont été° championnes olympiques.

laquelle *which* **plusieurs** *several* **ont été** *have been*

GAME Activités

PROPS: Transparency 43: *Les activités sportives*
With the overhead projector turned off, have one student come to the front and write an "X" by one of the activities on the transparency. Students at their desks try to guess which activity the student has chosen.
Tu fais de la natation? [Non, je ne fais pas de natation.]
Tu fais du ski? [Oui, je fais du ski.]
The student at the front verifies the correct guess by turning on the overhead projector. The student who guesses then comes forward, turns off the projector, erases the "X," chooses another activity, and the game continues.

Realia note

Mont Ste-Anne is a popular ski and snowboard resort in Beaupré, Quebec. It is about 400 miles from Boston, MA and 575 miles from New York, NY. There are more than 55 trails covering 40+ miles of terrain. The mountain's highest elevation is 2,625 feet. Mont-Ste-Anne has an average season of over 160 days. The mountain is also a popular summer destination that offers golf **(le golf)**, mountain biking **(le vélo de montagne)**, hiking **(la randonnée pedestre)**, and paragliding **(le parapente)** to its visitors.

Language note

le snowboard: the French also may say: **le surf des neiges**
Also:
le surf *(ocean surfboarding)*
un surf *(surfboard)*
VTT = vélo tout terrain

Note culturelle

Culture notes

- Mardi Gras is the last Tuesday before Lent (**le Carême**), which begins on Ash Wednesday (**le mercredi des cendres**). Traditionally, Lent (the 40 days before Easter) was a period of penance and fasting, and so Mardi gras – or fat Tuesday – was the last day to eat and be merry. In France (and areas with historic ties to France: **le Québec, Haïti, la Nouvelle Orléans,** etc.), this day is known as **Carnaval** and is celebrated with parades, floats, and masked balls.
- **Le 14 juillet** commemorates the beginning of the French Revolution (1789–1799). The holiday is celebrated with fireworks (**des feux d'artifice**) and dancing in the streets (**des bals populaires**).
- **Le onze novembre** commemorates the 1918 signing of the Armistice ending World War I. It is the day on which the French remember their veterans and those who died for their country.

Teaching Resource Options

PRINT 

Workbook PE, pp. 181–186
Unit 7 Resource Book
Communipak, pp. 148–170
Video Activities, pp. 25–26
Videoscript, p. 28
Workbook TE, pp. 1–6

VIDEO PROGRAM

VIDÉO DVD

MODULE 21

21.8 Vignette culturelle: La planche à voile (5:00–6:21 min.)

4 COMMUNICATION describing one's vacation preferences

1. Mes vacances préférés sont (les grands vacances).
2. Pendant les grands vacances, je préfère (aller à la mer).
3. En été, je vais à la plage spécialement pour (nager).
4. Je voudrais aller dans le Colorado pour (faire du ski).
5. Je voudrais aller à la Martinique principalement pour (faire de la plongée).
6. Mon sport préféré est (le snowboard).
7. Pour mon anniversaire, je préfère avoir (un VTT).
8. Avec mes copains, je préfère (faire du skate).
9. Quand je voyage pendant les vacances, je préfère voyager (avec ma famille).
10. Je voudrais aller à Paris et rester là-bas pendant (dix jours).

Cultural note Remind students that Martinique is a French island in the Caribbean.

Variation See variation for Act. 1, p. 311.

Challenge Have students give an original completion for each sentence. For example:

1. Mes vacances préférées sont [les vacances de "Thanksgiving".]

5 COMPREHENSION describing people's activities

1. Il fait du sport (du jogging).
2. Tu fais de la planche à voile (du ski nautique).
3. Nous faisons de l'escalade (du camping).
4. Tu fais du ski.
5. Ils font du camping (de la voile).
6. Elles font de la gymnastique.
7. Vous faites de la voile (du ski nautique, de la planche à voile).
8. Nous faisons de la planche à voile (de la voile, du ski nautique).
9. Nous faisons du jogging (du sport).
10. Je fais du ski nautique (de la voile, de la planche à voile).

4 Et toi?

PARLER/ÉCRIRE Indique tes préférences personnelles en complétant les phrases suivantes.

1. Mes vacances préférées sont …	• les vacances de Noël • les vacances de printemps	• les grandes vacances • … ?
2. Pendant les grandes vacances, je préfère …	• aller à la mer • aller à la montagne	• aller à la campagne • … ?
3. En été, je vais à la plage spécialement *(especially)* pour …	• nager • faire du ski nautique	• bronzer *(to get a tan)* • … ?
4. Je voudrais aller dans le Colorado pour …	• faire du ski • faire de l'escalade	• faire du VTT • … ?
5. Je voudrais aller à la Martinique principalement *(mainly)* pour …	• parler français • faire de la planche à voile	• faire de la plongée *(scuba diving)* • … ?

5 Leurs activités favorites

PARLER/ÉCRIRE Les personnes suivantes ont certaines activités favorites. Lisez où elles sont et dites ce qu'elles font. Pour cela choisissez une activité appropriée de la liste à droite.

▶ Anne est dans un studio de danse.
Elle fait de la danse moderne.

1. Jean-Pierre est au stade.
2. Je suis à la plage.
3. En juillet, nous allons dans le Colorado.
4. Tu passes les vacances de Noël en Suisse.
5. Mes copains passent les vacances à la campagne.
6. Pauline et Marie sont à la salle *(room)* de gymnastique.
7. Vous êtes à la mer.
8. Nous sommes à Tahiti.
9. Avant le dîner, nous allons au parc municipal.
10. Je suis à la Martinique.

la gymnastique
la danse moderne
le sport
le jogging
le camping
la voile
la planche à voile
le ski
le ski nautique
l'escalade

CLASSROOM MANAGEMENT Group practice

For Act. 4, divide the class into groups of 4 or 5 students. Name one person as recorder **(secrétaire)**.

For each question, members of the group each state their preferences, by selecting one of the completions.

The **secrétaires** tally the responses of their groups and report back to the entire class or hand results to the teacher.

La majorité préfère les grandes vacances. Pendant les grands vacances, la majorité préfère rester avec leur famille. ...

6. Mon sport préféré est ...	• la natation • le snowboard	• le roller • ... ?
7. Pour mon anniversaire, je préfère avoir ...	• un skate • des rollers	• un VTT • ... ?
8. Avec mes copains, je préfère ...	• faire du roller • faire du skate	• faire du jogging • ... ?
9. Quand je voyage pendant les vacances, je préfère voyager ...	• seul(e) • avec mes copains	• avec ma famille • ... ?
10. Je voudrais aller à Paris et rester là-bas pendant *(for)* ...	• dix jours • trois semaines	• six mois • ... ?

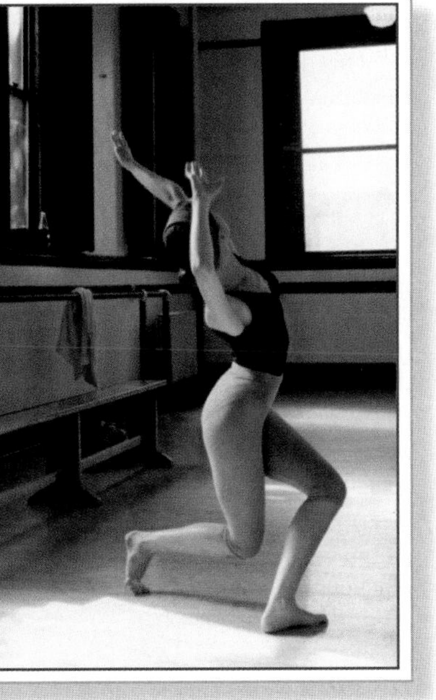

6 *Questions personnelles* PARLER/ÉCRIRE

1. En général, qu'est-ce que tu fais pendant les vacances de Noël?
2. Est-ce que tu vas voyager pendant les grandes vacances? Où vas-tu aller? Combien de temps *(How long)* est-ce que tu vas rester là-bas?
3. Qu'est-ce que tu aimes faire quand tu es à la plage?
4. Est-ce que tu voyages souvent? Comment voyages-tu?

COMMUNAUTÉS

During summer vacation, some American teenagers spend a month in a French-speaking region doing community service. At the same time they have the opportunity to meet other young people and to use their French skills.

You can go on the Internet to research some of the non-profit organizations that sponsor such exchanges. It is not too early to begin planning ahead.

6 COMMUNICATION answering personal questions

Answers will vary.

1. En général, pendant les vacances de Noël je reste avec ma famille et je rends visite à ma grand-mère.
2. Oui, je vais voyager pendant les grandes vacances. Je vais aller au Canada. Je vais passer trois semaines là-bas. (Non, je ne vais pas voyager pendant les grandes vacances.)
3. Quand je suis à la plage, j'aime nager et parler avec mes amis. J'aime aussi faire de la voile et du ski nautique.
4. Oui, je voyage souvent. Je voyage en avion. (Non, je ne voyage pas souvent.)

INCLUSION

Alphabetic/phonetic Review the pronunciation of activity vocabulary, calling out each item and having students repeat three times. Hold up pictures of various activities and have students identify each one by name. Check pronunciation. Then pair at-risk and stronger students and have them complete Activities 4 and 5.

À VOTRE TOUR

Main Topic
- Recapitulation and review

Teaching Resource Options

PRINT 

Workbook PE, pp. 181–186
Unit 7 Resource Book
Audioscript, p. 29
Communipak, pp. 148–170
Family Involvement, pp. 19–20
Workbook TE, pp. 1–6

Assessment
Lesson 21 Quiz, pp. 33–34
Portfolio Assessment, Unit 1 URB pp. 155–164
Audioscript for Quiz 21, pp. 31–32
Answer Keys, pp. 213–216

AUDIO & VISUAL 

Audio Program
CD 4 Tracks 1, 2, 3
CD 16 Track 1

TECHNOLOGY 

Test Generator CD-ROM/McDougal Littell Assessment System

1 ORAL COMPREHENSION

1. B	**2.** A	**3.** A	**4.** B
5. B	**6.** A	**7.** B	**8.** B
9. A	**10.** A	**11.** B	**12.** A

2 WRITTEN SELF-EXPRESSION

Answers will vary.
- Le week-end prochain, je vais ...
  –nettoyer ma chambre
  –regarder la télé
  –faire mes devoirs
  –aider mes parents
- Je vais ...
  –faire du jogging
  –jouer au basket
  –passer samedi après-midi avec mes amis au café
  –laver la voiture

Follow-up activity Have students in pairs compare their compositions. How many similar activities did they choose?

À votre tour!

OBJECTIFS
Now you can ...
- discuss your weekend and vacation plans
- talk about individual sports

1 Écoutez bien!

ÉCOUTER On weekends, you can stay in and take care of things at home, or you can go out and have fun. Listen carefully to what the people are saying. If they refer to an indoor activity, mark A. If they refer to an outdoor activity, mark B.

	1	2	3	4	5	6
A: À l'intérieur						
B: À l'extérieur						

A. À l'intérieur

B. À l'extérieur

2 Composition: Le week-end prochain

ÉCRIRE Make plans for next weekend. Prepare a list of activities describing ...

- four things that you are going to do at home
- four things that you are going to do outside

Samedi, je
vais ranger
ma chambre.
Après, je ...

3 Composition: Mes sports préférés

ÉCRIRE Describe two sports that you engage in during each of the following times of year.

- Pendant les vacances d'été
- En hiver
- En toute (*any*) saison

À VOTRE TOUR

Depending on your goals and objectives, you may or may not wish to assign all of the activities in the **À votre tour** section.

GROUP PRACTICE

In Act. 4 and 5, you may want to have students work in trios, with two performing and one consulting the Answer Key and acting as monitor.

4 Créa-dialogue

PARLER Des amis parlent de leurs projets. Avec un(e) camarade de classe, choisissez une scène et composez le dialogue correspondant.

▶ —Où vas-tu vendredi?
—Je vais en ville.
—Qu'est-ce que tu vas faire là-bas?
—Je vais faire des achats.

vendredi	en ville	

1. samedi matin		
2. samedi après-midi		
3. à Noël	à Aspen	
4. pendant les vacances de printemps	en Floride	
5. en juillet		
6. en août		
7. demain matin	?	
8. dimanche après-midi	?	?
9. cet été	?	?

5 Conversation dirigée

PARLER Avec un(e) camarade, composez un dialogue basé sur les instructions suivantes. Thomas demande à Hélène si elle a des projets de vacances.

Thomas		Hélène
asks Hélène where she is going this summer	→ ↙	says that she is going to the ocean with friends
asks her if they are going to travel by car	→ ↙	answers that they are going to travel by train because they do not have a car
asks her if she is going to go sailing	→ ↙	answers yes and says that she is also going to windsurf
says good-bye to Hélène and wishes her a good vacation **(Bonnes vacances!)**	→	answers good-bye

3 Written Self-Expression

Answers will vary.
Pendant les vacances d'été, je (nage et je fais de la planche à voile.)
En hiver, je (fais du ski et du snowboard).
En toute saison, je (fais du jogging et je fais du roller.)

4 Comprehension

Answers will vary.

1. –Où vas-tu samedi matin?
   –Je vais à la campagne.
   –Qu'est-ce que tu vas faire là-bas?
   –Je vais faire une promenade à vélo.
2. –Où vas-tu samedi après-midi?
   –Je vais à la campagne.
   –Qu'est-ce que tu vas faire là-bas?
   –Je vais faire un pique-nique.
3. –Où vas-tu à Noël?
   –Je vais à Aspen.
   –Qu'est-ce que tu vas faire là-bas?
   –Je vais faire du ski.
4. –Où vas-tu pendant les vacances de printemps?
   –Je vais en Floride.
   –Qu'est-ce que tu vas faire là-bas?
   –Je vais faire du ski nautique.
5. –Où vas-tu en juillet?
   –Je vais à la mer (plage).
   –Qu'est-ce que tu vas faire là-bas?
   –Je vais faire de la voile.
6. –Où vas-tu en août?
   –Je vais à la montagne.
   –Qu'est-ce que tu vas faire là-bas?
   –Je vais faire de l'escalade.
7. –Où vas-tu demain matin?
   –Je vais (au parc).
   –Qu'est-ce que tu vas faire là-bas?
   –Je vais faire du jogging.
8. –Où vas-tu dimanche après-midi?
   –Je vais (à la piscine).
   –Qu'est-ce que tu vas faire là-bas?
   –Je vais (nager).
9. –Où vas-tu cet été?
   –Je vais (à la campagne).
   –Qu'est-ce que tu vas faire là-bas?
   –Je vais (faire du camping).

5 Guided Oral Expression

JP: Où vas-tu cet été?
H: Je vais à la mer avec des amis.
JP: Est-ce que vous allez voyager en voiture?
H: (Non,) nous allons voyager en train parce que nous n'avons pas de voiture.
JP: Est-ce que tu vas faire de la voile?
H: Oui, et je vais faire de la planche à voile aussi.
JP: Au revoir, Hélène. Bonnes vacances!
H: Au revoir!

Portfolio Assessment

You will probably select only one speaking activity and one writing activity to go into the students' portfolios for Unit 7.

In this lesson, you might suggest that students do their own variations of Act. 5 as an oral portfolio recording. **Pre-AP skill:** Respond to questions with thorough answers.

Inclusion

Cumulative Prepare students for Activity 5 by reviewing the essential vocabulary. Call out the vocabulary mentioned in the direction line (this summer, by car, the ocean, etc.) and have students call back the French words. Then, have them do the activity.

Leçon 22

Main Topic Describing what happened last weekend

Teaching Resource Options

PRINT 

Workbook PE, pp. 187–194
Activités pour tous PE, pp. 115–117
Block Scheduling Copymasters, pp. 169–175
Unit 7 Resource Book
- *Activités pour tous* TE, pp. 43–45
- Audioscript, pp. 67, 68–70
- Communipak, pp. 148–170
- Lesson Plans, pp. 46–47
- Block Scheduling Lesson Plans, pp. 48–50
- Absent Student Copymasters, pp. 51–56
- Video Activities, pp. 59–64
- Videoscript, pp. 65–66
- Workbook TE, pp. 35–42

AUDIO & VISUAL 

Audio Program
CD 4 Tracks 4, 5
CD 11 Tracks 7–12

TECHNOLOGY 

Online Workbook

VIDEO PROGRAM

MODULE 22
Mercredi après-midi

TOTAL TIME: 6:13 min.
DVD Disk 2
Videotape 4 (COUNTER: 6:35 min.)

22.1 Introduction: Listening
– Mercredi après-midi
(6:46–7:57 min.)

22.2 Dialogue: L'examen de maths
(7:58–8:28 min.)

22.3 Mini-scenes: Listening
– Qu'est-ce que vous avez fait hier?
(8:29–9:53 min.)

22.4 Mini-scenes: Listening
– Est-ce que tu as joué au tennis?
(9:54–10:45 min.)

22.5 Mini-scenes: Speaking
– Est-ce que tu as joué au tennis?
(10:46–11:45 min.)

22.6 Vignette culturelle: Le cinéma
(11:46–12:48 min.)

Comprehension practice Play the entire module through as an introduction to the lesson.

LEÇON 22

Vive le week-end!

AUDIO

Le week-end, nous avons nos occupations préférées. Certaines personnes aiment aller en ville et rencontrer leurs amis.

D'autres préfèrent rester à la maison et bricoler. *Others / do things around the house*
Qu'est-ce que les personnes suivantes ont fait *did ... do*
le week-end dernier? *last*

Le week-end	**Le week-end dernier**

J'aime acheter des vêtements.

J'ai acheté des vêtements. *bought*

Tu aimes réparer ton vélo.

Tu as réparé ton vélo. *fixed*

M. Lambert aime travailler dans le jardin.

Il a travaillé dans le jardin. *worked*

Nous aimons organiser des boums.

Nous avons organisé une boum. *organized*

SETTING THE SCENE

In this lesson, the video module is independent of the opening text. However, the opening scenes are narrated in Section 1 of the audio program.

The video first shows how Jean-Claude and Nathalie spent the day on Wednesday. Then it shows them talking on Thursday morning when Jean-Claude realizes that he has forgotten about his math test.

To set the scene, ask students if they have ever forgotten about a test **(oublier la date d'un examen).** If so, how did they perform on the exam?

Teaching note Arrange to have a native French speaker from your community visit your class to talk about his or her native country. You can have students prepare questions ahead of time.

Le week-end	Le week-end dernier
 Vous aimez jouer au foot.	 Vous <u>avez joué</u> au foot. *played*
 Pluton et Philibert aiment rencontrer leurs amis.	 Ils <u>ont rencontré</u> leurs amis. *met*

Et toi?

Indique si oui ou non tu as fait les choses suivantes le week-end dernier. Pour cela complète les phrases suivantes.

1. (J'ai/Je n'ai pas) … acheté des vêtements.
2. (J'ai/Je n'ai pas) … réparé mon vélo.
3. (J'ai/Je n'ai pas) … travaillé dans le jardin.
4. (J'ai/Je n'ai pas) … organisé une boum.
5. (J'ai/Je n'ai pas) … joué au foot.
6. (J'ai/Je n'ai pas) … rencontré mes amis.

NOTE culturelle

Le week-end

Le week-end ne commence pas° le vendredi soir pour tout le monde.° Dans beaucoup d'écoles françaises, les élèves ont classe le samedi matin. Pour eux, le week-end commence seulement° le samedi à midi.

Que font les jeunes Français le samedi? Ça dépend. Beaucoup° vont en ville. Ils vont dans des magasins pour écouter les nouveaux CD ou pour regarder, essayer° et parfois° acheter des vêtements. Ils vont au café ou au cinéma avec leurs copains. Certains° préfèrent louer un film et rester chez eux ou aller chez des copains. Parfois

ils vont à une soirée. Là on écoute de la musique, on mange des sandwichs et on danse …

En général, le dimanche est réservé aux activités familiales.° Un week-end, on invite des cousins. Un autre° week-end, on rend visite aux grands-parents … Le dimanche, on déjeune° et on dîne en famille.° Le soir, on regarde la télé et souvent on fait ses devoirs pour les classes du lundi matin.

ne commence pas *does not begin* **tout le monde** *everyone* **seulement** *only* **Beaucoup** *Many* **essayer** *try on* **parfois** *sometimes* **Certains** *Some of them* **activités familiales** *family activities* **Un autre** *Another* **déjeune** *has lunch* **en famille** *at home (with the family)*

Et toi?

Answers will vary.

1. J'ai acheté des vêtements. (Je n'ai pas acheté de vêtements.)
2. J'ai réparé mon vélo. (Je n'ai pas réparé mon vélo.)
3. J'ai travaillé dans le jardin. (Je n'ai pas travaillé dans le jardin.)
4. J'ai organisé une boum. (Je n'ai pas organisé de boum.)
5. J'ai joué au foot. (Je n'ai pas joué au foot.)
6. J'ai rencontré mes amis. (Je n'ai pas rencontré mes amis.)

Expansion Ask for more information. Have students give only short answers unless they have been practicing the passé composé.

1. **Où? Quels vêtements?**
2. **Quand?**
3. **Quel jour? Avec qui?**
4. **Quand? Où?**
5. **Où?**
6. **Où?**

CROSS-CULTURAL OBSERVATION

The **Vignette culturelle** of the video presents one of the favorite pastimes of French young people: going to the movies.

Have students watch to see whether they have the same taste in films as the students who were interviewed in Paris.

The **Vignette** shows two short interviews, the first with two young boys and the second with a girl. The boys like going to see "L'Ours." The first boy likes **les films d'adventures**; his friend's favorite actress is Kim Basinger in "Batman." The girl's favorite actress is Marilyn Monroe.

SECTION A

Communicative function
Expressing thirst, hunger, and other feelings

Teaching Resource Options

PRINT 

Workbook PE, pp. 187–194
Unit 7 Resource Book
Audioscript, p. 67
Communipak, pp. 148–170
Workbook TE, pp. 35–42

AUDIO & VISUAL 

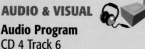

Audio Program
CD 4 Track 6

Overhead Transparencies
44 Expressions with ***avoir***

TECHNOLOGY 

Power Presentations

Re-entry and review
The purpose of this section is to have students review **avoir** before practicing the passé composé. Students have already learned **avoir faim/soif** (Lesson 10).

Teaching strategy Introduce the **avoir** expressions using appropriate gestures. For example:
avoir faim *(pointing to stomach)*
avoir soif *(pointing to throat)*
avoir tort *(wagging index finger)*
avoir de la chance *(extending arms in a "youpie!" manner)*
See **Comprehension** activity, p. 74.

Supplementary vocabulary
avoir sommeil *to be (feel) sleepy*
avoir peur *to be scared, afraid*

1 COMPREHENSION evaluating actions of others

1. Elle a raison!
2. Nous avons raison!
3. Tu as raison!
4. Vous avez tort!
5. Ils ont raison!
6. Il a tort!
7. Il a tort!
8. Ils ont tort!
9. Vous avez raison!
10. Elle a raison!

A Les expressions avec *avoir*

Note the use of **avoir** in the following sentences:

J'ai **faim.** — ***I am hungry.***
Brigitte **a soif.** — *Brigitte* ***is thirsty.***

French speakers use **avoir** in many expressions where English speakers use the verb *to be.*

VOCABULAIRE Expressions avec *avoir* 

avoir chaud	*to be (feel) warm*	Quand j'**ai chaud** en été, je vais à la plage.
avoir froid	*to be (feel) cold*	Est-ce que tu **as froid?** Voici ton pull.
avoir faim	*to be hungry*	Tu **as faim?** Est-ce que tu veux une pizza?
avoir soif	*to be thirsty*	J'**ai soif.** Je voudrais une limonade.
avoir raison	*to be right*	Est-ce que les profs **ont** toujours **raison?**
avoir tort	*to be wrong*	Marc ne fait pas ses devoirs. Il **a tort!**
avoir de la chance	*to be lucky*	J'**ai de la chance.** J'ai des amis sympathiques.

1 Tort ou raison?

PARLER/ÉCRIRE Informez-vous sur les personnes suivantes et dites si, à votre avis, elles ont tort ou raison.

▶ Les élèves ne font pas leurs devoirs.
Ils ont tort!

▶ Tu écoutes le prof.
Tu as raison!

1. Catherine est généreuse avec ses copines.
2. Nous aidons nos parents.
3. Tu fais tes devoirs.
4. Vous êtes très impatients avec vos amis.
5. Mes copains étudient le français.
6. Jean-François dépense son argent inutilement *(uselessly)*.
7. M. Legros mange trop *(too much)*.
8. Alain et Nicolas sont impolis *(impolite)*.
9. Vous rangez votre chambre.
10. Léa est polie *(polite)* avec les voisins.

2 De bonnes questions

PARLER/ÉCRIRE Étudiez ce que font les personnes suivantes. Ensuite, posez une question logique sur chaque personne. Pour cela, utilisez l'une des expressions suivantes:

avoir faim — avoir soif — avoir chaud — avoir froid — avoir de la chance

▶ Philippe va au restaurant.
Est-ce que Philippe a faim?

1. Tu veux un soda.
2. Jean-Pierre mange une pizza.
3. Cécile porte un manteau.
4. Vous gagnez à la loterie.
5. Vous faites des sandwichs.
6. Tu mets ton blouson.
7. Mes copains vont aller à la piscine.
8. Ces élèves n'étudient pas beaucoup, mais ils réussissent toujours à leurs examens.
9. Tu as des grands-parents très généreux.

WARM-UP Quel âge as-tu?

Quickly review the forms of **avoir** by asking students how old they are.
Quel âge as-tu, X? [J'ai [treize] ans.]
Dis, Y, quel âge a X? [X a treize ans.]
Et Z, quel âge as-tu? [J'ai treize ans.]
Comme X! Alors, Z et X, quel âge avez-vous? [Nous avons treize ans.]
Eh bien, tout le monde, quel âge ont X et Z? [Ils ont treize ans.]

Expansion: Hold up magazine ads and have the class estimate the people's ages.

B Le passé composé des verbes en *-er*

The sentences below describe past events. In the French sentences, the verbs are in the PASSÉ COMPOSÉ. Note the forms of the passé composé and its English equivalents.

Hier j'**ai réparé** mon vélo.	*Yesterday I **fixed** my bicycle.*
Le week-end dernier, Marc **a organisé** une boum.	*Last weekend, Marc **organized** a party.*
Pendant les vacances, nous **avons visité** Paris.	*During vacation, we **visited** Paris.*

FORMS

The PASSÉ COMPOSÉ is composed of two words. For most verbs, it is formed as follows:

PRESENT of **avoir** + PAST PARTICIPLE

Note the forms of the passé composé for **visiter.**

PASSÉ COMPOSÉ		PRESENT OF avoir + PAST PARTICIPLE		
J'**ai visité**	Québec.	j'	**ai**	**visité**
Tu **as visité**	Paris.	tu	**as**	
Il/Elle/On **a visité**	Montréal.	il/elle/on	**a**	
Nous **avons visité**	Genève.	nous	**avons**	
Vous **avez visité**	Strasbourg.	vous	**avez**	
Ils/Elles **ont visité**	Fort-de-France.	ils/elles	**ont**	

→ For all **-er** verbs, the past participle is formed by replacing the **-er** of the infinitive by **-é**.

jouer	→	**joué**	Nous **avons joué** au tennis.
parler	→	**parlé**	Éric **a parlé** à Nathalie.
téléphoner	→	**téléphoné**	Vous **avez téléphoné** à Cécile.

LEARNING ABOUT LANGUAGE

The PASSÉ COMPOSÉ, as its name indicates, is a "past" tense "composed" of two parts. It is formed like the present perfect tense in English.

AUXILIARY VERB + PAST PARTICIPLE of the main verb

Nous **avons** **travaillé**.
We have worked.

USES

The passé composé is used to describe past actions and events. It has several English equivalents.

J'ai visité Montréal. — *I **visited** Montreal.* / *I **have visited** Montreal.* / *I **did visit** Montreal.*

Profitez de cette offre imbattable et venez visiter les grandes attractions de Montréal
Découvrez
Montréal
La Ronde

COMPREHENSION Past activities

Review the gestures your class developed for the verbs on pp. 94-95.

Tout le monde: dansez.
Chantez. Téléphonez. Nagez.

Have an individual act out an activity.

X, joue au tennis. C'est bien. Merci.

Then describe what the student did.

Qu'est-ce que X a fait?
Il a joué au tennis.

Then have two students act out an activity.

Y et Z, dansez. Voilà, c'est très bien.

Describe what the students did.

Qu'est-ce que Y et Z ont fait?
Ils ont dansé.

2 COMPREHENSION asking logical questions

1. Est-ce que tu as soif?
2. Est-ce qu'il a faim?
3. Est-ce qu'elle a froid?
4. Est-ce que vous avez de la chance?
5. Est-ce que vous avez faim?
6. Est-ce que tu as froid?
7. Est-ce qu'ils ont chaud (ont de la chance)?
8. Est-ce qu'ils ont de la chance?
9. Est-ce que tu as de la chance?

SECTION B

Communicative function
Talking about what happened in the past

Language note/Looking ahead
In English, the auxiliary verb is always *to have.* In French, the auxiliary verb is usually, but not always, **avoir.**
The passé composé with **être** is presented in Lesson 24.

Teaching strategy If you have been practicing the passé composé orally, this material will be familiar to the students. You will want to focus particularly on the written forms.

Realia notes

- With a population of over two million people, **Montréal** is a bustling commercial and industrial center as well as the artistic and intellectual capital of Quebec. Its inland port, located on an island in the St. Lawrence river, ranks among the busiest in North America. Below the skyscrapers of downtown Montreal is a honeycomb of shopping malls connected to one another and to the various subway stations by underground pedestrian tunnels. This way, in the ice and cold of the Canadian winter, shoppers have easy access to their favorite stores.
- **La Ronde,** an amusement park in Montreal (the largest one in Quebec), is located on a man-made island (**Ile Ste-Hélène**) on the St. Lawrence River. La Ronde is part of the **Parc Jean-Drapeau,** a park which includes other attractions such as the Biosphere. The Parc Jean-Drapeau resides on two islands: **Ile Ste-Hélène** and **Ile Notre-Dame.** There are over 30 rides for thrill-seekers visiting the La Ronde. Also hosted here is the annual Montreal International Fireworks Competition in the summer. The exciting displays can be seen from the nearby Jacques Cartier Bridge which is closed to traffic for this purpose.

Teaching Resource Options

PRINT 

Workbook PE, pp. 187–194
Unit 7 Resource Book
  Communipak, pp. 148–170
  Workbook TE, pp. 35–42

3 DESCRIPTION saying what people bought

1. Pauline a acheté un jean.
2. J'ai acheté une montre.
3. Tu as acheté une guitare.
4. Vous avez acheté des chemises.
5. Nous avons acheté une chaîne stéréo.
6. Stéphanie et Isabelle on acheté des chaussures.
7. Patrick et Jean-Paul ont acheté des livres.
8. M. et Mme Dupont ont acheté une voiture.

4 ROLE PLAY talking about past activities

1. –J'ai acheté des CD.
   –Eh bien, moi, j'ai acheté des magazines.
2. –J'ai dîné au restaurant.
   –Eh bien, moi, j'ai dîné chez moi.
3. –J'ai invité mon cousin.
   –Eh bien, moi, j'ai invité un ami.
4. –J'ai téléphoné à ma tante.
   –Eh bien, moi, j'ai téléphoné à mon grand-père.
5. –J'ai aidé ma mère.
   –Eh bien, moi, j'ai aidé mon père.
6. –J'ai nettoyé la cuisine.
   –Eh bien, moi, j'ai nettoyé le garage.
7. –J'ai réparé ma mobylette.
   –Eh bien, moi, j'ai réparé mon vélo.
8. –J'ai assisté à un match de foot.
   –Eh bien, moi, j'ai assisté à un concert.
9. –J'ai lavé mes tee-shirts.
   –Eh bien, moi, j'ai lavé mes jeans.
10. –J'ai regardé un film.
    –Eh bien, moi, j'ai regardé une comédie.
11. –J'ai rangé ma chambre.
    –Eh bien, moi, j'ai rangé le salon.
12. –J'ai loué un DVD.
    –Eh bien, moi, j'ai loué une cassette vidéo.

5 ROLE PLAY asking about past actions

–Tu as ... ?
–Mais oui, j'ai ...

1. préparé les sandwichs
2. rangé le salon
3. réparé la chaîne hi-fi
4. apporté un DVD
5. invité nos copains
6. téléphoné aux voisins

Variation Have students ask and answer questions in the plural.
– Vous avez acheté des sodas?
– Mais oui, nous avons acheté des sodas.

3 Achats

PARLER/ÉCRIRE Samedi dernier *(Last Saturday)*, les personnes suivantes ont fait des achats. Dites ce que chaque personne a acheté.

▶ Philippe (des CD)
Philippe a acheté des CD.

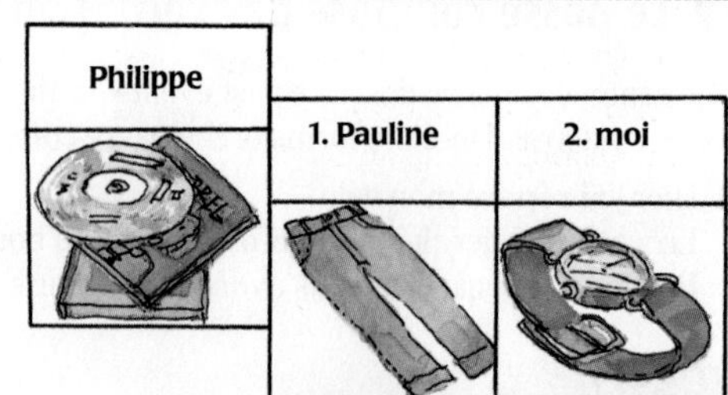

3. toi	4. vous	5. nous	6. Stéphanie et Isabelle	7. Patrick et Jean-Paul	8. M. et Mme Dupont

4 Vive la différence!

PARLER Caroline et Jean-Pierre sont des copains, mais ils aiment faire des choses différentes. Ils parlent de ce qu'ils ont fait ce week-end.

J'ai joué au volley.
Eh bien, moi, j'ai joué au tennis.

▶ jouer au volley (au tennis)

1. acheter des CD (des magazines)
2. dîner au restaurant (chez moi)
3. inviter mon cousin (un ami)
4. téléphoner à ma tante (à mon grand-père)
5. aider ma mère (mon père)
6. nettoyer la cuisine (le garage)
7. réparer ma mobylette (mon vélo)
8. assister à un match de foot (à un concert)
9. laver mes tee-shirts (mes jeans)
10. regarder un film (une comédie)
11. ranger ma chambre (le salon)
12. louer un DVD (une cassette vidéo)

5 La boum

PARLER Anne et Éric organisent une boum ce week-end. Anne demande à Éric s'il a fait les choses suivantes. Il répond oui.

▶ acheter des sodas? **—Tu as acheté des sodas?**
—Mais oui, j'ai acheté des sodas.

1. préparer les sandwichs?
2. ranger le salon?
3. réparer la chaîne hi-fi?
4. apporter un DVD?
5. inviter nos copains?
6. téléphoner aux voisins?

GAME Samedi dernier

You can treat Act. 6 as a team game.
Divide the class into teams of three.
Each team picks a person from column A and decides what that subject did last Saturday. All three team members must then write the same sentence down correctly.

Then the team formulates another sentence using elements of columns A, B, and C, and again all three members write it down.

The game is played against the clock. The team whose three members have written the greatest number of correct sentences in five minutes is the winner.

6 Un jeu

PARLER/ÉCRIRE Décrivez ce que certaines personnes ont fait samedi dernier. Pour cela, faites des phrases logiques en utilisant les éléments des Colonnes A, B et C.

▶ **Vous avez assisté à un concert de jazz.**

A	B	C
nous	acheter	une boum
vous	assister	un musée
Marc	dîner	des vêtements
Hélène et Juliette	jouer	un film
Éric et Stéphanie	organiser	aux jeux vidéo
mes copains	louer	dans le jardin
les voisins	travailler	dans un restaurant vietnamien
	visiter	à un concert de jazz

VOCABULAIRE Expressions pour la conversation

▶ ***How to indicate the order in which actions take place:***

d'abord	*first*	**D'abord,** nous avons invité nos copains à la boum.
après	*after, afterwards*	**Après,** tu as préparé des sandwichs.
ensuite	*then, after that*	**Ensuite,** Jacques a acheté des jus de fruit.
enfin	*at last*	**Enfin,** vous avez décoré le salon.
finalement	*finally*	**Finalement,** j'ai apporté ma radiocassette.

7 Dans quel ordre?

PARLER/ÉCRIRE Décrivez ce que les personnes suivantes ont fait dans l'ordre logique.

▶ nous (manger / préparer la salade / acheter des pizzas)
D'abord, nous avons acheté des pizzas.
Après, nous avons préparé la salade.
Ensuite, nous avons mangé.

1. Alice (travailler / trouver un job / acheter une moto)
2. les touristes canadiens (voyager en avion / visiter Paris / réserver les billets [*tickets*])
3. tu (assister au concert / acheter un billet / acheter le programme)
4. vous (danser / apporter des CD / inviter des copains)
5. nous (payer l'addition [*check*]/dîner / trouver un restaurant)

6 COMPREHENSION making logical statements about past events

Answers will vary.
Nous avons (acheté des vêtements).
Vous avez (assisté à un concert de jazz).
Marc a (dîné dans un restaurant vietnamien).
Hélène et Juliette ont (joué aux jeux vidéo).
Éric et Stéphanie ont (organisé une boum).
Mes copains ont (loué un film).
Les voisins ont (travaillé dans le jardin).
Nous avons (visité un musée).

Realia note
Le Jazz en France
The poster reads **"Nice, l'arène du jazz"** *(Nice, the arena of jazz)*. When said aloud, it could be interpreted as **"Nice, la reine du jazz"** *(Nice, the queen of jazz)*.
Jazz has always been popular in France, especially after the creation of the **Hot Club de France** in 1932. Festivals are regularly organized in many cities, attracting both French and American musicians.

7 COMPREHENSION narrating past events in logical sequence

Answers will vary.
1. D'abord, Alice a trouvé un job.
   Après, elle a travaillé.
   Ensuite, elle a acheté une moto.
2. D'abord, les touristes canadiens ont réservé les billets.
   Après, ils ont voyagé en avion.
   Ensuite, ils ont visité Paris.
3. D'abord, tu as acheté un billet.
   Après, tu as acheté le programme.
   Ensuite, tu as assisté au concert.
4. D'abord, vous avez invité des copains.
   Après, vous avez apporté des CD.
   Ensuite, vous avez dansé.
5. D'abord, nous avons trouvé un restaurant.
   Après, nous avons dîné.
   Ensuite, nous avons payé l'addition.

Teaching strategy Note that several logical sequences are sometimes possible.

SECTION C

Communicative function
Talking about what did not happen in the past

Teaching Resource Options

PRINT

Workbook PE, pp. 187–194
Unit 7 Resource Book
Communipak, pp. 148–170
Video Activities, pp. 59–60
Videoscript, p. 65
Workbook TE, pp. 35–42

TECHNOLOGY 

Power Presentations

VIDEO PROGRAM

VIDÉO DVD

MODULE 22

22.1 Introduction: Mercredi après-midi (6:46–7:57 min.)

22.2 Dialogue: L'examen de maths (7:58–8:28 min.)

Teaching strategy Point out to students that if the English sentence contains *did not* or *didn't,* the equivalent French sentence will use the negative passé composé.

8 ROLE PLAY talking about what one did not do

1. –Tu as réparé ta chaîne hi-fi?
   –Euh, non ... Je n'ai pas réparé ma chaîne hi-fi.
2. –Tu as apporté tes livres?
   –Euh, non ... Je n'ai pas apporté mes livres.
3. –Tu as étudié?
   –Euh, non ... Je n'ai pas étudié.
4. –Tu as téléphoné à ta tante?
   –Euh, non ... Je n'ai pas téléphoné à ma tante.
5. –Tu as invité tes copains?
   –Euh, non ... Je n'ai pas invité mes copains.
6. –Tu as rangé ta chambre?
   –Euh, non ... Je n'ai pas rangé ma chambre.
7. –Tu as lavé tes chemises?
   –Euh, non ... Je n'ai pas lavé mes chemises.
8. –Tu as loué un film?
   –Euh, non ... Je n'ai pas loué de film.
9. –Tu as aidé ta mère?
   –Euh, non ... Je n'ai pas aidé ma mère.
10. –Tu as nettoyé le garage?
    –Euh, non ... Je n'ai pas nettoyé le garage.
11. –Tu as cherché le programme de télé?
    –Euh, non ... Je n'ai pas cherché le programme de télé.

C Le passé composé: forme négative

Compare the affirmative and negative forms of the passé composé in the sentences below.

AFFIRMATIVE	NEGATIVE	
Alice **a travaillé.**	Éric **n'a pas travaillé.**	*Éric **has not worked.*** *Éric **did not work.***
Nous **avons visité** Paris.	Nous **n'avons pas visité** Lyon.	*We **have not visited** Lyon.* *We **did not visit** Lyon.*

In the negative, the passé composé follows the pattern:

negative form of **avoir** + PAST PARTICIPLE

Note the negative forms of the passé composé of **travailler.**

PASSÉ COMPOSÉ (NEGATIVE)	PRESENT of **avoir** (NEGATIVE) + PAST PARTICIPLE	
Je **n'ai pas travaillé.**	je **n'ai pas**	**travaillé**
Tu **n'as pas travaillé.**	tu **n'as pas**	
Il/Elle/On **n'a pas travaillé.**	il/elle/on **n'a pas**	
Nous **n'avons pas travaillé.**	nous **n'avons pas**	
Vous **n'avez pas travaillé.**	vous **n'avez pas**	
Ils/Elles **n'ont pas travaillé.**	ils/elles **n'ont pas**	

8   **Oublis** *(Things forgotten)*

PARLER Nicole demande à Jean-Marc s'il a fait *(did)* les choses suivantes. Jean-Marc a oublié *(forgot)*.

▶ acheter *Paris-Match*?

1. réparer ta chaîne hi-fi?
2. apporter tes livres?
3. étudier?
4. téléphoner à ta tante?
5. inviter tes copains?
6. ranger ta chambre?
7. laver tes chemises?
8. louer un film?
9. aider ta mère?
10. nettoyer le garage?
11. chercher le programme de télé?
12. trouver ton livre?

Tu as acheté *Paris Match*?
Euh, non ... Je n'ai pas acheté *Paris Match.*
librairie . galerie

INCLUSION

Structured Review the **passé composé** and the negative formation of present tense sentences. Have students write parts of sentences on cards: **ne (n'), pas, ai, travaillé,** etc. Read sentences out loud and have them place the cards in order. Have them work in pairs to manipulate the cards to create negative sentences in the **passé composé**.

9 Quel mauvais temps!

PARLER/ÉCRIRE Ce week-end, il a fait mauvais et les personnes suivantes sont restées *(stayed)* chez elles. Dites qu'elles n'ont pas fait les choses suivantes.

▶ nous/nager
Nous n'avons pas nagé.

1. vous/jouer au tennis
2. Philippe/rencontrer ses copains à la plage
3. Nathalie/dîner en ville
4. les voisins/travailler dans le jardin
5. Mlle Lacaze/laver sa voiture
6. mes copains/organiser un pique-nique
7. nous/assister au match de foot
8. toi/visiter le musée

10 Une question d'argent

PARLER/ÉCRIRE Les personnes suivantes n'ont pas beaucoup d'argent. Décrivez leur choix. Pour cela, dites ce qu'elles ont fait et ce qu'elles n'ont pas fait.

▶ nous/dîner au restaurant ou chez nous?
Nous avons dîné chez nous.
Nous n'avons pas dîné au restaurant.

1. Philippe/acheter un tee-shirt ou une chemise?
2. vous/manger un steak ou un sandwich?
3. nous/assister au concert ou au match de foot?
4. les touristes/voyager en car ou en avion?
5. mes voisins/louer une petite maison ou un grand appartement?
6. Marc/passer dix jours ou trois semaines à Paris?

11 Impossibilités

PARLER/ÉCRIRE Sans *(Without)* certaines choses il n'est pas possible de faire certaines activités. Expliquez cela logiquement en choisissant une personne de la Colonne A, un objet de la Colonne B et une activité de la Colonne C.

▶ **Je n'ai pas d'aspirateur. Je n'ai pas nettoyé le salon.**

A	B	C
je	une raquette	surfer sur l'Internet
vous	un billet *(ticket)*	voyager en Europe
nous	un passeport	nettoyer le salon
Frédéric	un ordinateur	regarder la comédie
Éric et Olivier	une télé	assister au concert
Claire et Caroline	un aspirateur *(vacuum cleaner)*	jouer au tennis

9 PRACTICE describing what people didn't do

1. Vous n'avez pas joué au tennis.
2. Philippe n'a pas rencontré ses copains à la plage.
3. Nathalie n'a pas dîné en ville.
4. Les voisins n'ont pas travaillé dans le jardin.
5. Mlle Lacaze n'a pas lavé sa voiture.
6. Mes copains n'ont pas organisé de pique-nique.
7. Nous n'avons pas assisté au match de foot.
8. Tu n'as pas visité le musée.

Teaching note Be sure students use **pas de** in item 6.

Realia note
La météo (short for **météorologie**) is the French word for weather report.

10 COMPREHENSION describing what did and did not happen

1. Philippe a acheté un tee-shirt. Il n'a pas acheté de chemise.
2. Vous avez mangé un sandwich. Vous n'avez pas mangé de steak.
3. Nous avons assisté au match de foot. Nous n'avons pas assisté au concert.
4. Les touristes ont voyagé en car. Ils n'ont pas voyagé en avion.
5. Mes voisins ont loué une petite maison. Ils n'ont pas loué un grand appartement.
6. Marc a passé dix jours à Paris. Il n'a pas passé trois semaines à Paris.

Teaching note Be sure students use **pas de** in items 1, 2, and 5.

11 COMPREHENSION drawing conclusions about what did not happen

Answers will vary.
1. Je n'ai pas (de raquette. Je n'ai pas joué au tennis.)
2. Vous n'avez pas (de billets. Vous n'avez pas assisté au concert.)
3. Nous n'avons pas (de passeport. Nous n'avons pas voyagé en Europe.)
4. Frédéric n'a pas (d'ordinateur. Il n'a pas surfé sur l'Internet.)
5. Éric et Olivier n'ont pas (de télé. Ils n'ont pas regardé la comédie.)
6. Claire et Caroline n'ont pas (d'aspirateur. Elles n'ont pas nettoyé le salon.)

Teaching note Remind students to use **pas de** with the items in Column B.

Variation (game format) See how many logical sentences teams of students can construct within a given time limit.

See **Game: Samedi dernier** on p. 322.

SECTION D

Communicative function
Asking questions about the past

Teaching Resource Options

PRINT 

Workbook PE, pp. 187–194
Unit 7 Resource Book
- Audioscript, p. 67
- Communipak, pp. 148–170
- Workbook TE, pp. 35–42

AUDIO & VISUAL 

Audio Program
CD 4 Track 7

TECHNOLOGY

Power Presentations

Teaching strategy Remind students that in French, unlike English, interrogative expressions cannot be separated. Compare:
Pour qui as-tu travaillé?
For whom did you work?
Who(m) did you work for?

Expansion You may want to present inversion with **il/elle/on** for recognition.
A-t-il téléphoné?
A-t-elle téléphoné?
A-t-on téléphoné?

12 EXCHANGES discussing past activities

–Est-ce que tu as ... ?
–Oui, j'ai ... (Non, je n'ai pas ...)

1. visité le Tibet
2. voyagé en Alaska
3. piloté un (d')avion
4. dîné dans un restaurant vietnamien
5. mangé des (d')escargots
6. gagné à la loterie
7. assisté à un match de catch
8. rencontré un (de) fantôme

Teaching note
Remind students to use **pas de** in items 3, 5, and 8.

Variation Have students ask and answer the questions in the plural.
– Est-ce que vous avez visité Paris?
– Oui, nous avons visité Paris. (Non, nous n'avons pas visité Paris.)

13 PRACTICE asking questions about past events

1. Quand est-ce qu'il a visité Québec?
2. À quelle heure est-ce qu'elle a téléphoné?
3. Comment est-ce qu'elle a voyagé en Italie?
4. Où est-ce qu'elle a acheté une (sa) robe?
5. Où est-ce qu'elle a rencontré sa copine?
6. Avec qui est-ce qu'elle a visité Genève?
7. Où est-ce qu'il a trouvé un job?
8. Dans quel restaurant est-ce qu'ils on dîné?
9. Quand est-ce qu'ils ont téléphoné?

D Les questions au passé composé

Compare the statements and questions in the passé composé.

STATEMENT	QUESTION	
Tu as travaillé.	Tu as travaillé? **Est-ce que** tu as travaillé?	*Did you work?*
Philippe a voyagé cet été.	**Quand est-ce que** Philippe a voyagé? **Où est-ce qu'**il a voyagé?	*When did Philippe travel?* *Where did he travel?*

For most verbs, questions in the passé composé are formed as follows:

interrogative form of **avoir** + PAST PARTICIPLE

	YES/NO QUESTIONS	INFORMATION QUESTIONS
WITH INTONATION	Tu as voyagé? Paul a téléphoné?	– –
WITH est-ce que	**Est-ce que** tu as voyagé? **Est-ce qu'**Alice a téléphoné?	**Avec qui est-ce que** tu as voyagé? **À qui est-ce qu'**Alice a téléphoné?

→ When the subject is a pronoun, questions in the passé composé can also be formed by inversion.

As-tu assisté au match de foot? *Did you go to the soccer game?*
Avec qui **avez-vous joué** au foot? *With whom did you play soccer?*
Who(m) did you play soccer with?

12  

PARLER Demandez à vos camarades s'ils ont déjà *(already)* fait les choses suivantes.

▶ visiter Paris?

Est-ce que tu as visité Paris?
Oui, j'ai visité Paris.
(Non, je n'ai pas visité Paris.)

1. visiter le Tibet?
2. voyager en Alaska?
3. piloter un avion?
4. dîner dans un restaurant vietnamien?
5. manger des escargots *(snails)*?
6. gagner à la loterie?
7. assister à un match de catch *(wrestling)*?
8. rencontrer un fantôme *(ghost)*?

13  

PARLER Lisez ce que les personnes suivantes ont fait et posez des questions sur leurs activités.

▶ Paul a joué au tennis. (avec qui?)
Avec qui est-ce qu'il a joué au tennis?

1. Thomas a visité Québec. (quand?)
2. Corinne a téléphoné. (à quelle heure?)
3. Nathalie a voyagé en Italie. (comment?)
4. Marthe a acheté une robe. (où?)
5. Léa a rencontré sa copine. (où?)
6. Michèle a visité Genève. (avec qui?)
7. Philippe a trouvé un job. (où?)
8. Éric et Véronique ont dîné en ville. (dans quel restaurant?)
9. Les voisins ont téléphoné. (quand?)

CASUAL FRENCH

Information questions using intonation may be formed by placing the interrogative expression in the same position in the sentence as the corresponding answer. Usually, but not always, this is at the end.

Paul a voyagé avec qui?
Paul a voyagé avec ses parents.

Vous avez téléphoné quand?
J'ai téléphoné à cinq heures.

Claire a amené qui à la boum?
Elle a amené Bruno à la boum.

Jérôme et Valérie

PARLER Jérôme est très curieux. Il veut toujours savoir ce que Valérie a fait. Valérie répond à ses questions.

▶ où/dîner? (dans un restaurant italien)
JÉRÔME: **Où est-ce que tu as dîné?**
VALÉRIE: **J'ai dîné dans un restaurant italien.**

1. avec qui / jouer au tennis? (avec Marc)
2. quand / assister au concert? (samedi après-midi)
3. qui / inviter au café? (ma copine Nathalie)
4. où / rencontrer Pierre? (dans la rue)
5. où / acheter ta veste? (au Bon Marché)
6. combien / payer ce CD? (10 euros)
7. à qui / téléphoner? (à ma grand-mère)
8. chez qui / passer le week-end? (chez une amie)

Conversation

PARLER Demandez à vos camarades ce qu'ils ont fait hier.

▶ à quelle heure / dîner?

1. avec qui / dîner?
2. à qui / téléphoner?
3. quel programme / regarder à la télé?
4. quel programme / écouter à la radio?
5. qui / rencontrer après les classes?
6. quand / étudier?

Dis, Hélène, à quelle heure est-ce que tu as dîné?
J'ai dîné à six heures.

PRONONCIATION ain = /ɛ̃/ aine = /ɛn/ in = /ɛ̃/ ine = /in/

Les lettres «ain» et «in»

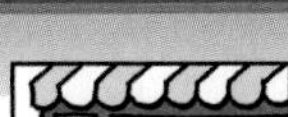

sa m<u>ain</u> **sem<u>aine</u>** **magas<u>in</u>** **magaz<u>ine</u>**

When the letters "**ain**," "**aim**," "**in**," "**im**" are at the end of a word or are followed by a *consonant,* they represent the nasal vowel /ɛ̃/.

REMEMBER: Do not pronounce an /n/ after the nasal vowel /ɛ̃/.

Répétez: /ɛ̃/ **dem<u>ain</u> f<u>aim</u> tr<u>ain</u> m<u>ain</u> vois<u>in</u> cous<u>in</u> jard<u>in</u> magas<u>in</u> m<u>ain</u>tenant <u>in</u>telligent <u>in</u>téressant <u>im</u>portant**

When the letters "**ain**," "**aim**," "**in(n)**," "**im**" are followed by a *vowel,* they do NOT represent a nasal sound.

Répétez: /ɛn/ **sem<u>aine</u> améric<u>aine</u>**
/ɛm/ **j'<u>aime</u>**
/in/ **vois<u>ine</u> cous<u>ine</u> cuis<u>ine</u> magaz<u>ine</u> c<u>iné</u>ma Cor<u>inne</u> f<u>inir</u>**
/im/ **t<u>imi</u>de d<u>im</u>anche M<u>imi</u> cent<u>ime</u>**

Al<u>ain</u> M<u>inime</u> a un rendez-vous <u>im</u>portant dem<u>ain</u> mat<u>in</u>, avenue du M<u>aine</u>.

INCLUSION

Multisensory Model the sound of words ending in **aim, ain, in** and **im** when they are at the end of the word and when they are followed by a vowel. Ask students to practice the sounds, noting the placement of their tongue (touching the roof of their mouth when the **n** is followed by a vowel, but not when it is at the end of the word or followed by a consonant). Provide a list of easy words and ask students to pronounce them as a group. Then have students pair off, practice, and put the list in their notebooks.

14 ROLE PLAY asking and answering questions about past events

1. **J:** Avec qui est-ce qu tu as joué au tennis?
   V: J'ai joué au tennis avec Marc.
2. **J:** Quand est-ce que tu as assisté au concert?
   V: J'ai assisté au concert samedi après-midi.
3. **J:** Qui est-ce que tu as invité au café?
   V: J'ai invité ma copine Nathalie au café.
4. **J:** Où est-ce que tu as rencontré Pierre?
   V: J'ai rencontré Pierre dans la rue.
5. **J:** Où est-ce que tu as acheté ta veste?
   V: J'ai acheté ma veste au Bon Marché.
6. **J:** Combien est-ce que tu as payé ce CD?
   V: J'ai payé ce CD dix euros.
7. **J:** À qui est-ce que tu as téléphoné?
   V: J'ai téléphoné à ma grand-mère.
8. **J:** Chez qui est-ce que tu as passé le week-end?
   V: J'ai passé le week-end chez une amie.

Variation (inversion) **Où as-tu dîné?**

15 EXCHANGES talking about yesterday

Answers will vary.

1. –Dis, (Léa), avec qui est-ce qu tu as dîné?
   –J'ai dîné avec (mes parents, mes amis).
2. –Dis, (Jean-Paul), à qui est-ce que tu as téléphoné?
   –J'ai téléphoné à (ma copine, à Roger).
3. –Dis, (Anne), quel programme est-ce que tu as regardé à la télé?
   –J'ai regardé (un film, une comédie).
4. –Dis, (Julie), quel programme est-ce que tu as écouté à la radio?
   –J'ai écouté (un concert de jazz).
5. –Dis, (Nancy), qui est-ce que tu as rencontré après les classes?
   –J'ai rencontré (Luc et Léa, un copain).
6. –Dis, (Luc), quand est-ce que tu as étudié?
   –J'ai étudié à (6 heures, après le dîner).

Teaching strategy Encourage students to give only affirmative answers, since they have not yet learned the negative forms **ne...rien, ne...personne.** These forms will be introduced in Lesson 24.

PRONUNCIATION

Teaching strategy Before doing the **pronunciation** section, have students practice minimal pairs containing /ɛ̃/ /ɛ̃n/ and /ɛ̃/, /in/.

/ɛ̃/	/ɛ̃n/
certain	**certaine**
américain	**américaine**
musicien	**musicienne**

/ɛ̃/	/in/
cousin	**cousine**
voisin	**voisine**
Martin	**Martine**

Point out that **maintenant, intelligent,** etc. all end in the sound /ã/. Be sure students do not pronounce the final "n" or "t."

À VOTRE TOUR

Teaching Resource Options

PRINT 

Workbook PE, pp. 187–194
Unit 7 Resource Book
Audioscript, p. 68
Communipak, pp. 148–170
Family Involvement, pp. 57–58
Workbook TE, pp. 35–42

Assessment
Lesson 22 Quiz, pp. 72–73
Portfolio Assessment, Unit 1 URB pp. 155–164
Audioscript for Quiz 22, p. 71
Answer Keys, pp. 213–216

AUDIO & VISUAL 

Audio Program
CD 4 Tracks 8, 9
CD 16 Track 2

TECHNOLOGY

Test Generator CD-ROM/McDougal Littell Assessment System

1 COMPREHENSION

1. À quelle heure est-ce que tu as dîné hier soir? (e) À sept heures et demie.
2. Et après, tu as regardé la télé? (d) Oui, mais d'abord j'ai aidé ma mère.
3. Qu'est-ce que tu as regardé après? (a) Le match Marseille-Nice.
4. Qui a gagné? (b) Nice. Par un score de trois à un.
5. Dis, tu as préparé la leçon pour demain? (c) Mais oui! J'ai étudié avant le dîner.

2 ORAL COMPREHENSION

- J'ai travaillé à la maison.
- J'ai préparé mes devoirs.
- J'ai regardé un film à la télé.
- Je n'ai pas joué au basket.
- Je n'ai pas acheté de CD.
- Je n'ai pas organisé de boum.

Teaching strategy If students want to use some of the expressions listed in the text, encourage them to vary them in some way.

Expansion Last Saturday I was in town with your friends but we did not see you. You probably were busy at home. Answer my questions in French. Please tell me . . .

- Did you help your parents?
- Did you clean your room?
- Did you wash the car?
- Did you phone your friends?
- What else did you do?

À votre tour!

OBJECTIFS

Now you can ...
- talk with friends about what you did and did not do last weekend
- talk about past events in general

1 Allô!

PARLER Reconstituez la conversation entre Alain et Christine. Pour cela, faites correspondre les réponses de Christine avec les questions d'Alain.

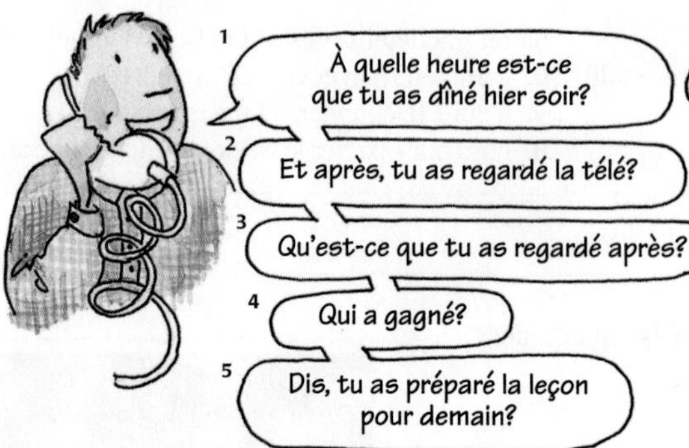
1 À quelle heure est-ce que tu as dîné hier soir?
2 Et après, tu as regardé la télé?
3 Qu'est-ce que tu as regardé après?
4 Qui a gagné?
5 Dis, tu as préparé la leçon pour demain?
a Le match Marseille-Nice.
b Nice. Par un score de trois à un.
c Mais oui! J'ai étudié avant le dîner.
d Oui, mais d'abord j'ai aidé ma mère.
e À sept heures et demie.

2 Dis-moi ...

PARLER *I will tell you a few things that I did yesterday after school and a few things that I did not do, then you will tell me what you did and did not do.*

- J'ai étudié.
- J'ai dîné avec mes parents.
- J'ai téléphoné à une copine.
- Je n'ai pas rangé ma chambre.
- Je n'ai pas rencontré mes copains.
- Je n'ai pas regardé la télé.

Et maintenant, dis-moi ...

3 Créa-dialogue

PARLER Demandez à vos camarades s'ils ont fait les choses suivantes le week-end dernier. En cas de réponse affirmative, continuez la conversation.

▶ —Est-ce que tu as dîné au restaurant?
—Oui, j'ai dîné au restaurant.
—Avec qui?
—Avec mes cousins.
—Où est-ce que vous avez dîné?
—Nous avons dîné Chez Tante Lucie (à l'Hippopotamus, etc.).

MENU
▶ avec qui?
où?

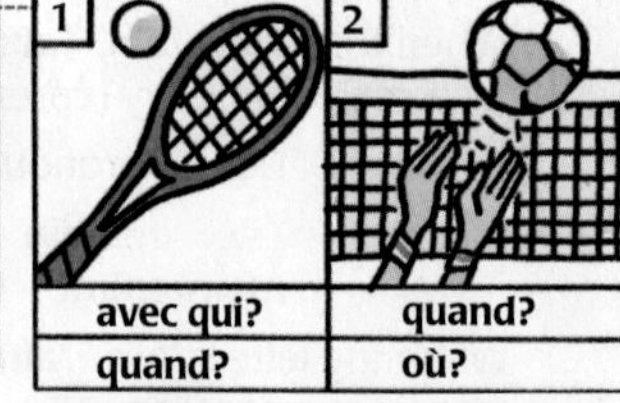
1 avec qui?
quand?
2 quand?
où?

3 quand?
pourquoi?
4 quand?
où?
5 quand?
avec qui?

À VOTRE TOUR

Depending on your goals and objectives, you may or may not want to assign all of the activities in the **À votre tour** section.

PAIR PRACTICE

In Act. 1 and 3, you may want to have students work in trios, with two performing and one consulting the Answer Key and acting as monitor.

4 Composition: Hier soir *(Last night)*

ÉCRIRE In one or two paragraphs describe what you did yesterday evening. You may wish to use the following suggestions:

- étudier (quoi?)
- dîner (à quelle heure?)
- manger (quoi?)
- téléphoner (à qui?)
- parler (de quoi?)
- écouter (quel type de musique?)
- regarder (quel programme à la télé?)
- aider (qui? comment?)
- ranger (quoi?)

STRATEGY Writing

Narrating the past When you write about past events, it is helpful to indicate the order in which these events occurred. In your composition, you can indicate the sequence in which you did certain things last night by using expressions such as **d'abord, après, ensuite, enfin,** and **finalement**.

COMMENT DIT-ON ...?

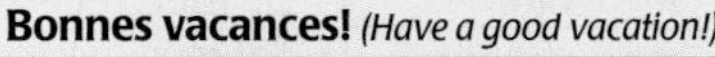

How to wish somebody a nice time:

Bon week-end! *(Have a nice weekend!)*

Bonnes vacances! *(Have a good vacation!)*

Bonne journée! *(Have a nice day!)*

Bon voyage! *(Have a good trip!)*

PORTFOLIO ASSESSMENT

You will probably select only one speaking activity and one writing activity to go into the students' portfolios for Unit 7.

3 GUIDED ORAL EXPRESSION

Answers will vary.

1. –Est-ce que tu as joué au tennis?
   –Oui, j'ai joué au tennis.
   –Avec qui?
   –Avec (Jean, Luc et Karine).
   –Quand est-ce que tu as joué au tennis?
   –(Dimanche après-midi.) (Non, je n'ai pas joué au tennis.)
2. –Est-ce que tu as joué au volley?
   –Oui, j'ai joué au volley.
   –Quand?
   –(Samedi matin.)
   –Où est-ce que tu as joué au volley?
   –(Au stade.)
3. –Est-ce que tu as nettoyé ta chambre?
   –Oui, j'ai nettoyé ma chambre.
   –Quand est-ce que tu as nettoyé ta chambre?
   –(Vendredi après-midi.)
   –Pourquoi?
   –(Parce que je vais inviter mes copains.) (Non, je n'ai pas nettoyé ma chambre.)
4. –Est-ce que tu as rencontré tes (des) amis?
   –Oui, j'ai rencontré mes (des) amis.
   –Quand?
   –(Samedi après-midi.)
   –Où est-ce que tu as rencontré tes (des) amis?
   – (Au café.)
   (Non, je n'ai pas rencontré mes amis.)
5. –Est-ce que tu as dansé?
   –Oui, j'ai dansé.
   –Quand est-ce que tu as dansé?
   –(Samedi soir.)
   –Avec qui est-ce que tu as dansé?
   –Avec (Dominique).
   (Non, je n'ai pas dansé.)

Teaching strategy Have pairs of students each choose and prepare one of the dialogues and present it to the class.

4 WRITTEN SELF-EXPRESSION

Answers will vary.
Hier soir, j'ai étudié avant le dîner. Après le dîner, j'ai aidé mon père dans la cuisine. Après, j'ai téléphoné à ma copine. Nous avons parlé des devoirs. Ensuite, j'ai écouté du rock et j'ai regardé un film à la télé.

Supplementary vocabulary

Amuse-toi bien! *Have a good time*
Amusez-vous bien!

Language note In Quebec, the traditional term for *weekend* is **fin de semaine: Bonne fin de semaine!** *(Have a nice weekend!)*

Leçon 23

Main Topic Describing past events

Teaching Resource Options

PRINT 

Workbook PE, pp. 195–200
Activités pour tous PE, pp. 119–121
Block Scheduling Copymasters, pp. 177–184
Unit 7 Resource Book
- *Activités pour tous* TE, pp. 81–83
- Audioscript, pp. 102, 103–105
- Communipak, pp. 148–170
- Lesson Plans, pp. 84–85
- Block Scheduling Lesson Plans, pp. 86–87
- Absent Student Copymasters, pp. 88–91
- Video Activities, pp. 94–99
- Videoscript, pp. 100–101
- Workbook TE, pp. 75–80

AUDIO & VISUAL 

Audio Program
CD 4 Tracks 10, 11
CD 11 Tracks 13–18

TECHNOLOGY 

Online Workbook

VIDEO PROGRAM

MODULE 23
Pas de chance!

TOTAL TIME: 5:08 min.
DVD Disk 2
Videotape 4 (COUNTER: 13:06 min.)

23.1 Dialogue: Pas de chance! (13:24–14:40 min.)

23.2 Mini-scenes: Listening – Qu'est-ce que vous avez fait? (14:41–15:19 min.)

23.3 Mini-scenes: Speaking – Est-ce qu'ils ont perdu? (15:20–16:28 min.)

23.4 Vignette culturelle: La télé (16:29–18:14 min.)

Comprehension practice Play the entire module through as an introduction to the lesson.

Challenge activity Have students consult a French-English dictionary and try to find out the meanings of the suspects' last names.
filou *(dishonest person, thief)*
la roulette *(roulette wheel)*
l'escroc *(crook)*
malin *(shrewd, cunning)*

LEÇON 23 L'alibi

AUDIO

l'inspecteur Leflic

Êtes-vous bon (bonne) détective? Pouvez-vous trouver la solution du mystère suivant? — *Can / following*

Samedi dernier à deux heures de l'après-midi, il y a eu une panne d'électricité dans la petite ville de Marcillac-le-Château. La panne a duré une heure. Pendant la panne, un cambrioleur a pénétré dans la Banque Populaire de Marcillac-le-Château. Bien sûr, l'alarme n'a pas fonctionné et c'est seulement lundi matin que le directeur de la banque a remarqué le cambriolage: un million d'euros. — *there was / power failure / lasted; burglar / entered; only; noticed / burglary*

Lundi après-midi, l'inspecteur Leflic a interrogé quatre suspects, mais chacun a un alibi. — *police detective; each one*

Sophie Filou

Euh, … excusez-moi, Monsieur l'Inspecteur.
Ma mémoire n'est pas très bonne.
Voyons, qu'est-ce que j'ai fait samedi après-midi? — *Let's see / did I do*
Ah oui, j'ai fini un livre. — *finished*
Le titre du livre? *Le crime ne paie pas!* — *title*

Marc Laroulette

Qu'est-ce que j'ai fait samedi?
J'ai rendu visite à mes copains. — *visited*
Nous avons joué aux cartes.
C'est moi qui ai gagné!

Patrick Lescrot

Voyons, samedi dernier …
Ah oui … cet après-midi-là, j'ai invité des amis chez moi.
Nous avons regardé la télé.
Nous avons vu le match de foot France-Allemagne. — *saw / Germany*
Quel match! Malheureusement, c'est la France qui a perdu! — *Unfortunately / lost*
Dommage!

Pauline Malin

Ce n'est pas moi, Monsieur l'Inspecteur!
Samedi j'ai fait un pique-nique à la campagne avec une copine.
Nous avons choisi un coin près d'une rivière. — *chose / spot*
Ensuite, nous avons fait une promenade à vélo.
Nous avons eu de la chance! — *were lucky*
Il a fait un temps extraordinaire! — *The weather was great!*

Lisez attentivement les quatre déclarations. À votre avis, qui est le cambrioleur ou la cambrioleuse? Pourquoi? (Vous pouvez comparer votre réponse avec la réponse de l'inspecteur à la page 337.) — *carefully*

CLASSROOM MANAGEMENT Group reading

Since this is a longer story, you may want to use it as a recapitulation at the end of the lesson.

Divide the class into groups of three or four. Have each group read the story, without turning to p. 337 to see the solution.

The recorder **(secrétaire)** of each group writes down the solution: who is the guilty one and why. **Qui est le coupable et pourquoi?**

After all the recorders have given their reports to the class, the students may read the solution in the text.

Compréhension

Certains événements ont eu lieu *(took place)* samedi dernier. Indiquez si oui ou non les événements suivants ont eu lieu.

1. Le directeur de la banque a vu *(saw)* le cambrioleur.
2. Un cambriolage a eu lieu *(took place)* à Marcillac-le-Château.
3. L'inspecteur Leflic a arrêté *(arrested)* quatre personnes.
4. Sophie Filou a vu le film *Le crime ne paie pas* à la télé.
5. Marc Laroulette a perdu un million d'euros.
6. L'Allemagne a gagné un match de foot.
7. Pauline Malin a fait une promenade à vélo à la campagne.
8. Il a fait beau.

Et toi?

Dis si oui ou non tu as fait les choses suivantes le week-end dernier.

1. (J'ai/Je n'ai pas) … rendu visite à mes copains.
2. (J'ai/Je n'ai pas) … vu un match de foot à la télé.
3. (J'ai/Je n'ai pas) … fini un livre.
4. (J'ai/Je n'ai pas) … fait une promenade à vélo.
5. (J'ai/Je n'ai pas) … fait un pique-nique.

NOTE culturelle

france 3

france 5

arte

Les jeunes Français et la télé

Combien d'heures par° jour est-ce que tu regardes la télé? Une heure? deux heures? trois heures? plus? moins? En général, les jeunes Français regardent la télé moins souvent et moins longtemps° que les jeunes Américains: en moyenne° 1 heure 15 les jours d'école et 2 heures 15 les autres° jours (mercredi, samedi et dimanche). Dans beaucoup de familles, les parents contrôlent l'usage° de la télé. Souvent ils exigent° que leurs enfants finissent leurs devoirs avant de regarder la télé. Ainsi,° beaucoup de jeunes regardent la télé seulement° après le dîner.

Quels sont leurs programmes favoris? Les jeunes Français aiment surtout° les films, les programmes de sport, les variétés et les jeux télévisés,° comme «Qui veut gagner° des millions?». Les séries américaines sont aussi très populaires.

par *per* **moins longtemps** *for a shorter time* **en moyenne** *on an average of* **autres** *other* **usage** *use* **exigent** *insist* **Ainsi** *Thus* **seulement** *only* **surtout** *especially* **jeux télévisés** *game shows* **gagner** *to win*

SETTING THE SCENE

Video Module 23 opens with **Pas de chance!** *(out of luck),* a humorous series of dialogues. Philippe has had a bad day, and in these conversations he explains what happened.

The **Vignette culturelle** focuses on French television and expands on the cultural note in the student text.

Compréhension
Answers

1. Non, le directeur de la banque n'a pas vu le cambrioleur.
2. Oui, le cambriolage a eu lieu à Marcillac-le-Château.
3. Non, l'inspecteur n'a pas arrêté quatre personnes. Il a interrogé quatre personnes.
4. Non, Sophie Filou n'a pas vu le film *Le crime ne paie pas* à la télé. Elle a lu le livre.
5. Non, Marc Laroulette n'a pas perdu un million d'euros. Il a gagné à un jeu de cartes.
6. Oui, l'Allemagne a gagné le match de foot.
7. Oui, Pauline Malin a fait une promenade à vélo à la campagne.
8. Oui, il a fait beau.

Et toi?

Answers will vary.

1. J'ai rendu visite à mes copains. (Je n'ai pas rendu visite à mes copains.
2. J'ai vu un match de foot à la télé. (Je n'ai pas vu de match de foot à la télé.)
3. J'ai fini un livre. (Je n'ai pas fini de livre.)
4. J'ai fait une promenade à vélo. (Je n'ai pas fait de promenade à vélo.)
5. J'ai fait un pique-nique. (Je n'ai pas fait de pique-nique.)

Realia note

La Coupe de France
The French national soccer tournament is called **La Coupe de France.**

This TV ad is for a game early in the playoffs where 32 teams are in competition and playing in 16 games around the country **(les seizièmes de finale).**

Note culturelle

Teaching strategy For more information on French TV channels, see p. 118.

SECTION A

Communicative function
Talking about what one sees

Teaching Resource Options

PRINT 

Workbook PE, pp. 195–200
Unit 7 Resource Book
  Audioscript, p. 102
  Communipak, pp. 148–170
  Workbook TE, pp. 75–80

AUDIO & VISUAL 

Audio Program
CD 4 Track 12

TECHNOLOGY

Power Presentations

Pronunciation Be sure students maintain the sound /vwa/ in all forms of the verb, especially in:
nous voyons /vwajɔ̃/
vous voyez /vwaje/

1 PRACTICE seeing sights in Paris

1. Nous voyons le musée d'Orsay.
2. Tu vois l'Arc de Triomphe.
3. Je vois le Centre Pompidou.
4. Sophie voit le Quartier latin.
5. Vous voyez la pyramide du Louvre.
6. Les touristes japonais voient le musée Picasso.

Teaching strategy Tell students that **voir** is another "boot" verb.

je vois	**nous voyons**
tu vois	**vous voyez**
il voit	**ils voient**

2 COMMUNICATION answering personal questions

Answers will vary.

1. Oui, je vois bien. Non, je ne porte pas de lunettes. (Non, je ne vois pas bien. Oui, je porte des lunettes.)
2. Oui, je vois mes amis pendant les vacances. (Non, je ne vois pas mes amis pendant les vacances.) Oui, je vois mes professeurs. (Non, je ne vois pas mes professeurs.)
3. Oui, je vois souvent mes cousins. (Non, je ne vois pas souvent mes cousins.) Oui, je vois mes cousins pendant les vacances. (Non, je ne vois pas mes cousins pendant les vacances.) Oui, je vois mes cousins à Noël. (Non, je ne vois pas mes cousins à Noël.)
4. Je préfère voir un match de football à la télé. (Je préfère voir un match de baseball à la télé.)
5. Quand je vais au cinéma, j'aime voir (les comédies).

A Le verbe *voir* 

The verb **voir** *(to see)* is irregular. Note the forms of **voir** in the present tense.

INFINITIVE	voir	
PRESENT	Je **vois** Marc. Tu **vois** ton copain. Il/Elle/On **voit** un accident.	Nous **voyons** un film. Vous **voyez** un match de baseball. Ils/Elles **voient** le professeur.

1 Week-end à Paris

PARLER/ÉCRIRE Les personnes suivantes passent le week-end à Paris. Décrivez ce que chacun voit.

▶ Olivier   **Olivier voit Notre-Dame.**

Notre-Dame

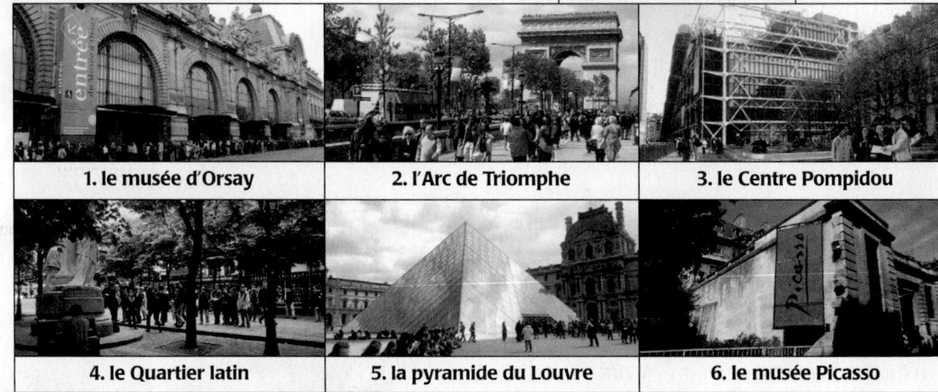

1. le musée d'Orsay 2. l'Arc de Triomphe 3. le Centre Pompidou 4. le Quartier latin 5. la pyramide du Louvre 6. le musée Picasso

1. nous
2. toi
3. moi
4. Sophie
5. vous
6. les touristes japonais

2 Questions personnelles PARLER/ÉCRIRE

1. Est-ce que tu vois bien? Est-ce que tu portes des lunettes?
2. Est-ce que tu vois tes amis pendant les vacances? Est-ce que tu vois tes professeurs?
3. Est-ce que tu vois souvent tes cousins? Est-ce que tu vois tes cousins pendant les vacances? à Noël?
4. Qu'est-ce que tu préfères voir à la télé? un match de football ou un match de baseball?
5. Quand tu vas au cinéma, quels films aimes-tu voir? les comédies? les films d'aventures? les films policiers *(detective movies)*?

B Le passé composé des verbes réguliers en *-ir* et *-re*

Note the passé composé of the verbs below, paying special attention to the ending of the past participle.

choisir	J'ai **choisi** cette casquette.	Je **n'ai pas choisi** cette chemise.
finir	Nous **avons fini** le magazine.	Nous **n'avons pas fini** le livre.
vendre	Tu **as vendu** ton vélo.	Tu **n'as pas vendu** ta moto.
attendre	Jacques **a attendu** Paul.	Il **n'a pas attendu** François.
répondre	**J'ai répondu** au professeur.	Tu **n'as pas répondu** à la question.

The past participle of regular **-ir** and **-re** verbs is formed as follows:

-ir	→	-i	-re	→	-u
chois**ir**	→	chois**i**	vend**re**	→	vend**u**
fin**ir**	→	fin**i**	attend**re**	→	attend**u**

3 Besoins d'argent *(Money needs)*

PARLER/ÉCRIRE Parce qu'elles ont besoin d'argent, les personnes suivantes ont vendu certains objets. Dites ce que chaque personne a vendu.

▶ Philippe/sa guitare **Philippe a vendu sa guitare.**

1. M. Roche/sa voiture
2. mes copains/leur chaîne hi-fi
3. moi/mon appareil-photo
4. toi/ton skate
5. les voisins/leur piano
6. nous/nos livres
7. vous/votre ordinateur
8. François et Vincent/ leurs CD

4 Bravo!

PARLER/ÉCRIRE Les personnes suivantes méritent *(deserve)* des félicitations *(congratulations)*. Expliquez pourquoi.

▶ les élèves/réussir à l'examen **Les élèves ont réussi à l'examen.**

1. M. Bedon/maigrir
2. Mlle Legros/perdre dix kilos
3. Florence/gagner le match de tennis
4. les élèves/finir la leçon
5. moi/ranger ma chambre
6. nous/choisir une classe difficile
7. toi/finir les exercices
8. Marc/rendre visite à un copain à l'hôpital
9. vous/attendre vos copains
10. les élèves/répondre en français

SECTION B

Communicative function
Talking about the past

Teaching strategy Point out that like **-er** verbs, most **-ir** and **-re** verbs form the passé composé with **avoir.** Note the endings of the past participle.

3 PRACTICE describing what people sold

1. M. Roche a vendu sa voiture.
2. Mes copains ont vendu leur chaîne hi-fi.
3. J'ai vendu mon appareil-photo.
4. Tu as vendu ton skate.
5. Les voisins ont vendu leur piano.
6. Nous avons vendu nos livres.
7. Vous avez vendu votre ordinateur.
8. François et Victor ont vendu leurs CD.

Variation (in the negative) **Philippe n'a pas vendu sa guitare.**

4 PRACTICE describing people's accomplishments

1. M. Bedon a maigri.
2. Mlle Legros a perdu dix kilos.
3. Florence a gagné le match de tennis.
4. Les élèves ont fini la leçon.
5. J'ai rangé ma chambre.
6. Nous avons choisi une classe difficile.
7. Tu as fini les exercises.
8. Marc a rendu visite à un copain à l'hôpital.
9. Vous avez attendu vos copains.
10. Les élèves ont répondu en français.

Variation (in the negative) **Les élèves n'ont pas réussi à l'examen.**

Realia note
à vendre *for sale*

INCLUSION

Synthetic/Analytic After teaching the passé composé of **-ir** and **-re** verbs, draw verb ending charts on the board. Have students copy the charts in their notebooks. Ask them to repeat the verb endings on each chart several times while looking at the endings. Then have them work in pairs, one person gives an infinitive and the other answers with the correct form of the past participle.

Teaching Resource Options

PRINT 

Workbook PE, pp. 195–200
Unit 7 Resource Book
 Communipak, pp. 148–170
 Video Activities, pp. 95–96
 Videoscript, pp. 100–101
 Workbook TE, pp. 75–80

TECHNOLOGY

Power Presentations

VIDEO PROGRAM

VIDÉO DVD

MODULE 23

23.2 Mini-scenes: Qu'est-ce que vous avez fait? (14:41–15:19 min.)

23.3 Mini-scenes: Est-ce qu'ils ont perdu? (15:20–16:28 min.)

5 ROLE PLAY talking about past events

1. –Tu as étudié ce week-end?
 –Non! J'ai rendu visite à un copain.
2. –Tu as acheté un DVD?
 –Non! J'ai choisi un CD.
3. –Tu as fini ce livre?
 –Non! J'ai regardé la télé.
4. –Tu as vendu ta guitare?
 –Non! J'ai vendu mon appareil-photo.
5. –Tu as téléphoné à Marc?
 –Non! J'ai rendu visite à son cousin.
6. –Tu as maigri?
 –Non! J'ai grossi.
7. –Tu as répondu à la lettre?
 –Non! J'ai téléphoné.

6 DESCRIPTION contrasting present and past events

1. téléphone/j'ai téléphoné
2. finis/as fini
3. mangeons/avons mangé
4. choisit/a choisi
5. réussissent/ont réussi
6. vend/a vendu
7. rendent/ont rendu
8. attendent/ont attendu

7 ROLE PLAY explaining why one did not do certain things

–Tu as ... ?
–Non, je n'ai pas ...
–Pourquoi est-ce que tu n'as pas ... ?
–Parce que ...

1. travaillé/j'ai joué au foot
2. répondu/je n'ai pas entendu la question
3. joué au tennis/j'ai perdu ma raquette
4. acheté une veste/acheté de veste/j'ai choisi un blouson
5. fini le livre/j'ai regardé la télé
6. rendu visite à Marc/j'ai étudié
7. réussi à l'examen/j'ai perdu mes notes
8. écouté tes CD/écouté mes CD/écouté tes CD/j'ai vendu mon baladeur

5  *Non!*

PARLER Jean-Louis répond négativement aux questions de Béatrice. Jouez les deux rôles.

Tu as gagné le match?
Non! J'ai perdu!

▶ gagner le match/perdre

1. étudier ce week-end/rendre visite à un copain
2. acheter un DVD/choisir un CD
3. finir ce livre/regarder la télé
4. vendre ta guitare/vendre mon appareil-photo
5. téléphoner à Marc/rendre visite à son cousin
6. maigrir/grossir
7. répondre à la lettre/téléphoner

6 *Aujourd'hui et hier*

PARLER/ÉCRIRE Dites ce que les personnes suivantes font aujourd'hui et ce qu'elles ont fait hier.

▶ Paul/acheter un blouson/un pantalon
Aujourd'hui, Paul achète un blouson.
Hier, il a acheté un pantalon.

1. moi/téléphoner à mon cousin/à mes copains
2. toi/finir ce livre/ce magazine
3. nous/manger des sandwichs/une pizza
4. Mélanie/choisir une jupe/un chemisier
5. les élèves/réussir à l'examen de français/à l'examen d'anglais
6. Philippe/vendre sa chaîne hi-fi/ses vieilles cassettes
7. Philippe et Jean-Pierre/rendre visite à leurs cousins/à leur grand-mère
8. les touristes/attendre le train/le car

7   *Excuses*

PARLER Quand Michel ne fait pas une chose, il a toujours une excuse. Jouez le dialogue entre Michel et sa soeur Laure.

▶ étudier/perdre mon livre

1. travailler/jouer au foot
2. répondre/entendre la question
3. jouer au tennis/perdre ma raquette
4. acheter une veste/choisir un blouson
5. finir le livre/regarder la télé
6. rendre visite à Marc/étudier
7. réussir à l'examen/perdre mes notes
8. écouter tes CD/vendre mon baladeur

COMPREHENSION Past and present

Teach students gestures for present and past.

Montrez-moi le présent. [index finger pointing to floor]

Montrez-moi le passé. [thumb pointing back over shoulder]

Now read sentences aloud containing the present or the passé composé and have students identify the tense by using the appropriate gesture.

Est-ce que c'est le présent ou le passé?

- **Tu finis la leçon de natation.** [P]
- **J'ai fini la leçon de ski nautique.** [PC]
- **Paul a eu un accident de ski.** [PC]

C Le passé composé des verbes *être, avoir, faire, mettre* et *voir*

The verbs **être, avoir, faire, mettre,** and **voir** have irregular past participles.

être	→	**été**	Nous **avons été** à Paris.
avoir	→	**eu**	M. Lambert **a eu** un accident.
faire	→	**fait**	Qu'est-ce que tu **as fait** hier?
mettre	→	**mis**	Nous **avons mis** des jeans.
voir	→	**vu**	J'**ai vu** un bon film.

→ In the passé composé, the verb **être** has two different meanings:

Mme Lebrun **a été** malade.	*Mme Lebrun **has been** sick.*
Elle **a été** à l'hôpital.	*She **was** in the hospital.*

8  Dialogue

PARLER Demandez à vos camarades s'ils ont fait les choses suivantes récemment *(recently)*.

▶ faire une promenade?
—Est-ce que tu as fait une promenade récemment?
—Oui, j'ai fait une promenade. (Non, je n'ai pas fait de promenade.)

1. faire un pique-nique?
2. faire une promenade en voiture?
3. être malade *(sick)*?
4. avoir la grippe *(flu)*?
5. avoir une dispute *(fight)* avec ton copain?
6. avoir une bonne surprise?
7. avoir un «A» en français?
8. voir un film?
9. voir tes cousins?
10. mettre des affiches dans ta chambre?

9   Pourquoi?

PARLER Avec vos camarades de classe, parlez des personnes suivantes.

▶ Fabrice est content.
(avoir un «A» à l'examen)

1. Mes copains sont furieux. (avoir un «F» à l'examen)
2. Pauline est très contente. (voir son copain)
3. Mon père n'est pas content. (avoir une dispute avec son chef [*boss*])
4. Philippe est pâle. (voir un accident)
5. Juliette est fatiguée *(tired)*. (faire du jogging)
6. Alice et Laure sont bronzées *(tanned)*. (être à la mer)
7. Mon frère est fatigué. (faire de la gymnastique [*to work out*])
8. Patrick et Marc sont contents. (voir un bon film)
9. Isabelle est très élégante. (mettre une jolie robe)

SECTION C

Communicative function
Talking about the past

Language note Point out that the passé composé of most irregular verbs is formed with **avoir.**

Pronunciation Be sure students pronounce the past participle **eu** /y/, as in **tu.**

8 COMMUNICATION asking about past activities

Answers will vary.
–Est-ce que tu as ... récemment?
–Oui, j'ai ... (Non, je n'ai pas ...)

1. fait un pique-nique/je n'ai pas fait de pique-nique
2. fait une promenade en voiture/je n'ai pas fait de promenade
3. été malade
4. eu la grippe
5. eu une dispute avec ton copain/j'ai eu une (je n'ai pas eu de) dispute avec mon copain
6. eu une bonne surprise /je n'ai pas eu de bonne surprise
7. eu un «A» en français/je n'ai pas eu de «A» en français
8. vu un film/je n'ai pas vu de film
9. vu tes cousins/vu mes cousins
10. mis des affiches dans ta chambre/je n'ai pas mis d'affiches dans ma chambre

Pronunciation **récemment** /resamã/

Teaching note Remind students to use **pas de** in items 1, 2, 5, 6, 7, and 8 if they choose to answer in the negative.

9 EXCHANGES explaining people's looks and moods

1. –Mes copains sont furieux.
–Ah bon? Pourquoi?
–Ils ont eu un «F» à l'examen.
2. –Pauline est très contente.
–Ah bon? Pourquoi?
–Elle a vu son copain.
3. –Mon père n'est pas content.
–Ah bon? Pourquoi?
–Il a eu une dispute avec son chef.
4. –Philippe est pâle.
–Ah bon? Pourquoi?
–Il a vu un accident.
5. –Juliette est fatiguée.
–Ah bon? Pourquoi?
–Elle a fait du jogging.
6. –Alice et Laure sont bronzées.
–Ah bon? Pourquoi?
–Elles ont été à la mer.
7. –Mon frère est fatigué.
–Ah bon? Pourquoi?
–Il a fait de la gymnastique.
8. –Patrick et Marc sont contents.
–Ah bon? Pourquoi?
–Ils ont vu un bon film.
9. –Isabelle est très élégante.
–Ah bon? Pourquoi?
–Elle a mis une jolie robe.

- **Nous sommes à la mer.** [P]
- **Sophie fait de l'escalade.** [P]
- **Marc a fait de la planche à voile.** [PC]
- **Vous avez acheté un vélo.** [PC]
- **J'ai grossi cet été.** [PC]
- **Nous passons les vacances à la mer.** [P]
- **Mes cousins ont vu un match de tennis.** [PC]
- **Stéphanie met son maillot de bain.** [P]

INCLUSION

Repetitive Review the irregular past participles of **être**, **avoir**, **faire**, **mettre**, and **voir**, then write each infinitive on the board. Have 5 students go to the board and write the past participles under the infinitive forms as other students do this exercise in their notebooks. Then have 5 students go to the board to create sentences in the **passé composé**.

Teaching Resource Options

PRINT 

Workbook PE, pp. 195–200
Unit 7 Resource Book
Audioscript, pp. 102–103
Communipak, pp. 148–170
Video Activities, p. 94
Videoscript, p. 100
Workbook TE, pp. 75–80

AUDIO & VISUAL 

Audio Program
CD 4 Track 13

VIDEO PROGRAM

VIDÉO DVD

MODULE 23

23.1 Dialogue: Pas de chance! (13:24–14:40 min.)

10 COMPREHENSION describing what people did and did not do

1. Élodie a été à la montagne. Elle n'a pas nagé. Elle a fait du VTT.
2. Nous avons été à la campagne. Nous n'avons pas visité de monuments. Nous avons fait du camping.
3. Vous avez été à Paris. Vous n'avez pas parlé italien. Vous avez vu la tour Eiffel.
4. J'ai été à la mer. J'ai fait de la planche à voile. Je n'ai pas travaillé.
5. Mes parents ont été en Égypte. Ils ont vu les pyramides. Ils n'ont pas visité Paris.
6. Vous avez été dans un club de sport. Vous avez fait de la gymnastique. Vous n'avez pas grossi.
7. Christine a été à la plage. Elle a mis des lunettes de soleil. Elle n'a pas joué au tennis.

Realia note
Villages vacances

Most French employees get at least five weeks of paid vacation. One popular option is to go to a "vacation village" **(un village vacances).**

In this ad, the Viva group announces that they have a network **(un réseau)** of such "villages" and that, in addition to room and board, they offer sports instruction and numerous social events **(les villages sont "animés").**

Supplementary vocabulary

cette année *this year*
l'année dernière
l'année prochaine

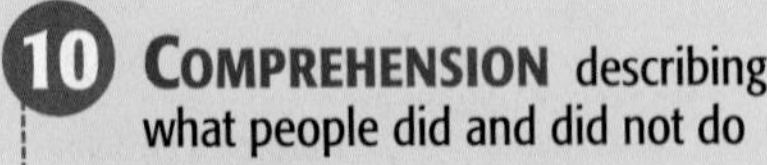

10 *Vive les vacances!*

PARLER/ÉCRIRE Dites où les personnes suivantes ont été pendant les vacances. Dites aussi si oui ou non elles ont fait les choses entre parenthèses. Soyez logique *(Be logical)*.

▶ Christophe: à la piscine (étudier/nager)
Christophe a été à la piscine. Il n'a pas étudié. Il a nagé.

1. Élodie: à la montagne (nager/faire du VTT)
2. nous: à la campagne (visiter des monuments/faire du camping)
3. vous: à Paris (parler italien/voir la tour Eiffel)
4. moi: à la mer (faire de la planche à voile/travailler)
5. mes parents: en Égypte (voir les pyramides/visiter Paris)
6. vous: dans un club de sport (faire de la gymnastique/grossir)
7. Christine: à la plage (mettre des lunettes de soleil/jouer au tennis)

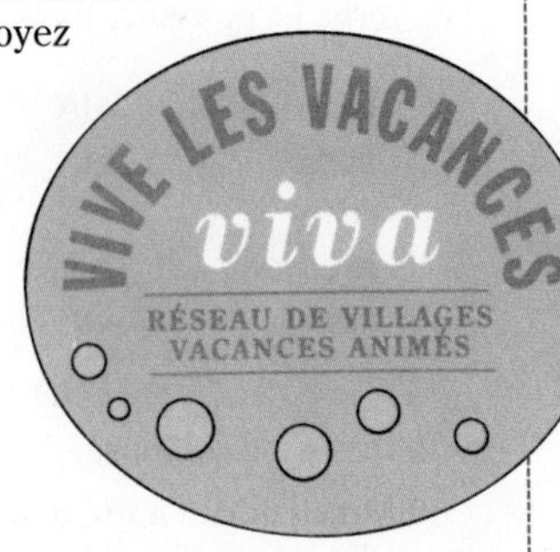

VIVE LES VACANCES
viva
RÉSEAU DE VILLAGES
VACANCES ANIMÉS

VOCABULAIRE *Quand?*

	maintenant	avant	après
le jour	**aujourd'hui**	**hier**	**demain**
le matin	**ce matin**	**hier matin**	**demain matin**
l'après-midi	**cet après-midi**	**hier après-midi**	**demain après-midi**
le soir	**ce soir**	**hier soir**	**demain soir**
le jour	**samedi**	**samedi dernier** *(last)*	**samedi prochain** *(next)*
le week-end	**ce week-end**	**le week-end dernier**	**le week-end prochain**
la semaine	**cette semaine**	**la semaine dernière**	**la semaine prochaine**
le mois	**ce mois-ci**	**le mois dernier**	**le mois prochain**

11   *Quand?*

PARLER Demandez à vos camarades quand ils ont fait les choses suivantes. Ils vont répondre en utilisant une expression du **Vocabulaire.**

▶ faire tes devoirs?

1. faire des achats?
2. ranger ta chambre?
3. rencontrer tes voisins?
4. voir ton copain?
5. voir un film?
6. avoir un examen?
7. faire une promenade à pied?
8. être en ville?
9. mettre *(set)* la table?

Quand est-ce que tu as fait tes devoirs?
J'ai fait mes devoirs hier après-midi.
(vendredi soir, le week-end dernier, ...)

GAME Moi aussi

For homework, have students write out their answers to Act. 12.

In class, students share their responses with one another. The object of the game is to find ten classmates who wrote the same answers.

One student reads the first statement, without showing the text to his/her partner.

The partner then reads his/her first statement.
X: Ce matin, j'ai regardé la télé. Et toi?
Y: Moi aussi. Ce matin, j'ai regardé la télé.

The answers match, so each one writes the other's name next to #1. Then they both read their responses to the next item.

12 Le passé et le futur

PARLER/ÉCRIRE Décrivez ce que vous avez fait (phrases 1 à 5) et ce que vous allez faire (phrases 6 à 10). Dites la vérité ... ou utilisez votre imagination!

1. Ce matin, j'ai ...
2. Hier matin, j'ai ...
3. Samedi après-midi, j'ai ...
4. La semaine dernière, j'ai ...
5. Le mois dernier, j'ai ...
6. Ce soir, je vais ...
7. Demain soir, je vais ...
8. Vendredi soir, je vais ...
9. Le week-end prochain, je vais ...
10. La semaine prochaine, je vais ...

13 Questions personnelles PARLER/ÉCRIRE

1. En général, est-ce que tu étudies avant ou après le dîner?
2. En général, est-ce que tu regardes la télé avant ou après le dîner?
3. À quelle heure est-ce que tu as dîné hier soir?
4. Quel programme de télé est-ce que tu as regardé hier après-midi?
5. Qu'est-ce que tu vas faire le week-end prochain?
6. Où vas-tu aller le week-end prochain?

PRONONCIATION gn = /ɲ/

Les lettres «gn»

The letters "**gn**" represent a sound similar to the "**ny**" in *canyon*.
First, practice with words you know.

Répétez: **espagnol gagner mignon**
la montagne la campagne

¡HOLA! ¿QUÉ TAL?

espagnol

Now try saying some new words. Make them sound French!

Répétez: **Champagne Espagne** *(Spain)* **un signe**
la vigne *(vineyard)* **la ligne** *(line)* **un signal**
la dignité ignorer magnétique magnifique Agnès

Agnès Mignard a gagné son match. C'est magnifique!

(L'alibi, p. 330)

LA RÉPONSE DE L'INSPECTEUR:

C'est Patrick Lescrot le cambrioleur. Samedi après-midi, il y a eu une panne d'électricité. Patrick Lescrot n'a pas pu *(was not able to)* regarder la télé. Son alibi n'est pas valable *(valid)*.

Often the answers will not be the same:
X: Hier matin, j'ai étudié. Et toi?
Y: Hier matin, j'ai joué au tennis.

Here the answers do not match, so they continue with #3. If time remains when they have shared the ten responses with one another, they may talk to another partner to try to find the missing matches.

At the end of the time limit, the student who has found the most matches wins.

11 COMMUNICATION finding out when past events took place

Answers will vary.
1. –Quand est-ce que tu as fait des achats?
   –J'ai fait des achats (hier soir).
2. –Quand est-ce que tu as rangé ta chambre?
   –J'ai rangé ma chambre (hier matin).
3. –Quand est-ce que tu as rencontré tes voisins?
   –J'ai rencontré mes voisins (la semaine dernière).
4. –Quand est-ce que tu as vu ton copain?
   –J'ai vu mon copain (hier après-midi).
5. –Quand est-ce que tu as vu un film?
   –J'ai vu un film (samedi dernier).
6. –Quand est-ce que tu as eu un examen?
   –J'ai eu un examen (le mois dernier).
7. –Quand est-ce que tu as fait une promenade à pied?
   –J'ai fait une promenade à pied (dimanche dernier).
8. –Quand est-ce que tu as été en ville?
   –J'ai été en ville (le week-end dernier).
9. –Quand est-ce que tu as mis la table?
   –J'ai mis la table (hier soir).

12 COMMUNICATION describing past events and future plans

Answers will vary.
1. Ce matin, j'ai (été à l'école).
2. Hier matin, j'ai (eu un examen).
3. Samedi après-midi, j'ai (fait des achats).
4. La semaine dernière, j'ai (fait de l'escalade).
5. Le mois dernier, j'ai (acheté un vélo).
6. Ce soir, je vais (retrouver mes amis au café).
7. Demain soir, je vais (faire mes devoirs de français).
8. Vendredi soir, je vais (aller à un concert de rock).
9. Le week-end prochain, je vais (faire du ski).
10. La semaine prochaine, je vais (organiser une boum).

13 COMMUNICATION answering personal questions

Answers will vary.
1. En général, j'étudie après (avant) le dîner.
2. En général, je regarde la télé avant (après) le dîner.
3. Hier soir, j'ai dîné à (sept heures et demie).
4. Hier après-midi, j'ai regardé (un match de baseball).
5. Le week-end prochain, je vais (rendre visite à mes grands-parents).
6. Le week-end prochain, je vais aller (en ville).

À VOTRE TOUR

Main Topic
- Recapitulation and review

Teaching Resource Options

PRINT 

Workbook PE, pp. 195–200
Unit 7 Resource Book
Audioscript, p. 103
Communipak, pp. 148–170
Family Involvement, pp. 57–58
Workbook TE, pp. 75–80

Assessment
Lesson 23 Quiz, pp. 107–108
Portfolio Assessment, Unit 1 URB pp. 155–164
Audioscript for Quiz 23, p. 106
Answer Keys, pp. 213–216

AUDIO & VISUAL 

Audio Program
CD 4 Tracks 14, 15
CD 16 Track 3

TECHNOLOGY

Test Generator CD-ROM/McDougal Littell Assessment System

1 COMPREHENSION

1. Tu as fini tes devoirs de français?
   (b) Non, je n'ai pas étudié cet après-midi.
2. Qu'est-ce que tu as fait alors?
   (d) J'ai joué au tennis avec Caroline.
3. Tu as gagné?
   (a) Non, j'ai perdu.
4. Mais d'habitude tu joues bien?
   (c) C'est vrai, mais aujourd'hui, je n'ai pas eu de chance ...
5. Peut-être que Caroline a joué mieux que toi?
   (e) Tu as raison. Elle a joué comme une championne.

2 GUIDED ORAL EXPRESSION

Answers will vary.
- J'ai rencontré des amis au café. J'ai mangé une très bonne glace.
- La semaine dernière, j'ai été à un concert de rock. J'ai beaucoup aimé le concert.
- Samedi dernier, j'ai fait une promenade à la campagne avec des amis. Il a fait très beau.

À votre tour!

OBJECTIFS

Now you can ...
- talk about what you did last week
- find out what others did recently

1 Allô!

PARLER Reconstituez la conversation entre Robert et Julien. Pour cela, faites correspondre les réponses de Julien avec les questions de Robert.

1. Tu as fini tes devoirs de français?
2. Qu'est-ce que tu as fait alors?
3. Tu as gagné?
4. Mais d'habitude *(usually)* tu joues bien?
5. Peut-être que Caroline a joué mieux *(better)* que toi?

a. Non, j'ai perdu!
b. Non, je n'ai pas étudié cet après-midi.
c. C'est vrai, mais aujourd'hui, je n'ai pas eu de chance ...
d. J'ai joué au tennis avec Caroline.
e. Tu as raison. Elle a joué comme une championne.

2 Dis-moi ...

PARLER *I will tell you about some nice things that happened to me recently; then you will tell me about three nice things that happened to you.*

- J'ai réussi à mon examen d'anglais. (J'ai eu un «A».)
- J'ai eu un rendez-vous avec une personne très intéressante.
- J'ai vu un très bon film.

Et maintenant, dis-moi ...

3 Créa-dialogue

PARLER Avec vos camarades, discutez de ce que vous avez fait récemment *(recently)*. Vous pouvez utiliser les expressions et les activités suggérées. Continuez la conversation avec des questions supplémentaires.

Quand?	
dimanche après-midi	lundi dernier
hier soir	la semaine dernière
samedi soir	le mois dernier
le week-end dernier	

Quoi?	
jouer aux jeux vidéo	dîner au restaurant
faire des achats	voir un film
faire du skate	avoir un rendez-vous
voir mes cousins	rendre visite à un copain
	faire du roller

▶ **—Qu'est-ce que tu as fait dimanche après-midi?**
—J'ai joué au tennis avec ma soeur.
—Est-ce que tu as gagné?
—Non, j'ai perdu.
—Dommage!

À VOTRE TOUR

Depending on your goals and objectives, you may or may not wish to assign all of the activities in the **À votre tour** section.

GROUP PRACTICE

In Act. 1 and 3, you may want to have students work in trios, with two performing and one acting as monitor.

4 Le week-end dernier

ÉCRIRE Write a short composition in which you describe what you did last weekend. You may adopt some of the following suggestions. Do not use **aller.**

- voir (qui? où? quand?)
- voir (quel film? où?)
- faire (de quel sport? de quelle activité? avec qui?)
- jouer (à quel jeu? à quel sport?)
- jouer (de quel instrument? où?)
- avoir un rendez-vous (avec qui?)
- faire une promenade (où? avec qui?)
- dîner (où? avec qui?)
- être (à quel endroit? avec qui? quand?)
- faire des achats (où? quand?)
- acheter (quoi? pourquoi?)
- regarder (quel programme de télé? quel DVD?)
- assister (à quel match? à quel concert?)

COMMENT DIT-ON ...?

How to wish someone good luck or give encouragement:

Bonne chance!

Bon courage!

PORTFOLIO ASSESSMENT

You will probably select only one speaking activity and one writing activity to go into the students' portfolios for Unit 7.

In this lesson, Act. 3 lends itself well to oral portfolio recordings.

3 GUIDED ORAL EXPRESSION

Answers will vary.

- –Qu'est-ce que tu as fait hier soir?
  –J'ai eu un rendez-vous.
  –Avec qui est-ce que tu as eu un rendez-vous?
  –Avec Thomas, mon meilleur ami.
  –C'est chouette!
- –Qu'est-ce que tu as fait samedi soir?
  –J'ai dîné au restaurant.
  –Est-ce que tu as aimé le dîner?
  –Oui, c'est un très bon restaurant.
  –Mmmh, j'ai faim.
- –Qu'est-ce que tu as fait le week-end dernier?
  –J'ai fait du skate.
  –Est-ce qu'il a fait bon?
  –Non, il a fait très froid.
  –Dommage!
- –Qu'est-ce que tu as fait lundi dernier?
  –J'ai vu mes cousins.
  –Est-ce que tu as dîné chez eux?
  –Oui, et on a joué aux jeux vidéo. J'ai gagné!
  –Super!
- –Qu'est-ce que tu as fait la semaine dernière?
  –J'ai fait des achats.
  –Qu'est-ce que tu as acheté?
  –J'ai acheté ce tee-shirt.
  –Il est extra!
- –Qu'est-ce que tu as fait le mois dernier?
  –J'ai rendu visite à un copain.
  –Est-ce que vous avez fait du sport?
  –Oui, on a joué au basket.
  –Super!

Culture note

Le tennis The French not only love to play tennis, they are avid tennis fans. It was a national event when France won the Davis Cup in 2001.

Roland Garros is the tennis stadium near Paris which hosts the annual French Open **(Les Internationaux de France)**. The stadium was named in memory of Roland Garros (1888–1918), a World War I fighter pilot and the first aviator to cross the Mediterranean (1913).

4 WRITTEN SELF-EXPRESSION

Answers will vary.
Vendredi soir, j'ai vu le film *Casablanca* au Palace avec mon copain. Après, nous avons pris un chocolat au café.

Samedi matin, mes amis et moi, nous avons eu des cours. J'ai aussi étudié. Samedi après-midi, nous avons fait du roller au parc.

Dimanche après-midi, ma famille et moi, nous avons rendu visite à ma grand-mère. Nous avons dîné chez elle. Dimanche soir, j'ai fini mes devoirs.

Leçon 24

Main Topic Describing where people went

Teaching Resource Options

PRINT 

Workbook PE, pp. 201–208
Activités pour tous PE, pp. 123–125
Block Scheduling Copymasters, pp. 185–191
Unit 7 Resource Book
- *Activités pour tous* TE, pp. 117–119
- Audioscript, pp. 139, 140–142
- Communipak, pp. 148–170
- Lesson Plans, pp. 120–121
- Block Scheduling Lesson Plans, pp. 122–124
- Absent Student Copymasters, pp. 125–128
- Video Activities, pp. 131–136
- Videoscript, pp. 137–138
- Workbook TE, pp. 109–116

AUDIO & VISUAL 

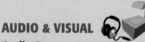

Audio Program
CD 4 Tracks 16, 17
CD 11 Tracks 19–25

TECHNOLOGY 

Online Workbook

VIDEO PROGRAM

MODULE 24
Un bon week-end

TOTAL TIME: 6:23 min.
DVD Disk 2
Videotape 4 (COUNTER: 18:30 min.)

24.1 Dialogue: Un bon week-end (18:41–20:19 min.)

24.2 Mini-scenes: Listening – Où êtes-vous allé? Et qu'est-ce que vous avez fait? (20:20–22:08 min.)

24.3 Mini-scenes: Speaking – Où est-ce qu'ils sont allés? (22:09–23:20 min.)

24.4 Vignette culturelle: La musique (23:21–24:53 min.)

Comprehension practice Play the entire module through as an introduction to the lesson.

LEÇON 24 Qui a de la chance?

AUDIO

VENDREDI APRÈS-MIDI

Anne et Valérie parlent de leurs projets pour le week-end.

Anne: Qu'est-ce que tu vas faire samedi soir?
Valérie: Je vais aller au cinéma avec Jean-Pierre.
Anne: Tu as de la chance! Moi, je dois rester à la maison.
Valérie: Mais pourquoi?
Anne: Les amis de mes parents viennent chez nous ce week-end. Mon père insiste pour que je reste pour le dîner. Quelle barbe! — *that / What a pain!*
Valérie: C'est vrai! Tu n'as pas de chance!

LUNDI MATIN

Anne et Valérie parlent de leur week-end.

Anne: Alors, tu as passé un bon week-end?
Valérie: Euh non, pas très bon.
Anne: Mais tu es sortie avec Jean-Pierre! — *went out*
Valérie: C'est vrai. Je suis allée au cinéma avec lui … — *went*
Nous avons vu un très, très mauvais film! Après le film, j'ai eu une dispute avec Jean-Pierre. Et, en plus, j'ai perdu mon porte-monnaie … et je suis rentrée chez moi à pied! Et toi, tu es restée chez toi? — *quarrel / in addition / wallet / went back / stayed*
Anne: Non.
Valérie: Comment? Les amis de tes parents ne sont pas venus? — *didn't come*
Anne: Si, si, ils sont venus … avec leur fils!
Valérie: Et alors?
Anne: Eh bien, c'est un garçon très sympa et très amusant … — *sympa = sympathique*

Après le dîner, nous sommes allés au Zénith.* Nous avons assisté à un concert de rock absolument extraordinaire. Après, nous sommes allés dans un café et nous avons fait des projets pour le week-end prochain. — *went*
Valérie: Qu'est-ce que vous allez faire?
Anne: Nous allons faire une promenade à la campagne dans la nouvelle voiture de sport de Thomas. (C'est le nom de mon nouveau copain!)
Valérie: Toi, vraiment, tu as de la chance!

*Une salle *(hall)* de concert à Paris, parc de la Villette.

CLASSROOM MANAGEMENT Pair reading

Since this is a longer story, you may want to use it as a recapitulation at the end of the lesson.

Have students read the title. Then, in pairs, have them read the story and write out brief answers to the following questions:
Qui a de la chance? Pourquoi?
Qui n'a pas de chance? Pourquoi?

Compréhension

1. Qu'est-ce que Valérie va faire samedi soir?
2. Pourquoi est-ce qu'Anne doit *(must)* rester à la maison?
3. Est-ce que Valérie a aimé le film?
4. Qu'est-ce qu'elle a perdu?
5. Comment est-ce qu'elle est rentrée chez elle?
6. Où et avec qui est-ce qu'Anne a dîné?
7. Où est-ce qu'elle est allée après le dîner?
8. Qu'est-ce qu'elle va faire le week-end prochain?
9. Comment s'appelle son nouveau copain?

Et toi?

Dis si oui ou non tu as fait les choses suivantes samedi dernier.

1. (Je suis/Je ne suis pas) ... allé(e) en ville.
2. (Je suis/Je ne suis pas) ... allé(e) au cinéma.
3. (Je suis/Je ne suis pas) ... allé(e) à un concert.
4. (Je suis/Je ne suis pas) ... rentré(e) chez moi pour le dîner.
5. (Je suis/Je ne suis pas) ... resté(e) chez moi le soir.

Les jeunes Français et la musique

«Pour moi, la musique c'est tout!»° déclare Anne, une jeune Française de quinze ans. Sa copine Hélène est d'accord: «Aujourd'hui, on ne peut pas° vivre° sans° musique.»

Comme les jeunes Américains, les jeunes Français sont des «fanas»° de la musique. Ils aiment particulièrement le rock, le rap français ou américain, la techno, le pop, le reggae et le ska, mais certains préfèrent la musique classique. En semaine, ils écoutent leur musique préférée sur leurs baladeurs et leurs chaînes hi-fi. Le week-end, ils vont au concert écouter les stars de la chanson° française, anglaise ou américaine.

Le 21 juin de chaque année, les jeunes célèbrent la «Fête de la Musique» avec tous° les Français. C'est une grande fête nationale avec des concerts publics gratuits° dans toutes les villes et tous les villages de France. Ce jour-là, 800 000 musiciens jouent pour 60 millions de spectateurs. Pour la «Fête de la Musique» tout le monde° fait de la musique.

tout *everything* **ne peut pas** *cannot* **vivre** *live* **sans** *without* **fanas = fanatiques** **chanson** *song* **tous** *all* **gratuits** *free* **tout le monde** *everyone*

COMPARAISONS CULTURELLES

- Do you think American teenagers would agree with Anne: **"On ne peut pas vivre sans musique?"** Explain.
- Do French and American teenagers listen to the same types of music?
- Do you think that the United States should declare a national music day like the French "**Fête de la Musique**"? Why or why not?

SETTING THE SCENE

The opening scene of **Video Module 24** presents two girls who are at a café talking about where they went last Saturday. At the end, the conversation takes an unexpected twist.

The **Vignette culturelle** of the video expands on the culture note in the text. French young people are interviewed about their tastes in music.

Compréhension

Answers

1. Elle va aller au cinéma avec Jean-Pierre.
2. Des amis de ses parents viennent chez eux.
3. Non, elle n'a pas aimé le film.
4. Elle a perdu son porte-monnaie.
5. Elle est rentrée chez elle à pied.
6. Anne a dîné à la maison avec ses parents, les amis de ses parents et leur fils.
7. Elle est allée au Zenith (à un concert de rock) et dans un café.
8. Le week-end prochain, elle va faire une promenade à la campagne avec Thomas (dans sa nouvelle voiture de sport).
9. Il s'appelle Thomas.

Et toi?

Answers will vary.

1. Je suis allé(e) en ville. (Je ne suis pas allé(e) en ville.)
2. Je suis allé(e) au cinéma. (Je ne suis pas allé(e) au cinéma.)
3. Je suis allé(e) au concert. (Je ne suis pas allé(e) au concert.)
4. Je suis rentré(e) chez moi pour le dîner. (Je ne suis pas rentré(e) chez moi pour le dîner.)
5. Je suis resté(e) chez moi le soir. (Je ne suis pas resté(e) chez moi le soir.)

Teaching suggestion American music has a strong influence on many French radio stations. Have students go online to various French radio station websites, and ask them to find out which American songs are popular in France.

SECTION A

Communicative function
Talking about the past

Teaching Resource Options

PRINT 

Workbook PE, pp. 201–208
Unit 7 Resource Book
Communipak, pp. 148–170
Video Activities, pp. 132–133
Videoscript, pp. 137–138
Workbook TE, pp. 109–116

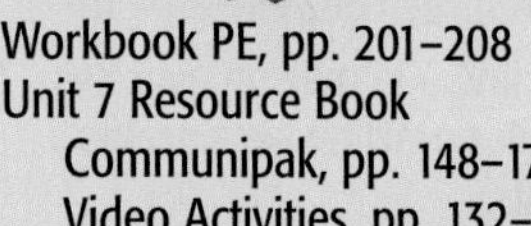

TECHNOLOGY 

Power Presentations

VIDEO PROGRAM

VIDÉO DVD

MODULE 24

24.2 Mini-scenes: Où êtes-vous allé? Et qu'est-ce que vous avez fait?
(20:20–22:08 min.)

24.3 Où est-ce qu'ils sont allés?
(22:09–23:20 min.)

Pronunciation In spoken French, the four forms of **allé** sound the same.

PRACTICE describing who went where

1. Claire est
2. Olivier est
3. Éric et Jacques sont
4. Anne et Monique sont
5. Olivier est
6. Éric et Jacques sont
7. Olivier est
8. Anne et Monique sont

Teaching note Have students consult the website for the nearest French consulate to find out about cultural events that are happening in your area.

A Le passé composé avec *être*

Note the forms of the passé composé of **aller** in the sentences below, paying attention to the endings of the past participle **(allé).**

Jean-Paul **est allé** au cinéma.	*Jean-Paul **went** to the movies.*
Mélanie **est allée** à la plage.	*Mélanie **went** to the beach.*
Éric et Patrick **sont allés** en ville.	*Éric and Patrick **went** downtown.*
Mes copines **sont allées** à la campagne.	*My friends **went** to the country.*

The passé composé of **aller** and certain verbs of motion is formed with **être** according to the pattern:

PRESENT of **être** + PAST PARTICIPLE

→ When the passé composé of a verb is conjugated with **être** (and not with **avoir**), the PAST PARTICIPLE *agrees* with the SUBJECT in gender and number.

INFINITIVE	aller	
PASSÉ COMPOSÉ	je **suis** **allé** tu **es** **allé** il **est** **allé**	je **suis** **allée** tu **es** **allée** elle **est** **allée**
	nous **sommes** **allés** vous êtes **allés** ils **sont** **allés**	nous **sommes** **allées** vous êtes **allées** elles **sont** **allées**
NEGATIVE	je **ne suis pas** **allé**	je **ne suis pas** **allée**
INTERROGATIVE	est-ce que tu **es** **allé?** tu **es** **allé?** (es-tu **allé?**)	est-ce que tu **es** **allée?** tu **es** **allée?** (es-tu **allée?**)

→ When **vous** refers to a single person, the past participle is in the singular:

Mme Mercier, est-ce que vous êtes **allée** au concert hier soir?

WARM-UP AND REVIEW

As a preparation for the passé composé of **aller,** have students review the forms of **être,** together with the expression **chez.**

You will indicate what people are doing, and the students will let you know whether those people are at home or not.

Paul joue au foot. [Il n'est pas chez lui.]
Je regarde la télé. [Je suis chez moi.]
Nous étudions. [Nous sommes chez nous.]
Mes copains dînent. [Ils sont chez eux.]
Tu fais de la voile. [Tu n'es pas chez toi.]
Sophie nettoie sa chambre. [Elle est chez elle.]
Elles font du ski. [Elles ne sont pas chez elles.]
Vous voyagez. [Vous n'êtes pas chez vous.]

1 À Paris

PARLER/ÉCRIRE Des amis sont allés à Paris samedi dernier. Chacun est allé à un endroit différent. Dites qui est allé aux endroits suivants. Complétez chaque phrase avec le sujet approprié et la forme correspondante du verbe **aller.**

Olivier Éric et Jacques Claire Anne et Monique

▶ **Anne et Monique sont allées au Louvre.**

1. … allée à la tour Eiffel.
2. … allé au Centre Pompidou.
3. … allés au Stade de France.
4. … allées aux Galeries Lafayette.
5. … allé à la Villette.
6. … allés au Zénith.
7. … allé au musée d'Orsay.
8. … allées au Quartier latin.

2 Conversation

PARLER Demandez à vos camarades s'ils sont allés aux endroits suivants.

▶ ce matin/à la bibliothèque?

1. hier matin/à l'école?
2. hier soir/au cinéma?
3. dimanche dernier/au restaurant?
4. samedi dernier/dans les magasins?
5. l'été dernier/chez tes cousins?
6. le week-end dernier/à la campagne?
7. le mois dernier/à un concert?
8. la semaine dernière/chez le coiffeur *(barber, hairdresser)*?
9. les vacances dernières/à la mer?

Ce matin, est-ce que tu es allé à la bibliothèque?
Oui, je suis allé à la bibliothèque.
(Non, je ne suis pas allé à la bibliothèque.)

3 Le week-end dernier

PARLER/ÉCRIRE Dites ce que les personnes de la Colonne A ont fait en choisissant une activité de la Colonne B. Puis dites où ces personnes sont allées en choisissant un endroit de la Colonne C. Soyez logiques!

A	B	C
je	voir des clowns	à la campagne
tu	nager	au zoo
nous	dîner en ville	dans un magasin de chaussures
Catherine	regarder les éléphants	à la bibliothèque
vous	choisir des livres	à la plage
mon petit frère	faire un pique-nique	au restaurant
André et Thomas	acheter des sandales	au cirque *(circus)*
les filles	faire du roller	dans la rue

▶ **J'ai nagé. Je suis allé(e) à la plage.**

INCLUSION

Metacognitive, Gifted & Talented Review the forms of the verb **être**. Have students write the forms in their notebooks. Then, write sentences on the board using the verb **aller**, with blank spaces for the verb **être**. Ask students to go to the board and fill in the blanks with the verb form and explain their choice of verb. Then, create 5 simple questions using **être + passé composé** and ask students to answer and explain their choices.

2 COMMUNICATION finding out where people went

1. –Hier matin, est-ce que tu es allé(e) à l'école.
   –Oui, je suis allé(e) à l'école. (Non, je ne suis pas allé(e) à l'école.)
2. –Hier soir, est-ce que tu es allé(e) au cinéma?
   –Oui, je suis allé(e) au cinéma. (Non, je ne suis pas allé(e) au cinéma.)
3. –Dimanche dernier, est-ce que tu es allé(e) au restaurant?
   –Oui, je suis allé(e) au restaurant. (Non, je ne suis pas allé(e) au restaurant.)
4. –Samedi dernier, est-ce que tu es allé(e) dans les magasins?
   –Oui, je suis allé(e) dans les magasins. (Non, je ne suis pas allé(e) dans les magasins.)
5. –L'été dernier, est-ce que tu es allé(e) chez tes cousins?
   –Oui, je suis allé(e) chez mes cousins. (Non, je ne suis pas allé(e) chez mes cousins.)
6. –Le week-end dernier, est-ce que tu es allé(e) à la campagne?
   –Oui, je suis allé(e) à la campagne. (Non, je ne suis pas allé(e) à la campagne.)
7. –Le mois dernier, est-ce que tu es allé(e) à un concert?
   –Oui, je suis allé(e) à un concert. (Non, je ne suis pas allé(e) à un concert.)
8. –La semaine dernière, est-ce que tu es allé(e) chez le coiffeur?
   –Oui, je suis allé(e) chez le coiffeur. (Non, je ne suis pas allé(e) chez le coiffeur.)
9. –Les vacances dernières, est-ce que tu es allé(e) à la mer?
   –Oui, je suis allé(e) à la mer. (Non, je ne suis pas allé(e) à la mer.)

Vocabulary update:
la bibliothèque *municipal library*
le CDI (Centre de documentation et d'information) *school library*
Students in school would say: "Je suis allé au CDI."

3 COMPREHENSION describing where people went to do certain things

Answers will vary.

1. J'ai vu des clowns. Je suis allé(e) au cirque.
2. Tu as nagé. Tu es allé(e) à la plage.
3. Nous avons dîné en ville. Nous sommes allé(e)s au restaurant.
4. Catherine a regardé les éléphants. Elle est allée au zoo.
5. Vous avez choisi des livres. Vous êtes allé(e)(s) à la bibliothèque.
6. Mon petit frère a fait une promenade. Il est allé à la campagne.
7. André et Thomas ont acheté des sandales. Ils sont allés dans un magasin de chaussures.
8. Les filles ont fait du roller. Elles sont allées dans la rue.

Pronunciation
clown /klun/
zoo /zo/ or /zoo/

Teaching note This activity may be done in a game format. See Teaching note, p. 272.

Teaching Resource Options

PRINT 

Workbook PE, pp. 201–208
Unit 7 Resource Book
Communipak, pp. 148–170
Workbook TE, pp. 109–116

AUDIO & VISUAL 

Overhead Transparencies
16 Subject pronouns

TECHNOLOGY 

Power Presentations

4 ROLE PLAY talking about last weekend

1. –Où est-ce que tu es allé(e)?
–Je suis allé(e) au stade.
–Ah bon! Qu'est-ce que tu as fait?
–J'ai regardé un match de foot.
2. –Où est-ce que tu es allé(e)?
–Je suis allé(e) à la plage.
–Ah bon! Qu'est-ce que tu as fait?
–J'ai joué au volley.
3. –Où est-ce que tu es allé(e)?
–Je suis allé(e) à une boum.
–Ah bon! Qu'est-ce que tu as fait?
–J'ai dansé.
4. –Où est-ce que tu es allé(e)?
–Je suis allé(e) à la campagne.
–Ah bon! Qu'est-ce que tu as fait?
–J'ai fait une promenade à pied.
5. –Où est-ce que tu es allé(e)?
–Je suis allé(e) au Bon Marché.
–Ah bon! Qu'est-ce que tu as fait?
–J'ai acheté un blouson.
6. –Où est-ce que tu es allé(e)?
–Je suis allé(e) dans un restaurant italien.
–Ah bon! Qu'est-ce que tu as fait?
–J'ai mangé des spaghetti.

Looking ahead If you wish to present the other verbs conjugated with **être,** you can have students refer to the Appendix, page R11. These verbs will be formally introduced in Book Two.

Extra practice Use Transparency Subject pronouns to do rapid substitution drills. Give the model sentence and then point to various subject pronouns.

Je suis venu(e) hier.
[tu] Tu es venu(e) hier.
Je suis arrivé(e) à midi.
Je suis rentré(e) à minuit.

Realia note
This is an ad for **Sport Magazine.** The word **infos** is a shortened form of **informations,** meaning news and background information.

4  *Week-end*

PARLER Des amis parlent de leur week-end. Jouez ces dialogues.

▶ en ville / acheter des vêtements

1. au stade / regarder un match de foot
2. à la plage / jouer au volley
3. à une boum / danser
4. à la campagne / faire une promenade à pied
5. au Bon Marché / acheter un blouson
6. dans un restaurant italien / manger des spaghetti

VOCABULAIRE Quelques verbes conjugués avec *être* au passé composé

INFINITIVE	PAST PARTICIPLE		
aller	**allé**	*to go*	Nous **sommes allés** en ville.
arriver	**arrivé**	*to arrive*	Vous **êtes arrivés** à midi.
rentrer	**rentré**	*to return, go back, come back*	Nous **sommes rentrés** à la maison à onze heures.
rester	**resté**	*to stay*	Les touristes **sont restés** à l'hôtel Ibis.
venir	**venu**	*to come*	Qui **est venu** hier?

5 *Qui est resté à la maison?*

PARLER/ÉCRIRE Samedi après-midi, les personnes suivantes ont fait certaines choses. Dites si oui ou non elles sont restées à la maison.

▶ Paul a regardé la télé. **Il est resté à la maison.**
▶ Mélanie a fait des achats. **Elle n'est pas restée à la maison.**

1. Mlle Joly a lavé sa voiture.
2. Nous avons fait une promenade à vélo.
3. Tu as nettoyé le garage.
4. Éric et Olivier ont joué aux jeux vidéo.
5. Christine et Isabelle ont travaillé dans le jardin.
6. Vous avez fait du roller.
7. Mes cousins ont fait de la voile.
8. J'ai fait du jogging.

COMPREHENSION Destinations and arrival times

PROPS: Map (or transparency) of France, clock with movable hands

Imagine that the class is visiting France.
Je suis allé(e) à Nice. [point to Nice]
Je suis arrivé(e) à midi. [move clock to 12]

Have pairs of students come up to show where they went and when they arrived.

X et Y, vous êtes allé(e)s à Lyon.
Vous êtes arrivé(e)s à 1h20.
Venez nous montrer la ville et l'heure.

Follow-up questions:
Où est-ce que X et Y sont allé(e)s?
À quelle heure sont-ils(elles) arrivé(e)s?

6 La journée de Sandrine

PARLER/ÉCRIRE Pendant les vacances, Sandrine travaille dans une agence de tourisme. Le soir, elle raconte *(tells about)* sa journée à son père.

▶ aller au bureau *(office)*

1. arriver à neuf heures
2. téléphoner à un client anglais
3. parler avec des touristes japonais
4. aller au restaurant à midi et demi
5. rentrer au bureau à deux heures
6. copier des documents
7. préparer des billets *(tickets)* d'avion
8. rester jusqu'à *(until)* six heures
9. dîner en ville
10. rentrer à la maison à neuf heures

Je suis allée au bureau.

7 Une question de circonstances *(A matter of circumstances)*

PARLER/ÉCRIRE Nos activités dépendent souvent des circonstances. Dites si oui ou non les personnes suivantes ont fait les choses indiquées.

MARDI
3

▶ On est mardi aujourd'hui.
- les élèves/rester à la maison?

Les élèves ne sont pas restés à la maison.

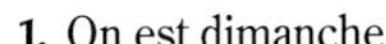

1. On est dimanche.
   - M. Boulot/travailler?
   - nous/aller à l'école?
   - vous/dîner à la cantine *(school cafeteria)*?
2. Il fait très beau aujourd'hui.
   - moi/aller à la campagne?
   - mes copines/regarder la télé?
   - toi/venir à la piscine avec nous?
3. Il fait très mauvais!
   - Marc/faire un pique-nique?
   - Hélène et Juliette/rester à la maison?
   - ma mère/rentrer à la maison à pied?
4. Mes copains et moi, nous n'avons pas beaucoup d'argent.
   - toi/aller dans un restaurant cher?
   - mes copains/venir chez moi en taxi?
   - moi/acheter des vêtements?

5 COMPREHENSION concluding who stayed home and who did not

1. Elle est restée à la maison.
2. Nous ne sommes pas resté(e)s à la maison.
3. Tu es resté(e) à la maison.
4. Ils ne sont pas restés à la maison. (Ils sont restés à la maison.)
5. Elles sont restées à la maison.
6. Vous n'êtes pas resté(e)(s) à la maison.
7. Ils ne sont pas restés à la maison.
8. Je ne suis pas resté(e) à la maison.

Variation Have students respond using **chez** plus stress pronouns.

Paul est resté chez lui.
Mélanie n'est pas restée chez elle.

6 ROLE PLAY narrating the day's events

1. Je suis arrivée à neuf heures.
2. J'ai téléphoné à un client anglais.
3. J'ai parlé avec des touristes japonais.
4. Je suis allée au restaurant à midi et demi.
5. Je suis rentrée au bureau à deux heures.
6. J'ai copié des documents.
7. J'ai préparé des billets d'avion.
8. Je suis restée jusqu'à six heures.
9. J'ai dîné en ville.
10. Je suis rentré(e) à la maison à neuf heures.

Variation (using other subjects)

[elle] Elle est allée au bureau.
[nous] Nous sommes allés au bureau.
[Élisabeth et sa soeur Alice (elles)] Elles sont allées au bureau.

7 COMPREHENSION drawing conclusions about past actions

1. M. Boulot n'a pas travaillé.
   Nous ne sommes pas allé(e)s à l'école.
   Vous n'avez pas dîné à la cantine.
2. Je suis allé(e) à la campagne.
   Mes copines n'ont pas regardé la télé.
   Tu es venu(e) à la piscine avec nous.
3. Marc n'a pas fait de pique-nique.
   Hélène et Juliette sont restées à la maison.
   Ma mère n'est pas rentrée à la maison à pied.
4. Tu n'es pas allé(e) dans un restaurant cher.
   Mes copains ne sont pas venus chez moi en taxi.
   Je n'ai pas acheté de vêtements.

Teaching note Remind students to use **pas de** in items 3 and 4:

3. Marc n'a pas fait de pique-nique.
4. Je n'ai pas acheté de vêtements.

Expansion Have students write an original affirmative and negative sentence for each item.

Nous avons eu un examen de français.
Je n'ai pas regardé la télé ce matin.

SECTION B

Communicative function
Saying that one never does something

Teaching Resource Options

PRINT 

Workbook PE, pp. 201–208
Unit 7 Resource Book
- Audioscript, p. 139
- Communipak, pp. 148–170
- Video Activities, p. 131
- Videoscript, p. 137
- Workbook TE, pp. 109–116

AUDIO & VISUAL

Audio Program
CD 4 Track 18

TECHNOLOGY

Power Presentations

VIDEO PROGRAM

VIDÉO DVD

MODULE 24

24.1 Dialogue: Un bon week-end
(18:41–20:19 min.)

Teaching strategy Point out that the pattern with **ne ... jamais** in the passé composé is the same as with **ne ... pas.**

8 PRACTICE talking about what one never does

1. Le dimanche, elle n'étudie jamais.
2. Le dimanche, il ne travaille jamais.
3. Le dimanche, nous ne parlons jamais français.
4. Le dimanche, vous n'allez jamais à la bibliothèque.
5. Le dimanche, il ne va jamais en ville.
6. Le dimanche, ils ne mangent jamais à la cantine.
7. Le dimanche, tu ne rends jamais visite à tes copains.
8. Le dimanche, vous ne dînez jamais chez vous.
9. Le dimanche, je ne range jamais ma chambre.
10. Le dimanche, je ne lave jamais la voiture.

B La construction négative *ne ... jamais*

Compare the following negative constructions.

Éric **ne** parle **pas** à Paul.	*Éric does **not** speak to Paul.*
Éric **ne** parle **jamais** à Paul.	*Éric **never** speaks to Paul.*
Nous **n'**étudions **pas** le dimanche.	*We do **not** study on Sundays.*
Nous **n'**étudions **jamais** le dimanche.	*We **never** study on Sundays.*

To say that one NEVER does something, French speakers use the construction **ne ... jamais,** as follows:

SUBJECT	+	ne	+	VERB	+	jamais ...
Nous		**ne**		regardons		**jamais** la télé.

→ **Ne** becomes **n'** before a vowel sound.

Nous **n'**allons **jamais** à l'opéra.

→ Note the use of **ne ... jamais** in the passé composé:

Nous **n'**avons **jamais** visité Québec.	*We **never** visited Quebec.*
Je **ne** suis **jamais** allé à Genève.	*I **never** went to Geneva.*

8 Jamais le dimanche

PARLER/ÉCRIRE Le dimanche les personnes suivantes ne font jamais ce qu'elles font pendant la semaine. Exprimez cette situation.

▶ François va à l'école.
Le dimanche, il ne va jamais à l'école.

1. Anne étudie.
2. Marc travaille.
3. Nous parlons français.
4. Vous allez à la bibliothèque.
5. M. Bernard va en ville.
6. Les élèves mangent à la cantine.
7. Tu rends visite à tes copains.
8. Vous dînez chez vous.
9. Je range ma chambre.
10. Je lave la voiture.

9 Et toi?

PARLER/ÉCRIRE Dites si vous avez jamais *(ever)* fait les choses suivantes.

▶ aller en France
Oui, je suis allé(e) en France.
Non, je ne suis jamais allé(e) en France.

1. aller en Chine?
2. visiter Paris?
3. voyager en limousine?
4. voir un opéra?
5. voir un fantôme *(ghost)*?
6. téléphoner au Président?
7. surfer sur l'Internet en français?
8. dîner dans un restaurant vietnamien?
9. jouer aux échecs?
10. faire une promenade en scooter?

Les expressions *quelqu'un, quelque chose* et leurs contraires

Compare the affirmative and negative constructions in heavy print.

—Tu attends **quelqu'un?**	*Are you waiting for* ***someone (anyone)?***
—Non, je **n'**attends **personne.**	*No, I'm* ***not*** *waiting for* ***anyone.***
—Vous faites **quelque chose** ce soir?	*Are you doing* ***something (anything)*** *tonight?*
—Non, nous **ne** faisons **rien.**	*No, we're* ***not*** *doing* ***anything.***
	No, we're doing ***nothing.***

To refer to unspecified people or things, French speakers use the following expressions:

quelqu'un	someone, anyone somebody, anybody	**ne ... personne**	no one, not anyone nobody, not anybody
quelque chose	something, anything	**ne ... rien**	nothing, not anything

→ Like all negative expressions, **personne** and **rien** require **ne** before the verb.

→ In short answers, **personne** and **rien** may be used alone.

Qui est là? **Personne.**
Qu'est-ce que tu fais? **Rien.**

Florence est malade

PARLER Florence est malade *(sick)* aujourd'hui. Elle répond négativement aux questions de Paul.

Tu dînes avec quelqu'un?

Non, je ne dîne avec personne.

▶ dîner avec quelqu'un?

1. inviter quelqu'un?
2. faire quelque chose ce soir?
3. manger quelque chose à midi?
4. regarder quelque chose à la télé?
5. attendre quelqu'un ce matin?
6. voir quelqu'un cet après-midi?
7. préparer quelque chose pour le dîner?
8. rencontrer quelqu'un après le dîner?

PRONONCIATION

qu = /k/

Les lettres «qu»

The letters "**qu**" represent the sound /k/.

Répétez: **qui quand quelque chose quelqu'un quatre quatorze Québec Monique Véronique sympathique un pique-nique le ski nautique**

Véronique pense que Monique aime la musique classique.

un bouquet

INCLUSION

Alphabetic/phonetic Model pronunciation of words with a "**qu**" combination. Ask students to say words three times and write them in their notebooks with phonetic transcriptions.

9 COMMUNICATION answering personal questions

Answers will vary.

1. Oui je suis allé(e) en Chine. (Non, je ne suis jamais allé(e) en Chine.)
2. Oui, j'ai visité Paris. (Non, je n'ai jamais visité Paris.)
3. Oui, j'ai voyagé en limousine. (Non, je n'ai jamais voyagé en limousine.)
4. Oui, j'ai vu un opéra. (Non, je n'ai jamais vu d'opéra.)
5. Non, je n'ai jamais vu de fantôme. (Oui, j'ai vu un fantôme.)
6. Non, je n'ai jamais téléphoné au Président. (Oui, j'ai téléphoné au Président.)
7. Oui, j'ai surfé sur l'Internet en français. (Non, je n'ai jamais surfé sur l'Internet en français.)
8. Oui, j'ai dîné dans un restaurant vietnamien. (Non, je n'ai jamais dîné dans un restaurant vietnamien.)
9. Non, je n'ai jamais joué aux échecs. (Oui, j'ai joué aux échecs.)
10. Non, je n'ai jamais fait de promenade en scooter. (Oui, j'ai fait une promenade en scooter.)

SECTION C

Communicative function
Identifying people and things

Language note Word order with **ne... personne** and **ne... rien** is presented in Book Two. In general, **personne** and **rien** have the same position in the sentence as **quelqu'un** and **quelque chose:**
Quelqu'un a téléphoné?
Non, personne n'a téléphoné.

Exception: In the passé composé **rien** comes between the auxiliary and the past participle:
Tu as acheté quelque chose?
Non, je n'ai rien acheté.

Teaching strategy Point out that **pas** is never used together with **personne** or **rien.**

10 ROLE PLAY giving negative responses

1. –Tu invites quelqu'un?
   –Non, je n'invite personne.
2. –Tu fais quelque chose ce soir?
   –Non, je ne fais rien.
3. –Tu manges quelque chose à midi?
   –Non, je ne mange rien à midi.
4. –Tu regardes quelque chose à la télé?
   –Non, je ne regarde rien à la télé.
5. –Tu attends quelqu'un ce matin?
   –Non, je n'attends personne ce matin.
6. –Tu vois quelqu'un cet après-midi?
   –Non, je ne vois personne cet après-midi.
7. –Tu prépares quelque chose pour le dîner?
   –Non, je ne prépare rien pour le dîner.
8. –Tu rencontres quelqu'un après le dîner?
   –Non, je ne rencontre personne après le dîner.

À votre tour!

OBJECTIFS

Now you can ...
- say where you went and when you came back
- talk about things you have never done

1 Allô!

PARLER Reconstituez la conversation entre Sophie et Charlotte. Pour cela, faites correspondre les réponses de Charlotte avec les questions de Sophie.

1. Tu es restée chez toi samedi soir?
2. Qu'est-ce que vous avez vu?
3. Qu'est-ce que vous avez fait ensuite?
4. Vous avez mangé quelque chose?
5. À quelle heure es-tu rentrée chez toi?

a. Oui, des sandwichs.
b. À onze heures et demie.
c. Un vieux western avec Gary Cooper.
d. Nous sommes allées dans un café sur le boulevard Saint Michel.
e. Non! J'ai téléphoné à une copine et nous sommes allées au cinéma.

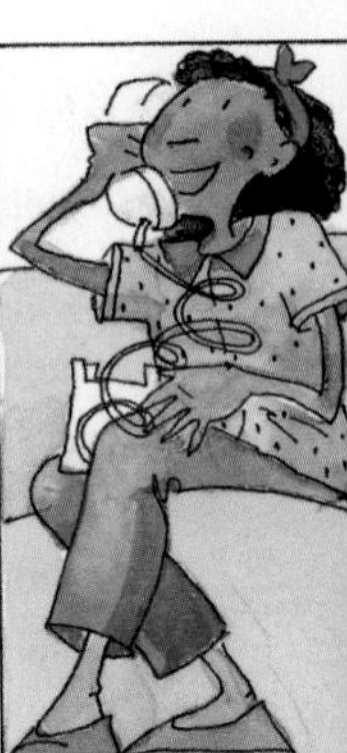

2 Dis-moi ...

PARLER *I will tell you about some places I have never visited. Then you will tell me about a few places where you have been.*

- Je ne suis jamais allée à la Martinique.
- Je n'ai jamais vu la Statue de la Liberté.
- Je n'ai jamais été à New York.
- Je n'ai jamais visité San Francisco.

Et maintenant, dis-moi ...

3 Créa-dialogue

PARLER Avec vos copains, discutez de ce que vous avez fait récemment *(recently)*. Utilisez les suggestions suivantes.

▶ —Tu es resté(e) chez toi hier matin?
—Oui, je suis resté(e) chez moi.
—Qu'est-ce que tu as fait?
—J'ai rangé ma chambre.

▶ —Tu es resté(e) chez toi hier matin?
—Non, je ne suis pas resté(e) chez moi.
—Qu'est-ce que tu as fait?
—Je suis allé(e) à l'école.

▶	1.	2.	3.
rester chez toi	aller en ville	rentrer chez toi	rester à la maison
hier matin	samedi après-midi	vendredi soir	samedi matin
??	??	??	??

À VOTRE TOUR

Main Topic
- Recapitulation and review

Teaching Resource Options

PRINT 

Workbook PE, pp. 201–208
Unit 7 Resource Book
Audioscript, pp. 139–140
Communipak, pp. 148–170
Family Involvement, pp. 129–130
Workbook TE, pp. 109–116

Assessment
Lesson 24 Quiz, pp. 144–145
Portfolio Assessment, Unit 1 URB pp. 155–164
Audioscript for Quiz 24, p. 143
Answer Keys, pp. 213–216

AUDIO & VISUAL 

Audio Program
CD 4 Tracks 19, 20
CD 16 Track 4

TECHNOLOGY 

Test Generator CD-ROM/McDougal Littell Assessment System

1 COMPREHENSION

1. Tu es restée chez toi samedi soir?
(e) Non! J'ai téléphoné à une copine et nous sommes allées au cinéma.
2. Qu'est-ce que vous avez vu?
(c) Un vieux western avec Gary Cooper.
3. Qu'est-ce que vous avez fait ensuite?
(d) Nous sommes allées dans un café sur le boulevard Saint Michel.
4. Vous avez mangé quelque chose?
(a) Oui, des sandwichs.
5. À quelle heure es-tu rentrée chez toi?
(b) À onze heures et demie.

2 GUIDED ORAL EXPRESSION

Answers will vary.
- Je suis allé(e) en France.
- J'ai vu l'Arc de Triomphe.
- J'ai visité Québec.
- Je suis allé(e) à Montréal.

Expansion I did not see you last weekend. Please answer my questions in French. Tell me:
- Did you stay home Saturday morning?
- What did you do?
- Where did you go Saturday afternoon?
- What did you do there?
- Did you meet your friends?
- If so, what did you do together?

À VOTRE TOUR

Depending on your goals and objectives, you may or may not wish to assign all of the activities in the **À votre tour** section.

GROUP PRACTICE

In Act. 1 and 3, you may want to have students work in trios, with two performing and one acting as monitor.

Composition: Samedi dernier

ÉCRIRE Read what Céline did last Saturday. Then write a short composition in the **passé composé** telling how a friend of yours (real or imaginary) spent the day. Use only familiar vocabulary.

Le matin, Céline est restée à la maison. Elle a rangé sa chambre et après elle a fini ses devoirs.

L'après-midi, elle est allée au cinéma avec son copain Trinh. Ils ont vu une comédie. Ensuite ils sont allés dans un magasin de vêtements. Céline a acheté un tee-shirt et Trinh a acheté une nouvelle casquette. Finalement, Céline est rentrée chez elle.

Le soir, elle a dîné avec ses parents. Après, elle est restée dans sa chambre. Elle a surfé sur l'Internet et elle a téléchargé de la musique reggae. Elle adore la musique reggae!

STRATEGY Writing

Narration in the *passé composé* Read the description of Céline's activities again. Note that the author wrote **Céline est restée, elle est allée,** and **Céline est rentrée,** adding a final "e" to the past participles because the subject, **Céline/elle** is feminine. In referring to Céline and Trinh, the author wrote **ils sont allés** and added a final "s" to **allé** because the subject, **ils,** is plural.

When you are writing in the passé composé, it is important to go back over your composition and check all the verb forms. If you have used the verbs **aller, venir, arriver, rester,** or **rentrer,** look to be sure that you formed the passé composé with **être,** rather than **avoir,** and that in each case the past participle agrees with the subject.

4. aller à la plage	5. aller à la campagne	6. aller à une boum	7. faire un voyage	8. travailler
dimanche dernier	le week-end dernier	la semaine dernière	le mois dernier	l'été dernier
??	??	??	??	??

COMMENT DIT-ON ...?

How to celebrate a happy occasion:

Bon anniversaire!

Bonne année!

PORTFOLIO ASSESSMENT

You will probably select only one speaking activity and one writing activity to go into the students' portfolios for Unit 7.

In this lesson, Act. 4 offers an excellent writing portfolio topic.

3 GUIDED ORAL EXPRESSION

Answers will vary.

1. –Tu es allé(e) en ville samedi après-midi?
   –Oui, je suis allé(e) en ville samedi après-midi. (Non, je suis pas allé(e) en ville.)
   –Qu'est-ce que tu as fait?
   –J'ai fait des achats. (Je suis allé[e] à la plage.)
2. –Tu es rentré(e) chez toi vendredi soir?
   –Oui, je suis rentré(e) chez moi vendredi soir. (Non, je ne suis pas rentré(e) chez moi.)
   –Qu'est-ce que tu as fait?
   –J'ai regardé la télé. (Je suis allé[e] à une boum avec des copains.)
3. –Tu es resté(e) à la maison samedi matin?
   –Oui, je suis resté(e) à la maison samedi matin. (Non, je ne suis pas resté[e] à la maison.
   –Qu'est-ce que tu as fait?
   –J'ai nettoyé ma chambre. (Je suis allé[e] au parc.)
4. –Tu es allé[e] à la plage dimanche dernier?
   –Oui, je suis allé(e) à la plage dimanche dernier. (Non, je ne suis pas allé(e) à la plage.)
   –Qu'est-ce que tu as fait?
   –J'ai nagé. (Je suis allé[e] au cinéma.)
5. –Tu es allé(e) à la campagne le week-end dernier?
   –Oui, je suis allé(e) à la campagne le week-end dernier. (Non, je ne suis pas allé(e) à la campagne.)
   –Qu'est-ce que tu as fait?
   –J'ai fait une promenade à vélo. (J'ai fait mes devoirs de maths!)
6. –Tu es allé(e) à une boum la semaine dernière?
   –Oui, je suis allé(e) à une boum la semaine dernière. (Non, je ne suis pas allé(e) à une boum.)
   –Qu'est-ce que tu as fait?
   –J'ai dansé! (Je suis allé[e] au restaurant avec des amis.)
7. –Tu as fait un voyage le mois dernier?
   –Oui, j'ai fait un voyage le mois dernier. (Non, je n'ai pas fait de voyage.)
   –Qu'est-ce que tu as fait?
   –Je suis allé(e) aux Bahamas! (Je suis resté[e] à la maison.)
8. –Tu as travaillé l'été dernier?
   –Oui, j'ai travaillé l'été dernier. (Non, je n'ai pas travaillé.)
   –Qu'est-ce que tu as fait?
   –J'ai travaillé dans un magasin. (J'ai fait beaucoup de sports.)

4 WRITTEN SELF-EXPRESSION

Answers will vary.
Le matin, mon ami Kevin n'est pas resté à la maison. Il a fait du jogging et après il a joué au basket avec ses cousins. L'après-midi, il est allé à la plage et il a nagé. Le soir, il est allé dans un restaurant avec ses parents et son frère. Ils ont mangé un bon dîner.

TESTS DE CONTRÔLE

Teaching Resource Options

PRINT

Unit 7 Resource Book
Communipak, pp. 148–170

Assessment
Unit 7 Test, pp, 179–187
Portfolio Assessment, Unit 1 URB pp. 155–164
Multiple Choice Test Items, pp. 200–208
Listening Comprehension Performance Test, pp. 188–189
Reading Performance Test, pp. 194–196
Speaking Performance Test, pp. 190–193
Writing Performance Test, pp. 197–199
Test Scoring Tools, p. 209
Audioscript for Tests, pp. 210–212
Answer Keys, pp. 213–216

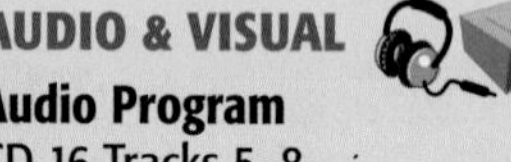

AUDIO & VISUAL

Audio Program
CD 16 Tracks 5–8

TECHNOLOGY

Test Generator CD-ROM/McDougal Littell Assessment System

1 COMPREHENSION

1. c
2. a
3. b
4. a
5. c
6. b
7. c
8. a
9. b
10. b
11. b
12. a

2 COMPREHENSION

1. avons loué
2. ont joué
3. a rangé
4. avez fini
5. as vendu
6. a eu
7. ont fait
8. ai été
9. as vu
10. a mis

Tests de contrôle

By taking the following tests, you can check your progress in French and also prepare for the unit test. Write your answers on a separate sheet of paper.

Review...
new words and expressions
- verbs: p. 310
- sports: pp. 312, 313
- expressions with **avoir**: p. 320
- expressions of time: p. 336
- **quelqu'un** and **quelque chose**: p. 347

1 The right choice

Choose the expressions (a), (b), or (c) which best complete the following sentences.

1. Céline va au cinéma. Elle va — une comédie.
   a. aider **b.** rencontrer **c.** voir
2. Thomas va au stade. Il va — un match de foot.
   a. assister à **b.** attendre **c.** nettoyer
3. Mathieu va rester à la maison. Il va — la voiture de sa mère.
   a. aider **b.** laver **c.** rencontrer
4. Charlotte va au café. Elle va — ses copines.
   a. rencontrer **b.** assister à **c.** louer
5. Julien est à la mer. Il fait —.
   a. du ski **b.** du roller **c.** de la planche à voile
6. Léa est à la montagne. Elle fait —.
   a. de la voile **b.** de l'escalade **c.** ses devoirs
7. Clément met un pull parce qu'il a —.
   a. faim **b.** chaud **c.** froid
8. Mélanie commande (*orders*) un soda parce qu'elle a —.
   a. soif **b.** tort **c.** de la chance
9. Je suis allé au cinéma—.
   a. demain **b.** hier soir **c.** samedi prochain
10. Je vais aller à une boum —.
    a. hier matin **b.** demain après-midi **c.** la semaine dernière
11. Catherine est au café. Elle attend —.
    a. un **b.** quelqu'un **c.** personne
12. Pierre n'a pas faim. Il ne mange —.
    a. rien **b.** quelque chose **c.** une pizza

Review...
the **passé composé**
- **-er** verbs: p. 321
- **-ir** and **-re** verbs: p. 333
- irregular verbs: p. 335

2 The right verb

Complete the following sentences with the appropriate forms of the **passé composé** of the verbs in parentheses.

1. **(louer)** La semaine dernière, nous — un DVD.
2. **(jouer)** Hier après-midi, Céline et Thomas — au tennis.
3. **(ranger)** Samedi matin, Pauline — sa chambre.

4. **(finir)** Est-ce que vous — les exercices?
5. **(vendre)** À qui est-ce que tu — ton vélo?
6. **(avoir)** Monsieur Lescure — un accident avec sa nouvelle voiture.
7. **(faire)** Pendant les vacances, les élèves — un voyage au Canada.
8. **(être)** Moi, j'— à Paris l'année dernière.
9. **(voir)** Quel film est-ce que tu — mardi soir?
10. **(mettre)** Mathieu — un CD de rock.

3 Être or avoir?

Complete the following sentences with the **passé composé** forms of the verbs in parentheses. Be sure to use the appropriate forms of **être** or **avoir.**

1. **(acheter)** Nous — un livre sur Paris.
2. **(aller)** Marie — à la tour Eiffel.
3. **(rester)** Mes copains — à l'hôtel.
4. **(téléphoner)** Ils — à des amis.
5. **(arriver)** Pierre — à l'aéroport.
6. **(rentrer)** Nous — le 15 août.
7. **(visiter)** Tu — le musée d'Orsay.
8. **(venir)** Mes amis — avec nous.

Review...
- **passé composé with être:** pp. 342 and 344

4 Non!

Transform the statements below into **negative** sentences. Replace the underlined words with the expressions in parentheses.

1. Léa a voyagé <u>en bus</u>. **(en train)**
2. J'ai joué <u>au foot</u> hier. **(au basket)**
3. Tu es resté <u>à l'hôtel</u>. **(chez tes cousins)**
4. Éric a invité <u>sa cousine</u>. **(son copain)**

Review...
- the negative **passé composé:** p. 324

5 Composition: Thanksgiving

Write a short paragraph of five or six sentences about what you and your family did last Thanksgiving. Did you travel somewhere or did people come to your house? What did you do together? Use the **passé composé,** limiting yourself to words and expressions that you know in French.

STRATEGY Writing

a Make a list of the verbs you will use to describe your activities. Review which ones use **avoir** in the **passé composé** and which use **être.**

	avoir	être
<u>dîner</u> chez mes cousins	x	

b Organize your ideas and write your paragraph.

c Check the **passé composé** forms of all the verbs in your composition.

3 COMPREHENSION

1. avons acheté
2. est allée
3. sont restés
4. ont téléphoné
5. est arrivé
6. sommes rentré(e)s
7. as visité
8. sont venus

4 COMPREHENSION

1. Léa n'a pas voyagé en train.
2. Je n'ai pas joué au basket hier.
3. Tu n'es pas resté chez tes cousins.
4. Éric n'a pas invité son copain.

5 WRITTEN SELF-EXPRESSION

Answers will vary.
Le Thanksgiving dernier, ma famille est restée dans notre ville. Le matin, mon frère et moi, nous avons assisté au match de football américain de notre lycée. Notre équipe a gagné!

L'après-midi, mes parents, mon frère et moi, nous sommes allés chez ma tante. Nous avons mangé un grand dîner. J'ai joué aux jeux vidéo avec mon cousin.

Le soir, nous avons regardé un DVD. Ma famille est rentrée chez nous à dix heures.

VOCABULAIRE

Language Learning Benchmarks

FUNCTION

- Engage in conversations pp. 324, 334
- Obtain information pp. 326, 343
- Understand some ideas and familiar details pp. 344, 345
- Begin to provide information pp. 315, 324, 326, 332, 337

CONTEXT

- Converse in face-to-face social interactions pp. 322, 324, 326
- Listen to audio and video texts pp. 308-309, 318-319, 330, 341
- Use authentic materials when reading: posters pp. 312, 321, 323
- Use authentic materials when reading: charts p. 315
- Use authentic materials when reading: signs p. 333
- Use authentic materials when reading: short narratives pp. 358-359
- Write notes p. 329
- Write lists p. 316
- Write postcards p. 357

TEXT TYPE

- Use short sentences when speaking pp. 314, 320, 325
- Use short sentences when writing pp. 314, 322, 325, 346
- Use learned words and phrases when speaking pp. 311, 333, 336
- Use learned words and phrases when writing pp. 311, 333
- Use simple questions when speaking pp. 327, 335
- Use simple questions when writing pp. 320, 323
- Understand some ideas and familiar details presented in clear, uncomplicated speech when listening pp. 318-319, 341
- Understand short texts enhanced by visual clues when reading pp. 313, 319, 331, 341

Vocabulaire

POUR COMMUNIQUER

Talking about past activities

Qu'est-ce que tu as fait hier?	*What did you do yesterday?*
J'ai vu un film.	*I saw a film.*
Je suis allé au cinéma.	*I went to the movies.*
Je n'ai pas travaillé.	*I didn't work.*
Je ne suis pas allé à l'école.	*I didn't go to school.*

Explaining why

Pourquoi est-ce que tu es allé en ville?	*Why did you go downtown?*
Je suis allé en ville pour louer un DVD.	*I went downtown to rent a DVD.*

Talking about one's activities

Est-ce que tu fais	**du roller?**	*Do you do*	*in-line skating?*
	de la voile?		*sailing?*
	de l'escalade?		*rock climbing?*
Marc ne fait pas de sport.		*Marc doesn't do sports.*	

MOTS ET EXPRESSIONS

Activités sportives

le jogging	*jogging*	**l'escalade**	*rock climbing*
le roller	*in-line skating*	**la natation**	*swimming*
le skate	*skateboarding*	**la planche à voile**	*windsurfing*
le ski	*skiing*	**la voile**	*sailing*
le ski nautique	*water-skiing*		
le snowboard	*snowboarding*		
le sport	*sport(s)*		
le VTT	*mountain biking*		

Équipement sportif

des rollers	*in-line skates*
un skate	*skateboard*
un snowboard	*snowboard*
un VTT	*mountain bike*

Vacation travel

un autocar, un car	*touring bus*
un avion	*plane*
un bateau	*boat, ship*
un train	*train*

Vacation destinations

la campagne	*countryside*
la mer	*ocean, shore*
la montagne	*mountains*

Les contraires

souvent	*often*	**ne ... jamais**	*never*
quelque chose	*something, anything*	**ne ... rien**	*nothing, not anything*
quelqu'un	*someone, anyone, somebody*	**ne ... personne**	*no one, not anyone, nobody*

Verbes en *-er*

aider	*to help*
assister à	*to go to, to attend*
laver	*to wash*
louer	*to rent*
nettoyer	*to clean*
passer	*to spend*
préparer	*to prepare*
ranger	*to clean, to pick up*
rencontrer	*to meet*
réparer	*to fix*

Verbes irréguliers

avoir chaud/froid	*to be (feel) hot/cold*
avoir faim/soif	*to be hungry/thirsty*
avoir raison/tort	*to be right/wrong*
avoir de la chance	*to be lucky*
faire des achats	*to go shopping*
faire les devoirs	*to do homework*
faire un pique-nique	*to have a picnic*
voir	*to see*

Le passé composé avec *avoir*

parler	**j'ai parlé**	*I spoke*
finir	**j'ai fini**	*I finished*
vendre	**j'ai vendu**	*I sold*
avoir	**j'ai eu**	*I had*
être	**j'ai été**	*I was, I have been*
faire	**j'ai fait**	*I did*
mettre	**j'ai mis**	*I put*
voir	**j'ai vu**	*I saw*

Le passé composé avec *être*

aller	**je suis allé(e)**	*I went*
arriver	**je suis arrivé(e)**	*I arrived*
rentrer	**je suis rentré(e)**	*I came back*
rester	**je suis resté(e)**	*I stayed*
venir	**je suis venu(e)**	*I came*

Le calendrier

Noël	*Christmas*
un jour	*day*
un mois	*month*
l'après-midi	*afternoon*
le matin	*morning*
le soir	*evening*
le week-end	*weekend*
Pâques	*Easter*
une semaine	*week*
les vacances	*vacation*
les grandes vacances	*summer vacation*

Expressions pour indiquer quand

aujourd'hui	*today*
hier	*yesterday*
demain	*tomorrow*
prochain(e)	*next*
dernier (dernière)	*last*
d'abord	*first*
avant	*before*
pendant	*during*
après	*after, afterwards*
ensuite	*then, after that*
enfin	*at last*
finalement	*finally*

Expressions utiles

pour	*in order to*
seul(e)	*alone*

CONTENT

- Understand and convey information about leisure activities pp. 311, 314-315
- Understand and convey information about travel p. 315

ASSESSMENT

- Communicate effectively with some hesitation and errors, which do not hinder comprehension pp. 317, 339, 349, 351
- Demonstrate culturally acceptable behavior for engaging in conversations pp. 317, 328, 339
- Demonstrate culturally acceptable behavior for obtaining information pp. 317, 348
- Demonstrate culturally acceptable behavior for understanding some ideas and familiar details p. 317
- Demonstrate culturally acceptable behavior for providing information pp. 317, 339, 348
- Understand most important information pp. 316, 328, 338, 348

ENTRACTE 7

Objectives

- Reading skills development
- Re-entry of materials in the unit
- Development of cultural awareness

Le roller: un sport qui roule!

Objectives

- Reading at the paragraph level

Teaching Resource Options

 **PRINT** 

Workbook PE, pp. 209–212
Activités pour tous PE, pp. 127–129
Unit 7 Resource Book
Activités pour tous TE, pp. 171–173
Workbook TE, pp. 175–178

Le roller: un sport qui roule!°

Beaucoup de jeunes Français participent aux sports d'équipe° comme° le foot, le basket et le volley, mais certains préfèrent les sports individuels comme le jogging ou la natation. Aujourd'hui, beaucoup de jeunes pratiquent aussi les «sports de glisse»° comme le roller, le skate, la planche à voile (en été) et le ski et le snowboard (en hiver).

Le roller est particulièrement populaire parce qu'il peut être pratiqué en toute° saison et par les gens de tout âge. Deux millions de Français font régulièrement du roller, principalement dans les grandes villes et surtout° dans la région parisienne. «Pour moi,» dit Clément, 15 ans, «le roller est l'occasion° de me faire des nouveaux copains.» Mélanie, 17 ans, dit qu'elle fait du roller «parce que j'ai l'impression de vitesse,° d'indépendance et de liberté. Je suis libre° comme un oiseau.» Pour Charlotte, 21 ans, «le roller est un excellent moyen° de faire de l'exercice et de rester en bonne forme° physique.»

Pour certaines personnes qui habitent dans les grandes villes, le roller est un nouveau moyen de transport urbain. Philippe Tardieu, un jeune avocat° de la région parisienne, va à son bureau° en roller. «Le roller est plus économique, moins polluant° et souvent plus rapide que l'auto. Le roller, ça roule...!»

Le roller a beaucoup d'avantages, mais c'est aussi un sport qui peut être dangereux si on ne fait pas attention. Pour faire du roller, on doit être en bonne forme physique et avoir l'équipement nécessaire. On doit toujours porter un casque pour se protéger° la tête. On doit aussi porter des genouillières pour se protéger les genoux° et des protège-poignets pour se protéger les poignets.°

On peut faire du roller dans la rue ou sur toute surface plane, mais il est préférable de pratiquer ce sport dans les endroits réservés pour cette activité. Dans les grandes villes, il y a des «rollerparks» où les jeunes peuvent aussi faire du roller acrobatique et jouer au hockey sur roller.

À Paris, une association sportive nommée Pari-Roller organise tous les vendredis soirs° une grande randonnée° en roller dans les rues de la ville. Cette randonnée commence à dix heures du soir et finit à une heure du matin. Il y a souvent 12 000 (douze mille) participants de tout âge accompagnés de policiers en roller. Pendant cet événement, les rues du circuit sont interdites° aux voitures. Pour beaucoup de Parisiens, cet événement est l'occasion de redécouvrir° leur ville dans une ambiance° d'amitié, de bonne humeur et de fête populaire.

roule *rolls* **équipe** *team* **comme** *like* **glisse** *gliding* **toute** *any* **surtout** *above all* **occasion** *opportunity* **vitesse** *speed* **libre** *free* **moyen** *means* **forme** *shape* **avocat** *lawyer* **bureau** *office* **polluant** *polluting* **protéger** *to protect* **genoux** *knees* **poignets** *wrists* **tous les vendredis soirs** *every Friday evening* **randonnée** *long ride* **interdites** *closed* **redécouvrir** *to rediscover* **ambiance** *atmosphere*

PRE-READING

Have students look at the illustrations. Can they guess what the reading is about? [in-line skating]

L'équipement du roller

Compréhension

Faites correspondre *(Match)* les personnes et leurs opinions.

a. Clément
b. Mélanie
c. Charlotte
d. Philippe

1. «Le roller, ça roule!»
2. «Le roller est moins polluant que l'auto.»
3. «Quand je fais du roller, je suis libre comme un oiseau.»
4. «Le roller est l'occasion de me faire des nouveaux copains.»
5. «Le roller est un excellent moyen de faire de l'exercice.»
6. «Quand je fais du roller, j'ai l'impression de vitesse.»
7. «En ville, le roller est un bon moyen de transport.»

Et vous?

Classez *(Rank)* les avantages du roller par ordre d'importance personnelle — de 6 (plus important) à 1 (moins important). Comparez votre classement avec vos camarades.

Le roller, c'est ...

- un moyen de faire de l'exercice
- un moyen de rester en forme
- un moyen de rencontrer des copains
- un moyen de transport urbain
- l'impression d'indépendance
- l'impression de vitesse

Compréhension Answers

1. d
2. d
3. b
4. a
5. c
6. b
7. d

POST-READING

Using the advantages of in-line skating listed in **Et vous?**, have each student create a chart listing the six advantages vertically on the left and numbers 1–6 horizontally across the top. Have them rank the order of importance for themselves by writing **moi** in the corresponding boxes. Then, have them compare their rankings with a classmate's, writing the name of the classmate in the corresponding box.

Les activités du week-end

Objectives

- Reading at the paragraph level
- Building reading skills

Teaching Resource Options

PRINT  

Workbook PE, pp. 209–212
Activités pour tous PE, pp. 127–129
Unit 7 Resource Book
Activités pour tous TE, pp. 171–173
Workbook TE, pp. 175–178

Pronunciation **Karim** /karim/

Questions sur le texte

Pierre: Qu'est-ce que Pierre a fait le week-end dernier? (Il a fait un match de foot.)

Est-ce qu'il a gagné le match? (Non, il a perdu.)

Qu'est-ce qu'il a fait le soir? (Il est allé chez des copains et il a dansé.)

Aïcha: Où est allée Aïcha le week-end dernier? (Elle est allée chez son oncle Karim.)

Qui est-ce qu'elle a vu là-bas? (Elle a vu tous ses cousins et cousines.)

Élisabeth: Pourquoi est-ce qu'Élisabeth a acheté un cadeau? (Elle a acheté un cadeau pour l'anniversaire de son père.)

Où est-ce qu'elle est allée l'après-midi? (Elle est allée au ciné-club.)

Quel film est-ce qu'elle a vu? (Elle a vu *Les temps modernes.*)

Qu'est-ce qu'elle a fait après le film? (Elle est allée dans un café.)

Yvan: Qu'est-ce qu'Yvan a fait le matin? (Il est allé au rollerpark et il a joué au hockey avec des copains.)

À quelle heure est-ce qu'il est rentré chez lui? (Il est rentré chez lui à midi.)

Où est-ce qu'il a dîné? (Il a dîné au restaurant.)

Les activités du week-end

Qu'est-ce que vous faites le week-end? Qu'est-ce que vous avez fait le week-end dernier? Voici les réponses de quatre jeunes du monde° francophone.

Pierre
(16 ans)
Basse Terre, Guadeloupe

Le samedi, je joue généralement au foot. Je fais partie° de l'équipe° junior de mon village. Le week-end dernier, nous avons fait un match. Nous avons bien joué, mais nous avons perdu! Après le match, je suis allé à la plage. Le soir, je suis allé chez des copains. Nous avons mis de la musique et nous avons dansé.

Aïcha
(14 ans)
Casablanca, Maroc

Samedi dernier, nous avons eu une grande réunion de famille chez mon oncle Karim. Une centaine° de personnes sont venues. Nous avons fait un «méchoui». (C'est un repas° où on rôtit° un mouton° entier à la broche.°) J'ai eu l'occasion° de voir tous° mes cousins et cousines. On s'est bien amusé.°

Élisabeth
(15 ans)
Bruxelles, Belgique

Samedi matin, j'ai fait des achats. J'ai choisi un cadeau pour l'anniversaire de mon père. (J'ai acheté une cravate en soie.°) L'après-midi, je suis allée au ciné-club avec un copain. Nous avons vu *Les Temps modernes*, un vieux film de Charlie Chaplin. Après, nous sommes allés dans un café et nous avons rencontré d'autres° copains. J'ai passé la soirée° en famille.

Yvan
(14 ans)
Montréal, Québec

Le matin, je suis allé à un rollerpark avec des copains et nous avons joué au hockey. À midi, je suis rentré chez moi. L'après-midi, j'ai aidé mes parents à repeindre° la cuisine. Pour le dîner, nous sommes allés au restaurant.

monde *world* **fais partie** *am a member* **équipe** *team*
soie *silk* **d'autres** *other* **soirée** *evening*

une centaine *about 100* **repas** *meal* **rôtit** *roasts* **mouton** *sheep*
à la broche *on the spit* **occasion** *opportunity* **tous** *all*
On s'est bien amusé. *We had a good time.* **repeindre** *repaint*

CONNEXIONS

Pick one of the above French-speaking cities, and find out more about it on the Internet. Imagine that you will be spending a week in that city.

- What kinds of things would you like to do?
- What places would you like to visit?
- What would be the best season to go?

PRE-READING ACTIVITY

Have students glance over the reading quickly. What are the questions that were asked in the interview?

POST-READING ACTIVITY

Ask each student to decide which of the four people they would like to spend a weekend with and why.

Imaginez que vous avez la possibilité de passer un week-end avec un de ces jeunes. Qui allez-vous choisir? Pourquoi?

STRATEGY Reading

More cognate patterns
Here are two important cognate patterns that will help you read French more easily.

- French verbs in **-er** sometimes correspond to English verbs in *-ate*.

FRENCH	ENGLISH	FRENCH	ENGLISH
situer	*situate*	**situé**	*situated*
indiquer	*indicate*	**indiqué**	*indicated*

- The ending **-ment** usually corresponds to the English ending *-ly*.
généralement *generally*

Activité écrite: Une carte postale

Imaginez que vous avez passé le week-end avec l'une des quatre personnes: Pierre, Yvan, Élisabeth ou Aïcha. Dans une carte postale, décrivez ce week-end de votre point de vue personnel.

Chers amis,

J'ai passé le week-end avec Yvan. Nous avons ....

Writing Hint Be sure to use the **passé composé.**

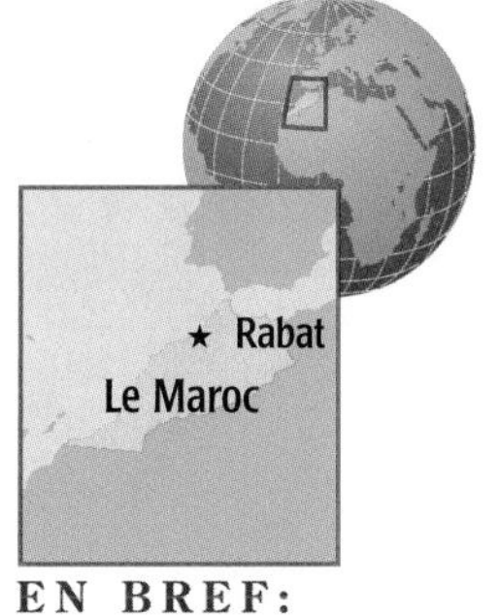

EN BREF: LE MAROC

Population: 30 millions
Capitale: Rabat
Langues: arabe, français, espagnol

Le Maroc est un pays° d'Afrique du Nord° situé entre la Méditerranée au nord, l'Atlantique à l'est° et le Sahara au sud.° Autrefois° administré par la France, ce pays est maintenant gouverné par un roi,° le roi Mohammed VI. Le sud du pays est habité par les Touareg, un peuple nomade qui traverse le Sahara en caravanes de chameaux.°

De culture islamique, le Maroc est un pays moderne avec une longue tradition intellectuelle et artistique. Les artisans marocains créent° des produits d'excellente qualité: textiles, céramiques et objets de cuir° et de cuivre.°

Il y a aujourd'hui un million de Marocains qui habitent en France où ils ont introduit le couscous, le thé à la menthe° et d'autres° spécialités de leur pays.

pays *country* **nord** *north* **est** *east* **sud** *south* **Autrefois** *In the past* **roi** *king* **chameaux** *camels* **créent** *create* **cuir** *leather* **cuivre** *copper* **menthe** *mint* **d'autres** *other*

Words with several meanings

passer *to pass [by], to spend time*
gagner *to earn, to win*
l'anniversaire *anniversary, birthday*

Activité écrite: Une carte postale

Answers will vary.

Chers amis,

J'ai passé le week-end avec Yvan. Nous avons joué au hockey avec ses copains à un rollerpark. À midi, nous sommes rentrés chez lui. L'après-midi, nous avons aidé ses parents à repeindre la cuisine. Pour le dîner, nous sommes allés au restaurant.

À la semaine prochaine!

Paul

Bruxelles

Brussels is an important center for the 15-member European Union **(l'Union européenne)**. It is the seat of the Council of Ministers and houses the working committees of the European Parliament.

Photo cultural note

The photo shows typical goods found at the Marrakesh market in Morocco.

Teaching Suggestions

- The influence of Moroccan food specialties in France is seen in the popularity of **le couscous** and **le thé à la menthe**. Have students do research to find out which other Moroccan food specialties are popular in France.
- Encourage students to seek out local concerts which showcase French music. They can contact their nearest French Consulate, **Alliance française** or the Cultural Services of the French Embassy.

Note culturelle

Tell students that one of the traditional foods of the nomadic Touareg people is *taguella*, a kind of flat bread that is dipped into stews. Have small groups of students discuss how the Touareg can bake their bread in the desert without an oven! (The bread dough is buried under the sand and hot charcoal is placed on top to provide the heat for baking.)

Les quatre erreurs de Sophie

Objectives

- Reading for fun
- Logical thinking: finding errors of fact

Teaching Resource Options

PRINT

Workbook PE, pp. 209–212
Activités pour tous PE, pp. 127–129
Unit 7 Resource Book
Activités pour tous TE, pp. 171–173
Workbook TE, pp. 175–178

Les quatre erreurs de Sophie
Answers

Marrakech, le 10 juillet
Erreur: Le Maroc est un pays d'Afrique du nord.

Québec, le 25 juillet
Erreur: Ottawa est la capitale du Canada.

Fort-de-France, le 3 août
Erreur: La Martinique est une île de la mer des Caraïbes.

Port-au-Prince, le 14 août
Erreur: Les gens d'Haïti parlent créole et français.

Photo culture notes

Leather market Leather bags at the market "Souq" in the medina of "Fès El-Bali" (old town).

Citadelle Massive entry gate at the Citadel with Sentry guard.

Les quatre erreurs de Sophie

Pendant les vacances, Sophie Lambert, une jeune Française, a fait un grand voyage dans les pays° francophones. Dans chaque° pays où elle est allée, elle a écrit° des cartes postales à ses copains. Dans chaque carte postale, Sophie a fait une erreur.° Quelle est cette erreur? (Les erreurs de Sophie concernent la géographie ou les gens.) Lisez attentivement chaque carte et cherchez l'erreur que Sophie a faite.

pays *countries* **chaque** *each* **a écrit** *wrote* **erreur** *error, mistake*

Marrakech, le 10 juillet

Ma chère Pauline,

Je suis au Maroc. C'est un pays d'Afrique du Sud° où on parle arabe et où beaucoup de gens parlent aussi français. Samedi, je suis allée à la «médina» qui est le vieux quartier° de Marrakech. Là, j'ai acheté un beau sac de cuir° à un artisan local.

Amitiés,
Sophie

Sud *south* **quartier** *district* **cuir** *leather*

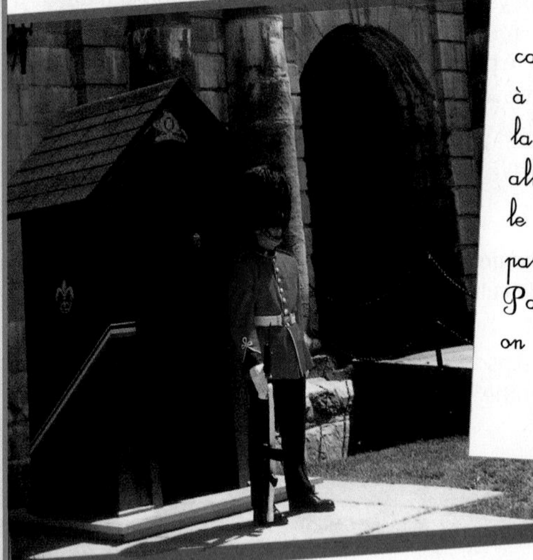

Québec, le 25 juillet

Mon cher Guillaume,

Je passe une semaine à Québec, la capitale du Canada. Hier j'ai téléphoné à une copine et nous sommes allées dans la vieille ville. Ensuite, nous sommes allées à la Citadelle et nous avons vu le changement de la garde.° Ici, les gens parlent un français un peu ancien.° Par exemple, pour dire «au revoir», on dit° «bonjour». C'est amusant, non?

Amicalement,
Sophie

changement de la garde *changing of the guard* **ancien** *old* **dit** *says*

PRE-READING ACTIVITY

Have students look at each of the postcards and read the descriptions of the places pictured. Then have them locate the four cities on a map.

POST-READING ACTIVITY

Have students imagine that they had been able to accompany Sophie on one part of her trip. Which part would they have chosen and why?

Fort-de-France, le 3 août

Ma chère Élodie,

Un grand bonjour de la Martinique qui est une petite île° de l'Océan Pacifique. Je suis arrivée ici la semaine dernière. Ici, il fait toujours chaud et les gens vont à la plage toute l'année!° Hier j'ai acheté un maillot de bain et des lunettes de soleil dans une boutique de l'hôtel. Ensuite, j'ai nagé et j'ai fait de la planche à voile et de la plongée sous-marine.° J'ai vu des poissons de toutes les couleurs!

Affectueusement,

Sophie

île *island* **toute l'année** *all year long*
plongée sous-marine *scuba diving*

Port-au-Prince, le 14 août

Mon cher Mathieu,

Je suis arrivée à Haïti dimanche dernier. J'ai trouvé une chambre dans une pension° à Port-au-Prince, la capitale du pays. Les gens d'ici parlent créole et espagnol. Hier soir, je suis allée écouter un orchestre de musique «compas». Génial! J'aime aussi la cuisine créole. C'est épicé,° mais c'est très bon!

Amitiés,

Sophie

pension *boarding house* **épicé** *spicy, hot*

Les 4 erreurs:

1. *Le Maroc est en Afrique du Nord (et non pas en Afrique du Sud).*
2. *La capitale du Canada est Ottawa (et non pas Québec).*
3. *La Martinique est dans l'Océan Atlantique (et non pas dans l'Océan Pacifique).*
4. *À Haïti, on parle créole et français (et non pas espagnol).*

CLASSROOM MANAGEMENT Pair writing practice

Ask students to bring in local postcards. Divide the class into small groups.

Each group of students writes a postcard in French. In the text, however, they introduce an error of history or geography.

Then let groups exchange cards and try to find the errors.

Expansion activities PLANNING AHEAD

Games

• Dessinez!

Have students work in small groups. Each student will draw a table place setting, with all the items in the wrong place. Then, students will describe their drawings to the other players, who will try to reproduce the drawing as best they can. Award points for the most accurate reproduction at each round.

Pacing Suggestion: Upon completion of Leçon 25.

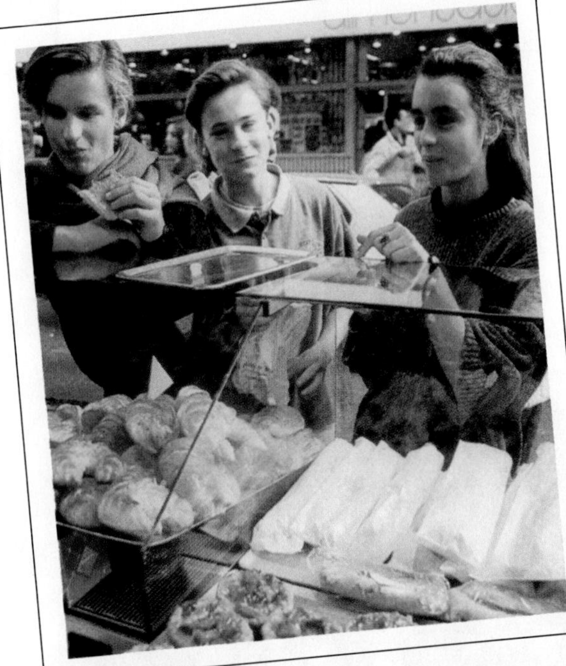

Projects

• Au marché

Have students work in pairs or small groups to write and perform a shopping scene at a French market. In each scene, students will ask for several items, inquire about the price, and pay for their items. Encourage students to incorporate props into their scenes to make them more realistic. Have groups exchange dialogues and proofread one another's work. Students should rehearse the finished dialogues and present them to the class. As an alternative, you could change the setting to a restaurant or cafeteria and have students practice using verbs with the partitive.

Pacing Suggestion: Upon completion of Leçon 26.

• Un menu

Each student will create a menu for a French restaurant. First, have students research on the Internet to identify items they would typically find on the menu of a French restaurant. Have them make a list of appetizers, main dishes, desserts, and beverages. Then have students name their restaurant and design their menu, choosing the dishes that will be served in it. Each student will ask a classmate to proofread the first draft of his or her menu. Finally, students will create a final draft of their respective menus. You may want to grade the menus on accuracy, variety of vocabulary used, creativity, neatness, and visual appeal. As an alternative, students might create menus for a francophone restaurant.

Pacing Suggestion: Upon completion of Leçon 27.

Bulletin Boards

• La nourriture

Students will work in small groups to create a poster for a certain category of food: *les fruits, les légumes, les boissons, la viande, les desserts,* and so on. Assign these a day or two in advance so that each group can find photographs or create illustrations of items that fit their category. Have students lay out the images on a poster board, making sure to leave room for a title and descriptive captions for each item. You may also want to have students show where their category of food is located in a standard food pyramid.

Pacing Suggestion: Upon completion of Leçon 25.

• Les articles partitifs, les articles indéfinis

Students will make posters illustrating the use of the partitive article and the indefinite article. See pages 378–379 for examples. First, have each student select a food item to illustrate. Then, have students create an illustration of the whole item and caption it using the indefinite article. Next to the first illustration and caption, have students create an illustration of a portion of the food item (a slice, a piece, and so on) and caption it using the partitive article.

Pacing Suggestion: Upon completion of Leçon 26.

Music

• L'hymne national

Teach your students *La Marseillaise,* the national anthem of France. You can download the music from the Internet. The lyrics are provided below in French. You may also want to give students a list of vocabulary words from the song in English.

- *La Marseillaise* was written during the French Revolution by an engineer and amateur musician, Rouget de Lisle. It was first adopted as the French national anthem in 1795.

La Marseillaise

Allons enfants de la patrie,
Le jour de gloire est arrivé
Contre nous de la tyrannie
L'étendard sanglant est levé
Entendez vous dans les campagnes,
Mugir ces féroces soldats?
Ils viennent jusque dans nos bras
Egorger nos fils, nos compagnes!

(Refrain)
Aux armes, citoyens!
Formez vos bataillons!
Marchons! Marchons!
Qu'un sang impur
Abreuve nos sillons!

Pacing Suggestion: Upon completion of Leçon 28.

Storytelling

• Une mini-histoire

Create a brief story in dialogue format about a funny or a difficult customer in a restaurant or at a market. Pass out copies of your scripted dialogue to students. Repeat the conversation with pauses, allowing students to repeat after you, or to fill in the words. Then have them work in pairs to develop their own conflict based on the scripted tale. Ask students to write out their expanded conversations, practice them aloud for intonation, and perform them for the class.

Pacing Suggestion: Upon completion of Leçon 28.

Recipe

• Tapioca banane

Many recipes from the islands of the Caribbean incorporate the tropical fruits that are native to the area. This simple dessert uses bananas and coconut milk.

Pacing Suggestion: Upon completion of Leçon 27.

Tapioca banane

Ingrédients	*Ingredients*
• 1 litre d'eau	• approx. 4 cups water
• 200 g de tapioca	• approx. 7 oz. tapioca
• 2 bananes, coupées en rondelles	• 2 bananas, cut up
• 1/2 bol de lait de coco	• approx. 3/4 cups coconut milk
• 1/2 bol de sucre	• approx. 3/4 cups sugar
• 100 g de cacahuètes pilées	• approx. 3.5 oz. crushed peanuts

Préparation

1. Faites bouillir l'eau.
2. Ajoutez le tapioca.
3. Mélangez bien et puis ajoutez les bananes.
4. Ajoutez le sucre et le lait de coco.
5. Remuez et cuisez pendant quelques minutes à feu doux.
6. Servez lorsque le tapioca est gonflé.
7. Si vous voulez, saupoudrez avec des cacahuètes pilées.

Directions

1. Boil the water.
2. Add the tapioca.
3. Mix well and add the banana slices.
4. Add the sugar and coconut milk.
5. Stir and cook for several minutes at low heat.
6. The tapioca is ready to serve when it puffs up.
7. Serve topped with crushed peanuts.

Hands-on Crafts

• Un paysage créole

Students will create a three dimensional tableau representing a Caribbean scene. First have students decide what kind of scene they want to create. They may wish to look for photographs or videos of Martinique, Guadeloupe, and Haiti for inspiration. Have them bring in small cardboard boxes and cut away all but the bottom and one side of their box. They should paint or color the background before they begin attaching items to the bottom, or "floor." Students can use pieces of the rest of the box as backing to stand up human figures and whatever else they want to place in their tableau. Have them cut these figures out of construction paper and decorate them with seashells, toothpicks, and other items, each to a cardboard backing, and place them at intervals on the "floor" of the box in order to create a multi-layered image.

Pacing Suggestion: Upon completion of Leçon 28.

Mangez chaque jour ...
du fromage, de la viande,
des fruits et du pain.
Santé et Bien-être social Canada
Health and Welfare Canada

End of Unit

• Le dîner français

Students will prepare and eat a typical French meal. Have the class vote and select several courses: 1–2 appetizers, 1–2 main dishes, and 1–2 desserts. Then, divide the class into groups, one group for each dish. Have each group prepare a dish and bring it to class. Remind students that all conversation during the meal should be in French! Encourage everyone to sample all the dishes. This would be a great time to discuss differences in French and American mealtime behavior. As an alternative, students could bring simple, inexpensive dishes (crêpes, salads, and so on) from a local French restaurant.

Rubric

A = 13–15 pts. **B** = 10–12 pts. **C** = 7–9 pts. **D** = 4–6 pts. **F** = < 4 pts.

Criteria	Scale
Vocabulary Use	1 2 3 4 5
Grammar/Spelling Accuracy	1 2 3 4 5
Creativity	1 2 3 4 5

Planning Guide CLASSROOM MANAGEMENT

OBJECTIVES

Communication
- Talk about your favorite foods *pp. 366–367, 370–371*
- Describe the different meals of the day *pp. 364, 375*
- Prepare a shopping list and do the grocery shopping *pp. 366–367, 370–371, 376, 378–379*
- Order a meal in a restaurant *pp. 376, 378–379*
- Set the table *p. 364*
- Ask people to do things for you *pp. 389, 392*

Grammar
- Le verbe *vouloir p. 376*
- Le verbe *prendre p. 377*
- L'article partitif: *du, de la pp. 378–379*
- L'article partitif dans les phrases négatives *p. 381*
- Le verbe *boire p. 383*
- Les pronoms compléments *me, te, nous, vous p. 388*
- Les pronoms compléments à l'impératif *p. 390*
- Les verbes *pouvoir* et *devoir p. 392*
- Le verbe connaître *p. 398*
- Les pronoms compléments: *le, la, les p. 399*
- La place des pronoms à l'impératif *p. 401*
- Les pronoms compléments: *lui, leur p. 402*
- Les verbes *dire* et *écrire p. 404*

Vocabulary
- Les repas et la table *p. 364*
- La nourriture et les boissons *pp. 366–367*
- Les fruits et les légumes *pp. 370–371*
- Verbes comme *prendre p. 377*
- Les services personnels *p. 389*
- Verbes suivis d'un complément indirect *p. 403*

Pronunciation
- Les lettres «ou» et «u» *p. 383*
- Les lettres «s» et «ss» *p. 393*
- Les lettres «on» et «om» *p. 405*

Culture
- Le marché *p. 371*
- À la cantine *p. 375*
- Les restaurants français et la cuisine française *p. 387*
- Un pique-nique français *p. 397*
- La cuisine créole *p. 415*

PROGRAM RESOURCES

Print

- Workbook PE, *pp. 213–249*
- *Activités pour tous* PE, *pp. 131–149*
- Block Scheduling Copymasters *pp. 193–224*
- *Français pour hispanophones*
- *Lectures pour tous*
- Teacher to Teacher Copymasters
- Teaching Proficiency through Reading and Storytelling
- Unit 8 Resource Book
  - Lessons 25–28 Resources
    - Workbook TE
    - *Activités pour tous* TE
    - Family Letter
    - Absent Student Copymasters
    - Family Involvement
    - Video Activities
    - Videoscripts
    - Audioscripts
    - Assessment Program
  - Unit 8 Resources
    - Communipak
    - *Activités pour tous* TE Reading
    - Workbook TE Reading and Culture Activities
    - Assessment Program
    - Answer Keys

Audiovisual

- Audio Program PE CD 4 Tracks 21–43
- Audio Program Workbook CD 12 Tracks 1–27
- *Chansons* Audio CD
- Sing Along: Grammar and Vocabulary Songs CD
- Video Program Modules 25, 26, 27, 28
- Warm-Up Transparencies
- Overhead Transparencies
  - 45 Table setting;
  - 46a, 46b *La nourriture et les boissons;*
  - 47 *Les fruits et les légumes*
  - 48 *Au marché*
  - 49 *Le partitif (du, de la)*

Technology

- Online Workbook
- ClassZone.com
- McDougal Littell Assessment System/ Test Generator CD-ROM
- EasyPlanner CD-ROM
- Power Presentations on CD-ROM
- Take-Home Tutor CD-ROM

Assessment Program Options

Lesson Quizzes
Portfolio Assessment
Unit Test Form A
Unit Test Form B
Unit Test Part III (Alternate) Cultural Awareness
Listening Comprehension Performance Test
Speaking Performance Test
Reading Comprehension Performance Test
Writing Performance Test
Multiple Choice Test Items
Test Scoring Tools
Audio Program CD 16 Tracks 9–16
Answer Keys
McDougal Littell Assessment System/ Test Generator CD-ROM

Pacing Guide SAMPLE LESSON PLAN

DAY	DAY	DAY	DAY	DAY
1 Unité 8 Opener Leçon 25 • Vocabulaire et Culture–Les repas et la nourriture • Vocabulaire–Les repas et la table	**2** Leçon 25 • Vocabulaire–La nourriture et les boissons	**3** Leçon 25 • Vocabulaire–Les fruits et les légumes • Note culturelle–Le marché	**4** Leçon 25 • À votre tour!	**5** Leçon 26 • Conversation et Culture–À la cantine • Note culturelle–À la cantine • Le verbe *vouloir*
6 Leçon 26 • Le verbe *prendre* • Vocabulaire–Verbes comme *prendre* • L'article partitif: *du, de la*	**7** Leçon 26 • L'article partitif dans les phrases négatives	**8** Leçon 26 • Le verbe *boire* • Prononciation–Les lettres «ou» et «u»	**9** Leçon 26 • À votre tour!	**10** Leçon 27 • Conversation et Culture–Un client difficile • Note culturelle–Les restaurants français et la cuisine française • Les pronoms compléments *me, te, nous, vous*
11 Leçon 27 • Vocabulaire–Les services personnels • Les pronoms compléments à l'impératif	**12** Leçon 27 • Les verbes *pouvoir* et *devoir* • Prononciation–Les lettres «s» et «ss»	**13** Leçon 27 • À votre tour!	**14** Leçon 28 • Conversation et Culture–Pique-nique • Note culturelle–Un pique-nique français • Le verbe *connaître*	**15** Leçon 28 • Les pronoms compléments: *le, la, les*
16 Leçon 28 • La place des pronoms à l'impératif	**17** Leçon 28 • Les pronoms compléments: *lui, leur* • Vocabulaire–Verbes suivis d'un complément indirect	**18** Leçon 28 • Vocabulaire–Verbes suivis d'un complément indirect *(continued)* • Les verbes *dire* et *écrire* • Prononciation–Les lettres «on» et «om»	**19** Leçon 28 • À votre tour!	**20** • Tests de contrôle
21 • Unit 8 Test	**22** • Entracte–Lecture et culture			

Student Text Listening Activity Scripts
AUDIO PROGRAM

▶ LEÇON 25 LE FRANÇAIS PRATIQUE Les repas et la nourriture

À votre tour!

• Écoutez bien! *p. 372* CD 4, TRACK 21

Pauline et Thomas ont fait les courses dans deux supermarchés différents. Écoutez bien les phrases. Si vous entendez le nom d'un produit acheté par Pauline, marquez A. Si vous entendez le nom d'un produit acheté par Thomas, marquez B. Écoutez bien. Chaque phrase va être répétée. Commençons.

1. Où est la mayonnaise? #
2. Est-ce que tu as acheté des pommes de terre? #
3. J'aime bien le jus de pomme. #
4. Il y a un poulet pour le dîner. #
5. Les tomates coûtent deux euros la livre. #
6. Est-ce que tu aimes le gâteau? #
7. Le thon est mon poisson préféré. #
8. Passe-moi la confiture, s'il te plaît. #
9. Est-ce que tu aimes le saucisson? #
10. Pour le dessert, il y a une tarte. #
11. Les pommes sont bon marché. #
12. Au petit déjeuner, nous mangeons des céréales. #
13. Voici les oeufs. #
14. Où as-tu mis le lait? #
15. L'eau minérale est sur la table. #
16. Combien coûte la salade? #
17. Où as-tu acheté les poires? #
18. Combien de pamplemousses as-tu acheté? #
19. Passe-moi le jus d'orange, s'il te plaît. #
20. Mets le jambon au réfrigérateur. #
21. Mon petit frère n'aime pas les carottes. #
22. Tiens, voilà le pain. #

• Conversation dirigée *p. 372* CD 4, TRACK 22

Listen to the conversation. Écoutez la conversation entre Marc et Juliette.

Marc: Est-ce que tu as faim, Juliette?
Juliette: Oui, j'ai très faim.
Marc: Est-ce que tu veux déjeuner?
Juliette: Oui, je veux déjeuner, merci.
Marc: Est-ce que tu aimes la cuisine italienne?
Juliette: Je préfère la cuisine française.
Marc: Est-ce que tu aimes la viande?
Juliette: Oui, j'aime la viande, mais j'aime aussi les légumes.
Marc: Est-ce que tu veux aller à La Campagne?
Juliette: Oui, d'accord.

• Créa-dialogue *p. 373* CD 4, TRACK 23

Listen to the sample *Créa-dialogues.* Écoutez les conversations.

Modèle: –Tu aimes la viande? –Non, je n'aime pas la viande.
–Tu aimes les légumes? –Non, je n'aime pas les légumes.
–Tu aimes le poisson? –Oui, j'aime beaucoup le poisson.
–On déjeune à La Marine? –D'accord.

Maintenant écoutez le dialogue numéro 1.

–Tu aimes le poisson? –Non, je n'aime pas beaucoup le poisson.
–Tu aimes la viande? –J'aime un peu la viande.
–Tu aimes les spaghetti? –Oui, j'aime beaucoup les spaghetti!
–Alors, on déjeune Chez Rigoletto? –D'accord!

▶ LEÇON 26 À la cantine

• À la cantine *p. 374*

A. Compréhension orale CD 4, TRACK 24

Please turn to page 374 for complete *Compréhension orale* text.

B. Écoutez et répétez. CD 4, TRACK 25

You will now hear a paused version of the dialog. Listen to the speaker and repeat right after he or she has completed the sentence.

• Grammaire *p. 376* CD 4, TRACK 26

Le verbe *vouloir*

Repeat the sentences after the speaker.

Je **veux** aller au café. #
Il **veut** dîner. #
Vous **voulez** des spaghetti. #
J'ai voulu dîner chez Maxim's. #
Tu **veux** déjeuner. #
Nous **voulons** une glace. #
Elles **veulent** des frites. #

• Grammaire *p. 377* CD 4, TRACK 27

Le verbe *prendre*

Je **prends** une pizza. #
Elle **prend** une salade. #
Vous **prenez** l'avion. #
J'ai pris un steak. #
Tu **prends** un sandwich. #
Nous **prenons** le train. #
Ils **prennent** des photos. #

• Prononciation *p. 383* CD 4, TRACK 28

Les lettres «ou» et «u»

Écoutez: la p<u>ou</u>le le p<u>u</u>ll

The letters "**ou**" always represent the sound /u/.

Répétez: /u/ # v<u>ou</u>s # n<u>ou</u>s # p<u>ou</u>let # s<u>ou</u>pe # f<u>ou</u>rchette # c<u>ou</u>teau # d<u>ou</u>zaine #

The letter "**u**" always represents the sound /y/.

Répétez: /y/ # t<u>u</u> # d<u>u</u> # <u>u</u>ne # lég<u>u</u>me # j<u>u</u>s # s<u>u</u>cre # bien s<u>û</u>r # aven<u>u</u>e # m<u>u</u>sée #

Now distinguish between the two vowel sounds:

Répétez: /u/ – /y/ # p<u>ou</u>le–p<u>u</u>ll # r<u>ou</u>e–r<u>u</u>e # v<u>ou</u>s–v<u>u</u>e # je j<u>ou</u>e–le j<u>u</u>s #
V<u>ou</u>s b<u>u</u>vez d<u>u</u> j<u>u</u>s de pamplem<u>ou</u>sse. Je v<u>ou</u>drais de la s<u>ou</u>pe, d<u>u</u> p<u>ou</u>let et d<u>u</u> j<u>u</u>s de raisin. #

À votre tour!

• Allô! *p. 384* CD 4, TRACK 29

Listen to the conversation. Écoutez la conversation entre Frédéric et Sandrine.

Frédéric: Tu dînes au restaurant ce soir?
Sandrine: Non, j'ai invité mon copain Fabien à dîner chez moi.
Frédéric: Tu as fait les courses?
Sandrine: Oui, je suis allée au supermarché ce matin.
Frédéric: Qu'est-ce que tu as acheté?
Sandrine: Du riz, des oeufs, de la salade et du fromage.
Frédéric: Tu n'as pas acheté de viande?
Sandrine: Mais non, tu sais bien que Fabien est végétarien.
Frédéric: C'est vrai. Et pour le dessert, tu as acheté de la glace?
Sandrine: Non, j'ai pris un gâteau au chocolat.

• Créa-dialogue *p. 384* CD 4, TRACK 30

Listen to some sample *Créa-dialogues.* Écoutez les conversations.

Modèle: –Où es-tu allée? –Je suis allée au supermarché.
–Qu'est-ce que tu as acheté? –J'ai acheté du pain, du lait et de la confiture.

Maintenant, écoutez le dialogue numéro 1.

–Où es-tu allé? –Je suis allé à la cantine.
–Qu'est-ce que tu as mangé? –J'ai mangé du rosbif, de la salade et de la glace.

pause for oral response

▶ LEÇON 27 Un client difficile

• Un client difficile *p. 386*

A. Compréhension orale CD 4, TRACK 31

Please turn to page 386 for complete *Compréhension orale* text.

B. Écoutez et répétez. CD 4, TRACK 32

You will now hear a paused version of the dialog. Listen to the speaker and repeat right after he or she has completed the sentence.

• Vocabulaire *p. 389* CD 4, TRACK 33

Les services personnels

Repeat the sentences after the speaker. Répétez les phrases.

aider quelqu'un #	J'**aide** mes copains avec les devoirs. #
amener quelqu'un #	Le taxi **amène** les touristes à la gare. #
apporter quelque chose **à** quelqu'un #	Le serveur **apporte** le menu **aux** clients. #
donner quelque chose **à** quelqu'un #	Mme Marin **donne** 10 euros **à** sa fille. #
montrer quelque chose **à** quelqu'un #	Est-ce que tu **montres** tes photos **à** ton copain? #
prêter quelque chose **à** quelqu'un #	Est-ce que tu **prêtes** tes disques **à** tes amis? #

• Grammaire *p. 392* CD 4, TRACK 34

Les verbes *pouvoir* et *devoir*

Repeat the sentences after the speaker. Répétez les phrases.

Je **peux** venir. #	Je **dois** rentrer avant midi. #
Tu **peux** travailler. #	Tu **dois** gagner de l'argent. #
Elle **peut** voyager. #	Elle **doit** visiter Paris. #
Nous **pouvons** dîner ici. #	Nous **devons** regarder le menu. #
Vous **pouvez** rester. #	Vous **devez** finir vos devoirs. #
Ils **peuvent** aider. #	Ils **doivent** mettre la table. #
J'**ai pu** étudier. #	J'**ai dû** faire mes devoirs. #

• Prononciation *p. 393* CD 4, TRACK 35

Les lettres «s» et «ss»

Écoutez: poison poisson

Be sure to distinguish between "**s**" and "**ss**" in the middle of a word.

Répétez: /z/ # mauvaise # cuisine # fraise # mayonnaise # quelque chose # magasin #
/s/ # poisson # saucisson # dessert # boisson # assiette # pamplemousse #
/z/ – /s/ # poison–poisson # désert–dessert #
Comme dessert nous choisissons une tarte aux fraises. #

À votre tour!

• Allô! *p. 394* CD 4, TRACK 36

Listen to the conversation. Écoutez la conversation entre Corinne et Philippe.

Corinne: Dis, Philippe, j'ai besoin d'un petit service.
Philippe: Qu'est-ce que je peux faire pour toi?
Corinne: Prête-moi ta mobylette, s'il te plaît.
Philippe: Ah, je ne peux pas. Je dois aller en ville cet après-midi.
Corinne: Dans ce cas, apporte-moi *Paris-Match.*
Philippe: D'accord! Je vais aller à la librairie Duchemin.
Corinne: Alors, achète-moi aussi le nouvel album d'Astérix.
Philippe: Écoute, je n'ai pas assez d'argent.
Corinne: Je t'ai prêté vingt euros hier!
Philippe: C'est vrai . . . Bon, je t'achète tout ça.

• Créa-dialogue *p. 394* CD 4, TRACK 37

Listen to the sample *Créa-dialogues.* Écoutez les conversations.

Modèle: –S'il te plaît, prête-moi ton vélo!
–Pourquoi?
–Parce que je voudrais faire une promenade à la campagne.
–D'accord, je te prête mon vélo.

Maintenant, écoutez le dialogue numéro 1.

–S'il te plaît, prête-moi ta raquette!
–Pourquoi?
–Parce que je voudrais jouer au tennis.
–D'accord, je te prête ma raquette.

▶ LEÇON 28 Pique-nique

• Pique-nique *p. 396* CD 4, TRACK 38

A. Compréhension orale

Please turn to page 396 for complete *Compréhension orale* text.

B. Écoutez et répétez. CD 4, TRACK 39

You will now hear a paused version of the dialog. Listen to the speaker and repeat right after he or she has completed the sentence.

• Grammaire *p. 398* CD 4, TRACK 40

Le verbe *connaître*

Écoutez et répétez.

Je **connais** Stéphanie. #	Tu **connais** son cousin? #
Elle **connaît** ces garçons. #	Nous **connaissons** Paris. #
Vous **connaissez** Montréal? #	Ils **connaissent** ce café. #

J'**ai connu** ton frère pendant les vacances. #

• Prononciation *p. 405* CD 4, TRACK 41

Les lettres «on» et «om»

Écoutez: lion lionne

Be sure to distinguish between the nasal and non-nasal vowel sounds.

REMEMBER: Do not pronounce an /n/ or /m/ after the nasal vowel /ɔ̃/.

Répétez: /ɔ̃/ # mon # ton # son # bon # avion # montrer # répondre # invitons # blouson #
/ɔn/ # téléphone # Simone # donner # connais # mayonnaise # personne # bonne #
/ɔm/ # fromage # promenade # tomate # pomme # dommage # comment #
/ɔ̃/ – /ɔn/ # lion–lionne # bon–bonne # Simon–Simone # Yvon–Yvonne #
Monique donne une pomme à Raymond. #
Simone connaît mon oncle Léon. #

À votre tour!

• Allô! *p. 406* CD 4, TRACK 42

Listen to the conversation. Écoutez la conversation entre Olivier et Sophie.

Olivier: Qu'est-ce que tu fais ce week-end?
Sophie: J'organise une fête.
Olivier: Tu m'invites?
Sophie: Bien sûr, je t'invite.
Olivier: Et Catherine? Tu l'invites aussi?
Sophie: Catherine? Je ne la connais pas. Qui est-ce?
Olivier: C'est ma nouvelle copine.
Sophie: Ah oui, je vois qui c'est maintenant. Eh bien, d'accord! Je l'invite.
Olivier: Tu veux son numéro de téléphone?
Sophie: Oui, je ne l'ai pas.
Olivier: C'est le 01.44.32.28.50.
Sophie: Je lui téléphone tout de suite.

• Créa-dialogue *p. 406* CD 4, TRACK 43

Listen to some sample *Créa-dialogues.* Écoutez les conversations.

Modèle: –Tu regardes la télé?	–Oui, je la regarde.
–À quelle heure est-ce que tu la regardes?	–À huit heures.

Maintenant, écoutez le dialogue numéro 1.

–Tu invites tes amis?	–Oui, je les invite.
–Quand est-ce que tu les invites?	–Je les invite ce week-end.
–À quelle occasion est-ce que tu les invites?	–Je les invite pour mon anniversaire.

Complete videoscripts, plus Workbook and Assessment audioscripts, are available in the Unit Resource Books.

Main Theme
- Food and meals

COMMUNICATION
- Talking about favorite foods
- Describing meals
- Preparing a shopping list
- Doing the grocery shopping
- Ordering a meal in a restaurant
- Setting the table
- Asking people to do things for you

CULTURES
- Learning about French meals
- Learning about the market
- Learning about French school cafeterias and what they serve
- Learning about French restaurants
- Learning about French cuisine
- Learning about French picnics
- Learning about creole cuisine

CONNECTIONS
- Connecting to Math: Calculating quantities and prices
- Connecting to English: Recognizing English cooking terms that were borrowed from French
- Connecting to Cooking: Making crêpes

COMPARISONS
- Learning about the use of French food terms in the English language
- Comparing school cafeterias in France and the U.S.
- Comparing meals in France and the U.S.
- Finding out about the influence of French food products in American grocery stores

continued on next page

UNITÉ 8

Les repas

THÈME ET OBJECTIFS

Food and meals

Eating well is not only essential for our health, it should be an enjoyable experience as well.

In this unit, you will learn ...

- to talk about your favorite foods
- to describe the different meals of the day
- to prepare a shopping list and do the grocery shopping
- to order a meal in a restaurant
- to set the table

You will also be able ...

- to ask people to do things for you

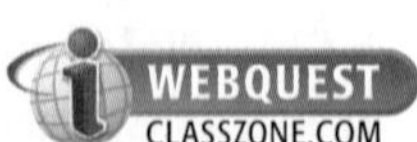

UNIT OVERVIEW

- **Communication Goals:** Students will be able to buy food and order a meal.
- **Linguistic Goals:** Students will learn to express quantities and use object pronouns.
- **Critical Thinking Goals:** Students will begin to understand the concept of the partitive and to observe the differences between object pronouns in French and English.
- **Cultural Goals:** Students will learn about French meals, restaurants, and cafeterias as well as grocery shopping habits in France.

STANDARDS *continued*

COMMUNITIES

- Conversing in French while enjoying a French meal in the classroom
- Finding French foods at the local supermarket
- Using French to order in a restaurant

Teaching Resource Options

PRINT 

Unit 8 Resource Book
  Family Letter p. 17
Français pour hispanophones
  Conseils, pp. 17–18
  Vocabulaire, pp. 52–53

AUDIO & VISUAL 

Audio Program
Chansons CD

TECHNOLOGY 

EasyPlanner CD-ROM

PACING

Your pacing of Unit 8 will depend on where you are in the academic year.

Since this material is reintroduced in **Discovering French, *Nouveau!–Blanc,*** you may want to present the material primarily for student recognition. However, if you have the time, present all four lessons of Unit 8 so that students have a solid introduction to object pronouns.

For further suggestions on pacing, see the general discussion in the Front Matter.

Leçon 25

Main Topic Meals and foods

Teaching Resource Options

PRINT 

Workbook PE, pp. 213–220
Activités pour tous PE, pp. 131–133
Block Scheduling Copymasters, pp. 193–200
Unit 8 Resource Book
- *Activités pour tous* TE, pp. 9–11
- Audioscript, pp. 33–34
- Communipak, pp. 152–173
- Lesson Plans, pp. 12–13
- Block Scheduling Lesson Plans, pp. 14–16
- Absent Student Copymasters, pp. 18–21
- Video Activities, pp. 24–29
- Videoscript, pp. 30–31
- Workbook TE, pp. 1–8

AUDIO & VISUAL 

Audio Program
CD 12 Tracks 1–7

TECHNOLOGY 

Online Workbook

VIDEO PROGRAM

MODULE 25
Le français pratique:
Les repas et la nourriture

TOTAL TIME: 6:53 min.
DVD Disk 2
Videotape 4 (COUNTER: 25:07 min.)

25.1 Introduction: Listening
– Où allez-vous quand vous avez faim? (25:17–26:10 min.)

25.2 Mini-scenes: Listening
– Qu'est-ce que vous aimez manger? (26:11–27:09 min.)

25.3 Mini-scenes: Listening
– Vous préférez les frites ou les spaghetti? (27:10–27:35 min.)

25.4 Mini-scenes: Speaking
– Qu'est-ce que vous préférez? (27:36–28:26 min.)

25.5 Dialogue: Au marché
(28:27–30:03 min.)

25.6 Vignette culturelle: Les courses
(30:04–32:00 min.)

Comprehension practice Play the entire module through as an introduction to the lesson.

LEÇON 25

Les repas et la nourriture

LE FRANÇAIS PRATIQUE
VIDÉO DVD AUDIO

Accent sur ... Les repas français

For the French, a meal is more than just food served on a plate. It is a happy social occasion where people gather around a table to enjoy one another's company. Dinner is the most important family time of the day. Parents and children sit down together and talk about the day's events and topics of common interest. Special events are celebrated by more elaborate meals.

In traditional homes, children do not go to the refrigerator to fix their own sandwiches nor do they help themselves to snacks. They are expected to sit down at the table with everyone else at mealtime, eat what is served, join in the conversation, and not ask to be excused until the adults are finished.

Le petit déjeuner (*breakfast*)

Le petit déjeuner français traditionnel est un repas simple: tartines° de pain avec du beurre° et de la confiture° et un grand bol de café au lait ou de chocolat chaud. Dans les familles modernes, les enfants mangent «à l'américaine»: ils prennent° des céréales et du jus d'orange.

tartines *slices* **beurre** *butter* **confiture** *jam* **prennent** *have*

Le déjeuner (*lunch*)

Le déjeuner est généralement servi entre° midi et demi et une heure et demie. Il se compose de hors-d'oeuvre divers (saucisson,° radis,° salade de concombres, etc.), d'un plat principal (viande° ou poisson° avec des légumes°), d'une salade verte, d'un fromage° et d'un dessert (gâteau,° fruits ou glace). Le café est toujours servi à la fin du repas.

entre *between* **saucisson** *salami* **radis** *radishes* **viande** *meat* **poisson** *fish* **légumes** *vegetables* **fromage** *cheese* **gâteau** *cake*

USING THE VIDEO

Ask students whether they prefer to eat in restaurants, cafés, or fast-food places. What do they usually order there? What kinds of foods do they eat at home? Where do their families shop for groceries?

Then show the Video Module 25 and have students look for similarities and differences in eating and grocery shopping habits in France and the U.S.

In the first part, French people are eating out in cafés and restaurants. Then diners express their preferences for various foods in an interview situation. The *Vignette culturelle* shows French shoppers purchasing fruits and vegetables at an open-air market.

Le goûter (afternoon snack)

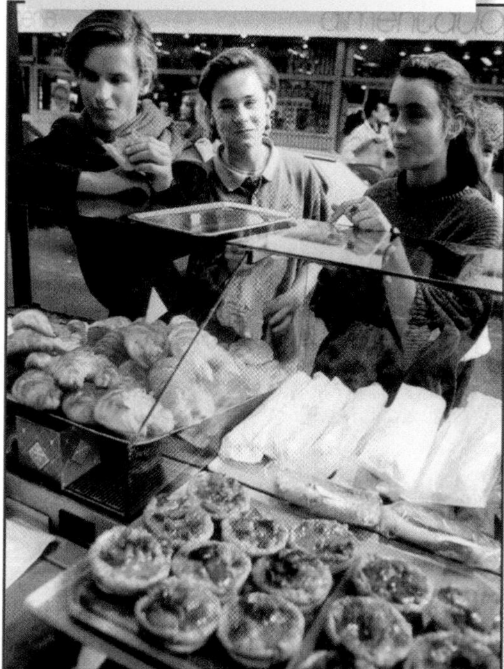

Après les cours, beaucoup de jeunes vont à la pâtisserie. Là, ils achètent un pain au chocolat,° un croissant ou un éclair.

pain au chocolat *chocolate croissant*

Le dîner (dinner)

Le dîner est le repas familial principal. Il est servi entre huit heures et neuf heures avec tout le monde° présent. C'est un repas simple qui se compose d'une soupe, d'un plat principal (viande ou poisson, omelette ou pâtes°), d'une salade et d'un dessert léger° (yaourt ou fruit).

tout le monde *everybody*
pâtes *pasta* **léger** *light*

TEACHING NOTE

Break the class into pairs and have the students examine each photo. Tell them to look for similarities and differences between meals in the French homes pictured here and their homes. Note their ideas on the board, and share the **Photo cultural notes** with them.

Photo culture notes

Le petit déjeuner
This French breakfast mixes traditional elements **(des biscottes, du pain, du beurre, de la confiture)** with modern foods **(des céréales).**

Note that the coffee is served in deep bowls **(un bol).**

Note also the open cupboard **(le buffet)** in the back of the room. It is used to display decorative dishes.

Le déjeuner
In summer, lunches are lighter and may consist of cold cuts **(des viandes froides)**, salad, and fruit.

Note the bottle of mineral water which is almost always present on a French table.

Le goûter
Many department stores have snack counters where one can buy sandwiches, croissants, mini-pizzas, and light pastries.

Le dîner
Note the basket of fruit on the table. In France, it is typical to serve fruit at the end of the meal.

Note also the wardrobe **(l'armoire)** against the wall.

Cultural note

Eating habits in Quebec are a blend between those in France and English-speaking Canada. Like other Canadians, the **Québécois** have bacon, eggs, toast, and cereal for breakfast. But, like the French, they enjoy wine, mineral water, and croissants. Ethnic food, particularly in Montreal, is also very popular. People eat out in cafés, restaurants, and fast-food places. **Le casse-croûte** *(snack bar)* is a favorite place for a quick lunch.

SECTION A

Communicative function
Discussing meals and food

Teaching Resource Options

PRINT

Workbook PE, pp. 213–220
Unit 8 Resource Book
Communipak, pp. 152–173
Video Activities, p. 24
Videoscript, p. 30
Workbook TE, pp. 1–8

AUDIO & VISUAL

Overhead Transparencies
45 Table setting

VIDEO PROGRAM

VIDÉO DVD

MODULE 25

25.1 Introduction: Où allez-vous quand vous avez faim? (25:17–26:10 min.)

Looking ahead The verb **prendre** is formally presented in Lesson 26. Here students will be using only the **je** and **tu** forms.

Language notes

- Remind students that **la cuisine** is also *the kitchen.*
- In Quebec, meals of the day are:
  le déjeuner *(breakfast)*
  le dîner *(lunch)*
  le souper *(dinner)*
- **Un fast-food** (in official French, **un restaurant rapide**) is a restaurant that serves hamburgers, pizza, etc.

Cultural note In setting the table in France, the spoon is usually placed above the plate.

Supplementary vocabulary
une nappe *tablecloth*
une soucoupe *saucer*
le couvert *place setting*
mettre le couvert *to set the table (putting out the dishes, glasses, silverware)*

A VOCABULAIRE Les repas et la table

▶ ***How to talk about meals:***

–En général, à quelle heure est-ce que tu **prends le petit déjeuner** *(have breakfast)*?
–Je prends le petit déjeuner à sept heures et demie.
–Où est-ce que tu vas **déjeuner** *(to have lunch)* aujourd'hui?
–Je vais déjeuner à **la cantine de l'école** *(school cafeteria).*

À quelle heure est-ce que tu prends le petit déjeuner?
Je prends le petit déjeuner à sept heures et demie.

Les repas et la nourriture

NOMS		VERBES	
un repas	*meal*		
le petit déjeuner	*breakfast*	**prendre le petit déjeuner**	*to have breakfast*
le déjeuner	*lunch*	**déjeuner**	*to have lunch*
le dîner	*dinner*	**dîner**	*to have dinner*
la nourriture	*food*		
la cuisine	*cooking, cuisine*		

–Tu peux **mettre** *(set)* la table?
–D'accord. Je vais mettre la table.

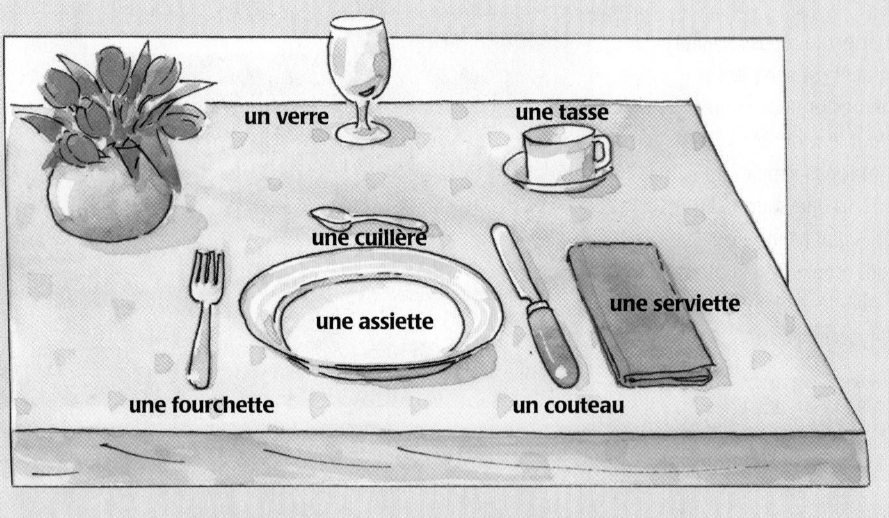
un verre
une tasse
une cuillère
une assiette
une serviette
une fourchette
un couteau

COMPREHENSION Table setting

PROPS: Plastic dishes and place settings

Present the new vocabulary.
Voici une cuillère. Voici une assiette. ...
X, viens ici. Montre-nous la serviette.

Have students pass around the items.
X, donne le verre à Y et la tasse à Z.

Have students manipulate the items.
X, mets la tasse sur l'assiette.
Puis, mets le couteau sur l'assiette et la cuillère dans la tasse.
Ouvre la serviette et mets-la sur la tasse. ...

1 Et toi?

PARLER/ÉCRIRE Exprime tes préférences. Pour cela complète les phrases suivantes.

1. Mon repas préféré est …
   - le petit déjeuner
   - le déjeuner
   - le dîner
2. Je préfère déjeuner …
   - chez moi
   - dans un fast-food
   - à la cantine de l'école
   - …?
3. En général, la nourriture de la cantine de l'école est …
   - excellente
   - mauvaise
   - bonne
   - …?
4. Je préfère dîner …
   - chez moi
   - au restaurant
   - chez mes copains
   - …?
5. Je préfère la nourriture …
   - mexicaine
   - chinoise
   - italienne
   - …?
6. Quand je dois aider pour le dîner, je préfère …
   - préparer la salade
   - laver les assiettes
   - mettre la table
   - …?

2 Questions personnelles PARLER/ÉCRIRE

1. À quelle heure est-ce que tu prends ton petit déjeuner le lundi? Et le dimanche?
2. En général, à quelle heure est-ce que tu dînes?
3. Où est-ce que tu déjeunes pendant la semaine? le samedi? le dimanche?
4. Où est-ce que tu as déjeuné hier? Avec qui?
5. Où est-ce que tu vas dîner ce soir? Avec qui?
6. Est-ce que tu vas souvent au restaurant? Quand? Avec qui? Quel est ton restaurant préféré?
7. Est-ce que tu as jamais *(ever)* déjeuné dans un restaurant français? (dans un restaurant mexicain? dans un restaurant italien? dans un restaurant chinois? dans un restaurant vietnamien?) Quand et avec qui?
8. Est-ce que tu mets la table chez toi? Qui a mis la table pour le petit déjeuner? Et pour le dîner?

3  Au restaurant

PARLER Vous êtes dans un restaurant français. Vous avez commandé *(ordered)* les choses suivantes. Le serveur a oublié *(forgot)* d'apporter le nécessaire (les ustensiles, etc.).

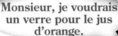

Monsieur, je voudrais un verre pour le jus d'orange.
Pardon. Voici un verre.

▶ pour le jus d'orange

1. pour l'eau minérale *(mineral water)*
2. pour le thé
3. pour la soupe
4. pour les frites
5. pour le steak
6. pour le gâteau *(cake)*

INCLUSION

Multisensory To reinforce table setting vocabulary, have students draw and make cutouts of the objects (or use props). Ask them to label with phonetic transcriptions. Then, have them work in pairs, pretending they are having a meal, asking for various objects (**–Donne-moi l'assiette, s'il vous plaît. –Voici l'assiette. –Merci.**).

1 COMMUNICATION expressing opinions about food

Answers will vary.

1. Mon repas préféré est (le petit déjeuner).
2. Je préfère déjeuner (chez mes copains).
3. En général, la nourriture de la cantine de l'école est (bonne).
4. Je préfère dîner (chez ma grand-mère).
5. Je préfère la nourriture (française).
6. Quand je dois aider avec le dîner, je préfère (préparer la salade).

2 COMMUNICATION answering personal questions

Answers will vary.

1. Le lundi, je prends mon petit déjeuner à (sept heures et demie). Le dimanche, je prends mon petit déjeuner à (neuf heures et demie).
2. En général, je dîne à (sept heures).
3. Pendant la semaine, je déjeune (à la cantine de l'école). Le samedi, je déjeune (chez des copains). Le dimanche, je déjeune (chez mes grands-parents).
4. Hier, j'ai déjeuné (à la cantine de l'école, avec mes copains Paul et Anne).
5. Ce soir, je vais dîner (à la maison, avec mes parents et ma soeur).
6. Oui, je vais souvent au restaurant. (Non, je ne vais pas souvent au restaurant.) Je vais au restaurant (le dimanche, avec mes parents). (Je vais au restaurant pour mon anniversaire, avec mes grands-parents.) Mon restaurant préféré est (un restaurant français, Chez Nous).
7. (Oui, j'ai déjeuné dans un restaurant français. (Le mois dernier, avec mes parents) (Non, je n'ai jamais déjeuné dans un restaurant français.)
   - (Oui, j'ai déjeuné dans un restaurant mexicain. (Samedi dernier, avec mes amis) (Non, je n'ai jamais déjeuné dans un restaurant mexicain.)
   - (Oui, j'ai déjeuné dans un restaurant italien. (Vendredi dernier, avec mes copains) (Non, je n'ai jamais déjeuné dans un restaurant italien.)
   - (Oui, j'ai déjeuné dans un restaurant chinois. (Le mois dernier, avec mes cousins) (Non, je n'ai jamais déjeuné dans un restaurant chinois.)
   - (Oui, j'ai déjeuné dans un restaurant vietnamien. (La semaine dernière, avec ma copine) (Non, je n'ai jamais déjeuné dans un restaurant vietnamien.)
8. Oui, je mets la table chez moi. (Non, je ne mets pas la table chez moi.) (Ma mère) a mis la table pour le petit déjeuner. (Mon frère et moi) avons mis la table pour le dîner.

3 ROLE PLAY asking for missing utensils

–Monsieur, je voudrais ...
–Pardon. Voici ...

1. un verre pour l'eau minérale/un verre
2. une tasse (une cuillère) pour le thé/une tasse (une cuillère)
3. une cuillère pour la soupe/une cuillère
4. une fourchette pour les frites/une fourchette
5. un couteau (une fourchette) pour le steak/un couteau (une fourchette)
6. une fourchette pour le gâteau/une fourchette

SECTION B

Communicative function
Talking about food and beverages

Teaching Resource Options

PRINT 

Workbook PE, pp. 213–220
Unit 8 Resource Book
- Communipak, pp. 152–173
- Video Activities, pp. 25–26
- Videoscript, pp. 30–31
- Workbook TE, pp. 1–8

AUDIO & VISUAL 

Overhead Transparencies
46a, 46b *La nourriture et les boissons (a) (b)*

VIDEO PROGRAM

VIDÉO DVD

MODULE 25

25.2 Mini-scenes: Qu'est-ce que vous aimez manger? (26:11–27:09 min.)

25.3 Mini-scenes: Vous préférez les frites ou les spaghetti? (27:10–27:35 min.)

25.4 Mini scenes: Qu'est-ce que vous préférez? (27:36–28:26 min.)

Pronunciation

- **l'oeuf** /lœf/
- **les oeufs** /lezø/

Supplementary vocabulary

LE PETIT DÉJEUNER
les oeufs brouillés *scrambled eggs*
les oeufs sur le plat *fried eggs*
le beurre de cacahuète *peanut butter*

LA VIANDE
le rôti *roast*
l'agneau *lamb*
le boeuf *beef*
le porc *pork*
une côtelette *chop, cutlet*

LE POISSON
le saumon *salmon*
la morue *cod*
la perche *perch*

B VOCABULAIRE La nourriture et les boissons

How to express food preferences:

—Est-ce que tu aimes **le poisson** *(fish)*?
—Oui, j'aime le poisson mais je préfère **la viande** *(meat)*.
—Quelle viande est-ce que tu aimes?
—J'aime **le rosbif** *(roast beef)* et **le poulet** *(chicken)*.

TEACHING STRATEGY Foods and beverages

Use Transparencies 46a and 46b: *La nourriture et les boissons* to present the various foods and beverages. Since the partitive will not be introduced until Lesson 26, ask questions about students' likes and dislikes using the definite article.

X, est-ce que tu préfères le poulet ou le jambon?
Y, est-ce que tu aimes les céréales?
Z, est-ce que W aime la confiture? etc.

aimer	*to like*	Alice **aime** le poulet.
préférer	*to prefer*	Philippe **préfère** le rosbif.
détester	*to hate*	Paul **déteste** le poisson.

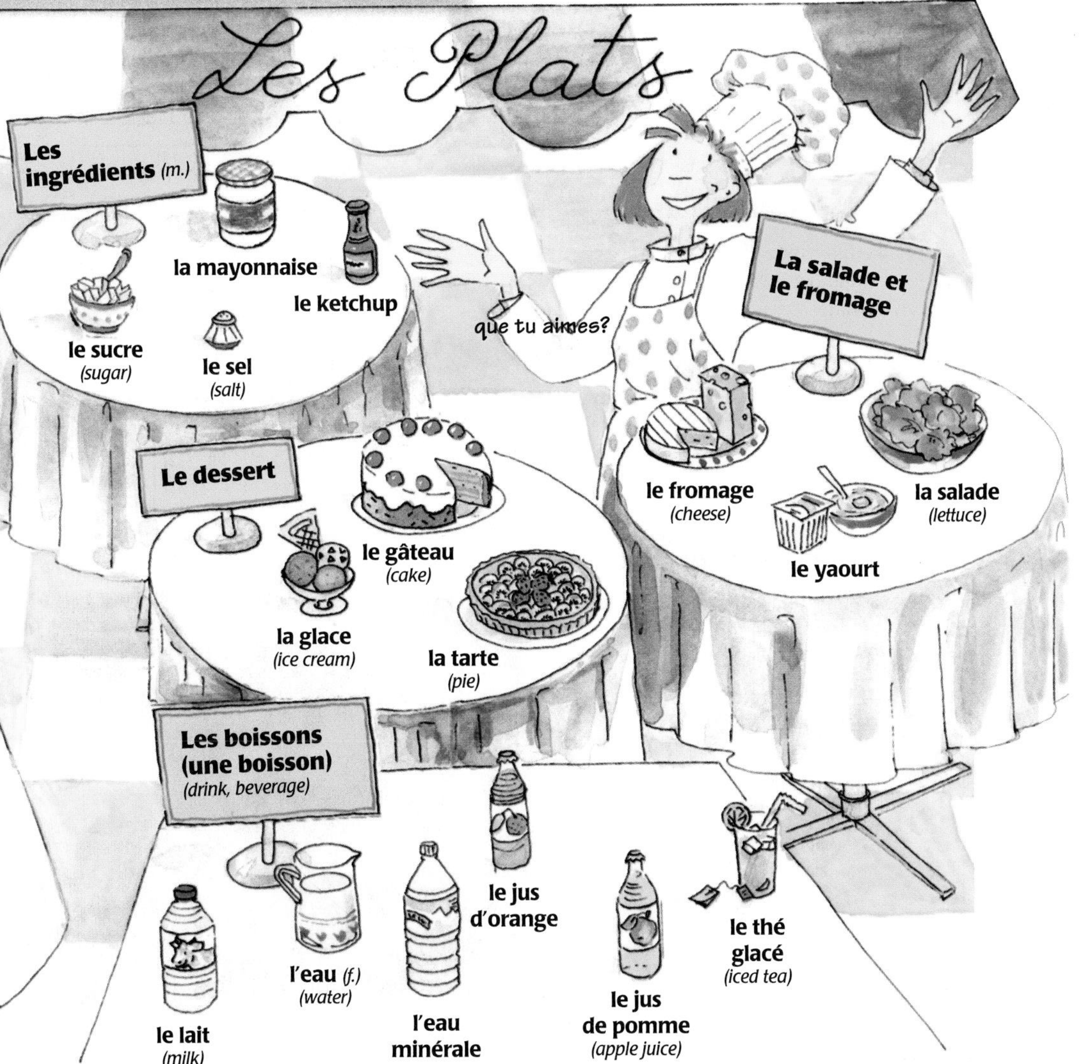

CRITICAL THINKING The French connection

Ask students: Which of the above food names have English cognates?

dessert < **dessert**
salad < **salade**
poultry < **poulet**
tart < **tarte**
juice < **jus**
sole < **sole**
soup < **soupe**

Which food names has English borrowed from French? [hors d'oeuvre, mayonnaise]

Which food names has French borrowed from English? **[le rosbif, le ketchup]**

Photo culture note

Le rayon de charcuterie
Many French supermarkets have a deli counter **(un rayon de charcuterie)** where one can buy salami **(du saucisson)**, sausages **(des saucisses)**, slices of ham **(des tranches de jambon)**, and all types of **pâtés.**

Looking ahead Vegetables and fruits are activated in the next section of this lesson.

Pronunciation

- **le yaourt** /jaurt/
- **la mayonnaise** /majɔnɛz/
- **le ketchup** /kɛtʃœp/

Supplementary vocabulary

LES INGRÉDIENTS
le poivre *pepper*
l'huile *oil*
le vinaigre *vinegar*
la moutarde *mustard*
la sauce tomate
la margarine

At your discretion, you may want to introduce some common adult beverages:
le vin *wine*
la bière *beer*
le cidre *cider*

Cultural note Soft drinks are usually ordered by brand name. All are masculine.

Language note

In Quebec:
le yogourt /yogurt/ *yogurt*
un breuvage *beverage*
la crème glacée *ice cream*

Teaching note The packages of many products that are sold throughout North America are printed in both French and English. Ask students to look for such products in a grocery store and to make a list of what they find. If possible, they could bring some of the products to class.

Teaching Resource Options

PRINT 

Workbook PE, pp. 213–220
Unit 8 Resource Book
Communipak, pp. 152–173
Workbook TE, pp. 1–8

4 COMMUNICATION expressing food preferences

Answers will vary.

1. (J'aime [beaucoup]) le poulet. (Je n'aime pas/Je déteste le poulet.)
2. (J'aime [beaucoup]) les frites. (Je n'aime pas/Je déteste les frites.)
3. (J'aime [beaucoup] l'eau minérale.) (Je n'aime pas/Je déteste l'eau minérale.)
4. (J'aime [beaucoup] les oeufs.) (Je n'aime pas/Je déteste les oeufs.)
5. (J'aime [beaucoup] le yaourt.) (Je n'aime pas/Je déteste le yaourt.)
6. (J'aime [beaucoup] les spaghetti.) (Je n'aime pas/Je déteste les spaghetti.)
7. (J'aime [beaucoup] le jambon.) (Je n'aime pas/Je déteste le jambon.)
8. (J'aime [beaucoup] le thon.) (Je n'aime pas/Je déteste le thon.)
9. (J'aime [beaucoup] le gâteau.) (Je n'aime pas/Je déteste le gâteau.)
10. (J'aime [beaucoup] le thé glacé.) (Je n'aime pas/Je déteste le thé glacé.)
11. (J'aime [beaucoup] le poisson.) (Je n'aime pas/Je déteste le poisson.)
12. (J'aime [beaucoup] le riz.) (Je n'aime pas/Je déteste le riz.)
13. (J'aime [beaucoup] les céréales.) (Je n'aime pas/Je déteste les céréales.)
14. (J'aime [beaucoup] le rosbif.) (Je n'aime pas/Je déteste le rosbif.)

Re-entry and review You may wish to review the use of the definite article in the general sense; see page 158.

5 ROLE PLAY asking a friend to pass you food

–S'il te plaît, André, passe-moi ...
–Tiens. Voilà ...
–Merci.

1. le sel
2. le sucre
3. le beurre
4. le lait
5. le fromage
6. la confiture
7. l'eau

6 ROLE PLAY choosing food

Answers will vary.
–Vous avez choisi?
–Oui, j'ai choisi ...

- la viande (le poisson)
- le poulet (le veau)
- la sole (le thon)
- les frites (les spaghetti)
- le fromage (la salade)
- le yaourt (la glace)
- la tarte (le gâteau)
- le thé (le café)

4 Vous aimez ça?

PARLER/ÉCRIRE Dites si oui ou non vous aimez les choses suivantes.

- J'aime ...
- J'aime beaucoup ...
- Je n'aime pas ...
- Je déteste ...

▶ **J'aime le fromage. (Je n'aime pas le fromage.)**

5 Dîner avec André

PARLER Vous dînez avec André, un ami canadien. Demandez à André de vous passer les choses suivantes.

▶ **—S'il te plaît, André, passe-moi le pain.**
—Tiens. Voilà le pain.
—Merci.

6 La Petite Marmite

PARLER Vous dînez au restaurant français La Petite Marmite. Le garçon demande ce que vous préférez. Répondez-lui.

▶ 

7 Dans le réfrigérateur ou sur la table?

PARLER Choisissez un produit et demandez à vos camarades où est le produit. Ils vont dire si le produit est dans le réfrigérateur ou sur la table.

▶ Où est la confiture?
Elle est sur la table.
RIZ

8 Les préférences

PARLER/ÉCRIRE Indiquez les préférences culinaires des personnes suivantes en complétant les phrases.

1. J'aime …
2. Je déteste …
3. Ma mère aime …
4. Mon petit frère (ma petite soeur) déteste …
5. Mon copain aime …
6. Ma copine déteste …
7. Les enfants aiment …
8. En général, les Italiens aiment …
9. En général, les Japonais aiment …

9 Les courses *(Food shopping)*

ÉCRIRE Vous passez les vacances en France avec votre famille. Faites la liste des courses pour les repas suivants.

▶ un repas végétarien

1. un pique-nique à la campagne
2. un bon petit déjeuner
3. un repas d'anniversaire
4. le dîner de ce soir
5. le déjeuner de demain
6. un repas de régime *(diet)*

LISTE

▶ *Un repas végétarien:*
— oeufs
— salade
— fromage
— pain
— yaourt
— eau minérale

CLASSROOM MANAGEMENT Groups

Have groups of 3 or 4 students work together to compose a shopping list for one of the meals suggested in Act. 9.

Each recorder **(secrétaire)** then reads aloud the shopping list that the group has prepared. The rest of the class tries to guess the corresponding menu.

7 EXCHANGES asking where certain foods are

- –Où sont les oeufs?
  –Ils sont dans le réfrigérateur.
- –Où est le yaourt?
  –Il est dans le réfrigérateur.
- –Où est le beurre?
  –Il est dans le réfrigérateur.
- –Où est le lait?
  –Il est dans le réfrigérateur.
- –Où est le jambon?
  –Il est dans le réfrigérateur.
- –Où est la mayonnaise?
  –Elle est dans le réfrigérateur.
- –Où est le gâteau?
  –Il est dans le réfrigérateur.
- –Où est le poulet?
  –Il est sur la table.
- –Où est l'eau minérale?
  –Elle est est sur la table.
- –Où sont les céréales?
  –Elles sont sur la table.
- –Où est le sel?
  –Il est sur la table.
- –Où est le riz?
  –Il est sur la table.
- –Où est le pain?
  –Il est sur la table.
- –Où est le ketchup?
  –Il est sur la table.
- –Où est la confiture?
  –Elle est sur la table.

Language note In France, a refrigerator is often referred to as **un frigo** or **un frigidaire.**

8 COMMUNICATION expressing preferences

Answers will vary.
1. J'aime (la glace).
2. Je déteste (le saucisson).
3. Ma mère aime (le fromage).
4. Mon petit frère (ma petite soeur) déteste (le poisson).
5. Mon copain aime (le rosbif).
6. Ma copine déteste (la sole).
7. Les enfants aiment (les gâteaux).
8. En général, les Italiens aiment (les spaghetti).
9. En général, les Japonais aiment (le riz/le poisson).

9 COMMUNICATION writing shopping lists

Answers will vary.
1. Un pique-nique à la campagne: oeufs, pain, jambon, thon, rosbif, salade, saucisson, jus de pomme, eau minérale
2. Un bon petit déjeuner: céréales, lait, jambon, oeufs, pain, fromage, confiture, jus d'orange, thé
3. Un repas d'anniversaire: gâteau, glace, jus de pomme, thé glacé, pain, jambon, fromage, moutarde, thon, rosbif
4. Le dîner de ce soir: soupe, sole, salade, spaghetti, fromage, jus de pomme, tarte
5. Le déjeuner de demain: salade, yaourt, poulet, frites, fromage, glace
6. Un repas de régime: soupe, salade, yaourt, poulet, jus d'orange, eau minérale

SECTION C

Communicative function
Talking about fruits and vegetables

Teaching Resource Options

PRINT  

Workbook PE, pp. 213–220
Unit 8 Resource Book
Communipak, pp. 152–173
Video Activities, pp. 27–29
Videoscript, p. 31
Workbook TE, pp. 1–8

AUDIO & VISUAL

Overhead Transparencies
47 *Les fruits et les légumes*
48 *Au marché*

VIDEO PROGRAM

VIDÉO DVD

MODULE 25

25.5 Dialogue: Au marché (28:27–30:03 min.)

25.6 Vignette culturelle: Les courses (30:04–32:00 min.)

Pronunciation There is no liaison (or elision) before **haricot: des haricots (le haricot)**

10 COMMUNICATION indicating food preferences

Answers will vary.
1. Je préfère une pamplemousse (une banane).
2. Je préfère une pomme (une poire).
3. Je préfère des petits pois (des haricots verts).
4. Je préfère des pommes de terre (des carottes).
5. Je préfère une salade de tomates (une salade de concombres).
6. Je préfère une tarte aux poires (une tarte aux cerises).
7. Je préfère une glace à la fraise (une glace à la vanille).

11 EXCHANGES describing food purchases

—Qu'est-ce que tu as acheté au marché?
—J'ai acheté ...
1. des bananes et des poires
2. des carottes et des pommes de terre
3. des petits pois et des pamplemousses
4. des oranges et des pommes
5. des fraises et des cerises
6. des haricots verts et des carottes

C VOCABULAIRE Les fruits et les légumes *(Fruits and vegetables)*

▶ ***How to shop for food:***

À la maison

—Où vas-tu?
—Je vais au **marché.**
Je vais **faire les courses** *(to do the food shopping).*
—Qu'est-ce que tu vas acheter?
—Je vais acheter des **tomates** et des **oranges.**

Au marché

—Pardon, madame. Combien coûtent les **pommes?**
—Elles coûtent un euro cinquante le kilo.
—Donnez-moi deux **kilos de** pommes, s'il vous plaît.
—Voilà. Ça fait trois euros.

10 Qu'est-ce que vous préférez?

PARLER/ÉCRIRE Indiquez vos préférences.

▶ pour le petit déjeuner: (un oeuf ou des céréales?) **Je préfère des céréales.**

1. pour le petit déjeuner: (un pamplemousse ou une banane?)
2. après le déjeuner: (une pomme ou une poire?)
3. avec le poulet: (des haricots verts ou des petits pois?)
4. avec le steak: (des pommes de terre ou des carottes?)
5. comme *(as)* salade: (une salade de tomates ou une salade de concombres *(cucumbers)*?)
6. pour le dessert: (une tarte aux cerises ou une tarte aux poires?)
7. comme glace: (une glace à la vanille ou une glace à la fraise?)

11  Les achats

PARLER Vos copains reviennent du marché. Demandez ce qu'ils ont acheté.

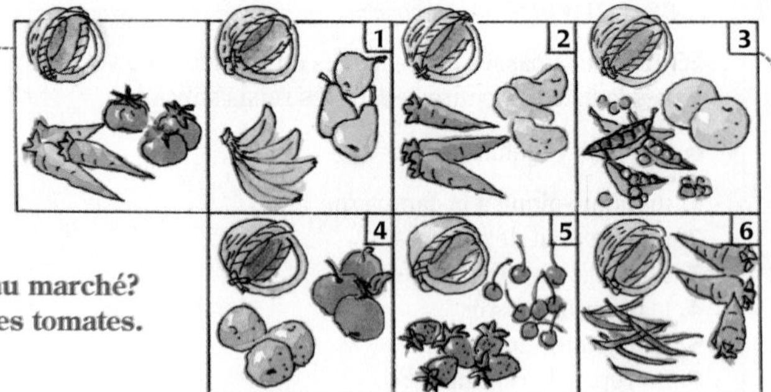

▶ **—Qu'est-ce que tu as acheté au marché?**
—J'ai acheté des carottes et des tomates.

COMPREHENSION Fruits and vegetables

PROPS: Plastic fruits and vegetables

Place the items on a desk ("market stand"). Have students "buy" and distribute them.
X, viens au marché et achète une pomme.
Maintenant, donne la pomme à Y.

Frequently ask who has what.
Qui a la pomme? [Y] Qui a l'orange? [Z]

Optional: If the fruits and vegetables are light in weight and if the class is well behaved, manipulate the props as follows:
Y, donne-moi la pomme, s'il te plaît.
Attention, je vais lancer la pomme à X.

[Toss the apple to X.]
Qui a l'orange? X? Bien, lance l'orange à Y.

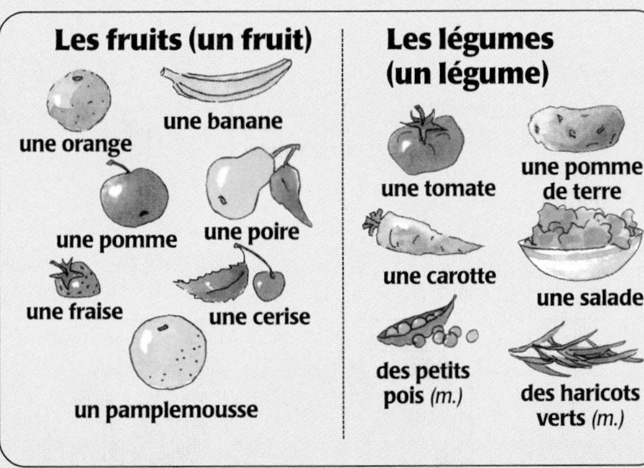

NOTE culturelle

Le marché

In France, as in the United States, most people do their food shopping at the supermarket **(le supermarché).** However, to have fresher fruits and vegetables, many people still go to the local open-air market **(le marché)** where farmers come to sell their produce.

LES QUANTITÉS

une livre (de) *pound*
un kilo (de) *kilo (2.2 pounds)*
une douzaine (de) *dozen*

Donnez-moi | **une livre** de tomates. **un kilo de** pommes. **une douzaine d'**oeufs.

12 Au marché

PARLER Vous êtes au marché. Demandez au vendeur combien coûtent certaines choses. Dites aussi quelle quantité vous voulez acheter.

INCLUSION

Alphabetic/phonetic Model the pronunciation of fruit and vegetable vocabulary. Pay special attention to the "**h aspiré**" of **haricots verts** (no liaison). Write the vocabulary on the board and ask students to pronounce the words as a group. Then have students pair off and practice. Have them put the list in their notebooks.

Supplementary vocabulary

Les fruits
un ananas /anana/ or /ananas/
un citron
un melon
le raisin *grapes*
une cerise
une pastèque *watermelon*
une pêche

Les légumes
un champignon *mushroom*
un chou-fleur *cauliflower*
un concombre
des épinards (m.) *spinach*
un oignon *onion*
un poivron *pepper*
une aubergine *eggplant*
une laitue
une salade

Cultural notes

- In general, farmers come to sell their produce on a given day of the week **(le jour du marché).** These open-air markets exist in large cities as well as in small villages.
- French people often buy food in speciality shops, such as:
  la boulangerie *(bakery)*
  la pâtisserie *(pastry shop)*
  la boucherie *(butcher shop)*
  la charcuterie *(delicatessen)*
  la crémerie *(dairy shop)*
  l'épicerie *(grocery store)*
- In the metric system, a pound **(une livre)** equals 500 grams or 1.1 U.S. pounds.

12 ROLE PLAY Purchasing food at the market

Teaching note The cues for this activity are written on the ends of the "boxes" at the bottom of the illustration.

–Pardon, monsieur. Combien coûtent les ...
–... coûtent ...
–Alors, donnez-moi ..., s'il vous plaît.
–Voici. Ça fait ...

- oeufs/trois euros la douzaine/une douzaine d'oeufs/trois euros
- fraises/trois euros la livre/une livre de fraises/trois euros
- oranges/deux euros le kilo/trois kilos d'oranges/six euros
- haricots verts/deux euros cinquante le kilo/deux kilos d'haricots verts/cinq euros
- petits pois/deux euros vingt-cinq la livre/une livre de petits pois/deux euros vingt-cinq
- pommes/un euro cinquante le kilo/trois kilos de pommes/quatre euros cinquante
- poires/un euro cinquante le kilo/un kilo de poires/un euro cinquante
- cerises/trois euros la livre/une livre de cerises/trois euros

À votre tour!

OBJECTIFS

Now you can ...
- talk about what you like to eat and drink
- prepare a shopping list

1 Écoutez bien!

ÉCOUTER Pauline et Thomas ont fait les courses dans deux supermarchés différents. Écoutez bien les phrases. Si vous entendez le nom d'un produit acheté par Pauline, marquez A. Si vous entendez le nom d'un produit acheté par Thomas, marquez B.

	1	2	3	4	5	6
A: Pauline						
B: Thomas						

A. Pauline

B. Thomas

2 Conversation dirigée

PARLER Avec un(e) camarade, composez un dialogue basé sur les instructions suivantes. C'est samedi aujourd'hui. Ce matin Marc et Juliette ont fait des achats en ville. Il est midi et demi maintenant.

Marc		Juliette
asks Juliette if she is hungry	→ ←	says she is very hungry
asks her if she wants to have lunch	→ ←	answers yes
asks if she likes Italian cooking **(la cuisine italienne)**	→ ←	says that she prefers French cooking
asks her if she likes meat	→ ←	says she does, but that she also likes vegetables
suggests they go to La Campagne	→	accepts

À VOTRE TOUR

Main Topic
- Recapitulation and review

Teaching Resource Options

PRINT  

Workbook PE, pp. 213–220
Unit 8 Resource Book
Audioscript, p. 32
Communipak, pp. 152–173
Family Involvement, pp. 22–23
Workbook TE, pp. 1–8

Assessment
Lesson 25 Quiz, pp. 36–37
Portfolio Assessment, Unit 1 URB pp. 155–164
Audioscript for Quiz 25, p. 35
Answer Keys, pp. 218–221

AUDIO & VISUAL 

Audio Program
CD 4 Tracks 21, 22, 23
CD 16 Track 9

TECHNOLOGY 

Test Generator CD-ROM/McDougal Littell Assessment System

1 Listening Comprehension

1. A 2. B 3. A 4. B 5. B
6. A 7. A 8. B 9. A 10. B
11. A 12. B 13. B 14. B 15. B
16. B 17. B 18. A 19. A 20. A
21. A 22. A

2 Guided Oral Expression

M: Est-ce que tu as faim, Juliette?
J: Oui, j'ai très faim.
M: Est-ce que tu veux déjeuner?
J: Oui, je veux déjeuner, merci.
M: (Est-ce que) tu aimes la cuisine italienne?
J: Je préfère la cuisine française.
M: (Est-ce que) tu aimes la viande?
J: Oui, j'aime la viande, mais j'aime aussi les légumes.
M: Est-ce que tu veux aller (déjeuner) à La Campagne?
J: Oui, d'accord.

À VOTRE TOUR

Depending on your goals and objectives, you may or may not wish to assign all of the activities in the **À votre tour** section.

PAIR/GROUP PRACTICE

Act. 2 and 3 lend themselves to pair practice. They can also be done in trios, with two students performing and the third acting as monitor.

Créa-dialogue

PARLER Vous êtes à Deauville avec un(e) ami(e). Essayez de découvrir *(try to discover)* ce que votre ami(e) aime manger. Proposez à votre ami(e) de déjeuner dans le restaurant correspondant à ses préférences.

▶ **—Tu aimes la viande?**
—Non, je n'aime pas la viande. ▶
—Tu aimes les légumes?
—Non, je n'aime pas les légumes.
—Tu aimes le poisson?
—Oui, j'aime beaucoup le poisson.
—On déjeune à La Marine?
—D'accord.

1 

2

3 

4 

5 

6 

7 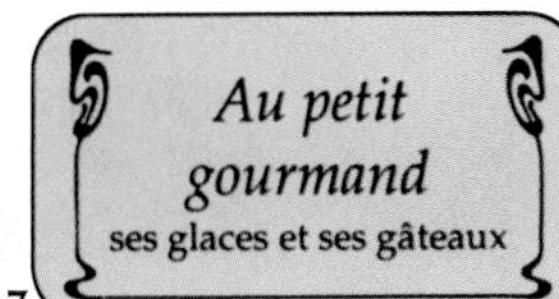

Comparaisons

ÉCRIRE Avec un(e) camarade de classe, préparez le menu de trois repas américains et trois repas français typiques. Comparez ces menus.

Repas américains	Repas français
• **petit déjeuner** ____________	• **petit déjeuner** ____________
• **déjeuner** ____________	• **déjeuner** ____________
• **dîner** ____________	• **dîner** ____________

CONNEXIONS

La France exporte beaucoup de produits alimentaires *(food products)*, en particulier des fromages et des eaux minérales.

Allez dans votre supermarché local et visitez le rayon *(department)* de ces produits.

- Est-ce qu'il y a des fromages français? Quelles sortes de fromage?
- Est-ce qu'il y a des eaux minérales françaises? Quelles marques *(brands)*?

PORTFOLIO ASSESSMENT

You will probably select only one speaking activity and one writing activity to go into the students' portfolios for Unit 8.

In this lesson, Act. 3 can be used as an oral portfolio recording. Activity 4 is an excellent topic for a written portfolio piece.

3 COMPREHENSION

Answers will vary.
–Tu aimes ...?
–Non, je n'aime pas ...
–Tu aimes ...?
–Je ...
–Tu aimes ...?
–Oui, j'aime ...
–Alors, on déjeune ... ?
–D'accord!

1. le poisson/beaucoup le poisson/la viande/J'aime un peu la viande/les spaghetti/beaucoup les spaghetti/Chez Rigoletto
2. le poisson/le poisson/la viande/n'aime pas la viande/les desserts/beaucoup les desserts/au Palais des Glaces
3. la glace/la glace/la salade/n'aime pas la salade/le fromage/beaucoup le fromage/Ah, enfin! Alors, on déjeune À la Normandie
4. les spaghetti/beaucoup les spaghetti/la viande/déteste la viande/la salade/j'adore la salade/À la Campagne
5. le poisson/le poisson/le poulet/n'aime pas le poulet/le jambon/beaucoup le jambon/à L'Auvergnat?
6. le fromage/le fromage/le poisson/déteste le poisson/la viande/j'adore la viande/Chez Obélix
7. la viande/la viande/les légumes/déteste les légumes/les desserts/j'adore les desserts/Au petit gourmand

Culture note

La Marine
"La Marine" is a seafood restaurant located in the harbor section of **Deauville,** an Atlantic Ocean resort on the coast of Normandy.

Teaching strategy As a preparation for Act. 3, have students name the types of foods that might be on the menu in each of the restaurants. This list of foods could function as a point of departure for the dialogues.

4 WRITTEN SELF-EXPRESSION

Answers will vary.

Repas américains
- petit déjeuner
  oeufs
  pain grillé
  saucisson
  café
  jus d'orange
- déjeuner
  sandwich
  pomme
  lait
- dîner
  poulet
  pomme de terre
  carottes

Repas français
- petit déjeuner
  pain
  confiture
  café / chocolat chaud
- déjeuner
  hors-d'oeuvre
  viande
  légumes
  salade verte
  fromage
  dessert
- dîner
  soupe
  omelette / viande / poisson
  salade
  dessert léger (yaourt ou fruit)

Leçon 26

Main Topic Talking about food

Teaching Resource Options

PRINT  

Workbook PE, pp. 221–228
Activités pour tous PE, pp. 135–137
Block Scheduling Copymasters, pp. 201–208
Unit 8 Resource Book
- *Activités pour tous* TE, pp. 47–49
- Audioscript, pp. 71, 72–74
- Communipak, pp. 152–173
- Lesson Plans, pp. 50–51
- Block Scheduling Lesson Plans, pp. 52–54
- Absent Student Copymasters, pp. 55–60
- Video Activities, pp. 63–68
- Videoscript, pp. 69–70
- Workbook TE, pp. 39–46

AUDIO & VISUAL 

Audio Program
CD 4 Tracks 24, 25
CD 12 Tracks 8–17

TECHNOLOGY 

Online Workbook

VIDEO PROGRAM

VIDÉO DVD 

MODULE 26
Les courses

TOTAL TIME: 6:48 min.
DVD Disk 2
Videotape 4 (COUNTER: 32:15 min.)

26.1 Dialogue: Le pique-nique (32:24–34:42 min.)

26.2 Mini-scenes: Listening – Voici du pain (34:43–36:06 min.)

26.3 Mini-scenes: Listening – Je prends du beurre? (36:07–36:32 min.)

26.4 Mini-scenes: Speaking – Tu veux du pain? (36:33–37:58 min.)

26.5 Vignette culturelle: Le petit déjeuner (37:59–39:03 min.)

Comprehension practice Play the entire module through as an introduction to the lesson.

LEÇON 26

À la cantine

AUDIO

Il est midi et demi. Suzanne va à la cantine. Elle rencontre Jean-Marc.

Suzanne: Est-ce que tu veux déjeuner avec moi?
Jean-Marc: Ça dépend. Qu'est-ce qu'il y a aujourd'hui?
Suzanne: Il y a du poisson!
Jean-Marc: Du poisson?
Suzanne: Oui, du poisson.
Jean-Marc: Quelle horreur! Bon, aujourd'hui, je ne veux pas déjeuner. — *How disgusting!*
Suzanne: Il y a aussi du gâteau.
Jean-Marc: Du gâteau! Hm …
Suzanne: Et de la glace!
Jean-Marc: Une minute … je vais prendre un plateau. — *to take / tray*

Compréhension

1. À quelle heure est-ce que Suzanne va déjeuner?
2. Qui est-ce qu'elle rencontre?
3. Est-ce que Jean-Marc aime le poisson?
4. Qu'est-ce qu'il aime?
5. Est-ce qu'il va déjeuner avec Suzanne? Pourquoi?

SETTING THE SCENE

Ask questions about the school cafeteria.
Est-ce que vous déjeunez à la cantine de l'école?
Si oui, levez la main.
Est-ce que vous aimez la nourriture?
Qu'est-ce que vous aimez particulièrement?
Qu'est-ce que vous détestez?

Then have students read the opening text and the *Note culturelle* to find out what foods and beverages French students are served at school and what their reactions are.

Et toi?

1. En général, où est-ce que tu déjeunes?
2. À quelle heure est-ce que tu déjeunes?
3. En général, est-ce que tu aimes la nourriture de la cantine?
4. Qu'est-ce que tu fais quand tu n'aimes pas la nourriture de la cantine?

NOTE culturelle

À la cantine

Où est-ce que tu déjeunes pendant la semaine? Quand on habite près de l'école, on peut° rentrer à la maison. Quand on habite loin, on déjeune à la cantine. À midi, beaucoup de jeunes Français déjeunent à la cantine de leur école.

À la cantine, chacun° prend° un plateau et va chercher° sa nourriture. Cette nourriture est généralement bonne, abondante° et variée. Le menu change chaque° jour de la semaine. Un repas typique inclut° les plats suivants:

- **un hors-d'oeuvre**
  salade de concombres,
  salade de pommes de terre,
  carottes râpées,° jambon ...
- **un plat principal° chaud**
  poulet, steak, côtelette de porc°
- **une garniture°**
  spaghetti, frites, petits pois,
  purée de pommes de terre°
- **une salade verte**
- **du fromage**
- **un dessert**
  glace ou fruit
- **une boisson**
  eau minérale, limonade, jus de fruit

Où est-ce que tu préférerais° déjeuner? À ton école ou dans une école française?

peut *can* **chacun** *each one* **prend** *takes* **chercher** *to get* **abondante** *plentiful* **chaque** *each* **inclut** *includes* **râpées** *grated* **principal** *main* **côtelette de porc** *pork chop* **garniture** *side dish* **purée de pommes de terre** *mashed potatoes* **est-ce que tu préférerais** *would you prefer*

USING THE VIDEO

In the opening segment of Video Module 26, a father and son are sent to the supermarket to get food for a picnic. Students will see what a French supermarket looks like.

In the middle segments, people talk about various foods, often in contexts where they naturally use the partitive article.

The *Vignette culturelle* is filmed at Nathalie Aubin's house. The family members each explain what they usually have for breakfast.

Compréhension

Answers

1. Suzanne va déjeuner à midi et demi.
2. Elle rencontre Jean-Marc.
3. Non, Jean-Marc n'aime pas le poisson.
4. Il aime le gâteau et la glace.
5. Oui, il va déjeuner avec Suzanne parce qu'il aime les desserts au menu (le gâteau et la glace).

Et toi?

Answers will vary.

1. En général, je déjeune (à la cantine de mon école).
2. Je déjeune à (midi).
3. En général, je (n'aime pas la nourriture de la cantine).
4. Quand je n'aime pas la nourriture de la cantine, (j'apporte un sandwich de chez moi).

Cultural notes

- **une salade de concombres** thinly sliced cucumbers served with an oil and vinegar dressing
- **une salade verte** lettuce and vinaigrette, served after the main course
- **du fromage** cheese is served as a separate course, after the salad

Photo cultural note

À la cantine

In school cafeterias in France, there are two ways of serving meals:

- family style: the cafeteria personnel brings the dishes to the table and students serve themselves. There is no choice of menu.
- cafeteria style (as shown on the bottom photo): students take a tray **(un plateau)** and select what they want to eat.

SECTION A

Communicative function
Talking about what one wants

Teaching Resource Options

PRINT

Workbook PE, pp. 221–228
Unit 8 Resource Book
- Audioscript, p. 71
- Communipak, pp. 152–173
- Workbook TE, pp. 39–46

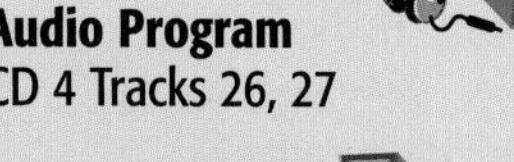

AUDIO & VISUAL

Audio Program
CD 4 Tracks 26, 27

TECHNOLOGY

Power Presentations

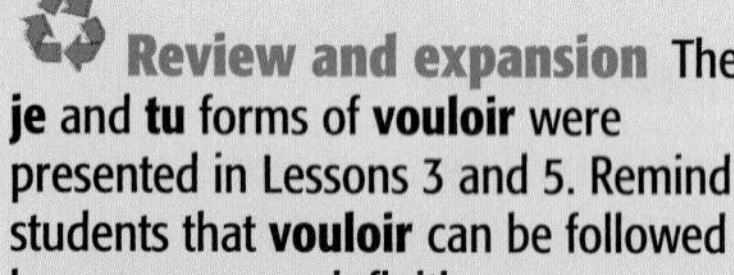

Review and expansion The **je** and **tu** forms of **vouloir** were presented in Lessons 3 and 5. Remind students that **vouloir** can be followed by a noun or an infinitive.

Looking ahead The verbs **pouvoir** and **devoir** are presented in Lesson 27.

Supplementary vocabulary

vouloir dire *to mean*
Qu'est-ce que vous voulez dire? *What do you mean?*
Qu'est-ce que ce mot veut dire? *What does that word mean?*

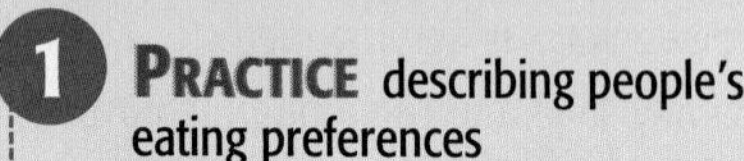

1 PRACTICE describing people's eating preferences

1. Nous voulons ...
2. Tu veux ...
3. Vous voulez ...
4. Je veux ...
5. Ils veulent ...
6. Isabelle veut ...

2 COMPREHENSION indicating what people want to do

Answers will vary.
1. Non, Éric ne veut pas jouer au foot.
2. Oui, mes copains veulent aller à la plage.
3. Non, vous ne voulez pas déjeuner à la cantine.
4. Oui, je veux dîner. (Non, je ne veux pas dîner.)
5. Oui, tu veux regarder la télé. (Non, tu ne veux pas regarder la télé.)
6. Non, nous ne voulons pas travailler.

3 COMMUNICATION describing what one wants and does not want to do

Answers will vary.
1. (aller à la plage/nettoyer ma chambre)
2. (jouer au tennis/faire de jogging)
3. (écouter la radio/regarder la télé)
4. (avoir des amis/être seul[e])

A Le verbe *vouloir*

Note the forms of the irregular verb **vouloir** *(to want)*.

INFINITIVE	vouloir		
PRESENT	Je **veux** aller au café.		Nous **voulons** une glace.
	Tu **veux** déjeuner.		Vous **voulez** des spaghetti.
	Il/Elle/On **veut** dîner.		Ils/Elles **veulent** des frites.
PASSÉ COMPOSÉ	J'**ai voulu** dîner chez Maxim's.		

➔ When making a request, French speakers often use **je voudrais** *(I would like)*, which is more polite than **je veux** *(I want)*.

Je voudrais un café. — ***I would like*** *a cup of coffee.*
Je voudrais dîner. — ***I would like*** *to have dinner.*

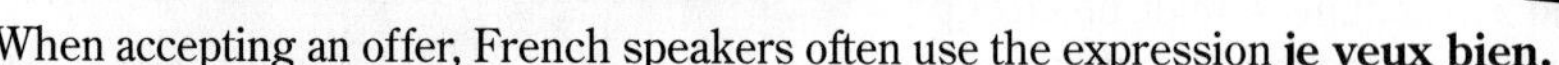

➔ When accepting an offer, French speakers often use the expression **je veux bien.**

— Est-ce que tu veux déjeuner avec moi? *Do you want to have lunch with me?*
— Oui, **je veux bien.** *Yes, **I do.** (Yes, **I want to.**)*

1 Vive la différence!

PARLER/ÉCRIRE Nous sommes samedi. Des amis vont en ville. Pour le déjeuner, chacun veut faire des choses différentes.

▶ Cécile/aller dans un café
Cécile veut aller dans un café.

1. nous/manger des frites
2. toi/manger une pizza
3. vous/aller dans un restaurant italien
4. moi/aller dans un restaurant chinois
5. Patrick et Alain/déjeuner à midi
6. Isabelle/déjeuner à une heure

2 Oui ou non?

PARLER/ÉCRIRE Dites si oui ou non les personnes entre parenthèses veulent faire les choses indiquées.

▶ Il est midi. (nous/déjeuner?)
Oui, nous voulons déjeuner.

▶ C'est samedi. (les élèves/étudier?)
Non, les élèves ne veulent pas étudier.

1. Il fait froid. (Éric/jouer au foot?)
2. Il fait beau. (mes copains/aller à la plage?)
3. La nourriture est mauvaise. (vous/déjeuner à la cantine?)
4. Il y a des spaghetti. (moi/dîner?)
5. Il y a une excellente comédie. (toi/regarder la télé?)
6. C'est dimanche. (nous/travailler)

3 Expression personnelle

PARLER/ÉCRIRE Complétez les phrases suivantes avec une expression personnelle.

1. Ce week-end, je voudrais ...
   Je ne veux pas ...
2. Cet été, je voudrais ...
   Je ne veux pas ...
3. Après l'école, je voudrais ...
   Je ne veux pas ...
4. Dans la vie *(life)*, je voudrais ...
   Je ne veux pas ...

INCLUSION

Cumulative Have students look at and repeat the forms of **vouloir** three times. Then, tell them to write the forms three times. Write the forms on the board and call on a student ask a question using **vouloir** (**Tu veux un café, Jean?**). The student will answer. Then ask another student to tell you what the answer was (**–Est-ce que Jean veut un café? –Oui, il veut un café**).

B Le verbe *prendre* 

Note the forms of the irregular verb **prendre** *(to take)*.

INFINITIVE	prendre	
PRESENT	Je **prends** une pizza. Tu **prends** un sandwich. Il/Elle/On **prend** une salade.	Nous **prenons** le train. Vous **prenez** l'avion. Ils/Elles **prennent** des photos.
PASSÉ COMPOSÉ	J'**ai pris** un steak.	

→ The singular forms follow the pattern of regular **-re** verbs. The plural forms are irregular.

VOCABULAIRE Verbes comme *prendre*

prendre	*to take*	Nous **prenons** le métro.
	to have (food)	Est-ce que tu **prends** un café?
apprendre	*to learn*	Nous **apprenons** le français.
apprendre à + *infinitive*	*to learn how to*	Sophie **apprend à** jouer de la guitare.
comprendre	*to understand*	Est-ce que vous **comprenez** l'espagnol?

4 Qu'est-ce qu'ils prennent?

PARLER/ÉCRIRE Dites ce que les personnes suivantes prennent. Pour cela, choisissez une expression logique de la liste.

un bateau, un taxi, le bus, des photos, une salade, une limonade, un steak-frites

▶ Philippe a faim. **Il prend un steak-frites.**

1. J'ai très soif.
2. Vous n'avez pas très faim.
3. Hélène a un nouvel appareil-photo.
4. Tu vas à l'aéroport.
5. Nous allons à l'école.
6. Les touristes vont à la Statue de la Liberté.

5 Questions personnelles **PARLER/ÉCRIRE**

1. À quelle heure est-ce que tu prends le petit déjeuner le lundi? Et le dimanche?
2. Est-ce que tu prends le bus pour aller à l'école? Et tes copains?
3. Est-ce que tu prends des photos? Avec quel appareil?
4. Quand tu fais un grand voyage, est-ce que tu prends l'autocar? le train? l'avion?
5. Est-ce que tu apprends le français? l'italien? l'espagnol? Et ton copain?
6. Est-ce que tu apprends à jouer du piano? à jouer de la guitare? à faire du snowboard? à faire de la planche à voile?
7. Où as-tu appris à nager? À quel âge?
8. Est-ce que tu comprends quand le prof parle français? Et les autres *(other)* élèves?
9. À ton avis, est-ce que les adultes comprennent les jeunes? Est-ce que les jeunes comprennent les adultes?

COMPREHENSION Choosing foods

PROPS: Pictures of various foods: salad, hamburger, sandwich, ice cream, etc.

Hold up the foods and pick one.
J'ai faim. Qu'est-ce que je vais prendre?
Bien, je prends un hamburger.

Have individual students select foods.
X, viens ici. Qu'est-ce que tu prends?

[X picks ice cream] **Ah, X prend une glace.**

Similarly present plural forms of prendre.
Y et Z, qu'est-ce que vous prenez? [salad] **Ah bon, ils prennent une salade.**
Tiens, Y et Z prennent une salade.
Moi aussi, je vais prendre une salade.
Nous trois, nous prenons une salade.

SECTION B

Communicative function
Describing daily activities

Pronunciation You may point out that **prendre** has three stems, all pronounced differently:
prend- /prɑ̃/
je prends, tu prends, il prend
pren- /prən/
nous prenons, vous prenez
prenn- /prɛn/
ils prennent
Note: The "d" is silent in all the singular forms, and is dropped in the plural forms.

Language note Remind students that *to take* a person somewhere is **amener.** (Also: *to take* a test is **passer** un examen.)

4 COMPREHENSION describing what people are doing

1. Je prends une limonade.
2. Vous prenez une salade.
3. Elle prend des photos.
4. Tu prends un taxi.
5. Nous prenons le bus.
6. Ils prennent un bateau.

5 COMMUNICATION answering personal questions

Answers will vary.
1. Le lundi, je prends le petit déjeuner à (sept heures et demie). Le dimanche, je prends le petit déjeuner à (neuf heures et demie).
2. Oui, je prends le bus pour aller à l'école. (Non, je ne prends pas le bus pour aller à l'école.) Oui, mes copains prennent le bus pour aller à l'école. (Non, ils ne prennent pas le bus pour aller à l'école.)
3. Oui, je prends des photos avec l'appareil-photo (de mon frère). (Non, je ne prends pas de photos.)
4. Quand je fais un grand voyage, je prends (le train / l'avion / l'autocar).
5. Oui, j'apprends le français (l'espagnol / l'italien). (Non, je n'apprends pas [l'italien / l'espagnol].) Oui, mon copain apprend le français (l'espagnol / l'italien). (Non, mon copain n'apprend pas le français [l'espagnol / l'italien].)
6. Oui, j'apprends à jouer (du piano / de la guitare). (Non, je n'apprends pas à [jouer du piano / de la guitare].) Oui, j'apprends à faire (du snowboard / de la planche à voile). (Non, je n'apprends pas à faire [du snowboard / de la planche à voile].)
7. J'ai appris à nager (à la plage à l'âge de 5 ans).
8. Oui, je comprends quand le prof parle français. (Non, je ne comprends pas quand le prof parle français.) Oui, les autres élèves comprennent quand le prof parle français. (Non, ils ne comprennent pas quand le prof parle français.)
9. À mon avis, les adultes ne comprennent pas les jeunes. (À mon avis, les adultes comprennent les jeunes.) Non, les jeunes ne comprennent pas les adultes. (Oui, les jeunes comprennent les adultes.)

SECTION C

Communicative function
Discussing quantities

Teaching Resource Options

PRINT 

Workbook PE, pp. 221–228
Unit 8 Resource Book
- Communipak, pp. 152–173
- Video Activities, pp. 63–65
- Videoscript, 69–70
- Workbook TE, 39–46

AUDIO & VISUAL 

Overhead Transparencies
49 *Le partitif (du, de la)*

TECHNOLOGY 

Power Presentations

VIDEO PROGRAM

VIDÉO DVD

MODULE 26

26.1 Dialogue: Le pique-nique (32:24–34:42 min.)

26.2 Mini-scenes: – Voici du pain (34:43–36:06 min.)

26.3 Mini-scenes: – Je prends du beurre? (36:07–36:32 min.)

26.4 Mini-scenes: – Tu veux du pain? (36:33–37:58 min.)

Looking ahead This section introduces the forms and basic uses of the partitive article. This concept is further developed in Book Two.

C L'article partitif: *du, de la*

LEARNING ABOUT LANGUAGE

The pictures on the left represent *whole* items: a whole chicken, a whole cake, a whole head of lettuce, a whole fish. The nouns are introduced by INDEFINITE ARTICLES: **un, une.**

The pictures on the right represent a *part* or *some quantity* of these items: a serving of chicken, a slice of cake, some leaves of lettuce, a piece of fish. The nouns are introduced by PARTITIVE ARTICLES: **du, de la.**

Voici ... | Voilà ...

un poulet  **du poulet** 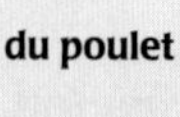 

un gâteau **du gâteau** 

une salade **de la salade** 

une sole **de la sole** 

FORMS

The PARTITIVE ARTICLE is used to refer to A CERTAIN QUANTITY or A CERTAIN AMOUNT OF SOMETHING and corresponds to the English *some* or *any*. It has the following forms:

MASCULINE	**du**	*some*	**du** fromage, **du** pain
FEMININE	**de la**	*some*	**de la** salade, **de la** limonade

→ Note that **du** and **de la** become **de l'** before a vowel sound.

de l'eau minérale

TEACHING STRATEGY

PROP: Transparency 49: *Le partitif (du, de la)*

Use Transparency 49 to present the differences between the indefinite article and the partitive article.

Help students notice the difference between *a whole item* **(un/une)** and *a part or amount of something* **(du/de la).**

Voici un poulet. [pointing to transparency]
Voici du poulet. [pointing to transparency]

Then have various students come up and point to the corresponding items as you mention them randomly in sentences. Meanwhile, students at their desks point to the illustrations in their books. Begin slowly, and then speak more rapidly.

Voici un poulet.
Je voudrais du gâteau.

USES

Note how the partitive article is used in the sentences below.

Philippe mange **du** fromage.	*Philippe is eating (some) cheese.*
Nous prenons **de la** salade.	*We are having (some) salad.*
—Est-ce que tu veux **du** lait?	*Do you want (any, some) milk?*
—Non, mais je voudrais **de l'**eau.	*No, but I would like some water.*

➔ While the words *some* or *any* are often omitted in English, the articles **du** and **de la** must be used in French.

➔ Partitive articles may also be used with nouns designating things other than foods and beverages. For example:

Tu as **de l'argent?**	*Do you have (any) money?*

Partitive articles are often, but not always, used after the following expressions and verbs.

voici	**Voici du** pain.	*Here is (some) bread.*
voilà	**Voilà de la** mayonnaise.	*Here is (some) mayonnaise.*
il y a	Est-ce qu'**il y a de la** salade?	*Is there (any) salad?*
acheter	Nous **achetons du** fromage.	*We are buying (some) cheese.*
avoir	Est-ce que tu **as de la** limonade?	*Do you have (any) lemon soda?*
manger	Marc **mange du** rosbif.	*Marc is eating (some) roast beef.*
prendre	Est-ce que vous **prenez du** café?	*Are you having (any) coffee?*
vouloir	Est-ce que tu **veux de la** glace?	*Do you want (any) ice cream?*

Voici un gâteau.

Voici du gâteau.

6 Le menu

PARLER/ÉCRIRE Vous avez préparé un dîner pour le Club Français. Dites à un(e) camarade ce qu'il y a au menu.

▶ la viande **Il y a de la viande.**

1. le rosbif
2. le poulet
3. la salade
4. le fromage
5. la glace
6. la tarte
7. l'eau minérale
8. le jus d'orange

If students ask

The plural partitive article **des** is used with plural "mass nouns":

des spaghetti
des épinards *(spinach)*
des oeufs brouillés *(scrambled eggs)*
des carottes râpées *(grated carrots)*

Language notes

- Depending on the context, these expressions (**voici, voilà, il y a,** etc.) can also be followed by definite and indefinite articles:
  Voici **le gâteau.**
  Voici **un gâteau.**
  Voici **du gâteau.**

  Since these distinctions sometimes tend to be confusing, they are not developed until Book Two. At this point, the important thing is that students become familiar with the partitive and its uses.
- The partitive article is also used with **boire,** which is taught in section E of this lesson.

6 PRACTICE describing a menu

1. Il y a du rosbif.
2. Il y a du poulet.
3. Il y a de la salade.
4. Il y a du fromage.
5. Il y a de la glace.
6. Il y a de la tarte.
7. Il y a de l'eau minérale.
8. Il y a du jus d'orange.

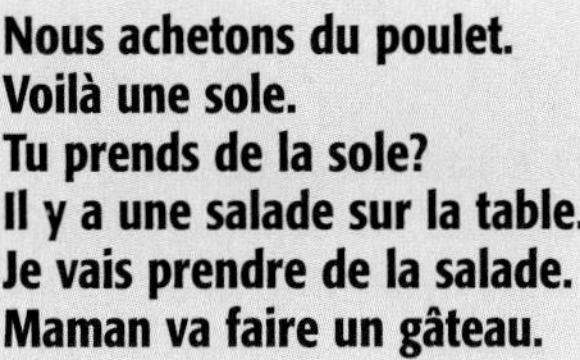

Nous achetons du poulet.
Voilà une sole.
Tu prends de la sole?
Il y a une salade sur la table.
Je vais prendre de la salade.
Maman va faire un gâteau.

INCLUSION

Metacognitive, Gifted & Talented Write a chart for the forms of the partitive article on the board. Ask students to copy it in their notebooks. To reinforce the idea of a whole versus a part, show them pictures and ask them to repeat the appropriate article after you (**un poulet, du poulet**). Then, show them the pictures and ask them to say the articles. Ask them to describe the difference in purpose between the indefinite and the partitive articles.

Teaching Resource Options

PRINT

Workbook PE, pp. 221–228
Unit 8 Resource Book
    Communipak, pp. 152–173
    Workbook TE, pp. 39–46

TECHNOLOGY 

Power Presentations

7 EXCHANGES offering food and beverages

Answers will vary.

1. –Tu veux de la soupe ou de la salade?
   –Je voudrais de la soupe (de la salade).
2. –Tu veux du poisson ou de la viande?
   –Je voudrais du poisson (de la viande).
3. –Tu veux du rosbif ou du poulet?
   –Je voudrais du rosbif (du poulet).
4. –Tu veux du ketchup ou de la mayonnaise?
   –Je voudrais du ketchup (de la mayonnaise).
5. –Tu veux du fromage ou du yaourt?
   –Je voudrais du fromage (du yaourt).
6. –Tu veux du beurre ou de la margarine?
   –Je voudrais du beurre (de la margarine).
7. –Tu veux du gâteau ou de la tarte?
   –Je voudrais du gâteau (de la tarte).
8. –Tu veux du jus d'orange ou du jus de pomme?
   –Je voudrais du jus d'orange (du jus de pomme).

8 COMPREHENSION/PRACTICE using the partitive

Answers will vary.

1. du sucre (du lait, de la crème)
2. du sucre (du lait, de la crème)
3. du sel
4. de la mayonnaise (de la moutarde, du jambon)
5. du ketchup
6. de la moutarde (du ketchup)
7. du lait (du sucre)
8. du beurre (de la confiture)

Variation (dialogue format)

– Qu'est-ce que tu mets sur le pain?
– Je mets du beurre (de la confiture).

9 DESCRIPTION describing food purchases

1. Il a acheté de la confiture.
2. Il a acheté de l'eau minérale.
3. Il a acheté du beurre.
4. Il a acheté du café.
5. Il a acheté du fromage.
6. Il a acheté du poisson.
7. Il a acheté du lait.

7  *Au choix*

PARLER Vous déjeunez avec votre famille. Offrez aux membres de votre famille le choix entre les choses suivantes. Ils vont indiquer leurs préférences.

▶ le jus ou l'eau minérale?

Tu veux du jus ou de l'eau minérale?
Je voudrais de l'eau minérale.

1. la soupe ou la salade?
2. le poisson ou la viande?
3. le rosbif ou le poulet?
4. le ketchup ou la mayonnaise?
5. le fromage ou le yaourt?
6. le beurre ou la margarine?
7. le gâteau ou la tarte?
8. le jus d'orange ou le jus de pomme?

8 *Qu'est-ce qu'on met?*

PARLER/ÉCRIRE Dites quels produits de la liste on met dans ou sur les choses suivantes.

▶ **On met du beurre (de la confiture) sur le pain.**

1. On met … dans le café.
2. On met … dans le thé.
3. On met … dans la soupe.
4. On met … dans un sandwich.
5. On met … sur un hamburger.
6. On met … sur un hot dog.
7. On met … dans les céréales.
8. On met … sur un toast.

le fromage
le jambon
le beurre
la confiture
le ketchup
la mayonnaise
le sel
la crème
le sucre
la moutarde (*mustard*)
le lait

9 *Les courses*

PARLER/ÉCRIRE M. Simon a fait les courses. Dites ce qu'il a acheté.

▶ **Il a acheté de la viande.**

10 *Le Cochon d'Or*

LIRE/PARLER Émilie est allée au restaurant. Voici l'addition. Dites ce qu'elle a pris.

▶ **Émilie a pris de la salade de tomates.**

RESTAURANT
Le Cochon d'Or

▶ salade de tomates	3€
poulet	4€
salade	3€
fromage	3€50
glace	2€50
eau minérale	
	19 €

TEACHING PROJECT Les repas

PROPS: One large paper plate per student

Have students illustrate their paper plates with drawings or pictures of at least five food items for one meal of the day. (They should write their names on the back of the plate.) Then in small groups, students take turns telling what they have for the particular meal.

As a follow-up activity, collect the plates and redistribute them so that each student has another student's plate. Then have them write what this person is having. For example:

Pierre prend un hot dog, des frites avec du ketchup et de la salade. Comme dessert, il prend du gâteau et de la glace.

11  *Au café*

PARLER Au café, une cliente commande *(orders)* les choses suivantes. Le serveur apporte ces choses.

S'il vous plaît, monsieur, je voudrais de la limonade.
Voici de la limonade, mademoiselle.

12 *Menus*

PARLER/ÉCRIRE Préparez des menus pour les personnes suivantes. Dites ce que vous allez acheter pour chaque personne.

▶ une personne qui aime manger
Je vais acheter du rosbif, du fromage, de la glace ...

1. une personne malade *(sick)*
2. un(e) athlète
3. un petit enfant
4. un végétarien (une végétarienne)
5. une personne qui veut maigrir
6. un invité *(guest)* japonais
7. une invitée française
8. un invité américain

D L'article partitif dans les phrases négatives

Note the forms of the partitive articles in the negative sentences below.

AFFIRMATIVE	NEGATIVE	
Tu manges **du jambon?**	Non, je **ne** mange **pas de jambon.**	*No, I don't eat ham.*
Tu veux **de la salade?**	Non, merci, je **ne** veux **pas de salade.**	*Thanks, I don't want any salad.*
Il y a **de l'eau minérale?**	Non, il **n'y** a **pas d'eau minérale.**	*No, there is no mineral water.*

In negative sentences, the PARTITIVE ARTICLE follows the pattern:

du, de la (de l')	→	**ne ... pas de (d')**
Marc prend **du** café.		Éric **ne** prend **pas de** café.
Sophie prend **de la** limonade.		Alain **ne** prend **pas de** limonade.
Anne prend **de l'**eau.		Nicole **ne** prend **pas d'**eau.

GAME Menus

Prepare slips of paper numbered 1 to 8. Divide the class into eight groups, and distribute the numbered slips.

Each group prepares a menu for the corresponding guest in Act. 12 (e.g., group 2 sets up a menu for **un(e) athlète**).

The recorder **(secrétaire)** of each group then reads the menu:

Nous allons servir du rosbif, ...

The rest of the class tries to identify the guest.

10 DESCRIPTION describing food purchases

1. Émilie a pris du poulet.
2. Émilie a pris de la salade.
3. Émilie a pris du fromage.
4. Émilie a pris de la glace.
5. Émilie a pris de l'eau minérale.

Expansion Have students say how much was paid for each item.
Jacqueline a pris une salade de tomates. Elle a payé 3 euros.

Variation Have students choose only three items at the **Cochon d'Or** and say how much they paid.

J'ai pris du fromage, de la salade et de l'eau minérale. J'ai payé 8 euros 50.

11 ROLE PLAY asking for things in a restaurant

–S'il vous plaît, monsieur, je voudrais ...
–Voici ..., mademoiselle.

1. du pain/du pain
2. du sucre/du sucre
3. du beurre/du beurre
4. du yaourt/du yaourt
5. du thé/du thé
6. de l'eau/de l'eau
7. du jus d'orange/du jus d'orange
8. du sel/du sel
9. de la glace/de la glace

12 COMPREHENSION preparing special menus

1. Je vais acheter (du riz, du pain, de la soupe).
2. Je vais acheter (de la viande, des légumes, du poisson, des fruits).
3. Je vais acheter (de la soupe, des hamburgers, de la salade, de la glace).
4. Je vais acheter (de la salade, des oeufs, du pain, de la confiture, du yaourt, des fruits).
5. Je vais acheter (du yaourt, de la salade, de la soupe).
6. Je vais acheter (des spaghetti, du riz, du poisson, de la viande).
7. Je vais acheter (du pain, de la sole, de la salade, des légumes, du fromage, un dessert).
8. Je vais acheter (du pain, de la salade, du rosbif, des carottes, des pommes de terre, un gâteau).

SECTION D

Communicative function
Making negative statements

Language note The same pattern occurs with **ne... jamais.** Je **ne** prends **jamais de** sucre avec le café.

Teaching Resource Options

PRINT 

Workbook PE, pp. 221–228
Unit 8 Resource Book
Audioscript, p. 71
Communipak, pp. 152–173
Workbook TE, pp. 39–46

AUDIO & VISUAL 

Audio Program
CD 4 Track 28

TECHNOLOGY 

Power Presentations

13 ROLE PLAY explaining one doesn't have certain foods

–Est-ce que vous avez ...
–Je regrette, mademoiselle, mais nous n'avons pas de (d')...

1. du jambon/jambon
2. du melon/melon
3. du thon/thon
4. de la sole/sole
5. du veau/veau
6. du yaourt/yaourt
7. du jus de pamplemousse/jus de pamplemousse
8. de l'eau minérale/eau minérale
9. de la tarte aux pommes/tartes aux pommes
10. du gâteau au chocolat/gâteau au chocolat

14 PRACTICE negative sentences with the partitive

1. Non, il ne prend pas de mayonnaise.
2. Non, elle ne veut pas de gâteau.
3. Non, il ne mange pas de glace.
4. Non, elle ne prend pas de beurre.
5. Non, il ne veut pas de tarte.
6. Non, elle ne met pas de crème dans son café.

15 EXCHANGES talking about what one does and does not eat

–Est-ce que tu manges souvent ...
–Oui, je mange souvent ... (Non, je ne mange pas souvent de ...

1. de la confiture/de la confiture/confiture
2. du veau/du veau/veau
3. du pain français/du pain français/pain français
4. du fromage français/du fromage français/fromage français
5. de la tarte aux fraises/de la tarte aux fraises/tarte aux fraises
6. de la soupe/de la soupe/soupe
7. du rosbif/du rosbif/rosbif
8. du poulet/du poulet/poulet
9. du thon/du thon/thon
10. de la glace/de la glace/glace

Photo culture note

À la cantine In the cafeteria, French students eat directly from the tray. On the table you will note a pitcher of water **(un pichet).**

13  *Un mauvais restaurant*

PARLER Une cliente demande au serveur s'il y a certaines choses au menu. Le serveur répond négativement.

▶ le rosbif

1. le jambon
2. le melon
3. le thon
4. la sole
5. le veau
6. le yaourt
7. le jus de pamplemousse
8. l'eau minérale
9. la tarte aux pommes
10. le gâteau au chocolat

14  *Au régime* (On a diet)

PARLER Les personnes suivantes sont au régime parce qu'elles veulent maigrir. Répondez négativement aux questions suivantes.

▶ —Est-ce qu'Anne mange du pain?
—Non, elle ne mange pas de pain.

1. Est-ce que Marc prend de la mayonnaise?
2. Est-ce que Pauline veut du gâteau?
3. Est-ce que Jean-Pierre mange de la glace?
4. Est-ce qu'Alice prend du beurre?
5. Est-ce que Monsieur Ledodu veut de la tarte?
6. Est-ce que Mademoiselle Poix met de la crème dans son café?

15   *Conversation*

PARLER Demandez à vos camarades s'ils mangent souvent les choses suivantes.

▶ du poisson

1. de la confiture
2. du veau
3. du pain français
4. du fromage français
5. de la tarte aux fraises
6. de la soupe
7. du rosbif
8. du poulet
9. du thon
10. de la glace

16   *Dans le réfrigérateur*

PARLER Vous préparez le dîner. Demandez à un(e) camarade s'il y a les choses suivantes dans le réfrigérateur.

▶ le lait **—Est-ce qu'il y a du lait?**
—Non, il n'y a pas de lait.

1. le jus d'orange?
2. le pain?
3. la glace?
4. le beurre?
5. le jambon?
6. l'eau minérale?
7. le jus de pomme?
8. le fromage?
9. la mayonnaise?
10. le ketchup?

GAME Qu'est-ce qu'il y a?

PROPS: Vocabulary cards of food items

Divide the class in half–Team A and Team B. Place 5 cards backwards on the chalkledge so that students cannot see the pictures. Player A-1 guesses a food item:

Est-ce qu'il y a du pain?
[Oui, il y a du pain. (Non, ...)]

If A-1 guesses correctly, his/her team wins a point. The teacher replaces the appropriate card with another one and the student guesses again. If not, player B-1 gets a chance to guess, etc. The team with the most points at the end of the game wins.

Note: It is easier to remember the position of the cards if you alphabetize them as you place them on the chalkledge.

E Le verbe *boire*

Note the forms of the irregular verb **boire** *(to drink)*.

INFINITIVE	boire	
PRESENT	Je **bois** du lait. Tu **bois** de l'eau. Il/Elle/On **boit** du soda.	Nous **buvons** du café. Vous **buvez** du thé glacé. Ils/Elles **boivent** du jus d'orange.
PASSÉ COMPOSÉ	J'**ai bu** du jus de tomate.	

17 Les boissons

PARLER/ÉCRIRE Philippe et ses amis ont soif. Chacun *(Each person)* boit quelque chose de différent.

▶ **Philippe boit de l'eau.**

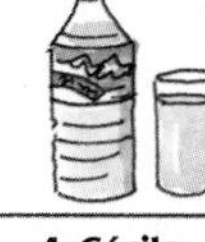

▶ Philippe	1. nous	2. toi	3. vous	4. Cécile	5. mes copains	6. moi

18 Expression personnelle

PARLER/ÉCRIRE Complétez les phrases suivantes avec la forme appropriée du verbe **boire** et une expression de votre choix. Attention: utilisez le passé composé dans les phrases 6 à 8.

1. Au petit déjeuner, je …
2. Au petit déjeuner, mes parents …
3. À la cantine de l'école, nous …
4. Quand il fait chaud, on …
5. Quand il fait froid, on …
6. Hier soir au dîner, j' …
7. Hier matin, au petit déjeuner, ma mère …
8. À la dernière boum, nous …

PRONONCIATION

Les lettres «ou» et «u»

ou = /u/ **u** = /y/

la poule

le pull

The letters "**ou**" always represent the sound /u/.
Répétez: /u/ **vous nous poulet soupe fourchette couteau douzaine**

The letter "**u**" always represents the sound /y/.
Répétez: /y/ **tu du une légume jus sucre bien sûr avenue musée**

Now distinguish between the two vowel sounds:
Répétez: /u/ – /y/ **poule** *(hen)* – **pull** **roue** *(wheel)* – **rue** **vous** – **vue** *(view)* **je joue** – **le jus**

Vous buvez du jus de pamplemousse. Je voudrais de la soupe, du poulet et du jus de raisin.

COMPREHENSION Drinking beverages

PROPS: Vocabulary cards of beverages
Hold up the beverages and pick one.
J'ai soif. Qu'est-ce que je vais boire? [gesture "drinking" milk]
Normalement je bois du lait.
Have individual students select beverages.
X, viens ici. Qu'est-ce que tu bois?
[X picks water] **Ah, X boit de l'eau.**

Similarly present plural forms of **boire.**
Y et Z, qu'est-ce que vous buvez? [coffee]
Tiens, Y et Z boivent du café.
Moi aussi, je vais boire du café.
Nous trois, nous buvons du café.

16 EXCHANGES describing which foods are available and which are not

1. –Est-ce qu'il y a du jus d'orange?
–Oui, il y a du jus d'orange.
2. –Est-ce qu'il y a du pain?
–Non, il n'y a pas de pain.
3. –Est-ce qu'il y a de la glace?
–Oui, il y a de la glace.
4. –Est-ce qu'il y a du beurre?
–Non, il n'y a pas de beurre.
5. –Est-ce qu'il y a du jambon?
–Oui, il y a du jambon.
6. –Est-ce qu'il y a de l'eau minérale?
–Non, il n'y a pas d'eau minérale.
7. –Est-ce qu'il y a du jus de pomme?
–Oui, il y a du jus de pomme.
8. –Est-ce qu'il y a du fromage?
–Non, il n'y a pas de fromage.
9. –Est-ce qu'il y a de la mayonnaise?
–Non, il n'y a pas de mayonnaise.
10. –Est-ce qu'il y a du ketchup?
–Non, il n'y a pas de ketchup.

Variation Ask students whether these items are in their refrigerators at home.
– Et chez toi, est-ce qu'il y a du lait dans le réfrigérateur?
– Oui, il y a du lait. (Non, il n'y a pas de lait.)

SECTION E

Communicative function
Talking about what one is drinking

17 PRACTICE describing what people are drinking

1. Nous buvons du jus de raisin.
2. Tu bois de la limonade.
3. Vous buvez du thé glacé.
4. Cécile boit de l'eau minérale.
5. Mes copains boivent du jus de pomme.
6. Je bois du jus d'orange.

Variation Have students give sentences in the negative.
Philippe ne boit pas d'eau.

18 COMMUNICATION describing beverage choices

Answers will vary.
1. Au petit déjeuner, je bois (du lait).
2. ... mes parents boivent (du thé).
3. ... nous buvons (de l'eau).
4. Quand il fait chaud, on boit (du thé glacé).
5. ... on boit (du chocolat chaud).
6. ... j'ai bu (du jus de pomme).
7. ... ma mère a bu (du café au lait).
8. ... nous avons bu (du jus de raisin).

PRONUNCIATION

Teaching strategy If your students still have trouble pronouncing /y/, be sure they pronounce the vowel as /i/.

Then have them repeat the word, rounding their lips as if to whistle.

For example, to pronounce **du,** first say **di.** Then repeat **di** with rounded lips. The resulting word will be quite close to **du.**

À VOTRE TOUR

Main Topic
- Recapitulation and review

Teaching Resource Options

PRINT 

Workbook PE, pp. 221–228
Unit 8 Resource Book
Audioscript, p. 72
Communipak, pp. 152–173
Family Involvement, pp. 61–62
Workbook TE, pp. 39–46

Assessment
Lesson 26 Quiz, pp. 76–77
Portfolio Assessment, Unit 1 URB pp. 155–164
Audioscript for Quiz 26, p. 75
Answer Keys, pp. 218–221

AUDIO & VISUAL 

Audio Program
CD 4 Tracks 29, 30
CD 16 Track 10

TECHNOLOGY

Test Generator CD-ROM/McDougal Littell Assessment System

VIDEO PROGRAM

VIDÉO DVD

MODULE 26

26.5 Vignette culturelle: Le petit déjeuner (37:59–39:03 min.)

1 COMPREHENSION

1. Tu dînes au restaurant ce soir?
   (d) Non, j'ai invité mon copain Fabien à dîner chez moi.
2. Tu as fait les courses?
   (a) Oui, je suis allée au supermarché ce matin.
3. Qu'est-ce que tu as acheté?
   (b) Du riz, des oeufs, de la salade et du fromage.
4. Tu n'as pas acheté de viande?
   (e) Mais non, tu sais bien que Fabien est végétarien.
5. C'est vrai. Et pour le dessert, tu as acheté de la glace?
   (c) Non, j'ai pris un gâteau au chocolat.

2 GUIDED ORAL EXPRESSION

Answers will vary.
- J'ai dîné à (sept heures).
- J'ai mangé (du poulet, des frites, et de la salade).
  J'ai aussi mangé (une pomme et de la glace).
- J'ai bu (du jus de pomme).

À votre tour!

OBJECTIFS

Now you can ...
- describe what you eat and drink at meals
- talk about food shopping

1 Allô!

PARLER Reconstituez la conversation entre Frédéric et Sandrine. Pour cela, faites correspondre les réponses de Sandrine avec les questions de Frédéric.

a. Oui, je suis allée au supermarch
ce matin.
b. Du riz, des oeufs, de la salade e
du fromage.
c. Non, j'ai pris un gâteau au choc
d. Non, j'ai invité mon copain Fabi
à dîner chez moi.
e. Mais non, tu sais *(know)* bien q
Fabien est végétarien.

2 Dis-moi ...

I will tell you about my breakfast this morning.

- J'ai pris le petit déjeuner à sept heures.
- J'ai mangé du pain avec du beurre et de la confiture.
- J'ai bu du jus d'orange.

PARLER *Now choose one of the meals you had yesterday and tell me ...*

- *at what time you had that meal*
- *what you ate*
- *what you drank*

3 Créa-dialogue

PARLER Avec vos camarades, décrivez où vous êtes allé(e)s et ce que vous avez fait aux endroits suivants.

▶ **au supermarché**
acheter

À VOTRE TOUR

Depending on your goals and objectives, you may or may not wish to assign all of the activities in the **À votre tour** section.

PAIR/GROUP PRACTICE

Act. 1 and 2 lend themselves to pair practice. Act. 3 can be done in trios, with two students performing and the third acting as monitor.

4 Composition: Un bon repas

Imaginez que vous êtes allé(e) *(went)* dans un bon restaurant pour une occasion spéciale. Décrivez le repas. Voici quelques suggestions:

- Dans quel restaurant êtes-vous allé(e)?
- Avec qui et pour quelle occasion?
- Qu'est-ce que vous avez mangé comme *(as)* hors d'oeuvre?
- Comme plat principal?
- Comme dessert?
- Qu'est-ce que vous avez bu?
- Qu'est-ce que les autres *(other)* personnes ont mangé et bu?
- Est-ce que tout le monde *(everyone)* a aimé le repas?

STRATEGY Writing

Writing about food When you are writing in French about what you ate and drank at a recent meal, you have to decide whether you had a whole item (for example, **une pizza**) or whether you had a portion of that item (for example, **de la pizza**).

Before you begin your composition, make a list of the foods and beverages that you and your friends had. Then, next to each item, write the appropriate article (**un**/**une** or **du**/**de la**/**de l'**). Use this list as you write your composition.

un steak
du poulet

COMMENT DIT-ON ...?

How to show your appreciation for good food:

Hm ... C'est délicieux!

C'est exquis!

C'est fameux!

1. à la cantine manger	2. au restaurant manger	3. au marché acheter	4. à la boum boire

5. à la cuisine prendre	6. au café boire	7. dans un restaurant chinois ??
	? ?	? ?

LESSON REVIEW
CLASSZONE.COM

3 GUIDED ORAL EXPRESSION

Answers will vary.

1. –Où es-tu allé(e)?
 –Je suis allé(e) à la cantine.
 –Qu'est-ce que tu as mangé?
 –J'ai mangé du rosbif, de la salade et de la glace.
2. –Où es-tu allé(e)?
 –Je suis allé(e) au restaurant.
 –Qu'est-ce que tu as mangé?
 –J'ai mangé du poulet, du fromage et du yaourt.
3. –Où es-tu allé(e)?
 –Je suis allé(e) au marché.
 –Qu'est-ce que tu as acheté?
 –J'ai acheté du fromage, du lait et du thon.
4. –Où es-tu allé(e)?
 –Je suis allé(e) à la boum.
 –Qu'est-ce que tu as bu?
 –J'ai bu de l'eau minérale et du jus de raisin.
5. –Où es-tu allé(e)?
 –Je suis allé(e) à la cuisine.
 –Qu'est-ce que tu as pris?
 –J'ai pris de la glace et du jus d'orange.
6. –Où es-tu allé(e)?
 –Je suis allé(e) au café.
 –Qu'est-ce que tu as bu?
 –J'ai bu (du chocolat chaud).
7. –Où es-tu allé(e)?
 –Je suis allé(e) dans un restaurant chinois.
 –Qu'est-ce que tu as (mangé)?
 –J'ai (mangé du poulet et du riz).

4 WRITTEN SELF-EXPRESSION

Answers will vary.
Pour mon anniversaire, ma famille et moi, nous sommes allés au restaurant Le Bon Repas. Comme hors d'oeuvre, j'ai mangé de la salade et ma soeur a mangé de la soupe. Comme plat principal, ma soeur et moi, nous avons pris du poulet, mais nos parents ont pris du rosbif. Comme dessert, tout le monde a mangé du gâteau au chocolat avec de la glace. J'ai bu du lait, ma soeur a bu de l'eau minérale, et mes parents ont bu du café au lait. Tout le monde a aimé le repas!

Teaching strategy You may suggest supplementary vocabulary, such as:

la dinde *(turkey)*
le maïs */mais/* *(corn)*
le homard *(lobster)*
le rôti *(roast)*

PORTFOLIO ASSESSMENT

You will probably select only one speaking activity and one writing activity to go into the students' portfolios for Unit 8.

In this lesson, Act. 2 and 3 can be adapted as oral portfolio recordings.

Act. 4 is an excellent topic for a written portfolio piece.

Leçon 27

Main Topic Ordering food in a restaurant

Teaching Resource Options

PRINT

Workbook PE, pp. 229–236
Activités pour tous PE, pp. 139–141
Block Scheduling Copymasters, pp. 209–216
Unit 8 Resource Book
- *Activités pour tous* TE, pp. 87–89
- Audioscript, pp. 108, 109–111
- Communipak, pp. 152–173
- Lesson Plans, pp. 90–91
- Block Scheduling Lesson Plans, pp. 92–94
- Absent Student Copymasters, pp. 95–97
- Video Activities, pp. 100–105
- Videoscript, pp. 106–107
- Workbook TE, pp. 79–86

AUDIO & VISUAL

Audio Program
CD 4 Tracks 31, 32
CD 12 Tracks 18–21

TECHNOLOGY

Online Workbook

VIDEO PROGRAM

MODULE 27
Un client difficile

TOTAL TIME: 7:34 min.
DVD Disk 2
Videotape 4 (COUNTER: 39:16 min.)

27.1 Dialogue: Un client difficile (39:41–41:57 min.)

27.2 Mini-scenes: Listening – Apportez-moi du poulet (41:58–43:21 min.)

27.3 Mini-scenes: Speaking – Qu'est-ce que tu veux? (43:22–44:13 min.)

27.4 Vignette culturelle: La recette des crêpes (44:14–46:50 min.)

Comprehension practice Play the entire module through as an introduction to the lesson.

Language note Tell the students the meaning of **un ronchon** *(grouch).*

Un client difficile

VIDÉO DVD AUDIO

M. Ronchon a beaucoup d'appétit … mais pas beaucoup de patience. En fait, M. Ronchon est rarement de bonne humeur. Et quand il est de mauvaise humeur, c'est un client difficile. Aujourd'hui, par exemple, au restaurant …

En fait: As a matter of fact / in fact; de bonne humeur: a good mood; par exemple: for instance

—Garçon! — *Waiter!*
—J'arrive! — *I'm coming!*
—Qu'est-ce que vous avez comme hors-d'oeuvre? — *comme: as, for*
—Nous avons du jambon et du saucisson.
—Apportez-moi tout ça … avec du pain et du beurre! — *all of that*
—Bien, monsieur.

—Et comme boisson, qu'est-ce que je vous apporte?
—Donnez-moi de l'eau minérale … Dépêchez-vous! J'ai soif! — *Hurry up!*

—Apportez-moi du poulet et des frites … Vite! J'ai très faim! — *Fast!*
—Je vous apporte ça tout de suite. — *right away*

—Et apportez-moi aussi du fromage, de la glace, de la tarte aux pommes et de la tarte aux abricots … Mais, qu'est-ce que vous attendez? — *apricots*
—Tout de suite, monsieur, tout de suite.

—Mais qu'est-ce que vous m'apportez?
—Je vous apporte l'addition! — *check*

SETTING THE SCENE

This comic scene is much more effective if presented by video. If this is not possible, play the corresponding audio segment which has been taken from the video soundtrack.

MAKING CRÊPES

The *Vignette culturelle,* Part 4 of Video Module 27, shows how to make **crêpes.** If students ask, a **crêpe** recipe can be found at the end of Entracte 8, pp. 416–417.

Compréhension

1. En général, est-ce que M. Ronchon est de bonne humeur ou de mauvaise humeur?
2. Qu'est-ce qu'il va prendre comme hors-d'oeuvre?
3. Qu'est-ce qu'il va prendre comme plat principal *(main course)*?
4. Qu'est-ce qu'il va boire?
5. Qu'est-ce qu'il va manger comme dessert?
6. Qu'est-ce que le garçon apporte après le dessert?
7. Quelle est la réaction de M. Ronchon? Est-ce qu'il est de bonne humeur ou de mauvaise humeur?

Et toi?

1. En général, est-ce que tu es de bonne humeur?
2. Et aujourd'hui, est-ce que tu es de bonne ou de mauvaise humeur?
3. En général, est-ce que tu as beaucoup d'appétit?
4. Est-ce que tu es une personne patiente?
5. Quand tu vas au restaurant avec un copain (une copine), qui paie l'addition?

NOTE culturelle

Les restaurants français et la cuisine française

Les Français aiment manger chez eux, mais ils aiment aussi aller au restaurant. Pour les gens pressés,° il y a la restauration rapide° et les pizzerias.

Pour les gens qui veulent faire un bon repas, il y a toutes° sortes de restaurants spécialisés: auberges,° restaurants régionaux, restaurants de poisson, … Il y a aussi les «grands restaurants» où la cuisine est extraordinaire … et très chère!

La cuisine française a une réputation internationale. Pour beaucoup de personnes, c'est la meilleure° cuisine du monde.°

Les Américains ont emprunté° un grand nombre de mots° au vocabulaire de la cuisine française. Est-ce que tu connais les mots suivants: **soupe, sauce, mayonnaise, omelette, filet mignon, tarte, purée, soufflé?** Est-ce que tu aimes **les croissants? les crêpes? la mousse au chocolat?**

pressés *in a hurry* **restauration rapide** *fast food* **toutes** *all* **auberges** *country inns* **meilleure** *best* **du monde** *in the world* **ont emprunté** *have borrowed* **mots** *words*

INTERNET ACTIVITY

Go to the sites of restaurants in France and read their menus. Which menu/restaurant do you find tempting?

TEACHING SUGGESTION

Knowledge of French can come in very useful for many careers. Poll your students to see how many of them are interested in a career in the culinary arts. Mention the internationally acclaimed school **Le Cordon Bleu**, headquartered in Paris. Here, techniques and methods of cooking, pastry and bread baking which have been systematized in France over the last half-century are taught to those interested in a career in the culinary arts. Ask students to brainstorm other careers in which knowing French would be beneficial.

Compréhension

Answers.

1. Il est de mauvaise humeur.
2. Comme hors d'oeuvre, il va prendre du jambon, du saucisson, du pain et du beurre.
3. Comme plat principal, il va prendre du poulet et des frites.
4. Il va boire de l'eau minérale.
5. Comme dessert, il va manger du fromage, de la glace, de la tarte aux pommes et de la tarte aux abricots.
6. Après le dessert, le garçon apporte l'addition.
7. Il est de mauvaise humeur.

Et toi?

Answers will vary.

1. Oui, en général, je suis de bonne humeur. (Non, en général, je ne suis pas de bonne humeur.)
2. Aujourd'hui, je suis de bonne humeur (de mauvaise humeur).
3. Oui, en général, j'ai beaucoup d'appétit. (Non, en général, je n'ai pas beaucoup d'appétit.)
4. Oui, je suis une personne patiente. (Non, je ne suis pas une personne patiente.)
5. Quand je vais au restaurant avec un copain (une copine), je paie l'addition (ma copine/mon copain paie l'addition).

Note culturelle

Teaching strategy First, have the students pronounce the borrowed French words in boldface type as we do in English. Then have them try to pronounce the words "sounding French."

Photo culture note

La cuisine française

Most people who appreciate fine cooking consider French cuisine to be the best in the world. French chefs **(un chef)** like to create new dishes that will enhance their reputations. In France the top chefs enjoy the status of superstars.

SECTION A

Communicative function
Referring to oneself and to those one is addressing

Teaching Resource Options

PRINT 
Workbook PE, pp. 229–236
Unit 8 Resource Book
Audioscript, p. 108
Communipak, pp. 152–173
Workbook TE, pp. 79–86

AUDIO & VISUAL 
Audio Program
CD 4 Track 33

TECHNOLOGY 
Power Presentations

1 EXCHANGES asking friends to do things for you

1. –Tu me téléphones demain?
   –D'accord, je te téléphone demain.
2. –Tu m'attends après la classe?
   –D'accord, je t'attends après la classe.
3. –Tu m'invites à ta fête (soirée)?
   –D'accord, je t'invite à ma fête (soirée).
4. –Tu m'invites à dîner?
   –D'accord, je t'invite à dîner.
5. –Tu me rends visite ce week-end?
   –D'accord, je te rends visite ce week-end.
6. –Tu me rends visite cet été?
   –D'accord, je te rends visite cet été.
7. –Tu m'achètes une glace?
   –D'accord, je t'achète une glace.
8. –Tu m'apportes un sandwich?
   –D'accord, je t'apporte un sandwich.
9. –Tu me vends ton baladeur?
   –D'accord, je te vends mon baladeur.
10. –Tu m'écoutes?
    –D'accord, je t'écoute.

Variation (response in the negative)
Non, je ne te téléphone pas.

Variation (in the plural)
– Tu nous téléphones?
– Oui, je vous téléphone.

Realia note
Le cahier de texte
French students are often required to buy special notebooks of the type pictured here **(un cahier de texte)** in which they write down their daily homework assignments.

A Les pronoms compléments *me, te, nous, vous*

In the sentences below, the pronouns in heavy print are called OBJECT PRONOUNS. Note the form and the position of these pronouns in the sentences below.

Anne **me** parle.	Elle **m'**invite.	*Anne talks* ***to me.***	*She invites* ***me.***
Mes amis **te** parlent.	Ils **t'**invitent.	*My friends talk* ***to you.***	*They invite* ***you.***
Tu **nous** parles.	Tu **nous** invites.	*You talk* ***to us.***	*You invite* ***us.***
Je **vous** parle.	Je **vous** invite.	*I am talking* ***to you.***	*I invite* ***you.***

FORMS

The OBJECT PRONOUNS that correspond to the subject pronouns **je, tu, nous, vous** are:

me ↓ **m'** (+ VOWEL SOUND)	*me, to me*	**nous**	*us, to us*
te ↓ **t'** (+ VOWEL SOUND)	*you, to you*	**vous**	*you, to you*

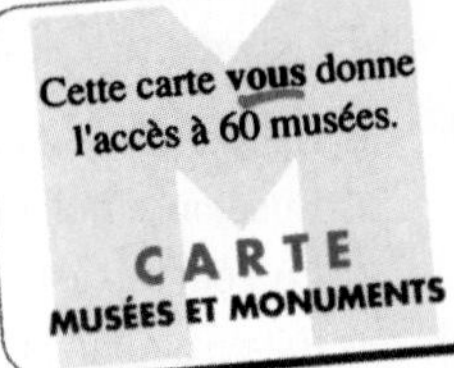

Cette carte vous donne l'accès à 60 musées.
CARTE
MUSÉES ET MONUMENTS

POSITION

In French, object pronouns usually come before the verb, according to the following patterns:

AFFIRMATIVE			NEGATIVE				
SUBJECT + OBJECT PRONOUN + VERB ...			SUBJECT + **ne** + OBJECT PRONOUN + VERB + **pas** ...				
Paul	**nous**	invite.	Éric	**ne**	**nous**	invite	**pas.**

1   ***D'accord!***

PARLER Demandez à vos camarades de faire les choses suivantes pour vous. Ils sont d'accord pour faire ces choses.

▶ téléphoner ce soir?

1. téléphoner demain?
2. attendre après la classe?
3. inviter à ta fête/soirée?
4. inviter à dîner?
5. rendre visite ce week-end?
6. rendre visite cet été?
7. acheter une glace?
8. apporter un sandwich?
9. vendre ton baladeur?
10. écouter?

TEACHING STRATEGY Object pronouns

The introduction of **me, te, nous, vous** before **le, la, les, lui, leur** serves two purposes:

- ▶ These pronouns are very useful in conversation.
- ▶ Students can practice sentence word order with these pronouns without having to make the distinction between direct and indirect objects. The third person pronouns are presented in Lesson 28.

INCLUSION

Synthetic/analytic Write 2 columns on the board; one for the subject pronouns and one for the corresponding object pronouns. Ask students to read words in each column. Then point to the subject pronouns from column 1 and have students say the object pronouns in column 2. Have students write the information in their notebooks.

Pauvre Chloé!

PARLER Charlotte a de la chance. Sa copine Chloé n'a pas de chance. Jouez les deux rôles.

▶ mon copain/inviter

1. ma tante/inviter au restaurant
2. mes cousins/téléphoner souvent
3. mon frère/écouter
4. mes parents/comprendre
5. mes voisins/inviter à dîner
6. ma copine/aider avec mes devoirs
7. mon grand-père/acheter des cadeaux *(gifts)*
8. mes amis/attendre après la classe

Mon copain m'invite.
Tu as de la chance. Mon copain ne m'invite pas.
SELECT HO

VOCABULAIRE Les services personnels 

aider quelqu'un	*to help*	J'**aide** mes copains avec les devoirs.
amener quelqu'un	*to bring*	Le taxi **amène** les touristes à la gare *(train station)*.
apporter quelque chose **à** quelqu'un	*to bring*	Le serveur **apporte** le menu **aux** clients.
donner quelque chose **à** quelqu'un	*to give*	Mme Marin **donne** 10 euros **à** sa fille.
montrer quelque chose **à** quelqu'un	*to show*	Est-ce que tu **montres** tes photos **à** ton copain?
prêter quelque chose **à** quelqu'un	*to lend, loan*	Est-ce que tu **prêtes** tes CD **à** tes amis?

Questions personnelles

PARLER/ÉCRIRE Réponds affirmativement ou négativement aux questions suivantes.

1. Est-ce que tes copains t'aident avec tes devoirs?
2. Est-ce que ta mère ou ton père t'aide avec les devoirs de français?
3. Est-ce que ton père ou ta mère te prête sa voiture?
4. Est-ce que ton frère ou ta soeur te prête ses CD?
5. Est-ce que tes profs te donnent des conseils *(advice)*?
6. Est-ce que ton copain te montre ses photos?
7. Est-ce que tes cousins t'apportent des cadeaux *(gifts)* quand ils viennent chez toi?
8. Est-ce que tes parents t'amènent au restaurant pour ton anniversaire?

SAMEDI devoirs

MATIÈRES	pour le	TEXTES
histoire	lundi	questions 1-15 page 475
français	mardi	examen chapitre 8

2 ROLE PLAY describing others' actions

1. –Ma tante m'invite au restaurant.
   –Tu as de la chance. Ma tante ne m'invite pas au restaurant.
2. –Mes cousins me téléphonent souvent.
   –Tu as de la chance. Mes cousins ne me téléphonent pas souvent.
3. –Mon frère m'écoute.
   –Tu as de la chance. Mon frère ne m'écoute pas.
4. –Mes parents me comprennent.
   –Tu as de la chance. Mes parents ne me comprennent pas.
5. –Mes voisins m'invitent à dîner.
   –Tu as de la chance. Mes voisins ne m'invitent pas à dîner.
6. –Ma copine m'aide avec mes devoirs.
   –Tu as de la chance. Ma copine ne m'aide pas avec mes devoirs.
7. –Mon grand-père m'achète des cadeaux.
   –Tu as de la chance. Mon grand-père ne m'achète pas de cadeaux.
8. –Mes amis m'attendent après la classe.
   –Tu as de la chance. Mes amis ne m'attendent pas après la classe.

Teaching note Remind students to use **pas de** in item 7.

Variation (with **ne... jamais**) **Mon copain ne m'invite jamais.**

Language note The verbs **donner, montrer,** and **prêter** are new.

Re-entry and review You may want to review the conjugation of **amener**:
j'amène, nous amenons, etc.
Remind students of the distinction between **amener** *(to bring people)* and **apporter** *(to bring things)*.

3 COMMUNICATION answering personal questions

Answers will vary.

1. Oui, mes copains m'aident avec mes devoirs. (Non, mes copains ne m'aident pas avec mes devoirs.)
2. Oui, ma mère (mon père) m'aide avec mes devoirs de français. (Non, ma mère [mon père] ne m'aide pas avec mes devoirs de français.)
3. Oui, mon père (ma mère) me prête sa voiture. (Non, mon père [ma mère] ne me prête pas sa voiture.)
4. Oui, mon frère (ma soeur) me prête ses CD. (Non, mon frère [ma soeur] ne me prête pas ses CD.)
5. Oui, mes profs me donnent des conseils. (Non, mes profs ne me donnent pas de conseils.)
6. Oui, mon copain me montre ses photos. (Non, mon copain ne me montre pas ses photos.)
7. Oui, mes cousins m'apportent des cadeaux quand ils viennent chez moi. (Non, mes cousins ne m'apportent pas de cadeaux quand ils viennent chez moi.)
8. Oui, mes parents m'amènent au restaurant pour mon anniversaire. (Non, mes parents ne m'amènent pas au restaurant pour mon anniversaire.)

Teaching Resource Options

PRINT 

Workbook PE, pp. 229–236
Unit 8 Resource Book
Communipak, pp. 152–173
Video Activities, pp. 101–102
Videoscript, pp. 106–107
Workbook TE, pp. 79–86

TECHNOLOGY 

Power Presentations

VIDEO PROGRAM

VIDÉO DVD

MODULE 27

27.2 Mini-scenes: Apportez-moi du poulet (41:58–43:21 min.)

27.3 Mini-scenes: Qu'est-ce que tu veux? (43:22–44:13 min.)

4 PRACTICE describing what people do for others

1. nous
2. t'
3. vous
4. me
5. te
6. nous
7. vous
8. nous
9. m'

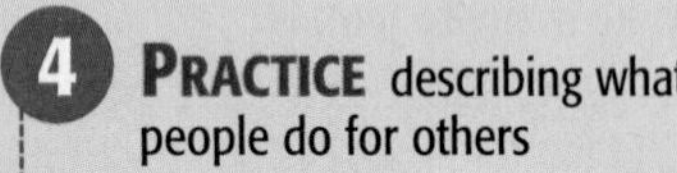

SECTION B

Communicative function
Giving orders

Language note The only time the pronoun follows the verb is the affirmative imperative:

Téléphone-moi.

5 EXCHANGES borrowing things from friends

1. –Prête-moi ton appareil-photo!
–Tiens, voilà mon appareil-photo.
–Merci.
2. –Prête-moi ta veste!
–Tiens, voilà ma veste.
–Merci.
3. –Prête-moi ton ordinateur!
–Tiens, voilà mon ordinateur.
–Merci.
4. –Prête-moi ta raquette!
–Tiens, voilà ma raquette.
–Merci.
5. –Prête-moi ton vélo!
–Tiens, voilà mon vélo.
–Merci.
6. –Prête-moi ton skate!
–Tiens, voilà mon skate.
–Merci.

4 Bons services

PARLER/ÉCRIRE Informez-vous sur les personnes suivantes. Dites ce que leurs amis ou leurs parents font pour eux. Pour cela, complétez les phrases avec les pronoms **me (m'), te (t'), nous** ou **vous.**

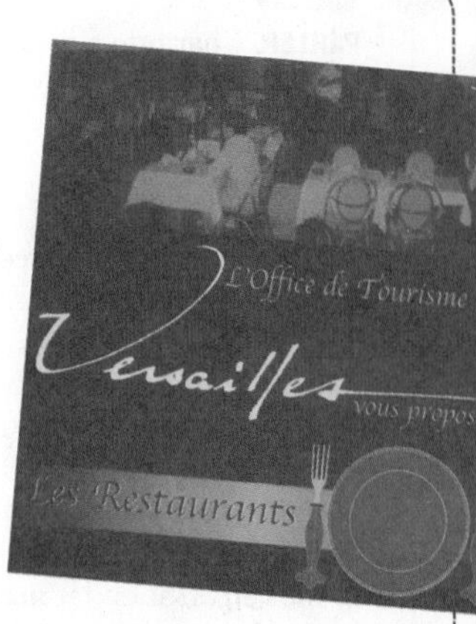

▶ J'organise une boum. — **Ma soeur me prête ses CD.**
▶ Nous avons faim. — **Cécile nous apporte des sandwichs.**

1. Nous organisons un pique-nique. Nos copains … aident.
2. Tu as soif. Je … apporte un soda.
3. Vous préparez l'examen. Le prof … donne des conseils *(advice)*.
4. J'ai besoin d'argent. Mon cousin … prête vingt euros.
5. Tu es chez les voisins. Ils … montrent leur appartement.
6. Nous sommes à l'hôpital. Nos amis … rendent visite.
7. Vous êtes sympathiques. Je … invite chez moi.
8. Nous allons prendre l'avion. Le taxi … amène à l'aéroport.
9. Je nettoie le garage. Mon frère … aide.

B Les pronoms compléments à l'impératif

Compare the position and the form of the object pronouns when the verb is in the imperative.

AFFIRMATIVE	NEGATIVE
Téléphone-**moi** ce soir!	Ne **me** téléphone pas demain!
Invite-**moi** samedi!	Ne **m'**invite pas dimanche!
Apporte-**nous** du thé!	Ne **nous** apporte pas de café!

When the IMPERATIVE verb is AFFIRMATIVE, the object pronouns come *after* the verb.

→ **me** becomes **moi**

When the imperative verb is negative, the object pronouns come *before* the verb.

5 Prêts *(Loans)*

PARLER Demandez à vos copains de vous prêter les choses suivantes. Ils vont accepter.

COMPREHENSION Showing and distributing things

PROPS: Miscellaneous objects from Lesson 25 (plastic fruits and vegetables; picnicware)

Place the objects on a table. Show and give the class certain items but not others.

Je vous montre une tasse. [hold up cup]
Je ne vous montre pas le verre. [hide glass]

Then call on students.

X, viens ici. Montre-nous la pomme.
Ne nous montre pas l'orange.
Y, viens ici et donne-moi le couteau.
Ne me donne pas la fourchette.
Donne la fourchette à Z.
Z, ne me montre pas la fourchette.
Passe la fourchette à W. ...

6 À Paris

PARLER/ÉCRIRE Vous visitez Paris. Demandez certains services aux personnes suivantes.

▶ au garçon de café *(waiter)*
- apporter un sandwich

S'il vous plaît, apportez-moi un sandwich.

1. au garçon de café
   - apporter de l'eau
   - apporter une limonade
   - donner un croissant
2. à la serveuse *(waitress)* du restaurant
   - montrer le menu
   - donner du pain
   - apporter l'addition *(check)*
3. au chauffeur de taxi *(cab driver)*
   - amener au musée d'Orsay
   - montrer Notre-Dame
   - aider avec les bagages
4. à un copain parisien
   - téléphoner ce soir
   - donner ton adresse
   - prêter ton plan *(map)* de Paris

7 Quel service?

PARLER Demandez à vos camarades certains services. Pour cela complétez les phrases en utilisant ces verbes.

aider	amener	apporter
donner	montrer	prêter

▶ J'ai soif. … de la limonade.
S'il te plaît, apporte-moi (donne-moi) de la limonade.

▶ J'ai faim. … un sandwich
S'il te plaît, apporte-moi (donne-moi) un sandwich.

1. Je ne comprends pas les devoirs de maths. … avec le problème.
2. Je voudrais téléphoner à ta cousine. … son numéro de téléphone.
3. Je n'ai pas d'argent pour aller au cinéma. … dix dollars.
4. Je voudrais voir tes photos. … tes photos.
5. J'ai soif. … de l'eau minérale.
6. J'organise une boum. … tes CD.
7. Je vais peindre *(to paint)* ma chambre. … avec ce projet.
8. Je vais à l'aéroport. … là-bas avec ta voiture.
9. Je ne sais pas où tu habites. … ton adresse.

8 Non!

PARLER Proposez à vos camarades de faire les choses suivantes pour eux. Ils vont refuser et donner une explication.

▶ téléphoner ce soir (Je ne suis pas chez moi.)

1. téléphoner demain soir (Je dois faire mes devoirs.)
2. inviter ce week-end (Je vais à la campagne.)
3. inviter dimanche (Je dîne chez mes cousins.)
4. attendre après la classe (Je dois rentrer chez moi.)
5. prêter mes CD (Je n'ai pas de chaîne hi-fi.)
6. acheter un sandwich (Je n'ai pas faim.)
7. rendre visite ce soir (Je vais au cinéma.)

Je te téléphone ce soir?
Non, ne me téléphone pas. Je ne suis pas chez moi.

6 ROLE PLAY asking for services

1. S'il vous plaît, apportez-moi de l'eau.
   S'il vous plaît, apportez-moi une limonade.
   S'il vous plaît, donnez-moi un croissant.
2. S'il vous plaît, montrez-moi le menu.
   S'il vous plaît, donnez-moi du pain.
   S'il vous plaît, apportez-moi l'addition.
3. S'il vous plaît, amenez-moi au musée d'Orsay.
   S'il vous plaît, montrez-moi Notre-Dame.
   S'il vous plaît, aidez-moi avec les bagages.
4. S'il te plaît, téléphone-moi ce soir.
   S'il te plaît, donne-moi ton adresse.
   S'il te plaît, prête-moi ton plan de Paris.

Teaching note Have students use the **vous** form in items 1, 2, and 3; and the **tu** form in item 4.

Expansion Have students make original requests to the people in items 1–4. Sample answers:

1. S'il vous plaît, apportez-moi le menu.
2. S'il vous plaît, apportez-moi (donnez-moi) du beurre.
3. S'il vous plaît, amenez-moi au musée du Louvre.
4. S'il te plaît, montre-moi la tour Eiffel.

7 COMPREHENSION asking for appropriate services

Answers will vary.

1. S'il te plaît, aide-moi avec le problème.
2. S'il te plaît, donne-moi (montre-moi) son numéro de téléphone.
3. S'il te plaît, prête-moi (donne-moi) dix dollars.
4. S'il te plaît, montre-moi tes photos.
5. S'il te plaît, donne-moi (apporte-moi) de l'eau minérale.
6. S'il te plaît, prête-moi tes CD.
7. S'il te plaît, aide-moi avec ce projet.
8. S'il te plaît, amène-moi là-bas avec ta voiture.
9. S'il te plaît, donne-moi ton adresse.

8 EXCHANGES asking friends not to do things

1. –Je te téléphone demain soir?
   –Non, ne me téléphone pas. Je dois faire mes devoirs.
2. –Je t'invite ce week-end?
   –Non, ne m'invite pas. Je vais à la campagne.
3. –Je t'invite dimanche?
   –Non, ne m'invite pas. Je dîne chez mes cousins.
4. –Je t'attends après la classe?
   –Non, ne m'attends pas. Je dois rentrer chez moi.
5. –Je te prête mes CD?
   –Non, ne me prête pas tes CD. Je n'ai pas de chaîne hi-fi.
6. –Je t'achète un sandwich?
   –Non, ne m'achète pas de sandwich. Je n'ai pas faim.
7. –Je te rends visite ce soir?
   –Non, ne me rends pas visite. Je vais au cinéma.

Teaching note Remind students to use **pas de** in item 6.

SECTION C

Communicative function
Saying what one can and must do

Teaching Resource Options

PRINT 

Workbook PE, pp. 229–236
Unit 8 Resource Book
Audioscript, pp. 108–109
Communipak, pp. 152–173
Workbook TE, pp. 79–86

AUDIO & VISUAL 

Audio Program
CD 4 Tracks 34, 35

TECHNOLOGY 

Power Presentations

Review and expansion
The **je** form of **devoir** and the **je** and **tu** forms of **pouvoir** were introduced in Lesson 5.

Teaching strategy Have students note how the forms of **pouvoir** are similar to those of **vouloir.**

Language notes

- In writing, the accent circonflexe appears on the past participle **dû** to distinguish it from the partitive article **du**.
- **Devoir** + noun means *to owe.* **Je dois** dix euros à Hélène.

9 COMPREHENSION
determining shopping options

Answers will vary.
1. Elles peuvent acheter un CD.
2. Je peux acheter une veste (un appareil-photo, une raquette).
3. Tu peux acheter un pantalon. (des lunettes de soleil, des livres, et un CD).
4. Vous pouvez acheter un appareil-photo.
5. Elle peut acheter des chaussures.
6. Nous pouvons acheter une raquette.
7. Il peut acheter des livres.

C Les verbes *pouvoir* et *devoir*  

FORMS

Note the forms of the irregular verbs **pouvoir** *(can, may, be able)* and **devoir** *(must, have to)*.

INFINITIVE	pouvoir		devoir	
PRESENT	Je **peux**	venir.	Je **dois**	rentrer avant midi.
	Tu **peux**	travailler.	Tu **dois**	gagner de l'argent.
	Il/Elle/On **peut**	voyager.	Il/Elle/On **doit**	visiter Paris.
	Nous **pouvons**	dîner ici.	Nous **devons**	regarder le menu.
	Vous **pouvez**	rester.	Vous **devez**	finir vos devoirs.
	Ils/Elles **peuvent**	aider.	Ils/Elles **doivent**	mettre la table.
PASSÉ COMPOSÉ	J'ai **pu**	étudier.	J'ai **dû**	faire mes devoirs.

USES

- **Pouvoir** has several English equivalents.

can	Est-ce que tu **peux** venir au pique-nique?	***Can*** *you come to the picnic?*
may	Est-ce que je **peux** prendre la voiture?	***May*** *I take the car?*
to be able	Jacques ne **peut** pas réparer sa mobylette.	*Jacques* ***is*** *not* ***able*** *to fix his moped.*

- **Devoir** is used to express an OBLIGATION.

must	Vous **devez** faire vos devoirs.	*You* ***must*** *do your homework.*
to have to	Est-ce que je **dois** ranger ma chambre?	***Do*** *I* ***have to*** *pick up my room?*

➔ **Devoir** is usually followed by an infinitive. It cannot stand alone.

Est-ce que tu **dois étudier** ce soir?	*Do you* ***have to study*** *tonight?*
Oui, je **dois étudier.**	*Yes, I* ***have to (study).***
Non, je **ne dois pas étudier.**	*No, I* ***don't have to (study).***

9 Le coût de la vie *(The cost of living)*

PARLER/ÉCRIRE Décrivez ce que les personnes suivantes peuvent acheter avec leur argent.

▶ Philippe a quinze euros.
Il peut acheter des lunettes de soleil.

1. Alice et Françoise ont vingt euros.
2. J'ai cent euros.
3. Tu as soixante euros.
4. Vous avez quatre-vingts euros.
5. Ma copine a soixante-cinq euros.
6. Nous avons cinquante euros.
7. Mon frère a vingt-cinq euros.

INCLUSION

Repetitive Make flashcards and review conjugations for **pouvoir** and **devoir**. Then ask students to work in pairs to form sentences with the different verb forms. One student reads a verb infinitive and the other student creates a sentence in the present tense. Then have students reverse roles.

10  Obligations?

PARLER Demandez à vos camarades s'ils doivent faire les choses suivantes.

▶ étudier?

1. étudier ce soir?
2. ranger ta chambre?
3. mettre la table?
4. réussir à l'examen?
5. aller chez le dentiste cette semaine?
6. parler au professeur après la classe?
7. être poli(e) *(polite)* avec tes voisins?
8. rentrer chez toi après la classe?

11 Excuses

PARLER/ÉCRIRE Thomas demande à ses amis de repeindre *(to repaint)* sa chambre avec lui, mais chacun a une excuse. Dites que les personnes suivantes ne peuvent pas aider Thomas. Dites aussi ce qu'elles doivent faire.

▶ Hélène (étudier)
Hélène ne peut pas aider Thomas. Elle doit étudier.

1. nous (faire les courses)
2. Lise et Rose (acheter des vêtements)
3. moi (aider ma mère)
4. toi (nettoyer le garage)
5. Alice (rendre visite à sa grand-mère)
6. vous (déjeuner avec vos cousins)
7. mon frère et moi (laver la voiture)
8. Nathalie et toi (préparer l'examen)

12 Expression personnelle

PARLER/ÉCRIRE Complétez les phrases suivantes avec vos idées personnelles.

1. Chez moi, je peux …
   Je ne peux pas …
2. À l'école, nous devons …
   Nous ne devons pas …
3. À la maison, je dois …
   Mes frères (Mes soeurs) doivent …
4. Quand on est riche, on peut …
   On doit …
5. Quand on est malade *(sick)*, on doit …
   On ne doit pas …
6. Quand on veut maigrir, on doit …
   On ne peut pas …

PRONONCIATION

Les lettres «s» et «ss» s = /z/ ss = /s/

Be sure to distinguish between "**s**" and "**ss**" in the middle of a word.

Répétez: /z/ **mauvaise cuisine fraise mayonnaise quelque chose magasin**

/s/ **poisson saucisson dessert boisson assiette pamplemousse**

/z/–/s/ **poison – poisson désert** *(desert)* **– dessert**

Comme dessert nous choisissons une tarte aux fraises.

poison poisson

10 EXCHANGES finding out what friends have to do and don't have to do

1. –Est-ce que tu dois étudier ce soir?
   –Oui, je dois étudier ce soir. (Non, je ne dois pas étudier ce soir.)
2. –Est-ce que tu dois ranger ta chambre?
   –Oui, je dois ranger ma chambre. (Non, je ne dois pas ranger ma chambre.)
3. –Est-ce que tu dois mettre la table?
   –Oui, je dois mettre la table. (Non, je ne dois pas mettre la table.)
4. –Est-ce que tu dois réussir à l'examen?
   –Oui, je dois réussir à l'examen. (Non, je ne dois pas réussir à l'examen.)
5. –Est-ce que tu dois aller chez le dentiste cette semaine?
   –Oui, je dois aller chez le dentiste cette semaine. (Non, je ne dois pas aller chez le dentiste cette semaine.)
6. –Est-ce que tu dois parler au professeur après la classe?
   –Oui, je dois parler au professeur après la classe. (Non, je ne dois pas parler au professeur après la classe.)
7. –Est-ce que tu dois être poli(e) avec tes voisins?
   –Oui, je dois être poli(e) avec mes voisins. (Non, je ne dois pas être poli[e] avec mes voisins.)
8. –Est-ce que tu dois rentrer chez toi après la classe?
   –Oui, je dois rentrer chez moi après la classe. (Non, je ne dois pas rentrer chez moi après la classe.)

11 PRACTICE making excuses

1. Nous ne pouvons pas aider Thomas. Nous devons faire les courses.
2. Lise et Rose ne peuvent pas aider Thomas. Elles doivent acheter des vêtements.
3. Je ne peux pas aider Thomas. Je dois aider ma mère.
4. Tu ne peux pas aider Thomas. Tu dois nettoyer le garage.
5. Alice ne peut pas aider Thomas. Elle doit rendre visite à sa grand-mère.
6. Vous ne pouvez pas aider Thomas. Vous devez déjeuner avec vos cousins.
7. Mon frère et moi, nous ne pouvons pas aider Thomas. Nous devons laver la voiture.
8. Nathalie et toi, vous ne pouvez pas aider Thomas. Vous devez préparer l'examen.

Teaching note Help students choose correct pronouns for items 7 and 8: **nous lavons ..., vous préparez ...**

12 COMMUNICATION talking about what one can and should do

Answers will vary.

1. Chez moi, je peux (écouter la radio). Je ne peux pas (regarder la télé après onze heures).
2. À l'école, nous devons (écouter le prof). Nous ne devons pas (lire des bandes dessinées en classe).
3. À la maison, je dois (ranger ma chambre). Mes frères (Mes soeurs) doivent (laver la voiture).
4. Quand on est riche, on peut (faire de grands voyages). On doit (aider les pauvres).
5. Quand on est malade, on doit (rester au lit). On ne doit pas (faire de promenade à vélo).
6. Quand on veut maigrir, on doit (manger beaucoup de salade). On ne peut pas (manger beaucoup de glace).

À VOTRE TOUR

Main Topic

- Recapitulation and review

Teaching Resource Options

PRINT 

Workbook PE, pp. 229–236
Unit 8 Resource Book
- Audioscript, p. 109
- Communipak, pp. 152–173
- Family Involvement, pp. 98–99
- Workbook TE, pp. 79–86

Assessment
- Lesson 27 Quiz, pp. 112–113
- Portfolio Assessment, Unit 1 URB pp. 155–164
- Audioscript for Quiz 27, p. 111
- Answer Keys, pp. 218–221

AUDIO & VISUAL 

Audio Program
CD 4 Tracks 36, 37
CD 16 Track 11

TECHNOLOGY 

Test Generator CD-ROM/McDougal Littell Assessment System

1 COMPREHENSION

1. Dis, Philippe, j'ai besoin d'un petit service.
   (e) Qu'est-ce que je peux faire pour toi?
2. Prête-moi ta mobylette, s'il te plaît.
   (d) Ah, je ne peux pas. Je dois aller en ville cet après-midi.
3. Dans ce cas, apporte-moi *Paris Match.*
   (b) D'accord, je vais aller à la librairie Duchemin.
4. Alors, achète-moi aussi le nouvel album d'Astérix.
   (c) Écoute, je n'ai pas assez d'argent.
5. Je t'ai prêté vingt euros hier.
   (a) C'est vrai ... Bon, je t'achète tout ça.

Culture note

In addition to bookstores **(des librairies)** many French cities have a **Maison de la presse** that sells magazines and newspapers as well as books.

À votre tour!

OBJECTIFS

Now you can ...
- ask people for favors
- say what your friends do for you

1 Allô!

PARLER Reconstituez la conversation entre Corinne et Philippe. Pour cela, faites correspondre les réponses de Philippe avec ce que dit Corinne.

Corinne

1. Dis, Philippe, j'ai besoin d'un petit service.
2. Prête-moi ta mobylette, s'il te plaît.
3. Dans ce cas, apporte-moi Paris-Match.
4. Alors, achète-moi aussi le nouvel album d'Astérix.
5. Je t'ai prêté vingt euros hier!

Philippe

a. C'est vrai ... Bon, je t'achète tout ça *(all that)*.
b. D'accord! Je vais aller à la librairie *(bookstore)* Duchemin.
c. Écoute, je n'ai pas assez d'argent.
d. Ah, je ne peux pas. Je dois aller en ville cet après-midi.
e. Qu'est-ce que je peux faire pour toi?

2 Créa-dialogue

PARLER Demandez certains services à vos camarades. Ils vont vous demander pourquoi. Répondez à leurs questions. Ils vont accepter le service.

▶ —S'il te plaît, prête-moi ton vélo!
—Pourquoi?
—Parce que je voudrais faire une promenade à la campagne.
—D'accord, je te prête mon vélo.

	▶ prêter	1. prêter	2. prêter	3. apporter	4. prêter	5. donner	6. donner
QUEL SERVICE?					$1.00	$5.00	??
POURQUOI?	faire une promenade à la campagne	jouer au tennis	organiser une boum	prendre des photos	acheter une glace	??	??

À VOTRE TOUR

Depending on your goals and objectives, you may or may not wish to assign all of the activities in the **À votre tour** section.

PAIR/GROUP PRACTICE

Act. 1 and 2 lend themselves to pair practice. They can also be done in trios, with two students performing and the third acting as monitor.

3 Au restaurant

PARLER Avec un(e) camarade, préparez un dialogue original correspondant à la situation suivante.

You are having dinner at a French restaurant called Sans-Souci. You have a friendly but inexperienced waiter/waitress (played by your classmate) who forgets to bring you what you need. However, whenever you mention something, he/she agrees to bring it right away **(tout de suite).**

Tell your waiter/waitress ...

- to please show you the menu **(le menu)**
- to please give you some water
- to bring you a napkin
- to give you a beverage (of your choice)
- to bring you a dessert (of your choice)
- to bring you the silverware that you need for eating the dessert

COMMENT DIT-ON ...?

How to show your reaction to bad food:

Pouah! ... C'est infect! ... C'est dégoûtant! C'est infâme!

4 Composition: Bonnes relations

ÉCRIRE Select a person you like (a friend, a neighbor, a relative, a teacher) and write a short paragraph mentioning at least four things this person does for you. You may want to use some of the following verbs:

acheter amener aider
donner inviter montrer
prêter rendre visite téléphoner

J'ai une bonne copine. Elle s'appelle Stéphanie. Elle est très sympathique. Elle me téléphone souvent et le week-end, elle m'invite chez elle. Elle est très intelligente et quand je ne comprends pas, elle m'aide avec mes devoirs de français. Elle me donne toujours des conseils (advice) excellents.

Now tell me about a friend of yours and let me know some of the things this friend does for you.

LESSON REVIEW
CLASSZONE.COM

PORTFOLIO ASSESSMENT

You will probably select only one speaking activity and one writing activity to go into the students' portfolios for Unit 8.

In this lesson, Act. 3 can be used as the basis for oral portfolio recordings. Act. 4 could be used as written portfolio topic.

2 GUIDED ORAL EXPRESSION

1. –S'il te plaît, prête-moi ta raquette!
   –Pourquoi?
   –Parce que je voudrais jouer au tennis.
   –D'accord, je te prête ma raquette.
2. –S'il te plaît, prête-moi ta chaîne hi-fi!
   –Pourquoi?
   –Parce que je voudrais organiser une boum.
   –D'accord, je te prête ma chaîne hi-fi.
3. –S'il te plaît, apporte-moi ton appareil-photo!
   –Pourquoi?
   –Parce que je voudrais prendre des photos.
   –D'accord, je t'apporte mon appareil-photo.
4. –S'il te plaît, prête-moi un dollar!
   –Pourquoi?
   –Parce que je voudrais acheter une glace.
   –D'accord, je te prête un dollar.
5. –S'il te plaît, donne-moi cinq dollars!
   –Pourquoi?
   –Parce que je voudrais (acheter un magazine).
   –D'accord, je te donne cinq dollars.
6. –S'il te plaît, donne-moi (ton livre de français)!
   –Pourquoi?
   –Parce que je voudrais (faire mes devoirs).
   –D'accord, je te donne (mon livre de français).

3 GUIDED ORAL EXPRESSION

- –Mademoiselle (Monsieur), montrez-moi le menu, s'il vous plaît.
  –Je vous apporte le menu tout de suite, monsieur (mademoiselle).
- –Mademoiselle (Monsieur), donnez-moi (apportez-moi) de l'eau (minérale), s'il vous plaît.
  –Je vous donne (apporte) de l'eau (minérale) tout de suite, monsieur (mademoiselle).
- –Mademoiselle (Monsieur), apportez-moi une serviette, s'il vous plaît.
  –Je vous apporte une serviette tout de suite, monsieur (mademoiselle).
- –Mademoiselle (Monsieur), apportez-moi (du jus de pomme), s'il vous plaît.
  –Je vous apporte (du jus de pomme) tout de suite, monsieur (mademoiselle).
- –Mademoiselle (Monsieur), apportez-moi (du gâteau).
  –Je vous apporte (du gâteau) tout de suite, monsieur (mademoiselle).
- –Mademoiselle (Monsieur), donnez-moi (apportez-moi) (une fourchette) pour le dessert, s'il vous plaît.
  –Je vous donne (apporte) (une fourchette) tout de suite, monsieur (mademoiselle).

4 WRITTEN SELF-EXPRESSION

Answers will vary.
Ma meilleure amie s'appelle Karine. Elle habite à Montréal. Elle me téléphone souvent et j'aime beaucoup parler avec elle. Quand elle me rend visite, je l'amène au parc et au stade. Elle me prête ses CD. Elle m'aide avec les devoirs de maths, et elle me montre comment faire un très bon gâteau au chocolat. Mmm ... Vous aimez le gâteau au chocolat?

Leçon 28

Main Topic Talking about friends and acquaintances

Teaching Resource Options

PRINT 

Workbook PE, pp. 237–243
Activités pour tous PE, pp. 143–145
Block Scheduling Copymasters, pp. 217–224
Unit 8 Resource Book
- *Activités pour tous* TE, pp. 123–125
- Audioscript, pp. 144, 145–147
- Communipak, pp. 152–173
- Lesson Plans, pp. 126–127
- Block Scheduling Lesson Plans, pp. 128–130
- Absent Student Copymasters, pp. 131–135
- Video Activities, pp. 138–141
- Videoscript, pp. 142–143
- Workbook TE, pp. 115–121

AUDIO & VISUAL 

Audio Program
CD 4 Tracks 38, 39
CD 12 Tracks 22–27

TECHNOLOGY 

Online Workbook

VIDEO PROGRAM

VIDÉO DVD

MODULE 28
Sur la plage

TOTAL TIME: 5:48 min.
DVD Disk 2
Videotape 4 (COUNTER: 47:05 min.)

28.1 Dialogue: Sur la plage (48:16–49:30 min.)

28.2 Mini-scenes: Listening – Tu le connais? (49:31–50:32 min.)

28.3 Mini-scenes: Listening – On va lui parler? (50:33–51:34 min.)

28.4 Vignette culturelle: À la plage de Deauville (51:35–52:53 min.)

Comprehension practice Play the entire module through as an introduction to the lesson.

LEÇON 28

Pique-nique

AUDIO

Mélanie et Jean-Marc organisent un pique-nique ce week-end. Ils préparent la liste des invités. Qui vont-ils inviter? — *guests*

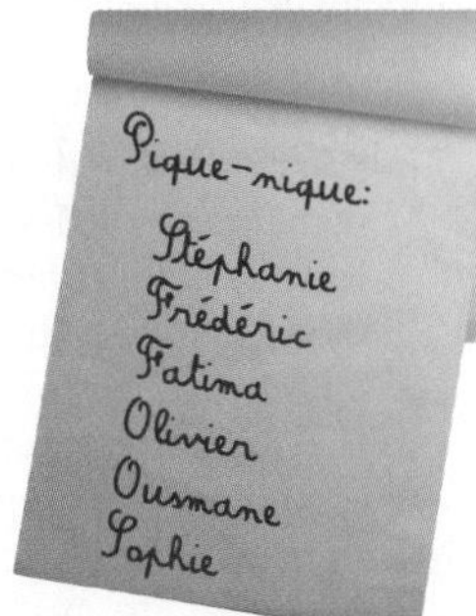

Mélanie: Tu connais Stéphanie?
Jean-Marc: Oui, je la connais. C'est une copine.
Mélanie: Je l'invite au pique-nique?
Jean-Marc: Bien sûr. Invite-la.
Mélanie: Et son cousin Frédéric, tu le connais?
Jean-Marc: Oui, je le connais un peu.
Mélanie: Je l'invite aussi?
Jean-Marc: Non, ne l'invite pas. Il est trop snob.
Mélanie: Comment? Tu le trouves snob? Moi, je le trouve intelligent et sympathique. Et puis, il a une voiture et nous avons besoin d'une voiture pour transporter tout le monde ...
Jean-Marc: Mélanie, tu es géniale ... C'est vrai, Frédéric n'est pas aussi snob que ça ... Téléphonons-lui tout de suite et invitons-le au pique-nique!

Comment? = *What?*; *puis* = *also*; *tout le monde* = *everyone*; *géniale* = *brilliant*; *aussi snob que ça* = *that snobbish*; *tout de suite* = *right away*

SETTING THE SCENE

Ask students if they go on picnics with family or friends.
Est-ce que vous faites des pique-niques avec votre famille/vos copains?

Where do they go? What do they do?
Où allez-vous? Qu'est-ce que vous faites?

And what do they eat and drink?
Qu'est-ce que vous mangez? Qu'est-ce que vous buvez?

NOTE culturelle

Un pique-nique français

Quand ils vont à la campagne, les Français adorent faire des pique-niques. Un pique-nique est un repas froid assez simple. Il y a généralement du poulet froid et des oeufs durs° et aussi du jambon, du saucisson ou du pâté* pour les sandwichs. Quand on a l'équipement nécessaire, on peut aussi faire des grillades° sur un barbecue. Comme dessert, il y a des fruits (bananes, oranges, pommes, poires, raisin°). Comme boisson, il y a de l'eau minérale, des sodas et des jus de fruit.

*The French have created dozens of varieties of **pâté**, ranging from the expensive and refined **foie gras** (made from the livers of fattened geese) to the everyday **pâté de campagne** (a type of cold meat loaf served in thin slices with bread).

durs *hard-boiled* **grillades** *grilled meat* **raisin** *grapes* *(Note that* **raisin** *is always in the singular.)*

Compréhension

1. Qui est Stéphanie?
2. Qui est Frédéric?
3. Est-ce que Jean-Marc a une bonne ou une mauvaise opinion de Frédéric? Pourquoi?
4. Et Mélanie, comment est-ce qu'elle trouve Frédéric?
5. Finalement, est-ce que Jean-Marc va inviter Frédéric au pique-nique? Pourquoi?

Et toi?

1. Est-ce que tu aimes faire des pique-niques?
2. Quand tu fais un pique-nique avec des copains, où allez-vous?
3. Qui invites-tu?
4. En général, qu'est-ce qu'on mange à un pique-nique américain?
5. Qu'est-ce qu'on boit?
6. Dans ta famille, est-ce qu'on fait des barbecues? Où? Qui est le «chef»? Qu'est-ce qu'on mange et qu'est-ce qu'on boit?

USING THE VIDEO

Video Module 28 was filmed in Normandy at the resort town of Deauville. In the dialogue scenes, two boys on vacation are trying to figure out how to introduce themselves to a girl at the beach.

In the *Vignette culturelle,* other young people are interviewed about their vacation activities. The theme of the module provides an appropriate point for wishing your students a relaxing summer vacation.

Photo cultural note

In the photo, French youngsters are having a picnic on the grass **(un pique-nique sur l'herbe)** in a park. Note that they have simply spread a tablecloth **(une nappe)** on the ground. In France, public picnic grounds with tables are mainly found at the rest areas along the superhighways **(les autoroutes)**.

Compréhension

Answers

1. C'est une copine de Jean-Marc.
2. C'est le cousin de Stéphanie.
3. Il a une mauvaise opinion de Frédéric. Il pense qu'il est trop snob.
4. Elle le trouve intelligent et sympa.
5. Oui, parce qu'il a une voiture.

Et toi?

Answers will vary.

1. Oui, j'aime faire des pique-niques.
2. Nous allons (à la plage, à la campagne).
3. J'invite (ma soeur, mes amis).
4. En général, on mange (des sandwichs et des fruits).
5. On boit (de l'eau minérale, du soda, du jus de fruits).
6. Dans ma famille, on fait des barbecues. (Mon père) est le chef. On mange (des hamburgers et des hot dogs). On boit (du soda et du jus de raisin).

Pronunciation The expression **un barbecue** /barb kju/ has been borrowed from the English. It refers to the meal as well as to the grill on which it was cooked.

Supplementary vocabulary

PICNIC FOODS

du poulet frit *fried chicken*
du poulet rôti *roast chicken*
des chips (m.) /ʃip/ or /ʃips/
des côtes (f.) **de porc** *spare ribs*
de la salade de pommes de terre *potato salad*
de la salade de chou *cole slaw*

SECTION A

Communicative function
Talking about whom one knows

Teaching Resource Options

PRINT 

Workbook PE, pp. 237–243
Unit 8 Resource Book
- Audioscript, p. 144
- Communipak, pp. 152–173
- Video Activities, pp. 138–139
- Videoscript, p. 142
- Workbook TE, pp. 115–121

AUDIO & VISUAL 
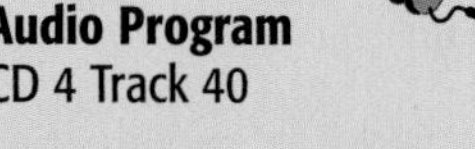

Audio Program
CD 4 Track 40

TECHNOLOGY 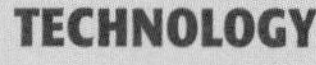
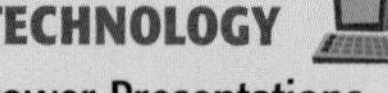

Power Presentations

VIDEO PROGRAM

VIDÉO DVD

MODULE 28

28.2 Mini-scenes: Tu le connais?
(49:31–50:32 min.)

Spelling hint The circumflex appears on the "î" of **connaître** only when the next letter is a "t."

Supplementary vocabulary The verb **reconnaître** *(to recognize)* is conjugated like **connaître.**

Teaching strategy This is a simplified explanation of the distinction between **connaître** and **savoir.** The more complex differences are presented formally in Book Two, e.g., **Je connais la leçon** *(I know which one it is)* vs. **Je sais la leçon** *(I know it because I have studied it).* For the complete conjugation of **savoir**, see Appendix, p. R10.

1 PRACTICE describing whom or what people know

1. Nous connaissons Paul. Nous ne connaissons pas ses copains.
2. Vous connaissez le prof d'anglais. Vous ne connaissez pas le prof de maths.
3. Je connais les voisins. Je ne connais pas leurs amis.
4. Tu connais Paris. Tu ne connais pas Bordeaux.
5. Les touristes connaissent le Louvre. Ils ne connaissent pas le musée d'Orsay.
6. Mon copain connaît ce café. Il ne connaît pas ce restaurant.

A Le verbe *connaître* 

Note the forms of the irregular verb **connaître** *(to know)*.

INFINITIVE	connaître	
PRESENT	Je **connais** Stéphanie. Tu **connais** son cousin? Il/Elle/On **connaît** ces garçons.	Nous **connaissons** Paris. Vous **connaissez** Montréal? Ils/Elles **connaissent** ce café.
PASSÉ COMPOSÉ	J'ai **connu** ton frère pendant les vacances.	

→ In the passé composé, **connaître** means *to meet for the first time.*

→ The French use **connaître** to say that they *know* or *are acquainted with people or places.* To say that they *know information,* they use **je sais, tu sais.** Compare:

PEOPLE/PLACES	INFORMATION
Je **connais** Éric.	Je **sais** où il habite.
Tu **connais** Frédéric.	Tu **sais** à quelle heure il vient?
Je **connais** un bon restaurant.	Je **sais** qu'il est près du théâtre.

Je connais Éric.

Je sais où il habite.

1 On ne peut pas tout connaître

PARLER/ÉCRIRE Les personnes suivantes connaissent la première personne ou la première chose entre parenthèses. Elles ne connaissent pas la deuxième.

▶ Philippe (Isabelle/sa soeur)
Philippe connaît Isabelle.
Il ne connaît pas sa soeur.

1. nous (Paul/ses copains)
2. vous (le prof d'anglais/le prof de maths)
3. moi (les voisins/leurs amis)
4. toi (Paris/Bordeaux)
5. les touristes (le Louvre/le musée d'Orsay)
6. mon copain (ce café/ce restaurant)

2 Questions personnelles PARLER/ÉCRIRE

1. Est-ce que tu connais New York? Chicago? San Francisco? Montréal? Quelles villes est-ce que tu connais bien?
2. Dans ta ville est-ce que tu connais un bon restaurant? Comment est-ce qu'il s'appelle? Est-ce que tu connais un supermarché? un centre commercial? un magasin de CD? Comment est-ce qu'ils s'appellent?
3. Est-ce que tu connais des monuments à Paris? Quels monuments?
4. Est-ce que tu connais bien tes voisins? Est-ce qu'ils sont sympathiques? Est-ce que tu connais personnellement le directeur (la directrice) de ton école? Est-ce qu'il (elle) est strict(e)?
5. Quels acteurs de cinéma est-ce que tu connais? Quelles actrices? Quels musiciens? Quels athlètes professionnels?

COMPREHENSION Direct object pronouns

PROPS: 3 pictures of known personalities: a man, a woman, a couple

Tape the 3 pictures on the chalkboard.

Point to the picture of the man:
Vous le connaissez? [write **le** on board]
Bien sûr, vous le connaissez. C'est ...

Present the other 2 pictures (writing **la, les**).

Have students point to the right picture.
X, tu le connais? [X points to man]
Tu ne la connais pas? [X points to woman]
Tu les connais? [X points to couple]

B Les pronoms compléments: *le, la, les*

In the questions below, the nouns in heavy type follow the verb directly. They are the DIRECT OBJECTS of the verb. Note the forms and position of the DIRECT OBJECT PRONOUNS which are used to replace those nouns in the answers.

Tu connais **Éric?**	Oui, je **le** connais. Je **l'**invite souvent.	*Yes, I know **him.*** *I invite **him** often.*
Tu connais **Stéphanie?**	Oui, je **la** connais. Je **l'**invite aussi.	*Yes, I know **her.*** *I invite **her** also.*
Tu connais **mes copains?**	Je **les** connais bien. Je **les** invite.	*I know **them** well.* *I invite **them.***
Tu connais **mes amies?**	Je **les** connais aussi. Je **les** invite souvent.	*I know **them** too.* *I invite **them** often.*

FORMS AND USES

Direct object pronouns have the following forms:

	SINGULAR		PLURAL
MASCULINE	**le** ↓ **l'** (+ VOWEL SOUND)	*him, it*	**les** *them*
FEMININE	**la** ↓ **l'** (+ VOWEL SOUND)	*her, it*	

Qui le vend?
Qui le répare?

On le trouve dans les pages jaunes!

LA POSTE

→ The direct object pronouns **le, la, l', les** can refer to either people or things.

Tu vois **Nicole?**	Oui, je **la** vois.	*Yes, I see **her.***
Tu vois **ma voiture?**	Oui, je **la** vois.	*Yes, I see **it.***
Tu comprends **le professeur?**	Oui, je **le** comprends.	*Yes, I understand **him.***
Tu comprends **ce mot** *(word)*?	Oui, je **le** comprends.	*Yes, I understand **it.***

POSITION

Direct object pronouns generally come *before* the verb according to the following patterns:

	AFFIRMATIVE			NEGATIVE				
	SUBJECT	+ **le/la/les**	+ VERB ...	SUBJECT	+ **ne**	+ **le/la/les**	+ VERB	+ **pas** ...
Éric?	Je	**le**	connais bien.	Tu	**ne**	**le**	connais	**pas.**
Ces filles?	Nous	**les**	invitons.	Vous	**ne**	**les**	invitez	**pas.**

Vary the verbs (beginning with consonants).
Y, tu la vois souvent? [Y points to woman]
Tu les trouves intéressants? [points to couple]

Once students are comfortable with **le, la, les,** you may wish to introduce verbs beginning with vowels.
Z, tu les admires? [Z points to couple]
Tu l'admires aussi? [Z is confused]
Point to the man, addressing the entire class:
Cet homme, est-ce que vous l'admirez?

Write **l'** under the man's picture.
Et cette femme, vous l'admirez? Oui?

Write **l'** under the woman's picture.

2 COMMUNICATION answering personal questions

Answers will vary.
1. Oui, je connais (New York). Je connais bien (New York).
2. Oui, je connais un bon restaurant dans ma ville. Il s'appelle (Chez Nous). Oui, je connais un supermarché. Il s'appelle (Shopi). Non, je ne connais pas de centre commercial. Non, je ne connais pas de magasin de CD.
3. Oui, je connais des monuments à Paris. Je connais (l'Arc de Triomphe et le musée d'Orsay).
4. Oui, je connais bien mes voisins. Oui, ils sont sympathiques. Non, je ne connais pas personnellement la directrice de mon école. Oui, elle est stricte.
5. Je connais (Matt Damon et Ben Affleck). Je connais (Reese Witherspoon). Je connais (Dave Matthews et John Mayer). Je connais (Tom Brady et Nomar Garciaparra).

Language note In item 5, **connaître** means *to know* in the sense of *to know of* or *to know by reputation.* Students should be able to name one person in each category.

SECTION B

Communicative function
Talking about people and things

Pronunciation Be sure students make the liaison when the next word begins with a vowel sound.

Language notes
- Point out that direct object pronouns, in French as in English, replace the entire noun group: article (possessive, demonstrative, number), noun, adjective.
- Direct object pronouns are NOT used to replace nouns introduced by **un, une, des, du, de la.**
- The pronoun **en** is introduced in Book Two.

Teaching strategy The following common verbs take direct objects in French. You may want to write them on the board.
- with people: **aider, inviter, rencontrer,**
- with things: **acheter, avoir, laver, nettoyer, prendre, vendre**
- with people or things: **aimer, connaître, trouver, voir**

Point out that while **attendre, écouter,** and **regarder** take direct objects in French, the English equivalents have prepositions: *to wait for, to listen to, to look at.*

Teaching Resource Options

PRINT 

Workbook PE, pp. 237–244
Unit 8 Resource Book
Communipak, pp. 152–173
Workbook TE, pp. 115–121

TECHNOLOGY 

Power Presentations

3 ROLE PLAY indicating whether one knows people

–Tu connais ... ?
–Oui, je ... connais.
–Et toi, Lise?
–Non, je ne ... connais pas.

1. Christophe/le/le
2. Jacqueline/la/la
3. Anne et Valérie/les/les
4. Jérôme et Jean-François/les/les
5. la fille là-bas/la/la
6. cette étudiante/la/la
7. ma cousine/la/la
8. les cousins de Véronique/les/les
9. la copine de Jacques/la/la
10. ses frères/les/les

4 EXCHANGES answering questions using pronouns

–Tu prends ... ?
–Oui, je ... prends. (Non, je ne ... prends pas.)

1. tes CD/les/les
2. ton livre de français/le/le
3. ta guitare/la/la
4. ton baladeur/le/le
5. ta chaîne hi-fi/la/la
6. ton maillot de bain/le/le
7. ton skate/le/le
8. tes tee-shirts/les/les
9. tes sandales/les/les

5 ROLE PLAY/COMPREHENSION asking about activities

Answers will vary.

- –Quand est-ce que tu vois ta cousine?
  –Je la vois pendant les vacances.
- –Où est-ce que tu regardes la télé?
  –Je la regarde dans le salon.
- –À quelle heure est-ce que tu regardes la télé?
  –Je la regarde à neuf heures du soir.
- – Quand est-ce que tu regardes la télé?
  –Je la regarde le week-end (pendant les vacances, le samedi matin).
- – Quand est-ce que tu ranges ta chambre?
  –Je la range le samedi matin.
- –À quelle heure est-ce que tu ranges ta chambre?
  –Je la range à huit heures du matin.
- –Où est-ce que tu fais les courses?
  –Je les fais dans un supermarché.
- –Quand est-ce que tu fais les courses?
  –Je les fais le week-end.
- –À quelle heure est-ce que tu fais les courses?
  –Je les fais à neuf heures du matin.
- –Où est-ce que tu achètes tes CD?
  –Je les achète à la Boîte à Musique.
- –Quand est-ce que tu achètes tes CD?
  –Je les achète le week-end (pendant les vacances).
- –Où est-ce que tu achètes tes vêtements?
  –Je les achète à Mod'Shop.
- –Quand est-ce que tu achètes tes vêtements?
  –Je les achète le week-end (le samedi matin).
- –Où est-ce que tu prends le petit déjeuner?
  –Je le prends dans la cuisine.

3 À la boum de Delphine

PARLER Pierre connaît tous les invités *(all the guests)* à la boum de Delphine, mais Lise ne les connaît pas. Jouez les trois rôles.

▶ ces garçons?

Tu connais ces garçons?
Oui, je les connais.
Et toi, Lise?
Non, je ne les connais pas.

1. Christophe?
2. Jacqueline?
3. Anne et Valérie?
4. Jérôme et Jean-François?
5. la fille là-bas?
6. cette étudiante?
7. ma cousine?
8. les cousins de Véronique?
9. la copine de Jacques?
10. ses frères?

4 Un choix difficile

PARLER Vous allez passer le mois de juillet en France. Vous êtes limité(e) à 20 kilos de bagages. Un(e) camarade demande si vous allez prendre les choses suivantes. Répondez affirmativement ou négativement.

▶ ta raquette?
—Tu prends ta raquette?
—Oui, je la prends.
(Non, je ne la prends pas.)

1. tes CD?
2. ton livre de français?
3. ta guitare?
4. ton baladeur?
5. ta chaîne hi-fi?
6. ton maillot de bain?
7. ton skate?
8. tes tee-shirts?
9. tes sandales?

5 Questions et réponses

PARLER Julien pose des questions à Luc en utilisant les éléments des colonnes A et B. Jérôme répond logiquement en utilisant les éléments des colonnes B et C et un pronom complément. Avec un(e) camarade, jouez les deux rôles.

A	B	C
où	rencontrer tes copains	le samedi matin
quand	voir ta cousine	à 8 heures du matin
à quelle heure	regarder la télé	à 9 heures du soir
	ranger ta chambre	à la Boîte à Musique
	faire les courses	à Mod' Shop
	acheter tes CD	au café Le Pont Neuf
	acheter tes vêtements	dans un supermarché
	prendre le petit déjeuner	le week-end
		pendant les vacances
		dans la cuisine
		dans le salon

Où est-ce que tu rencontres tes copains?
MUSEE NATIONAL PICASSO
Je les rencontre au café Le Pont Neuf.

C La place des pronoms à l'impératif

Note the position of the object pronoun when the verb is in the imperative.

	AFFIRMATIVE COMMAND	NEGATIVE COMMAND
J'invite **Frédéric?**	Oui, invite-**le!**	Non, ne **l'**invite pas!
Je prends **la guitare?**	Oui, prends-**la!**	Non, ne **la** prends pas!
J'achète **les sandales?**	Oui, achète-**les!**	Non, ne **les** achète pas!

In AFFIRMATIVE COMMANDS, the object pronoun comes *after* the verb and is joined to it by a hyphen.
In NEGATIVE COMMANDS, the object pronoun comes *before* the verb.

6 Invitations

PARLER/ÉCRIRE Vous préparez une liste de personnes à inviter à une boum. Vous êtes limité(e)s à quatre *(4)* des personnes suivantes. Faites vos suggestions d'après les modèles.

▶ Caroline est sympathique.
Invitons-la!
▶ Jean-Louis est pénible.
Ne l'invitons pas!

1. Sylvie est très sympathique.
2. Cécile et Anne aiment danser.
3. Jacques est stupide.
4. Robert joue bien de la guitare.
5. Ces filles sont intelligentes.
6. Martin et Thomas sont snobs.
7. Nicolas n'est pas mon ami.
8. Ces garçons sont pénibles.
9. Cette fille est gentille.
10. Tes copains sont méchants.

7  Le pique-nique

PARLER Élodie demande à Mathieu si elle doit prendre certaines choses pour le pique-nique.

▶ ma guitare (oui)

1. la limonade (oui)
2. les sandwichs (non)
3. la salade (oui)
4. le lait (non)
5. le gâteau (non)
6. mon appareil-photo (oui)
7. mes lunettes de soleil (oui)
8. les impers (non)

8  Oui ou non?

PARLER Votre petit cousin de Québec passe deux semaines chez vous. Il vous demande s'il doit ou peut faire les choses suivantes. Répondez affirmativement ou négativement.

1. Je fais les courses?
2. Je regarde tes photos?
3. Je range ma chambre?
4. J'achète le journal *(newspaper)*?
5. J'invite les voisins à déjeuner?
6. Je prépare le dîner?
7. Je prends ton vélo?
8. Je loue les DVD?
9. J'aide ta mère?
10. Je mets la télé?

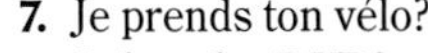

INCLUSION

Structured On the board, write a chart detailing the position of the object pronoun. Ask students to copy it in their notebooks. Ask them to repeat after you as you say sentences using the object pronoun, first in affirmative and then in negative commands. Then, ask students questions and have them generate sentences with the object pronoun, both in the affirmative and in the negative.

SECTION C

Communicative function
Giving orders

6 COMPREHENSION making suggestions about whom to invite

1. Invitons-la!
2. Invitons-les!
3. Ne l'invitons pas!
4. Invitons-le!
5. Invitons-les!
6. Ne les invitons pas!
7. Ne l'invitons pas!
8. Ne les invitons pas!
9. Invitons-la!
10. Ne les invitons pas!

Variation (dialogue format) With a classmate, decide if you will invite the following people.

Caroline est sympathique.
– J'invite Caroline?
– Oui, invite-la.

Jean-Louis est pénible.
– J'invite Jean-Louis?
– Non, ne l'invite pas.

7 ROLE PLAY offering and accepting or refusing services

1. –Est-ce que je prends de la limonade?
–Oui, prends-la!
2. –Est-ce que je prends les sandwichs?
–Non, ne les prends pas!
3. –Est-ce que je prends la salade?
–Oui, prends-la!
4. –Est-ce que je prends le lait?
–Non, ne le prends pas!
5. –Est-ce que je prends le gâteau?
–Non, ne le prends pas!
6. –Est-ce que je prends mon appareil-photo?
–Oui, prends-le!
7. –Est-ce que je prends mes lunettes de soleil?
–Oui, prends-les!
8. –Est-ce que je prends les impers?
–Non, ne les prends pas!

8 ROLE PLAY telling a friend what to do and not to do

1. Oui, fais-les. (Non, ne les fais pas.)
2. Oui, regarde-les. (Non, ne les regarde pas.)
3. Oui, range-la. (Non, ne la range pas.)
4. Oui, achète-le. (Non, ne l'achète pas.)
5. Oui, invite-les à déjeuner. (Non, ne les invite pas à déjeuner.)
6. Oui, prépare-le. (Non, ne le prépare pas.)
7. Oui, prends-le. (Non, ne le prends pas.)
8. Oui, loue-les. (Non, ne les loue pas.)
9. Oui, aide-la. (Non, ne l'aide pas.)
10. Oui, mets-la. (Non, ne la mets pas.)

SECTION D

Communicative function
Talking about others

Teaching Resource Options

PRINT 

Workbook PE, pp. 237–243
Unit 8 Resource Book
- Communipak, pp. 152–173
- Video Activities, p. 139
- Videoscript, pp. 142–143
- Workbook TE, pp. 115–121

TECHNOLOGY 

Power Presentations

VIDEO PROGRAM

VIDÉO DVD 

MODULE 28

28.3 Mini-scenes: On va lui parler?
(50:33–51:34 min.)

9 EXCHANGES asking friends whom they're telephoning

1. –Tu téléphones à ton copain?
   –Oui, je lui téléphone. (Non, je ne lui téléphone pas.)
2. –Tu téléphones à tes cousins?
   –Oui, je leur téléphone. (Non, je ne leur téléphone pas.)
3. –Tu téléphones à ta grand-mère?
   –Oui, je lui téléphone. (Non, je ne lui téléphone pas.)
4. –Tu téléphones à ton prof de français?
   –Oui, je lui téléphone. (Non, je ne lui téléphone pas.)
5. –Tu téléphones à tes voisins?
   –Oui, je leur téléphone. (Non, je ne leur téléphone pas.)
6. –Tu téléphones à ta tante favorite?
   –Oui, je lui téléphone. (Non, je ne lui téléphone pas.)

Variation (in the plural)

– Vous téléphonez à votre copine?
– Oui, nous lui téléphonons. (Non, nous ne lui téléphonons pas.)

D Les pronoms compléments *lui, leur*

In the questions below, the nouns in heavy type are INDIRECT OBJECTS. These nouns represent PEOPLE and are introduced by **à.**

Note the forms and position of the corresponding INDIRECT OBJECT PRONOUNS in the answers on the right.

Tu téléphones **à Philippe?**	Oui, je **lui** téléphone.
Tu parles **à Juliette?**	Non, je ne **lui** parle pas.
Tu téléphones **à tes amis?**	Oui, je **leur** téléphone.
Tu prêtes ton vélo **à tes cousines?**	Non, je ne **leur** prête pas mon vélo.

FORMS

INDIRECT OBJECT PRONOUNS replace **à** + noun representing people. They have the following forms:

	SINGULAR		PLURAL	
MASCULINE/FEMININE	**lui**	*to him, to her*	**leur**	*to them*

POSITION

Like other object pronouns, **lui** and **leur** come before the verb, except in affirmative commands.

Voici Henri. Parle-**lui!** Prête-**lui** ton vélo!

→ In negative sentences, **lui** and **leur,** like other object pronouns, come between **ne** and the verb.

Voici Éric.	Je ne **lui** téléphone pas.
Voici mes voisins.	Je ne **leur** parle pas.

9 Au téléphone

PARLER Demandez à vos camarades s'ils téléphonent aux personnes suivantes.

▶ ta copine

pharmacie
cosmetologie
herb
homéopathie
Tu téléphones à ta copine?
Oui, je lui téléphone.
(Non, je ne lui téléphone pas.)

1. ton copain
2. tes cousins
3. ta grand-mère
4. ton prof de français
5. tes voisins
6. ta tante favorite

VOCABULAIRE Verbes suivis *(followed)* d'un complément indirect

parler à	*to speak, talk (to)*	Je **parle à** mon copain.
rendre visite à	*to visit*	Nous **rendons visite à** nos voisins.
répondre à	*to answer*	Tu **réponds au** professeur.
téléphoner à	*to phone, call*	Jérôme **téléphone à** Juliette.
demander à	*to ask*	Je ne **demande** pas d'argent **à** mes frères.
donner à	*to give (to)*	Tu **donnes** ton adresse **à** ta copine.
montrer à	*to show (to)*	Nous **montrons** nos photos **à** nos amis.
prêter à	*to lend, loan (to)*	Je ne **prête** pas mon baladeur **à** ma soeur.

→ **Répondre** is a regular **-re** verb.
Je réponds à François. **J'ai répondu** à Catherine.

→ The verbs **téléphoner, répondre**, and **demander** take indirect objects in French, but not in English. Compare:

téléphoner

Nous **téléphonons**	**à**	Paul.	Nous **lui téléphonons.**
*We **are calling***	…	*Paul.*	*We **are calling him.***

répondre

Tu **réponds**	**à**	tes parents.	Tu **leur réponds.**
*You **answer***	…	*your parents.*	*You **answer them.***

demander

Je **demande**	**à**	Sylvie	…	son stylo.	Je **lui demande** son stylo.
*I **am asking***	…	*Sylvie*	*for*	*her pen.*	*I **am asking her** for her pen.*

10  Les copains de Léa

PARLER/ÉCRIRE Léa a beaucoup de copains. Décrivez ce que chacun fait pour elle. Complétez les phrases avec **Léa** ou **à Léa.**

▶ **Françoise invite Léa.**
Patrick rend visite à Léa.

1. Marc téléphone …
2. Jean-Paul voit … samedi prochain.
3. Sophie prête son vélo …
4. Mélanie écoute …
5. François donne son adresse …
6. Philippe regarde … pendant la classe.
7. Antoine attend … après la classe.
8. Nathalie parle …
9. Pauline invite … au concert.
10. Pierre répond …
11. Céline montre ses photos …
12. Thomas demande … son numéro de téléphone.
13. Éric rend visite …

Language note Point out that **rendre visite** takes an indirect object because the expression literally means *render a visit to someone.*

Extra practice Have students reword the sample sentences using object pronouns.
Je lui parle.
Nous leur rendons visite. etc.

10 PRACTICE distinguishing between direct and indirect objects

1. à Léa
2. Léa
3. à Léa
4. Léa
5. à Léa
6. Léa
7. Léa
8. à Léa
9. Léa
10. à Léa
11. à Léa
12. à Léa
13. à Léa

Expansion (using object pronouns)
Léa, C'est une fille!
Françoise l'invite.
Patrick lui rend visite.

Teaching Resource Options

PRINT 

Workbook PE, pp. 237–243
Unit 8 Resource Book
 Audioscript, p. 144
 Communipak, pp. 152–173
 Workbook TE, pp. 115–121

AUDIOVISUAL 

Audio Program
CD 4 Track 41

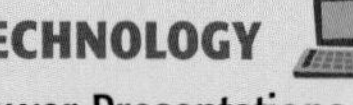

TECHNOLOGY

Power Presentations

11 EXCHANGES talking about giving presents

Answers will vary.

1. Je lui donne ...
2. Je lui donne ...
3. Je lui donne ...
4. Je lui donne ...
5. Je leur donne ...
6. Je lui donne ...
7. Je leur donne ...

12 COMMUNICATION answering personal questions

Answers will vary.

1. Oui, le week-end, je leur rends visite. Non, je ne lui rends pas visite.
2. Oui, je lui prête mes CD. (Non, je ne lui prête pas mes CD.) Oui, je leur prête mes CD. (Non, je ne leur prête pas mes CD.)
3. Oui, je lui demande de l'argent. (Non, je ne lui demande pas d'argent.)
4. Oui, je leur demande des conseils. (Non, je ne leur demande pas de conseils.)
5. Oui, je leur donne de bons conseils.
6. Oui, je lui montre mes photos. (Non, je ne lui montre pas mes photos.) Oui, je leur montre mes photos. (Non, je ne leur montre pas mes photos.)
7. Oui, je lui réponds en français. (Non, je ne lui réponds pas en français.)
8. Oui, je leur parle de mon problème. (Non, je ne leur parle pas [de mon problème].) Oui, je lui parle. (Non, je ne lui parle pas.)

SECTION E

Communicative function
Describing what people say and write

Re-entry and review Ask students which two other verbs have **vous** forms ending in **-tes**: **vous êtes, vous faites.**

Looking ahead The verb **lire** is not introduced until Book Two. If you wish to present the forms quickly for recognition, have students turn to the Appendix, page R10.

11 *Joyeux anniversaire!*

PARLER Choisissez un cadeau d'anniversaire pour les personnes suivantes. Un(e) camarade va vous demander ce que vous donnez à chaque personne.

▶ à ton copain

1. à ton petit frère
2. à ta mère
3. à ta grand-mère
4. à ta copine
5. à tes cousins
6. à ton (ta) prof
7. à tes copains

Cadeaux
un pull
un jeu vidéo
une cravate
un livre
des billets *(tickets)* de théâtre
un magazine
ma photo
une boîte *(box)* de chocolats
un gâteau
??

12 *Questions personnelles*

PARLER/ÉCRIRE Réponds aux questions suivantes. Utilise **lui** ou **leur** dans tes réponses.

1. Le week-end, est-ce que tu rends visite à tes copains? à ton oncle?
2. Est-ce que tu prêtes tes CD à ta soeur? à ton frère? à tes copains?
3. Est-ce que tu demandes de l'argent à ton père? à ta mère?
4. Est-ce que tu demandes des conseils *(advice)* à tes parents? à tes professeurs?
5. Est-ce que tu donnes de bons conseils à tes copains?
6. Est-ce que tu montres tes photos à ton frère? à ta soeur? à ta copine? à ton copain? à tes cousins?
7. En classe, est-ce que tu réponds en français à ton professeur?
8. Quand tu as un problème, est-ce que tu parles à tes copains? à ton professeur? à tes grands-parents? à tes parents?

E Les verbes *dire* et *écrire*

Note the forms of the irregular verbs **dire** *(to say, tell)* and **écrire** *(to write)*.

INFINITIVE	dire	écrire
PRESENT	je **dis**	j' **écris**
	tu **dis**	tu **écris**
	il/elle/on **dit**	il/elle/on **écrit**
	nous **disons**	nous **écrivons**
	vous **dites**	vous **écrivez**
	ils/elles **disent**	ils/elles **écrivent**
PASSÉ COMPOSÉ	j'ai **dit**	j'ai **écrit**

→ Note the use of **que/qu'** *(that)* after **dire** and **écrire.**

Florence **dit que** Frédéric est sympathique. — *Florence **says (that)** Frédéric is nice.*
Alain **écrit qu'**il est allé à un pique-nique. — *Alain **writes (that)** he went on a picnic.*

→ **Décrire** *(to describe)* follows the same pattern as **écrire.**

13 *Correspondance*

PARLER/ÉCRIRE Pendant les vacances, on écrit beaucoup de lettres. Dites à qui les personnes suivantes écrivent.

▶ Juliette/à Marc
Juliette écrit à Marc.

1. nous/à nos copains
2. toi/à ta cousine
3. moi/à ma grand-mère
4. Nicolas/à ses voisins
5. vous/à vos parents
6. les élèves/au professeur

14 *La boum*

PARLER/ÉCRIRE Des amis sont à une boum. Décrivez ce que chacun dit.

▶ toi/la musique est super
Tu dis que la musique est super.

1. Nicole/les sandwichs sont délicieux
2. nous/les invités *(guests)* sont sympathiques
3. Pauline/Jérôme danse bien
4. moi/ces garçons dansent mal
5. vous/vous n'aimez pas ce CD
6. mes copains/ils vont organiser une soirée le week-end prochain

15 *Questions personnelles* PARLER/ÉCRIRE

1. Est-ce que tu aimes écrire?
2. Pendant les vacances, est-ce que tu écris à tes copains? à tes voisins? à ton(ta) meilleur(e) *(best)* ami(e)?
3. À Noël, est-ce que tu écris des cartes *(cards)*? À qui?
4. À qui as-tu écrit un mail récemment *(recently)*?
5. Est-ce que tu dis toujours la vérité *(truth)*?
6. À ton avis, est-ce que les journalistes disent toujours la vérité? Et les politiciens?

PRONONCIATION

Les lettres «on» et «om»

on = /ɔ̃/ **on(n)e = /ɔ/**

lion **lionne**

Be sure to distinguish between the nasal and non-nasal vowel sounds.

REMEMBER: Do not pronounce an /n/ or /m/ after the nasal vowel /ɔ̃/.

Répétez:

/ɔ̃/	**mon ton son bon avion montrer répondre invitons blouson**
/ɔn/	**téléphone Simone donner connais mayonnaise personne bonne**
/ɔm/	**fromage promenade tomate pomme dommage comment**
/ɔ̃/–/ɔn/	**lion–lionne bon–bonne Simon–Simone Yvon–Yvonne**

Monique donne une pomme à Raymond.
Simone connaît mon oncle Léon.

INCLUSION

Alphabetic/phonetic Model the sounds of words ending in **on** and **om**. Ask students to practice the sounds, noting the placement of their tongue for the **m** and **n** sound, and for the nasal. Provide a list of easy words and ask students to pronounce them as a group. Have students pair off and practice. Then have them put the list in their notebooks.

13 PRACTICE telling whom people are writing

1. Nous écrivons à nos copains.
2. Tu écris à ta cousine.
3. J'écris à ma grand-mère.
4. Nicolas écrit à ses voisins.
5. Vous écrivez à vos parents.
6. Les élèves écrivent au professeur.

Variation (dialogue format, reviewing **lui, leur**)

– Est-ce que Juliette écrit à Marc?
– Oui, elle lui écrit.

Variation (in the passé composé)

Juliette a écrit à Marc.

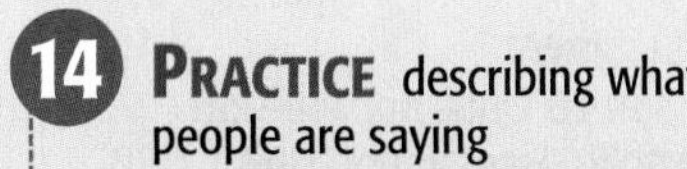

14 PRACTICE describing what people are saying

1. Nicole dit que les sandwichs sont délicieux.
2. Nous disons que les invités sont sympathiques.
3. Pauline dit que Jérôme danse bien.
4. Je dis que ces garçons dansent mal.
5. Vous dites que vous n'aimez pas ce CD.
6. Mes copains disent qu'ils vont organiser une soirée le week-end prochain.

15 COMMUNICATION answering personal questions

Answers will vary.

1. Oui, j'aime écrire. (Non, je n'aime pas écrire.)
2. Oui, pendant les vacances, j'écris à mes copains (à mes voisins, à mon [ma] meilleur[e] ami[e]). (Non, pendant les vacances, je n'écris pas à mes copains [à mes voisins, à mon (ma) meilleur(e) ami(e)].)
3. Oui, à Noël, j'écris des cartes. J'écris à (mes grands-parents, mes amis, mes professeurs, mes cousins, et mes voisins). (Non, à Noël, je n'écris pas de cartes.)
4. J'ai écrit un mail à (ma tante Marie) récemment.
5. Oui, je dis toujours la vérité. (Non, je ne dis pas toujours la vérité.)
6. Oui, à mon avis, les journalistes disent toujours la vérité. (Non, à mon avis, les journalistes ne disent pas toujours la vérité.) Oui, à mon avis, les politiciens disent toujours la vérité. (Non, à mon avis, les politiciens ne disent pas toujours la vérité.)

PRONUNCIATION

Remind students that the letters "on" and "om" represent a nasal vowel when they occur at the end of a word or when they are followed by a consonant. When these letters are followed by a vowel, they do not represent a nasal sound.

Additional practice

/ɔ̃/	/ɔn/
champion	**championne**
mignon	**mignonne**

À votre tour!

OBJECTIFS

Now you can …
- talk about people you know and don't know
- use pronouns to refer to people and things

1 Allô!

PARLER Reconstituez la conversation entre Olivier et Sophie. Pour cela, faites correspondre les réponses de Sophie avec les questions d'Olivier.

1 Qu'est-ce que tu fais ce week-end?
2 Tu m'invites?
3 Et Catherine? Tu l'invites aussi?
4 C'est ma nouvelle copine.
5 Tu veux son numéro de téléphone?
6 C'est le 01.44.32.28.50.

a. Je lui téléphone tout de suite *(right away)*.
b. Oui, je ne l'ai pas.
c. Bien sûr, je t'invite.
d. J'organise une fête.
e. Catherine? Je ne la connais pas. Qui est-ce?
f. Ah oui, je vois qui c'est maintenant. Eh bien, d'accord! Je l'invite.

2 Créa-dialogue

PARLER Avec vos camarades, discutez de certaines choses que vous faites. Posez plusieurs questions sur chaque activité.

Tu regardes la télé?
Oui je la regarde.
À quelle heure est-ce que tu la regardes?
À huit heures.

▶ regarder la télé?	1. inviter tes amis?	2. voir tes cousins?
à quelle heure?	quand? à quelle occasion?	quand? où?

3. faire les courses?	4. aider ta mère?	5. faire tes devoirs?	6. téléphoner à tes copains?	7. rendre visite à ta grand-mère?	8. écrire à ton cousin?
quand? où?	quand? comment?	quand? où?	quand? pourquoi?	quand? pourquoi?	pourquoi?

À VOTRE TOUR

Main Topic
- Recapitulation and review

Teaching Resource Options

PRINT 

Workbook PE, pp. 237–244
Unit 8 Resource Book
- Audioscript, p. 145
- Communipak, pp. 152–173
- Family Involvement, pp. 136–137
- Workbook TE, pp. 151–121

Assessment
- Lesson 28 Quiz, pp. 149–150
- Portfolio Assessment, Unit 1 URB pp. 155–164
- Audioscript for Quiz 28, p. 148
- Answer Keys, pp. 218–221

AUDIO & VISUAL 

Audio Program
CD 4 Tracks 42, 43
CD 16 Track 12

TECHNOLOGY

Test Generator CD-ROM/McDougal Littell Assessment System

1 COMPREHENSION

1. Qu'est-ce que tu fais ce week-end?
   (d) J'organise une fête.
2. Tu m'invites?
   (c) Bien sûr, je t'invite.
3. Et Catherine? Tu l'invites aussi?
   (e) Catherine? Je ne la connais pas. Qui est-ce?
4. C'est ma nouvelle copine.
   (f) Ah oui, je vois qui c'est maintenant. Eh bien, d'accord! Je l'invite.
5. Tu veux son numéro de téléphone?
   (b) Oui, je ne l'ai pas.
6. C'est le 01.44.32.28.50.
   (a) Je lui téléphone tout de suite.

À VOTRE TOUR

Depending on your goals and objectives, you may or may not wish to assign all of the activities in the **À votre tour** section.

PAIR/GROUP PRACTICE

Act. 1 lends itself to pair practice. It can also be done in trios, with two students performing and the third acting as monitor.

3  Composition: Les personnes dans ma vie *(life)*

Select three people from the list and write a short paragraph about each one. Give their names, say when you see them, and describe several things you do for them as well as one thing that you can't do. In your descriptions use the suggested verbs … and your imagination!

- un cousin/une cousine
- un frère/une soeur
- un copain/une copine
- un voisin/une voisine
- mon meilleur *(best)* ami
- ma meilleure amie
- un professeur de français (d'anglais, de maths, d'histoire)

téléphoner	voir	prêter	inviter
écrire	connaître	donner	rendre visite
répondre	parler	aider	

▶ 

COMMENT DIT-ON …?

How to tell someone to leave you alone:

Laisse-moi tranquille!

Fiche-moi la paix!

PORTFOLIO ASSESSMENT

You will probably select only one speaking activity and one writing activity to go into the students' portfolios for Unit 8.

In this lesson, Act. 3 can be used as the basis for a written portfolio entry.

2 GUIDED ORAL EXPRESSION

Answers will vary.

1. –Tu invites tes amis?
   –Oui, je les invite.
   –Quand est-ce que tu les invites?
   –Je les invite (ce week-end).
   –À quelle occasion est-ce que tu les invites?
   –Je les invite (pour mon anniversaire).
2. –Tu vois tes cousins?
   –Oui, je les vois (souvent).
   –Quand est-ce que tu les vois?
   –Je les vois (le dimanche).
   –Où est-ce que tu les vois?
   –Je les vois (chez ma grand-mère).
3. –Tu fais les courses?
   –Oui, je les fais.
   –Quand est-ce que tu les fais?
   –Je les fais (samedi matin).
   –Où est-ce que tu les fais?
   –Je les fais (au supermarché).
4. –Tu aides ta mère?
   –Oui, je l'aide.
   –Quand est-ce que tu l'aides?
   –Je l'aide (le soir).
   –Comment est-ce que tu l'aides?
   –Je (mets la table).
5. –Tu fais tes devoirs?
   –Oui, je les fais.
   –Quand est-ce que tu les fais?
   –Je les fais (avant le dîner).
   –Où est-ce que tu les fais?
   –Je les fais (dans ma chambre).
6. –Tu téléphones à tes copains?
   –Oui, je leur téléphone.
   –Quand est-ce que tu leur téléphones?
   –Je leur téléphone (le soir et le week-end).
   –Pourquoi est-ce que tu leur téléphones?
   –Je leur téléphone (pour organiser le week-end).
7. –Tu rends visite à ta grand-mère?
   –Oui, je lui rends visite.
   –Quand est-ce que tu lui rends visite?
   –Je lui rends visite (le dimanche).
   –Pourquoi est-ce que tu lui rends visite?
   –Parce que (j'aime lui parler).
8. –Tu écris à ton cousin?
   –Oui, je lui écris.
   –Pourquoi est-ce que tu lui écris?
   –(Pour lui parler de mon nouveau copain.)

3 WRITTEN SELF-EXPRESSION 

Answers will vary.

- Mon copain s'appelle Thomas. Je lui téléphone souvent. Il veut maigrir, alors je ne lui apporte jamais de glace. Je lui apporte des fruits!
- Mes voisins s'appellent Georges et Céline. Je les vois le matin et le soir. Je leur parle beaucoup. Je les aide dans leur jardin de temps en temps. Je ne leur rend pas visite le dimanche parce qu'ils vont en ville le dimanche.
- Mon amie s'appelle Rénée. Je déjeune toujours avec elle. On est dans la même classe, mais je ne lui parle jamais pendant la classe. Je l'aide avec ses devoirs.

TESTS DE CONTRÔLE

Teaching Resource Options

PRINT 

Unit 8 Resource Book
Communipak, pp. 252–273

Assessment
Unit 8 Test, pp. 184–192
Portfolio Assessment, Unit 1 URB pp. 155–164
Multiple Choice Test Items, pp. 205–213
Listening Comprehension Performance Test, pp. 193–194
Reading Performance Test, pp. 199–201
Speaking Performance Test, pp. 195–198
Writing Performance Test, pp. 202–204
Test Scoring Tools, p. 214
Audioscript for Tests, pp. 215–217
Answer Keys, pp. 218–221

AUDIO & VISUAL 

Audio Program
CD 16 Tracks 13–16

TECHNOLOGY 

Test Generator CD-ROM/McDougal Littell Assessment System

1 COMPREHENSION

1. de l'eau
2. du lait
3. du poulet
4. du jambon
5. du thé glacé
6. du fromage
7. du beurre
8. de la glace
9. du pain
10. du gâteau

2 COMPREHENSION

1. montre
2. déjeune
3. fait
4. apprend
5. donnent
6. écrit
7. comprends
8. bois
9. prend
10. prête

Tests de contrôle

By taking the following tests, you can check your progress in French and also prepare for the unit test. Write your answers on a separate sheet of paper.

1 Foods and beverages

Review...
- foods and beverages: pp. 366-367
- partitive article: pp. 378-379

Give the names of the foods and beverages you see on the table. With each one, be sure to use the appropriate partitive article: **du, de la,** or **de l'**.

Sur la table, il y a ...

1. — **3.** — **5.** — **7.** — **9.** —
2. — **4.** — **6.** — **8.** — **10.** —

2 The right choice

Review...
- new verbs: pp. 364, 370, 377, 383, 389, and 404

Complete each of the following sentences with the appropriate forms of the verbs in the box. Be logical in your choice of verbs and do not use the same word more than once.

apprendre
boire
comprendre
déjeuner
donner
écrire
faire
montrer
prendre
prêter

1. Caroline — ses photos de vacances à sa copine.
2. Madame Durand — au restaurant La Marmite.
3. Monsieur Lemaire — les courses au supermarché Prisunic.
4. À la piscine, mon petit frère — à nager.
5. Les gens généreux — de l'argent aux pauvres *(poor people)*.
6. Nicolas — un mail à sa cousine.
7. Est-ce que tu — bien quand le professeur parle français?
8. Au petit déjeuner, je — du jus d'orange.
9. Pauline — des photos avec son nouvel appareil-photo.
10. Catherine — souvent son vélo à sa soeur.

3 The right verb

Complete the following sentences with the appropriate forms of the present tense of the verb in parentheses.

(vouloir) 1. Cécile — voyager. Ses copines — visiter Paris.

(prendre) 2. Les touristes — le train. Nous — le bus.
(apprendre) 3. Élodie — l'anglais. Ses copains — l'espagnol.

(boire) 4. Nous — du thé. Les enfants — du lait.

(pouvoir) 5. Mes amis — venir à la boum. Est-ce que vous — rester?
(devoir) 6. Éric — étudier. Nous — aider nos parents.

(connaître) 7. Isabelle — Céline. Nous — ses copains.

(écrire) 8. Tu — une lettre. Mes cousins — un mail.
(dire) 9. Je — «oui». Mais vous, vous — «non».

Review...
- irregular verbs: pp. 376, 377, 383, 392, 398, and 404

4 The right pronoun

Complete the following sentences with the appropriate pronoun in parentheses that replaces the underlined words.

▶ Je connais Céline. Je **la** connais. **(le, la)**

1. Nous invitons Pierre. Nous — invitons à la boum. **(l', le)**
2. Tu écris à Charlotte. Tu — écris. **(la, lui)**
3. J'aide mes parents. Je — aide. **(l', les)**
4. Vous téléphonez à Mathieu. Vous — téléphonez souvent. **(le, lui)**
5. J'écoute mes CD. Je — écoute. **(les, leur)**
6. Nous parlons à nos amis. Nous — parlons. **(les, leur)**
7. Tu regardes ces photos. Tu — regardes avec Léa. **(les, leur)**
8. Vous lavez la voiture. Vous — lavez. **(la, lui)**

Review...
- object pronouns: pp. 399 and 402

5 Composition: Mon repas d'anniversaire

Write a short paragraph of five or six sentences describing what you would like for a special birthday dinner. Use only vocabulary and expressions that you know in French.

STRATEGY Writing

a First write out your menu.

b Then plan your paragraph, perhaps explaining why you are choosing certain items.

c Read over your composition to check that you are using the correct article with each food item.

hors d'oeuvre: ______________
viande ou poisson: ______________
autres plats: ______________
____
dessert: ______________
boissons: ______________

3 COMPREHENSION

1. veut / veulent
2. prennent / prenons
3. apprend / aprennent
4. buvons / boivent
5. peuvent / pouvez
6. doit / devons
7. connaît / connaissons
8. écris / écrivent
9. dis / dites

4 COMPREHENSION

1. l'
2. lui
3. les
4. lui
5. les
6. leur
7. les
8. la

5 WRITTEN SELF-EXPRESSION

Answers will vary.
Pour mon anniversaire, je veux dîner au restaurant Le Bon Temps. Comme hors d'oeuvre, je voudrais de la salade et de la soupe. Comme viande, je voudrais du poulet parce que j'aime le poulet! Comme autres plats, je voudrais des petits pois et des carottes. Je vais boire du lait. Après le dîner, je vais manger de la tarte aux pommes parce que c'est mon dessert préféré!

Language Learning Benchmarks

FUNCTION

- Engage in conversations pp. 370, 380, 390
- Express likes and dislikes pp. 368, 369
- Make requests pp. 365, 367, 371, 381, 391
- Begin to provide information pp. 365, 377, 398

CONTEXT

- Converse in face-to-face social interactions pp. 390, 391, 400, 402
- Listen to audio and video texts pp. 362-363, 374, 386, 396
- Use authentic materials when reading: schedules p. 389
- Use authentic materials when reading: signs p. 373
- Use authentic materials when reading: short narratives p. 412
- Write notes p. 395
- Write lists pp. 369, 373, 409

TEXT TYPE

- Use short sentences when speaking pp. 376, 383, 405
- Use short sentences when writing pp. 376, 383
- Use learned words and phrases when speaking pp. 365, 379
- Use learned words and phrases when writing pp. 365, 380
- Use simple questions when speaking pp. 369, 382, 393, 404
- Use simple questions when writing p. 389
- Use commands when speaking p. 401
- Use commands when writing p. 401
- Understand some ideas and familiar details presented in clear, uncomplicated speech when listening pp. 372, 397
- Understand short texts enhanced by visual clues when reading pp. 375, 387, 416-417

Vocabulaire

POUR COMMUNIQUER

Saying where you will eat

Je vais déjeuner	**à la maison.**	*I will have lunch*	*at home.*
	à la cantine (de l'école)		*at the (school) cafeteria*
	au restaurant		*at the restaurant*

Planning a meal

Il faut ...	
aller au marché	*go to the market*
faire les courses	*do the food shopping*
acheter la nourriture	*buy the food*
choisir les boissons	*choose the beverages*
préparer le repas	*fix the meal*
faire la cuisine	*do the cooking*
mettre le couvert	*set the table*

Saying what foods you like and dislike

J'aime [le rosbif].	*I like roast beef.*
Je préfère [la glace].	*I prefer ice cream.*
Je déteste [les frites].	*I detest French fries.*

Shopping for food, asking for certain quantities

Je voudrais ...		**une livre de beurre**	*a pound of butter*
du beurre	*(some) butter*	**un kilo de sole**	*a kilo (2.2 pounds) of sole*
de la sole	*(some) sole*	**une douzaine d'oeufs**	*a dozen eggs*
des oeufs	*(some) eggs*		

MOTS ET EXPRESSIONS

Les repas *(Meals)*

le petit déjeuner	*breakfast*	**prendre le petit déjeuner**	*to have breakfast*
le déjeuner	*lunch*	**déjeuner**	*to have lunch*
le dîner	*dinner*	**dîner**	*to have dinner*

Le couvert *(Place settings)*

un couteau	*knife*	**une assiette**	*plate*
un verre	*glass*	**une cuillère**	*spoon*
		une fourchette	*fork*
		une serviette	*napkin*
		une tasse	*cup*

La nourriture et les plats

un dessert	*dessert*	**le poulet**	*chicken*	**les céréales**	*cereal*
le fromage	*cheese*	**le riz**	*rice*	**les frites**	*French fries*
le gâteau	*cake*	**le rosbif**	*roast beef*	**la glace**	*ice cream*
un hors-d'oeuvre	*appetizer*	**le saucisson**	*salami*	**la nourriture**	*food*
le jambon	*ham*	**les spaghetti**	*spaghetti*	**la salade**	*salad*
le pain	*bread*	**le thon**	*tuna*	**la sole**	*sole*
un plat	*dish*	**le veau**	*veal*	**la soupe**	*soup*
le poisson	*fish*	**le yaourt**	*yogurt*	**la tarte**	*pie*
				la viande	*meat*

Les fruits et les légumes

un fruit	*fruit*	**une banane**	*banana*	**une poire**	*pear*
des haricots verts	*green beans*	**une carotte**	*carrot*	**une pomme**	*apple*
un légume	*vegetable*	**une cerise**	*cherry*	**une pomme de terre**	*potato*
un pamplemousse	*grapefruit*	**une fraise**	*strawberry*	**une salade**	*(head of) lettuce*
des petits pois	*peas*	**une orange**	*orange*	**une tomate**	*tomato*

Les ingrédients

le beurre	*butter*	**la confiture**	*jam*
le ketchup	*ketchup*	**la mayonnaise**	*mayonnaise*
un oeuf	*egg*		
le sel	*salt*		
le sucre	*sugar*		

Les boissons

le jus d'orange	*orange juice*	**une boisson**	*beverage*
le jus de pomme	*apple juice*	**l'eau**	*water*
le lait	*milk*	**l'eau minérale**	*mineral water*
le thé glacé	*iced tea*		

Interacting with others

Est-ce que Paul	**me**	**connaît?**	*Does Paul know*	*me ?*
	te			*you?*
	nous			*us?*
	vous			*you?*
	le			*him?*
	la			*her?*
	les			*them?*
Est-ce que Sophie	**me**	**parle?**	*Is Sophie talking*	*to me?*
	te			*to you?*
	nous			*to us?*
	vous			*to you?*
	lui			*to him/her?*
	leur			*to them?*

Verbes réguliers

aider	*to help*
amener	*to bring (people)*
apporter	*to bring (things)*
demander (à)	*to ask*
donner (à)	*to give (to)*
montrer (à)	*to show (to)*
prêter (à)	*to lend, to loan (to)*
répondre (à)	*to answer*

Verbes irréguliers

apprendre	*to learn*
apprendre à + *infinitive*	*to learn how to*
boire	*to drink*
comprendre	*to understand*
connaître	*to know*
décrire	*to describe*
devoir	*must, to have to*
dire	*to say, to tell*
écrire (à)	*to write (to)*
pouvoir	*can, may, to be able*
prendre	*to take, to have (a meal)*
vouloir	*to want*

FLASHCARDS AND MORE!

CONTENT

- Understand and convey information about likes and dislikes pp. 368, 369
- Understand and convey information about prices pp. 371, 413
- Understand and convey information about size and quantity pp. 371, 413
- Understand and convey information about food and customs p. 365

ASSESSMENT

- Communicate effectively with some hesitation and errors, which do not hinder comprehension pp. 373
- Demonstrate culturally acceptable behavior for engaging in conversations pp. 372, 385, 395, 406
- Demonstrate culturally acceptable behavior for making requests p. 394
- Understand most important information pp. 373, 394, 406

ENTRACTE 8

Objectives

- Reading skills development
- Re-entry of material in the unit
- Development of cultural awareness

Teaching Resource Options

PRINT  

Workbook PE, pp. 245–249
Activités pour tous PE, pp. 147–149
Unit 8 Resource Book
Activités pour tous TE, pp. 175–177
Workbook TE, pp. 179–183

Bon appétit, Aurélie!

Objectives

- Reading at the paragraph level
- Reading for cultural information about French foods and eating habits

Questions sur le texte

1. Où est-ce qu'Aurélie mange à midi? le soir? [à la cantine de l'école/à la maison]
2. Qui fait les courses chez Aurélie? [sa mère]
3. Qui prépare le dîner chez Aurélie? [son père]
4. Qu'est-ce qu'il y a comme dessert chez Aurélie? [du yaourt ou un fruit]
5. Quel type de restaurant est-ce qu'il y a dans le quartier d'Aurélie? [vietnamien]
6. Quel type de pizza est-ce qu'Aurélie préfère? [une pizza avec du fromage, des olives et des anchois]
7. Qu'est-ce qu'Aurélie boit avec la pizza? [un soda]

Comparaisons culturelles
Answers

- À la maison, Aurélie mange une salade de concombres ou de tomates, de la viande, des légumes, parfois du cassoulet en boîte, une salade verte et des fromages et un dessert.
- Au restaurant avec la famille, Aurélie mange du riz avec des crevettes et des petits pois.
- Au restaurant avec les copains, Aurélie mange une pizza avec du fromage, des olives et des anchois.

Bon appétit, Aurélie!

Nous avons demandé à Aurélie de décrire ses repas. Voici sa réponse.

À midi, je mange à la cantine de l'école et le soir à la maison. C'est ma mère qui fait les courses et c'est mon père qui prépare le dîner. Il adore ça! Il fait une cuisine assez traditionnelle, mais bien équilibrée°. En général, on commence par une salade de concombres ou de tomates. Ensuite, il y a de la viande, par exemple, un bifteck ou du poulet, avec des haricots verts ou des pommes de terre. Parfois, on mange du cassoulet° en boîte°. Après, il y a une salade verte et des fromages divers. Comme dessert, il y a du yaourt ou un fruit. Avec le repas, on boit de l'eau minérale.

Quand mon père n'a pas envie de faire la cuisine, on va au restaurant. Dans notre quartier, il y a un restaurant vietnamien que nous aimons bien. Mon plat préféré, c'est le riz avec des crevettes° et des petits pois.

Quand je sors avec mes copains, on va dans les fast-food. J'aime bien aller dans les pizzerias parce qu'on peut choisir ses ingrédients. En général, je prends une pizza avec du fromage, des olives et des anchois. Avec la pizza, je bois souvent un soda.

équilibrée *balanced*
cassoulet *bean stew with pork or duck*
en boîte *canned* **crevettes** *shrimp*

COMPARAISONS CULTURELLES

Comparez les repas d'Aurélie avec vos repas. Qu'est-ce que vous mangez pour le dîner? Faites une liste des similarités et des différences.

	AURÉLIE	LES SIMILARITÉS AVEC MOI	LES DIFFÉRENCES AVEC MOI
À la maison	________	________	________
Au restaurant avec la famille	________	________	________
Au restaurant avec les copains	________	________	________

ALLOpizza

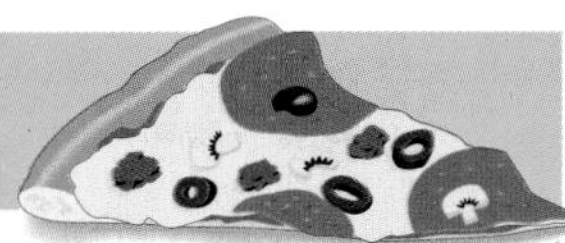

MENU

		26 cm. 1 pers.	31 cm. 2/3 pers.	40 cm. 3/4 pers.
ITALIENNE	sauce tomate, origan, mozzarella, anchois, olives	7,50 €	12 €	15 €
4 SAISONS	sauce tomate, mozzarella, crème, olives, tomates fraîches, champignons	7,50 €	12 €	15 €
3 FROMAGES	sauce tomate, mozzarella, origan, chèvre, Roquefort	8 €	13 €	17 €
PESCATORE	sauce tomate, mozzarella, origan, oignons, saumon, champignons	8 €	13 €	17 €
ANGLAISE	sauce tomate, mozzarella, origan, bacon, oeuf, pommes de terre	9 €	14 €	20 €
TEXANE	sauce tomate, mozzarella, origan, boeuf épicé, pepperoni, oignons	9 €	14 €	20 €

02-47-66-89-89

Petit dictionnaire

anchois	*anchovies*
frais/fraîche	*fresh*
boeuf épicé	*spicy beef*
oignon	*onion*
champignon	*mushroom*
origan	*oregano*
chèvre	*goat cheese*
saumon	*salmon*

Et vous?

Formez un groupe de 4 à 5 personnes. Imaginez que vous êtes en France. Vous voulez dîner et vous avez décidé de commander des pizzas. Faites une liste de ce que chacun veut commander.

NOM	TYPE DE PIZZA	DIMENSION	PRIX
John	Texane	31 cm.	14 €
•			
•			
•			
•			
•			

PRE-READING

Have students look quickly at the menu and decide what meal is presented.

How can they tell? **Pre-AP skill:** Skim and scan.

ALLOpizza

Objectives

- Reading authentic documents
- Vocabulary expansion

Et vous?

Answers will vary.

Sara	Italienne	26 cm.	7,50 euros
Josh	Pescatore	31 cm.	13 euros
Emma	Anglaise	26 cm.	9 euros
Noah	4 Saisons	40 cm.	15 euros
Alex	3 Fromages	31 cm.	13 euros

Supplementary vocabulary

Here are some other popular toppings on pizzas in France:

de l'ananas *pineapple*
des artichauts *artichokes*
de l'aubergine *eggplant*
des câpres *capers*
du jambon *ham*
des lardons *diced bacon*
du maïs *corn*
de la persillade *parsley vinaigrette*
des poivrons *peppers*
du poulet fumé *smoked chicken*
du saumon *salmon*
du thon *tuna*

Culture notes

- The French often have an egg on their pizza. The egg **(l'oeuf)** is broken on top of the pizza just before baking.
- Pizza in France generally does not come sliced as it does here in the United States. It arrives as a complete pizza, and the cutting is left to the customer.
- Many pizzerias in France have websites from which customers can order pizza to be picked up **(pizza à emporter)** or to be delivered **(la livraison)**.

Le petit déjeuner

Objectives

- Reading at the paragraph level
- Building reading skills

Teaching Resource Options

PRINT

Workbook PE, pp. 245–249
Activités pour tous PE, pp. 147–149
Unit 8 Resource Book
Activités pour tous TE, pp. 175–177
Workbook TE, pp. 179–183

Questions sur le texte

1. Qu'est-ce que Fabrice met sur son pain? (Il met du beurre et de la confiture sur son pain.)
2. Qu'est-ce qu'il boit? (Il boit un grand bol de café au lait.)
3. Pourquoi est-ce que Mathieu dit qu'il prend le petit déjeuner «à l'américaine»? (Parce qu'il prend des céréales et il boit du jus d'orange.)
4. Qu'est-ce que Sandrine boit au petit déjeuner? (Elle boit du lait chaud ou du chocolat avec beaucoup de sucre.)
5. Quel jour est-ce qu'elle mange des croissants? (Elle mange des croissants le dimanche.)
6. Pourquoi est-ce que Sylvie ne mange pas beaucoup au petit déjeuner? (Elle n'a pas très faim le matin.)
7. Qu'est-ce qu'elle prend avec elle pour manger avant la première classe? (Elle prend une barre de céréales ou une barre chocolatée.)
8. De quelle origine est Stéphanie? (Elle est martiniquaise.)
9. En général, qu'est-ce qu'elle mange au petit déjeuner? (Elle mange du pain et de la confiture.)
10. Qu'est-ce qu'elle mange avec le blaff de poisson? (Elle mange des bananes vertes cuites.)

Comparaisons culturelles

Answers will vary.

- Mathieu a le petit déjeuner le plus semblable parce qu'il mange des céréales et il boit du jus d'orange.
- Stéphanie a le petit déjeuner le plus different parce qu'elle mange du poisson!

Activité écrite

Answers will vary.
Pendant la semaine, le petit déjeuner est normal. Je mange des céréales et je bois du jus d'orange ou du chocolat chaud. Mais, le dimanche matin, ma famille et moi, nous allons dans un restaurant. Je mange une omelette avec du fromage et des champignons et du pain grillé. J'aime le dimanche!

Le petit déjeuner *en France*

«Qu'est-ce que vous prenez au petit déjeuner?» Aux États-Unis, le petit déjeuner est généralement un repas abondant.° En France, c'est un repas simple.

Fabrice (13 ans)

Chez nous, nous sommes très traditionnels. Je mange du pain avec du beurre et de la confiture. Je bois un grand bol° de café au lait.

Mathieu (16 ans)

Chez nous, on prend le petit déjeuner «à l'américaine». Je mange des céréales et je bois du jus d'orange.

Sandrine (16 ans)

Je mange des tartines de pain° grillé° et je bois du lait chaud ou du chocolat avec beaucoup de sucre. Le dimanche, il y a parfois° des croissants. (Ça dépend si quelqu'un veut faire les courses!)

Sylvie (15 ans)

Le matin, je n'ai pas très faim. En général, je mange une tartine, c'est tout.° Je prends avec moi une barre de céréales ou une barre chocolatée que je mange avant° la première classe.

abondant *abundant, copious* **bol** *deep bowl* **tartines de pain** *slices of bread* **grillé** *toasted* **parfois** *sometimes* **tout** *all* **avant** *before*

COMPARAISONS CULTURELLES

Comparez le petit déjeuner des cinq jeunes Français avec votre petit déjeuner.

- Qui a le petit déjeuner le plus semblable *(most similar)*? Expliquez.
- Qui a le petit déjeuner le plus différent? Expliquez.

Activité écrite

Décrivez le petit déjeuner chez vous:

- pendant la semaine
- le dimanche matin

PRE-READING

Have students glance over the reading quickly. What is the question that was asked in the interview?

POST-READING

Ask each student to decide which of the five people they would like to have breakfast with and why.

Chez qui veux-tu prendre le petit déjeuner? Pourquoi?

Questions personnelles

Answers will vary.

1. Est-ce que tu bois du jus de fruit le matin? Quel jus de fruit?
[Oui, je bois du jus de fruit. Je bois du jus d'orange. (Non, je ne bois pas de jus de fruit.)]
2. Est-ce que tes parents boivent du café? Sinon, qu'est-ce qu'ils boivent?
[Oui, mes parents boivent du café. (Non, mes parents ne boivent pas de café. Ils boivent du thé.)]
3. Est-ce que tu manges souvent des croissants? Quand? Oui, je mange souvent des croissants. Je mange des croissants le week-end.
[Non, je ne mange pas souvent de croissants. Je mange des croissants quand je suis à Paris.]
4. Est-ce que tu aimes la confiture? Quelle est ta confiture préférée?
[Oui, j'aime la confiture. Ma confiture préférée est la confiture aux fraises. (Non, je n'aime pas la confiture.)]
5. Est-ce que tu manges des céréales? De quelles sortes?
[Oui, je mange des céréales. Je mange des céréales sucrés. (Non, je ne mange pas de céréales.)]
6. Est-ce que tu préfères le petit déjeuner français ou le petit déjeuner américain? Pourquoi?
[Je préfère le petit déjeuner américain parce que j'aime les omelettes. (Je préfère le petit déjeuner français parce qu'il est plus léger.)]

Stéphanie (13 ans)

Je suis martiniquaise. En général, je mange du pain et de la confiture comme° tout le monde.° Parfois ma mère prépare un petit déjeuner martiniquais typique. On mange du blaff de poisson° et des bananes vertes cuites.° On mange aussi des ananas,° des papayes et de la gelée de goyave.° C'est délicieux!

comme *like* **tout le monde** *everyone* **blaff de poisson** *fish stew* **cuites** *cooked* **ananas** *pineapple* **gelée de goyave** *guava jelly*

NOTE culturelle

La cuisine créole

La cuisine créole est une cuisine régionale typique de la Martinique et de la Guadeloupe. C'est une cuisine assez épicée° qui utilise les produits locaux,° principalement les produits de la mer° et les fruits exotiques.

Voici certaines spécialités:

boudin créole	*spicy sausage*
colombo	*rice with spicy meat sauce*
blaff de poisson	*fish stew*
matoutou crabes	*stewed crabs served with rice*
crabes farcis	*stuffed crabs*
langoustes grillées	*(small) lobsters, broiled*

épicée *hot (spicy)* **locaux** *local* **mer** *sea*

DÉCOUVREZ LA MARTINIQUE
au
TYPIC BELLEVUE
LE PLUS TYPIQUE DES RESTAURANTS
UN CHOIX UNIQUE DE SPÉCIALITÉS CRÉOLES
Boulevard de la Marne Tél. 05.96.71.68.87
FORT-DE-FRANCE
Parking Boulevard de Verdun
** RELAIS CRÉOLE **
Menu du jour et à la carte
Ouvert midi et soir sauf dimanche

LA VILLA CRÉOLE
La Bonne Cuisine Française et Créole
ANSE-MITAN
TROIS-ILETS
66.05.53

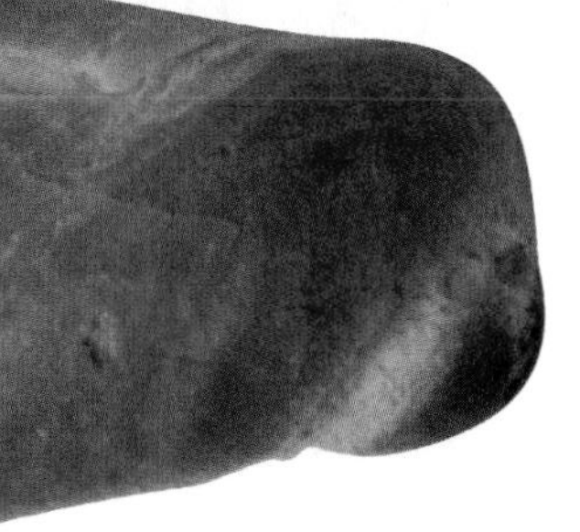

Realia note
Le menu
At the **Typic Bellevue** one can either select the **prix fixe** menu **(le menu du jour)** or order dishes from the main menu **(à la carte).**

Realia note
La Villa Créole is a small Martinique restaurant on the beach at Anse-Mitan (**anse** = bay) in the town of Trois Îlets (**îlet** = small island)

CONNEXIONS

Haitian people have their own creole cuisine which is somewhat different from that of Martinique. Find out about Haitian cuisine by visiting a local Haitian restaurant or by surfing the Internet.

- What products do Haitians use in their cooking?
- What are some typical dishes?

Les crêpes

Objectives
- Reading for information
- Understanding and following instructions

Teaching Resource Options

PRINT

Workbook PE, pp. 245–249
Activités pour tous PE, pp. 147–149
Unit 8 Resource Book
Activités pour tous TE, pp. 175–177
Workbook TE, pp. 179–183

VIDEO PROGRAM

MODULE 28

28.4 Vignette culturelle: La recette des crêpes (51:35–52:53 min.)

Photo culture note

Une cuisine française
French kitchens are smaller than American kitchens, but they are usually equipped in the same way.

Note in the background:
- the counter **(le comptoir)**
- the cabinets **(les placards)**
- the sink **(l'évier)**
- pots and pans **(les casseroles)**
- the microwave oven **(le four à micro-ondes)**

Les crêpes

Les crêpes sont d'origine bretonne.° Aujourd'hui, on vend les crêpes dans les «crêperies». On peut aussi faire des crêpes à la maison. Voici une recette° très simple.

les ingrédients

3 oeufs
3 cuillères à soupe de sucre
une pincée° de sel
2 tasses de lait
1 tasse de farine°
1 cuillère à soupe d'huile°
du beurre

les ustensiles

un petit bol

un grand bol

un fouet

une poêle

STRATEGY Reading

Using illustrations When you are reading, the context is not only the printed word. Sometimes the illustrations can help you understand the text. As you read the recipe, try guessing the meanings of the new words by studying the pictures.

D'abord: Pour faire la pâte°

Mettez les oeufs dans le petit bol. Battez-les° bien avec le fouet.

Ajoutez° le sucre, le sel et un peu de lait.

Mettez la farine dans le grand bol. Versez° le contenu° du petit bol dans le grand bol.

Ajoutez l'huile et le reste du lait. Mélangez° bien la pâte. Attendez deux heures.

bretonne *from Brittany* **recette** *recipe* **pincée** *pinch* **farine** *flour* **huile** *oil* **pâte** *batter* **Battez-les** *Beat them* **Ajoutez** *Add* **Versez** *Pour* **contenu** *contents* **Mélangez** *Mix, Stir*

PRE-READING

Have students identify the type of reading. [a recipe: **une recette**]

What kinds of verb forms are used in this recipe? [commands]

optional: Show the *Vignette culturelle* of Video Module 28 which demonstrates the making of crêpes.

Ensuite: Pour faire les crêpes

Chauffez° la poêle. Mettez du beurre dans la poêle.

Mettez une cuillère de pâte dans la poêle.

Agitez° la poêle pour étendre° la pâte.

Retournez° la crêpe quand elle est dorée.°

Si vous êtes adroit(e), faites sauter° la crêpe en l'air. Si vous n'êtes pas adroit(e), abstenez-vous!°

Enfin: Pour servir les crêpes

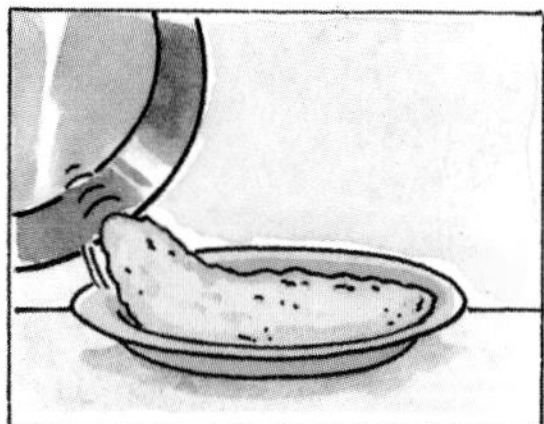

Mettez la crêpe sur une assiette chaude. Faites les autres° crêpes.

Mettez du sucre ou de la confiture sur chaque° crêpe.

Au choix, roulez-la° ou pliez-la° en quatre.

Chauffez *Heat* **Agitez** *Shake* **étendre** *spread* **Retournez** *Turn over* **dorée** *golden brown* **faites sauter** *flip* **abstenez-vous** *don't try* **autres** *other* **chaque** *each* **roulez-la** *roll it* **pliez-la** *fold it*

TEACHING STRATEGY Les crêpes

You might want to cooperate with the home economics department and let the students learn to make **crêpes** in the school kitchen.

Tête à tête Pair Activities

CONTENTS

Teaching note All of the **Tête à tête** activities are done in pairs as **Élève A** and **Élève B**. Quickly divide the class into **Élève A** and **Élève B** by going around the classroom and counting off: A…B…A…B. Then, have the "A" students pair up with the nearest "B" students. Instruct "B" students to turn their books upside down in order to begin the activity.

Teaching hint For additional pair activities, and for other communicative activities for Unité 1, please go to the **Communipak** section of the **Unit 1 Resource Book**, pp. 128–144.

Teaching tip Have students review NATIONALITY VOCABULARY by referring them to p. 19 in the textbook. Alternately, you can use **Overhead Transparency** 4 to review this vocabulary.

Answers

Élève A: Comment s'appelle ton amie?
Élève B: Elle s'appelle Alice.

Élève A: Quel âge a ton amie?
Élève B: Elle a 15 ans.

Élève A: Elle est française ou américaine?
Élève B: Elle est américaine.

Élève A: Comment s'appelle ton ami?
Élève B: Il s'appelle David.

Élève A: Quel âge a ton ami?
Élève B: Il a 14 ans.

Élève A: Il est français ou américain?
Élève B: Il est français.

Élève B: Comment s'appelle ton amie?
Élève A: Elle s'appelle Pauline.

Élève B: Quel âge a ton amie?
Élève A: Elle a 16 ans.

Élève B: Elle est française ou américaine?
Élève A: Elle est française.

Élève B: Comment s'appelle ton ami?
Élève A: Il s'appelle Patrick.

Élève B: Quel âge a ton ami?
Élève A: Il a 15 ans.

Élève B: Il est français ou américain?
Élève A: Il est américain.

? *Answers will vary.*

L'École franco-américaine — Élève B

You and your partner are both enrolled in a French-American school, but you are in different classes and have different friends.

- The pictures on the right show your two best friends: one a girl, the other a boy.
- Your partner has pictures of his/her two best friends.

▶ Ask each other questions to find out more about each other's friends:

- name
  Comment s'appelle ton ami(e)?
- age
  Quel âge a ton ami(e)?
- nationality
  Il est français ou américain?
  Elle est française ou américaine?

? *Do any of your friends have the same name? the same age? the same nationality?*

David – 14 ans

Alice – 15 ans

L'École franco-américaine — Élève A

You and your partner are both enrolled in a French-American school, but you are in different classes and have different friends.

- The pictures on the right show your two best friends: one a girl, the other a boy.
- Your partner has pictures of his/her two best friends.

▶ Ask each other questions to find out more about each other's friends:

- name
  Comment s'appelle ton ami(e)?
- age
  Quel âge a ton ami(e)?
- nationality
  Il est français ou américain?
  Elle est française ou américaine?

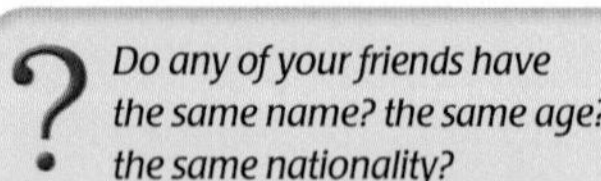
? *Do any of your friends have the same name? the same age? the same nationality?*

Pauline – 16 ans

Patrick – 15 ans

Au restaurant — Élève B

You are at a French restaurant with your partner.

- Your menu has the prices for the beverages.
- Your partner's menu has the prices for the food items.

▶ Ask each other questions to find out the cost of the various foods and beverages.

Élève A: **Combien coûte le café?**
Élève B: **Le café coûte deux euros dix.**

Élève B: **Combien coûte la pizza?**
Élève A: **La pizza coûte ...**

What is the most expensive food?
What is the least expensive food?

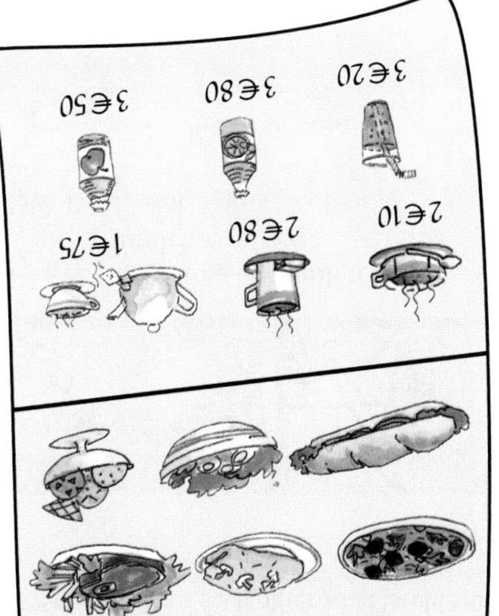

Au restaurant — Élève A

You are at a French restaurant with your partner.

- Your menu has the prices for the food items.
- Your partner's menu has the prices for the beverages.

▶ Ask each other questions to find out the cost of the various foods and beverages.

Élève A: **Combien coûte le café?**
Élève B: **Le café coûte deux euros dix.**

Élève B: **Combien coûte la pizza?**
Élève A: **La pizza coûte ...**

menu

5€40 4€80 10€80

3€70 3€30 2€50

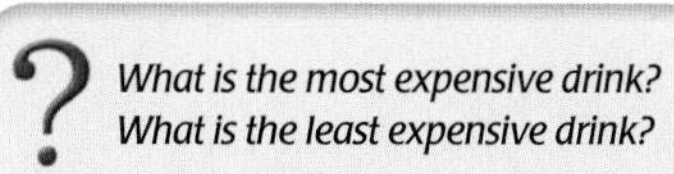

What is the most expensive drink?
What is the least expensive drink?

TÊTE À TÊTE

Teaching hint For additional pair activities, and for other communicative activities for **Unité 2**, please go to the **Communipak** section of the **Unit 2 Resource Book**, pp. 132–153.

Teaching tip Have students review FOOD and BEVERAGE VOCABULARY by referring them to pp. 45 and 49 in the textbook. Alternately, you can use Overhead Transparencies S7, 3A, 3B, and 3C to review this vocabulary.

Answers

Élève A: Combien coûte le chocolat?
Élève B: Le chocolat coûte deux euros quatre-vingts.

Élève A: Combien coûte le thé?
Élève B: Le thé coûte un euro soixante-quinze.

Élève A: Combien coûte le soda?
Élève B: Le soda coûte trois euros vingt.

Élève A: Combien coûte le jus d'orange?
Élève B: Le jus d'orange coûte trois euros quatre-vingts.

Élève A: Combien coûte le jus de pomme?
Élève B: Le jus de pomme coûte trois euros cinquante.

Élève B: Combien coûte la pizza?
Élève A: La pizza coûte cinq euros quarante.

Élève B: Combien coûte l'omelette?
Élève A: L'omelette coûte quatre euros quatre-vingts.

Élève B: Combien coûte le steak-frites?
Élève A: Le steak-frites coûte dix euros quatre-vingts.

Élève B: Combien coûte le sandwich?
Élève A: Le sandwich coûte trois euros soixante-dix.

Élève B: Combien coûte la salade?
Élève A: La salade coûte trois euros trente.

Élève B: Combien coûte la glace?
Élève A: La glace coûte deux euros cinquante.

? *The most expensive drink is the orange juice. The least expensive drink is the tea. The most expensive food is the steak and French fries. The least expensive food is the ice cream.*

Teaching hint For additional pair activities, and for other communicative activities for Unité 3, please go to the **Communipak** section of the **Unit 3 Resource Book**, pp. 128–141.

Teaching tip Have students review WEEKLY ACTIVITY VOCABULARY by referring them to pp. 74-75 in the textbook. Alternately, you can use **Overhead Transparencies** 14a and 14b to review this vocabulary.

Answers

Élève A: Qu'est-ce que Julien fait mardi?
Élève B: Mardi, il regarde la télé.

Élève B: Et Sophie, qu'est-ce qu'elle fait mardi?
Élève A: Elle chante.

Élève A: Qu'est-ce que Julien fait mercredi?
Élève B: Mercredi, il travaille.

Élève B: Et Sophie, qu'est-ce qu'elle fait mercredi?
Élève A: Elle joue aux jeux vidéo.

Élève A: Qu'est-ce que Julien fait jeudi?
Élève B: Jeudi, il joue aux jeux vidéo.

Élève B: Et Sophie, qu'est-ce qu'elle fait jeudi?
Élève A: Elle écoute la radio.

Élève A: Qu'est-ce que Julien fait vendredi?
Élève B: Vendredi, il danse.

Élève B: Et Sophie, qu'est-ce qu'elle fait vendredi?
Élève A: Elle danse.

Élève A: Qu'est-ce que Julien fait samedi?
Élève B: Samedi, il joue au basketball.

Élève B: Et Sophie, qu'est-ce qu'elle fait samedi?
Élève A: Elle dîne au restaurant.

Élève A: Qu'est-ce que Julien fait dimanche?
Élève B: Dimanche, il nage.

Élève B: Et Sophie, qu'est-ce qu'elle fait dimanche?
Élève A: Elle étudie.

? *Vendredi - Ils dansent.*

UNITÉ 3 Pair Activity

Activités de la semaine — Élève B

Sophie and Julien have each planned their activities for the week.

- You have Julien's calendar and your partner has Sophie's calendar.

▶ Take turns asking each other what Sophie and Julien are doing each day.

La semaine de Julien

Élève A: Qu'est-ce que Julien fait lundi?
Élève B: Lundi, il joue au foot.

Élève B: Et Sophie, qu'est-ce qu'elle fait lundi?
Élève A: Elle joue au tennis.

? *Is there any day when Sophie and Julien are both doing the same thing?*

Activités de la semaine — Élève A

Sophie and Julien have each planned their activities for the week.

- You have Sophie's calendar and your partner has Julien's calendar.

▶ Take turns asking each other what Sophie and Julien are doing each day.

La semaine de Sophie

Élève A: Qu'est-ce que Julien fait lundi?
Élève B: Lundi, il joue au foot.

Élève B: Et Sophie, qu'est-ce qu'elle fait lundi?
Élève A: Elle joue au tennis.

? *Is there any day when Sophie and Julien are both doing the same thing?*

Deux chambres — Élève B

Mélanie and Marc are brother and sister.

- You have a picture of Marc's room. Your partner has a picture of Mélanie's room.

▶ Take turns asking each other questions to determine which objects or furniture can be found in each of the rooms.

Élève A: **Est-ce que Marc a un bureau?**
Élève B: **Non, il n'a pas de bureau.**

Élève B: **Est-ce que Mélanie a une radiocassette?**
Élève A: **Non, elle n'a pas de radiocassette.**

? *Which items are the same in both rooms?*

La chambre de Marc

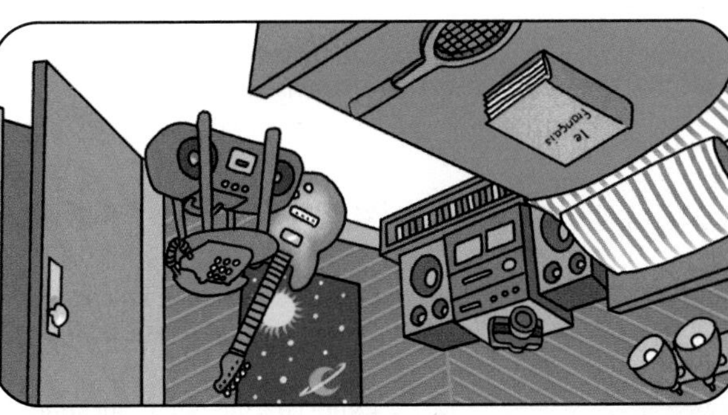

Deux chambres — Élève A

Mélanie and Marc are brother and sister.

- You have a picture of Mélanie's room. Your partner has a picture of Marc's room.

▶ Take turns asking each other questions to determine which objects or furniture can be found in each of the rooms.

La chambre de Mélanie

Élève A: **Est-ce que Marc a un bureau?**
Élève B: **Non, il n'a pas de bureau.**

Élève B: **Est-ce que Mélanie a une radiocassette?**
Élève A: **Non, elle n'a pas de radiocassette.**

? *Which items are the same in both rooms?*

TÊTE À TÊTE

Teaching hint For additional pair activities, and for other communicative activities for **Unité 4**, please go to the **Communipak** section of the **Unit 4 Resource Book**, pp. 140–157.

Teaching tip Have students review OBJECTS and FURNITURE VOCABULARY by referring them to pp. 140, 142, and 144 in the textbook. Alternately, you can use **Overhead Transparencies** 20-22 to review this vocabulary.

Answers *Sample answers*

Élève A: Est-ce que Marc a une raquette?
Élève B: Oui, il a une raquette.
Élève A: Est-ce que Marc a un lit?
Élève B: Oui, il a un lit.
Élève A: Est-ce que Marc a un livre?
Élève B: Oui, il a un livre.
Élève A: Est-ce que Marc a un ordinateur?
Élève B: Non, il n'a pas d'ordinateur.
Élève A: Est-ce que Marc a une lampe?
Élève B: Oui, il a une lampe.
Élève A: Est-ce que Marc a une chaise?
Élève B: Non, il n'a pas de chaise.
Élève A: Est-ce que Marc a une fenêtre?
Élève B: Non, il n'a pas de fenêtre.
Élève A: Est-ce que Marc a un baladeur?
Élève B: Non, il n'a pas de baladeur.
Élève A: Est-ce que Marc a un appareil-photo?
Élève B: Oui, il a un appareil-photo.

Élève B: Est-ce que Mélanie a une affiche?
Élève A: Non, elle n'a pas d'affiche.
Élève B: Est-ce que Mélanie a une raquette?
Élève A: Oui, elle a une raquette.
Élève B: Est-ce que Mélanie a un lit?
Élève A: Oui, elle a un lit.
Élève B: Est-ce que Mélanie a une guitare?
Élève A: Non, elle n'a pas de guitare.
Élève B: Est-ce que Mélanie a un appareil-photo?
Élève A: Oui, elle a un appareil-photo.
Élève B: Est-ce que Mélanie a un portable?
Élève A: Oui, elle a un portable.
Élève B: Est-ce que Mélanie a une lampe?
Élève A: Oui, elle a une lampe.
Élève B: Est-ce que Mélanie a une table?
Élève A: Non, elle n'a pas de table.
Élève B: Est-ce que Mélanie a un livre?
Élève A: Oui, elle a un livre.
Élève B: Est-ce que Mélanie a une chaîne hi-fi?
Élève A: Non, elle n'a pas de chaîne hi-fi.

? *un lit, une raquette, un livre, une lampe, un appareil-photo*

Teaching hint For additional pair activities, and for other communicative activities for **Unité 5**, please go to the Communipak section of the **Unit 5 Resource Book**, pp. 140–160.

Teaching tip Have students review GAME and INSTRUMENT VOCABULARY by referring them to p. 220 in the textbook.

Answers *Answers will vary.*

Élève A: Jean-Paul joue du piano. Et Stéphanie?
Élève B: Oui, Stéphanie joue du piano aussi.
Élève A: Jean-Paul joue de la guitare. Et Stéphanie?
Élève B: Stéphanie ne joue pas de la guitare, mais elle joue de la batterie.
Élève A: Jean-Paul joue aux échecs. Et Stéphanie?
Élève B: Oui, Stéphanie joue aux échecs aussi.
Élève A: Jean-Paul joue aux dames. Et Stéphanie?
Élève B: Oui, Stéphanie joue aux dames aussi.
Élève A: Jean-Paul joue au tennis. Et Stéphanie?
Élève B: Non, Stéphanie ne joue pas au tennis, mais elle joue au ping-pong.
Élève A: Jean-Paul joue au ping-pong. Et Stéphanie?
Élève B: Oui, Stéphanie joue au ping-pong aussi.
Élève A: Jean-Paul joue du violon. Et Stéphanie?
Élève B: Non, Stéphanie ne joue pas du violon, mais elle joue du piano.

Élève B: Stéphanie joue au basket. Et Jean-Paul?
Élève A: Non, Jean-Paul ne joue pas au basket, mais il joue au tennis.
Élève B: Stéphanie joue aux échecs. Et Jean-Paul?
Élève A: Jean-Paul joue aux échecs aussi.
Élève B: Stéphanie joue de la clarinette. Et Jean-Paul?
Élève A: Non, Jean-Paul ne joue pas de la clarinette, mais il joue de la flûte.
Élève B: Stéphanie joue du piano. Et Jean-Paul?
Élève A: Jean-Paul joue du piano aussi.
Élève B: Stéphanie joue de la batterie. Et Jean-Paul?
Élève A: Non, Jean-Paul ne joue pas de la batterie, mais il joue de la guitare.
Élève B: Stéphanie joue aux cartes. Et Jean-Paul?
Élève A: Non, Jean-Paul ne joue pas aux cartes, mais il joue aux dames.
Élève B: Stéphanie joue au ping-pong. Et Jean-Paul?
Élève A: Jean-Paul joue au ping-pong aussi.
Élève B: Stéphanie joue aux dames. Et Jean-Paul?
Élève A: Jean-Paul joue aux dames aussi.

? *Ils jouent du piano, aux échecs, aux dames et au ping-pong.*

Sports, jeux et musique — Élève B

Jean-Paul and Stéphanie are very active.

- Look at the illustrations on the right to find out about Stéphanie's pastimes. (Your partner has similar illustrations showing Jean-Paul's pastimes.)

▶ Take turns asking each other questions to discover which games and instruments Jean-Paul and Stéphanie play.

Élève A: Jean-Paul joue de la flûte. Et Stéphanie?

Élève B: Stéphanie ne joue pas de la flûte, mais elle joue de la clarinette. Est-ce que Jean-Paul joue aux échecs? ...

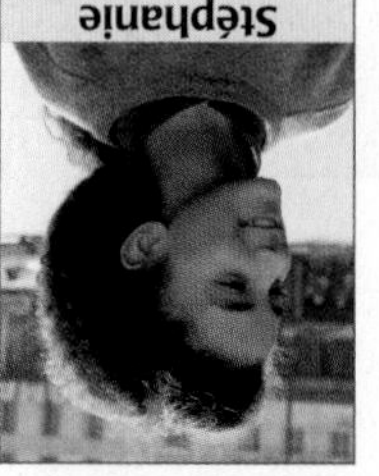
Stéphanie

? *Which pastimes do Jean-Paul and Stéphanie have in common?*

Sports, jeux et musique — Élève A

Jean-Paul and Stéphanie are very active.

- Look at the illustrations on the right to find out about Jean-Paul's pastimes. (Your partner has similar illustrations showing Stéphanie's pastimes.)

▶ Take turns asking each other questions to discover which games and instruments Jean-Paul and Stéphanie play.

Élève A: Jean-Paul joue de la flûte. Et Stéphanie?

Élève B: Stéphanie ne joue pas de la flûte, mais elle joue de la clarinette. Est-ce que Jean-Paul joue aux échecs? ...

Jean-Paul

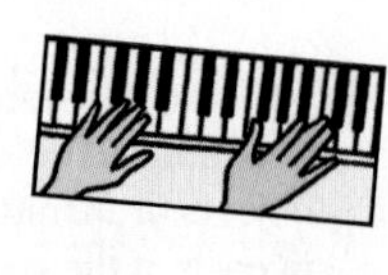

? *Which pastimes do Jean-Paul and Stéphanie have in common?*

Vêtements — Élève A

You and your partner are shopping for clothes.

- You each have a maximum of 250 euros to spend.
- Choose five (5) different items from the picture on the right.

▶ Ask each other questions to find out what each of you is planning to buy.
Also find out the color and price of the five items your partner is buying.

Élève A: Est-ce que tu vas acheter une chemise?
Élève B: Oui, je vais acheter une chemise. [Non, je ne vais pas acheter de chemise.]
Élève A: De quelle couleur?
Élève B: Je vais acheter une chemise bleue.
Élève A: Combien est-ce qu'elle coûte?
Élève B: Elle coûte 35 euros.

? *How many similar items are the two of you going to buy?*

Vêtements — Élève B

You and your partner are shopping for clothes.

- You each have a maximum of 250 euros to spend.
- Choose five (5) different items from the picture on the right.

▶ Ask each other questions to find out what each of you is planning to buy.
Also find out the color and price of the five items your partner is buying.

Élève A: Est-ce que tu vas acheter une chemise?
Élève B: Oui, je vais acheter une chemise. [Non, je ne vais pas acheter de chemise.]
Élève A: De quelle couleur?
Élève B: Je vais acheter une chemise bleue.
Élève A: Combien est-ce qu'elle coûte?
Élève B: Elle coûte 35 euros.

How many similar items are the two of you going to buy?

TÊTE À TÊTE

Teaching hint For additional pair activities, and for other communicative activities for **Unité 6**, please go to the **Communipak** section of the **Unit 6 Resource Book**, pp. 140–156

Teaching tip Have students review CLOTHING and ACCESSORY VOCABULARY by referring them to pp. 258-260 in the textbook. Alternately, you can use **Overhead Transparencies** 35-36 to review this vocabulary.

Answers *Sample answers*

Élève A: Est-ce que tu vas acheter un pull (une veste, etc.)?
Élève B: Oui, je vais acheter un pull (une veste, etc.). [Non, Je ne vais pas acheter de pull (de veste, etc.).]

Élève A: De quelle couleur?
Élève B: Je vais acheter un pull noir (une veste grise et verte, etc.).

Élève A: Combien est-ce qu'il (qu'elle) coûte?
Élève B: Il coûte 57 euros. (Elle coûte 75 euros., etc.)

Élève B: Est-ce que tu vas acheter un short (une jupe, etc.)?
Élève A: Oui, je vais acheter un short (une jupe, etc.). [Non, je ne vais pas acheter de short (de jupe, etc.).]

Élève B: De quelle couleur?
Élève A: Je vais acheter un short marron (une jupe rose, etc.).

Élève B: Combien est-ce qu'il (qu'elle) coûte?
Élève A: Il coûte 20 euros. (Elle coûte 48 euros., etc.)

? *une veste grise et verte, un jean bleu, un short marron, des chaussures marron et une chemise bleue*

Teaching hint For additional pair activities, and for other communicative activities for **Unité 7**, please go to the **Communipak** section of the **Unit 7 Resource Book**, pp. 148–168.

Teaching tip Have students review WEEKEND ACTIVITY VOCABULARY by referring them to pp. 310, 312-313 in the textbook. Alternately, you can use **Overhead Transparencies** 42-43 to review this vocabulary.

Answers *Sample answers*

Élève A: Où es-tu allé(e) mardi?
Élève B: Mardi je suis allé(e) à la piscine.
Élève A: Et qu'est-ce que tu as fait là-bas?
Élève B: J'ai … [nagé / fait de la natation …].

Élève A: Où es-tu allé(e) mercredi?
Élève B: Mercredi je suis allé(e) au club de sport.
Élève A: Et qu'est-ce que tu as fait là-bas?
Élève B: J'ai … [fait du jogging / fait du VTT / joué au basket …].

Élève A: Où es-tu allé(e) jeudi?
Élève B: Jeudi je suis allé(e) à la mer.
Élève A: Et qu'est-ce que tu as fait là-bas?
Élève B: J'ai … [nagé / fait de la voile / fait du ski nautique …].

Élève B: Où es-tu allé(e) jeudi?
Élève A: Jeudi je suis allé(e) au cinéma.
Élève B: Et qu'est-ce que tu as fait là-bas?
Élève A: J'ai … [vu un film / rencontré mes amis …].

Élève B: Où es-tu allé(e) vendredi?
Élève A: Vendredi je suis allé(e) au centre commercial.
Élève B: Et qu'est-ce que tu as fait là-bas?
Élève A: J'ai … [acheté un cadeau pour ma mère / fait des achats / loué un film …].

Élève B: Où es-tu allé(e) samedi?
Élève A: Samedi je suis allé(e) à la campagne.
Élève B: Et qu'est-ce que tu as fait là-bas?
Élève A: J'ai … [fait un pique-nique avec mes amis / fait une promenade à pied / fait du vélo …].

Élève B: Où es-tu allé(e) dimanche?
Élève A: Dimanche je suis allé(e) à la piscine.
Élève B: Et qu'est-ce que tu as fait là-bas?
Élève A: J'ai … [fait de la natation / nagé …].

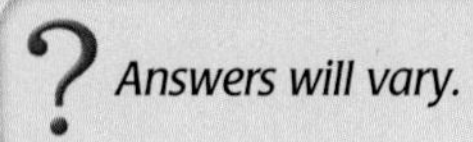
Answers will vary.

Vacances en France — Élève B

Is there any day on which you did the same activity?

Last July, you and your partner spent a week in France, but you were each in different cities. You went to Nice on the French Riviera.

- The calendar on the right shows where you went each day.
- On a separate piece of paper, complete the calendar with an activity that corresponds logically to each place.

▶ Then find out where your partner went each day and what he/she did there. Your partner will ask you similar questions.

Élève A: Où es-tu allé(e) lundi?
Élève B: Lundi je suis allé(e) au stade.
Élève A: Et qu'est-ce que tu as fait là-bas?
Élève B: J'ai … [joué au foot / fait du jogging/assisté à un match de foot …]

	Où?	Activité
lundi	le stade	?
mardi	la piscine	?
mercredi	le club de sport	?
jeudi	la mer	?
vendredi	les magasins	?
samedi	la campagne	?
dimanche	la plage	?

Vacances en France — Élève A

Last July, you and your partner spent a week in France, but you were each in different cities. You went to Annecy which is on a lake in the Alps.

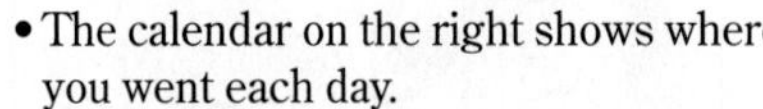
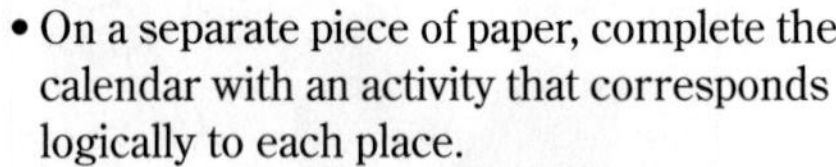

- The calendar on the right shows where you went each day.
- On a separate piece of paper, complete the calendar with an activity that corresponds logically to each place.

▶ Then find out where your partner went each day and what he/she did there. Your partner will ask you similar questions.

Élève A: Où es-tu allé(e) lundi?
Élève B: Lundi je suis allé(e) au stade.
Élève A: Et qu'est-ce que tu as fait là-bas?
Élève B: J'ai … [joué au foot / fait du jogging /assisté à un match de foot …]

	Où?	Activité
lundi	le club de sport	?
mardi	la plage	?
mercredi	la montagne	?
jeudi	le cinéma	?
vendredi	le centre commercial	?
samedi	la campagne	?
dimanche	la piscine	?

Is there any day on which you did the same activity?

TÊTE À TÊTE

Au supermarché — Élève B

You and your partner have been food shopping in two different supermarkets. On the right are the items you brought home.

▶ Find out about your partner's purchases by asking what he/she bought in the following categories:

- viande?
- poisson?
- dessert?
- fruits?
- légumes?
- boissons?

Your partner will ask you similar questions.

Élève A: **Est-ce que tu as acheté de la viande?**
Élève B: **Oui, j'ai acheté du jambon. Et toi, est-ce que tu as acheté de la viande aussi?**
Élève A: **Moi, j'ai acheté ...**

Which items did you buy that were the same?

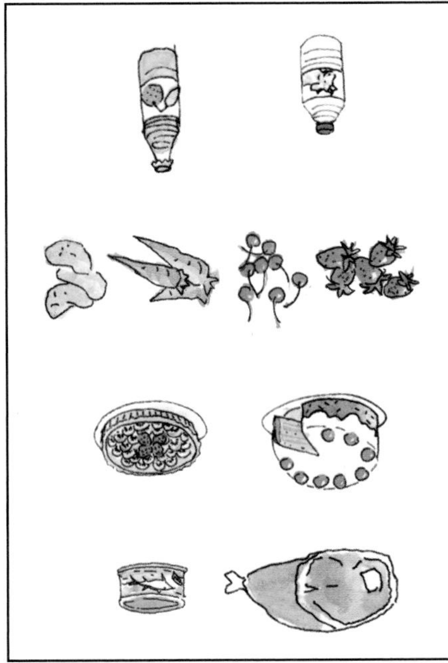

Au supermarché — Élève A

You and your partner have been food shopping in two different supermarkets. On the right are the items you brought home.

▶ Find out about your partner's purchases by asking what he/she bought in the following categories:

- viande?
- poisson?
- dessert?
- fruits?
- légumes?
- boissons?

Your partner will ask you similar questions.

Élève A: **Est-ce que tu as acheté de la viande?**
Élève B: **Oui, j'ai acheté du jambon. Et toi, est-ce que tu as acheté de la viande aussi?**
Élève A: **Moi, j'ai acheté ...**

? *Which items did you buy that were the same?*

Teaching hint For additional pair activities, and for other communicative activities for Unité 8, please go to the Communipak section of the Unit 8 Resource Book, pp. 152–170.

Teaching tip Have students review FOOD and BEVERAGE VOCABULARY by referring them to pp. 366-367, and 371 in the textbook. Alternately, you can use **Overhead Transparencies** 46a, 46b, and 47 to review this vocabulary. Students can also review the PARTITIVE ARTICLE on p. 378 of the textbook, and on **Overhead Transparency** 49.

Answers

Élève A: Est-ce que tu as acheté du poisson?
Élève B: Oui, j'ai acheté du thon.
Et toi, est-ce que tu as acheté du poisson aussi?
Élève A: Moi, j'ai acheté du thon aussi.

Élève A: Est-ce que tu as acheté du dessert?
Élève B: Oui, j'ai acheté une tarte et du gâteau.
Et toi, est-ce que tu as acheté du dessert aussi?
Élève A: Moi, j'ai acheté de la glace et du gâteau.

Élève A: Est-ce que tu as acheté des fruits?
Élève B: Oui, j'ai acheté des cerises et des fraises.
Et toi, est-ce que tu as acheté des fruits aussi?
Élève A: Moi, j'ai acheté des bananes et des poires.

Élève A: Est-ce que tu as acheté des légumes?
Élève B: Oui, j'ai acheté des pommes de terres et des carottes.
Et toi, est-ce que tu as acheté des légumes aussi?
Élève A: Moi, j'ai acheté des carottes et des haricots verts.

Élève A: Est-ce que tu as acheté des boissons?
Élève B: Oui, j'ai acheté du jus d'orange et du lait.
Et toi, est-ce que tu as acheté des boissons aussi?
Élève A: Moi, j'ai acheté de l'eau minérale et du lait.

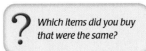

? *du lait, du thon, du gâteau, des carottes*

Reference Section

CONTENTS

APPENDIX 1

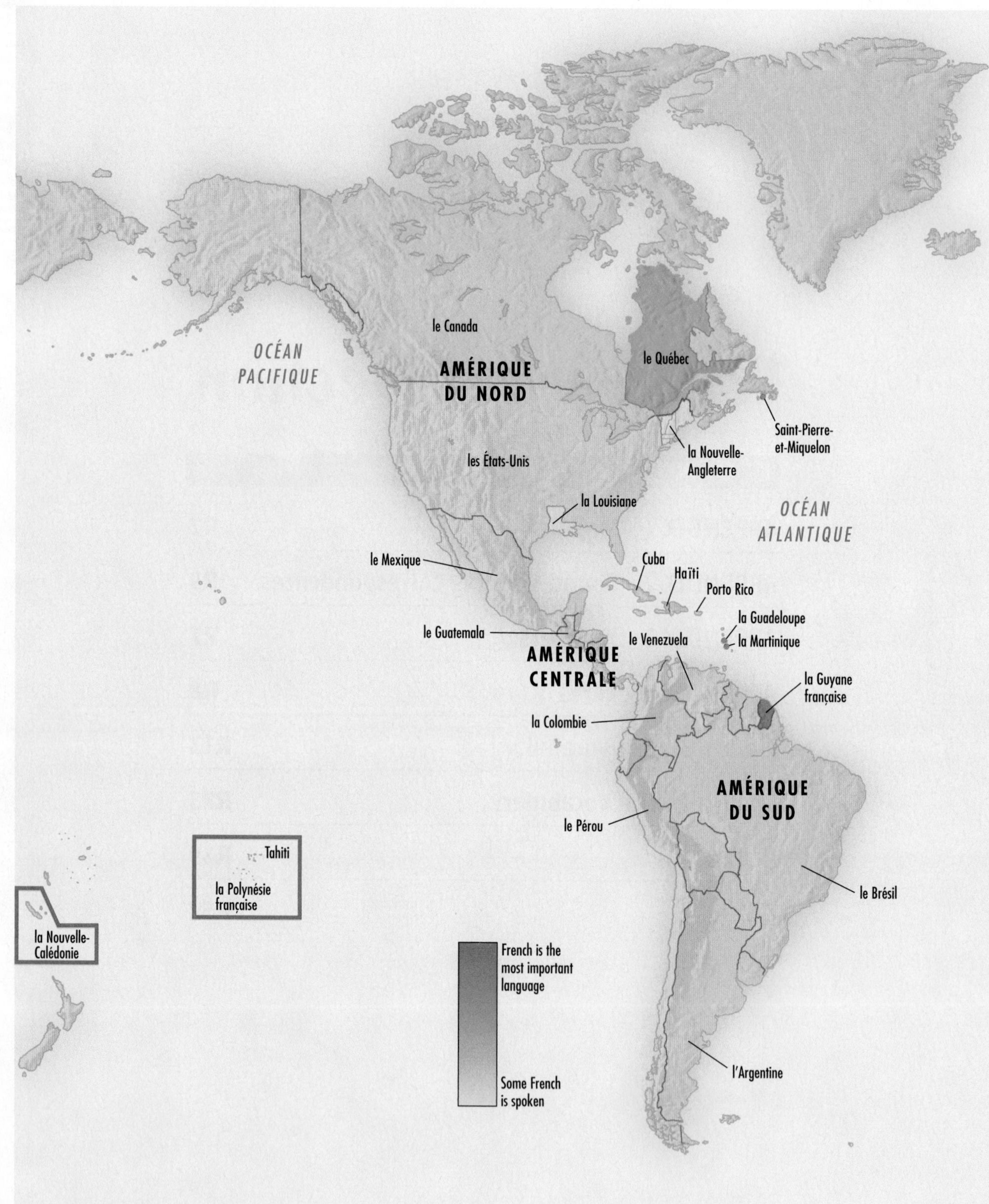

le Canada
OCÉAN PACIFIQUE
AMÉRIQUE DU NORD
le Québec
Saint-Pierre-et-Miquelon
la Nouvelle-Angleterre
les États-Unis
la Louisiane
OCÉAN ATLANTIQUE
le Mexique
Cuba
Haïti
Porto Rico
la Guadeloupe
la Martinique
le Guatemala
le Venezuela
AMÉRIQUE CENTRALE
la Guyane française
la Colombie
AMÉRIQUE DU SUD
le Pérou
Tahiti
la Polynésie française
le Brésil
la Nouvelle-Calédonie
French is the most important language
Some French is spoken
l'Argentine

Map The French-Speaking World

la Russie
la Belgique
le Luxembourg
la Suisse
Monaco
la France
EUROPE
ASIE
l'Italie
le Maroc
Israël
le Liban
la Chine
la Tunisie
l'Algérie
l'Egypte
OCÉAN PACIFIQUE
l'Inde
le Laos
la Mauritanie
le Mali
le Niger
le Tchad
le Sénégal
le Viêt-Nam
la Guinée
AFRIQUE
le Cambodge
le Burkina Faso
la République Centrafricaine
la Côte d'Ivoire
le Togo
le Bénin
le Rwanda
le Cameroun
le Gabon
le Burundi
la République du Congo
OCÉAN INDIEN
la République démocratique du Congo
l'île Maurice
la Réunion
AUSTRALIE
Madagascar
OCÉAN ATLANTIQUE

APPENDIX 1

Maps R3

Map France

[1]Also known as Île-de-France

[2]Also known as Nord-Pas-de-Calais

[3]Also known as Provence-Alpes-Côte d'Azur (Bottin 1989)

Sound-Spelling Correspondences

VOWELS

Sound	Spelling	Examples
/a/	**a, à, â**	Madame, là-bas, théâtre
/i/	**i, î**	visite, Nice, dîne
	y (initial, final, or between consonants)	Yves, Guy, style
/u/	**ou, où, oû**	Toulouse, où, août
/y/	**u, û**	tu, Luc, sûr
/o/	**o** (final or before silent consonant)	piano, idiot, Margot
	au, eau	jaune, Claude, beau
	ô	hôtel, drôle, Côte d'Ivoire
/ɔ/	**o**	Monique, Noël, jolie
	au	Paul, restaurant, Laure
/e/	**é**	Dédé, Québec, télé
	e (before silent final **z, t, r**)	chez, et, Roger
	ai (final or before final silent consonant)	j'ai, mai, japonais
/ɛ/	**è**	Michèle, Ève, père
	ei	seize, neige, tour Eiffel
	ê	tête, être, Viêt-nam
	e (before two consonants)	elle, Pierre, Annette
	e (before pronounced final consonant)	Michel, avec, cher
	ai (before pronounced final consonant)	française, aime, Maine
/ə/	**e** (final or before single consonant)	je, Denise, venir
/ϕ/	**eu, oeu**	deux, Mathieu, euro, oeufs
	eu (before final **se**)	nerveuse, généreuse, sérieuse
/œ/	**eu** (before final pronounced consonant except /z/)	heure, neuf, Lesieur
	oeu	soeur, coeur, oeuf
	oe	oeil

NASAL VOWELS

Sound	Spelling	Examples
/ɑ̃/	**an, am**	France, quand, lampe
	en, em	Henri, pendant, décembre
/ɔ̃/	**on, om**	non, Simon, bombe
/ɛ̃/	**in, im**	Martin, invite, impossible
	yn, ym	syndicat, sympathique, Olympique
	ain, aim	Alain, américain, faim
	(o) + in	loin, moins, point
	(i) + en	bien, Julien, viens
/œ̃/	**un, um**	un, Lebrun, parfum

APPENDIX 2

Sound-Spelling Correspondences *continued*

SEMI-VOWELS

Sound	*Spelling*	*Examples*
/j/	**i, y** (before vowel sound)	bien, piano, Lyon
	-il, -ill (after vowel sound)	oeil, travaille, Marseille, fille
/ɥ/	**u** (before vowel sound)	lui, Suisse, juillet
/w/	**ou** (before vowel sound)	oui, Louis, jouer
/wa/	**oi, oî**	voici, Benoît
	oy (before vowel)	voyage

CONSONANTS

Sound	*Spelling*	*Examples*
/b/	**b**	Barbara, banane, Belgique
/k/	**c** (before **a, o, u,** or consonant)	casque, cuisine, classe
	ch(r)	Christine, Christian, Christophe
	qu, q (final)	Québec, qu'est-ce que, cinq
	k	kilo, Kiki, ketchup
/ʃ/	**ch**	Charles, blanche, chez
/d/	**d**	Didier, dans, médecin
/f/	**f**	Félix, franc, neuf
	ph	Philippe, téléphone, photo
/g/	**g** (before **a, o, u,** or consonant)	Gabriel, gorge, légumes, gris
	gu (before **e, i, y**)	vague, Guillaume, Guy
/ɲ/	**gn**	mignon, champagne, Allemagne
/ʒ/	**j**	je, Jérôme, jaune
	g (before **e, i, y**)	rouge, Gigi, gymnastique
	ge (before **a, o, u**)	orangeade, Georges, nageur
/l/	**l, ll**	Lise, elle, cheval
/m/	**m**	Maman, moi, tomate
/n/	**n**	banane, Nancy, nous
/p/	**p**	peu, Papa, Pierre
/r/	**r, rr**	arrive, rentre, Paris
/s/	**c** (before **e, i, y**)	ce, Cécile, Nancy
	ç (before **a, o, u**)	ça, garçon, déçu
	s (initial or before consonant)	sac, Sophie, reste
	ss (between vowels)	boisson, dessert, Suisse
	t (before **i** + vowel)	attention, Nations Unies, natation
	x	dix, six, soixante
/t/	**t**	trop, télé, Tours
	th	Thérèse, thé, Marthe
/v/	**v**	Viviane, vous, nouveau
/gz/	**x**	examen, exemple, exact
/ks/	**x**	Max, Mexique, excellent
/z/	**s** (between vowels)	désert, Louise, télévision
	z	Suzanne, zut, zéro

A. CARDINAL NUMBERS

0 zéro
1 un (une)
2 deux
3 trois
4 quatre
5 cinq
6 six
7 sept
8 huit
9 neuf
10 dix
11 onze
12 douze
13 treize
14 quatorze
15 quinze
16 seize
17 dix-sept
18 dix-huit
19 dix-neuf
20 vingt
21 vingt et un (une)
22 vingt-deux
23 vingt-trois
30 trente
31 trente et un (une)
32 trente-deux
40 quarante
41 quarante et un (une)
50 cinquante
60 soixante
70 soixante-dix
71 soixante et onze
72 soixante-douze
80 quatre-vingts
81 quatre-vingt-un (une)
82 quatre-vingt-deux
90 quatre-vingt-dix
91 quatre-vingt-onze
100 cent
101 cent un (une)
102 cent deux
200 deux cents
201 deux cent un
300 trois cents
400 quatre cents
500 cinq cents
600 six cents
700 sept cents
800 huit cents
900 neuf cents
1 000 mille
2 000 deux mille
1 000 000 un million

Notes:
1. The word **et** occurs only in the numbers 21, 31, 41, 51, 61, and 71: **vingt et un**, **soixante et onze**
2. **Un** becomes **une** before a feminine noun: **trente et une filles**
3. **Quatre-vingts** becomes **quatre-vingt** before another number: **quatre-vingt-cinq**
4. **Cents** becomes **cent** before another number: **trois cent vingt**
5. **Mille** never adds an **-s:** **quatre mille**

B. ORDINAL NUMBERS

1er (ère)^	**premier (première)**	5^e^	**cinquième**	9^e^	**neuvième**
2^e^	**deuxième**	6^e^	**sixième**	10^e^	**dixième**
3^e^	**troisième**	7^e^	**septième**	11^e^	**onzième**
4^e^	**quatrième**	8^e^	**huitième**	12^e^	**douzième**

Note: Premier becomes **première** before a feminine noun: **la première histoire**

C. METRIC EQUIVALENTS

1 gramme	= 0.035 ounces	1 ounce	= **28,349 grammes**
1 kilogramme	= 2.205 pounds	1 pound	= **0,453 kilogrammes**
1 litre	= 1.057 quarts	1 quart	= **0,946 litres**
1 mètre	= 39.37 inches	1 foot	= **30,480 centimètres**
1 kilomètre	= 0.62 miles	1 mile	= **1,609 kilomètres**

Numbers R7

APPENDIX 4

A. REGULAR VERBS

Infinitive	***Present***		***Passé Composé***	
parler *(to talk, speak)*	je **parle** tu **parles** il **parle**	nous **parlons** vous **parlez** ils **parlent**	j'**ai parlé** tu **as parlé** il **a parlé**	nous **avons parlé** vous **avez parlé** ils **ont parlé**
	IMPERATIVE: **parle, parlons, parlez**			
finir *(to finish)*	je **finis** tu **finis** il **finit**	nous **finissons** vous **finissez** ils **finissent**	j'**ai fini** tu **as fini** il **a fini**	nous **avons fini** vous **avez fini** ils **ont fini**
	IMPERATIVE: **finis, finissons, finissez**			
vendre *(to sell)*	je **vends** tu **vends** il **vend**	nous **vendons** vous **vendez** ils **vendent**	j'**ai vendu** tu **as vendu** il **a vendu**	nous **avons vendu** vous **avez vendu** ils **ont vendu**
	IMPERATIVE: **vends, vendons, vendez**			

B. *-er* VERBS WITH SPELLING CHANGES

Infinitive	***Present***		***Passé Composé***
acheter *(to buy)*	j'**achète** tu **achètes** il **achète**	nous **achetons** vous **achetez** ils **achètent**	j'**ai acheté**
	Verb like **acheter:** amener *(to bring, take along)*		
espérer *(to hope)*	j'**espère** tu **espères** il **espère**	nous **espérons** vous **espérez** ils **espèrent**	j'**ai espéré**
	Verbs like **espérer:** célébrer *(to celebrate)*, préférer *(to prefer)*		
commencer *(to begin, start)*	je **commence** tu **commences** il **commence**	nous **commençons** vous **commencez** ils **commencent**	j'**ai commencé**
manger *(to eat)*	je **mange** tu **manges** il **mange**	nous **mangeons** vous **mangez** ils **mangent**	j'**ai mangé**
	Verbs like **manger:** nager *(to swim)*, voyager *(to travel)*		
payer *(to pay, pay for)*	je **paie** tu **paies** il **paie**	nous **payons** vous **payez** ils **paient**	j'**ai payé**
	Verbs like **payer:** nettoyer *(to clean)*		

R8 Appendix 4

C. IRREGULAR VERBS

INFINITIVE	PRESENT		PASSÉ COMPOSÉ
avoir *(to have, own)*	j'ai tu **as** il **a**	nous **avons** vous **avez** ils **ont**	j'ai **eu**
	IMPERATIVE: **aie, ayons, ayez**		
être *(to be)*	je **suis** tu **es** il **est**	nous **sommes** vous **êtes** ils **sont**	j'ai **été**
	IMPERATIVE: **sois, soyons, soyez**		
aller *(to go)*	je **vais** tu **vas** il **va**	nous **allons** vous **allez** ils **vont**	je **suis allé(e)**
	IMPERATIVE: **va, allons, allez**		
boire *(to drink)*	je **bois** tu **bois** il **boit**	nous **buvons** vous **buvez** ils **boivent**	j'ai **bu**
connaître *(to know)*	je **connais** tu **connais** il **connaît**	nous **connaissons** vous **connaissez** ils **connaissent**	j'ai **connu**
devoir *(to have to, should, must)*	je **dois** tu **dois** il **doit**	nous **devons** vous **devez** ils **doivent**	j'ai **dû**
dire *(to say, tell)*	je **dis** tu **dis** il **dit**	nous **disons** vous **dites** ils **disent**	j'ai **dit**
dormir *(to sleep)*	je **dors** tu **dors** il **dort**	nous **dormons** vous **dormez** ils **dorment**	j'ai **dormi**
écrire *(to write)*	j'**écris** tu **écris** il **écrit**	nous **écrivons** vous **écrivez** ils **écrivent**	j'ai **écrit**
	Verb like **écrire:** décrire *(to describe)*		
faire *(to make, do)*	je **fais** tu **fais** il **fait**	nous **faisons** vous **faites** ils **font**	j'ai **fait**

APPENDIX 4

Verbs R9

C. IRREGULAR VERBS *continued*

INFINITIVE	PRESENT		PASSÉ COMPOSÉ
lire *(to read)*	je **lis** tu **lis** il **lit**	nous **lisons** vous **lisez** ils **lisent**	**j'ai lu**
mettre *(to put, place)*	je **mets** tu **mets** il **met**	nous **mettons** vous **mettez** ils **mettent**	**j'ai mis**
	Verb like **mettre:** promettre *(to promise)*		
ouvrir *(to open)*	j'**ouvre** tu **ouvres** il **ouvre**	nous **ouvrons** vous **ouvrez** ils **ouvrent**	**j'ai ouvert**
	Verbs like **ouvrir:** découvrir *(to discover)*, offrir *(to offer)*		
partir *(to leave)*	je **pars** tu **pars** il **part**	nous **partons** vous **partez** ils **partent**	je **suis parti(e)**
pouvoir *(to be able, can)*	je **peux** tu **peux** il **peut**	nous **pouvons** vous **pouvez** ils **peuvent**	**j'ai pu**
prendre *(to take)*	je **prends** tu **prends** il **prend**	nous **prenons** vous **prenez** ils **prennent**	**j'ai pris**
	Verbs like **prendre:** apprendre *(to learn)*, comprendre *(to understand)*		
savoir *(to know)*	je **sais** tu **sais** il **sait**	nous **savons** vous **savez** ils **savent**	**j'ai su**
sortir *(to go out, get out)*	je **sors** tu **sors** il **sort**	nous **sortons** vous **sortez** ils **sortent**	je **suis sorti(e)**
venir *(to come)*	je **viens** tu **viens** il **vient**	nous **venons** vous **venez** ils **viennent**	je **suis venu(e)**
	Verb like **venir:** revenir *(to come back)*		
voir *(to see)*	je **vois** tu **vois** il **voit**	nous **voyons** vous **voyez** ils **voient**	**j'ai vu**

R10 Appendix 4

C. IRREGULAR VERBS *continued*

Infinitive	*Present*		*Passé composé*
vouloir *(to want)*	je **veux** tu **veux** il **veut**	nous **voulons** vous **voulez** ils **veulent**	**j'ai voulu**

D. VERBS WITH *ÊTRE* IN THE *PASSÉ COMPOSÉ*

aller *(to go)*	je **suis allé(e)**	**passer** *(to go by, through)*	je **suis passé(e)**
arriver *(to arrive, come)*	je **suis arrivé(e)**	**rentrer** *(to go home)*	je **suis rentré(e)**
descendre *(to go down)*	je **suis descendu(e)**	**rester** *(to stay)*	je **suis resté(e)**
entrer *(to enter, go in)*	je **suis entré(e)**	**revenir** *(to come back)*	je **suis revenu(e)**
monter *(to go up)*	je **suis monté(e)**	**sortir** *(to go out, get out)*	je **suis sorti(e)**
mourir *(to die)*	il/elle **est mort(e)**	**tomber** *(to fall)*	je **suis tombé(e)**
naître *(to be born)*	je **suis né(e)**	**venir** *(to come)*	je **suis venu(e)**
partir *(to leave)*	je **suis parti(e)**		

APPENDIX 4

Verbs R11

FRENCH-ENGLISH VOCABULARY

French-English Vocabulary

The French-English vocabulary contains active and passive words from the text, as well as the important words of the illustrations used within the units. Obvious passive cognates have not been listed.

The numbers following an entry indicate the lesson in which the word or phrase is activated. (**I** stands for the list of classroom expressions at the end of the first **Images** section; **E** stands for **Entracte.**)

Nouns: If the article of a noun does not indicate gender, the noun is followed by *m.* (*masculine*) or *f.* (*feminine*). If the plural (*pl.*) is irregular, it is given in parentheses.

Adjectives: Adjectives are listed in the masculine form. If the feminine form is irregular, it is given in parentheses. Irregular plural forms (*pl.*) are also given in parentheses.

Verbs: Verbs are listed in the infinitive form. An asterisk (*) in front of an active verb means that it is irregular. (For forms, see the verb charts in Appendix 4C.) Irregular present tense forms are listed when they are used before the verb has been activated. Irregular past participle (*p.p.*) forms are listed separately.

Words beginning with an **h** are preceded by a bullet (•) if the **h** is aspirate; that is, if the word is treated as if it begins with a consonant sound.

A

a: il y a there is, there are **9**
à at, in, to **6, 14**
à côté next door; next to
à demain see you tomorrow **4B**
à droite on (to) the right **13**
à gauche on (to) the left **13**
à la mode popular; in fashion; fashionable **17**
à mon avis in my opinion **19**
à partir de as of, beginning
à pied on foot **14**
à samedi! see you Saturday! **4B**
à vélo by bicycle **14**
abolir to abolish
abondant plentiful, copious, large
abord: d'abord (at) first **22**
un **abricot** apricot
absolument absolutely
un **accent** accent mark, stress
accepter to accept
des **accessoires** *m.* accessories **17**
un **accord** agreement
d'accord okay, all right **5**
être d'accord to agree **6**
un **achat** purchase
faire des achats to go shopping **21**
acheter to buy **17, 18**
acheter + du, de la *(partitive)* to buy (some) **26**
un **acteur, une actrice** actor, actress
une **activité** activity
l' **addition** *f.* check
adorer to love
une **adresse** address **13**
quelle est ton adresse? what's your address? **13**
adroit skilled, skillful
un(e) **adulte** adult
aéronautique aeronautic, aeronautical
un **aéroport** airport
affectueusement affectionately *(at the end of a letter)*
une **affiche** poster **9**
affirmativement affirmatively
l' **Afrique** *f.* Africa
l' **âge** *m.* age
quel âge a-t-il/elle? how old is he/she? **9**
quel âge as-tu? how old are you? **2C**
quel âge a ton père/ta mère? how old is your father/your mother? **2C**
âgé old
une **agence** agency
une agence de tourisme tourist office
une agence de voyages travel agency
agiter to shake
agité agitated
ah! ah!, oh!
ah bon? oh? really? **8**
ah non! ah, no!
ai (*see* **avoir**): **j'ai** I have **9**
j'ai... ans I'm ... (years old) **2C**
aider to help **21, 27**
une **aile** wing
aimer to like **7, 25**
est-ce que tu aimes...? do you like ...? **5**
j'aime... I like ... **5**
j'aimerais I would like
je n'aime pas... I don't like ... **5**
ainsi thus
aîné older
un frère aîné older brother
une soeur aînée older sister
ajouter to add
l' **Algérie** *f.* Algeria *(country in North Africa)*
algérien (algérienne) Algerian
l' **Allemagne** *f.* Germany
allemand German
* **aller** to go **14**
aller + *inf.* to be going to + *inf.* **14**
allez (*see* **aller**): **allez-vous-en** go away!
allez-y come on!, go ahead!, do it!
comment allez-vous? how are you? **1C**
allô! hello! *(on the telephone)*
allons (*see* **aller**): **allons-y** let's go! **14**

R14 French-English Vocabulary

alors so, then **11**
une **alouette** lark
les **Alpes** *f.* (the) Alps
l' **alphabet** *m.* alphabet
l' **Alsace** *f.* Alsace *(province in eastern France)*
amener to bring *(a person)* **18, 27**
américain American **1B, 11**
à l'américaine American-style
un **Américain, une Américaine** American person
l' **Amérique** *f.* America
un **ami, une amie** (close) friend **2A**
amicalement love *(at the end of a letter)*
l' **amitié** *f.* friendship
amitiés best regards *(at the end of a letter)*
amusant funny, amusing **11**
amuser to amuse
s'amuser to have fun
on s'est bien amusé! we had a good time!
un **an** year
avoir... ans to be ... (years old) **10**
il/elle a... ans he/she is ... (years old) **2C**
j'ai... ans I'm ... (years old) **2C**
l'an dernier last year
par an per year
un **ananas** pineapple
ancien (ancienne) former, old, ancient
un **âne** donkey
un **ange** angel
anglais English **1B, 11**
un **Anglais, une Anglaise** English person
un **animal** (*pl.* **animaux**) animal
une **animation** live entertainment
animé animated, lively
une **année** year **4B**
Bonne année! Happy New Year! **24**
toute l'année all year long
un **anniversaire** birthday **4B**
bon anniversaire! happy birthday! **24**
c'est quand, ton anniversaire? when is your birthday? **4B**
mon anniversaire est le (2 mars) my birthday is (March 2nd) **4B**
un **annuaire** telephone directory
un **anorak** ski jacket
les **antiquités** *f.* antiquities, antiques
août *m.* August **4B**
un **appareil-photo** (*pl.* **appareils-photo**) (still) camera **9**
un **appartement** apartment **13**
s' **appeller** to be named, called
comment s'appelle...? what's ...'s name? **2B**
comment s'appelle-t-il/elle? what's his/her name? **9**
comment t'appelles-tu? what's your name? **1A**
il/elle s'appelle... his/her name is ... **2B**
je m'appelle... my name is ... **1A**
apporter to bring *(things)* **18**
apporter quelque chose à quelqu'un to bring something to someone **27**
apporte-moi (apportez-moi) bring me **I**
* **apprendre (à)** + *inf.* to learn (to) **26**
apprécier to appreciate
approprié appropriate
après after **21**; after, afterwards **22, 23**
d'après according to
l' **après-midi** *m.* afternoon **21**
cet après-midi this afternoon **23**
de l'après-midi in the afternoon, P.M. **4A**
demain après-midi tomorrow afternoon **23**
hier après-midi yesterday afternoon **23**
l' **arabe** *m.* Arabic *(language)*
un **arbre** tree
un arbre généalogique family tree
l' **arche** *f.* **de Noé** Noah's Ark
l' **argent** *m.* money **20**
l' argent de poche allowance, pocket money
arrêter to arrest; to stop
arriver to arrive, come **14**
j'arrive! I'm coming!
une **arrivée** arrival
un **arrondissement** district
un **artifice: le feu d'artifice** fireworks
un **artiste, une artiste** artist
as (*see* **avoir**): **est-ce que tu as...?** do you have ...? **9**
un **ascenseur** elevator
un **aspirateur** vacuum cleaner
asseyez-vous! sit down! **I**
assez rather **11**; enough
assieds-toi! sit down! **I**
une **assiette** plate **25**
assister à to go to, attend **21**
associer to associate
l' **Atlantique** *m.* Atlantic Ocean
attendre to wait, wait for **20**
attention *f.*: **faire attention** to be careful, pay attention **8**
attentivement carefully
au (à + le) to (the), at (the), in (the) **6, 14**
au revoir! good-bye! **1C**
une **auberge** inn
une auberge de campagne country inn **27**
aucun: ne... aucun none, not any
aujourd'hui today **4B, 23**
aujourd'hui, c'est... today is ... **4B**
aussi also, too **1B, 7**
aussi... que as ... as **19**
une **auto (automobile)** car, automobile **9**
une auto-école driving school
un **autobus** bus
un **autocar** touring bus **21**
l' **automne** *m.* autumn, fall
en automne in (the) autumn, fall **4C**
autre other **25**
d'autres others
un(e) autre another
aux (à + les) to (the), at (the), in (the) **14**
avant before **21**
avant hier the day before yesterday
en avant let's begin
avantageux (avantageuse) reasonable, advantageous
avec with **6**

FRENCH-ENGLISH VOCABULARY

French-English Vocabulary R15

avec moi, avec toi with me, with you **5**
avec qui? with who(m)? **8**
une **avenue** avenue **13**
un **avion** airplane, plane **21**
en avion by airplane **21**
un **avis** opinion
avis de recherche missing person's bulletin
à mon avis in my opinion **19**
à votre avis in your opinion
* **avoir** to have **10**
avoir... ans to be ... (years old) **10**
avoir besoin de to need **20**
avoir chaud to be warm, hot **22**
avoir de la chance to be lucky **22**
avoir envie de to feel like, want **20**
avoir faim to be hungry **10**
avoir froid to be cold **22**
avoir lieu to take place
avoir raison to be right **22**
avoir soif to be thirsty **10, 22**
avoir tort to be wrong **22**
avril *m.* April **4B**

B

le **babyfoot** tabletop soccer game
le **babysitting: faire du babysitting** to baby-sit
les **bagages** *m.* bags, baggage
bain: un maillot de bain bathing suit **17**
un **baladeur** portable player **9**
une **banane** banana **25**
une **bande dessinée** comic strip
des bandes dessinées comics
la **Bannière étoilée** Star-Spangled Banner
une **banque** bank
une **barbe: quelle barbe!** what a pain! *(colloq.)*
bas: en bas downstairs **13**
au bas at the bottom
le **baseball** baseball **15**
basé based
le **basket (basketball)** basketball **15**
jouer au basket to play basketball **5**
des **baskets** *m.* hightops (sneakers) **17**
un **bateau** boat, ship **21**
un bateau-mouche sightseeing boat
la **batterie** drums **15**
battre to beat
bavard talkative
beau (bel, belle; *m.pl.* **beaux)** handsome, good-looking, beautiful **9, 12, 19**
il est beau he is good-looking, handsome **9**
il fait beau it's beautiful (nice) out **4C**
un **beau-frère** stepbrother, brother-in-law
un **beau-père** stepfather, father-in-law
beaucoup (de) much, very much, many, a lot **7**
la **beauté** beauty
un **bec** beak
bel (*see* **beau**) beautiful, handsome **19**
belge Belgian
la **Belgique** Belgium
belle (*see* **beau**) beautiful **9, 12, 19**
elle est belle she is beautiful **9**
une **belle-mère** stepmother, mother-in-law
une **belle-soeur** stepsister, sister-in-law
les **Bermudes** *f.* Bermuda
le **besoin** need
avoir besoin de to need, to have to **20**
des besoins d'argent money needs
bête dumb, silly **11**
le **beurre** butter **25**
une **bibliothèque** library **13**
une **bicyclette** bicycle **9**
bien well, very well, carefully **7**
bien sûr of course **5**
ça va bien everything's fine (going well) **1C**
ça va très bien I'm (everything's) very well **1C**
c'est bien that's good (fine) **12**
eh bien! well! **18**
je veux bien (...) I'd love to (...), I do, I want to **5, 26**
oui, bien sûr... yes, of course ... **5**
très bien very well **7**
bientôt: à bientôt! see you soon!
bienvenue welcome
le **bifteck** steak
un bifteck de tortue turtle steak
bilingue bilingual
un **billet** bill, paper money **20**; ticket
la **biologie** biology
une **biscotte** dry toast
blaff de poisson *m.* fish stew
blanc (blanche) white **E1, 12**
Blanche-Neige Snow White
blanchir to blanch, turn white
bleu blue **E1, 12**
blond blonde **9**
il/elle est blond(e) he/she is blond **9**
un **blouson** jacket **17**
* **boire** to drink **26**
une **boisson** drink, beverage **3B, 25**
une **boîte** box
un **bol** deep bowl
bon (bonne) good **12**
bon marché *(inv.)* inexpensive **17**
ah bon? oh, really? **8**
de bonne humeur in a good mood
il fait bon the weather's good (pleasant) **4C**
le **bonheur** happiness
bonjour hello **1A, 1C**
une **botte** boot **17**
une **bouche** mouth **E2**
une **boucherie** butcher shop
le **boudin** sausage
une **boulangerie** bakery
un **boulevard** boulevard **13**
une **boum** party *(colloq.)* **14**
une **boutique** boutique, shop **17**
boxe: un match de boxe boxing match
un **bras** arm **E2**
brésilien (brésilienne) Brazilian
la **Bretagne** Brittany *(province in northwestern France)*
bricoler to do things around the house
broche: à la broche on the spit
bronzé tan

R16 French-English Vocabulary

un **bruit** noise
brun brown, dark-haired **9**
il/elle est brun(e) he/she has dark hair **9**
brunir to turn brown
Bruxelles Brussels
le **bulletin de notes** report card
un **bureau** desk **I, 9;** office
un **bus** bus
en bus by bus **14**
un **but** goal; end

ça that, it
ça fait combien? ça fait... how much is that (it)? that (it) is ... **3C**
ça, là-bas that (one), over there **9**
ça va? how's everything? how are you? **1C**
ça va everything's fine, I'm OK **1C**
ça va (très) bien, ça va bien everything's going very well, everything's fine (going well) **1C**
ça va comme ci, comme ça everything's (going) so-so **1C**
ça va (très) mal things are going (very) badly **1C**
regarde ça look at that **9**
une **cabine d'essayage** fitting room
les **cabinets** *m.* toilet
un **cadeau** (*pl.* **cadeaux**) gift, present
cadet (cadette) younger
un frère cadet (a) younger brother
une soeur cadette (a) younger sister
le **café** coffee **3B**
un café au lait coffee with hot milk
un **café** café *(French coffee shop)* **6**
au café to (at) the café **6**
un **cahier** notebook **I, 9**
une **calculatrice** calculator **9**
un **calendrier** calendar
un **camarade, une camarade** classmate **9**
le **Cambodge** Cambodia *(country in Asia)*
un **cambriolage** burglary
un **cambrioleur** burglar
une **caméra** movie camera
la **campagne** countryside **21**
à la campagne to (in) the countryside **21**
une auberge de campagne country inn
le **Canada** Canada
canadien (canadienne) Canadian **1B, 11**
un **Canadien, une Canadienne** Canadian person
un **canard** duck
la **cantine de l'école** school cafeteria **25**
un **car** touring bus **21**
un car scolaire school bus
une **carotte** carrot **25**
des carottes râpées grated carrots
un **carré** square
le Vieux Carré *the French Quarter in New Orleans*
une **carte** map **I;** card
une carte postale postcard
les cartes *f.* (playing) cards **15**
jouer aux cartes to play cards **15**
un **cas** case
en cas de in case of
une **casquette** (baseball) cap **17**
une **cassette** cassette tape
une **cassette vidéo** videotape **9**
le **catch** wrestling
une **cathédrale** cathedral
une **cave** cellar
un **CD** CD, compact disc **9**
ce (c') this, that, it
ce n'est pas that's/it's not **12**
ce que what
ce sont these are, those are, they are **12**
c'est it's, that's **2A, 9, 12**
c'est + *day of the week* it's ... **4B**
c'est + *name or noun* it's ... **2A**
c'est bien/mal that's good/bad **12**
c'est combien? how much is that/it? **3C**
c'est le (12 octobre) it's (October 12) **4B**
qu'est-ce que c'est? what is it? what's that? **9**
qui est-ce? who's that/this? **9**
ce (cet, cette; ces) this, that, these, those **18**
ce... -ci this... (over here) **18**
ce mois-ci this month **23**
ce n'est pas it's (that's) not **12**
ce soir this evening, tonight **23**
un **cédérom (un CD-ROM)** CD-ROM
une **cédille** cedilla
une **ceinture** belt **17**
cela that
célèbre famous
cent one hundred **2B, 17**
cent un, cent deux 101, 102 **17**
deux cents, trois cents, ... neuf cents 200, 300, ... 900 **17**
une **centaine** about a hundred
un **centime** centime *(1/100 of a euro)*
un **centre** center
un centre commercial shopping center **13**
les **céréales** *f.* cereal **25**
une **cerise** cherry **25**
certain certain
certains some of them
ces (*see* **ce**) these, those **18**
c'est (*see* **ce**)
cet (*see* **ce**) this, that **18**
cette (*see* **ce**) this, that **18**
chacun each one, each person
une **chaise** chair **I, 9**
une **chaîne** (TV) channel
une **chaîne hi-fi** stereo set **9**
une mini-chaîne compact stereo
la **chaleur** heat, warmth
une **chambre** bedroom **9, 13**
un **champion, une championne** champion
la **chance** luck
avoir de la chance to be lucky **22**
bonne chance! good luck! **23**
une **chanson** song
chanter to sing **5, 7**
un **chanteur, une chanteuse** singer

French-English Vocabulary R17

un **chapeau** (*pl.* **chapeaux**) hat **17**
chaque each, every
charmant charming
un **chat** cat **2C, E4**
un **château** (*pl.* **châteaux**) castle
chatter to chat (online)
chaud warm, hot
avoir chaud to be warm (hot) *(people)* **22**
il fait chaud it's warm (hot) *(weather)* **4C**
chauffer to warm, heat up
un **chauffeur** driver
une **chaussette** sock **17**
une **chaussure** shoe **17**
un **chef** boss; chef
une **chemise** shirt **17**
un **chemisier** blouse **17**
cher (chère) expensive; dear **17**
chercher to look for, to get, to find **17**
je cherche... I'm looking for... **17**
un **cheval** (*pl.* **chevaux**) horse **E4**
les **cheveux** *m.* hair **E2**
chez + *person* at (to) someone's house **14;** at (to) the office of
chez moi (toi, lui...) (at) home **15**
chic *(inv.)* nice; elegant, in style
une chic fille a great girl
un **chien** dog **2C**
la **chimie** chemistry
chinois Chinese **11**
le **chinois** Chinese *(language)*
le **chocolat** hot chocolate, cocoa **3B**
une glace au chocolat chocolate ice cream
choisir to choose **19**
un **choix** choice
au choix choose one, your choice
une **chorale** choir
une **chose** thing **9**
quelque chose something **24**
chouette great, terrific **12, 17**
le **cidre** cider
un **cinéaste, une cinéaste** film maker
un **cinéma** movie theater **13**
le cinéma the movies
au cinéma to (at) the movies, movie theater **6**

cinq five **1A**
cinquante fifty **1C**
cinquième fifth **16**
une **circonstance** circumstance
cité: la Cité Interdite Forbidden City
une **clarinette** clarinet **15**
une **classe** class
en classe in class **6**
classique classical
un **clavier** keyboard **15**
un **client, une cliente** customer
un **clip** music video
un **cochon** pig
un **coiffeur, une coiffeuse** hairdresser
un **coin** spot
une **coïncidence** coincidence
le **Colisée** the Coliseum *(a large stadium built by the Romans)*
des **collants** *m.* (pair of) tights, pantyhose **17**
un **collège** junior high school
une **colonie** colony
une **colonne** column
combien how much **20**
combien coûte...? how much does...cost? **3C, 17**
combien de how much, how many **20**
combien de temps? how long?
combien d'heures? how many hours?
ça fait combien? how much is this (it)? **3C**
c'est combien? how much is this (it)? **3C**
combinaison spatiale space suit
commander to order
comme like, as, for
comme ci, comme ça so-so
ça va comme ci, comme ça everything's so-so **1C**
commencer to begin, start
comment? how? **8;** what?
comment allez-vous? how are you? **1C**
comment est-il/elle? what's he/she like? what does he/she look like? **9**
comment dit-on... en français? how do you say ... in French? **I**
comment lire reading hints

comment s'appelle...? what's...'s name? **2B**
comment s'appelle-t-il/elle? what's his/her name? **9**
comment t'appelles-tu? what's your name? **1A**
comment trouves-tu...? what do you think of...? **17**
comment vas-tu? how are you? **1C**
un **commentaire** comment, commentary
commercial: un centre commercial shopping center **13**
le **commérage** gossip
communiquer to communicate
un **compact (disc), un CD** compact disc, CD **9**
complément object
compléter to complete
* **comprendre** to understand **26**
je (ne) comprends (pas) I (don't) understand **I**
compter to count (on); to expect, intend
concerne: en ce qui concerne as for
un **concert** concert **14**
un **concombre** cucumber
la **confiture** jam **25**
confortable comfortable **13**
une **connaissance** acquaintance
faire connaissance (avec) to become acquainted (with)
* **connaître** to know, be acquainted with; *(in passé composé)* to meet for the first time **28**
tu connais...? do you know...? are you acquainted with...? **2B**
connu (*p.p. of* **connaître**) knew, met **28**
un **conseil** piece of advice, counsel
des conseils *m.* advice
un **conservatoire** conservatory
une **consonne** consonant
se **contenter** to limit oneself
le **contenu** contents
continuer to continue **13**
une **contradiction** disagreement
une **contravention** (traffic) ticket
cool cool, neat

R18 French-English Vocabulary

un **copain, une copine** friend, pal **2A**
un petit copain, une petite copine boyfriend, girlfriend
copier to copy
une **copine** friend **2A**
coréen (coréenne) Korean
un **corps** body
correspondant corresponding
correspondre to correspond, agree
la **Corse** Corsica *(French island off the Italian coast)*
un **costume** man's suit
la **Côte d'Azur** Riviera *(southern coast of France on the Mediterranean)*
la **Côte d'Ivoire** Ivory Coast *(French-speaking country in West Africa)*
côté: à côté (de) next door; next to
une **côtelette de porc** pork chop
le **cou** neck **E2**
une **couleur** color **12**
de quelle couleur ...? what color ...? **12**
un **couloir** hall, corridor
coup: dans le coup with it
courage: bon courage! good luck! **23**
courageux (courageuse) courageous
le **courrier électronique** e-mail, electronic mail
une **course** race
faire les courses to go shopping *(for food)* **25**
court short **17**
un **cousin, une cousine** cousin **2C, 16**
le **coût: le coût de la vie** cost of living
un **couteau** (*pl.* **couteaux**) knife **25**
coûter to cost
combien coûte...? how much does...cost? **3C, 17**
il (elle) coûte... it costs...**3C**
un **couturier, une couturière** fashion designer
un **couvert** place setting **25**
un **crabe** crab
des matoutou crabes stewed crabs with rice
la **craie** chalk
un morceau de craie piece of chalk **I**
une **cravate** tie **17**
un **crayon** pencil **I, 9**
créer to create
un **crétin** idiot
une **crêpe** crepe (pancake) **3A**
une **crêperie** crepe restaurant
une **crevaison** flat tire
une **croisade** crusade
un **croissant** crescent (roll) **3A**
une **cuillère** spoon **25**
une cuillère à soupe soup spoon
la **cuisine** cooking **25**
une **cuisine** kitchen **13**
cuit cooked
culturel (culturelle) cultural
curieux (curieuse) curious, strange
la **curiosité** curiosity
le **cybercafé** internet café
un **cyclomoteur** moped

d'abord (at) first **22**
d'accord okay, all right
être d'accord to agree **6**
oui, d'accord yes, okay **5**
une **dame** lady, woman *(polite term)* **2A**
les **dames** *f.* checkers *(game)* **15**
dangereux (dangereuse) dangerous
dans in **9**
danser to dance **5, 7**
la **date** date **4B**
quelle est la date? what's the date? **4B**
de (d') of, from, about **6, 15**
de l'après-midi in the afternoon **4A**
de quelle couleur...? what color ...? **12**
de qui? of whom? **8**
de quoi? about what?
de temps en temps from time to time
pas de not any, no **10, 26**
débarquer to land
décembre *m.* December **4B**
décider (de) to decide (to)
une **déclaration** statement
décoré decorated
* **découvrir** to discover
* **décrire** to describe
décrivez... describe...
un **défaut** shortcoming
un **défilé** parade
dégoûtant: c'est dégoûtant! it's (that's) disgusting **27**
dehors outside
en dehors de outside of
déjà already; ever
déjeuner to eat (have) lunch **25**
le **déjeuner** lunch **25**
le petit déjeuner breakfast **25**
délicieux (délicieuse) delicious **26**
demain tomorrow **4B**
à demain! see you tomorrow! **4B**
demain, c'est... (jeudi) tomorrow is ... (Thursday) **4B**
demander (à) to ask **28**
demandez ... ask ...
un **demi-frère** half-brother
une **demi-soeur** half-sister
demi: ... heures et demie half past ... **4A**
midi et demi half past noon **4A**
minuit et demi half past midnight **4A**
démodé out of style, unfashionable **17**
un **démon** devil
une **dent** tooth
un **départ** departure
se **dépêcher: dépêchez-vous!** hurry up!
dépend: ça dépend that depends
une **dépense** expense
dépenser to spend (money) **20**
dernier (dernière) last **23**
derrière behind, in back of **9**
des some, any **10;** of (the), from (the), about (the) **15**
le **désert** desert
désirer to wish, want
vous désirez? what would you like? may I help you? **3B, 17**

French-English Vocabulary R19

désolé sorry
le **dessert** dessert **25**
le **dessin** art, drawing
un dessin animé cartoon
détester to hate, detest **1C**
deux two **1A**
deuxième second **16**
le deuxième étage third floor
devant in front of **9**
développer to develop
deviner to guess
* **devoir** to have to, should, must **27**
un **devoir** homework assignment **I**
les **devoirs** *m.* homework
faire mes devoirs to do my homework **21**
d'habitude usually
différemment differently
différent different
difficile hard, difficult **12**
la **dignité** dignity
dimanche *m.* Sunday **4B**
dîner to have dinner **7, 25**
dîner au restaurant to have dinner at a restaurant **5**
le dîner dinner, supper **25**
* **dire** to say, tell **28**
que veut dire...? what does...mean? **I**
directement straight
un **directeur, une directrice** director, principal
dirigé directed, guided
dis! (*see* **dire**) say!, hey! **12**
dis donc! say there!, hey there! **12**
discuter to discuss
une **dispute** quarrel, dispute
distrait absent-minded
dit (*p.p. of* **dire**) said
dit (*see* **dire**): **comment dit-on... en français?** how do you say...in French? **I**
dites... (*see* **dire**) say..., tell...
dix ten **1A, 1B**
dix-huit eighteen **1B**
dixième tenth **16**
dix-neuf nineteen **1B**
dix-sept seventeen **1B**
un **docteur** doctor
dois (*see* **devoir**): **je dois** I have to (must) **5**
domestique domestic
les animaux *m.* **domestiques** pets **2C**
dommage! too bad! **7**
donner (à) to give (to) **27, 28**
donne-moi... give me... **3A, I**
donnez-moi... give me **3B, I**
s'il te plaît, donne-moi... please, give me... **3B**
doré golden brown
* **dormir** to sleep
le **dos** back **E2**
une **douzaine** dozen **25**
douze twelve **1B**
douzième twelfth **16**
droit: tout droit straight **13**
droite right
à droite to (on) the right **13**
drôle funny **12**
du (de + le) of (the), from (the) **15**; some, any **26**
du matin in the morning, A.M. **4A**
du soir in the evening, P.M. **4A**
dû (*p.p. of* **devoir**) had to **27**
dur hard
des oeufs *(m.)* **durs** hard-boiled eggs
durer to last
un **DVD** DVD **9**
dynamique dynamic

E

l' **eau** *f.* (*pl.* **eaux**) water **25**
l'eau minérale mineral water **25**
un **échange** exchange
les **échecs** *m.* chess **15**
une **éclosion** hatching
une **école** school **13**
économiser to save money
écouter to listen to **I, 7**
écouter la radio to listen to the radio **5**
écouter des CD to listen to CDs **21**
l' **écran** *m.* screen (computer)
* **écrire** to write **28**
l' **éducation** *f.* education
l'éducation civique civics
l'éducation physique physical education
une **église** church **13**
égyptien (égyptienne) Egyptian
eh bien! well! **18**
électronique: une guitare électrique electric guitar
élégant elegant **17**
un **éléphant** elephant **E4**
un **élève, une élève** pupil, student **9**
élevé high
elle she, it **3C, 6, 10**; her **15**
elle coûte... it costs ... **3C**
elle est (canadienne) she's (Canadian) **2B**
elle s'appelle... her name is ... **2B**
embrasser: je t'embrasse love and kisses *(at the end of a letter)*
un **emploi du temps** time-table *(of work)*
emprunter à to borrow from
en in, on, to, by
en avion by airplane, plane **21**
en bas (haut) downstairs (upstairs) **13**
en bus (métro, taxi, train, voiture) by bus (subway, taxi, train, car) **14**
en ce qui concerne as for
en face opposite, across (the street)
en fait in fact
en famille at home
en plus in addition
en scène on stage
en solde on sale
va-t'en! go away! **14**
un **endroit** place **14**
un **enfant, une enfant** child **16**
enfin at last **22**
ensuite then, after that **22**
entendre to hear **20**
entier (entière) entire
l' **entracte** *m.* interlude
entre between
une **entrée** entry *(of a house)*
un **entretien** discussion
envers toward
l' **envie** *f.* envy; feeling
avoir envie de to want; to feel like, want to **20**
envoyer to send
envoyer un mail to send an e-mail

R20 French-English Vocabulary

épicé hot (spicy)
une **épicerie** grocery store
les **épinards** *m.* spinach
une **équipe** team
une **erreur** error, mistake
es (*see* **être**)
tu es + *nationality* you are … **1B**
tu es + *nationality?* are you …? **1B**
tu es de…? are you from …? **1B**
l' **escalade** *f.* rock climbing **21**
faire de l'escalade to go rock climbing **21**
un **escalier** staircase
un **escargot** snail
l' **Espagne** *f.* Spain
espagnol Spanish **11**
parler espagnol to speak Spanish **5**
espérer to hope **18**
un **esprit** spirit
essayer to try on, to try
l' **essentiel** *m.* the important thing
est (*see* **être**)
est-ce que (qu')…? *phrase used to introduce a question* **6**
c'est… it's …, that's … **2A, 2C, 12**
c'est le + date it's … **4B**
il/elle est + nationality he/she is … **2B**
n'est-ce pas…? isn't it? **6**
où est…? where is …? **6**
quel jour est-ce? what day is it? **4B**
qui est-ce? who's that (this)? **2A, 9**
l' **est** *m.* east
et and **1B, 6**
et demi(e), et quart half past, quarter past **4A**
et toi? and you? **1A**
établir to establish
un **étage** floor of a building, story
les **États-Unis** *m.* United States
été (*p.p. of* **être**) been, was **23**
l' **été** *m.* summer
en été in (the) summer **4C**
l'heure d'été daylight savings time
étendre to spread

une **étoile** star
étrange strange
étranger (étrangère) foreign
* **être** to be **6**
être à to belong to
être d'accord to agree **6**
une **étude** study
un **étudiant, une étudiant(e)** (college) student **9**
étudier to study **5, 7**
eu (*p.p. of* **avoir**) had **23**
il y a eu there was
euh… er …, uh …
euh non… well, no
un **euro** euro; monetary unit of Europe
européen (européenne) European
eux they, them **15**
eux-mêmes themselves
un **événement** event **14**
un **examen** exam, test
réussir à un examen to pass an exam, a test
excusez-moi excuse me **13**
un **exemple** example
par exemple for instance
un **exercice** exercise
faire des exercices to exercise
exiger to insist
expliquer to explain
expliquez… explain …
exprimer to express
exquis: c'est exquis! it's exquisite! **26**
extérieur: à l'extérieur outside
extraordinaire extraordinary
il a fait un temps extraordinaire! the weather was great!

face: en face (de) opposite, across (the street) from
facile easy **12**
faible weak
la **faim** hunger
avoir faim to be hungry **22**
j'ai faim I'm hungry **3A**
tu as faim? are you hungry? **3A**
* **faire** to do, make **8**

faire attention to pay attention, be careful **8**
faire de + *activity* to do, play, study, participate in **21**
faire des achats to go shopping **21**
faire les courses to go shopping **25**
faire mes devoirs to do my homework **21**
faire les magasins to go shopping (browsing from store to store)
faire partie de to be a member of
faire sauter to flip
faire un match to play a game (match) **8**
faire un pique-nique to have a picnic **21**
faire un voyage to take a trip **8**
faire une promenade to take a walk **8**
faire une promenade à pied (à vélo, en voiture) to take a walk (a bicycle ride, a drive) **14**
fait (*p.p. of* **faire**) did, done, made **23**
fait: en fait in fact
fait (*see* **faire**): **ça fait combien?** how much is that (it)? **3C**
ça fait… euros that's (it's) … euros **3C**
il fait (beau, etc.) it's (beautiful, etc.) *(weather)* **4C**
quel temps fait-il? what (how) is the weather? **4C**
fameux: c'est fameux! it's superb! **26**
familial with the family
une **famille** family **2C, 16**
en famille at home
un **fana, une fana** fan *(person)*
un **fantôme** ghost
la **farine** flour
fatigué tired
faux (fausse) false **12**
favori (favorite) favorite
les **félicitations** *f.* congratulations
une **femme** woman **9**; wife **16**
une **fenêtre** window **I, 9**

French-English R21 Vocabulary

fermer to close **I**
une **fête** party, holiday
le **feu d'artifice** fireworks
une **feuille** sheet, leaf **I**
  une feuille de papier sheet of paper **I**
un **feuilleton** series, serial story *(in newspaper)*
février *m.* February **4B**
fiche-moi la paix! leave me alone! *(colloq.)* **28**
la **fièvre** fever
une **fille** girl **2A;** daughter **16**
un **film** movie **14, 21**
  un film policier detective movie
un **fils** son **16**
la **fin** end
finalement finally **22**
fini (*p.p. of* **finir**) over, finished **23**
finir to finish **19**
flamand Flemish
un **flamant** flamingo
une **fleur** flower
un **fleuve** river
un **flic** cop *(colloq.)*
une **flûte** flute **15**
une **fois** time
  à la fois at the same time
la **folie: à la folie** madly
folklorique: une chanson folklorique folksong
fonctionner to work, function
fondé founded
le **foot (football)** soccer **15**
  le football américain football
  jouer au foot to play soccer **5**
une **forêt** forest
formidable great!
fort strong
  plus fort louder **I**
un **fouet** whisk
une **fourchette** fork **25**
la **fourrure** fur
  un manteau de fourrure fur coat
frais: il fait frais it's cool *(weather)* **4C**
une **fraise** strawberry **25**
un **franc** franc *(former monetary unit of France)* **3C**
  ça fait... francs that's (it's) ... francs **3C**
français French **1B, 11**
  comment dit-on... en français? how do you say... in French? **I**
  parler français to speak French **5**
le **français** French *(language)*
un **Français, une Française** French person
la **France** France **6**
  en France in France **6**
francophone French-speaking
un **frère** brother **2C, 16**
des **frites** *f.* French fries **25**
  un steak-frites steak and French fries **3A**
froid cold
  avoir froid to be (feel) cold *(people)* **22**
  il fait froid it's cold out *(weather)* **4C**
le **fromage** cheese **25**
  un sandwich au fromage cheese sandwich
un **fruit** fruit **25**
furieux (furieuse) furious
une **fusée** rocket

gagner to earn, to win **20**
un **garage** garage **13**
un **garçon** boy **2A;** waiter
une **gare** train station
une **garniture** side dish
un **gâteau** (*pl.* **gâteaux**) cake **25**
gauche left
  à gauche to (on) the left **13**
une **gelée** jelly
généralement generally
généreux (généreuse) generous
la **générosité** generosity
génial brilliant; terrific **12**
des **gens** *m.* people **10**
gentil (gentille) nice, kind **11;** sweet
la **géographie** geography
une **girafe** giraffe **E4**
une **glace** ice cream **3A, 25;** mirror, ice
glacé iced
  un thé glacé iced tea **25**
un **goûter** afternoon snack
une **goyave** guava
grand tall **9;** big, large **12;** big *(size of clothing)* **17**
  un grand magasin department store **17**
  une grande surface big store, self-service store
grandir to get tall; to grow up
une **grand-mère** grandmother **2C, 16**
un **grand-père** grandfather **2C, 16**
les **grands-parents** *m.* grandparents **16**
grec (grecque) Greek
un **grenier** attic
une **grillade** grilled meat
une **grille** grid
grillé: le pain grillé toast
  une tartine de pain grillé buttered toast
la **grippe** flu
gris gray **12**
gros (grosse) fat, big
grossir to gain weight, get fat **19**
la **Guadeloupe** Guadeloupe *(French island in the West Indies)*
une **guerre** war
une **guitare** guitar **9, 15**
un **gymnase** gym

H

habillé dressed
habiter (à) to live (in + *city*) **7**
Haïti Haiti *(French- and Creole-speaking country in the West Indies)*
un • **hamburger** hamburger **3A**
les • **haricots** *m.* **verts** green beans **25**
la • **hâte** haste
  en hâte quickly
• **haut** high
  en haut upstairs **13**
  plus haut above
• **hélas!** too bad!
hésiter to hesitate
l' **heure** *f.* time, hour; o'clock **4A**
  ... heure(s) (dix) (ten) past ... **4A**
  ... heure(s) et demie half past ... **4A**
  ... heure(s) et quart quarter past ... **4A**

R22 French-English Vocabulary

... heure(s) moins (dix) (ten) of ... **4A**
... heure(s) moins le quart quarter to ... **4A**
à... heures at ... o'clock **6**
à quelle heure...? at what time ...? **8**
à quelle heure est...? at what time is ...? **4A**
il est... heure(s) it's ... o'clock **4A**
par heure per hour, an hour
quelle heure est-il? what time is it? **4A**
heureux (heureuse) happy
hier yesterday **23**
avant-hier the day before yesterday
un **hippopotame** hippopotamus **E4**
une **histoire** story, history
l' **hiver** *m.* winter **4C**
en hiver in (the) winter **4C**
• **hollandais** Dutch
un **homme** man **9**
honnête honest
un **hôpital** (*pl.* **hôpitaux**) hospital **13**
une **horreur** horror
quelle horreur! what a scandal! how awful!
un • **hors-d'oeuvre** appetizer **25**
un • **hot dog** hot dog **3A**
un **hôte, une hôtesse** host, hostess
un **hôtel** hotel **13**
un hôtel de police police department
l' **huile** *f.* oil
• **huit** eight **1A**
huitième eighth **16**
l' **humeur** *f.* mood
de bonne humeur in a good mood
un **hypermarché** shopping center

ici here **6**
une **idée** idea
c'est une bonne idée! it's (that's) a good idea! **20**
ignorer to be unaware of
il he, it **3C, 6, 10**
il est it is **12**
il/elle est + *nationality* he/she is ... **2B**
il y a there is, there are **9**
il y a + du, de la *(partitive)* there is (some) **26**
il y a eu there was
il n'y a pas de... there is/are no ... **10**
est-ce qu'il y a...? is there, are there ...? **9**
qu'est-ce qu'il y a...? what is there ...? **9**
une **île** island
illustré illustrated
un **immeuble** apartment building **13**
un **imper (imperméable)** raincoat **17**
l' **impératif** *m.* imperative (command) mood
impoli impolite
l' **importance** *f.* importance
ça n'a pas d'importance it doesn't matter
importé imported
impressionnant impressive
l' **imprimante** *f.* printer
inactif (inactive) inactive
inclure to include
l' **indicatif** *m.* area code
indiquer to indicate, show
indiquez... indicate ...
infâme: c'est infâme! that's (it's) awful! **27**
infect: c'est infect! that's revolting! *(colloq.)* **27**
les **informations** *f.* news
l' **informatique** *f.* computer science
s' **informer (de)** to find out about
un **ingénieur** engineer
un **ingrédient** ingredient **25**
un **inspecteur, une inspectrice** police detective
un **instrument** instrument **15**
intelligent intelligent **11**
intéressant interesting **11**
l' **intérieur** *m.* interior, inside
l' **Internet** *m.* the Internet
surfer sur l'Internet (sur le Net) to surf the Internet
interroger to question
interviewer to interview
inutilement uselessly
un **inventaire** inventory
un **invité, une invitée** guest
inviter to invite **7**
israélien (israélienne) Israeli
italien (italienne) Italian **11**
un **Italien, une Italienne** Italian person

j' (*see* **je**)
jamais ever; never
jamais le dimanche! never on Sunday!
ne... jamais never **24**
la **Jamaïque** Jamaica
une **jambe** leg **E2**
un **jambon** ham **25**
janvier *m.* January **4B**
japonais Japanese **11**
un **jardin** garden **13**
jaune yellow **E1, 12**
jaunir to turn yellow
je I **6**
un **jean** pair of jeans **15**
un **jeu** (*pl.* **jeux**) game **17**
les jeux d'ordinateur computer games
les jeux télévisés TV game shows
les jeux vidéo video games
jeudi *m.* Thursday **4B**
jeune young **9**
les **jeunes** *m.* young people
un **job** (part-time) job
le **jogging** jogging **21**
faire du jogging to jog 21
un **jogging** jogging suit **25**
joli pretty *(for girls, women* **17**; *(for clothing)* **17**
plus joli(e) que prettier than
jouer to play **7**
jouer à + *game, sport* to play a game, sport **15**
jouer aux jeux vidéo to play video games **5**
jouer au tennis (volley, basket, foot) to play tennis (volleyball, basketball, soccer) **5**
jouer de + *instrument* to play a musical instrument **15**
un **jour** day **4B, 21**
le Jour de l'An New Year's Day
par jour per week, a week

French-English Vocabulary R23

quel jour est-ce? what day is it? **8**
un **journal** (*pl.* **journaux**) newspaper
une **journée** day, whole day
bonne journée! have a nice day!
joyeux (joyeuse) happy
juillet *m.* July **4B**
le quatorze juillet Bastille Day *(French national holiday)*
juin *m.* June **4B**
un **jumeau** (*pl.* **jumeaux**), **une jumelle** twin
une **jupe** skirt **17**
le **jus** juice
le jus d'orange orange juice **3B, 25**
le jus de pomme apple juice **3B, 25**
le jus de raisin grape juice **3B**
le jus de tomate tomato juice **3B**
jusqu'à until
juste right, fair
le mot juste the right word

K

un **kangourou** kangaroo **E4**
le **ketchup** ketchup **25**
un **kilo** kilogram
un kilo (de) a kilogram (of) **25**

L

l' (*see* **le, la**)
la the **2B, 10;** her, it **28**
là here, there **6**
là-bas over there **6**
ça, là-bas that (one), over there **9**
ce... -là that ... (over there) **18**
oh là là! uh, oh!; oh, dear!; wow!; oh, yes!
laid ugly
laisser (un message) to leave (a message)
laisser: laisse-moi tranquille! leave me alone! **28**
le **lait** milk **25**
une **lampe** lamp **9**
une **langue** language
large wide
laver to wash **21**
se laver to wash (oneself), wash up
le the **2B, 10;** him, it **28**
le + *number* + *month* the ... **4B**
le (lundi) on (Mondays) **10**
une **leçon** lesson
un **légume** vegetable **25**
lent slow
les the **10;** them **28**
une **lettre** letter
leur(s) their **16**
leur (to) them **28**
se **lever: lève-toi!** stand up! **I**
levez-vous! stand up! **I**
un **lézard** lizard **E4**
le **Liban** Lebanon *(country in the Middle East)*
libanais Lebanese
libéré liberated
une **librairie** bookstore
libre free
un **lieu** place, area
avoir lieu to take place
une **ligne** line
limité limited
la **limonade** lemon soda **3B**
un **lion** lion **E4**
* **lire** to read
comment lire reading hints
lisez... (*see* **lire**) read ... **I**
une **liste** list
une liste des courses shopping list
un **lit** bed **9**
un **living** living room *(informal)*
un **livre** book **I, 9**
une **livre** metric pound **25**
local (*m.pl.* **locaux**) local
une **location** rental
logique logical
logiquement logically
loin far **13**
loin d'ici far (from here)
le **loisir** leisure, free time
un **loisir** leisure-time activity
Londres London
long (longue) long **17**
longtemps (for) a long time
moins longtemps que for a shorter time
le **loto** lotto, lottery, bingo
louer to rent **21**
un **loup** wolf **E4**
lui him **15;** (to) him/her **28**
lui-même: en lui-même to himself
lundi *m.* Monday **4B**
des **lunettes** *f.* glasses **17**
des lunettes de soleil sunglasses **17**
le **Luxembourg** Luxembourg
un **lycée** high school

M

m' (*see* **me**)
M. (monsieur) Mr. (Mister) **1C**
ma my **2C, 16**
et voici ma mère and this is my mother **2C**
ma chambre my bedroom **9**
une **machine** machine
une machine à coudre sewing machine
Madagascar Madagascar *(French-speaking island off of East Africa)*
Madame (Mme) Mrs., ma'am **1C**
Mademoiselle (Mlle) Miss **1C**
un **magasin** store, shop **13, 17**
faire les magasins to go shopping (browsing from store to store)
un grand magasin department store **17**
magnétique magnetic
un **magnétophone** tape recorder
un **magnétoscope** VCR (videocassette recorder)
magnifique magnificent
mai *m.* May **4B**
maigre thin, skinny
maigrir to lose weight, get thin **19**
un **mail** e-mail
un **maillot de bain** bathing suit **17**
une **main** hand **E2**
maintenant now **7, 23**
mais but **6**
j'aime..., mais je préfère... I like ..., but I prefer ... **5**

R24 French-English Vocabulary

je regrette, mais je ne peux pas... I'm sorry, but I can't ... **5**
mais oui! sure! **6**
mais non! of course not! **6**
une **maison** house **13**
à la maison at home **6**
mal badly, poorly **1C, 7**
le **mal** evil
ça va mal things are going badly **1C**
ça va très mal things are going very badly **1C**
c'est mal that's bad **12**
malade sick
malheureusement unfortunately
malin clever
manger to eat **7**
j'aime manger I like to eat **5**
manger + du, de la *(partitive)* to eat (some) **26**
une salle à manger dining room **13**
un **manteau** (*pl.* **manteaux**) overcoat **17**
un manteau de fourrure fur coat
un **marchand, une marchande** merchant, shopkeeper, dealer
un **marché** open-air market **25**
un marché aux puces flea market
bon marché *(inv.)* inexpensive **17**
marcher to work, to run *(for objects)* **9;** to walk *(for people)* **9**
il/elle (ne) marche (pas) bien it (doesn't) work(s) well **9**
est-ce que la radio marche? does the radio work? **9**
mardi *m.* Tuesday **4B**
le **Mardi gras** Shrove Tuesday
un **mari** husband **16**
le **mariage** wedding, marriage
marié married
une **marmite** covered stew pot
le **Maroc** Morocco *(country in North Africa)*
une **marque** brand (name)
une **marraine** godmother
marrant fun
marron *(inv.)* brown **12**
mars *m.* March **4B**
martiniquais from Martinique
la **Martinique** Martinique *(French island in the West Indies)*
un **match** game, (sports) match **14**
faire un match to play a game, (sports) match **8**
les **maths** *f.* math
le **matin** morning **21**
ce matin this morning **23**
demain matin tomorrow morning **23**
du matin in the morning, A.M. **4A**
hier matin yesterday morning **23**
le matin in the morning
des **matoutou crabes** *m.* stewed crabs with rice
mauvais bad **12**
c'est une mauvaise idée that's a bad idea
il fait mauvais it's bad *(weather)* **4C**
la **mayonnaise** mayonnaise **25**
me (to) me **27**
méchant mean, nasty **11**
un **médecin** doctor
un médecin de nuit doctor on night duty
la **Méditerranée** Mediterranean Sea
meilleur(e) better, best **19**
un **mél** e-mail
mélanger to mix, stir
même same; even
eux-mêmes themselves
les mêmes choses the same things
une **mémoire** memory
mentionner to mention
la **mer** ocean, shore **21**
à la mer to (at) the sea **21**
merci thank you **1C**
oui, merci yes, thank you **5**
mercredi *m.* Wednesday **4B**
une **mère** mother **2C, 16**
mériter to deserve
mes my **16**
la **messagerie vocale** voice mail
le **métro** subway
en métro by subway **14**
* **mettre** to put on, to wear **17;** to put, to place, to turn on **18**
mettre la table to set the table **25**
mexicain Mexican **11**
midi *m.* noon **4A**
mieux better
mignon (mignonne) cute **11**
militaire military
mille one thousand **2B, 17**
minérale: l'eau *f.* **minérale** mineral water **25**
une **mini-chaîne** compact stereo **9**
minuit *m.* midnight **4A**
mis (*p.p. of* **mettre**) put, placed **23**
mixte mixed
Mlle Miss **1C**
Mme Mrs. **1C**
une **mob (mobylette)** motorbike, moped **9**
moche plain, ugly **17**
la **mode** fashion
à la mode popular; in fashion; fashionable **17**
moderne modern **13**
moi me **1A, 15;** (to) me **27**
moi, je m'appelle (Marc) me, my name is (Marc) **1A**
avec moi with me **5**
donne-moi give me **3A**
donnez-moi give me **3B**
excusez-moi... excuse me ... **13**
prête-moi... lend me ... **3C**
s'il te plaît, donne-moi... please give me ... **3B**
un **moine** monk
moins less
moins de less than
moins... que less ... than **19**
... heure(s) moins (dix) (ten) of ... **4A**
... heure(s) moins le quart quarter of ... **4A**
un **mois** month **4B, 21**
ce mois-ci this month **23**
le mois dernier last month **23**
le mois prochain next month **23**
par mois per month, a month
mon (ma; mes) my **2C, 16**
mon anniversaire est le... my birthday is the ... **4B**
voici mon père this is my father **2C**

FRENCH-ENGLISH VOCABULARY

French-English Vocabulary R25

le **monde** world
du monde in the world
tout le monde everyone
la **monnaie** money; change
Monsieur (M.) Mr., sir **1C**
un **monsieur** (*pl.* **messieurs**) gentleman, man *(polite term)* **2A**
une **montagne** mountain **21**
à la montagne to (at) the mountains **21**
une **montre** watch **9**
montrer à to show ... to **27, 28**
montre-moi (montrez-moi) show me **I**
un **morceau** piece
un morceau de craie piece of chalk **I**
un **mot** word
une **moto** motorcycle **9**
la **moutarde** mustard
un **mouton** sheep
moyen (moyenne) average, medium
en moyenne on the average
un **moyen** means
muet (muette) silent
le **multimédia** multimedia
un **musée** museum **13**
la **musique** music **15**

N

n' (*see* **ne**)
nager to swim **7**
j'aime nager I like to swim **5**
une **nationalité** nationality **1B**
nautique: le ski nautique water-skiing **21**
ne (n')
ne... aucun none, not any
ne... jamais never **24**
ne... pas not **6**
ne... personne nobody **24**
ne... plus no longer
ne... rien nothing **24**
n'est-ce pas? right?, no?, isn't it (so)?, don't you?, aren't you? **6**
né born
nécessaire necessary
négatif (négative) negative
négativement negatively
la **neige** snow
neiger to snow
il neige it's snowing **4C**
le **Net** the Internet
nettoyer to clean **21**
neuf nine **1A**
neuvième ninth **16**
un **neveu** (*pl.* **neveux**) nephew
un **nez** nose **E2**
une **nièce** niece
un **niveau** (*pl.* **niveaux**) level
Noël *m.* Christmas
à Noël at Christmas **21**
noir black **E1, 12**
un **nom** name; noun
un **nombre** number
nombreux (nombreuses) numerous
nommé named
non no **1B, 6**
non plus neither
mais non! of course not! **6**
le **nord** north
le nord-est northeast
normalement normally
nos our **16**
une **note** grade
notre (*pl.* **nos**) our **16**
la **nourriture** food **25**
nous we **6**; us **15**; (to) us **27**
nouveau (nouvel, nouvelle; *m.pl.* **nouveaux)** new **19**
la **Nouvelle-Angleterre** New England
la **Nouvelle-Calédonie** New Caledonia *(French island in the South Pacific)*
novembre *m.* November **4B**
le onze novembre Armistice Day
la **nuit** night
un **numéro** number

O

objectif (objective) objective
un **objet** object **9**
une **occasion** occasion; opportunity
occupé occupied
un **océan** ocean
octobre *m.* October **4B**
une **odeur** odor
un **oeil** (*pl.* **yeux**) eye **E2**
un **oeuf** egg **25**
officiel (officielle) official
offert (*p.p. of* **offrir**) offered
* **offrir** to offer, to give
oh là là! uh,oh!, oh, dear!, wow!, oh, yes!
un **oiseau** (*pl.* **oiseaux**) bird
une **omelette** omelet **3A**
on one, they, you, people **20**
on est... today is ...
on va dans un café? shall we go to a café?
on y va let's go
comment dit-on... en français? how do you say ... in French? **I**
un **oncle** uncle **2C, 16**
onze eleven **1B**
opérer to operate
l' **or** *m.* gold
orange *(inv.)* orange *(color)* **E1, 12**
une **orange** orange *(fruit)*
le jus d'orange orange juice **3B, 25**
un **ordinateur** computer **9**
un ordinateur portable laptop computer
une **oreille** ear **E2**
organiser to organize **7**
originairement originally
l' **origine** *f.* origin, beginning
d'origine bretonne from Brittany
orthographiques: les signes *m.* **orthographiques** spelling marks
ou or **1B, 6**
où where **6, 8**
où est...? where is ...? **6**
où est-ce? where is it? **13**
d'où? from where? **15**
oublier to forget
l' **ouest** *m.* west
oui yes **1B, 6**
oui, bien sûr... yes, of course ... **5**
oui, d'accord... yes, okay ... **5**
oui, j'ai... yes, I have ... **9**
oui, merci... yes, thank you ... **5**
mais oui! sure! **6**
un **ouragan** hurricane
un **ours** bear **E4**
ouvert open

* **ouvrir** to open
ouvre... (ouvrez...) open ... **I**

P

le **pain** bread **25**
pâle pale
un **pamplemousse** grapefruit **25**
une **panne** breakdown
une panne d'électricité power failure
un **pantalon** pants, trousers **17**
une **panthère** panther
une **papaye** papaya
le **papier** paper
une feuille de papier a sheet (piece) of paper **I**
Pâques *m.* Easter **21**
à Pâques at Easter **21**
par per
par exemple for example
par jour per day
un **parc** park **13**
un parc public city park
parce que (parce qu') because **8**
pardon excuse me **13, 17**
les **parents** *m.* parents, relatives **16**
paresseux (paresseuse) lazy
parfait perfect
rien n'est parfait nothing is perfect
parfois sometimes
parisien (parisienne) Parisian
parler to speak, talk **I, 7**
parler à to speak (talk) to **28**
parler (français, anglais, espagnol) to speak (French, English, Spanish) **5**
un **parrain** godfather
une **partie** part
* **partir** to leave
à partir de as of, beginning
partitif (partitive) partitive
pas not
ne... pas not **6**
pas de not a, no, not any **10, 26**
pas du tout not at all, definitely not **15**
pas possible not possible
pas toujours not always **5**
pas très bien not very well

le **passé composé** compound past tense
passer to spend (time) **21**; to pass by
passionnément passionately
une **pâte** dough
patient patient
le **patinage** ice skating, roller skating
une **patinoire** skating rink
une **pâtisserie** pastry, pastry shop
une **patte** foot, paw *(of bird or animal)*
pauvre poor **20**
payer to pay, pay for **20**
un **pays** country
un **PC portable** laptop computer
la **peau** skin, hide
* **peindre** to paint
peint painted
une **pellicule** film (camera)
pendant during **21**
pénétrer to enter
pénible bothersome, a pain **12**
penser to think **17**
penser de to think of **17**
penser que to think that **17**
qu'est-ce que tu penses de...? what do you think of ...? **17**
une **pension** inn, boarding house
Pentecôte *f.* Pentecost
perdre to lose, to waste **20**
perdu (*p.p. of* **perdre**) lost
un **père** father **2C, 16**
* **permettre** to permit
un **perroquet** parrot
personne (de) nobody **24**
ne... personne nobody, not anybody, not anyone **24**
une **personne** person **2A**
personnel (personnelle) personal
personnellement personally
péruvien (péruvienne) Peruvian
petit small, short **9, 12, 17**
il/elle est petit(e) he/she is short **9**
un petit copain, une petite copine boyfriend, girlfriend
plus petit(e) smaller
le **petit déjeuner** breakfast **25**

prendre le petit déjeuner to have breakfast **25**
le **petit-fils, la petite-fille** grandson, granddaughter
les **petits pois** *m.* peas **25**
peu little, not much
un peu a little, a little bit **7**
un peu de a few
peut (*see* **pouvoir**)
peut-être perhaps, maybe **6**
peux (*see* **pouvoir**)
est-ce que tu peux...? can you ...? **5**
je regrette, mais je ne peux pas... I'm sorry, but I can't ... **5**
la **photo** photography
une **phrase** sentence **I**
la **physique** physics
un **piano** piano **15**
une **pie** magpie **E4**
une **pièce** coin **20**; room
un **pied** foot **E2**
à pied on foot **14**
faire une promenade à pied to take a walk **14**
piloter to pilot (a plane)
une **pincée** pinch
le **ping-pong** Ping-Pong **15**
un **pique-nique** picnic **14**
faire un pique-nique to have a picnic **21**
une **piscine** swimming pool **13**
une **pizza** pizza **3A**
un **placard** closet
une **plage** beach **13**
plaît: s'il te plaît please *(informal)* **3A**; excuse me (please)
s'il te plaît, donne-moi... please, give me ... **3B**
s'il vous plaît please *(formal)* **3B**; excuse me (please)
un **plan** map
la **planche à voile** windsurfing **21**
faire de la planche à voile to windsurf **21**
une **plante** plant
un **plat** dish, course *(of a meal)* **25**
le plat principal main course
un **plateau** tray
pleut: il pleut it's raining **4C**
plier to fold

French-English Vocabulary R27

plumer to pluck
plus more
plus de more than
plus joli que prettier than
plus... que more ... than, ... -er than **19**
en plus in addition
le plus the most
ne... plus no longer, no more
non plus neither
plusieurs several
une **poche** pocket
l'argent *m.* **de poche** allowance, pocket money
une **poêle** frying pan
un **point de vue** point of view
une **poire** pear **25**
pois: les petits pois *m.* peas **25**
un **poisson** fish **E4, 25**
un poisson rouge goldfish
blaff de poisson fish stew
poli polite
un **politicien, une politicienne** politician
un **polo** polo shirt **17**
une **pomme** apple
le jus de pomme apple juice **3B, 25**
une **pomme de terre** potato **25**
une purée de pommes de terre mashed potatoes
le **porc: une côtelette de porc** pork chop
un **portable** cell phone **9**
une **porte** door **I, 9**
un **porte-monnaie** change purse, wallet
porter to wear **17**
portugais Portuguese
poser: poser une question to ask a question
une **possibilité** possibility
la **poste** post office
pouah! yuck! yech!
une **poule** hen **E4**
le **poulet** chicken **25**
pour for **6;** in order to **21**
pour que so that
pour qui? for whom? **8**
le **pourcentage** percentage
pourquoi why **8**
* **pouvoir** to be able, can, may **27**
pratique practical
pratiquer to participate in
des **précisions** *f.* details
préféré favorite
préférer to prefer **18;** to like (in general)
je préfère I prefer **5**
tu préférerais? would you prefer?
premier (première) first **16**
le premier de l'an New Year's Day
le premier étage second floor
le premier mai Labor Day *(in France)*
c'est le premier juin it's June first **4B**
* **prendre** to take, to have *(food)* **I, 26**
prendre + du, de la *(partitive)* to have (some) **26**
prendre le petit déjeuner to have breakfast **25**
un **prénom** first name
préparer to prepare; to prepare for **21**
près nearby **13**
près d'ici nearby, near here
tout près very close
une **présentation** appearance
la présentation extérieure outward appearance
des **présentations** *f.* introductions
presque almost
pressé in a hurry
prêt ready
un **prêt** loan
prêter à to lend to, to loan **27, 28**
prête-moi... lend me... **3C**
principalement mainly
le **printemps** spring **4C**
au printemps in the spring **4C**
pris (*p.p. of* **prendre**) took **26**
un **prix** price
quel est le prix ...? what's the price ...? **17**
un **problème** problem
prochain next **21, 23**
le week-end prochain next weekend **21**
un **produit** product
un **prof, une prof** teacher *(informal)* **2A, 9**
un **professeur** teacher **9**
professionnel (professionnelle) professional
un **programme** program
un **projet** plan
une **promenade** walk
faire une promenade à pied to go for a walk **8, 14**
faire une promenade à vélo to go for a ride (by bike) **14**
faire une promenade en voiture to go for a drive (by car) **14**
* **promettre** to promise
une **promo** special sale
proposer to suggest
propre own
un **propriétaire, une propriétaire** landlord/landlady, owner
la **Provence** Provence *(province in southern France)*
pu (*p.p. of* **pouvoir**) could, was able to **27**
n'a pas pu was not able to
public: un parc public city park
un jardin public public garden
la **publicité** commercials, advertising, publicity
une **puce** flea
un marché aux puces flea market
puis then, also
puisque since
un **pull** sweater, pullover **17**
les **Pyrénées** (the) Pyrenees *(mountains between France and Spain)*

Q

qu' (*see* **que**)
une **qualité** quality
quand when **8**
c'est quand, ton anniversaire? when is your birthday? **4B**
une **quantité** quantity **25**
quarante forty **1C**
un **quart** one quarter
... heure(s) et quart quarter past ... **4A**
... heure(s) moins le quart quarter of ... **4A**

R28 French-English Vocabulary

un **quartier** district, neighborhood 13
un joli quartier a nice neighborhood 13
quatorze fourteen 1B
quatre four 1A
quatre-vingt-dix ninety 2B
quatre-vingts eighty 2B
quatrième fourth 16
que that, which
que veut dire...? what does ... mean? I
qu'est-ce que (qu') what *(phrase used to introduce a question)* 8
qu'est-ce que c'est? what is it? what's that? 9
qu'est-ce que tu penses de...? what do you think of ...? 17
qu'est-ce que tu veux? what do you want? 3A
qu'est-ce qu'il y a? what is there? 9; what's the matter?
qu'est-ce qui ne va pas? what's wrong?
un **Québécois, une Québécoise** person from Quebec
québécois from Quebec
quel (quelle) what, which, what a 18
quel (quelle)...! what a...!
quel âge a ta mère/ton père? how old is your mother/your father? 2C
quel âge a-t-il/elle? how old is he/she? 9
quel âge as-tu? how old are you? 2C
quel est le prix...? what is the price ...? 17
quel jour est-ce? what day is it? 4B
quel temps fait-il? what's (how's) the weather? 4C
quelle est la date? what's the date? 4B
quelle est ton adresse? what's your address? 13
quelle heure est-il? what time is it? 4A
à quelle heure? at what time? 4A
à quelle heure est...? at what time is ...? 4A
de quelle couleur...? what color is ...? 12
quelqu'un someone 24
quelque chose something 24
quelques some, a few 9
une **question** question
une **queue** tail
qui who, whom 8
qui est-ce? who's that (this)? 2A, 9
qui se ressemble... birds of a feather ...
à qui? to whom? 8
avec qui? with who(m)? 8
c'est qui? who's that? *(casual speech)*
de qui? about who(m)? 8
pour qui? for who(m)? 8
quinze fifteen 1B
quoi? what? 9
quotidien (quotidienne) daily
la **vie quotidienne** daily life

raconter to tell about
une **radio** radio 9
écouter la radio to listen to the radio 5
une radiocassette boom box 9
une radiocassette/CD boom box with CD
raisin: le jus de raisin grape juice 3B
une **raison** reason
avoir raison to be right 22
ranger to pick up 21
rapidement rapidly
un **rapport** relationship
une **raquette** racket 9
une raquette de tennis tennis racket 15
rarement rarely, seldom 7
un **rayon** department *(in a store)*
réalisé made, directed
récemment recently
une **recette** recipe
recherche: un avis de recherche missing person's bulletin
un **récital** (*pl.* **récitals**) (musical) recital
reconstituer to reconstruct
un **réfrigérateur** refrigerator
refuser to refuse
regarder to look at, watch I, 7
regarde ça look at that 9
regarder la télé to watch TV 5
un **régime** diet
être au régime to be on a diet
régional (*m.pl.* **régionaux**) regional
regretter to be sorry
je regrette, mais... I'm sorry, but ... 5
régulier (régulière) regular
une **reine** queen
rencontrer to meet 21
une **rencontre** meeting, encounter
un **rendez-vous** date, appointment 14
j'ai un rendez-vous à... I have a date, appointment at ... 4A
rendre visite à to visit, come to visit 20, 28
la **rentrée** first day back at school in fall
rentrer to go back, come back 14; to return, go back, come back 24
réparer to fix, repair 21
un **repas** meal 25
* **repeindre** to repaint
répéter to repeat I
répondre (à) to answer, respond (to) I, 28
répondez-lui (moi) answer him (me)
répondre que oui to answer yes
une **réponse** answer
un **reportage** documentary
représenter to represent
réservé reserved
une **résolution** resolution
un **restaurant** restaurant 13
au restaurant to (at) the restaurant 6
dîner au restaurant to have dinner at a restaurant 5
un restaurant trois étoiles three star restaurant

FRENCH-ENGLISH VOCABULARY

French-English Vocabulary R29

rester to stay **14, 24**
retard: **un jour de retard** one day behind
en retard late
retourner to return; to turn over
réussir to succeed **19**
réussir à un examen to pass an exam **19**
* **revenir** to come back **15**
revoir: au revoir! good-bye! **1C**
le **rez-de-chaussée** ground floor
un **rhinocéros** rhinoceros **E4**
riche rich **20**
rien (de) nothing **24**
rien n'est parfait nothing is perfect
ne... rien nothing **24**
une **rive** (river) bank
une **rivière** river, stream
le **riz** rice **25**
une **robe** dress **17**
le **roller** in-line skating **21**
faire du roller to go in-line skating **21**
des **rollers** in-line skates **21**
romain Roman
le **rosbif** roast beef **25**
rose pink **12**
rosse nasty *(colloq.)*
une **rôtie** toast *(Canadian)*
rôtir to roast
une **roue** wheel
rouge red **E1, 12**
rougir to turn red
rouler to roll
roux (rousse) red-head
une **rue** street **13**
dans la rue (Victor Hugo) on (Victor Hugo) street **13**
russe Russian

S

sa his, her **16**
un **sac** book bag, bag **I**; bag, handbag **9**
sais (*see* **savoir**)
je sais I know **I, 9, 28**
je ne sais pas I don't know **I, 9**
tu sais you know **28**
une **saison** season **4C**
toute saison all year round (any season)
une **salade** salad **3A, 25;** lettuce **25**
un **salaire** salary
une **salle** hall, large room
une salle à manger dining room **13**
une salle de bains bathroom **13**
une salle de séjour informal living room
un **salon** formal living room **13**
salut hi!, good-bye! **1C**
une **salutation** greeting
samedi Saturday **4B, 23**
samedi soir Saturday night
à samedi! see you Saturday! **4B**
le samedi on Saturdays **10**
une **sandale** sandal **17**
un **sandwich** sandwich **3A**
sans without
des **saucisses** *f.* sausages
le **saucisson** salami **25**
* **savoir** to know *(information)*
je sais I know **I, 9, 28**
je ne sais pas I don't know **I, 9**
tu sais you know **28**
un **saxo (saxophone)** saxophone **15**
une **scène** scene, stage
les **sciences** *f.* **économiques** economics
les **sciences** *f.* **naturelles** natural science
un **scooter** motor scooter **9**
second second
seize sixteen **1B**
un **séjour** stay; informal living room
le **sel** salt **25**
selon according to
selon toi in your opinion
une **semaine** week **4B, 21**
cette semaine this week **23**
la semaine dernière last week **23**
la semaine prochaine next week **23**
par semaine per week, a week
semblable similar
le **Sénégal** Senegal *(French-speaking country in Africa)*
sensationnel (sensationnelle) sensational
séparer to separate
sept seven **1A**
septembre *m.* September **4B**
septième seventh **16**
une **série** series
sérieux (sérieuse) serious
un **serveur, une serveuse** waiter, waitress
servi served
une **serviette** napkin **25**
ses his, her **16**
seul alone, only; by oneself **21**
seulement only, just
un **short** shorts **17**
si if, whether
si! so, yes! *(to a negative question)* **10**
un **signal** (*pl.* **signaux**) signal
un **signe** sign
un signe orthographique spelling mark
un **singe** monkey **E4**
situé situated
six six **1A**
sixième sixth **16**
le **skate** skateboarding **21**
un **skate** skateboard **21**
faire du skate to go skateboarding **21**
le **ski** skiing
le ski nautique water-skiing **21**
faire du ski to ski **21**
faire du ski nautique to go water-skiing **21**
skier to ski
snob snobbish
le **snowboard** snowboarding **21**
faire du snowboard to go snowboarding **21**
un **snowboard** snowboard **21**
la **Société Nationale des Chemins de Fer (SNCF)** *French railroad system*
une **société** society
un **soda** soda **3B**
une **soeur** sister **2C, 16**
la **soie** silk
la **soif** thirst
avoir soif to be thirsty **22**
j'ai soif I'm thirsty **3B**
tu as soif? are you thirsty? **3B**

R30 French-English Vocabulary

un **soir** evening **21**
ce soir this evening, tonight **23**
demain soir tomorrow night (evening) **21, 23**
du soir in the evening, P.M. **4A**
hier soir last night **23**
le soir in the evening
une **soirée** (whole) evening; (evening) party
soixante sixty **1C, 2A**
soixante-dix seventy **2A**
un **soldat** soldier
un **solde** (clearance) sale
en solde on sale
la **sole** sole *(fish)* **25**
le **soleil** sun
les lunettes *f.* **de soleil** sunglasses **17**
sommes (*see* **être**)
nous sommes... it is, today is ... *(date)*
son (sa; ses) his, her **16**
un **sondage** poll
une **sorte** sort, type, kind
* **sortir** to leave, come out
un **souhait** wish
la **soupe** soup **25**
une **souris** mouse *(computer)*
sous under **9**
le **sous-sol** basement
souvent often **7**
soyez (*see* **être**): **soyez logique** be logical
les **spaghetti** *m.* spaghetti **25**
spécialement especially
spécialisé specialized
une **spécialité** specialty
le **sport** sports **15, 21**
faire du sport to play sports **21**
des vêtements *m.* **de sport** sports clothing **17**
une voiture de sport sports car **15**
sportif (sportive) athletic **11**
un **stade** stadium **13**
un **stage** sports training camp; internship
une **station-service** gas station
un **steak** steak **3A**
un **steak-frites** steak and French fries **3A**
un **stylo** pen **I, 9**
le **sucre** sugar **25**
le **sud** south
suggérer to suggest
suis (*see* **être**)
je suis + *nationality* I'm ... **1B**
je suis de... I'm from ... **1B**
suisse Swiss **11**
la **Suisse** Switzerland
suivant following
suivi followed
un **sujet** subject, topic
super terrific **7;** great **12, 17**
un **supermarché** supermarket **13**
supersonique supersonic
supérieur superior
supplémentaire supplementary, extra
sur on **9;** about
sûr sure, certain
bien sûr! of course! **6**
oui, bien sûr... yes, of course ...! **5**
tu es sûr(e)? are you sure? **16**
sûrement surely
la **surface: une grande surface** big store, self-service store
surfer to go snowboarding
surfer sur l'Internet (sur le Net) to surf the Internet
surtout especially
un **survêtement** jogging or track suit **17**
un **sweat** sweatshirt **17**
une **sweaterie** shop specializing in sweatshirts and sportswear
sympa nice, pleasant *(colloq.)*
sympathique nice, pleasant **11**
une **synagogue** Jewish temple or synagogue
un **synthétiseur** electronic keyboard, synthesizer

t' (*see* **te**)
ta your **2C, 16**
une **table** table **I, 9**
mettre la table to set the table **25**
un **tableau** (*pl.* **tableaux**) chalkboard **I**
Tahiti Tahiti *(French island in the South Pacific)*
une **taille** size
de taille moyenne of medium height or size
un **tailleur** woman's suit
se **taire: tais-toi!** be quiet!
une **tante** aunt **2C, 16**
la **tarte** pie **25**
une **tasse** cup **25**
un **taxi** taxi
en taxi by taxi **14**
te (to) you **27**
un **tee-shirt** T-shirt **17**
la **télé** TV **9**
à la télé on TV
regarder la télé TV **5**
télécharger to download
un **téléphone** telephone **9**
téléphoner (à) to call, phone **5, 7, 28**
télévisé: des jeux *m.* **télévisés** TV game shows
un **temple** Protestant church
le **temps** time; weather
combien de temps? how long?
de temps en temps from time to time
quel temps fait-il? what's (how's) the weather? **4C**
tout le temps all the time
le **tennis** tennis **15**
jouer au tennis to play tennis **5**
des **tennis** *m.* tennis shoes, sneakers **17**
un **terrain de sport** (playing) field
une **terrasse** outdoor section of a café, terrace
la **terre** earth
une pomme de terre potato **25**
terrifiant terrifying
tes your **16**
la **tête** head **E2**
le **thé** tea **3B**
un thé glacé iced tea **25**
un **théâtre** theater **13**
le **thon** tuna **25**
tiens! look!, hey! **2A, 10**
un **tigre** tiger **E4**
timide timid, shy **11**
le **tissu** fabric
un **titre** title

FRENCH-ENGLISH VOCABULARY

French-English Vocabulary R31

toi you **15**
avec toi with you **5**
et toi? and you? **1A**
les **toilettes** *f.* bathroom, toilet **13**
un **toit** roof
une **tomate** tomato **25**
le jus de tomate tomato juice **3B**
un **tombeau** tomb
ton (ta; tes) your **2C, 16**
c'est quand, ton anniversaire? when's your birthday? **4B**
tort: avoir tort to be wrong **22**
une **tortue** turtle **E4**
un bifteck de tortue turtle steak
toujours always **7**
je n'aime pas toujours... I don't always like ... **5**
un **tour** turn
à votre tour it's your turn
la **Touraine** Touraine *(province in central France)*
tourner to turn **13**
la **Toussaint** All Saints' Day *(November 1)*
tout (toute; tous, toutes) all, every, the whole
tous les jours every day
tout ça all that
tout le monde everyone
tout le temps all the time
toutes sortes all sorts, kinds
tout completely, very
tout droit straight **13**
tout de suite right away
tout près very close
tout all, everything
pas du tout not at all **15**
un **train** train **21**
tranquille quiet
laisse-moi tranquille! leave me alone! 28
un **travail** (*pl.* **travaux**) job
travailler to work **5, 7**
une **traversée** crossing
treize thirteen **1B**
trente thirty **1C**
un **tréma** diaeresis *(accent mark)*
très very **11**
très bien very well **7**
ça va très bien things are going very well **1C**
ça va très mal things are going very badly **1C**
trois three **1A**
troisième third **16;** *9th grade in France*
trop too, too much **17**
trouver to find, to think of **17**
comment trouves-tu...? what do you think of ...? how do you find ...? **17**
s'y trouve is there
tu you **6**
la **Tunisie** Tunisia *(country in North Africa)*

U

un, une one **1A;** a, an **2A, 10**
unique only
uniquement only
une **université** university, college
l' **usage** *m.* use
un **ustensile** utensil
utile useful
utiliser to use
en utilisant (by) using
utilisez... use ...

V

va (*see* **aller**)
va-t'en! go away! **14**
ça va? how are you? how's everything? **1C**
ça va! everything's fine (going well); fine, I'm OK **1C**
on va dans un café? shall we go to a café?
on y va let's go
les **vacances** *f.* vacation
bonnes vacances! have a nice vacation!
en vacances on vacation **6**
les grandes vacances summer vacation **21**
une **vache** cow
vais (*see* **aller**): **je vais** I'm going **14**
la **vaisselle** dishes
faire la vaisselle to do the dishes
valable valid
une **valise** suitcase
vanille: une glace à la vanille vanilla ice cream
varié varied
les **variétés** *f.* variety show
vas (see **aller**)
comment vas-tu? how are you? **1C**
vas-y! come on!, go ahead!, do it! **14**
le **veau** veal **25**
une **vedette** star
un **vélo** bicycle **9**
à vélo by bicycle **14**
faire une promenade à vélo to go for a bicycle ride **14**
un **vélo tout terrain (un VTT)** mountain bike
un **vendeur, une vendeuse** salesperson
vendre to sell **20**
vendredi *m.* Friday **4B**
vendu (*p.p. of* **vendre**) sold **23**
• **venir** to come **15**
le **vent** wind
une **vente** sale
le **ventre** stomach **E2**
venu (*p.p. of* **venir**) came, come **24**
vérifier to check
la **vérité** truth
un **verre** glass **25**
verser to pour
vert green **E1, 12**
les • haricots *m.* **verts** green beans **25**
une **veste** jacket **17**
des **vêtements** *m.* clothing **17**
des vêtements de sport sports clothing **17**
veut (*see* **vouloir**): **que veut dire...?** what does ... mean? **I**
veux (*see* **vouloir**)
est-ce que tu veux...? do you want ...? **5**
je ne veux pas... I don't want ... **5**
je veux... I want ... **5, 26**
je veux bien... I'd love to, I do, I want to ... **5, 26**
qu'est-ce que tu veux? what do you want? **3A**
tu veux...? do you want ...? **3A**

R32 French-English Vocabulary

la viande meat **25**
la vie life
la vie quotidienne daily life
viens (*see* **venir**)
viens... come ... **I**
oui, je viens yes, I'm coming along with you
vieux (vieil, vieille; *m.pl.* **vieux)** old **19**
le Vieux Carré *the French Quarter in New Orleans*
le Viêt-nam Vietnam *(country in Southeast Asia)*
vietnamien (vietnamienne) Vietnamese
une vigne vineyard
un village town, village **13**
un petit village small town **13**
une ville city
en ville in town **6**
une grande ville big city, town **13**
le vin wine
vingt twenty **1B, 1C**
violet (violette) purple, violet **E1**
un violon violin **15**
une visite visit
rendre visite à to visit *(a person)* **20, 28**
visiter to visit *(places)* **23, 20**
vite! fast!, quick!
vive: vive les vacances! three cheers for vacation!
* **vivre** to live
le vocabulaire vocabulary
voici... here is, this is..., here come(s) ... **2A**
voici + du, de la *(partitive)* here's some **26**
voici mon père/ma mère here's my father/my mother **2C**
voilà... there is ..., there come(s) ... **2A**
voilà + du, de la *(partitive)* there's some **26**
la voile sailing **21**
faire de la voile to sail **21**
la planche à voile windsurfing **21**
* **voir** to see **21, 23**
voir un film to see a movie **21**
un voisin, une voisine neighbor **9**
une voiture car **9**
une voiture de sport sports car **15**
en voiture by car **14**
faire une promenade en voiture to go for a drive by car **14**
une voix voice
le volley (volleyball) volleyball **15**
un volontaire, une volontaire volunteer
comme volontaire as a volunteer
vos your **16**
votre (*pl.* **vos**) your **16**
voudrais (*see* **vouloir**)**: je voudrais** I'd like **3A, 3B, 5, 26**
* **vouloir** to want **26**
vouloir + du, de la *(partitive)* to want some (of something) **26**
vouloir dire to mean **26**
voulu (*p.p. of* **vouloir**) wanted **26**
vous you **6;** (to) you **27**
vous désirez? what would you like? may I help you? **3B, 17**
s'il vous plaît please **3B**
un voyage trip
bon voyage! have a nice trip!
faire un voyage to take a trip **8**
voyager to travel **5, 7**
vrai true, right, real **12**
vraiment really **15**
le VTT mountain biking **21**
faire du VTT to go mountain biking **21**
un VTT mountain bike **21**
vu (*p.p. of* **voir**) saw, seen **23**
une vue view
un point de vue point of view

W

les WC *m.* toilet
un week-end weekend **21, 23**
bon week-end! have a nice weekend!
ce week-end this weekend **21, 23**
le week-end on weekends
le week-end dernier last weekend **23**
le week-end prochain next weekend **21, 23**

Y

y there
il y a there is, there are **9**
est-ce qu'il y a...? is there ...?, are there ...? **9**
qu'est-ce qu'il y a? what is there? **9**
allons-y! let's go! **14**
vas-y! come on!, go ahead!, do it! **14**
le yaourt yogurt **25**
des yeux *m.* (*sg.* **oeil**) eyes **E2**

Z

un zèbre zebra
zéro zero **1A**
zut! darn! **1C**

FRENCH-ENGLISH VOCABULARY

French-English Vocabulary R33

ENGLISH-FRENCH VOCABULARY

ENGLISH-FRENCH VOCABULARY

English-French Vocabulary

The English-French vocabulary contains only active vocabulary.

The numbers following an entry indicate the lesson in which the word or phrase is activated. (**I** stands for the list of classroom expressions at the end of the first **Images** section; **E** stands for **Entracte.**)

Nouns: If the article of a noun does not indicate gender, the noun is followed by *m.* (*masculine*) or *f.* (*feminine*). If the plural (*pl.*) is irregular, it is given in parentheses.

Verbs: Verbs are listed in the infinitive form. An asterisk (*) in front of an active verb means that it is irregular. (For forms, see the verb charts in Appendix 4C.)

Words beginning with an **h** are preceded by a bullet (•) if the **h** is aspirate; that is, if the word is treated as if it begins with a consonant sound.

a, an un, une **2A, 10**
a few quelques **25**
a little (bit) un peu **7**
a lot beaucoup **7**
able: to be able (to) *pouvoir **27**
about de **15**
about whom? de qui? **8**
accessories des accessoires *m.* **17**
acquainted: to be acquainted with *connaître **28**
are you acquainted with ...? tu connais...? **2B**
address une adresse **13**
what's your address? quelle est ton adresse? **13**
after après **21, 22**
after that ensuite **22**
afternoon l'après-midi *m.* **21**
in the afternoon de l'après-midi **4A**
this afternoon cet après-midi **23**
tomorrow afternoon demain après-midi **23**
yesterday afternoon hier après-midi **23**
afterwards après **22**
to **agree** *être d'accord **6**
airplane un avion **21**
by airplane en avion **21**
all tout
all right d'accord **5**
not at all pas du tout **15**
alone seul **21**
leave me alone! laisse-moi tranquille! **28**
also aussi **1B, 7**
always toujours **7**
not always pas toujours **5**
A.M. du matin **4A**
am (*see* **to be**)
I am ... je suis + *nationality* **1B**
American américain **1B, 11**
I'm American je suis américain(e) **1B**
amusing amusant **11**
an un, une **2A, 10**
and et **1B, 6**
and you? et toi? **1A**
annoying pénible **12**
another un(e) autre
to **answer** répondre (à) **28**
any des **10**; du, de la, de l', de **26**
not any pas de **10, 26**
anybody: not anybody ne... personne **24**
anyone quelqu'un **24**
anything quelque chose **24**
not anything ne... rien **24**
apartment un appartement **13**
apartment building un immeuble **13**
appetizer un • hors-d'oeuvre **25**
apple une pomme
apple juice le jus de pomme **3B, 25**
appointment un rendez-vous **14**
I have an appointment at... j'ai un rendez-vous à... **4A**
April avril *m.* **4B**
are (*see* **to be**)
are there? est-ce qu'il y a? **9**
are you...? tu es + *nationality?* **1B**
there are il y a **9**
these/those/they are ce sont **12**
arm un bras **E2**
to **arrive** arriver **14**
as ... as aussi... que **19**
to **ask** demander (à) **28**
at à **6**; chez **14**
at (the) au, à la, à l', aux **14**
at ...'s house chez ... **14**
at ... o'clock à ... heure(s) **6**
at home à la maison **6**
at last enfin **22**
at the restaurant au restaurant **6**
at what time? à quelle heure? **4A, 8**
at what time is ...? à quelle heure est ...? **4A**
athletic sportif (sportive) **11**
to **attend** assister à **21**
attention: to pay attention *faire attention **8**
August août *m.* **4B**
aunt une tante **2C, 16**
automobile une auto, une voiture **9**
autumn l'automne *m.* **4C**
in (the) autumn en automne **4C**
avenue une avenue **13**
away: go away! va-t'en! **14**

back le dos **E2**
back: to come back rentrer **14, 24**; *revenir **15**
to go back rentrer **14, 24**
in back of derrière **9**

R36 English-French Vocabulary

bad mauvais **12**
I'm/everything's (very) bad ça va (très) mal **1C**
it's bad (weather) il fait mauvais **4C**
that's bad c'est mal **12**
too bad! dommage! **7**
badly mal **1C**
things are going (very) badly ça va (très) mal **1C**
bag un sac **I, 9**
banana une banane **25**
banknote un billet **20**
baseball le baseball **15**
basketball le basket (basketball) **15**
bathing suit un maillot de bain **17**
bathroom une salle de bains **13**
to **be** *être **6**
to be ... (years old) *avoir... ans **10**
to be able (to) *pouvoir **27**
to be acquainted with *connaître **28**
to be active in *faire de + *activity* **21**
to be careful *faire attention **8**
to be cold (*people*) *avoir froid **22;** (*weather*) il fait froid **4C**
to be going to (*do something*) *aller + *inf.* **14**
to be hot (*people*) *avoir chaud **22**
to be hungry *avoir faim **10, 22**
to be lucky *avoir de la chance **22**
to be present at assister à **21**
to be right *avoir raison **22**
to be supposed to *devoir **27**
to be thirsty *avoir soif **10, 22**
to be warm (*people*) *avoir chaud **22, 23**
to be wrong *avoir tort **22**
beach une plage **13**
beans: green beans les •haricots *m.* verts **25**
beautiful beau (bel, belle; *m.pl.* beaux) **9**
it's beautiful (nice) weather il fait beau **4C**
because parce que (qu') **8**
bed un lit **9**
bedroom une chambre **9, 13**
been été (*p.p. of* *être) **23**
before avant **21, 23**
behind derrière **9**
below en bas **13**
belt une ceinture **17**
best meilleur **19**
better meilleur **19**
beverage une boisson **3B, 25**
bicycle un vélo, une bicyclette **9**
by bicycle à vélo **14**
take a bicycle ride *faire une promenade à vélo **14**
big grand **9, 12**
bill (*money*) un billet **20**
birthday un anniversaire **4B**
my birthday is (March 2) mon anniversaire est le (2 mars) **4B**
when is your birthday? c'est quand, ton anniversaire? **4B**
bit: a little bit un peu **7**
black noir **E1, 12**
blond blond **9**
blouse un chemisier **17**
blue bleu **E1, 12**
boat un bateau (*pl.* bateaux) **21**
book un livre **I1, 9**
boom box une radiocassette **9**
boots des bottes *f.* **17**
bothersome pénible **12**
boulevard un boulevard **13**
boutique une boutique **17**
boy le garçon **2A, 2B**
boyfriend un petit copain
bread le pain **25**
breakfast le petit déjeuner **25**
to have breakfast prendre le petit déjeuner **25**
to **bring** (*a person*) amener **18;** (*things*) apporter **27**
to bring something to someone apporter quelque chose à quelqu'un **27**
brother un frère **2C, 16**
brown brun **9;** marron (*inv.*) **12**
building: apartment building un immeuble **13**
bus un bus
by bus en bus **14**
touring bus un autocar, un car **21**
but mais **5**
butter le beurre **25**
to **buy** acheter **33, 34**
to buy (some) acheter + du, de la (*partitive*) **26**
by: by airplane, plane en avion **21**
by bicycle à vélo **14**
by bus en bus **14**
by car en voiture **14**
by oneself seul(e) **21**
by subway en métro **14**
by taxi en taxi **14**
by train en train **14**

café un café **6**
at (to) the café au café **6**
cafeteria: school cafeteria la cantine de l'école **25**
cake un gâteau (*pl.* gâteaux) **25**
calculator une calculatrice **9**
to **call** téléphoner **7**
came venu (*p.p. of* *venir) **23**
camera un appareil-photo (*pl.* appareils-photo) **9**
can *pouvoir **27**
can you ...? est-ce que tu peux...? **5**
I can't je ne peux pas **5**
Canada le Canada
Canadian canadien (canadienne) **1B, 11**
he's/she's (Canadian) il/elle est (canadien/canadienne) **2B**
cannot: I cannot je ne peux pas **5**
I'm sorry, but I cannot je regrette, mais je ne peux pas **5**
cap (*baseball*) une casquette **17**
car une auto, une voiture **9**
by car en voiture **14**
card une carte **(playing) cards** des cartes *f.* **15**
careful: to be careful *faire attention **8**
carrot une carotte **25**
cassette tape une cassette
cat un chat **2C**

ENGLISH-FRENCH VOCABULARY

English-French Vocabulary R37

CD un CD, un compact (disc) **9**
CD-ROM un cédérom (un CD-ROM)
cell phone un portable **9**
cereal les céréales *f.* **25**
chair une chaise **I, 9**
chalk la craie **I**
  piece of chalk un morceau de craie **I**
chalkboard un tableau (*pl.* tableaux) **I**
to **chat (online)** chatter
checkers les dames *f.* **15**
cheese le fromage **25**
cherry une cerise **25**
chess les échecs *m.* **15**
chicken le poulet **25**
child un (une) enfant **16**
  children des enfants *m.* **16**
Chinese chinois **11**
chocolate: hot chocolate un chocolat **3B**
to **choose** choisir **19**
chose, chosen choisi (*p.p. of* choisir) **23**
Christmas Noël **21**
  at Christmas à Noël **21**
church une église **13**
cinema le cinéma **6**
  to the cinema au cinéma **6**
city une ville **13**
  in the city en ville **6**
clarinet une clarinette **15**
class une classe **6**
  in class en classe **6**
classmate un (une) camarade **9**
to **clean** nettoyer **21**
clothing des vêtements *m.* **17**
  sports clothing des vêtements *m.* de sport **17**
coffee le café **3B, 13**
coin une pièce **20**
cold le froid
  to be (feel) cold *avoir froid **22**
  it's cold (*weather*) il fait froid **4C**
college student un étudiant, une étudiante **9**
color une couleur **12**
  what color? de quelle couleur? **12**
to **come** arriver **14;** *venir **15**
  come on! vas-y! **14**
  here comes ... voici... **2A**
  to come back rentrer **14, 24;** *revenir **15**
  to come to visit rendre visite à **20, 28**
comfortable confortable **13**
compact disc un compact (disc), un CD **9**
computer un ordinateur, un PC **9**
  computer game un jeu d'ordinateur (*pl.* les jeux d'ordinateur)
concert un concert **14**
to **continue** continuer **13**
cooking la cuisine **25**
cool: it's cool (*weather*) il fait frais **4C**
cost le coût **17**
to **cost** coûter
  how much does ... cost? combien coûte...? **3C, 17**
  it costs ... il/elle coûte... **3C**
country(side) la campagne **21**
  to (in) the country(side) à la campagne **21**
course: of course! bien sûr! **5;** mais oui! **6**
  of course not! mais non! **6**
cousin un cousin, une cousine **2C, 16**
crepe une crêpe **3A**
croissant un croissant **3A**
cuisine la cuisine **25**
cup une tasse **25**
cute mignon (mignonne) **11**

to **dance** danser **5, 7**
dark-haired brun **9**
darn! zut! **1C**
date la date **4B;** un rendez-vous **14**
  I have a date at ... j'ai un rendez-vous à... **4A**
  what's the date? quelle est la date? **4B**
daughter une fille **16**
day un jour **4B, 21**
  what day is it? quel jour est-ce? **4B**
  whole day une journée
dear cher (chère) **17**
December décembre *m.* **4B**
department store un grand magasin **17**
to **describe** *décrire
  describe ... décrivez...
desk un bureau **I, 9**
dessert le dessert **25**
to **detest** détester **25**
did fait (*p.p. of* *faire) **23**
difficult difficile **12**
dining room une salle à manger **13**
dinner le dîner **25**
  to have (eat) dinner dîner **7, 25**
  to have dinner at a restaurant dîner au restaurant **5**
dish (*course of a meal*) un plat **25**
to **do** *faire **8**
  do it! vas-y! **14**
  I do je veux bien **26**
  to do + *activity* *faire de + *activity* **21**
  to do my homework *faire mes devoirs **21**
dog un chien **2C**
door une porte **I, 9**
done fait (*p.p. of* *faire) **23**
to **download** télécharger
downstairs en bas **13**
downtown en ville **6**
dozen une douzaine **25**
dress une robe **17**
drink une boisson **3B, 25**
to **drink** *boire **26**
drive: to take a drive *faire une promenade en voiture **14**
drums une batterie **15**
dumb bête **11**
during pendant **21**
DVD un DVD **9**

e-mail un mail, un mél
ear une oreille **E2**
to **earn** gagner **20**
Easter Pâques *m.* **21**
  at Easter à Pâques **21**
easy facile **12**
to **eat** manger **7**
  I like to eat j'aime manger **5**

R38 English-French Vocabulary

to eat breakfast *prendre le petit déjeuner **25**
to eat dinner dîner **7, 25**
to eat lunch déjeuner **25**
to eat (some) manger + du, de la *(partitive)* **26**
egg un oeuf **25**
eight •huit **1A**
eighteen dix-huit **1B**
eighth •huitième **16**
eighty quatre-vingts **2B**
elegant élégant **17**
elephant un éléphant **E4**
eleven onze **1B, 3C**
eleventh onzième **16**
England l'Angleterre *f.*
English anglais(e) **1B, 11**
errand: to run errands *faire les courses **25**
euro un euro
evening un soir **21**
in the evening du soir **4A**
this evening ce soir **23**
tomorrow evening demain soir **21, 23**
event un événement **14**
everything tout
everything's going (very) well ça va (très) bien **1C**
everything's (going) so-so ça va comme ci, comme ça **1C**
how's everything? ça va? **1C**
exam un examen
to pass an exam réussir à un examen **19**
excuse me excusez-moi **13**
expensive cher (chère) **17**
to **explain** expliquer
eye un oeil (*pl.* yeux) **E2**

fall l'automne **4C**
in (the) fall en automne **4C**
false faux (fausse) **12**
family une famille **2C, 16**
far (from) loin (de) **13**
fashion la mode
in fashion (fashionable) à la mode **17**
fat: to get fat grossir **19**
father un père **16**
this is my father voici mon père **2C**
February février *m.* **4B**
to **feel like** *avoir envie de + *inf.* **20**
few: a few quelques **9**
fifteen quinze **1B**
fifth cinquième **16**
fifty cinquante **1C**
film un film **14, 21**
finally finalement **22**
to **find** trouver **17**
fine ça va **1C**
fine! d'accord **5**
everything's fine ça va bien **1C**
that's fine c'est bien **12**
to **finish** finir 19
finished fini (*p.p. of* finir) **23**
first d'abord **22;** premier (première) **16**
it's (June) first c'est le premier (juin) **4B**
fish un poisson **25**
five cinq **1A**
to **fix** réparer **21**
flute une flûte **15**
food la nourriture **25**
foot un pied **E2**
on foot à pied **14**
for pour **6**
for whom? pour qui? **8**
fork une fourchette **25**
forty quarante **1C**
four quatre **1A**
fourteen quatorze **1B**
fourth quatrième **16**
franc *(former monetary unit of France)* un franc **3C**
that's (it's) ... francs ça fait...francs **3C**
France la France **6**
in France en France **6**
French français(e) **1B, 11**
how do you say ... in French? comment dit-on... en français? **I**
French fries des frites *f.* **25**
steak and French fries un steak-frites **3A**
Friday vendredi *m.* **4B**
friend un ami, une amie **2A;** un copain, une copine **2A**
boyfriend, girlfriend un petit copain, une petite copine
school friend un (une) camarade **9**
from de **22**
from (the) du, de la, de l', des **15**
from where? d'où? **15**
are you from ...? tu es de...? **1B**
I'm from ... je suis de... **1B**
front: in front of devant **9**
fruit(s) des fruits *m.* **25**
funny amusant **11;** drôle **12**

to **gain weight** grossir **19**
game un jeu (*pl.* jeux) **15;** un match **14**
to play a game (match) *faire un match **8**
to play a game jouer à + *game* **15**
garage un garage **13**
garden un jardin **13**
gentleman un monsieur (*pl.* messieurs) **2A**
to **get: to get fat** grossir **19**
to get thin maigrir **19**
girl une fille **2A**
girlfriend une petite copine
to **give (to)** donner (à) **27, 28**
give me donne-moi, donnez-moi **3A, 3B**
please give me s'il te plaît donne-moi **3B**
glass un verre **25**
glasses des lunettes *f.* **17**
sunglasses des lunettes *f.* de soleil **17**
to **go** *aller **14**
go ahead! vas-y! **14**
go away! va-t'en! **14**
to go (come) back rentrer **14, 24;** *revenir **15**
to go by bicycle *aller en vélo **14**
to go by car, by train ... *aller en auto, en train... **14**
to go food shopping *faire les courses **25**
to go rock climbing *faire de l'escalade **21**
to go shopping *faire des achats **21**
to go to assister à **21**

ENGLISH-FRENCH VOCABULARY

English-French Vocabulary R39

gone allé(e) (*p.p. of* *aller) **24**
good bon (bonne) **12**
  good morning (afternoon) bonjour **1A**
  that's good c'est bien **12**
  the weather's good (pleasant) il fait bon **4C**
good-bye! au revoir!, salut! **1C**
good-looking beau (bel, belle; *m.pl.* beaux) **9, 12, 19**
grandfather un grand-père **2C, 16**
grandmother une grand-mère **2C, 16**
grandparents les grandsparents *m.* **16**
grape juice le jus de raisin **3B**
grapefruit un pamplemousse **25**
gray gris **12**
great super **12, 17**
green vert **E1, 12**
  green beans les •haricots *m.* verts **25**
guitar une guitare **9, 15**

had eu (*p.p. of* *avoir) **23**
hair les cheveux *m.* **E2, 15**
  he/she has dark hair il/elle est brun(e) **9**
half: half past ... ... heure(s) et demie **4A**
  half past midnight minuit et demi **4A**
  half past noon midi et demi **4A**
ham le jambon **25**
hamburger un hamburger **3A**
hand une main **E2**
handbag un sac **9**
handsome beau (bel, belle; *m.pl.* beaux) **9, 12, 19**
hard difficile **12**
hat un chapeau (*pl.* chapeaux) **17**
to **hate** détester **25**
to **have** *avoir **10**; (*food*) *prendre **26**
  do you have ...? est-ce que tu as...? **9**
  I have j'ai **9**
  I have to (must) je dois **5**
  to have (some) *avoir + du, de la (*partitive*); *prendre + du, de la (*partitive*) **26**
  to have a picnic *faire un pique-nique **21**
  to have breakfast *prendre le petit déjeuner **25**
  to have dinner dîner **25**
  to have dinner at a restaurant dîner au restaurant **5**
  to have to *avoir besoin de + *inf.* **20**; *devoir **27**
he il **3C, 6, 10**; lui **15**
  he/she is ... il/elle est + *nationality* **2B**
head la tête **E2**
to **hear** entendre **20**
hello bonjour **1A, 1C**
to **help** aider **21, 27**
  may I help you? vous désirez? **3B, 17**
her elle **15**; son, sa; ses **16**; la **28**
  (to) her lui **28**
  her name is ... elle s'appelle... **2B**
  what's her name? comment s'appelle-t-elle? **9**
here ici **6**
  here comes, here is voici **2A**
  here's my mother/father voici ma mère/mon père **2C**
  here's some voici + du, de la (*partitive*) **26**
  this ... (over here) ce... -ci **18**
hey! dis! **12**; tiens! **2A, 10**
  hey there! dis donc! **12**
hi! salut! **1C**
high school student un (une) élève **9**
him lui **15**; le **28**
  (to) him lui **28**
his son, sa; ses **16**
  his name is ... il s'appelle... **2B**
  what's his name? comment s'appelle-t-il? **9**
home, at home à la maison **6**; chez (moi, toi...) **15**
  to go home rentrer **14, 24**
homework les devoirs *m.* **21**
  homework assignment un devoir **I**
  to do my homework *faire mes devoirs **21**
to **hope** espérer **18**
horse un cheval (*pl.* chevaux) **E4**
hospital un hôpital **13**
hot chaud **4C, 23**
  hot chocolate un chocolat **3B**
  hot dog un •hot dog **3A**
  to be hot (*people*) *avoir chaud **22**
  it's hot (*weather*) il fait chaud **4C**
hotel un hôtel **13**
house une maison **13**
  at someone's house chez + *person* **14**
how? comment? **8**
  how are you? comment allez-vous?, comment vas-tu?, ça va? **1C**
  how do you find ...? comment trouves-tu...? **17**
  how do you say ... in French? comment dit-on... en français? **I**
  how much? combien (de)? **20**
  how much does ... cost? combien coûte...? **3C, 17**
  how much is that/this/it? c'est combien?, ça fait combien? **3C**
  how old are you? quel âge as-tu? **2C**
  how old is he/she? quel âge a-t-il/elle? **9**
  how old is your father/mother? quel âge a ton père/ta mère? **2C**
  how's everything? ça va? **1C**
  how's the weather? quel temps fait-il? **4C**
  to learn how to *apprendre à **26**
hundred cent **2B, 17**
hungry avoir faim **3A**
  are you hungry? tu as faim? **3A**
  I'm hungry j'ai faim **3A**
  to be hungry avoir faim **10, 22**
husband un mari **16**

R40 English-French Vocabulary

I je 6, moi 15
I don't know je ne sais pas I, 9
I have a date/appointment at ... j'ai un rendez-vous à... 4A
I know je sais I, 9, 28
I'm fine/okay ça va 1C
I'm (very) well/so-so/(very) bad ça va (très) bien/comme ci, comme ça/(très) mal 1C
ice la glace 3A, 25
ice cream une glace 3A, 25
iced tea un thé glacé 25
idea une idée 20
it's (that's) a good idea c'est une bonne idée 20
if si
in à 6, 14; dans 9
in (Boston) à (Boston) 6
in class en classe 6
in front of devant 9
in order to pour 21
in the afternoon de l'après-midi 4A
in the morning/evening du matin/soir 4A
in town en ville 6
in (the) au, à la, à l', aux 14
to indicate indiquer
inexpensive bon marché (*inv.*) 17
ingredient un ingrédient 25
in-line skating le roller 21
in-line skates des rollers 21
to go in-line skating faire du roller 21
instrument un instrument 15
to play a musical instrument jouer de + *instrument* 15
intelligent intelligent 25
interesting intéressant 11
to invite inviter 7
is (*see* to be)
is there? est-ce qu'il y a? 9
isn't it (so)? n'est-ce pas? 6
there is il y a 9
there is (some) il y a + du, de la (*partitive*) 26
it il, elle 6, 10; le, la 28
it's ... c'est... 2A
it's ... (o'clock) il est... heure(s) 4A
it's ... euros ça fait... euros 3C
it's fine/nice/hot/cool/cold/bad (*weather*) il fait beau/bon/chaud/frais/froid/mauvais 4C
it's (June) first c'est le premier (juin) 4B
it's not ce n'est pas 12
it's raining il pleut 4C
it's snowing il neige 4C
what time is it? quelle heure est-il? 4A
who is it? qui est-ce? 2A, 9
its son, sa; ses 16
Italian italien, italienne 11

jacket un blouson, une veste 17
jam la confiture 25
January janvier *m.* 4B
Japanese japonais(e) 1
jeans: pair of jeans un jean 17
to jog *faire du jogging 21
jogging le jogging 21
jogging suit un jogging, un survêtement 17
juice le jus
apple juice le jus de pomme 3B, 25
grape juice le jus de raisin 3B
orange juice le jus d'orange 3B, 25
tomato juice le jus de tomate 3B
July juillet *m.* 4B
June juin *m.* 4B

ketchup le ketchup 25
keyboard un clavier 15
kilogram un kilo (de) 25
kind gentil (gentille) 11
kitchen une cuisine 13
knife un couteau 25
to know *connaître 36
do you know ...? tu connais...? 2B
I (don't) know je (ne) sais (pas) I, 9, 28
you know tu sais 28

lady une dame 2A
lamp une lampe 9
laptop computer un ordinateur portable
large grand 9, 12
last dernier (dernière) 23
last month le mois dernier 23
last night hier soir 23
last Saturday samedi dernier 23
at last enfin 22
to learn (how to) *apprendre (à) + *inf.* 26
left gauche
on (to) the left à gauche 13
leg une jambe E2
lemon soda la limonade 3B
to lend prêter (à) 27, 28
lend me prête-moi 3C
less ... than moins... que 19
let's go! allons-y! 14
lettuce la salade 25
library une bibliothèque 13
like: what does he/she look like? comment est-il/elle? 9
what's he/she like? comment est-il/elle? 9
to like aimer 7
do you like? est-ce que tu aimes? 5
I also like j'aime aussi 5
I don't always like je n'aime pas toujours 5
I don't like je n'aime pas 5
I like j'aime 5
I like ..., but I prefer ... j'aime..., mais je préfère... 5
I'd like je voudrais 3A, 3B, 5
what would you like? vous désirez? 3B, 17
to listen écouter 7
to listen to CDs écouter des CD 21

ENGLISH-FRENCH VOCABULARY

English-French Vocabulary R41

to listen to the radio écouter la radio **5**
little petit **9, 12, 17**
a little (bit) un peu **7**
to **live** habiter **7**
living room (*formal*) un salon **13**
to **loan** prêter (à) **27, 28**
long long (longue) **17**
to **look (at)** regarder **7**
look! tiens! **2A, 10**
look at that regarde ça **9**
I'm looking for ... je cherche... **17**
to look for chercher **17**
what does he/she look like? comment est-il/elle? **9**
to **lose** perdre **20**
to lose weight maigrir **19**
lot: a lot beaucoup **7**
to **love: I'd love to** je veux bien **5**
luck la chance **22**
to be lucky *avoir de la chance **22**
lunch le déjeuner **25**
to have (eat) lunch déjeuner **25**

made fait (*p.p. of* *faire) **23**
to **make** *faire **8**
man un homme **9;** un monsieur (*polite term*) **2A**
many beaucoup (de) **7**
how many combien de **20**
map une carte **I**
March mars *m.* **4B**
match un match **8**
to play a match *faire un match **8**
May mai *m.* **4B**
may *pouvoir **27**
maybe peut-être **6**
mayonnaise la mayonnaise **25**
me moi **1A, 27**
excuse me pardon **13, 17**
(to) me me, moi **27**
meal un repas **25**
mean méchant **11**
to **mean** *vouloir dire **26**
what does ... mean? que veut dire...? **I**
meat la viande **25**
to **meet** rencontrer **21**
to **meet for the first time** *connaître (*in passé composé*) **28**
Mexican mexicain(e) **11**
midnight minuit *m.* **4A**
milk le lait **25**
mineral water l'eau *f.* minérale **25**
Miss Mademoiselle (Mlle) **1C**
modern moderne **13**
Monday lundi *m.* **4B**
money l'argent *m.* **21**
month un mois **4B, 19**
last month le mois dernier **23**
next month le mois prochain **23**
this month ce mois-ci **23**
moped une mob (mobylette) **9**
more ... than plus... que **19**
morning le matin **21**
good morning bonjour **1A**
in the morning du matin **4A**
this morning ce matin **21**
tomorrow morning demain matin **23**
yesterday morning hier matin **23**
mother une mère **2C, 16**
this is my mother voici ma mère **2C**
motorbike une mob (mobylette) **9**
motorcycle une moto **9**
motorscooter un scooter **9**
mountain une montagne **21**
mountain bike un VTT **21**
mountain biking le VTT **21**
to do mountain biking faire du VTT **21**
to (at/in) the mountain(s) à la montagne **21**
mouse une souris
mouth une bouche **E2**
movie un film **14, 21**
movie theater un cinéma **6**
movies le cinéma **13**
at (to) the movies au cinéma **6**
Mr. Monsieur (M.) **1C**
Mrs. Madame (Mme) **1C**
much, very much beaucoup **7**
how much? combien? **20**
how much does ... cost? combien coûte...? **3C, 17**
how much is it? ça fait combien?, c'est combien? **3C**
too much trop **17**
museum un musée **13**
music la musique **15**
must *devoir **27**
I must je dois **5**
my mon, ma; mes **2C, 16**
my birthday is (March 2) mon anniversaire est le (2 mars) **4B**
my name is ... je m'appelle... **1A**

name: his/her name is ... il/elle s'appelle... **2B**
my name is ... je m'appelle... **1A**
what's ...'s name? comment s'appelle...? **2B**
what's his/her name? comment s'appelle-t-il/elle? **9**
what's your name? comment t'appelles-tu? **1A**
napkin une serviette **25**
nasty méchant **11**
nationality la nationalité **1B**
nearby près **13**
neat chouette **12**
neck le cou **E2**
to **need** *avoir besoin de **20**
neighbor un voisin, une voisine **9**
neighborhood un quartier **13**
a nice neighborhood un joli quartier **13**
never ne... jamais **24**
new nouveau (nouvel, nouvelle; *m.pl.* nouveaux) **19**
next prochain **21, 23**
next week la semaine prochaine **23**
nice gentil (gentille), sympathique **11**
it's nice (beautiful) weather il fait beau **4C**
night: tomorrow night demain soir **4A**

last night hier soir **23**
nine neuf **1A**
nineteen dix-neuf **1B**
ninety quatre-vingt-dix **2B**
ninth neuvième **16**
no non **1B, 6**
no ... pas de **10, 26**
no? n'est-ce pas? **6**
nobody ne... personne, personne **24**
noon midi *m.* **4A**
nose le nez **E2**
not ne... pas **6**
not a, not any pas de **10, 26**
not always pas toujours **5**
not anybody ne... personne **24**
not anything ne... rien **24**
not at all pas du tout **15**
it's (that's) not ce n'est pas **12**
of course not! mais non! **6**
notebook un cahier **I, 9**
nothing ne... rien, rien **24**
November novembre *m.* **4B**
now maintenant **7, 23**

O

o'clock heure(s)
at ... o'clock à... heures **4A**
it's ... o'clock il est... heure(s) **4A**
object un objet **9**
ocean la mer **21**; l'océan *m.*
to (at) the oceanside à la mer **21**
October octobre *m.* **4B**
of de **6**
of (the) du, de la, de l', des **15**
of course not! mais non! **6**
of course! bien sûr! **5**
of whom de qui **8**
often souvent **7**
oh: oh, really? ah, bon? **8**
okay d'accord **5**
I'm okay ça va **1C**
old vieux (vieil, vieille; *m.pl.* vieux) **19**
he/she is ... (years old) il/elle a... ans **2C**
how old are you? quel âge as-tu? **2C**
how old is he/she? quel âge a-t-il/elle? **9**
how old is your father/ mother? quel âge a ton père/ta mère? **2C**
I'm ... (years old) j'ai... ans **2C**
to be ... (years old) *avoir ... ans **10**
omelet une omelette **3A**
on sur **9**
on foot à pied **14**
on Monday lundi **10**
on Mondays le lundi **10**
on vacation en vacances **6**
one un, une **1**; (*we, they, people*) on **20**
oneself: by oneself seul **21**
only seul **21**
open *ouvrir
open ... ouvre... (ouvrez...) **I**
opinion: in my opinion à mon avis **19**
or ou **1B, 6**
orange (*color*) orange (*inv.*) **E1, 12**
orange (*fruit*) une orange **25**
orange juice le jus d'orange **3B, 25**
order: in order to pour **21**
to **organize** organiser **7**
other autre **25**
our notre; nos **16**
out of style démodé **17**
over: over (at) ...'s house chez... **15**
over there là-bas **6**
that (one), over there ça, là-bas **9**
overcoat un manteau (*pl.* manteaux) **17**
to **own** *avoir **10**

P

P.M. du soir **4A**
pain: a pain pénible **12**
pants un pantalon **17**
pantyhose des collants *m.* **17**
paper le papier **I**
sheet of paper une feuille de papier **I**
parents les parents *m.* **16**
park un parc **13**
party (*informal*) une fête, une soirée, une boum **14**
to **pass a test (an exam)** réussir à un examen **19**
past: half past ... ... heure(s) et demie **4A**
quarter past ... ... heure(s) et quart **4A**
to **pay (for)** payer **20**
to pay attention *faire attention **8**
pear une poire **25**
peas les petits pois *m.* **25**
pen un stylo **I, 9**
pencil un crayon **I, 9**
people des gens *m.* **10**; on **20**
perhaps peut-être **6**
person une personne **2A, 9**
pet un animal (*pl.* animaux) domestique **2C**
to **phone** téléphoner **7**
piano un piano **15**
to **pick up** ranger **21**
picnic un pique-nique **14**
to have a picnic *faire un pique-nique **21**
pie une tarte **25**
piece: piece of chalk un morceau de craie **I**
ping-pong le Ping-Pong **15**
pink rose **12**
pizza une pizza **3A**
place un endroit **14**
place setting un couvert **25**
to **place** *mettre **18**
placed mis (*p.p. of* *mettre) **23**
plain moche **17**
plane un avion **21**
by plane en avion **21**
plate une assiette **25**
to **play** jouer **7**
to play a game jouer à + *game* **15**
to play a game (match) *faire un match **8**
to play a musical instrument jouer de + *instrument* **15**
to play basketball (soccer, tennis) jouer au basket (au foot, au tennis) **5**
pleasant sympathique **11**
it's pleasant (good) weather il fait bon **4C**
please s'il vous plaît (*formal*) **3B**; s'il te plaît (*informal*) **3A**
please give me ... s'il te plaît, donne-moi... **3B**

English-French Vocabulary R43

polo shirt un polo **17**
pool: swimming pool une piscine **13**
poor pauvre **20**
poorly mal **1C**
popular à la mode **17**
poster une affiche **9**
potato une pomme de terre **25**
pound une livre (de) **25**
to **prefer** préférer **18, 25**
I prefer je préfère + *inf.* **5**
I like ..., but I prefer ... j'aime..., mais je préfère... **5**
to **prepare** préparer **21**
pretty joli **9, 17**
price un prix **17**
what's the price? quel est le prix? **17**
printer une imprimante
pullover un pull **17**
pupil un (une) élève **9**
to **purchase** acheter **21**
purple violet (violette) **E1**
to **put** *mettre **18**
to put on *mettre **18**

quantity une quantité **25**
quarter un quart
quarter of ... ... heure(s) moins le quart **4A**
quarter past ... ... heure(s) et quart **4A**

racket une raquette **9**
radio une radio **9**
to listen to the radio écouter la radio **5**
rain: it's raining il pleut **4C**
raincoat un imper (imperméable) **17**
rarely rarement **7**
rather assez **11**
really: oh, really? ah, bon? **8**
really?! vraiment?! **15**
red rouge **E1, 12**
relatives les parents *m.* **16**
to **rent** louer **21**
to **repair** réparer **21**
to **respond** répondre **28**
restaurant un restaurant **13**
at (to) the restaurant au restaurant **6**
have dinner at a restaurant dîner au restaurant **5**
to **return** rentrer **24**; *revenir **15**
rice le riz **25**
rich riche **20**
ride: to take a bicycle ride *faire une promenade à vélo **14**
right vrai **12**; droite
right? n'est-ce pas? **6**
all right d'accord **5**
to be right *avoir raison **22**
to (on) the right à droite **13**
roast beef le rosbif **25**
rock climbing l'escalade *f.* **21**
to do rock climbing *faire de l'escalade **21**
room une chambre **9**; une salle **13**
bathroom une salle de bains **13**
dining room une salle à manger **13**
formal living room un salon **13**
to **run** (*referring to objects*) marcher **9**

sailing la voile **21**
salad une salade **3A, 25**
salami le saucisson **25**
salt le sel **25**
sandal une sandale **17**
sandwich un sandwich **3A**
Saturday samedi *m.* **4B, 23**
see you Saturday! à samedi! **4B**
last Saturday samedi dernier **23**
next Saturday samedi prochain **23**
saw vu (*p.p. of* *voir) **23**
saxophone un saxo (saxophone) **15**
say *dire **28**
say ... dites...
say! dis (donc)! **12**
how do you say ... in French? comment dit-on... en français? **I**
school une école **13**
school cafeteria la cantine de l'école **25**
school friend un (une) camarade **9**
screen *(computer)* un écran
sea la mer **21**
to (at) the sea à la mer **21**
season une saison **4C**
second deuxième **16**
to **see** *voir **21**
see you tomorrow! à demain! **4B, 21**
seen vu (*p.p. of* *voir) **23**
seldom rarement **7**
to **sell** vendre **20**
to **send** envoyer
to send an e-mail envoyer un mail
September septembre *m.* **4B**
to **set the table** *mettre la table **25**
seven sept **1A**
seventeen dix-sept **1B**
seventh septième **16**
seventy soixante-dix **2A**
she elle **6, 10, 15**
sheet of paper une feuille de papier **I**
ship un bateau (*pl.* bateaux) **21**
shirt une chemise **17**
shoe une chaussure **17**
tennis shoes des tennis *m.* **17**
shop une boutique **17**
shopping: shopping center un centre commercial **13**
to go food shopping *faire les courses **25**
to go shopping *faire des achats **21**
shore la mer **21**
short court **17**; petit **9, 12, 17**
he/she is short il/elle est petit(e) **9**
shorts un short **17**
should *devoir **27**
to **show** indiquer; montrer à **27, 28**
to **shut** fermer **I**
shy timide **11**
silly bête **11**
to **sing** chanter **5, 7**
sir Monsieur (M.) **1C**
sister une soeur **2C, 16**
six six **1A**

R44 English-French Vocabulary

sixteen seize **1B**
sixth sixième **16**
sixty soixante **1C, 2A**
skateboard un skate
  skateboarding le skate **21**
  to go skateboarding faire du skate **21**
to **ski** *faire du ski **21**
  skiing le ski **21**
skirt une jupe **17**
small petit **9, 12, 17**
sneakers des tennis *m.* **17**
  hightop sneakers des baskets *m.* **17**
snow: it's snowing il neige **4C**
snowboard un snowboard, un surf (des neiges) **21**
  snowboarding le snowboard, le surf (des neiges) **21**
  to go snowboarding faire du snowboard **21**
so alors **7**
  so-so comme ci, comme ça **1C**
  everything's (going) so-so ça va comme ci, comme ça **1C**
soccer le foot (football) **15**
sock une chaussette **17**
soda un soda **3B**
  lemon soda une limonade **3B**
sold vendu (*p.p. of* vendre) **23**
sole (*fish*) la sole **25**
some des **10;** du, de la, de l' **26;** quelques **9**
somebody quelqu'un **24**
someone quelqu'un **24**
something quelque chose **24**
son un fils **16**
sorry: to be sorry regretter
  I'm sorry, but (I cannot) je regrette, mais (je ne peux pas) **5**
soup la soupe **25**
spaghetti les spaghetti *m.* **25**
Spanish espagnol(e) **11**
to **speak** parler **7**
  to speak (French, English, Spanish) parler (français, anglais, espagnol) **5**
  to speak to parler à **28**
to **spend** (*money*) dépenser **20;** (*time*) passer **21**
spoon une cuillère **25**
sports le sport **21**
  to play a sport *faire du sport **21;** jouer à + *sport* **15**
  sports clothing des vêtements *m.* de sport **17**
spring le printemps **4C**
  in the spring au printemps **4C**
stadium un stade **13**
to **stay** rester **14**
steak un steak **3A**
  steak and French fries un steak-frites **3A**
stereo set une chaîne hi-fi **9**
stomach le ventre **E2**
store un magasin **13, 17**
  department store un grand magasin **17**
straight tout droit **13**
strawberry une fraise **25**
street une rue **13**
student (*high school*) un (une) élève **9;** (*college*) un étudiant, une étudiante **9**
to **study** étudier **5, 7**
stupid bête **11**
style: in style à la mode **17**
  out of style démodé **17**
subway le métro **14**
  by subway en métro **14**
to **succeed** réussir **19**
sugar le sucre **25**
summer l'été *m.* **4C**
  summer vacation les grandes vacances **21**
  in the summer en été **4C**
sun le soleil **17**
Sunday dimanche *m.* **4B**
sunglasses des lunettes *f.* de soleil **17**
supermarket un supermarché **13**
supper le dîner **25**
  to have (eat) supper dîner **7, 25**
sure bien sûr **5**
  sure! mais oui! **6**
  are you sure? tu es sûr(e)? **16**
to **surf the Internet** surfer sur l'Internet
sweater un pull **17**
sweatshirt un sweat **17**
to **swim** nager **7**
  I like to swim j'aime nager **5**
swimming pool une piscine **13**
swimsuit un maillot de bain **17**
Swiss suisse **11**

T

table une table **I, 9**
  to set the table *mettre la table **25**
to **take** *prendre **I, 26**
  to take along amener **18, 27**
  to take a bicycle ride *faire une promenade à vélo **14**
  to take a drive *faire une promenade en voiture **14**
  to take a trip *faire un voyage **8**
  to take a walk *faire une promenade à pied **14**
to **talk** parler **7**
  to talk to parler à **28**
tall grand **9, 12**
tape: cassette tape une cassette
taxi un taxi **14**
  by taxi en taxi **14**
tea le thé **3B**
  iced tea un thé glacé **25**
teacher un (une) prof **2A, 9;** un professeur **9**
telephone un téléphone **9**
to **telephone** téléphoner **7**
television la télé **9**
  to watch television regarder la télé **5**
to **tell** *dire **28**
ten dix **1A, 1B**
tennis le tennis **15**
  tennis racket une raquette de tennis **15**
  tennis shoes des tennis *m.* **17**
  to play tennis jouer au tennis **5**
tenth dixième **16**
terrific génial **12;** super **12, 17**
test un examen
  to pass a test réussir à un examen **19**
than que **19**
thank you merci **1C**
that que **17;** ce, cet, cette **18**
  that is ... c'est... **9, 12**
  that (one), over there ça, là-bas **9**

ENGLISH-FRENCH VOCABULARY

English-French Vocabulary R45

that's … c'est… **2A, 9, 12;** voilà **2A**
that's … euros ça fait… euros **3C**
that's bad c'est mal **12**
that's a good idea! c'est une bonne idée! **20**
that's good (fine) c'est bien **12**
that's not … ce n'est pas… **12**
what's that? qu'est-ce que c'est? **9**
the le, la, l' **2B, 10;** les **10**
theater un théâtre **13**
movie theater un cinéma **13**
their leur, leurs **16**
them eux, elles **15;** les **28**
(to) them leur **28**
themselves eux-mêmes
then alors **11;** ensuite **22**
there là **6**
there is (are) il y a **9**
there is (here comes someone) voilà **2A**
there is (some) il y a + du, de la (*partitive*) **26**
there's some voilà + du, de la (*partitive*) **26**
over there là-bas **6**
that (one), over there ça, là-bas **9;** ce…-là **18**
what is there? qu'est-ce qu'il y a? **9**
these ces **18**
these are ce sont **12**
they ils, elles **6;** eux **15;** on **20**
they are ce sont **12**
thin: to get thin maigrir **19**
thing une chose
things are going (very) badly ça va (très) mal **1C**
to **think** penser **17**
to think of penser de, trouver **17**
to think that penser que **17**
what do you think of …? comment trouves-tu…?, qu'est-ce que tu penses de…? **17**
third troisième **16**
thirsty: to be thirsty *avoir soif **22**
are you thirsty? tu as soif? **3B**
I'm thirsty j'ai soif **3B**
thirteen treize **1B**
thirty trente **1C**
3:30 trois heures et demie **4A**
this ce, cet, cette **18**
this is … voici… **2A**
those ces **18**
those are ce sont **12**
thousand mille **2B, 17**
three trois **1A**
Thursday jeudi *m.* **4B**
tie une cravate **17**
tights des collants *m.* **17**
time: at what time is …? à quelle heure est…? **4A**
at what time? à quelle heure? **4A**
what time is it? quelle heure est-il? **4A**
to à **6, 14;** chez **14, 15**
to (the) au, à la, à l', aux **14**
in order to pour **21**
to class en classe **6**
to someone's house chez + *person* **14**
to whom à qui **8**
today aujourd'hui **4B, 23**
today is (Wednesday) aujourd'hui, c'est (mercredi) **4B**
toilet les toilettes **13**
tomato une tomate
tomato juice le jus de tomate **3B**
tomorrow demain **4B**
tomorrow afternoon demain après-midi **23**
tomorrow is (Thursday) demain, c'est (jeudi) **4B**
tomorrow morning demain matin **23**
tomorrow night (evening) demain soir **23**
see you tomorrow! à demain! **4B, 21**
tonight ce soir **23**
too aussi **1B, 7;** trop **17**
too bad! dommage! **7**
touring bus un autocar, un car **21**
tourist: tourist office office (*m.*) de tourisme
town un village **13**
in town en ville **6**
track suit un survêtement **17**
train un train **21**
by train en train **14, 21**
to **travel** voyager **5, 7**
trip: to take a trip *faire un voyage **8**
trousers un pantalon **17**
true vrai **12**
T-shirt un tee-shirt **17**
Tuesday mardi *m.* **4B**
tuna le thon **25**
to **turn** tourner **13**
to turn on *mettre **18**
TV la télé **9**
to watch TV regarder la télé **5**
twelfth douzième **16**
twelve douze **1B**
twenty vingt **1B, 1C**
two deux **1A**

ugly moche **17**
uncle un oncle **2C, 16**
under sous **9**
to **understand** *comprendre **26**
I (don't) understand je (ne) comprends (pas) **I**
unfashionable démodé **17**
United States les États-Unis *m.*
upstairs en • haut **13**
us nous **15**
(to) us nous **27**
to **use** utiliser

vacation les vacances *f.* **21**
on vacation en vacances **6**
summer vacation les grandes vacances **21**
VCR (videocassette recorder) un magnétoscope
veal le veau **25**
vegetable un légume **25**
very très **11**
very well très bien **7**
very much beaucoup **7**
video game un jeu vidéo (*pl.* des jeux vidéo)
videotape une cassette vidéo **9**
violin un violon **15**

R46 English-French Vocabulary

to visit (*place*) visiter **7, 20;** (*people*) rendre visite à **20, 28**
volleyball le volley (volleyball) **15**

to wait (for) attendre **20**
walk une promenade **14**
to take (go for) a walk *faire une promenade à pied **8, 14**
to walk *aller à pied **14;** marcher **9**
to want *avoir envie de **20;** *vouloir **26**
do you want ...? tu veux...? **3A**
do you want to ...? est-ce que tu veux...? **5**
I don't want ... je ne veux pas... **5**
I want ... je veux... **5, 26**
I want to je veux bien **26**
what do you want? qu'est-ce que tu veux? **3A;** vous désirez? **3B, 17**
wanted voulu (*p.p. of* *vouloir) **26**
warm chaud **4C, 23**
to be warm (*people*) *avoir chaud **22**
it's warm (*weather*) il fait chaud **4C**
was été (*p.p. of* *être) **23**
to wash laver **21**
to waste perdre **20**
watch une montre **9**
to watch regarder **7**
to watch TV regarder la télé **5**
water l'eau *f.* **25**
mineral water l'eau minérale **25**
to water-ski *faire du ski nautique **21**
water-skiing le ski nautique **21**
we nous **6, 15;** on **20**
to wear *mettre **18;** porter **17**
weather: how's (what's) the weather? quel temps fait-il? **4C**
it's ... weather il fait... **4C**
Wednesday mercredi *m.* **4B**
week une semaine **4B, 21**
last week la semaine dernière **23**
next week la semaine prochaine **23**
this week cette semaine **23**
weekend un week-end **21**
last weekend le week-end dernier **23**
next weekend le week-end prochain **21, 23**
this weekend ce week-end **23**
weight: to gain weight grossir **19**
well bien **7**
well! eh bien! **18**
well then alors **11**
everything's going (very) well ça va (très) bien **1C**
went allé (*p.p. of* *aller) **24**
what comment? quoi? **17;** qu'est-ce que **8**
what color? de quelle couleur? **12**
what day is it? quel jour est-ce? **4B**
what do you think of ...? comment trouves-tu...?, qu'est-ce que tu penses de...? **17**
what do you want? qu'est-ce que tu veux? **3A;** vous désirez? **3B, 17**
what does ... mean? que veut dire...? **I**
what does he/she look like? comment est-il/elle? **9**
what is it? qu'est-ce que c'est? **9**
what is there? qu'est-ce qu'il y a? **9**
what time is it? quelle heure est-il? **4A**
what would you like? vous désirez? **3B, 17**
what's ...'s name? comment s'appelle...? **2B**
what's he/she like? comment est-il/elle? **9**
what's his/her name? comment s'appelle-t-il/elle? **9**
what's that? qu'est-ce que c'est? **9**
what's the date? quelle est la date? **4B**
what's the price? quel est le prix? **17**
what's the weather? quel temps fait-il? **4C**
what's your address? quelle est ton adresse? **13**
what's your name? comment t'appelles-tu? **1A**
at what time is ...? à quelle heure est...? **4A**
at what time? à quelle heure? **4A, 8**
when quand **8**
when is your birthday? c'est quand, ton anniversaire? **4B**
where où **6, 8**
where is ...? où est...? **6**
where is it? où est-ce? **13**
from where? d'où? **15**
whether si
which quel (quelle) **18**
white blanc (blanche) **E1,12**
who qui **8**
who's that/this? qui est-ce? **2A, 9**
about whom? de qui? **8**
for whom? pour qui? **8**
of whom? de qui? **8**
to whom? à qui? **8**
with whom? avec qui? **8**
why pourquoi **8**
wife une femme **16**
to win gagner **20**
window une fenêtre **I, 9**
to windsurf *faire de la planche à voile **21**
windsurfing la planche à voile **21**
winter l'hiver *m.* **4C**
in the winter en hiver **4C**
with avec **6**
with me avec moi **5**
with you avec toi **5**
with whom? avec qui? **8**
woman une dame (*polite term*) **2A;** une femme **9**
to work travailler **5, 7;** (*referring to objects*) marcher **9**
does the radio work? est-ce que la radio marche? **9**
it (doesn't) work(s) well il/elle (ne) marche (pas) bien **9**

ENGLISH-FRENCH VOCABULARY

English-French Vocabulary R47

English-French Vocabulary *continued*

would: I'd like je voudrais **3A, 3B, 5**
to **write** *écrire **28**
wrong faux (fausse) **12**
to be wrong *avoir tort **22**

year un an, une année **4B**
he/she is ... (years old) il/elle a... ans **2C**
I'm ... (years old) j'ai... ans **2C**
to be ... (years old) *avoir... ans **10**
yellow jaune **E1, 12**
yes oui **1B, 6;** (*to a negative question*) si! **10**
yes, of course oui, bien sûr **5**
yes, okay (all right) oui, d'accord **5**
yes, thank you oui, merci **5**
yesterday hier **23**
yesterday afternoon hier après-midi **23**
yesterday morning hier matin **23**
yogurt le yaourt **25**
you tu, vous **6, 15;** on **20**
you are ... tu es + *nationality* **1B**
and you? et toi? **1A**
(to) you te, vous **27**
your ton, ta; tes **2C;** votre; vos **16**
what's your name? comment t'appelles-tu? **1A**
young jeune **9**

zero zéro **1A**

R48 English-French Vocabulary

Index

A

B

C

Index R49

M

R50 Index

Index R51

Credits

Front Cover
Background Eiffel Tower illuminated at night, Paris, France, Paul Hardy/Corbis
Inset Digital Vision/Getty Images

Back Cover
Level 1a: *background* Palace of Versailles, Versailles, France, Fernand Ivaldi/Getty Images; *inset* PhotoDisc/Getty Images

Level 1b: *background* Martinique, Jake Rajs/Getty Images; *inset* PhotoDisc/Getty Images

Level 1: *background* Eiffel Tower illuminated at night, Paris, France, Paul Hardy/Corbis; *inset* Digital Vision/Getty Images

Level 2: *background* Chateau Frontenac, Quebec Old Town, Quebec, Canada, nagelestock.com/Alamy; *inset* AGE Fotostock

Level 3: *background* Port Al-Kantaoui, Sousse, Tunisia, José Fuste Raga/zefa/Corbis; *inset* PhotoDisc/Getty Images

Illustration
Tim Foley: 74, 75 *(t)*, 80, 101, 142, 145 *(t)*, 146 *(t)*, 148, 154, 160 *(br)*, 161 *(b)*, 182, 230, 258, 264 *(t)*, 316, 372, 390 392, 408

All other illustration by:
Yves Clarnou
Jean-Pierre Foissy
Elisabeth Schlossberg

Photography
All photos by Lawrence Migdale/PIX except the following: **1** Pierre Valette **5** *(tl)* Larry Prosor/SuperStock; *(bl)* Catherine Secula/Photolibrary/ PictureQuest; *(br)* Robert Fried; **14** *(bl, br)* Owen Franken; **15** *(t)* Owen Franken; **16** *(tl, tr)* copyright ©Albert Rene Editions; *(all others except cr)* Owen Franken; **18** Owen Franken; **19** *(b)* Mick Roessler/ Index Stock; **22** Owen Franken; **24** *(cr, cl)* Owen Franken; **26** *(t)* VPG/Woods; *(b)* Owen Franken; **30** Owen Franken; **31** *(t)* Owen Franken; *(b)* Canstock/Index Stock; **32** Owen Franken; **34** Owen Franken; **38** *(bl)* Owen Franken; *(br)* Carol Palmer-Andrew Brilliant, D.C. Heath; **44** J. Charlas; **56** Owen Franken; **58** *(tr)* Owen Franken; **60** Owen Franken; **58** *(t)* Owen Franken; **60** Owen Franken; **62** *(t)* Owen Franken; **64** Owen Franken; **66** *(tr)* Adine Sagalyn; **139** *(tr)* PhotoDisc; *(br)* Comstock; *all others* Corbis; **105** *(tr)* Beryl Goldberg; *(cl)* Andrea Comas/Reuters; *(cr)* Chip & Maria de la Cueva; *(bl)* School Division, Houghton Mifflin Co.; **104** Yves Levy; **110** Yves Levy; **123** *(t)* Robert Fried; *(b)* Beryl Goldberg; **124** Sophie Reiter; **125** *(br)* Yves Levy; *all others* Patrick Pipard; **126** *(t) Self Portrait* (1835), Jean-Baptiste Camille Corot. Oil on canvas. Uffizi, Florence, Italy. Photography ©Scala/Art Resource; *(b) View from Chatelaine*, Jean-Camille Corot. Musee d'Art et d'Histoire, Geneva, Switzerland. Photography ©Francis G. Mayer/Corbis; **127** Yves Levy; **129** *(b)* Michael Newman/PhotoEdit; *all others* Stockbyte; **131** Yves Levy; **151** *(t)* Andre Jenny/ ImageState; **151** *(b)* Manu Sassoonian/Art Resource; **162** Yves Levy; **172** Owen Franken; **177** Patrick Pipard; **189** courtesy of MBK Europe; **195** *(t)* Robert Fried; *(c)* N. Hautemaniere/On Location; *(c)* courtesy Touraine Val de Loire; *(b)* Rebecca Valette;
196 Tim O'Hara/Corbis; **205** *(t)* William Tenney; **224** Owen Franken; **227** *(bl)* PhotoDisc, Inc.; **227** *(br)* PhotoDisc, Inc.; **235** Owen Franken; **242** copyright ©Casterman; **243** copyright ©Casterman; **245** Parrot Pascal/Corbis Sygma; **247** Adine Sagalyn; **252** Adine Sagalyn; **265** Adine Sagalyn; **266** *(tl)* Patrick Pipard; **267** Patrick Pipard; **274** Owen Franken; **277** Owen Franken; **282** Owen Franken; **285** Owen Franken; **294** Yves Levy; **305** Chris Barton/Lonely Planet Images; **309** *(b)* Kirk Anderson/ImageState; **309** *(t)* Andre Jenny/Focus Group/PictureQuest; **313** Pictor International/PictureQuest; **315** Rick Hornick/Index Stock Imagery; **317** *(br)* Owen Franken; **341** Gail Mooney/Corbis; **356** *(tl, bl, br)* PhotoDisc; *(tr)* Mitch Diamond/ImageState; **357** Ellen Rooney/ImageState; **358** *(t)* Robert Fried; *(b)* Lee Snider/Photo Images; **359** Daniel Morel/AP Wide World Photo; **362** *(t)* Owen Franken; *(b)* J. Charlas; *(background)* courtesy of Perspectives; **372** Owen Franken; **384** *(t)* Yves Levy; **386** Patrick Pipard; **394** Owen Franken; **416** Owen Franken; *(background)* courtesy of Perspectives

R52 Credits